Dewey Decimal Classification
and Relative Index

Dewey Decimal Classification and Relative Index

Devised by Melvil Dewey

EDITION 20

Edited by

John P. Comaromi, Editor

Julianne Beall, Assistant Editor

Winton E. Matthews, Jr., Assistant Editor

Gregory R. New, Assistant Editor

VOLUME 4

Relative Index ■ Manual

FOREST PRESS

A Division of

OCLC Online Computer Library Center, Inc.

ALBANY, NEW YORK

1989

Library of Congress Cataloging-in-Publication Data
Dewey, Melvil, 1851-1931.
    Dewey decimal classification and relative index / devised by Melvil Dewey. -- Ed. 20 / edited by John P. Comaromi, Julianne Beall, Winton E. Matthews, Jr., Gregory R. New.
    Contents: v. 1. Introduction. Tables -- v. 2-3. Schedules -- v.4. Relative index. Manual.
    1. Classification, Dewey decimal. I. Comaromi, John P. (John Phillip), 1937-   . II. Beall, Julianne, 1946-   . III. Matthews, Winton E. IV. New, Gregory R. V. Forest Press. VI. Title.
Z696.D519 1989   025.4'31--dc19   88-24629

The paper used in this publication meets the minimum requirements of American National Standard for Information Science - Permanence of Paper for Printed Library Materials. ANSI Z39.48-1984.

ISBN: (set) 0-910608-37-7; v. 1 0-910608-38-5; v. 2 0-910608-39-3; v. 3 0-910608-40-7; v. 4 0-910608-41-5

Contents

Volume 1

v

Contents

Volume 2

Volume 3

Volume 4

Relative Index

Use of the Relative Index

Full instructions on the use of the Relative Index are found in the Introduction to the Dewey Decimal Classification in Volume 1.

Alphabeting is word by word. A hyphenated word is filed as two words. Abbreviations are filed as spelled.

Digits are printed in groups of three purely for ease in reading and copying. The spaces are not part of the numbers, and the groups are not related to the segmentation shown in DDC numbers on Library of Congress cataloging records.

Abbreviations Used in the Index

T1	Table 1	Standard Subdivisions	T3C	Table 3–C	Notation to Be Added Where Instructed in Table 3-B and in 808-809
T2	Table 2	Geographic Areas, Historical Periods, Persons			
T3	Table 3	Subdivisions for Individual Literatures, for Specific Literary Forms	T4	Table 4	Subdivisions of Individual Languages
			T5	Table 5	Racial, Ethnic, National Groups
T3A	Table 3–A	Subdivisions for Works by or about Individual Authors	T6	Table 6	Languages
			T7	Table 7	Groups of Persons
T3B	Table 3–B	Subdivisions for Works by or about More than One Author			

A.C.T.	Australian Capital Territory		N.S.	Nova Scotia
A.S.S.R.	Autonomous Soviet Socialist Republic		N.S.W.	New South Wales
Ala.	Alabama		N.T.	Northern Territory
Alta.	Alberta		N.W.T.	Northwest Territories
Ariz.	Arizona		N.Y.	New York
Ark.	Arkansas		N.Z.	New Zealand
B.C.	Before Christ		Neb.	Nebraska
	British Columbia		Nev.	Nevada
Calif.	California		Okla.	Oklahoma
Colo.	Colorado		Ont.	Ontario
Conn.	Connecticut		Or.	Oregon
D.C.	District of Columbia		P.E.I.	Prince Edward Island
Del.	Delaware		P.R.	Puerto Rico
Dept.	Department		Pa.	Pennsylvania
Fla.	Florida		Qld.	Queensland
Ga.	Georgia		R.I.	Rhode Island
Ill.	Illinois		R.S.F.S.R.	Russian Soviet Federated Socialist Republic
Inc.	Incorporated		S. Aust.	South Australia
Ind.	Indiana		S.C.	South Carolina
Kan.	Kansas		S.D.	South Dakota
Ky.	Kentucky		S.S.R.	Soviet Socialist Republic
La.	Louisiana		Sask.	Saskatchewan
Man.	Manitoba		Tas.	Tasmania
Mass.	Massachusetts		Tenn.	Tennessee
Md.	Maryland		Tex.	Texas
Me.	Maine		U.K.	United Kingdom
Mich.	Michigan		U.S.	United States of America
Minn.	Minnesota		U.S.S.R.	Union of Soviet Socialist Republics
Miss.	Mississippi		V.I.	Virgin Islands
Mo.	Missouri		Va.	Virginia
Mont.	Montana		Vic.	Victoria
N.B.	New Brunswick		Vt.	Vermont
N.C.	North Carolina		W.A.	Western Australia
N.D.	North Dakota		W.Va.	West Virginia
N.H.	New Hampshire		Wash.	Washington
N.J.	New Jersey		Wis.	Wisconsin
N.M.	New Mexico		Wyo.	Wyoming
			Yukon	Yukon Territory

A

A.B.M. (Missiles)	358.174 82
military engineering	623.451 94
military equipment	358.174 82
A.C.T. (College testing program)	378.166 2
A.C.T.H. (Hormone)	
pharmacology	615.363
production	
human physiology	612.492
see also Endocrine system	
A.D.P. (Computing)	004
A.F.D.C. (Social welfare)	362.713
A.F.L. (Labor)	331.883 209 7
A.F.L.-C.I.O. (Labor)	331.880 97
A.I.D.S. (Disease)	362.196 979 2
medicine	616.979 2
social services	362.196 979 2
see also AIDS (Disease)	
A.M. radio stations	384.545 3
engineering	621.384
facilities	384.545 3
organizations	384.540 65
A.M. radio systems	621.384 153
A.M.V.E.T.S. (Veterans)	369.186 2
A.N.C. (African National	
Congress)	324.268 083
A.P. ammunition	623.451 8
A.S.E.A.N. (Alliance)	341.247 3
Aabenraa amt (Denmark)	T2—489 5
Aabenraa-Sonderborg amt	
(Denmark)	T2—489 5
Aachen (Germany)	T2—435 511
Aalborg amt (Denmark)	T2—489 5
Aardvarks	599.75
Aardwolves	599.744 26
Aargau (Switzerland)	T2—494 56
Aarhus amt (Denmark)	T2—489 5
Abaca	584.21
fiber crop	633.571
Abacus	513.028
Abandoned children	305.906 945
	T1—086 945
social group	305.906 945
social services	362.73
Abau (Papua New Guinea)	T2—954 6
Abbeville County (S.C.)	T2—757 35
Abbeys	
architecture	726.7
Abbotsford (B.C.)	T2—711 37
Abbott, John J. C., Sir	
Canadian history	971.055
Abbreviated longhand	653.2
Abbreviation dictionaries	413.1
specific languages	T4—31
specific subject	T1—014 8

Abbreviations	411
specific languages	T4—11
specific subject	T1—014 8
Abdias (Biblical book)	224.91
Abdication of monarchs	
public administration	351.003 6
Abdomen	591.104 2
animal physiology	591.104 2
human anatomy	611.95
human physiology	612.95
regional medicine	617.55
surgery	617.550 59
Abdominal hernia	
regional medicine	617.559
surgery	617.559 059
Abdominal muscles	
human anatomy	611.736
see also Musculoskeletal system	
Abduction	364.154
law	345.025 4
Abdul Rahman, Tunku, Putra	
Al-Haj	
Malaysian history	959.505 1
Abdul Razak bin Dato' Hussein,	
Tun Haji	
Malaysian history	959.505 2
Abelian categories	512.55
Abelian groups	512.2
Aberconwy (Wales :	
Borough)	T2—429 27
Aberdeen (Scotland)	T2—412 35
Aberdeen (South Africa :	
District)	T2—687 15
Aberdeen Angus cattle	
animal husbandry	636.223
zoology	599.735 8
Aberdeenshire (Scotland)	T2—412 32
Aberration	
astronomy	522.9
Abhidhammapitaka	294.382 4
Abidjan (Ivory Coast)	T2—666 8
Ability grouping in education	371.254
Ability testing	153.93
education	371.26
personnel selection	658.311 25
Abiogenesis	577
Abitibi (Quebec : Regional	
County Municipality)	T2—714 13
Abitibi, Lake (Ont. and	
Quebec)	T2—713 142
Abitibi-Ouest (Quebec :	
Regional County	
Municipality)	T2—714 13
Abitibi-Témiscamingue	
(Quebec : Administrative	
region)	T2—714 13
Abitibi-Témiscamingue	
Region (Quebec)	T2—714 13

Abitibi Territory (Quebec)	T2—714 115
Abkhaz A.S.S.R. (Georgian S.S.R.)	T2—479 5
Abkhàzskaia A.S.S.R. (Georgian S.S.R.)	T2—479 5
ABM (Missiles)	358.174 82
military engineering	623.451 94
military equipment	358.174 82
Abnormal psychology	616.89
see also Mental illness	
Abnormalities	
human teratology	616.043
physical anthropology	573.8
Abolition	326
political science	326
sociology	306.362
United States history	973.711 4
Abominable snowman	001.944
Aborigines	306.089
legal status	342.087 2
social group	306.089
Abortion	363.46
criminology	364.185
demographic effect	304.667
ethics	179.76
religion	291.569 76
Buddhism	294.356 976
Christianity	241.697 6
Hinduism	294.548 697 6
Islam	297.5
Judaism	296.385 697 6
law	344.041 92
social problem	363.46
surgery	618.88
Abra (Philippines)	T2—599 1
Abrading tools	621.92
Abrasions	
medicine	617.13
Abrasive materials	553.65
economic geology	553.65
Abreaction	
psychology	154.2
Abrupt variations	575.29
plants	581.159
Abruzzi (Italy)	T2—457 1
Absaroka Range (Mont. and Wyo.)	T2—787 4
Abscission (Plant physiology)	581.31
Absentee ownership	
land economics	333.4
Absentee voting	324.65
law	342.075
Absenteeism	331.259 8
labor economics	331.259 8
personnel management	658.314
public administration	350.164
central governments	351.164
local governments	352.005 164

Absenteeism (continued)	
sociology	306.361
Absinthe	641.255
commercial processing	663.55
Absolute (Philosophy)	111.6
Absolute monarchy	321.6
Absolute rights	323.01
Absolute temperature	536.5
Absolution (Christian rite)	234.166
public worship	265.64
Absorbency	
skin	
human physiology	612.791
see also Skin	
Absorber oil	665.538 4
Absorption	541.33
chemical engineering	660.284 23
chemistry	541.33
gaseous state physics	530.43
nutrition	574.13
human physiology	612.38
see also Digestive system	
Absorption of heat	536.34
Absorption of light	
meteorology	551.566
Absorption of sound	
physics	534.208
Abstinence	178
religious practice	291.447
Buddhism	294.344 47
Christianity	248.47
Hinduism	294.544 7
Abstract algebra	512.02
Abstract expressionism	709.040 52
painting	759.065 2
sculpture	735.230 452
Abstract harmonic analysis	515.785
Abstract spaces	516.1
Abstract thought	153.24
philosophy	128.3
psychology	153.24
Abstracting techniques	
information science	025.402 8
rhetoric	808.062
Abstractionism	709.040 52
painting	759.065 2
sculpture	735.230 452
Abstracts of title	346.043 8
Abu Daud Sulayman ibn al-Ashath al-Sijistani	
Hadith	297.124 2
Abu Dhabi (United Arab Emirates : Emirate)	T2—535 7
Abu Zaby (United Arab Emirates : Emirate)	T2—535 7
Abuja (Federal Capital Territory, Nigeria)	T2—669 68

Abuse of laws	
civil rights issue	323.49
Abuse of power	
law	345.023 2
public administration	350.991
central governments	351.991
local governments	352.002
Abused children	305.906 945
	T1—086 945
social group	305.906 945
social welfare	362.76
see also Child abuse	
Abutments	721.3
architecture	721.3
construction	690.13
structural engineering	624.16
Abydos (Egypt : Ancient city)	T2—32
Abyssinia	T2—63
Abyssinian cat	
animal husbandry	636.826
see also Cats	
Abyssinians	T5—928
Acacia	583.321
Academic costume	378.28
Academic degrees	378.2
Academic freedom	371.104
higher education	378.121
law	342.085 3
Academic libraries	027.7
administration	025.197 7
collection development	025.218 77
use studies	025.587 7
Academic placement	371.264
Academic year	371.23
law	344.079 2
Academicians	
occupational group	T7—090 1
Academies (Organizations)	060
Acadia	971.601
	T2—716
Acadia National Park (Me.)	T2—741 45
Acadia Parish (La.)	T2—763 56
Acadians	T5—41
Acadians in Canada	T5—114
expulsion of	971.018 7
Acanthaceae	583.81
Acanthobdellida	595.145
Acanthocephala	595.13
paleozoology	565.1
Acanthodii	567.2
Acanthopterygii	597.58
paleozoology	567.5
Acanthuses	583.81
Acari	595.42
paleozoology	565.4
Acariformes	595.42
Acarina	595.42

Acarnania (Greece)	T2—495 1
ancient	T2—383
Acceleration	
biophysics	574.191 34
human	612.014 414
classical mechanics	531.112
Acceleration of particles	539.73
Accelerator effect	
(Macroeconomics)	339.41
Accelerometers	
aircraft	629.135 2
Accent (Linguistics)	414.6
specific languages	T4—16
Accent (Poetry)	808.1
Acceptances (Commercial paper)	332.77
exchange medium	332.55
law	346.096
Access control (Computers)	005.8
management	658.478
Access points (Cataloging)	025.322
Access to information	
civil right	323.445
Accessories (Clothing)	391.44
care	646.6
commercial technology	687.19
customs	391.44
home economics	646.3
home sewing	646.48
see also Clothing	
Accident insurance	368.384
commercial law	346.086 384
government-sponsored	368.42
industrial casualty	368.7
social law	344.022
see also Insurance	
Accidents	363.1
personal safety	613.69
psychology	155.936
social services	363.1
law	344.047
public administration	350.783
central governments	351.783
local governments	352.3
tort law	346.032 2
Accidents (Philosophy)	111.1
Accipitridae	598.916
Acclimation	
health	613.1
Acclimatization	
animals	591.542
biology	574.542
plants	581.542
Accomack County (Va.)	T2—755 16
Accommodation	
disorders of eye	
incidence	614.599 7
optometry	617.755
see also Eyes	

Accompaniment
  musical technique | 781.47
Accomplices | 345.03
Accordions | 788.86
  see also Woodwind instruments
Account security
  credit management | 658.88
Accountability
  Christian doctrines | 233.4
  ethics | 170
  legal ethics | 340.112
Accountability in executive
  management | 658.402
Accountability in public
  administration | 350.9
  central governments | 351.9
  local governments | 352.002
Accountability in public
  education | 379.154
Accountability of teachers | 371.144
Accountants | 657.092
  occupational group | T7—657
Accounting | 657
  corporation law | 346.066 48
  home economics | 640.42
  law | 346.063
  management policy | 658.151 1
  public administration | 350.723 1
    central governments | 351.723 1
    local governments | 352.171
Accounting for inflation | 657.48
Accounts payable
  accounting | 657.74
  financial management | 658.152 6
Accounts receivable | 657.72
  accounting | 657.72
  financial management | 658.152 44
Accra (Ghana) | T2—667
Acculturation | 303.482
Accumulators
  hydraulic | 621.254
Accuracy drills and tests
  shorthand | 653.15
  typing | 652.307
Aceraceae | 583.28
Acetabularia | 589.47
Acetals | 668.423
Acetates | 668.423
Acetobacteriaceae | 589.95
Acetylene | 547.413
  chemical engineering | 661.814
  gas technology | 665.85
Achaea (Greece) | T2—495 2
  ancient | T2—387
Achaia (Greece) | T2—495 2
  ancient | T2—387
Achariaceae | 583.456
Achatocarpaceae | 583.138

Achievement tests | 371.264
Achromatiaceae | 589.96
Acid mine drainage | 363.738 4
  environmental protection | 363.738 4
  preventive technology | 622.5
  water-supply engineering | 628.168 32
Acid precipitation | 363.738 6
  see also Acid rain
Acid rain | 363.738 6
  international law | 341.762 3
  law | 344.046 34
  meteorology | 551.577 1
  pollution technology | 628.532
  social welfare | 363.738 6
  see also Pollution
Acid rock | 781.66
Acid soil conditioners | 631.821
  chemical engineering | 668.64
  use | 631.821
Acidimetric analysis | 545.22
Acidity
  soil science | 631.42
Acids | 546.24
  chemical engineering | 661.2
  chemistry | 546.24
  organic chemistry | 547.037
    applied | 661.86
  toxicology | 615.921
  see also Chemicals
Acidulous salts | 546.342
  chemical engineering | 661.4
Acipenseriformes | 597.44
  paleozoology | 567.4
Acklins Island | T2—729 6
Acne
  medicine | 616.53
  see also Skin
Acoela (Platyhelminthes) | 595.123
Acoelea (Mollusks) | 594.36
  paleozoology | 564.36
Acoli (African people) | T5—965
Acoli language | 496.5
| T6—965
Aconcagua (Chile) | T2—832 4
Aconcagua (Chile : Region) | T2—832 4
Aconite | 583.111
Acorns
  coffee substitute
    commercial processing | 663.97
Acoustical communications
  engineering | 621.382 8
Acoustical engineering | 620.2
Acoustical engineers | 620.209 2
  occupational group | T7—620 2
Acoustical insulation
  buildings | 693.834
Acoustical pattern recognition | 006.45
  engineering | 621.399

Acoustical properties	
materials science	620.112 94
Acoustical prospecting	622.159 2
Acoustics	534
architectural design	729.29
engineering	620.2
Acousto-optical communications	
engineering	621.382 8
Acquired immune deficiency	
syndrome	362.196 979 2
medicine	616.979 2
social services	362.196 979 2
see also AIDS (Disease)	
Acquisition of corporations	
law	346.066 26
management	658.16
Acquisition of public lands	
law	343.025 2
Acquisition of real property	
law	346.043 62
Acquisition of territory	325.32
law	341.42
Acquisitions (Libraries)	025.2
Acquisitions (Museums)	069.51
Acrasida	593.115
Acre (Brazil)	T2—811 2
Acreage allotments	338.18
law	343.076
Acrobatics	796.47
circuses	791.34
sports	796.47
Acrobats	796.470 92
circus	791.340 92
circus group	T7—791 3
sports	796.470 92
sports group	T7—796 4
Acromegaly	
medicine	616.47
see also Endocrine system	
Acronym dictionaries	413.1
specific languages	T4—31
specific subject	T1—014 8
Acronyms	411
specific languages	T4—11
specific subject	T1—014 8
Acrostics	793.73
Acrothoracica	595.35
paleozoology	565.35
Acrylic painting	751.426
Acrylics	668.423 2
textiles	677.474 2
see also Textiles	
Acrylonitrile rubber	678.72
ACT (College testing program)	378.166 2
Act of Union, 1840	971.039
ACTH (Hormone)	
pharmacology	615.363

ACTH (Hormone) (continued)	
production	
human physiology	612.492
see also Endocrine system	
Acting	792.028
motion pictures	791.430 28
radio	791.440 28
stage	792.028
television	791.450 28
Actinide series	669.292
chemistry	546.42
metallurgy	669.292
see also Chemicals, Metals	
Actinidiaceae	583.166
Actinium	
chemistry	546.421
metallurgy	669.292 1
see also Chemicals, Metals	
Actinomycetales	589.92
Actinopoda	593.13
Actinopterygii	597.5
paleozoology	567.5
Actinotherapy	
medicine	615.842
Action	
philosophical anthropology	128.4
psychology	150
Action games	
indoor	793.4
Action toys	
manufacturing technology	688.728
see also Toys	
Activated carbon	662.93
water treatment	628.166
Activated sludge process	628.354
Activation analysis	543.088 2
Activity therapy	
medicine	615.851 5
Acton (Quebec : Regional	
County Municipality)	T2—714 525
Actors	792.028 092
motion picture	791.430 280 92
occupational group	T7—791 4
occupational group	T7—792 1
radio	791.440 280 92
occupational group	T7—791 4
stage	792.028 092
occupational group	T7—792 1
television	791.450 280 92
occupational group	T7—791 4
Acts of the Apostles	226.6
pseudepigrapha	229.92
Actual grace	234.1
Actuarial science	368.01
Acuity (Visual perception)	
psychology	152.142 2
Acupressure	
therapeutics	615.822

Acupuncture	
medicine	615.892
Acylation	547.21
chemical engineering	660.284 41
Ad-Dakhla (Morocco :	
Province)	T2—648
Ada County (Idaho)	T2—796 28
Adages	398.9
Adair County (Iowa)	T2—777 73
Adair County (Ky.)	T2—769 675
Adair County (Mo.)	T2—778 264
Adair County (Okla.)	T2—766 89
Adamawa languages	496.36
	T6—963 6
Adams, John	
United States history	973.44
Adams, John Quincy	
United States history	973.55
Adams County (Colo.)	T2—788 81
Adams County (Idaho)	T2—796 26
Adams County (Ill.)	T2—773 44
Adams County (Ind.)	T2—772 73
Adams County (Iowa)	T2—777 76
Adams County (Miss.)	T2—762 26
Adams County (N.D.)	T2—784 89
Adams County (Neb.)	T2—782 397
Adams County (Ohio)	T2—771 86
Adams County (Pa.)	T2—748 42
Adams County (Wash.)	T2—797 34
Adams County (Wis.)	T2—775 56
Adams Lake (B.C.)	T2—711 72
Adams River (B.C.)	T2—711 75
Adana Ili (Turkey)	T2—564
Adaptability	
psychology	155.24
old persons	155.672
situational	155.9
Adaptation (Ecology)	574.5
animals	591.5
plants	581.5
Adaptive control systems	
automation engineering	629.836
Added-value tax	336.271 4
law	343.055
public administration	350.724 7
central governments	351.724 7
local governments	352.135
public finance	336.271 4
Adder's-tongue fern	587.33
Addiction	362.29
customs	394.14
medicine	616.86
personal health	613.8
social theology	291.178 322 9
Christianity	261.832 29
social welfare	362.29
see also Substance abuse	
Addictive drugs	
pharmacodynamics	615.78
Addington, Lennox and (Ont.)	T2—713 59
Addis Ababa (Ethiopia)	T2—633
Addison County (Vt.)	T2—743 5
Addison's disease	
medicine	616.45
see also Endocrine system	
Addition	512.92
algebra	512.92
arithmetic	513.211
Addition (Chemical reaction)	541.393
organic chemistry	547.2
applied	660.284 4
Additive processes	
color photography	778.65
Additive properties	512.73
Addo Elephant National Park	T2—687 5
Addresses	080
Addressing machines	
office use	651.759
Adelaide (S. Aust.)	T2—942 31
Adelaide (South Africa :	
District)	T2—687 5
Adelbert Range	T2—957 3
Aden	T2—533 5
Aden, Gulf of	551.467 32
	T2—165 32
Adenoids	
surgery	617.532
Adenomas	
medicine	616.993
see also Diseases (Human)	
Adenoviruses	576.648 4
Adephaga	595.762
Adhesion	541.33
chemical engineering	660.293
Adhesiveness	
materials science	620.112 92
Adhesives	668.3
building materials	691.99
foundation materials	624.153 99
manufacturing technology	668.3
materials science	620.199
structural engineering	624.189 9
Adi Granth (Sikhism)	294.682
Adipose tissues	
human histology	611.018 2
Adirondack Mountains (N.Y.)	T2—747 5
Adiyaman Ili (Turkey)	T2—565
Adjudication	347.07
competitions	T1—079
criminal law	345.07
international law	341.55
Adjustment (Insurance)	368.014
Adjustment (Psychology)	155.24
Adlerian psychology	150.195 3

Afghan literature	891.593
Afghan rugs	
arts	746.758 1
see also Rugs	
Afghanistan	958.1
	T2—581
Afghans	T5—915 93
Afghans (Coverlets)	643.53
arts	746.97
home sewing	646.21
household equipment	643.53
AFL (Labor)	331.883 209 7
AFL-CIO	331.880 97
Aflatoxins	
toxicology	615.952 923
Africa	960
	T2—6
Africa, Black	T2—67
Africa, Central	967
	T2—67
Africa, East	967.6
	T2—676
Africa, Negro	T2—67
Africa, North	961
	T2—61
ancient	939.7
	T2—397
Africa, Southern	968
	T2—68
Africa, Sub-Saharan	967
	T2—67
Africa, West	966
	T2—66
African languages	496
	T6—96
African literature	808.898 96
history and criticism	809.889 6
in African languages	896
African Methodist Episcopal Church	287.83
see also Methodist Church	
African Methodist Episcopal Zion Church	287.83
see also Methodist Church	
African National Congress	324.268 083
African religions	299.6
African sleeping sickness	
incidence	614.533
medicine	616.936 3
see also Communicable diseases (Human)	
African violets	583.81
floriculture	635.933 81
Africans	T5—96
Afrihili (Artificial language)	499.99
	T6—999 9
Afrikaans language	439.36
	T6—393 6

Afrikaans literature	839.36
Afrikaners	T5—393 6
Afro-American cooking	641.592 960 73
Afro-American Methodist churches	287.8
see also Methodist Church	
Afro-Americans	305.896 073
	T5—960 73
military troops	
World War II	940.540 3
social aspects	305.896 073
Afro-Asian bloc	T2—171 65
Afro-Asiatic languages	492
	T6—92
non-Semitic	493
	T6—93
Afro-Asiatic literatures	892
non-Semitic	893
Afro-Cuban jazz	781.657
Afrohili (Artificial language)	T6—999 9
After-dinner speeches	
literature	808.851
history and criticism	809.51
specific literatures	T3B—501
individual authors	T3A—5
rhetoric	808.51
Afterimages	
psychology	152.148
Afternoon music	781.523
Afyon-Karahisar Ili (Turkey)	T2—562
Agadir (Morocco : Province)	T2—646
Agalega Island	T2—698 2
Agapes (Christian rites)	265.9
Agaricales	589.222
Agavales	584.43
Agave	584.43
fiber crop	633.577
Agdestidaceae	583.913
Age discrimination in employment	331.398
law	344.013 98
Age groups	305.2
	T1—083—084
	T7—05
Age-hardening metals	671.36
Aged persons	305.26
	T1—084 6
see also Old persons	
Agency law	346.029
Agent Orange	
toxicology	615.951 37
Aggadah	296.19
Aggeus (Biblical book)	224.97
Agglutination	
human immunology	616.079 5
immunology	574.295

Agriculture	
applied science	630
economics	338.1
enterprises	338.763
law	343.076
public administration	351.823 3
cabinet departments	351.082 33
Agriculture and state	338.18
Agrigento (Sicily : Province)	T2—458 22
Agroforestry	634.99
Agromyzidae	595.774
Agronomy	630
Agrosteae	584.93
Aguadilla (P.R. : District)	T2—729 54
Aguascalientes (Mexico : State)	T2—724 2
Agulhas, Cape	T2—687 3
Ahimsa	294.548 697
Buddhism	294.356 97
Hinduism	294.548 697
Ahmadiyya movement	297.86
Ahom (India)	T5—959 1
Ahom language	495.919
	T6—959 19
Ahom literature	895.919
Ahuachapán (El Salvador : Dept.)	T2—728 411
Ahvenanmaa (Finland)	T2—489 73
Aichi-ken (Japan)	T2—521 67
Aid to families with dependent children	362.713
AIDS (Disease)	362.196 979 2
church work with patients	259.4
incidence	614.599 3
medicine	616.979 2
nursing	610.736 99
pediatrics	618.929 792
social services	362.196 979 2
social theology	291.178 321 969 792
Christianity	261.832 196 979 2
Aiken County (S.C.)	T2—757 75
Aikido	796.815 4
physical fitness	613.714 8
Ailanthuses	583.24
Ailerons	629.134 33
Ain (France)	T2—444 4
Ain Chok-Hay Hassani (Morocco : Prefecture)	T2—643
Ainu	T5—946
Ainu language	494.6
	T6—946
Ainu literature	894.6
Air	
gas technology	665.82
health	613.19
Air bags	
automobile	629.276
Air bases	358.417
military engineering	623.66
Vietnamese War	959.704 348
World War I	940.443
World War II	940.544 3
Air circulation equipment	
buildings	697.932 5
Air-compression engines	
automotive	629.250 7
Air-compression-powered automobiles	
engineering	629.229 4
Air-compression-powered locomotives	385.365
engineering	625.265
transportation services	385.365
see also Rolling stock	
Air compression technology	621.51
Air conditioning	
aircraft	629.134 42
automobile	629.277
buildings	697.93
health	613.5
household management	644.5
library buildings	022.8
mining	622.42
museums	069.29
plant management	658.25
ships	623.853 7
Air conditioning engineers	
building trades	697.930 92
occupational group	T7—697
Air currents	551.517
aeronautics	629.132 4
Air-cushion vehicles	388.35
engineering	629.3
military engineering	623.748
transportation services	388.35
Air engines	621.42
Air force personnel	358.400 92
occupational group	T7—358
role and function	358.413 3
Air forces	358.4
Air freight	387.744
airport services	387.736 4
international law	341.756 78
law	343.097 8
Air guns	683.4
art metalwork	739.73
Air holes	
aeronautics	629.132 327
Air mail	383.144
see also Postal service	
Air masses	551.551 2
Air mechanics	533.6
aeronautics	629.132
engineering	620.107
Air-mileage indicators	629.135 1

Air transportation workers	387.709 2	Airline employees	387.709 2
occupational group	T7—387 7	occupational group	T7—387 7
Air warfare	358.4	Airlines	387.7
Vietnamese War	959.704 348	law	343.097 8
World War I	940.44	Airplane accidents	363.124
World War II	940.544	*see also* Transportation safety	
Airborne infantry	356.166	Airplane-banner advertising	659.134 4
Airbrush drawing	741.29	Airplane hijacking	364.155 2
Airbrush painting	751.494	international law	341.772
Aircraft	387.73	law	345.025 52
engineering	629.133	Airplane piloting	
international law	341.756 75	international law	341.756 75
law	343.097 5	Airplanes	387.733 4
military engineering	623.746	engineering	629.133 34
military equipment	358.418 3	military engineering	623.746
piloting	629.132 52	piloting	629.132 521
psychological influence	155.965	transportation services	387.733 4
sanitation services	363.729 3	*see also* Aircraft	
see also Waste control		Airport facilities	387.736 2
sports	797.5	*see also* Airports	
transportation services	387.73	Airport police	363.287 6
operation	387.740 44	Airports	387.736
Aircraft accidents	363.124	architecture	725.39
see also Transportation safety		area planning	711.78
Aircraft carriers	359.948 35	engineering	629.136
design	623.812 55	international law	341.756 77
engineering	623.825 5	law	343.097 7
naval equipment	359.948 35	military engineering	623.66
naval units	359.943 5	public administration	350.877 736
Aircraft detection	358.414	central governments	351.877 736
civil defense	363.35	local governments	352.917 736
see also Civil defense		transportation services	387.736
Aircraft engineers	629.130 092	*see also* Aircraft	
occupational group	T7—629 1	Airships	387.732 4
Aircraft failures	363.124 16	engineering	629.133 24
public safety	363.124 16	military engineering	623.743
wreckage studies	629.132 55	piloting	629.132 522
see also Transportation safety		transportation services	387.732 4
Aircraft gunnery	623.555	*see also* Aircraft	
Aircraft navigators	629.132 510 92	Airspace (International law)	341.46
occupational group	T7—629 1	Airstrips	387.736
Aircraft noise	363.741	engineering	629.136 12
engineering	629.132 3	military engineering	623.661 2
social welfare	363.741	transportation services	387.736
see also Noise		*see also* Airports	
Aircraft operation		Aisén (Chile : Province)	T2—836 22
transportation services	387.740 44	Aisén del General Carlos	
Aircraft piloting		Ibáñez del Campo	
international law	341.756 75	(Chile : Region)	T2—836 2
Aircraft racing	797.52	Aisne (France)	T2—443 45
Aire River	T2—428 15	Aitape (Papua New Guinea)	T2—957 7
Airedale terriers		Aiti-ken (Japan)	T2—521 67
animal husbandry	636.755	Aitkin County (Minn.)	T2—776 72
see also Dogs		Aitōlia kai Akarnania	
Airflow		(Greece)	T2—495 1
aeronautics	629.132 32	Aix-la-Chapelle (Germany)	T2—435 511
Airfoils	629.134 32	Aizoaceae	583.152
Airframes	629.134 31		

Albert, Lake	T2—676 1
Albert Falls and Nature Reserve	T2—684 75
Albert I, King of the Belgians Belgian history	949.304 1
Albert II, Emperor of Germany German history	943.028
Alberta	971.23
	T2—712 3
Alberton (South Africa : District)	T2—682 2
Albigensians	284.4
heresy	273.6
persecution of	272.3
religious group	T7—244
see also Christian denominations	
Albinism	
medicine	616.55
see also Skin	
Albokas	788.37
see also Woodwind instruments	
Albumin glue	668.32
Albumins	574.192 452
biochemistry	574.192 452
chemistry	547.752
see also Proteins	
Albuminuria	
medicine	616.63
see also Urinary system	
Albuquerque (N.M.)	T2—789 61
Albury (N.S.W.)	T2—944 8
Alcae	598.33
Alcedine	598.892
Alchemy	540.112
Alcidae	598.33
Alcohol	
pharmacodynamics	615.782 8
Alcohol abuse	362.292
law	344.044 61
medicine	616.861
personal health	613.81
social welfare	362.292
see also Substance abuse	
Alcoholic beverages	641.21
commercial processing	663.1
cooking with	641.62
customs	394.13
ethics	178.1
see also Ethical problems	
home preparation	641.874
public control	363.41
public administration	350.761
central governments	351.761
local governments	352.936 1
Alcoholics Anonymous	362.292 86
Alcoholism	362.292
law	344.044 61

Alcoholism (continued)	
medicine	616.861
personal health	613.81
social theology	291.178 322 92
Christianity	261.832 292
social welfare	362.292
see also Substance abuse	
Alcohols	547.031
aromatic chemistry	547.631
chemical engineering	661.82
chemistry	547.031
fuel	662.669
cooking	641.585
toxicology	615.951 31
Alcona County (Mich.)	T2—774 79
Alcorn County (Miss.)	T2—762 993
Alcyonaria	593.6
Aldabra Island (Seychelles)	T2—696
Aldehydes	547.036
aromatic chemistry	547.636
chemical engineering	661.85
Alder	583.976
Alderney (England)	T2—423 43
Alderney cattle	
animal husbandry	636.224
zoology	599.735 8
Ale	641.23
commercial processing	663.42
cooking with	641.623
home preparation	641.873
Aleatory composition	
music	781.32
Aleksei Mikhailovich, Czar of Russia	
Russian history	947.048
Alemán, Miguel	
Mexican history	972.082 7
Alemanni literatures	839
Alentejo (Portugal)	T2—469 5
Aleppo (Syria : Province)	T2—569 13
Alessandrí Rodriguez, Jorge	
Chilean history	983.064 4
Alessandria (Italy : Province)	T2—451 4
Alethopteris	561.597
Aleurone grains	574.874
Aleut	T5—971
Aleut language	497.1
	T6—971
Aleutian Islands (Alaska)	T2—798 4
Aleutian Range	T2—798 4
Alexander County (Ill.)	T2—773 999
Alexander County (N.C.)	T2—756 795
Alexander I, Emperor of Russia	
Russian history	947.072
Alexander II, Emperor of Russia	
Russian history	947.081
Alexander III, Emperor of Russia	
Russian history	947.082

Alkalis	546.32	Allen County (Ky.)	T2—769 732
chemical engineering	661.3	Allen County (Ohio)	T2—771 42
toxicology	615.922	Allen Parish (La.)	T2—763 58
Alkaloidal plants	581.63	Allendale County (S.C.)	T2—757 77
agriculture	633.7	Allende Gossens, Salvador	
botany	581.63	Chilean history	983.064 6
Alkaloids	574.192 42	Allentiac language	498.4
biochemistry	574.192 42		T6—984
human	612.015 72	Allerdale (England : District)	T2—427 87
chemistry	547.72	Allergenic plants	
pharmacognosy	615.321	botany	581.67
Alkanes	547.411	Allergies	
chemical engineering	661.814	cooking for	641.563 1
Alkenes	547.412	incidence	614.599 3
chemical engineering	661.814	medicine	616.97
Alkylation	547.21	pediatrics	618.929 7
chemical engineering	660.284 41	see also Diseases (Human)	
Alkynes	547.413	Alliaceous plants	584.324
chemical engineering	661.814	Alliances	327.116
All-cargo plane services	387.744	Allied fire insurance lines	368.12
All-risk insurance coverage	368.09	see also Insurance	
All-star games (Baseball)	796.357 648	Allier (France : Dept.)	T2—445 7
All-terrain vehicles	388.34	Allies	355.031
driving	629.283 042	military forces	355.356
engineering	629.220 42	World War I	940.332
military engineering	623.747	World War II	940.533 2
repair	629.287 042	Alligator pear	583.931
transportation services	388.34	agriculture	634.653
see also Automotive vehicles		Alligators	597.98
All-volunteer army	355.223 62	big game hunting	799.279 8
All-year school	371.236	farming	639.398
Allamakee County (Iowa)	T2—777 33	Alliopteris	561.597
Allanridge (South Africa)	T2—685 3	Allocation of staff	658.312 8
Allegan County (Mich.)	T2—774 14	public administration	350.14
Allegany County (Md.)	T2—752 94	central governments	351.14
Allegany County (N.Y.)	T2—747 84	local governments	352.005 14
Alleghany County (N.C.)	T2—756 832	Allodium	333.323 2
Alleghany County (Va.)	T2—755 816	Alloeocoela	595.123
Allegheny County (Pa.)	T2—748 85	Allopathy	610
Allegheny Mountains	T2—748 7	therapeutic system	615.531
Pennsylvania	T2—748 7	Allorhythmia	
West Virginia	T2—754 8	medicine	616.128
Allegheny River (Pa. and		see also Cardiovascular system	
N.Y.)	T2—748 6	Allotheria	569.17
Allegheny spurge	583.394	Alloy binary systems	
Allegory		metallurgy	669.94
art representation	704.946	Alloys	669
Biblical	220.68	chemistry	546.3
literature	808.801 5	foundation materials	624.153 6
history and criticism	809.915	materials science	620.16
specific literatures	T3B—080 15	metallography	669.95
history and criticism	T3B—091 5	metallurgy	669
paintings	753.6	ship design	623.818 2
Alleles	575.2	shipbuilding	623.820 7
Allemanskraal Dam	T2—685 3	structural engineering	624.182
Allen, Bog of	T2—418 5	Allspice	583.42
Allen County (Ind.)	T2—772 74	agriculture	633.83
Allen County (Kan.)	T2—781 94	Alluvial mining	622.292 7

Alto voices (continued)
men's   782.86
  choral and mixed voices   782.86
  single voices   783.86
women's   782.68
  choral and mixed voices   782.68
  single voices   783.68
Altoona (Pa.)   T2—748 75
Altos, Los (Guatemala :
  Province)   T2—728 18
Altotau (Papua New Guinea)   T2—954 1
Altruism
  ethical systems   171.8
  personality trait   155.232
Alumina   553.67
  economic geology   553.67
  technology   666.72
Aluminum   669.722
  architectural construction   721.044 772 2
  building construction   693.772 2
  building material   691.872 2
  chemical engineering   661.067 3
  chemistry   546.673
  decorative arts   739.57
  economic geology   553.492 6
  foundation materials   624.153 86
  materials science   620.186
  metallography   669.957 22
  metallurgy   669.722
  metalworking   673.722
  mining   622.349 26
  physical metallurgy   669.967 22
  ship design   623.818 26
  shipbuilding   623.820 7
  structural engineering   624.182 6
  toxicology   615.925 673
  see also Chemicals, Metals
Aluminum lithography   763.23
Aluminum soaps   668.125
Alumni
  social group   T7—379
Alunite
  mineralogy   549.755
Alveolar abscesses
  dentistry   617.632
  see also Dentistry
Alvsborgs lan (Sweden)   T2—486
Alwa (Kingdom)   962.620 22
Alyn and Deeside (Wales)   T2—429 36
Alzheimer's disease   362.196 831
  geriatrics   618.976 831
  medicine   616.831
  social services   362.196 831
  see also Nervous system
AM radio stations   384.545 3
  engineering   621.384
  facilities   384.545 3
  organizations   384.540 65

AM radio systems   621.384 153
Amador County (Calif.)   T2—794 42
Amalgamations of corporations   338.83
Amalgams
  dentistry   617.675
  see also Dentistry
Amambay (Paraguay)   T2—892 137
Amanoris   589.41
Amanzimtoti (South Africa)   T2—684 55
Amapá (Brazil : Territory)   T2—811 6
Amaranth   583.913
Amaranthaceae   583.913
Amaryllidales   584.25
Amaryllis   584.25
Amasya Ili (Turkey)   T2—563
Amateur circuses   791.3
Amateur motion pictures   791.433
  performing arts   791.433
  photography   778.534 9
    cinematography   778.534 9
    projection   778.554 9
Amateur radio   384.54
  communication services   384.54
  engineering   621.384 16
  international law   341.757 7
  law   343.099 45
  public administration   351.874 54
Amateur theater   792.022 2
Amateur workshops   684.08
Amateurs
  social group   T7—090 9
Amatole Range   T2—687 92
Amaurotic idiocy
  medicine   616.858 845
  see also Mental retardation
Amazon River   T2—811
  Brazil   T2—811
  Peru   T2—854 3
Amazonas (Brazil)   T2—811 3
Amazonas (Colombia)   T2—861 7
Amazonas (Peru)   T2—854 6
Amazonas (Venezuela :
  Territory)   T2—876 4
Ambari hemp   583.17
  fiber crop   633.56
Ambassadors   327.209 2
  occupational group   T7—352 2
Amber   553.29
  carving   736.6
  economic geology   553.29
Amber Valley (England :
  District)   T2—425 16
Ambition
  social psychology   302.54
Amblypygi   595.453 6
Amblystomoidea   597.65
Ambulance services   362.188
  armed forces   355.345

Ambulance services (continued)
  South African War   968.048 7
  Spanish-American War, 1898   973.897 5
  Vietnamese War   959.704 37
  World War I   940.475 3
  World War II   940.547 53
  see also Health services
Ambulances   362.188
  driving   629.283 34
  engineering   629.222 34
  health services   362.188
    see also Health services
  military engineering   623.747 24
  military equipment   355.83
  repair   629.287 234
  sanitation services   363.729 7
    see also Waste control
Ambulatory services   362.12
  see also Health services
Ambush tactics   355.422
Amebiasis
  incidence   614.53
  medicine   616.936
  see also Communicable
    diseases (Human)
Amebic dysentery
  incidence   614.516
  medicine   616.935 3
  see also Communicable
    diseases (Human)
Amele language   499.12
    T6—991 2
Amelia County (Va.)   T2—755 634
Amenhetep IV, King of Egypt
  Egyptian history   932.014
Amenhotep, King of Egypt
  Egyptian history   932.014
Amenorrhea
  gynecology   618.172
  see also Female genital system
Amens
  music   782.295
American Arctic seawaters   551.468 7
    T2—163 27
American Baptist Association   286.136
  see also Baptists
American Baptist Churches in the
  U.S.A.   286.131
  see also Baptists
American Baptist Convention   286.131
  see also Baptists
American buffalo   599.735 8
  animal husbandry   636.292
American College Testing
  Program   378.166 2
American English dialects   427.97
    T6—21
American English pronunciation   421.54

American English spelling   421.54
American Evangelical Lutheran
  Church   284.133 2
  see also Lutheran church
American Falls Reservoir   T2—796 49
American Federation of Labor   331.883 209 7
American Federation of Labor
  and Congress of Industrial
  Organizations   331.880 97
American football   796.332
American hemp (Malvalceae)   583.17
  fiber crop   633.56
American Independent Party   324.273 3
American Indian languages   497
    T6—97
  South America   498
    T6—98
American Indian literatures   897
  South America   898
American Indians   305.897
    T5—97
  South America   T5—98
  see also American native
    peoples
American Legion   369.186 1
American literature (English)   810
American Lutheran Church   284.131
  see also Lutheran church
American Muslim Mission   297.87
American native languages   497
    T6—97
  South America   498
    T6—98
American native literatures   897
  South America   898
American native peoples   305.897
    T5—97
  military troops
    United States Revolutionary
      War   973.343
    War of 1812   973.524 2
    World War II   940.540 3
  social aspects   305.897
  South America   T5—98
American Nazi Party   324.273 38
American organs   786.55
  see also Keyboard instruments
American Party (U.S.)   324.273 2
American Reformed Church   285.7
  see also Reformed Church
    (American Reformed)
American revised version Bible   220.520 4
American Revolution   973.3
American saddle horse
  animal husbandry   636.13
  zoology   599.725
American Samoa   996.13
    T2—961 3

American standard version Bible 220.520 4
American Veterans of World
   War II, Korea, and Vietnam 369.186 2
American Whig Party 324.273 23
Americans (U.S.) T5—13
Americas T2—181 2
Americium 546.441
  see also Chemicals
Amerindians 305.897
                            T5—97
  South America T5—98
  see also American native
    peoples
Amersfoort (South Africa :
  District) T2—682 7
Amethysts 553.87
Amhara (African people) T5—928
Amharic language 492.87
                            T6—928 7
Amharic literature 892.87
Amherst (N.S.) T2—716 11
Amherst, William Pitt, Earl
  Indian history 954.031 3
Amherst County (Va.) T2—755 496
Ami (Taiwan people) T5—992 5
Amiante (Quebec) T2—714 573
Amides 547.042
  chemical engineering 661.894
Amiiformes 597.41
  paleozoology 567.4
Amin, Idi
  Ugandan history 967.610 4
Amination 547.25
  chemical engineering 660.284 45
Amindivi Island T2—548 1
Amines 547.042
  chemical engineering 661.894
Amino acids 574.192 45
  biochemistry 574.192 45
    human 612.015 75
  chemistry 547.75
  see also Proteins
Aminoglycosides
  pharmacology 615.329
Amirante Islands T2—696
Amish churches 289.73
  see also Mennonite Church
Amish cooking 641.566
Amite County (Miss.) T2—762 24
Amitosis 574.876 22
Amman (Jordan : District) T2—569 58
Ammeters 621.374 4
Ammonia 546.711 22
  chemical engineering 661.34
Ammonite language 492.6
                            T6—926
Ammonitoidea 564.53
Ammonium chlorate 662.27

Ammonium fertilizers 631.841
  chemical engineering 668.624 1
  use 631.841
Ammonium hydroxide 546.711 22
  chemical engineering 661.34
Ammonium nitrate fertilizer 631.842
  chemical engineering 668.624 2
  use 631.842
Ammonium picrate 662.27
Ammonium salts 546.711 22
  chemical engineering 661.5
Ammunition 355.825
  military 355.825
    engineering 623.45
    use 355.825
  small arms engineering
    military 623.451
  small arms manufacturing
    technology 683.406
Amnesia
  medicine 616.852 32
  see also Mental illness
Amnesty 364.65
  penology 364.65
Amniocentesis
  obstetrics 618.320 42
Amniotic fluid
  human diseases
    obstetrics 618.34
  human physiology 612.63
Amoebiasis
  incidence 614.53
  medicine 616.936
  see also Communicable
    diseases (Human)
Amoebic dysentery
  incidence 614.516
  medicine 616.935 3
  see also Communicable
    diseases (Human)
Amoebida 593.117
Amorites T5—921
Amorphous solids 530.413
Amos (Biblical book) 224.8
Amoy dialect 495.17
                            T6—951 7
Ampere-hour meters 621.374 4
Amphetamine abuse 362.299
  medicine 616.864
  personal health 613.84
  social welfare 362.299
  see also Substance abuse
Amphibia 597.6
  see also Amphibians
Amphibians 597.6
  art representation 704.943 2
  commercial hunting 639.13
  drawing 743.676

Amphibians (continued)	
farming	639.37
paleozoology	567.6
resource economics	333.957
small game hunting	799.257 6
Amphibious air-cushion vehicles	
engineering	629.325
military engineering	623.748 5
Amphibious operations	355.46
marine forces	359.964 6
Amphibious planes	387.733 48
engineering	629.133 348
transportation services	387.733 48
see also Aircraft	
Amphiboles	553.672
mineralogy	549.66
Amphineura	594.19
paleozoology	564.19
Amphipoda	595.371
paleozoology	565.37
Amphissa (Greece)	T2—383
Amphitheaters	796.068
architecture	725.827
Amphoteric salts	546.342
chemical engineering	661.4
Amplifiers	621.381 535
electronic circuits	621.381 535
radio engineering	621.384 12
Amplitude-modulation radio	
systems	621.384 153
Amplitude modulators	
electronic circuits	621.381 536 2
Amplitude of sound	534.3
Amputation of limbs	
surgery	617.580 59
Amsterdam (Netherlands)	T2—492 352
Amsterdam Island	969.9
	T2—699
Amulets	133.44
numismatics	737.23
religious significance	291.37
Islam	297.33
Amundsen Sea	551.469 4
	T2—167 4
Amur (R.S.F.S.R.)	T2—577
Amur River (China and	
R.S.F.S.R.)	T2—577
Amusement parks	791.068
architecture	725.76
area planning	711.558
landscape architecture	712.5
recreation	791.068
Amusements	790
journalism	070.444
law	344.099
see also Recreation	
AMVETS (Veterans)	369.186 2

Amyl nitrite abuse	362.299
medicine	616.86
personal health	613.8
social welfare	362.299
see also Substance abuse	
Amylases	574.192 54
see also Enzymes	
Amyloidosis	
medicine	616.399 5
see also Digestive system	
Amytrophic lateral sclerosis	
medicine	616.83
see also Nervous system	
An-Najaf (Iraq : Province)	T2—567 5
An-Nil (Sudan : Province)	T2—625
An-Nil al-Abyad (Sudan :	
Province)	T2—626 4
An-Nil al-Azraq (Sudan)	T2—626 4
Anabaptists	284.3
religious group	T7—243
see also Christian	
denominations	
Anabolism	574.133
see also Metabolism	
Anacardiaceae	583.28
fruit crops	634.44
Anaerobic digestion	628.354
Anaerobic respiration	574.128
animals	591.128
plants	581.128
Anaesthetics	
pharmacodynamics	615.781
Anagrams	793.73
Anahim Lake (B.C.)	T2—711 75
Analgesic abuse	362.299
medicine	616.86
personal health	613.8
social welfare	362.299
see also Substance abuse	
Analgesics	
pharmacodynamics	615.783
see also Nervous system	
Analog circuits	
electronics	621.381 5
Analog communications	621.382
Analog computers	004.19
electronic	004.19
engineering	621.391 9
nonelectronic	004.9
Analog instruments	
technology	681.1
Analog-to-digital converters	004.64
engineering	621.398 14
Analogy	
logic	169
Analysis (Mathematics)	515
Analysis of covariance	519.538
Analysis of variance	519.538

Analysis situs	514
Analytic curves	516.362
Analytic functions	515.73
Analytic geometry	516.3
Analytic number theory	512.73
Analytic spaces	515.223
Analytic surfaces	516.362
Analytic topology	514.7
Analytic trigonometry	516.34
Analytical accounting	657.48
Analytical bibliography	010.42
Analytical biochemistry	574.192 85
human	612.015 85
Analytical chemistry	543
organic	547.3
Analytical guides	
music	780.15
Analytical mechanics	531.015 15
Analytical philosophy	146.4
Anambra State (Nigeria)	T2—669 48
Ananda Mahidol, King of	
Thailand	
Thai history	959.304 3
Anaphrodisiacs	
pharmacodynamics	615.766
see also Genital system	
Anapsida	
paleozoology	567.92
Anapsidea (Mollusks)	
paleozoology	564.37
Anarchism	335.83
economics	335.83
political ideology	320.57
Anarchist communities	
economics	335.9
Anarchists	335.830 92
political group	T7—335
Anarcho-syndicalism	335.82
economics	335.82
political ideology	320.57
Anarchy	
political system	321.07
Anaspidacea	595.379
Anatidae	598.41
Anatolia	T2—561
Anatolian languages	491.998
	T6—919 98
Anatomic embryology	
human	611.013
Anatomy	574.4
animal embryology	591.332
animals	591.4
domestic animals	636.089 1
drawing	
animals	743.6
human	743.49
embryology	574.332
human	611
Anatomy (continued)	
microorganisms	576.14
plant embryology	581.332
plants	581.4
Anaxagorean philosophy	182.8
Anbar (Iraq : Province)	T2—567 4
ANC (African National	
Congress)	324.268 083
Ancash (Peru)	T2—852 1
Ancestors	T1—085 3
	T7—043
family relationships	306.874
religious worship	291.213
Ancestry	929.1
Anchor ice	551.344
Anchorages	387.1
engineering	627.22
see also Ports	
Anchors	623.862
Anchovy	597.55
fishing	639.275 5
Ancienne-Lorette (Quebec)	T2—714 471
Ancient Arabic Order of the	
Nobles of the Mystic Shrine	
for North America	366.16
Ancient architecture	722
Ancient civilization	930
Ancient Egyptians	T5—931
Ancient government	321.14
Ancient Greeks	T5—81
Ancient history	930
	T1—090 1
Ancient law	340.53
Ancient philosophy	180
Ancient remedies	
therapeutics	615.899
Ancient sculpture	732
Ancient world	T2—3
Ancistrocladaceae	583.167
Ancona (Italy : Province)	T2—456 71
Ancyclostomiasis	
incidence	614.555 4
medicine	616.965 4
see also Communicable	
diseases (Human)	
Andalusia (Spain)	T2—468
Andalusite	
mineralogy	549.62
Andaman and Nicobar Islands	T2—548 8
Andaman Sea	551.467 65
	T2—165 65
Andamanese	T5—991 1
Andean-Equatorial languages	498.3
	T6—983
Andean languages	498.32
	T6—983 2
Anderson County (Kan.)	T2—781 672
Anderson County (Ky.)	T2—769 463

Anglican Communion (continued)
theology | 230.3
Anglican sacred music | 781.713
  public worship | 782.322 3
    music | 782.322 3
    religion | 264.030 2
Anglicans
  biography | 283.092
  religious group | T7—23
Angling | 799.12
Anglo-Boer War, 1880-1881 | 968.204 6
Anglo-Boer War, 1899-1902 | 968.048
Anglo-Dutch Wars, 1652-1653 | 949.204
Anglo-Egyptian Sudan | 962.403
  | T2—624
Anglo-Indians | T5—914 11
Anglo-Irish War, 1919-1921 | 941.508 21
Anglo-Saxon language | 429
  | T6—29
Anglo-Saxon literature | 829
Anglo-Saxons | T5—2
Anglo-Spanish War, 1739-1741 | 946.055
Angola | 967.3
  | T2—673
Angolans | T5—967 3
Angolese | T5—967 3
Angoni (African people) | T5—963 98
Angoni language | T6—963 98
Angora cat
  animal husbandry | 636.83
  see also Cats
Angora goats
  animal husbandry | 636.398 5
  zoology | 599.735 8
Angora Ili (Turkey) | T2—563
Angoram (Papua New
  Guinea) | T2—957 5
Angoulême, House of (French
  history) | 944.028
Angoumois (France) | T2—446 5
Angra do Heroísmo (Azores :
  District) | T2—469 9
Anguilla | 972.973
  | T2—729 73
Anguilliformes | 597.51
Angular momentum (Nuclear
  physics) | 539.725
Angus (Scotland) | T2—412 6
Angus cattle
  animal husbandry | 636.223
  zoology | 599.735 8
Anhalt (Germany) | T2—431 84
Anhidrosis
  medicine | 616.56
Anhimidae | 598.41
Anhui Sheng (China) | T2—512 25
Anhwei Province (China) | T2—512 25

Anhydrite
  mineralogy | 549.752
Anhydrous sulfates
  mineralogy | 549.752
Animal babies | 591.3
  domestic animals | 636.07
  mammals | 599.03
Animal behavior | 591.51
  comparative psychology | 156
Animal black | 662.93
Animal body disposal | 363.78
Animal combat sports | 791.8
  ethics | 175.6
    see also Recreation—ethics
  performing arts | 791.8
Animal communication | 591.59
Animal-derived drugs
  pharmacology | 615.36
Animal-derived poisons
  toxicology | 615.94
Animal diseases | 591.2
  agricultural economics | 338.14
  agriculture | 636.089 6
Animal fats | 665.2
  food technology | 664.3
  home cooking | 641.66
  home economics | 641.36
  industrial | 665.2
Animal feeds | 636.085 5
  commercial processing | 664.76
  use | 636.085 5
Animal fibers | 338.476 773
  materials science | 620.197
  production economics | 338.476 773
  textiles | 677.3
    arts | 746.043
    see also Textiles
Animal food
  manufacturing technology | 664.66
Animal glue | 668.32
Animal hospitals | 636.083 2
Animal husbandry | 636
  equipment manufacturing
    technology | 681.763 6
  production economics | 338.176
  public administration | 351.823 36
Animal industry | 338.176
  law | 343.076 6
  public administration | 351.823 36
Animal intelligence | 156.39
Animal judging | 636.081 1
Animal magnetism | 154.72
Animal manures | 631.86
  agricultural use | 631.86
  waste technology | 628.746 6
Animal neuston | 592.092
Animal oils | 665.2
  home cooking | 641.66

Annexation of territory	320.12	Anostraca	595.32
government	320.12	paleozoology	565.32
local government	320.859	Anschluss (Austrian history)	943.605 22
law	342.041 3	Anseriformes	598.41
Annihilation (Nuclear particles)	539.75	paleozoology	568.4
Annihilationism	236.23	Anson County (N.C.)	T2—756 753
Anniversaries	394.2	Answers	
see also Celebrations		books of miscellaneous facts	030
Annobón (Equatorial Guinea)	T2—671 86	study and teaching	T1—076
Annonaceous fruit	583.115	Ant lions	595.747
agriculture	634.41	Antacids	
Annonales	583.115	pharmacodynamics	615.73
Annotations to cases	348.047	see also Digestive system	
Annotations to laws	348.027	Antakya Ili (Turkey)	T2—564
Announcements		Antalya Ili (Turkey)	T2—564
etiquette	395.4	Antananarivo (Madagascar :	
Announcing		Province)	T2—691
radio performances	791.443	Antarctic regions	T2—989
television performances	791.453	Antarctic waters	551.469
Annual publications	050		T2—167
	T1—05	Antarctica	T2—989
almanacs	030	Antártica Chilena (Chile :	
encyclopedia yearbooks	030	Province)	T2—836 48
publishing	070.572	Ante-Nicene church	270.1
Annual variations		Anteaters	599.31
air temperatures	551.525 3	Antelope County (Neb.)	T2—782 55
Annual wages	331.216 2	Antelopes	599.735 8
Annuals (Plants)		big game hunting	799.277 358
floriculture	635.931 2	Antennas	621.382 4
see also Plants		communications engineering	621.382 4
Annuals (Publications)	050	radar engineering	621.384 83
	T1—05	radio engineering	621.384 135
almanacs	030	satellite communication	621.382 54
encyclopedia yearbooks	030	television engineering	621.388 35
publishing	070.572	Antenuptial contracts	346.016
Annuities		Anterior chambers (Eyes)	
insurance	368.37	human physiology	612.841
see also Insurance		see also Eyes	
tax law	343.064	Anthelmintics	
Annulment	346.016 6	pharmacodynamics	615.733
Annunciation to Mary	232.912	Anthems	782.265
Anodynes		choral and mixed voices	782.526 5
pharmacodynamics	615.783	single voices	783.092 65
see also Nervous system		Anthers	
Anointing of the sick	234.167	anatomy	582.130 446 3
public worship	265.7	Anthocerotae	588.32
Anoka County (Minn.)	T2—776 65	Anthologies	080
Anomochloeae	584.93	literature	808.8
Anomura	595.384 4	specific literatures	T3B—08
Anonymous works		Anthozoa	593.6
bibliographies	014	paleozoology	563.6
Anopla	595.124	Anthracenes	547.616
Anoplura	595.751 2	chemical engineering	661.816
paleozoology	565.75	Anthracite coal	553.25
Anorexia nervosa	362.25	economic geology	553.25
medicine	616.852 62	mining	622.335
social welfare	362.25	properties	662.622 5
see also Mental illness			

Antineutrons	539.721 3
Antinomianism	273.6
Antioch (Turkey)	T2—564
ancient	939.43
	T2—394 3
Antione-Labelle (Quebec)	T2—714 225
Antioquia (Colombia : Dept.)	T2—861 26
Antiparticles	539.72
Antipersonnel devices	623.451 4
Antipodes Islands	T2—931 1
Antiprotons	539.721 2
Antipyretics	
pharmacodynamics	615.75
Antique (Philippines)	T2—599 5
Antique furniture	749.1
Antiques	745.1
Antiquities	930.1
international law	341.767 7
law	344.094
Antisepsis	
obstetrics	618.89
public health	614.48
surgery	617.910 1
Antisocial personality disorders	
medicine	616.858 2
see also Mental illness	
Antisocial persons	305.906 92
	T1—086 92
Antispasmodics	
pharmacodynamics	615.784
see also Nervous system	
Antisubmarine reconnaissance	
(Air warfare)	358.45
Antisubmarine warfare	359.93
World War I	940.451 6
World War II	940.545 16
Antisynclines	551.86
Antitank artillery forces	358.12
Antitoxins	
pharmacology	615.375
Antitrust law	343.072 1
Antitrust policies	338.8
Antitrust violations	364.168
Antlerite	
mineralogy	549.755
Antofagasta (Chile : Province)	T2—831 38
Antofagasta (Chile : Region)	T2—831 3
Antoniaceae	583.74
Antonines	255.18
church history	271.18
Antonym dictionaries	413.1
specific languages	T4—31
specific subjects	T1—03
Antrim (Northern Ireland : Borough)	T2—416 12
Antrim (Northern Ireland : County)	T2—416 1
Antrim County (Mich.)	T2—774 85
Ants	595.796
Antsiranana (Madagascar : Province)	T2—691
Antwerp (Belgium)	T2—493 222
Antwerp (Belgium : Province)	T2—493 22
Anura	597.8
paleozoology	567.8
Anus	
human anatomy	611.35
human diseases	
medicine	616.35
human physiology	612.36
surgery	617.555
see also Digestive system	
Anvers (Belgium)	T2—493 222
Anvers (Belgium : Province)	T2—493 22
Anvil Island (B.C. : Island)	T2—711 31
Anvils	682
blacksmithing	682
music	786.884 3
see also Percussion instruments	
Anxiety	152.46
Anxiety neuroses	
medicine	616.852 23
see also Mental illness	
Anyi (African people)	T5—963 385
Anyi language	496.338 5
	T6—963 385
Anzoátegui (Venezuela : State)	T2—875 2
Aomori-ken (Japan)	T2—521 12
Aorta	
human anatomy	611.13
human diseases	
medicine	616.138
human physiology	612.133
see also Cardiovascular system	
Aortic valve	
human anatomy	611.12
human diseases	
medicine	616.125
human physiology	612.17
see also Cardiovascular system	
Aosta (Italy)	T2—451 1
Aosta, Valle d'	T2—451 1
AP ammunition	623.451 8
Apache County (Ariz.)	T2—791 37
Apache Indians	T5—972
Apache languages	497.2
	T6—972
Apachean languages	497.2
	T6—972
Apalachicola River (Fla.)	T2—759 92
Apartheid	
political ideology	320.560 968
Apartment-house districts	
area planning	711.58

Appenzell Inner-Rhoden
(Switzerland)   T2—494 714
Apperception
   psychology   153.73
Appetite
   philosophical anthropology   128.3
Appetite disorders
   medicine   616.852 6
   see also Digestive system,
     Mental illness
Appetizers   641.812
Apple blossom (Escalloniaceae)   583.397
Apples   641.341 1
   botany   583.372
   commercial processing   664.804 11
   cooking   641.641 1
   orchard crop   634.11
Appleton layers   538.767 4
Application generators   005.13
Application programming   005.1
Application programs   005.3
Applied chemistry   660
Applied ethics   170
   see also Ethical problems
Applied geology   553
Applied linguistics   418
     T1—014
   specific languages   T4—8
Applied mathematics   519
Applied mechanics   620.1
Applied numerical analysis   519.4
Applied nutrition
   animal husbandry   636.085 2
   health   613.2
   home economics   641.1
Applied physics   621
Applied psychology   158
Applied sciences   600
Applied sociology   360
Appling County (Ga.)   T2—758 784
Appliqué
   textile arts   746.445
Appointment power (Legislative
   bodies)   328.345 5
Appomattox County (Va.)   T2—755 625
Apportionment (Legislatures)   328.334 5
   law   342.053
Appraisals
   land economics   333.332
Appreciation
   arts   701.1
   literature   801
   music   781.17
Apprentices
   economics   331.55
Apprenticeship
   economics   331.259 22
     union control   331.889 4

Apprenticeship training
   secondary education   373.27
Approach piloting   623.892 9
Appropriate technology
   economics   338.927
Appropriation of public funds   350.722 36
   central governments   351.722 36
   local governments   352.123 6
Approval plans
   library acquisitions   025.233
Approximation (Mathematics)   511.4
   algebra   512.924
   arithmetic   513.24
Apraxia
   medicine   616.855 2
   see also Communicative
     disorders
Apricots   641.342 1
   botany   583.372
   commercial processing   664.804 21
   cooking   641.642 1
   orchard crop   634.21
Aprons   391.44
   commercial technology   687.19
     leather   685.22
   see also Accessories (Clothing)
Apses
   Christian church architecture   726.593
Aptandraceae   583.26
Apterous insects   595.751
   paleozoology   565.75
Apterygiformes   598.54
   paleozoology   568.5
Apterygota   595.71
   paleozoology   565.71
Aptitude tests   153.94
   education   371.262
   personnel selection   658.311 25
Aptitudes
   psychology   153.9
Apulia (Italy)   T2—457 5
   ancient   T2—377
Apure (Venezuela)   T2—874 2
Apurímac (Peru)   T2—852 94
Aqaba, Gulf of   551.467 33
     T2—165 33
Aqaid (Islam)   297.2
Aquaculture   639.8
Aquariums   597.007 4
   fish culture   639.34
Aquatic biological resources   333.952
   public administration   351.823 28
Aquatic biology   574.92
Aquatic ecology   574.526 3
Aquatic exercises   613.716
Aquatic gardens   635.967 4
Aquatic plants   581.92
   floriculture   635.967 4

Arborvitae	585.2
Arbuckle Mountains (Okla.)	T2—766 5
Arc furnace practice	669.142 4
Arc length	
calculus	515.43
integral geometry	516.362
Arc lighting	621.325
Arc welding	671.521 2
Arcade games	794.822
Arcades	721.41
architecture	721.41
construction	690.141
Arcadia (Greece)	T2—495 2
ancient	T2—388
Arcellinida	593.118
Arch bridges	388
construction	624.6
see also Bridges	
Archaeobacteria	589.9
Archaeoceti	569.5
Archaeocyatha	563.47
Archaeologists	930.109 2
occupational group	T7—93
Archaeology	930.1
ancient places	931–939
Bible	220.93
law	344.094
modern places	940–990
Archaeology and religion	291.175
Christianity	261.55
natural theology	215.8
Archaeopteris	561.597
Archaeornithes	568.22
Archaeostraca	565.36
Archaisms (Linguistics)	417.7
specific languages	T4—7
Archangel (R.S.F.S.R. :	
Oblast)	T2—472 3
Archangiaceae	589.98
Archean era	551.712
geology	551.712
Arched harps	787.94
see also Stringed instruments	
Archeogastropoda	594.32
paleozoology	564.32
Archeology	930.1
see also Archaeology	
Archeozoic era	551.712
geology	551.712
paleontology	560.171
Archer County (Tex.)	T2—764 543
Archer River	T2—943 8
Archerfish	597.58
Archers	799.320 92
sports group	T7—799 3
Archery	799.32

Arches (Structural element)	721.41
architecture	721.41
construction	690.141
structural engineering	624.177 5
concrete	624.183 45
Arches (Structures)	725.96
Arches National Park (Utah)	T2—792 58
Archiacanthocephala	595.13
Archiannelida	595.142
Archipelago of the Recherche	T2—941 7
Architarbi	565.49
Architects	720.92
occupational group	T7—72
Architectural acoustics	
construction	690.2
Architectural decoration	729
Architectural design	729
Architectural drawing	720.284
Architectural drawings	720.222
Architectural orders	721.36
architecture	721.36
construction	690.13
Architectural schools and styles	720.9
ancient	722
construction details	721
design and decoration	729
Architectural structure	721
Architecture	720
art representation	704.944
landscapes	712
naval	623.81
painting	758.7
religious significance	291.37
Christianity	246.9
see also Arts—religious	
significance	
see also Arts	
Architecture (Computer science)	004.22
computers	004.22
databases	005.74
engineering	621.392
network	004.65
Archival materials	
cataloging	025.341 4
library treatment	025.171 4
records management	651.56
Archive buildings	
architecture	725.15
Archives	027
law	344.092
operations	025
public records management	350.714 6
central governments	351.714 6
local governments	352.164 6
publishing	070.594
relationships	021
Archosauria	
paleozoology	567.97

Armed services	355
cooking	641.57
law	343.013
libraries	027.65
life insurance	368.364
see also Insurance	
relation to state	322.5
reserves	355.37
law	343.012
Armenia	T2—566 2
ancient	T2—395 5
Turkey	T2—566 2
USSR	T2—479 2
Armenian Church	281.62
see also Eastern churches	
Armenian language	491.992
	T6—919 92
Biblical texts	220.49
Armenian literature	891.992
Armenian S.S.R.	T2—479 2
Armenians	T5—919 92
Armidale (N.S.W.)	T2—944 4
Armies (Military units)	355.31
Arminians	284.9
religious group	T7—249
see also Christian	
denominations	
Armistice	
law	341.66
World War I	940.439
Armor (Wearable)	623.441
art metalwork	739.75
Armor-piercing ammunition	623.451 8
Armored cavalry	358.18
Armored forces	358.18
Armored personnel carriers	358.183
engineering	623.747 5
military equipment	358.183
Armored vehicles	358.183
engineering	623.747 5
military equipment	358.183
Armored warfare	358.18
Armorial bearings	929.82
Armories	355.75
architecture	725.18
Arms (Human)	612.97
human physiology	612.97
regional medicine	617.574
surgery	617.574 059
see also Upper extremities	
(Human)	
Arms (Military)	355.82
art metalwork	739.7
customs	399
engineering	623.4
military science	355.82
Arms (Small firearms)	683.4
civil rights issue	323.43

Arms (Small firearms) (continued)	
manufacturing technology	683.4
see also Gun control	
Arms control	327.174
international politics	327.174
law	341.733
military science	355.03
verification of specific weapons	355.82
Armstrong (B.C.)	T2—711 5
Armstrong County (Pa.)	T2—748 88
Armstrong County (Tex.)	T2—764 833
Army engineer corps	358.22
Arnhem (Netherlands)	T2—492 18
Arnhem Land (N.T.)	T2—942 95
Arnold, Benedict	
treason	973.382
Arnsberg (Germany :	
Regierungsbezirk)	T2—435 63
Aromatic compounds	547.6
chemical engineering	661.8
Aromatic hydrocarbons	
toxicology	615.951 1
Aromatic teas	641.357
home preparation	641.877
see also Herb teas, Tea	
Aromatization	547.21
chemical engineering	660.284 41
Aroostook County (Me.)	T2—741 1
Aroostook River (Me.)	T2—741 1
Arpad dynasty (Hungarian	
history)	943.902
Arpeggiones	787.6
see also Stringed instruments	
Arpeggios	781.252
Arraignment	345.072
Arrangement (Music)	781.37
Array processing	004.35
Array processors	004.35
Arrest	363.232
law	345.052 7
police services	363.232
Arrhythmia	
medicine	616.128
see also Cardiovascular system	
Arrondissements	
government	320.83
public administration	352.007 3
Arrow grass	584.744
Arrow Lakes (B.C.)	T2—711 62
Arrowhead (Plant)	584.721
Arrowroot	584.21
food technology	664.23
starch crop	633.68
Arrows	
manufacturing technology	
military equipment	623.441
Arrowworm	595.186
Ars antiqua	780.902

Ars nova	780.902	Arteries (continued)	
Arsenals	355.7	surgery	617.413
architecture	725.18	*see also* Cardiovascular system	
Arsenates		Arteriosclerosis	
mineralogy	549.72	medicine	616.136
Arsenic	669.75	*see also* Cardiovascular system	
chemical engineering	661.071 5	Artesian wells	
chemistry	546.715	engineering	628.114
economic geology	553.47	hydrology	551.498
metallography	669.957 5	Arthabaska (Quebec : County)	T2—714 565
metallurgy	669.75	Arthabaska (Quebec :	
mining	622.347	Regional County	
organic chemistry	547.057 15	Municipality)	T2—714 565
applied	661.895	Arthritis	
physical metallurgy	669.967 5	medicine	616.722
toxicology	615.925 715	*see also* Musculoskeletal system	
see also Chemicals, Metals		Arthrochirotida	563.96
Arsenides		Arthropoda	595.2
mineralogy	549.32	*see also* Arthropods	
Arson	364.164	Arthropods	595.2
law	345.026 4	culture	639.7
Art	700	paleozoology	565.2
investment economics	332.63	Arthroscopy	617.472 059
sociology	306.47	*see also* Musculoskeletal system	
therapeutics	615.851 56	Arthur, Chester Alan	
see also Arts		United States history	973.84
Art and religion	291.175	Arthur, King	
Christianity	261.57	English history	942.014
Art appreciation	701.1	Arthur County (Neb.)	T2—782 785
Art deco	709.040 12	Arthur Range	T2—946 2
sculpture	735.230 412	Arthur River (Tas.)	T2—946 5
Art galleries	708	Artibonite (Haiti : Dept.)	T2—729 44
architecture	727.7	Artichokes	641.353 2
law	344.093	botany	583.55
Art libraries	026.7	commercial processing	664.805 32
Art metalwork	739	cooking	641.653 2
Art metalworkers	739.092	garden crop	635.32
occupational group	T7—739	Articles of Confederation (United	
Art museums	708	States history)	973.318
architecture	727.7	Articulata	593.91
Art music	781.68	paleozoology	563.91
non-Western	781.69	Articulation (Education)	371.218
Western	781.68	Articulation disorders	
Art needlework	746.4	medicine	616.855
Art nouveau	709.034 9	*see also* Communicative	
architecture	724.6	disorders	
decoration	745.444 1	Articulations	
Art paper	676.282 5	human anatomy	611.72
Art therapy		human physiology	612.75
medicine	615.851 56	*see also* Musculoskeletal system	
psychiatry	616.891 656	Artificial arms	
see also Mental illness		manufacturing technology	681.761
Arta (Greece)	T2—495 3	medicine	617.574
Arteries		Artificial environments	
human anatomy	611.13	health	613.5
human diseases		Artificial flies (Fishing)	
medicine	616.13	angling	799.12
human physiology	612.133	making	688.791 2

Artificial flower arrangements	745.92
Artificial flowers	
handicrafts	745.594 3
Artificial gems	666.88
Artificial harbors	387.1
hydraulic engineering	627.2
military engineering	623.64
see also Ports	
Artificial heart	
surgery	617.412 059 2
see also Cardiovascular system	
Artificial insemination	
animal husbandry	636.082 45
ethics	176
see also Reproduction—ethics	
gynecology	618.178
health	613.94
see also Female genital system	
Artificial intelligence	006.3
	T1—028 563
engineering	621.399
Artificial islands	627.98
Artificial languages	499.99
	T6—999 9
literatures	899.99
Artificial legs	
manufacturing technology	685.38
medicine	617.58
Artificial-light photography	778.72
Artificial limbs	
manufacturing technology	681.761
medicine	617.58
Artificial minerals	666.86
Artificial modification of weather	551.68
Artificial organs	
plastic surgery	617.95
Artificial radioactivity	
physics	539.753
Artificial recharge of	
groundwater	627.56
Artificial respiration	
medicine	617.18
Artificial road surfaces	625.8
Artificial satellites	
engineering	629.46
flight	629.434
weather reporting	551.635 4
Artificial satellites in telecommunication	
international law	341.757 7
law	343.099 4
Artificial stone	666.89
architectural construction	721.044 4
building construction	693.4
building materials	691.3
foundation materials	624.153 39
materials science	620.139

Artificial teeth	
dentistry	617.69
see also Dentistry	
Artificial tissue	
plastic surgery	617.95
Artigas (Uruguay : Dept.)	T2—895 36
Artillery	355.821
art metalwork	739.742
military engineering	623.41
military equipment	355.821
Artillery ballistics	623.51
Artillery forces	358.12
Artillery installations	355.73
Artillery plant (Botany)	583.962
Artillery projectiles	623.451 3
Artiodactyla	599.73
paleozoology	569.73
Artisans	609.2
labor economics	331.794
occupational group	T7—6
see also Handicrafters	
Artistic étude form	784.189 49
Artistic lettering	745.61
Artistic principles	700.1
Artistic themes	
folklore	398.27
sociology	398.357
Artists	700.92
labor economics	331.761 7
occupational group	T7—7
Artists' books	700
fine arts	702.81
Artists' marks	702.78
	T1—027 8
Artists' sketches	
criminal investigation	363.258
Artois (France)	T2—442 7
Arts	700
decorative	745
elementary education	372.5
influence on crime	364.254
law	344.097
public administration	350.854
central governments	351.854
local governments	352.945 4
religious significance	291.37
Buddhism	294.343 7
Christianity	246
Hinduism	294.537
Islam	297.3
Judaism	296.4
sociology	306.47
study and teaching	700.7
Arts and crafts	745
sociology	306.489
Artvin Ili (Turkey)	T2—566 2
Aruba	T2—729 86
Arum	584.64

Arun (England : District)	T2—422 67	Ascomycetes	589.23
Arunachal Pradesh (India)	T2—541 63	Ascoseirales	589.45
Arundineae	584.93	Ascothoracica	595.35
Arundinelleae	584.93	paleozoology	565.35
Arusha Region (Tanzania)	T2—678 26	ASEAN	341.247 3
Arusi (Ethiopia)	T2—632	Asellota	595.372
Arya-Samaj	294.556 3	Asepsis	
Aryan languages (Indo-		obstetrics	618.89
European)	410	public health	614.48
	T6—1	surgery	617.910 1
Aryan languages (Indo-Iranian)	491.1	Asexual reproduction	574.162
	T6—911	Ash-Shamaliyah (Sudan :	
Aryan literatures (Indo-Iranian)	891.1	Province)	T2—625
As-Sulaymaniyah (Iraq :		Ash trays	
Province)	T2—567 2	automobile	629.277
Asante (Empire)	966.701 8	manufacturing	688.4
	T2—667	Ash tree	583.74
Asbesberg Range	T2—687 11	Ashante language	496.338 5
Asbestos	553.672		T6—963 385
building material	691.95	Ashanti	966.701 8
economic geology	553.672		T2—667
materials science	620.195	Ashanti (African people)	T5—963 385
mining	622.367 2	Ashburton River	T2—941 3
public safety	363.179 1	Ashe County (N.C.)	T2—756 835
technology	666.72	Asheville (N.C.)	T2—756 88
textiles	677.51	Ashfield (England)	T2—425 25
see also Textiles		Ashford (England : Borough)	T2—422 392
toxicology	615.925 392 24	Ashland County (Ohio)	T2—771 29
Asbestos paper	676.289	Ashland County (Wis.)	T2—775 21
Asbestosis		Ashley County (Ark.)	T2—767 83
medicine	616.244	Ashmore Island	T2—948
workers' compensation law	344.021 8	Ashoka, King of Magadha	
see also Respiratory system		Indian history	934.045
Ascariasis		Ashtabula County (Ohio)	T2—771 34
incidence	614.555 4	Ashur (Ancient city)	T2—35
medicine	616.965 4	Asia	950
see also Communicable			T2—5
diseases (Human)		Asia, Central	958
Ascension Island (Atlantic			T2—58
Ocean)	T2—973	Asia, Southeastern	959
Ascension of Jesus Christ	232.97		T2—59
Ascension of Mary	232.914	Asia Minor	956.1
Ascension Parish (La.)	T2—763 19		T2—561
Ascensiontide	263.9	ancient	939.2
music	781.728		T2—392
Asceticism	291.447	Asian Arctic seawaters	551.468 5
Buddhism	294.344 47		T2—163 25
Christianity	248.47	Asians	T5—95
Hinduism	294.544 7	Asiatic cholera	
Islam	297.447	incidence	614.514
Judaism	296.74	medicine	616.932
Aschaffenburg (Germany)	T2—433 31	see also Communicable	
Aschelminthes	595.18	diseases (Human)	
paleozoology	565.1	Āsmera (Ethiopia)	T2—635
Ascidiacea	596.2	Asnam (Algeria : Dept.)	T2—653
Asclepiadaceae	583.72	Asocial persons	305.568
Ascoli Piceno (Italy :			T1—086 92
Province)	T2—456 75		

Aśoka, King of Magadha

Indian history	934.045
Asotin County (Wash.)	T2—797 42
Asparagus	641.353 1
botany	584.324
commercial processing	664.805 31
cooking	641.653 1
garden crop	635.31
Aspects (Astrology)	133.53
Aspen	583.981
Aspergillus	589.23
Asphalt	553.27
building materials	691.96
economic geology	553.27
materials science	620.196
mining	622.337
petroleum product	665.538 8
processing	665.4
Asphalt concrete	666.893
Asphalt pavements	625.85
road engineering	625.85
sidewalk engineering	625.885
Asphaltite	553.27
see also Asphalt	
Asphyxiating gases	
toxicology	615.91
Asphyxiation	
medicine	617.18
Aspidochirotida	593.96
Aspidogastrea	595.122
Aspirin	615.313 7
Aspleniaceae	587.31
Assam (India)	T2—541 62
Assamese	T5—914 5
Assamese language	491.451
	T6—914 51
Assamese literature	891.451
Assassination	364.152 4
law	345.025 24
Assateague Island (Md. and Va.)	T2—752 21
Assault and battery	364.155 5
law	345.025 55
torts	346.033
Assaying	
metallurgy	669.92
Assemblage	
arts	702.814
Assemblers (Computer programs)	005.456
Assemblies (Legislative bodies)	328.3
Assemblies of God	289.94
see also Christian denominations	
Assembling machines	670.427
Assembling products	670.42
factory engineering	670.42
production management	658.533

Assembly	
civil right	323.47
Assembly languages	005.136
Assembly-line processes	670.42
production management	658.533
technology	670.42
Assens amt (Denmark)	T2—489 4
Assertiveness training	
applied psychology	158.2
Asses	
animal husbandry	636.18
zoology	599.725
Assessment tests	
educational use	371.264
Assimilation (Physiology)	574.133
human	612.39
see also Digestive system, Metabolism	
Assimilation (Sociology)	303.482
Assiniboine River (Sask. and Man.)	T2—712 73
Associate-degree nurses	610.730 92
role and function	610.730 692
see also Nurses	
Association	302.3
civil right	323.47
Association analysis	519.537
Association football	796.334
electronic games	794.863 34
Association of ideas	
psychology	153.22
Association of South East Asian Nations	341.247 3
Associationism	
psychological system	150.194 4
Associations	060
fraternal organizations	366
see also Organizations	
Associations for religious work	291.65
Christianity	267
Judaism	296.67
Associative algebras	512.24
Associative learning	
psychology	153.152 6
Associative memory	004.5
Associative processing	004.35
Associative processors	004.35
engineering	621.391
Assumption of Mary	232.914
Assumption Parish (La.)	T2—763 43
Assurance	368
see also Insurance	
Assyria	935.03
	T2—35
Mesopotamian history	935.03
Palestinian history	933.03
Assyrian dialect	492.1
	T6—921

Athens (Ga.)	T2—758 18
Athens (Greece)	T2—495 12
ancient	T2—385
Athens County (Ohio)	T2—771 97
Atheriniformes	597.53
Atherosclerosis	
medicine	616.136
see also Cardiovascular system	
Atherton (Qld.)	T2—943 6
Athletes	796.092
health	613.711
occupational ethics	174.979 6
physical fitness	613.711
sports group	T7—796
Athlete's foot	
medicine	616.57
see also Skin	
Athletic club buildings	
architecture	725.85
Athletic fields	796.420 68
area planning	711.558
Athletic games	796
Athletic garments	796
commercial technology	687.16
customs	391
home sewing	646.47
use	796
see also Clothing	
Athletic gloves and mitts	
manufacturing technology	685.43
Athletic injuries	
medicine	617.102 7
Athletic services	
armed forces	355.346
Athletic sports	796
Athos (Greece)	T2—495 6
Athos, Mount (Greece)	T2—495 6
Atitlán (Guatemala :	
Province)	T2—728 16
Atkinson County (Ga.)	T2—758 822
Atlanta (Ga.)	T2—758 231
Atlantic City (N.J.)	T2—749 85
Atlantic Coast (Nicaragua)	T2—728 53
Atlantic Coastal Plain	T2—75
Maryland	T2—752 1
North Carolina	T2—756 1
South Carolina	T2—757 6
United States	T2—75
Virginia	T2—755 1
Atlantic County (N.J.)	T2—749 84
Atlantic international	
organizations	341.243
Atlantic Ocean	551.461
	T2—163
Atlantic Ocean islands	997
	T2—97
Atlantic Provinces	971.5
	T2—715
Atlantic Region	T2—182 1
Atlántico (Colombia : Dept.)	T2—861 15
Atlántida (Honduras)	T2—728 312
Atlantis	001.94
folklore	398.234
sociology	398.42
literature	808.803 72
history and criticism	809.933 72
specific literatures	T3B—080 372
history and criticism	T3B—093 72
mystery	001.94
Atlas Mountains	T2—64
Atlases	912
	T1—022 3
cataloging	025.346
geography	912
library treatment	025.176
pictorial	T1—022 2
Atmosphere	551.5
	T2—161
meteorology	551.5
Atmospheric disturbances	551.55
Atmospheric electricity	551.563
Atmospheric entry	
manned space flight	629.458 8
Atmospheric formations	551.551
Atmospheric ionization	538.767
Atmospheric optics	551.565
Atmospheric pressure	551.54
physics	533.6
Atmospheric radiation	
meteorology	551.527 3
Atmospheric thermodynamics	
space flight	629.415 2
Atoka County (Okla.)	T2—766 66
Atolls	551.424
	T2—142
geography	910.914 2
geomorphology	551.424
physical geography	910.021 42
Atomic bonds	541.244
Atomic energy	333.792 4
economics	333.792 4
law	343.092 5
physics	539.7
Atomic number	541.242
Atomic physics	539.7
Atomic properties	
materials science	620.112 99
Atomic structure	539.14
chemistry	541.24
Atomism	146.5
Atoms	539.7
theoretical chemistry	541.24
Atonality	781.267
Atonement	291.22
Christianity	234.5
Islam	297.22

Audiovisual materials (continued)
  cataloging   025.347
  Christian religious education   268.635
  education   371.335
  library treatment   025.177
  reviews   028.137
Audiovisual treatment   T1—020 8
Auditing   657.45
  accounting   657.45
    government accounts   657.835 045
  public administration   350.723 2
    central governments   351.723 2
    local governments   352.172
Auditoriums
  architecture   725.83
Auditory canals
  human physiology   612.851
  otology   617.83
  see also Ears
Auditory memory   153.133
Auditory perception
  psychology   152.15
Audits   657.45
  see also Auditing
Audrain County (Mo.)   T2—778 332
Audubon County (Iowa)   T2—777 486
Aughrabies Falls   T2—687 12
Aughrabies National Park   T2—687 12
Auglaize County (Ohio)   T2—771 43
Augsburg (Germany)   T2—433 75
Augsburg, War of the League of,
  1688-1697   940.252 5
  North American history   973.25
Augsburg Confession   238.41
Augusan del Norte
  (Philippines : Province)   T2—599 7
Augusan del Sur
  (Philippines : Province)   T2—599 7
Augusta (Ga.)   T2—758 64
Augusta (Me.)   T2—741 6
Augusta County (Va.)   T2—755 916
Augustana Evangelical Lutheran
  Church   284.133 3
  see also Lutheran church
Augustinians   255.4
  church history   271.4
Auks   598.33
Aunis (France)   T2—446 4
Aunts   306.87
   T1—085
   T7—046
  family relationships   306.87
Aura (Human)   133.8
  physiology   612.014 2
Aural nervous system
  human anatomy   611.85
  human diseases
    incidence   614.599 8

Aural nervous system
  human diseases (continued)
    otology   617.886
  human physiology   612.85
  see also Ears
Aural techniques
  music   781.424
Aurangzeb, Emperor of
  Hindustan
  Indian history   954.025 8
Aurich (Germany : Landkreis)   T2—435 917
Auricles (Ears)
  human anatomy   611.85
  human diseases
    incidence   614.599 8
    otology   617.82
  human physiology   612.851
  see also Ears
Auricles (Heart)
  human anatomy   611.12
  human physiology   612.17
  see also Cardiovascular system
Aurora County (S.D.)   T2—783 375
Auroras (Geomagnetism)   538.768
Ausdehnungslehre   512.5
Aust-Agder fylke (Norway)   T2—482
Austin (Tex.)   T2—764 31
Austin, Lake   T2—941 3
Austin County (Tex.)   T2—764 252
Austral Islands   T2—962 2
Australasia   T2—9
Australia   994
   T2—94
Australian aboriginal languages   499.15
   T6—991 5
Australian aboriginal literatures   899.15
Australian aborigines   T5—991 5
Australian Alps   T2—944
Australian Capital Territory   T2—947
Australian cattle dog
  animal husbandry   636.737
  see also Dogs
Australian Country Party   324.294 04
Australian football   796.336
Australian Labour Party   324.294 07
Australian languages   499.15
   T6—991 5
Australian Liberal Party   324.294 05
Australian literature (English)   820
Australian native peoples   T5—991 5
Australian pitcher-plant   583.38
Australians   T5—24
Australoid race   T5—991 5
Australopithicus   569.9
Austria   943.6
   T2—436
Austrian Empire   943.604
   T2—436

Automation (continued)
social effects 303.483 4
Automation engineers 629.809 2
occupational group T7—629 8
Automation training
personnel management 658.312 43
Automatons 629.8
engineering 629.8
Automobile bodies 629.26
Automobile cars (Railroad) 385.34
engineering 625.24
see also Rolling stock
Automobile driving 629.283
international law 341.756 86
law 343.094 6
Automobile engineers 629.209 2
occupational group T7—629 2
Automobile industry
law 343.078 629 2
Automobile insurance 368.092
inland marine 368.232
law 346.086 092
liability 368.572
see also Insurance
Automobile noise 363.741
social welfare 363.741
see also Noise
Automobile parking 388.474
see also Parking facilities
Automobile racers 796.720 92
sports group T7—796 7
Automobile racing 796.72
electronic games 794.867 2
Automobile rallies 796.73
Automobile registration 350.878 34
international law 341.756 84
law 343.094 4
public administration 350.878 34
Automobile safety 363.125
law 343.094 4
Automobile theft 364.162
law 345.026 2
Automobile transportation 388.321
engineering 629.2
international law 341.756 8
law 343.094
transportation services 388.321
Automobiles 388.342
engineering 629.222
international law 341.756 84
law 343.094 4
military engineering 623.747 2
production economics 338.476 292 22
public administration 350.878 34
central governments 351.878 34
local governments 352.918 34
repair 629.287 2
sports 796.7

Automobiles (continued)
transportation services 388.342
urban 388.413 21
Automorphic functions 511.33
calculus 515.9
number theory 512.7
Automorphisms
geometry 516.1
topological algebras 512.55
Automotive industry 338.476 292
Automotive vehicles 388.34
engineering 629.2
international law 341.756 84
law 343.094 4
military engineering 623.747
production economics 338.476 292
public administration 350.878 34
central governments 351.878 34
local governments 352.918 34
repair 629.287
safety engineering 629.204 2
safety services 363.125
sports 796.7
transportation services 388.34
Autonomic nervous system
human anatomy 611.83
human diseases
medicine 616.88
human physiology 612.89
see also Nervous system
Autonomous authorities
public administration 350.009 1
central governments 351.009 1
local governments 352.009 2
Autonomy of states 320.15
Autopilots
aircraft 629.135 2
Autopsy
forensic medicine 614.1
medicine 616.075 9
Autumn
music 781.524 6
natural history 508
see also Seasons
Autumn-flowering plants
floriculture 635.953
Auvergne (France) T2—445 9
Auxiliaries (Foreign troops) 355.359
Auxiliary power systems
spacecraft 629.474 4
unmanned spacecraft 629.464 4
Auxiliary procedures T1—028
Auxiliary routes
marine 387.523
Auxiliary storage
computer science 004.56
engineering 621.397 6
Auxiliary techniques T1—028

Auxins	
chemistry	547.734 2
physiology	581.31
Auyuittuq National Park	
(N.W.T.)	T2—719 5
Available light photography	778.76
Avalanches	551.307
snow	551.578 48
Avant-garde jazz	781.656
Avant-garde music	780.904
Ave Maria	242.74
Aveiro (Portugal : District)	T2—469 35
Avellino (Italy : Province)	T2—457 21
Aveneae	584.93
Average costs	338.514 2
management	658.155 3
Averaging	519.533
Averrhoaceae	583.24
Avery County (N.C.)	T2—756 862
Aves	598
see also Birds	
Avesta (Zoroastrianism)	295.82
Avestan language	491.52
	T6—915 2
Avestan literature	891.52
Aveyron (France)	T2—447 4
Aviary birds	
animal husbandry	636.68
see also Birds	
Aviation	387.7
Aviation fuel	665.538 25
Aviation insurance	368.093
inland marine	368.24
liability	368.576
see also Insurance	
Aviation law	343.097
Aviation medicine	616.980 213
Aviation meteorology	629.132 4
Aviation psychology	155.965
Avignon (France)	T2—449 22
Avignon (Quebec)	T2—714 78
Avila (Spain : Province)	T2—463 59
Avila Camacho, Manuel	
Mexican history	972.082 6
Avionics	629.135
military aircraft	623.746 049
Avitaminosis	
medicine	616.39
see also Digestive system	
Avocado	641.346 53
agriculture	634.653
botany	583.931
commercial processing	664.804 653
cooking	641.646 53
Avocets	598.33
Avon (England)	T2—423 9
Avon River (Gloucestershire-	
Avon, England)	T2—423 9

Avon River (Leicestershire-	
Gloucestershire, England)	T2—424 4
Avon River (Wiltshire-Dorset,	
England)	T2—423 19
Avoyelles Parish (La.)	T2—763 71
Awadhi dialect	491.49
	T6—914 9
Awadhi literature	891.49
Awards	929.81
	T1—079
genealogy	929.81
research	001.44
Awnings	645.3
household management	645.3
manufacturing technology	684
Axes	621.93
art metalwork	739.72
Axinite	
mineralogy	549.64
Axiology	121.8
Axiomatic set theory	511.3
Axioms	160
mathematical logic	511.3
Axis Powers (World War II)	940.533 4
Axles	621.823
automotive	629.245
railroad engineering	625.21
Axons	
human histology	611.018 8
see also Nervous system	
Axum (Kingdom)	963.501
	T2—635
Ayacucho (Peru : Dept.)	T2—852 92
Ayatollahs	297.092
role and function	297.61
specific sects	297.8
Aydin Ili (Turkey)	T2—562
Aye-ayes	599.81
Ayers Rock	T2—942 91
Ayers Rock-Mount Olga	
National Park	T2—942 91
Aylesbury Vale (England)	T2—425 93
Aylmer (Quebec)	T2—714 221
Ayr (Qld.)	T2—943 6
Ayrshire (Scotland)	T2—414 6
Ayrshire cattle	
animal husbandry	636.225
zoology	599.735 8
Aysen (Chile : Province)	T2—836 22
Ayub Khan, Mohammad	
Pakistani history	954.904 5
Ayurveda	615.53
Ayutthaya period (Thai history)	959.302 3
Azad Kashmir	T2—549 13
Azalea	583.62
floriculture	635.933 62
Azarbayjan-i Bakhtari (Iran :	
Province)	T2—554

Azarbayjan-i Khavari (Iran)	T2—553
Azerbaijan (Iran)	T2—553
Azerbaijan S.S.R.	T2—479 1
Azerbaijani	T5—943
Azerbaijani language	494.361
	T6—943 61
Azerbaijani literature	894.361
Azilal (Morocco : Province)	T2—644
Azimuth	526.63
Azlon	677.472
see also Textiles	
Azo compounds	547.043
chemical engineering	661.894
Azo-oxy dyes	667.253
Azo-tetrazo dyes	667.253
Azores	T2—469 9
Azotobacteraceae	589.95
Azov, Sea of (Ukraine and	
R.S.F.S.R.)	551.462 9
	T2—163 89
Aztec calendar	529.329 784
Aztec language	497.45
	T6—974 5
Azteco-Tanoan Indians	T5—974
Azteco-Tanoan languages	497.45
	T6—974 5
Aztecs	T5—974
Mexican history	972.018
Azua (Dominican Republic :	
Province)	T2—729 372
Azuay (Ecuador)	T2—866 24
Azurite	
mineralogy	549.785

B

B cells	596.029
human immunology	616.079
vertebrate immunology	596.029
B-flat horns	788.974
see also Brass instruments	
Baalbek (Lebanon)	T2—394 4
Bab el Mandeb	551.467 32
	T2—165 32
Babanango (South Africa :	
District)	T2—684 2
Babangida, Ibrahim Badamosi	
Nigerian history	966.905 3
Babenbergs (Austrian history)	943.602 3
Babergh (England : District)	T2—426 48
Babies	305.232
	T1—083 2
health	613.043 2
pediatrics	618.92
see also Infants	
Bābil (Iraq : Province)	T2—567 5
Babine language	497.2
	T6—972

Babism	297.92
Babists	
biography	297.920 92
religious group	T7—297 8
Baboons	599.82
Babouvism (Socialist school)	335.2
Babur, Emperor of Hindustan	
Indian history	954.025 2
Baby animals	591.3
domestic animals	636.07
mammals	599.03
Baby blue-eyes (Flower)	583.76
Baby food	641.308 32
commercial preparation	664.62
cooking	641.562 2
feeding	649.3
Baby sitters' handbooks	649.102 48
Babylon (Ancient city)	T2—35
Babylonia	935.02
	T2—35
Mesopotamian history	935.02
Palestinian history	933.03
Babylonian dialect	492.1
	T6—921
Babylonian literature	892.1
Babylonian Talmud	296.125
Babylonians	T5—921
Baby's breath (Flower)	583.152
Baca County (Colo.)	T2—788 99
Bacau (Romania : Judet)	T2—498 1
Baccarat	795.42
Bacchus Marsh (Vic.)	T2—945 2
Bachelors	305.389 652
	T1—086 52
social group	305.389 652
Bacillaceae	589.95
Bacillariophyceae	589.481
Bacillary diseases	
incidence	614.512
medicine	616.931
see also Communicable	
diseases (Human)	
Bacillary dysentery	
incidence	614.516
medicine	616.935 5
see also Communicable	
diseases (Human)	
Back muscles	
human anatomy	611.731
see also Musculoskeletal system	
Backache	
medicine	617.564
Backgammon	795.15
Background investigation	
personnel selection	658.311 2
public administration	350.132 5
central governments	351.132 5
local governments	352.005 132 5

Bahr al Ahmar (Sudan :	
Province)	T2—625
Bahr al Ghazal (Sudan :	
Region)	T2—629 4
Bahrain	953.65
	T2—536 5
Bahraini	T5—927 536 5
Bahrein	T2—536 5
Bahreini	T5—927 536 5
Bail (Law)	345.056
Bailey bridges	388
construction	624.37
see also Bridges	
Bailey County (Tex.)	T2—764 844
Bailments	346.025
Bairnsdale (Vic.)	T2—945 6
Bait casting	799.12
Baixo Alentejo (Portugal)	T2—469 55
Baja California (Mexico)	T2—722
Baja California (State)	T2—722 3
Baja California Norte	
(Mexico)	T2—722 3
Baja California Sur (Mexico)	T2—722 4
Baja California Sur (Mexico :	
Territory)	T2—722 4
Baja Verapaz (Guatemala :	
Dept.)	T2—728 152
Baker County (Fla.)	T2—759 13
Baker County (Ga.)	T2—758 967
Baker County (Or.)	T2—795 75
Baker Island	T2—969 9
Baker Lake (N.W.T.)	T2—719 4
Bakery goods	641.815
commercial processing	664.752
home preparation	641.815
Bakhtiari va Chahar Mahall	
(Iran : Province)	T2—559 5
Baking	
commercial food preparation	664.02
home cooking	641.71
Baking powder	664.68
Baking soda	546.382 22
food technology	664.68
Bakongo (Kingdom)	967.320 1
	T2—673 2
Balaenicipites	598.34
Balalaikas	787.875
see also Stringed instruments	
Balance of payments	382.17
international banking	332.152
international commerce	382.17
Balance of power	327.112
Balance of trade	382.17
Balance sheets	657.3
accounting	657.3
financial management	658.151 2
investment analysis	332.632 042
Balancing machinery	621.816

Balanitaceae	583.214
Balanoglossida	593.993
Balanophoraceae	583.94
Balanopsidales	583.961
Balcones Escarpment	T2—764 88
Balconies	721.84
architecture	721.84
construction	690.184
Balcony furniture	645.8
see also Outdoor furniture	
Balcony gardening	635.967 1
Bald cypress	585.2
Bald Mountains	T2—768 91
Baldachins	
church architecture	726.529 3
Baldness	
medicine	616.546
see also Hair	
Baldwin County (Ala.)	T2—761 21
Baldwin County (Ga.)	T2—758 573
Balē (Ethiopia)	T2—632
Balē kifle hāger (Ethiopia)	T2—632
Bâle-Ville (Switzerland)	T2—494 32
Baleares	T2—467 5
Balearic Islands	T2—467 5
Balearic Sea	551.462 2
	T2—163 82
Baleen whales	599.51
Balelesberg Range	T2—684 1
Balfour (South Africa :	
District)	T2—682 7
Bali Island (Indonesia)	T2—598 6
Bali Sea	551.465 74
	T2—164 74
Balikesir Ili (Turkey)	T2—562
Balimo (Papua New Guinea)	T2—954 9
Balinese language	499.22
	T6—992 2
Balinese literature	899.22
Baling crops	631.56
equipment manufacturing	
technology	681.763 1
Balkan Mountains (Bulgaria)	T2—497 7
Balkan Peninsula	949.6
	T2—496
Balkan States	949.6
	T2—496
Balkan Wars	949.6
Balkars	T5—942
Ball bearings	621.822
Ball games	796.3
equipment technology	688.763
indoor	794.7
outdoor	796.3
Ball lightning	551.563 4
Ballad operas	782.14
music	782.14
stage presentation	792.6

Ballade	784.189 6	Baltic languages	491.9	
Ballads			T6—919	
literature	808.814 4	Baltic literatures	891.9	
history and criticism	809.144	Baltic Sea	551.461 34	
specific literatures	T3B—104 4		T2—163 34	
individual authors	T3A—1	Baltic States	T2—474	
music	782.43	Baltimore (Md.)	T2—752 6	
Ballarat (Vic.)	T2—945 7	Baltimore County (Md.)	T2—752 71	
Ballard County (Ky.)	T2—769 96	Balto-Finnic languages	494.54	
Ballast (Railroad)	625.141		T6—945 4	
Ballet	792.8	Balto-Slavic languages	491.8	
Ballet dancers	792.802 809 2		T6—918	
occupational group	T7—792 8	Balto-Slavic literatures	891.8	
Ballet music	781.556	Baluchi	T5—915 9	
Ballet skiing	796.937	Baluchi language	491.59	
Balletts	782.43		T6—915 9	
Ballina (N.S.W.)	T2—944 3	Baluchi literature	891.59	
Ballistic missile forces	358.17	Baluchistan	T2—549 15	
Ballistic missiles	358.171 82	Iran	T2—558 3	
military engineering	623.451 95	Pakistan	T2—549 15	
military equipment	358.171 82	Baluchistan (Pakistan)	T2—549 15	
Ballistics	531.55	Baluchistan va Sistan (Iran :		
criminal investigation	363.256 2	Province)	T2—558 3	
engineering	620.105	Balustrades	721.8	
military engineering	623.51	architecture	721.8	
physics	531.55	artistic ironwork	739.48	
Ballistocardiography		construction	690.18	
medicine	616.120 754	Bamako (Mali)	T2—662 3	
see also Cardiovascular system		Bambara (African people)	T5—963 4	
Balloons		Bambara language	496.34	
engineering	629.133 22		T6—963 4	
military engineering	623.742	Bamberg (Germany)	T2—433 18	
piloting	629.132 522	Bamberg County (S.C.)	T2—757 78	
sports	797.51	Bamboo	584.93	
see also Aircraft		basketwork crops	633.58	
Ballots	324.65	handicrafts	745.51	
Ballroom dancing	793.33	textiles	677.54	
Balls (Dances)	793.38	*see also* Textiles		
Balls (Recreational equipment)	796.3	Bamboo pulp	676.14	
manufacturing technology	688.763	Bambuseae	584.93	
Ballymena (Northern Ireland :		Bambute (African people)	T5—963 94	
Borough)	T2—416 13	Bambute language	496.394	
Ballymoney (Northern			T6—963 94	
Ireland : Borough)	T2—416 14	Bamileke (African people)	T5—963 6	
Balms	583.24	Bamileke languages	496.36	
Burseraceae	583.24		T6—963 6	
Labiatae	583.87	Bamun language	496.36	
Balneotherapy			T6—963 6	
medicine	615.853	Bana (African people)	T5—963 6	
Balong language	496.396	Bana language	496.36	
	T6—963 96		T6—963 6	
Balqa (Jordan : District)	T2—569 55	Banaba Island	T2—968 1	
Balranald (N.S.W.)	T2—944 8	Banach algebras	512.55	
Balsa	583.19	Banach groups	512.55	
Balsam fig	583.163	Banach spaces	515.732	
Balsaminaceae	583.216	Bananas	641.347 72	
Balsams	583.216	botany	584.21	
		commercial processing	664.804 772	

Bananas (continued)	
cooking	641.647 72
horticulture	634.772
Banat	T2—498 4
Romania	T2—498 4
Yugoslavia	T2—497 1
Banbridge (Northern Ireland :	
District)	T2—416 57
Band leaders	784.092
occupational group	T7—784
Banda (African people)	T5—963 6
Banda, H. Kamuzu (Hastings	
Kamuzu)	
Malawian history	968.970 4
Banda languages	496.36
	T6—963 6
Banda Sea	551.465 74
	T2—164 74
Bandages	677.8
manufacturing technology	677.8
surgical use	617.93
Bandera County (Tex.)	T2—764 885
Bandicoots	599.2
Bandjoun language	496.36
	T6—963 6
Bandoneons	788.84
see also Woodwind instruments	
Bands	784
Bandundu (Zaire)	T2—675 116
Banff (Alta.)	T2—712 332
Banff and Buchan (Scotland)	T2—412 25
Banff National Park (Alta.)	T2—712 332
Bangalore torpedoes	623.454 5
Banghazi (Libya)	T2—612
Bangi-Ntumba languages	496.396 8
	T6—963 968
Bangiales	589.41
Bangladesh	954.92
	T2—549 2
Bangladesh people	T5—914 126
Bangladeshis	T5—914 126
Bangor (Me.)	T2—741 3
Bang's disease	636.208 969 57
Bangui (Central African	
Republic)	T2—674 1
Banjoists	787.880 92
occupational group	T7—787
Banjos	787.88
see also Stringed instruments	
Banjul (Gambia)	T2—665 1
Bank accounts	332.175 2
Bank deposit insurance	368.854
law	346.086 854
see also Insurance	
Bank failures	332.1
Bank for International	
Settlements	332.155
Bank holding companies	332.16

Bank mergers	332.16
Bank notes	332.404 4
central banking	332.112
Bank reserves	332.1
macroeconomic policy	339.53
requirements	332.113
Bankers	332.109 2
occupational group	T7—332
Banking	332.1
international law	341.751
law	346.082
public administration	351.825 2
Banking cooperatives	334.2
Banking services	332.17
Bankruptcy	332.75
economics	332.75
law	346.078
public finance	336.368
Banks (Finance)	332.1
accounting	657.833 3
credit regulation	
law	346.082
macroeconomic policy	339.53
international law	341.751
public administration	351.825 2
Banks County (Ga.)	T2—758 143
Banks Island (N.W.T.)	T2—719 6
Bann River	T2—416
Banned books	098.1
Banner County (Neb.)	T2—782 975
Banners	929.92
armed forces	355.15
Bannock County (Idaho)	T2—796 47
Bannock Range	T2—796 47
Bannockburn, Battle of, 1314	941.102
Banquets	642.4
Banstead, Reigate and	
(England)	T2—422 17
Bansuris	788.35
see also Woodwind instruments	
Bantams	
animal husbandry	636.587 1
see also Chickens	
Bantoid languages	496.36
	T6—963 6
Bantu languages	496.39
	T6—963 9
Bantu literatures	896.39
Bantu-speaking peoples	T5—963 9
Bantustans	T2—682 9
Cape of Good Hope	T2—687 9
Natal	T2—684 9
Orange Free State	T2—685 9
Transvaal	T2—682 9
see also Homelands (South	
Africa)	
Banyan	583.962
Baobab	583.19

Baritone voices	782.88	Baroque sculpture	735.21
choral and mixed voices	782.88	Barotse kingdoms (Zambian	
single voices	783.88	history)	968.940 1
Baritones (Horns)		Barraba (N.S.W.)	T2—944 4
American	788.975	Barracks	355.71
see also Brass instruments		architecture	725.18
British	788.974	military housing	355.71
see also Brass instruments		Barracuda	597.58
Barium	669.725	Barrage balloons	
chemical engineering	661.039 5	military engineering	623.744
chemistry	546.395	Barrages	
metallurgy	669.725	engineering	627.123
physical metallurgy	669.967 25	Barrels	688.8
see also Chemicals		wooden	674.82
Bark	582.047	Barren County (Ky.)	T2—769 72
forest product	634.985	Barrier islands	551.423
Bark beetle	595.768		T2—142
Barkerville (B.C.)	T2—711 75	geography	910.914 2
Barking and Dagenham		geomorphology	551.423
(London, England)	T2—421 75	physical geography	910.021 42
Barkley, Lake (Ky. and		Barrine, Lake	T2—943 6
Tenn.)	T2—769 79	Barron County (Wis.)	T2—775 18
Barkly East (South Africa :		Barrow County (Ga.)	T2—758 195
District)	T2—687 6	Barrow-in-Furness (England :	
Barkly Tableland	T2—942 95	Borough)	T2—427 81
Barkly West (South Africa :		Barrow Island National Park	T2—941 3
District)	T2—687 11	Barrow River (Ireland)	T2—418
Barlee, Lake	T2—941 6	Barry County (Mich.)	T2—774 16
Barley	641.331 6	Barry County (Mo.)	T2—778 76
botany	584.93	Bars (Drinking places)	647.95
cooking	641.631 6	architecture	725.72
food crop	633.16	home economics	643.4
forage crop	633.256	public household management	647.95
Barlow, George, Sir		Bars (Engineering)	624.177 4
Indian history	954.031 2	Bars (Musical instrument)	786.82
Barmera (S. Aust.)	T2—942 33	concussed	786.873
Barnabites	255.52	friction	786.863
church history	271.52	set	786.863
Barnacles	595.35	single	786.888
paleozoology	565.35	percussed	786.843
Barnes County (N.D.)	T2—784 32	set	786.843
Barnet (London, England)	T2—421 87	single	786.884 3
Barnouic (England)	T2—423 49	plucked	786.85
Barns	631.22	set	786.85
architecture	728.922	single	786.887
construction	690.892 2	*see also* Percussion instruments	
use	631.22	Bartenders' manuals	641.874
Barnsley (England :		Barter instruments	332.5
Metropolitan Borough)	T2—428 25	Bartholomew County (Ind.)	T2—772 24
Barnstable County (Mass.)	T2—744 92	Barton County (Kan.)	T2—781 52
Barnwell County (S.C.)	T2—757 76	Barton County (Mo.)	T2—778 71
Barometric leveling	526.37	Bartow County (Ga.)	T2—758 365
Barometric pressure	551.54	Baruch (Bible)	229.5
Baroque architecture	724.16	Barwon River	T2—944 9
Baroque art	709.032	Baryons	539.721 64
Baroque decoration	745.443	Barytons	787.6
Baroque music	780.903 2	*see also* Stringed instruments	
Baroque painting	759.046	Bas-Rhin (France)	T2—443 835

Bas-Richelieu (Quebec)	T2—714 51
Bas-Saint-Laurent-Gaspésie (Quebec : Administrative region)	T2—714 77
Bas-Zaïre (Zaire)	T2—675 114
Basa (Cameroon people)	T5—963 96
Basa (Liberian people)	T5—963 3
Basa languages	496.396
	T6—963 96
Basal body	574.876 4
Basal ganglia	
human diseases	
medicine	616.83
see also Nervous system	
Basalts	552.26
Bascule bridges	388
construction	624.82
see also Bridges	
Base lines	
geodetic surveying	526.33
Base running	
baseball	796.357 27
Baseball	796.357
electronic games	794.863 57
equipment manufacturing	688.763 57
gloves and mitts	685.43
Baseball players	796.357 092
sports group	T7—796 35
Baseband computer equipment	004.64
engineering	621.398 1
Baseband local-area networks	004.68
see also Computer communications	
Basel (Switzerland : Canton)	T2—494 32
Basel-Stadt (Switzerland)	T2—494 32
Basellaceae	583.913
Baselland (Switzerland)	T2—494 33
Basements	
home economics	643.5
Basenji	
animal husbandry	636.753
see also Dogs	
Bases (Chemicals)	546.32
chemical engineering	661.3
see also Chemicals	
Bases (Military installations)	355.7
international law	341.725
law	343.01
Bashfulness	155.232
Bashkir A.S.S.R. (R.S.F.S.R.)	T2—478 7
Bashkir language	494.3
	T6—943
Bashkirskaia A.S.S.R. (R.S.F.S.R.)	T2—478 7
Basic Christian communities	250
ecclesiology	262.26
Basic education	370.11
adults	374.012
Basic English	428
Basic races	T5—03
Basic skills education	370.11
Basic sulfates	
mineralogy	549.755
Basic training (Military)	355.54
living conditions	355.129 2
Basidiomycetes	589.22
Basil	583.87
Basil III, Czar of Russia	
Russian history	947.042
Basilan (Philippines : Province)	T2—599 7
Basilan Island	T2—599 7
Basildon (England)	T2—426 772
Basilians	255.17
church history	271.17
Basilicata (Italy)	T2—457 7
ancient	T2—377
Basilisks (Folklore)	398.245 4
sociology	398.469
Basingstoke and Deane (England : Borough)	T2—422 71
Basket star	593.94
Basketball	796.323
electronic games	794.863 23
Basketball players	796.323 092
sports group	T7—796 32
Basketry	
handicrafts	746.412
Basketwork plants	
agriculture	633.58
Basommatophora	594.38
paleozoology	564.38
Basotho	T5—968 85
Basotho-Qwaqwa (South Africa)	T2—685 91
Basque language	499.92
	T6—999 2
Basque literature	899.92
Basque Provinces (Spain)	T2—466
Basques	T5—999 2
Basques (Quebec : Regional County Municipality)	T2—714 76
Basrah (Iraq : Province)	T2—567 5
Bass	597.58
commercial fishing	639.275 8
Bass clarinets	788.65
see also Woodwind instruments	
Bass drums	786.95
see also Percussion instruments	
Bass flutes	788.34
see also Woodwind instruments	
Bass recorders	788.367
see also Woodwind instruments	
Bass saxophones	788.75
see also Woodwind instruments	

Bass Strait	551.467 76
	T2—165 76
Bass viols	787.65
see also Stringed instruments	
Bass voices	782.89
choral and mixed voices	782.89
single voices	783.89
Bassa (Cameroon people)	T5—963 96
Bassa (Liberian people)	T5—963 3
Bassa language (Cameroon)	496.396
	T6—963 96
Bassa language (Liberia)	496.33
	T6—963 3
Bassari (Senegal-Guinea people)	T5—963 2
Bassari (Togo-Ghana people)	T5—963 5
Bassari language	496.32
	T6—963 2
Bassarisks	599.744 43
Basse-Normandie (France)	T2—442
Basse-taille	
ceramic arts	738.4
Basses (Stringed instruments)	787.5
see also Stringed instruments	
Basses-Alpes (France)	T2—449 5
Basses-Pyrénées (France)	T2—447 9
Bassetlaw (England : District)	T2—425 21
Bassoons	788.58
see also Woodwind instruments	
Basswood	583.19
forestry	634.972 77
lumber	674.142
Bast fibers	
textiles	677.1
see also Textiles	
Bastiat, Frédéric	
economic school	330.153
Bastrop County (Tex.)	T2—764 32
Basutoland	968.850 2
	T2—688 5
Bat flies	595.774
Bat games	796.35
Bat tick flies	595.774
Bataan (Philippines : Province)	T2—599 1
Batan Islands	T2—599 1
Batanes (Philippines : Province)	T2—599 1
Batangas (Philippines : Province)	T2—599 1
Batavian Republic	949.205
Batch processing	004.3
Batemans Bay (N.S.W.)	T2—944 7
Bates County (Mo.)	T2—778 43
Bath (England)	T2—423 98
Bath County (Ky.)	T2—769 555
Bath County (Va.)	T2—755 87

Bath mitzvah	296.443
customs	392.14
etiquette	395.24
music	781.583
Bathhouses	
domestic	
architecture	728.9
public	
architecture	725.73
Bathing	613.41
child training	649.63
customs	391.64
health	613.41
personal care	646.71
therapeutics	615.853
Bathrooms	643.52
home economics	643.52
plumbing	696.182
residential interior decoration	747.78
Baths	
therapeutic use	615.853
Bathurst (N.B.)	T2—715 12
Bathurst (N.S.W.)	T2—944 5
Bathurst (South Africa : District)	T2—687 5
Bathurst Inlet (N.W.T.)	T2—719 7
Bathurst Island	T2—942 95
Bathynellacea	595.379
Bathyscaphes and bathyspheres	387.27
design	623.812 7
engineering	623.827
transportation services	387.27
see also Ships	
Batidaceae	583.913
Batik	746.662
Bating leather	675.22
Batna (Algeria : Dept.)	T2—655
Batoidea	597.35
paleozoology	567.3
Baton Rouge (La.)	T2—763 18
Batracoidiformes	597.53
Bats	599.4
paleozoology	569.4
Bats (Baseball)	796.357 26
manufacturing technology	688.763 57
Batswana (Ethnic group)	T5—963 977 5
Batswana (National group)	T5—968 83
Battalions (Military units)	355.31
Battered wives	362.829 2
criminal law	345.025 553
criminology	364.155 53
social welfare	362.829 2
see also Family violence	
Batteries (Artillery units)	358.123
Batteries (Electric)	621.312 42
automotive	629.254 2

Bearded collie	
animal husbandry	636.737
see also Dogs	
Bearing walls	721.2
architecture	721.2
construction	690.12
see also Walls (Building	
element)	
Bearings	621.822
clockwork	681.112
machine engineering	621.822
railroad engineering	625.21
Béarn (France)	T2—447 9
Bears	599.744 46
big game hunting	799.277 444 6
Bearsden and Milngavie	
(Scotland : District)	T2—414 34
Beasts of burden	
care and maintenance	636.088 2
Beatification of saints	235.24
Beating metals	
decorative arts	739.14
sculpture	731.41
Beatitudes	226.93
Christian moral theology	241.53
Beatrice (Neb.)	T2—782 286
Beatrix, Queen of the	
Netherlands	
Dutch history	949.207 3
Beauce-Sartigan (Quebec)	T2—714 71
Beaudesert (Qld.)	T2—943 2
Beaufort County (N.C.)	T2—756 186
Beaufort County (S.C.)	T2—757 99
Beaufort Sea	551.468 7
	T2—163 27
Beaufort West (South Africa :	
District)	T2—687 15
Beauharnois (Quebec :	
County)	T2—714 32
Beauharnois-Salaberry	
(Quebec)	T2—714 32
Beauport (Quebec)	T2—714 471
Beauregard Parish (La.)	T2—763 59
Beauticians	646.720 92
Beauty	111.85
philosophy	111.85
Beauty shops	646.72
personal care	646.72
sanitation services	363.729 9
see also Waste control	
Beaver County (Okla.)	T2—766 14
Beaver County (Pa.)	T2—748 92
Beaver County (Utah)	T2—792 46
Beaverhead County (Mont.)	T2—786 69
Beaverhead Mountains	T2—796 78
Beavers	599.323 2
Bebop	781.655

Bécancour (Quebec :	
Regional County	
Municipality)	T2—714 55
Béchar (Algeria : Dept.)	T2—657
Bechuanaland	968.830 2
	T2—688 3
Becker County (Minn.)	T2—776 84
Beckham County (Okla.)	T2—766 43
Becoming	
philosophy	116
Bed and breakfasts	647.94
Bed-wetting	
medicine	616.849
pediatrics	618.928 49
see also Nervous system	
Bedclothing	643.53
arts	746.97
commercial technology	684.3
home sewing	646.21
household equipment	643.53
Bedford (South Africa :	
District)	T2—687 5
Bedford (Va.)	T2—755 676
Bedford County (Pa.)	T2—748 71
Bedford County (Tenn.)	T2—768 583
Bedford County (Va.)	T2—755 675
Bedfordshire (England)	T2—425 6
Bedrooms	643.53
home economics	643.53
interior decoration	747.77
Beds (Furniture)	645.4
manufacturing technology	684.15
see also Furniture	
Bedsores	
medicine	616.545
see also Skin	
Bedspreads	643.53
arts	746.97
home sewing	646.21
household equipment	643.53
Bedworth, Nuneaton and	
(England : Borough)	T2—424 83
Bee balm	583.87
Bee County (Tex.)	T2—764 117
Bee eaters	598.892
Bee flies	595.771
Bee keeping	638.1
Bee lice	595.774
Bee venom	
toxicology	615.942
Beech	583.976
forestry	634.972 5
lumber	674.142
Beechworth (Vic.)	T2—945 5
Beef	641.362
commercial processing	
economics	338.476 649 2
technology	664.92

Beef (continued)
  cooking 641.662
Beef cattle
  agricultural economics 338.176 213
  animal husbandry 636.213
  zoology 599.735 8
Beefwood 583.975
Beekeepers 638.109 2
  occupational group T7—638
Beer 641.23
  commercial processing 663.42
  cooking with 641.623
  home preparation 641.873
Bees 595.799
  agriculture 638.1
Beeswax
  apiculture processing 638.17
Beet sugar
  commercial processing 664.123
  see also Sugar
Beet syrup
  commercial processing 664.123
Beetles 595.76
  paleozoology 565.76
Beetling textiles 677.028 25
Beets 641.351 1
  botany 583.913
  commercial processing 664.805 11
  cooking 641.651 1
  garden crop 635.11
  sugar crop 633.63
Bega (N.S.W.) T2—944 7
Beganas 787.78
  see also Stringed instruments
Begēmdir (Ethiopia) T2—634
Beggar's-lice 583.322
Beggiatoaceae 589.96
Begheli dialect 491.49
  T6—914 9
Beginner cooking 641.512
Beginners
  social group T7—090 9
Begonia 583.46
Begoniaceae 583.46
Begonias
  floriculture 635.933 46
Behavior
  animals 591.51
  biology 574.5
  comparative psychology 156
  educational psychology 370.153
  general psychology 150
  plants 581.5
  social psychology 302
Behavior modification 153.85
  home child care 649.64
  teaching method 371.393

Behavior therapy
  psychiatry 616.891 42
  see also Mental illness
Behavioral genetics 155.7
Behavioral pharmacology 615.78
  see also Mental illness
Behavioral sciences 300
  psychology 150
Behaviorism 150.194 3
Beheira (Egypt) T2—621
Beijing (China) T2—511 56
Beijing dialect 495.17
  T6—951 7
Being 111
Beira (Portugal) T2—469 3
Beira Alta (Portugal) T2—469 31
Beira Baixa (Portugal) T2—469 33
Beira Litoral (Portugal) T2—469 35
Beirut (Lebanon) T2—569 25
Beja (Portugal : District) T2—469 55
Beja language 493.5
  T6—935
Bejaia (Algeria : Dept.) T2—655
Bekes Megye (Hungary) T2—439 9
Bekhterev, Vladimir
  Mikhailovich
  psychological system 150.194 4
Bel and the Dragon (Bible) 229.6
Belau 996.6
  T2—966
Belfast (Northern Ireland) T2—416 7
Belfast (South Africa :
  District) T2—682 7
Belfort (France : Territory) T2—444 55
Belgian Congo 967.510 24
  T2—675 1
Belgian horse
  animal husbandry 636.15
  zoology 599.725
Belgian literature
  Flemish 839.31
  French 840
Belgian malinois
  animal husbandry 636.737
  see also Dogs
Belgian tervuren
  animal husbandry 636.737
  see also Dogs
Belgians T5—393 2
Belgica T2—364
Belgium 949.3
  T2—493
Belgorod (R.S.F.S.R. :
  Oblast) T2—473 5
Belgorodskaia oblast
  (R.S.F.S.R.) T2—473 5
Belgrade (Serbia) T2—497 1

Belief	
epistemology	121.6
Belief and doubt	
epistemology	121.6
Belief systems	
social control	303.372
Belize	972.82
	T2—728 2
Belize (Belize : District)	T2—728 22
Belknap County (N.H.)	T2—742 45
Bell County (Ky.)	T2—769 123
Bell County (Tex.)	T2—764 287
Bell-jar gardening	
floriculture	635.985
Bell magpies	598.8
Bell peppers	641.356 43
see also Sweet peppers	
Bell towers	
architecture	725.97
Bella Coola (B.C.)	T2—711 1
Bella Coola language	497.9
	T6—979
Bella Coola River (B.C.)	T2—711 1
Belladonna	583.79
pharmacology	615.323 79
Belle Fourche River	T2—787 13
Bellechasse (Quebec :	
County)	T2—714 733
Bellechasse (Quebec :	
Regional County	
Municipality)	T2—714 733
Bellenden Ker National Park	T2—943 6
Belles-lettres	800
history and criticism	809
Bellflower	583.57
Belligerency	341.62
Belligerent countries	T2—171 82
Bellingshausen Sea	551.469 4
	T2—167 4
Bells	786.884 8
see also Percussion instruments	
Belluno (Italy : Province)	T2—453 7
Bellville (South Africa :	
District)	T2—687 35
Belly dancing	793.3
Belmont County (Ohio)	T2—771 93
Beloit (Wis.)	T2—775 87
Belorussia	T2—476 5
Belorussian language	491.799
	T6—917 99
Belorussian literature	891.799
Belorussians	T5—917 99
Belt buckles	391.7
customs	391.7
making	739.278
see also Jewelry	
Belt conveyors	621.867 5
Beltrami County (Minn.)	T2—776 82

Belts	
power transmission	621.852
Belts (Clothing)	391.44
commercial technology	687.19
leather	685.22
see also Accessories (Clothing)	
Beltways	388.122
see also Roads	
Belugas	599.53
Bemba (African people)	T5—963 915
Bemba kingdoms (Zambian	
history)	968.940 1
Bemba languages	496.391 5
	T6—963 915
Bemba literature	896.391 5
Bembe-Kabwari languages	496.394
	T6—963 94
Ben Hill County (Ga.)	T2—758 852
Ben Lomond (Tas.)	T2—946 4
Ben Lomond National Park	T2—946 4
Ben Msik-Sidi Othmane	
(Morocco : Prefecture)	T2—643
Ben Slimane (Morocco :	
Province)	T2—643
Bena-Kinga languages	496.391
	T6—963 91
Benalla (Vic.)	T2—945 5
Bench marks	526.32
Bench-scale plants	
chemical engineering	660.280 71
Bendel State (Nigeria)	T2—669 3
Bendigo (Vic.)	T2—945 4
Bending metals	
decorative arts	739.14
sculpture	731.41
Bending stress	531.38
materials science	620.112 44
Bending tools	621.982
Bendjedid, Chadli	
Algerian history	965.05
Bends	
medicine	616.989 4
see also Environmental diseases	
(Human)	
Benedictines	255.1
church history	271.1
women	255.97
church history	271.97
Benedictus	264.36
music	782.323 2
Beneficial animals	591.61
Beneficial microorganisms	576.162
Beneficial organisms	
biology	574.61
Beneficial plants	581.61
Beneficiation (Ore dressing)	622.7
Benefit societies	334.7
economics	334.7

Berkshire (England)	T2—422 9	Bessarabskaia guberniia	
Berkshire County (Mass.)	T2—744 1	(Russia)	T2—477 5
Berkshire Hills (Mass.)	T2—744 1	Bessel function	515.53
Berlin (Germany)	T2—431 55	Bessemer steel	669.142 3
Berlin (Germany : East)	T2—431 552	Best books	
Berlin (Germany : West)	T2—431 554	bibliographies	011.73
Berlin Reservoir (Ohio)	T2—771 37	Beta decay	539.752 3
Bermuda	972.99	Beta functions	515.52
	T2—729 9	Beta Israel	T5—924
Bermuda Islands	972.99	Beta particles	539.721 12
	T2—729 9	Beta radiation	
Bermuda Triangle	001.94	biophysics	574.191 56
Bermudians	T5—969 729 9	human	612.014 486
Bern (Switzerland)	T2—494 542	Betatron-synchrotrons	539.735
Bern (Switzerland : Canton)	T2—494 54	Betatrons	539.734
Bernalillo County (N.M.)	T2—789 61	Betel nut	584.5
Bernese mountain dog		Bethal (South Africa :	
animal husbandry	636.73	District)	T2—682 7
see also Dogs		Bethlehem (South Africa :	
Bernese Oberland	T2—494 54	District)	T2—685 1
Bernier and Dorre Islands		Bethulie (South Africa :	
National Park	T2—941 3	District)	T2—685 7
Berri (S. Aust.)	T2—942 33	Betrothal	392.4
Berrien County (Ga.)	T2—758 862	customs	392.4
Berrien County (Mich.)	T2—774 11	etiquette	395.22
Berries	582.130 416 6	music	781.586
anatomy	582.130 446	social aspects	306.81
commercial processing	664.804 7	Betsimisaraka (Kingdom)	969.101
cooking	641.647		T2—691
food	641.347	Better business bureaus	381.34
horticulture	634.7	Betting	306.482
physiology	582.130 416 6	ethics	175.9
Berry (France)	T2—445 5	*see also* Recreation—ethics	
Berry Islands	T2—729 6	*see also* Gambling—sociology	
Berseem	583.322	Betting systems	795.01
forage crop	633.327	Betulaceae	583.976
Berthier (Quebec : County)	T2—714 43	Bevel gears	621.833 2
Bertie County (N.C.)	T2—756 163	Beverage containers	
Berwick-upon-Tweed		disposal	363.728 8
(England : Borough)	T2—428 89	*see also* Waste control	
Berwickshire (Scotland :		Beverage technologists	663.092
District)	T2—413 95	occupational group	T7—663
Beryl		Beverage technology	663
mineralogy	549.64	Beverages	641.2
Beryllium	669.724	commercial processing	663
chemical engineering	661.039 1	cooking with	641.62
chemistry	546.391	health	613.3
economic geology	553.492 3	home economics	641.2
materials science	620.189 4	home preparation	641.87
metallography	669.957 24	product safety	363.192 9
metallurgy	669.724	*see also* Food—product safety	
metalworking	673.724	Beverley (England : Borough)	T2—428 36
mining	622.349 23	Bexar County (Tex.)	T2—764 35
physical metallurgy	669.967 24	Bexley (London, England)	T2—421 77
toxicology	615.925 391	Bhagavad Gita	294.592 4
see also Chemicals, Metals		Bhakti Yoga	294.543
Bessarabia (Russia)	T2—477 5	Bhedabheda (Philosophy)	181.484 2

Big Sandy River (Ky. and W. Va.)	T2—754 47
Kentucky	T2—769 2
West Virginia	T2—754 47
Big Sioux River (S.D. and Iowa)	T2—783 39
Iowa	T2—777 1
South Dakota	T2—783 39
Big Stone County (Minn.)	T2—776 432
Bigamy	364.183
law	345.028 3
Bigfoot	001.944
Bignoniales	583.54
Bihar (India)	T2—541 2
Bihari	T5—914 5
Bihari language	491.454
	T6—914 54
Bihari literature	891.454
Bihor (Romania)	T2—498 4
Bikeways	388.12
see also Bicycle paths	
Bikini Atoll (Marshall Islands)	T2—968 3
Bilateral schools (United Kingdom)	373.25
Bilateral trade agreements	382.9
Bilateral treaties	341.1
texts	341.026 6
Bilbao (Spain)	T2—466 3
Bile	
human physiology	612.35
see also Digestive system	
Bile acids	596.013 2
biochemistry	
human	612.015 737
chemistry	547.737
physiology	596.013 2
Bile ducts	
human anatomy	611.36
human diseases	
medicine	616.365
human physiology	612.35
surgery	617.556
see also Digestive system	
Bilecik Ili (Turkey)	T2—563
Bilharziasis	
incidence	614.553
medicine	616.963
see also Communicable diseases (Human)	
Biliary tract	
human anatomy	611.36
human diseases	
medicine	616.36
human physiology	612.35
surgery	617.556
see also Digestive system	
Bilinear forms	512.944
algebraic geometry	516.35
Bilingual education	371.97
Bilingual phrase books	T4—834
Bilingual programs	
public administration	351.85
Bilingualism	306.446
linguistics	404.2
specific languages	T4—042
sociology	306.446
Bill collection	658.88
law	346.077
Billboards	659.134 2
land use law	346.045
outdoor advertising	659.134 2
Billiard players	794.720 92
sports group	T7—794 7
Billiards	794.72
equipment technology	688.747 2
Billiatt Conservation Park	T2—942 33
Billings County (N.D.)	T2—784 94
Bills (Legislative)	328.37
texts	348.01
United States	348.731
Bills of exchange	332.77
exchange medium	332.55
law	346.096
Bills of lading	
law	343.087 8
Biloela (Qld.)	T2—943 5
Bimetallic monetary standards	332.423
Bimini Islands (Bahamas)	T2—729 6
Binary form	781.822 2
instrumental	784.182 2
Binary numbers	513.52
Binary salts	546.342
chemical engineering	661.4
Binary stars	523.841
Binary system	513.52
Bingham County (Idaho)	T2—796 51
Binghamton (N.Y.)	T2—747 75
Bingo	795.3
Bingol Ili (Turkey)	T2—566 7
Bini language	496.33
	T6—963 3
Binocular imbalance	
ophthalmology	617.762
see also Eyes	
Binocular-vision photography	778.4
Binoculars	681.412
Binomial equations	512.942
algebra	512.942
calculus	515.252
Binuclear family	306.89
Bío Bío (Chile : Province)	T2—834 3
Bío Bío (Chile : Region)	T2—834 1
Bioastronautics	574.191 9
human	612.014 5

Bira-Huku languages	496.394
	T6—963 94
Birational transformations	
algebraic geometry	516.35
Birch	583.976
forestry	634.972 6
Birchip (Vic.)	T2—945 9
Birchir	597.42
Bird dogs	
animal husbandry	636.752
see also Dogs	
Bird lice	595.751 4
Bird pest control	
sanitary engineering	628.968
Bird watching	598.072 34
Birdbanding	598.072 32
Birds	598
agricultural pests	632.68
air transportation hazard	363.124 12
animal husbandry	636.5
art representation	704.943 2
commercial hunting	639.12
conservation technology	639.978
disease carriers	614.434
drawing	743.68
paleozoology	568
resource economics	333.958
sports hunting	799.24
Bird's-eye fabrics	677.615
Bird's-nest fungi	589.221
Birds of paradise	598.865
Birds of prey	598.91
Biremes	387.21
design	623.812 1
engineering	623.821
handling	623.882 1
transportation services	387.21
see also Ships	
Birmingham (Ala.)	T2—761 781
Birmingham (England)	T2—424 96
Birth	
customs	392.12
etiquette	395.24
folklore	
sociology	398.354
literature	808.803 54
history and criticism	809.933 54
specific literatures	T3B—080 354
history and criticism	T3B—093 54
music	781.582
obstetrics	618.2
Birth control	363.96
crime prevention	364.4
see also Crime prevention	
demographic effect	304.666
ethics	176
religion	291.566
Buddhism	294.356 6
Birth control	
ethics	
religion (continued)	
Christianity	241.66
Hinduism	294.548 66
Islam	297.5
Judaism	296.385 66
health	613.94
law	344.048
public administration	351.815
central governments	351.815
local governments	352.941 5
social services	363.96
social theology	291.178 366 66
Christianity	261.836 666
Birth of Jesus Christ	232.921
Birth order	306.87
environmental psychology	155.924
family relationships	306.87
Birthday books	
astrology	133.540 42
Birthday parties	
cooking	641.568
Birthdays	
customs	394.2
Birthmarks	
capillary hemangiomas	
medicine	616.993 15
medicine	616.55
see also Skin	
Births	
certification	
public administration	350.816
central governments	351.816
local governments	352.941 6
demography	304.63
Birthwort	583.922
Bisa-Lamba languages	496.391
	T6—963 91
Bisayan Islands (Philippines)	T2—599 5
Biscay (Spain)	T2—466 3
Biscay, Bay of	551.461 38
	T2—163 38
Biscayne Bay (Fla.)	551.461 48
	T2—163 48
Biscayne National Park (Fla.)	T2—163 48
Biscuit mixes	664.753
Biscuits (Breads)	641.815
commercial processing	664.752
cooking	641.815
Biscuits (Cookies)	641.865 4
commercial processing	664.752 5
home preparation	641.865 4
Bisexuality	306.765
medicine	616.858 34
psychology	155.334
Bisexuals	305.906 63
	T1—086 63

Black lung disease	362.196 244
medicine	616.244
social services	362.196 244
workers' compensation law	344.021 8
see also Respiratory system	
Black magic	133.4
Black mangrove	583.88
Black mass	133.422
Black Methodist churches	287.8
see also Methodist Church	
Black moss	588.2
Black Muslim religion	297.87
Black Muslims	
biography	297.870 92
religious group	T7—297 7
Black pepper	
botany	583.925
cooking with	641.638 4
see also Hot spices	
Black powder	662.26
Black River (Ark.)	T2—767 2
Black River (S.C.)	T2—757 8
Black Rock Desert	T2—793 54
Black Sea	551.462 9
	T2—163 89
Black shale	553.283
economic geology	553.283
mining	622.338 3
processing	665.4
Black vultures	598.912
Black Welsh cattle	
animal husbandry	636.223
zoology	599.735 8
Blackall (Qld.)	T2—943 5
Blackberries	641.347 13
commercial processing	664.804 713
cooking	641.647 13
horticulture	634.713
Blackberry	583.372
Blackberry lily	584.24
Blackbirds (American)	598.881
Blackburn (England :	
Borough)	T2—427 623
Blackdown Hills	T2—423 87
Blackford County (Ind.)	T2—772 68
Blackheads	
medicine	616.53
see also Skin	
Blackjack (Game)	795.42
Blacklands (Tex.)	T2—764 26
Blacklisting (Labor)	331.894
law	344.018 94
Blackmail	364.165
law	345.026 5
Blackouts	
electrical engineering	621.319
military engineering	623.77
Blackpool (England)	T2—427 65

Blacks (United States)	T5—960 73
Blacks as consumers	
marketing management	658.834 8
Blacksmithing	682
Blacksmiths	682.092
occupational group	T7—682
Blackwater River (Ireland)	T2—419 5
Blackwood River (W.A.)	T2—941 2
Bladder (Urinary)	
human anatomy	611.62
human diseases	
medicine	616.62
human physiology	612.467
surgery	617.462
see also Urinary system	
Bladdernut	583.28
Bladderwort	583.81
Bladen County (N.C.)	T2—756 32
Blaenau Gwent (Wales)	T2—429 95
Blagoevgrad (Bulgaria :	
Okrug)	T2—497 74
Blagoevgradski okrug	
(Bulgaria)	T2—497 74
Blaine County (Idaho)	T2—796 32
Blaine County (Mont.)	T2—786 15
Blaine County (Neb.)	T2—782 772
Blaine County (Okla.)	T2—766 31
Blair County (Pa.)	T2—748 75
Blanche, Lake	T2—942 37
Blanco County (Tex.)	T2—764 64
Bland County (Va.)	T2—755 765
Blanket orders	
library acquisitions	025.233
Blankets	643.53
arts	746.97
home sewing	646.21
household equipment	643.53
manufacturing technology	677.626
Blantyre (Malawi)	T2—689 7
Blasphemy	291.569 5
criminology	364.188
ethics	179.5
see also Ethical problems	
law	345.028 8
Blast-furnace gas	665.772
Blast-furnace practice	669.141 3
Blast injuries	
medicine	617.19
Blast-resistant construction	624.176
buildings	693.854
Blasting	624.152
excavation	624.152
mining	622.23
underwater engineering	627.74
Blastoidea	563.92
Blattaria	595.722
paleozoology	565.72

Blazers	391	Blister beetle	595.767
commercial technology	687.113	Blitz tactics	355.422
customs	391	Blizzards	551.555
home sewing	646.433	Block books	092
see also Clothing		Block diagramming	
Blazonry	929.6	program design	005.120 28
Bleaching clothes and related		Block Island (R.I.)	T2—745 8
materials	667.14	Block printing	761
home economics	648.1	textile arts	746.62
Bleaching oils and gases	665.028 3	Blockades	355.44
Bleckley County (Ga.)	T2—758 525	Civil War (United States)	973.75
Bledsoe County (Tenn.)	T2—768 76	international law	341.584
Bleeding		law of war	341.63
therapeutics	615.899	military operations	355.44
Bleeding heart	583.122	World War I	940.452
Blekinge lan (Sweden)	T2—486	World War II	940.545 2
Blended waxes	665.19	Blockbusters (Ammunition)	623.451 7
Blenders		Blocking	
use in cooking	641.589	American football	796.332 26
Blending oils and gases	665.028 3	Blocks (Musical instrument)	786.82
Blending petroleum distillates	665.534	see also Bars (Musical	
Blenny	597.58	instrument)	
Blepharitis		Bloemfontein (South Africa)	T2—685 4
medicine	617.771	Bloemfontein (South Africa :	
see also Eyes		District)	T2—685 4
Blepharoplasts	574.873 4	Bloemhof (South Africa :	
Blida (Algeria : Dept.)	T2—653	District)	T2—682 4
Blighted areas		Bloemhof Dam	T2—685 3
area planning	711.5	Blood	
Blimps (Airships)	387.732 7	cancer	
engineering	629.133 27	medicine	616.994 18
military engineering	623.743 7	see also Cancer	
see also Aircraft		human histology	611.018 5
Blind-deaf persons	305.908 161	human physiology	612.11
	T7—081 61	puerperal diseases	
see also Blind persons		obstetrics	618.77
Blind man's buff	793.4	see also Cardiovascular system	
Blind persons	305.908 161	Blood analysis	
	T1—087 1	criminal investigation	363.256 2
	T7—081 61	medicine	616.075 61
education	371.911	Blood banks	362.178 4
library services	027.663	law	344.041 94
social group	305.908 161	see also Health services	
social welfare	362.41	Blood chemistry	
Blind play (Chess)	794.17	human physiology	612.12
Blindman's buff	793.4	see also Cardiovascular system	
Blindness		Blood coagulation	
incidence	614.599 7	human diseases	
ophthalmology	617.712	medicine	616.157
social welfare	362.41	human physiology	612.115
see also Eyes		see also Cardiovascular system	
Blinds	645.3	Blood diseases	
architecture	721.82	medicine	616.15
construction	690.182	see also Cardiovascular system	
household management	645.3	Blood-forming system	591.14
manufacturing technology	684	animal physiology	591.14
Bliss's Bibliographic			
Classification	025.434		

Blood-forming system (continued)
   cancer   362.196 994 41
      medicine   616.994 41
      social services   362.196 994 41
      see also Cancer
   geriatrics   618.976 41
   human anatomy   611.41
   human diseases   362.196 41
      incidence   614.594 1
      medicine   616.41
      social services   362.196 41
   human physiology   612.41
   pediatrics   618.924 1
   pharmacodynamics   615.718
   see also Bone marrow
Blood plasma
   human histology   611.018 5
   see also Cardiovascular system
Blood plasma banks   362.178 4
   see also Health services
Blood pressure
   human physiology   612.14
   see also Cardiovascular system
Blood River   T2—684 1
Blood River, Battle of, 1838   968.404 2
Blood transfusion   362.178 4
   law   344.041 94
   pharmacology   615.39
   social service   362.178 4
Blood types
   human physiology   612.118 25
   see also Cardiovascular system
Blood vessels
   human anatomy   611.13
   human diseases
      medicine   616.13
   human physiology   612.13
   surgery   617.413
   see also Cardiovascular system
Bloodletting
   therapeutics   615.899
Bloodroot   583.122
Bloodwort   584.29
Blotting paper   676.284 4
Blount County (Ala.)   T2—761 72
Blount County (Tenn.)   T2—768 885
Blouses   391.2
   commercial technology   687.115
   customs   391.2
   home sewing   646.435
   see also Clothing
Blow flies   595.774
Blowers   621.61
Blowing glass   666.122
   decorative arts   748.202 82
Blown glassware
   decorative arts   748.2
Blowpipe analysis   543.086

Blowpipes (Chemical apparatus)   542.5
Blowpipes (Weapons)
   sports   799.202 82
Blue-collar workers   305.562
       T1—086 23
   labor economics   331.79
   labor unions   331.880 42
   personnel management   658.304 4
   social class   305.562
   training
      personnel management   658.312 45
   see also Laboring classes
Blue Earth County (Minn.)   T2—776 21
Blue-green algae   589.46
Blue Mountains (N.S.W.)   T2—944 5
Blue Mountains (Or. and
   Wash.)   T2—795 7
   Oregon   T2—795 7
   Washington   T2—797 46
Blue Mountains National Park   T2—944 5
Blue Nile Province (Sudan)   T2—626 4
Blue Nile River   T2—626 4
Blue Ridge Mountains   T2—755
   Georgia   T2—758 2
   North Carolina   T2—756 8
   South Carolina   T2—757 2
   Virginia   T2—755
Blue whales   599.51
Bluebell (Boraginaceae)   583.77
Bluebell (Campanulaceae)   583.57
Bluebell (Liliaceae)   584.324
Blueberries   641.347 37
   botany   583.62
   commercial processing   664.804 737
   cooking   641.647 37
   horticulture   634.737
Bluebonnet   583.322
Bluefish   597.58
   commercial fishing   639.275 8
   sports fishing   799.175 8
Bluegrass   584.93
   forage crop   633.21
Bluegrass music   781.642
Bluegrass region (Ky.)   T2—769 3
Blueprints   604.25
   building construction   692.1
   printing technology   686.42
   technical drawing   604.25
Blues   781.643
Bluestone   553.53
   economic geology   553.53
   quarrying   622.353
Blyde River Canyon   T2—682 6
Blyth Valley (England :
   Borough)   T2—428 84
Bo tree
   Buddhism   294.343 5
Boaco (Nicaragua : Dept.)   T2—728 526

Boiling		Bomb disposal units	
home cooking	641.73	armed forces	358.23
Boiling points	536.44	Bombacaceae	583.19
Boils		Bombala (N.S.W.)	T2—944 7
medicine	616.523	Bombardment	
see also Skin		military science	355.4
Boina (Kingdom)	969.101	particle physics	539.73
	T2—691	solid state physics	530.416
Bois-Francs Region (Quebec)	T2—714 565	Bombay (India)	T2—547 923
Boise (Idaho)	T2—796 28	Bombers	358.428 3
Boise County (Idaho)	T2—796 74	engineering	623.746 3
Bojutsu	796.86	military equipment	358.428 3
Bok choy	641.353	Bombing forces	358.42
botany	583.123	Bombs	623.451
cooking	641.653	Bombsights	623.46
garden crop	635.3	Bombycillidae	598.852
Bokhara rugs		Bombycoidea	595.781
arts	746.758 7	Bombyliidae	595.771
see also Rugs		Bon (Tibetan religion)	299.54
Bokkeveld Range	T2—687 17	Bon Homme County (S.D.)	T2—783 395
Bokmal language	439.82	Bonaire	T2—729 86
	T6—398 2	Bonaparte Archipelago	T2—941 4
Bokmal literature	839.82	Bonaparte River (B.C.)	T2—711 72
Boksburg (South Africa :		Bonaventure (Quebec :	
District)	T2—682 2	County)	T2—714 78
Boland	T2—687 3	Bonaventure (Quebec :	
Bolas		Regional County	
sports	799.202 82	Municipality)	T2—714 78
Boletes	589.222	Bond (Employee)	368.83
Bolívar (Colombia : Dept.)	T2—861 14	insurance	368.83
Bolívar (Ecuador : Province)	T2—866 16	law	346.086 83
Bolívar (Venezuela : State)	T2—876 3	personnel management	658.314
Bolívar, Simón		public administration	350.132 44
South American history	980.02	central governments	351.132 44
Bolivar County (Miss.)	T2—762 43	local governments	352.005 132 44
Bolivia	984	Bond (Law)	345.056
	T2—84	Bond County (Ill.)	T2—773 873
Bolivia (Game)	795.418	Bond paper	676.282 3
Bolivian literature	860	Bonded fabrics	677.69
Bolivians	T5—688 4	*see also* Textiles	
Bollinger County (Mo.)	T2—778 94	Bonding metals	671.58
Bolobedu (South Africa :		Bonds (Chemical forces)	541.224
District)	T2—682 93	Bonds (Securities)	332.632 3
Bologna (Italy : Province)	T2—454 1	accounting	657.75
Bolsena (Italy)	T2—456 25	corporate law	346.066 6
ancient	T2—376	financial management	
Bolshevik International	324.175	capital procurement	658.152 24
Bolshevik parties	324.217 5	debt management	658.152 6
Bolsover (England : District)	T2—425 15	income tax law	343.052 46
Bolton (England :		investment economics	332.632 3
Metropolitan Borough)	T2—427 37	law	346.092 2
Bolts (Locks)	683.31	Bône (Algeria : Dept.)	T2—655
Bolts and nuts	621.882	Bone carving	736.6
Boltzmann statistics	530.132	Bone char	662.93
Bolu Ili (Turkey)	T2—563	Bone marrow	596.014
Bolyai geometry	516.9	animal physiology	596.014
Bolzano (Italy : Province)	T2—453 83	human diseases	
Bomaderry (N.S.W.)	T2—944 7	incidence	614.594 1

Boone Lake	T2—768 96
Boosters (Detonators)	662.4
Boothferry (England :	
Borough)	T2—428 35
Boothia Peninsula (N.W.T.)	T2—719 7
Bootlegging	364.133
law	345.023 3
Boots	391.413
customs	391.413
manufacturing technology	685.31
see also Clothing	
Bop	781.655
Bophuthatswana (South	
Africa)	T2—682 94
Boquerón (Paraguay : Dept.)	T2—892 24
Boracite	
mineralogy	549.735
Borage	583.77
Boraginales	583.77
Borates	553.633
economic geology	553.633
mineralogy	549.735
mining	622.363 3
Borax	553.633
economic geology	553.633
mineralogy	549.735
mining	622.363 3
Bordeaux (France)	T2—447 14
Borden, Robert Laird, Sir	
Canadian history	971.061 2
Borden County (Tex.)	T2—764 853
Border Country	T2—413 7
Border defense	355.45
Border patrols	363.285
Border region (South Africa)	T2—687 5
Borderline personality disorder	
medicine	616.858 52
see also Mental illness	
Borders (Floriculture)	635.963
Borders Region (Scotland)	T2—413 7
Bordertown (S. Aust.)	T2—942 34
Boring	
mining	622.24
Boring tools	621.952
Boris Fyodorovich Godunov,	
Czar of Russia	
Russian history	947.044
Bornean languages	499.22
	T6—992 2
Borneo	T2—598 3
Indonesia	T2—598 3
Malaysia	T2—595 3
Bornholm (Denmark)	T2—489 2
Bornholms amt (Denmark)	T2—489 2
Borno State (Nigeria)	T2—669 85
Bornu (Kingdom)	966.980 1
	T2—669 8

Boron	553.6
chemical engineering	661.067 1
chemistry	546.671
economic geology	553.6
organic chemistry	547.056 71
applied	661.895
see also Chemicals	
Boron fuels	662.86
Borrelia	589.99
Borrowing	332.041 54
capital management	658.152 24
public finance	336.34
administration	350.726
central governments	351.726
local governments	352.14
Borsod-Abauj-Zemplen	
Megye (Hungary)	T2—439 9
Borstals	365.42
see also Correctional	
institutions	
Borzoi	
animal husbandry	636.753
see also Dogs	
Bose-Einstein statistics	530.133 2
Boshof (South Africa :	
District)	T2—685 8
Bosnia and Hercegovina	T2—497 42
Bosnia and Herzegovina,	
(Federated Republic,	
1945)	T2—497 42
Bosons	539.721
Bosporus	551.462 9
	T2—163 89
Bosque County (Tex.)	T2—764 518
Bosses (Geology)	551.88
Bossier Parish (La.)	T2—763 97
Boston (England : Borough)	T2—425 37
Boston (Mass.)	T2—744 61
Boston ivy	583.279
Boston Massacre, 1770	973.311 3
Boston Mountains	T2—767 1
Arkansas	T2—767 1
Oklahoma	T2—766 8
Boston Port Bill, 1774	973.311 6
Boston Tea Party, 1773	973.311 5
Boston terrier	
animal husbandry	636.72
see also Dogs	
Bosworth, Hinckley and	
(England)	T2—425 49
Bot flies	595.774
Botanic medicine	
therapeutic system	615.53
Botanical drugs	
pharmacology	615.32
Botanical gardens	580.744
architecture	727.658
landscape architecture	712.5

Bowlers	794.609 2
sports group	T7—794 6
Bowling (Cricket)	796.358 22
Bowling (Game)	794.6
equipment technology	688.746
Bowling alleys	794.6
architecture	725.84
Bowman County (N.D.)	T2—784 92
Bowron Lake Provincial Park	
(B.C.)	T2—711 75
Bows	
art metalwork	739.73
manufacturing technology	688.792
military equipment	623.441
shooting game	799.215
sports use	799.202 85
target shooting	799.32
Bowutu Mountains	T2—957 1
Box Butte County (Neb.)	T2—782 94
Box elder	583.28
Box Elder County (Utah)	T2—792 42
Box-girder bridges	388
construction	624.4
see also Bridges	
Box lily	584.42
Box lunches	642.4
Boxcars	385.34
engineering	625.24
see also Rolling stock	
Boxer (Dog)	
animal husbandry	636.73
see also Dogs	
Boxer Rebellion (Chinese	
history)	951.035
Boxers (Pugilists)	796.830 92
sports group	T7—796 8
Boxes	688.8
paperboard	676.32
Boxing	796.83
ethics	175.6
see also Recreation—ethics	
law	344.099
Boxwood	583.394
Boy Scout camps	796.542 2
Boy Scouts	369.43
Boyacá (Colombia)	T2—861 37
Boycott	
international politics	327.117
international law	341.582
labor economics	331.893
law	344.018 93
restraint of trade	338.604 8
law	343.072 3
Boyd County (Ky.)	T2—769 27
Boyd County (Neb.)	T2—782 723
Boyer Ahmadi-ye Sardir va	
Kohkiluyeh (Iran :	
Province)	T2—556

Boyer River	T2—777 4
Boyle County (Ky.)	T2—769 523
Boyne River (Ireland)	T2—418 22
Boys	305.23
	T1—083
criminal offenders	364.36
health	613.042 32
home care	649.132
journalism for	070.483 26
psychology	155.432
publications for	
bibliographies	011.624 1
recreation	790.194
indoor	793.019 4
outdoor	796.019 4
sex hygiene	613.953
social aspects	305.23
Boys' clubs	369.42
Boys' societies	369.42
Boysenberries	641.347 18
botany	583.372
commercial processing	664.804 718
cooking	641.647 18
horticulture	634.718
Bozcaada Island	T2—562
Brabant (Belgium)	T2—493 3
Bracelets	391.7
customs	391.7
making	739.278
see also Jewelry	
Brachiopoda	594.8
paleozoology	564.8
Brachycephalidae	597.87
Brachyura	595.384 2
Bracing equipment	
aircraft	629.134 37
Bracken (Fern)	587.31
Bracken County (Ky.)	T2—769 325
Bracket fungi	589.222 5
Brackish waters	T2—169
Bracknell (England : District)	T2—422 98
Bracknell Forest (England :	
Borough)	T2—422 98
Bradford (England : City)	T2—428 17
Bradford County (Fla.)	T2—759 15
Bradford County (Pa.)	T2—748 57
Bradley County (Ark.)	T2—767 63
Bradley County (Tenn.)	T2—768 873
Bradyodonti	567.3
Braga (Portugal : District)	T2—469 12
Bragança (Portugal : District)	T2—469 2
Braganza, House of (Portuguese	
history)	946.903
Brahma Samaj	294.556 2
Brahmanas	294.592 1
Brahmanism	294.5
Brahmans	
biography	294.509 2

Braunschweig (South Africa)	T2—687 92
Braxton County (W. Va.)	T2—754 66
Brayer painting	751.49
Braziers	
ceramic arts	738.8
heating buildings	697.1
Brazil	981
	T2—81
Brazil nut	641.345 75
agriculture	634.575
botany	583.42
cooking	641.645 75
Brazilian literature	869
Brazilian Portuguese dialects	469.798
	T6—69
Brazilians	T5—698
Brazing	671.56
decorative arts	739.14
sculpture	731.41
Brazoria County (Tex.)	T2—764 137
Brazos County (Tex.)	T2—764 242
Brazos River (Tex.)	T2—764
Brazzaville (Congo)	T2—672 4
Breach of contract	346.022
Bread	641.815
commercial baking	664.752 3
home baking	641.815
Bread-dough handicrafts	745.5
Bread molds (Fungi)	589.258
Breadfruit	583.962
orchard crop	634.39
Break dancing	793.3
Break-even analysis	658.155 4
Breakfast	642
cooking	641.52
customs	394.15
Breakfast foods	
commercial processing	664.756
Breakfast rooms	643.4
home economics	643.4
Breaking	
materials science	620.112 6
Breaks (Rest periods)	
labor economics	331.257 6
personnel management	658.312 1
Breakwaters	
engineering	627.24
Bream	597.58
Breast	
human anatomy	611.49
human diseases	
medicine	618.19
men	616.49
surgery	618.19
women's physiology	612.664
Breast cancer	
medicine	616.994 49
see also Cancer	
Breast feeding	649.33
child rearing	649.33
health	613.26
human physiology	612.664
Breathing	591.12
animals	591.12
health	613.192
human physiology	612.2
musical technique	781.48
instrumental	784.193 2
see also Respiratory system	
Breathitt County (Ky.)	T2—769 19
Brechou (England)	T2—423 47
Breckinridge County (Ky.)	T2—769 854
Breckland (England : District)	T2—426 14
Brecknock (Wales : Borough)	T2—429 56
Breconshire (Wales)	T2—429 56
Brecqhou (England)	T2—423 47
Bredasdorp (South Africa : District)	T2—687 3
Breë River	T2—687 3
Breeder reactors	621.483 4
Breeding	
animal husbandry	636.082
plant cultivation	631.53
Breeding stock	636.088 1
animals	636.088 1
plants	631.52
Bremen (Germany)	T2—435 2
Bremer County (Iowa)	T2—777 34
Bremerhaven (Germany)	T2—435 21
Bremsstrahlung	539.722 2
Brent (London, England)	T2—421 85
Brentwood (England : District)	T2—426 76
Brescia (Italy : Province)	T2—452 6
Brest (Belorussian S.S.R. : Oblast)	T2—476 52
Brestskaia oblast (Byelorussian S.S.R.)	T2—476 52
Bretagne (France)	T2—441
Breton language	491.68
	T6—916 8
Breton literature	891.68
Bretons	T5—916 8
Brevard County (Fla.)	T2—759 27
Breviaries	264.1
Roman Catholic	264.020 1
texts	264.024
Brewarrina (N.S.W.)	T2—944 9
Brewed alcoholic beverages	641.23
commercial processing	663.3
cooking with	641.62
home preparation	641.873
Brewed nonalcoholic beverages	641.26
commercial processing	663.9
home preparation	641.877
Brewster County (Tex.)	T2—764 932

British Commonwealth of Nations	T2—171 241
British Empire	T2—171 241
British Guiana	T2—881
British Honduras	T2—728 2
British Isles	941
	T2—41
ancient	936.1
	T2—361
British Kaffraria	T2—687 5
British New Guinea	995.402 1
British North America Act, 1867	971.049
British Open (Golf)	796.352 66
British pronunciation	421.55
British Solomon Islands	T2—959 3
British Somaliland	T2—677 3
British spelling	421.55
British system (Measurement)	530.813
physics	530.813
social aspects	389.15
British Virgin Islands	T2—729 725
British western seawaters	551.461 37
	T2—163 37
Britons	T5—21
Brits (South Africa : District)	T2—682 3
Britstown (South Africa : District)	T2—687 13
Brittany (France)	T2—441
Brittany vizsla	
animal husbandry	636.752
see also Dogs	
Brittle star	593.94
Brittleness	
materials science	620.112 6
Broaching tools	621.954
Broad beans	583.322
garden crop	635.651
Broad-gage railroads	385
engineering	625.1
transportation services	385
see also Railroad transportation	
Broad jump	796.432
Broad River (S.C.)	T2—757 4
Broadband computer equipment	004.64
engineering	621.398 1
Broadband local-area networks	004.68
see also Computer communications	
Broadcast advertising	659.14
Broadcast drama	
radio programs	791.447
television	791.457
Broadcast media	
journalism	070.19
Broadcast videotex	004.69
communication services	384.352
see also Computer communications	

Broadcasters	384.540 92
occupational group	T7—384
Broadcasting	384.54
law	343.099 4
public administration	351.874
Broadcasting channels	384.545 2
radio	384.545 2
television	384.552 1
Broadcasting networks	384.545 5
radio	384.545 5
television	384.552 3
Broadcasting stations	384.545 3
radio	384.545 3
engineering	621.384
facilities	384.545 3
organizations	384.540 65
television	384.552 2
facilities	384.552 2
organizations	384.550 65
Broadford (Vic.)	T2—945 3
Broadland (England)	T2—426 17
Broads, The (England)	T2—426 17
Broadsides	
cataloging	025.342
direct advertising	659.133
library treatment	025.172
Broadwater County (Mont.)	T2—786 664
Brocade	677.616
Brocatelle	677.616
Broccoli	641.353 5
botany	583.123
commercial processing	664.805 35
cooking	641.653 5
garden crop	635.35
Broiling	641.76
Broken Hill (N.S.W.)	T2—944 9
Broken homes	362.829 4
social services	362.829 4
sociology	306.89
see also Families—social welfare	
Brokers (Securities)	332.62
law	346.092 6
public administration	351.825 8
Brokopondo (Surinam : District)	T2—883 9
Brome (Quebec : County)	T2—714 64
Brome-Missisquoi	T2—714 62
Bromegrass	584.93
Bromeliales	584.22
floriculture	635.934 22
Bromine	
chemical engineering	661.073 3
chemistry	546.733
economic geology	553.6
organic chemistry	547.02
applied	661.891
see also Chemicals	

Brunswick County (N.C.)	T2—756 29	Buckingham County (Va.)	T2—755 623
Brunswick County (Va.)	T2—755 575	Buckinghamshire (England)	T2—425 9
Bruny Island (Tas.)	T2—946 2	Buckles	391.7
Brush disposal methods		customs	391.7
silviculture	634.955	making	739.278
Brush drawing	741.26	*see also* Jewelry	
Brush turkey	598.612	Bucks County (Pa.)	T2—748 21
Brushes	679.6	Bucks County chickens	
Brushes (Generator parts)	621.316	animal husbandry	636.581
Brussels (Belgium)	T2—493 32	*see also* Chickens	
Brussels griffon		Buckthorn	583.279
animal husbandry	636.76	Buckwheat	641.331 2
see also Dogs		botany	583.917
Brussels sprouts	641.353 6	commercial processing	664.725
botany	583.123	cooking	641.631 2
commercial processing	664.805 36	food crop	633.12
cooking	641.653 6	Bucuresti (Romania)	T2—498 2
garden crop	635.36	Budapest (Hungary)	T2—439 12
Bruttium	T2—377	Buddha	294.363
Bryales	588.2	art representation	704.948 943 63
Bryan County (Ga.)	T2—758 732	Buddhism	294.3
Bryan County (Okla.)	T2—766 62	art representation	704.948 943
Bryansk (R.S.F.S.R. : Oblast)	T2—476 2	Buddhist architecture	720.95
Bryce Canyon National Park		Buddhist calendar	529.324 3
(Utah)	T2—792 52	religion	294.343 6
Bryophyta	588	Buddhist ethics	294.35
paleobotany	561.8	Buddhist holidays	294.343 6
pharmacology	615.322	customs	394.268 294 3
Bryozoa	594.7	Buddhist monasteries	
paleozoology	564.7	architecture	726.784 3
Brythonic languages	491.6	Buddhist philosophy	181.043
	T6—916	Buddhist regions	T2—176 43
Bubble memory	004.56	Buddhist sacred music	781.743
engineering	621.397 63	public worship	782.343
Bubbles	530.427 5	music	782.343
chemical engineering	660.293	religion	294.343 8
chemistry	541.33	religion	294.343 7
physics	530.427 5	Buddhist sculpture	730.95
Bube-Benga languages	496.396	Buddhist temples and shrines	294.343 5
	T6—963 96	architecture	726.143
Bubonic plague		Buddhists	
incidence	614.573 2	biography	294.309 2
medicine	616.923 2	religious group	T7—294 3
see also Communicable		Budding bacteria	589.94
diseases (Human)		Buddleiaceae	583.74
Bucerotidae	598.892	Budgerigars	598.71
Buchan, Banff and (Scotland)	T2—412 25	animal husbandry	636.686 4
Buchan Caves	T2—945 6	Budget	
Buchanan, James		law	343.034
United States history	973.68	military administration	355.622
Buchanan County (Iowa)	T2—777 382	public administration	350.722 52
Buchanan County (Mo.)	T2—778 132	central governments	351.722 52
Buchanan County (Va.)	T2—755 752	local governments	352.125 2
Bucharest (Romania)	T2—498 2	Budget deficits	
Bücher, Karl		macroeconomic policy	339.523
economic school	330.154 2		
Buck beans	583.75		
Buckeye	583.28		

Budget digests
  public administration — 350.722 53
    central governments — 351.722 53
    local governments — 352.125 3
Budget estimates
  public administration — 350.722 25
    central governments — 351.722 25
    local governments — 352.122 5
Budget manuals
  public administration — 350.722 202 02
    central governments — 351.722 202 02
    local governments — 352.122 020 2
Budget messages — 350.722 56
  central governments — 351.722 56
  local governments — 352.125 6
Budget surpluses
  macroeconomic policy — 339.523
Budgeting — 658.154
  public administration — 350.722
    central governments — 351.722
    local governments — 352.12
Budgets (Home economics) — 640.42
Buds
  plant propagation — 631.533
Buena Vista (Va.) — T2—755 851
Buena Vista County (Iowa) — T2—777 18
Buenos Aires (Argentina) — T2—821 1
Buenos Aires (Argentina :
  Province) — T2—821 2
Buffalo — 599.735 8
  animal husbandry — 636.293
  big game hunting — 799.277 358
  hunting — 639.117 358
Buffalo (Bison) — 599.735 8
  animal husbandry — 636.292
Buffalo (N.Y.) — T2—747 97
Buffalo, Mount — T2—945 5
Buffalo berries — 583.279
  horticulture — 634.74
Buffalo County (Neb.) — T2—782 45
Buffalo County (S.D.) — T2—783 31
Buffalo County (Wis.) — T2—775 48
Buffalo River — T2—684 1
Buffels River — T2—687 15
Buffers
  railroad engineering — 625.25
Buffing metals — 671.72
Buffing tools — 621.922
Bufonoidea — 597.87
  paleozoology — 567.8
Buganda (Kingdom) — 967.610 1
  — T2—676 1
Bugey (France) — T2—444 4
Bugles — 788.95
  see also Brass instruments
Buhayrah (Egypt) — T2—621
Buhayrah (Sudan : Region) — T2—629 4
Buhid (Philippine people) — T5—992 1

Buhid language — 499.21
  — T6—992 1
Builders — 690.092
  occupational group — T7—69
Building
  enterprises — 338.769
    restrictive practices — 338.826 9
      economics — 338.826 9
  government control — 350.824 2
    central governments — 351.824 2
    local governments — 352.922
  production economics — 338.476 9
  technology — 690
Building and loan associations — 332.32
  law — 346.082 32
Building codes — 343.078 69
  enforcement — 363.233
Building construction services
  (Armed forces) — 358.22
Building cooperatives — 334.1
  economics — 334.1
Building engineering services — 696
Building industries — 338.476 9
  public administration
    local governments — 352.942 42
Building management — 658.2
  public administration — 350.713 3
    central governments — 351.713 3
    local governments — 352.163 3
Building materials — 691
  architectural construction — 721.044
  construction — 691
  synthetic — 666.89
Building paper — 676.289
Building remodeling
  home economics — 643.7
Building safety violations
  criminology — 364.142
  law — 345.024 2
Buildings — 720
  architecture — 720
  area planning — 711.6
  art representation — 704.944
  capital procurement — 658.152 42
  construction — 690
  economics
    sale and rental — 333.338
  investment economics — 332.632 43
  landscape architecture — 717
  management — 658.2
    public administration — 350.713 3
      central governments — 351.713 3
      local governments — 352.163 3
  planning
    museums — 069.22
  public procurement — 350.712 3
    central governments — 351.712 3
    local governments — 352.162 3

Built-in furniture	645.4
decorative arts	749.4
manufacturing technology	684.16
see also Furniture	
Bujumbura (Burundi)	T2—675 72
Buka Island	T2—959 2
Bukhara rugs	
arts	746.758 7
see also Rugs	
Bukhari, Muhammad ibn Ismail	
Hadith	297.124 1
Bukidnon (Philippines)	T2—599 7
Bukovina	T2—498 4
Romania	T2—498 4
Ukraine	T2—477 18
Bulacan (Philippines)	T2—599 1
Bulawayo (Zimbabwe)	T2—689 1
Bulbs (Plants)	584.041 65
anatomy	584.044 6
floriculture	635.944
nursery production	631.526
plant propagation	631.532
Bulganin, Nikolay Aleksandrovich	
Russian history	947.085 2
Bulgaria	949.77
	T2—497 7
ancient	939.8
	T2—398
Bulgarian Empire, 680-1014	949.770 13
Bulgarian Empire, 1185-1396	949.770 14
Bulgarian language	491.81
	T6—918 11
Bulgarian literature	891.81
Bulgarian Macedonia	T2—497 74
Bulgarian Thrace	T2—497 78
Bulgarians	T5—918 11
Bulimia	
medicine	616.852 63
see also Mental illness	
Bulk carriers (Ships)	387.245
engineering	623.824 5
see also Ships	
Bulk mailings	383.124
see also Postal service	
Bulk modulus	531.381
Bulkley-Nechako (B.C.)	T2—711 82
Bulkley River (B.C.)	T2—711 82
Bull mastiff	
animal husbandry	636.73
see also Dogs	
Bull Moose Party (U.S.)	324.273 27
Bull-roarers	788.29
see also Wind instruments	
Bull Shoals Lake (Ark. and Mo.)	T2—767 193

Bulldog	
animal husbandry	636.72
see also Dogs	
Bulldozers	624.152
engineering	629.225
repair	629.287 5
Bulletin boards	
education	371.335 6
management use	658.455
Bulletin boards (Computer)	004.693
see also Computer communications	
Bullets	
military engineering	623.455
Bullfighting	791.82
ethics	175.6
see also Recreation—ethics	
performing arts	791.82
Bullis fever	
incidence	614.526 6
medicine	616.922 6
see also Communicable diseases (Human)	
Bullitt County (Ky.)	T2—769 453
Bulloch County (Ga.)	T2—758 766
Bullock County (Ala.)	T2—761 483
Bullroarers	788.29
see also Wind instruments	
Bulrush (Cyperaceae)	584.84
Bulrush (Typhaceae)	584.613
Bultfontein (South Africa : District)	T2—685 3
Bumpers	
automobile	629.276
Bunbury (W.A.)	T2—941 2
Buncombe County (N.C.)	T2—756 88
Bundaberg (Qld.)	T2—943 2
Bundi (New Guinea people)	T5—991 2
Bundi language	499.12
	T6—991 2
Bundling (Customs)	392.4
Bungalows	
architecture	728.373
Bunker Hill, Battle of, 1775	973.331 2
Bunker oils	665.538 8
Bunsen burners (Chemical apparatus)	542.4
Bunt	589.227
disease of wheat	633.119 427
Buntings	598.883
Bunun (Taiwan people)	T5—992 5
Bunya Mountains	T2—943 2
Bunya Mountains National Park	T2—943 2
Bunyaviruses	576.648 4
Bunyoro (Kingdom)	967.610 1
	T2—676 1

Bus terminals (continued)	
transportation services	388.33
urban	388.473
Bus transportation	388.322
international law	341.756 882
law	343.094 82
public administration	350.878 322
central governments	351.878 322
local governments	352.918 322
transportation services	388.322
urban	388.413 22
law	343.098 2
public administration	350.878 413 22
central governments	351.878 413 22
local governments	352.918 413 22
Buses	388.342 33
driving	629.283 33
engineering	629.222 33
law	343.094 4
military engineering	623.747 23
operation	388.322 044
repair	629.287 233
sanitation services	363.729 3
see also Waste control	
Bush babies	599.81
Bush clover	583.322
forage crop	633.364
Bushehr (Iran : Province)	T2—557 5
Bushman languages	496.1
	T6—961
Bushmanland	T2—687 2
Bushman's River	T2—684 7
Bushmen (African people)	T5—961
Bushveld (South Africa)	T2—682 5
Business	650
Business cards	
illustration	741.685
Business crime	364.168
law	345.026 8
Business cycles	
economics	338.542
Business districts	307.333
area planning	711.552 2
Business enterprises	338.7
economics	338.7
initiation	658.11
	T1—068 1
international law	341.753
law	346.065
location	338.09
economic rationale	338.604 2
economics	338.09
law	346.07
management	658.11
	T1—068 1
see also Plant location—	
management	
relations with government	322.3

Business ethics	174.4
see also Ethical problems	
Business etiquette	395.52
Business forecasting	338.544
Business forecasts	338.544 3
Business forms	651.29
Business income tax	336.241 7
public administration	350.724 4
central governments	351.724 4
local governments	352.135
public finance	336.241 7
Business insurance	368.81
see also Insurance	
Business intelligence	
management use	658.47
Business interruption insurance	368.815
see also Insurance	
Business law	346.07
Business libraries	027.69
Business losses	
tax economics	336.241 7
tax law	343.052 36
Business machines	651.2
manufacturing technology	681.14
office services	651.2
Business management	658
	T1—068
Business names	929.97
property law	346.048
Business organizations	
social welfare	361.765
Business records	
law	346.065
Business relationships (Personal)	650.13
Business security	
management	658.47
Business success	650.1
Business tax	336.207
law	343.068
public administration	350.724
central governments	351.724
local governments	352.13
public finance	336.207
Businesses	338.7
see also Business enterprises	
Businessmen	338.092
occupational group	T7—338
Busing (School desegregation)	370.193 42
law	344.079 8
Busing students (Transportation)	371.872
Buskerud fylke (Norway)	T2—482
Busoga (Kingdom)	967.610 1
	T2—676 1
Bustards	598.31
Busts (Sculpture)	731.74
Butadiene-styrene rubber	678.72
Butane	665.773
Butcher paper	676.287

C.D.-R.O.M. (Computer
  memory)   004.56
  engineering   621.397 6
C.D.s (Compact discs)
  sound reproduction   621.389 32
C.E.N.T.O. (Alliance)   355.031 095 6
C.I.A. (Intelligence agency)   327.127 3
C.I.M. (Manufacturing)   670.285
C.I.O. (Labor)   331.883 309 73
C.I.P. (Cataloging)   025.3
C.O.D. mail   383.184
  see also Postal service
C.O.D.A.S.Y.L. databases   005.754
C.O.M. devices   004.77
  manufacturing technology   681.6
C.O.M.E.C.O.N. (Economic
    organization)   341.242 7
  international commerce   382.914 7
  international economics   337.147
  international law   341.242 7
C.O.N.S.E.R. Project   025.343 2
C.P.M. (Management)   658.403 2
C.P.R. (Resuscitation)
  medicine   616.102 5
  see also Cardiovascular system
C.P.U. (Central processor)   004
  engineering   621.39
C.T. (Tomography)
  medicine   616.075 72
Caaguazú (Paraguay : Dept.) T2—892 134
Caazapá (Paraguay)   T2—892 127
Cabacas   786.885
  see also Percussion instruments
Cabala   296.16
  Jewish mysticism
    experience   296.712
    movement   296.833
  Judaistic sources   296.16
  occultism   135.4
Cabañas (El Salvador)   T2—728 426
Cabaret shows   792.7
Cabarrus County (N.C.)   T2—756 72
Cabbage   641.353 4
  botany   583.123
  commercial processing   664.805 34
  cooking   641.653 4
  garden crop   635.34
Cabell County (W. Va.)   T2—754 42
Cabin pressurization
  aircraft   629.134 42
Cabinda (Angola : Province) T2—673 1
Cabinet members
  occupational group   T7—352 1
Cabinet organs   786.55
  see also Keyboard instruments
Cabinet system   321.804 3
Cabinetmakers   684.100 92
Cabinetmaking   684.16

Cabinets (Furniture)
  decorative arts   749.3
  manufacturing technology   684.16
Cabinets (Government councils)
  public administration   351.004
Cabins   643.1
  architecture   728.73
  home economics   643.1
Cabins (Aircraft)   629.134 45
Cable communication systems   384.6
  see also Telephone
Cable railways   385.6
  engineering   625.5
  transportation services   385.6
  see also Railroad transportation
Cable television   384.555
  engineering   621.388 57
  law   343.099 46
  public administration   350.874 555
    central governments   351.874 555
    local governments   352.914 555
  see also Television
Cables
  computer science   004.64
    engineering   621.398 1
  electrical circuits   621.319 34
  knotting and splicing   623.888 2
  metal   671.84
  structural engineering   624.177 4
Cabo Delgado (Mozambique :
    District)   T2—679 8
Cabo Gracias a Dios
    (Nicaragua : Territory) T2—728 532
Cabombaceae   583.111
Cabooses   385.32
  engineering   625.22
  transportation services   385.32
  see also Rolling stock
Cabs   388.342 32
  driving   629.283 32
  engineering   629.222 32
  repair   629.287 232
  transportation services   388.342 32
  urban   388.413 214
  see also Automobiles
Cacao   583.19
  agriculture   633.74
  see also Cocoa
Cacao butter   665.354
  see also Cocoa butter
Cáceres (Spain : Province) T2—462 8
Cachapoal (Chile : Province) T2—833 2
Cache County (Utah)   T2—792 12
Cache Creek (B.C.)   T2—711 72
Cachets (Philately)   769.567
Cactales   583.47
Cactus   583.47
  floriculture   635.933 47

Calcium soaps	668.125
Calculators	681.14
manufacturing technology	681.14
mathematics	510.28
Calculus	515
Calculus of finite differences	515.62
Calculus of variations	515.64
Calcutta (India)	T2—541 47
Caldas (Colombia : Dept.)	T2—861 35
Calderdale (England)	T2—428 12
Caldwell County (Ky.)	T2—769 815
Caldwell County (Mo.)	T2—778 185
Caldwell County (N.C.)	T2—756 845
Caldwell County (Tex.)	T2—764 33
Caldwell Parish (La.)	T2—763 76
Caledon (South Africa :	
District)	T2—687 3
Caledon River	T2—685 6
Caledonia County (Vt.)	T2—743 34
Calendar reform	529.5
Calendars	529.3
chronology	529.3
illustration	741.682
religion	291.36
Christianity	263.9
Calendars (Liturgical books)	264
Anglican	264.031
Roman Catholic	264.021
Calendering paper	676.234
Calendering rubber	678.27
Calendering textiles	677.028 25
Calgary (Alta.)	T2—712 338
Calhoun County (Ala.)	T2—761 63
Calhoun County (Ark.)	T2—767 64
Calhoun County (Fla.)	T2—759 943
Calhoun County (Ga.)	T2—758 956
Calhoun County (Ill.)	T2—773 853
Calhoun County (Iowa)	T2—777 43
Calhoun County (Mich.)	T2—774 22
Calhoun County (Miss.)	T2—762 81
Calhoun County (S.C.)	T2—757 72
Calhoun County (Tex.)	T2—764 121
Calhoun County (W. Va.)	T2—754 29
Calibration	681.2
electrical instruments	621.372
California	979.4
	T2—794
California, Gulf of (Mexico)	551.466 1
	T2—164 1
California, Southern	T2—794 9
California myrtle	583.931
Californium	546.448
see also Chemicals	
Caligoida	595.34
paleozoology	565.34
Caliphate	297.24
Islamic organization	297.65
Caliphs	297.092
role and function	297.61
specific sects	297.8
Calisthenics	613.714
child care	649.57
therapeutics	615.824
Calitzdorp (South Africa :	
District)	T2—687 16
Call	332.645
multiple forms of investment	332.645
stocks	332.632 28
Calla lily	584.64
Callabonna, Lake	T2—942 37
Callahan County (Tex.)	T2—764 726
Callao (Peru : Province)	T2—852 6
Callaway County (Mo.)	T2—778 335
Calles, Plutarco Elías	
Mexican history	972.082 3
Calligraphy	745.61
Callipteris	561.597
Callithricidae	599.82
Callitrichaceae	583.44
Callixylon	561.55
Callosities	
medicine	616.544
see also Skin	
Calloway County (Ky.)	T2—769 92
Caloosahatchee River (Fla.)	T2—759 48
Calorie counters	641.104 2
Calories	
home economics	641.104 2
Calorimeters	
manufacturing technology	681.2
Calorimetry	536.6
Caltanissetta (Sicily :	
Province)	T2—458 21
Calumet County (Wis.)	T2—775 66
Calvados (France)	T2—442 2
Calvert County (Md.)	T2—752 44
Calvinia (South Africa :	
District)	T2—687 17
Calvinistic Baptists	286.1
see also Baptists	
Calvinistic churches	284.2
see also Reformed Church	
Calvinists	
biography	284.209 2
religious group	T7—242
Calycanthaceae	583.374
Calyceraceae	583.53
Calyxes	
anatomy	582.130 446 3
CAM (Manufacturing)	670.427
Camagüey (Cuba : Province)	T2—729 156
Camarines Norte (Philippines)	T2—599 1
Camarines Sur (Philippines)	T2—599 1
Camas County (Idaho)	T2—796 31
Cambistry	332.45

Campus police	363.289
Cams	621.838
Canaanite language	492.6
	T6—926
Canaanite literature	892.6
Canaanites	T5—926
Canaanitic languages	492.6
	T6—926
Canaanitic literatures	892.6
Canada	971
	T2—71
Canada, Eastern	T2—713
Canada, Western	T2—712
Canadian Arctic	T2—719
Canadian County (Okla.)	T2—766 39
Canadian football	796.335
Canadian language	
English	420.971
	T6—21
French	440.971
	T6—41
Canadian literature	
English	810
French	840
Inuit	897.1
Canadian Pacific seawaters	551.466 33
	T2—164 33
Canadian pronunciation (English language)	421.52
Canadian pronunciation (French language)	441.52
Canadian River	T2—766
Canadian River, North (Okla.)	T2—766 1
Canadian Shield	T2—714
Canada	T2—714
Manitoba	T2—712 72
Ontario	T2—713 1
Canadian spelling (English language)	421.52
Canadian spelling (French language)	441.52
Canadians	T5—11
Canaigre	583.143
agriculture	633.87
Canakkale Ili (Turkey)	T2—562
Europe	T2—496 1
Canal transportation	386.4
transportation services	386.4
see also Inland waterway transportation	
Canal Zone	T2—728 75
Canalboats	
freight services	386.244
power-driven	386.224 36
design	623.812 436
engineering	623.824 36
transportation services	386.224 36

Canalboats (continued)	
towed	386.229
design	623.812 9
engineering	623.829
transportation services	386.229
see also Ships	
Canalized rivers	
engineering	627.13
Canals	
engineering	627.13
international law	341.446
irrigation	
engineering	627.52
Canandaigua Lake (N.Y.)	T2—747 86
Canapés	641.812
Cañar (Ecuador : Province)	T2—866 23
Canarese	T5—948 14
Canaries	598.883
animal husbandry	636.686 2
Canary grass	584.93
Canary Islands	964.9
	T2—649
Canasta	795.418
Canberra (A.C.T.)	T2—947 1
Cancellations (Philately)	769.567
Cancer	362.196 994
geriatrics	618.976 994
incidence	614.599 9
medicine	616.994
nursing	610.736 98
pediatrics	618.929 94
social services	362.196 994
surgery	616.994 059
veterinary medicine	636.089 699 4
zoology	591.2
Candelilla wax	665.12
Candleberry wax	665.12
Candler County (Ga.)	T2—758 773
Candles	621.323
handicrafts	745.593 32
Candlesticks	621.323
ceramic arts	738.8
handicrafts	745.593 3
Candlewood	583.158
Candy	641.853
commercial processing	664.153
home preparation	641.853
Candytuft	583.123
Cane fruit	583.372
horticulture	634.71
Cane sugar	
commercial processing	664.122
see also Sugar	
Cane syrup	
commercial processing	664.122
Cane textiles	677.54
see also Textiles	
Canea (Greece : Nome)	T2—499 8

Cape Agulhas	T2—687 3
Cape Barren Island	T2—946 7
Cape Breton (N.S. : County)	T2—716 95
Cape Breton Highlands National Park (N.S.)	T2—716 91
Cape Breton Island (N.S.)	T2—716 9
Cape Cod (Mass.)	T2—744 92
Cape Cod Bay (Mass.)	551.461 45
	T2—163 45
Cape Dorset (N.W.T.)	T2—719 5
Cape Douglas	T2—798 3
Cape Fear River (N.C.)	T2—756 2
Cape Flats (South Africa : District)	T2—687 35
Cape Girardeau County (Mo.)	T2—778 96
Cape Hatteras (N.C.)	T2—756 175
Cape Le Grand National Park	T2—941 7
Cape May County (N.J.)	T2—749 98
Cape of Good Hope (South Africa)	968.7
	T2—687
Cape of Good Hope (South Africa : Cape)	T2—687 35
Cape of Good Hope Nature Reserve	T2—687 35
Cape Peninsula (South Africa : Cape)	T2—687 35
Cape Range National Park	T2—941 3
Cape Town (South Africa)	T2—687 355
Cape Verde	966.58
	T2—665 8
Cape Verde Islands	T2—665 8
Cape Verdeans	T5—966 58
Cape York Peninsula (Qld.)	T2—943 8
Caper (Plant)	583.131
Capets (French history)	944.021
Capillaries	
human anatomy	611.15
human diseases	
medicine	616.148
human physiology	612.135
surgery	617.415
see also Cardiovascular system	
Capillarity	541.33
chemical engineering	660.293
physics	530.427
Capillary circulation	
human physiology	612.135
see also Cardiovascular system	
Capital	332.041
distribution	
macroeconomics	339.21
financial economics	332.041
management	658.152
Capital (B.C.)	T2—711 28
Capital accounting	657.76

Capital budgets	658.154
public administration	350.722 253 4
central governments	351.722 253 4
local governments	352.122 534
Capital cities	
area planning	711.45
Capital District (Paraguay)	T2—892 121
Capital formation	332.041 5
agriculture	338.13
economics	332.041 5
financial management	658.152 2
macroeconomics	339.43
mineral industries	338.23
secondary industries	338.43
Capital gains tax	336.242 4
law	343.052 45
public administration	351.724 4
public finance	336.242 4
Capital management	658.152
Capital punishment	364.66
ethics	179.7
religion	291.569 7
Buddhism	294.356 97
Christianity	241.697
Hinduism	294.548 697
Islam	297.5
Judaism	296.385 697
law	345.077 3
penology	364.66
social theology	291.178 336 6
Christianity	261.833 66
Capital sources	332.041 54
financial management	658.152 2
Capital transactions (Balance of payments)	
international banking	332.152
international commerce	382.173
Capitalism	330.122
economics	330.122
sociology	306.342
Capitalization (Finance)	658.152
Capitals (Architecture)	721.3
Capitán Prat (Chile : Province)	T2—836 28
Capitol Reef National Park (Utah)	T2—792 54
Capitols	
architecture	725.11
Capiz (Philippines : Province)	T2—599 5
Cappadocia	T2—393 4
Capparidales	583.131
Capraia Island	T2—455 6
Caprellidea	595.371
Capri Island (Italy)	T2—457 3
Caprifoliaceae	583.52
Caprimulgi	598.99
Caprimulgiformes	598.99
paleozoology	568.9
Capstans	621.864

Card players	795.409 2
sports group	T7—795
Card readers (Computer)	004.76
engineering	621.398 6
Card tricks	795.438
Card weaving	
arts	746.14
Cardamom	584.21
Cardboard	676.288
Cárdenas, Lázaro	
Mexican history	972.082 5
Cardiac arrest	
medicine	616.123 025
see also Cardiovascular system	
Cardiac muscle tissue	
human histology	611.018 6
Cardiff (Wales)	T2—429 87
Cardigans	391
commercial technology	687.146
customs	391
home sewing	646.454
see also Clothing	
Cardiganshire (Wales)	T2—429 61
Cardinal sins	241.3
Cardinals (Birds)	598.883
Cardinals (Clergy)	282.092
ecclesiology	262.135
Carding textiles	677.028 21
arts	746.11
manufacturing technology	677.028 21
Cardiology	616.12
see also Cardiovascular system	
Cardiopteridaceae	583.271
Cardiopulmonary resuscitation	
medicine	616.102 5
see also Cardiovascular system	
Cardiovascular agents	
pharmacodynamics	615.71
see also Cardiovascular system	
Cardiovascular diseases	
medicine	616.1
see also Cardiovascular system	
Cardiovascular organs	591.11
human physiology	612.1
see also Cardiovascular system	
Cardiovascular system	591.11
anesthesiology	617.967 41
animal anatomy	591.41
animal diseases	591.211
animal histology	591.824
animal physiology	591.11
cancer	362.196 994 1
medicine	616.994 1
social services	362.196 994 1
see also Cancer	
geriatrics	618.976 1
human anatomy	611.1
Cardiovascular system (continued)	
human diseases	362.196 1
incidence	614.591
medicine	616.1
social services	362.196 1
human histology	611.018 91
human physiology	612.1
nursing	610.736 91
pediatrics	618.921
perinatal medicine	618.326 1
pharmacodynamics	615.71
surgery	617.41
veterinary medicine	636.089 61
Cards (Games)	795.4
manufacturing technology	688.754
CARE (Firm)	361.763
Career education	370.113
adult education	374.013
curriculums	375.008 6
secondary level	373.246
Career guidance	
education	371.425
Career opportunities	331.702
	T1—023
economics	331.702
Carey, Lake	T2—941 6
Cargados Carajos Shoals	T2—698 2
Cargo airplanes	
military engineering	623.746 5
Cargo handling	388.044
port services	387.164
engineering	623.888 1
equipment	623.867
onboard	627.34
shipboard	623.867
see also Freight services	
Cargo insurance	368.2
see also Insurance	
Cargo ships	387.245
petroleum technology	665.543
power-driven	387.245
design	623.812 45
engineering	623.824 5
wind-driven	387.224
design	623.812 24
engineering	623.822 4
see also Merchant ships, Ships	
Caria	T2—392 4
Cariamae	598.31
Carib Indians	T5—984
Carib languages	498.4
	T6—984
Caribbean Area	972.9
	T2—729
Caribbean Islands	T2—729
Caribbean Sea	551.463 5
	T2—163 65
Caribbees	T2—729

Cariboo (B.C. : Regional District)	T2—711 75
Cariboo Mountains (B.C.)	T2—711 7
Caribou	599.735 7
big game hunting	799.277 357
Caribou County (Idaho)	T2—796 45
Caricaceae	583.46
Caricatures	741.5
drawing	741.5
Caries	
dentistry	617.67
incidence	614.599 6
see also Dentistry	
Carillons	786.64
see also Mechanical musical instruments	
Carinthia (Austria)	T2—436 6
Carleton (N.B. : County)	T2—715 52
Carletonville (South Africa)	T2—682 2
Carlisle (England : City)	T2—427 89
Carlisle County (Ky.)	T2—769 97
Carlow (Ireland : County)	T2—418 82
Carlsbad Caverns National Park (N.M.)	T2—789 42
Carlton County (Minn.)	T2—776 73
Carmarthen (Wales : District)	T2—429 65
Carmelite Nuns	255.971
church history	271.971
Carmelites	255.73
church history	271.73
women	255.971
church history	271.971
Carnallite	553.636
mineralogy	549.4
Carnarvon (South Africa : District)	T2—687 17
Carnarvon (W.A.)	T2—941 3
Carnarvon National Park (Qld.)	T2—943 5
Carnation pinks	583.75
Carnations	583.152
floriculture	635.933 152
Carnauba wax	665.12
Carnegie, Lake	T2—941 6
Carnivals	791.1
customs	394.25
performing arts	791.1
Carnivora	599.74
paleozoology	569.74
Carnot cycle	536.71
Caro, Joseph	
Judaistic sources	296.182
Carob	583.322
orchard crop	634.46
Carolina (South Africa : District)	T2—682 7
Caroline County (Md.)	T2—752 31
Caroline County (Va.)	T2—755 362

Caroline Island	T2—964
Caroline Islands	T2—966
Carolingian calligraphy	745.619 74
Carolingian dynasty (French history)	944.014
Carolingian dynasty (German history)	943.014
Carolingian dynasty (Italian history)	945.02
Carols	782.28
choral and mixed voices	782.528
single voices	783.092 8
Carotid glands	
human anatomy	611.47
human diseases medicine	616.48
human physiology	612.492
see also Endocrine system	
Carp	597.52
commercial fishing	639.275 2
culture	639.375 2
sports fishing	799.175 2
Carpals	
human anatomy	611.717
see also Musculoskeletal system	
Carpathian Mountains	T2—477 18
Carpathos Island (Greece)	T2—499 6
Carpels	
anatomy	582.130 446 3
Carpentaria, Gulf of	551.465 75
	T2—164 75
Carpenter Lake (B.C.)	T2—711 31
Carpenters	694.092
occupational group	T7—694
Carpentry	694
ship hulls	623.844
Carpeting	
building construction	698.9
Carpetmakers	746.792
occupational group	T7—746
Carpets	645.1
arts	746.7
household management	645.1
interior decoration	747.5
manufacturing technology	677.643
nonwoven felts	677.632
Carranza, Venustiano	
Mexican history	972.082 1
Carrera, Rafael	
Guatemalan history	972.810 44
Carriacou Island	972.984 5
	T2—729 845
Carriage horses	
animal husbandry	636.14
zoology	599.725
Carriages	388.341
manufacturing technology	688.6
Carrick (England : District)	T2—423 78

Carrick, Kyle and (Scotland)	T2—414 64
Carrickfergus (Northern Ireland : Borough)	T2—416 17
Carrier language	497.2
	T6—972
Carriers (Common carriers)	388.041
law	343.093
see also Passenger services	
Carriers (Pneumatic)	621.54
Carrion beetle	595.764 2
Carrion flower	584.323
Carroll County (Ark.)	T2—767 17
Carroll County (Ga.)	T2—758 39
Carroll County (Ill.)	T2—773 345
Carroll County (Ind.)	T2—772 94
Carroll County (Iowa)	T2—777 465
Carroll County (Ky.)	T2—769 373
Carroll County (Md.)	T2—752 77
Carroll County (Miss.)	T2—762 633
Carroll County (Mo.)	T2—778 225
Carroll County (N.H.)	T2—742 42
Carroll County (Ohio)	T2—771 67
Carroll County (Tenn.)	T2—768 25
Carroll County (Va.)	T2—755 714
Carrots	641.351 3
botany	583.48
commercial processing	664.805 13
cooking	641.651 3
garden crop	635.13
Carrying cases	
cameras	771.38
Cars (Automobiles)	388.342
driving	629.283
engineering	629.222
repair	629.287 2
transportation services	388.342
see also Automobiles	
Carson City (Nev.)	T2—793 57
Carson County (Tex.)	T2—764 826
Cartagena (Spain)	T2—467 7
Cartago (Costa Rica : Province)	T2—728 62
Cartan geometry	516.376
Cartels	338.87
economics	338.87
international	338.88
Carter, James Earl	
United States history	973.926
Carter, Jimmy	
United States history	973.926
Carter County (Ky.)	T2—769 28
Carter County (Mo.)	T2—778 892
Carter County (Mont.)	T2—786 36
Carter County (Okla.)	T2—766 58
Carter County (Tenn.)	T2—768 984
Carteret County (N.C.)	T2—756 197
Cartesian coordinate system	516.16
Carthage	939.73
	T2—397 3
Carthaginian architecture	722.32
Carthaginian period (Spanish history)	936.602
Carthusians	255.71
church history	271.71
women	255.97
church history	271.97
Cartier, Jacques	
Quebec history	971.401 2
Cartier Island	T2—948
Cartilaginous fishes	597.3
Cartilaginous ganoids	597.44
Cartilaginous tissue	
human histology	611.018 3
see also Musculoskeletal system	
Cartographers	526.092
occupational group	T7—526
Cartographic materials	
cataloging	025.346
library treatment	025.176
Cartography	526
military engineering	623.71
Cartomancy	133.324 2
Cartonemataceae	584.38
Cartons	688.8
paperboard	676.32
Cartoon fiction	741.5
Cartoons	741.5
	T1—022
drawing	741.5
humorous	741.5
	T1—020 7
journalism	
comics	070.444
editorial	070.442
Cartridge tapes (Computer)	004.56
engineering	621.397 6
Cartridges (Ammunition)	683.406
manufacturing technology	683.406
military engineering	623.455
Carts	388.341
manufacturing technology	688.6
Carver County (Minn.)	T2—776 53
Carving	736
architectural decoration	729.5
decorative arts	736
sculpture	731.46
Carving (Meats)	642.6
Caryocaraceae	583.166
Caryophyllales	583.152
Casaba melon	641.356 117
botany	583.46
garden crop	635.611 7
Casablanca (Morocco)	T2—643
Casablanca-Anfa (Morocco : Prefecture)	T2—643

Castlereagh (Northern
   Ireland : Borough)   T2—416 51
Castlereagh River   T2—944 9
Castles
   architecture   728.81
   domestic
      architecture   728.81
   military
      architecture   725.18
Castles (Chessmen)   794.143
Castor oil   665.353
Castor-oil plant   583.95
Castrato voices   782.86
   choral and mixed voices   782.86
   single voices   783.86
Castro, Cipriano
   Venezuelan history   987.063 12
Castro, Fidel
   Cuban history   972.910 64
Castro County (Tex.)   T2—764 837
Castroism   335.434 7
   economics   335.434 7
   political ideology   320.532 309 729 1
Casual clothes   391
   see also Clothing
Casual workers
   economics   331.544
Casualty insurance   368.5
   law   346.086 5
   see also Insurance
Casuariiformes   598.53
   paleozoology   568.5
Casuarinales   583.975
Casuistry
   ethical systems   171.6
Caswell County (N.C.)   T2—756 575
CAT (Air transportation hazard)   363.124 12
Cat brier   584.323
Cat Island   T2—729 6
CAT scan
   medicine   616.075 72
Catabolism   574.133
   see also Metabolism
Catahoula Parish (La.)   T2—763 74
Catalan language   449.9
    T6—499
Catalan literature   849.9
Catalans   T5—49
Catalases   574.192 58
   see also Enzymes
Cataloging
   library science   025.3
   museology   069.52
Cataloging in publication   025.3
Catalogs   T1—021 6
   postal handling   383.124
      see also Postal service

Catalogs (Bibliographic
   materials)   025.31
   bibliography   017
   library science   025.31
Catalogs of exhibits   069.52
    T1—074
   museology   069.52
Catalonia (Spain)   T2—467
Catalpa   583.54
Cataluña (Spain)   T2—467
Catalysis   541.395
   chemical engineering   660.299 5
Catalytic cracking   665.533
Catamarca (Argentina :
   Province)   T2—824 5
Catanduanes Island   T2—599 1
Catanduanes Province
   (Philippines)   T2—599 1
Catania (Sicily : Province)   T2—458 13
Catanzaro (Italy : Province)   T2—457 81
Catapults   623.441
Cataracts
   ophthalmology   617.742
   see also Eyes
Catastrophes   904
   see also Disasters
Catastrophes (Mathematics)   514.74
Catastrophic health insurance   368.382
   government-sponsored   368.42
   law   344.022
   see also Insurance
Catawba County (N.C.)   T2—756 785
Catawba River (N.C. and
   S.C.)   T2—757 45
Catbirds   598.841
Catch-as-catch-can wrestling   796.812 3
Catch basins
   sewers   628.25
Catchers' mitts
   manufacturing technology   685.43
Catching
   baseball   796.357 23
Catchword indexing   025.486
Catechetics   268
Catechisms   291.2
   Christianity   238
Catechists   268.092
   role and function   268.3
Catechols   547.633
Catechumenate   265.13
Categories (Mathematics)   511.3
   topological algebras   512.55
Catered meals   642.4
Caterers   642.409 2
   occupational group   T7—642
Catering   642.4
   armed forces   355.341
Caterpillars   595.780 43

Cavan (Ireland : County)	T2—416 98
Caves	551.447
	T2—144
exploring	796.525
geography	910.914 4
geomorphology	551.447
physical geography	910.021 44
psychological influence	155.964
Cavies	599.323 4
Caviomorpha	599.323 4
Cavitation	532.059 5
air mechanics	533.62
engineering	620.106 4
fluid mechanics	532.059 5
gas mechanics	533.295
liquid mechanics	532.595
Cavite Province (Philippines)	T2—599 1
Cavities (Teeth)	
dentistry	617.67
incidence	614.599 6
see also Dentistry	
Cavity resonators	621.381 332
Cayenne (French Guiana)	T2—882
Cayenne peppers	583.79
Cayman Islands	972.921
	T2—729 21
Cayo (Belize : District)	T2—728 25
Cayuga County (N.Y.)	T2—747 68
Cayuga Lake (N.Y.)	T2—747 68
CB radio	384.53
communication services	384.53
engineering	621.384 54
CBR warfare	358.3
law	341.735
CCF (Machine-readable format)	025.316
CD-ROM (Computer memory)	004.56
engineering	621.397 6
CDs	
sound reproduction	621.389 32
Ceará (Brazil : State)	T2—813 1
Cebidae	599.82
Cebu (Philippines)	T2—599 5
Cebu Island (Philippines)	T2—599 5
Cebuano language	499.21
	T6—992 1
Cecil County (Md.)	T2—752 38
Cecum	
human anatomy	611.345
human physiology	612.33
surgery	617.554 5
see also Digestive system	
Cedar	585.2
forestry	634.975 6
lumber	674.144
Cedar County (Iowa)	T2—777 66
Cedar County (Mo.)	T2—778 743
Cedar County (Neb.)	T2—782 58
Cedar River	T2—777 6

Cedarberg Range	T2—687 2
Ceiling coverings	
household management	645.2
Ceilings	721.7
architecture	721.7
construction	690.17
interior decoration	747.3
Celandine	583.122
Celastrales	583.271
Celebes (Indonesia)	T2—598 4
Celebes Sea	551.465 73
	T2—164 73
Celebrations	394.2
armed forces	355.16
Civil War (United States)	973.76
cooking	641.568
customs	394.2
Mexican War	973.626
public administration	350.859
central governments	351.859
local governments	352.945 9
South African War	968.048 6
Spanish-American War, 1898	973.896
United States Revolutionary War	973.36
Vietnamese War	959.704 36
War of 1812	973.526
World War I	940.46
World War II	940.546
Celeriac	641.351 28
botany	583.48
cooking	641.651 28
garden crop	635.128
Celery	641.355 3
botany	583.48
commercial processing	664.805 53
cooking	641.655 3
garden crop	635.53
Celery root	641.351 28
see also Celeriac	
Celestas	786.83
see also Percussion instruments	
Celestial bodies	523
folklore	398.26
sociology	398.362
Celestial coordinates	522.7
Celestial mechanics	521
engineering	629.411
Celestial navigation	527
nautical	623.89
Celestial sphere	522.7
Celestines	255.16
church history	271.16
Celestite	
mineralogy	549.752
Celibacy	306.732
customs	392.6

Central African Federation	968.903
	T2—689
Central African Republic	967.41
	T2—674 1
Central African Republic	
people	T5—967 41
Central Africans (National	
group)	T5—967 41
Central America	972.8
	T2—728
Central America (Federal	
Republic : 1823-1840)	972.804
	T2—728
Costa Rican history	972.860 42
Guatemalan history	972.810 42
Honduran history	972.830 4
Nicaraguan history	972.850 42
Salvadoran history	972.840 42
Central American native	
languages	497
	T6—97
Central American native	
literatures	897
Central American native	
peoples	T5—97
Central Asia	958
	T2—58
ancient	939.6
	T2—396
Central Auckland (N.Z.)	T2—931 22
Central Australia	T2—942
Central banks	332.11
Central Bantu languages	496.391
Central Black Earth Region	
(R.S.F.S.R.)	T2—473 5
Central business district	
community redevelopment	307.342
Central Chernozem Region	
(R.S.F.S.R.)	T2—473 5
Central Coast (B.C.)	T2—711 1
Central District (Guatemala)	T2—728 11
Central Dravidian languages	494.82
	T6—948 2
Central Dravidian literatures	894.82
Central Dravidians	T5—948 2
Central Europe	943
	T2—43
Central Fraser Valley (B.C.)	T2—711 37
Central governments	351
law	342.042
Central heating	697.03
Central Intelligence Agency	327.127 3
Central Islands (Solomon	
Islands : Province)	T2—959 35
Central Islands and Santa	
Isabel Province (Solomon	
Islands)	T2—959 35
Central Kootenay (B.C.)	T2—711 62

Central Lowlands (Scotland)	T2—413
Central nervous system	591.188
human anatomy	611.81
human diseases	
medicine	616.8
human physiology	612.82
see also Nervous system	
Central Okanagan (B.C.)	T2—711 5
Central Pacific Basin	551.465 9
	T2—164 9
Central Pacific islands	T2—96
Central Powers (World War I)	940.334
Central processing units	004
engineering	621.39
Central Province (Kenya)	T2—676 26
Central Province (Papua New	
Guinea)	T2—954 6
Central Province (Zambia)	T2—689 4
Central Region (Scotland)	T2—413 1
Central Saanich (B.C.)	T2—711 28
Central-Southern Region	
(China)	T2—512
Central stations	
steam engineering	621.19
Central Treaty Organization	355.031 095 6
Central Valley (Calif. :	
Valley)	T2—794 5
Centrales	589.481
Centralization	
library systems	021.6
public administration	350.007 3
central governments	351.007 3
local governments	352.000 473
Centralized databases	005.75
Centralized processing	004.3
Centre (France)	T2—445
Centre County (Pa.)	T2—748 53
Centre-de-la-Mauricie	
(Quebec)	T2—714 451
Centrifugal blowers	621.63
Centrifugal casting	
metals	671.254
Centrifugal fans	621.63
Centrifugal force	531.113
fluid mechanics	532.05
liquid mechanics	532.5
mechanics	531.113
solid mechanics	531.35
Centrifugal pumps	621.67
hydraulic	621.252
Centrifugation	
sewage treatment	628.34
Centrifuging latex	678.522
Centripetal force	531.113
fluid mechanics	532.05
liquid mechanics	532.5
mechanics	531.113
solid mechanics	531.35

Cerium
  chemistry 546.412
  see also Rare earths
Cerium-group metals
  chemistry 546.41
  economic geology 553.494 3
  see also Rare earths
Cerro Gordo County (Iowa) T2—777 25
Cerro Largo (Uruguay) T2—895 23
Certainty
  epistemology 121.63
Certhiidae 598.823
Certificates of deposit 332.175 2
Certificates of indebtedness
  public finance 336.32
Certification
  public administration 350.8
    central governments 351.8
    local governments 352.8
Certitude
  epistemology 121.63
Cerussite
  mineralogy 549.785
Cervical caps
  health 613.943 5
  see also Birth control, Female
    genital system
Cervical vertebrae
  human diseases
    medicine 616.73
  see also Musculoskeletal system
Cervicitis
  gynecology 618.142
  see also Female genital system
Cervix (Uterine)
  gynecology 618.14
  human anatomy 611.66
  human physiology 612.62
  surgery 618.145
  see also Female genital system
Cervoidea 599.735 7
César, El (Colombia : Dept.) T2—861 23
Cesarean section
  obstetrical surgery 618.86
Cesium 669.725
  chemical engineering 661.038 5
  chemistry 546.385
  metallurgy 669.725
  see also Chemicals
Cessnock (N.S.W.) T2—944 2
Cestoda 595.121
Cestodaria 595.121
Cestode-caused diseases
  medicine 616.964
Cetacea 599.5
  paleozoology 569.5
Cetewayo, King of Zululand
  Natal history 968.404 5

Ceuta (Spain) T2—642
Cévennes Mountains (France) T2—448
Ceylon T2—549 3
Ceylonese T5—914 13
Chabad Lubavitch Hasidism 296.833 22
Chachalacas 598.614
Chaco (Argentina) T2—823 4
Chaco (Paraguay : Dept.) T2—892 26
Chaco Boreal (Paraguay and
  Bolivia) T2—892 2
Chaco War, 1933-1935 989.207 1
Chaconne form 781.827
  instrumental 784.182 7
Chad 967.43
   T2—674 3
Chadians T5—967 43
Chadic languages 493.7
   T6—937
Chadic literatures 893
Chaetognatha 595.186
  paleozoology 565.1
Chaetophorales 589.47
Chaffee County (Colo.) T2—788 47
Chafing dish cooking 641.58
Chaga languages 496.395
   T6—963 95
Chagas' disease
  incidence 614.533
  medicine 616.936 3
  see also Communicable
    diseases (Human)
Chagatai language 494.3
   T6—943
Chagos Islands 969.7
   T2—697
Chailletiaceae 583.373
Chain banking 332.16
Chain drives 621.859
Chain gangs 365.65
  penology 365.65
Chain hoists 621.863
Chain indexing 025.482
Chain reactions
  chemical engineering 660.299 3
  chemistry 541.393
  nuclear engineering 621.483 1
  nuclear physics 539.761
  organic chemistry 547.139 3
Chain-stitch fabrics 677.66
  see also Textiles
Chain stores 381.12
  management 658.870 2
  see also Commerce
Chains
  power transmission 621.859
Chair cars 385.33
  engineering 625.23
  see also Rolling stock

Chaouen (Morocco : Province)	T2—642
Chaparral ecology	574.526 52
Chapbooks	398.5
Chapels	
architecture	726.4
Chaperonage	
customs	392.6
Chaplain services (Military)	355.347
Civil War (United States)	973.778
Mexican War	973.627
South African War	968.048 7
Spanish-American War, 1898	973.897
United States Revolutionary War	973.37
Vietnamese War	959.704 37
War of 1812	973.527
World War I	940.478
World War II	940.547 8
Chapping	
medicine	616.58
see also Skin	
Chapter houses	
architecture	726.69
Characins	597.52
Character	155.2
children	155.418 2
psychology	155.418 2
influence on crime	364.24
psychology	155.2
Character disorders	
medicine	616.858
see also Mental illness	
Character education	370.114
Character recognition	006.4
computer engineering	621.399
Character training	
home child care	649.7
Characters (Fictitious persons)	808.802 7
history and criticism	809.927
specific literatures	T3B—080 27
history and criticism	T3B—092 7
Characters (Symbols)	
printing	686.21
Charades	793.24
Charadrii	598.33
Charadriidae	598.33
Charadriiformes	598.33
paleozoology	568.3
Charales	589.47
Charbon	
incidence	614.561
medicine	616.956
see also Communicable diseases (Human)	
Charcoal	
chemical engineering	662.74
Charcoal cooking	641.58

Charcoal drawing	741.22
Chard	641.354 2
botany	583.913
cooking	641.654 2
garden crop	635.42
Charente (France)	T2—446 5
Charente-Inférieure (France)	T2—446 4
Charente-Maritime (France)	T2—446 4
Charente River	T2—446 5
Charge of particles (Nuclear physics)	539.725
Chari-Nile languages	496.5
	T6—965
Charismatic gifts	234.13
Charismatic movement	270.82
Charismatic spiritual renewal	269
Charitable donations	
financial management	658.153
tax law	343.052 32
Charitable trusts	
law	346.064
social welfare	361.763 2
tax law	343.066 8
Charities	361.7
see also Welfare services	
Chariton County (Mo.)	T2—778 25
Chariton River (Iowa and Mo.)	T2—778 2
Charity	
ethics	177.7
see also Virtues	
Charles City County (Va.)	T2—755 44
Charles County (Md.)	T2—752 47
Charles I, King of England	
British history	941.062
English history	942.062
Scottish history	941.106 2
Charles I, King of Spain	
Spanish history	946.042
Charles II, King of England	
British history	941.066
English history	942.066
Scottish history	941.106 6
Charles II, King of Spain	
Spanish history	946.053
Charles III, King of Spain	
Spanish history	946.057
Charles IV, King of France	
French history	944.024
Charles IV, King of Spain	
Spanish history	946.058
Charles Mix County (S.D.)	T2—783 382
Charles River (Mass.)	T2—744 4
Charles V, Holy Roman Emperor	
German history	943.031
Spanish history	946.042
Charles V, King of France	
French history	944.025

Charles VI, Holy Roman
  Emperor
    German history   943.052
Charles VI, King of France
  French history   944.026
Charles VII, Holy Roman
  Emperor
    German history   943.054
Charles VII, King of France
  French history   944.026
Charles VIII, King of France
  French history   944.027
Charles IX, King of France
  French history   944.029
Charles X, King of France
  French history   944.062
Charlesbourg (Quebec)   T2—714 471
Charleston (S.C.)   T2—757 915
Charleston (W. Va.)   T2—754 37
Charleston County (S.C.)   T2—757 91
Charleville (Qld.)   T2—943 4
Charlevoix (Quebec :
  Regional County
  Municipality)   T2—714 49
Charlevoix County (Mich.)   T2—774 86
Charlevoix-Est (Quebec)   T2—714 49
Charlevoix-Est (Quebec :
  Regional County
  Municipality)   T2—714 49
Charlevoix-Ouest (Quebec)   T2—714 49
Charlotte (N.B.)   T2—715 33
Charlotte (N.C.)   T2—756 76
Charlotte County (Fla.)   T2—759 49
Charlotte County (Va.)   T2—755 65
Charlottesville (Va.)   T2—755 481
Charlottetown (P.E.I.)   T2—717 5
Charlottetown Conference, 1864   971.049
Charlton (Vic.)   T2—945 4
Charlton County (Ga.)   T2—758 752
Charm
  personal living   646.76
Charms (Occultism)   133.44
Charnwood (England)   T2—425 47
Charter services
  air   387.742 8
Chartered banks   332.122
Chartered surveyors (United
  Kingdom)
    economics   333.08
Charters
  administrative law   342.066
  constitutional law   342.02
  private law   346.06
  public administration   350.8
    central governments   351.8
    local governments   352.8
Charters Towers (Qld.)   T2—943 6

Charts   912
  aeronautics   629.132 54
  diagrammatic   T1—022 3
  geography   912
  pictorial   T1—022 2
Charts (Statistical presentations)   001.422 6
Chase (B.C.)   T2—711 72
Chase County (Kan.)   T2—781 59
Chase County (Neb.)   T2—782 87
Chasing metals
  decorative arts   739.15
Chasms   551.442
                 T2 111
  geography   910.914 4
  geomorphology   551.442
  physical geography   910.021 44
Chassis   629.24
Chastity
  ethics   176
    religion   291.566
      Buddhism   294.356 6
      Christianity   241.66
      Hinduism   294.548 66
      Islam   297.5
      Judaism   296.385 66
    religious practice   291.447
      Buddhism   294.344 47
      Christianity   248.47
      Hinduism   294.544 7
Chateau Clique   971.038
Châteauguay (Quebec :
  County)   T2—714 33
Chateaux
  architecture   728.8
Chatham County (Ga.)   T2—758 724
Chatham County (N.C.)   T2—756 59
Chatham Islands   T2—931 1
Chatsworth (South Africa :
  District)   T2—684 5
Chattahoochee County (Ga.) T2—758 476
Chattahoochee River   T2—758
Chattanooga (Tenn.)   T2—768 82
Chattel mortgages   346.074
Chattisgarhi dialect   491.49
                 T6—914 9
Chattisgarhi literature   891.49
Chattooga County (Ga.)   T2—758 344
Chaudière River (Quebec)   T2—714 71
Chaunceys Line Reserve
  National Park   T2—942 32
Chausey Islands (England)   T2—423 48
Chautauqua County (Kan.) T2—781 918
Chautauqua County (N.Y.) T2—747 95
Chaves County (N.M.)   T2—789 43
Chayahuita language   498.32
                 T6—983 2
Cheat River   T2—754 8
Cheatham County (Tenn.)   T2—768 462

Cheating	179.8
see also Vices	
Cheboygan County (Mich.)	T2—774 87
Chebyshev polynomials	515.55
Chechaouen (Morocco :	
Province)	T2—642
Chechen	T5—999 6
Chechen-Ingush A.S.S.R.	
(R.S.F.S.R.)	T2—479 7
Chechen language	499.96
	T6—999 6
Checheno-Ingushskaia	
A.S.S.R. (R.S.F.S.R.)	T2—479 7
Checkers	794.2
Checking accounts	332.175 2
Checklists	T1—021 6
Checkoff (Union dues)	331.889 6
Checks	332.76
law	346.096
Cheddar cheese	641.373 54
cooking	641.673 54
processing	637.354
Cheeks	
human anatomy	611.318
human physiology	612.31
see also Digestive system	
Cheerfulness	179.9
see also Virtues	
Cheerleading	791.64
Cheese	641.373
cooking	641.673
processing	637.3
Cheese foods	641.373 58
cooking	641.673 58
processing	637.358
Cheese pies	641.824
cooking	641.824
Cheetahs	599.744 28
animal husbandry	636.89
Cheilostomata	594.71
Chekiang Province (China)	T2—512 42
Chelan County (Wash.)	T2—797 59
Chelates	541.225 3
Cheliabinskaia oblast	
(R.S.F.S.R.)	T2—478 7
Chelicerata	595.39
paleozoology	565.39
Chelmsford (England :	
Borough)	T2—426 752
Chelmsford, Frederic John	
Napier Thesiger, Viscount	
Indian history	954.035 7
Chelonia	597.92
paleozoology	567.92
Chelsea, Kensington and	
(London, England)	T2—421 34
Cheltenham (England)	T2—424 16

Chelyabinsk (R.S.F.S.R. :	
Oblast)	T2—478 7
Chemical analysis	543
Chemical compounds	546
engineering	660
Chemical contraceptives	
health	613.943 2
pharmacodynamics	615.766
see also Birth control, Genital	
system	
Chemical crystallography	548.3
Chemical diagnosis	
medicine	616.075 6
Chemical engineering	660
Chemical engineers	660.092
occupational group	T7—66
Chemical fire extinction	628.925 4
Chemical forces (Armed	
services)	358.34
Chemical industries	338.476 6
technology	660
Chemical instruments	542
manufacturing technology	681.754
Chemical laboratories	542.1
Chemical lasers	621.366 4
Chemical metallurgy	669.9
Chemical mineralogy	549.13
Chemical mutagens	575.131
Chemical physics	539
Chemical pollution	363.738
Chemical preservation of food	664.028 6
home economics	641.46
Chemical projectiles	623.451 6
Chemical propulsion	621.435
aircraft	629.134 353
spacecraft	629.475 2
unmanned spacecraft	629.465 2
Chemical seasoning	
lumber	674.386
Chemical senses	591.182 6
animal physiology	591.182 6
human physiology	612.86
Chemical sensory perception	
psychology	152.16
Chemical technologists	660.092
occupational group	T7—66
Chemical technology	660
Chemical warfare	358.34
civil defense	363.35
see also Civil defense	
Chemical waste disposal	363.728 8
see also Waste control	
Chemical wastes	
water-pollution engineering	628.168 36
Chemical weapons	
law	341.735
military engineering	623.445

Chesterfield Inlet (N.W.T.)   T2—719 4
Chestnut   641.345 3
  agriculture   634.53
Chestnut bean   641.356 57
  see also Chick-peas
Chestnut Ridge   T2—748 84
Chestnut tree   583.976
  forestry   634.972 4
  lumber   674.142
Chests (Furniture)   645.4
  manufacturing technology   684.16
  see also Furniture
Chetahs   599.744 28
Cheviot Hills   T2—428 8
Chevrotains   599.735 5
Chewa (African people)   T5—963 918
Chewa language   496.391 8
              T6—963 918
Chewing
  human physiology   612.311
  see also Digestive system
Chewing gum   641.338
  commercial processing   664.6
Chewong (Malaysian people)   T5—95
Cheyenne (Wyo.)   T2—787 19
Cheyenne County (Colo.)   T2—788 92
Cheyenne County (Kan.)   T2—781 112
Cheyenne County (Neb.)   T2—782 96
Cheyenne River   T2—783 5
Chhattisgarhi dialect   491.49
              T6—914 9
Chhattisgarhi literature   891.49
Chi-square test   519.56
Chiapas (Mexico)   T2—727 5
Chiaroscuro   701.8
Chiba-ken (Japan)   T2—521 37
Chibcha Indians   T5—982
Chibchan languages   498.2
              T6—982
  North America   497.8
              T6—978
Chibougamau (Quebec)   T2—714 115
Chibougamau Wildlife
  Reserve (Quebec)   T2—714 14
Chicago (Ill.)   T2—773 11
Chicago breakdown   781.653
Chicago school of economics   330.15
Chicanos   T5—687 207 3
Chich   641.356 57
  see also Chick-peas
Chichester (England :
  District)   T2—422 62
Chichewa language   496.391 8
              T6—963 918
Chick-peas   641.356 57
  botany   583.322
  commercial processing   664.805 657
  cooking   641.656 57

Chick-peas (continued)
  garden crop   635.657
Chickadees   598.824
Chickamauga Lake   T2—768 82
Chickasaw County (Iowa)   T2—777 315
Chickasaw County (Miss.)   T2—762 942
Chicken meat   641.365
  agricultural economics   338.176 513
  commercial processing
    economics   338.476 649 3
    technology   664.93
  cooking   641.665
Chicken pox
  incidence   614.525
  medicine   616.914
  pediatrics   618.929 14
  see also Communicable
    diseases (Human)
Chickens   598.617
  agricultural economics   338.176 5
  animal husbandry   636.5
  experimental animals
    medicine   619.5
Chickweed   583.152
Chicle   583.685
Chicory   583.55
Chicory (Beverage)   641.337 8
  agriculture   633.78
  botany   583.55
  commercial processing   663.97
  cooking with   641.637 8
  home preparation   641.877
Chicory (Salad green)   641.355 4
  agriculture   635.54
  botany   583.55
  commercial processing   664.805 54
  cooking   641.655 4
Chicot County (Ark.)   T2—767 84
Chicoutimi (Quebec : County)   T2—714 16
Chicozapote
  orchard crop   634.43
Chief executives
  executive management   658.42
  public administration   350.003
    central governments   351.003
    local governments   352.008
Chieti (Italy : Province)   T2—457 13
Chiga (African people)   T5—963 956
Chiga language   496.395 6
              T6—963 956
Chiggers   595.42
Chihuahua (Dog)
  animal husbandry   636.76
  see also Dogs
Chihuahua (Mexico : State)   T2—721 6
Chilako River (B.C.)   T2—711 82

Children's clothing	391.3	Chimborazo (Ecuador)	T2—866 17
child rearing	649.4	Chimbu Province (Papua New	
commercial technology	687.083	Guinea)	T2—956 7
home economics	646.36	Chimera	597.38
home sewing	646.406	Chimes	786.848
see also Clothing		*see also* Percussion instruments	
Children's diseases		Chimneys	721.5
medicine	618.92	architecture	721.5
Children's Hearings (Scotland)	345.411 08	buildings	697.8
Children's homes	362.732	steam furnaces	621.183
social welfare	362.732	Chimpanzees	599.884 4
see also Children—social		animal husbandry	636.988 44
welfare		Ch'in and Chin dynasties	
Children's hospitals	362.198 92	(Chinese history)	931.04
see also Health care facilities,		China	951
Health services			T2—51
Children's libraries	027.625	ancient	931
administration	025.197 625		T2—31
collection development	025.218 762 5	China (Republic : 1949-)	951.249 05
use studies	025.587 625		T2—512 49
Children's literature	808.899 282	China cabinets	645.4
history and criticism	809.892 82	manufacturing technology	684.16
rhetoric	808.068	*see also* Furniture	
specific literatures	T3B—080 928 2	China jute	583.17
history and criticism	T3B—099 282	fiber crop	633.56
Children's parties	793.21	Chinaberry	583.25
Children's theater	792.022 6	Chinandega (Nicaragua :	
Children's voices	782.7	Dept.)	T2—728 511
choral and mixed voices	782.7	Chinchilla (Qld.)	T2—943 3
single voices	783.7	Chinchilla cat	
Childress County (Tex.)	T2—764 754	animal husbandry	636.83
Chile	983	*see also* Cats	
	T2—83	Chinchillas	599.323 4
Chile saltpeter	553.64	animal husbandry	636.932 34
chemistry	546.382 24	Chinese	T5—951
economic geology	553.64	Chinese artichoke	583.87
mineralogy	549.732	Chinese calendar	529.329 51
Chilean literature	860	religion	299.51
Chileans	T5—688 3	Chinese calligraphy	745.619 951
Chili		Chinese chess	794.18
botany	583.79	Chinese communism	335.434 5
cooking with	641.638 4	economics	335.434 5
see also Hot spices		political ideology	320.532 309 51
Chili con carne	641.823	Chinese evergreen	584.64
cooking	641.823	Chinese flower arrangements	745.922 51
Chilko River (B.C.)	T2—711 75	Chinese ink painting	751.425 1
Chilled dishes		Chinese language	495.1
cooking	641.79		T6—951
Chilliwack (B.C.)	T2—711 37	Chinese literature	895.1
Chiloé (Chile)	T2—835 6	Chinese rugs	
Chilopoda	595.62	arts	746.751
paleozoology	565.62	*see also* Rugs	
Chiltern (England)	T2—425 97	Chinese Shar-Pei	
Chiltern Hill (England)	T2—425	animal husbandry	636.72
Chilterns (England)	T2—425	*see also* Dogs	
Chilton County (Ala.)	T2—761 81	Chinese water chestnut	584.84
Chimaltenango (Guatemala :		Chinese wood oil	665.333
Dept.)	T2—728 161	Ch'ing dynasty (Chinese history)	951.03

Choice of vocation	331.702
	T1—023
economics	331.702
Choir lofts	
architecture	726.593
Choir stalls	247.1
architecture	726.529 3
Chokeberry	583.372
Chokwe (African people)	T5—963 99
Chokwe language	496.399
	T6—963 99
Chokwe-Luchazi languages	496.399
	T6—963 99
Cholera	
incidence	614.514
medicine	616.932
see also Communicable	
diseases (Human)	
Cholesterol	574.192 431
biochemistry	574.192 431
chemistry	547.731
Cholic acids	596.013 2
chemistry	547.737
physiology	596.013 2
Cholla	583.47
Choltí language	497.415
	T6—974 15
Choluteca (Honduras : Dept.)	T2—728 351
Chondrichthyes	597.3
paleozoology	567.3
Chondrodite	
mineralogy	549.62
Chondrophora	593.71
Chondrostei	597.44
paleozoology	567.4
Chong-kie	794.18
Chongqing Shi (China)	T2—513 8
Chonos Archipelago	T2—836 22
Chontales (Nicaragua)	T2—728 527
Chopi (African people)	T5—963 97
Chopi languages	496.397
	T6—963 97
Choptank River (Del. and Md.)	T2—752 31
Choral music	782.5
Choral speaking	808.855
literature	808.855
history and criticism	809.55
specific literatures	T3B—505
individual authors	T3A—5
music	782.96
rhetoric	808.55
Chorale form	784.189 925
Chorale prelude form	784.189 92
Chordariales	589.45
Chordata	596
paleozoology	566

Chordophones	787
see also Stringed instruments	
Chords (Music)	781.252
Chorea	
medicine	616.851
see also Nervous system	
Choreographers	792.820 92
occupational group	T7—792 8
Choreography	792.82
musical plays	792.62
Choreology	792.82
Chorionic villus biopsy	
obstetrics	618.320 42
Chorley (England : Borough)	T2—427 615
Choroids	
human physiology	612.842
see also Eyes	
Chou dynasty (Chinese history)	931.03
Chouteau County (Mont.)	T2—786 293
Chow chow	
animal husbandry	636.72
see also Dogs	
Chowan County (N.C.)	T2—756 147
Chowan River (N.C.)	T2—756 15
Christchurch (England : Borough)	T2—423 39
Christchurch (N.Z.)	T2—931 55
Christening	265.1
customs	392.12
music	781.582
Christian art	
religious significance	246
Christian Brothers	255.78
church history	271.78
Christian calendars	529.4
religion	263.9
Christian church	260
Christian Church (Disciples of Christ)	286.63
see also Disciples of Christ	
Christian church buildings	
architecture	726.5
religious significance	246.9
Christian County (Ill.)	T2—773 81
Christian County (Ky.)	T2—769 78
Christian County (Mo.)	T2—778 792
Christian democratic parties	324.218 2
international organizations	324.182
Christian denominations	280
church government	262.01–.09
parishes	254.01–.09
church law	262.98
doctrines	230.1–.9
catechisms and creeds	238.1–.9
general councils	262.51–.59
guides to Christian life	248.48
missions	266.1–.9
moral theology	241.04

Chromium group
  chemical engineering 661.053
  chemistry 546.53
Chromolithography 764.2
Chromoproteins 574.192 454
  biochemistry 574.192 454
  chemistry 547.754
  see also Proteins
Chromosomes 574.873 22
Chromosphere of sun 523.75
Chronic obstructive pulmonary
  disease
  medicine 616.24
  see also Respiratory system
Chronic pain
  symptomatology 616.047 2
Chronicles 900
  see also History
Chronicles (Biblical books) 222.6
Chronobiology 574.188 2
Chronographs
  astronomy 522.5
  technology 681.118
Chronologies 902.02
  T1—020 2
Chronologists 529.092
Chronology 529
Chronometers
  astronomy 522.5
  technology 681.118
Chronoscopes
  technology 681.118
Chroococcales 589.46
Chrysanthemums 583.55
  floriculture 635.933 55
Chrysoberyl
  mineralogy 549.528
Chrysocapsales 589.487
Chrysocolla
  mineralogy 549.64
Chrysomeloidea 595.764 8
Chrysomonadales 589.487
Chrysomonadida 593.18
Chrysophyceae 589.487
Chrysophyta 589.48
Chrysosphaerales 589.487
Chrysotrichales 589.487
Chub 597.52
Chūbu Region (Japan) T2—521 6
Chubut (Argentina) T2—827 4
Chuckchee Sea 551.468 5
  T2—163 25
Chucks 621.992
Chūgoku Region (Japan) T2—521 9
Chukchee-Kamchatkan
  languages 494.6
  T6—946

Chukchi National Okrug
  (R.S.F.S.R.) T2—577
Chukchi Sea 551.468 5
  T2—163 25
Chukotskii natsionalnyi okrug
  (R.S.F.S.R.) T2—577
Chulalongkorn, King of Siam
  Thai history 959.303 5
Chulupí language 498.4
  T6—984
Ch'ung-ch'ing shih (China) T2—513 8
Chungking (China) T2—513 8
Chuquisaca (Bolivia) T2—842 4
Church and education 377.1
Church and state 322.1
  social theology 291.177
    Buddhism 294.337 7
    Christianity 261.7
    Hinduism 294.517 7
    Islam 297.197 7
    Judaism 296.387 7
Church and the poor 261.834 56
Church authority 262.8
Church buildings
  architecture 726.5
  landscape architecture 712.7
  management 254.7
  religious significance 246.9
Church calendar 263.9
  chronology 529.44
Church camps 796.542 2
Church etiquette 395.53
Church fathers 270.092
  religious group T7—211
Church finance 262.006 81
  local 254.8
Church furniture 247.1
Church government 262
  local church 254
Church growth
  local 254.5
Church history 270
  specific denominations 280
Church holidays 263.9
  customs 394.268 28
Church law 262.9
  Christian moral theology 241.57
Church membership
  local 254.5
Church modes 781.263
Church music 781.71
Church of Christ, Scientist 289.5
  see also Christian
    denominations
Church of England 283.42
  see also Anglican Communion

Ciliophora	593.17
paleozoology	563.17
CIM (Manufacturing)	670.285
Cimarron County (Okla.)	T2—766 132
Cimarron River	T2—766 3
Cimbaloms	787.74
see also Stringed instruments	
Cimicoidea	595.754
Cincinnati (Ohio)	T2—771 78
Cincinnati, Society of the	369.13
Cinclidae	598.832
Cinder blocks	
building construction	693.4
building materials	691.3
manufacturing technology	666.894
materials science	620.139
structural engineering	624.183 2
Cinematography	778.53
Cinemax	384.555 4
see also Television	
Cinnabar	
mineralogy	549.32
Cinnamon	583.931
agriculture	633.83
Cinque Ports (England)	T2—422 352
Cinquefoil	583.372
CIO (Labor)	331.883 309 73
CIP (Cataloging)	025.3
Ciphers (Cryptography)	652.8
computer science	005.82
Circadian rhythms	574.188 2
plants	581.188 2
Circaeasteraceae	583.117
Circassian languages	499.96
	T6—999 6
Circassians	T5—999 6
Circle geometry	516.184
Circle-squaring	516.204
Circles	516.15
Circuit breakers	621.317
Circuit courts	347.02
Circuit switching	621.381 537
computer communications	004.66
engineering	621.398 1
Circuits	621.319 2
computer engineering	621.395
electronics	621.381 5
microwave electronics	621.381 32
radio engineering	621.384 12
Circular buildings	720.48
architectural construction	721.042
architecture	720.48
Circulars	
direct advertising	659.133
postal handling	383.124
see also Postal service	
Circulation (Biology)	
animal physiology	591.11
brain	
human physiology	612.824
see also Nervous system	
human physiology	612.1
physiology	574.11
plant physiology	581.11
see also Cardiovascular system	
Circulation (Meteorology)	551.517
Circulation services	
library science	025.6
museology	069.13
Circulation theory (Economics)	332.401
Circulatory fluids	574.113
human physiology	612.1
plants	581.113
see also Cardiovascular system	
Circulatory organs	
anatomy	574.41
animal anatomy	591.41
human anatomy	611.1
human physiology	612.1
physiology	574.116
plant anatomy	581.41
plants	581.116
see also Cardiovascular system	
Circumcision	392.1
customs	392.1
Jewish rites	296.442 2
music	781.582
surgery	617.463
see also Male genital system	
Circumcision of Jesus Christ	232.924
Circumnutation	
plant physiology	581.185
Circumstantial evidence	347.064
criminal investigation	363.25
criminal law	345.06
law	347.064
Circumterrestrial flights	
manned	629.454
unmanned	629.435 2
Circus animals	791.32
care and training	636.088 8
Circus performers	791.309 2
occupational group	T7—791 3
Circuses	791.3
Cire perdue casting	
metals	671.255
Cirques (Geologic land forms)	551.315
Cirrhosis	
medicine	616.362 4
see also Digestive system	
Cirripedia	595.35
paleozoology	565.35
Ciskei (South Africa)	T2—687 92
Cistaceae	583.138

Civil rights	323	Civil war	
government programs	350.811	social theology (continued)	
central governments	351.811	Judaism	296.387 7
local governments	352.941 1	Civil War	
international law	341.481	Spanish history	946.081
law	342.085	United States history	973.7
legal theory	340.112	Civilian manpower (Armed	
political science	323	forces)	355.23
social theology	291.177	Civilian workers	
Buddhism	294.337 7	armed forces	
Christianity	261.7	management	355.61
Hinduism	294.517 7	labor economics	331.79
Islam	297.197 7	labor force	331.119 042
Judaism	296.387 7	labor market	331.129 042
social welfare	361.614	Civilization	909
Civil rights leaders	323.092	Bible	220.95
Civil rights violations	364.132 2	history	909
law	345.023 22	ancient	930
public administration	350.996	specific places	930–990
central governments	351.996	*see also* History	
local governments	352.002	painting	758.99
Civil rights workers	323.092	sociology	306
occupational group	T7—323	Clackamas County (Or.)	T2—795 41
Civil service	350.6	Clackmannan (Scotland :	
central governments	351.6	District)	T2—413 15
investigation	350.992	Cladding	
central governments	351.992	buildings	698
local governments	352.002	nuclear engineering	621.483 35
law	342.068	Cladding metals	671.73
local governments	352.005 6	Cladocera	595.32
Civil service examinations	350.3	paleozoology	565.32
	T1—076	Cladocopa	595.33
central governments	351.3	paleozoology	565.33
local governments	352.005 3	Cladophorales	589.47
Civil service lists	350.2	Cladoselachii	567.3
central governments	351.2	Claiborne County (Miss.)	T2—762 285
local governments	352.005 2	Claiborne County (Tenn.)	T2—768 944
Civil service pensions	331.252 913 5	Claiborne Parish (La.)	T2—763 94
administration	350.5	Claiming	
central governments	351.5	library acquisitions	025.236
local governments	352.005 5	Claims (Customer)	
Civil service workers	351.000 92	marketing management	658.812
see also Government workers		Claims (Insurance)	368.014
Civil war	355.021 8	Claims adjustment	
ethics	172.1	insurance	368.014
religion	291.562 1	Claims against government	
Buddhism	294.356 21	public administration	350.91
Christianity	241.621	central governments	351.91
Hinduism	294.548 621	local governments	352.002
Islam	297.5	Claims courts	347.04
Judaism	296.385 621	Claims settlement	
international law	341.68	government contracts	350.711 3
social conflict	303.64	central governments	351.711 3
social theology	291.177	local governments	352.161 3
Buddhism	294.337 7	Clairaudience	133.85
Christianity	261.7	Clairvoyance	133.84
Hinduism	294.517 7	Clairvoyants	133.840 92
Islam	297.197 7	occupational group	T7—13

Clallam County (Wash.)	T2—797 99
Clam shrimp	595.32
Clamming	639.44
sport	799.254 11
Clamps	621.992
Clams	594.11
cooking	641.694
fisheries	639.44
food	641.394
commercial processing	664.94
sports clamming	799.254 11
Clandestine publications	
bibliographies	011.56
Clanwilliam (South Africa : District)	T2—687 2
Clare (Ireland : County)	T2—419 3
Clare (S. Aust.)	T2—942 32
Clare County (Mich.)	T2—774 71
Clarence River	T2—944 3
Clarendon County (S.C.)	T2—757 81
Clarinet concertos	784.286 2
Clarinetists	788.620 92
occupational group	T7—788
Clarinets	788.62
see also Woodwind instruments	
Clarion County (Pa.)	T2—748 69
Clark, Charles Joseph	
Canadian history	971.064 5
Clark, Joe	
Canadian history	971.064 5
Clark County (Ark.)	T2—767 49
Clark County (Idaho)	T2—796 57
Clark County (Ill.)	T2—773 71
Clark County (Ind.)	T2—772 185
Clark County (Kan.)	T2—781 77
Clark County (Ky.)	T2—769 54
Clark County (Mo.)	T2—778 343
Clark County (Nev.)	T2—793 13
Clark County (Ohio)	T2—771 49
Clark County (S.D.)	T2—783 22
Clark County (Wash.)	T2—797 86
Clark County (Wis.)	T2—775 28
Clarke County (Ala.)	T2—761 245
Clarke County (Ga.)	T2—758 18
Clarke County (Iowa)	T2—777 856
Clarke County (Miss.)	T2—762 673
Clarke County (Va.)	T2—755 98
Clarke Island	T2—946 7
Clarke Range	T2—943 6
Clarkia	583.44
Clarksburg (W. Va.)	T2—754 57
Class actions	347.053
Class groups (Mathematics)	512.74
Class numbers	512.74
Class schedules	371.242 1
Class struggle	305.5
influence on crime	364.256
Marxian theory	335.411

Class struggle theory of unions	331.880 1
Classed catalogs	
bibliography	017
library science	025.315
Classes	
museum services	069.15
Classes (Education)	371.25
Classical architecture	722.6
Classical conditioning	153.152 6
Classical economics	330.153
Classical Greek language	480
	T6—81
Classical Greek literature	880
Classical languages	480
	T6—8
Classical literatures	880
Classical mechanics	531
Classical music	781.68
Classical physics	530
Classical religion	292
temples and shrines	
architecture	726.12
Classical revival	709.034 1
Classical revival architecture	724.2
Classical revival decoration	745.444 1
Classical revival painting	759.051
Classical revival sculpture	735.22
Classical statistical mechanics	530.132
Classical typology (Psychology)	155.262
Classicism	
literature	808.801 42
history and criticism	809.914 2
specific literatures	T3B—080 142
history and criticism	T3B—091 42
music	780.903 3
Classification	001.012
	T1—012
information science	025.42
knowledge	001.012
military personnel	355.223 6
Classified catalogs	
bibliography	017
library science	025.315
Classroom control	371.102 4
Classroom discipline	371.102 4
Classrooms	371.621
Clatsop County (Or.)	T2—795 46
Claves	786.872
see also Percussion instruments	
Clavichords	786.3
see also Keyboard instruments	
Clavicipitales	589.23
Clavicles	
human anatomy	611.717
see also Musculoskeletal system	
Clay	553.61
building materials	691.4
economic geology	553.61

Clay (continued)

materials science	620.191
mineralogy	549.6
mining	622.361
petrology	552.5
pottery	666.42
arts	738.12
technology	666.42
sculpture material	731.2
Clay County (Ala.)	T2—761 58
Clay County (Ark.)	T2—767 995
Clay County (Fla.)	T2—759 16
Clay County (Ga.)	T2—758 927
Clay County (Ill.)	T2—773 795
Clay County (Ind.)	T2—772 44
Clay County (Iowa)	T2—777 153
Clay County (Kan.)	T2—781 275
Clay County (Ky.)	T2—769 145
Clay County (Minn.)	T2—776 92
Clay County (Miss.)	T2—762 945
Clay County (Mo.)	T2—778 16
Clay County (N.C.)	T2—756 985
Clay County (Neb.)	T2—782 357
Clay County (S.D.)	T2—783 393
Clay County (Tenn.)	T2—768 49
Clay County (Tex.)	T2—764 542
Clay County (W. Va.)	T2—754 67
Clay pigeons	799.313
Clayton County (Ga.)	T2—758 432
Clayton County (Iowa)	T2—777 36
Cleaning	
pneumatic engineering	621.54
technology	667.1
Cleaning crops	631.56
Cleaning house	648.5
Cleaning metals	671.7
Cleanliness	613.4
personal customs	391.64
personal grooming	646.71
personal health	613.4
Cleansing tissues	676.284 2
Clear-air turbulence	
transportation hazard	363.124 12
Clear Creek County (Colo.)	T2—788 61
Clearance (Banking)	332.178
central banking	332.113
commercial banking service	332.178
Clearfield County (Pa.)	T2—748 61
Clearing banks	332.12
Clearing houses (Banking)	332.12
Clearing land	
agriculture	631.61
Clearwater County (Idaho)	T2—796 88
Clearwater County (Minn.)	T2—776 83
Clearwater Mountains	T2—796 82
Clearwater River (B.C.)	T2—711 72
Clearwater River (Idaho)	T2—796 85

Cleavage	
crystals	548.843
geology	551.84
mineralogy	549.121
Cleburne County (Ala.)	T2—761 64
Cleburne County (Ark.)	T2—767 285
Cleethorpes (England :	
Borough)	T2—428 33
Clematis	583.111
Clemency	364.65
law	345.077
penology	364.65
Cleopatra, Queen of Egypt	
Egyptian history	932.021
Clerestories	
Christian church architecture	726.594
Clergy	291.092
Christian	270.092
ecclesiology	262.1
occupational ethics	241.641
pastoral theology	253
personal religion	248.892
specific denominations	280
occupational ethics	174.1
religion	291.564 1
occupational group	T7—2
role and function	291.61
Clerical services	651.37
public administration	350.714
central governments	351.714
local governments	352.164
Clerihews	808.817
history and criticism	809.17
specific literatures	T3B—107
individual authors	T3A—1
Clerks	651.370 92
occupational group	T7—651
office services	651.37
Clerks regular	255.5
church history	271.5
Clerks Regular of Somaschi	255.54
church history	271.54
Clerks Regular of the Mother of	
God	255.57
church history	271.57
Clermont (Qld.)	T2—943 5
Clermont County (Ohio)	T2—771 794
Clethraceae	583.62
Cleveland (England)	T2—428 5
Cleveland (Ohio)	T2—771 32
Cleveland, Grover	
United States history	973.85
1885-1889	973.85
1893-1897	973.87
Cleveland bay horse	
animal husbandry	636.14
zoology	599.725
Cleveland County (Ark.)	T2—767 69

Closed shop	331.889 2
labor economics	331.889 2
Closed stacks	025.81
Closets	643.5
home economics	643.5
Closing (Real estate)	346.043 73
Clostridium	589.95
Cloth	
ship design	623.818 97
shipbuilding	623.820 7
Cloth covers	
bookbinding	686.343
Clothes dryers	667.13
home economics	648.1
manufacturing technology	683.88
Clothing	391
armed forces	355.81
costume	355.14
arts	746.92
commercial manufacturing	
instruments	681.767 7
commercial technology	687
leather and fur	685.2
customs	391
health	613.482
home economics	646.3
home sewing	646.4
product safety	363.19
law	344.042 35
see also Product safety	
psychological influence	155.95
social welfare	362.042 5
Clothing care	
home economics	646.6
Clothing construction	646.4
commercial technology	687
home sewing	646.4
Clothing workers	687.092
occupational group	T7—687
Cloud colors	551.567
Cloud County (Kan.)	T2—781 25
Cloud particle formation	551.574 1
Cloud seeding	551.687 6
Clouds	551.576
aeronautics	629.132 4
weather modification	551.687 6
Clove	583.42
agriculture	633.83
Clover	583.322
forage crop	633.32
Clowns	791.33
occupational group	T7—791 3
Club cars	385.33
engineering	625.23
see also Rolling stock	
Club fungi	589.222 5
Club games	796.35
Club moss	587.9
paleobotany	561.79
Club rush	584.84
Clubhouse buildings	
architecture	728.4
Clubmen	367.92
social group	T7—367
Clubs	367
household management	647.94
Clubwomen	367.92
social group	T7—367
Cluj (Romania : Judet)	T2—498 4
Cluniacs	255.14
church history	271.14
Clupeiformes	597.55
Clupeomorpha	
paleozoology	567.5
Clusiaceae	583.163
Cluster analysis	519.53
Cluster headache	
symptomatology	
neurological diseases	616.849 1
see also Nervous system	
Cluster-type variables (Stars)	523.844 25
Clusters of stars	523.85
Clutches (Machine parts)	621.825
Clwyd (Wales)	T2—429 3
Clyde, Firth of (Scotland)	551.461 37
	T2—163 37
Clyde River (Scotland)	T2—414 1
Clydebank (Scotland : District)	T2—414 32
Clydesdale (Scotland : District)	T2—414 69
Clydesdale horse	
animal husbandry	636.15
zoology	599.725
Cneoraceae	583.271
Cnidaria	593.5
paleozoology	563.5
Cnidospora	593.19
Co-dependence	362.29
medicine	616.86
social welfare	362.29
Coach dogs	
animal husbandry	636.72
see also Dogs	
Coach horses	
animal husbandry	636.14
zoology	599.725
Coaches (Railroad cars)	385.33
engineering	625.23
see also Rolling stock	
Coaches (Sports)	796.092
occupational group	T7—796
Coaching (Driving)	
recreation	798.6

Cobb County (Ga.)	T2—758 245
Cobbling	685.31
Cobourg Peninsula Fauna Reserve	T2—942 95
Cobourg Peninsula National Park	T2—942 95
Cobourg Peninsula Wildlife Sanctuary and Fauna Reserve	T2—942 95
Coburg (Germany)	T2—433 11
Coca	583.214
Cocaine abuse	362.298
medicine	616.864 7
personal health	613.84
social welfare	362.298
see also Substance abuse	
Coccidia	593.19
Coccidiosis	
incidence	614.53
medicine	616.936
see also Communicable diseases (Human)	
Coccinellidae	595.769
Coccoidea	595.752
Cochabamba (Bolivia : Dept.)	T2—842 3
Cochineal culture	638.3
Cochineal dyes	667.26
Cochise County (Ariz.)	T2—791 53
Cochleas	
human anatomy	611.85
human physiology	612.858
see also Ears	
Cochlospermaceae	583.138
Cochoas	598.842
Cochran County (Tex.)	T2—764 845
Cochrane (Ont. : District)	T2—713 142
Cockatoos	598.71
animal husbandry	636.686 5
Cocke County (Tenn.)	T2—768 895
Cockfighting	791.8
Cockney dialect	427.1
	T6—21
Cockroaches	595.722
paleozoology	565.72
Cocks (Mechanisms)	621.84
Cockscomb (Plant)	583.913
Cocksfoot (Grass)	584.93
forage crop	633.22
Coclé (Panama : Province)	T2—728 721
Cocoa	641.337 4
beverage	
commercial processing	663.92
cooking with	641.637 4
home preparation	641.877
Cocoa bean	583.19
agriculture	633.74
Cocoa butter	665.354
chemical technology	665.354

Cocoa butter (continued)	
cooking with	641.637 4
food	641.337 4
food technology	664.3
Coconino County (Ariz.)	T2—791 33
Coconut	584.5
cooking	641.646 1
fiber crop	633.58
food	641.346 1
food crop	634.61
textiles	677.18
see also Textiles	
Coconut milk	
commercial processing	663.64
Coconut oil	665.355
Coconuts	
commercial processing	664.804 61
Cocoparra National Park	T2—944 8
Cocos (Keeling) Islands	969.9
	T2—699
Cod	597.53
commercial fishing	639.275 3
sports fishing	799.175 3
Cod, Cape (Mass.)	T2—744 92
Cod-liver oil	
pharmacology	615.34
COD mail	383.184
see also Postal service	
CODASYL databases	005.754
Code generators	
computer science	005.45
Code of Manu	294.592 6
Code telegraphy	384.14
wireless	384.524
see also Telegraphy	
Codes	
computer science	005.72
Codes (Law)	348.023
United States	348.732 3
Codes of conduct	
moral theology	291.5
Christianity	241.5
Codex iuris canonici (1917)	262.93
Codex iuris canonici (1983)	262.94
Codification	348.004
international law	341.026 7
United States	348.730 4
Coding data	005.72
Coding programs	005.13
Coding theory	003.54
Codington County (S.D.)	T2—783 23
Codium	589.47
Coeducation	376
Coefficient of expansion	536.41
Coefficient of restitution	531.382
Coelacanth	597.46
Coelenterata	593.5
paleozoology	563.5

Cold weather	
health	613.111
Cold-weather cooking	641.591 1
Cold-weather diseases	
medicine	616.988 1
see also Environmental diseases	
(Human)	
Cold-weather photography	778.75
Cold-working operations	
metals	671.3
Coldwater River (B.C.)	T2—711 72
Cole County (Mo.)	T2—778 55
Coleman County (Tex.)	T2—764 725
Colemanite	
mineralogy	549.735
Colenso (South Africa)	T2—684 7
Coleoidea	594.5
Coleoptera	595.76
paleozoology	565.76
Coleraine (Northern Ireland :	
Borough)	T2—416 27
Coleraine (Vic.)	T2—945 7
Coles County (Ill.)	T2—773 72
Colesberg (South Africa :	
District)	T2—687 13
Colfax County (N.M.)	T2—789 22
Colfax County (Neb.)	T2—782 532
Colic	
gastrointestinal disorder	
pediatrics	618.923 3
regional medicine	617.55
Coligny (South Africa :	
District)	T2—682 4
Coliiformes	598.75
paleozoology	568.7
Colima (Mexico : State)	T2—723 6
Colitis	
medicine	616.344 7
see also Digestive system	
Collage	702.812
Collage painting	751.493
Collagen	591.185
chemistry	547.753
physiology	591.185
see also Proteins	
Collagen diseases	
medicine	616.77
see also Musculoskeletal system	
Collagenous tissues	
human histology	611.018 2
see also Musculoskeletal system	
Collards	641.353 47
botany	583.123
cooking	641.653 47
garden crop	635.347

Collateral kinsmen	306.87
	T1—085
	T7—046
family relationships	306.87
Collected biography	920
	T1—092 2
Collecting	T1—075
biological specimens	579.6
descriptive research	001.433
museology	069.4
recreation	790.132
Collecting of accounts	658.88
law	346.077
Collection analysis	
library science	025.21
Collection development	
library science	025.21
Collection maintenance	
library operations	025.8
library science	025.21
Collection management	
library science	025.21
Collection-on-delivery mail	383.184
see also Postal service	
Collections	080
description	T1—074
museology	069.5
preparation	T1—075 3
Collective bargaining	331.89
economics	331.89
law	344.018 9
personnel management	658.315 4
public administration	350.174
central governments	351.174
local governments	352.005 174
public administration	351.832
women workers	331.479
Collective security	327.116
Collectivism	335
economics	335
political ideology	320.53
Collectors	
social group	T7—090 9
College administrators	378.009 2
occupational group	T7—371
role and function	378.112
College attendance	
sociology	370.193 41
College buildings	
architecture	727.3
College costs	378.38
College education	378
see also Higher education	
College Entrance Examination	
Board	378.166 2
College entrance examinations	378.166 2
College graduates	
choice of vocation	331.702 3

Colorado Desert	T2—794 99
Colorado Plateau	T2—791 3
Arizona	T2—791 3
Colorado	T2—788 1
Utah	T2—792 5
Colorado River (Colo.-	
Mexico)	T2—791 3
Arizona	T2—791 3
Colorado	T2—788 17
Utah	T2—792 5
Colorado River (Tex.)	T2—764
Colorado Springs (Colo.)	T2—788 56
Colorado tick fever	
incidence	614.574 2
medicine	616.924 2
see also Communicable	
diseases (Human)	
Colorimetric analysis	543.085 2
Coloring oils and gases	665.028 3
Coloring paper	676.234
Colors (Flags)	929.92
armed forces	355.15
Colossians (Biblical book)	227.7
Colostomy	617.554 7
Colquitt County (Ga.)	T2—758 975
Columbae	598.65
Columbia (S.C.)	T2—757 71
Columbia County (Ark.)	T2—767 59
Columbia County (Fla.)	T2—759 83
Columbia County (Ga.)	T2—758 635
Columbia County (N.Y.)	T2—747 39
Columbia County (Or.)	T2—795 47
Columbia County (Pa.)	T2—748 38
Columbia County (Wash.)	T2—797 46
Columbia County (Wis.)	T2—775 81
Columbia River	T2—797
British Columbia	T2—711 6
Oregon	T2—795 4
Washington	T2—797
Columbia-Shuswap (B.C.)	T2—711 68
Columbiana County (Ohio)	T2—771 63
Columbiformes	598.65
paleozoology	568.6
Columbine	583.111
Columbite	
mineralogy	549.528
Columbium	669.79
chemistry	546.524
see also Chemicals, Niobium	
Columbus (Ohio)	T2—771 57
Columbus, Christopher	
North American history	970.015
South American history	980.013
Columbus County (N.C.)	T2—756 31
Columelliaceae	583.81
Column chromatography	543.089 4
Columnar epithelia	
human histology	611.018 7

Columns	721.3
architecture	721.3
construction	690.13
structural engineering	624.177 2
concrete	624.183 42
Colusa County (Calif.)	T2—794 33
Colwyn (Wales : Borough)	T2—429 31
Colydioidea	595.769
Colymbiformes	598.443
paleozoology	568.4
COM devices	004.77
manufacturing technology	681.6
Coma	
symptomatology	
neurological diseases	616.849
see also Nervous system	
Comal County (Tex.)	T2—764 887
Comanche County (Kan.)	T2—781 79
Comanche County (Okla.)	T2—766 48
Comanche County (Tex.)	T2—764 554
Comayagua (Honduras :	
Dept.)	T2—728 372
Comb jellies	593.8
Combat aircraft	358.418 3
military engineering	623.746
military equipment	358.418 3
Combat fatigue	
medicine	616.852 12
see also Mental illness	
Combat groups (Air force)	358.413 1
Combat readiness	355.033 2
Combat sports	796.8
ethics	175.6
see also Recreation—ethics	
Combat squadrons (Air force)	358.413 1
Combat vehicles	355.83
engineering	623.747 5
military equipment	355.83
Combatants and noncombatants	
law of war	341.67
Combination systems	
air conditioning	
buildings	697.934 4
Combinations (Enterprises)	338.8
accounting	657.96
economics	338.8
international law	341.753
management	658.046
initiation	658.114 6
see also International	
enterprises	
Combinations (Mathematics)	511.64
algebra	512.925
arithmetic	513.25
number theory	512.72
Combinatorial analysis	511.6
Combinatorial geometry	516.13
Combinatorial probabilities	519.2

Commercial catalogs	T1—029 4
Commercial circulars	T1—029 4
Commercial credit	332.742
Commercial crimes	364.168
law	345.026 8
Commercial fishing	639.2
Commercial gardening	635
Commercial land use	333.77
community sociology	307.333
economics	333.77
Commercial languages	401.3
Commercial law	346.07
international	341.754
Commercial leases	346.043 462
Commercial miscellany	T1—029
Commercial paper	332.77
exchange medium	332.55
Commercial policy	380.13
domestic commerce	381.3
international commerce	382.3
Commercial property	333.77
taxation	336.225
Commercial publishers	070.592
Commercial revenues	
public finance	336.1
Commercial vehicles	
(Automotive)	388.34
engineering	629.22
transportation services	388.34
see also Automotive vehicles	
Commercials	659.14
broadcast advertising	659.14
radio performances	791.443
television performances	791.453
Commewijne (Surinam :	
District)	T2—883 7
Commission government	
cities	320.854
Commissioned officers	355.009 2
occupational group	T7—355
role and function	355.332
Commissioners	350.009 092
occupational group	T7—352 3
Commissioning	
military personnel	355.223 6
Commissions	
libraries	021.82
public administration	350.009
central governments	351.009
local governments	352.009
Committees	302.34
legislative bodies	328.365
social psychology	302.34
Commodities	338.02
investment economics	332.632 8
public administration	351.826
production	338.02
speculation	332.632 8

Commodity brokers	332.62
public administration	351.826
Commodity exchanges	332.644
architecture	725.25
international law	341.752 44
law	343.08
public administration	351.826
Commodity futures	332.632 8
Commodity futures markets	332.644
Commodity options	332.632 8
Commodity options markets	332.644
Commodity standards	332.42
Commodores	359.009 2
role and function	359.331
Common buzzards	598.916
Common carriers	388.041
truck	388.324 3
see also Freight services,	
Passenger services	
Common cold	
medicine	616.205
see also Respiratory system	
Common Communication Format	025.316
Common land	
economics	333.2
landscape architecture	712.5
Common law	340.57
Common-law marriage	306.84
law	346.016
Common Market	341.242 2
see also European Economic	
Community	
Common of the mass	264.36
music	782.323 2
choral and mixed voices	782.532 32
single voices	783.093 232
Common people	
customs	390.24
dress	391.024
Common stocks	332.632 23
speculation	332.632 28
Commons	
land economics	333.2
landscape architecture	712.5
Commonwealth of Nations	T2—171 241
Commonwealth of the	
Northern Mariana Islands	T2—967
Communal land	
economics	333.2
Communalism	302.14
Communauté régionale de	
l'Outaouais (Quebec)	T2—714 221
Communauté urbaine de	
Montréal (Quebec)	T2—714 28
Communauté urbaine de	
Québec (Quebec)	T2—714 471
Communes	307.774

Communicable diseases
  (Animals) 591.23
  veterinary medicine 636.089 69
Communicable diseases (Human) 362.196 9
  geriatrics 618.976 9
  incidence 614.5
  medicine 616.9
  nursing 610.736 99
  pediatrics 618.929
  social services 362.196 9
Communication 302.2
                        T1—014
  animals 591.59
  civil rights issues 323.448 2
  management 658.45
    see also Communication in
      management
  office services 651.7
  psychology 153.6
  sociology 302.2
Communication devices
  computer science 004.64
  engineering 621.398 1
Communication equipment
  military equipment 355.85
Communication facilities
  area planning 711.8
  military resources 355.27
  misuse 364.147
  railroads 385.316
Communication forces
  air warfare 358.46
Communication in management 658.45
  public administration 350.714 2
    central governments 351.714 2
    local governments 352.164 2
Communication law 343.099
Communication satellites 384.51
  engineering 621.382 5
  international law 341.757 7
  law 343.099 4
  radio 384.545 6
  television 384.552
Communication services
  armed forces 358.24
  naval forces 359.983
  police services 363.24
Communication skills
  elementary education 372.6
Communication systems
  ships 623.856
  spacecraft 629.474 3
  unmanned spacecraft 629.464 3
Communications 384
  computer science 004.6
    see also Computer
      communications

Communications (continued)
  engineering 621.382
    see also Communications
      engineering
  international law 341.757
  law 343.099
  public administration 350.874
    central governments 351.874
    local governments 352.914
  social effects 303.483 3
Communications buildings
  architecture 725.23
Communications engineering 621.382
  manned space flight 629.457
  military 623.73
  space flight 629.457
  unmanned space flight 629.437
Communications engineers 621.382 092
  occupational group T7—621 3
Communications media
  accounting 657.84
  influence on crime 364.254
  use by local Christian church 254.3
Communications media and
  religion 291.175
  Christianity 261.52
Communications network
  architecture 004.65
  engineering 621.398 1
Communications protocols
  computer science 004.62
Communications systems
  engineering 621.382
Communications workers 384.092
  occupational group T7—384
Communicative disorders 362.196 855
  geriatrics 618.976 855
  incidence 614.598 55
  medicine 616.855
  pediatrics 618.928 55
  social services 362.196 855
Communion (Part of service) 264.36
  music 782.323 5
Communion of saints 262.73
Communion service 264.36
  music 782.323
Communism 335.4
  Christian polemics 239.9
  economics 335.4
  political ideology 320.532
Communism and Christianity 261.21
Communist bloc T2—171 7
Communist ethics 171.7
Communist front organizations
  political science 324.3
Communist government 321.92
Communist Information Bureau 324.175
Communist International 324.175

Communist manifesto	335.422
Communist parties	324.217 5
international organizations	324.175
Communist Party of the United	
States of America	324.273 75
Communists	335.430 92
political group	T7—335
Communities	307
psychological influence	155.94
Communities (Ecology)	574.524 7
animals	591.524 7
plants	581.524 7
Community action	
social welfare	361.8
Community and school	370.193 1
Community antenna television	
systems	384.554 6
law	343.099 46
see also Television	
Community-based corrections	365.6
Community centers	
architecture	727.9
area planning	711.55
recreation centers	790.068
Community chests	361.8
Community colleges	378.052
Community development	307.14
law	346.045
Community education	
sociology	370.194
Community health services	362.12
see also Health services	
Community information services	
libraries	021.28
Community mental health	
services	362.22
see also Mental health services	
Community nursing	
medicine	610.734 3
Community planning	307.12
Community property	346.042
Community schools	371.03
Community service	
penology	364.68
Community suppers	642.4
Commutation of sentence	364.65
penology	364.65
Commutative algebra	512.24
Commutative groups	512.2
Commuter services	388.042
urban	388.4
see also Urban transportation	
see also Passenger services	
Como (Italy : Province)	T2—452 3
Comorans	T5—969 694
Comoro Islands	T2—694
Comoros	969.4
	T2—694

Comox-Strathcona (B.C.)	T2—711 2
Compact discs	384
communication services	384
sound reproduction	621.389 32
Compact disk read-only memory	004.56
engineering	621.397 6
Compact disks (Computer)	004.56
engineering	621.397 6
Compact groups	512.55
Compact spaces	514.32
Companies	338.7
law	346.066
Companies (Military units)	355.31
Company law	346.066
Company meetings	
law	346.066 45
Company of New France	
(Canadian history)	971.016 2
Company records	
law	346.066 4
Company towns	307.767
Company unions	331.883 4
Comparable worth	331.215 3
labor law	344.012 153
Comparative advantage	
economics	338.604 6
international commerce	382.104 2
Comparative cytology	574.87
Comparative education	370.195
Comparative government	320.3
Comparative grammar	415
Comparative law	340.2
Comparative librarianship	020.9
Comparative linguistics	410
Comparative literature	809
Comparative psychology	156
Comparative religion	291
Comparison shopping	381.33
	T1—029 7
consumer products	640.73
Comparisons of products	T1—029 6
Comparisons of services	T1—029 6
Compass variations	
astronomy	522.7
Compatibility	
computer science	004
hardware	004
engineering	621.39
software	005
Compendiums	T1—020 2
Compensation	331.21
economics	331.21
income distribution	339.21
labor law	344.012 1
legislators	328.333
personnel management	658.32
	T1—068 3
armed forces	355.64

Condemnation (Law)	343.025 2
Condemnation of Jesus Christ	232.962
Condensation	536.44
Condensation (Chemical	
reaction)	541.393
chemical engineering	660.284 48
organic chemistry	547.28
Condensation of moisture	
buildings	693.893
meteorology	551.574
Condensed matter	
physics	530.41
Condensed milk	641.371 424
cooking	641.671 424
processing	637.142 4
Condensers (Electrical)	621.315
radio engineering	621.384 133
Condensers (Steam)	621.197
Condiments	641.338 2
commercial processing	664.5
cooking with	641.638 2
Conditional equations	515.254
calculus	515.254
Conditional immortality	236.23
Conditional sales	
law	346.074
tax law	343.055 2
Conditioned reflexes	
psychology	152.322 4
animals	156.232 24
Conditions of employment	331.2
economics	331.2
law	344.012
personnel management	658.312
public administration	350.16
central governments	351.16
local governments	352.005 16
Conditions of employment	
(Physical)	331.25
see also Work environment	
Condobolin (N.S.W.)	T2—944 9
Condominiums	643.2
home economics	643.2
law	346.043 3
Condors	598.912
Conduct of election campaigns	324.7
Conduct of life	
armed forces	355.133
ethics	170.44
religion	291.5
Christianity	241
etiquette	395
parapsychology	131
personal religion	291.44
Buddhism	294.344 4
Christianity	248.4
Hinduism	294.544
Islam	297.44

Conduct of life	
personal religion (continued)	
Judaism	296.74
psychology	158.1
Conducting	781.45
Conducting scores	780
treatises	780.264
Conduction of electricity	537.62
Conduction of heat	536.23
Conduction of heat in fluids	536.25
Conductivity (Electrodynamics)	537.62
Conductivity of heat	
material property	536.201 2
Conductometric analysis	543.087 11
Conduits	
road engineering	625.734
Condylarthra	569.75
Conecuh County (Ala.)	T2—761 263
Conejos County (Colo.)	T2—788 33
Cones	516.15
Confections	641.86
home preparation	641.86
Confederate States of America	973.713
	T2—75
Confederate sympathizers	
(United States history)	973.718
Confederated Benedictines	255.11
church history	271.11
Confederation of the Rhine	943.06
Confederations	321.02
Conference calls	384.64
see also Telephone	
Conference committees	
legislative bodies	328.365 7
Conference on Data Systems	
Languages databases	005.754
Conferences	060
Confession (Christian rite)	234.166
public worship	265.62
Confession (Law)	345.06
Confessionals	247.1
architecture	726.529 1
Confessions of faith	291.2
Christianity	238
public worship	264.5
Confidential communications	323.448
civil right	323.448
law	342.085 8
Confinement (Childbirth)	392
music	781.582
Confirmation (Religious rite)	
Christianity	234.162
public worship	265.2
etiquette	395.24
Judaism	296.442 4
women's	296.443
music	781.583

Conflict	303.6
international politics	327.16
social groups	305
sociology	303.6
subconscious psychology	154.24
Conflict management	303.69
Conflict of interest	
law	342.068 4
occupational ethics	174
political ethics	172
public administration	350.995
central governments	351.995
local governments	352.002
Conflict of laws	340.9
domestic	342.042
Conflict resolution	303.69
international relations	327.17
sociology	303.69
Conflicts of duties	
ethical systems	171.6
Conformal mapping	516.36
calculus	515.9
differential geometry	516.36
Conformal projections	526.82
Conformal transformations	516.35
Conformity	303.32
psychology	153.854
Confraternities	248.06
Confraternity Bible	220.520 5
Confucianism	299.512
art representation	704.948 995 12
philosophy	181.112
religion	299.512
Confucianist holidays	299.512 36
customs	394.268 299 512
Confucianist sacred music	781.795 12
public worship	782.395 12
music	782.395 12
religion	299.512 38
religion	299.512 37
Confucianists	
biography	299.512 092
religious group	T7—299 512
Congenital diseases	
medicine	616.043
Congestion (Mathematics)	519.82
Congleton (England :	
Borough)	T2—427 13
Conglomerates	338.804 2
management	658.046
production economics	338.804 2
Congo (Brazzaville)	967.24
	T2—672 4
Congo (Democratic Republic)	T2—675 1
Congo, French (Brazzaville)	T2—672 4
Congo Free State	967.510 22
	T2—675 1
Congo-Kordofanian languages	496.3
	T6—963
Congo language	496.393 1
	T6—963 931
Congo River	T2—675 1
Congolese (Brazzaville)	T5—967 24
Congolese (Kinshasa)	T5—967 51
Congregational Christian	
Churches of the United	
States	285.833
see also Congregationalism	
Congregational Churches of the	
United States	285.832
see also Congregationalism	
Congregational Methodist	
Church	287.2
see also Methodist Church	
Congregational systems	
Christian ecclesiology	262.4
Congregationalism	285.8
church government	262.058
parishes	254.058
church law	262.985 8
doctrines	230.58
catechisms and creeds	238.58
general councils	262.558
guides to Christian life	248.485 8
missions	266.58
moral theology	241.045 8
public worship	264.058
religious associations	267.185 8
religious education	268.858
seminaries	207.115 8
theology	230.58
Congregationalists	
biography	285.809 2
religious group	T7—258
Congregations	
local church	250
papal administration	262.136
Congress of Industrial	
Organizations (U.S.)	331.883 309 73
Congresses	060
Congresses (Legislative bodies)	328.3
Congruences	
Euclidean geometry	516.2
number theory	512.72
Conic sections	516.15
Conies	599.62
Coniferales	585.2
paleobotany	561.52
Conifers	585.2
forestry	634.975
ornamental arboriculture	635.977 52
paleobotany	561.52
Conjugales (Zygnematales)	589.47
Conjugated carbohydrates	574.192 483
biochemistry	574.192 483

Conjugated carbohydrates (continued)
chemistry	547.783

see also Carbohydrates

Conjugated proteins	574.192 454
biochemistry	574.192 454
chemistry	547.754

see also Proteins

Conjugation (Grammar)	415
specific languages	T4—5
Conjugation (Sexual)	574.166 2
animals	591.166 2
plants	581.166 2
Conjunctions (Grammar)	415
specific languages	T4—5

Conjunctiva
human anatomy	611.84
human physiology	612.841
ophthalmology	617.77

see also Eyes

Conjunctivitis
incidence	614.599 7
ophthalmology	617.773

see also Eyes

Conjuring
recreation	793.8
Connacht (Ireland)	T2—417 1
Connaraceae	583.28
Connecticut	974.6
	T2—746
Connecticut Lakes (N.H.)	T2—742 1
Connecticut River	T2—74
Connecticut	T2—746
Massachusetts	T2—744 2
New Hampshire	T2—742
Vermont	T2—743
Connecting rods	621.827
internal-combustion engines	621.437
machine engineering	621.827
Connections (Mathematics)	516.35
Connective tissue	591.185 2
animal anatomy	591.47
animal physiology	591.185 2
human anatomy	611.74

human diseases
medicine	616.77
human histology	611.018 2
human physiology	612.75

see also Musculoskeletal system

Connors Range	T2—943 5
Conodonts	562.2

Conrad I, Holy Roman Emperor
German history	943.022
Conscience	170
civil rights issues	323.442
ethical systems	171.6
religion	291.5
Buddhism	294.35
Christianity	241.1

Conscience
religion (continued)
Hinduism	294.548
Islam	297.5
Judaism	296.385
Conscientious objection	355.224
ethics	172.42

see also War—ethics

law	343.012 6
social theology	291.178 73
Buddhism	294.337 873
Christianity	261.873
Hinduism	294.517 873
Islam	297.197 873
Judaism	296.387 873
Conscientious objectors	355.224

see also Conscientious
objection

Conscious mental processes	153
animals	156.3
children	155.413
Consciousness	153
children	155.413
philosophy	126
Consciousness-raising groups	305
Conscription (Draft)	355.223 63
law	343.012 2
Consecrations (Christian rites)	265.92

Consequential loss
insurance	368.08

Consequentialism
ethics	171.5
CONSER Project	025.343 2

Conservation
arts	702.88
bibliographic materials	025.84
museology	069.53
Conservation law	346.044
international	341.762
Conservation of energy (Physics)	531.62

Conservation of mass-energy
(Physics)	531.62
Conservation of natural resources	333.72
international law	341.762
law	346.044
public administration	350.823 2
central governments	351.823 2
local governments	352.942 32
technology	639.9
Conservation tillage	631.451
Conservationists	333.720 92
occupational group	T7—333
of biological resources	333.950 92
occupational group	T7—333
technologists	639.909 2
occupational group	T7—639 9

Conservatism
political ideology	320.52

Control devices (continued)
transportation 388.041
  engineering 629.042
  transportation services 388.041
  see also Signals
Control mechanisms (Biology) 574.188
  animal physiology 591.188
  human physiology 612.022
  plant physiology 581.188
Control of usage
  natural resources 333.717
Control rods
  nuclear reactors 621.483 5
Control theory 629.831 2
  automation engineering 629.831 2
  mathematics 519.4
Controlled-environment
  agriculture 631.583
  floriculture 635.982
Controlled market price
  determination 338.523
Controlled money 332.427
Controlled subject vocabularies 025.49
Controlled transmission
  television 384.556
  see also Television
Controllers
  computer science 004.64
  engineering 621.398 1
  control engineering 629.895
Controls
  export trade 382.64
  see also Export trade
Controversial knowledge 001.9
Contusions
  medicine 617.13
Contwoyto Lake (N.W.T.) T2—719 7
Conulariida 563.73
Conurbations 307.764
  government 320.85
  public administration 352.009 4
Convalescent homes 362.16
  see also Health care facilities,
    Health services
Convalescent serums
  pharmacology 615.375
Convalescents 305.908 14
  T1—087 7
  see also Sick persons
Convection of heat 536.25
Convection-oven cooking 641.58
Convective heating
  buildings 697.2
Convenience stores 381.147
  management 658.87
  see also Commerce
Convent education 376.5

Convention centers
  architecture 725.91
Conventional housing
  architecture 728
  construction 690.8
Conventional war 355.02
Conventions 060
  labor unions 331.874
Conventions (Treaties) 341.37
  texts 341.026
Convents
  architecture 726.7
Conventuals 255.37
  church history 271.37
Convergence 515.24
Conversation
  ethics 177.2
    see also Ethical problems
  etiquette 395.59
  literature 808.856
    history and criticism 809.56
    specific literatures T3B—506
      individual authors T3A—5
  rhetoric 808.56
  social psychology 302.346
Converse County (Wyo.) T2—787 16
Conversion (Law) 346.036
Conversion (Religious
  experience) 291.42
  Christianity 248.24
Conversion tables (Measurement) 530.81
Conversion to metric system 389.16
  executive management 658.406 2
Converter substations
  electrical engineering 621.312 6
Converters
  electrical engineering 621.313
  electronic circuits 621.381 532 2
Convertible tops 629.26
Convertiplanes
  engineering 629.133 35
Convex programming 519.76
Convex sets
  geometry 516.08
Convex surfaces 516.362
Conveyancing 346.043 8
Conveying equipment 621.867
  mining 622.66
  pneumatic engineering 621.54
Conveyor belts 621.867 5
  manufacturing technology 678.36
  materials handling 621.867 5
Convict labor 365.65
  economics 331.51
  law 344.035 65
  penology 365.65
Convicts 365.6
  T1—086 92

Copiapó (Chile : Province)	T2—831 45	Coquimbo (Chile : Region)	T2—832 3
Copies		Coquitlam (B.C.)	T2—711 33
arts	702.872	Cor pulmonale	
paintings	751.5	medicine	616.12
technical drawing	604.25	*see also* Cardiovascular system	
Copolymerization		Coraciidae	598.892
chemical engineering	660.284 48	Coraciiformes	598.892
chemistry	547.28	paleozoology	568.8
Copper	669.3	Coracles	386.229
architectural construction	721.044 73	design	623.812 9
building construction	693.73	engineering	623.829
building material	691.83	transportation services	386.229
chemical engineering	661.065 2	Coral fungi	589.222 5
chemistry	546.652	Coral Harbour (N.W.T.)	T2—719 4
decorative arts	739.511	Coral reef biology	574.91
economic geology	553.43	Coral reefs	T2—142
foundation materials	624.153 82	geography	910.914 2
materials science	620.182	physical geography	910.021 42
metallography	669.953	Coral Sea	551.465 76
metallurgy	669.3		T2—164 76
metalworking	673.3	Coral vine	583.917
mining	622.343	Coralbells	583.38
organic chemistry	547.056 52	Corals	593.6
applied	661.895	harvesting	639.736
physical metallurgy	669.963	paleozoology	563.6
structural engineering	624.182 2	Corangamite, Lake	T2—945 7
toxicology	615.925 652	Corby (England : District)	T2—425 51
see also Chemicals, Metals		Corchorus	583.19
Copper Age	930.15	Cordage	
Copper-aluminum alloys	669.3	ship gear	623.862
see also Copper		textiles	677.71
Copper-beryllium alloys	669.3	Cordaitales	561.55
see also Copper		Cordaiteae	561.55
Copper soaps	668.125	Cordials	641.255
Copper sulfate water treatment	628.166 2	commercial processing	663.55
Copperbelt Province (Zambia)	T2—689 4	Cordierite	
Copperleaf	583.95	mineralogy	549.64
Coppermine (N.W.T.)	T2—719 7	Cordillera (Paraguay)	T2—892 135
Copra	665.355	Cordite	662.26
Coptic Church	281.7	military engineering	623.452 6
see also Eastern churches		Córdoba	T2—825 4
Coptic language	493.2	Córdoba (Colombia : Dept.)	T2—861 12
	T6—932	Córdoba (Spain : Province)	T2—468 4
Biblical texts	220.49	Cordoba caliphate (Spanish	
Coptic literature	893.2	history)	946.02
Coptic people	T5—932	Cords (Textiles)	677.76
Coptic period (Egyptian history)	932.023	textile arts	746.27
Copts	T5—932	Corduroy	677.617
Copulation		Core memory	004.53
sociology	306.77	engineering	621.397 3
Copyright	346.048 2	Core of earth	551.112
international law	341.758 2	Coreoidea	595.754
law	346.048 2	Corfu (Greece : Nome)	T2—495 5
public administration	351.824	Coriander	583.48
Copyright deposits		Coriariales	583.29
library acquisitions	025.26	Corinth (Greece : Nome)	T2—495 2
Coquet River	T2—428 87	ancient	T2—387
Coquihalla River (B.C.)	T2—711 37		

Corporate mergers (continued)
  management 658.16
Corporate organization
  law 346.066 2
Corporate ownership
  land economics 333.324
Corporate profits
  income distribution 339.21
Corporate reorganization 338.74
  credit economics 332.75
  law 346.066 26
  management 658.16
  production economics 338.74
  tax law 343.067
Corporate retail chains 381.12
  management 658.870 2
  see also Commerce
Corporate securities 332.632 044
Corporate state
  political system 321.94
Corporation meetings
  law 346.066 45
Corporation records
  law 346.066 4
Corporation tax 336.207
  law 343.067
Corporations 338.74
  accounting 657.95
  economics 338.74
  law 346.066
  management 658.045
    initiation 658.114 5
Corps (Military units) 355.31
Corps of engineers 358.22
Corpus Christi (Tex.) T2—764 113
Corpus iuris canonici 262.923
Corpus striatum
  human physiology 612.825
  see also Nervous system
Corpuscular radiation
  meteorology 551.527 6
Corpuscular theory of electricity 537.14
Corpuscular theory of light 535.12
Correctional institutions 365
  area planning 711.556
  buildings 365.5
    architecture 725.6
  law 344.035
  psychological influence 155.962
  public administration 350.849 5
    central governments 351.849 5
    local governments 352.944 95
  reform 365.7
Corrections 364.6
  law 345.077
  public administration 350.849
    central governments 351.849
    local governments 352.944 9

Corrections (Astronomy) 522.9
Correlation analysis 519.537
Correspondence (Letters) T1—092
  biography 920
Correspondence (Mathematics) 511.33
Correspondence courses 374.4
  T1—071 54
Correspondence schools 374.4
Corrèze (France : Dept.) T2—446 7
Corrientes (Argentina :
  Province) T2—822 2
Corrodentia 595.732
  paleozoology 565.73
Corrosion 620.112 23
Corrosion-resistant construction
  ship hulls 623.848
Corrosive materials 363.179
  public safety 363.179
  technology 604.7
  see also Hazardous materials
Corrugated paperboard boxes 676.32
Corruption in government 364.132 3
  law 345.023 23
  public administration 350.994
    central governments 351.994
    local governments 352.002
Corryong (Vic.) T2—945 5
Cors anglais 788.53
  see also Woodwind instruments
Corsages 745.923
Corse (Region) T2—449 45
Corse-de-Sud (France) T2—449 452
Corsiaceae 584.13
Corsica (Region) T2—449 45
  ancient T2—379
Corsicans T5—58
Corson County (S.D.) T2—783 52
Cortés (Honduras : Dept.) T2—728 311
Cortes Island (B.C.) T2—711 1
Cortex
  human anatomy 611.81
  human physiology 612.825
  see also Nervous system
Cortin 596.014 2
  chemistry 547.734 5
  physiology 596.014 2
Cortisone
  pharmacology 615.364
  see also Endocrine system
Cortland County (N.Y.) T2—747 72
Coruh Ili (Turkey) T2—566 2
Corum Ili (Turkey) T2—563
Coruña, La (Spain : Province) T2—461 1
Corundum 553.65
  materials science 620.198
  mineralogy 549.523
Corvidae 598.864
Coryell County (Tex.) T2—764 515

Cottbus (Germany : Bezirk)	T2—431 51
Cotters	621.883
Cottle County (Tex.)	T2—764 751
Cotton	583.17
agricultural economics	338.173 51
fiber crop	633.51
textiles	677.21
arts	746.042 1
see also Textiles	
Cotton County (Okla.)	T2—766 49
Cotton grass	584.84
Cottonseed meal	664.726
Cottonseed oil	
food technology	664.363
Cottonwood	583.981
Cottonwood County (Minn.)	T2—776 28
Cotylosauria	567.92
Couches	645.4
manufacturing technology	684.12
see also Furniture	
Couching	
arts	746.44
Cough remedies	
pharmacodynamics	615.72
see also Respiratory system	
Coulometers	621.374 4
Coulometric analysis	543.087 4
Council for Mutual Economic	
Assistance	341.242 7
international commerce	382.914 7
international economics	337.147
international law	341.242 7
Council housing	363.585
law	344.063 635
see also Housing	
Council-manager government	
cities	320.854
Council of Europe	T2—4
law	341.242
Councillors of state	
occupational group	T7—352 1
Councils	
Christian ecclesiology	262.5
Councils of state	351.004
Coundres Island (Quebec)	T2—714 49
Counsel (Gift of the Holy Spirit)	234.12
Counseling	361.323
armed forces	355.347
crime prevention	364.48
education	371.4
law	344.079 4
pastoral theology	291.61
Christianity	253.5
personnel management	658.385
public administration	350.16
central governments	351.16
local governments	352.005 16

Counseling (continued)	
prisoner services	365.66
psychology	158.3
social work	361.323
old persons	362.66
Counted thread embroidery	746.443
Counter displays	
advertising	659.157
Counter-Reformation	270.6
German history	943.03
Counterattacks (Military tactics)	355.422
Counterculture	306.1
Counterfactuals	
logic	160
Counterfeit cancellations	
philately	769.562
Counterfeit coins	
numismatics	737.4
Counterfeit covers	
philately	769.562
Counterfeit paper money	
arts	769.55
Counterfeit postage stamps	
philately	769.562
Counterfeiting	364.133
economics	332.9
law	345.023 3
Counterglow (Astronomy)	523.59
Counterintelligence	327.12
armed forces	355.343 3
see also Espionage	
Countermining	623.31
Countermonopoly theory of	
unions	331.880 1
Counterpoint	781.286
Counters	
numismatics	737.3
Countersubjects	
musical element	781.248
Countertenor voices	782.86
choral and mixed voices	782.86
single voices	783.86
Counties	
government	320.83
public administration	352.007 3
Counting	513.211
Counting circuits	621.381 534
Counting machines	
manufacturing technology	681.14
Counting-out rhymes	398.84
Counting rhymes	398.84
Country clubs	
landscape architecture	712.7
Country music	781.642
Country Party (Australia)	324.294 04

Cowpeas (continued)
 garden crop   635.659 2
Cowpox
 incidence   614.521
 medicine   616.913
 see also Communicable
  diseases (Human)
Cowra (N.S.W.)   T2—944 5
Cowries   594.32
Cows
 animal husbandry   636.2
 see also Cattle
Cowslip   583.672
Coyotes   599.744 42
Coypus   599.323 4
CPM (Management)   658.403 2
CPR (Resuscitation)
 medicine   616.102 5
 see also Cardiovascular system
CPU (Central processor)   004
 engineering   621.39
Crab apples   583.372
Crabbing
 economics   338.372 538 42
 fisheries   639.542
Crabgrass   584.92
Crabs   595.384 2
 cooking   641.695
 fisheries   639.542
 fisheries economics   338.372 538 42
 food   641.395
  commercial processing   664.94
Cracidae   598.614
Crack abuse   362.298
 medicine   616.864 7
 personal health   613.84
 social welfare   362.298
 see also Substance abuse
Crack resistance (Engineering)
 materials science   620.112 6
Crackers   641.815
 commercial processing   664.752
 cooking   641.815
Cracking processes
 petroleum   665.533
Cradle Mountain (Tas.)   T2—946 3
Cradle Mountain-Lake Saint
  Clair National Park (Tas.)   T2—946 3
Cradock (South Africa :
  District)   T2—687 14
Craft (Ships)   387.2
 see also Ships
Craft unions   331.883 2
Crafts   680
 arts   745
 sociology of recreation   306.489
Craftsmen's marks   T1—027 8
Craig County (Okla.)   T2—766 98

Craig County (Va.)   T2—755 795
Craigavon (Northern Ireland :
  Borough)   T2—416 64
Craighead County (Ark.)   T2—767 98
Cranberries   641.347 6
 botany   583.62
 commercial processing   664.804 76
 cooking   641.647 6
 horticulture   634.76
Cranbrook (B.C.)   T2—711 65
Crane County (Tex.)   T2—764 915
Crane flies   595.771
Cranes (Birds)   598.31
Cranes (Hoisting machinery)   621.873
Cranial nerves
 human diseases
  medicine   616.87
 human physiology   612.819
 see also Nervous system
Craniata   596
 paleozoology   566
Craniology
 physical anthropology   573.7
Craniotomy
 obstetrical surgery   618.83
Cranks (Mechanisms)   621.827
Crape myrtle   583.44
Crappie   597.58
Craps   795.12
Crash injuries
 medicine   617.102 8
Crassulaceae   583.38
Crater Lake National Park
  (Or.)   T2—795 915
Craters (Depressions)   551.21
                                    T2—144
 geography   910.914 4
 geology   551.21
 physical geography   910.021 44
Craters of the Moon National
  Monument (Idaho)   T2—796 59
Crates
 wooden   674.82
Craven (England : District)   T2—428 41
Craven County (N.C.)   T2—756 192
Crawfish   595.384 1
 fisheries   639.541
Crawford County (Ark.)   T2—767 35
Crawford County (Ga.)   T2—758 562
Crawford County (Ill.)   T2—773 75
Crawford County (Ind.)   T2—772 28
Crawford County (Iowa)   T2—777 45
Crawford County (Kan.)   T2—781 98
Crawford County (Mich.)   T2—774 77
Crawford County (Mo.)   T2—778 62
Crawford County (Ohio)   T2—771 27
Crawford County (Pa.)   T2—748 97
Crawford County (Wis.)   T2—775 74

Cretaceous period (continued)
paleontology 560.176 6
Crete 949.98
T2—499 8
ancient 939.18
T2—391 8
Crete, Sea of 551.462 8
T2—163 88
Cretinism
medicine 616.858 848
see also Mental retardation
Creuse (France) T2—446 8
Creutzfeldt-Jakob disease
medicine 616.83
see also Nervous system
Crewe and Nantwich
(England : Borough) T2—427 12
Crewelwork 746.446
Crib death
pediatrics 618.92
Cribbage 795.41
Criblé engraving 765.6
Cricket (Game) 796.358
Cricket players 796.358 092
sports group T7—796 35
Crickets 595.726
Cries (Rhymes) 398.87
Crime 364
correction 364.6
social theology 291.178 33
Christianity 261.833
Crime insurance 368.82
government-sponsored 368.48
see also Insurance
Crime prevention 364.4
criminology 364.4
public administration 350.849 2
central governments 351.849 2
local governments 352.944 92
individual action 362.88
management 658.473
penology 364.601
police services 363.23
public administration 350.75
central governments 351.75
local governments 352.935
Crime victims 362.88
see also Victims of crime
Crimea (Ukraine : Oblast) T2—477 17
Crimean War, 1853-1856 947.073
Crimes 364.1
law 345.02
Crimes against humanity 364.135
law 345.023 5
Crimes against peace 364.135
law 345.023 5
Crimes against the state 364.131
law 345.023 1

Crimes without victims 364.1
law 345.02
Criminal abortion 364.185
law 345.028 5
Criminal anthropology 364.2
Criminal courts 345.01
England 345.420 1
Scotland 345.411 01
Criminal Division of Courts of
Appeal (Great Britain) 345.420 18
Criminal intent 345.04
Criminal investigation 363.25
armed forces 355.133 23
law 345.052
police services 363.25
Criminal jurisdiction 345.01
international law 341.488
Criminal justice information
systems 025.063 64
Criminal law 345
international 341.77
Criminal liability 345.04
Criminal offenses 364.1
insurance against 368.82
government-sponsored 368.48
see also Insurance
law 345.02
Criminal practice
law 345.05
Criminal procedure 345.05
Criminal psychology 364.3
Criminal responsibility 345.04
Criminal trial practice 345.075
Criminal trials 345.07
Criminal usury 364.168
law 345.026 8
Criminalistics 363.25
see also Criminal investigation
Criminally insane persons 364.38
correctional institutions 365.46
see also Correctional
institutions
Criminals 364.3
T1—086 92
law 345.03
see also Offenders
Criminologists 364.092
occupational group T7—364
Criminology 364
Crimson clover 583.322
forage crop 633.327
Crinoidea 593.91
paleozoology 563.91
Crippled persons 305.908 166
T1—087 3
see also Motor-impaired
persons

Crossing over (Genetics)	575.29
Crossings (Railroad)	385.312
engineering	625.163
transportation services	385.312
Crossopterygii	597.46
paleozoology	567.4
Crossosomataceae	583.112
Crossroads (South Africa)	T2—687 35
Crossword puzzles	793.732
Croton	583.95
Croup	
medicine	616.201
pediatrics	618.922 01
see also Respiratory system	
Crow Indians	T5—975
Crow language	497.5
	T6—975
Crow Wing County (Minn.)	T2—776 71
Crowbars	621.93
Crowberry	583.271
Crowd control	363.32
Crowds	302.33
Crowley County (Colo.)	T2—788 94
Crown Counsel (Scotland)	345.411 01
Crown Court (Great Britain)	345.420 14
Crown of thorn (Plant)	583.95
Crownest Pass (Alta.)	T2—712 34
Crowns (Dentistry)	617.692
see also Dentistry	
Crows	598.864
Croydon (London, England)	T2—421 91
Crozet Islands	969.9
	T2—699
Cruciales	583.123
Crucible steel	669.142 9
Crucibles (Chemical apparatus)	542.2
Cruciferae	583.123
Crucifixes	
religious significance	246.558
Crucifixion of Jesus Christ	232.963
Crude drugs	
pharmacognosy	615.321
Crude gelatin	668.34
Cruelty	
ethics	179
see also Ethical problems	
Cruelty to animals	
criminal law	345.028 7
criminology	364.187
ethics	179.3
religion	291.569 3
Buddhism	294.356 93
Christianity	241.693
Hinduism	294.548 693
Islam	297.5
Judaism	296.385 693
Cruisers	359.835 3
design	623.812 53

Cruisers (continued)	
engineering	623.825 3
naval equipment	359.835 3
naval units	359.325 3
Crumhorns	788.5
see also Woodwind instruments	
Crusades	909.07
Church history	270.4
European history	940.18
history	909.07
Crushed stone pavements	625.82
road engineering	625.82
sidewalk engineering	625.882
Crushers (Agricultural tools)	
manufacturing technology	681.763 1
Crushing	
chemical engineering	660.284 22
ores	622.73
Crushing tools	621.914
Crust of earth	551.13
compression	551.82
Crustaceans	595.3
cooking	641.695
culture	639.5
fisheries	639.5
food	641.395
commercial processing	664.94
paleozoology	565.3
Crutches	
manufacturing technology	685.38
Crwths	787.78
see also Stringed instruments	
Cryobiology	574.191 67
human	612.014 467
Cryogenic engineering	621.59
Cryogenic engineers	621.590 92
occupational group	T7—621
Cryogenics	536.56
biophysics	574.191 67
human	612.014 467
materials science	620.112 16
Cryolite	
mineralogy	549.4
synthetic	666.86
Cryometry	536.54
Cryosurgery	617.05
Cryotherapy	
medicine	615.832 9
Cryptanalysis	652.8
armed forces	355.343 2
Crypteroniaceae	583.44
Cryptobranchoidea	597.65
Cryptococcales	589.24
Cryptodira	597.92
Cryptogamia	586
paleobotany	561.6

Cultural influence
  psychology   155.92
Cultural institutions   306.4
Cultural levels (Social classes)   305.906 3
      T1—086 3
Cultural programs (Libraries)   021.26
Cultural property
  historic preservation   363.69
    international law   341.767 7
    law   344.094
Cultural relations   303.482
  international law   341.767
Cultural resources
  law   344.09
Cultural Revolution (Chinese
  history)   951.056
Culturally disadvantaged children
  home care   649.156 7
Culturally disadvantaged persons
  education   371.967
Culture   306
  law   344.09
  public administration   350.85
    central governments   351.85
     cabinet departments   351.085
    local governments   352.945
  sociology   306.4
Cultured skim milk   641.371 476
  cooking   641.671 476
  processing   637.147 6
Cultured whole milk   641.371 46
  cooking   641.671 46
  processing   637.146
Culverts (Drainage)   625.734 2
Cumacea   595.381
  paleozoology   565.38
Cumberland (England)   T2—427 8
Cumberland (Md.)   T2—752 94
Cumberland (N.S. : County)   T2—716 11
Cumberland, Lake   T2—769 63
Cumberland County (Ill.)   T2—773 73
Cumberland County (Ky.)   T2—769 683
Cumberland County (Me.)   T2—741 91
Cumberland County (N.C.)   T2—756 373
Cumberland County (N.J.)   T2—749 94
Cumberland County (Pa.)   T2—748 43
Cumberland County (Tenn.)   T2—768 75
Cumberland County (Va.)   T2—755 615
Cumberland Gap   T2—768 944
Cumberland Mountains   T2—769 1
  Kentucky   T2—769 1
  Tennessee   T2—768 944
Cumberland Plateau   T2—768 7
  Kentucky   T2—769 1
  Tennessee   T2—768 7
Cumberland Presbyterian Church   285.135
  see also Presbyterian Church

Cumberland River (Ky. and
  Tenn.)   T2—768 5
Cumbernauld and Kilsyth
  (Scotland : District)   T2—414 38
Cumbria (England)   T2—427 8
Cumbrian Mountains   T2—427 8
Cumin   583.48
Cuming County (Neb.)   T2—782 232
Cumnock and Doon Valley
  (Scotland : District)   T2—414 67
Cuna Indians   T5—982
Cuna language   498.2
      T6—982
Cundinamarca (Colombia)   T2—861 46
Cuneo (Italy : Province)   T2—451 3
Cunnamulla (Qld.)   T2—943 4
Cunninghame (Scotland)   T2—414 61
Cunoniales   583.397
Cup fungi   589.23
Cup games
  soccer   796.334 64
Cupolas   721.5
  architecture   721.5
  construction   690.15
Cuprammonium rayon   677.462
  see also Textiles
Cupressaceae   585.2
  paleobotany   561.52
Cuprite
  mineralogy   549.522
Cups
  paper   676.34
Curaçao   T2—729 86
Curassows   598.614
Curbs   625.888
Curculionoidea   595.768
Curfew
  crime prevention   364.4
  see also Crime prevention
Curia Romana   262.136
Curicó (Chile : Province)   T2—833 4
Curium   546.442
  see also Chemicals
Curlews   598.33
Curling (Sport)   796.96
Currants   641.347 21
  botany   583.397
  cooking   641.647 21
  horticulture   634.721
Currency   332.4
  see also Money
Currency convertibility   332.45
Currency movements
  international commerce   382.174
Currency paper   676.282 6
Current assets
  accounting   657.72

Cyanite	
mineralogy	549.62
Cyanobacteria	589.46
Cyanophyta	589.46
Cyatheaceae	587.31
Cybernetics	003.5
	T1—011 5
Cybernetics and religion	291.175
natural theology	215
Cycad	585.9
Cycadales	585.9
paleobotany	561.591
Cycadeoidaceae	561.592
Cycadeoidales	561.592
Cyclades (Greece)	T2—499
ancient	T2—391 5
Cyclamen	583.672
Cyclanthales	584.62
Cycles (Vehicles)	388.347
engineering	629.227
repair	629.287 7
riding	629.284 7
transportation services	388.347
Cyclic compounds	547.5
chemical engineering	661.8
Cyclic groups	512.2
Cyclical unemployment	331.137 047
Cycling	796.6
Cycling paths	388.12
see also Bicycle paths	
Cyclists	796.609 2
sports group	T7—796 6
Cyclo rubber	678.68
Cycloacetylenes	547.513
chemical engineering	661.815
Cyclones (Meteorology)	551.551 3
Cyclonite	662.27
Cycloolefins	547.512
chemical engineering	661.815
Cycloparaffins	547.511
chemical engineering	661.815
Cyclopedias	030
Cyclopoida	595.34
paleozoology	565.34
Cyclops (Zoology)	595.34
Cyclopteris	561.597
Cycloramas	745.8
decorative arts	745.8
painting	751.74
Cyclorrhapha	595.774
Cyclosilicates	
mineralogy	549.64
Cyclostomata (Bryozoa)	594.7
Cyclostomata (Jawless fish)	597.2
paleozoology	567.2
Cyclotomy (Number theory)	512.72
Cyclotrons	539.733
Cygnet (Tas.)	T2—946 2

Cylinder recordings	
sound reproduction	621.389 32
Cylinders (Engine parts)	621.437
Cylinders (Shape)	516.15
Cylinders (Structural elements)	624.177 2
concrete	624.183 42
Cylindrical bark beetle	595.769
Cymbals	786.873
see also Percussion instruments	
Cymbidium	584.15
Cymric language	491.66
	T6—916 6
Cymric literature	891.66
Cymry	T5—916 6
Cynewulf	829.4
Cynic philosophy	183.4
Cynocrambaceae	583.913
Cynomorium	583.94
Cynon Valley (Wales : Borough)	T2—429 73
Cyperales	584.84
Cypress	585.2
forestry	634.975 5
lumber	674.144
Cypress Hills (Alta. and Sask.)	T2—712 43
Cypriniformes	597.52
Cyprinodontes	597.53
Cypriot architecture	
Phoenician	722.32
Cypriots	T5—895
Cyprus	956.45
	T2—564 5
ancient	939.37
	T2—393 7
Cyrenaic philosophy	183.5
Cyrenaica	T2—397 5
ancient	939.75
Cyrillaceae	583.271
Cyrillic alphabet	
printing	686.219 18
Cyrillic calligraphy	745.619 918
Cystic fibrosis	
medicine	616.37
see also Digestive system	
Cystitis	
medicine	616.623
see also Urinary system	
Cystobacteriaceae	589.98
Cystoidea	563.97
Cytinaceae	583.922
Cytochemistry	574.876 042
Cytodiagnosis	
medicine	616.075 82
Cytogenetics	574.873 22
Cytokinesis	
cytology	574.876 2

Cytological examination	
medicine	616.075 82
Cytology	574.87
see also Cells	
Cytopathology	574.876 5
human	611.018 15
Cytoplasm	574.873 4
Cytoskeleton	574.873 4
Czech language	491.86
	T6—918 6
Czech literature	891.86
Czechoslovak Republic	943.703 2
	T2—437
Czechoslovakia	943.7
	T2—437
Czechoslovaks	T5—918 6
Czechs	T5—918 6
Czestochowa (Poland :	
Voivodeship)	T2—438 5

D

D.A.R. (Patriotic society)	369.135
D.A.T. (Digital audio)	
sound reproduction	621.389 3
D.A.V. (Veterans)	369.186 3
D.B.S. systems	384.552
D.N.A. (Genetics)	574.873 282
D.P. (Displaced persons)	325.21
see also Refugees	
D.P.I. (Macroeconomics)	339.32
D region (Ionosphere)	538.767 2
Da capo form	781.822 5
instrumental	784.182 2
Daba language	493.7
	T6—937
Dacca District (Bangladesh)	T2—549 22
Dachshund	
animal husbandry	636.753
see also Dogs	
Dacia	T2—398
Dacian language	491.993
	T6—919 93
Dacorum (England : District)	T2—425 84
Dactylopteriformes	597.58
Dadaism	709.040 62
painting	759.066 2
sculpture	735.230 462
Daddy longlegs	595.43
Dade County (Fla.)	T2—759 38
Dade County (Ga.)	T2—758 342
Dade County (Mo.)	T2—778 745
Dādra and Nagar Haveli	
(India)	T2—547 96
Daffodils	584.25
floriculture	635.934 25
Dafur al-Janubiyah (Sudan :	
Province)	T2—627

Dafur al-Shamaliyah (Sudan :	
Province)	T2—627
Dagari (African people)	T5—963 5
Dagari language	496.35
	T6—963 5
Dagenham, Barking and	
(London, England)	T2—421 75
Dagestan A.S.S.R.	
(R.S.F.S.R.)	T2—479 7
Dagestanskaia A.S.S.R.	
(R.S.F.S.R.)	T2—479 7
Daggers	623.441
art metalwork	739.72
military engineering	623.441
Daggett County (Utah)	T2—792 15
Daghestan A.S.S.R.	
(R.S.F.S.R.)	T2—479 7
Dagomba language	496.35
	T6—963 5
Daguerreotype process	772.12
Dahlak Archipelago	T2—635
Dahlias	583.55
floriculture	635.933 55
Dahomeans	T5—966 83
Dahomey	966.83
	T2—668 3
Dahomey (Kingdom)	966.830 18
	T2—668 3
Dahuk (Iraq : Province)	T2—567 2
Dai language (Chad)	493.7
	T6—937
Daily devotions	291.446
Christianity	242.2
Judaism	296.72
Dairy cattle	
animal husbandry	636.214 2
Dairy cooperatives	334.683 7
economics	334.683 7
Dairy farmers	636.214 209 2
occupational group	T7—637
Dairy farming	636.214 2
Dairy industry	338.176 214 2
law	343.076 621 42
public administration	351.823 37
Dairy processing	637
Dairy processing industry	338.476 37
Dairy processors	637.092
occupational group	T7—637
Dairy products	641.37
cooking	641.67
product safety	363.192 9
see also Food—product safety	
Dairymen	636.214 209 2
occupational group	T7—637
Daisy	583.55
Dajabón (Dominican	
Republic : Province)	T2—729 345
Dakar (Senegal)	T2—663

Dakhla (Morocco : Province)   T2—648
Dakota County (Minn.)   T2—776 56
Dakota County (Neb.)   T2—782 224
Dakota Indians   T5—975
Dakota language   497.5
    T6—975
Dakota literature   897.5
Dalby (Qld.)   T2—943 3
Dale County (Ala.)   T2—761 33
Dale Hollow Lake   T2—768 49
Dalhousie, James Andrew Broun,
   Marquess
   Indian history   954.031 6
Dallam County (Tex.)   T2—764 812
Dallas (Tex.)   T2—764 281 2
Dallas County (Ala.)   T2—761 45
Dallas County (Ark.)   T2—767 67
Dallas County (Iowa)   T2—777 57
Dallas County (Mo.)   T2—778 813
Dallas County (Tex.)   T2—764 281 1
Dalmatia (Croatia)   T2—497 2
Dalmatian (Dog)
   animal husbandry   636.72
   see also Dogs
Dalmatian language (Romance)   457.994 972
    T6—57
Dalmatian language (Slavic)   491.82
    T6—918 2
Dalmatian literature (Romance)   850
Dalmatian literature (Slavic)   891.82
Dalmatians   T5—57
Dalmato-Romanic language   T6—57
Daly River (N.T.)   T2—942 95
Daly River Wildlife Sanctuary   T2—942 95
Daly Waters (N.T.)   T2—942 95
Damages (Law)   347.077
Damascening   739.15
Damascus (Syria)   T2—569 144
   ancient   T2—394 3
Damascus (Syria : Province)   T2—569 14
Damask   677.616
Damietta (Egypt)   T2—621
Dampier Archipelago   T2—941 3
Damping
   aeronautics   629.132 364
Damping of sound
   physics   534.208
Dampness control
   construction
    buildings   693.893
Dams   627.8
   agricultural use   631.28
   public administration   351.867
Damselfish   597.58
Damselfly   595.733
Damson plum   583.372
   orchard crop   634.227
Dan (African people)   T5—963 4

Dan language   496.34
    T6—963 4
Dance   792.8
   see also Dancing
Dance bands   784.48
Dance flies   595.771
Dance forms   784.188
Dance halls
   architecture   725.86
Dance music   781.554
Dance orchestras   784.48
Dance therapy
   medicine   615.851 55
Dancers   792.802 809 2
   occupational group   T7—792 8
Dances of the suite form   784.188 3
Dancing   792.8
   customs   394.3
   elementary education   372.66
   ethics   175.3
    see also Recreation—ethics
   etiquette   395.3
   musical plays   792.62
   religious significance   291.37
    Christianity   246.7
    see also Arts—religious
     significance
   sociology   306.484
Dancing games   796.13
Dandelions   583.55
   garden crop   635.51
Dandruff
   medicine   616.546
   see also Skin
Dane County (Wis.)   T2—775 83
Danes   T5—398 1
Daniel (Biblical book)   224.5
Daniels County (Mont.)   T2—786 213
Danish language   439.81
    T6—398 1
Danish literature   839.81
Danish pastry   641.865 9
   commercial processing   664.752 5
   home preparation   641.865 9
Danish people   T5—398 1
Dannhauser (South Africa :
   District)   T2—684 1
Dano-Norwegian language   439.82
    T6—398 2
Dano-Norwegian literature   839.82
Danube River   T2—496
   Germany   T2—433
Danville (Va.)   T2—755 666
Danzig (Germany)   T2—438 2
Daphne   583.933
Daphniphyllaceae   583.394
Daqahliya (Egypt :
   Governorate)   T2—621

Dating (Social customs)	306.73	Day language (Chad)	493.7
customs	392.6		T6—937
personal living	646.77	Day lilies	584.324
sociology	306.73	floriculture	635.934 324
Datiscaceae	583.46	Day of Atonement	
Daughters	306.874	customs	394.268 296 432
	T1—085 4	Day of the Lord	
	T7—044 1	Christianity	236.9
family relationships	306.874	Judaism	296.33
Daughters of Rebekah	366.38	Day schools	373.222
Daughters of Rebekah members	366.380 92	Daydreams	
social group	T7—366 3	psychology	154.3
Daughters of the American		Daylesford (Vic.)	T2—945 3
Revolution	369.135	Daylight savings time	389.17
Dauphin County (Pa.)	T2—748 18	law	343.07
Dauphiné (France)	T2—449 6	Daymarks	387.155
Dauplin (Man.)	T2—712 72	construction	627.924
D'Autray (Quebec)	T2—714 43	navigation aids	623.894 4
DAV (Veterans)	369.186 3	transportation services	387.155
Davao del Norte (Philippines)	T2—599 7	Days	529.1
Davao del Sur (Philippines)	T2—599 7	folklore	398.236
Davao Oriental (Philippines)	T2—599 7	sociology	398.33
Davenport (Iowa)	T2—777 69	music	781.522
Davenport Range	T2—942 91	Dayton (Ohio)	T2—771 73
Davenports	645.4	Daza (African people)	T5—965
see also Furniture		Daza language	496.5
Daventry (England : District)	T2—425 56		T6—965
David, King of Israel		DBS systems	384.552
Palestinian history	933.02	De Aar (South Africa :	
Davidson County (N.C.)	T2—756 68	District)	T2—687 13
Davidson County (Tenn.)	T2—768 55	De Baca County (N.M.)	T2—789 44
Davie County (N.C.)	T2—756 69	De facto government	
Daviess County (Ind.)	T2—772 385	international law	341.26
Daviess County (Ky.)	T2—769 864	De Kalb County (Ala.)	T2—761 66
Daviess County (Mo.)	T2—778 183	De Kalb County (Ga.)	T2—758 225
Davis County (Iowa)	T2—777 97	De Kalb County (Ill.)	T2—773 28
Davis County (Utah)	T2—792 27	De Kalb County (Ind.)	T2—772 77
Davis Strait	551.461 42	De Kalb County (Mo.)	T2—778 153
	T2—163 42	De Kalb County (Tenn.)	T2—768 532
Davison County (S.D.)	T2—783 374	De Soto County (Fla.)	T2—759 59
Dawes County (Neb.)	T2—782 93	De Soto County (Miss.)	T2—762 87
Dawn	525.7	De Soto Parish (La.)	T2—763 63
literature	808.803 3	De Witt County (Ill.)	T2—773 585
history and criticism	809.933 3	De Witt County (Tex.)	T2—764 259
specific literatures	T3B—080 33	Deacons	270.092
history and criticism	T3B—093 3	ecclesiology	262.14
Dawson (Yukon)	T2—719 1	*see also* Clergy—Christian	
Dawson County (Ga.)	T2—758 263	Dead	
Dawson County (Mont.)	T2—786 24	disposal	363.75
Dawson County (Neb.)	T2—782 46	customs	393
Dawson County (Tex.)	T2—764 854	music	781.588
Dawson Creek (B.C.)	T2—711 87	*see also* Undertaking	
Day camps	796.542 3	(Mortuary)	
Day care	362.712	religious worship	291.213
educational centers	372.21	Dead animal disposal	363.78
social welfare	362.712	Dead letter services	383.186
Day County (S.D.)	T2—783 142	*see also* Postal service	
		Dead nettles	583.87

...tinued)	
	781.584
...ania	745.74
... (Crustaceans)	595.384
...ology	565.38
...a (Mollusks)	594.58
...zoology	564.58
... County (Ga.)	T2—758 993
... County (Ind.)	T2—772 16
... County (Iowa)	T2—777 875
...r County (Kan.)	T2—781 143
...ir County (Tenn.)	T2—768 32
...	
...terials science	620.112 2
...y (Sound)	
...usical element	781.235
...ay schemes (Nuclear physics)	539.752
...can (India)	T2—548
...celeration	
...iophysics	574.191 34
...human	612.014 414
...centralization	
executive management	658.402
public administration	350.007 3
central governments	351.007 3
local governments	352.000 473
Deception	001.95
military operations	355.41
Decidability	511.3
Decimal numbers	513.55
Decimal system	513.55
Decimalization of currency	332.404 8
Decision analysis	
management use	658.403 54
Decision making	
executive management	658.403
	T1—068 4
political science	320.019
production management	658.503 6
psychology	153.83
public administration	350.007 25
central governments	351.007 25
local governments	352.000 472 5
social psychology	302.3
Decision tables	
program design	005.120 28
Decision theory	003.56
	T1—011 56
Decision theory (Mathematics)	519.542
Decks (Buildings)	721.84
architecture	721.84
construction	690.184
Declaration of Independence, 1776	973.313
Declaratory judgments	347.077
Declension (Grammar)	415
specific languages	T4—5
...ecolorizing carbons	662.93

Decomposition	
materials science	620.112 2
Decomposition analysis	544.1
Decomposition method	519.4
Decompression sickness	
medicine	616.989 4
see also Environmental diseases (Human)	
Decoration	745.4
arts	745.4
automobile	629.26
Decorations (Awards)	929.81
armed forces	355.134 2
genealogy	929.81
numismatics	737.223
Decorative arts	745
see also Arts	
Decorative coloring	745.7
Decorative lettering	745.61
Decorative sculpture	731.72
Decorative treatment	
glass	748.6
metals	739.15
pottery	666.45
arts	738.15
technology	666.45
sculpture	731.4
Decorative values	701.8
drawing	741.018
Decoupage	745.546
Decoys	
handicrafts	745.593 6
Decubitus ulcers	
medicine	616.545
see also Skin	
Dedications (Christian rites)	265.92
Deductive mathematics	511.24
Deductive reasoning	162
logic	162
psychology	153.433
Dee River	T2—412 4
Deeds	346.043 8
conveyancing	346.043 8
Deep-freezing foods	664.028 53
commercial preservation	664.028 53
home preservation	641.453
Deep-sea diving	627.72
Deep-sea fishing	639.22
commercial	639.22
sports	799.16
Deep-sea surveys	551.460 7
Deer	599.735 7
agricultural pests	632.697 357
animal husbandry	636.294
big game hunting	799.277 357
Deer flies	595.771
Deer Lodge County (Mont.)	T2—786 87
Deeside, Alyn and (Wales)	T2—429 36

Delinquent children	364.36
see also Juvenile delinquents	
Delinquent persons	305.906 92
	T1—086 92
Delinquent students	371.93
Delmarva Peninsula	T2—752 1
Maryland	T2—752 1
Virginia	T2—755 1
Delmas (South Africa :	
District)	T2—682 2
Deloraine (Tas.)	T2—946 3
Delos Island (Greece)	T2—499
Delphi (Greece)	T2—383
Delta (B.C.)	T2—711 33
Delta Amacuro (Venezuela)	T2—876 2
Delta County (Colo.)	T2—788 18
Delta County (Mich.)	T2—774 94
Delta County (Tex.)	T2—764 273
Deltas	551.456
	T2—146
geography	910.914 6
geomorphology	551.456
physical geography	910.021 46
Delusions	001.96
Delyn (Wales : Borough)	T2—429 33
Demand	
communication industry	384.041
forecasts	338.02
agricultural economics	338.17
production economics	338.02
secondary industries	338.47
foreign exchange rate	
determination	332.456 2
microeconomics	338.521 2
natural resources	333.712
transportation services	388.049
Demand deposits	332.175 2
Dematerialization (Spiritualism)	133.92
Demineralization	
sewage treatment	628.358
water-supply treatment	628.166 6
Demobilization (Military	
science)	355.29
Democratic centralism	335.43
economics	335.43
Democratic government	321.8
Democratic Labour Party	
(Australia)	324.294 06
Democratic Party (U.S.)	324.273 6
Democratic Republic of the	
Congo	T2—675 1
Democratic Republican Party	
(U.S.)	324.273 6
Democratic socialism	335.5
economics	335.5
political ideology	320.531 5
Democritean philosophy	182.7

Demodulation	
electronics	621.381 536
Demodulators	
electronic circuits	621.381 536
Demography	304.6
DeMolay (Secret order)	366.17
DeMolay members	366.170 92
social group	T7—366 1
Demolition (Military)	623.27
Demolition charges	
military engineering	623.454 5
Demolition operations (Military)	358.23
underwater	359.984
Demoniac possession	133.426
occultism	133.426
religion	291.42
Demonology	133.42
religion	291.216
Demons	133.42
religion	291.216
Demonstrations (Advertising)	659.15
Demonstrative evidence	347.064
Demospongiae	593.46
paleozoology	563.4
Demotic (Modern Greek	
language)	489.3
	T6—89
Demotic Egyptian language	493.1
	T6—931
Demotic literature (Modern	
Greek)	889
Demotion	
armed forces	355.112
personnel management	658.312 7
employee discipline	658.314 4
public administration	350.14
central governments	351.14
local governments	352.005 14
Demulcents (Digestive)	
pharmacodynamics	615.735
see also Digestive system	
Demythologizing (Bible)	220.68
Denali National Park and	
Preserve (Alaska)	T2—798 3
Denbighshire (Wales)	T2—429 3
Dendrobatidae	597.87
Dendrobiums	584.15
floriculture	635.934 15
Dendrochirotida	593.96
Dendrologists	582.160 092
occupational group	T7—58
Dendrology	582.16
Denendeh	T2—719 2
Dengue fever	
incidence	614.571
medicine	616.921
see also Communicable	
diseases (Human)	

Depressant abuse	362.299
medicine	616.86
personal health	613.8
social welfare	362.299
see also Substance abuse	
Depression (Mental state)	362.25
medicine	616.852 7
social welfare	362.25
see also Mental illness	
Depressions (Economic)	
economic cycles	338.542
personal finance	332.024 02
Depressions (Physiography)	551.44
	T2—144
geography	910.914 4
geomorphology	551.44
physical geography	910.021 44
Depressive reactions	
medicine	616.895
see also Mental illness	
Deputy chief executives	
occupational group	T7—351 2
public administration	350.003 18
central governments	351.003 18
local governments	352.008
Deputy prime ministers	
occupational group	T7—351 3
public administration	351.003 18
Dera (Syria : Province)	T2—569 14
Dera Ismāīl Khān (Pakistan : District)	T2—549 124
Derbesiales	589.47
Derby (England)	T2—425 17
Derby (W.A.)	T2—941 4
Derbyshire (England)	T2—425 1
Derbyshire Dales (England : District)	T2—425 13
Derivation (Linguistics)	412
specific languages	T4—2
Derived spaces	514.320 3
Dermaptera	595.721
paleozoology	565.72
Dermatitis	
medicine	616.51
see also Skin	
Dermatitis (Atopic)	
medicine	616.521
see also Skin	
Dermatological allergies	
medicine	616.973
see also Diseases (Human)	
Dermatology	616.5
see also Skin	
Dermoptera	599.34
paleozoology	569.34
Derricks	621.872
Derry (Northern Ireland)	T2—416 21
Derry (Northern Ireland : County)	T2—416 2
Dervishes	
Islam	297.42
Derwent River	T2—946 2
Derwent River (Derbyshire, England)	T2—425 1
Derwent River (Yorkshire, England)	T2—428 4
Derwentside (England)	T2—428 68
Des Allemands, Lake	T2—763 32
Des Moines (Iowa)	T2—777 58
Des Moines County (Iowa)	T2—777 96
Des Moines River	T2—777
Des Plaines River	T2—773 2
Desai, Morarji Ranchodji	
Indian history	954.052
Desalinization	628.167
Descant recorders	788.364
see also Woodwind instruments	
Descant viols	787.62
see also Stringed instruments	
Descendants	T1—085 4
	T7—044
family relationships	306.874
Descent into hell of Jesus Christ	232.967
Deschutes County (Or.)	T2—795 87
Deschutes River (Or.)	T2—795 62
Description	
literature	808.802 2
history and criticism	809.922
specific literatures	T3B—080 22
history and criticism	T3B—092 2
Descriptive bibliography	010.42
Descriptive cataloging	025.32
Descriptive forms	
music	784.189 6
Descriptive geometry	516.6
applied	604.201 516 6
Descriptive government	320.4
Descriptive linguistics	410
Descriptive research	001.433
	T1—072 3
Descriptive statistics	519.53
Descriptors (Information science)	025.49
Desegregation	
educational sociology	370.193 42
Desert ecology	574.526 52
Desert tactics	355.423
Desertification	333.736
geomorphology	551.415
land economics	333.736
Desertion (Family)	306.88
Deserts	T2—154
geomorphology	551.415
Desha County (Ark.)	T2—767 85

Deux-Montagnes (Quebec :
  County) T2—714 25
Deux-Montagnes (Quebec :
  Regional County
  Municipality) T2—714 25
Deux-Sèvres (France) T2—446 2
Devaluation of currency 332.414
  foreign exchange 332.452
Developable surfaces 516.362
Developed regions T2—172 2
Developing (Photography) 771.4
Developing apparatus
  photography 771.49
Developing regions T2—172 4
Developing solutions
  photography 771.54
Development (Biology) 574.3
  see also Developmental biology
Development (History) 900
  see also History
Development (Improvement) 338.9
  expenditure estimates
    public administration 350.722 253 6
      central governments 351.722 253 6
      local governments 352.122 536
    natural resources 333.715
    production economics 338.9
    public administration 350.007 8
      central governments 351.007 8
      local governments 352.000 478
Development banks 332.153
  domestic 332.28
  international 332.153
Developmental biology 574.3
  animals 591.3
  cells 574.876 1
  human 612.6
  microorganisms 576.13
  plants 581.3
Developmental linguistics 401.93
Developmental psychology 155
  animals 156.5
Developmental reading 418.4
  specific languages T4—843
Developmentally disabled
  persons 305.908 16
    T1—087 5
    T7—081 6
  education 371.92
  social group 305.908 16
  social services 362.196 8
    mental retardation 362.3
    physical illness 362.196 8
    see also Health services
Developmentally disabled
  workers
  economics 331.59
Deveron River T2—412 25

Deviation 519.534
  social psychology 302.542
Devil 291.216
  art representation 704.948 7
  Christianity 235.4
  Islam 297.216
  Judaism 296.316
  literature 808.803 82
    history and criticism 809.933 82
    specific literatures T3B—080 382
      history and criticism T3B—093 82
  occultism 133.422
Devil worship 291.216
  occultism 133.422
Devolution, War of, 1667-1668 944.033
Devon (England) T2—423 5
Devon cattle
  animal husbandry 636.226
  zoology 599.735 8
Devonian period 551.74
  geology 551.74
  paleontology 560.172 6
Devonport (Tas.) T2—946 5
Devotional calendars 242.2
Devotional literature 291.43
  Buddhism 294.344 3
  Christianity 242
  Hinduism 294.543
  Islam 297.43
  Judaism 296.72
Devotional theology 291.4
  Buddhism 294.344
  Christianity 240
  Hinduism 294.54
  Islam 297.4
  Judaism 296.7
Dew 551.574 4
Dew points 536.44
Dewberries 641.347 17
  botany 583.372
  cooking 641.647 17
  horticulture 634.717
Dewdney-Alouette (B.C) T2—711 37
Dewetsdorp (South Africa :
  District) T2—685 6
Dewey County (Okla.) T2—766 18
Dewey County (S.D.) T2—783 54
Dewey Decimal Classification 025.431
Dewey shorthand system
  1922 653.425
  1936 653.428
Dexter shorthorn cattle
  animal husbandry 636.225
  zoology 599.735 8
Dextrans 574.192 482
  biochemistry 574.192 482
  chemistry 547.782
  see also Carbohydrates

Diazotype processes	773.7
Dice games	795.1
Dichapetalaceae	583.37
Dichotomosiphonales	589.47
Dickens County (Tex.)	T2—764 741
Dickenson County (Va.)	T2—755 745
Dickey County (N.D.)	T2—784 54
Dickinson County (Iowa)	T2—777 123
Dickinson County (Kan.)	T2—781 56
Dickinson County (Mich.)	T2—774 955
Dickson County (Tenn.)	T2—768 44
Diclidantheraceae	583.686
Dicotyledons	583
forestry	634.972
paleobotany	561.3
Dictation (Office practice)	651.74
shorthand	653.14
Dictators	
political group	T7—351 4
public administration	351.003 16
Dictatorship	321.9
Diction	418
applied linguistics	418
specific languages	T4—81
rhetoric	808
Dictionaries	413
specific languages	T4—3
specific subject	T1—03
Dictionary catalogs	025.315
bibliography	019
library science	025.315
Dictyosiphonales	589.45
Dictyotales	589.45
Didactic poetry	808.815
history and criticism	809.15
specific literatures	T3B—105
individual authors	T3A—1
Didana Range	T2—954 2
Didiereaceae	583.28
Didjeridu	783.99
Die casting	671.253
Diefenbaker, John G.	
Canadian history	971.064 2
Diefenbaker, Lake (Sask.)	T2—712 42
Dieffenbachia	584.64
Dielectric materials	
materials science	620.195
Dielectrics	537.24
Diencephalon	
human anatomy	611.81
human physiology	612.826 2
see also Nervous system	
Dies (Tools)	621.984
Diesel-electric locomotives	385.366 2
engineering	625.266 2
transportation services	385.366 2
see also Rolling stock	
Diesel engines	621.436
automotive	629.250 6
ships	623.872 36
Diesel fuel	665.538 4
Diesel-hydraulic locomotives	385.366 4
engineering	625.266 4
transportation services	385.366 4
see also Rolling stock	
Diesel locomotives	385.366
engineering	625.266
transportation services	385.366
see also Rolling stock	
Diesel submarines	359.938 32
design	623.812 572
engineering	623.825 72
naval equipment	359.938 32
Diet	
elementary education	372.37
health	613.7
Diet cooking	641.563
Dietary laws	
Judaism	296.73
Dietary limitations	
cooking for	641.563
Dietary regimens	
health	613.26
Dietetic salts	
food technology	664.4
Dietetics	613.2
Dietotherapy	
medicine	615.854
Difaqane (South African history)	968.041
Difference algebras	512.56
Difference equations	515.625
Differentiable manifolds	516.36
Differentiable mappings	515.352
Differential algebras	512.56
Differential calculus	515.33
Differential diagnosis	
medicine	616.075
Differential-difference equations	515.38
Differential equations	515.35
Differential forms	515.37
Differential gear	621.833
automotive	629.245
Differential geometry	516.36
Differential inequalities	515.36
Differential invariants	515.37
Differential operators	515.724 2
Differential psychology	155
animals	156.5
education	370.151
Differential topology	514.72
Differentials (Mathematics)	515.33
Differentiated staffing	371.141 23
Differentiation	
cytology	574.876 12
Diffraction crystallography	548.83

Diminishing marginal returns	338.512
Diminishing marginal utility	338.521 2
Dimitrovo, Bulgaria (Okrug)	T2—497 73
Dimitrovski okrug (Bulgaria)	T2—497 73
Dimmit County (Tex.)	T2—764 455
Dimorphism	
crystallography	548.3
Dimouts	
military engineering	623.77
Dinagat Island	T2—599 7
Dinefwr (Wales : Borough)	T2—429 68
Dingaan, King of the Zulus	
Natal history	968.404 1
Dingoes	599.744 42
Dining car cooking	641.576
Dining cars	385.33
engineering	625.23
see also Rolling stock	
Dining halls	
architecture	727.38
Dining rooms	643.4
home economics	643.4
interior decoration	747.76
Dinka (African people)	T5—965
Dinka language	496.5
	T6—965
Dinner	642
cooking	641.54
customs	394.15
Dinnerware	
table setting	642.7
Dinocapsales	589.43
Dinocerata	569.6
Dinococcales	589.43
Dinoflagellates	589.43
Dinoflagellida	593.18
Dinophysidales	589.43
Dinornithiformes	568.5
Dinosaur National Monument	
(Colo. and Utah)	T2—788 12
Dinosaurs	567.91
Dinotrichales	589.43
Dinwiddie County (Va.)	T2—755 582
Dioceses	
Christian ecclesiology	262.3
Diodes	
semiconductor	621.381 522
Diola (African people)	T5—963 2
Diola language	496.32
	T6—963 2
Diomedeidae	598.42
Diophantine analysis	512.74
Diophantine approximations	512.73
Diophantine equations	512.72
Dioramas	745.8
decorative arts	745.8
painting	751.74
Diorites	552.3
Dioscoreales	584.27
Diouf, Abdou	
Senegalese history	966.305
Diourbel (Senegal : Region)	T2—663
Dioxin	
toxicology	615.951 2
Dipentodontaceae	583.26
Diphenyl hydrocarbons	547.613
chemical engineering	661.816
Diphenylmethane dyes	667.254
Diphtheria	
incidence	614.512 3
medicine	616.931 3
see also Communicable	
diseases (Human)	
Diphthongs (Phonology)	414.6
specific languages	T4—16
Diploid cells	574.333
Diplomacy	327.2
customs	399
international law	341.33
Diplomas	371.291 2
prints	769.5
Diplomatic causes of war	355.027 2
Diplomatic customs	399
Diplomatic history	327.09
Civil War (United States)	973.72
Mexican War	973.622
South African War	968.048 2
Spanish-American War, 1898	973.892
United States Revolutionary	
War	973.32
Vietnamese War	959.704 32
War of 1812	973.522
World War I	940.32
World War II	940.532
Diplomatic immunities	327.2
international law	341.33
Diplomatic languages	401.3
Diplomatic law	342.041 2
international law	341.33
Diplomatic privileges	327.2
international law	341.33
Diplomats	327.209 2
occupational group	T7—352 2
Diplopia	
ophthalmology	617.762
see also Eyes	
Diplopoda	595.61
paleozoology	565.61
Diplura	595.714
paleozoology	565.71
Dipnoi	597.48
paleozoology	567.4
Dipole moments	537.243
Dipped latex	678.533
Dipped rubber	678.36
Dippers (Birds)	598.832

Disabled veterans	362.408 697	Disciples of Christ (continued)	
legal status	343.011 6	religious group	T7—266
social welfare	362.408 697	seminaries	207.116 6
Disadvantaged workers		theology	230.66
public administration	350.836	Discipline	
central governments	351.836	armed forces	355.13
local governments	352.943 6	law	343.014
Disarmament	327.174	education	371.5
ethics	172.4	home child care	649.64
religion	291.562 4	labor economics	331.259 8
Christianity	241.624	labor unions	331.873
see also Political ethics		legislators	328.366
international politics	327.174	personnel management	658.314
law	341.733	public administration	350.147
military science	355.03	central governments	351.147
social theology	291.178 7	local governments	352.005 147
Christianity	261.87	prisons	365.643
Disassembling tools	621.93	Disco dancing	793.33
Disaster insurance	368.122	Discoglossidea	
see also Insurance		paleozoology	567.8
Disaster nursing		Discoglossoidea	597.84
medicine	610.734 9	Discographies	011.38
Disaster relief	363.348	Discount	332.84
law	344.053 4	Discount rates	332.84
Disasters	904	economics	332.84
international law	341.766	central banking	332.113
law	344.053 4	macroeconomic policy	339.53
management aspects	658.477	Discount stores	381.149
personal safety	613.69	management	658.879
psychology	155.935	see also Commerce	
social effects	303.485	Discourse analysis	
social services	363.34	linguistics	401.41
public administration	350.754	specific languages	T4—014 1
central governments	351.754	rhetoric	808.001 4
local governments	352.935 4	Discoveries in geography	910.9
Disc recordings		Discoveries in natural history	508
sound reproduction	621.389 32	Discoveries in science	509
Discarding		Discovery	
library collections	025.216	archaeological technique	930.102 82
museology	069.51	Discovery (Law)	347.072
Discarnate spirits	133.9	criminal law	345.072
Discharge (Military personnel)	355.114	Discrete-time systems	003.83
Discharged offenders	364.8	Discriminant analysis	519.535
labor economics	331.51	Discriminants	
Discifloral plants	583.2	number theory	512.74
Disciples of Christ	286.6	Discrimination	305
biography	286.609 2	ethics	177.5
church government	262.066	see also Ethical problems	
parishes	254.066	social theology	291.178 34
church law	262.986 6	Christianity	261.834
doctrines	230.66	Discrimination (Psychology)	152.1
catechisms and creeds	238.66	quantitative studies	152.82
guides to Christian life	248.486 6	Discrimination in education	370.193 4
missions	266.66	law	344.079 8
moral theology	241.046 6	Discrimination in employment	331.133
public worship	264.066	labor unions	331.873 2
religious associations	267.186 6	law	344.011 33
religious education	268.866	Discrimination in housing	363.51

Disposal of dead	363.75
see also Undertaking (Mortuary)	
Disposal of government property	
public administration	350.713 045
central governments	351.713 045
local governments	352.163 045
Disposal of public lands	
economics	333.16
Dispute resolution	303.69
international relations	327.17
law	347.09
sociology	303.69
Disruptive discharges	537.52
Disruptive students	371.93
Dissent	303.484
social action	361.23
Dissenters (Protestant churches)	280.4
see also Protestantism	
Dissertation requirements	378.242
Dissertations	
bibliographies	011.75
rhetoric	808.02
Dissociative reactions	
medicine	616.852 3
see also Mental illness	
Dissonance	
musical element	781.239
Distance races	796.424
Distant prospection (Parapsychology)	133.323 9
Distillation	
alcoholic beverages	663.16
desalinization	628.167 2
Distilled liquor	641.25
commercial processing	663.5
cooking with	641.625
home preparation	641.874
Distomatosis	
incidence	614.553
medicine	616.963
see also Communicable diseases (Human)	
Distributed databases	005.758
Distributed-parameter systems	003.78
Distributed processing	004.36
Distribution channels	
marketing management	658.84
Distribution management	658.8
	T1—068 8
Distribution theory (Mathematics)	515.782
Distribution theory of prime numbers	512.73
Distributions (Mathematics)	512.924
algebra	512.924
arithmetic	513.25

Distributive justice	340.115
ethics	172.2
religion	291.562 2
Buddhism	294.356 22
Christianity	241.622
Hinduism	294.548 622
Islam	297.5
Judaism	296.385 622
Distributor brands	
sales promotion	658.827
District Court (Scotland)	345.411 012
District courts	347.02
United States	347.732 2
District heating	697.03
hot water	697.4
steam	697.54
District nursing	
medicine	610.734 3
District of Columbia	975.3
	T2—753
Districting (Legislatures)	328.334 5
law	342.053
Districts	
government	320.83
public administration	352.007 3
Distrito Especial de Bogotá (Colombia)	T2—861 48
Distrito Federal (Brazil)	T2—817 4
Distrito Federal (Mexico)	T2—725 3
Distrito Federal (Venezuela)	T2—877
Distrito Nacional (Dominican Republic)	T2—729 375
Ditches	
agriculture	631.62
road engineering	625.734
Ditsobotla (South Africa : District)	T2—682 94
Diuretics	
pharmacodynamics	615.761
see also Urinary system	
Diurnal variations	
air temperatures	551.525 3
geomagnetism	538.742
Divehi language	491.487
	T6—914 8
Divers	627.720 92
springboard sports	797.240 92
springboard sports group	T7—797 2
underwater sports	797.230 92
underwater sports group	T7—797 2
underwater technologists	627.720 92
occupational group	T7—627
Diversification	
production management	658.503 8
Divertimento form	784.185 2
Divestment	
management	658.16
Divide County (N.D.)	T2—784 71

Doctors (continued)	
role and function	610.695 2
Doctrinal controversies	
Christian church history	273
Doctrinal theology	291.2
Buddhism	294.342
Christianity	230
Hinduism	294.52
Islam	297.2
Judaism	296.3
natural theology	210
Document delivery services	025.6
Documentary evidence	347.064
criminal investigation	363.256 5
law	347.064
Documentary films	
journalism	070.18
Documentation	025
Documents	
cataloging	025.343 4
Dodder	583.76
Doddridge County (W. Va.)	T2—754 56
Dodecanese	T2—499 6
Dodecaphony	781.268
Dodge County (Ga.)	T2—758 532
Dodge County (Minn.)	T2—776 153
Dodge County (Neb.)	T2—782 235
Dodge County (Wis.)	T2—775 82
Dodoma Region (Tanzania)	T2—678 26
Dodos	598.65
Doe, Samuel K. (Samuel Kanyon)	
Liberian history	966.620 3
Dog cabbage	583.913
Dog pounds	363.78
see also Pest control	
Dog racing	798.8
Dog sled racing	798.8
Dogbane	583.72
Dogmatism	
philosophy	148
Dogon (African people)	T5—963 5
Dogon language	496.35
	T6—963 5
Dogs	599.744 42
animal husbandry	636.7
experimental animals	
medicine	619.7
pest control technology	628.969 7
Dogwood	583.687
Dohuk (Iraq : Province)	T2—567 2
Doilies	642.7
arts	746.96
home sewing	646.21
table setting	642.7
Doldrums (Meteorology)	551.518 3
Dolerites	552.3
Dolj (Romania)	T2—498 4

Doll clothing	688.722 1
handicrafts	745.592 21
manufacturing technology	688.722 1
see also Toys	
Doll furniture	688.723
handicrafts	745.592 3
manufacturing technology	688.723
see also Toys	
Dollhouses	688.723
handicrafts	745.592 3
manufacturing technology	688.723
see also Toys	
Dolls	688.722 1
handicrafts	745.592 21
manufacturing technology	688.722 1
see also Toys	
Dolomite	553.516
economic geology	553.516
mineralogy	549.782
petrology	552.58
Dolores County (Colo.)	T2—788 26
Dolphins	599.53
Domaine-du-Roy (Quebec)	T2—714 14
Dombes (France)	T2—444 4
Dombras	787.85
see also Stringed instruments	
Domes	721.46
architecture	721.46
construction	690.146
structural engineering	624.177 5
concrete	624.183 45
Domestic animals	636
agriculture	636
source species	636.082 1
Domestic architecture	728
Domestic arts	640
Domestic cats	636.8
Domestic commerce	381
law	343.088
public administration	350.826
central governments	351.826
cabinet departments	351.082 6
local governments	352.942 6
Domestic Court of Magistrates Court (Great Britain)	347.420 23
Domestic customs	392.3
Domestic economic assistance	
law	343.074
Domestic employees	640.46
Domestic industries	338.634
Domestic investment	332.672
Domestic law	
relation to international law	341.04
Domestic medicine	616.024
Domestic relations (Family)	306.8
law	346.015
Domestic safety	363.13
see also Safety	

Dosage determination	
pharmacology	615.14
Dosimetry	
biophysics	
human	612.014 48
physics	539.77
Dotted swiss embroidery	677.77
Douala (Cameroon)	T2—671 1
Douay Bible	220.520 2
Double basses	787.5
see also Stringed instruments	
Double bassoons	788.59
see also Woodwind instruments	
Double jeopardy	345.04
Double-reed bagpipes	788.49
see also Woodwind instruments	
Double-reed instruments	788.5
see also Woodwind instruments	
Double salts	546.343
chemical engineering	661.4
Double sulfides	
mineralogy	549.35
Double taxation	336.294
international law	341.484 4
law	343.052 6
public finance	336.294
Doubles (Literature)	808.802 7
history and criticism	809.927
specific literatures	T3B—080 27
history and criticism	T3B—092 7
Doubles (Tennis)	796.342 28
Doubling the cube	516.204
Doubs (France : Dept.)	T2—444 6
Doubt	
epistemology	121.5
Dougherty County (Ga.)	T2—758 953
Douglas (South Africa)	T2—687 11
Douglas, Cape	T2—798 3
Douglas County (Colo.)	T2—788 86
Douglas County (Ga.)	T2—758 243
Douglas County (Ill.)	T2—773 68
Douglas County (Kan.)	T2—781 65
Douglas County (Minn.)	T2—776 45
Douglas County (Mo.)	T2—778 832
Douglas County (Neb.)	T2—782 254
Douglas County (Nev.)	T2—793 59
Douglas County (Or.)	T2—795 29
Douglas County (S.D.)	T2—783 383
Douglas County (Wash.)	T2—797 31
Douglas County (Wis.)	T2—775 11
Douglas Lake	T2—768 924
Douro Litoral (Portugal)	T2—469 15
Dove River (England)	T2—425 13
Dover (Del.)	T2—751 4
Dover (England : District)	T2—422 352
Dover, Strait of	551.461 36
	T2—163 36
Doves	598.65

Dowayo (African people)	T5—963 6
Down (Northern Ireland : County)	T2—416 5
Down (Northern Ireland : District)	T2—416 56
Downhill skiing	796.935
Downs (Qld. : District)	T2—943 3
Down's syndrome	
medicine	616.858 842
see also Mental retardation	
Downtown	307.333 16
area planning	711.552 2
community redevelopment	307.342
community sociology	307.333 16
Downy mildews	589.252
Dowry	392.5
Dowsing	133.323
Doxologies	
private prayer	
Christianity	242.721
Doyayo language	496.36
	T6—963 6
DP (Displaced persons)	325.21
see also Refugees	
DPI (Macroeconomics)	339.32
Dracaena	584.43
Draft (Conscription)	355.223 63
law	343.012 2
Draft animals	
care and maintenance	636.088 2
Draft horses	
animal husbandry	636.15
zoology	599.725
Draft registration	355.223 6
Draft resistance	355.224
law	343.012 2
Drafted labor	331.117 32
Drafting (Drawing)	604.2
	T1—022 1
Drafts (Credit)	332.77
exchange medium	332.55
law	346.096
Draftsmen	604.209 2
occupational group	T7—604
Drag	
aeronautics	629.132 34
Dragonfish	597.58
Dragonfly	595.733
Dragons	
folklore	398.245 4
sociology	398.469
literature	808.803 7
history and criticism	809.933 7
specific literatures	T3B—080 37
history and criticism	T3B—093 7
Dragoons	357.1
Drainage	
agriculture	631.62

Dresses (continued)	
home sewing	646.432
see also Clothing	
Dressing	
child training	649.63
Dressing leather	675.24
Dressmakers	646.400 92
commercial	687.112 092
occupational group	T7—687
occupational group	T7—646 4
Dressmaking	646.404
commercial technology	687.112
home sewing	646.404
Drew County (Ark.)	T2—767 825
Dried eggs	641.375 4
cooking	641.675 4
processing	637.54
Dried foods	
cooking	641.614
Dried milk	641.371 43
cooking	641.671 43
processing	637.143
Dried skim milk	641.371 473
cooking	641.671 473
processing	637.147 3
Driers	
home laundry	648.1
manufacturing technology	683.88
Driers (Paints)	667.622
Drift mining	622.2
Driftwood arrangements	745.925
Drill (Military training)	355.54
Drilling	
gas wells	622.338 1
mining	622.23
oil wells	622.338 1
underwater engineering	627.75
Drilling platforms	627.98
petroleum extraction	622.338 19
Drilling ships	
design	623.812 8
engineering	623.828
petroleum extraction	622.338 19
Drilling tools	621.952
Drinking	
customs	394.12
Drinking age	363.41
law	344.054 1
Drinking glasses	
decorative arts	748.83
Drinking places	647.95
architecture	725.72
household management	647.95
sanitation services	363.729 6
see also Waste control	
Drinks	641.2
commercial processing	663
home preparation	641.87

Drip-dry fabrics	677.68
see also Textiles	
Drive shafts	
automotive	629.245
Driver information	
highway services	388.312 4
urban	388.413 124
Drivers' licenses	343.094 6
international law	341.756 86
Drives (Computer devices)	004.56
engineering	621.397 6
Drives (Psychology)	153.8
physiological	152.5
Driveways	625.889
Driving belts	621.852
rubber technology	678.36
Driving family cars	629.283
recreation	796.78
Driving horses (Breeds)	
animal husbandry	636.14
zoology	599.725
Driving horses (Recreation)	798.6
Driving motor vehicles	629.283
recreation	796.7
Driving sports cars	629.283
recreation	796.77
Drogheda (Ireland)	T2—418 256
Drôme (France)	T2—449 8
Dromedaries	599.736
animal husbandry	636.295
Drones (Aircraft)	
control systems	629.132 6
military engineering	623.746 9
Dronten (Netherlands)	T2—492 2
Dropouts (Education)	371.291 3
Drops	530.427
technology	620.43
Droseraceae	583.121
Drosophilidae	595.774
Droughts	
agricultural economics	338.14
agriculture	632.12
meteorology	551.577 3
plant husbandry	632.12
social services	363.349 2
economics	338.18
see also Disasters	
Drug abuse	362.29
medicine	616.86
personal health	613.8
social theology	291.178 322 9
Christianity	261.832 29
social welfare	362.29
see also Substance abuse	
Drug adulteration	363.194
criminology	364.142
law	345.024 2

Dual personalities
  medicine   616.852 36
  see also Mental illness
Duala (African people)   T5—963 96
Duala languages   496.396
         T6—963 96
Dualism
  philosophy   147.4
    Hindu   181.484
Dualism (Concept of God)   211.33
  comparative religion   291.14
Duality (Mathematics)   515.782
Duarte (Dominican Republic)   T2—729 367
Dubai (United Arab
  Emirates : Emirate)   T2—535 7
Dubayy (United Arab
  Emirates : Emirate)   T2—535 7
Dubbo (N.S.W.)   T2—944 5
Dublin (Ireland)   T2—418 35
Dublin (Ireland : County)   T2—418 3
Dubois County (Ind.)   T2—772 37
Dubuque County (Iowa)   T2—777 39
Ducane Range   T2—946 3
Duchesne County (Utah)   T2—792 22
Ducie Island   T2—961 8
Duck meat   641.365 97
  commercial processing   664.93
  cooking   641.665 97
Duck River (Tenn.)   T2—768 434
Ducks   598.41
  animal husbandry   636.597
  sports hunting   799.248 41
Duckweed   584.64
Duct flutes   788.35
  see also Woodwind instruments
Ductility
  materials science   620.112 5
Dude farming   796.56
Dude ranching   796.56
Dudley (England :
  Metropolitan Borough)   T2—424 93
Due process of law   347.05
  civil right   323.422
Dueling   394.8
  customs   394.8
  ethics   179.7
Duets
  chamber music   785.12
  vocal music   783.12
Dufferin (Ont. : County)   T2—713 41
Dufferin and Ava, Frederick
  Temple Blackwood, Marquis
  of
    Indian history   954.035 4
Dugongs   599.55
Duikers   599.735 8
Duisburg (Germany)   T2—435 536
Duke of York Group   T2—958 5

Dukes County (Mass.)   T2—744 94
Dukhobors   289.9
  see also Christian
    denominations
Dulcea (Romania : Judet)   T2—498 3
Dulcians   788.58
  see also Woodwind instruments
Dulcimers   787.74
  see also Stringed instruments
Duluth (Minn.)   T2—776 771
Dumb cane   584.64
Dumbarton (Scotland :
  District)   T2—414 25
Dumfries and Galloway
  (Scotland)   T2—414 7
Dumfriesshire (Scotland)   T2—414 8
Dumortierite
  mineralogy   549.62
Dumping (Trade)
  law   343.087
Dumps (Solid waste)   363.728 5
  technology   628.445 62
  see also Waste control
Dumyati (Egypt)   T2—621
Dún Laoghaire (Ireland)   T2—418 38
Dundee (Scotland)   T2—412 7
Dundee (South Africa :
  District)   T2—684 1
Dundy County (Neb.)   T2—782 86
Dune buggies
  engineering   629.222
Dune ecology   574.526 5
Dune stabilization   631.64
  shore protection   627.58
Dunedin (N.Z.)   T2—931 57
Dunes   551.375
Dunfermline (Scotland :
  District)   T2—412 98
Dung beetle   595.764 9
Dung flies   595.774
Dungannon (Northern
  Ireland : District)   T2—416 45
Dungog (N.S.W.)   T2—944 2
Dunkers   286.5
  see also Baptists
Dunklin County (Mo.)   T2—778 993
Dunn County (N.D.)   T2—784 82
Dunn County (Wis.)   T2—775 43
Duodecimal system   513.56
Duodenal ulcers
  medicine   616.343 3
  see also Digestive system
Duodenitis
  medicine   616.344
  see also Digestive system
Duodenum
  human anatomy   611.341
  human physiology   612.33

Duodenum (continued)
surgery 617.554 1
see also Digestive system
Duplex houses
architecture 728.312
Duplex-process steel 669.142 3
Duplicating machines
library services 025.12
manufacturing technology 681.6
office use 652.4
Duplin County (N.C.) T2—756 382
Dupuit, Jules-Juvénal
economic school 330.154 3
Durability engineering 620.004 54
Durable press fabrics 677.68
Durango (Mexico : State) T2—721 5
Durazno (Uruguay : Dept.) T2—895 24
Durban (South Africa) T2—684 55
Durban-Pinetown industrial
area T2—684 55
Duress 345.04
Durham (England) T2—428 6
Durham (England : City) T2—428 65
Durham (Ont. : Regional
municipality) T2—713 56
Durham County (N.C.) T2—756 563
Durham mission (Canadian
history) 971.039
Duroc-Jersey swine
animal husbandry 636.483
zoology 599.734
Duroc swine
animal husbandry 636.483
zoology 599.734
Durra 584.92
food crop 633.174 7
forage crop 633.257 47
Durvilleales 589.45
Düsseldorf (Germany) T2—435 534
Düsseldorf (Germany :
Regierungsbezirk) T2—435 53
Dust
meteorology 551.511 3
technology 620.43
Dust control
buildings 697.932 4
mining 622.83
Dust storms 551.559
social services 363.349 2
see also Disasters
Dusting
agricultural pest control 632.94
housecleaning 648.5
Dusting-on processes
photographic printing 773.2
Dusty miller (Plant) 583.152
Dutch T5—393 1
Dutch Antilles T2—729 86

Dutch East India Company
(Indonesian history) 959.802 1
Dutch East Indies 959.802 2
T2—598
Dutch Guiana T2—883
Dutch language 439.31
T6—393 1
Dutch literature 839.31
Dutch Reformed Church in North
America 285.732
see also Reformed Church
(American Reformed)
Dutch Republic 949.204
T2—492
Dutch West Indies T2—729 86
Dutchess County (N.Y.) T2—747 33
Dutchman's breeches (Plants) 583.122
Duties (Tariff) 382.7
see also Customs (Tariff)
Duties of chief executives 350.003 2
central governments 351.003 2
local governments 352.008
Duties of citizens 323.65
Dutra, Eurico Gaspar
Brazilian history 981.061
Duty
religion 291.5
Buddhism 294.35
Christianity 241
Hinduism 294.548
Islam 297.5
Judaism 296.385
Duval County (Fla.) T2—759 12
Duval County (Tex.) T2—764 463
Duvalier, François
Haitian history 972.940 72
Duvalier, Jean-Claude
Haitian history 972.940 72
Dvaita (Philosophy) 181.484 1
Dvaitadvaita (Philosophy) 181.484 3
Dvoynices 788.37
see also Woodwind instruments
Dwarf pea 641.356 57
see also Chick-peas
Dwarfism (Pituitary)
medicine 616.47
see also Endocrine system
Dwarfs
physical anthropology 573.8
Dwellings 643.1
architecture 728
customs 392.36
health 613.5
home economics 643.1
literature 808.803 55
history and criticism 809.933 55
specific literatures T3B—080 355
history and criticism T3B—093 55

Dwyfor (Wales : District)	T2—429 23	Dyslexia (continued)	
Dye lasers	621.366 4	pediatrics	618.928 553
Dye-producing insects		see also Communicative	
culture	638.3	disorders	
Dye-producing plants		Dysmenorrhea	
agriculture	633.86	gynecology	618.172
Dyeing	667.3	see also Female genital system	
home economics	648.1	Dyspepsia	
textile arts	746.6	medicine	616.332
Dyeing leather	675.25	see also Digestive system	
Dyeing yarns		Dysphasia	
arts	746.13	medicine	616.855 2
Dyer County (Tenn.)	T2—768 15	see also Communicative	
Dyes	547.86	disorders	
chemistry	547.86	Dyspnea	
technology	667.2	medicine	616.2
Dyfed (Wales)	T2—429 6	see also Respiratory system	
Dying	306.9	Dyspraxia	
music	781.588	medicine	616.855 2
psychology	155.937	see also Communicative	
social aspects	306.9	disorders	
Dying patients	362.175	Dysprosium	
social theology	291.178 321 75	chemistry	546.417
Christianity	261.832 175	see also Rare earths	
social welfare	362.175	Dystocia	
see also Terminal care		obstetrics	618.5
Dynamic programming	519.703	Dyula language	496.34
Dynamic psychology	150.193		T6—963 4
Dynamic systems	003.85	Dzanani (South Africa :	
Dynamical systems		District)	T2—682 91
(Mathematics)	515.352		
Dynamics	531.11		
air	533.62	**E**	
engineering	620.107 4		
engineering	620.104	E.C.G. (Medicine)	616.120 754 7
fluids	532.05	see also Cardiovascular system	
engineering	620.106 4	E.D.P. (Computing)	004
gases	533.2	E.E.C. (Economic organization)	341.242 2
engineering	620.107 4	see also European Economic	
liquids	532.5	Community	
engineering	620.106 4	E.F.T.A. (Economic	
meteorology	551.515 3	organization)	341.242
particles	531.163	international commerce	382.914 3
engineering	620.43	international economics	337.143
physics	531.11	international law	341.242
solids	531.3	E-flat horns	788.974
engineering	620.105 4	see also Brass instruments	
Dynamite	662.27	E.K.G. (Medicine)	616.120 754 7
military engineering	623.452 7	see also Cardiovascular system	
Dynamos	621.313 2	E layers (Ionosphere)	538.767 3
Dysentery		E.N.D.O.R. (Physics)	538.362
incidence	614.516	E.P.R. (Physics)	538.364
medicine	616.935	E region (Ionosphere)	538.767 3
see also Communicable		E.S.P. (Extrasensory perception)	133.8
diseases (Human)		Eagle County (Colo.)	T2—788 44
Dyslexia		Eagles	598.916
education	371.914 4	Ealing (London, England)	T2—421 84
medicine	616.855 3	Ear training	781.424
		Eared seals	599.746

East Friesian cattle
  animal husbandry   636.234
  zoology   599.735 8
East Friesland (Germany)   T2—435 917
East Frisian Islands
  (Germany)   T2—435 917
East Germanic languages   439.9
                                         T6—399
East Germanic literatures   839.9
East Germany (Democratic
  Republic)   943.108 7
                                         T2—431
East Hampshire (England)   T2—422 74
East Hertfordshire (England :
  District)   T2—425 83
East India Company (Indian
  history)   954.031
East Indo-European languages   491
                                         T6—91
East Iranian languages
  (Ancient)   T6—915 2
East Iranian literatures (Ancient)   891.52
East Kilbride (Scotland :
  District)   T2—414 54
East Kootenay (B.C.)   T2—711 65
East Lansing (Mich.)   T2—774 27
East Lindsey (England :
  District)   T2—425 32
East London (South Africa :
  District)   T2—687 55
East Lothian (Scotland)   T2—413 6
East Makian language   499.5
                                         T6—995
East New Britain Province
  (Papua New Guinea)   T2—958 5
East Northamptonshire
  (England : District)   T2—425 54
East Orange (N.J.)   T2—749 33
East Pakistan (Pakistan)   954.920 4
                                         T2—549 2
East Prussia (Germany)   T2—438 3
East Punjab (India)   T2—545 5
East Rand (South Africa)   T2—682 2
East Redonda Island (B.C.)   T2—711 1
East Riding of Yorkshire
  (England)   T2—428 3
East Scandinavian languages   439.5
                                         T6—395
East Scandinavian literatures   839.5
East Scandinavians   T5—397–398
East Semites   T5—921
East Semitic languages   492.1
                                         T6—921
East Semitic literatures   892.1
East Sepik Province (Papua
  New Guinea)   T2—957 5
East Siberian Sea   551.468 5
                                         T2—163 25

East Slavic languages   491.7
                                         T6—917
East Slavic literatures   891.7
East Slavs   T5—917
East Staffordshire (England)   T2—424 65
East Suffolk (England)   T2—426 46
East Sussex (England)   T2—422 5
East Texas   T2—764 14
East Thurlow Island (B.C.)   T2—711 1
East York (Ont.)   T2—713 541
East Yorkshire (England :
  Borough)   T2—428 39
Eastbourne (England)   T2—422 58
Easter   263.93
  customs   394.268 283
  devotional literature   242.36
  sermons   252.63
Easter eggs   394.268 283
  customs   394.268 283
  handicrafts   745.594 4
Easter Island   T2—961 8
Easter music   781.727
Easter Rebellion, 1916   941.508 21
Eastern Aramaic languages   492.3
                                         T6—923
Eastern Aramaic literatures   892.3
Eastern Austronesian languages   499.4
                                         T6—994
Eastern Canada   T2—713
Eastern churches   281.5
  church government   262.015
    parishes   254.015
  church law   262.981 5
  doctrines   230.15
    catechisms and creeds   238.19
  general councils   262.515
  guides to Christian life   248.481 5
  liturgy   264.015
  missions   266.15
  moral theology   241.041 5
  public worship   264.015
  religious associations   267.181 5
  religious education   268.815
  seminaries   207.111 5
  theology   230.15
Eastern Desert (Egypt)   T2—623
Eastern Empire   949.501
Eastern Equatoria Province
  (Sudan)   T2—629 5
Eastern Europe   947
                                         T2—47
Eastern front
  World War I   940.414 7
Eastern Hemisphere   T2—181 1
Eastern Highlands Province
  (Papua New Guinea)   T2—956 9
Eastern Hindi languages   491.49
                                         T6—914 9

Echoes	
physics	534.204
Echography	
diagnosis	616.075 43
Echoi	781.264
Echols County (Ga.)	T2—758 814
Echuca (Vic.)	T2—945 4
Eckankar	299.93
Eclairs	641.865 9
commercial processing	664.752 5
home preparation	641.865 9
Eclampsia	
puerperal diseases	
obstetrics	618.75
Eclectic medicine	
therapeutic system	615.53
Eclectic philosophy	
ancient	186.3
Eclecticism	
architecture	724.5
philosophy	148
Eclipses	523.99
moon	523.38
sun	523.78
Eclipsing binaries (Stars)	523.844 4
Ecological anthropology	304.2
Ecological niches	574.524 7
Ecological succession	574.5
Ecology	574.5
animals	591.5
elementary education	372.357
ethics	179.1
religion	291.569 1
Buddhism	294.356 91
Christianity	241.691
Hinduism	294.548 691
Judaism	296.385 691
microorganisms	576.15
physical anthropology	573
plants	581.5
social theology	291.178 362
Christianity	261.836 2
sociology	304.2
Econometrics	330.015 195
management decision making	658.403 3
Economic advisors	
public administration	350.820 422
central governments	351.820 422
local governments	352.942
Economic aggregates	
macroeconomics	339.3
Economic anthropology	306.3
Economic assistance	
international law	341.759
international politics	327.111
law	343.074
public administration	350.72
central governments	351.72

Economic assistance	
public administration (continued)	
local governments	352.1
Economic biology	574.6
Economic botany	581.6
Economic causes of war	355.027 3
Economic classes	305.5
	T1—086 2
	T7—062
civil rights	323.322
customs	390.1
dress	391.01
relations with government	323.322
Economic concentration	338.8
Economic conditions	330.9
Economic cooperation	
international economics	337.1
Economic development	338.9
international banking	332.153
production economics	338.9
public administration	350.82
central governments	351.82
cabinet departments	351.082
local governments	352.942
Economic fluctuations	338.54
Economic geography	330.9
Economic geology	553
Economic growth	338.9
macroeconomic policy	339.5
production economics	338.9
Economic history	330.9
Economic integration	
international economics	337.1
Economic microbiology	576.16
Economic planning	338.9
Economic policy	338.9
Economic power (Legislative	
bodies)	328.341 3
Economic rent	
land economics	333.012
Economic rights	323.46
Economic services for workers	331.255
see also Conditions of	
employment	
Economic situation	330.9
Economic sociology	306.3
Economic stabilization	
law	343.034
macroeconomic policy	339.5
Economic strikes	331.892 2
see also Strikes (Work	
stoppages)	
Economic systems	330.12
Economic zoology	591.6
Economics	330
information systems	025.063 3
international politics	327.111

Education at home	
child care	649.68
Education of employees	331.259 2
economics	331.259 2
personnel management	658.312 4
	T1—068 3
public administration	350.15
central governments	351.15
local governments	352.005 15
Educational aid to foreign	
countries	370.196 5
Educational anthropology	370.19
Educational areas	
area planning	711.57
Educational buildings	371.62
architecture	727
construction	690.7
household management	647.99
interior decoration	747.87
Educational equalization	370.193 42
Educational exchanges	370.196
international law	341.767 3
law	344.08
Educational films	
instructional use	371.335 23
journalism	070.18
Educational games	371.397
classroom use	371.307 8
Educational guidance	371.422
Educational institutions	371
accounting	657.832 7
Educational law	344.07
Educational leave	331.257 63
labor economics	331.257 63
Educational policy	379.2
Educational psychology	370.15
Educational requirements	
personnel management	
public administration	350.132 3
central governments	351.132 3
local governments	352.005 132 3
Educational sociology	370.19
Educational technology	371.307 8
Educational tests	371.26
Educational therapy	
medicine	615.851 6
Educational toys	
classroom use	371.307 8
manufacturing technology	688.725
see also Toys	
Educators	370.92
law	344.078
occupational group	T7—37
Edward, Lake	T2—675 17
Edward I, King of England	
English history	942.035
Edward II, King of England	
English history	942.036
Edward III, King of England	
English history	942.037
Edward IV, King of England	
English history	942.044
Edward River (N.S.W.)	T2—944 8
Edward the Confessor, King of	
England	
English history	942.019
Edward the Elder, King of	
England	
English history	942.016 5
Edward the Martyr, King of	
England	
English history	942.017 3
Edward V, King of England	
English history	942.045
Edward VI, King of England	
English history	942.053
Edward VII, King of Great	
Britain	
British history	941.082 3
English history	942.082 3
Scottish history	941.108 23
Edward VIII, King of Great	
Britain	
British history	941.084
English history	942.084
Scottish history	941.108 4
Edwards County (Ill.)	T2—773 791
Edwards County (Kan.)	T2—781 782
Edwards County (Tex.)	T2—764 882
Edwards Plateau (Tex.)	T2—764 87
Edwy, King of England	
English history	942.017 2
EEC (Economic organization)	341.242 2
see also European Economic	
Community	
Eelgrass	584.743
Eels	597.51
commercial fishing	639.275 1
culture	639.375 1
Eerstehoek (South Africa :	
District)	T2—682 96
Effect	
philosophy	122
Efficiency	
agricultural economics	338.16
communication industry	384.041
economics	338.06
mineral industries	338.26
personnel management	658.314
public administration	350.147
central governments	351.147
local governments	352.005 147
production management	658.515
secondary industries	338.45
transportation services	388.049
Effigial slabs	736.5

Elastomers (continued)
  manufacturing technology — 678
    equipment manufacture — 681.766 8
    materials science — 620.194
    structural engineering — 624.189 4
Elastoplastics — 678.73
Elateroidea — 595.765
Elatinaceae — 583.152
Elazig Ili (Turkey) — T2—566 7
Elba (Italy) — T2—455 6
Elbert County (Colo.) — T2—788 87
Elbert County (Ga.) — T2—758 163
Elblag (Poland : Voivodeship) — T2—438 2
Elbows — 612.97
  human physiology — 612.97
  regional medicine — 617.574
  surgery — 617.574
  see also Upper extremities
    (Human)
Elcho Island — T2—942 95
Elder (Plant) — 583.52
Elderberries — 583.52
  horticulture — 634.74
Elderly persons — 305.26
   — T1—084 6
  see also Old persons
Eldon Range — T2—946 6
Eleatic philosophy — 182.3
Election (Christian doctrines) — 234
Election campaign finance — 324.78
Election campaigns — 324.9
  nominations — 324.5
  techniques — 324.7
Election districts — 328.334 5
Election fraud — 324.66
  law — 345.023 24
Election law — 342.07
Election officials — 324.65
Election procedures — 324.6
  law — 342.075
Election returns — 324.9
Election systems — 324.6
Electioneering — 324.7
  law — 342.078
Elections — 324
  labor unions — 331.874
Elective courses
  curriculums — 375.004
Electoral colleges — 324.63
Electoral fraud — 364.132 4
Electoral power (Legislative
  bodies) — 328.345 4
Electoral systems — 324.63
Electrets — 537.24
Electric arcs — 537.52
Electric automobiles
  engineering — 629.229 3
Electric charge — 537.21

Electric clocks
  technology — 681.116
Electric control — 629.804 3
Electric cooking — 641.586
Electric currents
  measurement — 621.374 4
  physics — 537.6
Electric eel — 597.52
Electric energy — 333.793 2
  see also Electric power
Electric eyes — 621.381 542
Electric furnace practice — 669.142 4
Electric generators — 621.313
Electric heating — 621.402 8
  buildings — 697.045
Electric lighting — 621.32
  mining — 622.474
  ships — 623.852
Electric locomotives — 385.363
  engineering — 625.263
  transportation services — 385.363
  see also Rolling stock
Electric meters — 621.373
  watt-hour usage — 621.374 5
Electric motors — 621.46
  ships — 623.872 6
Electric potential — 537.21
  measurement — 621.374 3
Electric power — 333.793 2
  area planning — 711.8
  economics — 333.793 2
  law — 343.092 9
  measurement — 621.374 5
  mining — 622.48
  public administration — 350.872 2
    central governments — 351.872 2
    local governments — 352.912 2
Electric power generation — 621.312 1
  nuclear steam generation — 621.483
Electric power measurement — 621.374 6
Electric power plants
  automotive — 629.250 2
Electric power systems
  spacecraft — 629.474 45
  unmanned spacecraft — 629.464 45
Electric propulsion — 621.46
  spacecraft — 629.475 5
Electric railroads
  electrification — 621.33
Electric shavers
  manufacturing technology — 688.5
Electric shock therapy
  psychiatry — 616.891 22
  see also Mental illness
Electric signs
  advertising — 659.136
Electric slow cooking — 641.588 4

Electromagnetic induction	621.34
Electromagnetic interaction	
(Nuclear particles)	539.754 6
Electromagnetic phenomena	
stars	523.82
Electromagnetic radiations	539.2
Electromagnetic spectrum	539.2
Electromagnetic theory	530.141
Electromagnetic theory of light	535.14
Electromagnetic wave theory of	
matter	530.141
Electromagnetic waves	539.2
Electromagnetism	537
biophysics	574.191 7
engineering	621.3
Electromagnets	621.34
generator parts	621.316
Electrometallurgy	669.028 4
Electrometers	621.374 3
Electromyography	616.740 754 7
see also Musculoskeletal system	
Electron acceleration	539.737 12
Electron arrangement	
crystallography	548.81
solid state physics	530.411
Electron ballistics	537.532
Electron magnetic resonance	538.364
Electron metallography	669.950 282
Electron microscopes	502.825
manufacturing technology	681.413
Electron microscopy	502.825
biology	578.45
Electron-nuclear double	
resonance	538.362
Electron optics	
physics	537.56
Electron paramagnetic resonance	538.364
Electron-ray tubes	621.381 542
Electron spin resonance	538.364
Electronic aids	
marine navigation	623.893
Electronic bands	784.6
Electronic bugging devices	621.389 28
Electronic bulletin boards	004.693
communication services	384.33
see also Computer	
communications	
Electronic circuits	621.381 5
Electronic communications	
engineering	621.382
Electronic components	621.381 5
Electronic computers	004
see also Computers	
Electronic control	629.89
Electronic data processing	004
	T1—028 5
Electronic digital computers	004
see also Computers	
Electronic eavesdropping devices	621.389 28
Electronic engineering	621.381
Electronic engineers	621.381 092
occupational group	T7—621 3
Electronic equipment	
use in chemistry	542.8
Electronic flash photography	778.72
Electronic funds transfer	
law	346.082 1
Electronic games	794.8
Electronic interference	621.382 24
Electronic mail	004.692
communication services	384.34
office services	651.79
see also Computer	
communications	
Electronic media	
sociology	302.234
Electronic music	786.74
Electronic musical instruments	786.7
see also Electrophones	
Electronic noise	621.382 24
Electronic organs	786.59
see also Keyboard instruments	
Electronic properties	
materials science	620.112 97
Electronic spreadsheets	005.3
Electronic surveillance	
criminal investigation	363.252
engineering	621.389 28
law	345.052
Electronic systems	
aircraft	629.135 5
automotive	629.254 9
internal-combustion engines	621.437
ships	623.850 4
Electronic therapy	
medicine	615.845
Electronic toys	790.133
manufacturing technology	688.728
recreation	790.133
see also Toys	
Electronic tubes	621.381 51
Electronics	
military engineering	623.043
physics	537.5
technology	621.381
Electrons	539.721 12
Electrooptical devices	
military communication	
engineering	623.731 4
Electrophones	786.7
bands and orchestras	784
chamber ensembles	785
mixed	785.2–.5
single type	785.67
construction	786.719 23
by hand	786.719 23

Elkhorn River	T2—782 5
Elko County (Nev.)	T2—793 16
Elks (Animals)	599.735 7
Elks (Fraternal order)	366.5
members	366.509 2
social group	T7—366 5
Ellenborough, Edward Law, Earl of	
Indian history	954.031 5
Ellesmere Port and Neston (England)	T2—427 17
Ellice Islands	T2—968 2
Elliot (South Africa : District)	T2—687 6
Elliotdale (South Africa : District)	T2—687 91
Elliott County (Ky.)	T2—769 255
Ellipses	516.15
Elliptic equations	515.353
Elliptic functions	515.983
Elliptic operators	515.724 2
Ellis County (Kan.)	T2—781 19
Ellis County (Okla.)	T2—766 155
Ellis County (Tex.)	T2—764 281 5
Ellisras (South Africa : District)	T2—682 5
Ellsworth County (Kan.)	T2—781 535
Ellsworth Land (Antarctic regions)	T2—989
Elm	583.962
forestry	634.972 8
lumber	674.142
ornamental arboriculture	635.977 396 2
Elmbridge (England)	T2—422 145
Elmira (N.Y.)	T2—747 78
Elmore County (Ala.)	T2—761 52
Elmore County (Idaho)	T2—796 29
Elocution	808.5
Elopiformes	597.51
Elopomorpha	597.51
paleozoology	567.5
Elqui (Chile : Province)	T2—832 32
Ely, Isle of (England)	T2—426 53
Emaciation	
medicine	616.396
see also Digestive system	
Emae language	499.4
	T6—994
Emancipation of slaves	326
Emancipation Proclamation, 1863	973.714
Emanuel County (Ga.)	T2—758 684
Embalming	
biological specimens	579.2
customs	393.3
Embankments	
road engineering	625.733
structural engineering	624.162

Embargoes	
international commerce	382.53
see also Import trade	
international law	341.582
Embarrassment	152.4
Embassies	327.2
architecture	725.17
public administration	351.892
Embellishments	
musical element	781.247
Embezzlement	364.162
law	345.026 2
Embioptera	595.737
paleozoology	565.73
Embolisms	
arteries	
medicine	616.135
veins	
medicine	616.145
see also Cardiovascular system	
Embossing leather	675.25
Embouchure	784.193 4
Embrithopoda	569.6
Embroidered rugs	
arts	746.74
see also Rugs	
Embroidery	
arts	746.44
Embryo	
human physiology	612.646
Embryo transplant	
ethics	176
see also Reproduction—ethics	
gynecology	618.178 059
see also Female genital system	
Embryological anatomy	574.332
Embryological physiology	574.333
Embryology	574.33
animals	591.33
human physiology	612.64
plants	581.33
Embryotomy	
obstetrical surgery	618.83
Embumbulu (South Africa : District)	T2—684 91
Emden (Lower Saxony, Germany)	T2—435 917
Emerald (Qld.)	T2—943 5
Emeralds	553.86
economic geology	553.86
jewelry	739.27
mining	622.386
Emergency care nursing	
medicine	610.736 1
Emergency labor	331.117 32
Emergency legislation	343.01

Employee selection
personnel management   658.311 2
    T1—068 3
    libraries   023.9
    public administration   350.132
      central governments   351.132
      local governments   352.005 132
Employee separation
personnel management   658.313
    public administration   350.18
      central governments   351.18
      local governments   352.005 18
Employees   331.11
    bonding
      personnel management   658.314
      public administration   350.132 44
        central governments   351.132 44
        local governments   352.005 132 44
    economics   331.11
    household   640.46
    journalism for   070.486
    malfeasance
      prevention
        personnel management   658.314
Employer-employee relationships
personnel management   658.315
    libraries   023.9
    public administration   350.17
      central governments   351.17
      local governments   352.005 17
Employers' liability
law   346.031
Employers' liability insurance   368.56
see also Insurance
Employment   331.125
civil rights issues   323.46
Employment agencies   331.128
see also Employment services
Employment conditions   331.2
see also Conditions of
    employment
Employment law   344.01
Employment rights   323.46
Employment security   331.259 6
law   344.012 596
public administration   351.834
Employment services   331.128
economics   331.128
physically ill
    social services   362.178 6
public administration   350.833
    central governments   351.833
    local governments   352.943 3
social services   362.042 5
    labor law   344.015 9
    mentally retarded   362.384
    old persons   362.64
    physically handicapped   362.404 84
    welfare law   344.032 042 5

Employment subsidies   331.120 42
Emporia (Va.)   T2—755 573
Empumalanga (South Africa :
    District)   T2—684 91
Emulsins   574.192 54
Emulsions   541.345 14
    chemical engineering   660.294 514
    colloid chemistry   541.345 14
    see also Enzymes
Emulsions (Pharmaceuticals)
    practical pharmacy   615.45
Emus   598.53
Emzumbe (South Africa :
    District)   T2—684 91
Ena language   496.394
    T6—963 94
Enactment of budgets   350.722 3
    public administration   350.722 3
      central governments   351.722 3
      local governments   352.123
Enactment of laws   328.37
Enameling glass
arts   748.6
Enamels   666.2
    architectural decoration   729.6
    ceramic arts   738.4
    materials science   620.146
    technology   666.2
Enargite
    mineralogy   549.35
Encampment
    military operations   355.412
    military training   355.544
Encaustic painting   751.46
Encephalitis
    medicine   616.832
    see also Nervous system
Enclosure
    land economics   333.2
Encoding
    computer science   005.72
Encounter groups
    social psychology   302.14
    social work   361.323
Encryption   652.8
    computer science   005.82
Encyclicals   262.91
Encyclopedia yearbooks   030
Encyclopedias   030
    T1—03
Encyclopedists
    biography   030.92
    Christian polemics   239.6
    occupational group   T7—093
End-blown flutes   788.35
    see also Woodwind instruments
End games
    chess   794.124

Energy conservation (continued)
  public administration — 350.823 2
    central governments — 351.823 2
    local governments — 352.942 32
  see also Energy
Energy development — 333.791 5
  law — 346.046 791 5
  see also Energy
Energy engineering — 621.042
  buildings — 696
Energy law — 346.046 791 6
Energy levels (Nuclear physics) — 539.725
Energy management — 658.2
  T1—068 2
Energy metabolism
  human physiology — 612.39
  see also Digestive system
Energy phenomena
  solid state physics — 530.416
Energy policy — 333.79
  law — 346.046 79
  see also Energy
Energy production — 333.79
  economics — 333.79
Energy resources — 333.79
  economic geology — 553.2
  extraction — 622.33
    economics — 338.2
  law — 346.046 791 1
  see also Energy
Energy supply — 333.791 1
  see also Energy
Enets language — 494.4
  T6—944
Enewetak Atoll (Marshall Islands) — T2—968 3
Enfield (London, England) — T2—421 89
Enga Province (Papua New Guinea) — T2—956 3
Engaged persons — 306.734
  T1—085 23
  T1—086 523
  social group — 305.906 523
  social relationships — 306.734
Engagement
  customs — 392.4
  etiquette — 395.22
Engcobo (South Africa : District) — T2—687 91
Engineering — 620
  accounting — 657.834
Engineering analysis
  structures — 624.171
Engineering and religion — 291.175
  Christianity — 261.56
  natural religion — 215.9
Engineering design — 620.004 2
Engineering drawing — 604.2

Engineering geology — 624.151
  railroads — 625.122
  roads — 625.732
Engineering graphics — 604.2
Engineering installations (Armed forces) — 355.74
Engineering materials — 620.11
Engineering mechanics — 620.1
Engineering optics — 621.36
Engineering services (Armed forces) — 358.22
  air force — 358.47
  navy — 359.982
Engineering systems
  ships — 623.85
Engineers — 620.009 2
  occupational group — T7—62
Engines — 621.4
  air-cushion vehicles — 629.314
  aircraft — 629.134 35
  automotive — 629.25
  military aircraft — 623.746 049
  ships — 623.87
  spacecraft — 629.475
England — 942
  T2—42
  ancient — 936.2
  T2—362
England, Northern — T2—427
English (People) — T5—21
English Channel — 551.461 36
  T2—163 36
English creole languages — 427.9
  T6—21
English horns — 788.53
  see also Woodwind instruments
English ivy — 583.687
English language — 420
  T6—21
  rhetoric — 808.042
English-language shorthand systems — 653.42
English literature — 820
English longhorn cattle
  animal husbandry — 636.226
  zoology — 599.735 8
English peas — 641.356 56
  botany — 583.322
  commercial processing — 664.805 656
  cooking — 641.656 56
  garden crop — 635.656
English revised version Bible — 220.520 4
English sparrows — 598.873
English system (Measurement) — 530.813
  physics — 530.813
  social aspects — 389.15

Entrepreneurship	338.04
income distribution	339.21
management	658.421
production economics	338.04
Entropy	536.73
Enugu (Nigeria)	T2—669 48
Enumeration (Combinatorial	
analysis)	511.62
Enumerative geometry	516.35
Enuresis	
medicine	616.849
pediatrics	618.928 49
see also Nervous system	
Environment	333.7
architectural consideration	720.47
economics	333.7
ethics	179.1
religion	291.569 1
Buddhism	294.356 91
Christianity	241.691
Hinduism	294.548 691
Judaism	296.385 691
Environment versus heredity	
psychology	155.234
Environmental abuse	363.7
social effects	304.28
social problem	363.7
social theology	291.178 362 8
Christianity	261.836 28
Environmental control	
spacecraft	629.477
unmanned spacecraft	629.467
Environmental design	
arts	711
crime prevention	364.49
ergonomics	620.82
Environmental diseases	
(Biology)	574.24
agriculture	632.1
animal husbandry	636.089 698
animals	591.24
plant husbandry	632.1
plants	581.24
veterinary medicine	636.089 698
Environmental diseases (Human)	362.196 98
geriatrics	618.976 98
incidence	614.59
medicine	616.98
pediatrics	618.929 8
social services	362.196 98
Environmental engineering	628
buildings	696
sanitary engineering	628
work environment	620.8
Environmental engineers	628.092
occupational group	T7—628
Environmental factors	
physical ethnology	572.3

Environmental factors (continued)	
plant genetics	581.152
Environmental health	
engineering	628
Environmental injuries	
agriculture	632.1
plant husbandry	632.1
Environmental law	344.046
Environmental medicine	616.98
see also Environmental diseases	
(Human)	
Environmental pollution	363.73
see also Pollution	
Environmental protection	363.7
engineering	628
executive management	658.408
international law	341.762
law	344.046
public administration	351.823 21
social services	363.7
Environmental psychology	155.9
Environmental sanitation	363.72
see also Waste control	
Environmental studies	
curriculums	375.008 3
elementary education	372.357
Environmental toxicology	615.902
Environmentalist parties	324.218
international organizations	324.18
Environments (Art style)	709.040 74
Envoys	327.209 2
occupational group	T7—352 2
Envy	152.4
Enzyme technology	660.634
Enzymes	574.192 5
biochemistry	574.192 5
animals	591.192 5
human	612.015 1
plants	581.192 5
chemistry	547.758
pharmacology	615.35
Eoacanthocephala	595.13
Eocene epoch	551.784
geology	551.784
paleontology	560.178
Eolithic Age	930.11
Eosuchia	567.94
Epacridaceae	583.62
Epeirogeny	551.8
Ephedra	585.1
Ephedrales	585.1
Ephedrine abuse	362.299
medicine	616.864
personal health	613.84
social welfare	362.299
see also Substance abuse	
Ephemerides	528
astrology	133.55

Equatoria (Sudan : Region)	T2—629 5
Equatorial Guinea	967.18
	T2—671 8
Equatorial Guineans	T5—967 18
Equatorial Islands	T2—964
Equatorial languages	498.3
	T6—983
Equatorial telescopes	
astronomy	522.4
Equestrian performers	791.320 92
occupational group	T7—791 3
Equestrian sculpture	731.81
Equestrian sports	798
equipment technology	688.78
Equestrian sportsmen	798.092
sports group	T7—798
Equidae	599.725
animal husbandry	636.1
Equilibrium	
astronomy	521
chemical engineering	660.299 2
chemistry	541.392
macroeconomic policy	339.5
Equinia	
incidence	614.564
medicine	616.954
see also Communicable	
diseases (Human)	
Equipment	T1—028
armed forces	355.8
educational use	T1—078
local Christian parishes	254.7
plant management	658.27
Equipment management	658.27
	T1—068 2
public administration	350.713 4
central governments	351.713 4
local governments	352.163 4
Equipment procurement	658.72
public administration	350.712 4
central governments	351.712 4
local governments	352.162 4
Equipment research	
production management	658.577
Equipment sheds	
agricultural use	631.25
Equisetales	587.2
paleobotany	561.72
Equitable remedies	347.077
Equity	346.004
Equivalent projections	
maps	526.85
Érable (Quebec)	T2—714 575
Eragrosteae	584.93
Erath County (Tex.)	T2—764 551
Erbil (Iraq : Province)	T2—567 2

Erbium	
chemistry	546.418
see also Rare earths	
Eremitical religious orders	255.02
church history	271.02
women's	255.902
church history	271.902
Eremosynaceae	583.38
Eretrian philosophy	183.7
Erewash (England)	T2—425 18
Erfenis Dam	T2—685 3
Erfurt (Germany : Bezirk)	T2—432 24
Ergodic theory	515.42
Ergonomics	620.82
computers	004.019
engineering	621.398 4
Ergosterol	581.192 431
biochemistry	581.192 431
chemistry	547.731
Ergot	589.23
Ericales	583.62
Erie, Lake	T2—771 2
Ohio	T2—771 2
Ontario	T2—713 3
Erie County (N.Y.)	T2—747 96
Erie County (Ohio)	T2—771 22
Erie County (Pa.)	T2—748 99
Eriocaulales	584.81
Eritrea (Ethiopia)	T2—635
Erlangen (Germany)	T2—433 22
Ermelo (South Africa :	
District)	T2—682 7
Erogeneity	155.31
Erosion	551.302
agriculture	631.45
by glaciers	551.313
by water	551.352
by wind	551.372
engineering	627.5
geology	551.302
Erosions	
uterus and cervix	
gynecology	618.143
see also Female genital	
system	
Erotic art	704.942 8
Erotic literature	808.803 538
history and criticism	809.933 538
specific literatures	T3B—080 353 8
history and criticism	T3B—093 538
Erotic painting	757.8
Errachidia (Morocco :	
Province)	T2—645
Errantia	595.147
Error analysis (Mathematics)	511.43
Error-correcting codes	005.72
Error correctors	
automation engineering	629.831 5

Espionage (continued)
law	345.023 1
law of war	341.63
social theology	291.178 7
Christianity	261.87
Espírito Santo (Brazil : State)	T2—815 2
Esquimalt (B.C.)	T2—711 28

Essaouira (Morocco :
Province)	T2—646

Essayists (Literature)
Essayists (Literature)	809.4
collected biography	809.4
specific literatures	T3B—400 9
individual biography	T3A—4
occupational group	T7—84
Essays	080

Essays (Literature)
Essays (Literature)	808.84
criticism	809.4
theory	801.954
history	809.4
rhetoric	808.4
specific literatures	T3B—4
individual authors	T3A—4
Essen (Germany)	T2—435 538
Essence (Philosophy)	111.1

Essences
commercial processing	664.52
Essenes	296.81

Essential hypertension
medicine	616.132
see also Cardiovascular system	

Essential oils
Essential oils	581.192
biochemistry	581.192
chemical engineering	661.806
chemistry	547.71
Essequibo (Guyana : District)	T2—881 2

Essequibo Islands (Guyana :
District)	T2—881 3
Essex (England)	T2—426 7
Essex (Ont. : County)	T2—713 31
Essex County (Mass.)	T2—744 5
Essex County (N.J.)	T2—749 31
Essex County (N.Y.)	T2—747 53
Essex County (Va.)	T2—755 34
Essex County (Vt.)	T2—743 25
Essonne (France)	T2—443 65

Estate planning
Estate planning	332.024 01
inheritance law	346.052
tax law	343.053

Estate tax
Estate tax	336.276
law	343.053
public administration	351.724 76
public finance	336.276

Estates (Financial)
accounting	657.47
administration	346.056

Estates (Grounds)
landscape architecture	712.6
Estates-General (French history)	944.041

Estcourt (South Africa :
District)	T2—684 7
Estelí (Nicaragua : Dept.)	T2—728 524
Esterases	574.192 53
see also Enzymes	

Esterification
Esterification	547.24
chemical engineering	660.284 44

Esters
Esters	547.038
aromatic chemistry	547.638
chemical engineering	661.83
Esther (Biblical book)	222.9
Esther (Deuterocanonical book)	229.27
Esthonia	T2—474 1

Esthonian language
Esthonian language	494.545
	T6—945 45
Esthonians	T5—945 45
Estill County (Ky.)	T2—769 59

Estimates
Estimates	T1—029 9
building construction	692.5

Estimation theory
Estimation theory	519.5
probabilities	519.287
statistical mathematics	519.544
Estonia	T2—474 1

Estonian language
Estonian language	494.545
	T6—945 45
Estonian literature	894.545

Estonian Soviet Socialist
Republic	T2—474 1
Estonians	T5—945 45

Estrelleta, La (Dominican
Republic : Province)	T2—729 343

Estremadura (Portugal)
historic province	T2—469 4
modern province	T2—469 42
Estremadura (Spain)	T2—462 6

Estrie (Quebec :
Administrative region)	T2—714 6

Estuaries
Estuaries	551.460 9
engineering	627.124
resource economics	333.916 4
Estuarine ecology	574.526 365
Etchemins (Quebec)	T2—714 72

Etching
graphic arts	767.2

Etching glass
arts	748.6

Eternity
philosophy	115
religion	
Christianity	236.21
Islam	297.23
Judaism	296.33

Ethelbald, King of England
English history	942.016 3

Ethelbert, King of England
English history	942.016 3

Ethelred I, King of England
English history	942.016 3

Euboea Island (Greece)	T2—495 1
ancient	T2—384
Eucalyptus	583.42
Eucarida	595.384
Eucestoda	595.121
Eucharist	234.163
public worship	264.36
Anglican	264.030 36
texts	264.03
Roman Catholic	264.020 36
texts	264.023
Euclidean geometry	516.2
metric differential	516.372
Eucommiaceae	583.394
Eucryphiaceae	583.163
Eudorina	589.47
Euechinoidea	593.95
paleozoology	563.95
Eugenics	363.92
crime prevention	364.4
see also Crime prevention	
health	613.94
medical ethics	174.25
see also Medical ethics	
population control	363.98
social services	363.92
sterilization services	363.97
Euglenales	589.44
Euglenamorphales	589.44
Euglenida	593.18
Euglenoids	589.44
Euglenophyta	589.44
Eulerian integrals	515.52
Eumalacostraca	595.37
paleozoology	565.37
Eumycetes	589.2
Eumycetozoida	593.115
Eumycophyta	589.2
Eungella National Park	T2—943 6
Euphausiacea	595.385
paleozoology	565.38
Euphoniums	788.975
see also Brass instruments	
Euphorbiales	583.95
Eupomatiaceae	583.115
Eurasia	T2—5
Eurasians	T5—042
Eure (France)	T2—442 4
Eure-et-Loir (France)	T2—445 1
Eureka County (Nev.)	T2—793 32
Euroa (Vic.)	T2—945 5
Eurobonds	
public finance	336.31
Eurocommunism	
political ideology	320.532 309 4
Eurocurrency market	332.45
Eurodollar market	332.45
Europe	940
	T2—4
ancient	936
	T2—36
Europe, Eastern	947
	T2—47
Europe, Northern	948
	T2—48
ancient	936
	T2—36
Europe, Southeastern	949.6
	T2—496
ancient	939.8
	T2—398
Europe, Southern	940
	T2—4
ancient	938
	T2—38
Europe, Western	940
	T2—4
ancient	936
	T2—36
European Arctic seawaters	551.468 4
	T2—163 24
European Common Market	341.242 2
see also European Economic Community	
European Community	341.242 2
see also European Economic Community	
European Economic Community	341.242 2
commerce	382.914 2
economics	337.142
international law	341.242 2
economic functions	341.750 614
European federation	
political science	321.040 94
European Free Trade Association	341.242
international commerce	382.914 3
international economics	337.143
law	341.242
European Investment Bank	
economics	332.153 4
European Parliament	341.242 4
Europium	
chemistry	546.415
see also Rare earths	
Euryapsida	567.93
Eurypterida	565.391
Eurypygae	598.31
Eurytania (Greece)	T2—495 1
Eurytanias Nomos (Greece)	T2—495 1
Eusporangiated ferns	587.33
paleobotany	561.73
Eustachian tubes	
human anatomy	611.85
human physiology	612.854

Evidence (Law)	347.06
criminal law	345.06
law	347.06
Evidence procurement	
criminal investigation	363.252
Evil (Concept)	111.84
ethics	170
religion	291.5
Christianity	241.3
religion	291.2
Christianity	230
freedom of choice	233.7
natural theology	216
Evil eye	133.425
Evil spirits	133.423
religion	291.216
Evolutes	516.362
Evolution	575
animals	591.38
biology	575
ethical systems	171.7
humankind	573.2
microorganisms	576.138
philosophy	116
plants	581.38
social process	303.4
Evolution (Mathematics)	512.923
Evolution of stars	523.88
Evolution versus creation	291.24
Christianity	231.765
Judaism	296.34
natural theology	213
Evolutional psychology	155.7
Evolutionary cycles	575.7
Evolutionism	
philosophy	146.7
Evora (Portugal : District)	T2—469 52
Evreiskaia avtonomnaia	
oblast (R.S.F.S.R.)	T2—577
Evros (Greece)	T2—495 7
Ewe (African people)	T5—963 374
Ewe language	496.337 4
	T6—963 374
Ewe literature	896.337 4
Ewell, Epsom and (England)	T2—422 15
Ewings Morass Fauna	
Reserve	T2—945 6
Ewondo language	496.396
	T6—963 96
Ex-convicts	364.8
labor economics	331.51
Examination of witnesses	347.075
criminal investigation	363.254
criminal law	345.075
Examinations	T1—076
education	371.271
military personnel	355.223 6

Exanthems	
incidence	614.52
medicine	616.91
see also Communicable	
diseases (Human)	
Excavation	624.152
archaeological technique	930.102 83
mining	622.2
road engineering	625.733
Excelsior	674.84
Excelsior (South Africa :	
District)	T2—685 5
Exceptional children	
home care	649.15
psychology	155.45
Exceptional students	371.9
Excess profits tax	336.243 2
law	343.052 44
public administration	351.724 4
public finance	336.243 2
Exchange buildings	
architecture	725.25
Exchange rates	
foreign exchange	332.456
Exchange work (Libraries)	
government relationships	021.8
Exchanges	
library acquisitions	025.26
Excise tax	336.271
law	343.055 3
public administration	350.724 71
central governments	351.724 71
local governments	352.135
public finance	336.271
Excitation	
solid state physics	530.416
Excited states	
solid state physics	530.416
Excluded classes	305.568
	T1—086
Exclusionary rule	347.062
Excretion	574.14
animals	591.149
cytology	574.876 4
human physiology	612.46
plants	581.14
Excretory organs	574.14
anatomy	574.44
animal anatomy	591.44
human anatomy	611.61
human physiology	612.46
physiology	574.14
plant anatomy	581.44
Exe River	T2—423 5
Execution of wills	346.056
Executions of judgment	347.077
Executive agencies	350
see also Executive departments	

Extramarital relations	306.736
ethics	176
social problem	363.48
social theology	291.178 357 36
Christianity	261.835 736
see also Sexual relations	
Extrasensory perception	133.8
Extraterrestrial biophysics	574.191 9
human	612.014 5
Extraterrestrial civilization	999
Extraterrestrial engineering	620.419
Extraterrestrial life	577
natural theology	215.24
Extraterrestrial rovers	
engineering	629.295
Extraterrestrial worlds	999
	T2—99
Extraterritoriality	
international law	341.4
Extrauterine pregnancy	
obstetrics	618.31
Extravehicular activity (Manned	
space flight)	629.458 4
Extremadura (Spain)	T2—462 6
Extreme cold	536.56
Extreme unction	234.167
public worship	265.7
Extremities	
bones	
human anatomy	611.718
human physiology	612.75
medicine	616.71
surgery	617.471
fractures	
medicine	617.158
human anatomy	611.98
human physiology	612.98
joints	
medicine	616.72
surgery	617.58
muscles	
human anatomy	611.738
orthopedics	617.39
regional medicine	617.58
surgery	617.580 59
see also Musculoskeletal system	
Extrinsic variables (Stars)	523.844 4
Extroversion	155.232
educational psychology	370.153
personality trait	155.232
Extruded latex	678.538
Extruded rubber	678.35
Extruding metals	671.34
decorative arts	739.14
sculpture	731.41
Extruding plastics	668.413
Extruding rubber	678.27

Eyadéma, Gnassingbé	
Togolese history	966.810 4
Eyak language	497.2
	T6—972
Eye banks	362.178 3
see also Health services	
Eyeballs	
human anatomy	611.84
human physiology	612.84
ophthalmology	617.74
see also Eyes	
Eyeglasses	
customs	391.44
manufacturing technology	681.411
optometry	617.752 2
see also Eyes	
Eyelids	
human physiology	612.847
ophthalmology	617.771
see also Eyes	
Eyes	591.182 3
anesthesiology	617.967 71
animal anatomy	591.48
animal diseases	591.218 23
animal histology	591.824
animal physiology	591.182 3
geriatrics	618.977 7
human anatomy	611.84
human diseases	362.197 7
incidence	614.599 7
ophthalmology	617.7
social services	362.197 7
human physiology	612.84
nursing	610.736 77
pediatrics	618.920 977
personal care	646.726
surgery	617.71
Eyre, Lake	T2—942 38
Eyre Creek	T2—943 5
Eyre Peninsula (S. Aust.)	T2—942 38
Ezekiel (Biblical book)	224.4
Ezingolweni (South Africa :	
District)	T2—684 91
Ezo (Japan : Island)	T2—524
Ezo-ken (Japan)	T2—524
Ezra (Biblical book)	222.7

F

F layers (Ionosphere)	538.767 4
F.M. radio stations	384.545 3
engineering	621.384
facilities	384.545 3
organizations	384.540 65
F.M. radio systems	621.384 152
F region (Ionosphere)	538.767 4
Fabaceae	583.322

Fabian socialism	335.14
political ideology	320.531 2
Fabric furnishings	645.046
commercial technology	684.3
see also Furnishings	
Fabricating equipment	621.9
Fabrics	677.028 64
home economics	646.11
home furnishings	645.046
home sewing	646.11
textile technology	677.028 64
see also Textiles	
Facades	
architectural design	729.1
Face	
human anatomy	611.92
human physiology	612.92
personal care	646.726
regional medicine	617.52
surgery	617.520 59
Facial bones	
fractures	
medicine	617.156
human anatomy	611.716
human physiology	612.75
medicine	616.71
orthopedics	617.371
surgery	617.471
see also Musculoskeletal system	
Facility management	658.2
Facsimile transmission	384.14
engineering	621.382 35
postal service	383.141
see also Postal service	
wireless	384.524
see also Telegraphy	
Facsimiles	
bibliographies	011.47
Fact books	030
Fact-finding bodies	
public administration	350.009 3
central governments	351.009 3
local governments	352.009
Factor algebras	512.57
Factor analysis	519.535 4
Factoral proportions	
economics	338.512
Factorial series	515.243
Factories	
architecture	725.4
landscape architecture	712.7
manufacturing industries	338.476 7
manufacturing technology	670
organization of production	338.65
Factoring	512.923
algebra	512.923
arithmetic	513.23

Factorization	
number theory	512.74
Factors of production	338.01
agricultural economics	338.14
income distribution	339.21
microeconomics	338.512
mineral industries	338.26
secondary industries	338.45
Factory operations engineering	670.42
Factory outlets	381.15
see also Outlet stores	
Factory ships	387.248
design	623.812 48
engineering	623.824 8
transportation services	387.248
see also Ships	
Factory system	
economics	338.65
Facts (Philosophy)	111
Facultae	523.74
Faculty	371.1
higher education	378.12
Faculty meetings	371.146
Faculty psychology	150.192
Faeroe Islands	949.15
	T2—491 5
Faeroes	949.15
	T2—491 5
Faeroese dialect	439.699
	T6—396 99
Faeroese literature	839.699
Faeroese people	T5—396 9
Fagales	583.976
Failure (Education)	371.28
Failure (Materials science)	620.112
Fair employment	331.133
see also Equal employment opportunity	
Fair linens	
arts	746.96
Fair organs	786.68
see also Mechanical musical instruments	
Fair trade	338.522
law	343.07
Fairbanks North Star Borough (Alaska)	T2—798 6
Fairfax (Va.)	T2—755 292
Fairfax County (Va.)	T2—755 291
Fairfield County (Conn.)	T2—746 9
Fairfield County (Ohio)	T2—771 58
Fairfield County (S.C.)	T2—757 49
Fairgrounds	
area planning	711.552 2
landscape architecture	712.5

Fairies
folklore	398.21
literature	808.803 75
history and criticism	809.933 75
specific literatures	T3B—080 375
history and criticism	T3B—093 75

Fairness doctrine (Broadcasting)
law	343.099 4

Fairs
customs	394.6
distribution channels	381.18
management	658.84
see also Commerce	
see also Exhibitions	

Fairways (Navigation) 387.1
engineering	627.23
see also Ports	

Fairy chess	794.18
Fairy shrimp	595.32
Fairy tales	398.21
folklore	
sociology	398.45

Faisal I
Iraqi history	956.704 1

Faisal II
Iraqi history	956.704 2

Faith	121.7
epistemology	121.7
religion	291.22
Christianity	234.2
knowledge of God	231.042
private prayer	242.723
Islam	297.22
Judaism	296.32
natural theology	218

Faith and reason
Christianity	231.042

Faith healing
medicine	615.852

Faiyum (Egypt : Governorate)	T2—622
Fal River	T2—423 78

Falangism
economics	335.6
political ideology	320.533

Falasha	T5—924
Falcón (Venezuela)	T2—872 4
Falconidae	598.918
Falconiformes	598.91
paleozoology	568.9
Falconry	799.232
Falcons	598.918
Faliscan languages	479.4
	T6—794
Falkirk (Scotland : District)	T2—413 18
Falkland Islands	T2—971 1
Falklands	T2—971 1

Fall
music	781.524 6

Fall (continued)
natural history	508
see also Seasons	
Fall of humankind	233.14
Fall River County (S.D.)	T2—783 97
Fallacies	001.96
logic	165
Falling bodies	531.14
solid mechanics	531.5
Fallon County (Mont.)	T2—786 35

Fallopian tubes
gynecology	618.12
human anatomy	611.65
human physiology	612.62
surgery	618.12
see also Female genital system	

Fallowing	631.581 2
Falls Church (Va.)	T2—755 293
Falls County (Tex.)	T2—764 286
False arrest	346.033
False hemp	583.46
False imprisonment	346.033
False mermaid	583.216
False scorpion	595.47
Falsetto voices	782.86
choral and mixed voices	782.86
single voices	783.86
Falster (Denmark)	T2—489 3

Families
	306.85
applied psychology	158.24
guides to Christian living	248.4
histories	929.2
influence on crime	364.253
law	346.015
pastoral theology	291.61
Christianity	259.1
psychological influence	155.924
recreation	790.191
indoor	793.019 1
outdoor	796.019 1
social theology	291.178 358 5
Christianity	261.835 85
social welfare	362.82
public administration	350.848 2
central governments	351.848 2
local governments	352.944 82
sociology	306.85
welfare law	344.032 82
worship	291.43
Christianity	249
Judaism	296.4

Families of clergymen
pastoral theology	
Christianity	253.2

Family	306.85
see also Families	
Family abuse	362.829 2
see also Family violence	

Family cars
driving   629.283
   recreation   796.78
engineering   629.222
repair   629.287 2
Family Compact (Canadian
   history)   971.038
Family corporations
law   346.066 8
Family counseling   362.828 6
   see also Families—social
     welfare
Family dissolution   306.88
Family ethics   173
religion   291.563
   Buddhism   294.356 3
   Christianity   241.63
   Hinduism   294.548 63
   Islam   297.5
   Judaism   296.385 63
Family histories   929.2
Family law   346.015
Family life   306.85
applied psychology   158.24
customs   392.3
home economics   646.78
psychological influence   155.924
Family living   646.7
Family meals   642.1
Family names   929.42
Family planning   363.96
health   613.94
law   344.048
   see also Birth control
Family psychotherapy
psychiatry   616.891 56
   see also Mental illness
Family relationships   306.87
home economics   646.78
Family rooms   643.55
home economics   643.55
interior decoration   747.791
Family size
demography   304.634
Family socialization   303.323
Family state (System of
   government)   321.12
Family violence   362.829 2
criminal law   345.025 55
criminology   364.155 5
psychiatry   616.858 22
social theology   291.178 32
   Christianity   261.832
social welfare   362.829 2
   see also Families—social
     welfare, Mental illness
Famine   363.8
social welfare   363.8

Famous problems (In geometry)   516.204
Fan-jet engines
aircraft   629.134 353 7
Fan vaults   721.45
architecture   721.45
construction   690.145
Fancy forms (Music)   784.187 6
Fancy-weave fabrics   677.61
   see also Textiles
Fanfare form   784.189 24
Fang (African people)   T5—963 96
Fang language   496.396
    T6—963 96
Fannin County (Ga.)   T2—758 293
Fannin County (Tex.)   T2—764 265
Fanning Island   T2—964
Fans (Machinery)   621.61
Fans (Ornamental)   391.44
customs   391.44
handicrafts   745.594
Fantastic fiction   808.838 766
history and criticism   809.387 66
specific literatures   T3B—308 766
   individual authors   T3A—3
Fantasy   154.3
literature   808.801 5
   history and criticism   809.915
   specific literatures   T3B—080 15
    history and criticism   T3B—091 5
psychology   154.3
Fantasy fiction   808.838 766
history and criticism   809.387 66
specific literatures   T3B—308 766
   individual authors   T3A—3
Fantasy games   793.93
Fante language   496.338 5
    T6—963 385
Fanti language   496.338 5
    T6—963 385
Far East   950
    T2—5
Far East international
   organizations   341.247 3
Far Western Rand (South
   Africa)   T2—682 2
Farces
literature   808.825 23
   history and criticism   809.252 3
   specific literatures   T3B—205 23
    individual authors   T3A—2
Fareham (England)   T2—422 775
Fares
transportation services   388.049
Fargo (N.D.)   T2—784 13
Faribault County (Minn.)   T2—776 22
Farm accounting   657.863
Farm advertising   659.131 5

Farm buildings	
construction	690.892
use	631.2
Farm costs	338.13
Farm cottages	
architecture	728.6
Farm forestry	634.99
Farm income	338.13
Farm investment	338.13
Farm law	343.076
Farm loans	332.71
law	346.073
Farm manure	
agricultural use	631.861
Farm-owner insurance	368.096
see also Insurance	
Farm pests	632.6
plant husbandry	632.6
Farm prices	338.13
Farm production quotas	
law	343.076
Farm profits	338.13
Farm property	333.76
resource economics	333.76
taxation	336.225
law	343.054 2
Farm roads	
use	631.28
Farm tenancy	333.335 53
economics	333.335 53
law	346.043 48
Farm valuation	333.335 2
real estate economics	333.335 2
tax economics	336.225
tax law	343.054 2
Farmers	630.92
occupational group	T7—631
social class	305.555
Farmhouses	631.21
architecture	728.6
construction	690.867
Farming	630
Farmowner-ranchowner	
insurance	368.096
see also Insurance	
Farms	630
animal husbandry	636.01
Faro (Game)	795.42
Faro (Portugal : District)	T2—469 6
Faroe Islands	949.15
	T2—491 5
Farquhar Islands	T2—696
Farr (Scotland)	T2—411 65
Fars (Iran)	T2—557 2
Farsi language	491.55
	T6—915 5
Farsi literature	891.55

Faruk I, King of Egypt	
Egyptian history	962.052
Fasciae	
human anatomy	611.74
human diseases	
medicine	616.75
human physiology	612.75
see also Musculoskeletal system	
Fascism	
economics	335.6
political ideology	320.533
Fascist government	321.94
Fascist parties	324.213 8
Fascist period (Italian history)	945.091
Fashion	391
arts	746.92
customs	391
Fashion design	746.92
Fashion designers	746.920 92
occupational group	T7—746
Fashion drawing	741.672
Fashion modeling	746.92
advertising	659.152
Fast days	291.36
Christianity	263.9
cooking	641.567
customs	394.2
see also Holy days	
Fasteners	621.88
buildings	721.8
architecture	721.8
construction	690.18
Fastening equipment	621.97
Fasting	
health	613.25
Islamic moral theology	297.53
religious practice	291.447
Buddhism	294.344 47
Christianity	248.47
Hinduism	294.544 7
Fatalism	
philosophy	149.8
Fate	
philosophy	123
Father (God)	
Christian doctrines	231.1
Father and child	306.874 2
Fatherhood	306.874 2
Fathers	306.874 2
	T1—085 1
	T7—043 1
family relationships	306.874 2
psychology	155.646 2
Fatigue (Human)	
muscle tissue	
physiology	612.744
see also Musculoskeletal system	

Federal-state systems	321.023
Federal statutes (Compilations)	348.022
United States	348.732 2
Federal systems	321.02
law	342.042
Federalist Party (U.S.)	324.273 22
Federation of Arab Republics	T2—62
Federation of Rhodesia and	
Nyasaland	968.903
	T2—689
Federation of South Arabia	T2—533 5
Fee simple	346.043 2
land economics	333.323 2
Feeblemindedness	
medicine	616.858 8
see also Mental retardation	
Feedback circuits	
electronics	621.381 535
Feedback control systems	629.83
Feeding animals	636.084
Feeding-bottle nipples	
latex technology	678.533
Feeding children	649.3
Feedlot runoff	
water-pollution engineering	628.168 46
Feeds	
animal husbandry	636.085 5
commercial processing	664.66
grain and seeds	
commercial processing	664.76
Feelings	152.4
educational psychology	370.153
Fees	
public administration	350.726
central governments	351.726
local governments	352.14
public revenues	336.16
Feet	612.98
human physiology	612.98
regional medicine	617.585
surgery	617.585 059
see also Lower extremities	
(Human)	
Fe'fe' (Cameroon people)	T5—963 6
Fe'fe' language	496.36
	T6—963 6
Fejer Megye (Hungary)	T2—439 7
Feldspar	
materials science	620.198
mineralogy	549.68
synthetic	666.86
Felidae	599.744 28
animal husbandry	636.8
Felling trees	634.98
Fellowships	371.22
	T1—079
higher education	378.33
research	001.44

Feloidea	599.744 2
Felt	677.63
see also Textiles	
Felting textiles	677.028 24
manufacturing technology	677.028 24
Female genital organs	
human physiology	612.62
see also Female genital system	
Female genital system	591.166
anesthesiology	617.968 1
animal physiology	591.166
cancer	362.196 994 65
medicine	616.994 65
social services	362.196 994 65
see also Cancer	
geriatrics	618.978 1
gynecology	618.1
human anatomy	611.65
human diseases	362.198 1
incidence	614.599 2
social services	362.198 1
nursing	610.736 78
pediatrics	618.920 98
surgery	618.105 9
Female sexual disorders	
gynecology	618.17
see also Female genital system	
Females (Human)	305.4
	T1—082
grooming	646.704 2
guides to Christian life	248.843
health	613.042 4
religion	291.082
Christianity	208.2
social theology	261.834 4
social theology	291.178 344
see also Women	
Femininity	155.333
Feminism	305.42
social aspects	305.42
social theology	291.178 344 2
Christianity	261.834 42
Femurs	
human anatomy	611.718
see also Musculoskeletal system	
Fencers	796.860 92
sports group	T7—796 8
Fences	631.27
agricultural use	631.27
landscape architecture	717
Fencing (Offense)	364.162
law	345.026 2
Fencing (Swordplay)	796.86
Fenders	
automobile	629.26
Fenians (Canadian history)	971.048
Fenland (England : District)	T2—426 53
Fennel	583.48

Fetus	
human physiology	612.647
Feudal Age (European history)	940.14
Feudal land tenure	
economics	333.322
Feudal law	340.55
Feudal system	
political science	321.3
Feuds	
influence on crime	364.256
Fever	
result of injury	
medicine	617.22
symptomatology	616.047
Fever blisters	
medicine	616.52
see also Skin	
Fever therapy	
medicine	615.832 5
Fever tree	583.52
Feverbush	583.982
Few-bodies problem	530.14
Fez (Morocco : Province)	T2—643
Fianarantsoa (Madagascar :	
Province)	T2—691
Fiat money	332.427
Fiber bundles	514.224
combinatorial topology	514.224
integral geometry	516.362
Fiber crops	633.5
Fiber glass	666.157
materials science	620.144
sculpture material	731.2
ship design	623.818 38
ship hulls	623.845 8
shipbuilding	623.820 7
textiles	677.52
arts	746.045 2
see also Textiles	
Fiber optics	621.369 2
Fiber spaces	514.224
combinatorial topology	514.224
integral geometry	516.362
Fiberboards	676.183
Fibers	
materials science	620.197
textile materials	677.028 32
Fibers (Histology)	
human	611.018 2
Fibonacci numbers	512.72
Fibrin	
human physiology	612.115
see also Cardiovascular system	
Fibrinolytic agents	
pharmacodynamics	615.718
see also Cardiovascular system	

Fibrinoplastin	
human physiology	612.115
see also Cardiovascular system	
Fibrocartilage	
human histology	611.018 3
see also Musculoskeletal system	
Fibrous cartilage	
human histology	611.018 3
see also Musculoskeletal system	
Fibrous tunics	
human physiology	612.841
see also Eyes	
Fibulas	
human anatomy	611.718
see also Musculoskeletal system	
Ficksburg (South Africa :	
District)	T2—685 1
Ficoidaceae	583.152
Fiction	808.83
criticism	809.3
theory	801.953
folklore	398.2
history	809.3
rhetoric	808.3
specific literatures	T3B—3
individual authors	T3A—3
Fiction writers	809.3
collected biography	809.3
specific literatures	T3B—300 9
individual biography	T3A—3
occupational group	T7—83
Fictions	
logic	165
Ficus	583.962
Ficus elastica	
agriculture	633.895 2
Fidelity bonds	
insurance	368.83
see also Insurance	
Fiduciary accounting	657.47
Fiduciary trusts	
law	346.059
tax law	343.064
Field artillery	358.128 2
military engineering	623.412
military equipment	358.128 2
Field artillery forces	358.12
Field athletics	796.43
Field crops	633
animal feed	636.086
Field-effect transistors	621.381 528 4
Field effects	
solid state physics	530.416
Field extensions	
number theory	512.74
Field glasses	
manufacturing technology	681.412
Field hockey	796.355

Fillings
  dentistry   617.675
    see also Dentistry
Fillmore, Millard
  United States history   973.64
Fillmore County (Minn.)   T2—776 16
Fillmore County (Neb.)   T2—782 342
Fills
  road engineering   625.733
Film music   781.542
Film reviews   791.437 5
Filmed programs
  television performances   791.453
Films (Photographic material)   771.532 4
  development   771.43
Films (Photographic records)
  cataloging   025.347 3
  library treatment   025.177 3
Filmslides
  bibliographies   011.37
  cataloging   025.347 3
  library treatment   025.177 3
Filmstrips   778.2
  bibliographies   011.37
  cataloging   025.347 3
  education   371.335 22
  library treatment   025.177 3
Filters
  air conditioning
    buildings   697.932 4
  cameras   771.356
  electronic circuits   621.381 532 4
  radio engineering   621.384 12
Filtration
  chemical engineering   660.284 245
  sewage treatment   628.352
  water-supply treatment   628.164
Finance   332
  agriculture   338.13
  communication industry   384.041
  ethics   174.4
    see also Ethical problems
  library operations   025.11
  local Christian church   254.8
  mineral industries   338.23
  production economics   338.604 1
  secondary industries   338.43
  transportation services   388.049
Finance departments (Public
  administration)   350.72
  central governments   351.72
    cabinet departments   351.02
  local governments   352.1
Financial accounting   657.48
Financial administration   658.15
  see also Financial management
Financial aid (Welfare)   361.05
  crime prevention   364.44

Financial clerks
  office services   651.37
Financial control
  management   658.151
Financial crime   364.168
  law   345.026 8
Financial decision making
  management   658.15
Financial economics   332
Financial futures   332.632
Financial independence (Personal
  finance)   332.024 01
Financial institutions   332.1
  accounting   657.833 3
  architecture   725.24
  public administration   351.825
Financial management   658.15
                                 T1—068 1
  armed services   355.622
  public administration   350.72
    central governments   351.72
      cabinet departments   351.02
    local governments   352.1
Financial patronage   T1—079
  research   001.44
Financial planning
  management   658.15
  personal finance   332.024
Financial power (Legislative
  bodies)   328.341 2
Financial reports
  accounting   657.3
  management   658.151 2
  see also Financial statements
Financial security
  personal finance   332.024 01
Financial statements   657.3
  accounting   657.3
  corporate law   346.066 48
  management   658.151 2
  public administration   350.723 1
    central governments   351.723 1
    local governments   352.171
Financial strength measurement
  accounting   657.48
Financial success   650.12
Financial support
  education   T1—07
Financial support by
  governments
  libraries   021.83
Financial support of
  individuals   T1—079
Financiers   332.092
  occupational group   T7—332
Finbacks   599.51
Finches   598.883
  animal husbandry   636.686 2

Fire prevention (continued)	
technology	628.922
see also Fire safety	
Fire prevention equipment	
aircraft	629.134 43
Fire-resistant clothing	391
commercial technology	687.16
customs	391
see also Clothing	
Fire-resistant construction	
ship hulls	623.848
Fire-resistant paints	667.69
Fire retardants	628.922 3
Fire safety	363.37
law	344.053 7
mining technology	622.82
public administration	350.782
central governments	351.782
local governments	352.3
schools	371.774
social services	363.37
technology	628.922
Fire stations	363.37
architecture	725.19
construction	690.519
Firearms	
art metalwork	739.74
control	363.33
law	344.053 3
military engineering	623.442
Fireclays	553.67
ceramic technology	666.72
economic geology	553.67
materials science	620.143
Fireflies	595.764 4
Fireless cooking	641.588
Firemen	363.370 92
occupational group	T7—363 3
Firenze (Italy : Province)	T2—455 1
Fireplaces	
architecture	721.8
construction	697.1
furniture arts	749.62
home economics	644.1
Fireproofing	628.922 3
buildings	693.82
Fires	363.37
see also Fire stations	
Fireweed	583.44
Fireworks	662.1
Firing artillery	623.558
Firing clays	
pottery	666.443
arts	738.143
technology	666.443
sculpture	731.47
Firing glass	666.126
Firing metallurgical furnaces	669.83
Firmware	
hardware	004
engineering	621.395
microprograms	005.6
Firmware development	005.6
Firnification	551.578 465
First aid	362.18
emergency surgery	617.026 2
health services	362.18
medicine	616.025 2
First aid stations	362.18
armed forces	355.72
First-class mail	383.122
see also Postal service	
First editions	094.4
First Empire (French history)	944.05
First International	324.17
First names	929.44
First Republic (French history)	944.042
First Republic (Spanish history)	946.073
Firth of Clyde (Scotland)	551.461 37
	T2—163 37
Firth of Forth	551.461 36
	T2—163 36
Fiscal policy	336.3
law	343.034
macroeconomics	339.52
public finance	336.3
Fiscal tariffs	382.72
see also Customs (Tariff)	
Fischer-Tropsch processes	662.662 3
Fish	597
animal feed	636.087 6
art representation	704.943 2
cooking	641.692
drawing	743.67
food	641.392
commercial processing	664.94
production economics	338.372 7
resource economics	333.956
public administration	351.823 28
Fish culture	639.3
economics	338.371 3
enterprises	338.763 93
Fish culturists	639.309 2
occupational group	T7—639 3
Fish hatcheries	639.311
Fish lice	595.31
Fish-liver oils	
pharmacology	615.34
Fish oil	665.2
industrial	665.2
Fisher County (Tex.)	T2—764 732
Fisheries	338.372 7
law	343.076 92
public administration	351.823 62
cabinet departments	351.082 362
technology	639.2

Flat-backed lutes	787.85
see also Stringed instruments	
Flat racing	
dogs	798.8
horses	798.4
Flatcars	385.34
engineering	625.24
see also Rolling stock	
Flatfish	597.58
fishing	639.275 8
Flathead County (Mont.)	T2—786 82
Flathead Lake	T2—786 832
Flats	
apartment house management	647.92
apartment management	643.2
architecture	728.314
Flattery	
ethics	177.3
see also Ethical problems	
Flatware	
table setting	642.7
Flatworms	595.12
Flavoring aids	
commercial processing	664.5
Flavoring-producing plants	
agriculture	633.82
Flavorings	641.338 2
cooking with	641.638 2
Flax	583.214
fiber crop	633.52
textiles	677.11
arts	746.041 1
see also Textiles	
Flaxseed oil	665.352
Flea-borne typhus	
incidence	614.526 2
medicine	616.922 2
see also Communicable	
diseases (Human)	
Flea markets	381.192
management	658.87
see also Commerce	
Fleabane	583.55
Fleas	595.775
disease carriers	614.432 4
Fleets (Naval units)	359.31
Fleming County (Ky.)	T2—769 56
Flemings	T5—393 2
Flemish	T5—393 2
Flemish dialect	439.31
	T6—393 1
Flemish literature	839.31
Flesh flies	595.774
Fleshing leather	675.22
Fleshy-finned fishes	597.48
Fleuve (Senegal : Region)	T2—663
Flevoland (Netherlands)	T2—492 2
Flexible algebras	512.24

Flexible polymers	
chemistry	547.843
Flexible working periods	
economics	331.257 2
Flexure	
effect on materials	620.112 44
Fliers	629.130 92
Flies	595.77
disease carriers	614.432 2
Flight	
aeronautics	629.13
animal physiology	591.185 2
literature	808.803 56
history and criticism	809.933 56
specific literatures	T3B—080 356
history and criticism	T3B—093 56
Flight attendants	387.742 092
occupational group	T7—387 7
Flight guides	
aeronautics	629.132 54
Flight instrumentation	
aircraft	629.135 2
Flight into Egypt	232.926
Flight navigators	629.132 510 92
Flight operations systems	
spacecraft	629.474 2
unmanned spacecraft	629.464 2
Flight simulators	
aeronautics	629.132 520 78
manned space flight	629.450 078
Flight tests	
aircraft	629.134 53
Flights (Air force units)	358.413 1
Flights (Naval air units)	359.943 4
Flin Flon (Man.)	T2—712 72
Flinders Chase National Park	T2—942 35
Flinders Island (Tas.)	T2—946 7
Flinders Ranges (S. Aust.)	T2—942 37
Flinders River	T2—943 7
Flint	553.65
Flint (Mich.)	T2—774 37
Flint Island	T2—964
Flint River (Ga.)	T2—758 9
Flint River (Mich.)	T2—774 37
Flintshire (Wales)	T2—429 33
Floater insurance	368.2
see also Insurance	
Floating airports	
engineering	629.136 1
Floating bridges	388
construction	624.87
see also Bridges	
Floating debts	
public finance	336.32
Floating dry docks	623.83
Floating exchange rates	332.456 2
Floating foundations	624.156

Flugelhorns 788.97
  see also Brass instruments
Fluid balance
  biochemistry
    human 612.015 22
Fluid mechanics 532
  engineering 620.106
Fluid phases
  fluid state physics 530.424
Fluid-power technology 620.106
Fluid-state lasers 621.366 2
Fluid-state physics 530.42
Fluid transmission 532.02
  gas mechanics 533.12
Fluidics 629.804 2
Fluidization
  chemical engineering 660.284 292
Fluidized nuclear reactors 621.483 4
Fluids
  biochemistry 574.192 12
    human 612.015 22
  heat transfer 536.25
  state of matter 530.42
Fluke-caused diseases
  incidence 614.553
  medicine 616.963
  see also Communicable
    diseases (Human)
Flukes (Worms) 595.122
Fluorescence 535.35
  physics 535.35
Fluorescent lighting 621.327 3
Fluoridation
  dental disease prevention 614.599 6
    see also Dentistry
  water-supply engineering 628.166 3
Fluorine 553.95
  chemical engineering 661.073 1
  chemistry 546.731
  economic geology 553.95
  organic chemistry 547.02
    applied 661.891
  see also Chemicals
Fluorite
  mineralogy 549.4
Fluorophotometric analysis 543.085 2
Fluoroscopy
  medicine 616.075 72
Fluorspar
  mineralogy 549.4
Flute concertos 784.283 2
Flute family 788.3
  see also Woodwind instruments
Flutes 788.32
  see also Woodwind instruments
Flutists 788.320 92
  occupational group T7—788

Flutter
  aeronautics 629.132 362
Fluvanna County (Va.) T2—755 47
Flux (Metallurgy) 669.84
Fly fishing 799.12
Fly River T2—954 9
Fly River Province (Papua
  New Guinea) T2—954 9
Fly tying (Fishing)
  technology 688.791 2
Flying
  aeronautics 629.132 5
  animal physiology 591.185 2
Flying discs (Game) 796.2
Flying fish 597.53
Flying jeeps
  engineering 629.133 35
  military engineering 623.746 047
Flying lemurs 599.34
Flying saucers 001.942
Flying techniques
  sports 797.5
Flytraps (Plants) 583.121
FM radio stations 384.545 3
  engineering 621.384
  facilities 384.545 3
  organizations 384.540 65
FM radio systems 621.384 152
Foam glass 666.157
Foam latex 678.532
Foamed plastics 668.493
Foams 541.345 14
  chemical engineering 660.294 514
  colloid chemistry 541.345 14
Foard County (Tex.) T2—764 748
Fochville (South Africa) T2—682 4
Focusing apparatus 771.37
Fodder grass 584.93
Foggia (Italy : Province) T2—457 57
Fogs 541.345 15
  colloid chemistry 541.345 15
    applied 660.294 515
  meteorology 551.575
Foils
  use in cooking 641.589
Foix (Ariège, France) T2—448 8
Folding boxes 676.32
Folds (Geology) 551.87
Foliage plants
  floriculture 635.975
Foliations 514.72
Folk arts 745
Folk beliefs
  folklore 398.41
Folk dancers 793.319 2
  social group T7—793 3
Folk dancing 793.31
Folk high schools 374.8

Foodstuffs	641.3
see also Food	
Foot forces (Military)	356
Foot warfare	356
Football	796.33
electronic games	794.863 3
equipment technology	688.763 3
Football players	796.330 92
sports group	T7—796 33
Football rattles	786.886
see also Percussion instruments	
Footings	
walls	721.2
construction	690.12
see also Walls (Building element)	
Footpaths	388.12
see also Pedestrian paths	
Footwear	391.413
commercial technology	685.3
customs	391.413
see also Clothing	
For-hire carriers	388.041
truck	388.324 3
see also Freight services, Passenger services	
Forage crops	633.2
Forage grasses	584.9
agriculture	633.2
Foraminifera	593.12
paleozoology	563.12
Forbes (N.S.W.)	T2—944 5
Force	
philosophy	118
Force (International politics)	327.117
Forces (Mechanics)	531.113
Forcing	
agriculture	631.583
Forcipulatida	593.93
paleozoology	563.93
Ford, Gerald R.	
United States history	973.925
Ford County (Ill.)	T2—773 62
Ford County (Kan.)	T2—781 76
Forearm techniques	
music	784.193 62
Forebrain	
human physiology	612.825
see also Nervous system	
Forecasting	003.2
	T1—011 2
business	338.544
investments	332.678
management decision making	658.403 55
marketing management	658.818
occultism	133.3
social change	303.49
weather	551.63
Forecasting methods	
economics	338.544 2
Forecasts	003.2
	T1—011 2
business	338.544 3
social change	303.49
Foreclosure	346.043 64
Forehand	
tennis	796.342 22
Foreign affairs	327
see also Foreign relations	
Foreign aid	338.91
economic law	343.074 8
economics	338.91
international law	341.759
international relations	327.111
law	342.041 2
military science	355.032
Foreign assistance	338.91
see also Foreign aid	
Foreign bodies	
removal from wounds	
medicine	617.146
Foreign commerce	
public administration	351.827
cabinet departments	351.082 7
Foreign departments (Public administration)	351.01
Foreign economic assistance	338.91
Foreign economic policies	337
Foreign economic relations	337
Foreign enterprises	
financial management	658.159 9
Foreign exchange	332.45
international law	341.751
law	343.032
Foreign income	
tax economics	336.24
tax law	343.052 48
Foreign investment	332.673
Foreign labor	
law	344.016 2
Foreign language groups	
journalism for	070.484
Foreign languages	
elementary education	372.65
Foreign legions	355.359
Foreign licensing	
management	658.18
Foreign loans	
international law	341.751
law	346.073
Foreign merchants	382.092
Foreign missions	
Christianity	266.023
Foreign news	
journalism	070.433 2
Foreign policy	327.1

Formations	
sports	
American football	796.332 22
soccer	796.334 22
Formentera (Spain)	T2—467 56
Formicidea	595.796
Formosa	951.249
	T2—512 49
Formosa (Argentina :	
Province)	T2—823 5
Formosa Strait	551.465 57
	T2—164 57
Formosan native peoples	T5—992 5
Forms	
design	
public administration	350.714 4
central governments	351.714 4
local governments	352.164 4
Forms (Law)	347.055
Forms (Mathematics)	512.944
Forms of address	
etiquette	395.4
Forms of music	781.8
instrumental	784.18
vocal	782
Formula feed	
animal husbandry	636.085 57
commercial processing	664.768
Formula plans	
investments	332.678
Formularies	
pharmacology	615.13
Formulas	T1—021 2
Forrest County (Miss.)	T2—762 18
Forster (N.S.W.)	T2—944 2
Forsyth County (Ga.)	T2—758 265
Forsyth County (N.C.)	T2—756 67
Fort Beaufort (South Africa :	
District)	T2—687 5
Fort Bend County (Tex.)	T2—764 135
Fort Franklin (N.W.T.)	T2—719 6
Fort Gibson Lake (Okla.)	T2—766 87
Fort Gibson Reservoir (Okla.)	T2—766 87
Fort Lauderdale (Fla.)	T2—759 35
Fort Loudon Lake	T2—768 85
Fort Macleod (Alta.)	T2—712 34
Fort McMurray (Alta.)	T2—712 32
Fort Nelson (B.C.)	T2—711 87
Fort Nelson River (B.C.)	T2—711 87
Fort Norman (N.W.T.)	T2—719 6
Fort Peck Lake	T2—786 17
Fort Qu'Appelle (Sask.)	T2—712 44
Fort Simpson (N.W.T.)	T2—719 3
Fort Smith (N.W.T.)	T2—719 3
Fort Smith (N.W.T. : Region)	T2—719 3
Fort St. John (B.C.)	T2—711 87
Fort Wayne (Ind.)	T2—772 74
Fort Worth (Tex.)	T2—764 531 5

Forth, Firth of	551.461 36
	T2—163 36
Forth River (Scotland)	T2—413 1
Forth River (Tas.)	T2—946 5
Fortification	
basic training	355.544
military engineering	623.1
Fortitude (Gift of the Holy Spirit)	234.12
Fortresses	
architecture	725.18
military engineering	623.1
Forts	
architecture	725.18
military engineering	623.1
military installations	355.7
Fortune-tellers	133.309 2
occupational group	T7—13
Fortune-telling	133.3
Fortune-telling by runes	133.33
Forty Hours devotion	
Roman Catholic liturgy	264.027 4
Forward exchange	332.45
Forward play	
sports	
rugby	796.333 23
soccer	796.334 23
Fossa	599.744 22
Fossil fuels	553.2
chemistry	547.82
economic geology	553.2
resource economics	333.82
Fossil gums	553.29
economic geology	553.29
mining	622.339
Fossil resins	553.29
economic geology	553.29
mining	622.339
Fossils	560
Foster children	306.874
	T1—085 4
	T7—044 1
family relationships	306.874
home care	649.145
psychology	155.445
Foster County (N.D.)	T2—784 516
Foster homes	362.733
crime prevention	364.44
social welfare	362.733
see also Children—social	
welfare	
Foster parents	306.874
	T1—085
	T7—043 1
family relationships	306.874
Fotonovelas	741.5
Foucault's pendulum	525.36

Francoaceae	583.38	Fraser-Cheam (B.C.)	T2—711 37
Franconia (Germany)	T2—433	Fraser-Fort George (B.C.)	T2—711 82
Franconian dialect	437.3	Fraser Island (Qld.)	T2—943 2
	T6—32	Fraser Plateau (B.C.)	T2—711 75
Franconian emperors (German		Fraser River (B.C.)	T2—711 3
history)	943.023	Fraserburg (South Africa :	
Franconian Jura (Germany)	T2—433	District)	T2—687 17
Frangipani	583.72	Fraternal insurance	368.363
Frankeniaceae	583.158	*see also* Insurance	
Frankfort (Ky.)	T2—769 432	Fraternal organizations	366
Frankfort (South Africa :		Fraternities	
District)	T2—685 1	education	371.855
Frankfurt am Main (Germany)	T2—434 164	Fraud	364.163
Frankfurt an der Oder		law	345.026 3
(Germany)	T2—431 532	occultism	133
Frankfurt an der Oder		prevention	
(Germany : Bezirk)	T2—431 53	management	658.473
Frankiaceae	589.92	Fraudulent advertising	
Frankincense	583.24	postal handling	383.120 5
Franking privileges	383.120 2	*see also* Postal service	
see also Postal service		Fraudulent claims	
Fränkische Alb (Germany)	T2—433	insurance	368.014
Frankish rule (Italian history)	945.02	Fraudulent elections	324.66
Frankland Range	T2—946 2	criminology	364.132 4
Franklin (N.W.T. : District)	T2—719 5	law	345.023 24
Franklin (State)	976.803	Fraudulent promotion	
	T2—768	postal handling	383.120 5
Franklin (Va.)	T2—755 553	*see also* Postal service	
Franklin County (Ala.)	T2—761 913	Frazil ice	551.344
Franklin County (Ark.)	T2—767 34	Freaks (Circuses)	791.35
Franklin County (Fla.)	T2—759 91	Frechet algebras	512.55
Franklin County (Ga.)	T2—758 135	Frederick, the Great	
Franklin County (Idaho)	T2—796 42	German history	943.053
Franklin County (Ill.)	T2—773 94	Frederick Barbarossa, Holy	
Franklin County (Ind.)	T2—772 15	Roman Emperor	
Franklin County (Iowa)	T2—777 28	German history	943.024
Franklin County (Kan.)	T2—781 66	Frederick County (Md.)	T2—752 87
Franklin County (Ky.)	T2—769 432	Frederick County (Va.)	T2—755 992
Franklin County (Mass.)	T2—744 22	Frederick I, Holy Roman	
Franklin County (Me.)	T2—741 72	Emperor	
Franklin County (Miss.)	T2—762 27	German history	943.024
Franklin County (Mo.)	T2—778 63	Frederick II, King of Prussia	
Franklin County (N.C.)	T2—756 54	German history	943.053
Franklin County (N.Y.)	T2—747 55	Frederick III, Emperor of	
Franklin County (Neb.)	T2—782 377	Germany	
Franklin County (Ohio)	T2—771 56	German history	943.028
Franklin County (Pa.)	T2—748 44	Frederick III, German Emperor	
Franklin County (Tenn.)	T2—768 63	German history	943.084
Franklin County (Tex.)	T2—764 213	Fredericksburg (Va.)	T2—755 366
Franklin County (Va.)	T2—755 68	Fredericton (N.B.)	T2—715 515
Franklin County (Vt.)	T2—743 13	Frederiksborg (Denmark)	T2—489 1
Franklin County (Wash.)	T2—797 33	Fredholm equations	515.45
Franklin D. Roosevelt Lake	T2—797 23	Free aerophones	788.29
Franklin Parish (La.)	T2—763 77	*see also* Wind instruments	
Franklinite		Free algebras	512.24
mineralogy	549.526	Free assistance	
Franz Josef Land (R.S.F.S.R.)	T2—985	social welfare	361.02
Fraser Canyon (B.C.)	T2—711 37		

Freight services (continued)

bus	388.322 2
international law	341.756 882
law	343.094 82
terminal services	388.33
ferries	386.6
ground	388.044
law	343.094
inland waterway	386.244
international law	341.756 68
law	343.096 8
port services	386.864
international law	341.756
law	343.093 2
marine	387.544
international law	341.756 68
law	343.096 8
port services	387.164
port services	387.164
public administration	351.875
railroad	385.24
international law	341.756 5
law	343.095 8
special purpose	385.5
terminal services	385.264
truck	388.324
international law	341.756 883
law	343.094 83
terminal services	388.33
urban	388.413 24
terminal services	388.473
Freight terminals	388.044
architecture	725.3
area planning	711.7
construction	690.53
inland waterway	386.853
ports	387.153
Freighters (Ships)	387.245
engineering	623.824 5
see also Ships	
Fremantle (W.A.)	T2—941 1
Fremont County (Colo.)	T2—788 53
Fremont County (Idaho)	T2—796 56
Fremont County (Iowa)	T2—777 77
Fremont County (Wyo.)	T2—787 63
French (People)	T5—41
French and Indian War, 1756-1763	940.253 4
North American history	973.26
French Broad River	T2—768 895
French bulldog	
animal husbandry	636.72
see also Dogs	
French Cameroons	T2—671 1
French-Canadian literature	840
French-Canadians	T5—114
French Community	T2—171 244
French Congo (Brazzaville)	T2—672 4

French creole languages	447.9
	T6—41
French dressing	
food technology	664.37
French Equatorial Africa	967.203
	T2—672
Central African history	967.410 3
Chadian history	967.430 2
Congolese history	967.240 3
Gabonese history	967.210 2
French Flanders	T2—442 8
French Guiana	988.2
	T2—882
French Guinea	966.520 3
	T2—665 2
French horns	788.94
see also Brass instruments	
French Indochina	959.703
	T2—597
Cambodian history	959.603
Laotian history	959.403
Vietnamese history	959.703
French Island	T2—945 2
French language	440
	T6—41
French literature	840
French pastry	641.865 9
commercial processing	664.752 5
home preparation	641.865 9
French Polynesia	T2—962
French Revolution	944.04
French Riviera (France)	T2—449
French Somaliland	967.710 32
	T2—677 1
French Sudan	966.230 3
	T2—662 3
French Territory of the Afars and Issas	967.710 34
	T2—677 1
French West Indies	T2—729 76
Frenchmans Cap National Park	T2—946 6
Frequency	
sound physics	534.32
Frequency allocation	
radio	384.545 2
television	384.552 1
Frequency bridges	
electric engineering	621.374 7
Frequency distributions	519.532
Frequency meters	
electric engineering	621.374 7
Frequency-modulation radio systems	621.384 152
Frequency modulators	
electronic circuits	621.381 536 3
Frequency synthesizers	621.381 548 6
Fresco painting	751.44

Fromm, Erich
  psychological system — 150.195 7
Fronds (Plants)
  anatomy — 581.497
  physiology — 581.104 27
Front axles
  automotive — 629.247
Front Range (Colo. and Wyo.) — T2—788 6
Front yards
  landscape architecture — 712.6
Frontenac (Ont.) — T2—713 71
Frontenac (Quebec : County) — T2—714 69
Frontier County (Neb.) — T2—782 835
Frontier defense — 355.45
Frontier troops — 355.351
Fronts (Meteorology) — 551.551 2
Frosinone (Italy : Province) — T2—456 22
Frost
  geologic agent — 551.38
Frost (Crystals) — 551.574 4
Frost (Temperatures) — 551.525 3
  weather forecasting — 551.642 53
  weather modification — 551.682 53
Frost injury
  agriculture — 632.11
  plant husbandry — 632.11
Frostbite
  medicine — 616.58
  see also Skin
Froths — 541.345 14
  chemical engineering — 660.294 514
  colloid chemistry — 541.345 14
Frottole — 782.43
Frozen desserts — 641.86
  home preparation — 641.86
  manufacturing — 637.4
Frozen foods
  cooking — 641.615 3
Frozen seawater
  geology — 551.343
Fructose — 574.192 481 3
  biochemistry — 574.192 481 3
  chemistry — 547.781 3
  see also Carbohydrates
Fruit — 582.130 416 6
  anatomy — 582.046 4
    flowering plants — 582.130 446
  animal feed — 636.087 4
  art representation — 704.943 4
  commercial preservation — 664.8
  cooking — 641.64
  drawing — 743.7
  food — 641.34
  forest products — 634.987
  home preservation — 641.4
  orchard crop — 634
  paleobotany — 561.14
  physiology — 582.130 416 6

Fruit arrangements — 745.924
Fruit culture — 634
Fruit flies — 595.774
Fruit growers — 634.092
  occupational group — T7—634
Fruit juices — 641.34
  commercial processing — 663.63
  cooking with — 641.64
  home preparation — 641.875
Frustration — 152.47
Frying — 641.77
Frying pans
  electric cooking — 641.586
Fuad I, King of Egypt
  Egyptian history — 962.051
Fuad II, King of Egypt
  Egyptian history — 962.052
Fucales — 589.45
Fuchsia — 583.44
  floriculture — 635.933 44
Fuel alcohols — 662.669
Fuel cells — 621.312 429
Fuel element materials
  nuclear engineering — 621.483 35
Fuel engineers — 662.609 2
  occupational group — T7—662
Fuel oils — 665.538 4
Fuel resources
  extraction
    economics — 338.2
  law — 346.046 82
  public administration — 351.823 27
Fuel systems
  automotive — 629.253
Fueling — 388.041
  aircraft — 387.736 4
  boats — 387.168
  buses — 388.33
    urban — 388.473
  ships — 387.168
  trains — 385.26
  trucks — 388.33
    urban — 388.473
Fuels — 662.6
  aircraft — 629.134 351
  automotive — 629.253 8
  chemical engineering — 662.6
  heat engineering — 621.402 3
  heating buildings — 697.04
  marine engines — 623.874
  metallurgical furnaces — 669.81
  military supplies — 355.83
  nuclear reactors — 621.483 35
  resource economics — 333.82
  spacecraft — 629.475
  steam engineering — 621.182
  unmanned spacecraft — 629.465

Fungicides	668.652
agricultural use	632.952
chemical engineering	668.652
Fungus diseases	574.232 6
agriculture	632.4
incidence in humans	614.559
medicine	616.969
plant husbandry	632.4
see also Communicable	
diseases (Human)	
Funicular railroads	385.6
engineering	625.32
transportation services	385.6
see also Railroad transportation	
Funj Sultanate	962.402 3
	T2—624
Funnies	741.5
drawing	741.5
journalism	070.444
Fur-bearing animals	
hunting	639.11
Fur clothing	391
commercial technology	685.24
customs	391
home sewing	646.4
see also Clothing	
Fur farming	636.9
Fur goods	
commercial technology	685
Fur processing	675.3
economics	338.476 753
Fur seals	599.746
Furans	547.592
chemical engineering	661.8
Furloughs	
armed forces	355.113
penology	365.643
Furnaces	
heat engineering	621.402 5
heating buildings	697.07
steam	697.507
steam engineering	621.183
Furnas County (Neb.)	T2—782 384
Furneaux Group	T2—946 7
Furnishings	645
commercial technology	684
customs	392.36
home cleaning	648.5
household management	645
libraries	022.9
Furniture	645.4
cleaning	648.5
customs	392.36
decorative arts	749
household management	645.4
libraries	022.9
manufacturing technology	684.1
office services	651.23

Furniture (continued)	
ships	623.866
Furniture arrangement	645.4
Furniture covers	645.4
home sewing	646.21
household management	645.4
textile arts	746.95
Furniture designers	749.2
occupational group	T7—749
Furniture makers	684.100 92
occupational group	T7—684
Furriers	675.309 2
occupational group	T7—675
Furs	
handicrafts	745.537
home sewing materials	646.1
processing	675.3
Further education	374
Furuncles	
medicine	616.523
see also Skin	
Fused aromatic compounds	547.615
chemical engineering	661.816
Fused heterocyclic compounds	547.596
Fuselages	
aircraft	629.134 34
Fuses (Detonators)	662.4
military engineering	623.454 2
Fuses (Electrical)	621.317
Fusibility	
crystals	548.86
Fusion	
heat physics	536.42
Fusion (Thermonuclear)	539.764
Fusion reactors	621.484
Futuna-Aniwa language	499.4
	T6—994
Futuna Islands	T2—961 6
Future interests (Law)	346.042
Futures	332.645
Futurism	709.040 33
painting	759.063 3
sculpture	735.230 433
Futurology	003.2
occultism	133.3
social change	303.49
Fuzzy sets	511.322
Fylde (England)	T2—427 662
Fylde (England : Borough)	T2—427 662
Fyn (Denmark)	T2—489 4
Fyns amt (Denmark)	T2—489 4

G

G.A.R. (Organization)	369.15
G.A.T.T. (Commerce)	382.92
law	341.754 3
G.D.P. (Macroeconomics)	339.31

Galleys (Ships) (continued)
   handling   623.882 1
   transportation services   387.21
   see also Ships
Galli   598.61
Gallia Cisalpina   T2—372
Gallia County (Ohio)   T2—771 89
Gallia Transalpina   T2—364
Galliard form   784.188 2
Gallican schismatic churches   284.8
   see also Old Catholic churches
Galliformes   598.61
   paleozoology   568.6
Gallinules   598.31
Gallionella   589.94
Gallium   669.79
   chemical engineering   661.067 5
   chemistry   546.675
   metallurgy   669.79
   see also Chemicals
Gallo-Roman period (French
   history)   936.402
Gallow cattle
   zoology   599.735 8
Galloway (Scotland : District)   T2—414 9
Galloway, Dumfries and
   (Scotland)   T2—414 7
Galloway cattle
   animal husbandry   636.223
Galls
   agricultural diseases   632.2
   botany   581.2
Galois theory   512.3
Galop form   784.188 4
Galvanic electromagnetic
   prospecting   622.154
Galvanometers   621.374 4
Galveston County (Tex.)   T2—764 139
Galway (Ireland)   T2—417 45
Galway (Ireland : County)   T2—417 4
Gama grass   584.93
Gambia   966.51
   T2—665 1
Gambia River   T2—665 1
Gambians   T5—966 51
Gambier Island (B.C.)   T2—711 31
Gambier Islands   T2—962 2
Gamblers   795.092
   occupational group   T7—795
Gambling   306.482
   criminal law   345.027 2
   criminology   364.172
   customs   394.3
   ethics   175.9
     see also Recreation—ethics
   horse racing   798.401
   law   344.054 2
   mathematics   519.2

Gambling (continued)
   occupational ethics   174.6
   public control   363.42
     public administration   350.76
       central governments   351.76
       local governments   352.936
   recreation   795
   sociology   306.482
Game animals
   cooking   641.691
   food   641.391
Game birds
   animal husbandry   636.63
   cooking   641.691
   food   641.391
   see also Birds
Game keepers   639.909 2
Game keeping   639.9
Game laws   346.046 954
Game resources   333.954
   economics   333.954
Game theory   519.3
Games
   camp sports   796.545
   cataloging   025.349 6
   customs   394.3
   educational use   371.307 8
   ethics   175.4
     see also Recreation—ethics
   folk literature   398.8
   indoor   793
   library treatment   025.179 6
   management decision making   658.403 53
   outdoor   796
   sociology   306.487
   see also Recreation
Games of chance   795
   equipment technology   688.75
   probabilities   519.2
Games of skill
   indoor   794
Gametes   574.32
Gametogenesis   574.32
   animals   591.32
   plants   581.32
Gaming
   education   371.397
Gamka River   T2—687 16
Gamma decay   539.752 4
Gamma functions   515.52
Gamma globulins
   pharmacology   615.39
Gamma particles   539.722 2
Gamma radiation
   biophysics   574.191 56
     human   612.014 486
Gamma-ray astronomy   522.686 2
Gamma-ray electronics   537.535

Garlic	641.352 6
botany	584.324
cooking	641.652 6
garden crop	635.26
pharmacology	615.324 324
Garment workers	687.092
occupational group	T7—687
Garments	391
see also Clothing	
Garnets	553.87
industrial	553.65
mineralogy	549.62
synthetic	666.88
Garnierite	
mineralogy	549.67
Garnishes	641.81
cooking	641.81
Garnishment	347.077
private law	346.077
Garo language	495.4
	T6—954
Garonne River (Spain and France)	T2—447
Garrard County (Ky.)	T2—769 525
Garrett County (Md.)	T2—752 97
Garrison Reservoir	T2—784 75
Garryales	583.982
Gars	597.47
commercial fishing	639.274 7
Garvin County (Okla.)	T2—766 56
Gary (Ind.)	T2—772 99
Garza County (Tex.)	T2—764 852
Gas analysis	
chemistry	543.08
Gas apparatus (Chemical apparatus)	542.7
Gas chromatography	543.089 6
chemical engineering	660.284 23
Gas content	
soil physics	631.433
Gas-detection prospecting	622.159
Gas engineering	665.7
equipment manufacturing technology	681.766 5
Gas engineers	665.709 2
occupational group	T7—665
Gas equipment	
household appliances	643.6
manufacturing technology	683.88
Gas exchange	
human physiology	612.22
see also Respiratory system	
Gas fitting	
buildings	696.2
Gas heating	
buildings	697.043
Gas hydrate desalinization	628.167 6
Gas lighting	621.324

Gas mechanics	533
engineering	620.107
soil physics	631.433
Gas oil	665.538 4
Gas pipes	
buildings	
installation	696.2
Gas supply	
public administration	350.872 3
central governments	351.872 3
local governments	352.912 3
public utilities	363.63
Gas supply facilities	
area planning	711.8
Gas tubes	
electronics	621.381 513
Gas-turbine engines	621.433
aircraft	629.134 353
automotive	629.250 3
ships	623.872 33
Gas-turbine locomotives	385.362
engineering	625.262
transportation services	385.362
see also Rolling stock	
Gas welding	671.522
Gascogne (France)	T2—447 7
Gasconade County (Mo.)	T2—778 61
Gascony (France)	T2—447 7
Gascoyne River	T2—941 3
Gaseous-state lasers	621.366 3
Gaseous-state physics	530.43
Gaseous wastes	
technology	628.53
Gases	
chemical engineering	660.043
chemistry	541.042 3
expansion and contraction	536.412
heat capacity	536.65
heat transfer	536.25
sound transmission	
physics	534.24
specific heats	536.65
state of matter	530.43
Gases (Fuels)	665.7
cooking	641.584
mine safety engineering	622.82
natural	553.285
see also Natural gas	
plant management	658.26
public safety	363.179 8
radiesthesia	133.323 7
see also Hazardous materials	
Gases (Noxious)	
mine safety engineering	622.82
pollution	363.738 7
see also Pollution	
toxicology	615.91
Gases in atmosphere	551.511 2

Gê language	498.4
	T6—984
Gê-Pano-Carib languages	498.4
	T6—984
Gear-cutting tools	621.944
Gear-driven hoists	
mining	622.67
Gears	621.833
clockwork	681.112
Geary County (Kan.)	T2—781 29
Geauga County (Ohio)	T2—771 336
Gedling (England)	T2—425 28
Geelong (Vic.)	T2—945 2
Geese	598.41
animal husbandry	636.598
sports hunting	799.248 41
Geez language	492.8
	T6—928
Geez literature	892.8
Gegenschein	
astronomy	523.59
Geiger-Müller counters	
nuclear physics	539.774
Geisel, Ernesto	
Brazilian history	981.063
Geissolomataceae	583.933
Gelatin process	
printing	686.232 5
Gelatins	641.864
commercial processing	664.26
home preparation	641.864
Gelderland (Netherlands)	T2—492 18
Gelidiales	589.41
Gels	541.345 13
chemical engineering	660.294 513
colloid chemistry	541.345 13
Gelsenkirchen (Germany)	T2—435 618
Gem County (Idaho)	T2—796 27
Gemini project	629.454
Gems	553.8
carving	736.2
economic geology	553.8
jewelry	739.27
materials science	620.198
mining	622.38
prospecting	622.188
synthetic	666.88
Gender identity	305.3
social aspects	305.3
Gene pools	575.15
Gene splicing	
biology	575.107 24
biotechnology	660.65
Genealogists	929.109 2
occupational group	T7—99
Genealogy	929.1

General Agreement on Tariffs	
and Trade (1947)	382.92
law	341.754 3
General anesthesia	
surgery	617.962
General Carrera (Chile :	
Province)	T2—836 25
General Conference Mennonite	
Church	289.73
see also Mennonite Church	
General paresis	
medicine	616.892
see also Nervous system	
General Society of Colonial Wars	
(U.S.)	369.12
General Society of Mayflower	
Descendants	369.12
General staffs	355.330 42
General stores	381.14
management	658.874
see also Commerce	
General strikes	322.2
economics	331.892 5
see also Strikes (Work	
stoppages)	
General television broadcasting	384.554
see also Television	
General topology	514.322
Generalized functions	515.782
Generalized system of preference	382.753
see also Customs (Tariff)	
Generals	355.009 2
role and function	355.331
Generating electricity	621.312 1
Generating functions	515.55
Generating machinery	
electrical engineering	621.313
Generating steam	621.18
Generation gap	305.2
Generation of sound	
physics	534.1
Generative grammar	415
specific languages	T4—5
Generative organs	
human anatomy	611.6
human physiology	612.6
see also Genital system	
Genes	574.873 22
animals	591.873 22
plants	581.873 22
Genesee County (Mich.)	T2—774 37
Genesee County (N.Y.)	T2—747 92
Genesee River (Pa. and N.Y.)	T2—747 88
Genesis (Bible)	222.11
Genetic control of population	363.98
see also Eugenics	
Genetic disorders	
medicine	616.042

Geography	910
Bible	220.91
elementary education	372.891
Geologic age measurements	551.701
Geologic time	551.701
Geological instruments	
manufacturing technology	681.755
Geological prospecting	622.12
Geologists	551.092
occupational group	T7—553
Geology	551
Geomagnetism	538.7
Geomancy	133.333
Geometric abstractionism	709.040 52
painting	759.065 2
sculpture	735.230 452
Geometric design	709.040 3
painting	759.063
sculpture	735.230 43
Geometric number theory	512.75
Geometric probability	519.2
Geometric progressions	512.93
algebra	512.93
arithmetic	513.4
Geometric shapes	516.15
Geometrical crystallography	548.81
Geometrical optics	535.32
Geometries over algebras	516.186
Geometries over groups	516.186
Geometries over rings	516.186
Geometroidea	595.781
Geometry	516
Geometry of numbers	512.75
Geomorphologists	551.410 92
occupational group	T7—553
Geomorphology	551.41
Geonavigation	
nautical	623.892
Geophysical prospecting	622.15
Geophysics	550
Geopolitics	320.12
international relations	327.101
George (South Africa :	
District)	T2—687 4
George, Lake (N.S.W.)	T2—944 7
George, Lake (N.Y.)	T2—747 51
George County (Miss.)	T2—762 165
George I, King of Great Britain	
British history	941.071
English history	942.071
Scottish history	941.107 1
George II, King of Great Britain	
British history	941.072
English history	942.072
Scottish history	941.107 2
George III, King of Great Britain	
British history	941.073
English history	942.073
Scottish history	941.107 3
George IV, King of Great Britain	
British history	941.074
English history	942.074
Scottish history	941.107 4
George Town (Tas.)	T2—946 4
George V, King of Great Britain	
British history	941.083
English history	942.083
Scottish history	941.108 3
George VI, King of Great Britain	
British history	941.084
English history	942.084
Scottish history	941.108 4
Georgetown (Guyana)	T2—881 5
Georgetown County (S.C.)	T2—757 89
Georgia	975.8
	T2—758
Georgia (Transcaucasia)	T2—479 5
Georgia, Strait of (B.C.)	551.466 33
	T2—164 33
Georgian architecture	724.19
Georgian Bay (Ont. : Bay)	T2—713 15
Georgian language	499.96
	T6—999 6
Georgian literature	899.96
Georgian S.S.R.	T2—479 5
Georgians (Transcaucasians)	T5—999 6
Georgina River	T2—943 5
Geosynclines	551.86
Geotectonics	551.8
Geothermal energy	333.88
economics	333.88
Geothermal engineering	621.44
Geothermal prospecting	622.159
Gephyrea	595.17
paleozoology	565.1
Gera (Germany : Bezirk)	T2—432 22
Geraldton (W.A.)	T2—941 2
Geraniales	583.216
Geraniums	583.216
floriculture	635.933 216
Gerbils	599.323 3
animal husbandry	636.932 33
Gere (African people)	T5—963 4
Gere language	496.34
	T6—963 4
Geriatric cardiology	618.976 12
see also Cardiovascular system	
Geriatric disorders	362.198 97
incidence	614.599 2
medicine	618.97
social services	362.198 97
Geriatric gynecology	618.978 1
see also Female genital system	

Geriatric nursing		Germanium (continued)	
medicine	610.736 5	metallurgy	669.79
Geriatric preventive measures	613.043 8	*see also* Chemicals	
Geriatric surgery	617.97	Germans	T5—31
Geriatric therapeutics	615.547	Germans (Dances)	793.35
Geriatricians	618.970 092	Germany	943
occupational group	T7—618		T2—43
role and function	618.970 232	Germany (East)	943.108 7
Geriatrics	618.97		T2—431
Germ cells	574.32	Germany (West)	943.087
Germ plasm			T2—43
agriculture	631.523	Germination	
animal breeding	636.082 1	plant biology	581.334
plant breeding	631.523	Germiston (South Africa :	
Germ warfare	358.38	District)	T2—682 2
see also Biological warfare		Gerona (Spain : Province)	T2—467 1
German Confederation	943.07	Gerontology	
German Democratic Republic	943.108 7	human physiology	612.67
	T2—431	social aspects	305.26
German Empire	943.083	Gerroidea	595.754
	T2 43	Gerrymandering	328.334 55
German historical school		Gers (France)	T2—447 71
(Economics)	330.154 2	Gesneriaceae	583.81
German language	430	Gestalt psychology	150.198 2
	T6—31	Gestalt therapy	
German literature	830	psychiatry	616.891 43
German measles		*see also* Mental illness	
incidence	614.524	Gestures	302.222
medicine	616.916	drama	792.028
pediatrics	618.929 16	motion pictures	791.430 28
see also Communicable		stage	792.028
diseases (Human)		television	791.450 28
German New Guinea	995.302 1	preaching	251.03
	T2—953	psychology	152.384
German police dog		social psychology	302.222
animal husbandry	636.737	Gettysburg, Battle of, 1863	973.734 9
see also Dogs		Geysers	551.23
German Pomerania	T2—431 7	Gezira (Sudan : Province)	T2—626 4
German Reformed Church (U.S.)	285.733	Ghaap Plateau	T2—687 11
see also Reformed Church		Ghana	966.7
(American Reformed)			T2—667
German shepherd		Ghana Empire	966.101 6
animal husbandry	636.737		T2—661
see also Dogs		Ghanaians	T5—966 7
Germania Inferior	T2—364	Gharbiya (Egypt :	
Germania Superior	T2—364	Governorate)	T2—621
Germanic languages	430	Ghazi I	
	T6—3	Iraqi history	956.704 2
Germanic literatures	830	Ghazni dynasty (Indian history)	954.022 3
Germanic people	T5—3	Ghent (Belgium)	T2—493 142
Germanic regions	943	Gherkins	583.46
	T2—43	Ghettos	307.336 6
ancient	936.3	Ghor dynasty (Indian history)	954.022 5
	T2—363	Ghosts	133.1
Germanic religion	293	fiction	808.838 733
Germanium		history and criticism	809.387 33
chemical engineering	661.068 4	specific literatures	T3B—308 733
chemistry	546.684	individual authors	T3A—3

Ghosts (continued)

folklore	398.25
sociology	398.47
occultism	133.1
Giannutri Island	T2—455 7
Giant fern	587.33

Giant schnauzer

animal husbandry	636.73

see also Dogs

Giant slalom skiing	796.935

Giants

folklore	398.21
sociology	398.45
physical anthropology	573.8
Giant's Castle Game Reserve	T2—684 7
Gibberellins	581.31
chemistry	547.734 2
physiology	581.31
Gibbons	599.882
Gibb's phase rule	541.363
Gibraltar	946.89
	T2—468 9
Gibraltar, Strait of	551.462 1
	T2—163 81
Gibraltar Range National Park	T2—944 3
Gibson County (Ind.)	T2—772 35
Gibson County (Tenn.)	T2—768 23
Gibson Desert (W.A.)	T2—941 5
Giessen (Germany : Regierungsbezirk)	T2—434 14

Gift revenues

public finance	336.16
Gift tax	336.276
law	343.053 5
public administration	351.724 76
public finance	336.276
Gift wrappings	745.54

Gifted children

home care	649.155
psychology	155.455
Gifted persons	305.908 29
	T1—087 9
	T7—082 9
Gifted students	371.95

Gifts

capital procurement	658.152 24
financial management	658.153
library acquisitions	025.26
military rewards	355.134 9
sales promotion	658.82
Gifts of the Holy Spirit	234.12
Gifu-ken (Japan)	T2—521 62

Gigantism (Pituitary)

medicine	616.47

see also Endocrine system

Gigartinales	589.41
Giglio Island (Italy)	T2—455 7
Gihu-ken (Japan)	T2—521 62

Gila County (Ariz.)	T2—791 55
Gila River (N.M. and Ariz.)	T2—791 7
Gilan (Iran : Province)	T2—551
Gilbert Islands	T2—968 1
Gilbert River	T2—943 7
Gilchrist County (Fla.)	T2—759 78

Gilding

bookbinding	686.36
decorative arts	745.75
Giles County (Tenn.)	T2—768 61
Giles County (Va.)	T2—755 782
Gilgandra (N.S.W.)	T2—944 5
Gill fungi	589.222

Gilles de la Tourette syndrome

medicine	616.83

see also Nervous system

Gillespie County (Tex.)	T2—764 65
Gilliam County (Or.)	T2—795 65
Gillingham (England)	T2—422 325
Gilmer County (Ga.)	T2—758 295
Gilmer County (W. Va.)	T2—754 27
Gilpin County (Colo.)	T2—788 62
Gilt-edged securities	332.632 044
Gilyak language	494.6
	T6—946
Gimps	677.76
Gin	641.255
commercial processing	663.55
Gin rummy	795.418
Ginger	584.21
agriculture	633.83

Ginger ales

commercial processing	663.62
Ginger lily	584.21

Gingivitis

dentistry	617.632

see also Dentistry

Ginkgo tree	585.7
Ginkgoales	585.7
paleobotany	561.57
Ginning cotton	677.212 1
Ginseng	583.687
agriculture	633.883 687
pharmacology	615.323 687
Gippsland (Vic.)	T2—945 6
Giraffes	599.735 7
big game hunting	799.277 357
Giraffoidea	599.735 7
Girder bridges	388
construction	624.37

see also Bridges

Girders	624.177 23
naval architecture	623.817 723
structural engineering	624.177 23
Giresun Ili (Turkey)	T2—565
Girl Guides Association	369.463
Girl Scout camps	796.542 2
Girl Scouts	369.463

Glazing leather	675.25
Glazing pottery	666.444
arts	738.144
technology	666.444
Glazing sculpture	731.4
Glazing windows	698.5
Gleicheniaceae	587.31
Glen Canyon National	
Recreation Area (Utah	
and Ariz.)	T2—792 59
Glen Innes (N.S.W.)	T2—944 4
Glencoe (South Africa :	
District)	T2—684 1
Glenelg River	T2—945 7
Glenn County (Calif.)	T2—794 31
Gliders (Aircraft)	387.733 3
engineering	629.133 33
piloting	629.132 523
transportation services	387.733 3
see also Aircraft	
Gliding	
aeronautics	629.132 31
sports	797.55
Gliding bacteria	589.96
Glires	599.32
paleozoology	569.32
Global analysis	515
topology	514.74
Global differential geometry	516.362
Globe daisy	583.87
Globular clusters (Stars)	523.855
Globulariaceae	583.87
Globulins	574.192 452
biochemistry	574.192 452
chemistry	547.752
see also Proteins	
Glockenspiels	786.843
see also Percussion instruments	
Glomerulonephritis	
medicine	616.612
see also Urinary system	
Gloria	264.36
music	782.323 2
Glorioso Islands	T2—691
Glossopteris	561.597
Glottis	
human anatomy	611.22
human diseases	
medicine	616.22
see also Respiratory system	
Gloucester (England)	T2—424 14
Gloucester (N.B.)	T2—715 12
Gloucester (N.S.W.)	T2—944 2
Gloucester County (N.J.)	T2—749 81
Gloucester County (Va.)	T2—755 32
Gloucestershire (England)	T2—424 1
Glove compartments	
automobile	629.277
Glove makers	685.409 2
occupational group	T7—685 4
Gloves	391.412
commercial technology	685.4
customs	391.412
home sewing	646.48
see also Clothing	
Glowworms	595.764 4
Gloxinia	583.81
Gluconobacter	589.95
Glucose	574.192 481 3
biochemistry	574.192 481 3
chemistry	547.781 3
see also Carbohydrates	
Glue	668.3
see also Adhesives	
Glue abuse	362.299
medicine	616.86
personal health	613.8
social welfare	362.299
see also Substance abuse	
Gluing	
bookbinding	686.35
Gluttony	178
see also Vices	
Glycerin	668.2
Glycogen	574.192 482
biochemistry	574.192 482
chemistry	547.782
see also Carbohydrates	
Glycosides	574.192 483
biochemistry	574.192 483
chemistry	547.783
see also Carbohydrates	
Glyndŵr (Wales)	T2—429 37
Glynn County (Ga.)	T2—758 742
Glyptics	736.2
Glyptographers	736.209 2
occupational group	T7—736
Gnathidea	595.372
Gnathobdellida	595.145
Gnats	595.771
Gneisses	552.4
Gnetacae	
paleobotany	561.51
Gnetales	585.1
Gneticae	585.1
Gnetum	585.1
Gnosticism	299.932
Christian heresy	273.1
GNP (Macroeconomics)	339.31
Go (Game)	794
Go-moku	794
Goa, Daman and Diu (India)	T2—547 99
Goajiro language	498.3
	T6—983
Goal posts	
American football	796.332 028

Gongs	786.884 3
see also Percussion instruments	
Goniotrichales	589.41
Gonorrhea	
incidence	614.547 8
medicine	616.951 5
see also Communicable	
diseases (Human)	
Gonorynchiformes	597.55
Gonystylaceae	583.19
Gonzales County (Tex.)	T2—764 257
Goochland County (Va.)	T2—755 455
Good and evil	111.84
ethics	170
religion	291.5
Christianity	241
religion	291.2
Christianity	230
freedom of choice	233.7
natural theology	216
Good Friday	263.92
devotional literature	242.35
music	781.726
sermons	252.62
Good Hope, Cape of (South	
Africa : Cape)	T2—687 35
Good luck spells and charms	133.443
Good News Bible	220.520 8
Goodeniales	583.58
Goodhue County (Minn.)	T2—776 14
Gooding County (Idaho)	T2—796 36
Goodness of God	214
Christianity	231.8
comparative religion	291.211
Goodwill	
property law	346.048
Goodwood (South Africa :	
District)	T2—687 35
Goondiwindi (Qld.)	T2—943 3
Goose Creek Mountains	T2—796 39
Gooseberries	583.397
horticulture	634.725
Goosefoot	583.913
Gorbachev, Mikhail Sergeevich	
Russian history	947.085 4
Gordioida	595.184
Gordon (Scotland : District)	T2—412 32
Gordon County (Ga.)	T2—758 362
Gordon River	T2—946 6
Gordonia (South Africa :	
District)	T2—687 12
Gorges	551.442
	T2—144
geography	910.914 4
geomorphology	551.442
physical geography	910.021 44
Gorgona Island	T2—455 6

Gorgonzola cheese	641.373 53
cooking	641.673 53
processing	637.353
Gorillas	599.884 6
big game hunting	799.278 846
Gorizia (Italy : Province)	T2—453 92
Gorj (Romania)	T2—498 4
Gorki (R.S.F.S.R. : Oblast)	T2—478 1
Gorkovskaia oblast	
(R.S.F.S.R.)	T2—478 1
Gorno-Altai Autonomous	
Oblast (R.S.F.S.R.)	T2—573
Gorno-Altaiskaia	
avtonomnaia oblast	
(R.S.F.S.R.)	T2—573
Gorno-Badakhshan	
Autonomous Oblast	
(Tajik S.S.R.)	T2—586
Goroka (Papua New Guinea)	T2—956 9
Gorzow Wielkopolski	
(Poland : Voivodeship)	T2—438 1
Gosford (N.S.W.)	T2—944 2
Goshen County (Wyo.)	T2—787 18
Gospels (Bible)	226
pseudepigrapha	229.8
Gosper County (Neb.)	T2—782 387
Gosport (England)	T2—422 78
Gossip	
ethics	177.2
see also Ethical problems	
social psychology	302.24
Gotaland (Sweden)	T2—486
Goteborgs och Bohus lan	
(Sweden)	T2—486
Gothic architecture	723.5
Gothic art	709.022
religious significance	246.1
Gothic calligraphy	745.619 75
Gothic decoration	745.442
Gothic fiction	808.838 729
history and criticism	809.387 29
specific literatures	T3B—308 729
individual authors	T3A—3
Gothic kingdom (Italian history)	945.01
Gothic language	439.9
	T6—399
literature	839.9
Gothic music	780.902
Gothic novels	808.838 729
history and criticism	809.387 29
specific literatures	T3B—308 729
individual authors	T3A—3
Gothic painting	759.022
Gothic revival architecture	724.3
Gothic sculpture	734.25
Gothic tracery	729.5
Gothic type	686.224 7
Goths (Germanic people)	T5—39

Government securities (continued)
  purchase
    central banking 332.114
Government service 350.1
  central governments 351.1
  local governments 352.005
Government spending 336.39
  law 343.034
  macroeconomic policy 339.522
  public finance 336.39
Government-sponsored insurance 368.4
  law 344.02
  public administration 351.825 6
  see also Insurance
Government subsidies
  production economics 338.922
Government work force
  public administration 350.4
    central governments 351.4
    local governments 352.005 4
Government workers 350.000 92
  administrative law 342.068
  biography 350.000 92
    central governments 351.000 92
    local governments 352.000 92
  labor economics 331.795
  labor force 331.119 042
  labor market 331.129 042
  lists 350.2
    central governments 351.2
    local governments 352.005 2
  occupational group T7—352 7
    local governments T7—354
  social group 305.553
Governmental institutions
  sociology 306.2
Governmental power
  law 342.041
Governmental social action 361.6
Governments-in-exile
  World War II 940.533 6
Governors (Control devices)
  internal-combustion engines 621.437
Governors (Executives) 351.003 13
  occupational group T7—351 8
Governors-general (Royal
  representatives)
  public administration 351.003 12
Graaff-Reinet (South Africa :
  District) T2—687 14
Grace (Religious doctrine) 291.22
  Christianity 234
Gracias a Dios (Honduras :
  Dept.) T2—728 32
Grade repetition 371.28
Grades (Education) 371.272 1
Grades (Military ranks) 355.33

Grading (Leveling)
  road engineering 625.733
Grading clothing
  commercial technology 687.042
Grading crops 631.567
Grading lumber 674.5
Gradual 264.36
  music 782.323 5
Graduate Record Examination 378.166 2
Graduate schools 378.155 3
Graduation 371.291 2
  customs 394.2
Grady County (Ga.) T2—758 986
Grady County (Okla.) T2—766 54
Graffiti 080
  literature 808.882
    specific literatures T3B—802
      individual authors T3A—8
  painting 751.73
Graft (Crime) 364.132 3
  law 345.023 23
  see also Corruption in
    government
Grafting
  plant propagation 631.541
    equipment manufacturing
      technology 681.763 1
Grafting (Surgery) 617.95
Grafton (N.S.W.) T2—944 3
Grafton County (N.H.) T2—742 3
Graham County (Ariz.) T2—791 54
Graham County (Kan.) T2—781 163
Graham County (N.C.) T2—756 97
Graham Land T2—989
Graham shorthand systems 653.424 4
Grahamstown (South Africa) T2—687 5
Grain (Cereal) 641.331
  animal feed 636.086
    commercial processing 664.762
  commercial processing 664.7
  cooking 641.631
Grain elevators
  agricultural use 633.104 68
Grain legumes
  field crop 633.3
Grain sorghums
  food crop 633.174
Grainger County (Tenn.) T2—768 932
Graining (Woodwork)
  buildings 698.32
Graminales 584.9
  paleobotany 561.49
Grammar 415
  applied linguistics 418
    specific languages T4—8
  education
    elementary 372.61

Grapes	641.348
botany	583.279
commercial processing	664.804 8
cooking	641.648
viticulture	634.8
Graph theory	511.5
Graphic artists	760.092
occupational group	T7—76
Graphic arts	760
Graphic arts paper	676.282
Graphic design arts	741.6
Graphic designers	741.609 2
Graphic expressions psychology	152.384 5
Graphic materials	T1—022
Graphic novels	741.5
Graphic representation	604.2
Graphic statics	
mechanics	531.12
solids	531.2
structural analysis	624.171 2
Graphics	
computer science	006.6
	T1—028 566
engineering	621.399
Graphics programming languages	006.66
Graphics terminals	006.62
Graphics utilities	006.68
Graphite	553.26
chemical engineering	662.92
economic geology	553.26
materials science	620.198
mining	622.336
synthetic	666.86
Graphitic anthracite coal	553.25
economic geology	553.25
properties	662.622 5
Graphology	155.282
criminal investigation	363.256 5
divination	137
personnel selection	658.311 2
Graphs	511.5
	T1—021
statistical presentations	001.422 6
Graptolitoidea	563.71
Graskop (South Africa)	T2—682 6
Grass skiing	796.2
Grass wax	665.12
Grasses	584.9
floriculture	635.964
forage crops	633.2
paleobotany	561.49
Grasshoppers	595.726
Grassland ecology	574.526 43
Grasslands	T2—153
Gratiot County (Mich.)	T2—774 49
Gratitude	179.9
see also Virtues	
Graubünden (Switzerland)	T2—494 73
Graubünden National Park	T2—494 73
Graupel (Soft hail)	551.578 7
Gravel	553.626
economic geology	553.626
materials science	620.191
quarrying	622.362 6
Gravel pavements road engineering	625.82
Graves County (Ky.)	T2—769 93
Graves registration service (Armed forces)	355.699
Gravesham (England)	T2—422 315
Gravestone inscriptions genealogy	929.5
Gravimetric analysis	543.083
Gravitation	531.14
see also Gravity	
Gravitational interaction	539.754
Gravitational prospecting	622.152
Gravity	531.14
biophysics	574.191 32
human	612.014 412
celestial mechanics	521.1
geologic work	551.39
mechanics	531.14
solid mechanics	531.5
Gravity concentration of ores	622.751
Gravity determinations geodesy	526.7
Gravity planes mining	622.66
Gray County (Kan.)	T2—781 74
Gray County (Tex.)	T2—764 827
Gray whales	599.51
Grayling	597.55
Grays Harbor County (Wash.)	T2—797 95
Grayson County (Ky.)	T2—769 842
Grayson County (Tex.)	T2—764 557
Grayson County (Va.)	T2—755 717
Grazing	
animal husbandry	636.084
forestry	634.99
Grazing lands	333.74
economics	333.74
GRE (Graduate Record Examination)	378.166 2
Great Abaco Island	T2—729 6
Great apes	599.884
Great Australian Bight	551.467 76
	T2—165 76
Great Barrier Reef (Qld.)	T2—943
Great Basin	979
	T2—79
Great Basin National Park	T2—793 15
Great Bear Lake (N.W.T.)	T2—719 3

Great Salt Lake Desert (Utah)	T2—792 43
Great Sand Dunes National Monument	T2—788 49
Great Sandy Desert	T2—941 5
Great schism (Christian church history)	270.38
Great Slave Lake (N.W.T.)	T2—719 3
Great Smoky Mountains (N.C. and Tenn.)	T2—768 89
North Carolina	T2—756 96
Tennessee	T2—768 89
Great Smoky Mountains National Park (N.C. and Tenn.)	T2—768 89
Great Trek (South African history)	968.042
Great Valley (Calif.)	T2—794 5
Great Victoria Desert	T2—941 5
Great War, 1914-1918	940.3
Great Western Mountains	T2—946 3
Great White Brotherhood	299.93
Great Yarmouth (England : Borough)	T2—426 18
Greater Anchorage Area Borough (Alaska)	T2—798 35
Greater Antilles	T2—729
Greater Manchester (England)	T2—427 3
Greater Vancouver (B.C.)	T2—711 33
Grebes	598.443
Greco-Roman wrestling	796.812 2
Greco-Turkish War, 1896-1897	949.506
Greece	949.5
	T2—495
ancient	938
	T2—38
Greed	178
see also Vices	
Greek architecture	722.8
Greek calligraphy	745.619 8
Greek language	480
	T6—8
Biblical texts	220.48
printing	686.218
Greek-letter societies	371.85
Greek literature	880
Greek literature (Modern)	889
Greek modes	781.264
Greek philosophy	180
modern	199.495
Greek religion	292.08
Greek revival architecture	724.23
Greek sculpture	733.3
Greeks (Ethnic group)	T5—8
ancient	T5—81
modern	T5—89
Greeks (National group)	T5—893
Greeley County (Kan.)	T2—781 413
Greeley County (Neb.)	T2—782 49

Green algae	589.47
Green bacteria	589.9
Green Bay	T2—775 63
Green County (Ky.)	T2—769 695
Green County (Wis.)	T2—775 86
Green fodder animal feed	636.085 51
Green integral	515.43
Green Lake County (Wis.)	T2—775 59
Green manures	631.874
Green Mountains (Vt.)	T2—743
Green peppers	641.356 43
see also Sweet peppers	
Green River (Ky. : River)	T2—769 8
Green River (Wyo.-Utah)	T2—792 5
Utah	T2—792 5
Wyoming	T2—787 85
Greenbrier	584.323
Greenbrier County (W. Va.)	T2—754 88
Greenbrier River (W. Va.)	T2—754 88
Greene County (Ala.)	T2—761 42
Greene County (Ark.)	T2—767 993
Greene County (Ga.)	T2—758 612
Greene County (Ill.)	T2—773 84
Greene County (Ind.)	T2—772 42
Greene County (Iowa)	T2—777 466
Greene County (Miss.)	T2—762 173
Greene County (Mo.)	T2—778 78
Greene County (N.C.)	T2—756 393
Greene County (N.Y.)	T2—747 37
Greene County (Ohio)	T2—771 74
Greene County (Pa.)	T2—748 83
Greene County (Tenn.)	T2—768 91
Greene County (Va.)	T2—755 375
Greenhouse agriculture	631.583
Greenhouse gardening	635.048 3
floriculture	635.982 3
Greenland	998.2
	T2—982
Greenland Sea	551.468 4
	T2—163 24
Greenlee County (Ariz.)	T2—791 51
Greenockite mineralogy	549.32
Greenough River (W.A.)	T2—941 2
Greensands petrology	552.5
Greensville County (Va.)	T2—755 572
Greenup County (Ky.)	T2—769 293
Greenville County (S.C.)	T2—757 27
Greenwich (London, England)	T2—421 62
Greenwood (B.C.)	T2—711 62
Greenwood County (Kan.)	T2—781 913
Greenwood County (S.C.)	T2—757 33
Greer County (Okla.)	T2—766 443

Ground-effect machines	
engineering	629.3
Ground forces (Military science)	355
Ground inspections	
aircraft	629.134 52
Ground ivy	583.87
Ground operations (Armed	
forces)	355.4
Ground photogrammetry	526.982 5
Ground substances (Histology)	
human	611.018 2
Ground surveying	526.9
photogrammetry	526.982 5
Ground testing facilities	
spacecraft	629.478
unmanned spacecraft	629.468
Ground tests	
aircraft	629.134 52
Ground transportation	388
engineering	629.049
military engineering	623.61
public administration	350.878
central governments	351.878
local governments	352.918
transportation services	388
urban	388.4
see also Urban	
transportation	
Ground transportation facilities	
area planning	711.7
Ground warfare	355
Ground wood process	676.122
Ground zithers	787.73
see also Stringed instruments	
Groundfish	
fishing	639.275 3
Groundhogs	599.323 2
Grounding devices	621.317
radio engineering	621.384 133
Grounding prevention	
sea safety	623.888 4
Groundnuts	641.356 596
see also Peanuts	
Grounds	
landscape architecture	712
prisons	365.5
Grounds management	658.2
libraries	022.1
museums	069.21
public administration	350.713 2
central governments	351.713 2
local governments	352.163 2
Groundwater	553.79
	T2—169 8
artificial recharge	627.56
economic geology	553.79
economics	333.910 4
hydrology	551.49

Groundwater (continued)	
water-supply engineering	628.114
Group banking	332.16
Group behavior	302.3
Group counseling	158.35
Group decision making	
management use	658.403 6
Group dynamics	302.3
Group homes	363.59
chronically ill persons	362.16
see also Health care facilities,	
Health services	
handicapped persons	362.404 85
homeless persons	362.5
maladjusted young people	362.74
mentally ill persons	362.223
see also Mental health	
services	
mentally retarded persons	362.385
old persons	362.61
see also Halfway houses	
Group insurance	368.3
see also Insurance	
Group practice	
medicine	610.65
Group relations training	
social psychology	302.14
Group sex	306.77
Group teaching	371.395
Group therapy	
prisoner services	365.66
psychiatry	616.891 52
see also Mental illness	
Group work	
social welfare	361.4
Grouper	597.58
Groupoids	512.2
Groups (Air force)	358.413 1
Groups (Biological populations)	574.524 6
Groups (Mathematics)	512.2
Groups (Naval air units)	359.943 4
Groups of figures	
art representation	704.942 6
painting	757.6
Grouse	598.616
Growlers (Ice formations)	551.342
Growth	574.31
animals	591.31
cells	574.876 1
developmental biology	574.31
human physiology	612.6
plants	581.31
Growth (Social development)	303.44
Growth movements	
plant physiology	581.183
Growth regulators	
agriculture	631.8
chemical engineering	668.6

Guidance systems	
spacecraft	629.474 2
unmanned spacecraft	629.464 2
Guidebooks	910.202
Guidebooks of exhibits	T1—074
Guided aircraft	
control systems	629.132 6
military engineering	623.746 9
Guided-light communication	621.382 75
Guided missile forces	358.17
in space	358.8
Guided missiles	358.171 82
military engineering	623.451 9
military equipment	358.171 82
Guided missiles in space	358.8
military engineering	623.451 98
military equipment	358.8
Guided-way systems	388.42
see also Local rail transit	
systems	
Guiding equipment (Tools)	621.992
Guild socialism	335.15
Guild system	338.632
Guildford (England :	
Borough)	T2—422 162
Guilford County (N.C.)	T2—756 62
Guilt	
Christianity	233.4
psychology	152.4
Guilt (Law)	345.04
Guinea	966.52
	T2—665 2
Guinea, Gulf of	551.464 73
	T2—163 73
Guinea-Bissau	966.57
	T2—665 7
Guinea-Bissauans	T5—966 57
Guinea fowl	598.618
animal husbandry	636.593
Guinea pigs	599.323 4
animal husbandry	636.932 34
experimental animals	
medicine	619.93
Guineans	T5—966 52
Guipúzcoa (Spain)	T2—466 1
Guiros	786.886
see also Percussion instruments	
Guitar concertos	784.278 7
Guitarfish	597.35
Guitarists	787.870 92
occupational group	T7—787
Guitars	787.87
see also Stringed instruments	
Guizhou Sheng (China)	T2—513 4
Gujar (South Asian people)	T5—914 7
Gujarat (India)	T2—547 5
Gujarati	T5—914 7

Gujarati language	491.47
	T6—914 71
Gujarati literature	891.47
Gulches	551.442
	T2—144
geography	910.914 4
geomorphology	551.442
physical geography	910.021 44
Gulf Coast (U.S.)	976
	T2—76
Gulf County (Fla.)	T2—759 947
Gulf Islands (B.C.)	T2—711 28
Gulf of Aden	551.467 32
	T2—165 32
Gulf of Alaska (Alaska)	551.466 34
	T2—164 34
Gulf of Aqaba	551.467 33
	T2—165 33
Gulf of Bothnia	551.461 34
	T2—163 34
Gulf of Cádiz	551.461 38
	T2—163 38
Gulf of California (Mexico)	551.466 1
	T2—164 1
Gulf of Carpentaria	551.465 75
	T2—164 75
Gulf of Corinth	551.462 6
	T2—163 86
Gulf of Darien	551.463 5
	T2—163 65
Gulf of Finland	551.461 34
	T2—163 34
Gulf of Guayaquil	551.466 1
	T2—164 1
Gulf of Guinea	551.464 73
	T2—163 73
Gulf of Honduras	551.463 5
	T2—163 65
Gulf of Lions	551.462 2
	T2—163 82
Gulf of Mannar	551.467 37
	T2—165 37
Gulf of Maracaibo	551.463 5
	T2—163 65
Gulf of Martaban	551.467 65
	T2—165 65
Gulf of Mexico	551.463 4
	T2—163 64
Gulf of Oman	551.467 36
	T2—165 36
Gulf of Panama	551.466 1
	T2—164 1
Gulf of Papua	551.465 76
	T2—164 76
Gulf of Paria	551.464 66
	T2—163 66
Gulf of Riga	551.461 34
	T2—163 34

Gurumis	787.82
see also Stringed instruments	
Gurus	291.092
Buddhist	294.309 2
role and function	294.361
specific sects	294.39
Hindu	294.509 2
role and function	294.561
specific sects	294.55
role and function	291.61
Sikh	294.609 2
role and function	294.663
Gusii (African people)	T5—963 95
Gusii language	496.395
	T6—963 95
Gustation	591.182 6
animal physiology	591.182 6
human physiology	612.87
Gustatory organs	591.182 6
animal physiology	591.182 6
human anatomy	611.87
Gustatory perception	
psychology	152.167
Gutenberg discontinuity	551.115
Guthrie, Edwin R. (Edwin Ray)	
psychological system	150.194 34
Guthrie County (Iowa)	T2—777 49
Gutta-percha	583.685
Gutters	
road engineering	625.734
Guttiferales	583.163
Guyana	988.1
	T2—881
Guyandotte River (W. Va.)	T2—754 4
Guyane	988.2
	T2—882
Guyanese	T5—914 1
Guyenne (France)	T2—447
Guysborough (N.S. : County)	T2—716 21
Guzmán Blanco, Antonio	
Venezuelan history	987.062
Gwent (Wales)	T2—429 9
Gwinnett County (Ga.)	T2—758 223
Gwydir River	T2—944 4
Gwynedd (Wales)	T2—429 2
Gyarung-Mishmi languages	495.49
	T6—954 9
Gyarung-Mishmi literatures	895.49
Gymnasiums (Secondary	
schools)	373.241
	T1—071 2
Gymnasiums (Sports)	796.406 8
architecture	725.85
educational use	371.624
sports	796.406 8
Gymnastic exercises	613.714
Gymnastics	796.44

Gymnasts	796.440 92
sports group	T7—796 4
Gymnodiniales	589.43
Gymnolaemata	594.71
Gymnophiona	597.7
paleozoology	567.7
Gymnosperms	585
forestry	634.975
paleobotany	561.5
Gympie (Qld.)	T2—943 2
Gynecologic cancer	
medicine	616.994 65
see also Cancer	
Gynecologic disorders	
incidence	614.599 2
Gynecologic nursing	
medicine	610.736 78
Gynecologic surgery	618.105 9
see also Female genital system	
Gynecologists	618.092
law	344.041 2
occupational group	T7—618 1
role and function	618.102 32
see also Female genital system	
Gynecology	618.1
anesthesiology	617.968 1
geriatrics	618.978 1
pediatrics	618.920 98
surgery	618.105 9
see also Female genital system	
Gynoplasty	618.105 9
see also Female genital system	
Gyor-Sopron Megye	
(Hungary)	T2—439 7
Gypsies	T5—914 97
Gypsum	553.635
economic geology	553.635
mineralogy	549.755
mining	622.363 5
petrology	552.5
Gypsum plasters	666.92
Gypsy language	491.499
	T6—914 99
Gypsy literature	891.499
Gyrinoidea	595.762
Gyrocompasses	
aircraft engineering	629.135 1
Gyrodynamics	531.34
Gyrohorizons	629.135 2
Gyropilots	629.135 2
Gyroscopes	
manufacturing technology	681.753
Gyrostemonaceae	583.913

H

H.B.O. (Television)	384.555 4
see also Television	

H.E.A.T. projectiles	623.451 7	Hafnium (continued)	
H.F. Verwoerd Dam (South		chemistry	546.514
Africa)	T2—687 13	metallurgy	669.79
H.I.V. (Viruses)	616.979 201	*see also* Chemicals	
H.M.O. (Social welfare)	362.104 25	Hagerstown (Md.)	T2—752 91
insurance	368.382	Hagfish	597.2
see also Health services		Haggadah (Passover)	296.437
H.M.T.D. (Explosives)	662.27	Haggai (Biblical book)	224.97
H.V.A.P. ammunition	623.451 8	Hagiographa (Bible)	221.042
Haakon County (S.D.)	T2—783 56	Hague (Netherlands)	T2—492 382
Haar integral	515.43	Hahnium	
Haarlem (Netherlands)	T2—492 35	chemistry	546.52
Habad Lubavitch Hasidism	296.833 22	*see also* Chemicals	
Habakkuk (Biblical book)	224.95	Haida Indians	T5—972
Habeas corpus	345.056	Haida language	497.2
civil right	323.422		T6—972
Habersham County (Ga.)	T2—758 125	Haifa (Israel : District)	T2—569 46
Habitat improvement		Haiku	808.814
animal conservation	639.92	history and criticism	809.14
Habitations		specific literatures	T3B—104
animals	591.564	individual authors	T3A—1
Habits		Hail	551.578 7
child training	649.6	Hail damage	
customs	390	agriculture	632.14
psychology	152.33	Hail Mary	242.74
Habituations	362.29	Haile Selassie I, Emperor of	
social welfare	362.29	Ethiopia	
see also Substance abuse		Ethiopian history	963.055
Habré, Hissein		as emperor	963.055
Chadian history	967.430 4	as regent and king	963.054
Habyarimana, Juvénal		Hailstones	
Rwandan history	967.571 04	formation	551.574 7
Hackberry	583.962	precipitation	551.578 7
Hackensack River	T2—749 21	Hailstorms	
Hackney (London, England)	T2—421 44	social services	363.349 2
Hackney horse		*see also* Disasters	
animal husbandry	636.14	Hainaut (Belgium)	T2—493 42
zoology	599.725	Haines Borough (Alaska)	T2—798 2
Hackney pony		Hair	599.018 58
animal husbandry	636.16	animal husbandry	636.088 45
zoology	599.725	geriatrics	618.976 546
Haddock	597.53	human anatomy	611.78
fishing	639.275 3	human diseases	
Haderslev amt (Denmark)	T2—489 5	incidence	614.595 46
Hades	291.23	medicine	616.546
literature	808.803 72	human physiology	612.799
history and criticism	809.933 72	mammalian physiology	599.018 58
specific literatures	T3B—080 372	pediatrics	618.925 46
history and criticism	T3B—093 72	personal care	646.724
see also Hell		pharmacodynamics	615.779
Hadith (Islamic sources)	297.124	surgery	617.477 9
Hadj	297.55	Hair analysis	
Hadrian's Wall	T2—428 81	criminal investigation	363.256 2
Hadrons	539.721 6	Hair dyeing	
Haemodorales	584.29	personal care	646.724 2
Haenertsburg (South Africa)	T2—682 5	Hair removal	
Hafnium	669.79	surgery	617.477 9
chemical engineering	661.051 4	*see also* Hair	

Hair styles	646.724 5
customs	391.5
Hair transplantation	617.477 9
see also Hair	
Hairdressers	646.724 209 2
occupational group	T7—646 7
Hairdressing	646.724 2
customs	391.5
Hairstyling	646.724 5
Hairworm	595.184
Hairy flies	595.771
Haiti	972.94
	T2—729 4
Haitian Creole	447.972 94
	T6—41
Haitian literature	840
Haitians	T5—969 729 4
Hajdu-Bihar Megye (Hungary)	T2—439 9
Hajj	297.55
Hake	597.53
fishing	639.275 3
Hakka dialect	495.17
	T6—951 7
Hakkari Ili (Turkey)	T2—566 2
Hala	584.611
Halakah	296.18
Haldimand-Norfolk (Ont.)	T2—713 36
Hale County (Ala.)	T2—761 43
Hale County (Tex.)	T2—764 842
Half-life periods (Nuclear physics)	539.752
Halfback play	
rugby	796.333 24
soccer	796.334 24
Halfbeak	597.53
Halfmoon (Fish)	597.58
Halftone cuts	
printing	686.232 7
Halfway houses	365.34
corrections	365.34
juvenile offenders	365.42
maladjusted young people	362.74
see also Correctional institutions, Group homes	
Halia language	499.5
	T6—995
Haliburton (Ont. : County)	T2—713 61
Halibut	597.58
commercial fishing	639.275 8
Halicarnassus (Ancient city)	T2—392 4
Halides	
mineralogy	549.4
Halifax (N.S.)	T2—716 225
Halifax (N.S. : County)	T2—716 22
Halifax, Edward Frederick Lindley Wood, Earl of	
Indian history	954.035 8

Halifax County (N.C.)	T2—756 48
Halifax County (Va.)	T2—755 661
Halifax Metropolitan Area (N.S.)	T2—716 225
Halite	
mineralogy	549.4
see also Salt	
Halkomelem language	497.3
	T6—973
Hall Beach (N.W.T.)	T2—719 5
Hall County (Ga.)	T2—758 272
Hall County (Neb.)	T2—782 41
Hall County (Tex.)	T2—764 753
Hall effects in semiconductors	537.622 6
Hallands lan (Sweden)	T2—486
Halle (Germany : Bezirk)	T2—431 84
Halley's comet	523.642
Hallmarks	929.9
	T1—027 8
Halloween	394.268 3
customs	394.268 3
Hallucinogen abuse	362.294
medicine	616.863 4
personal health	613.83
social welfare	362.294
see also Substance abuse	
Hallucinogenic drugs	
pharmacodynamics	615.788 3
Halobacteriaceae	589.95
Halocarbons	547.02
chemical engineering	661.891
toxicology	615.951 2
Halogen gases	
technology	665.83
Halogen salts	
chemical engineering	661.42
Halogenated compounds	
aromatic chemistry	547.62
chemical engineering	661.891
organic chemistry	547.02
toxicology	615.951 2
Halogenated rubber	678.68
Halogenation	547.223
chemical engineering	660.284 423
Halogens	
chemical engineering	661.073
chemistry	546.73
materials science	620.193
organic chemistry	547.02
applied	661.891
see also Chemicals	
Haloragidaceae	583.44
Halos	
meteorology	551.567
Halosphaerales	589.47
Halton (England : Borough)	T2—427 18
Halton (Ont.)	T2—713 533

Handguns	683.43
manufacturing technology	683.43
military engineering	623.443
Handicapped children	305.908 16
	T1—087
home care	649.151
see also Handicapped persons	
Handicapped persons	305.908 16
	T1—087
	T7—081 6
architecture for	720.42
clothing	
home sewing	646.401
education	371.91
law	344.079 11
footwear for	
manufacturing technology	685.38
institutional buildings	
architecture	725.54
legal status	346.013
libraries for	027.663
administration	025.197 663
collection development	025.218 766 3
use studies	025.587 663
museum services	069.17
publications for	
bibliographies	011.63
reviews	028.163
recreation	790.196
indoor	793.019 6
outdoor	796.019 6
self-help devices	617.03
social group	305.908 16
social welfare	362.4
public administration	350.844
central governments	351.844
local governments	352.944 4
Handicapped workers	305.908 16
	T1—087
economics	331.59
law	344.015 9
personnel management	658.304 5
public administration	350.836
central governments	351.836
local governments	352.943 6
Handicraft industries	
economics	338.477 455
production organization	338.642 5
Handicrafters	745.509 2
occupational group	T7—745
Handicrafts	680
arts	745.5
elementary education	372.55
Handkerchiefs	391.44
see also Accessories (Clothing)	
Handreading	133.6

Hands	612.97
human physiology	612.97
regional medicine	617.575
surgery	617.575 059
see also Upper extremities (Human)	
Handwork	
textile arts	746.4
Handwriting	652.1
education	372.634
Handwriting analysis	155.282
criminal investigation	363.256 5
divination	137
personnel selection	658.311 2
Hang gliders	
engineering	629.14
Hang gliding	
engineering	629.14
sports	797.55
Hangars	387.736 2
architecture	725.39
see also Airports	
Hangings	645.2
commercial technology	684.3
home sewing	646.21
household management	645.2
interior decoration	747.3
textile arts	746.3
Hankel functions	515.53
Hankey (South Africa : District)	T2—687 4
Hannover (Germany)	T2—435 954
Hannover (Germany : Regierungsbezirk)	T2—435 95
Hanover (South Africa : District)	T2—687 13
Hanover, House of (British history)	941.07
Hanover, House of (English history)	942.07
Hanover, House of (Scottish history)	941.107
Hanover County (Va.)	T2—755 462
Hansen's disease	
incidence	614.546
medicine	616.998
see also Communicable diseases (Human)	
Hansford County (Tex.)	T2—764 814
Hanson County (S.D.)	T2—783 373
Hants (England)	T2—422 7
Hants (N.S.)	T2—716 35
Hanukkah	296.435
customs	394.268 296 435
Haploid cells	574.32
Haplomi	597.53
Haplosclerida	593.46
Happenings (Art style)	709.040 74

Harp zithers	787.73	Harts Range	T2—942 91
see also Stringed instruments		Harts River	T2—687 11
Harpacticoida	595.34	Hartswater (South Africa :	
paleozoology	565.34	District)	T2—687 11
Harper County (Kan.)	T2—781 845	Hartz Mountains	T2—946 2
Harper County (Okla.)	T2—766 153	Hartz Mountains National	
Harpists	787.909 2	Park	T2—946 2
occupational group	T7—787	Harvest music	781.524 6
Harps	787.9	Harvesting	
see also Stringed instruments		production efficiency	338.163
Harpsichordists	786.409 2	Harvesting	631.55
occupational group	T7—786	equipment manufacturing	
Harpsichords	786.4	technology	681.763 1
see also Keyboard instruments		Harvestman (Arachnid)	595.43
Harquebuses		Harvey County (Kan.)	T2—781 85
art metalwork	739.744 25	Haryana (India)	T2—545 58
Harrier (Dog)		Harz Mountains (Germany)	T2—431 82
animal husbandry	636.753	Hasa (Saudi Arabia)	T2—538
see also Dogs		Haseke (Syria : Province)	T2—569 12
Harriers	598.916	Hashish	
Harris County (Ga.)	T2—758 466	agriculture	633.79
Harris County (Tex.)	T2—764 141	Hashish abuse	362.295
Harrisburg (Pa.)	T2—748 18	medicine	616.863 5
Harrismith (South Africa :		personal health	613.835
District)	T2—685 1	social welfare	362.295
Harrison, Benjamin		*see also* Substance abuse	
United States history	973.86	Hasidism	296.833 2
Harrison, William Henry		Haskell County (Kan.)	T2—781 732
United States history	973.58	Haskell County (Okla.)	T2—766 77
Harrison County (Ind.)	T2—772 21	Haskell County (Tex.)	T2—764 736
Harrison County (Iowa)	T2—777 47	Haskovo (Bulgaria : Okrug)	T2—497 75
Harrison County (Ky.)	T2—769 413	Hasmonean period (Palestinian	
Harrison County (Miss.)	T2—762 13	history)	933.04
Harrison County (Mo.)	T2—778 17	Hassan II, King of Morocco	
Harrison County (Ohio)	T2—771 68	Moroccan history	964.05
Harrison County (Tex.)	T2—764 192	Hastings (England)	T2—422 59
Harrison County (W. Va.)	T2—754 57	Hastings (Neb.)	T2—782 397
Harrison Lake (Fraser-Cheam,		Hastings (Ont. : County)	T2—713 585
B.C.)	T2—711 37	Hastings, Battle of, 1066	942.021
Harrisonburg (Va.)	T2—755 921	Hastings, Francis Rawdon-	
Harrogate (England :		Hastings, Marquess of	
Borough)	T2—428 42	Indian history	954.031 3
Harrow (London, England)	T2—421 86	Hastings, Warren	
Harrows		Indian history	954.029 8
manufacturing technology	681.763 1	Hastings Caves	T2—946 2
Harsha		Hatay Ili (Turkey)	T2—564
Indian history	934.07	Hatcheries	
Hart (England)	T2—422 723	fish culture	639.311
Hart County (Ga.)	T2—758 155	Hatha yoga	
Hart County (Ky.)	T2—769 715	health	613.704 6
Hartbees River	T2—687 12	Hatred	179.8
Hartbeespoort Dam (South		*see also* Vices	
Africa)	T2—682 3	Hats	391.43
Hartebeests	599.735 8	*see also* Headgear	
Hartford (Conn.)	T2—746 3	Hattah Lakes National Park	
Hartford County (Conn.)	T2—746 2	(Vic.)	T2—945 9
Hartlepool (England)	T2—428 57	Hatteras, Cape (N.C.)	T2—756 175
Hartley County (Tex.)	T2—764 823		

Headings (Cataloging)	025.322
Headmasters	371.200 92
personnel management	371.201 2
Heads of government	
occupational group	T7—351
Heads of state	
occupational group	T7—351
Headstart (Education)	372.21
Healesville (Vic.)	T2—945 2
Healing (Spiritual gift)	
Christianity	234.13
Health	613
child care	649.4
elementary education	372.37
medicine	613
sociology	306.461
Health care	362.1
see also Health services	
Health care facilities	362.1
architecture	725.5
law	344.032 1
safety	363.15
sanitation services	363.729 7
see also Waste control	
social welfare	362.1
see also Health services	
Health centers	362.12
see also Health care facilities,	
Health services	
Health cooking	641.563
Health foods	641.302
cooking	641.563 7
Health insurance	368.382
commercial law	346.086 38
government-sponsored	368.42
law	344.022
see also Insurance	
Health maintenance	
organizations	362.104 25
insurance	368.382
see also Insurance	
see also Health services	
Health promotion	
medicine	613
Health protection services	
public administration	350.77
central governments	351.77
local governments	352.4
Health resorts	
personal health	613.122
Health services	362.1
armed forces	355.345
Civil War (United States)	973.775
labor economics	331.255
law	344.032 1
Mexican War	973.627 5

Health services (continued)	
personnel management	658.382
public administration	350.16
central governments	351.16
local governments	352.005 16
prisoner services	365.66
public administration	350.841
central governments	351.841
local governments	352.944 1
social theology	291.178 321
Christianity	261.832 1
social welfare	362.1
South African War	968.048 7
Spanish-American War, 1898	973.897 5
United States Revolutionary	
War	973.375
Vietnamese War	959.704 37
War of 1812	973.527 5
World War I	940.475
World War II	940.547 5
see also Health care facilities	
Health surveys	614.42
Healthy persons	305.908 12
	T7—081 2
Heard County (Ga.)	T2—758 422
Hearing	591.182 5
animal physiology	591.182 5
human physiology	612.85
see also Ears	
Hearing devices	
audiology	617.89
see also Ears	
Hearing examiners (Law)	342.066 4
Hearing-impaired children	305.908 162
	T1—087 2
home care	649.151 2
see also Hearing-impaired	
persons	
Hearing-impaired persons	305.908 162
	T1—087 2
	T7—081 62
education	371.912
library services	027.663
social group	305.908 162
social welfare	362.42
Hearing impairment	
otology	617.8
see also Ears	
Hearsay evidence	347.064
Heart	
human anatomy	611.12
human physiology	612.17
see also Cardiovascular system	
Heart attacks	
medicine	616.123 025
myocardial infarction	616.123 7
see also Cardiovascular system	

Hebrew language (continued)
  printing — 686.219 24
  Talmudic texts — 296.120 4
Hebrew literature — 892.4
Hebrews — T5—924
Hebrews (Biblical book) — 227.87
Hebrides (Scotland) — T2—411 4
Hebron (Jordan : District) — T2—569 51
Hecate Strait (B.C.) — 551.466 33
  — T2—164 33
Heckelphones — 788.52
  see also Woodwind instruments
Hedge laurel — 583.141
Hedgehogs — 599.33
Hedges
  agricultural use — 631.27
  floriculture — 635.976
Hedging (Finance) — 332.645
Hedmark fylke (Norway) — T2—482
Hedonism
  ethical systems — 171.4
Heel-and-toe races — 796.429
Hei-Lung Chiang (China and
  R.S.F.S.R.) — T2—577
Heidelberg (Cape of Good
  Hope, South Africa :
  District) — T2—687 3
Heidelberg (Germany) — T2—434 645
Heidelberg (Transvaal, South
  Africa : District) — T2—682 1
Heidelberg man — 573.3
Heilbron (South Africa :
  District) — T2—685 2
Heilongjiang Sheng (China) — T2—518 4
Heilungkiang Province
  (China) — T2—518 4
Heisenberg representation — 530.122
Hejaz (Saudi Arabia) — T2—538
Helena (Mont.) — T2—786 615
Helicopters — 387.733 52
  engineering — 629.133 352
  military engineering — 623.746 047
  piloting — 629.132 525 2
  transportation services — 387.733 52
  see also Aircraft
Heliographs
  astronomy — 523.702 8
  military engineering — 623.731 2
  nautical engineering — 623.856 12
Heliornithes — 598.31
Heliostats
  astronomy — 523.702 8
Heliotherapy
  medicine — 615.831 4
Heliotrope (Plant) — 583.77
Heliozoa — 593.132
Heliports — 387.736
  engineering — 629.136 16

Heliports (continued)
  military engineering — 623.661 6
  see also Airports
Helium
  chemistry — 546.751
  economic geology — 553.97
  gas technology — 665.822
  see also Chemicals
Helium extraction — 665.73
Hell — 291.23
  Christianity — 236.25
  Islam — 297.23
  literature — 808.803 82
    history and criticism — 809.933 82
    specific literatures — T3B—080 382
     history and criticism — T3B—093 82
  see also Hades
Helleboraceae — 583.111
Hellenic languages — 480
  — T6—8
Hellenic literatures — 880
Hellenic sculpture — 733.3
Hellenistic Greek language — 487.4
  — T6—87
Hellenistic movement (Judaism) — 296.81
Hellenistic period (Egyptian
  history) — 932.021
Hellenistic period (Greek history) — 938.08
Hellenistic period
  (Mesopotamian history) — 935.06
Hellenistic period (Palestinian
  history) — 933.03
Hellenistic World — T2—38
Helmets (Armor) — 623.441
  art metalwork — 739.75
Helmets (Headgear) — 391.43
  see also Headgear
Helminthologists — 595.109 2
  occupational group — T7—595
Helminthology — 595.1
  agriculture — 632.651
  medicine — 616.962
  plant husbandry — 632.651
  veterinary medicine — 636.089 696 2
Helotiales — 589.23
Helotrephoidea — 595.754
Helping behavior — 158.3
Helsinki (Finland) — T2—489 71
Helvetic Republic — 949.405
  — T2—494
Hemangiomas
  medicine — 616.993 13
  see also Diseases (Human)
Hemapheresis
  pharmacology — 615.39
Hematheia (Greece) — T2—495 6
Hematite
  mineralogy — 549.523

Henry VI, King of England	
English history	942.043
Henry VII, King of England	
English history	942.051
Henry VIII, King of England	
English history	942.052
Hepatic jaundice	
medicine	616.362 5
see also Digestive system	
Hepaticae	588.33
Hepatitis	
medicine	616.362 3
Heptarchy (English history)	942.015
Heraclitean philosophy	182.4
Herakleion (Greece : Nome)	T2—499 8
Heraldic design	929.82
decorative arts	745.66
insignia	929.82
Heraldry	929.6
Hérault (France)	T2—448 4
Herb gardens	635.7
Herb teas	641.357
agriculture	635.7
commercial processing	663.96
cooking with	641.657
home preparation	641.877
Herbaceous flowering plants	582.13
Herbaceous plants	582.12
landscape architecture	716
Herbaceous shrubs	582.14
Herbaceous vines	582.14
Herbals	
pharmacognosy	615.321
Herbariums	580.742
Herbert (South Africa :	
District)	T2—687 11
Herbicides	668.654
agricultural use	632.954
chemical engineering	668.654
Herbs	581.63
botany	581.63
commercial processing	664.805 7
food	641.357
cooking	641.657
garden crop	635.7
pharmacognosy	615.321
Hercegovina	T2—497 42
Herculaneum (Ancient city)	T2—377
Herdbooks	636.082 2
Herding animals	
care and training	636.088 6
Herding dogs	
animal husbandry	636.737
see also Dogs	
Heredia (Costa Rica :	
Province)	T2—728 64
Hereditary diseases	
medicine	616.042
Hereditary societies	369.2
Hereditary society members	369.209 2
social group	T7—369 2
Heredity	575.1
animals	591.15
influence on crime	364.24
plants	581.15
psychology	155.7
evolutional psychology	155.7
individual psychology	155.234
Hereford (England)	T2—424 46
Hereford and Worcester	
(England)	T2—424 4
Hereford cattle	
animal husbandry	636.222
zoology	599.735 8
Herero (African people)	T5—963 99
Herero language	496.399
	T6—963 99
Heresy	
Christianity	262.8
in church history	273
criminology	364.188
law	345.028 8
Herkimer County (N.Y.)	T2—747 61
Herm (England)	T2—423 46
Hermanus (South Africa :	
District)	T2—687 3
Hermaphroditism	574.166 7
animals	591.166 7
human	
medicine	616.694
plants	581.166 7
Hermeneutics	121.68
sacred books	291.82
Bible	220.601
Koran	297.122 601
Talmud	296.120 601
Hermetism	135.4
Hermit crab	595.384 4
Hermit Islands	T2—958 1
Hermite polynomials	515.55
Hermitian spaces	515.73
Hernandiaceae	583.931
Hernando County (Fla.)	T2—759 71
Hernando Island (B.C.)	T2—711 31
Hernia	
abdominal surgery	617.559 059
regional medicine	617.559
Heroin abuse	362.293
law	344.044 63
medicine	616.863 2
personal health	613.83
social welfare	362.293
see also Substance abuse	
Heroism	
literature	808.803 53
history and criticism	809.933 53

High Court of Justice (Great
  Britain)   347.420 25
High Court of Justiciary
  (Scotland)   345.411 016
High-energy boron fuels   662.86
High-energy forming   671.3
High-energy physics   539.76
High-explosive ammunition   623.451 7
High explosives   662.27
High-fat cooking   641.563 8
High-fat diet
  health   613.28
High-fidelity systems
  sound reproduction   621.389 332
High jump   796.432
High-level languages   005.13
High-octane-rating gasoline   665.538 25
High Peak (England :
  Borough)   T2—425 11
High polymers
  chemistry   547.84
High-protein diet
  health   613.28
High-rise buildings   720.48
  architectural construction   721.042
  architecture   720.48
  fire hazards   363.379
  see also Fire stations
High school equivalency
  programs   373.238
High schools   373
    T1—071 2
High seas
  law   341.45
High-speed local networks   004.68
  see also Computer
    communications
High-speed photography   778.37
  motion pictures   778.56
High-styrene resins   678.73
High-talent workers
  personnel management   658.304 5
  public administration   350.1
   central governments   351.1
   local governments   352.005 1
High-temperature biology   574.191 62
High-temperature injury
  agriculture   632.12
  biology   574.24
  plant husbandry   632.12
High temperatures   536.57
  chemical engineering   660.296 87
  chemistry   541.368 7
  effect on materials   620.112 17
High-tension electric
  transmission   621.319 13
High Veld (South Africa)   T2—682

High-velocity armor-piercing
  ammunition   623.451 8
High voice   783.3
High-voltage accelerators   539.732
Higher education   378
    T1—071 1
  finance
   law   344.076 84
   private   378.100 681
   public   379.118
   student finances   378.3
  law   344.074
Highland County (Ohio)   T2—771 845
Highland County (Va.)   T2—755 89
Highland Region (Scotland)   T2—411 5
Highland Rim   T2—768 4
  Kentucky   T2—769 6
  Tennessee   T2—768 4
Highlands (Papua New Guinea)   995.6
    T2—956
Highlands (Scotland)   T2—411 5
Highlands County (Fla.)   T2—759 55
Highly volatile petroleum
  products   665.538 2
Highveld (South Africa)   T2—682
Highway accidents   363.125
  see also Transportation safety
Highway engineers   625.709 2
  occupational group   T7—625
Highway patrol   363.233 2
Highway post offices   383.42
  see also Postal service
Highway safety   363.125
  engineering   625.704 2
  law   343.094
  social services   363.125
  see also Transportation safety
Highway transportation   388.31
  see also Road transportation
Highways   388.1
  engineering   625.7
  transportation services   388.1
  see also Roads
Hijacking   364.155 2
  international law   341.772
  law   345.025 52
Hikers   796.510 92
  sports group   T7—796 5
Hiking   796.51
Hilbert spaces   515.733
Hilbert transform   515.723
Hildebrand, Bruno
  economic school   330.154 2
Hildesheim (Germany)   T2—435 958
Hill climbing   796.522
Hill County (Mont.)   T2—786 14
Hill County (Tex.)   T2—764 283
Hillingdon (London, England)   T2—421 83

Histophysiology	574.821
human	611.018
Historians	907.202
occupational group	T7—97
Historic buildings	
law	344.094
Historic political parties	324.212
Historic preservation	363.69
law	344.094
public administration	350.859
central governments	351.859
local governments	352.945 9
social services	363.69
Historic sites	
law	344.094
Historical bibliography	002
Historical books (Old Testament)	222
Historical books (Pseudepigrapha)	229.911
Historical criticism	
sacred books	291.82
Bible	220.67
Koran	297.122 67
Talmud	296.120 67
Historical drama	792.14
literature	808.825 14
history and criticism	809.251 4
specific literatures	T3B—205 14
individual authors	T3A—2
stage presentation	792.14
Historical events	900
art representation	704.949 9
literature	808.803 58
history and criticism	809.933 58
specific literatures	T3B—080 358
history and criticism	T3B—093 58
see also History	
Historical fiction	808.838 1
history and criticism	809.381
specific literatures	T3B—308 1
individual authors	T3A—3
Historical geography	911
Historical geology	551.7
Historical linguistics	417.7
specific languages	T4—7
Historical materialism	
Marxian theory	335.411 9
Historical novels	808.838 1
history and criticism	809.381
specific literatures	T3B—308 1
individual authors	T3A—3
Historical pageants	
performing arts	791.624
Historical periods	909
	T1—090 1–090 5
specific places	930–990
Historical remedies	
therapeutics	615.88

Historical research	001.432
	T1—072 2
Historical school (Economics)	330.154 2
Historical themes	
folklore	398.22
sociology	398.358
painting	758.99
Historical theory of folklore	398.01
Historical treatment	T1—09
Historicism	
philosophy	149
philosophy of history	901
Historicity of Jesus Christ	232.908
Historiographers	907.202
Historiography	907.2
church history	270.072
History	900
	T1—09
Biblical events	220.95
elementary education	372.89
public administration	350.859
central governments	351.859
local governments	352.945 9
specific places	930–990
world	909
History (Theology)	291.211
Christianity	231.76
Judaism	296.311
Hit-and-run tactics	355.422
Hitchcock County (Neb.)	T2—782 845
Hitler, Adolf	
German history	943.086
Hittite language	491.998
	T6—919 98
Hittite literature	891.998
Hittites	T5—919 9
HIV (Viruses)	616.979 201
Hives (Apiary equipment)	
use	638.142
Hives (Disease)	
medicine	616.51
see also Skin	
Hixkaryana language	498
	T6—98
Hjorring amt (Denmark)	T2—489 5
Hlabisa (South Africa : District)	T2—684 3
Hlanganani (South Africa : District)	T2—684 91
Hluhluwe Game Reserve	T2—684 91
HMO (Social welfare)	362.104 25
insurance	368.382
see also Health services	
Hmong (Asian people)	T5—95
Hmong language	495
	T6—95
Hmong literature	895
HMTD (Explosives)	662.27

Holstein-Friesian cattle	
animal husbandry	636.234
zoology	599.735 8
Holston River	T2—768 9
Holt County (Mo.)	T2—778 115
Holt County (Neb.)	T2—782 745
Holy Communion	234.163
public worship	264.36
Anglican	264.030 36
texts	264.03
Roman Catholic	264.020 36
texts	264.023
Holy day work	
economics	331.257 4
Holy days	291.36
Buddhism	294.343 6
Christianity	263.9
devotional literature	242.37
customs	394.268 2
Hinduism	294.536
Islam	297.36
Judaism	296.43
Holy Family	232.92
art representation	704.948 56
Holy Ghost	231.3
Holy Hours	264.7
Holy Orders	234.164
public worship	265.4
Holy Roman Empire	943
	T2—43
Church history	270
German history	943
Holy Spirit	231.3
baptism in	234.12
Holy war (Islam)	297.72
Holy Week	263.92
devotional literature	242.35
music	781.726
Roman Catholic liturgy	264.027 2
sermons	252.62
Home affairs departments	351.03
Home and school	370.193 1
Home-based education	
child care	649.68
Home-based enterprises	
management	658.041
Home Box Office	384.555 4
see also Television	
Home brewing	641.873
Home buying	643.12
Home care services	362.14
see also Health services	
Home Counties	T2—422
Home defense (Military science)	355.45
Home departments	351.03
Home economics	640
customs	392.3
elementary education	372.82

Home economists	640.92
occupational group	T7—64
Home finance	332.722
Home furnishings	645
household management	645
manufacturing technology	684
Home gardens	635
landscape architecture	712.6
Home guards	355.37
Home guards (Active units)	355.351
Home guards (Reserve units)	355.37
Home improvement	
home economics	643.7
Home libraries	643.58
home economics	643.58
interior decoration	747.73
Home loan associations	332.32
Home meals	642.1
Home medicine	616.024
Home missions	266.022
Home movies	791.433
Home nursing	
home economics	649.8
Home ownership	363.583
Home remedies	
therapeutics	615.88
Home rental	643.12
Home repairs	
home economics	643.7
Home reserves (Armed forces)	355.37
Home rule	
law	342.042
local government	320.8
Home safety	363.13
see also Safety	
Home selection	643.12
Home sites	
selection	643.12
Home video systems	621.388
Home workshops	684.08
Homelands (South Africa)	T2—682 9
Cape of Good Hope	T2—687 9
Natal	T2—684 9
Orange Free State	T2—685 9
Transvaal	T2—682 9
Homeless persons	305.569
	T1—086 942
law	344.032 5
social welfare	362.5
see also Poor people	
Homemakers	640.92
	T1—088 649
legal status	346.016 3
social group	T7—649
Homemaking	640
Homeomorphisms	514
Homeopathy	
therapeutic system	615.532

Honor
  literature | 808.803 53
    history and criticism | 809.933 53
    specific literatures | T3B—080 353
      history and criticism | T3B—093 53
Honor rolls (Military)
  Civil War (United States) | 973.76
  Mexican War | 973.626
  South African War | 968.048 6
  Spanish-American War, 1898 | 973.896
  United States Revolutionary
    War | 973.36
  Vietnamese War | 959.704 36
  War of 1812 | 973.526
  World War I | 940.467
  World War II | 940.546 7
Honor societies
  Greek letter | 371.852
Honor system
  education | 371.59
Honorary degrees | 378.25
Honorary insignia
  armed forces | 355.134 2
Honorary titles | T1—079
Honors
  awards | 929.81
  research | 001.44
Honors work | 371.394 2
Honshu (Japan) | T2—521
Hood, Mount (Or.) | T2—795 61
Hood County (Tex.) | T2—764 522
Hood River County (Or.) | T2—795 61
Hookahs | 688.4
Hooked rugs
  arts | 746.74
  see also Rugs
Hooker County (Neb.) | T2—782 777
Hooke's law | 531.382
Hookworm infestations
  incidence | 614.555 4
  medicine | 616.965 4
  see also Communicable
    diseases (Human)
Hoopoes | 598.892
Hoopstad (South Africa :
  District) | T2—685 3
Hoosic River (Mass.) | T2—744 1
Hoover, Herbert
  United States history | 973.916
Hop, step, and jump | 796.432
Hop tree | 583.24
Hope
  Christianity | 234.2
Hope (B.C.) | T2—711 37
Hope Island (B.C.) | T2—711 2
Hopefield (South Africa :
  District) | T2—687 3
Hopeh Province (China) | T2—511 52

Hopetoun (Vic.) | T2—945 9
Hopetown (South Africa :
  District) | T2—687 13
Hopewell (Va.) | T2—755 586
Hopf algebras | 512.55
Hopi Indians | T5—974
Hopi language | 497.45
  | T6—974 5
Hopkins County (Ky.) | T2—769 823
Hopkins County (Tex.) | T2—764 274
Hoplestigmataceae | 583.138
Hoplocarida | 595.382
  paleozoology | 565.38
Hoppers (Railroad cars) | 385.34
  engineering | 625.24
  see also Rolling stock
Hops | 583.962
  agriculture | 633.82
Horary astrology | 133.56
Hordaland fylke (Norway) | T2—483
Hordeeae | 584.93
Horehound | 583.87
Horizontal bars | 796.44
Horizontal combinations
  (Production economics) | 338.804 2
Horizontal property | 346.043 3
Hormic psychology | 150.193
Hormones | 574.192 7
  biochemistry | 574.192 7
    human | 612.405
  chemistry | 547.734
  human physiology | 612.405
  pharmacology | 615.36
  see also Endocrine system
Hormuz, Strait of | 551.467 35
  | T2—165 35
Horn carving | 736.6
Horn concertos | 784.289 4
Horn of Africa | T2—63
Horn players | 788.940 92
  occupational group | T7—788
Hornbeam | 583.976
Hornbills | 598.892
Hornby Island (B.C.) | T2—711 2
Horney, Karen
  psychological system | 150.195 7
Horns | 788.94
  English | 788.53
    see also Woodwind
      instruments
  French | 788.94
    see also Brass instruments
  see also Brass instruments
Hornsby (N.S.W.) | T2—944 1
Hornsby Shire (N.S.W.) | T2—944 1
Hornworts (Anthocerotae) | 588.32
Hornworts (Ceratophyllaceae) | 583.111
Horology | 529.7

Hugh Capet, King of France
French history — 944.021
Hughenden (Qld.) — T2—943 7
Hughes County (Okla.) — T2—766 72
Hughes County (S.D.) — T2—783 29
Huguenots — 284.5
  biography — 284.509 2
  persecution of — 272.4
  religious group — T7—245
  see also Christian
    denominations
Huíla (Angola) — T2—673 5
Huila (Colombia : Dept.) — T2—861 54
Huku language — 496.394
  — T6—963 94
Hukui-ken (Japan) — T2—521 55
Hukuoka-ken (Japan) — T2—522 2
Hukusima-ken (Japan) — T2—521 17
Hull (England) — T2—428 37
Hull (Quebec : County) — T2—714 221
Hull, Clark Leonard
  psychological system — 150.194 34
Hulls (Ships)
  engineering — 623.84
Humacao (P.R. : District) — T2—729 59
Human anatomy — 611
Human body
  folklore
    sociology — 398.353
Human chromosome
  abnormalities
  medicine — 616.042
Human-computer interaction — 004.019
  engineering — 621.398 4
Human ecology — 304.2
  social theology — 291.178 362
    Christianity — 261.836 2
Human engineering — 620.82
Human evolution — 573.2
Human experimentation in
    medicine — 619.98
  law — 344.041 96
Human-factors engineering — 620.82
  computers — 621.39
Human figures
  art representation — 704.942
  drawing — 743.4
  painting — 757
Human genetics — 573.21
Human geography — 304.2
Human immunodeficiency
    viruses — 616.979 201
Human life
  folklore — 398.27
    persons — 398.22
    sociology — 398.35

Human life (continued)
  origin
    religion — 291.22
      Christianity — 233.11
      natural theology — 213
Human physiology — 612
Human pigmentation
  physical anthropology — 573.5
Human qualities
  folklore
    sociology — 398.353
Human races
  physical ethnology — 572
Human relations
  government programs — 350.81
    central governments — 351.81
    local governments — 352.941
Human relations training
  personnel management — 658.312 44
    executives — 658.407 124 4
  public administration — 350.15
    central governments — 351.15
    local governments — 352.005 15
Human reproduction — 612.6
  see also Genital system
Human resources — 331.11
  armed forces — 355.22
  economics — 331.11
  utilization
    economics — 331.125
Human rights — 323
  international law — 341.481
  legal theory — 340.112
  see also Civil rights
Human settlement — 307.14
Human variation
  physical anthropology — 573.22
Humanism
  ethics — 171.2
  literature — 808.803 84
    history and criticism — 809.933 84
    specific literatures — T3B—080 384
      history and criticism — T3B—093 84
  natural religion — 211.6
  philosophy — 144
Humanistic education — 370.112
  curriculums — 375.008 8
Humanitarians — 361.740 92
  social group — T7—361
Humanities — 001.3
  law — 344.097
  public administration — 350.854
    central governments — 351.854
    local governments — 352.945 4
Humanity of Jesus Christ — 232.8
Humankind
  paleozoology — 569.9
  philosophy — 128

Hunting dogs (continued)	
sports	799.234
see also Dogs	
Hunting industries	
products	
commerce	380.143 2–.143 9
public administration	351.823 6
Hunting laws	346.046 954
Hunting lodges	
architecture	728.7
Huntingdon (Quebec : County)	T2—714 31
Huntingdon County (Pa.)	T2—748 73
Huntingdonshire (England : District)	T2—426 54
Huntington County (Ind.)	T2—772 71
Huntsville (Ala.)	T2—761 97
Huon Peninsula	T2—957 1
Huon River	T2—946 2
Huonville (Tas.)	T2—946 2
Hupeh Province (China)	T2—512 12
Hurdlers	796.426 092
sports group	T7—796 4
Hurdles (Race)	
horses	798.45
human	796.426
Hurdy-gurdies	787.69
see also Stringed instruments	
Huron (Ont. : County)	T2—713 22
Huron, Lake (Mich. and Ont.)	T2—774
Michigan	T2—774
Ontario	T2—713 2
Huron County (Mich.)	T2—774 44
Huron County (Ohio)	T2—771 25
Huron Indians	T5—975
Huron language	497.5
	T6—975
Hurrian languages	499.9
	T6—999
Hurricanes	
meteorology	551.552
social services	363.349 2
weather forecasting	551.645 2
weather modification	551.685 2
see also Disasters	
Husband and wife	306.872
law	346.016 3
Husbands	306.872
	T1—086 55
family relationships	306.872
Huskers	
manufacturing technology	681.763 1
Husking	631.56
Husky	
animal husbandry	636.73
see also Dogs	
Hussein Onn, Datuk	
Malaysian history	959.505 3
Hussite Wars, 1419-1436	943.702 24
Hussites	284.3
religious group	T7—243
see also Christian denominations	
Hutchinson County (S.D.)	T2—783 384
Hutchinson County (Tex.)	T2—764 821
Hutias	599.323 4
Hutterite Brethren	289.73
see also Mennonite Church	
HVAP ammunition	623.451 8
Hwang Ho (China)	T2—511
Hyacinth	584.324
Hyaenidae	599.744 27
Hyaline cartilage	
human histology	611.018 3
see also Musculoskeletal system	
Hyalospongiae	593.44
paleozoology	563.4
Hybrid computers	004.19
architecture	004.259
communications	004.619
programming	005.712 9
programs	005.713 9
engineering	621.391 9
graphics programming	006.679
graphics programs	006.689
interfacing	004.619
programming	005.712 9
programs	005.713 9
operating systems	005.449
performance evaluation	004.190 297
for improvement and design	004.259
peripherals	004.719
programming	005.29
programs	005.39
systems analysis	004.259
systems design	004.259
Hybrids	575.132
agriculture	631.523
animal husbandry	636.082 43
botany	581.158
genetics	575.132
plant breeding	631.523
zoology	591.158
Hydatid diseases	
incidence	614.554
medicine	616.964
see also Communicable diseases (Human)	
Hyde County (N.C.)	T2—756 184
Hyde County (S.D.)	T2—783 283
Hyderabad (India : State)	T2—548 4
Hyderabad District (Pakistan)	T2—549 182
Hydnaceae	589.222
Hydnoraceae	583.922
Hydrangea	583.397
Hydrangeaceae	583.397

Hydroxides	
mineralogy	549.53
Hydroxy compounds	547.03
aromatic chemistry	547.63
chemical engineering	661.8
Hydroxyketone dyes	667.256
Hydrozoa	593.71
paleozoology	563.71
Hyenas	599.744 27
Hyeniales	561.72
Hygiene	613
customs	391.64
elementary education	372.37
personal	613
veterinary medicine	636.089 3
Hygienists	613.092
Hylidae	597.87
Hylobatinae	599.882
Hymen	
gynecology	618.1
human anatomy	611.67
human physiology	612.62
see also Female genital system	
Hymenogastrales	589.221
Hymenoptera	595.79
paleozoology	565.79
Hymenostraca	565.36
Hymns	782.27
choral and mixed voices	782.527
religion	291.38
Christianity	264.2
private devotions	245
Judaism	296.4
private devotions	296.72
private devotions	291.43
single voices	783.092 7
Hyndburn (England :	
Borough)	T2—427 625
Hyōgo-ken (Japan)	T2—521 87
Hyperactive children	
home care	649.153
Hyperactive students	371.93
Hyperactivity	
medicine	616.858 9
pediatrics	618.928 589
see also Nervous system	
Hyperadrenalism	
medicine	616.45
see also Endocrine system	
Hyperbola	516.15
Hyperbolic equations	515.353
Hyperbolic geometry	516.9
Hyperboloids	516.15
Hyperborean languages	494.6
	T6—946
Hyperborean literatures	894.6
Hyperfunctions	515.9
Hypergeometric polynomials	515.55

Hypericaceae	583.163
Hyperiidea	595.371
Hyperkinesia	
medicine	616.858 9
see also Nervous system	
Hypermastigida	593.18
Hyperoliidae	597.89
Hyperons	539.721 64
Hyperparathyroidism	
medicine	616.445
see also Endocrine system	
Hyperpinealism	
medicine	616.48
see also Endocrine system	
Hypersensitivity	
incidence	614.599 3
medicine	616.97
see also Diseases (Human)	
Hypersonic flow	533.276
air mechanics	533.62
aeronautics	629.132 306
Hypertension	
medicine	616.132
see also Cardiovascular system	
Hyperthyroidism	
medicine	616.443
see also Endocrine system	
Hypertrichosis	
medicine	616.546
see also Hair	
Hypertrophic arthritis	
medicine	616.722 3
see also Musculoskeletal system	
Hypertrophies	
skin	
medicine	616.544
see also Skin	
Hyperventilation	
medicine	616.208
see also Respiratory system	
Hyphochytridiomycetes	589.258
Hyphomicrobium	589.94
Hypnotherapy	
medicine	615.851 2
Hypnotic regression	
occultism	133.901 3
Hypnotics	
pharmacodynamics	615.782
Hypnotism	154.7
parapsychology	133.8
Hypoadrenalism	
medicine	616.45
see also Endocrine system	
Hypochondria	
medicine	616.852 5
see also Mental illness	

Hypoglycemia
  medicine   616.466
  see also Endocrine system
Hypoparathyroidism
  medicine   616.445
  see also Endocrine system
Hypostatic union   232.8
Hypothalamus
  human anatomy   611.81
  human physiology   612.826 2
  see also Nervous system
Hypothermia
  medicine   616.989
  therapeutic use   615.832 9
Hypotheses
  logic   167
Hypotheses (Mathematics)   511.3
Hypothesis testing (Statistics)   519.56
Hypothyroidism
  medicine   616.444
  see also Endocrine system
Hypoxidaceae   584.29
Hyracoidea   599.62
  paleozoology   569.6
Hyraxes   599.62
Hyrcania   T2—396
Hyssop   583.87
Hysterectomies
  surgery   618.145 3
  see also Female genital system
Hysteresis (Magnetism)   538.3
Hysteria
  medicine   616.852 4
  see also Mental illness
Hystricomorpha   599.323 4

I

I.C.B.M. (Missiles)   358.175 482
  military engineering   623.451 954
  military equipment   358.175 482
I.L.O. (Labour office)
  law   341.763
I.M.F. (Fund)   332.152
  law   341.751
I.Q. tests   153.93
I.R.A. (Retirement account)   332.024 01
  tax law   343.052 33
I.R.B.M. (Missiles)   358.175 382
  military engineering   623.451 953
  military equipment   358.175 382
I Región (Chile)   T2—831 2
I.S.B.D. (Bibliographic
  description)   025.324
I.S.B.N. (Standard book number)   025.3
I.S.S.N. (Standard serial number)   025.343 2

I.U.D. (Contraceptive)
  health   613.943 5
  see also Birth control
I.W.W. (Labor)   331.886
IAkutskaia A.S.S.R.
  (R.S.F.S.R.)   T2—575
Ialomita (Romania)   T2—498 2
IAmbolski okrug (Bulgaria)   T2—497 78
IAroslavskaia oblast
  (R.S.F.S.R.)   T2—473 1
Iasi (Romania : Judet)   T2—498 1
Iatrogenic diseases
  medicine   615.5
Ibaraki-ken (Japan)   T2—521 31
Iberia (Georgian S.S.R.)   T2—395
Iberia Parish (La.)   T2—763 49
Iberian Peninsula   946
     T2—46
  ancient   936.6
     T2—366
Iberville (Quebec : County)   T2—714 61
Iberville Parish (La.)   T2—763 44
Ibibio (African people)   T5—963 6
Ibibio language   496.36
     T6—963 6
Ibises   598.34
Ibiza Island (Spain)   T2—467 56
Ibn Majah, Muhammad ibn
    Yazid
  Hadith   297.124 6
Ibo (African people)   T5—963 32
Ibo language   496.332
     T6—963 32
Ibo literature   896.332
Ica (Peru : Province)   T2—852 7
Icacinaceae   583.271
Icarianism (Socialist school)   335.2
ICBM (Missiles)   358.175 482
  military engineering   623.451 954
  military equipment   358.175 482
Ice   551.31
  building construction   693.91
  economic geology   553.7
  geology   551.31
  manufacturing technology   621.58
  mineralogy   549.522
Ice age   551.792
  geology   551.792
  paleontology   560.178
Ice carving   736.94
Ice control
  road engineering   625.763
Ice cream   641.862
  commercial processing   637.4
  home preparation   641.862
Ice crossings
  railroad engineering   625.147
  road engineering   625.792

Ice dancing	796.912
Ice fishing	799.12
Ice formation	
aeronautics	629.132 4
Ice games	796.96
Ice hockey	796.962
electronic games	794.869 62
Ice hockey players	796.962 092
sports group	T7—796 9
Ice milk	641.862
home preparation	641.862
manufacturing	637.4
Ice roads	388.12
engineering	625.792
see also Roads	
Ice skaters	796.910 92
sports group	T7—796 9
Ice skates	
manufacturing technology	685.361
Ice skating	796.91
Ice sports	796.9
equipment technology	688.769
Ice storms	551.559
Icebergs	551.342
Iceboating	796.97
Icebreakers	387.28
design	623.812 8
engineering	623.828
see also Ships	
Icebreaking services	387.54
Icel (Turkey : Province)	T2—564
Iceland	949.12
	T2—491 2
Icelanders	T5—396 1
Icelandic language	439.69
	T6—396 91
Icelandic literature	839.69
Icelandic people	T5—396 1
Ices	641.863
home preparation	641.863
manufacturing	637.4
Ichneumonoidea	595.79
Ichneumons	595.79
Ichthyologists	597.009 2
occupational group	T7—597
Ichthyology	597
Ichthyornithiformes	568.23
Ichthyosauria	567.93
Ichthyosis	
medicine	616.544
see also Skin	
Iconography	
arts	704.9
drawing	743.9
painting	753–758
Icons	
arts	704.948
Christianity	704.948 2

Icons (continued)	
religious significance	
Christianity	246.53
Icteridae	598.881
Id (Psychology)	154.22
Ida County (Iowa)	T2—777 422
Idaho	979.6
	T2—796
Idaho County (Idaho)	T2—796 82
Ideal states	
political system	321.07
Idealism	141
literature	808.801 3
history and criticism	809.913
specific literatures	T3B—080 13
history and criticism	T3B—091 3
Ideals (Mathematics)	512.4
algebra	512.4
number theory	512.74
Ideas	
epistemology	121.4
psychology	153.2
Ideation	
epistemology	121
psychology	153.2
Idée fixe	
musical element	781.248
Identification	
arts	702.87
Identification marks	929.9
	T1—027
Identification of criminals	363.258
Identity (Human)	155.2
philosophy	126
Identity (Principle of)	111.82
Ideographs	411
specific languages	T4—11
Ideologies (Political science)	320.5
political parties	324.23
Ideology	140
philosophical system	145
Idiophones	786.82
see also Percussion instruments	
Idlib (Syria : Province)	T2—569 13
Idocrase	
mineralogy	549.63
Idolatry	291.218
Idols	291.218
Idoma (African people)	T5—963 3
Idoma language	496.33
	T6—963 3
Idris I, King of Libya	
Libyan history	961.204 1
Idutywa (South Africa : District)	T2—687 91
Ife (Kingdom)	966.928 01
	T2—669 28
Ifrane (Morocco : Province)	T2—643

Ifugao (Philippines)	T2—599 1	Illegitimacy	306.874
Ig (Immunoglobulin)		law	346.017
human	616.079 3	Illegitimate children	305.906 945
Igala (African people)	T5—963 33		T1—086 945
Igala language	T6—963 33	family relationships	306.874
Igbo (African people)	T5—963 32	social group	305.906 945
Igbo language	496.332	social welfare	362.708 694 5
	T6—963 32	Illiciaceae	583.114
Igbo literature	896.332	Illicit distilling	364.133
Igloos		law	345.023 3
construction	693.91	Illinois	977.3
Igneous rocks	552.1		T2—773
Ignition	541.361	Illinois River (Ill.)	T2—773 5
chemical engineering	660.296 1	Illiteracy	302.224 4
chemistry	541.361	government policy	379.24
Ignition systems		sociology	302.224 4
automotive	629.254	Illiterate persons	305.906 33
internal-combustion engines	621.437		T1—086 33
Igoolik (N.W.T.)	T2—719 5	Illness	362.1
II Región (Chile)	T2—831 3	medicine	616
III Región (Chile)	T2—831 4	*see also* Diseases (Human)	
IJssel Lake (Netherlands)	T2—492 2	Illuminating engineering	621.32
IJssel River (Netherlands)	T2—492 18	Illumination	621.32
Ik (African people)	T5—965	*see also* Lighting	
Ikhnaton, King of Egypt		Illumination (Decorative arts)	745.67
Egyptian history	932.014	Illuminations (Performing arts)	791.6
Ilam (Iran : Province)	T2—555 2	Illusions	001.96
Ilamba-Irangi languages	496.394	psychology of perception	153.74
	T6—963 94	Illustration	
Île aux Grues (Quebec)	T2—714 735	arts	741.6
Ile-de-France (France)	T2—443 4	Illustrations	T1—022
Île de la Gonâve	T2—729 45	notable books	096.1
Île de la Tortue	T2—729 42	Illustrators	741.609 2
Île-de-Montréal (Quebec)	T2—714 27	occupational group	T7—74
Île d'Orléans (Quebec)	T2—714 48	Illyria	T2—398
Île-Jésus (Quebec)	T2—714 27	Illyrian languages	491.993
Ileitis			T6—919 93
medicine	616.344 5	Ilmenite	
see also Digestive system		mineralogy	549.523
Ileostomy	617.554 1	ILO (Labour office)	
Îles-de-la-Madeleine		law	341.763
(Quebec)	T2—714 797	Ilocos Norte (Philippines)	T2—599 1
Ileum		Ilocos Sur (Philippines)	T2—599 1
human anatomy	611.341	Iloilo (Philippines : Province)	T2—599 5
surgery	617.554 1	Iloko language	499.21
see also Digestive system			T6—992 1
Ilía (Greece)	T2—495 2	Ilorin (Nigeria)	T2—669 57
ancient	T2—388	Ilubabor (Ethiopia : Province)	T2—633
Iliamma Lake	T2—798 4	Image processing	621.367
Ilium (Ancient City)	T2—392 1	computer science	006.42
Ill persons	305.908 14	engineering	621.399
	T1—087 7	Imagery (Psychology)	153.32
		Images	
see also Sick persons		arts	704.9
Illawarra, Lake	T2—944 6	religious significance	291.37
Ille-et-Vilaine (France)	T2—441 5	Christianity	246.53
Illecebraceae	583.917	religious worship	291.218
Illecillewaet River (B.C.)	T2—711 68		

Imaginary wars	
military analysis	355.48
Imagination	153.3
education	370.157
philosophy	128.3
Imamat	297.24
Islamic organization	297.65
Imams	297.092
role and function	297.61
specific sects	297.8
Imathia (Greece)	T2—495 6
Imbabura (Ecuador)	T2—866 12
Imbibition processes	773.3
Imbros Island	T2—562
ancient	T2—391 1
IMF (Fund)	332.152
law	341.751
Imidazoles	547.593
chemical engineering	661.894
Imitation furs	675.3
Imitation-leather covers	
bookbinding	686.343
Imitation leathers	675.4
Imitative learning	
psychology	153.152 3
Immaculate Conception of Mary	232.911
Immigrants	
labor economics	331.62
Immigration	304.82
influence on crime	364.256
international law	341.484 2
law	342.082
political science	325.1
public administration	351.817
Immigration law	342.082
Immorality	170
religion	291.5
Christianity	241
Immortality	
philosophy	129
religion	291.23
Christianity	236.22
Islam	297.23
Judaism	296.33
Immune deficiency diseases	
incidence	614.599 3
medicine	616.979
see also Diseases (Human)	
Immune reactions	574.295
animals	591.295
human	616.079 5
plants	581.295
Immune system	
diseases	
medicine	616.97
see also Diseases (Human)	
Immunity	574.29
animals	591.29
Immunity (continued)	
humans	616.079
Immunity of legislators	328.348
Immunization	
disease control	614.47
law	344.043
Immunoassays	
medicine	616.075 6
Immunodiagnosis	
medicine	616.075 6
Immunogenetics	574.29
medicine	616.079
Immunoglobulins	574.293
human	616.079 3
Immunologic diseases	
medicine	616.97
see also Diseases (Human)	
Immunologic drugs	
pharmacology	615.37
Immunology	574.29
humans	616.079
plants	581.29
Immunosuppression	
medicine	616.079
Immunotherapy	615.37
Imo State (Nigeria)	T2—669 46
Impact strength	
materials science	620.112 5
Impact studies	333.714
environmental protection	363.7
law	344.046
natural resources	333.714
Impatiens	583.216
floriculture	635.933 216
Impeachment	
chief executives	
public administration	350.003 6
central governments	351.003 6
local governments	352.008
public administration	350.993
central governments	351.993
local governments	352.002
Impeachment power (Legislative bodies)	328.345 3
Impendle (South Africa : District)	T2—684 7
Imperia (Italy : Province)	T2—451 87
Imperial County (Calif.)	T2—794 99
Imperial system (Measurement)	530.813
physics	530.813
social aspects	389.15
Imperial Valley (Calif.)	T2—794 99
Imperialism	325.32
international relations	327.1
Impersonation	792.028
motion pictures	791.430 28
radio	791.440 28
stage	792.028

Incest (continued)
medicine	616.858 3
sociology	306.877
see also Mental illness	
Incidence geometry	516.12
Incidental dramatic music	781.552

Incineration
sewage sludge disposal	628.37
solid waste technology	628.445 7
waste disposal	363.728
see also Waste control	

Incisions (Wounds)
medicine	617.143
Inclined railroads	385.6
engineering	625.3
transportation services	385.6
see also Railroad transportation	

Inclines
canal engineering	627.135 3

Income
agriculture	338.13
analytical accounting	657.48
financial management	658.155 4
increase	
personal finance	332.024 01
labor economics	331.21
macroeconomics	339.3
mineral industries	338.23
secondary industries	338.43
transportation services	388.049

Income accounts
macroeconomics	339.3

Income-consumption relations
macroeconomics	339.41

Income distribution
macroeconomics	339.2

Income maintenance
social welfare	362.582

Income policy
macroeconomics	339.5

Income redistribution
macroeconomic policy	339.52

Income statements
financial management	658.151 2
Income tax	336.24
law	343.052
public administration	350.724 4
central governments	351.724 4
local governments	352.135
public finance	336.24

Income theory
monetary economics	332.401

Incompatibilities
logic	160

Incompressible airflow
aeronautics	629.132 322
Inconvertible money	332.427
Incorporated banks	332.122

Incorporation
law	346.066 22

Incorporation (Municipalities)
government	320.85

Incrustation
architectural decoration	729.6
Incubi	133.423
Incunabula	093
bibliographies	011.42
Indecent exposure	364.153
law	345.025 3

Indemnification
law of war	341.66

Indentured labor
sociology	306.363
Independence County (Ark.)	T2—767 26
Independence days	394.268 4

Independencia (Dominican Republic) | T2—729 325

Independent agencies
public administration	350.009
central governments	351.009
local governments	352.009

Independent Fundamental Churches of America | 289.95
see also Christian denominations

Independent Fundamentalist and Evangelical churches | 289.95
see also Christian denominations

Independent Methodists | 287.533
see also Methodist Church

Independent Order of Odd
Fellows	366.3
members	366.309 2
Independent retail stores	381.1
management	658.870 1
see also Commerce	
Independent schools	371.02
Independent study	371.394 3

Indeterminacy composition
music	781.32
Indeterminate equations	515.253
Indeterminate sentence	364.62
penology	364.62
Indeterminism	123
Index librorum prohibitorum	098.11
Index theorems	514.74
Indexing	025.3
information science	025.3
museology	069.52
subject	025.48
India	954
	T2—54
ancient	934
	T2—34
India-rubber tree	583.962

Induction of employees	
armed forces	355.223
personnel management	658.312 42
public administration	350.15
central governments	351.15
local governments	352.005 15
Induction welding	671.521 5
Inductive charging	
ores	622.77
Inductive mathematics	511.22
Inductive reasoning	
logic	161
psychology	153.432
Inductors	
radio engineering	621.384 133
Indulgences (Christian rite)	265.66
Indus River	T2—549 1
Industrial accidents	363.11
insurance	368.56
government-sponsored	368.41
see also Insurance	
see also Safety	
Industrial advertising	659.131 5
Industrial air conditioning	
buildings	697.931 6
Industrial arbitration	331.891 43
law	344.018 914 3
Industrial archaeology	
economic aspects	338.09
historical aspects	900
technological aspects	609
Industrial areas	
area planning	711.552 4
Industrial art	745.2
Industrial arts	600
Industrial banks	332.37
Industrial biochemistry	660.63
Industrial biology	660.6
Industrial botany	581.64
Industrial buildings	
architecture	725.4
construction	690.54
landscape architecture	712.7
sale and rental	333.338 7
Industrial casualty insurance	368.7
see also Insurance	
Industrial chemicals	661
toxicology	615.902
Industrial chemistry	660
Industrial chemists	660.092
occupational group	T7—661
Industrial cities	307.766
area planning	711.45
Industrial concentration	338.8
Industrial conditions	338.09
Industrial conflict	
sociology	306.34
Industrial credit	332.742
Industrial democracy	331.011 2
economics	331.011 2
Industrial democracy theory of	
unions	331.880 1
Industrial design	745.2
Industrial development	338.9
international banking	332.153
public administration	350.82
central governments	351.82
cabinet departments	351.082
local governments	352.942
Industrial diamonds	553.65
Industrial diseases	
health	613.62
medicine	616.980 3
see also Environmental diseases	
(Human)	
Industrial drawing	T1—022 1
Industrial economics	338
Industrial engineering	670.42
Industrial engineering	
(Production management)	658.5
Industrial espionage	364.16
law	343.072
management	658.472
Industrial fats	665
Industrial gases	665.7
equipment manufacturing	
technology	681.766 5
Industrial hazards	363.11
see also Safety	
Industrial health	613.62
Industrial insurance	368.3
accident	368.56
government-sponsored	368.41
life	368.362
see also Insurance	
Industrial land use	
community sociology	307.332
Industrial lands	333.77
economics	333.77
sale and rental	333.336
Industrial law	343.07
Industrial libraries	027.69
Industrial life insurance	368.362
see also Insurance	
Industrial medicine	616.980 3
Industrial microbiology	660.62
Industrial-military complex	355.021 3
military science	355.021 3
sociology	306.27
Industrial minerals	553.6
economic geology	553.6
Industrial mobilization	355.26
law	343.01
Industrial noise	363.741
see also Noise	

Inland water transportation
  workers | 386.092
  occupational group | T7—386
Inland waters
  hydrology | 551.48
Inland waterway transportation | 386
  engineering | 629.048
  law | 343.096 4
  public administration | 351.876
  transportation services | 386
Inland waterways
  engineering | 627.1
Inlay trim
  furniture arts | 749.5
  wood handicrafts | 745.51
Inlays
  dentistry | 617.675
  see also Dentistry
Inmates (Prisoners) | 365.6
| T1—086 92
Innate ideas | 121.4
Innate reflexes
  psychology | 152.322 3
Innate virtues (Christian
  doctrines) | 234
Inner ear
  human physiology | 612.858
  see also Internal ear
Inner Hebrides (Scotland) | T2—411 8
Inner House of Court of Session
  (Scotland) | 347.411 035
Inner Mongolia (China) | T2—517 7
Inner Mongolia Autonomous
  Region (China) | T2—517 7
Inner product spaces | 515.733
Inner tubes | 678.35
Innervation | 591.188
  human heart | 612.178
  human muscles | 612.743
  human physiology | 612.81
  human respiratory system | 612.28
  human skin | 612.798
  see also Nervous system
Innisfail (Qld.) | T2—943 6
Innocent passage | 341.4
Innomine form | 784.187 6
Innovation
  agent of social change | 303.484
  executive management | 658.406 3
Inns | 647.94
  see also Hotels
Innuit | T5—971
Innuit language | 497.1
| T6—971
Innuit literature | 897.1
Inoculation
  disease control | 614.47

Inonu, Ismet
  Turkish history | 956.102 5
Inorganic biochemistry | 574.192 14
  human | 612.015 24
Inorganic chemistry | 546
  applied | 660
Inorganic drugs
  pharmacology | 615.2
Inorganic poisons
  toxicology | 615.92
Inorganic substances
  metabolism | 574.133
    human physiology | 612.392
    see also Digestive system
Inosilicates
  mineralogy | 549.66
Input-output accounts
  macroeconomics | 339.23
Input-output peripherals | 004.75
  engineering | 621.398 5
Input peripherals | 004.76
  computer engineering | 621.398 6
Inquiry
  epistemology | 121.6
Inquisition (Church history) | 272.2
Insanity | 362.2
  legal defense | 345.04
  literature | 808.803 53
    history and criticism | 809.933 53
    specific literatures | T3B—080 353
      history and criticism | T3B—093 53
  see also Mental illness
Inscriptions
  architectural design | 729.19
  paleography | 411.7
    specific languages | T4—11
  prints | 769.5
  stone | 736.5
Insect control | 363.78
  home economics | 648.7
  sanitary engineering | 628.965 7
  social welfare | 363.78
  see also Pest control
Insect culture | 638
Insect culturists | 638.092
  occupational group | T7—638
Insect venom
  toxicology | 615.942
Insect waxes | 665.13
Insecta | 595.7
  see also Insects
Insecticide-producing plants
  agriculture | 633.898
Insecticides | 668.651
  agricultural economics | 338.162
  agricultural use | 632.951
  chemical engineering | 668.651

Insectivora	599.33
paleozoology	569.33
Insectivorous plants	583.121
Insects	595.7
agricultural pests	632.7
art representation	704.943 2
disease carriers	614.432
drawing	743.657
food	641.396
commercial processing	664.95
cooking	641.696
home preservation	641.495
paleozoology	565.7
plant crop pests	632.7
resource economics	333.955
Insider trading in securities	364.168
law	346.092
Insignia	929.9
armed forces	355.134 2
rank and service	355.14
religious significance	
Christianity	246.56
Insolvency	
law	346.078
Insomnia	
symptomatology	
neurological diseases	616.849 8
see also Nervous system	
Inspection	
engineering	620.004 4
military administration	355.63
production management	658.568
public administration	
external	350.009 1
central governments	351.009 1
local governments	352.009 2
internal	350.007 6
central governments	351.007 6
local governments	352.000 476
Inspection technology	670.425
Inspectors general (Armed forces)	355.63
Inspiration	
Bible	220.13
Instabilities in semiconductors	537.622 6
Installations (Armed forces)	355.7
Installment sales	
law	346.074
tax law	343.055 2
Instant cameras	771.32
Instant photography	770
Instantaneous systems	003.8
Instinctive movements	
psychology	152.324
Institutes (Adult education)	T1—071 52
Institutes (Roman law)	340.54
Institutional care	
social welfare	361.05
Institutional cooking	641.57
Institutional exemptions	
customs duties	382.782
see also Customs (Tariff)	
Institutional grounds	
landscape architecture	712.7
Institutional households	
household management	647.96
Institutional housekeeping	647
Institutional investment	332.671 54
domestic	332.672 54
international	332.673 14
Institutional investors	332.671 54
domestic	332.672 54
international	332.673 14
Institutional nursing	
medicine	610.733
Institutional publishers	070.594
Institutional school	
economics	330.155
Institutionalized children	
psychology	155.446
Institutions (Sociology)	306
Instruction	371.102
Instruction services	
museology	069.15
Instructional materials centers	371.307 8
Instructions to juries	347.075 8
criminal law	345.075
Instrument flying	629.132 521 4
Instrumental ensembles	784
Instrumental forms	784.18
Instrumentalism	144.5
Instrumentation	
aircraft	629.135
analytical chemistry	543.07
physics	530.7
weather reporting	551.635
Instruments	
music	784.19
Insulating materials	
building materials	691.95
materials science	620.195
Insulation	
building construction	693.83
electrical circuits	621.319 37
heat engineering	621.402 4
steam engineering	621.185
Insulators	
electrical circuits	621.319 37
Insulin	596.013 3
chemistry	547.734 5
human physiology	612.34
pharmacology	615.365
physiology	596.013 3
see also Digestive system, Endocrine system	

Insulin therapy
  psychiatry   616.891 2
  see also Mental illness
Insurance   368
  accounting   657.73
  financial management   658.153
  labor economics   331.255
  law   346.086
  personnel management   658.325 4
  public administration   351.825 5
Insurance agents   368.009 2
  occupational group   T7—368
Insurance companies   368.006 5
  accounting   657.836
  credit functions   332.38
  public administration   351.825 5
Insurance law   346.086
Insurance rates   368.011
Insured mail   383.182
  see also Postal service
Insurgency (Warfare)   355.021 8
Insurgent warfare   355.021 8
Intaglio printing   765
Intaglios   736.223
Intangible property   346.048
  international law   341.758
Intangible property risks   368.063
Integer programming   519.77
Integers   512.72
Integral calculus   515.43
Integral equations   515.45
Integral geometry   516.362
Integral inequalities   515.46
Integral operators   515.723
Integral transforms   511.33
Integrals   515.43
Integrated circuits   621.381 5
  computer engineering   621.395
Integrated optics   621.369 3
Integrated programs   005.3
Integration
  educational sociology   370.193 42
Integration (Mathematics)   515.43
Integration theory   515.42
Integro-differential equations   515.38
Integument   574.1
  anatomy   574.47
  animal anatomy   591.47
  animal physiology   591.185 8
  human anatomy   611.77
  human physiology   612.79
  physiology   574.1
  plant anatomy   581.47
  see also Skin
Intellectual freedom   323.44
  library policies   025.213
Intellectual guidance   371.422
Intellectual history   001.09

Intellectual life   001.1
  sociology   306.42
Intellectual processes   153
  children   155.413
Intellectual property   346.048
  international law   341.758
Intellectuals   305.552
        T1—086 31
  relations with government   323.323 1
Intelligence   153.9
  educational psychology   370.152
  philosophy   128.3
  psychology   153.9
  animals   156.39
Intelligence (Information)   327.12
  armed forces   355.343 2
  business management   658.47
  international relations   327.12
  military technology   623.71
Intelligence tests   153.93
Intelligentsia   305.552
        T1—086 31
Intensifying solutions
  photography   771.54
Intensity of light   535.22
Intensity of sound   534.3
Intensive care   362.174
  medicine   616.028
  nursing   610.736 1
  social welfare   362.174
  see also Health services
Intentionality
  philosophy   128
  psychology   153.8
Inter-American Development
  Bank   332.153 8
Interactive processing   004.33
Interactive videotex   004.69
  communication services   384.354
  see also Computer
    communications
Interamerican Development Bank   332.153 8
Interatomic forces
  chemistry   541.246
Intercellular respiration   574.124
  plants   581.124
Interception of communication
  civil rights issue   323.448 2
Interceptor missiles   358.174 82
  military engineering   623.451 94
  military equipment   358.174 82
Intercession of Jesus Christ   232.8
Interchangeability engineering   620.004 5
Interchangeability standards
  commerce   389.62
Intercoastal routes   387.522
Intercom systems
  office use   651.79

Intermolecular forces
  chemistry — 541.226
Intermunicipal authorities
  local public administration — 352.009 5
Internal auditing — 657.458
Internal-combustion engines — 621.43
  automotive — 629.25
  ships — 623.872 3
Internal commerce — 381
  see also Domestic commerce
Internal ear — 596.018 25
  human anatomy — 611.85
  human diseases
    incidence — 614.599 8
    otology — 617.882
  human physiology — 612.858
  see also Ears
Internal friction
  solid state physics — 530.416
Internal medicine — 616
Internal organization — 658.402
              T1—068 4
Internal respiration
  human physiology — 612.26
  see also Respiratory system
Internal revenue — 336.2
  law — 343.04
Internal storage (Computer) — 004.53
  engineering — 621.397 3
International administration — 354.1
International arbitration
  law — 341.522
International assistance
  economics — 338.91
  social welfare — 361.26
    governmental — 361.6
International Association of
  Rebekah Assemblies — 366.38
  members — 366.380 92
International Bank for
  Reconstruction and
  Development — 332.153 2
  law — 341.751
International banking — 332.15
  law — 346.082 15
International banks — 332.15
International borrowing — 336.343 5
  public administration — 351.72
  public finance — 336.343 5
International commerce — 382
  international law — 341.754
  law — 343.087
  public administration — 351.827
    cabinet departments — 351.082 7
International Committee of the
  Red Cross — 361.77
International Communist
  Congress — 324.175

International conflicts — 327.16
  law — 341.5
  see also Wars
International cooking — 641.59
International cooperation — 327.17
  law — 341.7
  political science — 327.17
International copyright law — 341.758 2
International Court of Justice — 341.552
International courts — 341.55
International crimes — 364.135
  law — 341.77
International Criminal Police
    Organization
  law — 341.77
International debt — 336.343 5
  public administration — 351.72
  public finance — 336.343 5
International development
  economics — 338.91
International Development
  Association — 332.153
International disputes — 327.16
  law — 341.5
International economic assistance — 338.91
International economic
  cooperation — 337
International economic
  development — 338.91
International economic law — 341.75
International economic planning — 337
International economic relations — 337
International economics — 337
International enterprises — 338.88
  financial management — 658.159 9
  management — 658.049
    initiation — 658.114 9
    organization — 658.18
International farm policies — 338.181
International finance — 332.042
  international law — 341.751
International Finance
  Corporation — 332.153
International fiscal law — 341.751
International grants
  public finance — 336.188
International investment — 332.673
International labor mobility — 331.127 91
  economics — 331.127 91
International Labour Office
  law — 341.763
International languages — 401.3
International law — 341
  relation to domestic law — 341.04
International mediation
  international law — 341.52
International migration — 304.82
  political science — 325

Interregional commerce 381.5
  see also Commerce
Interregnum (German history) 943.025
Interreligious marriage 306.843
  social theology 291.178 358 43
    Christianity 261.835 843
Interreligious relations 291.172
  Buddhism 294.337 2
  Christianity 261.2
  Hinduism 294.517 2
  Islam 297.197 2
  Judaism 296.387 2
Interrogation
  criminal investigation 363.254
  law 345.052
Intersections (Mathematics) 516.35
Intersections (Roads) 388.13
  engineering 625.7
  transportation services 388.13
  urban 388.411
Interstate agreements
  law 342.042
Interstate banking 332.16
Interstate commerce 381.5
  law 343.088
  see also Commerce
Interstate planning
  civic art 711.3
  economics 338.9
Interstate relations (Federal
  systems)
  law 342.042
  public administration 351.091
    United States 353.929 1
Interstellar matter 523.112 5
  Milky Way 523.113 5
Interstitial nerve tissue
  human histology 611.018 8
  see also Nervous system
Interurban railroads 385.5
  engineering 625.6
  transportation services 385.5
Interval analysis (Mathematics) 511.42
Intervals
  musical element 781.237
Intervention (International law) 341.584
Interventionism
  economics 330.126
Interviewing 158.39
  marketing research 658.83
  personnel selection 658.311 24
    public administration 350.132 5
      central governments 351.132 5
      local governments 352.005 132 5
  social work 361.322
Interviews 080
Intestinal obstructions
  medicine 616.342

Intestinal obstructions (continued)
  surgery 617.554
  see also Digestive system
Intestinal secretions
  human physiology 612.33
  see also Digestive system
Intestine
  human anatomy 611.34
  human diseases
    medicine 616.34
  human physiology 612.33
  surgery 617.554
  see also Digestive system
Intibucá (Honduras : Dept.) T2—728 381
Intimacy
  applied psychology 158.2
Intonation (Linguistics) 414.6
  specific languages T4—16
Intoxications 362.29
  medicine 616.86
  social welfare 362.29
  see also Substance abuse
Intractable pain
  symptomatology 616.047 2
Intrafamily relationships 306.87
Intragovernmental revenues
  public finance 336.18
Intramural sports 371.89
Intraocular lenses
  optometry 617.752 4
Intrauterine contraceptives
  health 613.943 5
  see also Birth control
Intravenous anesthesia
  surgery 617.962
Intravenous medication
  administering 615.6
Intravenous therapy
  medicine 615.855
Intrinsic differential geometry 516.363
Intrinsic variables (Stars) 523.844 2
Introductory forms
  music 784.189 2
Introit 264.36
  music 782.323 5
Introversion 155.232
  educational psychology 370.153
  personality trait 155.232
Intrusions (Geology) 551.88
Intuition 153.44
  epistemology 121.3
  ethical systems 171.2
  psychology 153.44
Intuitionism 143
Intuitive mathematics 511.22
Inuit T5—971
Inuit language 497.1
  T6—971

Ionian Sea	551.462 6
	T2—163 86
Ionic equilibriums	541.372 3
chemical engineering	660.297 23
Ionic philosophy	182.1
Ionization	
chemical engineering	660.297 22
chemistry	541.372 2
meteorology	551.561
Ionization chambers	
nuclear physics	539.772
Ionization of gases	530.43
electronic physics	537.532
gaseous-state physics	530.43
Ionization of the atmosphere	538.767
Ionized gases	
physics	530.44
Ionizing radiations	539.722
Ionosphere	538.767
	T2—161 4
meteorology	551.514 5
Ionospheric probes	
unmanned	629.435 2
Ions	541.372
chemical engineering	660.297 2
Iosco County (Mich.)	T2—774 74
Iowa	977.7
	T2—777
Iowa County (Iowa)	T2—777 653
Iowa County (Wis.)	T2—775 78
Iowa language	497.5
	T6—975
Iowa River	T2—777 6
Ipswich (England)	T2—426 49
Ipswich (Qld.)	T2—943 2
IQ tests	153.93
Iqaluit (N.W.T.)	T2—719 5
Iquique (Chile : Province)	T2—831 27
IRA (Retirement account)	332.024 01
tax law	343.052 33
Iran	955
	T2—55
ancient	935
	T2—35
Irangi (African people)	T5—963 94
Irangi language	496.394
	T6—963 94
Iranian-Iraqi Conflict, 1980-	955.054
Iranian languages	491.5
	T6—915
Iranian literatures	891.5
Iranians	T5—915
Iraq	956.7
	T2—567
ancient	935
	T2—35
Iraqi-Iranian Conflict, 1980-	955.054
Iraqis	T5—927 567
Irbid (Jordan : Province)	T2—569 54
Irbil (Iraq : Province)	T2—567 2
IRBM (Missiles)	358.175 382
military engineering	623.451 953
military equipment	358.175 382
Iredell County (N.C.)	T2—756 793
Ireland	941.7
	T2—417
Ireland (Island)	941.5
	T2—415
ancient	936.15
	T2—361 5
Irian Barat	T2—951
Irian Jaya (Indonesia)	995.1
	T2—951
Iridales	584.24
Iridium	669.7
chemical engineering	661.064 3
chemistry	546.643
metallography	669.957
metallurgy	669.7
metalworking	673.7
physical metallurgy	669.967
see also Chemicals	
Iringa Region (Tanzania)	T2—678 25
Irion County (Tex.)	T2—764 874
Iris (Plant)	584.24
floriculture	635.934 24
Irises (Eyes)	
human physiology	612.842
see also Eyes	
Irish	T5—916 2
Irish Free State	941.708 22
	T2—417
Irish Gaelic language	491.62
	T6—916 2
Irish Gaels	T5—916 2
Irish harps	787.95
see also Stringed instruments	
Irish language	491.62
	T6—916 2
Irish literature	
English	820
Gaelic	891.62
Irish Sea	551.461 37
	T2—163 37
Irkutsk (R.S.F.S.R. : Oblast)	T2—575
Irkutskaia oblast (R.S.F.S.R.)	T2—575
Iron	669.141
building construction	693.71
building material	691.7
chemical engineering	661.062 1
chemistry	546.621
economic geology	553.3
foundation materials	624.153 7
materials science	620.17
metallography	669.951 41
metallurgy	669.141

Islamic holidays	297.36
customs	394.268 297
Islamic law	340.59
Islamic philosophy	181.07
Islamic regions	T2—176 71
Islamic sacred music	781.771
public worship	782.371
music	782.371
religion	297.38
religion	297.3
Islamic schools	377.97
Islamic temples and shrines	297.35
architecture	726.2
Island biology	574.91
Island Carib Indians	T5—979
Island County (Wash.)	T2—797 75
Island ecology	574.526 7
Islands	551.42
	T2—142
geography	910.914 2
geomorphology	551.42
physical geography	910.021 42
Islands authorities (Scotland)	T2—411 2
Islands of Langerhans	
human anatomy	611.37
human diseases	
medicine	616.46
human physiology	612.34
surgery	617.557
see also Digestive system, Endocrine system	
Islands of the Arctic	T2—98
Canada	T2—719 5
Islands of the Atlantic	997
	T2—97
Islands of the Pacific	990
	T2—9
Islas de la Bahía (Honduras : Dept.)	T2—728 315
Isle au Haut (Me.)	T2—741 53
Isle of Anglesey (Wales)	T2—429 21
Isle of Capri (Italy)	T2—457 3
Isle of Ely (England)	T2—426 53
Isle of Man (England)	T2—427 9
Isle of Orléans (Quebec)	T2—714 48
Isle of Pines	T2—729 125
Isle of Wight (England)	T2—422 8
Isle of Wight County (Va.)	T2—755 54
Isle of Youth	T2—729 125
Isle Royale (Mich.)	T2—774 997
Isle Royale National Park (Mich.)	T2—774 997
Islington (London, England)	T2—421 43
Islwyn (Wales : Borough)	T2—429 93
Ismailia (Egypt : Governorate)	T2—621 5
Ismailis (Islamic sect)	297.822
Isobutylene rubber	678.72

Isochrysidales	589.487
Isoetales	587.1
paleobotany	561.71
Isolation	
disease control	614.45
social psychology	302.545
Isomers	541.225 2
Isometric exercises	613.714 9
Isometric projection	
technical drawing	604.245
Isometry	511.33
Isomorphism	
crystallography	548.3
Isonitriles	547.044
chemical engineering	661.894
Isopoda	595.372
paleozoology	565.37
Isoptera	595.736
paleozoology	565.73
Isospondylii	597.55
Isotope structure	539.74
Isotopes	
chemical engineering	660.298 8
radiochemistry	541.388
Isparta Ili (Turkey)	T2—564
Israel	956.94
	T2—569 4
ancient	933
	T2—33
Israel-Arab War, 1948-1949	956.042
Israel-Arab War, 1967	956.046
Israel-Arab War, 1973	956.048
Israel-Lebanon-Syria Conflict, 1982-1985	956.052
Israelis	T5—924
Israelites	T5—924
Issaquena County (Miss.)	T2—762 412
ISSN (Standard serial number)	025.343 2
Issuing houses	332.66
Istanbul (Turkey)	T2—496 18
ancient	T2—398
Istanbul Ili (Turkey)	T2—496 18
Asia	T2—563
Isthmus of Suez	T2—621 5
Istria (Croatia)	T2—497 2
ancient	T2—373
Italian greyhound	
animal husbandry	636.76
see also Dogs	
Italian language	450
	T6—51
Italian literature	850
Italian Peninsula	945
	T2—45
ancient	937
	T2—37
Italian Riviera (Italy)	T2—451 8
Italian Somaliland	T2—677 3

Italianate revivals	
architecture	724.52
Italians	T5—51
Italic calligraphy	745.619 77
Italic languages	470
	T6—7
Italic literatures	870
Italic peoples	T5—4
Italic type	686.224 7
Italo-Ethiopian War, 1935-1936	963.056
Italy	945
	T2—45
ancient	937
	T2—37
Italy, Southern	T2—457
ancient	T2—377
Itapúa (Paraguay)	T2—892 126
Itasca County (Minn.)	T2—776 78
Itawamba County (Miss.)	T2—762 982
Itch	
psychology	152.182 8
Iterative methods (Mathematics)	511.4
Ithaca (N.Y.)	T2—747 71
Ithaca Island (Greece)	T2—495 5
ancient	T2—383
Ithna Asharites (Islamic sect)	297.821
IUD (Contraceptive)	
health	613.943 5
see also Birth control	
IUgo-Osetinskaia	
avtonomnaia oblast	
(Georgian S.S.R.)	T2—479 5
IV Región (Chile)	T2—832 3
Ivan, the Terrible	
Russian history	947.043
Ivan III, Czar of Russia	
Russian history	947.041
Ivan IV, Czar of Russia	
Russian history	947.043
Ivan VI, Emperor of Russia	
Russian history	947.061
Ivano-Frankov (Ukraine :	
Oblast)	T2—477 18
Ivano-Frankovskaia oblast	
(Ukraine)	T2—477 18
Ivanovo (R.S.F.S.R. : Oblast)	T2—473 1
Ivanovskaia oblast	
(R.S.F.S.R.)	T2—473 1
Iviza Island (Spain)	T2—467 56
Ivorians	T5—966 68
Ivory	
manufacturing technology	679.43
Ivory carving	736.62
Ivory Coast	966.68
	T2—666 8
Ivory Coast people	T5—966 68
Ivy	583.687
Iwate ken (Japan)	T2—521 14

IWW (Labor)	331.886
IX Región (Chile)	T2—834 6
Ixonanthaceae	583.214
Ixopo (South Africa : District)	T2—684 7
Izabal (Guatemala : Dept.)	T2—728 131
Izabal (Guatemala : Province)	T2—728 13
Izard County (Ark.)	T2—767 27
Izmir Ili (Turkey)	T2—562

J

J. G. Strijdom Dam	T2—684 2
Jabim language	499.5
	T6—995
Jacamars	598.72
Jacanas	598.33
Jack (Fish)	597.58
Jack County (Tex.)	T2—764 544
Jack-in-the-pulpit	584.64
Jackals	599 744 42
Jackets (Clothing)	391
commercial technology	687 147
indoor garments	687.113
outdoor garments	687.147
customs	391
home sewing	646.457
indoor garments	646.433
outdoor garments	646.457
see also Clothing	
Jacks (Lifting mechanisms)	621.877
Jackson (Miss.)	T2—762 51
Jackson, Andrew	
United States history	973.56
Jackson County (Ala.)	T2—761 95
Jackson County (Ark.)	T2—767 97
Jackson County (Colo.)	T2—788 66
Jackson County (Fla.)	T2—759 93
Jackson County (Ga.)	T2—758 145
Jackson County (Ill.)	T2—773 994
Jackson County (Ind.)	T2—772 23
Jackson County (Iowa)	T2—777 64
Jackson County (Kan.)	T2—781 335
Jackson County (Ky.)	T2—769 183
Jackson County (Mich.)	T2—774 28
Jackson County (Minn.)	T2—776 235
Jackson County (Miss.)	T2—762 12
Jackson County (Mo.)	T2—778 41
Jackson County (N.C.)	T2—756 95
Jackson County (Ohio)	T2—771 85
Jackson County (Okla.)	T2—766 45
Jackson County (Or.)	T2—795 27
Jackson County (S.D.)	T2—783 572
Jackson County (Tenn.)	T2—768 51
Jackson County (Tex.)	T2—764 127
Jackson County (W. Va.)	T2—754 31
Jackson County (Wis.)	T2—775 51
Jackson Parish (La.)	T2—763 92
Jacksonville (Fla.)	T2—759 12
Jacobean architecture	720.942 090 32

Jacobi polynomials	515.55	James, William	
Jacobite Church	281.63	personality theory	155.264
see also Eastern churches		James Bay Region (Ont. and	
Jacob's ladder (Plant)	583.76	Quebec)	T2—714 115
Jacobsdal (South Africa :		James City County (Va.)	T2—755 425 1
District)	T2—685 8	James I, King of England	
Jacquard-weave fabrics	677.616	British history	941.061
see also Textiles		English history	942.061
Jacquard-weave rugs		Scottish history	941.106 1
arts	746.72	James I, King of Scotland	
see also Rugs		Scottish history	941.104
Jacques-Cartier (Quebec)	T2—714 47	James II, King of England	
Jacques-Cartier River		British history	941.067
(Quebec)	T2—714 47	English history	942.067
Jade	553.87	Scottish history	941.106 7
glyptics	736.24	James II, King of Scotland	
jewelry	739.27	Scottish history	941.104
Jade plant	583.38	James III, King of Scotland	
Jadida (Morocco : Province)	T2—643	Scottish history	941.104
Jaén (Spain : Province)	T2—468 3	James IV, King of Scotland	
Jagellonian dynasty (Polish		Scottish history	941.104
history)	943.802 3	James River	T2—783 3
Jagersfontein (South Africa :		North Dakota	T2—784 5
District)	T2—685 7	South Dakota	T2—783 3
Jahangir, Emperor of Hindustan		James River (Va.)	T2—755 4
Indian history	954.025 6	James V, King of Scotland	
Jahn-Teller effect (Physics)	530.416	Scottish history	941.104
Jail breaks	365.641	James VI, King of Scotland	
Jails	365.34	Scottish history	941.106 1
see also Correctional		1567-1603	941.105
institutions		1603-1625	941.106 1
Jain architecture	720.954	Jameson raid, 1895-1896	968.204 75
Jain philosophy	181.044	Jamesonite	
Jain sculpture	730.954	mineralogy	549.35
Jain temples and shrines	294.435	Jammu and Kashmir (India)	T2—546
architecture	726.144	Jamtlands lan (Sweden)	T2—488
Jainism	294.4	Jan Mayen Island	T2—983
art representation	704.948 944	Jansenism	284.84
Jains		in church history	273.7
biography	294.409 2	Jansenville (South Africa :	
religious group	T7—294 4	District)	T2—687 14
Jaipuri dialect	491.479 7	Jantars	787.72
	T6—914 79	*see also* Stringed instruments	
Jaipuri literature	891.479	Japan	952
Jakarta (Indonesia)	T2—598 22		T2—52
Jakun language	499.28	Japan, Sea of	551.465 54
	T6—992 8		T2—164 54
Jalapa (Guatemala : Dept.)	T2—728 142	Japan Current	551.475 5
Jalisco (Mexico)	T2—723 5	Japanese	T5—956
Jam	641.852	Japanese calendar	529.329 56
commercial processing	664.152	Japanese chess	794.18
home preparation	641.852	Japanese chin	
Jamaica	972.92	animal husbandry	636.76
	T2—729 2	*see also* Dogs	
Jamaican literature	810	Japanese flower arrangements	745.922 52
Jamaicans	T5—969 729 2	Japanese ink painting	751.425 2
James (Biblical book)	227.91	Japanese language	495.6
			T6—956

Jehovah's Witnesses	289.92
biography	289.920 92
religious group	T7—289
see also Christian	
denominations	
Jejunitis	
medicine	616.344
see also Digestive system	
Jejunum	
human anatomy	611.341
surgery	617.554 1
see also Digestive system	
Jelenia Gora (Poland :	
Voivodeship)	T2—438 5
Jelly	641.852
commercial processing	664.152
home preparation	641.852
Jelly fungi	589.225
Jellyfish	593.7
Jenkins County (Ga.)	T2—758 693
Jenkins' Ear, War of, 1739-1741	946.055
Jennings County (Ind.)	T2—772 17
Jenolan Caves	T2—944 5
Jerauld County (S.D.)	T2—783 32
Jerboas	599.323 3
Jeremiah (Biblical book)	224.2
Jerome County (Idaho)	T2—796 35
Jersey (England)	T2—423 41
Jersey Blue chickens	
animal husbandry	636.581
see also Chickens	
Jersey cattle	
animal husbandry	636.224
zoology	599.735 8
Jersey City (N.J.)	T2—749 27
Jersey County (Ill.)	T2—773 855
Jerusalem	T2—569 442
ancient	T2—33
sacred place	
Christianity	263.042 569 442
Islam	297.35
Judaism	296.4
Jerusalem (Israel : District)	T2—569 44
Jerusalem (Jordan : District)	T2—569 52
Jerusalem artichoke	583.55
agriculture	635.24
Jerusalem artichoke sugar	
commercial processing	664.139
see also Sugar	
Jerusalem artichoke syrup	
commercial processing	664.139
Jerusalem Bible	220.520 7
Jerusalem corn	584.92
food crop	633.174 7
forage crop	633.257 47
Jerusalem Talmud	296.124
Jessamine County (Ky.)	T2—769 483
Jesuits	255.53
church history	271.53
Jesus Christ	232
art representation	704.948 53
Jet (Coal)	553.22
economic geology	553.22
properties	662.622 2
Jet engines	621.435 2
aircraft	629.134 353
Jet fuel	665.538 25
Jet planes	387.733 49
engineering	629.133 349
military engineering	623.746 044
military equipment	358.418 3
transportation services	387.733 49
see also Aircraft	
Jet pumps	621.691
hydraulic	621.252
Jet skiing	797.37
Jet streams (Meteorology)	551.518 3
Jethou (England)	T2—423 47
Jetties	
engineering	627.24
Jevons, William Stanley	
economic school	330.157
Jewelers	739.270 92
occupational group	T7—739
Jewell County (Kan.)	T2—781 22
Jewelry	391.7
customs	391.7
making	739.27
costume jewelry	688.2
handicrafts	745.594 2
fine jewelry	739.27
Jewelweed	583.216
Jewish apocalypses	
pseudepigrapha	229.913
Jewish architecture	
ancient	722.33
Jewish Autonomous Oblast	
(R.S.F.S.R.)	T2—577
Jewish calendar	529.326
religion	296.43
Jewish Christians (Sects)	289.9
see also Christian	
denominations	
Jewish cooking	641.567 6
Jewish holidays	296.43
customs	394.268 296
Jewish philosophy	181.06
Jewish sculpture	732.3
Jews	T5—924
Jews (Religious group)	T7—296
biography	296.092
Jew's harps	786.887
see also Percussion instruments	
Jiangsu Sheng (China)	T2—511 36
Jiangxi Sheng (China)	T2—512 22

Johnston County (N.C.)	T2—756 41
Johnston County (Okla.)	T2—766 68
Johnston Island	T2—969 9
Johore	T2—595 1
Joinery	684.08
construction	694.6
ship hulls	623.844
woodworking	684.08
Joining equipment	621.97
Joining metals	671.5
decorative arts	739.14
sculpture	731.41
Joint chiefs of staff	355.330 42
Joint committees	
legislative bodies	328.365 7
Joint custody	346.017
Joint property	346.042
Joint stock companies	338.7
management	658.044
Joint tenancy	346.043 2
Joint ventures	338.7
law	346.068 2
management	658.044
Joints (Anatomical)	
diseases	
medicine	616.72
extremities	
surgery	617.58
human anatomy	611.72
human physiology	612.75
surgery	617.472
see also Musculoskeletal system	
Joints (Geology)	551.84
Jokes	
literature	808.882
specific literatures	T3B—802
individual authors	T3A—8
Joliette (Quebec : County)	T2—714 42
Joliette (Quebec : Regional	
County Municipality)	T2—714 42
Jonah (Biblical book)	224.92
Jonathan, Leabua	
Basotho history	968.850 3
Jones County (Ga.)	T2—758 567
Jones County (Iowa)	T2—777 63
Jones County (Miss.)	T2—762 55
Jones County (N.C.)	T2—756 21
Jones County (S.D.)	T2—783 577
Jones County (Tex.)	T2—764 733
Jongley (Sudan : Province)	T2—629 3
Jonkopings lan (Sweden)	T2—486
Jonquils	584.25
floriculture	635.934 25
Jordan	956.95
	T2—569 5
Jordan algebras	512.24
Jordan River	T2—569 4
Jordanians	T5—927 569 5
Jornada del Muerto	T2—789 67
Jos (Nigeria)	T2—669 52
Joseph, Saint	232.932
private prayers to	242.75
Joseph Bonaparte, King of Spain	
Spanish history	946.06
Joseph I, Emperor of Germany	
German history	943.051
Joseph II, Holy Roman Emperor	
German history	943.057
Josephine County (Or.)	T2—795 25
Josephson effect (Physics)	530.416
Joshua (Biblical book)	222.2
Joshua Tree National	
Monument (Calif.)	T2—794 97
Jost Van Dyke Island	T2—729 725
Joual	447.971
	T6—41
Joubertina (South Africa :	
District)	T2—687 4
Joule's law	536.71
Journalism	070.4
civil rights issues	323.445
sociology	302.23
Journalists	070.92
occupational ethics	174.909 7
occupational group	T7—097
Journals (Mechanisms)	621.821
Journals (Writings)	
literature	808.883
specific literatures	T3B—803
individual authors	T3A—8
sociology	302.232 4
Joysticks (Computer)	004.76
engineering	621.398 6
Ju-chen (Manchurian people)	T5—941
Ju-chen language	494.1
	T6—941
Juab County (Utah)	T2—792 44
Juan Carlos I, King of Spain	
Spanish history	946.083
Juan de Fuca Strait (B.C. and	
Washington)	551.466 32
	T2—164 32
Jubilees	
customs	394.4
Judaea	T2—33
Judah	T2—33
Judaic calendar	529.326
Judaic regions	T2—176 6
Judaic sacred music	781.76
public worship	782.36
music	782.36
religion	296.4
religion	296.4
Judaic temples and shrines	
architecture	726.3

Jurchen language	494.1	Jutland (Denmark)	T2—489 5
	T6—941	Juvenile courts	345.081
Juries	347.075 2	Juvenile delinquency	364.36
criminal law	345.075	Juvenile delinquents	364.36
Jurisdiction		church activities for	259.5
administrative law	342.08	home care	649.153
constitutional law	342.041 3	law	345.03
international law	341.4	penal institutions	365.42
Jurisdiction of courts	347.012	*see also* Correctional	
Jurisdictional strikes	331.892 2	institutions	
see also Strikes (Work		Juvenile justice	364.36
stoppages)		criminology	364.36
Jurisprudence	340	law	345.08
Juristic persons	346.013	Juvenile literature	808.899 282
Jurists	340.092	history and criticism	809.892 82
Jurists (Judges)	347.014 092	reviews	028.162 54
Jury instructions	347.075 8	rhetoric	808.068
Jury selection	347.075 2	specific literatures	T3B—080 928 2
Jury trial	347.052	history and criticism	T3B—099 282
civil right	323.422	Juvenile procedure	345.08
criminal law	345.056	Juventud, Isla de la	T2—729 125
Just war theory		Jyelings	788.52
ethics	172.42	*see also* Woodwind instruments	
Christianity	241.624 2		
Justice			
ethics	172.2	**K**	
religion	291.562 2		
Buddhism	294.356 22	K-mesons	539.721 62
Christianity	241.622	K-theory	
Hinduism	294.548 622	algebra	512.55
Islam	297.5	topology	514.23
Judaism	296.385 622	K.W.I.C. indexing	025.486
law	340.11	K.W.O.C. indexing	025.486
literature	808.803 53	Kabardino-Balkar A.S.S.R.	
history and criticism	809.933 53	(R.S.F.S.R.)	T2—479 7
specific literatures	T3B—080 353	Kabardino-Balkarskaia	
history and criticism	T3B—093 53	A.S.S.R. (R.S.F.S.R.)	T2—479 7
political science	320.011	Kabbalah	
public administration	351.88	Judaistic sources	296.16
cabinet departments	351.05	*see also* Cabala	
Justice departments	351.05	Kabuki theater	792.095 2
United States	353.5	Kabwari language	496.394
Justice of God	214		T6—963 94
Christianity	231.8	Kabyle language	493.3
comparative religion	291.211		T6—933
Justices of the peace	347.016	Kacem (Morocco : Province)	T2—643
occupational ethics	174.3	Kachin language	495.4
occupational group	T7—349		T6—954
Justification (Christian doctrine)	234.7	Kadarites (Islamic sect)	297.835
Jute	583.19	Kadina (S. Aust.)	T2—942 35
agricultural economics	338.173 54	Kaduna State (Nigeria)	T2—669 73
fiber crop	633.54	Kafir corn	584.92
textiles	677.13	food crop	633.174 7
arts	746.041 3	forage crop	633.257 47
economics	338.476 771 3	Kafir languages (Afghanistan)	491.499
see also Textiles			T6—914 99
Jute pulp	676.14	Kafiri languages	491.499
Jutiapa (Guatemala : Dept.)	T2—728 143		T6—914 99
		Kafiri literature	891.499

Kandiyohi County (Minn.)	T2—776 48
Kane County (Ill.)	T2—773 23
Kane County (Utah)	T2—792 51
Kanem (Kingdom)	967.430 1
	T2—674 3
Kanem-Bornu (Kingdom)	966.980 1
	T2—669 8
Kanembu (African people)	T5—965
Kanembu language	496.5
	T6—965
Kangaroo Island (S. Aust.)	T2—942 35
Kangaroo mice	599.323 2
Kangaroo rats	599.323 2
Kangaroos	599.2
animal husbandry	636.91
KaNgwane (South Africa)	T2—682 96
Kanis	787.73
see also Stringed instruments	
Kaniva (Vic.)	T2—945 8
Kankakee County (Ill.)	T2—773 63
Kankan (Guines)	T2—665 2
Kannada language	494.814
	T6—948 14
Kannada literature	894.814
Kano State (Nigeria)	T2—669 78
Kansas	978.1
	T2—781
Kansas City (Kan.)	T2—781 39
Kansas City (Mo.)	T2—778 411
Kansas City jazz	781.653
Kansas River (Kan.)	T2—781 3
Kansu Province (China)	T2—514 5
Kantianism	142.3
Kantō Mountains	T2—521 3
Kantō Region (Japan)	T2—521 3
Kaolin	553.61
economic geology	553.61
mining	622.361
Kaolinite	
mineralogy	549.67
Kaonde language	496.393
	T6—963 93
Kaons	539.721 62
Kapok	
materials science	620.195
textiles	677.23
see also Textiles	
Kaposi's sarcoma	
medicine	616.994 77
see also Cancer	
Kara-Kalpak Autonomous	
Soviet Socialist Republic	
(Uzbek S.S.R.)	T2—587
Kara Sea	551.468 5
	T2—163 25
Karachaevo-Cherkesskaia	
avtonomnaia oblast	
(R.S.F.S.R.)	T2—479 7

Karachai-Cherkess	
Autonomous Oblast	
(R.S.F.S.R.)	T2—479 7
Karachi District (Pakistan)	T2—549 183
Karagwe (Kingdom)	967.610 1
	T2—676 1
Karaites	296.81
Karak (Jordan : Muhafazah)	T2—569 56
Karakalpakskaia A.S.S.R.	
(Uzbek S.S.R.)	T2—587
Karakoram Range	T2—546
Karanga (African people)	T5—963 975
Karanga kingdoms (Zimbabwean	
history)	968.910 1
Karanga language	496.397 5
	T6—963 975
Karate	796.815 3
physical fitness	613.714 8
Karbala (Iraq : Province)	T2—567 5
Karditsa (Greece : Nome)	T2—495 4
Karelia (R.S.F.S.R.)	T2—472 5
Karelian Autonomous Soviet	
Socialist Republic	
(R.S.F.S.R.)	T2—472 5
Karelian language	494.54
	T6—945 4
Karelian literature	894.54
Karelians	T5—945 4
Karelskaia A.S.S.R.	
(R.S.F.S.R.)	T2—472 5
Karen (Asian people)	T5—95
Karen languages	495
	T6—95
Kari languages	496.39
	T6—963 9
Karimata Strait	551.465 72
	T2—164 72
Karkar Island	T2—957 3
Karl-Marx-Stadt (Germany)	T2—432 162
Karl-Marx-Stadt (Germany :	
Bezirk)	T2—432 16
Karlsruhe (Germany)	T2—434 643
Karlsruhe (Germany :	
Regierungsbezirk)	T2—434 64
Karluk languages	494.3
	T6—943
Karma	291.22
Buddhism	294.342 2
Hinduism	294.522
Karma yoga	294.544
Karnak (Egypt)	T2—32
Karnataka (India)	T2—548 7
Karnes County (Tex.)	T2—764 444
Karo, Joseph ben Ephraim	
Judaistic sources	296.182
Karoo	T2—687 15
Karoo, Great (South Africa)	T2—687 15
Karoo, Little	T2—687 16

Kegs	
wooden	674.82
Keimoes (South Africa)	T2—687 12
Keiskamma River	T2—687 92
Keiskammahoek (South	
Africa : District)	T2—687 92
Keith County (Neb.)	T2—782 89
Kejimkujik National Park	
(N.S.)	T2—716 33
Kekchi language	497.415
	T6—974 15
Kelaa-Srarhna (Morocco :	
Province)	T2—646
Kelantan	T2—595 1
Kele languages	496.396
	T6—963 96
Kelowna (B.C.)	T2—711 5
Kelp	589.45
Kemerovo (R.S.F.S.R. :	
Oblast)	T2—573
Kemerovskaia oblast	
(R.S.F.S.R.)	T2—573
Kemper County (Miss.)	T2—762 683
Kempo	796.815 9
Kempsey (N.S.W.)	T2—944 3
Kempton Park (South Africa :	
District)	T2—682 2
Kenaf	
fiber crop	633.56
Kenai Fjords National Park	
(Alaska)	T2—798 3
Kenai Peninsula (Alaska)	T2—798 3
Kenai Peninsula Borough	
(Alaska)	T2—798 3
Kendall County (Ill.)	T2—773 263
Kendall County (Tex.)	T2—764 886
Kendo	796.86
Kenedy County (Tex.)	T2—764 473
Kenhardt (South Africa :	
District)	T2—687 12
Kenitra (Morocco : Province)	T2—643
Kennebec County (Me.)	T2—741 6
Kennebec River (Me.)	T2—741 22
Kennedy, John F. (John	
Fitzgerald)	
United States history	973.922
Kennelly-Heaviside layers	538.767 3
Kennels (Dog housing)	636.708 31
Kennet (England : District)	T2—423 17
Kenora (Ont. : District)	T2—713 112
Patricia Portion	T2—713 1
Kenosha County (Wis.)	T2—775 98
Kensington and Chelsea	
(London, England)	T2—421 34
Kent (England)	T2—422 3
Kent (N.B. : County)	T2—715 22
Kent (Ont. : County)	T2—713 33
Kent County (Del.)	T2—751 4

Kent County (Md.)	T2—752 36
Kent County (Mich.)	T2—774 55
Kent County (R.I.)	T2—745 4
Kent County (Tex.)	T2—764 738
Kentani (South Africa :	
District)	T2—687 91
Kenton County (Ky.)	T2—769 35
Kentucky	976.9
	T2—769
Kentucky Lake	T2—769 895
Kentucky River	T2—769 3
Kenya	967.62
	T2—676 2
Kenyans	T5—967 62
Kenyatta, Jomo	
Kenyan history	967.620 4
Keogh plans	332.024 01
tax law	343.052 33
Keokuk County (Iowa)	T2—777 91
Kephallēnia (Greece)	T2—495 5
Kepler's laws	521.3
Kerala (India)	T2—548 3
Kerang (Vic.)	T2—945 4
Kerars	787.78
see also Stringed instruments	
Keratin	599.018 58
chemistry	547.753
mammalian physiology	599.018 58
see also Proteins	
Keratinous material products	679.4
Keratosis	
medicine	616.544
see also Skin	
Kerbela (Iraq : Province)	T2—567 5
Kerbs	625.888
Kerema (Papua New Guinea)	T2—954 7
Kerensky, Aleksandr	
Fyodorovich	
Russian history	947.084 1
Kerguelen Islands	969.9
	T2—699
Kerkyra (Greece)	T2—495 5
Kerman (Iran)	T2—558 2
Kermanshah (Iran)	T2—555 2
Kern County (Calif.)	T2—794 88
Kernite	
mineralogy	549.735
Kerosene	665.538 3
Kerosene lamps	621.323
Kerounés	787.82
see also Stringed instruments	
Kerr County (Tex.)	T2—764 884
Kerrier (England : District)	T2—423 76
Kerry (Ireland)	T2—419 6
Kerry cattle	
animal husbandry	636.225
zoology	599.735 8
Kershaw County (S.C.)	T2—757 61

Khoisan languages	496.1	Kielce (Poland : Voivodeship)	T2—438 4
	T6—961	Kieta (Papua New Guinea)	T2—959 2
Khoisan literatures	896.1	Kiev (Ukraine : Oblast)	T2—477 14
Khomeini, Ruhollah		Kievan period (Russian history)	947.02
Iranian history	955.054	Kievskaia oblast (Ukraine)	T2—477 14
Khond	T5—948 2	Kiga (Chiga) language	496.395 6
Khond language	494.824		T6—963 956
	T6—948 24	Kigali (Rwanda)	T2—675 71
Khond literature	894.824	Kigoma Region (Tanzania)	T2—678 28
Khorasan (Iran)	T2—559 2	Kikongo languages	496.393 1
Khotanese language	491.53		T6—963 931
	T6—915 3	Kikori (Papua New Guinea)	T2—954 7
Khotanese literature	891.53	Kikori River	T2—954 7
Khouribga (Morocco :		Kikuyu (African people)	T5—963 954
Province)	T2—643	Kikuyu-Kamba languages	496.395 3
Khowar language	491.499		T6—963 953
	T6—914 99	Kikuyu language	496.395 4
Khowar literature	891.499		T6—963 954
Khrushchev, Nikita Sergeevich		Kikuyu literature	896.395 4
Russian history	947.085 2	Kildare (Ireland : County)	T2—418 5
Khulna District (Bangladesh)	T2—549 25	Kilimanjaro, Mount	
Khurasan (Iran)	T2—559 2	(Tanzania)	T2—678 26
Khuzestan (Iran)	T2—556	Kilimanjaro National Park	
Khuzistan (Iran)	T2—556	(Tanzania)	T2—678 26
ki-Swahili language	496.392	Kilimanjaro Region	
	T6—963 92	(Tanzania)	T2—678 26
Kiama (N.S.W.)	T2—944 7	Kiliwa language	497.5
Kiangsi Province (China)	T2—512 22		T6—975
Kiangsu Province (China)	T2—511 36	Kilkenny (Ireland : County)	T2—418 9
Kibbutzim	307.776	Kilkís (Greece : Nome)	T2—495 6
Kicking		Killarney (Ireland)	T2—419 65
American football	796.332 27	Killer whales	599.53
Kidder County (N.D.)	T2—784 57	Killifish	597.53
Kidnap and ransom insurance	368.82	Kilmarnock and Loudoun	
see also Insurance		(Scotland : District)	T2—414 63
Kidnap insurance	368.82	Kilmore (Vic.)	T2—945 3
see also Insurance		Kiln drying lumber	674.384
Kidnapping	364.154	Kilns	666.43
law	345.025 4	decorative arts	738.13
Kidney beans	641.356 52	sculpture	731.3
botany	583.322	technology	666.43
commercial processing	664.805 652	Kilsyth, Cumbernauld and	
cooking	641.656 52	(Scotland : District)	T2—414 38
field crop	633.372	Kimbala languages	496.393
garden crop	635.652		T6—963 93
Kidney failure		Kimball County (Neb.)	T2—782 973
medicine	616.614	Kimbe (Papua New Guinea)	T2—958 7
see also Urinary system		Kimberley (B.C.)	T2—711 65
Kidney stones		Kimberley (South Africa :	
medicine	616.622	District)	T2—687 11
see also Urinary system		Kimberley (W.A.)	T2—941 4
Kidneys		Kimble County (Tex.)	T2—764 878
human anatomy	611.61	Kimbundu languages	496.393
human diseases			T6—963 93
medicine	616.61	Kinbasket Lake (B.C.)	T2—711 68
human physiology	612.463	Kincardine and Deeside	
surgery	617.461	(Scotland : District)	T2—412 4
see also Urinary system		Kindergarten	372.218

Kirkcaldy (Scotland : District) T2—412 95
Kirkcudbrightshire (Scotland :
  District) T2—414 92
Kirklareli Ili (Turkey) T2—496 1
Kirkless (England) T2—428 13
Kirkwood (South Africa :
  District) T2—687 5
Kirlian photography 778.3
  parapsychology 133.8
Kirman (Iran) T2—558 2
Kirov (R.S.F.S.R. : Oblast) T2—478 1
Kirovograd (Ukraine : Oblast) T2—477 14
Kirovogradskaia oblast
  (Ukraine) T2—477 14
Kirovskaia oblast (R.S.F.S.R.) T2—478 1
Kirsehir Ili (Turkey) T2—564
Kirstenbosch Botanic Gardens T2—687 355
Kisangani (Zaire) T2—675 15
Kiso Mountains T2—521 63
Kissi (African people) T5—963 2
Kissi language 496.32
  T6—963 2
Kissimmee River (Fla.) T2—759 53
Kissing
  customs 394
Kiswahili language 496.392
  T6—963 92
Kit Carson County (Colo.) T2—788 91
Kitchen linens
  household equipment 643.3
Kitchen utensils 641.502 8
  cooking 641.502 8
  manufacturing technology 683.82
Kitchener (Ont.) T2—713 45
Kitchens 643.3
  home economics 643.3
  plumbing 696.184
  residential interior decoration 747.797
Kites 629.133 32
  recreation 796.15
Kites (Birds) 598.916
Kitikmeot (N.W.T.) T2—719 7
Kitimat (B.C.) T2—711 1
Kitimat-Stikine (B.C.) T2—711 1
Kitsap County (Wash.) T2—797 76
Kitsch 709.034 8
Kittatinny Mountain T2—749 76
Kittitas County (Wash.) T2—797 57
Kittson County (Minn.) T2—776 99
Kiunga (Papua New Guinea) T2—954 9
Kiustendilski okrug
  (Bulgaria) T2—497 73
Kivu (Zaire) T2—675 17
Kivu, Lake (Rwanda and
  Zaire) T2—675 17
  Rwanda T2—675 71
  Zaire T2—675 17
Kiwanis International 369.5

Kiwanis International members 369.5
  social group T7—369 5
Kiwis 598.54
Kiyaka languages 496.393
  T6—963 93
Klamath County (Or.) T2—795 91
Klamath Mountains (Calif.
  and Or.) T2—795 2
  California T2—794 21
  Oregon T2—795 2
Kleberg County (Tex.) T2—764 472
Klebsiella 589.95
Kleptomania 362.27
  medicine 616.858 42
  social welfare 362.27
  see also Mental illness
Klerksdorp (South Africa :
  ·District) T2—682 4
Klickitat County (Wash.) T2—797 53
Klinefelter's syndrome
  medicine 616.680 42
  see also Male genital system
Klip River (South Africa :
  District) T2—684 7
Klystrons 621.381 333
Kneelers
  home sewing 646.21
  household management 645.4
  textile arts 746.95
Knees 612.98
  human physiology 612.98
  regional medicine 617.582
  ·surgery 617.582
  see also Lower extremities
    (Human)
Knies, Karl
  economic school 330.154 2
Knife combat
  military training 355.548
Knife fish 597.55
Knighthood
  genealogy 929.7
Knighthood orders 929.71
  Christian religious orders 255.791
    church history 271.791
Knights (Chessmen) 794.144
Knights Hospitalers of St. John
  of Jerusalem 255.791 2
  church history 271.791 2
Knights of Labor 331.883 309 7
Knights of Malta 255.791 2
  church history 271.791 2
Knights of Pythias 366.2
Knights of Pythias members 366.209 2
  social group T7—366 2
Knights Templars 255.791 3
  church history 271.791 3

Kongo (Kingdom)	967.511 401
	T2—675 114
Kongo language	496.393 1
	T6—963 931
Kongo literature	896.393 1
Konin (Poland : Voivodeship)	T2—438 4
Konjo languages	496.394
	T6—963 94
Konkani language	491.467
	T6—914 6
Konkani literature	891.46
Kono (African people)	T5—963 4
Kono language	496.34
	T6—963 4
Konya Ili (Turkey)	T2—564
Koochiching County (Minn.)	T2—776 79
Koodoos	599.735 8
Kootenai County (Idaho)	T2—796 94
Kootenay Boundary (B.C.)	T2—711 62
Kootenay Lake (B.C.)	T2—711 62
Kootenay National Park (B.C.)	T2—711 65
Kootenay River	T2—711 65
Kopparbergs lan (Sweden)	T2—487
Koppies (South Africa : District)	T2—685 2
Koran	297.122
Koras	787.98
see also Stringed instruments	
Kordestan (Iran)	T2—555 4
Kordofan (Sudan)	T2—628
Kordofanian languages	496.3
	T6—963
Korea	951.9
	T2—519
Korea (North)	T2—519 3
Korea (South)	T2—519 5
Korea Strait	551.465 54
	T2—164 54
Korean language	495.7
	T6—957
Korean literature	895.7
Korean War, 1950-1953	951.904 2
Koreans	T5—957
Korinthia (Greece : Nome)	T2—495 2
ancient	T2—387
Korumburra (Vic.)	T2—945 2
Koryak National Okrug (R.S.F.S.R.)	T2—577
Kos Island (Greece)	T2—499 6
Kosciusko, Mount	T2—944 7
Kosciusko County (Ind.)	T2—772 82
Kosciusko National Park (N.S.W.)	T2—944 7
Kosher cooking	641.567 6
Kosher observance	296.73
Kosi Lake	T2—684 91
Kosovo i Metohija (Serbia)	T2—497 1
Kosovo-Metohija (Serbia)	T2—497 1
Kosrae (Micronesia)	T2—966
Kossuth County (Iowa)	T2—777 21
Koster (South Africa : District)	T2—682 4
Kostroma (R.S.F.S.R. : Oblast)	T2—473 1
Kostromskaia oblast (R.S.F.S.R.)	T2—473 1
Kosygin, Aleksey Nikolayevich Russian history	947.085 3
Koszalin (Poland : Voivodeship)	T2—438 1
Kota language (Dravidian)	494.81
	T6—948 1
Kota literature	894.81
Koti-ken (Japan)	T2—523 3
Kougaberg Range	T2—687 4
Kountché, Seyni Nigerien (Niger) history	966.260 5
Kozánē (Greece : Nome)	T2—495 6
Kpelle (African people)	T5—963 4
Kpelle language	496.34
	T6—963 4
Kraai River	T2—687 6
Kraft process	676.126
Kraft wrapping paper	676.287
Krakow (Poland : Voivodeship)	T2—438 6
Krameriaceae	583.143
Kranskop (South Africa : District)	T2—684 7
Krasnodar (R.S.F.S.R. : Kray)	T2—479 7
Krasnodarskii krai (R.S.F.S.R.)	T2—479 7
Krasnoiarskii krai (R.S.F.S.R.)	T2—575
Krasnoyarsk (R.S.F.S.R. : Kray)	T2—575
Kratke Range	T2—956 9
Kretschmer, Ernst personality theory	155.264
Krio language	427.966 4
	T6—21
Kristianstads lan (Sweden)	T2—486
Kronobergs lan (Sweden)	T2—486
Kroonstad (South Africa : District)	T2—685 2
Krosno (Poland : Voivodeship)	T2—438 6
Kru (African people)	T5—963 3
Kru language	496.33
	T6—963 3
Kruger National Park	T2—682 6
Krugersdorp (South Africa : District)	T2—682 2
Krymskaia oblast (Ukraine)	T2—477 17

Kwanza Sul (Angola :
  Province)   T2—673 2
Kwara State (Nigeria)   T2—669 57
Kwashiorkor
  medicine   616.396
  see also Digestive system
KwaZulu (South Africa)   T2—684 91
Kweichow Province (China)   T2—513 4
Kwese language   496.393
     T6—963 93
KWIC indexing   025.486
KWOC indexing   025.486
Kyabram (Vic.)   T2—945 4
Kyanite
  mineralogy   549.62
Kyle and Carrick (Scotland)   T2—414 64
Kyloe cattle
  animal husbandry   636.223
  zoology   599.735 8
Kymi (Finland : Lääni)   T2—489 71
Kyneton (Vic.)   T2—945 3
Kyogle (N.S.W.)   T2—944 3
Kyoto (Japan)   T2—521 864
Kyoto (Japan : Prefecture)   T2—521 86
Kyrie   264.36
  music   782.323 2
Kythera Island (Greece)   T2—495 2
Kyūshū (Japan : Island)   T2—522
Kyūshū Region (Japan)   T2—522
Kyustendil (Bulgaria : Okrug)   T2—497 73
Kyusyu (Japan : Island)   T2—522
Kyusyu Region (Japan)   T2—522

L

L.E.D. (Diodes)   621.381 522
L.O.D. (Optical disks)   384.558
  see also Video recordings
L.P.T.V. stations   384.55
  see also Television
L.S.D. abuse   362.294
  medicine   616.863 4
  personal health   613.83
  social welfare   362.294
  see also Substance abuse
La Altagracia (Dominican
  Republic : Province)   T2—729 385
La Coruña (Spain : Province)   T2—461 1
La Côte-de-Beaupré (Quebec)   T2—714 48
La Côte-de-Gaspé (Quebec)   T2—714 79
La Crosse County (Wis.)   T2—775 71
La Estrelleta (Dominican
  Republic : Province)   T2—729 343
La Grange County (Ind.)   T2—772 79
La Guajira (Colombia : Dept.)   T2—861 17
La Haute-Côte-Nord
  (Quebec)   T2—714 17
La Haute-Yamaska (Quebec)   T2—714 63

La Jacques-Cartier (Quebec)   T2—714 47
La Libertad (El Salvador :
  Dept.)   T2—728 422
La Libertad (Peru : Dept.)   T2—851 6
La Mancha (Spain)   T2—464
La Matapédia (Quebec :
  Regional County
  Municipality)   T2—714 775
La Mitis (Quebec)   T2—714 771
La Moure County (N.D.)   T2—784 53
La Nouvelle-Beauce (Quebec)   T2—714 71
La Pampa (Argentina :
  Province)   T2—821 3
La Paz (Bolivia : Dept.)   T2—841 2
La Paz (El Salvador : Dept.)   T2—728 425
La Paz (Honduras : Dept.)   T2—728 36
La Paz County (Ariz.)   T2—791 72
La Pérouse Strait   551.465 53
     T2—164 53
La Plata (Viceroyalty)   982.024
     T2—82
La Plata County (Colo.)   T2—788 29
La Plata Estuary   551.464 68
     T2—163 68
La Porte County (Ind.)   T2—772 91
La Rioja (Argentina :
  Province)   T2—824 6
La Rioja (Spain)   T2—463 54
La Rivière-du-Nord (Quebec)   T2—714 24
La Romana (Dominican
  Republic : Province)   T2—729 383
La Salle County (Ill.)   T2—773 27
La Salle County (Tex.)   T2—764 453
La Salle Parish (La.)   T2—763 75
La Spezia (Italy : Province)   T2—451 83
La Trobe River   T2—945 6
La Unión (El Salvador : Dept)   T2—728 434
La Union (Philippines)   T2—599 1
La Vallée-de-la-Gatineau
  (Quebec)   T2—714 221
La Vallée-du-Richelieu
  (Quebec : Regional
  County Municipality)   T2—714 36
La Vega (Dominican
  Republic)   T2—729 369
La Vérendrye Provincial Park
  (Quebec)   T2—714 21
Laadi language   496.393 1
     T6—963 931
Laayoune (Morocco :
  Province)   T2—648
Labanotation   792.82
Labeling
  library materials   025.7
  production management   658.564
  regulation   343.082
Labelle (Quebec : County)   T2—714 225

Laboring classes
  social welfare
    public administration (continued)
      local governments   352.944 85
Laboulbeniales   589.23
Labour Party (Australia)   324.294 07
Labour Party (Great Britain)   324.241 07
Labrador (Nfld.)   971.82
    T2—718 2
Labrador Current   551.471 4
Labrador Sea   551.461 43
    T2—163 43
Labyrinthodontia   567.6
Labyrinths (Ears)
  human anatomy   611.85
  human physiology   612.858
  see also Ears
Lac la Biche (Alta.)   T2—712 33
Lac qui Parle County (Minn.)   T2—776 38
Lac-Saint-Charles (Quebec)   T2—714 471
Lac-Saint-Jean-Est (Quebec :
  Regional County
  Municipality)   T2—714 14
Lac-Saint-Jean Region
  (Quebec)   T2—714 14
Laccadive Islands   T2—548 1
Laccadive Sea   551.467 37
    T2—165 37
Laccoliths   551.88
Lacerations (Wounds)
  medicine   617.143
Laces   677.653
  arts   746.22
  manufacturing technology   677.653
Lacewings   595.747
Lachlan River (N.S.W.)   T2—944 9
Lacings   677.76
Lacistemataceae   583.925
Lackawanna County (Pa.)   T2—748 36
Laclede County (Mo.)   T2—778 815
Laconia (Greece)   T2—495 2
  ancient   T2—389
Lacquer tree   583.28
Lacquering
  decorative arts   745.726
  furniture arts   749.5
  woodwork
    buildings   698.34
Lacquers   667.75
Lacrimal mechanisms
  human physiology   612.847
  ophthalmology   617.764
  see also Eyes
Lacrosse (Game)   796.347
Lacrosse players   796.347 092
  sports group   T7—796 34
Lactation   599.03
  animal physiology   599.03

Lactation (continued)
  human diseases
    obstetrics   618.71
    human physiology   612.664
Lactobacteriaceae   589.95
Lactoridaceae   583.114
Lactose   599.019 248 15
  biochemistry   599.019 248 15
  chemistry   547.781 5
  see also Carbohydrates
Ladin language   459.9
    T6—599
Ladin literature   859.9
Ladino language   467.949 6
    T6—67
Ladino literature   860
Ladismith (South Africa :
  District)   T2—687 16
Ladoga Lake (R.S.F.S.R.)   T2—472 5
Ladrone Islands   T2—967
Lady Frere (South Africa :
  District)   T2—687 91
Lady Grey (South Africa :
  District)   T2—687 6
Ladybell   583.57
Ladybrand (South Africa :
  District)   T2—685 5
Ladybugs   595.769
Lady's slipper   584.15
Ladysmith (South Africa)   T2—684 7
Lae (Papua New Guinea)   T2—957 1
Lafayette County (Ark.)   T2—767 57
Lafayette County (Fla.)   T2—759 816
Lafayette County (Miss.)   T2—762 83
Lafayette County (Mo.)   T2—778 453
Lafayette County (Wis.)   T2—775 79
Lafayette Parish (La.)   T2—763 47
Lafourche Parish (La.)   T2—763 39
Lag b'Omer   296.439
  customs   394.268 296 439
Lagenidiales   589.251
Laghouat (Algeria : Dept.)   T2—657
Lagomorpha   599.322
  paleozoology   569.322
Lagoons   551.460 9
    T2—168
  freshwater ecology   574.526 322
  saltwater ecology   574.526 36
Lagos, Los (Chile : Region)   T2—835
Lagos State (Nigeria)   T2—669 1
LaGrange County (Ind.)   T2—772 79
Lagrange polynomials   515.55
Laguerre polynomials   515.55
Laguna (Philippines :
  Province)   T2—599 1
Lahn River (Germany)   T2—434 14
Lahnda language   491.419
    T6—914 19

Lake of the Woods	T2—776 81
Canada	T2—713 11
Minnesota	T2—776 81
Lake of the Woods County (Minn.)	T2—776 81
Lake Okeechobee (Fla.)	T2—759 39
Lake Onega (R.S.F.S.R.)	T2—472 5
Lake Ontario (N.Y. and Ont.)	T2—747 9
New York	T2—747 9
Ontario	T2—713 5
Lake Pedder National Park	T2—946 2
Lake Pepin	T2—776 13
Lake Pontchartrain (La.)	T2—763 34
Lake Powell (Utah and Ariz.)	T2—792 59
Lake Reeve Fauna Reserve	T2—945 6
Lake Rudolf (Kenya and Ethiopia)	T2—676 27
Lake Saint Clair (Mich. and Ont.)	T2—774 39
Michigan	T2—774 39
Ontario	T2—713 31
Lake Saint Clair (Tas.)	T2—946 3
Lake Saint Clair National Park	T2—946 3
Lake Saint Lucia	T2—684 3
Lake Saint Marys	T2—771 415
Lake Sakakawea	T2—784 75
Lake Salvador	T2—763 33
Lake Sibaya	T2—684 91
Lake Sorell	T2—946 3
Lake States	T2—77
Lake Superior	T2—774 9
Michigan	T2—774 9
Ontario	T2—713 12
Lake Tahoe (Calif. and Nev.)	T2—794 38
California	T2—794 38
Nevada	T2—793 57
Lake Tanganyika	T2—678 28
Lake temperatures meteorological effect	551.524 8
Lake Texoma (Okla. and Tex.)	T2—766 61
Lake Titicaca (Peru and Bolivia)	T2—841 2
Bolivia	T2—841 2
Peru	T2—853 6
Lake Torrens	T2—942 38
Lake transportation	386.5
see also Inland waterway transportation	
Lake Turkana (Kenya and Ethiopia)	T2—676 27
Lake Tyrell	T2—945 9
Lake Victoria	T2—678 27
Lake Victoria (N.S.W.)	T2—944 8
Lake Wallenpaupack (Pa.)	T2—748 23
Lake Wellington	T2—945 6
Lake Winnebago	T2—775 64
Lake Winnibigoshish	T2—776 78
Lake Winnipeg (Man.)	T2—712 72
Lake Winnipegosis (Man.)	T2—712 72
Lake Winnipesaukee (N.H.)	T2—742 4
Lakes	551.482
	T2—169 2
engineering	627.14
fish culture	639.312
hydrology	551.482
international law	341.444
recreational resources	333.784 4
recreational use	797
resource economics	333.916 3
water-supply engineering	628.112
Lakes Entrance (Vic.)	T2—945 6
Lakōnia (Greece)	T2—495 2
ancient	T2—389
Lakshadweep (India)	T2—548 1
Lamaism	294.392 3
Lamar County (Ala.)	T2—761 86
Lamar County (Ga.)	T2—758 446
Lamar County (Miss.)	T2—762 19
Lamar County (Tex.)	T2—764 263
Lamarckism	575.016 6
Lamb County (Tex.)	T2—764 843
Lamba language	496.391
	T6—963 91
Lambayeque (Peru : Dept.)	T2—851 4
Lambda calculus	511.3
Lambert's Bay (South Africa)	T2—687 2
Lambeth (London, England)	T2—421 65
Lamb's quarters	583.913
Lambton (Ont.)	T2—713 27
Lamé	677.616
Lamellibranchia	594.11
paleozoology	564.11
Lamentations (Bible)	224.3
Lamiales	583.87
L'Amiante (Quebec)	T2—714 573
Laminar flow	532.052 5
air mechanics	533.62
gas mechanics	533.215
liquid mechanics	532.515
Laminariales	589.45
Laminated fabrics	677.69
see also Textiles	
Laminated glass	666.154
Laminated plastic	668.492
Laminated wood	674.835
materials science	620.12
Laminating plastics	668.414
Lamington National Park	T2—943 2
Lammermuir Hills	T2—413 6
Lamoille County (Vt.)	T2—743 35
Lamoille River (Vt.)	T2—743 35
Lamp shells	594.8
paleozoology	564.8
Lampasas County (Tex.)	T2—764 513

Land tenure	333.3
economics	333.3
law	346.043 2
sociology	306.32
Land titles	346.043 8
conveyancing	346.043 8
Land transfer	
economics	333.33
law	346.043 6
Land transportation	388
engineering	629.049
military engineering	623.61
see also Ground transportation	
Land trusts	
law	346.068
Land use	333.73
agricultural surveys	631.47
community sociology	307.33
economics	333.73
law	346.045
public administration	350.823 26
central governments	351.823 26
local governments	352.96
Land valuation	333.332
Land vehicles	388
engineering	629.049
transportation services	388
see also Automotive vehicles	
Landed gentry	305.523 2
	T1—086 21
Lander County (Nev.)	T2—793 33
Landes (France : Dept.)	T2—447 72
Landing	
aeronautics	629.132 521 3
manned space flight	629.458 8
Landing (Military tactics)	355.422
Landing accidents	363.124 92
see also Transportation safety	
Landing craft	359.835 6
design	623.812 56
engineering	623.825 6
naval equipment	359.835 6
naval units	359.325 6
Landing fields	387.736
see also Airports	
Landing lights	629.135 1
Landing systems	
aircraft	629.134 381
spacecraft	629.474 2
unmanned spacecraft	629.464 2
Landkreise	
government	320.83
public administration	352.007 3
Landlord and tenant	
land economics	333.54
law	346.043 4
Landlords' liability insurance	368.56
see also Insurance	
Landowners	333.009 2
occupational group	T7—333
Landowning classes	305.523 2
	T1—086 21
Landscape architects	712.092
occupational group	T7—71
Landscape architecture	712
engineering aspects	624
Landscape design	712
Landscapes	
art representation	704.943 6
drawing	743.836
painting	758.1
Landshut (Germany)	T2—433 58
Landslides	
geology	551.307
Landsmal language	439.83
	T6—398 3
Landsmal literature	839.83
Lane County (Kan.)	T2—781 45
Lane County (Or.)	T2—795 31
Langbaurgh (England)	T2—428 54
Langbaurgh-on-Tees	
(England)	T2—428 54
Langberg Range	T2—687 11
Langeberg Range	T2—687 3
Langeland (Denmark)	T2—489 4
Langlade County (Wis.)	T2—775 354
Langley (B.C.)	T2—711 37
Language	400
	T1—014
cultural anthropology	306.44
elementary education	372.6
law	344.09
Language acquisition	401.93
Language arts	
elementary education	372.6
Language disorders	
medicine	616.855
see also Communicative	
disorders	
Language groups (Sociology)	305.7
Language planning	306.449
Language policy	306.449
Language programs	
public administration	351.85
Language regions	T2—175
Language textbooks	
audio-lingual approach	T4—83
for nonnative speakers	T4—834
formal approach	T4—82
for nonnative speakers	T4—824
Language translators	
engineering	621.389 4
Language usage	418
elementary education	372.61
specific languages	T4—8
Languages	400

Laser optical disks	384.558
see also Video recordings	
Laser printing	686.233
Laser surgery	617.05
Laser warfare	358.39
Laser weapons	
military engineering	623.446
Lasers	621.366
Lashley, Karl Spencer	
psychological system	150.194 32
Lasithion (Greece : Nome)	T2—499 8
Lasqueti Island (B.C.)	T2—711 31
Lassen County (Calif.)	T2—794 26
Lassen Volcanic National	
Park (Calif.)	T2—794 24
L'Assomption (Quebec :	
County)	T2—714 416
L'Assomption (Quebec :	
Regional County	
Municipality)	T2—714 416
Lassos	
sports	799.202 82
Last Judgment	
Christianity	236.9
Last Supper	232.957
Latah County (Idaho)	T2—796 86
Latakia (Syria : Province)	T2—569 13
Latches	683.31
Latent heat of fusion	536.42
Latent heats	541.362
chemical engineering	660.296 2
Laterality	
psychology	152.335
Latex biscuits	678.522
Latex paints	667.63
Latexes	
biochemistry	583.041 92
chemistry	547.842 5
manufacturing technology	678.5
Lathers	541.345 14
chemical engineering	660.294 514
colloid chemistry	541.345 14
Lathes	621.942
Lathing	693.6
architectural construction	721.044 6
Latimer County (Okla.)	T2—766 76
Latin America	980
	T2—8
Latin American literature	860
Latin American Spanish dialects	467.98
	T6—61
Latin Americans	T5—68
Latin calligraphy	745.619 7
Latin language	470
	T6—71
Biblical texts	220.47
Latin literature	870
Latin peoples	T5—4
Latin squares	511.64
Latina (Italy : Province)	T2—456 23
Latinian languages	479.4
	T6—794
Latitude	
celestial navigation	527.1
geodetic astronomy	526.61
Latium (Italy)	T2—456 2
ancient	T2—376
Latrobe (Tas.)	T2—946 5
Latter-Day Saints	
biography	289.309 2
religious group	T7—283
Latter-Day Saints Church	289.3
see also Mormon Church	
Lattice dynamics	
solid state physics	530.411
Lattice-girder bridges	388
construction	624.37
see also Bridges	
Lattice plant	584.743
Lattice point geometry	516.35
Lattices (Crystals)	548.81
Lattices (Mathematics)	511.33
number theory	512.7
Latvia	T2—474 3
Latvian language	491.93
	T6—919 3
Latvian literature	891.93
Latvian Soviet Socialist	
Republic	T2—474 3
Latvians	T5—919 3
Lauderdale, Ettrick and	
(Scotland : District)	T2—413 85
Lauderdale County (Ala.)	T2—761 99
Lauderdale County (Miss.)	T2—762 676
Lauderdale County (Tenn.)	T2—768 16
Lauds	264.1
music	782.324
Launceston (Tas.)	T2—946 5
Launch complexes	
spacecraft	629.478
unmanned spacecraft	629.468
Launch vehicles	
guided missiles	623.451 9
Launching	
manned space flight	629.452
space flight	629.41
unmanned space flight	629.432
Launching complexes	
guided missiles	623.451 9
Launderers	648.109 2
occupational group	T7—648
Laundering	667.13
home economics	648.1
Laundries	
plumbing	696.183

Laymen
  social group — 305.909 09
    T7—090 9
Laymen (Church members) — 262.15
  see also Laity (Church
    members)
Layoffs of employees
  economics
    conditions of employment — 331.25
    unemployment — 331.137
    union control — 331.889 4
  law — 344.012 596
  personnel management — 658.313 4
  public administration — 350.184
    central governments — 351.184
    local governments — 352.005 184
Layouts
  plant management — 658.23
Laz language — 499.96
    T6—999 6
Lazarists — 255.77
  church history — 271.77
Lazio (Italy) — T2—456 2
Lazulite
  mineralogy — 549.72
Lazurite
  mineralogy — 549.68
Le Bas-Richelieu (Quebec) — T2—714 51
Le Centre-de-la-Mauricie
  (Quebec) — T2—714 451
Le Chatelier's principle — 541.392
Le Domaine-du-Roy
  (Quebec) — T2—714 14
Le Fjord-du-Saguenay
  (Quebec) — T2—714 16
Le Flore County (Okla.) — T2—766 79
Le Granit (Quebec) — T2—714 69
Le Haut-Richelieu (Quebec) — T2—714 61
Le Haut-Saint-François
  (Quebec) — T2—714 68
Le Haut-Saint-Laurent
  (Quebec) — T2—714 31
Le Haut-Saint-Maurice
  (Quebec) — T2—714 45
Le Roux Dam (South Africa) — T2—687 13
Le Sueur County (Minn.) — T2—776 553
Le Val-Saint-François
  (Quebec) — T2—714 65
Lea County (N.M.) — T2—789 33
Leach mining wells — 622.22
Lead — 669.4
  architectural construction — 721.044 74
  building construction — 693.74
  building material — 691.84
  chemical engineering — 661.068 8
  chemistry — 546.688
  decorative arts — 739.54
  economic geology — 553.44

Lead (continued)
  materials science — 620.183
  metallography — 669.954
  metallurgy — 669.4
  metalworking — 673.4
  mining — 622.344
  organic chemistry — 547.056 88
    applied — 661.895
  physical metallurgy — 669.964
  pollution — 363.738 4
  public safety — 363.179 1
    see also Safety
  toxicology — 615.925 688
  see also Chemicals, Metals
Lead azide — 662.27
Lead picrate — 662.27
Lead soldiers
  handicrafts — 745.592 82
Leaded glass
  arts — 748.5
Leadership — 303.34
  armed forces — 355.330 41
  executive management — 658.409 2
  political parties — 324.22
  psychology — 158.4
  public administration — 350.007 4
    central governments — 351.007 4
    local governments — 352.000 474
  social control — 303.34
Leadership of chief executives
  public administration — 350.003 23
    central governments — 351.003 23
    local governments — 352.008
Leading windows
  buildings — 698.5
Leadwort — 583.672
Leaf beetle — 595.764 8
Leaf fish — 597.58
Leaf flies — 595.774
Leaf frog — 597.87
Leaf hoppers — 595.752
Leaf insect — 595.724
League of Arab States — 341.247 7
  finance — 336.091 68
League of Augsburg, War of the,
  1688-1697 — 940.252 5
  North American history — 973.25
League of Nations — 341.22
  finance — 336.091 62
  international law — 341.22
  public administration — 354.1
League of Nations treaties series — 341.026 1
League rugby — 796.333 8
Leake County (Miss.) — T2—762 653
Leapfrog (Game) — 796.14
Learned societies — 060
  libraries — 027.68
  publishing — 070.594

Leg muscles	
human anatomy	611.738
see also Musculoskeletal system	
Leg techniques	
music	784.193 8
Lega-Kalanga languages	496.394
	T6—963 94
Legal accounting	657.834
Legal aid	362.58
criminal law	345.01
law	347.017
social service	362.58
welfare law	344.032 58
Legal codes	348.023
United States	348.732 3
Legal counsel	
management use	658.12
Legal documents	347
Legal ethics	174.3
Legal malpractice	
torts	346.033
Legal officers	347.016
occupational group	T7—349
Legal positivism	340.112
Legal procedure	347.05
Legal process	347.05
Legal reasoning	340.11
Legal research	340.072
Legal responsibility	346.03
Legal schools	340.109
Legal systems	340.5
Legal tender	332.420 42
Legal theories	340.109
Legalism (Chinese philosophy)	181.115
Legations	
architecture	725.17
public administration	351.892
Legendary animals	
folklore	398.245 4
sociology	398.469
literature	808.803 75
history and criticism	809.933 75
specific literatures	T3B—080 375
history and criticism	T3B—093 75
Legendary places	
folklore	398.234
literature	808.803 72
history and criticism	809.933 72
specific literatures	T3B—080 372
history and criticism	T3B—093 72
Legendre function	515.53
Legendre polynomials	515.55
Legendre transform	515.723
Legends	
art representation	704.947
folklore	398.2
paintings	753.7

Leghorns (Chickens)	
animal husbandry	636.55
see also Chickens	
Legionella	589.95
Legionnaires' disease	
medicine	616.241
see also Respiratory system	
Legions (Military units)	355.31
Legislation (Compilations)	348.02
Legislation (Enactment and	
repeal)	328.37
Legislative Assembly (1791-	
1792) (French history)	944.041
Legislative bodies	328.3
bibliographies of publications	011.532
law	342.05
Legislative branch	328
law	342.05
Legislative budget	
public administration	350.722 3
central governments	351.722 3
local governments	352.123
Legislative buildings	
architecture	725.11
Legislative duties	328.3
law	342.052
Legislative-executive relations	328.345 6
law	342.044
Legislative functions	328.34
law	342.052
Legislative hearings	348.01
United States	348.731
Legislative histories	348.01
United States	348.731
Legislative institutions	
sociology	306.23
Legislative-judicial relations	
law	342.044
Legislative opposition	
party organization	328.369
Legislative organization	328.36
law	342.057
Legislative oversight	328.345 6
Legislative powers	328.34
chief executives	350.003 22
central governments	351.003 22
local governments	352.008
law	342.052
Legislative privileges (Members)	328.347
Legislative procedure	328
law	342.057
Legislative reference bureaus	027.65
Legislative representation	328.334
Legislators	328.092
law	342.055
occupational group	T7—328
office	328.33
personal immunities	328.348

Lepidobotryaceae	583.214
Lepidodendrales	561.79
Lepidoptera	595.78
paleozoology	565.78
Lepidosauria	597.94
paleozoology	567.94
Lepidosireniformes	597.48
Lepisosteidae	597.47
Lepospondyli	567.6
Leprosy	
incidence	614.546
medicine	616.998
see also Communicable	
diseases (Human)	
Leptis Magna (Ancient city)	T2—397 4
Leptodactylidae	597.87
Leptolepidimorpha	567.5
Leptomitales	589.251
Leptons	539.721 1
Leptospira	589.99
Leptostraca	595.36
paleozoology	565.36
Leptureae	584.93
L'Érable (Quebec)	T2—714 575
Lérida (Spain : Province)	T2—467 4
Lernaeopodoida	595.34
paleozoology	565.34
Les Basques (Quebec)	T2—714 76
Les Chutes-de-la-Chaudière	
(Quebec)	T2—714 59
Les Etchemins (Quebec)	T2—714 72
Les Îles-de-la-Madeleine	
(Quebec)	T2—714 797
Les Jardins-de-Napierville	
(Quebec)	T2—714 35
Les Laurentides (Quebec)	T2—714 24
Les Maskoutains (Quebec)	T2—714 523
Les Moulins (Quebec)	T2—714 24
Les Pays-d'en-Haut (Quebec)	T2—714 24
Les Saintes	T2—729 76
Lesbianism	306.766 3
Lesbians	305.489 664
	T1—086 643
Lesbos (Greece : Nome)	T2—499
Lesbos Island (Greece)	T2—499
ancient	T2—391 2
Leslie County (Ky.)	T2—769 152
Lesotho	968.85
	T2—688 5
Lesotho people	T5—968 85
Lespedeza	583.322
forage crop	633.364
Lesser Antilles	T2—729
Lesser Slave Lake (Alta.)	T2—712 31
Lesser Sunda Islands	
(Indonesia)	T2—598 6
Lesson plans	371.302 8

Leszno (Poland :	
Voivodeship)	T2—438 4
Letaba (South Africa :	
District)	T2—682 6
Letcher County (Ky.)	T2—769 163
Lethal gases	
toxicology	615.91
Lethbridge (Alta.)	T2—712 345
Lettering	T1—022 1
architectural design	729.19
bookbinding	686.36
decorative arts	745.61
prints	769.5
stone	736.5
technical drawing	604.243
Letterpress	
mechanical printing technique	686.231 2
Letters (Correspondence)	383.122
biography	920
direct advertising	659.133
etiquette	395.4
office services	651.75
postal handling	383.122
see also Postal service	
Letters (Literature)	808.86
criticism	809.6
theory	801.956
history	809.6
rhetoric	808.6
specific literatures	T3B—6
individual authors	T3A—6
Letters of credit	332.77
law	346.096
Letters rogatory	341.78
Lettish language	491.93
	T6—919 3
Letts	T5—919 3
Lettuce	641.355 2
botany	583.55
commercial processing	664.805 52
cooking	641.655 2
garden crop	635.52
Letzeburgesch	437.949 35
	T6—32
Leucite	
mineralogy	549.68
Leucocytes	
human histology	611.018 5
human physiology	612.112
see also Cardiovascular system	
Leucocytosis	
medicine	616.15
see also Cardiovascular system	
Leucopenia	
medicine	616.15
see also Cardiovascular system	
Leukas (Greece : Nome)	T2—495 5

Libraries and museums	021.3
Library acquisitions	025.2
Library administration	025.1
Library aide positions	023.3
Library and state	021.8
Library boards	021.82
Library bookbinding	686.303 2
Library buildings	
architecture	727.8
area planning	711.57
planning	022.3
Library catalogs	025.31
bibliography	017
library science	025.31
maintenance	025.317
Library collections	
maintenance	025.8
Library commissions	021.82
Library consortia	021.65
Library consultants	023.2
Library cooperation	021.64
Library economy	025
Library equipment	022.9
Library information networks	021.65
Library legislation	344.092
Library materials	
preservation	025.84
selection policy	025.21
Library networks	021.65
Library of Congress	027.573
Library of Congress Classification	025.433
Library orientation	025.56
Library relationships	021
Library science	020
Library systems	
cooperative	021.65
operations	025
Library trustees	021.82
Library use studies	025.58
Librettos	780
treatises	780.268
Libreville (Gabon)	T2—672 1
Libya	961.2
	T2—612
ancient	939.74
Libyan Desert	T2—612
Libyans	T5—927 612
Lice	595.751
disease carriers	614.432 4
License agreements	343.07
international law	341.758
License fees	
public revenues	336.16
License plates	929.9
Licensing	
economic law	343.07
enforcement	363.233

Licensing (continued)	
export trade	382.64
see also Export trade	
import trade	382.54
see also Import trade	
intangible property law	346.048
public administration	350.8
central governments	351.8
local governments	352.8
Licensing Appeals Court (Scotland)	347.411 04
Licensing Courts (Scotland)	347.411 04
Lichen	589.1
Lichfield (England : District)	T2—424 68
Lichtenburg (South Africa : District)	T2—682 4
Licking County (Ohio)	T2—771 54
Licking River	T2—769 3
Lie algebras	512.55
Lie detectors	363.254
civil rights	323.448
criminal investigation	363.254
law of privacy	342.085 8
law of self-incrimination	345.056
personnel management	658.314
public administration	350.147
central governments	351.147
local governments	352.005 147
selection procedures	658.311 2
public administration	350.132 5
central governments	351.132 5
local governments	352.005 132 5
Lie groups	512.55
Liechtenstein	T2—436 48
Liège (Belgium : Province)	T2—493 46
Liens	346.074
Liesegang rings	541.348 5
Lieutenant governors	
public administration	351.003 18
Life	
biological nature	577
civil rights issue	323.43
medical ethics	174.24
origin	577
philosophy	113.8
religion	291.24
Christianity	231.765
natural theology	213
philosophy	113.8
respect for	
ethics	179.1
religion	291.569 1
Buddhism	294.356 91
Christianity	241.691
Hinduism	294.548 691
Judaism	296.385 691
Life after death	
occultism	133.901 3

Lighters (Ships) (continued)
  engineering 623.823 2
  see also Ships
Lighthouses 387.155
  engineering 627.922
  navigation aid 623.894 2
  transportation services 387.155
Lighting 621.32
  airport engineering 629.136 5
  architectural design 729.28
  automobile 629.271
  customs 392.36
  dramatic performances 792.025
    motion pictures 791.430 25
    stage 792.025
    television 791.450 25
  engineering 621.32
  household management 644.3
  interior decoration 747.92
  library buildings 022.7
  mining 622.47
  motion-picture photography 778.534 3
  museums 069.29
  plant management 658.24
  public areas 628.95
  religious significance 291.37
    Christianity 246.6
Lighting fixtures 621.32
  ceramic arts 738.8
  church architecture 726.529 8
  furniture arts 749.63
  household management 645.5
  manufacturing technology 683.83
Lightning 551.563 2
Lightning arresters 621.317
Lightning injury
  agriculture 632.15
Lightning protection
  buildings 693.898
Lightships 387.28
  engineering 623.828
  navigation aids 623.894 3
  see also Ships
Lignin
  recovery from pulp 676.5
Lignin-derived plastics 668.45
Lignite 553.22
  economic geology 553.22
  mining 622.332
  properties 662.622 2
Lignum vitae 583.214
Liguria (Italy) T2—451 8
  ancient T2—371
Ligurian language 491.993
   T6—919 93
Ligurian Sea 551.462 2
   T2—163 82
Lihou (England) T2—423 49

Lihoumel (England) T2—423 49
Lij Yasu, Negus of Ethiopia
  Ethiopian history 963.053
Lilacs 583.74
Lilaeaceae 584.744
L' Île d'Orléans (Quebec) T2—714 48
Liliaceae 584.324
Liliales 584.32
Lilies 584.324
  floriculture 635.934 324
Lilies of the valley 584.324
Lille Baelt (Denmark) 551.461 34
   T2—163 34
Lillooet (B.C.) T2—711 31
Lillooet Lake (B.C.) T2—711 31
Lillooet River (B.C.) T2—711 3
Lilongwe (Malawi) T2—689 7
Lima (Peru : Dept.) T2—852 5
Lima beans 641.356 53
  botany 583.322
  commercial processing 664.805 653
  cooking 641.656 53
  garden crop 635.653
Limarí (Chile : Province) T2—832 35
Limavady (Northern Ireland :
  District) T2—416 25
Limbo 236.6
Limburg (Belgium : Province) T2—493 24
Limburg (Netherlands) T2—492 48
Limburger cheese 641.373 53
  cooking 641.673 53
  processing 637.353
Lime 553.68
  use as soil conditioner 631.821
Lime (Linden)
  forestry 634.972 77
Lime mortars 666.93
Limerick (Ireland) T2—419 45
Limerick (Ireland : County) T2—419 4
Limericks 808.818
  history and criticism 809.18
  specific literatures T3B—107 5
    individual authors T3A—1
Limes (Fruit) 641.343 37
  botany 583.24
  commercial processing 664.804 337
  cooking 641.643 37
  orchard crop 634.337
Limestone 553.516
  building material 691.2
  economic geology 553.516
  petrology 552.58
  quarrying 622.351 6
Limestone County (Ala.) T2—761 98
Limestone County (Tex.) T2—764 285
Liming leather 675.22
Limitation of actions 347.052
Limitation of rights 323.49

Lingerie	391.42
commercial technology	687.22
customs	391.42
home economics	646.34
home sewing	646.420 4
see also Clothing	
Lingua francas	401.3
Linguatula	593.992
paleozoology	563.992
Linguistic change	417.7
specific languages	T4—7
Linguistic groups (Sociology)	305.7
Linguistic philosophies	149.94
Linguistics	410
Linguists	409.2
language specialists	409.2
specific languages	T4—092
linguistics specialists	410.92
specific languages	T4—092
occupational group	T7—4
Linin network	574.873 2
Linkage editors	005.43
Links (Mathematics)	514.224
Linlithgow, Victor Alexander	
John Hope, Marquess of	
Indian history	954.035 9
Linn County (Iowa)	T2—777 62
Linn County (Kan.)	T2—781 69
Linn County (Mo.)	T2—778 24
Linn County (Or.)	T2—795 35
Linoleum	645.1
building construction	698.9
household management	645.1
Linoleum-block printing	761.3
Linopteris	561.597
Linotype	
manufacturing technology	681.61
Linotype composition	
automatic	686.225 44
manual	686.225 42
Linsangs	599.744 22
Linseed oil	665.352
Linters	
plastic technology	668.411
Lions	599.744 28
animal husbandry	636.89
big game hunting	799.277 442 8
Lions, Gulf of	551.462 2
	T2—163 82
Lions Bay (B.C.)	T2—711 33
Lions International	369.5
Lions International members	369.5
social group	T7—369 5
Lion's River (South Africa :	
District)	T2—684 7
Lip-reed instruments	788.9
see also Brass instruments	
Lipari Islands (Italy)	T2—458 11

Lipases	574.192 53
see also Enzymes	
Lipetsk (R.S.F.S.R. : Oblast)	T2—473 5
Lipetskaia oblast (R.S.F.S.R.)	T2—473 5
Lipid synthesis	
plant metabolism	581.133 46
Lipids	574.192 47
biochemistry	574.192 47
human	612.015 77
biosynthesis	574.192 93
human	612.015 43
chemistry	547.77
metabolism	574.133
human physiology	612.397
see also Digestive system	
metabolism disorders	
medicine	616.399 7
Lipolytic enzymes	574.192 53
see also Enzymes	
Lipoproteins	574.192 454
biochemistry	574.192 454
chemistry	547.754
see also Proteins	
Lipostraca	565.32
Liposuction	617.95
Lippe River	T2—435 6
Lippmann process	778.63
Lipreading	
education	371.912 7
Lips	
human anatomy	611.317
human physiology	612.31
speech	612.78
personal care	646.726
surgery	617.522
see also Digestive system	
Lipscomb County (Tex.)	T2—764 816
Liquefaction of air	
technology	665.82
Liquefaction of coal	
technology	662.662 2
Liquefaction of gases	
physics of heat	536.44
Liquefied-hydrocarbon gas	665.773
Liqueurs	641.255
commercial processing	663.55
Liquid chromatography	543.089 4
Liquid crystals	530.429
Liquid-drop model (Nuclear	
physics)	539.742
Liquid dynamics	532.5
Liquid-gas interface	
physics	530.427
Liquid mechanics	532
engineering	620.106
Liquid particle technology	620.43
Liquid phases	
liquid state physics	530.424

Lithuanian Soviet Socialist
  Republic | T2—475
Lithuanians | T5—919 2
Litigation | 347.053
Litopterna | 569.75
Little Belt (Denmark) | 551.461 34
  | T2—163 34
Little Colorado River (N.M.
  and Ariz.) | T2—791 33
Little Inagua Island | T2—729 6
Little Kanawha River (W.
  Va.) | T2—754 2
Little Karoo | T2—687 16
Little league (Baseball) | 796.357 62
Little Missouri River | T2—784 8
Little River County (Ark.) | T2—767 55
Little Rock (Ark.) | T2—767 73
Little Russia | T2—477 1
Little Sioux River | T2—777 1
Little Sisters of the Poor | 255.95
  church history | 271.95
Little Tennessee River | T2—768 863
Little theater | 792.022 3
Littoria, Italy (Province) | T2—456 23
Liturgical drama
  music | 782.298
    choral and mixed voices | 782.529 8
    single voices | 783.092 98
Liturgical music | 782.29
  instrumental forms | 784.189 93
  vocal forms | 782.29
    choral and mixed voices | 782.529
    single voices | 783.092 9
Liturgical renewal | 264.001
Liturgy | 291.38
  Christianity | 264
  music | 782.3
  see also Public worship
Live Oak County (Tex.) | T2—764 447
Live programs
  radio performances | 791.443
  television performances | 791.453
Liver
  human anatomy | 611.36
  human diseases
    medicine | 616.362
  human physiology | 612.35
  surgery | 617.556
  see also Digestive system
Liver extracts
  pharmacology | 615.367
  see also Digestive system
Liverpool (England) | T2—427 53
Liverpool (N.S.) | T2—716 24
Liverpool (N.S.W.) | T2—944 1
Liverworts | 588.33
Livestock liability insurance | 368.56
  see also Insurance

Livestock production | 636
Living chess | 794.17
Living conditions
  armed forces | 355.12
Living rooms | 643.54
  home economics | 643.54
  interior decoration | 747.75
Living standard
  macroeconomics | 339.47
Livingston County (Ill.) | T2—773 61
Livingston County (Ky.) | T2—769 895
Livingston County (Mich.) | T2—774 36
Livingston County (Mo.) | T2—778 223
Livingston County (N.Y.) | T2—747 85
Livingston Parish (La.) | T2—763 14
Livonia | T2—474 1
Livonian language | 494.54
  | T6—945 4
Livonian literature | 894.54
Livonian War, 1557-1582 | 947.043
Livonians | T5—945 4
Livorno (Italy : Province) | T2—455 6
Lizard fish | 597.55
Lizards | 597.95
  small game hunting | 799.257 95
Lizard's tail (Plant) | 583.925
Llama wool textiles | 677.32
  see also Textiles
Llamas | 599.736
  animal husbandry | 636.296
Llanelli (Wales : Borough) | T2—429 67
Llano County (Tex.) | T2—764 62
Llano Estacado | T2—764 8
  New Mexico | T2—789 3
  Texas | T2—764 8
Llanquihue (Chile : Province) | T2—835 4
Lliw Valley (Wales :
  Borough) | T2—429 83
Lloydminster (Sask. and
  Alta.) | T2—712 42
Lloyds of London | 368.012 060 421 2
Loa, El (Chile) | T2—831 35
Loach | 597.52
Loaders (Computer programs) | 005.43
Loading equipment
  port engineering | 627.34
  ships | 623.867
Loading operations
  materials management | 658.788 5
  ships | 623.888 1
Loads (Structural analysis) | 624.172
Loan brokers | 332.34
Loan collections
  museology | 069.56
Loan services
  library science | 025.6
  museology | 069.13

Locomotion	591.185 2	Logging	
animals	591.185 2	forestry	634.98
human physiology	612.76	Logic (Reasoning)	160
see also Musculoskeletal		Logic circuits	621.395
system		Logic design	
physiology	574.18	computer circuits	621.395
psychology	152.382	Logic operators	511.3
Locomotives	385.36	Logical atomism	146.5
engineering	625.26	Logical positivism	146.42
mining	622.66	Logistics	
transportation services	385.36	management	658.5
monorail	385.5	military operations	355.411
special purpose	385.5	Logos	
see also Rolling stock		Christian doctrines	232.2
Locomotor ataxia		Logroño (Spain : Province)	T2—463 54
medicine	616.838	Logs	
see also Nervous system		forestry	634.98
Locoweed	583.111	Loir-et-Cher (France)	T2—445 3
Locris (Greece)	T2—495 1	Loire (France : Dept.)	T2—445 81
ancient	T2—383	Loire-Atlantique (France)	T2—441 4
Locust (Plant)	583.322	Loire-Inférieure (France)	T2—441 4
orchard crop	634.46	Loire River (France)	T2—445
Locusts	595.726	Loiret (France)	T2—445 2
LOD (Optical disks)	384.558	Loja (Ecuador : Province)	T2—866 25
see also Video recordings		Lolland (Denmark)	T2—489 3
Loddon River	T2—945 4	Lollards	284.3
Lodes		Loloish languages	495.4
economic geology	553.19		T6—954
mineralogy	549.119	Lombard kingdom (Italian	
Lodi dynasty (Indian history)	954.024 5	history)	945.01
Lodz (Poland : Voivodeship)	T2—438 4	Lombardia (Italy)	T2—452
Lofoten (Norway)	T2—484 5	Lombardy (Italy)	T2—452
Lofoten Islands (Norway)	T2—484 5	Lombok (Indonesia)	T2—598 6
Lofting		Lomé (Togo)	T2—668 1
ship hulls	623.842	Lomond, Loch (Scotland)	T2—414 25
Logan County (Ark.)	T2—767 37	Lomza (Poland :	
Logan County (Colo.)	T2—788 75	Voivodeship)	T2—438 3
Logan County (Ill.)	T2—773 57	London (England)	T2—421
Logan County (Kan.)	T2—781 135	London (Ont.)	T2—713 26
Logan County (Ky.)	T2—769 76	Londonderry (Northern	
Logan County (N.D.)	T2—784 56	Ireland)	T2—416 21
Logan County (Neb.)	T2—782 795	Londonderry (Northern	
Logan County (Ohio)	T2—771 463	Ireland : County)	T2—416 2
Logan County (Okla.)	T2—766 33	Loneliness	155.92
Logan County (W. Va.)	T2—754 44	applied psychology	158.2
Loganberries	641.347 14	Long County (Ga.)	T2—758 762
botany	583.372	Long-distance service	384.64
cooking	641.647 14	see also Telephone	
horticulture	634.714	Long-haired cats	
Loganiales	583.74	animal husbandry	636.83
Logarithms	512.922	see also Cats	
algebra	512.922	Long Island (Bahamas)	T2—729 6
arithmetic	513.22	Long Island (N.Y.)	T2—747 21
Logbooks		Long Island (Papua New	
aeronautics	629.132 54	Guinea)	T2—957 3
Loggers	634.980 92	Long Island Sound (N.Y. and	
occupational group	T7—634	Conn.)	551.461 46
			T2—163 46

Lotbinière (Quebec : Regional
    County Municipality)   T2—714 58
Lothair II, Holy Roman Emperor
    German history   943.023
Lothian (Scotland)   T2—413 2
Lotteries
    occupational ethics   174.6
    use in advertising   659.17
Lottery income
    public administration   350.726
        central governments   351.726
        local governments   352.14
    public finance   336.17
Lotto   795.3
Loudness
    acoustical engineering   620.21
Loudon County (Tenn.)   T2—768 863
Loudoun, Kilmarnock and
    (Scotland : District)   T2—414 63
Loudoun County (Va.)   T2—755 28
Louga (Senegal : Region)   T2—663
Lough Neagh   T2—416
Louis Philippe, King of the
    French
    French history   944.063
Louis Trichardt (South
    Africa)   T2—682 5
Louis VI, King of France
    French history   944.022
Louis VII, King of France
    French history   944.022
Louis VIII, King of France
    French history   944.023
Louis IX, King of France
    French history   944.023
Louis X, King of France
    French history   944.024
Louis XI, King of France
    French history   944.027
Louis XII, King of France
    French history   944.027
Louis XIII, King of France
    French history   944.032
Louis XIV, King of France
    French history   944.033
Louis XV, King of France
    French history   944.034
Louis XVI, King of France
    French history   944.035
    1774-1789   944.035
    1789-1792   944.041
Louis XVIII, King of France
    French history   944.061
    1814-1815   944.05
    1815-1824   944.061
Louisa County (Iowa)   T2—777 926
Louisa County (Va.)   T2—755 465
Louisbourg (N.S.)   T2—716 955

Louisiade Archipelago   T2—954 1
Louisiana   976.3
        T2—763
Louisiana French Creole   447.976 3
        T6—41
Louisville (Ky.)   T2—769 44
Lounge cars   385.33
    engineering   625.23
    see also Rolling stock
Loup County (Neb.)   T2—782 767
Loup River   T2—782 4
Lourenço Marques
    (Mozambique : District)   T2—679 1
Louse-borne typhus
    incidence   614.526 2
    medicine   616.922 2
    see also Communicable
        diseases (Human)
Louse flies   595.774
Louth (Ireland)   T2—418 25
Louwsburg (South Africa)   T2—684 2
Love
    ethics   177.7
        religion   291.5
            Buddhism   294.35
            Christianity   241.4
            Hinduism   294.548
            Islam   297.5
            Judaism   296.385
    folklore
        sociology   398.354
    God's   212.7
        Christianity   231.6
        comparative religion   291.211
    literature   808.803 54
        history and criticism   809.933 54
        specific literatures   T3B—080 354
            history and criticism   T3B—093 54
    philosophy   128.4
    psychology   152.41
    social interaction   302.3
Love apples   583.79
Love County (Okla.)   T2—766 59
Love feasts
    Christian rites   265.9
Love spells and charms   133.442
Love stories   808.838 5
    history and criticism   809.385
    specific literatures   T3B—308 5
        individual authors   T3A—3
Lovebirds
    animal husbandry   636.686 4
Lovech okrug (Bulgaria)   T2—497 76
Loveshki okrug (Bulgaria)   T2—497 76
Loving County (Tex.)   T2—764 912
Loving cups   739.228 4
Low Archipelago   T2—963 2

LSD abuse (continued)
   social welfare   362.294
   see also Substance abuse
Luanda (Angola : Province)   T2—673 2
Luapala Province (Zambia)   T2—689 4
Luba (African people)   T5—963 93
Luba (Kingdom)   967.518 01
    T2—675 18
Luba languages   496.393
    T6—963 93
Lubang Islands   T2—599 3
Lubbock County (Tex.)   T2—764 847
Lubisi Dam   T2—687 91
Lublin (Poland : Voivodeship)   T2—438 4
Lubricants
   automobiles   629.255
   plastic technology   668.411
Lubricating grease   665.538 5
Lubricating oil   665.538 5
Lubrication   621.89
Lubumbashi (Zaire)   T2—675 18
Lucania (Italy)   T2—457 7
   ancient   T2—377
Lucas County (Iowa)   T2—777 863
Lucas County (Ohio)   T2—771 12
Lucazi language   496.399
    T6—963 99
Lucca (Italy : Province)   T2—455 3
Luce County (Mich.)   T2—774 925
Lucernariida   593.73
Lucerne (Plant)   583.322
   forage crop   633.31
Lucerne (Switzerland)   T2—494 55
Lucerne, Lake (Switzerland)   T2—494 55
Luchazi language   496.399
    T6—963 99
Luchu   T2—522 9
Lucifer
   Christianity   235.47
   Judaism   296.316
Ludwigshafen am Rhein
   (Germany)   T2—434 353
Luffa   583.46
Luganda language   496.395 7
    T6—963 957
Luganda literature   896.395 7
Lugano, Lake of   T2—494 78
Lugansk (Ukraine : Oblast)   T2—477 16
Luganskaia oblast (Ukraine)   T2—477 16
Lugbara (African people)   T5—965
Lugbara language   496.5
    T6—965
Lugdunensis   T2—364
Lugeing   796.95
Luggage
   manufacturing technology   685.51
Lugo (Spain : Province)   T2—461 3

Luhya language   496.395
    T6—963 95
Luke (Gospel)   226.4
Lumber   674
Lumber industry   338.476 74
   law   343.078 674
Lumber industry workers   674.092
   occupational group   T7—674
Lumbering   634.98
Lumberyards   674.32
Luminescence   535.35
   materials science   620.112 95
   physics   535.35
Luminism   709.034 4
   painting   759.054
Luminous paints   667.69
Luminous-tube lighting   621.327
Lumped-parameter systems   003.7
Lumpkin County (Ga.)   T2—758 273
Luna County (N.M.)   T2—789 68
Lunar flights   629.454
   manned   629.454
   unmanned   629.435 3
Lunch   642
   cooking   641.53
   customs   394.15
Lunch periods
   personnel management   658.312 1
Lunda (Kingdom)   967.340 1
    T2—673 4
Lunda languages   496.393
    T6—963 93
Lunda Norte (Angola :
   Province)   T2—673 4
Lunda Sul (Angola :
   Province)   T2—673 4
Lundu-Balong languages   496.396
    T6—963 96
Lüneburg (Germany :
   Regierungsbezirk)   T2—435 93
Lunenburg (N.S. : County)   T2—716 23
Lunenburg County (Va.)   T2—755 643
Lung cancer
   medicine   616.994 24
   see also Cancer
Lungfish   597.48
Lungs
   human anatomy   611.24
   human diseases
     medicine   616.24
   human physiology   612.2
   surgery   617.542
   see also Respiratory system
Luo (African people)   T5—965
Luo language (Africa)   496.5
    T6—965
Luorawetlin languages   494.6
    T6—946

Lyme disease	
medicine	616.92
see also Communicable	
diseases (Human)	
Lymph	
human histology	611.018 5
human physiology	612.42
see also Lymphatic system	
Lymph plasma	
human histology	611.018 5
see also Lymphatic system	
Lymphatic glands	
human anatomy	611.46
human physiology	612.42
see also Lymphatic system	
Lymphatic system	596.011
animal physiology	596.011
cancer	362.196 994 42
glands	616.994 46
medicine	616.994 42
social services	362.196 994 42
see also Cancer	
geriatrics	618.976 42
human anatomy	611.42
glands	611.46
human diseases	362.196 42
incidence	614.594 2
medicine	616.42
social services	362.196 42
human histology	611.018 5
human physiology	612.42
pediatrics	618.924 2
pharmacodynamics	615.74
surgery	617.44
Lymphatitis	
medicine	616.42
see also Lymphatic system	
Lymphocytes	
human histology	611.018 5
human immunology	616.079
see also Lymphatic system	
Lymphogranuloma venereum	
incidence	614.547
medicine	616.951 8
see also Communicable	
diseases (Human)	
Lymphokines	
human immunology	616.079
Lymphomatosis	
medicine	616.42
see also Lymphatic system	
Lynchburg (Va.)	T2—755 671
Lynches River	T2—757 6
Lynching	364.134
law	345.023 4
Lynn County (Tex.)	T2—764 851
Lyon (France)	T2—445 823
Lyon County (Iowa)	T2—777 114

Lyon County (Kan.)	T2—781 62
Lyon County (Ky.)	T2—769 813
Lyon County (Minn.)	T2—776 363
Lyon County (Nev.)	T2—793 58
Lyonnais (France)	T2—445 8
Lyres	787.78
see also Stringed instruments	
Lyric poetry	808.814
history and criticism	809.14
specific literatures	T3B—104
individual authors	T3A—1
Lyrics	780
treatises	780.268
Lysergic acid diethylamide abuse	362.294
medicine	616.863 4
personal health	613.83
social welfare	362.294
see also Substance abuse	
Lysosomes	574.874
Lythrales	583.44
Lytton (B.C.)	T2—711 72
Lytton, Edward Robert Bulwer	
Lytton, Earl of	
Indian history	954.035 3
Lzhedmitrii I, Czar of Russia	
Russian history	947.045
Lzhedmitrii II	
Russian history	947.045

M

M.A.R.C. system	
format	025.316
M.A.T.S. (Air transportation)	358.44
M.I.C.R. (Computer science)	006.4
engineering	621.399
M.O.S. memory	004.53
engineering	621.397 32
M.P. (Military police)	355.133 23
M.R.I. (Imaging)	
medicine	616.075 48
Maan (Jordan : District)	T2—569 57
Maas River	T2—492 4
Belgium	T2—493 46
Netherlands	T2—492 4
Maasai language	496.5
	T6—965
Maastricht (Netherlands)	T2—492 48
Macadam pavements	625.86
road engineering	625.86
sidewalk engineering	625.886
Macadamia nuts	641.345
agriculture	634.5
Macadamia tree	583.932
Macallister River	T2—945 6
Macao	951.26
	T2—512 6

Macquarie River	T2—944 9	Madhyamika Buddhism	294.392
Macramé	746.422 2	Madikwe (South Africa :	
Macro-Algonkian languages	497.3	District)	T2—682 94
	T6—973	Madison (Wis.)	T2—775 83
Macro-Carib languages	498.4	Madison, James	
	T6—984	United States history	973.51
Macro-Chibchan languages	498.2	Madison County (Ala.)	T2—761 97
	T6—982	Madison County (Ark.)	T2—767 15
North America	497.8	Madison County (Fla.)	T2—759 85
	T6—978	Madison County (Ga.)	T2—758 152
Macro-Gê languages	498.4	Madison County (Idaho)	T2—796 55
	T6—984	Madison County (Ill.)	T2—773 86
Macro-Khoisan languages	496.1	Madison County (Ind.)	T2—772 57
	T6—961	Madison County (Iowa)	T2—777 81
Macro-Otomanguean languages	497.6	Madison County (Ky.)	T2—769 53
	T6—976	Madison County (Miss.)	T2—762 623
Macro-Panoan languages	498.4	Madison County (Mo.)	T2—778 91
	T6—984	Madison County (Mont.)	T2—786 663
Macro-Penutian languages	497.4	Madison County (N.C.)	T2—756 875
	T6—974	Madison County (N.Y.)	T2—747 64
Macro processors	005.45	Madison County (Neb.)	T2—782 54
Macro-Sudanic languages	496.5	Madison County (Ohio)	T2—771 55
	T6—965	Madison County (Tenn.)	T2—768 27
Macro-Tucanoan languages	498.3	Madison County (Tex.)	T2—764 237
	T6—983	Madison County (Va.)	T2—755 38
Macroeconomic policy	339.5	Madison Parish (La.)	T2—763 81
Macroeconomic theory	339.3	Madness	362.2
Macroeconomics	339	social psychology	302.542
Macroinstructions		*see also* Mental illness	
programming	005.13	Madonna and Child	
programs	005.3	art representation	704.948 55
Macromolecular biochemicals	574.192	Madras (India : State)	T2—548 2
Macromolecular compounds		Madre de Dios (Peru : Dept.)	T2—854 2
biochemistry	574.192	Madrid (Spain : Province)	T2—464 1
chemistry	547.7	Madrid Hurtado, Miguel de la	
Macronutrient elements		Mexican history	972.083 4
plant metabolism	581.133 54	Madrigals	782.43
Macrophages		choral and mixed voices	782.543
human immunology	616.079	single voices	783.094 3
Macrosudanic languages	496.5	Madriz (Nicaragua)	T2—728 523
	T6—965	Madura Island (Indonesia)	T2—598 2
Macrotonality	781.265	Madurese language	499.22
Macrura	595.384 1		T6—992 2
Madadeni (South Africa :		Maffra, Australia (Victoria)	T2—945 6
District)	T2—684 91	Mafia	364.106
Madagascar	969.1	Mafia Island	T2—678 23
	T2—691	Mafikeng (South Africa)	T2—682 94
Madang Province (Papua New		Magadan (R.S.F.S.R.)	T2—577
Guinea)	T2—957 3	Magahi language	491.454 7
Madawaska (N.B. : County)	T2—715 54		T6—914 54
Madder	583.52	Magahi literature	891.454
Madeira Islands	T2—469 8	Magaliesberg Range (South	
Madeleine, Îles de la		Africa)	T2—682 3
(Quebec)	T2—714 797	Magallanes (Chile : Province)	T2—836 44
Madera County (Calif.)	T2—794 81	Magallanes y Antártica	
Madhvacharya (Philosophy)	181.484 1	Chilena (Chile)	T2—836 4
Madhya Bharat (India)	T2—543	Magar	T5—95
Madhya Pradesh (India)	T2—543		

Magnetization	
physics	538.3
Magnetochemistry	541.378
chemical engineering	660.297 8
Magnetohydrodynamic	
generation	621.312 45
Magnetohydrodynamic power	
systems	
spacecraft	629.474 45
unmanned spacecraft	629.464 45
Magnetohydrodynamic	
propulsion	
spacecraft	629.475 5
Magnetohydrodynamics	538.6
Magnetosphere (Earth)	538.766
meteorology	551.514
Magnetostriction	538.3
Magnetrons	621.381 334
Magnets	538.4
Magnitudes (Stars)	523.822
Magnoliales	583.114
Magnolias	583.114
Magoffin County (Ky.)	T2—769 215
Magpie larks	598.8
Magpies	598.864
Magsaysay, Ramon	
Philippine history	959.904 3
Magyar language	494.511
	T6—945 11
Magyar literature	894.511
Magyars	T5—945 11
Mah-jongg	795.3
Mahabharata	294.592 3
Mahajanga (Madagascar :	
Province)	T2—691
Maharashtra (India)	T2—547 92
Mahasanghika Buddhism	294.391
Mahaska County (Iowa)	T2—777 84
Mahathir bin Mohamad	
Malaysian history	959.505 4
Mahayana Buddhism	294.392
Mahé Island (Seychelles)	T2—696
Mahl language	491.487
	T6—914 8
Mahl literature	891.48
Mahlabatini (South Africa :	
District)	T2—684 91
Mahnomen County (Minn.)	T2—776 94
Mahogany	583.25
Mahomet the Prophet	297.63
Mahoning County (Ohio)	T2—771 39
Mahoning River (Ohio and	
Pa.)	T2—771 39
Mahratta	T5—948
Mahri	T5—929
Mahri language	492.9
	T6—929
Mahri literature	892.9

Maidenhair fern	587.31
Maidenhair tree	585.7
Maidenhead, Windsor and	
(England)	T2—422 96
Maidstone (England :	
Borough)	T2—422 375
Maiduguri (Nigeria)	T2—669 85
Mail	383
law	343.099 2
see also Postal service	
Mail art	709.04
Mail cars	385.33
engineering	625.23
see also Rolling stock	
Mail fraud	364.136
law	345.023 6
Mail handling	383.1
office services	651.759
Mail openers	
office use	651.759
Mail-order catalogs	T1—029 4
direct advertising	659.133
Mail-order houses	381.142
management	658.872
see also Commerce	
Mail sealers	
office use	651.759
Mail service	383.1
see also Postal service	
Maimonides, Moses	
Judaistic sources	296.172
Main Barrier Range	T2—944 9
Main dishes (Cooking)	641.82
Main memory (Computer)	004.53
engineering	621.397 3
Main River (Germany)	T2—434
Maine	974.1
	T2—741
Maine (France)	T2—441 6
Maine-et-Loire (France)	T2—441 8
Mainframe computers	004.12
architecture	004.252
communications	004.612
programming	005.712 2
programs	005.713 2
engineering	621.391 2
graphics programming	006.672
graphics programs	006.682
interfacing	004.612
programming	005.712 2
programs	005.713 2
operating systems	005.442
performance evaluation	004.120 297
for design and improvement	004.252
peripherals	004.712
programming	005.22
programs	005.32
systems analysis	004.252

Mainframe computers (continued)
  systems design 004.252
Mains
  water-supply engineering 628.15
Mainstream jazz 781.654
Mainstreaming in education 371.904 6
Mainstreaming in library services 027.663
Maintainability engineering 620.004 5
Maintenance 620.004 6
    T1—028 8
  plant management 658.202
    T1—068 2
    public administration 350.713 044
      central governments 351.713 044
      local governments 352.163 044
Maintenance (Domestic
  relations) 346.016 6
Maintenance cuttings
  silviculture 634.953
Maintenance facilities
  spacecraft 629.478
  unmanned spacecraft 629.468
Mainz (Rhineland-Palatinate,
  Germany) T2—434 351
Maithili language 491.454 7
    T6—914 54
Maithili literature 891.454
Maitland (N.S.W.) T2—944 2
Maitland (S. Aust.) T2—942 35
Maize 641.331 5
  see also Corn
Majingai dialect 496.5
    T6—965
Major County (Okla.) T2—766 29
Major surgery 617.025
Majorca (Spain) T2—467 54
Majority (Age)
  customs 392.15
  etiquette 395.24
  law 346.013 5
  music 781.584
Maka-Njem languages 496.396
    T6—963 96
Makasar Strait 551.465 73
    T2—164 73
Make-ahead meals
  cooking 641.555
Make-work arrangements
  economics 331.120 42
  unions 331.889 6
Makeup 646.72
  dramatic performances 792.027
  motion pictures 791.430 27
  stage 792.027
  television 791.450 27
  see also Cosmetics
Makhado (South Africa) T2—682 91
Makin Island T2—968 1

Makonde (African people) T5—963 97
Makonde language 496.397
    T6—963 97
Makua languages 496.397
    T6—963 97
Makula (Solomon Islands :
  Province) T2—959 39
Makula and Temotu Province
  (Solomon Islands) T2—959 39
Makurdi (Nigeria) T2—669 54
Malabo (Equatorial Guinea) T2—671 86
Malabsorption
  medicine 616.342 3
  see also Digestive system
Malacca (State) T2—595 1
Malacca, Strait of 551.467 65
    T2—165 65
Malachi (Biblical book) 224.99
Malachite
  mineralogy 549.785
Malacology 594
Malacostraca 595.37
  paleozoology 565.37
Maladjusted students 371.93
Maladjusted young people 305.908 24
    T1—087 4
    T7—082 4
  social group 305.908 24
  social welfare 362.74
Maladjustments
  international commerce 382.3
Málaga (Spain : Province) T2—468 5
Malagasy T5—993
Malagasy language 499.3
    T6—993
Malagasy literature 899.3
Malagasy Republic T2—691
Malaita Province (Solomon
  Islands) T2—959 37
Malalaua (Papua New
  Guinea) T2—954 7
Malamulele (South Africa :
  District) T2—682 92
Malan, Daniel François
  South African history 968.056
Malanje (Angola : Province) T2—673 4
Malaria
  incidence 614.532
  medicine 616.936 2
  see also Communicable
    diseases (Human)
Malaspina Peninsula (B.C.) T2—711 31
Malatya (Turkey : Province) T2—565
Malawi 968.97
    T2—689 7
Malawi (Kingdom) 968.970 1
    T2—689 7
Malawi, Lake T2—689 7

Malawi people	T5—968 97
Malawians	T5—968 97
Malay Archipelago	T2—598
Malay Archipelago inner seas	551.465 73
	T2—164 73
Malay language	499.28
	T6—992 8
Malay languages	499.2
	T6—992
Malay literature (Bahasa Malaysia)	899.28
Malay-Polynesian languages	499.2
	T6—992
Malaya	T2—595 1
Malayalam language	494.812
	T6—948 12
Malayalam literature	894.812
Malayalis	T5—948 12
Malayan languages	499.2
	T6—992
Malayan literatures	899.2
Malayo-Polynesian languages	499.2
	T6—992
Malayo-Polynesians	T5—992
Malays (Asian people)	T5—992
Malaysia	959.5
	T2—595
Malaysia, East	T2—595 3
Malaysians	T5—992
Malcolm Island (B.C.)	T2—711 2
Malden Island	T2—964
Maldive Islands	T2—549 5
Maldives	954.95
	T2—549 5
Maldivian language	491.487
	T6—914 8
Maldivian literature	891.48
Maldivians	T5—914 1
Maldon (England : District)	T2—426 756
Maldon (Vic.)	T2—945 3
Maldonado (Uruguay : Dept.)	T2—895 15
Male breast (Human)	
diseases	
medicine	616.49
surgery	617.549
Male genital system	591.166
anesthesiology	617.967 463
animal physiology	591.166
cancer	362.196 994 63
medicine	616.994 63
social services	362.196 994 63
see also Cancer	
human anatomy	611.63
human diseases	362.196 65
incidence	614.596 5
medicine	616.65
social services	362.196 65
human physiology	612.61
Male genital system (continued)	
surgery	617.463
Malenkov, Georgi	
Russian history	947.085 2
Males (Human)	305.31
	T1—081
grooming	646.704 4
health	613.042 3
see also Men	
Malesherbiaceae	583.456
Malfeasance by employees	
prevention	
personnel management	658.314
Malfeasance in office	364.132
see also Misconduct in office	
Malheur County (Or.)	T2—795 97
Mali	966.23
	T2—662 3
Mali Empire	966.201 7
	T2—662
Malians	T5—966 23
Malignant cholera	
incidence	614.514
medicine	616.932
see also Communicable diseases (Human)	
Malignant tumors	
medicine	616.994
see also Cancer	
Malikites (Islamic sect)	297.813
Malinke language	496.34
	T6—963 4
Malis (Greece)	T2—383
Mallacoota Inlet National Park	T2—945 6
Malleability	
materials science	620.112 5
Malleco (Chile)	T2—834 5
Mallee (Vic. : District)	T2—945 9
Mallet games	796.35
Malling, Tonbridge and (England)	T2—422 372
Mallophaga	595.751 4
paleozoology	565.75
Mallorca (Spain)	T2—467 54
Mallow	583.17
Malls (Shopping)	381.1
see also Shopping malls	
Malmesbury (South Africa : District)	T2—687 3
Malmohus lan (Sweden)	T2—486
Malnutrition	
medicine	616.39
see also Digestive system	
Malone shorthand system	653.426
Malpighiales	583.214
Malpractice	
torts	346.033

Manche (France)	T2—442 1	Manganese (continued)	
Manchester (England)	T2—427 33	toxicology	615.925 541
Manchester (N.H.)	T2—742 8	see also Chemicals, Metals	
Manchester terrier (Standard dog)		Manganese group	
animal husbandry	636.755	chemical engineering	661.054
see also Dogs		chemistry	546.54
Manchester terrier (Toy dog)		Manganite	
animal husbandry	636.76	mineralogy	549.53
see also Dogs		Mange	
Manchineel	583.95	medicine	616.57
Manchu	T5—941	see also Skin	
Manchu dynasty (Chinese		Mango	641.344 4
history)	951.03	botany	583.28
Manchu languages	494.1	cooking	641.644 4
	T6—941	orchard crop	634.44
Manchu literatures	894.1	Mangosteen	641.346 55
Manchuria	T2—518	agriculture	634.655
Manda languages	496.391	botany	583.163
	T6—963 91	cooking	641.646 55
Mandarin Chinese language	495.1	Mangroves	583.42
	T6—951 1	Mangue Indians	T5—976
Mandated states		Manguean languages	497.6
establishment			T6—976
World War I	940.314 26	Manhattan (New York, N.Y.)	T2—747 1
World War II	940.531 426	Manholes	
political science	321.08	sewers	628.25
Mandates		Manic-depressive psychoses	
international law	341.27	medicine	616.895
Mande (African people)	T5—963 4	see also Mental illness	
Mande languages	496.34	Manica (Mozambique :	
	T6—963 4	District)	T2—679 4
Mandekan languages	496.34	Manicheism	299.932
	T6—963 4	Christian heresy	273.2
Mandingo (African people)	T5—963 4	Manicouagan (Quebec :	
Mandingo languages	496.34	Regional County	
	T6—963 4	Municipality)	T2—714 17
Mandingo literatures	896.34	Manicure tools	
Mandini (South Africa)	T2—684 4	manufacturing technology	688.5
Mandinka languages	496.34	Manicuring	646.727
	T6—963 4	Manifold topology	514.3
Mandolins	787.84	Manifolds (Mathematics)	516.07
see also Stringed instruments		geometry	516.07
Mandrake	583.79	topology	514.223
Maneuvers (Military)	355.4	Manihiki Islands	T2—962 4
training	355.52	Manihot	583.95
Manganese	669.732	Manila (Philippines)	T2—599 16
chemical engineering	661.054 1	Manila hemp	584.21
chemistry	546.541	fiber crop	633.571
economic geology	553.462 9	Manila paper	676.287
materials science	620.189 32	Manioc	641.336 82
metallography	669.957 32	starch crop	633.682
metallurgy	669.732	see also Cassava	
metalworking	673.732	Manipur (India)	T2—541 7
mining	622.346 29	Manisa Ili (Turkey)	T2—562
organic chemistry	547.055 41	Manistee County (Mich.)	T2—774 62
applied	661.895	Manistee River	T2—774 6
physical metallurgy	669.967 32	Manitoba	971.27
			T2—712 7

Maple sugar	641.336 4
commercial processing	664.132
see also Sugar	
Maple syrup	641.336 4
agriculture	633.64
commercial processing	664.132
Maplewood (N.J.)	T2—749 33
Mapping services	
armed forces	355.343 2
Mappings (Mathematics)	511.33
topology	514
Maps	912
	T1—022 3
aeronautics	629.132 54
cartography	526
military engineering	623.71
cataloging	025.346
geography	912
library treatment	025.176
printing	686.283
publishing	070.579 3
Maps (Mathematics)	511.33
Mapulaneng (South Africa : District)	T2—682 93
Mapumulo (South Africa : District)	T2—684 91
Maputaland (South Africa)	T2—684 91
Maputo (Mozambique : District)	T2—679 1
Maputo River	T2—684 2
Mozambique	T2—679 1
South Africa	T2—684 2
Maqurrah (Kingdom)	962.502 2
	T2—625
Mar Thoma Church	281.5
see also Eastern churches	
Mara Region (Tanzania)	T2—678 27
Maracaibo, Gulf of	551.463 5
	T2—163 65
Maracaibo Lake (Venezuela)	T2—872 3
Maracas	786.885
see also Percussion instruments	
Marakwet (African people)	T5—965
Marakwet language	496.5
	T6—965
Maramures (Romania : Judet)	T2—498 4
Maranhão (Brazil)	T2—812 1
Marantaceae	584.21
Maras Ili (Turkey)	T2—565
Maratha	T5—948
Marathi language	491.46
	T6—914 6
Marathi literature	891.46
Marathon (Ancient city)	T2—385
Marathon County (Wis.)	T2—775 29
Marathon races	796.425
Marattiales	587.33
paleobotany	561.73

Marble	553.512
building material	691.2
economic geology	553.512
petrology	552.4
quarrying	622.351 2
Marbles (Game)	796.2
Marbling	
bookbinding	686.36
Marbling (Woodwork)	
buildings	698.32
MARC system	
format	025.316
Marcgraviaceae	583.166
March flies	595.771
March form	784.189 7
Marchantiaceae	588.33
Marche (France : Province)	T2—446 8
Marche (Italy)	T2—456 7
Marches (Italy)	T2—456 7
Marching bands	784.83
Marcos, Ferdinand E. (Ferdinand Edralin)	
Philippine history	959.904 6
Mardi Gras	394.25
customs	394.25
recreation	791.6
Mardin Ili (Turkey)	T2—566 7
Mareeba (Qld.)	T2—943 6
Maremma (Italy)	T2—455 7
Marengo County (Ala.)	T2—761 392
Mare's tail (Plant)	583.44
Marfan syndrome	
medicine	616.77
see also Musculoskeletal system	
Margarine	
food technology	664.32
Margate (South Africa)	T2—684 5
Margiana	T2—396
Margin	332.645
multiple forms of investment	332.645
stocks	332.632 28
Marginal costs	338.514 2
management	658.155 3
Marginal productivity theory	
land economics	333.012
wages	331.210 1
Marginal utility school (Economics)	330.157
Marginalist school (Economics)	330.157
Mari	T5—945 6
Mari A.S.S.R. (R.S.F.S.R.)	T2—478 1
Mari language	494.56
	T6—945 6
Mari literature	894.56
Maria-Chapdelaine (Quebec)	T2—714 14
Maria Island	T2—946 4

Maritime Kray (R.S.F.S.R.)	T2—577	Marowijne (Surinam :	
Maritime law	343.096	District)	T2—883 8
international law	341.756 6	Marquard (South Africa :	
Maritime Provinces	971.5	District)	T2—685 5
	T2—715	Marquesas Islands	T2—963 1
Marjoram	583.87	Marquetry	
Mark (Gospel)	226.3	furniture arts	749.5
Markazi (Iran : Province)	T2—552 5	wood handicrafts	745.51
Marker drawing	741.26	Marquette County (Mich.)	T2—774 96
Markerwaard (Netherlands)	T2—492 2	Marquette County (Wis.)	T2—775 58
Market analysis	658.83	Marquisettes	677.652
Market economies	330.122	Marrakesh (Morocco :	
Market research procedure	658.83	Province)	T2—646
Market research reports	380.1	Marriage	306.81
Marketing	380.1	citizenship issues	323.636
law	343.084	customs	392.5
management	658.8	ethics	173
see also Commerce		religion	291.563
Marketing firms	380.1	Buddhism	294.356 3
Marketing management	658.8	Christianity	241.63
	T1—068 8	Hinduism	294.548 63
Marketing managers	658.800 92	Islam	297.5
Marketing survey procedure	658.83	Judaism	296.385 63
Marketing survey reports	380.1	folklore	398.27
Markets	381	sociology	398.354
area planning	711.552 2	law	346.016
marketing management	658.84	literature	808.803 54
retail	381.1	history and criticism	809.933 54
management	658.87	specific literatures	T3B—080 354
see also Commerce		history and criticism	T3B—093 54
Markham River (Papua New		music	781.587
Guinea)	T2—957 1	personal religion	291.44
Markov chains	519.233	Buddhism	294.344 4
Markov processes	519.233	Christianity	248.4
Markov risk	519.287	Hinduism	294.544
Marks of identification	929.9	Islam	297.44
	T1—027	Judaism	296.74
Marlberry	583.677	public worship	291.38
Marlboro County (S.C.)	T2—757 64	Christianity	265.5
Marlborough County (N.Z.)	T2—931 52	Judaism	296.444
Marlin	597.58	*see also* Public worship	
sports fishing	799.175 8	religious doctrine	291.22
Marls	553.68	Buddhism	294.342 2
Marmalade	641.852	Christianity	234.165
commercial processing	664.152	Hinduism	294.522
home preparation	641.852	Islam	297.22
Marmara, Sea of (Turkey)	551.462 9	Judaism	296.32
	T2—163 89	social theology	291.178 358 1
Marmarica	T2—397 6	Christianity	261.835 81
ancient	939.76	Marriage counseling	
Marmosets	599.82	psychotherapy	616.891 56
Marmots	599.323 2	social welfare	362.828 6
Marne (France)	T2—443 2	*see also* Families—social	
Marne River (France)	T2—443	welfare	
Maronites	281.5	Married persons	306.872
Maronites (Religious order)	255.18		T1—086 55
church history	271.18	family relationships	306.872
		guides to Christian life	248.844

Mashona (African people)	T5—963 975
Mashonaland (Zimbabwe)	T2—689 1
Maskinongé (Quebec : County)	T2—714 44
Maskinongé (Quebec : Regional County Municipality)	T2—714 44
Maskoutains (Quebec)	T2—714 523
Masks	391.434
commercial technology	687.4
customs	391.434
home construction	646.478
see also Clothing	
Masks (Sculpture)	731.75
Masochism	
medicine	616.858 35
sociology	306.776
see also Mental illness	
Mason County (Ill.)	T2—773 553
Mason County (Ky.)	T2—769 323
Mason County (Mich.)	T2—774 61
Mason County (Tex.)	T2—764 66
Mason County (W. Va.)	T2—754 33
Mason County (Wash.)	T2—797 97
Masonry	693.1
Masonry (Secret order)	366.1
Masonry adhesives	666.9
building materials	691.5
foundation materials	624.153 5
materials science	620.135
Masonry dams	627.82
Masonry materials	
architectural construction	721.044 1
foundation engineering	624.153 3
materials science	620.13
structural engineering	624.183
Masons	693.109 2
occupational group	T7—693
Masons (Secret order)	366.1
Masques	782.15
literature	808.825
drama	
specific literatures	T3B—205
history and criticism	809.25
specific literatures	
individual authors	T3A—2
music	782.15
stage presentation	792.6
Mass (Christian rite)	264.36
Anglican	264.030 36
texts	264.03
music	782.323
choral and mixed voices	782.532 3
single voices	783.093 23
Roman Catholic	264.020 36
texts	264.023

Mass (Substance)	531.14
air mechanics	533.6
fluid mechanics	532.04
gas mechanics	533.15
liquid mechanics	532.4
solid mechanics	531.5
Mass action law	
chemistry	541.392
Mass communication	302.2
communication services	384
law	343.099
social aspects	302.2
Mass culture	306
Mass-energy conservation (Physics)	531.62
Mass-energy equivalence	530.11
Mass hysteria	302.17
Mass media	302.23
law	343.099
sociology	302.23
Mass media in election campaigns	324.73
Mass media music	781.54
Mass movement (Geology)	551.307
Mass of particles (Nuclear physics)	539.725
Mass spectrometry	
physics	539.602 87
Mass spectroscopy	543.087 3
chemical analysis	543.087 3
Mass transfer	530.475
chemical engineering	660.284 23
gaseous state physics	530.43
liquid state physics	530.425
physics	530.475
solid state physics	530.415
Mass transit	388.4
see also Urban transportation	
Mass transport (Physics)	530.475
see also Mass transfer	
Mass transportation	388.042
law	343.093 3
transportation services	388.042
urban	388.4
see also Urban transportation	
see also Passenger services	
Mass wasting (Geology)	551.307
Massa-Carrara (Italy : Province)	T2—455 4
Massa e Carrara (Italy : Province)	T2—455 4
Massac County (Ill.)	T2—773 997
Massachusetts	974.4
	T2—744
Massachusetts Bay	551.461 45
	T2—163 45
Massacre of innocents	232.925

Mathematical logic	511.3	Matting	
computer science	005.131	arts	746.41
Mathematical models	511.8	Mattresses	645.4
	T1—015 118	manufacturing technology	684.15
systems	003	*see also* Furniture	
	T1—011	Matumbi languages	496.397
Mathematical optimization	519.3		T6—963 97
Mathematical physics	530.15	Maturation	574.3
Mathematical programming	519.7	animals	591.3
management decision making	658.403 3	human	612.6
Mathematical recreations	793.74	plants	581.3
Mathematical school		Maturity	155.25
economics	330.154 3	human physiology	612.663
Mathematical systems	511.2	Maui (Hawaii)	T2—969 21
Mathematicians	510.92	Maui County (Hawaii)	T2—969 2
occupational group	T7—51	Maule (Chile : Region)	T2—833 5
Mathematics	510	Maumee River (Ind. and	
	T1—015 1	Ohio)	T2—771 1
elementary education	372.7	Maundy Thursday	263.92
Mathematics and religion	291.175	music	781.726
Christianity	261.55	Maurelle Island (B.C.)	T2—711 1
natural theology	215.1	Maurepas, Lake	T2—763 32
Mathews County (Va.)	T2—755 31	Mauretania	939.71
Mathieu functions	515.54		T2—397 1
Matins	264.1	Mauretania Caesariensis	T2—397 1
Anglican	264.030 1	Mauretania Tingitana	T2—397 1
texts	264.033	Mauricie Region (Quebec)	T2—714 45
music	782.324	Mauritania	966.1
Anglican church	782.325		T2—661
Mato Grosso (Brazil : State)	T2—817 2	Mauritanians	T5—966 1
Mato Grosso do Sul (Brazil)	T2—817 1	Mauritians	T5—914 1
Matriarchal family	306.859	Mauritius	969.82
Matriarchal state (Government)	321.12		T2—698 2
Matrices	512.943 4	Maury County (Tenn.)	T2—768 59
Matriculation	371.21	Mauryas (Indian history)	934.04
Matrilineal kinship	306.83	Maverick County (Tex.)	T2—764 435
Matrimony	306.81	Maxamed Siyaad Barre	
sacrament	234.165	Somali history	967.730 5
public worship	265.5	Maxima	511.66
see also Marriage		Maximilian, Emperor of Mexico	
Matrix algebra	512.943 4	Mexican history	972.07
Matrix mechanics	530.122	Maximilian I, Holy Roman	
Matruh (Egypt)	T2—621	Emperor	
Mats	642.7	German history	943.029
arts	746.96	Maximilian II, Emperor of	
home sewing	646.21	Germany	
table setting	642.7	German history	943.033
MATS (Air transportation)	358.44	Maxims	398.9
Matter	530	Maximum-security prisons	365.33
philosophy	117	*see also* Correctional	
physics	530	institutions	
structure	539.1	Maxwell's equations (Physics)	530.141
Matter at high temperatures	536.57	Maxwell's thermodynamic	
Matter at low temperatures	536.56	formulas	536.71
Matthew (Gospel)	226.2	May Day	394.268 3
Matthias, Holy Roman Emperor		Maya	T5—974
German history	943.035	history	972.810 16

Measles
 incidence 614.523
 medicine 616.915
 pediatrics 618.929 15
 see also Communicable
  diseases (Human)
Measure theory 515.42
 calculus 515.783
Measurement T1—028 7
Measurement systems 530.81
 physics 530.81
 social aspects 389.15
Measurement theory 530.16
Measures 530.81
 see also Weights and measures
Measuring instruments
 electric measurement 621.37
 electronics 621.381 548
 manufacturing technology 681.2
 physics 530.7
Meat 641.36
 animal feed 636.087 6
 commercial preservation
  technology 664.902 8
 commercial processing
  economics 338.476 649
  technology 664.9
 cooking 641.66
 home preservation 641.49
 product safety 363.192 9
 see also Food—product safety
Meat loaf 641.824
 commercial processing 664.92
 cooking 641.824
Meat pies 641.824
 commercial processing 664.92
 cooking 641.824
Meat processing industry 338.476 649
 see also Meat
Meath (Ireland) T2—418 22
Meatless high-protein foods
 technology 664.64
Meats 641.36
 see also Meat
Mecca (Saudi Arabia) T2—538
 Islamic religion 297.35
 pilgrimage 297.55
Mechanical bands 784.6
Mechanical barriers
 military engineering 623.31
Mechanical chess players 794.17
Mechanical conveyer systems
 office services 651.79
Mechanical deformation
 materials science 620.112 3
Mechanical drawing 604.2
Mechanical engineering 621
 military applications 623.045

Mechanical engineers 621.092
 occupational group T7—621
Mechanical forces 530
 biophysics 574.191 3
 human 612.014 41
 materials science 620.112 3
Mechanical musical instruments 786.6
 bands and orchestras 784
 chamber ensembles 785
 construction 786.619 23
  by hand 786.619 23
  by machine 681.866
 solo music 786.6
Mechanical pencils
 manufacturing technology 681.6
Mechanical processes
 printing 686.231
 wood pulp 676.122
Mechanical properties
 materials science 620.112 92
Mechanical separation
 ores 622.75
Mechanical stokers
 steam engineering 621.183
Mechanical systems
 ships 623.850 1
Mechanical toys 790.133
 manufacturing technology 688.728
 recreation 790.133
 see also Toys
Mechanical working
 metals 671.3
Mechanics 530
 classical physics 531
 engineering 620.1
 foundation soils 624.151 36
 meteorology 551.515
 physics 530
 quantum physics 530.12
 structures 624.171
Mechanics' liens 346.024
Mechanics of materials 620.112 3
Mechanics of particles
 classical physics 531.16
Mechanics of points 531.1
Mechanism (Philosophy) 146.6
Mechanisms
 engineering 621.8
Mechanization
 agricultural economics 338.161
 economics 338.064
 factory operations engineering 670.427
Mechanized bells 786.64
 see also Mechanical musical
  instruments
Mechanized cavalry 357.5
Mechanotherapy
 medicine 615.822

Medlar	641.341 5	Melastomataceae	583.42
botany	583.372	Melayu Asli languages	499.28
cooking	641.641 5		T6—992 8
orchard crop	634.15	Melbourne (Vic.)	T2—945 1
Medulla		Mele-Fila language	499.4
human histology	611.018 4		T6—994
see also Bone marrow		Meleagrididae	598.619
Medulla oblongata		Meliales	583.25
human anatomy	611.81	Melianthaceae	583.28
human physiology	612.828	Melilla (Spain)	T2—642
see also Nervous system		Melilot	583.322
Medullosaceae	561.595	forage crop	633.366
Medusagynaceae	583.166	Meliorism	
Medusandraceae	583.26	philosophy	149.5
Medusas	593.7	Mellette County (S.D.)	T2—783 63
Meeker County (Minn.)	T2—776 49	Melmoth (South Africa)	T2—684 3
Meetings		Melodeons	788.863
management use	658.456	*see also* Woodwind instruments	
Megachiroptera	599.4	Melodrama	792.27
paleozoology	569.4	literature	808.825 27
Megaloptera	595.742	history and criticism	809.252 7
Megalopteris	561.597	specific literatures	T3B—205 27
Mégantic (Quebec)	T2—714 575	individual authors	T3A—2
Megapodiidae	598.612	stage presentation	792.27
Megaric philosophy	183.6	Melody	781.24
Megaris (Greece)	T2—384	Meloidea	595.767
Meghalaya (India)	T2—541 64	Melons	641.356 1
Megillot (Bible)	221.044	botany	583.46
Mehedinti (Romania)	T2—498 4	commercial processing	664.805 61
Meighen, Arthur		cooking	641.656 1
Canadian history	971.061 3	garden crop	635.61
1920-1921	971.061 3	Melos Island (Greece)	T2—499
1926	971.062 2	Melting	536.42
Meigs County (Ohio)	T2—771 99	chemical engineering	660.284 296
Meigs County (Tenn.)	T2—768 836	Melting metals	671.24
Meiji period (Japanese history)	952.031	Melton (England : Borough)	T2—425 46
Meiosis	574.32	Melville (Sask.)	T2—712 44
Meirionnydd (Wales)	T2—429 29	Melville Island	T2—942 95
Mékinac (Quebec)	T2—714 45	Melville Peninsula (N.W.T.)	T2—719 5
Meknes (Morocco : Province)	T2—643	Membership lists	T1—06
Mekong River	T2—597	Membracoidea	595.752
Melaka (State)	T2—595 1	Membrane processes	
Melamines	668.422 4	chemical engineering	660.284 24
Melancholy		desalinization	628.167 4
literature	808.803 53	water-supply treatment	628.164
history and criticism	809.933 53	Membranes (Cytology)	574.875
specific literatures	T3B—080 353	Membranophones	786.9
history and criticism	T3B—093 53	*see also* Percussion instruments	
Melanconiales	589.24	Memoirs	920
Melanesia	995	Memorandums	
	T2—95	office use	651.755
Melanesian languages	499.5	Memorial buildings	725.94
	T6—995	*see also* Monuments	
Melanesian literatures	899.5	Memorizing	
Melanesians	T5—995	music training method	781.426
Melanoma		Memory	153.12
medicine	616.994 77	educational psychology	370.152 2
see also Cancer		human physiology	612.82

Memory (continued)
  philosophy   128.3
Memory (Computer)   004.5
  engineering   621.397
Memphis (Ancient city)   T2—32
Memphis (Tenn.)   T2—768 19
Memphrémagog (Quebec)   T2—714 64
Memphrémagog Lake
  (Quebec)   T2—714 64
Men   305.31
     T1—081
     T7—041

  art representation   704.942 3
  biography   920.71
  criminal offenders   364.373
  drawing   743.43
  etiquette   395.142
  grooming   646.704 4
  guides to Christian life   248.842
  health   613.042 34
  journalism for   070.483 46
  painting   757.3
  physical fitness   613.704 49
  psychology   155.632
  recreation   790.194
    indoor   793.019 4
    outdoor   796.019 4
  sex hygiene   613.952
  social aspects   305.31
  social theology   291.178 343 1
    Christianity   261.834 31
Menabe (Kingdom)   969.101
     T2—691
Ménage à trois   306.735
Menarche
  human physiology   612.662
  see also Female genital system
Menard County (Ill.)   T2—773 555
Menard County (Tex.)   T2—764 877
Mende (African people)   T5—963 4
Mende language   496.34
     T6—963 4
Mendelevium   546.449
  see also Chemicals
Mendel's laws   575.11
Mendi (Papua New Guinea)   T2—956 1
Mendicant religious orders   255.06
  church history   271.06
Mending books   025.7
Mending textiles
  home economics   646.2
  clothes   646.6
Mendip (England : District)   T2—423 83
Mendip Hills (England)   T2—423 83
Mendocino County (Calif.)   T2—794 15
Mendoza (Argentina :
  Province)   T2—826 4

Mendzans   786.843
  see also Percussion instruments
Menelik II, Negus of Ethiopia
  Ethiopian history   963.043
Menger, Carl
  economic school   330.157
Mengistu Haile-Mariam
  Ethiopian history   963.07
Menhaden   597.55
  fishing   639.275 5
Menière's disease   617.882
  see also Ears
Menifee County (Ky.)   T2—769 583
Menindee Lakes   T2—944 9
Meninges
  human anatomy   611.81
  human diseases
    medicine   616.82
  human histology   611.018 8
  human physiology   612.82
  see also Nervous system
Meningitis
  medicine   616.82
  see also Nervous system
Menispermaceae   583.117
Mennonite Church   289.7
  church government   262.097
    parishes   254.097
  church law   262.989 7
  doctrines   230.97
    catechisms and creeds   238.97
  general councils   262.597
  guides to Christian life   248.489 7
  missions   266.97
  moral theology   241.049 7
  public worship   264.097
  religious associations   267.189 7
  religious education   268.897
  seminaries   207.119 7
  theology   230.97
Mennonite cooking   641.566
Mennonites
  biography   289.709 2
  religious group   T7—287
Menominee County (Mich.)   T2—774 953
Menominee County (Wis.)   T2—775 356
Menominee River   T2—774 95
Menopause
  disorders
    gynecology   618.175
  human physiology   612.665
  see also Female genital system
Menorca (Spain)   T2—467 52
Menorrhagia
  gynecology   618.172
  see also Female genital system
Men's clothing   391.1
  commercial technology   687.081

Mercedarians	255.45
church history	271.45
Mercenary troops	355.35
Mercer County (Ill.)	T2—773 395
Mercer County (Ky.)	T2—769 485
Mercer County (Mo.)	T2—778 213
Mercer County (N.D.)	T2—784 83
Mercer County (N.J.)	T2—749 65
Mercer County (Ohio)	T2—771 415
Mercer County (Pa.)	T2—748 95
Mercer County (W. Va.)	T2—754 74
Mercerizing textiles	677.028 25
Merchandisers	380.109 2
occupational group	T7—381
Merchant marine	387.5
see also Ocean transportation	
Merchant seamen	387.509 2
occupational group	T7—387 5
technologists	623.880 92
Merchant ships	387.2
design	623.812
engineering	623.82
freight services	387.544
power-driven	387.24
design	623.812 4
engineering	623.824
transportation services	387.24
transportation services	387.2
wind-driven	387.224
design	623.812 24
engineering	623.822 4
handling	623.882 24
transportation services	387.224
see also Ships	
Merchants	380.109 2
Mercia supremacy (English history)	942.015 7
Mercury (Element)	669.71
chemical engineering	661.066 3
chemistry	546.663
economic geology	553.454
metallurgy	669.71
mining	622.345 4
organic chemistry	547.056 63
applied	661.895
physical metallurgy	669.967 1
toxicology	615.925 663
see also Chemicals, Metals	
Mercury (Planet)	523.41
	T2—992 1
unmanned flights to	629.435 41
Mercury (Plant)	583.95
Mercury fulminate	662.27
Mercury project	629.454
Mercury-vapor lighting	621.327 4
Mergansers	598.41
Mergers	338.83
accounting	657.96

Mergers (continued)	
banks	332.16
economics	338.83
law	346.066 26
management	658.16
Merging data	005.748
Mérida (Spain)	T2—462 7
Mérida (Venezuela : State)	T2—871 3
Meridian (Miss.)	T2—762 677
Meridians (Celestial coordinates)	
astronomy	522.7
Meridional instruments	522.3
use	522.3
Merina (Kingdom)	969.101
	T2—691
Merino sheep	
animal husbandry	636.36
zoology	599.735 8
Merioneth (Wales)	T2—429 29
Merit (Christian doctrines)	234
Merit awards	
personnel management	658.322 6
Merit system (Civil service)	350.6
central governments	351.6
local governments	352.005 6
Meriwether County (Ga.)	T2—758 455
Merkaz (Israel : District)	T2—569 47
Mermaids	
folklore	398.21
sociology	398.45
Mermen	
folklore	398.21
sociology	398.45
Meromorphic functions	515.982
Meropidae	598.892
Merovingian dynasty (French history)	944.013
Merovingian dynasty (German history)	943.013
Merreden (W.A.)	T2—941 2
Merrick County (Neb.)	T2—782 423
Merrimac, Battle of Monitor and, 1862	973.752
Merrimack County (N.H.)	T2—742 72
Merrimack River (N.H. and Mass.)	T2—742 72
Merritt (B.C.)	T2—711 72
Mersey River (England)	T2—427 5
Mersey River (Tas.)	T2—946 5
Merseyside (England)	T2—427 5
Merthyr Tydfil (Wales)	T2—429 75
Merton (London, England)	T2—421 93
Mesa County (Colo.)	T2—788 17
Mesa Verde National Park (Colo.)	T2—788 27
Mesabi Range (Minn.)	T2—776 77
Mescal	641.25
commercial processing	663.5

Metallurgical furnaces	669.8
Metallurgists	669.092
occupational group	T7—669
Metallurgy	669
equipment manufacturing	
technology	681.766 9
Metals	669
architectural construction	721.044 7
architectural decoration	729.6
building construction	693.7
building materials	691.8
chemical engineering	661.03
chemistry	546.3
decorative arts	739
economic geology	553.4
foundation materials	624.153 6
handicrafts	745.56
materials science	620.16
metallography	669.95
military resources	355.242
mineralogy	549.23
mining	622.34
organic chemistry	547.05
applied	661.895
prospecting	622.184
radiesthesia	133.323 3
sculpture material	731.2
ship design	623.818 2
shipbuilding	623.820 7
structural engineering	624.182
textiles	677.53
see also Textiles	
toxicology	615.925 3
see also Chemicals	
Metalworkers	669.092
metallurgy	669.092
metalworking	671.092
occupational group	T7—671
occupational group	T7—671
Metalworking	671
home workshops	684.09
production economics	338.476 71
ship hulls	623.843
technology	671
Metamathematics	510.1
Metamorphic rocks	552.4
Metamorphosis	591.334
Metaphysics	110
Metatarsals	
human anatomy	611.718
see also Musculoskeletal system	
Metcalfe, Charles Theophilus,	
Lord	
Indian history	954.031 4
Metcalfe County (Ky.)	T2—769 693
Metchosin (B.C.)	T2—711 28
Meteor showers	523.53
Meteorite craters	551.397
Meteorites	523.51
mineralogy	549.112
petrology	549.112
Meteoroids	523.51
	T2—993
effect on space flight	629.416
Meteorologists	551.509 2
occupational group	T7—551
Meteorology	551.5
	T1—015 515
aeronautics	629.132 4
agriculture	630.251 5
Meteors	523.51
Meter (Music)	781.226
Meter (Prosody)	808.1
Methane-producing bacteria	589.9
Methodist Church	287
church government	262.07
parishes	254.07
church law	262.987
doctrines	230.7
catechisms and creeds	238.7
guides to Christian life	248.487
missions	266.7
moral theology	241.047
public worship	264.07
religious associations	267.187
religious education	268.87
seminaries	207.117
theology	230.7
Methodist Church (U.S.)	287.631
see also Methodist Church	
Methodist Episcopal Church	287.632
see also Methodist Church	
Methodist Episcopal Church,	
South	287.633
see also Methodist Church	
Methodist New Connexion	287.53
see also Methodist Church	
Methodist Protestant Church	287.7
see also Methodist Church	
Methodist sacred music	781.717
public worship	782.322 7
music	782.322 7
religion	264.070 2
Methodists	
biography	287.092
religious group	T7—27
Methodology	T1—01
Metric differential geometries	516.37
Metric geometry	516.1
Euclidean	516.2
Metric system	530.812
law	343.075
physics	530.812
social aspects	389.15
Metric topology	514.3
Metrication	389.16

Microcomputers (continued)
graphics programs 006.686
interfacing 004.616
  programming 005.712 6
  programs 005.713 6
operating systems 005.446
performance evaluation 004.160 297
  for design and improvement 004.256
peripherals 004.716
programming 005.26
programs 005.36
systems analysis 004.256
systems design 004.256
Microeconomics 338.5
Microelectronic circuits 621.381 5
Microelectronics 621.381
social effects 303.483 4
Microfiche 302.23
bibliographies 011.36
see also Microforms
Microfilaments 574.873 4
Microfilms 302.23
bibliographies 011.36
see also Microforms
Microform catalogs 025.313
Microforms 302.23
bibliographies 011.36
cataloging 025.349 4
library treatment 025.179 4
production
  technology 686.43
publishing 070.579 5
Microlithography
electronics 621.381 531
Micrometeorology 551.66
Micrometers
astronomy 522.5
Micromorphology
soil physics 631.43
Micronesia T2—965
Micronesian languages 499.5
 T6—995
Micronesians T5—995
Micronutrient elements 574.192 14
see also Trace elements
Microorganisms 576
food technology 664.024
Microphones 621.382 84
radio engineering 621.384 133
Microphotography
technology 686.43
Microphysiology
botany 581.8
zoology 591.8
Microprocessors 004.16
see also Microcomputers
Microprogramming 005.6
 T1—028 556

Microprograms 005.6
 T1—028 556
Microreproduction
office records 651.58
Microreproductions 302.23
bibliographies 011.36
see also Microforms
Microscopes 502.82
manufacturing technology 681.413
Microscopic metallography 669.950 282
Microscopic objects
photography 778.31
Microscopic petrology 552.8
Microscopical analysis
chemistry 543.081 2
Microscopy 502.82
biology 578
medical diagnosis 616.075 8
natural sciences 502.82
Microstructure
materials science 620.112 99
Microsurgery 617.05
Microtomy 502.82
biology 578.6
Microtonality 781.269
Microtrabeculae 574.873 4
Microtubules 574.873 4
Microwave aids
marine navigation 623.893 3
Microwave cooking 641.588 2
Microwave electronics
engineering 621.381 3
physics 537.534 4
Microwave spectroscopes
manufacturing technology 681.414 8
Microwave spectroscopy 543.085 82
chemical analysis 543.085 82
engineering 621.361 5
physics 537.534 4
Microwave theory of electricity 537.123
Microwaves
biophysics 574.191 51
human 612.014 481
Mid Bedfordshire (England) T2—425 63
Mid Devon (England :
 District) T2—423 54
Mid Glamorgan (Wales) T2—429 7
Mid Suffolk (England) T2—426 45
Mid Sussex (England :
 District) T2—422 65
Mid Wales T2—429 5
Mid-Western State (Nigeria) T2—669 3
Midair collisions 363.124 92
see also Transportation safety
Midbrain
human anatomy 611.81
human physiology 612.826 4
see also Nervous system

Midwives	
law	344.041 5
role and function	618.202 33
Mie-ken (Japan)	T2—521 81
Mifflin County (Pa.)	T2—748 46
Mignonettes	583.124
Migraine	
medicine	616.857
see also Nervous system	
Migrant children	
education	371.967 5
Migrant workers	T1—086 24
economics	331.544
social class	305.562
social welfare	362.85
Migration	304.8
political science	325
Migration (Biology)	574.52
animals	591.525
plants	581.52
Mihai II, Viteazul, Voivode of Wallachia	
Romanian history	949.801 5
Mikhailovgradski okrug (Bulgaria)	T2—497 72
Mikhaylovgrad (Bulgaria : Okrug)	T2—497 72
Mikkeli (Finland)	T2—489 75
Milam County (Tex.)	T2—764 288
Milan (Italy : Province)	T2—452 1
Milano (Italy : Province)	T2—452 1
Mildew	589.25
agricultural disease	632.45
materials science	620.112 23
Mildura (Vic.)	T2—945 9
Miles (Qld.)	T2—943 3
Miletus (Ancient city)	T2—392 3
Milieu therapy	
psychiatry	616.891 44
see also Mental illness	
Militarism	355.021 3
ethics	172.42
see also War—ethics	
social theology	291.178 73
Buddhism	294.337 873
Christianity	261.873
Hinduism	294.517 873
Islam	297.197 873
Judaism	296.387 873
sociology	303.66
Military accounting	657.835
Military air transportation service	358.44
Military aircraft	358.418 3
armed forces equipment	358.418 3
engineering	623.746
Military alliances	355.031
Military arts	355

Military assistance	355.032
international law	341.728
law	342.041 2
Military attachés	355.032
Military bands	784.84
Military bases	355.7
international law	341.725
law	343.01
Military buildings	
architecture	725.18
Military capability	355.033 2
Military consultants	355.6
Military cooking	641.57
Military courts	343.014 3
Military customs	355.1
Military discipline	355.13
law	343.014
Military districts	355.31
Military engineering	623
Military engineers	623.092
occupational group	T7—623 1
Military geography	355.47
Military government	355.49
Military health	613.67
Military history	355.009
Civil War (United States)	973.73
Mexican War	973.623
South African War	968.048 4
Spanish-American War, 1898	973.893
United States Revolutionary War	973.33
Vietnamese War	959.704 34
War of 1812	973.523
World War I	940.4
World War II	940.54
Military housing	355.12
administration	355.67
Military hygiene	355.345
engineering	623.75
Military-industrial complex	355.021 3
military science	355.021 3
sociology	306.27
Military intelligence	355.343 2
technology	623.71
Military law	343.015
Military life	355.1
Civil War (United States)	973.783
Mexican War	973.628
South African War	968.048 8
Spanish-American War, 1898	973.898
United States Revolutionary War	973.38
Vietnamese War	959.704 38
War of 1812	973.528
World War I	940.483–.484
World War II	940.548 3–.548 4
Military maneuvers	355.4
training	355.52

Millet (continued)	
food crop	633.171
forage crop	633.257 1
Milliammeters	621.374 4
Milliners	646.504 092
occupational group	T7—646 5
Millinery	646.504
commercial technology	687.42
home construction	646.504
Milling grains	664.72
Milling metals	671.35
Milling plants	
ore dressing	622.79
Milling tools	621.91
Millipedes	595.61
paleozoology	565.61
Millmerran (Qld.)	T2—943 3
Mills	
architecture	725.4
Mills County (Iowa)	T2—777 74
Mills County (Tex.)	T2—764 512
Milne Bay Province (Papua	
New Guinea)	T2—954 1
Milngavie, Bearsden and	
(Scotland : District)	T2—414 34
Milo	584.92
food crop	633.174 7
forage crop	633.257 47
Milton Keynes (England)	T2—425 91
Milwaukee (Wis.)	T2—775 95
Milwaukee County (Wis.)	T2—775 94
Mimamsa (Philosophy)	181.42
Mimidae	598.841
Mimosa	583.321
Mimosaceae	583.321
Min dialect	495.17
	T6—951 7
Minarets	
architecture	726.2
Minas Gerais (Brazil)	T2—815 1
Mind	128.2
folklore	
sociology	398.353
philosophy	128.2
psychology	150
Mind reading	133.82
Mindanao Island (Philippines)	T2—599 7
Mindoro (Philippines)	T2—599 3
Mindoro Occidental	
(Philippines)	T2—599 3
Mindoro Oriental	
(Philippines)	T2—599 3
Mine clearance (Military)	623.26
Mine drainage	622.5
water-supply engineering	628.168 32
Mine health	363.119 622
social services	363.119 622
technology	622.8

Mine laying (Military)	623.26
Mine railroads	622.66
Mine safety	363.119 622
social services	363.119 622
technology	622.8
Mine shafts	622.25
Mine surveys	622.14
Mined lands	333.765
economics	333.765
reclamation technology	631.64
Minelayers	359.836 2
design	623.812 62
engineering	623.826 2
naval equipment	359.836 2
naval units	359.326 2
Miner County (S.D.)	T2—783 34
Miner flies	595.774
Mineral additives	
animal feed	636.087 7
Mineral commodities	338.27
investment economics	332.644 2
Mineral County (Colo.)	T2—788 38
Mineral County (Mont.)	T2—786 84
Mineral County (Nev.)	T2—793 51
Mineral County (W. Va.)	T2—754 94
Mineral deposits	
origin	553.1
Mineral drugs	
pharmacology	615.2
Mineral fertilizers	553.64
agriculture	631.8
see also Fertilizers	
Mineral industries	338.2
enterprises	338.762 2
law	343.077
products	
commerce	380.142
public administration	351.823 8
cabinet departments	351.082 38
Mineral oils	
processing	665.4
Mineral resources	
land economics	333.85
law	346.046 85
public administration	351.823 27
Mineral rights	346.043
public control law	346.046 8
fossil fuels	346.046 82
other minerals	346.046 85
public revenue	336.12
real estate law	346.043
sale and rental	333.339
Mineral springs	
health	613.122
therapeutic use	615.853
Mineral surveys	
prospecting	622.13

Mining (continued)
production economics	338.2
public administration	351.823 82
cabinet departments	351.082 382
Mining engineers	622.092
occupational group	T7—622
Mining equipment	
manufacturing technology	681.76
Mining law	343.077 5
Mining towns	307.766
Mining waterways	623.263
Ministates	
political science	321.06
Minister of justice's advisory	
opinions	348.05
Ministerial authority	262.8
Ministries (Government	
departments)	351.004
Minkowski geometry	516.374
Minks	599.744 47
animal husbandry	636.974 447
Minna (Nigeria)	T2—669 65
Minneapolis (Minn.)	T2—776 579
Minneapolis Metropolitan	
Area (Minn.)	T2—776 579
Minnedosa (Man.)	T2—712 73
Minnehaha County (S.D.)	T2—783 371
Minnesota	977.6
	T2—776
Minnesota River (S.D. and	
Minn.)	T2—776 3
Minnow	597.52
culture	639.375 2
Minoan architecture	722.61
Minoan Linear A	492.6
	T6—926
Minoan Linear B	487.1
	T6—87
Minor arts	745
see also Arts	
Minor Clerks Regular	255.56
church history	271.56
Minor prophets (Bible)	224.9
Minor surgery	617.024
obstetrics	618.85
Minorca (Spain)	T2—467 52
Minority enterprises	338.642 2
economics	338.642 2
financial management	658.159 208
management	658.022 08
Minority groups	305.56
	T1—086 93
civil rights	323.1
government programs	350.814
central governments	351.814
local governments	352.941 4
journalism for	070.484

Minority groups (continued)
labor	
economics	331.6
personnel management	658.304 1
public administration	350.836
central governments	351.836
local governments	352.943 6
legal status	342.087 3
libraries for	027.63
relation to government	323.1
social welfare	362.84
public administration	350.848 4
central governments	351.848 4
local governments	352.944 84
Minors	305.23
legal status	346.013 5
see also Young people	
Minquiers (England)	T2—423 48
Minsk (Belorussian S.S.R. :	
Oblast)	T2—476 52
Minskaia oblast (Byelorussian	
S.S.R.)	T2—476 52
Minstrel shows	791.12
Mint (Herb)	641.338 2
agriculture	633.82
botany	583.87
cooking with	641.638 2
Minting policies	332.46
Minto, Gilbert Elliot, Earl of	
Indian history	954.031 3
Minto, Gilbert John Murray	
Kynynmond Elliot, Earl of	
Indian history	954.035 6
Minuet form	784.188 35
Minufiya (Egypt)	T2—621
Minufiyah (Egypt)	T2—621
Minutes	
office records	651.77
Minya (Egypt : Governorate)	T2—622
Miocene epoch	551.787
geology	551.787
paleontology	560.178
Miquelon, Saint-Pierre and	
(France)	T2—718 8
Mirabel (Quebec : Regional	
County Municipality)	T2—714 25
Miracle plays	
literature	808.825 16
history and criticism	809.251 6
specific literatures	T3B—205 16
individual authors	T3A—2
stage presentation	792.16
Miracles	291.211
Christianity	231.73
spiritual gift	234.13
Islam	297.211
Judaism	296.311
natural theology	211

Mitchell County (Tex.)	T2—764 729
Mitchell River (Qld.)	T2—943 7
Mitchell River (Vic.)	T2—945 6
Mites	595.42
disease carriers	614.433
Mithraism	299.15
Mitis (Quebec)	T2—714 771
Mitochondria	574.873 42
Mitosis	574.876 23
Mitral valves	
human anatomy	611.12
human diseases	
medicine	616.125
human physiology	612.17
see also Cardiovascular system	
Mitta Mitta River	T2—945 5
Mittagong (N.S.W.)	T2—944 6
Mittelfranken (Germany)	T2—433 2
Mittelland	T2—494 5
Mitten makers	685.409 2
occupational group	T7—685 4
Mittens	391.412
commercial technology	685.4
customs	391.412
home sewing	646.48
see also Clothing	
Mixe language	497.41
	T6—974 1
Mixed-bloods (People)	T5—04
Mixed drinks	641.21
home preparation	641.874
Mixed economies	330.126
Mixed equations	512.942
algebra	512.942
Mixed marriage	306.84
Mixed-media arts	702.81
two-dimensional	760
Mixed voices	782.5
Mixes (Pastry)	664.753
Mixing	
chemical engineering	660.284 292
Mixing paints	
buildings	698.102 83
Mixtec Indians	T5—976
Mixtec language	497.6
	T6—976
Miyagi-ken (Japan)	T2—521 15
Miyazaki-ken (Japan)	T2—522 7
Miye-ken (Japan)	T2—521 81
Mizoram (India)	T2—541 66
Mkobola (South Africa : District)	T2—682 95
Mkomazi River	T2—684 5
Mkuze Game Reserve	T2—684 91
Mkuze River	T2—684 3
Mmabatho (South Africa)	T2—682 94
Mnemonics	153.14
Mnong (Indochinese people)	T5—959 3

Moab	939.46
	T2—394 6
Moabite language	492.6
	T6—926
Moats	
architecture	725.98
military engineering	623.31
Mobile County (Ala.)	T2—761 22
Mobile homes	643.2
architecture	728.79
automotive engineering	629.226
construction	690.879
home economics	643.2
property law	346.043
recreation	796.79
see also Motorized homes	
Mobile libraries	
public library use	027.4
Mobile River	T2—761 22
Mobile tactics	355.422
Mobiles	731.55
Mobilization	355.28
Civil War (United States)	973.73
Mexican War	973.623
South African War	968.048 4
Spanish-American War, 1898	973.893
United States Revolutionary War	973.33
Vietnamese War	959.704 34
War of 1812	973.523
World War I	940.402
World War II	940.540 2
Mobs	302.33
Mobs (Organized crime)	364.106
Mobutu Sese Seko	
Zairian history	967.510 3
Moçâmedes (Angola : Province)	T2—673 5
Mock oranges	583.397
Mockingbirds	598.841
Modality	
logic	160
Modality (Grammar)	415
specific languages	T4—5
Modder River	T2—685 4
Mode	519.533
Model aircraft	629.133 1
Model airplanes	
recreation	796.15
Model automobiles	629.221
Model cars	629.221
Model makers	688.109 2
occupational group	T7—688
Model trains	625.19
Modeling	
elementary education	372.53
sculpture	731.42
use in child care	649.51

Moi, Daniel Arap	
Kenyan history	967.620 4
Moism (Chinese philosophy)	181.115
Moisture	
meteorology	551.57
soil physics	631.432
Moistureproof construction	
buildings	693.893
Mojave Desert (Calif.)	T2—794 95
Mokerong (South Africa :	
District)	T2—682 93
Molasses	641.336
commercial processing	664.118
cooking with	641.636
Moldavia	T2—498 1
Romania	T2—498 1
USSR	T2—477 5
Moldavia (Principality)	949.801 4
	T2—498 1
Moldavian S.S.R	T2—477 5
Molded pulp	676.182
Molded rubber	678.34
Molding	
sculpture	731.43
Molding glass	666.125
Molding latex	678.527
Molding plastics	668.412
Molding rubber	678.27
Moldmaking	
metal casting	671.23
Molds (Fungi)	589.25
agricultural diseases	632.45
Molds (Tools)	621.984
Mole Creek Caves	T2—946 3
Mole rats	599.323 4
Mole Valley (England :	
District)	T2—422 165
Molecular biology	574.88
animals	591.88
plants	581.88
Molecular bonds	541.224
Molecular complexes	541.224 2
Molecular genetics	574.873 28
Molecular physics	539.6
Molecular properties	
materials science	620.112 99
Molecular sieve chromatographic	
analysis	543.089 2
Molecular spectra	539.6
Molecular structure	541.22
chemistry	541.22
physics	539.12
Molecular weights	541.222
Molecules	
chemistry	541.22
physics	539.6
Moles (Animals)	599.33
Moles (Disorder)	
medicine	616.55
see also Skin	
Molinism	273.7
persecution of	272.5
Molise (Italy : Region)	T2—457 19
Mollicutes	589.9
Molluginaceae	583.152
Mollusca	594
paleozoology	564
see also Mollusks	
Molluscoidea	594.6
paleozoology	564.6
Mollusks	594
cooking	641.694
culture	639.4
fisheries	639.4
fishing industry	338.372 4
food	641.394
commercial processing	664.94
paleozoology	564
Molokai (Hawaii)	T2—969 24
Molopo (South Africa :	
District)	T2—682 94
Molpadiida	593.96
Molteno (South Africa :	
District)	T2—687 6
Molucca Sea	551.465 73
	T2—164 73
Moluccas	T2—598 5
Molybdates	
mineralogy	549.74
Molybdenite	
mineralogy	549.32
Molybdenum	669.734
chemical engineering	661.053 4
chemistry	546.534
economic geology	553.464 6
materials science	620.189 34
metallography	669.957 34
metallurgy	669.734
metalworking	673.734
mining	622.346 46
organic chemistry	547.055 34
applied	661.895
physical metallurgy	669.967 34
see also Chemicals, Metals	
Momase region	995.7
	T2—957
Mombasa (Kenya)	T2—676 23
Moment distribution	
structural analysis	624.171 5
Moments of inertia	
aeronautics	629.132 364
Momentum	531.6
Momentum transfer	
chemical engineering	660.284 292

Momoyama period (Japanese history)	952.024	Mongo (African people)	T5—963 96
Mon-Khmer languages	495.93	Mongo-Nkundu languages	496.396
	T6—959 3		T6—963 96
Mon-Khmer literatures	895.93	Mongol dynasty (Chinese history)	951.025
Mon-Khmer peoples	T5—959 3	Mongol Empire	950.2
Mon language	495.93		T2—5
	T6—959 3	Mongolia	951.73
Monaco	944.949		T2—517 3
	T2—449 49	Mongolia (Region)	951.7
Monads			T2—517
ontology	111	Mongolian language	494.2
Monagas (Venezuela : State)	T2—875 6		T6—942
Monaghan (Ireland : County)	T2—416 97	Mongolian literature	894.2
Monarchist parties	324.213	Mongolian People's Republic	951.73
international organizations	324.13		T2—517 3
Monarchs		Mongolic languages	494.2
occupational group	T7—351 1		T6—942
public administration	351.003 12	Mongolic literatures	894.2
Monashee Mountains (B.C.)	T2—711 62	Mongolism	
Monasteries		medicine	616.858 842
architecture	726.7	*see also* Mental retardation	
Monastic schools	377.3	Mongoloid race	T5—035
Monasticism	291.657	Mongols	T5—942
Buddhism	294.365 7	Mongooses	599.744 22
Christianity	255	Monhegan Island (Me.)	T2—741 53
church history	271	Moniliales	589.24
personal religion	248.894	Monimiaceae	583.931
Monazite		Monism	
mineralogy	549.72	philosophy	147.3
Moncton (N.B.)	T2—715 235	Moniteau County (Mo.)	T2—778 52
Monera	589.9	Monitor and Merrimac, Battle of, 1862	973.752
Monetary law	343.032	Monitors (Computer)	
Monetary policy	332.46	control programs	005.43
economics	332.46	firmware	005.6
central banking	332.112	video display screens	004.77
international	332.456 6	engineering	621.398 7
international law	341.751	Monkeys	599.82
macroeconomics	339.53	animal husbandry	636.982
Monetary reform		Monklands (Scotland)	T2—414 46
international	332.456 6	Monks	291.657
Monetary stabilization	332.415	Buddhists	294.365 7
international banking	332.152	Christian	271.009 2
Monetary standards	332.42	ecclesiology	262.24
Monetary theory	332.401	Christianity	
Money	332.4	guides to Christian life	248.894 2
arts	737.4	Monkshood	583.111
economics	332.4	Monmouth (Wales : District)	T2—429 98
international law	341.751	Monmouth County (N.J.)	T2—749 46
law	343.032	Monmouthshire (Wales)	T2—429 9
public administration	351.822	Mono County (Calif.)	T2—794 48
Money market funds	332.632 7	Monochromatic photography	778.62
Money orders	332.76	motion pictures	778.534 2
law	346.096	Monocotyledons	584
Money-saving cooking	641.552	forestry	634.974
Money-saving interior decorating	747.1	paleobotany	561.4
Mongkut, King of Siam			
Thai history	959.303 4		

Monocycles
engineering	629.227 1
repair	629.287 71
riding	629.284 71
Monody	781.282
Monogamy	306.842 2
Monogenea	595.122

Monographs
cataloging	025.32
Monolithic circuits (Electronics)	621.381 5

Monologues (Drama)
literature	808.824 5
history and criticism	809.245
specific literatures	T3B—204 5
individual authors	T3A—2
Monometallic standards	332.422
Monomotapas (Kingdom)	968.910 1
	T2—689 1
Monona County (Iowa)	T2—777 44

Monongahela River (W. Va.
and Pa.)	T2—748 8
Pennsylvania	T2—748 8
West Virginia	T2—754 5
Monongalia County (W. Va.)	T2—754 52

Mononucleosis
incidence	614.575
medicine	616.925

see also Communicable
diseases (Human)
Monophonic electrophones	786.73

see also Electrophones
Monophysite churches	281.6

see also Eastern churches
Monoplacophora	594
Monopoly	338.82
economics	338.82
international economics	338.884
international law	341.753
law	343.072

Monopulse radar systems
engineering	621.384 85
Monorail railroads	385.5
engineering	625.103
transportation services	385.5
urban	388.44

see also Railroad transportation
Monorail rolling stock	385.5
engineering	625.28
transportation services	385.5
Monorail tracks	625.146
Monosaccharides	574.192 481 3
biochemistry	574.192 481 3
chemistry	547.781 3

see also Carbohydrates

Monosodium glutamate
food technology	664.4
Monotheism	211.34
Christianity	231

Monotheism (continued)
comparative religion	291.14
Islam	297.211
Judaism	296.311
natural theology	211.34

Monotony studies
production management	658.544
Monotremata	599.1
paleozoology	569.12
Monotropaceae	583.62

Monotype
manufacturing technology	681.61

Monotype composition
automatic	686.225 44
manual	686.225 42

Monroe, James
United States history	973.54
Monroe County (Ala.)	T2—761 25
Monroe County (Ark.)	T2—767 87
Monroe County (Fla.)	T2—759 41
Monroe County (Ga.)	T2—758 563
Monroe County (Ill.)	T2—773 91
Monroe County (Ind.)	T2—772 255
Monroe County (Iowa)	T2—777 865
Monroe County (Ky.)	T2—769 685
Monroe County (Mich.)	T2—774 32
Monroe County (Miss.)	T2—762 975
Monroe County (Mo.)	T2—778 325
Monroe County (N.Y.)	T2—747 88
Monroe County (Ohio)	T2—771 96
Monroe County (Pa.)	T2—748 25
Monroe County (Tenn.)	T2—768 883
Monroe County (W. Va.)	T2—754 78
Monroe County (Wis.)	T2—775 54
Monrovia (Liberia)	T2—666 2
Monserrat	972.975
Monsoons	551.518 4
Monstera	584.64

Monsters (Unexplained
phenomena)	001.944
Monstrilloida	595.34
paleozoology	565.34

Mont-Tremblant Provincial
Park (Quebec)	T2—714 4
Montage	702.813
Montagnais language	497.3
	T6—973

Montagnards (Vietnamese
people)	T5—959 3

Montagu (South Africa :
District)	T2—687 3
Montague County (Tex.)	T2—764 541
Montana	978.6
	T2—786
Montcalm (Quebec : County)	T2—714 415

Montcalm (Quebec : Regional
County Municipality)	T2—714 415
Montcalm County (Mich.)	T2—774 53

Mora County (N.M.)	T2—789 54
Moraceae	583.962
fruit crops	634.36
Moraines (Geologic land forms)	551.315
Moraines (Geologic material)	551.314
Moral determinants	
individual psychology	155.234
Moral education	370.114
Moral judgment	170
psychology	155.232
Moral offenses	
criminal law	345.027
criminology	364.17
moral theology	291.5
see also Moral theology	
social control	363.4
Moral philosophy	170
Moral Rearmament	267.16
Moral renewal (Christianity)	248.25
Moral sense	
ethical systems	171.2
Moral theology	291.5
Buddhism	294.35
Christianity	241
Hinduism	294.548
Islam	297.5
Judaism	296.385
Moral training	
home child care	649.7
Morale	
armed forces	355.123
personnel management	658.314
public administration	350.147
central governments	351.147
local governments	352.005 147
Morality	170
public control	363.4
criminal law	345.027
criminology	364.17
public administration	350.76
central governments	351.76
local governments	352.936
religion	291.5
see also Moral theology	
see also Ethics	
Morality plays	
literature	808.825 16
history and criticism	809.251 6
specific literatures	T3B—205 16
individual authors	T3A—2
stage presentation	792.16
Morals	170
Moravia (Czechoslovakia)	T2—437 2
Moravian Church	284.6
see also Christian	
denominations	
Moravian dialects	491.87
	T6—918 7

Moravian literature	891.87
Moravians	T5—918 7
Moravians (Religious group)	T7—246
biography	284.609 2
Moray (Scotland : District)	T2—412 23
Morays	597.51
Morazán (El Salvador : Dept.)	T2—728 433
Morbihan (France)	T2—441 3
Mordelloidea	595.767
Mordovian A.S.S.R.	
(R.S.F.S.R.)	T2—478 3
Mordovskaia A.S.S.R.	
(R.S.F.S.R.)	T2—478 3
Mordvin	T5—945 6
Mordvin language	494.56
	T6—945 6
Mordvin literature	894.56
Mordvinian A.S.S.R.	
(R.S.F.S.R.)	T2—478 3
Moré language	496.35
	T6—963 5
More og Romsdal fylke	
(Norway)	T2—483
Moreau River	T2—783 54
Moree (N.S.W.)	T2—944 4
Morehouse Parish (La.)	T2—763 84
Morel	589.23
Morelos (Mexico)	T2—724 9
Mores	306
customs	390
sociology	306
Moretele (South Africa :	
District)	T2—682 94
Morgan County (Ala.)	T2—761 93
Morgan County (Colo.)	T2—788 74
Morgan County (Ga.)	T2—758 595
Morgan County (Ill.)	T2—773 463
Morgan County (Ind.)	T2—772 513
Morgan County (Ky.)	T2—769 253
Morgan County (Mo.)	T2—778 53
Morgan County (Ohio)	T2—771 94
Morgan County (Tenn.)	T2—768 74
Morgan County (Utah)	T2—792 26
Morgan County (W. Va.)	T2—754 96
Morgan horse	
animal husbandry	636.17
zoology	599.725
Morgantown (W. Va.)	T2—754 52
Morgues	363.75
architecture	725.597
Morice Lake (B.C.)	T2—711 82
Morice River (B.C.)	T2—711 82
Moringaceae	583.131
Mormon Church	289.3
church government	262.093
parishes	254.093
church law	262.989 3

Moss animal	594.7
Moss Vale (N.S.W.)	T2—944 6
Mössbauer spectroscopy	543.085 86
chemical analysis	543.085 86
physics	537.535 2
Mossel Bay (South Africa :	
District)	T2—687 4
Mosses	588.2
paleobotany	561.8
Mossi (African people)	T5—963 5
Mossi (Kingdom)	966.250 1
	T2—662 5
Mossi languages	496.35
	T6—963 5
Mostaganem (Algeria : Dept.)	T2—651
Mosul (Iraq)	T2—567 4
Motacillidae	598.854
Motelkeepers	647.940 92
occupational group	T7—647
Motels	647.94
see also Hotels	
Motets	782.26
choral and mixed voices	782.526
single voices	783.092 6
Moth flies	595.771
Mother and child	306.874 3
Motherhood	306.874 3
Mothers	306.874 3
	T1—085 2
	T7—043 1
family relationships	306.874 3
psychology	155.646 3
Motherwell (Scotland :	
District)	T2—414 49
Moths	595.781
Motion	
celestial bodies	521
philosophy	116
physics	531.112
stars	523.83
Motion of particles (Nuclear	
physics)	539.725
Motion-picture directors	791.430 233 092
occupational group	T7—791 4
Motion-picture photography	778.53
Motion-picture	
photomicrography	778.56
Motion-picture plays	
literature	808.823
history and criticism	809.23
specific literatures	T3B—203
rhetoric	808.23
Motion-picture projection	778.55
Motion-picture scripts	
rhetoric	808.066 791

Motion pictures	791.43
adult education	374.27
bibliographies	011.37
communication services	384.8
drama	
presentation	791.43
education	371.335 23
influence on crime	364.254
journalism	070.18
performing arts	791.43
sociology	306.485
public administration	351.874 8
sociology	302.234 3
use in advertising	659.152
Motion sickness	
medicine	616.989 2
see also Environmental diseases	
(Human)	
Motion studies	
production management	658.542 3
psychology	152.3
Motions (Law)	347.052
Motivation	153.8
armed forces	355.123
education	370.154
personnel management	658.314
executives	658.407 14
public administration	350.147
central governments	351.147
local governments	352.005 147
psychology	
learning	153.153 4
Motivation research	
marketing management	658.834 2
Motley County (Tex.)	T2—764 752
Motmots	598.892
Motocross	796.756
Motor bicycles	388.347 5
engineering	629.227 5
see also Motorcycles	
Motor functions	
human physiology	612.7
localization in brain	612.825 2
physiology	574.18
psychology	152.3
see also Musculoskeletal system	
Motor horns	
music	786.99
see also Percussion	
instruments	
Motor-impaired children	
home care	649.151 6
Motor-impaired persons	305.908 166
	T1—087 3
	T7—081 66
education	371.916
social group	305.908 166
social welfare	362.43

Mount Hood (Or.)	T2—795 61
Mount Isa (Qld.)	T2—943 7
Mount Kaputar National Park	T2—944 4
Mount Kilimanjaro (Tanzania)	T2—678 26
Mount Kosciusko	T2—944 7
Mount Lofty Ranges	T2—942 32
Mount McKinley National Park (Alaska)	T2—798 3
Mount Morgan (Qld.)	T2—943 5
Mount Olga	T2—942 91
Mount Rainier National Park (Wash.)	T2—797 782
Mount Rescue Conservation Park	T2—942 33
Mount Revelstoke National Park (B.C.)	T2—711 68
Mount Robson Provincial Park (B.C.)	T2—711 82
Mount Spec National Park	T2—943 6
Mount Waddington (B.C.)	T2—711 2
Mount Whitney	T2—794 86
Mount Zeil	T2—942 91
Mountain climbing	796.522
equipment technology	688.765 22
Mountain ecology	574.526 4
Mountain laurel	583.62
Mountain lions	599.744 28
big game hunting	799.277 442 8
Mountain Province (Philippines)	T2—599 1
Mountain railroads	385.6
engineering	625.3
transportation services	385.6
see also Railroad transportation	
Mountain sickness	
medicine	616.989 3
see also Environmental diseases (Human)	
Mountain tactics	355.423
Mountain troops	356.164
Mountain tunnels	388
construction	624.192
see also Tunnels	
Mountain winds	551.518 5
Mountain Zebra National Park	T2—687 14
Mountaineering	796.522
Mountaineers	796.522 092
sports group	T7—796 5
Mountains	551.432
	T2—143
geography	910.914 3
geomorphology	551.432
health	613.12
land economics	333.73
physical geography	910.021 43
recreational resources	333.784
recreational use	796.522
Mountbatten of Burma, Louis Mountbatten, Earl	
Indian history	954.035 9
Mounted forces	357
Mountrail County (N.D.)	T2—784 74
Mourne, Newry and (Northern Ireland : District)	T2—416 58
Mourne Mountains (Northern Ireland)	T2—416 58
Mourning	393.9
music	781.588
Mouth	
human anatomy	611.31
human diseases	
medicine	616.31
human physiology	612.31
speech	612.78
surgery	617.522
see also Digestive system	
Mouth organs	788.82
see also Woodwind instruments	
Moutse (South Africa : District)	T2—682 95
Movable bridges	388
construction	624.8
see also Bridges	
Movable dams	627.84
Movable property	
international law	341.48
private ownership	346.047
public ownership	343.023
Movement	
arts	701.8
drawing	741.018
cytology	574.876 4
psychology	152.3
Movement disorders	
medicine	616.7
see also Musculoskeletal system	
Movement perception	
psychology	153.754
visual	152.142 5
Movements	
animals	591.18
human physiology	612.04
musculoskeletal system	612.7
see also Musculoskeletal system	
plants	581.18
Movements (Political ideologies)	320.5
Movie Channel, The	384.555 4
see also Television	
Moving and storage industry	388.044
law	343.093 2
Moving household goods	648.9
freight services	388.044
personnel management	658.383

Multilingualism	306.446
sociology	306.446
Multinational enterprises	338.88
accounting	657.96
Multiphase flow	
liquid mechanics	532.56
Multiple access systems	
computer communications	004.6
see also Computer	
communications	
processing modes	004.3
Multiple art	709.040 78
sculpture	735.230 478
Multiple banking	332.16
Multiple childbirth	
obstetrics	618.25
Multiple column tariffs	382.753
see also Customs (Tariff)	
Multiple deficiency states	
medicine	616.399
see also Digestive system	
Multiple dwellings	
architecture	728.31
Multiple flutes	788.37
see also Woodwind instruments	
Multiple-line insurance coverage	368.09
Multiple-loop systems	
automation engineering	629.833
Multiple personalities	
medicine	616.852 36
see also Mental illness	
Multiple pregnancy	
obstetrics	618.25
Multiple-purpose buildings	720.49
architecture	720.49
Multiple sclerosis	362.196 834
medicine	616.834
social services	362.196 834
see also Nervous system	
Multiple stars	523.841
Multiplexers	
computer communications	004.66
engineering	621.398 1
Multiplexing	
computer communications	004.66
engineering	621.398 1
Multiplication	512.92
algebra	512.92
arithmetic	513.213
Multiplicative properties	512.73
Multiplier effect	
macroeconomics	339.43
Multiprocessing	004.35
Multiprocessors	004.35
engineering	621.391
Multiprogramming	004.32
systems programs	005.43
Multistage programming	519.703
Multistory buildings	720.48
architectural construction	721.042
architecture	720.48
fire hazards	363.379
see also Fire stations	
Multistory houses	
architecture	728.372
Multituberculata	569.17
Multivariate analysis	519.535
Multnomah County (Or.)	T2—795 49
Mumesons	539.721 14
Mumps	
incidence	614.544
medicine	616.313
pediatrics	618.923 13
see also Digestive system	
München (Germany)	T2—433 64
Muncie (Ind.)	T2—772 65
Munda languages	495.95
	T6—959 5
Munda literatures	895.95
Mundane astrology	133.5
Mundari language (Munda)	495.95
	T6—959 5
Mundari literature	895.95
Mundas	T5—959 5
Mundubbera (Qld.)	T2—943 2
Mundurucu language	498.3
	T6—983
Munich (Germany)	T2—433 64
Municipal annexation	320.859
Municipal bankruptcy	336.368
Municipal bonds	332.632 33
law	346.092 2
Municipal charters	342.02
Municipal colleges	378.052
Municipal corporations	320.8
government	320.8
law	342.09
public administration	352.007 2
Municipal courts	347.02
Municipal engineering	628
Municipal engineers	628.092
occupational group	T7—628
Municipal finance	336.014
law	343.03
public administration	352.1
public finance	336.014
Municipal franchises	
public revenue	336.11
Municipal incorporation	
government	320.85
Municipal theater	792.022
Municipal universities	378.052
Municipal wastes	363.728
social services	363.728
see also Waste control	

Musculoskeletal system (continued)
geriatrics	618.976 7
human anatomy	611.7
human diseases	362.196 7
incidence	614.597
medicine	616.7
social services	362.196 7
human histology	611.018 97
human physiology	612.7
orthopedics	617.3
pediatrics	618.927
pharmacodynamics	615.77
sprains	
medicine	617.17
surgery	617.47
veterinary medicine	636.089 67
Museologists	069.092
occupational group	T7—096
Museology	069
	T1—075
Museum activities	069
	T1—075
Museum catalogs	069.52
	T1—074
Museum collections	069.5
	T1—074
Museum documentation	069.52
Museum equipment	069.3
Museum furnishings	
plant management	069.3
Museum furniture	
museology	069.33
Museum guidebooks	T1—074
Museum labels	069.53
Museum libraries	027.68
Museum objects	
circulation	069.132
selection	069.51
Museum registration methods	069.52
Museum science	069
Museum services	069.1
	T1—075 5
Museums	069
	T1—074
architecture	727.6
area planning	711.57
law	344.093
public administration	350.853
central governments	351.853
local governments	352.945 3
Museveni, Yoweri	
Ugandan history	967.610 4
Musgrave Ranges	T2—942 38
Mushrooms	589.222
agriculture	635.8
commercial processing	664.805 8
cooking	641.658
food	641.358
toxicology	615.952 922 2

Music	780
elementary education	372.87
literature	808.803 57
history and criticism	809.933 57
specific literatures	T3B—080 357
history and criticism	T3B—093 57
printing	686.284
public administration	350.854
central governments	351.854
local governments	352.945 4
publishing	070.579 4
religion	291.37
Buddhism	294.343 7
Christianity	246.7
Hinduism	294.537
Islam	297.3
Jainism	294.437
Judaism	296.4
public worship	291.38
Christianity	264.2
see also Public worship	
sociology	306.484
use in child care	649.51
Music appreciation	781.17
elementary education	372.872
Music boxes	786.65
see also Mechanical musical	
instruments	
Music hall presentations	792.7
Music halls	
architecture	725.81
Music libraries	026.78
Music theory	781
Music therapy	
medicine	615.851 54
Musical aptitude tests	153.947 8
Musical bows	787.92
see also Stringed instruments	
Musical chairs (Recreation)	793.4
Musical elements	781.2
Musical forms	781.8
instrumental	784.18
music	782
Musical glasses	786.866
see also Percussion instruments	
Musical instrument makers	784.192 309 2
craft producers	784.192 309 2
occupational group	T7—78
mass producers	681.809 2
occupational group	T7—681 8
occupational group	T7—78
Musical instruments	784.19
construction	784.192 3
by hand	784.192 3
by machine	681.8
Musical notation	780.148
Musical plays	782.14
music	782.14
stage presentation	792.6

Mynas	598.863	Mysticism	291.422
animal husbandry	636.68	Christianity	248.22
Myocardial infarction		comparative religion	291.422
medicine	616.123 7	Judaism	296.712
see also Cardiovascular system		philosophy	149.3
Myocarditis		medieval western	189.5
medicine	616.124	Myth	
see also Cardiovascular system		literature	808.801 5
Myocardium		history and criticism	809.915
human anatomy	611.12	specific literatures	T3B—080 15
human diseases		history and criticism	T3B—091 5
medicine	616.124	Mythological interpretation	
human physiology	612.17	Bible	220.68
see also Cardiovascular system		Mythology	398.2
Myodocopa	595.33	art representation	704.947
paleozoology	565.33	Christianity	204.5
Myomorpha	599.323 3	folklore	398.2
Myoporaceae	583.87	paintings	753.7
Myositis		religion	291.13
medicine	616.743	sources	291.8
see also Musculoskeletal system		Mythomania	
Myriapoda	595.6	medicine	616.858 45
paleozoology	565.6	*see also* Mental illness	
Myricales	583.974	Mytiloida	594.11
Myristicaceae	583.931	paleozoology	564.11
Myrobalan	583.42	Myxedemism	
Myrothamnaceae	583.394	medicine	616.858 848
Myrrh	583.24	*see also* Mental retardation	
Myrsinales	583.677	Myxobacterales	589.98
Myrtaceae		Myxococcaceae	589.98
fruit crop	634.42	Myxomycetes	589.29
Myrtales	583.42	Myxomycophyta	589.29
Myrtle	583.42	Myxoviruses	576.648 4
Myrtle (Lauraceae)	583.931	Myzondendraceae	583.94
Myrtle wax	665.12	Myzostomida	595.148
Myrtleford (Vic.)	T2—945 5	Mzimkulu River	T2—684 5
Mysia	T2—392 1	Mzimvubu River	T2—687 91
Mysidacea	595.383		
paleozoology	565.38		
Mysore (India : State)	T2—548 7	**N**	
Mystacocarida	595.31		
paleozoology	565.31	N.A.T.O. (Alliance)	355.031 091 821
Mysteries (Unexplained		N.I. (Macroeconomics)	339.32
phenomena)	001.94	N.M.R. (Physics)	538.362
Mystery films	791.436 55	N.M.R. imaging	
Mystery games	793.93	medicine	616.075 48
Mystery programs	791.446 55	N.M.S.Q.T. (Merit scholarship	
radio	791.446 55	test)	378.166 2
television	791.456 55	N.N.P. (Macroeconomics)	339.32
Mystery stories	808.838 72	N.O.W. accounts	332.175 2
history and criticism	809.387 2	N.Q.R. (Physics)	538.362
specific literatures	T3B—308 72	Na-Dene languages	497.2
individual authors	T3A—3		T6—972
Mystical body of Christ	262.77	Nabberu, Lake	T2—941 5
Mystical Judaism	296.833	Nablus (Jordan : District)	T2—569 53
Mysticeti	599.51	Naboomspruit (South Africa)	T2—682 5
paleozoology	569.5	Nacogdoches County (Tex.)	T2—764 182
		Nadgee Fauna Reserve	T2—944 7
		Nador (Morocco : Province)	T2—642

Naples (Italy)	T2—457 3	Narrative	
ancient	T2—377	literature	808.802 3
Naples (Italy : Province)	T2—457 3	history and criticism	809.923
Napo (Ecuador : Province)	T2—866 41	specific literatures	T3B—080 23
Napoleon I, Emperor of the		history and criticism	T3B—092 3
French		Narrative poetry	808.813
French history	944.05	history and criticism	809.13
Napoleon III, Emperor of the		specific literatures	T3B—103
French		individual authors	T3A—1
French history	944.07	Narrogin (W.A. : Shire)	T2—941 2
Napoleonic wars	940.27	Narrow-gage railroads	385.52
Napoli (Italy : Province)	T2—457 3	engineering	625.1
Nappes (Geology)	551.87	transportation services	385.52
Naqara	786.93	*see also* Railroad transportation	
see also Percussion instruments		Narwhals	599.53
Nara-ken (Japan)	T2—521 84	Nasai, Ahmad ibn Shuayb	
Naracoorte (S. Aust.)	T2—942 34	Hadith	297.124 5
Narbonensis	T2—364	Nasal sinuses	
Narcissism		human anatomy	611.21
medicine	616.858 5	human diseases	
see also Mental illness		medicine	616.212
Narcissus	584.25	human physiology	612.2
Narcolepsy		*see also* Respiratory system	
medicine	616.849 8	Nash County (N.C.)	T2—756 47
see also Nervous system		Nashville (Tenn.)	T2—768 55
Narcotic antagonists		Nasopharynx	
pharmacodynamics	615.782 2	human diseases	
Narcotics	362.29	medicine	616.212
customs	394.14	*see also* Respiratory system	
ethics	178.8	Nass River (B.C.)	T2—711 85
see also Ethical problems		Nassau (Bahamas)	T2—729 6
pharmacodynamics	615.782 2	Nassau County (Fla.)	T2—759 11
see also Drug traffic, Substance		Nassau County (N.Y.)	T2—747 245
abuse		Nasser, Gamal Abdel	
Narcotics abuse	362.293	Egyptian history	962.053
law	344.044 63	Nasser, Lake (Egypt and	
medicine	616.863 2	Sudan)	T2—623
personal health	613.83	Nastic movements	
social welfare	362.293	plant physiology	581.183 3
see also Substance abuse		Nasturtium	583.216
Narcotics traffic	363.45	Natal (South Africa)	968.4
international law	341.775		T2—684
law	345.027 7	Natalia	968.404 2
see also Drug traffic			T2—684
Nardeae	584.93	Natantia	595.384 3
Narellan (N.S.W.)	T2—944 6	Natchez (Miss.)	T2—762 26
Nariño (Colombia : Dept.)	T2—861 62	Natchitoches Parish (La.)	T2—763 65
Narooma (N.S.W.)	T2—944 7	Nathalia (Vic.)	T2—945 4
Narrabri (N.S.W.)	T2—944 4	Nation of Islam	297.87
Narragansett Bay (R.I.)	551.461 46	Nation River (B.C.)	T2—711 82
	T2—163 46	Nation-state	
Narration		political system	321.05
literature	808.802 3	National advertising	659.131 2
history and criticism	809.923	National Assembly (French	
specific literatures	T3B—080 23	history)	944.041
history and criticism	T3B—092 3	National bankruptcy	336.368
rhetoric	808	National banks	332.122 3

Nationalism (continued)
music — 780.903 4
political ideology — 320.54
Nationalist China — T2—512 49
Nationalist parties — 324.218 3
  international organizations — 324.183
Nationality — 323.6
  international law — 341.482
  law — 342.083
  political science — 323.6
Nationality clubs — 369.2
Nationalization of industry — 338.924
Nationalization of property
  international law — 341.484 6
  law — 343.025 2
Native American languages — 497
        T6—97
  South America — 498
        T6—98
Native American literatures — 897
  South America — 898
Native American peoples — 305.897
        T5—97
  South America — T5—98
  see also American native
    peoples
Native elements — 549.2
  see also Chemicals
Native metals — 549.23
  see also Metals
Native peoples — 306.08
  legal status — 342.087 2
Native plants
  floriculture — 635.951
Nativity of Jesus Christ — 232.921
NATO (Alliance) — 355.031 091 821
Natrona County (Wyo.) — T2—787 93
Natural childbirth
  obstetrics — 618.45
Natural dyes
  technology — 667.26
Natural environments
  health — 613.1
Natural gas — 553.285
  economic geology — 553.285
  extraction — 622.338 5
    law — 343.077 2
    public administration — 351.823 88
  extractive economics — 338.272 85
  pipeline transportation — 388.56
    engineering — 665.744
  prospecting — 622.182 85
  public utilities — 363.63
    law — 343.092 6
    see also Public utilities
  resource economics — 333.823 3
    law — 346.046 823 3
    public administration — 351.823 27

Natural gas (continued)
  technology — 665.7
    economics — 338.476 657
  see also Petroleum
Natural gas industry
  regulation — 343.077 2
Natural history — 508
Natural history and religion — 291.175
  Christianity — 261.55
  natural theology — 215.74
Natural landscapes
  landscape architecture — 719
Natural language processing
  computer science — 006.35
Natural law
  ethical systems — 171.2
  law — 340.112
  moral theology
    Christianity — 241.2
Natural leather — 675.2
Natural monuments
  landscape architecture — 719.32
Natural numbers — 513.2
  number theory — 512.72
Natural phenomena — 508
  see also Nature
Natural radioactivity — 539.752
Natural religion — 210
Natural resources — 333.7
  economics — 333.7
  law — 346.044
  public administration — 350.823 2
    central governments — 351.823 2
      cabinet departments — 351.082 32
    local governments — 352.942 32
  use of
    ethics — 178
      see also Ethical problems
Natural rights — 323.01
  international law — 341.481
  law — 340.112
Natural sciences — 500
  public administration — 351.855
Natural selection — 575.016 2
Natural stone — 553.5
  see also Stone
Natural theology — 210
Naturalism — 146
  arts — 709.034 3
  ethics — 171.2
  literature — 808.801 2
    history and criticism — 809.912
    specific literatures — T3B—080 12
      history and criticism — T3B—091 2
  painting — 759.053
Naturalization — 323.623
  law — 342.083
  political science — 323.623

Navy beans	583.322
field crop	633.372
Naxos Island (Greece)	T2—499
ancient	T2—391 5
Nayarit (Mexico)	T2—723 4
Nays	788.35
see also Woodwind instruments	
Nazi government	321.94
Nazi parties	324.213 8
Nazism	
political ideology	320.533 094 3
Nazko River (B.C.)	T2—711 75
Ndebele (African people)	T5—963 98
Ndebele (South Africa)	T2—682 95
Ndebele language	496.398
	T6—963 98
Ndonga languages	496.399
	T6—963 99
Ndumu Game Reserve	T2—684 91
Ndwanwe (Kingdom)	968.403 8
	T2—684
Ndwedwe (South Africa :	
District)	T2—684 91
Neagh, Lough	T2—416
Neales, The	T2—942 38
Neamt (Romania)	T2—498 1
Neanderthal man	573.3
Near-death experience	
occultism	133.901 3
Near East	956
	T2—56
Near-space exploration	
unmanned	629.435 2
Neath (Wales : Borough)	T2—429 84
Neat's-foot oil	665.2
Nebaliacea	595.36
Nebo (South Africa : District)	T2—682 93
Nebraska	978.2
	T2—782
Nebraska Panhandle	T2—782 9
Nebuchadnezzar II, King of	
Babylonia	
Mesopotamian history	935.04
Necessity	
philosophy	123.7
Nechako Plateau (B.C.)	T2—711 82
Nechako Reservoir (B.C.)	T2—711 82
Nechako River (B.C.)	T2—711 82
Neches River (Tex.)	T2—764 15
Neck	
fractures	
medicine	617.151
human anatomy	611.93
human physiology	612.93
orthopedics	617.371
regional medicine	617.53
surgery	617.530 59

Neck muscles	
human anatomy	611.733
see also Musculoskeletal system	
Necklaces	391.7
customs	391.7
making	739.278
see also Jewelry	
Necks (Geology)	551.88
Neckwear	391.41
see also Accessories (Clothing)	
Necrologies	920
Necromancy	133.9
Necropneumonia	
medicine	616.245
see also Respiratory system	
Nectarine	641.342 57
botany	583.24
cooking	641.642 57
orchard crop	634.257
Nederlandsche Oost-Indische	
Compagnie (Indonesian	
history)	959.802 1
Needle biopsy	
medicine	616.075 8
Needlefish	597.53
Needlepoint	746.442
Needlepoint laces	677.653
arts	746.224
manufacturing technology	677.653
Needlework	
textile arts	746.4
Ñeembucú (Paraguay : Dept.)	T2—892 124
Nefertiti, Queen of Egypt	
Egyptian history	932.014
Negation	
logic	160
Negative income tax	362.582
law	344.032 582
Negatives (Photography)	771.43
Negeri Sembilan	T2—595 1
Negev (Israel)	T2—569 49
Neglected children	
social welfare	362.76
see also Child abuse	
Negligence (Law)	346.032
Negotiable instruments	332.76
law	346.096
Negotiable order of withdrawal	
accounts	332.175 2
Negotiation	302.3
psychology	158.5
social psychology	302.3
Negro Africa	T2—67
Negro Methodist churches	287.8
see also Methodist Church	
Negro race	T5—036
Negroes	T5—96
Negroid race	T5—036

Nephews	306.87
	T1—085
	T7—046
family relationships	306.87
Nephritis	
medicine	616.612
see also Urinary system	
Nephrology	616.61
see also Urinary system	
Neptune (Planet)	523.481
	T2—992 8
unmanned flights to	629.435 481
Neptunium	546.432
see also Chemicals	
Nerve tissue	
human histology	611.018 8
see also Nervous system	
Nerves	
human anatomy	611.83
human physiology	612.81
surgery	617.483
see also Nervous system	
Nervous system	591.188
anesthesiology	617.967 48
animal anatomy	591.48
animal diseases	591.218 8
animal histology	591.824
animal physiology	591.188
cancer	362.196 994 8
medicine	616.994 8
social services	362.196 994 8
see also Cancer	
geriatrics	618.976 8
human anatomy	611.8
human diseases	362.196 8
incidence	614.598
medicine	616.8
social services	362.196 8
human histology	611.018 98
human physiology	612.8
see also Innervation	
pediatrics	618.928
perinatal medicine	618.326 8
pharmacodynamics	615.78
surgery	617.48
veterinary medicine	636.089 68
Neshoba County (Miss.)	T2—762 685
Nesosilicates	
mineralogy	549.62
Ness County (Kan.)	T2—781 46
Neston, Ellesmere Port and (England)	T2—427 17
Nestorian churches	281.8
see also Eastern churches	
Nests	591.564
Net fishing	
sports	799.13
Net national product	339.32
Net worth	
personal finance	332.024 01
Netball	796.32
Netherlanders	T5—393 1
Netherlandish languages	439.3
	T6—393
Netherlandish literatures	839.3
Netherlandish peoples	T5—393
Netherlands	949.2
	T2—492
Netherlands Antilles	T2—729 86
Netherlands New Guinea	T2—951
Nets (Fishing)	639.1
sports	799.202 82
use	639.1
Nets (Mathematics)	511.5
topology	514.223
Nets (Surveying)	526.33
Netsukes	736.68
Netted fabrics	677.664
see also Textiles	
Netting	
arts	746.422 4
Nettles	583.962
Labiatae	583.87
Urticaceae	583.962
Network affiliates	
television	384.550 65
Network analysis	
management use	658.403 2
telephony	621.385 1
Network architecture	004.65
Network databases	005.754
Network programs	791.443
radio performances	791.443
television performances	791.453
Network protocols	
computer science	004.62
Network topology	004.65
Networks (Communications facilities)	384.545 5
radio	384.545 5
television	384.552 3
Networks (Electrical)	621.319 2
Networks (Organizations)	384.540 65
radio	384.540 65
television	384.550 65
Neubrandenburg (Germany : Bezirk)	T2—431 72
Neuchâtel (Switzerland : Canton)	T2—494 38
Neuenburg (Switzerland : Canton)	T2—494 38
Neufchâtel cheese	641.373 53
cooking	641.673 53
processing	637.353
Neumann function	515.53
Neumes	780.148

New England Range	T2—944 4
New English Bible	220.520 6
New Forest (England : District)	T2—422 75
New France, Company of (Canadian history)	971.016 2
New Glasgow (N.S.)	T2—716 13
New Granada	986.102
	T2—861
Colombian history	986.102
Ecuadoran history	986.602
Venezuelan history	987.03
New Granada (Republic)	986.105 2
	T2—861
New Granada (Viceroyalty) Panamanian history	972.870 2
New Guinea	995
	T2—95
New Guinea (Territory)	995.302 2
	T2—953
New Hampshire	974.2
	T2—742
New Hanover (South Africa : District)	T2—684 7
New Hanover County (N.C.)	T2—756 27
New Hanover Island	T2—958 3
New Haven (Conn.)	T2—746 8
New Haven County (Conn.)	T2—746 7
New Hebrides	T2—959 5
New International Version (Bible)	220.520 8
New Ireland Province (Papua New Guinea)	T2—958 3
New Jersey	974.9
	T2—749
New Jerusalemites biography	289.409 2
religious group	T7—284
New Kent County (Va.)	T2—755 43
New Kingdom (Egyptian history)	932.014
New Land (R.S.F.S.R.)	T2—986
New left political ideology	320.53
New London County (Conn.)	T2—746 5
New Madrid County (Mo.)	T2—778 985
New Mexico	978.9
	T2—789
New nations establishment	
World War I	940.314 25
World War II	940.531 425
New Norfolk (Tas.)	T2—946 2
New Norse language	439.83
	T6—398 3
New Norse literature	839.83
New Orleans (La.)	T2—763 35
New Orleans, Battle of, 1814	973.523 9
New Orleans jazz	781.653

New product development management	658.575
New Providence Island (Bahamas)	T2—729 6
New Quebec (Quebec)	T2—714 11
New religions	291.046
New religious movements	291.046
New River (N.C.-W. Va.)	T2—754 7
North Carolina	T2—756 83
Virginia	T2—755 7
West Virginia	T2—754 7
New Siberian Islands (R.S.F.S.R.)	T2—988
New South Wales	T2—944
New Southwest	979
	T2—79
New Stone Age	930.14
New Testament	225
New Testament Greek language	487.4
	T6—87
New Testament pseudepigrapha	229.92
New Thought	299.93
Christian	289.98
see also Christian denominations	
New towns	307.768
area planning	711.45
New Valley (Egypt : Governorate)	T2—622
New Westminster (B.C.)	T2—711 33
New World monkeys	599.82
New World pitcher plant	583.121
New World vultures	598.912
New Year	394.268 3
customs	394.268 3
Jewish	394.268 296 431
Jewish	296.431
New York (N.Y.)	T2—747 1
New York (State)	974.7
	T2—747
New York Bay	551.461 46
	T2—163 46
New York County (N.Y.)	T2—747 1
New York jazz	781.653
New Zealand	993
	T2—93
New Zealand literature	820
New Zealanders	T5—23
Newar	T5—95
Newari language	495.49
	T6—954 9
Newari literature	895.49
Newark (N.J.)	T2—749 32
Newark and Sherwood (England : District)	T2—425 24
Newaygo County (Mich.)	T2—774 58
Newberry County (S.C.)	T2—757 39

Newborn infants
  pediatrics   618.920 1
Newbury (England : District) T2—422 91
Newcastle (N.S.W.) T2—944 2
Newcastle (South Africa :
  District)   T2—684 1
Newcastle Range (N.T.) T2—942 95
Newcastle-under-Lyme
  (England : Borough) T2—424 62
Newcastle upon Tyne
  (England)   T2—428 76
Newfoundland   971.8
                 T2—718

Newfoundland (Dog)
  animal husbandry   636.73
  see also Dogs
Newham (London, England) T2—421 76
Newport (R.I.) T2—745 7
Newport (Wales : Borough) T2—429 91
Newport County (R.I.) T2—745 6
Newport News (Va.) T2—755 416
Newry and Mourne (Northern
  Ireland : District) T2—416 58
News gathering   070.43
News media   070.1
News sources
  journalism   070.431
Newsletters   050
  journalism   070.175
Newspaper columns
  journalism   070.44
Newspaper illustration 741.65
Newspapers   070
           T1—05
  bibliographies   011.35
  journalism   070.172
  postal handling   383.123
    see also Postal service
  publishing   070.572 2
  sociology   302.232 2
Newsprint   676.286
Newsreel journalism 070.18
Newsreel photography 778.538 07
Newton County (Ark.) T2—767 16
Newton County (Ga.) T2—758 593
Newton County (Ind.) T2—772 974
Newton County (Miss.) T2—762 672
Newton County (Mo.) T2—778 732
Newton County (Tex.) T2—764 162
Newtownabbey (Northern
  Ireland : Borough) T2—416 18
Newts   597.65
Nez Perce County (Idaho) T2—796 85
Ngala languages   496.396 8
          T6—963 968
Nganasan language   494.4
          T6—944
Ngeleberg Range T2—684 6

Ngo language   496.36
          T6—963 6
Ngombe (African people) T5—963 96
Ngombe languages   496.396
          T6—963 96
Ngonde (African people) T5—963 91
Ngonde language   496.391
          T6—963 91
Ngondi languages   496.396
          T6—963 96
Ngoni (African people) T5—963 98
Ngoni language   496.398
          T6—963 98
Ngotshe (South Africa :
  District)   T2—684 2
Ngqeleni (South Africa :
  District)   T2—687 91
Ngundi languages   496.396
          T6—963 96
Nguni kingdoms (Natal history) 968.403 8
Nguni languages   496.398
          T6—963 98
Ngurus   788.38
  see also Woodwind instruments
Nhill (Vic.)   T2—945 8
NI (Macroeconomics) 339.32
Niagara (Ont. : Regional
  municipality)   T2—713 38
Niagara County (N.Y.) T2—747 98
Niagara Falls (N.Y. and Ont.) T2—713 39
  New York   T2—747 99
  Ontario   T2—713 39
Niagara River (N.Y. and Ont.) T2—713 38
  New York   T2—747 98
  Ontario   T2—713 38
Niamey (Niger)   T2—662 6
Niassa (Mozambique :
  District)   T2—679 9
Nicaragua   972.85
          T2—728 5
Nicaragua Canal   386.445
Nicaraguan literature 860
Nicaraguans   T5—687 285
Niccolite
  mineralogy   549.32
Nice (France)   T2—449 414
Nice (France : Region) T2—449 41
Nicene Creed   238.142
  private prayer   242.723
Niches   721.48
  architecture   721.48
  construction   690.148
Nichiren Shoshu   294.392 8
Nicholas County (Ky.) T2—769 417
Nicholas County (W. Va.) T2—754 69
Nicholas I, Emperor of Russia
  Russian history 947.073

Nicholas II, Emperor of Russia
  Russian history   947.083
Nickel   669.733 2
  building construction   693.773 32
  building material   691.873 32
  chemical engineering   661.062 5
  chemistry   546.625
  decorative arts   739.56
  economic geology   553.485
  materials science   620.188
  metallography   669.957 332
  metallurgy   669.733 2
  metalworking   673.733 2
  mining   622.348 5
  physical metallurgy   669.967 332
  toxicology   615.925 625
  see also Chemicals, Metals
Nickerie (Surinam : District)   T2—883 1
Nicobar Islands   T2—548 8
Nicola River (B.C.)   T2—711 72
Nicolet (Quebec : County)   T2—714 55
Nicolet-Yamaska (Quebec)   T2—714 54
Nicollet County (Minn.)   T2—776 32
Nicotine
  toxicology   615.952 379
Nidulariales   589.221
Nidwald (Switzerland)   T2—494 762
Nidwalden (Switzerland)   T2—494 762
Nieces   306.87
   T1—085
   T7—046
  family relationships   306.87
Niederbayern (Germany)   T2—433 5
Niederösterreich (Austria)   T2—436 12
Niedersachsen (Germany)   T2—435 9
Nielim language   496.36
   T6—963 6
Nielloing
  decorative arts   739.15
Nièvre (France)   T2—445 6
Nigde Ili (Turkey)   T2—564
Nigei Island (B.C.)   T2—711 2
Nigel (South Africa : District)   T2—682 2
Niger   966.26
   T2—662 6
Niger-Congo languages   496.3
   T6—963
Niger-Kordofanian languages   496.3
   T6—963
Niger people   T5—966 26
Niger River   T2—662
Niger State (Nigeria)   T2—669 65
Nigeria   966.9
   T2—669
Nigerian Civil War, 1967-1970   966.905 2
Nigerians   T5—966 9
Nigeriens (People of Niger)   T5—966 26

Night-blooming plants
  floriculture   635.953
Night flying   629.132 521 4
Night football   796.332 6
Night music   781.523
Night photography   778.719
Night schools   374.8
Night skies
  meteorology   551.566
Night work   331.257 4
Nightclothes   391.42
  commercial technology   687.165
  customs   391.42
  home sewing   646.475
  see also Clothing
Nightclub presentations   792.7
Nightshade   583.79
Nihilism
  philosophy   149.8
Niigata-ken (Japan)   T2—521 52
Niihau (Hawaii)   T2—969 42
Nijmegen (Netherlands)   T2—492 18
Nika language   496.395
   T6—963 95
Nikolaevskaia oblast
  (Ukraine)   T2—477 17
Nikolayev (Ukraine : Oblast)   T2—477 17
Nil (Sudan : Province)   T2—625
Nil al Abyad (Sudan :
  Province}   T2—626 4
Nil al Azraq (Sudan)   T2—626 4
Nile (Sudan : Province)   T2—625
Nile Delta   T2—621
Nile River   T2—62
Nilo-Hamitic peoples   T5—965
Nilo-Saharan languages   496.5
   T6—965
Nilotic-Kavirondo language   496.5
   T6—965
Nilotic languages   496.5
   T6—965
Nilotic peoples   T5—965
Nimbarka (Philosophy)   181.484 3
Ninawa (Iraq : Province)   T2—567 4
Nineveh (Ancient city)   T2—35
Nineveh (Iraq : Province)   T2—567 4
Ningsia Hui Autonomous
  Region (China)   T2—517 5
Ningxia Huizu Zizhiqu
  (China)   T2—517 5
Ninigo Islands   T2—958 1
Niobium   669.79
  chemical engineering   661.052 4
  chemistry   546.524
  metallurgy   669.79
  physical metallurgy   669.967 9
  see also Chemicals
Niobrara County (Wyo.)   T2—787 15

Nocardiaceae	589.92
Noctuoidea	595.781
Nocturne form	784.189 66
Nodaway County (Mo.)	T2—778 124
Nofretete, Queen of Egypt	
Egyptian history	932.014
Nograd Megye (Hungary)	T2—439 8
Noh plays	895.620 51
Noh theater	792.095 2
Noise	363.74
communications engineering	621.382 24
electronic engineering	621.382 24
engineering	620.23
environmental psychology	155.911 5
law	344.046 38
psychology	152.15
public administration	350.772
central governments	351.772
local governments	352.6
social welfare	363.74
Noise control equipment	
plant management	658.28
Nolan County (Tex.)	T2—764 728
Nolanaceae	583.79
Noltingham Island (N.W.T. :	
Island)	T2—719 5
Nomenclature	T1—014
Nominalism	
philosophy	149.1
Nominating conventions	
(Political parties)	324.56
Nomination (Political parties)	324.5
Nomograms (Statistical	
presentations)	001.422 6
Nomography	511.5
Non-Austronesian languages of	
Oceania	499.1
	T6—991
Non-Euclidean geometry	516.9
Non-Trinitarian concepts	
Christianity	
God	231.044
Jesus	232.9
Non-Western art music	781.69
Nonaffiliated commercial	
television	384.550 65
Nonalcoholic beverages	641.26
commercial processing	663.6
cooking with	641.62
home preparation	641.875
Nonassociative algebras	512.24
Nonaustronesian languages of	
Oceania	499.1
	T6—991
Nonbeing	111.5
Nonbook materials	
library treatment	025.17

Noncombat services (Armed	
forces)	355.34
Noncombatants	
law of war	341.67
World War I	940.316 1
World War II	940.531 61
Noncommissioned officers	355.009 2
role and function	355.338
Noncommissioned officers' clubs	355.346
Noncommunicable diseases	
incidence	614.59
medicine	616.98
see also Environmental diseases	
(Human)	
Nonconformists (British	
churches)	280.4
see also Protestantism	
Noncrystalline solids	530.413
Nondairy coffee whiteners	
commercial processing	663.64
Nondestructive testing	
materials science	620.112 7
Nondifferentiable functions	515.8
Nondisjunction (Genetics)	575.2
Nondominant groups	305.56
	T1—086 93
Nondramatic vocal forms	782.2
choral and mixed voices	782.52
Nonelectronic data processing	004.9
Nonets	
chamber music	785.19
vocal music	783.19
Nonexplosive ammunition	
military engineering	623.459
Nonferrous metals	669
architectural construction	721.044 7
building construction	693.72–.77
building materials	691.8
economic geology	553.4
foundation materials	624.153 8
materials science	620.18
metallography	669.95
metallurgy	669
metalworking	673
mining	622.34
physical metallurgy	669.96
ship design	623.818 2
shipbuilding	623.820 7
structural engineering	624.182 2–.182 9
see also Chemicals, Metals	
Nonflagellate molds	589.258
Nongoma (South Africa :	
District)	T2—684 91
Nongraded schools	371.254
Nonimpact printing	686.233
Nonlinear closed-loop systems	
automation engineering	629.836
Nonlinear differential equations	515.355

Nornalup National Park	T2—941 2
Norrbottens lan (Sweden)	T2—488
Norris Lake (Tenn.)	T2—768 935
Norrland (Sweden)	T2—488
Norseman (W.A.)	T2—941 7
Norte de Santander (Colombia)	T2—861 24
North Africa	961
	T2—61
ancient	939.7
	T2—397
North Africans	T5—93
North America	970
	T2—7
North American native languages	497
	T6—97
North American native literatures	897
North American native peoples	T5—97
North Americans	T5—1
North Arabic languages	492.7
	T6—927
North Arabic literatures	892.7
North Atlantic Ocean	551.461 1
	T2—163 1
North Atlantic Treaty Organization	355.031 091 821
law	341.72
North Battleford (Sask.)	T2—712 42
North Bedfordshire (England)	T2—425 61
North Borneo	T2—595 3
North Brabant (Netherlands)	T2—492 45
North Canadian River (Okla.)	T2—766 1
North Carolina	975.6
	T2—756
North Cascades National Park (Wash.)	T2—797 73
North Central State (Nigeria)	T2—669 73
North Central States	977
	T2—77
North Channel (Huron, Lake, Mich. and Ont.)	T2—713 132
North Channel (Ireland and Scotland)	551.461 37
	T2—163 37
North Coast (South Africa)	T2—684 4
North Cornwall (England : District)	T2—423 71
North Cotabato (Philippines : Province)	T2—599 7
North Dakota	978.4
	T2—784
North Devon (England : District)	T2—423 52
North Dorset (England)	T2—423 32
North Down (Northern Ireland)	T2—416 53
North Downs	T2—422 3
North Dravidian languages	494.83
	T6—948 3
North Dravidian literatures	894.83
North Dravidians	T5—948 3
North East Derbyshire (England)	T2—425 14
North East Fife (Scotland)	T2—412 92
North East Frontier Agency, India	T2—541 63
North East Polder	T2—492 16
North East Province (Kenya)	T2—676 22
North-Eastern Region (China)	T2—518
North-Eastern State (Nigeria)	T2—669 8
North Esk River	T2—946 4
North Friesland (Germany)	T2—435 12
North Frigid Zone	T2—113
North Frisian Islands (Denmark and Germany)	T2—435 12
North German Confederation	943.081
	T2—43
North Germanic languages	439.5
	T6—395
North Germanic literatures	839.5
North Hertfordshire (England)	T2—425 81
North Holland (Netherlands)	T2—492 35
North Island (N.Z.)	T2—931 2
North Kesteven (England : District)	T2—425 35
North Korea	T2—519 3
North Land (R.S.F.S.R.)	T2—987
North Norfolk (England : District)	T2—426 12
North Okanagan (B.C.)	T2—711 5
North Oset A.S.S.R. (R.S.F.S.R.)	T2—479 7
North Pacific Ocean	551.465 4
	T2—164 4
North Platte River	T2—787 16
North Polar Sea	551.468
	T2—163 2
North Pole	T2—163 2
North Queensland tick typhus incidence	614.526 6
medicine	616.922 6
see also Communicable diseases (Human)	
North Rhine-Westphalia (Germany)	T2—435 5
North Riding of Yorkshire (England)	T2—428 4
North Saanich (B.C.)	T2—711 28
North Saskatchewan River (Alta. and Sask.)	T2—712 33
North Sea	551.461 36
	T2—163 36
North Shropshire (England : District)	T2—424 53

Norton Sound (Alaska)	551.466 34
	T2—164 34
Norway	948.1
	T2—481
Norwegian language	439.82
	T6—398 2
Bokmal	439.82
	T6—398 2
New Norse	439.83
	T6—398 3
Norwegian literature	839.82
Bokmal	839.82
Landsmal	839.83
New Norse	839.83
Riksmal	839.82
Norwegian Sea	551.468 4
	T2—163 24
Norwegians	T5—398 2
Norwich (England)	T2—426 15
Nose	
fractures	
medicine	617.156
human anatomy	611.21
human diseases	
medicine	616.212
human physiology	612.2
smelling	612.86
speech	612.78
surgery	617.523
see also Respiratory system	
Nose flutes	788.3
see also Woodwind instruments	
Nostocales	589.46
Nostratic language	417.7
	T6—1
Nosu (Asian people)	T5—95
Notacanthiformes	597.51
Notaries	347.016
occupational group	T7—349
Notaspidea	594.36
paleozoology	564.36
Notched flutes	788.35
see also Woodwind instruments	
Note rows	781.268
Notes payable	
accounting	657.74
financial management	658.152 6
Nothingness	111.5
Notions	646.19
commercial technology	687.8
home sewing	646.19
Notodelphyoida	595.34
paleozoology	565.34
Notostraca	595.32
paleozoology	565.32
Notoungulata	569.75
Notre-Dame Mountains	
(Quebec)	T2—714 7

Nottingham (England)	T2—425 27
Nottinghamshire (England)	T2—425 2
Nottoway County (Va.)	T2—755 637
Nouakchott (Mauritania)	T2—661
Noupoort (South Africa :	
District)	T2—687 13
Nouveau-Québec (Quebec)	T2—714 11
Nouveau-Québec (Quebec :	
Administrative region)	T2—714 115
Nouvelle-Beauce (Quebec)	T2—714 71
Nova Scotia	971.6
	T2—716
Novaia Zemlia (R.S.F.S.R.)	T2—986
Novara (Italy : Province)	T2—451 6
Novas (Stars)	523.844 6
Novaya Zemlya (R.S.F.S.R.)	T2—986
Novelettes	808.83
history and criticism	809.3
specific literatures	T3B—3
individual authors	T3A—3
Novelists	809.3
collected biography	809.3
specific literatures	T3B—300 9
individual biography	T3A—3
occupational group	T7—83
Novellas	808.83
history and criticism	809.3
specific literatures	T3B—3
individual authors	T3A—3
Novels	808.83
history and criticism	809.3
specific literatures	T3B—3
individual authors	T3A—3
Novelties	
manufacturing technology	688.726
Novenas	264.7
Novgorod (R.S.F.S.R. :	
Oblast)	T2—474 5
Novices	
social group	305.909 09
	T7—090 9
Novitiate (Monastic life)	248.894 25
women	248.894 35
Novo Estado (Portuguese history)	946.904 2
Novogrodskaia oblast	
(R.S.F.S.R.)	T2—474 5
Novosibirsk (R.S.F.S.R. :	
Oblast)	T2—573
Novosibirskaia oblast	
(R.S.F.S.R.)	T2—573
NOW accounts	332.175 2
Nowata County (Okla.)	T2—766 97
Nowra (N.S.W.)	T2—944 7
Nowy Sacz (Poland :	
Voivodeship)	T2—438 6
Noxubee County (Miss.)	T2—762 955
Nqamakwe (South Africa :	
District)	T2—687 91

Nucleus	
cytology	574.873 2
Nucleus disintegration	539.752
Nuclide structure	
physics	539.74
Nuda	593.8
Nudes	
art representation	704.942 1
drawing	743.4
painting	757.22
Nudibranchia	594.36
paleozoology	564.36
Nudism	
health	613.194
Nueces County (Tex.)	T2—764 113
Nueces River (Tex.)	T2—764 11
Nuer (African people)	T5—965
Nuer language	496.5
	T6—965
Nueva Asunción (Paraguay : Dept.)	T2—892 25
Nueva Ecija (Philippines : Province)	T2—599 1
Nueva Esparta (Venezuela)	T2—875 4
Nueva Segovia (Nicaragua)	T2—728 521
Nueva Vizcaya (Philippines : Province)	T2—599 1
Nuguria Atoll	T2—959 2
Nuisance (Law)	346.036
Nukumanu Island	T2—959 2
Nullarbor Plain	T2—942 38
Nullification movement (United States history)	973.561
Numayri, Jafar Muhammad	
Sudanese history	962.404
Number systems	513.5
Numbers	513.2
Numeracy	513
elementary education	372.72
Numeration systems	513.5
Numerical algebra	512
Numerical analysis	515
applied	519.4
Numerical calculations	511
applied	519.4
Numerical control	
machine tools	621.902 3
Numerical differentiation	515.623
Numerical integration	515.624
Numerical interpretation	
Bible	220.68
Numerology	133.335
Numidia	939.72
	T2—397 2
Numididae	598.618
Numismatics	737
Numismatists	737.092
occupational group	T7—737

Numurkah (Vic.)	T2—945 4
Nunavut	T2—719 2
Nuneaton and Bedworth (England : Borough)	T2—424 83
Nunggubuyu language	499.15
	T6—991 5
Nuns	291.657
Buddhists	294.365 7
Christian	271.900 2
ecclesiology	262.24
guides to Christian life	248.894 3
Nuoro (Sardinia : Province)	T2—459 2
Nuove musiche	780.903 2
Nupe (African people)	T5—963 3
Nupe language	496.33
	T6—963 3
Nuremberg (Germany)	T2—433 24
Nuremberg war crime trials	341.690 268 43
Nuri (Afghanistan people)	T5—914 99
Nuristani languages	491.499
	T6—914 99
Nürnberg (Germany)	T2—433 24
Nurse and patient	610.730 699
Nurse and physician	610.730 699
Nurse practitioners	610.730 92
role and function	610.730 692
see also Nurses	
Nurseries (For children)	643.53
home economics	643.53
interior decoration	747.77
Nurseries (For plants)	631.52
floriculture	635.969
forestry	634.956 4
Nursery practice	631.52
floriculture	635.969
forestry	634.956 4
Nursery rhymes	398.8
Nursery schools	372.216
Nurses	610.730 92
health services	362.173
see also Health services	
law	344.041 4
occupational group	T7—613
role and function	610.730 69
Nurses' aides	610.730 92
role and function	610.730 698
see also Nurses	
Nursing	
home economics	649.8
law	344.041 4
medicine	610.73
Nursing (Breast feeding)	649.33
child rearing	649.33
health	613.26
human physiology	612.664
Nursing homes	362.16
law	344.032 16
mental illness	362.23

Nyunga language	499.15
	T6—991 5

O

O.A.S. (Alliance)	341.245
O.C.R. (Computer science)	006.424
O.T.C. market	332.643
Oadby and Wigston	
(England : Borough)	T2—425 43
Oahe, Lake	T2—783 5
Oahu (Hawaii)	T2—969 3
Oak	583.976
forestry	634.972 1
lumber	674.142
Oak Bay (B.C.)	T2—711 28
Oakey (Qld.)	T2—943 3
Oakland (Calif.)	T2—794 66
Oakland County (Mich.)	T2—774 38
OAS (Alliance)	341.245
Oaths of allegiance	
naturalization	323.623
Oaths of loyalty	
public personnel management	350.132 42
central governments	351.132 42
local governments	352.005 132 42
Oatlands (Tas.)	T2—946 3
Oats	641.331 3
botany	584.93
commercial processing	664.725
cooking	641.631 3
food crop	633.13
forage crop	633.253
Oaxaca (Mexico : State)	T2—727 4
Ob-Ugric languages	494.51
	T6—945 1
Obadiah (Biblical book)	224.91
Obas	787.73
see also Stringed instruments	
Obedience	
home child care	649.64
Obedience (Christian doctrine)	234.6
Obedience training (Pets)	636.088 7
Oberbayern (Germany)	T2—433 6
Oberfranken (Germany)	T2—433 1
Oberholzer (South Africa :	
District)	T2—682 2
Oberösterreich (Austria)	T2—436 2
Oberpfalz (Germany)	T2—433 4
Obesity	
health	613.25
low-calorie cooking	641.563 5
medicine	616.398
see also Digestive system	
Obiang Nguema Mbasogo,	
Teodoro	
Equatorial Guinean history	967.180 3
Obion County (Tenn.)	T2—768 13

Obituaries	920
Obituary sermons	
Christianity	252.9
Objectivity	
epistemology	121.4
Oblates	255.76
church history	271.76
women	255.97
church history	271.97
Obligations of citizens	323.65
Oblong books	099
Oboe concertos	784.285 2
Oboes	788.52
see also Woodwind instruments	
Obote, A. Milton (Apollo Milton)	
Ugandan history	967.610 4
Obregón, Alvaro	
Mexican history	972.082 2
O'Brien County (Iowa)	T2—777 14
Obscenity	
criminal law	345.027 4
criminology	364.174
ethics	176.7
law	344.054 7
postal handling	383.120 5
see also Postal service	
social problem	363.47
Observatories	
architecture	727.5
astronomy	522.1
Obsessive-compulsive neurosis	
medicine	616.852 27
see also Mental illness	
Obsidian	
glyptics	736.28
Obstacle courses (Military	
training)	355.544
Obstetrical disorders	
incidence	614.599 2
Obstetrical nursing	
medicine	610.736 78
Obstetrical surgery	618.8
Obstetricians	618.200 92
law	344.041 2
occupational group	T7—618 1
role and function	618.202 32
Obstetrics	618.2
anesthesiology	617.968 2
veterinary medicine	636.089 82
Obstructions	
intestine	
medicine	616.342
surgery	617.554
see also Digestive system	
Obstructive pulmonary disease	
medicine	616.24
see also Respiratory system	

Oceana County (Mich.)	T2—774 59
Oceania	995
	T2—95
Oceanic languages	499.4
	T6—994
Oceanographers	551.460 092
occupational group	T7—553
Oceanographic geology	551.460 8
Oceanography	551.46
Oceans	551.46
	T2—162
physical geology	551.46
resource economics	333.916 4
Ocelots	599.744 28
animal husbandry	636.89
Ochers	553.662
Ochil Hills	T2—412 8
Ochiltree County (Tex.)	T2—764 815
Ochnales	583.167
Ocmulgee River	T2—758 5
Oconee County (Ga.)	T2—758 193
Oconee County (S.C.)	T2—757 21
Oconee River	T2—758 6
Oconto County (Wis.)	T2—775 37
Ocotepeque (Honduras : Dept.)	T2—728 383
Ocotillo	583.158
OCR (Computer science)	006.424
Octal system (Numeration)	513.54
Octets	
chamber music	785.18
vocal music	783.18
Octoknemaceae	583.26
Octopoda	594.56
paleozoology	564.56
Octopus	594.56
cooking	641.694
fisheries	639.485 6
food	641.394
commercial processing	664.94
Ocular diagnosis	
medicine	616.075
Ocular neuromuscular mechanism	
human physiology	612.846
ophthalmology	617.762
see also Eyes	
Odd Fellows	366.3
Odd Fellows members	366.309 2
social group	T7—366 3
Odendaalsrus (South Africa : District)	T2—685 3
Odense amt (Denmark)	T2—489 4
Odes	808.814 3
history and criticism	809.143
specific literatures	T3B—104 3
individual authors	T3A—1
Odes of Solomon	229.912
Odessa (Ukraine : Oblast)	T2—477 17
Odesskaia oblast (Ukraine)	T2—477 17
Odi (South Africa : District)	T2—682 94
Odobenidae	599.747
Odonata	595.733
paleozoology	565.73
Odontoceti	599.53
paleozoology	569.5
Odontopteris	561.597
Odontopteryges	598.43
Oea (Libya)	T2—397 4
Oedongoniales	589.47
Oeno Island	T2—961 8
Off-road vehicles	388.34
driving	629.283 042
engineering	629.220 42
military engineering	623.747
repair	629.287 042
transportation services	388.34
see also Automotive vehicles	
Off-shore mining	622.295
Offaly (Ireland)	T2—418 6
Offenbach am Main (Germany)	T2—434 163
Offenders	364.3
	T1—086 92
criminology	364.3
law	345.03
punishment	364.6
welfare services	364.6
Offenses against military discipline	355.133 4
Offenses against property	364.16
law	345.026
Offenses against public morals	364.17
law	345.027
Offenses against public safety	364.142
law	345.024 2
Offenses against religion	364.188
law	345.028 8
Offenses against the person	364.15
law	345.025
Offensive arms	
art metalwork	739.7
customs	399
Offerings (Religion)	291.34
Offertory	264.36
music	782.323 5
Office buildings	
architecture	725.23
Office employees	651.309 2
see also Office workers	
Office equipment	
armed forces	355.81
office services	651.2
procurement	658.72
	T1—068 7
Office etiquette	395.52

Oil shale	553.283	Oklahoma City (Okla.)	T2—766 38
economic geology	553.283	Oklahoma County (Okla.)	T2—766 38
mining	622.338 3	Oklahoma Panhandle	T2—766 13
processing	665.4	Oklahoma Territory	T2—766 1
Oil-soluble paint	667.62	Okmulgee County (Okla.)	T2—766 83
Oil spills		Okpe language	496.33
water-pollution engineering	628.168 33		T6—963 3
Oil well flooding	622.338 2	Okra	583.17
Oil wells	622.338 2	commercial processing	664.805 648
Oilbirds	598.99	garden crop	635.648
Oiling		Oktibbeha County (Miss.)	T2—762 953
woodwork		Olacales	583.26
buildings	698.33	Olancho (Honduras)	T2—728 33
Oils		Oland (Sweden)	T2—486
hydraulic-power technology	621.204 24	Old-age and survivors' insurance	368.43
industrial	665	social law	344.023
materials science	620.198	*see also* Insurance	
Oils (Food)		Old age pensions	331.252
applied nutrition	613.28	*see also* Pensions	
home economics	641.14	Old Bulgarian language	491.817 01
food technology	664.3		T6—918 17
Oils (Paints)	667.622	Old Bulgarian literature	891.81
Oilseed plants		Old Castile (Spain)	T2—463 5
agriculture	633.85	Old Catholic churches	284.8
Ointments		church government	262.048
practical pharmacy	615.45	parishes	254.048
Oise (France)	T2—443 5	church law	262.984 8
Ōita-ken (Japan)	T2—522 8	doctrines	230.48
Ojibwa Indians	T5—973	catechisms and creeds	238.48
Ojibwa language	497.3	guides to Christian life	248.484 8
	T6—973	missions	266.48
Ojibwa literature	897.3	moral theology	241.044 8
Ojibway Indians	T5—973	public worship	264.048
Ojibway language	497.3	religious education	268.848
	T6—973	theology	230.48
Ojibway literature	897.3	Old Catholics	
Ok Tedi (Papua New Guinea)	T2—954 9	biography	284.8
Okaloacoochee Slough	T2—759 46	religious group	T7—248
Okaloosa County (Fla.)	T2—759 982	Old English language	429
Okanagan Lake (B.C.)	T2—711 5		T6—29
Okanagan-Similkameen		Old English literature	829
(B.C.)	T2—711 5	Old French language	447.01
Okanogan County (Wash.)	T2—797 28		T6—41
Okapis	599.735 7	Old Frisian language	439.1
Okayama-ken (Japan)	T2—521 94		T6—391
Okeechobee, Lake (Fla.)	T2—759 39	Old Frisian literature	839.1
Okeechobee County (Fla.)	T2—759 53	Old High German language	437.01
Okefenokee Swamp (Ga. and			T6—31
Fla.)	T2—758 752	Old Icelandic language	439.6
Okfuskee County (Okla.)	T2—766 73		T6—396 1
Okhahlamba (South Africa :		Old Icelandic literature	839.6
District)	T2—684 91	Old Indic language	491.2
Okhotsk, Sea of	551.465 53		T6—912
	T2—164 53	Old Indic literature	891.2
Okinawa Island (Japan)	T2—522 94	Old Italian language	457.01
Okinawa-ken (Japan)	T2—522 9		T6—51
Oklahoma	976.6	Old Kingdom (Egyptian history)	932.012
	T2—766		

Olfaction	591.182 6
animal physiology	591.182 6
human physiology	612.86
Olfactory organs	591.182 6
animal physiology	591.182 6
human anatomy	611.86
human physiology	612.86
Olfactory perception	
psychology	152.166
Olga, Mount	T2—942 91
Olifants River (Cape of Good	
Hope, South Africa)	
Little Karoo	T2—687 16
northwest	T2—687 2
Olifants River (Transvaal,	
South Africa)	T2—682 6
Olifants River Range	T2—687 2
Oligarchy	321.5
Oligocene epoch	551.785
geology	551.785
paleontology	560.178
Oligochaeta	595.146
Oligomenorrhea	
gynecology	618.172
see also Female genital system	
Oligopoly	338.82
economics	338.82
international economics	338.884
Oligosaccharides	574.192 481 5
biochemistry	574.192 481 5
chemistry	547.781 5
see also Carbohydrates	
Oliniaceae	583.44
Olive oil	641.346 3
cooking with	641.646 3
food technology	664.362
Oliver County (N.D.)	T2—784 843
Olives	641.346 3
agriculture	634.63
botany	583.74
commercial processing	664.804 63
cooking	641.646 3
Olivetans	255.13
church history	271.13
women	255.97
church history	271.97
Olivine	
mineralogy	549.62
Olmsted County (Minn.)	T2—776 155
Olsztyn (Poland :	
Voivodeship)	T2—438 3
Olt (Romania)	T2—498 2
Oltenia (Romania)	T2—498 4
Olympia (Greece : Ancient	
sanctuary)	T2—388
Olympia (Wash.)	T2—797 79
Olympic Games	796.48
summer	796.48
winter	796.98
Olympic Mountains (Wash.)	T2—797 94
Olympic Peninsula (Wash.)	T2—797 94
Olyreae	584.93
Omagh (Northern Ireland :	
District)	T2—416 47
Omaha (Neb.)	T2—782 254
Oman	953.53
	T2—535 3
Oman, Gulf of	551.467 36
	T2—165 36
Omanis	T5—927 535 3
Ombudsmen	350.91
law	342.066 7
legislative branch	328.345 2
public administration	350.91
central governments	351.91
local governments	352.002
Omens	133.334
religion	291.32
Omentum	
human anatomy	611.38
human physiology	612.33
surgery	617.558
see also Digestive system	
Omineca Mountains (B.C.)	T2—711 85
Omineca River (B.C.)	T2—711 82
Omissions insurance	368.564
see also Insurance	
Omnipotence of God	212.7
Christianity	231.4
comparative religion	291.211
Omniscience of God	212.7
Christianity	231.4
comparative religion	291.211
Omotic languages	493.5
	T6—935
Omotic peoples	T5—935
Omsk (R.S.F.S.R. : Oblast)	T2—573
Omskaia oblast (R.S.F.S.R.)	T2—573
On-the-job training	331.259 2
	T1—071 55
economics	331.259 2
personnel management	658.312 4
public administration	350.15
central governments	351.15
local governments	352.005 15
Onagraceae	583.44
Onchocerciasis	
incidence	614.555 2
medicine	616.965 2
see also Communicable	
diseases (Human)	
Oncidiums	
floriculture	635.934 15
Oncology	616.992

Operative gynecology	618.105 9
see also Female genital system	
Operative surgery	617.91
Operator algebras	512.55
Operator errors	363.120 1
see also Transportation safety	
Operator theory	515.724
Operators (Mathematics)	515.724
Operettas	782.12
music	782.12
stage presentation	792.5
Ophicleides	788.99
see also Brass instruments	
Ophioglossales	587.33
paleobotany	561.73
Ophiurida	593.94
paleozoology	563.94
Ophiuroidea	593.94
paleozoology	563.94
Ophthalmic nursing	
medicine	610.736 77
Ophthalmologists	617.709 2
occupational group	T7—617 7
role and function	617.702 32
Ophthalmology	617.7
anesthesiology	617.967 71
geriatrics	618.977 7
nursing	610.736 77
pediatrics	618.920 977
see also Eyes	
Opiliaceae	583.26
Opilioacariformes	595.42
Opilionea	595.43
paleozoology	565.4
Opisthobranchia	594.34
Opisthocomi	598.64
Opisthogoneata	595.62
paleozoology	565.62
Opisthopora	595.146
Opium	
pharmacodynamics	615.782 2
pharmacology	615.323 122
Opium abuse	362.293
law	344.044 63
medicine	616.863 2
personal health	613.83
social welfare	362.293
see also Substance abuse	
Opium War, 1840-1842	951.033
Opole (Poland : Voivodeship)	T2—438 5
Opossum rats	599.2
Opossum shrimp	595.383
Opossums	599.2
Oppland fylke (Norway)	T2—482
Opposition parties	
organization in legislatures	328.369
Optic nerves	
human anatomy	611.84

Optic nerves (continued)	
human diseases	
incidence	614.599 7
ophthalmology	617.73
human physiology	612.843
see also Eyes	
Optical analysis	
chemistry	543.085
Optical art	709.040 72
painting	759.067 2
sculpture	735.230 472
Optical character recognition	006.424
computer engineering	621.399
Optical coincidence card systems	025.484
Optical communications	621.382 7
Optical components	
cameras	771.35
Optical computers	
engineering	621.391
Optical crystallography	548.9
Optical data processing	621.367
computer science	006.42
engineering	621.399
Optical diagnosis	
medicine	616.075 45
Optical digital disks	004.56
engineering	621.397 67
Optical disc technology	621.382 7
Optical-fiber cable	
computer science	004.64
engineering	621.398 1
Optical-fiber communication	621.382 75
Optical glass	666.156
Optical illusions	
psychology	152.148
Optical instruments	
manufacturing technology	681.4
Optical metallography	669.950 282
Optical pattern recognition	
computer science	006.42
engineering	621.399
Optical properties	
materials science	620.112 95
Optical rotation	
chemistry	541.7
Optical scanning	
computer science	006.42
engineering	621.399
Optical spectroscopes	
manufacturing technology	681.414
Optical spectroscopy	
physics	535.84
Optical storage devices	004.56
engineering	621.397 67
Optical surgery	617.71
see also Eyes	
Opticians	681.409 2
occupational group	T7—681 4

Orchestras	784.2	Oregon County (Mo.)	T2—778 875
Orchestras with solo instruments	784.23	Orel (R.S.F.S.R. : Oblast)	T2—473 5
Orchestras with toy instruments	784.46	Orenburg (R.S.F.S.R. :	
Orchestras with vocal parts	784.22	Oblast)	T2—478 7
Orchestration	781.374	Orenburgskaia oblast	
Orchidales	584.15	(R.S.F.S.R.)	T2—478 7
Orchids	584.15	Orense (Spain : Province)	T2—461 5
floriculture	635.934 15	Ores	553
Ord River (W.A. : River)	T2—941 4	Oresund (Denmark and Sweden)	551.461 34
Order			T2—163 34
philosophy	117	Organ banks	362.178 3
Order of DeMolay	366.17	*see also* Health services	
Order of DeMolay members	366.170 92	Organ cases	
social group	T7—366 1	church architecture	726.529 7
Order of the Eastern Star	366.18	Organ concertos	784.265
Order of the Eastern Star		Organ culture	574.072 4
members	366.18	experimental botany	581.072 4
social group	T7—366 1	experimental zoology	591.072 4
Order of the Rainbow	366.18	human	612.028
Order statistics	519.5	Organ donation	
Ordered solids	530.413	law	344.041 94
Ordered systems	511.33	Organ transplants	362.197 95
Ordered topological spaces	514.32	law	344.041 94
Ordering	658.72	medical ethics	174.25
library acquisitions	025.23	*see also* Medical ethics	
Orderlies (Hospital)	610.730 92	social services	362.197 95
role and function	610.730 698	surgery	617.95
see also Nurses		Organelles	574.873 4
Orders (Rewards)		Organic chemicals	
armed forces	355.134 2	chemical engineering	661.8
numismatics	737.223	Organic chemistry	547
Orders (Societies)	366	applied	661.8
genealogy	929.81	Organic compounds	547
Orders of knighthood	929.71	biochemistry	574.192 4
Ordinances (Compilations)	348.02	human	612.015 7
Ordinary differential equations	515.352	Organic drugs	
Ordinary differentiation	515.33	pharmacology	615.3
Ordinary language philosophy	149.94	Organic evolution	575
Ordinary of the mass	264.36	Organic farming	631.584
music	782.323 2	Organic fertilizers	
Ordination of women	262.14	chemical engineering	668.63
Ordnance	355.82	use	631.86
military aircraft	623.746 1	Organic gardening	635.048 4
military engineering	623.4	floriculture	635.987
military equipment	355.82	Organic geochemistry	553.2
warships	623.825 1	Organic materials	
Ordos		materials science	620.117
Roman Catholic liturgy	264.021	Organic poisons	363.179 1
Ordovician period	551.731	public safety	363.179 1
geology	551.731	toxicology	615.95
paleontology	560.172 4	*see also* Hazardous materials	
Ordu Ili (Turkey)	T2—565	Organic solids	530.413
Orduña (Spain)	T2—466 9	Organically grown foods	641.302
Ore dressing	622.7	agriculture	631.584
Ore processing	622.7	home economics	641.302
Orebro lan (Sweden)	T2—487	Organismic psychology	150.193
Oregon	979.5	Organists	786.509 2
	T2—795	occupational group	T7—786

Ornamental nails	
ironwork	739.48
Ornamental plants	635.9
Ornamental woodwork	
furniture arts	749.5
handicrafts	745.51
Ornaments	
glass	
arts	748.8
handicrafts	745.594
manufacturing technology	688.726
musical element	781.247
stone	736.5
wood	736.4
Orne (France)	T2—442 3
Ornithischia	567.97
Ornithologists	598.092
occupational group	T7—598
Ornithology	598
Ornithopters	
engineering	629.133 36
Oro, El (Ecuador)	T2—866 31
Oro Province (Papua New	
Guinea)	T2—954 2
Orobanchaceae	583.81
Orogeny	551.82
Orominga language	493.5
	T6—935
Oromo (African people)	T5—935
Oromo language	493.5
	T6—935
Orphanages	362.732
Orphans	305.906 945
	T1—086 945
social group	305.906 945
social services	362.73
Orthochromatic photography	778.62
Orthodontics	617.643
see also Dentistry	
Orthodox Eastern Church	281.9
see also Eastern Orthodox	
Church	
Orthodox Judaism	296.832
Orthogenesis	
evolutionary biology	575.016 3
Orthogonal polynomials	515.55
Orthogonal series	515.243
Orthographic projection	
technical drawing	604.245
Orthography	411
applied linguistics	418
specific languages	T4—81
education	372.632
linguistics	411
specific languages	T4—152
Orthomorphic projections	
maps	526.82
Orthomyxoviruses	576.648 4

Orthopedic appliances	617.307
manufacturing technology	681.761
Orthopedic footwear	
manufacturing technology	685.38
Orthopedic nursing	
medicine	610.736 77
Orthopedic surgery	617.3
Orthopedics	617.3
anesthesiology	617.967 37
Orthoptera	595.726
paleozoology	565.72
Orthopters	
engineering	629.133 36
Orthoptics	617.762
see also Eyes	
Orthorrhapha	595.771
Ortiz Rubio, Pascual	
Mexican history	972.082 43
Oruro (Bolivia : Dept.)	T2—841 3
Oryx	599.735 8
Oryzeae	584.93
Osage County (Kan.)	T2—781 643
Osage County (Mo.)	T2—778 58
Osage County (Okla.)	T2—766 25
Osage oranges	583.962
Osaka (Japan)	T2—521 834
Osaka (Japan : Prefecture)	T2—521 83
Osborne County (Kan.)	T2—781 215
Oscan language	479.9
	T6—799
Oscans	T5—79
Osceola County (Fla.)	T2—759 25
Osceola County (Iowa)	T2—777 116
Osceola County (Mich.)	T2—774 69
Oscillations	
solid state physics	530.416
solids	531.32
Oscillators	
electronic circuits	621.381 533
radio engineering	621.384 12
Oscillographs	621.374 7
Oscilloscopes	621.381 548 3
Oscines	598.8
Osco-Umbrian languages	479.9
	T6—799
Osco-Umbrian literatures	879.9
Osco-Umbrians	T5—79
Oscoda County (Mich.)	T2—774 78
Osee (Biblical book)	224.6
Oshkosh (Wis.)	T2—775 64
Osier	
fiber crop	633.58
Osilinka River (B.C.)	T2—711 85
Oslo fylke (Norway)	T2—482 3
Osmanli language	494.35
	T6—943 5

Ottoman Empire (continued)
  Arabian history   953.03
  Egyptian history   962.03
  Iraqi history   956.703
  Jordanian history   956.950 3
  Lebanese history   956.920 34
  Libyan history   961.202
  North African history   961.023
  Palestinian history   956.940 3
  Syrian history   956.910 3
  Tunisian history   961.103
  Turkish history   956.101 5
Ottoman Turkish language   494.35
                  T6—943 5
Ouachita County (Ark.)   T2—767 66
Ouachita Mountains (Okla.
  and Ark.)   T2—766 6
  Arkansas   T2—767 4
  Oklahoma   T2—766 6
Ouachita Parish (La.)   T2—763 87
Ouachita River (Ark. and La.) T2—763 7
Ouagadougou (Burkina Faso) T2—662 5
Ouahran (Algeria : Dept.)   T2—651
Ouargla (Algeria : Dept.)   T2—657
Ouarzazate (Morocco :
  Province)   T2—646
Ouds   787.82
  see also Stringed instruments
Oudtshoorn (South Africa :
  District)   T2—687 16
Ouest (Haiti : Dept.)   T2—729 45
Ouija board messages   133.93
Oujda (Morocco : Province) T2—643
Oulu (Finland)   T2—489 76
Oum el Bouaghi (Algeria :
  Dept.)   T2—655
Ouray County (Colo.)   T2—788 22
Ouse River   T2—428 4
Out-of-body experience   133.9
Outagamie County (Wis.)   T2—775 39
Outaouais (Quebec :
  Administrative region)   T2—714 22
Outaouais Region (Quebec) T2—714 22
Outaouais Regional
  Community (Quebec)   T2—714 221
Outboard motorboats   387.231 3
  design   623.812 313
  engineering   623.823 13
  transportation services   387.231 3
  see also Ships
Outboard motors   623.872 34
Outbreeding
  animal husbandry   636.082 42
  genetics   575.132
Outcrops
  geology   551.85
Outdoor advertising   659.134 2
Outdoor cooking   641.578

Outdoor education   371.38
Outdoor furniture   645.8
  cleaning   648.5
  customs   392.36
  decorative arts   749.8
  household management   645.8
  manufacturing technology 684.18
Outdoor games   796
Outdoor life   796.5
  equipment technology   688.765
Outdoor markets   381.18
  management   658.87
  see also Commerce
Outdoor music   781.532
Outdoor photography   778.71
Outdoor recreation centers 790.068
Outdoor sports   796
  equipment technology   688.76
Outeniqua Range   T2—687 4
Outer Banks (N.C.)   T2—756 1
Outer ear
  human physiology   612.851
  see also External ear
Outer garments
  commercial technology
    leather and fur   685.2
Outer Hebrides (Scotland) T2—411 4
Outer House of Court of Session
  (Scotland)   347.411 024
Outer Mongolia   951.73
                  T2—517 3
Outer space   T2—19
  astronomy   523.111
  international law   341.47
Outfield play
  baseball   796.357 25
Outgroups   302.4
Outlaw strikes   331.892 4
  see also Strikes (Work
    stoppages)
Outlet stores   381.15
  retail   381.15
    management   658.870 5
  wholesale   381.2
    management   658.86
  see also Commerce
Outlets
  electrical engineering   621.319 24
Outlines   T1—020 2
Outpatient departments   362.12
  see also Health services
Outpatient surgery   617.024
Output peripherals   004.77
  computer engineering   621.398 7
Ouyen (Vic.)   T2—945 9
Ovaries
  gynecology   618.11
  human anatomy   611.65

Oyo (Kingdom)	966.925 01
	T2—669 25
Oyo State (Nigeria)	T2—669 25
Oyster catchers	598.33
Oyster shucking	
sport	799.254 11
Oysters	594.11
cooking	641.694
fisheries	639.41
food	641.394
commercial processing	664.94
Ozark County (Mo.)	T2—778 835
Ozark Mountains	T2—767 1
Arkansas	T2—767 1
Missouri	T2—778 8
Oklahoma	T2—766 8
Ozark Plateau	T2—767 1
Arkansas	T2—767 1
Missouri	T2—778 8
Oklahoma	T2—766 8
Ozarks	T2—767 1
Arkansas	T2—767 1
Oklahoma	T2—766 8
Ozarks, Lake of the (Mo.)	T2—778 493
Ozaukee County (Wis.)	T2—775 92
Ozobrome process	773.1
Ozokerite	553.27
economic geology	553.27
processing	665.4
Ozone	
gas technology	665.89
Ozone treatment	
water-supply engineering	628.166 2
Ozotype process	773.1

P

P.A.C.s (Action committees)	324.4
P-adic numbers	512.74
P.C.B. (Chemical)	
toxicology	615.951 2
P.C.P. abuse	362.294
medicine	616.863 4
personal health	613.83
social welfare	362.294
see also Substance abuse	
P.E.R.T. (Network analysis)	658.403 2
P.E.T. (Tomography)	616.075 75
P.E.T.N. (Explosives)	662.27
p.H.	541.372 8
chemical engineering	660.297 28
P.I. (Macroeconomics)	339.32
distribution	339.22
P.K. le Roux Dam (South Africa)	T2—687 13
P.M.S. (Syndrome)	
gynecology	618.172
see also Female genital system	

P.R.E.C.I.S. indexing	025.482
P.S.A.T. (Aptitude test)	378.166 2
P.T. boats	359.835 8
design	623.812 58
engineering	623.825 8
naval equipment	359.835 8
naval units	359.325 8
P.W.V. area (South Africa)	T2—682 2
Paarl (South Africa : District)	T2—687 3
Pabok (Quebec)	T2—714 79
Pacas	599.323 4
Pacemakers (Electronic cardiac)	
medicine	617.412 064 5
see also Cardiovascular system	
Pacific, War of the, 1879-1883	983.061
Pacific Area	T2—182 3
Pacific Coast (B.C.)	T2—711 1
Pacific Coast (North America)	979
	T2—79
Pacific County (Wash.)	T2—797 92
Pacific international	
organizations	341.246
Pacific Islands (Trust Territory)	996.5
	T2—965
Pacific Northwest	T2—795
Pacific Ocean	551.465
	T2—164
Pacific Ocean islands	990
	T2—9
Pacific Region	T2—182 3
Pacific Rim National Park (B.C.)	T2—711 2
Pacific settlement of international disputes	341.52
Pacifism	303.66
ethics	172.42
religion	291.562 42
Buddhism	294.356 242
Christianity	241.624 2
Hinduism	294.548 624 2
Islam	297.5
Judaism	296.385 624 2
social theology	291.178 73
Buddhism	294.337 873
Christianity	261.873
Hinduism	294.517 873
Islam	297.197 873
Judaism	296.387 873
Pacifists	303.660 92
international cooperation	327.170 92
Mexican War	973.621
South African War	968.048 1
Spanish-American War, 1898	973.891
Vietnamese War	959.704 31
War of 1812	973.521
World War I	940.316 2
World War II	940.531 62

Packaging	688.8
electronics	621.381 046
engineering	688.8
law	343.075
production management	658.564
sales promotion	658.823
Packers (Agricultural tools)	
manufacturing technology	681.763 1
Packet switching (Data	
transmission)	004.66
engineering	621.398 1
Packing clothes	
home economics	646.6
Packing crops	631.56
Packing for shipment	
materials management	658.788 4
PACs (Action committees)	324.4
Padded toys	
making	688.724
handicrafts	745.592 4
technology	688.724
see also Toys	
Paddle tennis	796.34
Paddlefish	597.44
Paddy rice	584.93
food crop	633.18
Padova (Italy : Province)	T2—453 2
Padre Island (Tex.)	T2—764 47
Padua (Italy : Province)	T2—453 2
Paelignian language	479.7
	T6—797
Paenungulata	599.6
paleozoology	569.6
Paeoniaceae	583.111
Paez Indians	T5—982
Paez language	498.2
	T6—982
Paezan languages	498.2
	T6—982
Pagalu (Equatorial Guinea)	T2—671 86
Paganism	292
Christian polemics	239.3
Islamic polemics	297.291
Page County (Iowa)	T2—777 78
Page County (Va.)	T2—755 94
Page design	
typesetting	686.225 2
Pageantry	
performing arts	791.6
Pageants	
customs	394.5
performing arts	791.62
Paging systems	
engineering	621.389 2
Pahang	T2—595 1
Pahari	T5—914 96
Pahari languages	491.49
	T6—914 9
Pahari literatures	891.49
Pahlavi language	491.53
	T6—915 3
Pahlavi literature	891.53
Pai language	497.5
	T6—975
Paici language	499.5
	T6—995
Paid assistance	
social welfare	361.04
Paid vacations	331.257 6
labor economics	331.257 6
personnel management	658.312 2
Pails	
manufacturing technology	683.82
Pain	
human physiology	612.88
symptomatology	616.047 2
neurological diseases	616.849
see also Nervous system	
Pain perception	
psychology	152.182 4
Paint	667.6
architectural decoration	729.4
household management	645.2
Paint removers	667.6
Paint thinners	667.624
Painted Desert	T2—791 33
Painted glass	
arts	748.5
Painters (Arts)	759
occupational group	T7—75
Painters (Building trades)	698.109 2
occupational group	T7—698
Painting	667.9
arts	750
buildings	698.1
woodwork	698.35
decorative arts	745.723
elementary education	372.52
interior decoration	747.3
literature	808.803 57
history and criticism	809.933 57
specific literatures	T3B—080 357
history and criticism	T3B—093 57
technology	667.9
textile arts	746.6
use in child care	649.51
Painting metals	
decorative arts	739.15
Painting pottery	666.45
arts	738.15
technology	666.45
Paintings	750
Paipai language	497.5
	T6—975
Pair skating	796.912
País Vasco (Spain)	T2—466

Paiwan (Taiwan people)	T5—992 5
Pakenham (Vic.)	T2—945 2
Pakenham Shire (Vic.)	T2—945 2
Pakistan	954.91
	T2—549 1
Pakistan (1947-1971)	954.9
	T2—549
Pakistanis	T5—914 122
Palaces	
official residences	
architecture	725.17
residential	
architecture	728.82
Palaeacanthocephala	595.13
Palaeanodonta	569.31
Palaeognathae	598.5
paleozoology	568.5
Palaeonisciformes	567.4
Palaic language	491.998
	T6—919 98
Palate	
human anatomy	611.315
human physiology	612.31
speech	612.78
surgery	617.522 5
see also Digestive system	
Palatinate (Germany)	T2—434 35
Palau	996.6
	T2—966
Palaung language	495.93
	T6—959 3
Palawan (Philippines)	T2—599 4
Palawan Island	T2—599 4
Palencia (Spain : Province)	T2—462 2
Paleo-Asiatics	T5—946
Paleobotanists	561.092
Paleobotany	561
Paleocene epoch	551.783
geology	551.783
paleontology	560.178
Paleoclimatology	551.69
Paleoecology	560.45
botanical	561.1
zoological	560.45
Paleogene period	551.782
geology	551.782
paleontology	560.178
Paleogeography	551.7
Paleography	411.7
specific languages	T4—11
Paleolithic Age	930.12
arts	709.011 2
painting	759.011 2
sculpture	732.22
Paleomagnetism	538.72
Paleontologists	560.9
occupational group	T7—56
Paleontology	560

Paleontology and religion	291.175
Christianity	261.55
natural theology	215.6
Paleopalynology	561.13
Paleosiberian languages	494.6
	T6—946
Paleosiberian literatures	894.6
Paleosiberian peoples	T5—946
Paleovolcanism	551.21
Paleozoic era	551.72
geology	551.72
paleontology	560.172
Paleozoology	560
Palermo (Sicily : Province)	T2—458 23
Palestine	956.94
	T2—569 4
ancient	933
	T2—33
Palestine Liberation Organization	322.420 956 94
Palestinian Arabs	T5—927 4
Palestinian architecture	
ancient	722.33
Palestinian sculpture	732.3
Palestinian Talmud	296.124
Palestinians	T5—927 4
Pali language	491.37
	T6—913 7
Pali literature	891.37
Palladium	669.7
chemical engineering	661.063 6
chemistry	546.636
metallography	669.957
metallurgy	669.7
metalworking	673.7
physical metallurgy	669.967
see also Chemicals	
Pallets	
wooden	674.82
Palm Beach County (Fla.)	T2—759 32
Palm reading	133.6
Palm Sunday	263.92
devotional literature	242.35
music	781.726
sermons	252.62
Palm Valley National Park	T2—942 91
Palma (Majorca)	T2—467 542
Palma de Mallorca (Majorca)	T2—467 542
Palmales	584.5
paleobotany	561.45
Palmer Peninsula	T2—989
Palmetto	584.5
Palmistry	133.6
Palmists	133.609 2
occupational group	T7—13
Palms	584.5
forestry	634.974 5
ornamental arboriculture	635.977 45
paleobotany	561.45

Panpipes 788.37
see also Woodwind instruments
Pans
  cooking 641.502 8
  manufacturing technology 683.82
Pansies 583.135
  floriculture 635.933 135
Pantelleria Island (Italy) T2—458 24
Pantheism 211.2
  comparative religion 291.14
  philosophy 147
Pantodonta 569.6
Pantomime 792.3
Pantotheria 569.18
Pants 391
  commercial technology 687.113
  customs 391
  home sewing 646.433
  see also Clothing
Papa Doc
  Haitian history 972.940 72
Papacy 262.13
Papago language 497.45
  T6—974 5
Papal administration 262.136
Papal bulls and decrees 262.91
Papal infallibility 262.131
Papal schism
  church history 270.5
Papal States T2—456
Papal systems (Ecclesiology) 262.3
Papaveraceae 583.122
Papaw 641.344 1
  botany 583.115
  cooking 641.644 1
  orchard crop 634.41
Papaya 641.346 51
  agriculture 634.651
  botany 583.46
  commercial processing 664.804 651
  cooking 641.646 51
Paper 676
  handicrafts 745.54
  manufacturing technology 676
  materials science 620.197
  photographic materials 771.532 3
  sculpture material 731.2
  textiles
    arts 746.045 7
Paper airplanes 745.592
Paper bags 676.33
Paper boxes 676.32
  handicrafts 745.54
Paper chromatography 543.089 52
Paper covers
  bookbinding 686.344
Paper cups 676.34
Paper cutting 736.98

Paper dolls 769.53
Paper folding 736.98
Paper industry workers 676.092
  occupational group T7—676
Paper money
  arts 769.55
  economics 332.404 4
  printing 686.288
Paper plates 676.34
Paper production 676.2
Paper recycling 676.142
Paper standard
  foreign exchange 332.454
Paper-tape devices 004.56
  engineering 621.397 6
Paper work
  child care 649.51
  elementary education 372.55
Paperbacks
  bibliographies 011.32
  publishing 070.573
  reviews 028.132
Paperboard 676.288
  materials science 620.197
  structural engineering 624.189 7
Paperboard boxes 676.32
  handicrafts 745.54
Paperhangers 698.609 2
  occupational group T7—698
Paperhanging 698.6
  interior decoration 747.3
Papermaking 676
  equipment manufacturing
    technology 681.767 6
Paperweights
  glass
    decorative arts 748.84
Paphlagonia T2—393 1
Papiamento dialect 467.972 986
  T6—68
Papiamento literature 860
Papier-mâché
  handicrafts 745.542
  sculpture material 731.2
Papilionaceae 583.322
Papilionoidea 595.789
Papillon (Dog)
  animal husbandry 636.76
  see also Dogs
Papineau (Quebec : County) T2—714 227
Papineau (Quebec : Regional
  County Municipality) T2—714 227
Papovaviruses 576.648 4
Pappophoreae 584.93
Paprika
  botany 583.79
  cooking with 641.638 4
  see also Hot spices

Papua	995.4	Paraíso, El (Honduras : Dept.)	T2—728 34
	T2—954	Parakeets	598.71
Papua (Territory)	995.402 2	animal husbandry	636.686 5
	T2—954	Parakeets (Lovebirds)	598.71
Papua, Gulf of	551.465 76	animal husbandry	636.686 4
	T2—164 76	Paralipomena (Biblical books)	222.6
Papua and New Guinea		Parallax corrections	522.9
(Territory)	995.304	Parallel bars	796.44
	T2—953	Parallel processing	004.35
Papua New Guinea	995.3	Parallel processors	004.35
	T2—953	engineering	621.391
Papuan languages	499.12	Paralympics	796.019 6
	T6—991 2	Paralysis	
Papuan literatures	899.12	symptomatology	
Papuans	T5—991 2	neurological diseases	616.842
Papular eruptions		*see also* Nervous system	
medicine	616.51	Paralysis agitans	
see also Skin		medicine	616.833
Papyrus	584.84	*see also* Nervous system	
Pará (Brazil : State)	T2—811 6	Paramagnetic resonance	538.364
Para (Surinam)	T2—883 4	Paramagnetic substances	538.43
Parables in the Gospels	226.8	Paramagnetism	538.43
Parabola	516.15	Paramaribo (Surinam :	
Parabolic equations	515.353	District)	T2—883 5
Parabolic functions	515.9	Parametric statistical methods	519.5
Paracanthopterygii	597.53	Paramyxoviruses	576.648 4
paleozoology	567.5	Paraná (Brazil : State)	T2—816 2
Parachute troops	356.166	Paraná River	T2—822
Parachutes	629.134 386	Argentina	T2—822
Parachuting		Brazil	T2—816
sports	797.56	Paranoia	
Parades		medicine	616.897
circuses	791.38	*see also* Mental illness	
customs	394.5	Paranormal arts	130
performing arts	791.6	Paranormal phenomena	130
Paradisaeidae	598.865	Paraphotic phenomena	535
Paradise	291.23	engineering	621.36
Christianity	236.24	physics	535
Paradoxes		Paraphotic spectroscopes	
logic	165	manufacturing technology	681.414
Paraffin (Kerosene)	665.538 3	Paraphotic spectroscopy	543.085 8
Paraffin (Wax)		chemical analysis	543.085 8
natural	665.4	physics	535.84
petroleum product	665.538 5	Paraphrase	
Paraffins (Compounds)	547.411	musical element	781.377
chemical engineering	661.814	musical forms	781.826
Paragraphs		instrumental	784.182 6
rhetoric	808	Paraplegia	
Paraguarí (Paraguay)	T2—892 123	medicine	616.837
Paraguay	989.2	*see also* Nervous system	
	T2—892	Parapsychologists	133.092
Paraguay River	T2—892	occupational group	T7—13
Paraguay tea	641.337 7	Parapsychology	133
see also Maté		Parapsychology and religion	291.175
Paraguayan literature	860	Christianity	261.51
Paraguayan War, 1865-1870	989.205	Pararthropoda	595.5
Paraguayans	T5—688 92	paleozoology	565.5
Paraíba (Brazil : State)	T2—813 3		

475

Parasitic diseases	574.23	Parent abuse	362.829 2
incidence	614.55	see also Family violence	
medicine	616.96	Parent and child	306.874
see also Communicable		law	346.017
diseases (Human)		sociology	306.874
Parasitic plants	581.524 9	Parent-teacher associations	370.193 12
agricultural pests	632.52	Parent-teacher relations	371.103
Parasitic skin diseases		Parental kidnapping	362.829 7
medicine	616.57	law	344.032 829 7
see also Skin		social welfare	362.829 7
Parasitiformes	595.42	see also Families—social	
Parasitism		welfare	
animals	591.524 9	Parental rights	346.017
ecology	574.524 9	Parenteral medication	
medicine	616.96	administering	615.6
see also Communicable		Parenteral therapy	
diseases (Human)		medicine	615.855
plants	581.524 9	Parenthood	
agriculture	632.52	child rearing	649.1
veterinary medicine	636.089 696	customs	392.3
Parasitology		Parenting	649.1
medicine	616.96	home economics	649.1
see also Communicable		sociology	306.874
diseases (Human)		Parents	306.874
Parasols			T1—085
customs	391.44		T7—043 1
Parasympathetic nervous system		family relationships	306.874
human diseases		guides to Christian life	248.845
medicine	616.88	psychology	155.646
human physiology	612.89	Pareto, Vilfredo	
see also Nervous system		economic school	330.154 3
Parathyroid extracts		Pari-mutuel betting	798.401
pharmacology	615.362	Paria, Gulf of	551.464 66
see also Endocrine system			T2—163 66
Parathyroid glands		Parianeae	584.93
human anatomy	611.44	Paridae	598.824
human diseases		Paris (France)	T2—443 61
medicine	616.445	Paris Commune, 1871	944.081 2
human physiology	612.44	Paris metropolitan area	
surgery	617.539	(France)	T2—443 6
see also Endocrine system		Parish houses	
Paratroops	356.166	architecture	726.4
Paratyphoid fever		Parish libraries	027.67
incidence	614.511 4	Parish missions	266.022
medicine	616.927 4	Parish welfare work	361.75
see also Communicable		Parishes	250
diseases (Human)		Christian ecclesiology	262.22
Parazoa	593.4	government and administration	254
paleozoology	563.4	Park buildings	
Parcels		architecture	725.7
postal handling	383.125	Park County (Colo.)	T2—788 59
see also Postal service		Park County (Mont.)	T2—786 661
Parchment papers	676.284 5	Park County (Wyo.)	T2—787 42
Parchments (Skins)		Park police	363.28
manufacturing technology	685	Park Range (Colo. and Wyo.)	T2—788 66
Pardon	364.65	Parke County (Ind.)	T2—772 465
law	345.077	Parker County (Tex.)	T2—764 553
penology	364.65	Parkersburg (W. Va.)	T2—754 22

Partial differential operators	515.724 2
Partial differentiation	515.33
Partially ordered sets	511.322
Participatory democracy	323.042
Participatory management	331.011 2
personnel management	658.315 2
see also Employee participation	
in management	
Particle acceleration	539.73
Particle beams	539.73
Particle board	674.836
Particle characteristics (Nuclear	
physics)	539.725
Particle colliders	539.73
Particle mechanics	
classical physics	531.16
Particle physics	539.72
Particle radiation	539.72
biophysics	574.191 56
human	612.014 486
ionization	539.722
Particles (Matter)	
classical mechanics	531.16
technology	620.43
Particles (Nuclear physics)	539.72
Particulates	
meteorology	551.511 3
Parties	
cooking	641.568
indoor amusements	793.2
interior decoration	747.93
Partita form	784.185 4
Partition (Territory)	
law	341.29
Partition chromatographic	
analysis	543.089 2
Partitions (Building element)	721.2
architecture	721.2
construction	690.12
see also Walls (Building	
element)	
Partitions (Mathematics)	
algebra	512.2
number theory	512.73
Partnership associations	
management	658.044
Partnerships	338.73
accounting	657.92
economics	338.73
law	346.068 2
management	658.042
initiation	658.114 2
tax law	343.066 2
Partridgeberry	583.52
Partridges	598.617
Parts of Holland (England)	T2—425 39
Parts of Kesteven (England)	T2—425 35
Parts of Lindsey (England)	T2—425 31
Parts of speech (Grammar)	415
specific languages	T4—5
Parturition	
disorders	
obstetrics	618.5
human physiology	612.63
obstetrics	618.4
Party costumes	
home sewing	646.478
see also Clothing	
Party finance	324.21
political science	324.21
Party leadership	
political science	324.22
Party organization	324.21
legislative bodies	328.369
sociology	306.26
Parulidae	598.872
Parys (South Africa : District)	T2—685 2
Pas, The (Man.)	T2—712 72
Pas-de-Calais (France)	T2—442 7
Pasadena (Calif.)	T2—794 93
Pasargadae (Ancient city)	T2—35
Pascagoula River	T2—762 12
Pasco (Peru : Dept.)	T2—852 3
Pasco County (Fla.)	T2—759 69
Pashto language	491.593
	T6—915 93
Pashto literature	891.593
Pashtoon	T5—915 93
Pashtun	T5—915 93
Pasquotank County (N.C.)	T2—756 142
Passacaglia form	781.827
instrumental	784.182 7
Passaic County (N.J.)	T2—749 23
Passaic River (N.J.)	T2—749 3
Passau (Germany)	T2—433 55
Passementerie	677.76
arts	746.27
Passenger automobiles	388.342
driving	629.283
engineering	629.222
military engineering	623.747 2
repair	629.287 2
transportation services	388.342
see also Automobiles	
Passenger services	388.042
air	387.742
airport services	387.736 4
international law	341.756 78
law	343.097 8
automobile	388.321
urban	388.413 21
bus	388.322 2
international law	341.756 882
law	343.094 82
terminal services	388.33

Pastries (continued)
home preparation 641.865
Pastry mixes 664.753
Pasture grasses 584.93
forage crop 633.202
Pasture lands 333.74
economics 333.74
sale and rental 333.335
forestry 634.99
Pasturing animals 636.084
Patagonia (Argentina and
Chile) T2—827
Patanjali's philosophy 181.452
Patchwork
arts 746.46
Patellas
human anatomy 611.718
see also Musculoskeletal system
Patent law 346.048 6
Patent leather 675.25
Patent medicines
therapeutics 615.886
Patents 346.048 6
international law 341.758 6
law 346.048 6
public administration 351.824
Patents (Collections) 608
T1—027 2
Paternity 346.017 5
Paternity leave 331.257 63
personnel management 658.312 2
Paternosters (England) T2—423 49
Paterson (N.J.) T2—749 23
Pâtés 641.812
Pathfinder Reservoir T2—787 86
Pathogenic microorganisms 576.165
medical microbiology 616.01
Pathogenicity 574.2
plants 581.2
Pathological anatomy
animals 591.22
human 616.07
Pathological physiology
animals 591.21
human 616.07
Pathological psychology 616.89
see also Mental illness
Pathology 574.2
animals 591.2
cytology 574.876 5
human 611.018 15
human 616.07
plants 581.2
surgery 617.07
Pathophysiology
human 616.07
Patience 179.9
see also Virtues

Patience (Game) 795.43
Patient compliance
medicine 615.5
Patients' libraries 027.662
Patinating
decorative arts 739.15
Patio furniture 645.8
see also Outdoor furniture
Patio gardening 635.967 1
Patio lighting 621.322 9
Patios 721.84
architecture 721.84
construction 690.184
domestic 643.55
architecture 728.9
construction 690.89
home economics 643.55
Patmos Island (Greece) T2—499 6
Patois 417.2
specific languages T4—7
Patriarchal family 306.858
Patriarchal state (Government) 321.12
Patriarchs 270.092
ecclesiology 262.13
specific denominations 280
Patricia Portion (Ont.) T2—713 1
Patrick County (Va.) T2—755 695
Patrilineal kinship 306.83
Patriotic holidays and events 394.268 4
customs 394.268 4
law 344.091
Patriotic music 781.599
Patriotic pageants
performing arts 791.624
Patriotic societies 369.2
Patriotic society members 369.209 2
social group T7—369 2
Patristic philosophy 189.2
Patristics (Christianity) 270
Patrol
military operation 355.413
police services 363.232
Patrol boats (Military) 359.835 8
design 623.812 58
engineering 623.825 8
naval equipment 359.835 8
naval units 359.325 8
Patrol boats (Police) 363.286
design 623.812 63
engineering 623.826 3
police services 363.286
Patron and client 306.2
Patronage 306.2
Patronage of individuals T1—079
Pattern lumber 674.43
Pattern perception
visual
psychology 152.142 3

Peace treaties	
law	341.66
Peaceful occupation	
international law	341.722
Peaceful settlement of disputes	303.69
international law	341.52
international relations	327.17
sociology	303.69
Peacekeeping forces	
international law	341.584
Peach County (Ga.)	T2—758 556
Peaches	641.342 5
botany	583.372
commercial processing	664.804 25
cooking	641.642 5
orchard crop	634.25
Peafowl	598.617
animal husbandry	636.595
Peak District (England)	T2—425 11
Peanut flour	664.726
Peanut meal	664.726
Peanut oil	
food technology	664.369
Peanuts	641.356 596
agricultural economics	338.175 659 6
botany	583.322
commercial processing	
economics	338.476 648 056 596
technology	664.805 659 6
cooking	641.656 596
field crop	633.368
garden crop	635.659 6
Pearl oysters	
culture	639.412
Pearl River (Miss. and La.)	T2—762 5
Pearl River County (Miss.)	T2—762 15
Pears	641.341 3
botany	583.372
commercial processing	664.804 13
cooking	641.641 3
orchard crop	634.13
Pearson, Lester B.	
Canadian history	971.064 3
Pearston (South Africa :	
District)	T2—687 14
Peas	641.356 5
agriculture	635.65
botany	583.322
commercial processing	664.805 65
cooking	641.656 5
field crop	633.3
garden crop	635.65
Peas (Pisum sativum)	641.356 56
commercial processing	664.805 656
cooking	641.656 56
garden crop	635.656
Peasants	305.563 3
	T1—086 24
Peasants' War, 1524-1525	943.031
Peat	553.21
economic geology	553.21
mining	622.331
properties	662.622 1
use as soil conditioner	631.826
Peat moss	588.1
Pecan	641.345 2
agriculture	634.52
botany	583.973
cooking	641.645 2
Peccaries	599.734
Pecopteris	561.597
Pecos County (Tex.)	T2—764 923
Pecos River (N.M. and Tex.)	T2—764 9
New Mexico	T2—789 4
Texas	T2—764 9
Pectins	574.192 482
biochemistry	574.192 482
chemistry	547.782
food technology	664.25
see also Carbohydrates	
Pectolite	
mineralogy	549.66
Pedaliaceae	583.54
Pedaling	
music	784.193 8
Pedalium	583.54
Peddie (South Africa :	
District)	T2—687 92
Pedernales (Dominican	
Republic : Province)	T2—729 323
Pedestals	721.3
architecture	721.3
construction	690.13
Pedestrian facilities	
area planning	711.74
landscape architecture	717
Pedestrian malls	388.411
area planning	711.74
landscape architecture	717
Pedestrian paths	388.12
area planning	711.74
law	343.098 1
use	388.12
local	388.411
Pedestrian traffic	388.41
law	343.098 1
Pedi (African people)	T5—963 977 1
Pedi language	496.397 71
	T6—963 977 1
Pediatric cardiology	618.921 2
see also Cardiovascular system	
Pediatric disorders	
incidence	614.599 2
medicine	618.92
Pediatric gynecology	618.920 98
see also Female genital system	

Penetration	
materials science	620.112 6
Penguin (Tas.)	T2—946 5
Penguins	598.441
Penicillin	
pharmacology	615.329 23
Penicillium	589.23
Peninsular Malaysia	T2—595 1
Peninsular War, 1807-1814	940.27
Penis	
human anatomy	611.64
human diseases	
medicine	616.66
human physiology	612.61
see also Male genital system	
Penitence	
private prayer	
Christianity	242.725
Penitentiaries	365.34
see also Correctional	
institutions	
Penmanship	652.1
education	372.634
Pennales	589.481
Pennines	T2—428
Pennington County (Minn.)	T2—776 965
Pennington County (S.D.)	T2—783 93
Pennsylvania	974.8
	T2—748
Pennsylvania Dutch	T5—310 748
Pennsylvania Dutch dialect	437.974 8
	T6—38
Pennsylvania German dialect	437.974 8
	T6—38
Pennsylvania Germans	T5—310 748
Pennsylvanian period	551.752
geology	551.752
paleontology	560.172 8
Penny stocks	332.632 23
speculation	332.632 28
Penny whistles	788.35
see also Woodwind instruments	
Pennyroyal	T2—769 6
Penobscot County (Me.)	T2—741 3
Penobscot River (Me.)	T2—741 3
Penology	364.6
public administration	350.849
central governments	351.849
local governments	352.944 9
Penrith (N.S.W.)	T2—944 1
Pens (Writing)	
manufacturing technology	681.6
Pensacola (Fla.)	T2—759 99
Pension funds	
investments by	332.671 54
domestic	332.672 54
Pension reform	331.252 2
see also Pensions	
Pension trusts	
labor law	344.012 52
tax law	343.064
Pensions	331.252
accounting	657.75
economics	331.252
law	344.012 52
personnel management	658.325 3
executives	658.407 253
public administration	351.835
Penstocks	
dam engineering	627.882
Pentadiplandraceae	583.271
Pentaerythrite tetranitrate	662.27
Pentane	665.773
Pentaphylacaceae	583.166
Pentastomida	593.992
paleozoology	563.992
Pentateuch	222.1
Pentatonicism	781.265
Pentecost	263.9
Jewish	296.438
customs	394.268 296 438
music	781.729 3
sermons	252.6
Pentecostal churches	289.94
see also Christian	
denominations	
Pentecostalism	270.82
spiritual renewal	269.4
Pentecostals	
biography	289.940 92
religious group	T7—289
Penthouse gardens	
landscape architecture	712.6
Penticton (B.C.)	T2—711 5
Pentland Hills	T2—413 5
Penutian languages	497.41
	T6—974 1
South America	498
	T6—98
Penutian peoples	T5—974
Penwith (England)	T2—423 75
Penza (R.S.F.S.R. : Oblast)	T2—478 3
Penzenskaia oblast	
(R.S.F.S.R.)	T2—478 3
Peonies	583.111
floriculture	635.933 111
Peons	305.56
	T1—086 25
see also Poor people	
People movers	
engineering	621.868
People's Democratic Republic	
of Korea	T2—519 3
People's Party of America	324.273 27
Peoria County (Ill.)	T2—773 52
Peperomia	583.925

PETN (Explosives)	662.27
Petorca (Chile : Province)	T2—832 48
Petra (Ancient city)	939.48
	T2—394 8
Petrels	598.42
Petrified Forest National Park	
(Ariz.)	T2—791 37
Petrified wood	561.21
Petrochemicals	
chemical engineering	661.804
toxicology	615.951
Petrogenesis	552.03
Petrography	552
Petrolatum	665.538 5
Petroleum	553.28
chemistry	547.83
economic geology	553.28
extraction	622.338
equipment manufacturing	
technology	681.766 5
law	343.077 2
public administration	351.823 88
cabinet departments	351.082 388
extractive economics	338.272 8
processing	665.5
economics	338.476 655
enterprises	338.766 55
prospecting	622.182 8
public administration	351.823 88
cabinet departments	351.082 388
radiesthesia	133.323 7
resource economics	333.823
public administration	351.823 27
see also Natural gas, Oil	
(Petroleum)	
Petroleum coke	665.538 8
Petroleum County (Mont.)	T2—786 28
Petroleum derived chemicals	
chemical engineering	661.804
Petroleum engineers	665.509 2
occupational group	T7—665
Petroleum gas	665.773
Petroleum geology	553.28
Petroleum industry	338.272 8
law	343.077 2
Petroleum resources	
law	346.046 823 2
Petrologists	552.009 2
occupational group	T7—552
Petrology	552
Petrosaviaceae	584.721
Petrusburg (South Africa :	
District)	T2—685 7
Pets	636.088 7
care and training	636.088 7
Pettis County (Mo.)	T2—778 48
Petty officers	359.009 2
role and function	359.338
Petunias	583.79
Pews	247.1
architecture	726.529 3
Pewter	
decorative arts	739.533
Peyote	583.47
Pezizales	589.23
pH	541.372 8
chemical engineering	660.297 28
Phaeophyta	589.45
Phaëthontes	598.43
Phages	576.648 2
Phagocytes	
human immunology	616.079
Phalaborwa (South Africa :	
District)	T2—682 6
Phalangers	599.2
Phalanges	
human anatomy	611.718
see also Musculoskeletal system	
Phalangida	595.43
paleozoology	565.4
Phalansterianism (Socialist	
school)	
economics	335.23
Phalanxes (Military units)	355.31
Phalarideae	584.93
Phalaropes	598.33
Phallales	589.221
Phanarists (Romanian history)	949.801 5
Phanerozoic eon	551.7
geology	551.7
paleontology	560.17
Phanerozonida	593.93
paleozoology	563.93
Phantasms	133.14
Phareae	584.93
Pharisees	296.812
Pharmaceutical chemistry	615.19
Pharmaceutical services	
social welfare	362.178 2
see also Health services	
Pharmacists	615.109 2
law	344.041 6
occupational group	T7—615
Pharmacodynamics	615.7
Pharmacognosy	615.321
Pharmacokinetics	615.7
Pharmacologists	615.109 2
occupational group	T7—615
Pharmacology	615.1
veterinary medicine	636.089 51
Pharmacopoeias	
pharmacology	615.11
Pharmacy	615.1
law	344.041 6

Philologists	409.2
linguistics	410.92
occupational group	T7—4
Philology	400
linguistics	410
Philosophers	
ancient	180
medieval western	189
modern	190
occupational group	T7—11
oriental	181
Philosopher's stone	540.112
folklore	398.26
sociology	398.465
Philosophical anthropology	128
Philosophy	100
	T1—01
literature	808.803 84
history and criticism	809.933 84
specific literatures	T3B—080 384
history and criticism	T3B—093 84
Philosophy and religion	291.175
Christianity	261.51
Philosophy of nature	113
Philosophy of science	501
Phlebitis	
medicine	616.142
see also Cardiovascular system	
Phlebotomy	
therapeutics	615.899
Phloem	
plant anatomy	581.41
Phlogiston theory	540.118
Phlorina (Greece : Nome)	T2—495 6
Phlox	583.76
Phobias	
medicine	616.852 25
see also Mental illness	
Phocidae	599.748
Phocis (Greece)	T2—383
Phocis (Greece : Nome)	T2—495 1
Phoenicia	939.44
	T2—394 4
Phoenician architecture	722.31
Phoenician language	492.6
	T6—926
Phoenician literature	892.6
Phoenician sculpture	732.944
Phoenicians	T5—926
Phoenicopteri	598.34
Phoenix	
folklore	398.245 4
sociology	398.469
Phoenix (Ariz.)	T2—791 73
Phoenix Islands	T2—968 1
Phoka (African people)	T5—963 91
Phoka language	496.391
	T6—963 91

Pholidophoriformes	567.4
Pholidota	599.31
paleozoology	569.31
Phonemics	414
specific languages	T4—15
Phonetic method	
reading instruction	372.414 5
Phonetic shorthand systems	
English language	653.423–.428
Phonetics	414
elementary education	372.622
specific languages	T4—15
Phonics	
reading instruction	372.414 5
Phonocardiography	
medicine	616.120 754 4
see also Cardiovascular system	
Phonodiscs	621.389 32
see also Sound recordings	
Phonograph records	621.389 32
see also Sound recordings	
Phonographs	621.389 33
education	371.333 2
Phonology	414
specific languages	T4—15
Phonons	
solid state physics	530.416
Phonorecords	621.389 32
see also Sound recordings	
Phoronidea	595.17
paleozoology	565.1
Phosphatases	574.192 53
see also Enzymes	
Phosphates	553.64
chemical engineering	661.43
economic geology	553.64
mineralogy	549.72
mining	622.364
Phosphenes	547.071
chemical engineering	661.87
Phosphinic acids	547.076
chemical engineering	661.87
Phosphoacids	547.074
chemical engineering	661.87
Phosphoalcohols	547.073
chemical engineering	661.87
Phosphoaldehydes	547.075
chemical engineering	661.87
Phosphoketones	547.075
chemical engineering	661.87
Phospholipids	574.192 47
see also Lipids	
Phosphonic acids	547.077
chemical engineering	661.87
Phosphonium compounds	547.071
chemical engineering	661.87
Phosphoproteins	574.192 454
biochemistry	574.192 454

Phraya Taksin, King of Siam
  Thai history   959.302 4
Phreatoicidea   595.372
Phrenology   139
Phrygia   T2—392 6
Phrygian language   491.993
    T6—919 93
Phrymacea   583.88
Phrynophiurida   593.94
  paleozoology   563.94
Phthiotis (Greece : Nome)   T2—495 1
Phuthaditjhaba (South Africa)   T2—685 91
Phutthalœtla Naphalai, King of
  Siam
  Thai history   959.303 2
Phutthayotfa Chulalok, King of
  Siam
  Thai history   959.303 1
Phycologists   589.309 2
  occupational group   T7—58
Phycology   589.3
Phycomycetes   589.25
Phylactolaemata   594.72
Phyllocarida   565.36·
Phyllosilicates
  mineralogy   549.67
Physarales   589.29
Physical allergies
  medicine   616.977
  see also Diseases (Human)
Physical anthropologists   573.092
  occupational group   T7—573
Physical anthropology   573
Physical biochemistry   574.192 83
  human   612.015 83
Physical chemistry   541.3
  applied   660.29
Physical conditions of work   331.25
  see also Work environment
Physical constants   530.81
Physical crystallography   548.8
Physical diagnosis
  medicine   616.075 4
Physical education   796.07
  elementary school   372.86
  health   613.7
Physical environment
  influence on crime   364.22
  psychological influence   155.91
Physical ethnologists   572.092
  occupational group   T7—572
Physical ethnology   572
Physical evidence
  criminal investigation   363.256 2
  criminal law   345.064
  law   347.064
Physical fitness   613.7
  health   613.7

Physical fitness (continued)
  public administration   350.773
    central governments   351.773
    local governments   352.4
Physical geodesy   526.7
Physical geology   551
Physical gerontology   612.67
Physical illness   362.1
  medicine   616
  see also Diseases (Human)
Physical instruments
  manufacturing technology   681.753
Physical metallurgy   669.9
Physical mineralogy   549.12
Physical oceanography   551.46
Physical operations
  chemical engineering   660.284 2
Physical optics   535.2
Physical sciences   500.2
Physical therapy
  medicine   615.82
  psychiatry   616.891 3
  see also Mental illness
Physical training
  health   613.7
Physical typology
  influence on crime   364.24
Physical units   530.81
Physical yoga
  health   613.704 6
Physically handicapped persons   305.908 16
    T1—087
    T7—081 6
  education   371.91
  social group   305.908 16
  social welfare   362.4
Physically healthy persons   305.908 12
    T7—081 2
Physician and patient   610.696
Physicians   610.92
  health services   362.172
    see also Health services
  law   344.041 2
  occupational group   T7—61
  role and function   610.695 2
Physicists   530.092
  occupational group   T7—53
Physics   530
  engineering   621
Physics and religion   291.175
  Christianity   261.55
  natural theology   215.3
Physiocracy (Economic school)   330.152
Physiognomy
  divination   138
Physiographic regions   T2—1
  folklore   398.23
    sociology   398.322

Piedmont (U.S. : Region) (continued)
North Carolina	T2—756 5
South Carolina	T2—757 3
Virginia	T2—755 6
Piemonte (Italy : Region)	T2—451
Pienaars River (South Africa)	T2—682 3
Pier foundations	624.158

Pierce, Franklin
United States history	973.66
Pierce County (Ga.)	T2—758 792
Pierce County (N.D.)	T2—784 591
Pierce County (Neb.)	T2—782 56
Pierce County (Wash.)	T2—797 78
Pierce County (Wis.)	T2—775 42
Pieria (Greece)	T2—495 6
Pierre (S.D.)	T2—783 29
Piers (Columns)	721.3
architecture	721.3
construction	690.13
structural engineering	624.16
Piers (Port facilities)	387.15
engineering	627.31

see also Port facilities
Pies	641.865 2
commercial processing	664.752 5
home preparation	641.865 2

Piet Retief (South Africa : District) T2—682 7
Pietermaritzburg (South Africa : District) T2—684 75
Pietersburg (South Africa : District) T2—682 5
Pietism	273.7
Piety (Gift of the Holy Spirit)	234.12

Piezodialysis
desalinization	628.167 46
Piezoelectricity	537.244 6
Piezomagnetism	538.3
Pig iron	669.141 3
Pigeon English	427.9
	T6—21
Pigeons	598.65
animal husbandry	636.596
Piggyback cargo services	385.72
public administration	351.875 72
Pigment materials	553.662
economic geology	553.662

Pigment processes
photographic printing	773

Pigmentation
human physiology	612.792 7

see also Skin
physical anthropology	573.5

Pigmented cells
human histology	611.018 2
Pigments	547.869
biochemistry	574.192 18
human	612.015 28

Pigments (continued)
biosynthesis	574.192 97
human	612.015 47
chemistry	547.869
paint technology	667.623

painting material
arts	751.2
technology	667.29
Pigs	599.734
animal husbandry	636.4
Pigweed	583.913
Pikas	599.322
Pike	597.53
sports fishing	799.175 3
Pike County (Ala.)	T2—761 35
Pike County (Ark.)	T2—767 485
Pike County (Ga.)	T2—758 453
Pike County (Ill.)	T2—773 453
Pike County (Ind.)	T2—772 36
Pike County (Ky.)	T2—769 23
Pike County (Miss.)	T2—762 23
Pike County (Mo.)	T2—778 36
Pike County (Ohio)	T2—771 847
Pike County (Pa.)	T2—748 24

Piketberg (South Africa : District) T2—687 3
Pila (Poland : Voivodeship)	T2—438 4
Pilanesberg Game Reserve	T2—682 94
Pilasters	721.3
architecture	721.3
construction	690.13
Pile foundations	624.154

Pile rugs
arts	746.75

see also Rugs
Pile-weave fabrics	677.617

see also Textiles
Pilgrimage to Mecca	297.55
Pilgrimages	291.446
Christianity	248.463

Pilgrim's Rest (South Africa : District) T2—682 6
Piling (Foundation engineering)	624.154
Pilipino language	499.211
	T6—992 11

Pillars of the faith
Islamic moral theology	297.5
Pillowcases	643.53
arts	746.97
home sewing	646.21
household equipment	643.53

Pills
practical pharmacy	615.43
Pills (Contraceptives)	615.766
health	613.943 2

see also Birth control, Genital system
Pilot ejection seats	629.134 386

Pipil language	497.45	Pitch (Sound)	534.32
	T6—974 5	musical element	781.232
Pipits	598.854	perception	
Pipoidea	597.84	psychology	152.152
paleozoology	567.8	physics	534.32
Piracy	364.164	Pitchblende	
international law	341.772	mineralogy	549.528
law	345.026 4	Pitcher plant	583.121
Piraeus (Greece)	T2—495 1	Asclepiadaceae	583.72
Piranha	597.52	New World	583.121
Pirate perch	597.53	Old World	583.922
Pirates' expeditions	910.45	Pitching (Aeronautics)	629.132 364
Pisa (Italy : Province)	T2—455 5	Pitching (Baseball)	796.357 22
Pisacha languages	491.499	Pitching (Golf)	796.352 34
	T6—914 99	Pitching games	796.24
Pisacha literatures	891.499	Pithecanthropus erectus	573.3
Piscataquis County (Me.)	T2—741 25	Pitkin County (Colo.)	T2—788 43
Pisces	597	Pitman shorthand systems	653.424
paleozoology	567	Pitt County (N.C.)	T2—756 44
sports fishing	799.1	Pitt Islands	T2—931 1
see also Fish		Pitt Meadows (B.C.)	T2—711 37
Pisé		Pitt River (B.C.)	T2—711 37
building construction	693.22	Pittosporales	583.141
Pisidia	T2—392 7	Pittsburg County (Okla.)	T2—766 75
Pistachio	641.345 74	Pittsburgh (Pa.)	T2—748 86
agriculture	634.574	Pittsworth (Qld.)	T2—943 3
botany	583.28	Pittsylvania County (Va.)	T2—755 665
commercial processing	664.804 574	Pituitary gland	
cooking	641.645 74	human anatomy	611.47
Pistils		human diseases	
anatomy	582.130 446 3	medicine	616.47
Pistoia (Italy : Province)	T2—455 2	human physiology	612.492
Pistols	683.432	*see also* Endocrine system	
art metalwork	739.744 3	Pituitary hormones	
manufacturing technology	683.432	pharmacology	615.363
military engineering	623.443	*see also* Endocrine system	
shooting game	799.213	Pityeae	561.55
sports	799.202 833	Piura (Peru : Dept.)	T2—851 3
target shooting	799.31	Piute County (Utah)	T2—792 53
Piston-driven airplanes	387.733 43	Pizza	641.824
engineering	629.133 343	cooking	641.824
transportation services	387.733 43	Place names	910.014
see also Aircraft		gazetters	910.3
Piston engines		Place settings	
aircraft	629.134 352	table service	642.6
Piston-turbine engines		Placebo effect	
aircraft	629.134 352	medicine	615.5
Pistons	621.84	Placement of workers	331.128
internal-combustion engines	621.437	economics	331.128
Pitakas	294.382	personnel management	658.312 8
Pitcairn Island	T2—961 8	public administration	350.14
Pitch (Aeronautics)	629.132 364	central governments	351.14
Pitch (Linguistics)	414.6	local governments	352.005 14
specific languages	T4—16	Placenta	599.03
Pitch (Natural asphalt)	553.27	animal physiology	599.03
mining	622.337	human diseases	
see also Asphalt		obstetrics	618.34
Pitch (Petroleum product)	665.538 8	human physiology	612.63

Plant location
- management 658.21
  - libraries 022.1
  - museums 069.21
  - *see also* Business enterprises— location
- Plant management 658.2
  - T1—068 2
  - libraries 022
  - museums 069.2
  - schools 371.6
- Plant nutrients 338.162
  - agricultural economics 338.162
- Plant-parasite diseases 574.232
- Plant pest control
  - sanitary engineering 628.97
- Plant propagation 631.53
  - botany 581.16
- Plant quarantine 632.93
- Plant resources 333.953
  - economics 333.953
  - public administration 351.823 28
- Plant sanitation 363.729 5
  - engineering 628.51
  - *see also* Waste control
- Plant supports
  - manufacturing technology 681.763 1
- Plant training 631.546
- Plant viruses 576.648 3
- Plantagenet, House of (English history) 942.03
- Plantagenet, House of (Irish history) 941.503
- Plantaginales 583.89
- Plantain (Fruit) 641.347 73
  - botany 584.21
  - commercial processing 664.804 773
  - cooking 641.647 73
  - horticulture 634.773
- Plantain (Weed) 583.89
- Plantain eaters 598.74
- Plantation crops 633
- Plantation houses
  - architecture 728.8
- Plantations
  - community sociology 307.72
  - system of production sociology 306.349
- Planting 631.53
  - equipment manufacturing technology 681.763 1
- Plants 581
  - agricultural pests 632.5
  - agriculture 630
  - art representation 704.943 4
  - botany 581
  - comparative psychology 156.9
  - conservation technology 639.99

Plants (continued)
- drawing 743.7
- folklore 398.242
  - sociology
    - legendary 398.468
    - real 398.368
- landscape architecture 716
- painting 758.5
- Plants (Buildings and equipment)
  - architecture 725.4
  - location
    - management 658.21
    - *see also* Business enterprises—location
  - management 658.2
    - T1—068 2
    - libraries 022
    - museums 069.2
    - prisons 365.5
- Plants in the Bible 220.858 1
- Plaquemines Parish (La.) T2—763 37
- Plasma (Blood)
  - human physiology 612.116
  - *see also* Cardiovascular system
- Plasma (Ionized gas)
  - chemical engineering 660.044
  - chemistry 541.042 4
- Plasma engineering 621.044
- Plasma membranes 574.875
- Plasma motors 621.466
- Plasma physics 530.44
- Plasma propulsion 629.475 5
- Plasma substitutes
  - pharmacology 615.39
- Plasma technology 660.044
- Plasma temperatures 536.57
- Plasmapheresis
  - pharmacology 615.39
- Plasmodiophorida 593.115
- Plasmodiophoromycetes 589.258
- Plasmodroma 593.1
  - paleozoology 563.1
- Plassey, Battle of, 1757 954.029 4
- Plaster casting
  - sculpture 731.452
- Plaster of paris 666.92
- Plasterers 693.609 2
  - occupational group T7—693
- Plastering 693.6
- Plasterwork
  - architectural construction 721.044 6
- Plastic arts 730
- Plastic deformation 531.38
  - *see also* Plasticity—physics
- Plastic fillings and inlays
  - dentistry 617.675
  - *see also* Dentistry
- Plastic films 668.495

Play	790
child care	649.5
psychology	155
children	155.418
recreation	790
sociology	306.481
see also Recreation	
Play-group movement	372.216
Play groups	
agent of socialization	303.327
social psychology	302.34
Player pianos	786.66
see also Mechanical musical	
instruments	
Playground equipment	
manufacturing technology	688.76
Playgrounds	796.068
outdoor sports	796.068
Playing cards	795.4
manufacturing technology	688.754
Playing time	
musical technique	781.432
Plays	
literature	808.82
see also Drama (Literature)	
music	
stage presentation	792.6
musical	782.14
music	782.14
Playwrights	809.2
collected biography	809.2
specific literatures	T3B—200 9
individual biography	T3A—2
Playwriting	808.2
Plazas	
area planning	711.55
Plea bargaining	345.072
Pleading (Law)	347.072
criminal law	345.072
Pleasant Island	996.85
	T2—968 5
Pleasants County (W. Va.)	T2—754 21
Pleasure	
ethical systems	171.4
sociology	306.481
Pleasure craft	387.204 23
design	623.812 042 3
engineering	623.820 23
handling	623.881 23
power-driven	387.231
design	623.812 31
engineering	623.823 1
handling	623.882 31
transportation services	387.231
transportation services	387.204 23
wind-driven	387.223
design	623.812 23
engineering	623.822 3

Pleasure craft	
wind-driven (continued)	
handling	623.882 23
transportation services	387.223
Pleasures of eating	641.013
Plecoptera	595.735
paleozoology	565.73
Plectral instruments	787.7
see also Stringed instruments	
Plectral lutes	787.8
see also Stringed instruments	
Pleinairism	709.034 4
painting	759.054
Pleisiopora	595.146
Pleistocene epoch	551.792
geology	551.792
paleontology	560.178
Pleosporales	589.23
Plettenberg Bay (South	
Africa)	T2—687 4
Pleura	
human anatomy	611.25
human diseases	
medicine	616.25
human physiology	612.2
surgery	617.543
see also Respiratory system	
Pleuracanthodii	567.3
Pleurocapsales	589.46
Pleurodira	597.92
Pleuromeiales	561.79
Pleuronectiformes	597.58
Pleven (Bulgaria : Okrug)	T2—497 76
Plevenski okrug (Bulgaria)	T2—497 76
Pliocene epoch	551.788
geology	551.788
paleontology	560.178
Ploceidae	598.873
Plock (Poland : Voivodeship)	T2—438 4
Plocospermaceae	583.72
Ploeisti (Romania)	T2—498 2
Ploesti (Romania)	T2—498 2
Plots	
literature	808.802 4
history and criticism	809.924
specific literatures	T3B—080 24
history and criticism	T3B—092 4
music	780
treatises	782.002 69
Plotters (Computer devices)	006.62
engineering	621.399
Plovdiv, Bulgaria (Okrug)	T2—497 75
Plovdivski okrug (Bulgaria)	T2—497 75
Plovers	598.33
Plowing	631.51
Plows	
manufacturing technology	681.763 1

Plucked board zithers 787.75
  see also Stringed instruments
Plucked drums 786.97
  see also Percussion instruments
Plucked idiophones 786.85
  set 786.85
  single 786.887
  see also Percussion instruments
Plum 641.342 2
  botany 583.372
  cooking 641.642 2
  orchard crop 634.22
Plumas County (Calif.) T2—794 29
Plumbaginaceae 583.672
Plumbago (Mineral) 553.26
Plumbers 696.109 2
  occupational group T7—696
Plumbing
  buildings 696.1
  government control 350.824 2
    central governments 351.824 2
    local governments 352.926
Plumerias
  ornamental arboriculture 635.977 372
Plural executives
  public administration 350.003 1
    central governments 351.003 1
    local governments 352.008
Pluralism
  philosophy 147.4
Pluriarcs 787.93
  see also Stringed instruments
Plush 677.617
Plush-capped finches 598.8
Pluto (Planet) 523.482
   T2—992 9
  unmanned flights to 629.435 482
Plutocracy 321.5
Plutonic rocks 552.3
Plutonium 669.293 4
  chemical engineering 661.043 4
  chemistry 546.434
  metallography 669.952 934
  metallurgy 669.293 4
  physical metallurgy 669.962 934
  toxicology 615.925 434
  see also Chemicals
Plymouth (England) T2—423 58
Plymouth Brethren 289.9
  see also Christian
    denominations
Plymouth County (Iowa) T2—777 16
Plymouth County (Mass.) T2—744 82
Plymouth Rocks (Chickens)
  animal husbandry 636.582
  see also Chickens
Plywood 674.834

PMS (Syndrome)
  gynecology 618.172
  see also Female genital system
Pneumatic clocks
  technology 681.115
Pneumatic construction 693.98
  architecture 721.044 98
Pneumatic control 629.804 5
Pneumatic conveyor systems
  library equipment 022.9
  office use 651.79
Pneumatic engineering 621.51
Pneumatic engineers 621.510 92
  occupational group T7—621
Pneumatic pumps 621.69
Pneumatic tools 621.904
Pneumatics
  physics 533.6
Pneumatotherapy
  medicine 615.836
Pneumoconiosis
  medicine 616.244
  see also Respiratory system
Pneumocystis carinii pneumonia
  medicine 616.241
  see also Respiratory system
Pneumonia
  medicine 616.241
  see also Respiratory system
Po River (Italy) T2—452
Poaceae 584.9
Poatina (Tas.) T2—946 3
Pocahontas County (Iowa) T2—777 19
Pocahontas County (W. Va.) T2—754 87
Pocket billiards 794.73
Pocket calculators 681.14
  mathematics 510.28
Pocket computers 004.16
  see also Microcomputers
Pocket gophers 599.323 2
Pocket scores 780
  treatises 780.265
Pocono Mountains (Pa.) T2—748 2
Podiatry 617.585
Podicipediformes 598.443
  paleozoology 568.4
Podoaceae 583.28
Podocarpaceae 585.2
  paleobotany 561.52
Podocopa 595.33
  paleozoology 565.33
Podophyllaceae 583.111
Podostemales 583.921
Poems 808.81
  music 780
    treatises 780.268
  see also Poetry

Poetic books (Old Testament)	223
pseudepigrapha	229.912
Poetic drama	
literature	808.82
history and criticism	809.2
specific literatures	
individual authors	T3A—2
specific literatures	T3B—2
Poetry	808.81
criticism	809.1
theory	801.951
history	809.1
rhetoric	808.1
specific literatures	T3B—1
individual authors	T3A—1
Poets	809.1
collected biography	809.1
specific literatures	T3B—100 9
individual biography	T3A—1
occupational group	T7—81
Pogolo (African people)	T5—963 91
Pogolo languages	496.391
	T6—963 91
Pohjois-Karjala (Finland)	T2—489 75
Poinsett County (Ark.)	T2—767 96
Poinsettia	583.95
Point Lookout (N.S.W.)	T2—944 3
Point-of-sale advertising	659.157
Point processes	519.2
Point set topology	514.322
Point sets	511.33
Pointe Coupee Parish (La.)	T2—763 454
Pointers (Dogs)	
animal husbandry	636.752
see also Dogs	
Pointillism	709.034 5
painting	759.055
Poison frog	597.87
Poison gas	
military engineering	623.459 2
Poison gas projectiles	623.451 6
Poison hemlock	583.48
Poison ivy	583.28
Poison oak	583.28
Poison sumac	583.28
Poisoning	
toxicology	615.9
Poisonous animals	591.69
toxicology	615.94
Poisonous fish	597.069
toxicology	615.945
Poisonous plants	581.69
toxicology	615.952
Poisons	363.179 1
public safety	363.179 1
toxicology	615.9
see also Hazardous materials	
Poisson integral	515.43

Poisson-Stieltjes integral	515.43
Poisson's ratio	531.381
Poitou (France)	T2—446
Poitou-Charentes (France)	T2—446
Poker (Game)	795.412
Pokeweed	583.913
Polabian language	491.89
	T6—918 9
Polabian literature	891.89
Poland	943.8
	T2—438
Poland China swine	
animal husbandry	636.482
zoology	599.734
Polar easterlies	551.518 3
Polarimeters	
manufacturing technology	681.416
Polarimetric analysis	543.085 6
Polarimetry	
astronomy	522.65
physical chemistry	541.702 87
Polaris missiles	358.981 782
military engineering	623.451 97
military equipment	358.981 782
Polariscopic analysis	543.085 6
Polarization of light	535.52
physics	535.52
Polarographic analysis	543.087 2
Polders	
engineering	627.54
Pole vaulting	796.434
Polecats	599.744 47
Polela (South Africa :	
District)	T2—684 7
Polemics	
Christianity	239
comparative religion	291.2
Islam	297.29
Polemoniales	583.76
Poles (People)	T5—918 5
Polesine (Italy)	T2—453 3
Police	363.2
law	344.052
sociology	306.28
Police boats	363.286
design	623.812 63
engineering	623.826 3
police services	363.286
Police buildings	
architecture	725.18
Police corruption	364.132 3
see also Corruption in	
government	
Police functions	363.23
Police law	344.052
Police officers	363.209 2
duties and functions	363.22
occupational group	T7—363 2

Politicians	324.209 2
characteristics	324.22
occupational group	T7—329
Politics	320
folklore	398.22
sociology	398.358
journalism	070.449 32
Politics and religion	322.1
see also Religion and politics	
Politics as a profession	324.22
Polk, James K. (James Knox)	
United States history	973.61
Polk County (Ark.)	T2—767 45
Polk County (Fla.)	T2—759 67
Polk County (Ga.)	T2—758 375
Polk County (Iowa)	T2—777 58
Polk County (Minn.)	T2—776 95
Polk County (Mo.)	T2—778 77
Polk County (N.C.)	T2—756 915
Polk County (Neb.)	T2—782 352
Polk County (Or.)	T2—795 38
Polk County (Tenn.)	T2—768 875
Polk County (Tex.)	T2—764 165
Polk County (Wis.)	T2—775 17
Polka form	784.188 44
Poll tax	336.25
law	343.062
public administration	350.724
central governments	351.724
local governments	352.135
public finance	336.25
qualification for voting	324.62
Pollack	597.53
fishing	639.275 3
Polled Durham cattle	
animal husbandry	636.226
zoology	599.735 8
Pollen	
anatomy	582.046 3
flowering plants	
anatomy	582.130 446 3
paleobotany	561.13
Pollen control	
air conditioning	
buildings	697.932 4
Pollenation	582.016 62
Polling	324.65
Pollutants	363.738
control	
public administration	350.823 23
central governments	351.823 23
local governments	352.942 323
see also Pollution	
Pollution	363.73
ecological effects	574.522 2
international law	341.762 3
law	344.046 32
social effects	304.28

Pollution (continued)	
social theology	291.178 362 8
Christianity	261.836 28
social welfare	363.73
toxicology	615.902
water-pollution engineering	628.168
Pollution-control technology	628.5
aircraft	629.134 35
automotive	629.25
dyeing processes	667.36
gas technology	665.78
glassmaking	666.14
paper manufacturing	676.042
petroleum	665.538 9
plastic technology	668.419 2
rubber manufacturing	678.29
sugars and syrups	664.119
textile manufacturing	677.029
wood products	674.84
Polo	796.353
Polo players	796.353 092
sports group	T7—796 35
Polonaise form	784.188 4
Polonium	
chemical engineering	661.072 8
chemistry	546.728
metallurgy	669.79
see also Chemicals	
Poltava (Ukraine : Oblast)	T2—477 15
Poltavskaia oblast (Ukraine)	T2—477 15
Poltergeists	133.14
Polyacrylics	668.423 2
textiles	677.474 2
see also Textiles	
Polyamides	668.423 5
textiles	677.473
see also Textiles	
Polyandry	306.842 3
Polyangiaceae	589.98
Polybasite	
mineralogy	549.35
Polybutadiene rubber	678.72
Polycarbonates	668.423
Polychaeta	595.147
Polychlorinated biphenyl	
toxicology	615.951 2
Polycladida	595.123
Polycyclic current transmission	621.319 16
Polycythemia	
medicine	616.153
see also Cardiovascular system	
Polyesters	668.422 5
textiles	677.474 3
see also Textiles	
Polyethers	668.423
Polyethylene	668.423 4
textiles	677.474 5
see also Textiles	

Pondicherry (India : Union Territory)	T2—548 6
Pondoland (South Africa)	T2—687 91
Ponds	551.482
	T2—169 2
fish culture	639.311
hydrology	551.482
resource economics	333.916 3
Pondweed	584.742
Pongidae	599.88
Ponginae	599.884
Pongola River	T2—684 2
Mozambique	T2—679 1
South Africa	T2—684 2
Pongos	599.884 2
Ponies	
animal husbandry	636.16
zoology	599.725
Pons Variolii	
human anatomy	611.81
human physiology	612.826 7
see also Nervous system	
Ponta Delgada (Azores : District)	T2—469 9
Pontchartrain, Lake (La.)	T2—763 34
Pontederiaceae	584.32
Pontevedra (Spain : Province)	T2—461 7
Pontiac (Quebec : County)	T2—714 21
Pontiac (Quebec : Regional County Municipality)	T2—714 21
Pontiac's Conspiracy, 1763-1764	973.27
Pontificale Romanum	264.025
Pontine Islands (Italy)	T2—456 23
Pontine Marshes (Italy)	T2—456 23
Pontoon bridges	388
construction	624.87
see also Bridges	
Pontotoc County (Miss.)	T2—762 932
Pontotoc County (Okla.)	T2—766 69
Pontus	T2—393 3
Ponza Islands (Italy)	T2—456 23
Poodle	
animal husbandry	636.72
see also Dogs	
Poodle (Toy dog)	
animal husbandry	636.76
see also Dogs	
Pooideae	584.93
forage crops	633.2
Pool (Game)	794.73
equipment technology	688.747 3
Pool halls	
architecture	725.84
Pool players	794.730 92
sports group	T7—794 7
Poole (England)	T2—423 37
Pools (Organizations)	338.87
economics	338.87

Pools (Water)	
landscape architecture	714
Poor Clares	255.973
church history	271.973
Poor laws	362.5
social aspects	362.5
Poor people	305.56
	T1—086 24
institutional buildings	362.585
social theology	291.178 345 6
Buddhism	294.337 834 56
Christianity	261.834 56
Hinduism	294.517 834 56
Islam	297.197 834 56
Judaism	296.387 834 56
social welfare	362.5
welfare law	344.032 5
see also Poverty	
Poor people (Destitute)	305.569
	T1—086 942
see also Poor people, Poverty	
Pop art	709.040 71
painting	759.067 1
sculpture	735.230 471
Popcorn	641.356 77
botany	584.92
commercial processing	664.805 677
cooking	641.656 77
garden crop	635.677
Pope County (Ark.)	T2—767 32
Pope County (Ill.)	T2—773 991
Pope County (Minn.)	T2—776 46
Popes	282.092
ecclesiology	262.13
Popguns	
music	786.99
see also Percussion instruments	
Poplar	583.981
forestry	634.972 3
lumber	674.142
Popoloca Indians	T5—976
Popoloca language	497.6
	T6—976
Popoluca language (Vera Cruz)	497.41
	T6—974 1
Popondetta (Papua New Guinea)	T2—954 2
Poppies	583.122
narcotic crop	633.75
Popular culture	306.4
Popular music	781.63
Population	304.6
social problems	363.9
social theology	291.178 366
Christianity	261.836 6
sociology	304.6

Port St. Johns (South Africa :
  District)   T2—687 91
Port Sudan (Sudan)   T2—625
Portability
  programs   005
Portable firearms
  military engineering   623.442
Portable flight vehicles
  engineering   629.14
Portable heaters
  buildings   697.24
Portable lights
  mining   622.473
  nautical equipment   623.86
Portable radios   621.384 5
Portable steam engines   621.15
Portable telephones   384.53
  communication services   384.53
  engineering   621.384 56
  see also Radiotelephony
Portage County (Ohio)   T2—771 37
Portage County (Wis.)   T2—775 53
Portage la Prairie (Man.)   T2—712 73
Portalegre (Portugal : District)   T2—469 52
Portals
  sculpture   731.542
Porter County (Ind.)   T2—772 98
Portes Gil, Emilio
  Mexican history   972.082 42
Portfolio analysis   332.6
Portfolio management   332.6
Portland (Me.)   T2—741 91
Portland (Or.)   T2—795 49
Portland (Vic.)   T2—945 7
Portland, Weymouth and
  (England : Borough)   T2—423 35
Portland cement   666.94
Portneuf (Quebec : County)   T2—714 46
Portneuf Wildlife Reserve
  (Quebec)   T2—714 46
Porto (Portugal : District)   T2—469 15
Porto-Novo (Benin)   T2—668 3
Portraits
  art representation   704.942
  drawing   743.42
  painting   757
Ports   387.1
  engineering   627.2
  inland waterway   386.8
    public administration   351.876 8
    transportation services   386.8
  law   343.096 7
  public administration   351.877 1
  transportation services   387.1
  see also Port facilities
Ports and Islands (Iran :
  Province)   T2—557 5
Portsmouth (England)   T2—422 792

Portsmouth (N.H.)   T2—742 6
Portsmouth (Va.)   T2—755 522
Portugal   946.9
     T2—469
Portuguesa (Venezuela)   T2—874 5
Portuguese   T5—691
Portuguese Guinea   966.570 2
     T2—665 7
Portuguese language   469
     T6—69
Portuguese literature   869
Portuguese man-of-war   593.71
Portuguese Timor   T2—598 6
Portuguese water dog
  animal husbandry   636.73
  see also Dogs
Portulacaceae   583.152
Posey County (Ind.)   T2—772 34
Posidoniaceae   584.744
Position (Location)
  geodetic astronomy   526.64
Position classification   658.306
Position-finding devices
  marine navigation   623.893
  radio engineering   621.384 191
Positional astronomy   526.6
Positives (Photography)   771.44
Positivism   146.4
  ethics   171.2
Positron emission tomography
  medicine   616.075 75
Positrons   539.721 4
Posology
  pharmacology   615.14
Post exchanges   355.341
Post-mortem examination
  medicine   616.075 9
Post offices   383.42
  architecture   725.16
  see also Postal service
Postage-due stamps
  prints   769.57
Postage meters
  office use   651.759
Postage stamps   383.23
  investment economics   332.63
  philately   769.56
  postal service   383.23
    see also Postal service
  printing   686.288
Postal cards   383.122
  see also Postal service
Postal clerks   383.492
  occupational group   T7—383
Postal communication   383
  see also Postal service
Postal insurance   368.2
  see also Insurance

Potatoes	641.352 1
agriculture	635.21
botany	583.79
commercial processing	664.805 21
cooking	641.652 1
Potchefstroom (South Africa : District)	T2—682 4
Potential energy	531.6
Potential offenders	
identification	364.41
Potential theory	515.9
Potentiometers	621.374 3
Potentiometric analysis	543.087 12
Potenza (Italy : Province)	T2—457 71
Potgietersrus (South Africa : District)	T2—682 5
Pothos	584.64
Potichomania	
handicrafts	745.546
Potomac River	T2—752
Maryland	T2—752
West Virginia	T2—754 9
Potoos	598.99
Potosí (Bolivia : Dept.)	T2—841 4
Pots	641.502 8
cooking	641.502 8
manufacturing technology	683.82
Potsdam (Germany)	T2—431 572
Potsdam (Germany : Bezirk)	T2—431 57
Potsdam (South Africa)	T2—687 92
Pottawatomie County (Kan.)	T2—781 32
Pottawatomie County (Okla.)	T2—766 36
Pottawattamie County (Iowa)	T2—777 71
Potted plants	
floriculture	635.965
Potted trees	
ornamental agriculture	635.977
Potter County (Pa.)	T2—748 55
Potter County (S.D.)	T2—783 19
Potter County (Tex.)	T2—764 825
Potters	738.092
occupational group	T7—738
Potter's wheels	666.43
decorative arts	738.13
sculpture	731.3
technology	666.43
Pottery	666.3
arts	738
technology	666.3
Poultry	598.61
agricultural economics	338.176 5
animal husbandry	636.5
Poultry meat	641.365
commercial processing	664.93
economics	338.476 649 3
cooking	641.665
home preservation	641.493

Poured concrete	624.183 4
building construction	693.5
with reinforcement	693.541
without reinforcement	693.521
structural engineering	624.183 4
Poverty	362.5
influence on crime	364.2
law	344.032 5
macroeconomics	339.46
religious practice	291.447
Buddhism	294.344 47
Christianity	248.47
Hinduism	294.544 7
social services	
institutional architecture	725.55
social theology	291.178 325
Christianity	261.832 5
social welfare	362.5
public administration	350.845
central governments	351.845
local governments	352.944 5
social welfare facilities	362.583
architecture	725.55
see also Poor people	
Poverty-stricken persons	305.569
	T1—086 942
see also Poor people, Poverty	
Powder iron	669.141 9
Powder metal products	671.87
Powder metallurgy	671.37
Powder processes	
photographic printing	773.2
Powder River County (Mont.)	T2—786 37
Powder rooms	643.52
home economics	643.52
interior decoration	747.78
Powder technology	620.43
Powdered eggs	641.375 4
cooking	641.675 4
processing	637.54
Powdered soaps	668.124
Powders	
practical pharmacy	615.43
Powdery mildew	589.23
Powell, Lake (Utah and Ariz.)	T2—792 59
Powell County (Ky.)	T2—769 585
Powell County (Mont.)	T2—786 86
Powell River (B.C.)	T2—711 31
Powell River (B.C. : Regional District)	T2—711 31
Power (Energy)	333.79
international law	341.755
see also Electricity, Energy	
Power (Social sciences)	303.3
international relations	327.101
political science	320.011
sociology	303.3
Power control devices	621.812

Prefabricated materials (continued)
  construction 693.97
Preferential hiring 331.889 2
  labor economics 331.889 2
  personnel management 658.311 2
    public administration 350.132 43
      central governments 351.132 43
      local governments 352.005 132 43
Preferred stocks 332.632 25
  speculation 332.632 28
Pregnancy 599.03
  animal physiology 599.03
  cooking for 641.563
  human physiology 612.63
  obstetrics 618.2
  psychology 155.646 3
  veterinary medicine 636.089 82
Prehistoric archaeology 930.1
Prehistoric humankind 573.3
Prehistoric religions 291.042
Prehnite
  mineralogy 549.63
Prejudice 303.385
  ethics 177.5
  social theology 291.178 34
    Christianity 261.834
  sociology 303.385
Preliminary hearings 345.072
Preliminary Scholastic Aptitude
  Test 378.166 2
Prelude form 784.189 28
Premarital counseling
  social welfare 362.828 6
  see also Families—social
    welfare
Premarital sexual relations 306.73
  customs 392.6
  social problem 363.48
  see also Sexual relations
Premature delivery
  obstetrics 618.397
Premature infants
  pediatrics 618.920 11
Premenstrual syndrome
  gynecology 618.172
  see also Female genital system
Premiers
  occupational group T7—351 3
  public administration 351.003 13
Premium television 384.555 4
  see also Television
Premonstratensians 255.19
  church history 271.19
Přemyslid dynasty
  (Czechoslovakian history) 943.702 23
Prenatal care
  obstetrics 618.24
Prentiss County (Miss.) T2—762 985

Prenuptial contracts 346.016
Preoperative care
  surgery 617.919
Prepaid health insurance 368.382
  see also Insurance
Preparation of food (Cooking) 641.5
Preparatory schools 373.222
Prepared doughs 664.753
Prepared ores 669.042
Prepared pianos 786.28
  see also Keyboard instruments
Prerelease guidance centers 365.34
  see also Correctional
    institutions
Prerelease programs
  prisoner services 365.66
Presbyterian Church 285
  church government 262.05
    parishes 254.05
  church law 262.985
  doctrines 230.5
    catechism and creeds 238.5
  general councils 262.33
  guides to Christian life 248.485
  missions 266.5
  moral theology 241.045
  public worship 264.05
  religious associations 267.185
  religious education 268.85
  seminaries 207.115
  theology 230.5
Presbyterian Church (U.S.A.) 285.137
  see also Presbyterian Church
Presbyterian Church in the
  United States 285.133
  see also Presbyterian Church
Presbyterian Church in the
  United States of America 285.132
  see also Presbyterian Church
Presbyterian Church of Wales 285.235
  see also Presbyterian Church
Presbyterian sacred music 781.715 1
  public worship 782.322 51
    music 782.322 51
    religion 264.050 2
Presbyterians
  biography 285.092
  religious group T7—251
Presbyteries
  Christian ecclesiology 262.4
Preschool children 305.233
                 T1—083 3
                 T7—054 3
  home care 649.123
  psychology 155.423
  social aspects 305.233
Preschool education 372
  see also Elementary education

Preschool teachers	372.210 92	Pressing textiles	677.028 25
Preschools	372.21	Pressure	
Prescott and Russell (Ont.)	T2—713 85	biophysics	574.191 35
Prescription drug abuse	362.299	human	612.014 415
medicine	616.86	mechanics	531.1
personal health	613.8	Pressure cooking	641.587
social welfare	362.299	Pressure distribution	
see also Substance abuse		aeronautics	629.132 35
Prescription filling	615.4	Pressure groups	324.4
Prescription writing	615.14	relation to government	322.43
Prescriptive linguistics	418	Pressure perception	
specific languages	T4—8	psychology	152.182 3
Preseli (Wales : District)	T2—429 62	Pressure regulators	
Presentation of Jesus Christ	232.928	steam engineering	621.185
Presentation religious orders	255.977	Pressure surge	
church history	271.977	engineering	620.106 4
Presentations (Parturition)		Pressure vessels	
obstetrics	618.42	manufacturing technology	681.760 41
Preservation		Pressure-volume-temperature	
arts	702.88	relationships	536.41
bibliographic materials	025.84	Pressurization	
biological specimens	579	aircraft	629.134 42
museology	069.53	manned spacecraft	629.477 5
negatives and transparencies	771.45	spacecraft	629.477 5
positives (Photography)	771.46	unmanned spacecraft	629.467 5
Preserved Context Indexing		Pressurizing oils and gases	665.028 2
System	025.482	Presswork	
Preserved foods		printing	686.23
cooking	641.61	Preston (England : Borough)	T2—427 665
home economics	641.4	Preston County (W. Va.)	T2—754 82
Preserves (Jams)	641.852	Prestressed concrete	624.183 412
commercial processing	664.152	building construction	693.542
home preparation	641.852	manufacturing technology	666.893
Preserves (Whole fruit)	641.34	materials science	620.137
cooking with	641.64	structural engineering	624.183 412
home preparation	641.4	Presumptions (Law)	347.064
Preservice training		Pretoria (South Africa :	
armed forces	355.223 2	District)	T2—682 35
Presidente Hayes (Paraguay :		Pretoria-Witwatersrand-	
Dept.)	T2—892 23	Vereeniging area (South	
Presidential system		Africa)	T2—682 2
democratic government	321.804 2	Pretrial procedure	347.072
Presidents of nations		criminal law	345.072
occupational group	T7—351 2	Pretrial release	345.072
public administration	351.003 13	Preventive dentistry	617.601
Presidio County (Tex.)	T2—764 933	see also Dentistry	
Presque Isle County (Mich.)	T2—774 82	Preventive detention	
Press	070	law	345.052 7
civil rights issues	323.445	Preventive medicine	613
influence on crime	364.254	personal	613
Press control	363.31	public	614.44
see also Censorship		administration	350.77
Press law	343.099 8	central governments	351.77
Pressing clothes		local governments	352.4
home economics	648.1	animal husbandry	636.089 444
Pressing equipment	621.98	Preveza (Greece : Nome)	T2—495 3
Pressing glass	666.123	Priapulida	595.17
Pressing metals	671.33		

Primitive weapons	
art metalwork	739.744 1
Primitivism	
literature	808.801 45
history and criticism	809.914 5
specific literatures	T3B—080 145
history and criticism	T3B—091 45
Primorski (R.S.F.S.R. : Kray)	T2—577
Primorskii krai (R.S.F.S.R.)	T2—577
Primrose	583.672
Primulales	583.672
Prince (P.E.I.)	T2—717 1
Prince Albert (Sask.)	T2—712 42
Prince Albert (South Africa :	
District)	T2—687 15
Prince Alexander Mountains	T2—957 5
Prince Edward (Ont.)	T2—713 587
Prince Edward County (Va.)	T2—755 632
Prince Edward Island	971.7
	T2—717
Prince Edward Islands	969.9
	T2—699
Prince George (B.C.)	T2—711 82
Prince George County (Va.)	T2—755 585
Prince George's County (Md.)	T2—752 51
Prince of Wales Island	
(N.W.T.)	T2—719 7
Prince Rupert (B.C.)	T2—711 1
Prince William County (Va.)	T2—755 273 2
Princeton (B.C.)	T2—711 5
Princeton (N.J.)	T2—749 65
Principal components analysis	519.535 4
Principals (Criminal law)	345.03
Principals (School)	371.200 92
personnel management	371.201 2
Print making	
graphic arts	760
Print media	
journalism	070.17
sociology	302.232
Print specimens	686.224
Printed advertising	659.132
Printed books	094
Printed circuits	621.381 531
Printed music	780
treatises	780.263
Printers	686.209 2
occupational group	T7—686 2
Printers (Equipment)	
computer science	004.77
manufacturing technology	681.62
Printing	686.2
photography	771.4
textile arts	746.62
textiles	667.38
Printing apparatus	
photography	771.49
Printing ink	667.5

Printing presses	
manufacturing technology	681.62
Printing solutions	
photography	771.54
Printing telegraphy	384.14
wireless	384.524
see also Telegraphy	
Printmakers	769.92
occupational group	T7—76
Prints	
arts	769
cataloging	025.347 1
library treatment	025.177 1
Priories	
architecture	726.7
Pripet Marshes (Byelorussian	
S.S.R. and Ukraine)	T2—476 5
Prisms	535.4
geometry	516.15
manufacturing technology	681.42
physics	535.4
Prison administrators	365.92
occupational group	T7—365
Prison camps	
military	365.48
see also Correctional	
institutions	
Prison chaplaincy	259.5
Prison discipline	365.643
law	344.035 643
Prison farms	365.34
see also Correctional	
institutions	
Prison libraries	027.665
administration	025.197 665
collection development	025.218 766 5
use studies	025.587 665
Prison life	365.6
Prison reform	365.7
Prison security	365.641
Prisoner discharge	365.647
Prisoner-of-war camps	355.71
Civil War (United States)	973.77
Mexican War	973.627
South African War	968.048 7
Spanish-American War, 1898	973.897
United States Revolutionary	
War	973.37
Vietnamese War	959.704 37
War of 1812	973.527
World War I	940.472
World War II	940.547 2
Prisoner release	365.647
Prisoners (Convicts)	365.6
	T1—086 92
labor economics	331.51
legal status	344.035 6
Prisoner's base	796.14

Probate law	346.052
Probation	364.63
law	345.077
penology	364.63
public administration	350.849 3
central governments	351.849 3
local governments	352.944 93
Probation after death	236.4
Probation of students	371.543
Probation of teachers	371.144
Problem of few bodies	530.14
Problem of *n* bodies	530.144
astronomy	521
Problem of three bodies	530.14
astronomy	521
Problem solving	153.43
educational psychology	370.152 4
executive management	658.403
psychology	153.43
Problems	
study and teaching	T1—076
Proboscidea	599.61
paleozoology	569.6
Procedural rights	323.422
Procedure (Law)	347.05
Procellaridae	598.42
Procellariiformes	598.42
paleozoology	568.4
Process analysis	
production management	658.5
Process control	003.5
	T1—011 5
chemical engineering	660.281 5
production management	658.5
Process design	
chemical engineering	660.281 2
Process metallurgy	669
Process philosophy	146.7
Process research	
production management	658.577
Process serving	347.072
Process theology	230.046
Processed cheese	641.373 58
cooking	641.673 58
manufacturing	637.358
Processing (Libraries)	025.02
Processing centers	
library operations	025.02
Processing modes	
computer science	004.3
	T1—028 543
Processions	
customs	394.5
performing arts	791.6
religious rites	
Christianity	265.9
Processors	
computer hardware	004
engineering	621.39
programming-language	
translators	005.45
Proctology	616.35
see also Digestive system	
Procurators fiscal	345.411 01
Procurement	658.72
	T1—068 7
military supplies	355.621 2
public administration	350.712
central governments	351.712
local governments	352.162
Procurement of capital	T1—068 1
Procyonidae	599.744 43
Producer brands	
sales promotion	658.827
Producer gas	665.772
Producers' cooperatives	334.6
Product comparison	T1—029 7
Product comparisons	T1—029 6
Product control	
law	344.042
see also Product safety	
Product design	
production management	658.575 2
Product development	
management	658.575
Product directories	T1—029 4
Product evaluation	T1—029 7
Product evaluations	T1—029 6
Product improvement research	
production management	658.576
Product liability	346.038
production management	658.56
Product liability insurance	368.562
see also Insurance	
Product life cycle	
management	658.5
Product listings	T1—029
Product management	658.5
marketing	658.8
production	658.5
Product planning	658.503 8
Product recall	
production management	658.56
Product returns	
marketing management	658.812
Product safety	363.19
international law	341.765
law	344.042
production management	658.56
social services	363.19
public administration	350.778
central governments	351.778
local governments	352.4

Professional services	338.46	Program documentation	
economics	338.46	preparation	005.15
Professional sports	796	text	005.3
law	344.099	Program evaluation techniques	
Professional workers	305.553	(Network analysis)	658.403 2
labor economics	331.712	Program languages	005.13
personnel management	658.304 4	Program maintenance	005.16
social class	305.553	Program music	781.56
training		Program notes	
personnel management	658.312 45	music	780.15
public administration	350.15	Program-performance budgeting	
central governments	351.15	public administration	350.722 204 2
local governments	352.005 15	central governments	351.722 204 2
Professional writing	808.066	local governments	352.122 042
Professionals	305.553	Program portability	005
	T1—086 22	Program reliability	005
social class	305.553	Program verification	005.14
Professions	331.712	Programmable calculators	510.285 41
	T1—023	Programmable controllers	
economics	331.712	control engineering	629.895
public administration	350.824 3	Programmed instruction	371.394 42
central governments	351.824 3		T1—077
local governments	352.942 43	electronic	371.334
Professors	378.120 92	non-electronic	371.394 42
occupational group	T7—372	Programmed learning	371.394 42
Profit and loss statements		electronic	371.334
financial management	658.151 2	nonelectronic	371.394 42
Profit sharing	331.216 4	Programming	
economics	331.216 4	dramatic performances	792.023 6
personnel management	658.322 5	motion pictures	791.430 236
Profitability measurement		radio	791.440 236
accounting	657.48	stage	792.023 6
Profits	338.516	television	791.450 236
agriculture	338.13	Programming (Mathematics)	519.7
financial management	658.155	Programming computers	005.1
income distribution	339.21		T1—028 551
mineral industries	338.23	graphics	006.66
production economics	338.516	Programming-language	
secondary industries	338.43	translators	005.45
taxes	336.243 2	Programming languages	005.13
law	343.052 44	Programs	
public administration	350.724 4	public administration	350
central governments	351.724 4	central governments	351
local governments	352.135	local governments	352
public finance	336.243 2	radiobroadcasting	384.544 3
Progeny	306.874	communications	384.544 3
	T1—085 4	performing arts	791.44
	T7—044	social action	361.25
family relationships	306.874	television broadcasting	384.553 2
Prognosis		communications	384.553 2
medicine	616.075	performing arts	791.45
Progoneata	595.6	Programs (Computer)	005.3
paleozoology	565.6		T1—028 553
Program auditing	657.453	coding	005.13
Program compatibility	005	graphics	006.68
Program design	005.12	Programs (Party platforms)	324.23
		Progreso, El (Guatemala : Dept.)	T2—728 153

Property insurance	368.1
see also Insurance	
Property law	346.04
Property loss insurance	368.1
see also Insurance	
Property management	
public administration	350.713
central governments	351.713
local governments	352.163
Property offenses	364.16
law	345.026
Property rights	323.46
civil rights issue	323.46
law	346.042
Property risks	368.06
Property systems	
sociology	306.32
Property tax	336.22
public administration	350.724 2
central governments	351.724 2
local governments	352.135 2
public finance	336.22
tax law	343.054
Prophecies	133.3
occultism	133.3
religion	291.32
Biblical	220.15
eschatological	291.23
Christianity	236
Judaism	296.33
Islam	297.32
messianic	
Christianity	232.12
Judaism	296.33
Prophecy (Concept)	291.211
Christianity	231.745
spiritual gift	234.13
in Bible	220.15
Islam	297.211
Judaism	296.311
Prophetic books (Old Testament)	224
Prophetic books	
(Pseudepigrapha)	229.913
Prophetic message	
Bible	220.15
Prophetic office of Jesus Christ	232.8
Prophets	291.63
Islam	297.24
Judaism	296.61
Prophets (Biblical books)	224
Prophylaxis	
public health	614.44
Propjet engines	
aircraft	629.134 353 2
Proportion	
architectural design	
horizontal plane	729.23
vertical plane	729.13

Proportion (Mathematics)	512.924
algebra	512.924
arithmetic	513.24
Proportional counters	
nuclear physics	539.773
Proportional representation	324.63
legislatures	328.334 7
law	342.053
Proportional taxation	336.293
Propositional calculus	511.3
Propositions	
logic	160
Proprietary libraries	027.2
Proprietor's income	
macroeconomics	339.21
Proprietorships	338.72
accounting	657.91
economics	338.72
management	658.041
initiation	658.114 1
Proprioceptive organs	
human anatomy	611.8
human physiology	612.88
see also Nervous system	
Proprioceptive perception	
psychology	152.188
Propulsion systems	621.4
air-cushion vehicles	629.314
spacecraft	629.475
unmanned spacecraft	629.465
Prorocentrales	589.43
Prose literature	808.888
specific literatures	T3B—808
individual authors	T3A—8
Prosecution	345.050 42
Prosencephalon	
human physiology	612.825
see also Nervous system	
Prosimii	599.81
paleozoology	569.8
Proso	584.92
food crop	633.171 7
forage crop	633.257 17
Prosobranchia	594.32
paleozoology	564.32
Prosodic analysis (Linguistics)	414.6
specific languages	T4—16
Prosody	808.1
Prosopora	595.146
Prospecting	622.1
Prospectors	622.109 2
occupational group	T7—622
Prosperity	
economics	338.542
Prostate	
human anatomy	611.63
human diseases	
medicine	616.65

Protons	539.721 2
Protoplasm	574.873
Prototheria	599.1
paleozoology	569.12
Protozoa	593.1
medical microbiology	616.016
paleozoology	563.1
Protozoan diseases	
agriculture	632.631
incidence	614.53
medicine	616.936
plant husbandry	632.631
see also Communicable	
diseases (Human)	
Protozoologists	593.109 2
occupational group	T7—593
Protungulata	569.75
Protura	595.712
paleozoology	565.71
Proustite	
mineralogy	549.35
Provençal language	449
	T6—491
Provençal literature	849
Provence (France)	T2—449
Provence-Côte d'Azur	
(France)	T2—449
Proverbs	398.9
Proverbs (Biblical book)	223.7
Providence (R.I.)	T2—745 2
Providence County (R.I.)	T2—745 1
Providence Islands	T2—696
Providence of God	214.8
Christianity	231.5
comparative religion	291.211
Providencia (Columbia)	T2—861 8
Provident societies	334.7
economics	334.7
Providential societies	
insurance	368
see also Insurance	
Province of Canada	971.04
	T2—71
Provinces (Central governments)	
public administration	351
Provinces (Local governments)	
administration	352.007 3
government	320.83
Provincial administration	
central governments	351
governments	352.007 3
Provincial banks	332.122 4
Provincial-local relations	
law	342.042
public administration	351.093
Provincial planning	
civic art	711.3
economics	338.9
Provincialisms	
linguistics	417.2
specific languages	T4—7
Provisional courts	342.062
Prowers County (Colo.)	T2—788 98
Proximity topology	514.323
Proxy	
law	346.066 6
Prudence	179.9
see also Virtues	
Pruning	631.542
equipment manufacturing	
technology	681.763 1
silviculture	634.953
Prussia	T2—43
Prussia, East (Poland)	T2—438 3
Prussia, West (Poland)	T2—438 2
Prussian language, Old	491.91
	T6—919 1
Prussian Saxony	T2—431 8
Prymnesiales	589.487
Przemysl (Poland :	
Voivodeship)	T2—438 6
Psalms	223.2
music	782.294
choral and mixed voices	782.529 4
single voices	783.092 94
Psalteries	787.75
see also Stringed instruments	
Psalters	264.1
Anglican	264.030 1
texts	264.038
Roman Catholic	264.020 1
texts	264.028
PSAT (Aptitude test)	378.166 2
Pseudepigrapha	229.9
Pseudo-Demetrius I, Czar of	
Russia	
Russian history	947.045
Pseudo-Demetrius II, Czar of	
Russia	
Russian history	947.045
Pseudo gospels	229.8
Pseudoanalytic functions	515.98
Pseudoborniales	561.72
Pseudomonadaceae	589.95
Pseudomorphism	
crystallography	548.3
Pseudonymous works	
bibliographies	014
Pseudoscorpiones	595.47
paleozoology	565.4
Psi phenomena	133.8
Psilomelane	
mineralogy	549.53
Psilophytales	561.74
Psilopsida	587.4
paleobotany	561.74

Pteropoda	594.35
paleozoology	564.35
Pterosauria	567.97
Pterostemonaceae	583.397
Pterygota	595.7
paleozoology	565.7
Ptilogonatidae	598.853
Ptolemies reign (Egyptian	
history)	932.021
Puberty	612.661
customs	392.14
etiquette	395.24
human physiology	612.661
music	781.583
Public accounting	657.61
see also Government	
accounting	
Public address systems	
engineering	621.389 2
office use	651.79
Public administration	350
armed forces	355.6
central governments	351
ethics	172.2
see also Political ethics	
local governments	352
Public administrators	350.000 92
biography	350.000 92
central governments	351.000 92
local governments	352.000 92
investigation	350.992
central governments	351.992
local governments	352.002
law	342.068
lists	350.2
central governments	351.2
local governments	352.005 2
occupational group	T7—35
Public behavior	
customs	390
etiquette	395.53
Public bills	
enactment	328.378
Public borrowing	336.34
see also Public debt	
Public buildings	
law	343.025 6
public works	350.862
central governments	351.862
local governments	352.5
Public carriers	
sanitation services	363.729 3
see also Waste control	
Public colleges	378.05
Public contracts	346.023
Public corporations	
law	346.067

Public credit	
public finance	336.3
Public debt	336.34
administration	350.72
central governments	351.72
local governments	352.1
law	343.037
macroeconomic policy	339.523
public finance	336.34
Public defenders	345.01
Public education	371.01
finance	379.11
government policy	379.2
government supervision	379.15
law	344.071
Public enterprise	338.62
organization of production	338.62
Public enterprises	338.74
production economics	338.74
public administration	350.009 2
central governments	351.009 2
local governments	352.009
public revenue source	336.19
Public entertainment	
ethics	175.1
see also Recreation—ethics	
music	781.55
Public expenditures	336.39
law	343.034
macroeconomic policy	339.522
public administration	350.72
central governments	351.72
local governments	352.1
public finance	336.39
Public expenditures limitation	
law	343.034
Public finance	336
administration	350.72
central governments	351.72
cabinet departments	351.02
local governments	352.1
economics	336
law	343.03
Public forests	
land economics	333.11
Public health	362.1
international law	341.765
law	344.04
medicine	614
public administration	350.841
central governments	351.841
local governments	352.944 1
social welfare	362.1
Public health law	344.04
Public health nursing	
medicine	610.734
Public health offenses	364.142
Public housekeeping	647

Public toilets	363.729 4
technology	628.45
Public transportation vehicles	388.34
driving	629.283 3
engineering	629.222 3
transportation services	388.34
Public universities	378.05
Public utilities	363.6
accounting	657.838
area planning	711.7
law	343.09
public administration	350.87
central governments	351.87
local governments	352.91
social services	363.6
Public utility workers	363.609 2
occupational group	T7—363 6
Public welfare	361.6
law	344.031 6
see also Welfare services	
Public works	363
public administration	350.86
central governments	351.86
cabinet departments	351.086
local governments	352.7
public law	343.025 6
social law	344.06
Public worship	291.38
Buddhism	294.343 8
Christianity	264
in Sunday schools	268.7
flower arrangements	745.926
Hinduism	294.538
Islam	297.38
Judaism	296.4
music	782.3
choral and mixed voices	782.53
single voices	783.093
see also Worship	
Publicity	659
Publishers	070.509 2
occupational ethics	174.909 7
occupational group	T7—097
relations with authors	070.52
Publishers' catalogs	015
Publishing	070.5
journalism	070.5
law	343.099 8
library services	025.12
Pubs	647.95
architecture	725.72
Puddings	641.864
home preparation	641.864
Puddling (Furnace practice)	669.141 4
Puebla (Mexico : State)	T2—724 8
Pueblo County (Colo.)	T2—788 55
Puerperal diseases	
obstetrics	618.7
Puerperal perticemia	
obstetrics	618.74
Puerperal pyemia	
incidence	614.545
obstetrics	618.74
Puerperal septicemia	
incidence	614.545
obstetrics	618.74
Puerperium	
obstetrics	618.6
Puerto Plata (Dominican Republic)	T2—729 358
Puerto Rican literature	860
Puerto Ricans	T5—687 295
Puerto Rico	972.95
	T2—729 5
Puffballs	589.221
Puffbirds	598.72
Puffer	597.58
Puffins	598.33
Pug (Dog)	
animal husbandry	636.76
see also Dogs	
Puget Sound (Wash.)	551.466 32
	T2—164 32
Puglia (Italy)	T2—457 5
ancient	T2—377
Pulaski County (Ark.)	T2—767 73
Pulaski County (Ga.)	T2—758 523
Pulaski County (Ill.)	T2—773 998
Pulaski County (Ind.)	T2—772 925
Pulaski County (Ky.)	T2—769 63
Pulaski County (Mo.)	T2—778 57
Pulaski County (Va.)	T2—755 775
Puli	
animal husbandry	636.737
see also Dogs	
Pullovers	391
commercial technology	687.146
customs	391
home sewing	646.454
see also Clothing	
Pulmonary embolisms	
medicine	616.249
see also Respiratory system	
Pulmonary tuberculosis	
incidence	614.542
medicine	616.995 24
see also Communicable diseases (Human)	
Pulmonary valve	
human anatomy	611.12
human diseases	
medicine	616.125
human physiology	612.17
see also Cardiovascular system	
Pulmonata	594.38
paleozoology	564.38

Pulp	676.1
Pulp industry workers	676.109 2
occupational group	T7—676
Pulpboards	676.183
Pulpit platforms	
architecture	726.593
Pulpits	
church architecture	726.529 2
Pulpwood	
forest products	634.983
Pulque	641.23
commercial processing	663.49
Pulsars (Stars)	523.887 4
Pulsating radio stars	523.887 4
Pulsating variables (Stars)	523.844 25
Pulsations (Geomagnetism)	538.744
Pulse	
human physiology	612.14
musical element	781.222
see also Cardiovascular system	
Pulse circuits	
electronic circuits	621.381 534
Pulse detectors	
electronic circuits	621.381 536 5
Pulse generators	
electronic circuits	621.381 534
Pulse-jet engines	
aircraft	629.134 353 6
Pulse-modulated radar systems	
engineering	621.384 85
Pulse modulators	
electronic circuits	621.381 536 5
Pulse processes	
electronics	621.381 534
Pumice	553.65
petrology	552.23
Pumping stations	
sewer engineering	628.29
water-supply engineering	628.144
Pumpkin	641.356 2
botany	583.46
commercial processing	664.805 62
cooking	641.656 2
garden crop	635.62
Pumps	621.69
hydraulic	621.252
ships	623.873
Punch cards	004.56
electronic data processing	004.56
nonelectronic data processing	004.9
Punched card readers	004.76
computer engineering	621.398 6
Punches	641.875
home preparation	641.875
Punching tools	621.96
Punctuation	411
specific languages	T4—11

Puncture wounds	
medicine	617.143
Punic language	492.6
	T6—926
Punic Wars, 264-146 B.C.	937.04
Punicaceae	583.44
Punishment	
armed services	355.133 25
law	345.077
penology	364.6
prisons	365.644
social control	303.36
social theology	291.178 336
Christianity	261.833 6
Punjab (India)	T2—545 52
Punjab (India : Province)	T2—545
Punjab (India : State, 1947-	
1966)	T2—545 5
Punjab (Pakistan)	T2—549 14
Punjabi language	491.42
	T6—914 2
Punjabis (South Asian people)	T5—914 2
Puno (Peru : Dept.)	T2—853 6
Puntarenas (Costa Rica :	
Province)	T2—728 67
Punting (Boating)	797.123
Punting (Kicking)	
American football	796.332 27
Punu language	496.396
	T6—963 96
Puppet films	791.433
Puppet masters	791.530 92
occupational group	T7—791 5
Puppet plays	
production scripts	791.538
Puppeteers	791.530 92
occupational group	T7—791 5
Puppetry	791.53
Christian religious education	268.67
Christian religious use	246.7
Puppets	791.53
making	688.722 4
handicrafts	745.592 24
technology	688.722 4
performing arts	791.53
Puranas	294.592 5
Purari River (Gulf Province,	
Papua New Guinea)	T2—954 7
Purbeck (England : District)	T2—423 36
Purcell Mountains (B.C. and	
Mont.)	T2—711 65
Purchase contracts	
accounting	657.75
materials management	658.723
Purchase of real property	
law	346.043 62
Purchasing	658.72
Purchasing manuals	T1—029 7

Purchasing power
  cost of living   339.42
  income-consumption relations   339.41
  value of money   332.41
Purchasing power parity   332.456
Pure food control   363.192
  see also Food—product safety
Pure Land Buddhism   294.392 6
Pure sciences   500
Purgatives
  pharmacodynamics   615.732
  see also Digestive system
Purgatory   291.23
  Christianity   236.5
Purification
  oils and gases   665.028 3
  petroleum distillates   665.534
Purified pulp   676.4
Purim   296.436
  customs   394.268 296 436
Purines   547.596
  chemical engineering   661.894
Puritanism   285.9
  doctrines   230.59
  moral theology   241.045 9
  persecution of others   272.8
Puritans
  biography   285.909 2
  religious group   T7—25
Purple bacteria   589.9
Purposive psychology   150.193
Purses   391.44
  customs   391.44
  manufacturing technology   685.51
Purslane   583.152
Pursuit (Law enforcement)   363.232
Pursuit forces (Air warfare)   358.43
Pursuit planes   358.428 3
  engineering   623.746 4
  military equipment   358.428 3
Push-button systems
  wireless   384.535
Push-button telephone systems
  communication services   384.65
Pushball   796.33
Pushmataha County (Okla.)   T2—766 65
Pushto language   491.593
                                           T6—915 93
Puss in corner   796.14
Pustular eruptions
  medicine   616.52
  result of injury
    medicine   617.22
  see also Skin
Put   332.645
  multiple forms of investment   332.645
  stocks   332.632 28

Put and call transactions   332.645
  multiple forms of investment   332.645
  stocks   332.632 28
Putnam County (Fla.)   T2—759 17
Putnam County (Ga.)   T2—758 576
Putnam County (Ill.)   T2—773 375
Putnam County (Ind.)   T2—772 49
Putnam County (Mo.)   T2—778 232
Putnam County (N.Y.)   T2—747 32
Putnam County (Ohio)   T2—771 18
Putnam County (Tenn.)   T2—768 67
Putnam County (W. Va.)   T2—754 35
Putonghua (Standard Chinese
    language)   495.1
                                           T6—951 1
Putters (Golf equipment)   796.352 35
Putting   796.352 35
Putumayo (Colombia :
    Intendancy)   T2—861 63
Puy-de-Dôme (France)   T2—445 91
Puzzles   793.73
PWV area (South Africa)   T2—682 2
Pycnodontiformes   567.4
Pycnogonida   595.394
  paleozoology   565.394
Pyelitis
  medicine   616.613
  see also Urinary system
Pyelocystitis
  medicine   616.613
  see also Urinary system
Pyelonephritis
  medicine   616.613
  see also Urinary system
Pyemia
  incidence   614.577
  medicine   616.944
  puerperal diseases
    incidence   614.545
    obstetrics   618.74
  see also Communicable
    diseases (Human)
Pygmies (African people)   T5—96
Pylorus
  human anatomy   611.33
  surgery   617.553
  see also Digestive system
Pyometra
  gynecology   618.142
  see also Female genital system
Pyorrhea
  dentistry   617.632
  see also Dentistry
Pyralididoidea   595.781
Pyramid power   001.94
Pyramids   516.15
Pyramids (Marketing)
  management   658.84

Qualifications of employees
  personnel management
    public administration (continued)
      local governments   352.005 132
Qualitative analysis   544
  organic   547.34
Quality control
  production management   658.562
  statistical mathematics   519.86
Quality engineering   620.004 5
Quality of life   306
Quality of work life   306.361
  labor economics   331.25
Quality standards
  commerce   389.63
Quangos   350.009
  central governments   351.009
  local governments   352.009
Quantitative analysis   545
  organic   547.35
Quantity
  philosophy   119
Quantity standards
  commerce   389.62
Quantity surveying   692.5
    T1—029 9
Quantity theory
  monetary economics   332.401
Quantock Hills   T2—423 85
Quantum chemistry   541.28
Quantum chromodynamics   539.754 8
Quantum electrodynamics   537.67
Quantum electronics   537.5
Quantum field theory   530.143
Quantum flavor   539.721 67
Quantum mechanics   530.12
Quantum physics   539
Quantum statistical mechanics   530.133
Quantum statistics   530.133
Quantum theory   530.12
Quantum theory of light   535.15
Quarantine
  disease control   614.46
  law   344.043
Quarks   539.721 67
Quarter (War)
  law   341.65
Quarter horse
  animal husbandry   636.133
  zoology   599.725
Quarters (Time interval)   529.2
Quarters for military personnel   355.71
Quartets
  chamber music   785.14
  vocal music   783.14
Quartic equations   512.942
  algebra   512.942
  calculus   515.252

Quartz
  materials science   620.198
  mineralogy   549.68
Quartzites   552.4
Quasars   523.115
Quasi-administrative bodies
  public administration   350.009
    central governments   351.009
    local governments   352.009
Quasi contract   346.029
Quasi-stellar sources   523.115
Quaternary period   551.79
  geology   551.79
  paleontology   560.178
Quaternions   512.5
Quay County (N.M.)   T2—789 26
Quays   387.15
  engineering   627.31
  see also Port facilities
Queanbeyan (N.S.W.)   T2—944 7
Quebec (Province)   971.4
    T2—714
Québec (Quebec)   T2—714 471
Québec (Quebec :
    Administrative region)   T2—714 47
Québec (Quebec : County)   T2—714 47
Quebec Act, 1774   971.022
Quebec Conference, 1864   971.049
Quebec Urban Community
  (Quebec)   T2—714 471
Quechua Indians   T5—983
Quechua language   498.323
    T6—983 23
Quechua literature   898.323
Quechumaran languages   498.323
    T6—983 23
Queen Anne architecture   720.942 090 33
Queen Anne's County (Md.)   T2—752 34
Queen Anne's lace   583.48
Queen Anne's War, 1701-1714   940.252 6
  North American history   973.25
Queen bees
  apiculture   638.145
Queen Charlotte Islands
  (B.C.)   T2—711 12
Queen Charlotte Sound (B.C.)   551.466 33
    T2—164 33
Queen Charlotte Strait (B.C.)   551.466 33
    T2—164 33
Queen Maud Land   T2—989
Queens (Chessmen)   794.146
Queens (N.B.)   T2—715 42
Queens (New York, N.Y.)   T2—747 243
Queens (P.E.I.)   T2—717 4
Queen's Bench Division of High
    Court of Justice (Great
    Britain)   347.420 27

R

R.H. factor
  human physiology   612.118 25
  incompatibility
    pediatrics   618.921 5
    perinatal medicine   618.326 1
  see also Cardiovascular system
R.I.F. (Personnel management)   658.313 4
  public administration   350.184
    central governments   351.184
    local governments   352.005 184
R.N.A. (Genetics)   574.873 283
R.O.M. (Computer memory)   004.53
  engineering   621.397 3
R.O.T.C. (Reserve training)   355.223 207 11
R.S.F.S.R. (Russia)   947
    T2—47
R.V. (Vehicle)   388.346
  engineering   629.226
  see also Motorized homes
Rababs   787.6
  see also Stringed instruments
Rabat (Morocco)   T2—643
Rabat-Sale (Morocco :
  Prefecture)   T2—643
Rabaul (Papua New Guinea)   T2—958 5
Rabbis   296.092
  role and function   296.61
  specific sects   296.8
Rabbit Ears Range   T2—788 65
Rabbit hair textiles   677.35
  see also Textiles
Rabbits   599.322
  agricultural pests   632.693 22
  animal husbandry   636.932 2
  small game hunting   799.259 322
Rabies
  incidence   614.563
  medicine   616.953
  see also Communicable
    diseases (Human)
Rabun County (Ga.)   T2—758 123
Raccoon River   T2—777 46
Raccoons   599.744 43
Race
  physical ethnology   572
Race discrimination   305.8
  law   342.087 3
Race discrimination in
  employment
  law   344.016
Race relations   305.8
  social theology   291.178 348
    Christianity   261.834 8
Race tracks
  animals
    horses   798.400 68
  architecture   725.89
  automobiles   796.720 68

Race walking   796.429
Racehorses
  animal husbandry   636.12
  zoology   599.725
Racemization   541.7
Races (Physical ethnology)   572
Races (Sports)   796
  see also Racing
Racial characteristics
  physical ethnology   572.2
Racial conflict   305.8
  influence on crime   364.256
Racial differences
  psychology   155.82
Racial discrimination   305.8
Racial groups   305.8
    T1—089
    T7—03
  legal status   342.087 3
  psychology   155.82
  see also Ethnic groups
Racial minorities   305.8
  see also Ethnic groups
Racine County (Wis.)   T2—775 96
Racing   796
  aircraft   797.52
  animals   798
    dogs   798.8
    horses   798.4
  automobiles   796.72
  bicycles   796.62
  boats   797.14
  ethics   175.7
    see also Recreation—ethics
  human   796.42
  midget cars   796.76
  motor scooters   796.75
  motor vehicles   796.7
  motorcycles   796.75
  soapboxes   796.6
Racing animals
  care and training   636.088 8
Racing cars   796.72
  driving   629.284 8
  engineering   629.228
  repair   629.287 8
  sports   796.72
  toys   790.133
    recreation   790.133
Racism   305.8
  ethics   177.5
    see also Ethical problems
  political ideology   320.56
  social theology   291.178 348
    Christianity   261.834 8

Radio drama
  literature   808.822 2
    history and criticism   809.222
    specific literatures   T3B—202 2
      individual authors   T3A—2
    rhetoric   808.222
Radio engineers   621.384 092
  occupational group   T7—621 3
Radio evangelism   269.26
Radio-frequency spectroscopes
  manufacturing technology   681.414 8
Radio-frequency spectroscopy
  engineering   621.361 5
  physics   537.534
Radio industry
  law   343.099 45
Radio music   781.544
Radio news   070.194
Radio plays
  literature   808.822 2
    history and criticism   809.222
    specific literatures   T3B—202 2
      individual authors   T3A—2
    rhetoric   808.222
Radio programs   384.544 3
  broadcasting   384.544 3
  performing arts   791.44
Radio relay
  telephone engineering   621.387 82
Radio scripts
  rhetoric   808.066 791
Radio stations   384.545 3
  engineering   621.384
  facilities   384.545 3
    architecture   725.23
  organizations   384.540 65
Radio telescopes
  astronomy   522.682
Radio towers
  architecture   725.23
Radio waves   537.534
  biophysics   574.191 51
    human   612.014 481
  physics   537.534
  propagation and transmission   621.384 11
Radioactivation analysis   543.088 2
Radioactive fallout   363.738
  physics   539.753
  social problem   363.738
  see also Pollution
Radioactive materials
  public safety   363.179 9
Radioactive wastes   363.728 9
  air pollution
    environmental engineering   628.535
  law   344.046 22
  social services   363.728 9
  technology   621.483 8

Radioactive wastes (continued)
  water pollution
    environmental engineering   628.168 5
  see also Waste control
Radioactivity   539.752
  physics   539.752
Radioactivity prospecting   622.159
Radiobiology   574.191 5
  human   612.014 48
Radiobroadcasting   384.54
  see also Radio
Radiochemical analysis   543.088
Radiochemistry   541.38
  chemical engineering   660.298
Radiocommunication   384.5
  see also Radio
Radioelements   539.752
Radiogenetics   575.131
  animals   591.159 2
  plants   581.159 2
Radiographic testing
  materials science   620.112 72
Radiography
  engineering   621.367 3
Radioimmunoassay
  medicine   616.075 7
Radioisotope scanning
  medicine   616.075 75
Radioisotopes   539.752
  chemical engineering   660.298 84
  chemistry   541.388 4
  physics   539.752
  technology   621.483 7
  therapeutic use   615.842 4
Radiolaria   593.14
  paleozoology   563.14
Radiology
  medicine   616.075 7
Radiology services   362.177
  see also Health services
Radiolysis
  chemical engineering   660.298 2
  radiochemistry   541.382
Radionuclides   539.752
Radios   621.384 18
  automobile   629.277
Radioscopic diagnosis
  medicine   616.075 7
Radioscopic urinalysis
  medicine   616.075 7
Radiosondes
  weather reporting   551.635 2
Radiotelegraphy   384.52
  communication services   384.52
  engineering   621.384 2
  military engineering   623.734 2
  see also Radio

Radiotelephony	384.53
communication services	384.53
engineering	621.384 5
military engineering	623.734 5
see also Radio	
Radiotherapy	
medicine	615.842
Radishes	641.351 5
botany	583.123
commercial processing	664.805 15
cooking	641.651 5
garden crop	635.15
Radium	669.725
chemical engineering	661.039 6
chemistry	546.396
economic geology	553.493
metallurgy	669.725
toxicology	615.925 396
see also Chemicals	
Radium therapy	
medicine	615.842 3
Radius (Bone)	
human anatomy	611.717
see also Musculoskeletal system	
Radnor (Wales)	T2—429 54
Radom (Poland : Voivodeship)	T2—438 4
Radon	
air pollution	363.738
see also Pollution	
air pollution technology	628.535
chemistry	546.756
economic geology	553.97
gas technology	665.822
see also Chemicals	
Rae (N.W.T.)	T2—719 3
Rae Lakes (N.W.T.)	T2—719 3
Raetia	T2—363
Raffia	584.5
fiber crop	633.58
textiles	677.54
see also Textiles	
Raffia work	
arts	746.41
Raft zithers	787.73
see also Stringed instruments	
Rafts	386.229
design	623.812 9
engineering	623.829
transportation services	386.229
Rag pulp	676.13
Rāgas	781.264
Ragoli-Kuria languages	496.395
	T6—963 95
Ragtime	781.64
Ragusa (Sicily : Province)	T2—458 15
Ragweed	583.55
Rahway (N.J.)	T2—749 36

Rail fastenings	
railroad engineering	625.15
Rail transit services	388.42
see also Local rail transit systems	
Railings	
church architecture	726.529 6
Railroad accidents	363.122
see also Transportation safety	
Railroad buildings	385.314
architecture	725.33
see also Railroad terminals	
Railroad construction workers	625.100 92
occupational group	T7—625
Railroad crossings	385.312
engineering	625.163
transportation services	385.312
Railroad engineers	625.100 92
occupational group	T7—625
Railroad freight stations	385.314
architecture	725.32
see also Railroad terminals	
Railroad insurance	
inland marine	368.233
see also Insurance	
Railroad law	343.095
Railroad mail	383.143
see also Postal service	
Railroad passenger stations	385.314
architecture	725.31
see also Railroad terminals	
Railroad police	363.287 4
Railroad post offices	383.42
see also Postal service	
Railroad safety	363.122
law	343.095
see also Transportation safety	
Railroad terminals	385.314
architecture	725.31
area planning	711.75
engineering	625.18
special purpose	625.3–.6
law	343.095 2
transportation services	385.314
special purpose	385.5
urban	388.472
Railroad ties	625.143
Railroad tracks	
engineering	625.14
Railroad transportation	385
engineering	625.1
international law	341.756 5
law	343.095
local transit	388.42
see also Local rail transit systems	
public administration	351.875
transportation services	385

Railroad transportation workers	385.092	Raleigh County (W. Va.)	T2—754 73
occupational group	T7—385	Rallies (Automobile sport)	796.73
Railroad workers	385.092	Ralls County (Mo.)	T2—778 355
construction	625.100 92	RAM (Computer memory)	004.53
occupational group	T7—625	engineering	621.397 3
occupational group	T7—385	Rama I, King of Siam	
Railroad yards	385.314	Thai history	959.303 1
engineering	625.18	Rama II, King of Siam	
law	343.095 2	Thai history	959.303 2
transportation services	385.314	Rama III, King of Siam	
Railroads	385	Thai history	959.303 3
electrification		Rama IV, King of Siam	
technology	621.33	Thai history	959.303 4
engineering	625.1	Rama V, King of Siam	
landscape architecture	713	Thai history	959.303 5
law	343.095	Rama VI, King of Siam	
military engineering	623.63	Thai history	959.304 1
mining	622.66	Rama VII, King of Siam	
transportation services	385	Thai history	959.304 2
Rails (Birds)	598.31	Rama VIII, King of Thailand	
Rails (Railroads)	625.15	Thai history	959.304 3
Railton (Tas.)	T2—946 5	Rama IX, King of Thailand	
Rain	551.577	Thai history	959.304 4
meteorology	551.577	Ramadan	297.36
weather forecasting	551.647 7	Islamic moral theology	297.53
weather modification	551.687 7	Ramakrishna movement	294.555
Rain damage		Raman effect	535.846
agriculture	632.16	Raman spectroscopes	
Rainbows	551.567	manufacturing technology	681.414 6
Raincoats	391	Raman spectroscopy	543.085 84
commercial technology	687.145	chemical analysis	543.085 84
customs	391	engineering	621.361 3
home sewing	646.453	physics	535.846
see also Clothing		Ramanujacharya (Philosophy)	181.483
Rainfall	551.577	Ramapithicus	569.9
Rains County (Tex.)	T2—764 275	Ramayana	294.592 2
Rainstorms		Rameses II, King of Egypt	
social services	363.349 2	Egyptian history	932.014
see also Disasters		Ramie	583.962
Rainy Lake	T2—776 79	fiber crop	633.55
Rainy River (Minn. and Ont.)	T2—776 79	textiles	677.15
Rainy River (Ont. : District)	T2—713 117	*see also* Textiles	
Raised-character publications		Ramjet engines	
cataloging	025.349 2	aircraft	629.134 353 5
library treatment	025.179 2	Ramos, Nereu	
publishing	070.579 2	Brazilian history	981.062
Rajasthan (India)	T2—544	Ramps	721.83
Rajasthani language	491.479	architecture	721.83
	T6—914 79	canal engineering	627.135 3
Rajasthani literature	891.479	construction	690.183
Rajasthani-speaking people	T5—914 7	Ramses II, King of Egypt	
Rajiformes	597.35	Egyptian history	932.014
paleozoology	567.3	Ramsey County (Minn.)	T2—776 58
Rājshāhi District		Ramsey County (N.D.)	T2—784 36
(Bangladesh)	T2—549 24	Ramu River	T2—957 3
Raleigh (N.C.)	T2—756 55	Ranales	583.111
Raleigh Bay	551.461 48	Ranch-style houses	
	T2—163 48	architecture	728.373

Ras Tafari
  Ethiopian history (continued)
    as regent and king   963.054
Ras Tafari movement   299.67
Raspberries   641.347 11
  botany   583.372
  commercial processing   664.804 711
  cooking   641.647 11
  horticulture   634.711
Rasps   621.924
Rastafari, Jah
  Ethiopian history   963.055
    as emperor   963.055
    as regent and king   963.054
Rat control   363.78
  social welfare   363.78
  technology   628.969 3
    agriculture   632.693 233
  see also Pest control
Ratchet wheels   621.837
Ratchets   621.837
  music   786.886
    see also Percussion
      instruments
Rates
  communication industry   384.041
  insurance   368.011
  transportation services   388.049
Rates (United Kingdom)   336.22
  law   343.054 2
  public finance   336.22
Ratio   512.924
  algebra   512.924
  arithmetic   513.24
Ration coupons
  prints   769.57
Rational functions   512.96
Rational psychology   150.192
Rationalism   149.7
  Christian polemics   239.7
  Islamic polemics   297.297
  natural religion   211.4
  philosophy   149.7
  political ideology   320.512
Rationality   121
  philosophical anthropology   128.3
Rationing   333.717
  law   343.07
  public administration   350.829
    central governments   351.829
    local governments   352.942
  social welfare   361.6
Ratites   598.5
  paleozoology   568.5
Rats   599.323 3
  animal husbandry   636.932 33
  experimental animals
    medicine   619.93

Rats (continued)
  pest control   363.78
    social welfare   363.78
    technology   628.969 3
      agriculture   632.693 233
    see also Pest control
Ratsiraka, Didier
  Malagasy history   969.105
Rattan   584.5
Rattan furniture   645.4
  manufacturing technology   684.106
  see also Furniture
Rattan textiles   677.54
  see also Textiles
Rattle drums   786.96
  see also Percussion instruments
Rattled idiophones   786.885
  see also Percussion instruments
Rattles   786.885
  see also Percussion instruments
Rattlesnake fern   587.33
Rauwolfia   583.72
  agriculture   633.883 72
Ravalli County (Mont.)   T2—786 89
Ravenna (Italy : Province)   T2—454 7
Ravens   598.864
Ravines   551.44
    T2—144
  geography   910.914 4
  geomorphology   551.44
  physical geography   910.021 44
Raw materials   333.7
  economics   333.7
  military resources   355.24
Rawalpindi District (Pakistan)   T2—549 142
Rawlings, Jerry J.
  Ghanaian history   966.705
Rawlins County (Kan.)   T2—781 125
Ray County (Mo.)   T2—778 19
Rayon
  textiles   677.46
    arts   746.044 6
    see also Textiles
Rays (Fish)   597.35
  commercial fishing   639.273 5
Rays (Nuclear physics)   539.722
Razgrad (Bulgaria : Okrug)   T2—497 77
Razgradski okrug (Bulgaria)   T2—497 77
Razing buildings   690.26
Razorback swine
  animal husbandry   636.484
  zoology   599.734
Razors
  manufacturing technology   688.5
RDX (Explosives)   662.27
Reaction cross sections (Nuclear
  particles)   539.75

Reasoning	153.43
educational psychology	370.152 4
logic	160
psychology	153.43
subconscious	154.24
Rebates	
law	343.072
Rebellion	364.131
law	345.023 1
Recall	324.68
chief executives	324.68
public administration	350.003 6
central governments	351.003 6
local governments	352.008
Recall (Information science)	025.04
Recall (Memory)	153.123
Recataloging	
library science	025.393
Receivership	
accounting	657.47
credit economics	332.75
law	346.078
Receiving operations	
materials management	658.728
Receiving sets	
radio	621.384 18
Recent epoch	551.793
geology	551.793
paleontology	560.178
Receptionists	
office services	651.374 3
Receptions	
meal service	642.4
Receptive processes (Psychology)	152.1
Recession (Economics)	338.542
Recherche, Archipelago of the	T2—941 7
Recidivists	364.3
	T1—086 92
law	345.03
see also Offenders	
Recipes	T1—021 2
cooking	641.5
Reciprocal equations	515.253
Reciprocal trade	382.9
law	343.087
Reciprocating engines	
aircraft	629.134 352
Reciprocating pumps	621.65
hydraulic	621.252
Reciprocating steam engines	621.164
Reciprocity (Mathematics)	
number theory	512.74
Recitals	
music	780.78
Recitation	
rhetoric	808.54
teaching method	371.37
Recitations	
literature	808.854
history and criticism	809.54
specific literatures	T3B—504
individual authors	T3A—5
Recklinghausen's disease	
medicine	616.993 83
see also Diseases (Human)	
Reclaimed rubber	678.29
Reclaimed water	
recharge of groundwater	627.56
Reclamation	
agriculture	631.6
hydraulic engineering	627.5
Reclamation from sea	
engineering	627.54
Reclassification	
library operations	025.396
Recognition (International law)	341.26
Recognition (Psychology)	153.124
Recognition of unions	331.891 2
Recoil	
military gunnery	623.57
Recombinant DNA	
biology	575.107 24
biotechnology	660.65
Recombination	
genetics	575.13
Reconciliation (Christian doctrine)	234.5
Reconnaissance (Military operations)	355.413
Reconnaissance aircraft	358.458 3
military engineering	623.746 7
military equipment	358.458 3
Reconnaissance forces (Air warfare)	358.45
Reconnaissance topography	
military engineering	623.71
Reconstruction (Aftermath of war)	355.028
United States history	973.8
World War I	940.314 4
World War II	940.531 44
Reconstructionist Judaism	296.834 4
Record buildings	
architecture	725.15
Recorded programs	
radio performances	791.443
Recorders (Musical instruments)	788.36
see also Woodwind instruments	
Recording	
accounting	657.2
music	781.49
Recording devices	621.382 34
physical quantities	530.7
manufacturing technology	681.2

Recordings
  communication services
    commercial — 384
Recordings (Sound) — 621.389 32
  bibliographies — 011.38
  cataloging — 025.348 2
  education — 371.333 2
  engineering — 621.389 32
  library treatment — 025.178 2
  music — 780
    cover illustration — 741.66
    treatises — 780.266
  reviews — 028.138
Records management — 651.5
  office services — 651.5
  public administration — 350.714
    see also Public records
Recovery
  economics — 338.542
Recovery (Law) — 346.043 2
Recreation — 790
  armed forces — 355.346
  child care — 649.5
  church work — 259.8
  crime prevention — 364.44
  ethics — 175
    religion — 291.565
      Christianity — 241.65
  human physiology — 612.044
  influence on crime — 364.25
  prisoner services — 365.66
  public administration — 350.858
    central governments — 351.858
    local governments — 352.945 8
  sociology — 306.48
Recreation centers — 790.068
  architecture — 725.804 2
  construction — 690.580 42
  recreation — 790.068
Recreation facilities — 790.068
  architecture — 725.8
  community redevelopment — 307.346
  construction — 690.58
  public works — 350.863 5
    central governments — 351.863 5
    local governments — 352.735
  recreation — 790.068
  sanitation services — 363.729 2
  social services — 363.68
Recreation leaders — 790.092
  occupational group — T7—79
Recreation safety — 363.14
  law — 344.047 6
Recreational areas — 643.55
  area planning — 711.558
  home economics — 643.55
  residential interior decoration — 747.791

Recreational arts — 790
  see also Arts, Recreation
Recreational equipment
  manufacturing technology — 688.7
Recreational equipment makers — 688.709 82
  occupational group — T7—688
Recreational land use
  community sociology — 307.334
Recreational lands — 333.78
  economics — 333.78
Recreational music — 781.594
Recreational reading — 790.138
  library science — 028.8
Recreational therapy
  medicine — 615.851 53
Recreational vehicles — 388.346
  engineering — 629.226
  pleasure driving — 796.79
  transportation services — 388.346
  see also Motorized homes
Recreational water resources — 333.784
Recreational waters
  hydraulic engineering — 627.046
Recruitment
  armed forces — 355.223
    law — 343.012
  personnel management — 658.311 1
    executives — 658.407 111
    libraries — 023.9
  public administration — 350.131
    central governments — 351.131
    local governments — 352.005 131
Rectal anesthesia
  surgery — 617.962
Rectifiers
  electrical engineering — 621.313 7
  electronic circuits — 621.381 532 2
  radio engineering — 621.384 12
Rectilinear propagation of light — 535.322
Rectum
  human anatomy — 611.35
  human diseases
    medicine — 616.35
  human physiology — 612.36
  surgery — 617.555
  see also Digestive system
Recurrent education — 374
Recursion theory — 511.35
Recursive functions — 511.35
Recurvirostridae — 598.33
Recycling paper — 676.142
Recycling technology — 628.445 8
Recycling waste — 363.728 2
  social services — 363.728 2
  see also Waste control
Red algae — 589.41
Red Cliffs (Vic.) — T2—945 9

Red clover	583.322
forage crop	633.327
Red corpuscles	
human histology	611.018 5
human physiology	612.111
see also Cardiovascular system	
Red Crescent	361.763 4
Red Cross	361.77
international	361.77
national	361.763 4
South African War	968.048 7
Vietnamese War	959.704 37
World War I	940.477 1
World War II	940.547 71
Red Cross nursing	
medicine	610.734
Red Deer (Alta.)	T2—712 33
Red Deer River (Alta. and	
Sask.)	T2—712 33
Red ironwood	583.167
Red jasmine	583.72
Red Lake County (Minn.)	T2—776 963
Red meats	641.36
commercial processing	664.92
home preservation	641.492
see also Meat	
Red peppers	583.79
Red River (Minn.-Man.)	T2—784 1
Manitoba	T2—712 74
Minnesota	T2—776 9
North Dakota	T2—784 1
Red River (Tex.-La.)	T2—766 6
Louisiana	T2—763 6
Oklahoma	T2—766 6
Red River County (Tex.)	T2—764 212
Red River of the North	T2—784 1
Manitoba	T2—712 74
Minnesota	T2—776 9
North Dakota	T2—784 1
Red River Parish (La.)	T2—763 64
Red River Rebellion, 1869-1870	971.051
Red Sea	551.467 33
	T2—165 33
Red Sea (Sudan : Province)	T2—625
Red Sea Province (Egypt)	T2—623
Red seaweed	589.41
Red tide	589.43
Red Willow County (Neb.)	T2—782 843
Red wine	641.222 3
commercial processing	663.223
sparkling	641.222 4
commercial processing	663.224
Redaction criticism (Bible)	220.66
Redbridge (London, England)	T2—421 73
Redbud	583.323
Reddersburg (South Africa :	
District)	T2—685 6
Redditch (England)	T2—424 43

Redemption	291.22
Christian doctrines	234.3
Christology	232.3
Judaism	296.32
Redemption (Public debt)	
public finance	336.363
Redemptorists	255.64
church history	271.64
Redevelopment	
community sociology	307.34
Redfish	597.58
fishing	639.275 8
Rediscount	332.84
Redistricting (Legislatures)	328.334 5
Redtop	584.93
forage crop	633.237
Reducing	
dietetics	613.25
for appearance	646.75
Reducing enzymes	574.192 58
see also Enzymes	
Reducing solutions	
photography	771.54
Reduction (Chemical reaction)	541.393
engineering	660.284 43
organic chemistry	547.23
Reduction in force	
economics	
conditions of employment	331.25
unemployment	331.137
law	344.012 596
personnel management	658.313 4
public administration	350.184
central governments	351.184
local governments	352.005 184
Reductionism (Psychology)	150.194
Reductive algebras	512.55
Reduvioidea	595.754
Redwood	585.2
forestry	634.975 8
lumber	674.144
Redwood County (Minn.)	T2—776 35
Redwood National Park	
(Calif.)	T2—794 12
Reed instruments	788.4
see also Woodwind instruments	
Reed organs	786.55
see also Keyboard instruments	
Reedfish	597.42
Reeds	584.9
fiber crop	633.58
Reef biology	574.91
Reef ecology	574.526 367
Reefs	551.424
	T2—142
geography	910.914 2
geomorphology	551.424
physical geography	910.021 42

Reformed Church (American
    Reformed) (continued)
  theology   230.57
Reformed Church in America   285.732
  see also Reformed Church
    (American Reformed)
Reformed Church in the United
  States   285.733
  see also Reformed Church
    (American Reformed)
Reformed Episcopal Church   283.3
  see also Anglican Communion
Reformed Hinduism   294.556
Reformed natural gas   665.773
Reformed Presbyterian churches   285.136
  see also Presbyterian Church
Reformed refinery gas   665.773
Refraction
  acoustical engineering   620.21
  astronomy
    corrections   522.9
Refraction errors
  optometry   617.755
    incidence   614.599 7
  see also Eyes
Refraction of heat   536.32
Refraction of light   535.324
Refractivity
  materials science   620.112 95
Refractometric analysis   543.085 3
Refractory materials   553.67
  economic geology   553.67
  materials science   620.143
  metallurgical furnaces   669.82
  technology   666.72
Refrigerants
  refrigeration engineering   621.564
Refrigerating foods   664.028 52
  commercial preservation   664.028 52
  home preservation   641.452
Refrigeration   621.56
  alcoholic beverages   663.15
  ships   623.853 5
Refrigeration engineers   621.560 92
  occupational group   T7—621
Refrigerator cars   385.34
  engineering   625.24
  see also Rolling stock
Refrigerators
  kitchen appliances   641.452 028
    manufacturing technology   683.88
  low-temperature engineering   621.57
Refugees   325.21
  citizenship law   342.083
  Civil War (United States)   973.715 9
  immigration law   342.082
  international law   341.486
  Mexican War   973.621

Refugees (continued)
  political science   325.21
  social welfare   362.87
  South African War   968.048 1
  Spanish-American War, 1898   973.891
  Vietnamese War   959.704 31
  War of 1812   973.521
  World War I   940.315 9
  World War II   940.531 59
Refugio County (Tex.)   T2—764 119
Refuse   363.728
  military sanitation   623.754
  waste technology   628.44
    rural   628.744
  see also Waste control
Regals   786.55
  see also Keyboard instruments
Regeneration   574.31
  animals   591.31
  cells   574.876 1
  developmental biology   574.31
  plants   581.31
Regeneration (Christian doctrine)   234.4
Regensburg (Germany)   T2—433 47
Regents
  occupational group   T7—351 1
  public administration   351.003 12
Reggae   781.64
Regge poles   539.721
Reggio di Calabria (Italy :
    Province)   T2—457 83
Reggio Emilia (Italy :
    Province)   T2—454 3
Reggio nell'Emilia (Italy :
    Province)   T2—454 3
Regiments (Military units)   355.31
Regina (Sask.)   T2—712 445
Région parisienne (France)   T2—443 6
Regional anatomy
  animals   591.49
  human   611.9
  plants   581.49
Regional anesthesia
  surgery   617.964
Regional bibliographies   015
Regional development
  law   343.074 6
  public administration   351.818
Regional international
    organizations
  public administration   354.104
Regional medicine   617.5
  geriatrics   618.977 5
  pediatrics   618.920 975
Regional physiology   574.104 2
  animals   591.104 2
  human   612.9
  plants   581.104 2

Remount services (Horse cavalry)	357.2
Removal from office recall elections	324.68
Renaissance architecture	724.12
Renaissance art	709.024
religious significance	246.4
Renaissance decoration	745.443
Renaissance music	780.903 1
Renaissance painting	759.03
Renaissance period (European history)	940.21
Italian history	945.05
Renaissance revival architecture	724.52
Renaissance sculpture	735.21
Renal disease	
medicine	616.61
see also Urinary system	
Renal failure	
medicine	616.614
see also Urinary system	
Renal hypertension	
medicine	616.132
see also Cardiovascular system	
Rendering oils and gases	665.028 2
Rendezvous	
manned space flight	629.458 3
Renewable energy resources	333.794
economics	333.794
engineering	621.042
Renewal theory	519.287
Renfrew (Ont. : County)	T2—713 81
Renfrew (Scotland : District)	T2—414 41
Rengao language	495.93
	T6—959 3
Renmark (S. Aust.)	T2—942 33
Reno (Nev.)	T2—793 55
Reno County (Kan.)	T2—781 83
Renovation	
home economics	643.7
Rensselaer County (N.Y.)	T2—747 41
Rent	
income distribution	
macroeconomics	339.21
land economics	333.012
law	346.043 44
public revenue	336.11
Rent control	
law	346.043 44
Rental collections	
museology	069.56
Rental libraries	027.3
Rental services	
museology	069.13
Rental subsidies	363.582
see also Housing	
Renting	
land economics	333.5

Renting homes	643.12
Renunciation of citizenship	323.623
Renville County (Minn.)	T2—776 34
Renville County (N.D)	T2—784 64
Reorganization	
management	658.16
public administration	350.007 3
central governments	351.007 3
local governments	352.000 473
Reorganized Church of Jesus Christ of Latter Day Saints	289.333
see also Mormon Church	
Repairs	620.004 6
	T1—028 8
library materials	025.7
Reparations	
law of war	341.66
revenue source	336.182
World War I	940.314 22
World War II	940.531 422
Reparative surgery	617.95
Repatriation	323.64
Repeal of laws	328.37
Repentance	291.22
Christianity	234.5
Islam	297.22
Judaism	296.32
Repetition learning	
psychology	153.152 2
Report literature	
cataloging	025.343 6
library treatment	025.173 6
Reporters	070.430 92
occupational group	T7—097
Reporting	
executive management	658.45
public administration	350.007 6
central governments	351.007 6
local governments	352.000 476
financial management	658.151 2
journalism	070.43
Reports	
audits	657.452
financial management	658.151 2
office records	651.78
Repoussé	
decorative arts	739.14
sculpture	731.41
Representation	324.63
electoral politics	324.63
political right	323.5
Representation in legislative bodies	328.334
Representation theory	515.722 3
Representations	
arts	704.9
number theory	512.72
Repression	323.044

Reserves (Capital management)	658.152 26
Reserves (Natural resources)	333.711
Reservoir engineering	
oil extraction	622.338 2
Reservoirs	627.86
flood control	627.44
landscape architecture	719.33
recreational resources	333.784 6
recreational use	797
water-supply engineering	628.132
Resettlement	
community sociology	307.2
housing services	363.583
see also Housing	
Residency (Training)	T1—071 55
Residential buildings	643.1
architecture	728
construction	690.8
economics	
sale and rental	333.338
home economics	643.1
interior decoration	747
sanitation services	363.729 8
see also Waste control	
Residential cities	
area planning	711.45
Residential finance	332.722
Residential land	333.77
area planning	711.58
community sociology	307.336
resource economics	333.77
taxation	336.225
Residents (Students)	
training	T1—071 55
Residues	
petroleum	665.538 8
wood	674.84
Residues (Mathematics)	512.72
Resignation (Military personnel)	355.114
Resignation of chief executives	
public administration	350.003 6
central governments	351.003 6
local governments	352.008
Resignation of employees	
personnel management	658.313
public administration	350.18
central governments	351.18
local governments	352.005 18
Resin-derived plastics	668.45
Resin-producing insects	
culture	638.3
Resin-producing plants	
agriculture	633.895
Resins	582.019 2
biochemistry	582.019 2
chemistry	547.843 4
commercial processing	668.37
fossil	553.29

Resins (continued)	
materials science	620.192 4
recovery from pulp	676.5
Resist-dyeing	
textile arts	746.66
Resistance	
materials science	620.112
Resistance meters	621.374 2
Resistance to electricity	537.62
Resistance to government	323.044
Resistance warfare	355.021 8
Resistance welding	671.521 3
Resistant construction	
buildings	693.8
ship hulls	623.848
Resistivity	
skin	
human physiology	612.791
see also Skin	
Resistivity in semiconductors	537.622 6
Resistivity prospecting	622.154
Resistivity to electricity	537.62
Resistors	
radio engineering	621.384 133
Resolute (N.W.T.)	T2—719 5
Resolutions (Legislation)	
enactment	328.377
Resonance	
musical technique	781.48
instrumental	784.193 2
Resonance accelerators	539.733
Resorcinols	547.633
Resource development	
international banking	332.153
natural resources	333.715
Resource recovery	363.728 2
see also Waste control	
Resources	
education	T1—07
military science	355.2
natural	333.7
see also Natural resources	
study and teaching	T1—07
Respiration	574.12
animals	591.12
cytology	574.876 4
human physiology	612.2
microorganisms	576.112
plants	581.12
see also Respiratory system	
Respiratory allergies	
medicine	616.202
see also Respiratory system	
Respiratory diseases	
medicine	616.2
see also Respiratory system	
Respiratory organs	574.12
anatomy	574.42

Respiratory organs (continued)
  animal anatomy   591.42
  human physiology   612.2
  physiology   574.12
  plant anatomy   581.42
  see also Respiratory system
Respiratory system   591.12
  animal anatomy   591.42
  animal diseases   591.212
  animal histology   591.824
  animal physiology   591.12
  cancer   362.196 994 2
    medicine   616.994 2
    social services   362.196 994 2
    see also Cancer
  geriatrics   618.976 2
  human anatomy   611.2
  human diseases   362.196 2
    incidence   614.592
    medicine   616.2
    social services   362.196 2
  human histology   611.018 92
  human physiology   612.2
  nursing   610.736 92
  pediatrics   618.922
  pharmacodynamics   615.72
  surgery   617.54
  veterinary medicine   636.089 62
Respiratory therapy
  medicine   615.836
Responsa
  Judaistic sources   296.179
Responses
  music   782.292
Responsibility
  executive management   658.402
  law   346.03
Responsive readings
  public worship
    Christianity   264.4
Rest
  human physiology   612.76
  physical fitness   613.79
Rest areas
  road engineering   625.77
Rest homes   362.16
  see also Health care facilities,
    Health services
Rest periods
  labor economics   331.257 6
Restaurant cooking   641.572
Restaurant meal service   642.5
Restaurants   647.95
  accounting   657.837
  architecture   725.71
  area planning   711.557
  household management   647.95

Restaurateurs   647.950 92
  occupational group   T7—642
Restigouche (N.B.)   T2—715 11
Restigouche River (N.B. and
  Quebec)   T2—715 11
Restionaceae   584.45
Restitution
  law of war   341.66
Restitution coefficient   531.382
Restoration
  arts   702.88
  museology   069.53
  natural resources   333.715 3
Restoration (British history)   941.066
Restoration (English history)   942.066
Restoration (French history)   944.06
Restoration (Scottish history)   941.106 6
Restoration of wooden furniture   684.104 42
Restorative surgery   617.95
Restoring torques
  aeronautics   629.132 364
Restormel (England .
  Borough)   T2—423 72
Restraint of trade (Competition)   338.604 8
  commercial law   343.072
    international   341.753
  criminal law   345.026 8
  criminology   364.168
  economics   338.604 8
  law   343.072 3
Restrictive environments
  psychology   155.96
Restrictive practices   338.82
  economics   338.82
  international economics   338.884
Rests (Music)   781.236
Resurfacing
  road maintenance   625.761
Resurrection   291.23
  Christianity   236.8
  Islam   297.23
  Judaism   296.33
Resurrection of Jesus Christ   232.5
  life   232.97
Resurrection plant   587.9
Resuscitation
  therapeutics   615.804 3
Retail advertising   659.131 4
Retail credit
  marketing management   658.883
Retail marketing   381.1
  management   658.87
  see also Commerce
Retail salesmanship   658.85
  etiquette   395.53

Retail trade	381.1	Retirement guides	
law	343.088 7	personal living	646.79
marketing management	658.87	Retirement income	
see also Commerce		pensions	331.252
Retail trade buildings		*see also* Pensions	
architecture	725.21	tax economics	336.242 8
Retained profits		tax law	343.052 4
capital formation	332.041 52	Retracts	514.24
Retaining walls	721.2	Retraining	
architecture	721.2	labor economics	331.259 24
construction	690.12	personnel management	658.312 43
railroad engineering	625.13	social welfare	362.042 5
structural engineering	624.164	Retreats (Military tactics)	355.422
see also Walls (Building		Retreats (Religion)	
element)		Christianity	269.6
Retalhuleu (Guatemala :		Retribution	
Dept.)	T2—728 183	penology	364.601
Retarded children	305.908 26	Retrieval of information	
	T1—087 4	computer science	005.74
Retarded persons	305.908 26	information science	025.524
	T1—087 4	Retrievers	
see also Mentally retarded		animal husbandry	636.752
persons		*see also* Dogs	
Retarding		Retrospective conversion	
agriculture	631.583	machine-readable catalog	
Retention (Memory)	153.122	records	025.317 3
Rethymnē (Greece : Nome)	T2—499 8	Retroviruses	576.648 4
Reticular tissues		medical microbiology	616.019 4
human histology	611.018 2	Returned merchandise	
Reticuloendothelial system		marketing management	658.812
human immunology	616.079	Réunion	969.81
Reticulosis			T2—698 1
medicine	616.156	Revegetation	631.64
see also Cardiovascular system		Revelation (Biblical book)	228
Retinas		Revelation of God	212.6
human anatomy	611.84	Bible	220.13
human diseases		Christianity	231.74
incidence	614.599 7	comparative religion	291.211
ophthalmology	617.73	Revelstoke (B.C.)	T2—711 68
human physiology	612.843	Revenue	336.02
see also Eyes		financial management	658.155 4
Retired persons	305.906 96	law	343.034
	T1—086 96	public administration	350.726
psychology	155.672	central governments	351.726
Retirement	306.38	local governments	352.14
armed forces	355.114	public finance	336.02
financial planning	332.024 01	Revenue cutters	363.286
personnel management	658.313 2	design	623.812 63
public administration	350.182	engineering	623.826 3
central governments	351.182	police services	363.286
local governments	352.005 182	Revenue estimates	
psychology	155.672	public administration	350.722 252
sociology	306.38	central governments	351.722 252
Retirement age		local governments	352.122 52
economics	331.252	Revenue offenses	364.133
Retirement benefits	331.252	law	345.023 3
Retirement enterprises			
management	658.041		

Rheumatic fever
  incidence — 614.597 23
  medicine — 616.991
  pediatrics — 618.929 91
  see also Communicable
    diseases (Human)
Rheumatic heart disease
  medicine — 616.127
  see also Cardiovascular system
Rheumatism
  medicine — 616.723
  see also Musculoskeletal system
Rheumatoid arthritis
  medicine — 616.722 7
  see also Musculoskeletal system
Rheumatology — 616.723
  see also Musculoskeletal system
Rhinbund — 943.06
Rhine, Confederation of the — 943.06
Rhine Province (Germany) — T2—434 3
Rhine River (Germany) — T2—434
Rhineland-Palatinate
  (Germany) — T2—434 3
Rhinencephalon
  human physiology — 612.825
  see also Nervous system
Rhinoceroses — 599.728
  big game hunting — 799.277 28
Rhinology — 616.212
  see also Respiratory system
Rhizobiaceae — 589.95
Rhizocephala — 595.35
  paleozoology — 565.35
Rhizochloridales — 589.486
Rhizochrysidales — 589.487
Rhizodiniales — 589.43
Rhizomastigida — 593.18
Rhizophoraceae — 583.42
Rhizopodea — 593.11
Rhizopus — 589.258
Rhizostomeae — 593.73
Rhode Island — 974.5
  T2—745
Rhode Island Reds
  animal husbandry — 636.584
  see also Chickens
Rhode Island Sound — 551.461 46
  T2—163 46
Rhodes (Greece : Island) — T2—499 6
  ancient — T2—391 6
Rhodesia (1964-1980) — 968.910 4
  T2—689 1
Rhodesia and Nyasaland — 968.903
  T2—689
Rhodesian man — 573.3
Rhodesian ridgeback
  animal husbandry — 636.753
  see also Dogs

Rhodesians — T5—968 91
Rhodium — 669.7
  chemical engineering — 661.063 4
  chemistry — 546.634
  metallography — 669.957
  metallurgy — 669.7
  metalworking — 673.7
  physical metallurgy — 669.967
  see also Chemicals
Rhodochaetales — 589.41
Rhodochrosite
  mineralogy — 549.782
Rhododendron — 583.62
  floriculture — 635.933 62
Rhodonite
  mineralogy — 549.66
Rhodope (Greece) — T2—495 7
Rhodope Mountains — T2—497 75
Rhodophyta — 589.41
Rhodymeniales — 589.41
Rhoeadales — 583.122
Rhoipteleaceae — 583.973
Rhondda (Wales) — T2—429 72
Rhône (France) — T2—445 82
Rhône-Alpes (France) — T2—445 8
Rhône River (Switzerland and
  France) — T2—445 8
Rhubarb — 641.354 8
  botany — 583.917
  commercial processing — 664.805 48
  cooking — 641.654 8
  garden crop — 635.48
Rhuddlan (Wales : Borough) — T2—429 32
Rhumb line course
  celestial navigation — 527.53
Rhyme — 808.1
Rhymes
  folk literature — 398.8
Rhyming — 808.1
Rhyming dictionaries — 413.1
  specific languages — T4—31
Rhyming games — 398.8
Rhymney Valley (Wales :
  District) — T2—429 76
Rhynchocephalia — 597.945
  paleozoology — 567.945
Rhynchocoela — 595.124
  paleozoology — 565.1
Rhynocheti — 598.31
Rhysodoidea — 595.762
Rhythm
  harmonic — 781.256
  musical element — 781.224
Rhythm (Linguistics) — 414.6
  specific languages — T4—16
Rhythm and blues — 781.643
Rhythm bands — 784.68

Riddles	398.6
folk literature	398.6
recreation	793.735
Ridesharing	388.413 212
Riding-club buildings	
architecture	725.88
Riding horses (Breeds)	
animal husbandry	636.13
zoology	599.725
Riding horses (Recreation)	798.23
Riel's Rebellion, 1869-1870	971.051
Riel's Rebellion, 1885	971.054
Riemann integral	515.43
Riemann surfaces	515.223
Riemannian geometry	516.373
Riemannian hypothesis	512.73
Riesz spaces	515.73
Riet River	T2—685 7
Rieti (Italy : Province)	T2—456 24
RIF (Personnel management)	658.313 4
public administration	350.184
central governments	351.184
local governments	352.005 184
Rif language	493.3
	T6—933
Rif Mountains (Morocco)	T2—642
Rifles	683.422
art metalwork	739.744 25
manufacturing technology	683.422
military engineering	623.442 5
military equipment	355.824 25
shooting game	799.213
sports	799.202 832
target shooting	799.31
Rift Valley Province (Kenya)	T2—676 27
Rift valleys	551.87
Rifts (Geology)	551.87
Riga, Gulf of	551.461 34
	T2—163 34
Rigging equipment	
aircraft	629.134 37
Right and wrong	170
religion	291.5
Christianity	241
Right-hand techniques	
music	784.193 67
Right of assembly	323.47
law	342.085 4
Right of association	323.47
Right of asylum	323.631
international law	341.488
law	342.083
Right of petition	323.48
law	342.085 4
Right of privacy	323.448
Right of way	346.043 5
Right to bear arms	323.43
Right to counsel	345.056

Right to die	
ethics	179.7
medical	174.24
see also Death—ethics	
law	344.041 97
Right to education	
law	344.079
Right to hold office	323.5
Right to information	323.445
law	342.066 2
Right to learn	
law	344.079
Right to life	323.43
Right to representation	323.5
Right to strike	331.892 01
Right to vote	324.62
law	342.072
Right to work	331.889 2
government policy	331.898
Right whales	599.51
Righteousness (Christian	
doctrines)	234
Rightist parties	324.213
international organizations	324.13
Rights of mankind	323
Rigid bodies	
mechanics	531
Rigidity	
materials science	620.112 5
Rigveda	294.592 12
Riksmal language	439.82
	T6—398 2
Riksmal literature	839.82
Riley County (Kan.)	T2—781 28
Rime	551.574 4
Rimouski (Quebec : County)	T2—714 771
Rimouski-Neigette (Quebec)	T2—714 771
Ringgold County (Iowa)	T2—777 873
Ringkobing amt (Denmark)	T2—489 5
Rings (Jewelry)	391.7
customs	391.7
making	739.278
see also Jewelry	
Rings (Mathematics)	512.4
number theory	512.74
Rings (Planets)	523.98
Ringworm	
medicine	616.57
see also Skin	
Rinks	
architecture	725.86
Rinzai	294.392 7
Rio Arriba County (N.M.)	T2—789 52
Rio Blanco County (Colo.)	T2—788 15
Rio Branco (Brazil :	
Territory)	T2—811 4
Rio de Janeiro (Brazil : State)	T2—815 3
Río de la Plata	982.024

Riveting	671.59	Roads (continued)	
decorative arts	739.14	public administration	350.864 2
sculpture	731.41	central governments	351.864 2
ship hulls	623.843 2	local governments	352.74
Riveting equipment	621.978	transportation services	388.1
Rivets	621.884	urban	388.411
Riviera	T2—449	use	
France	T2—449	urban	388.413 14
Italy	T2—451 8	Roadside areas	
Rivière-du-Loup (Quebec :		engineering	625.77
County)	T2—714 76	Roadside barriers	625.795
Rivière-du-Loup (Quebec :		Roadside shrines	
Regional County		architecture	726.9
Municipality)	T2—714 76	Roadside signs	
Rivière-du-Nord (Quebec)	T2—714 24	outdoor advertising	659.134 2
Rizal (Philippines : Province)	T2—599 1	Roadsteads	
Rize Ili (Turkey)	T2—566 2	hydraulic engineering	627.2
RNA (Genetics)	574.873 283	Roane County (Tenn.)	T2—768 84
Road accidents	363.125	Roane County (W. Va.)	T2—754 36
see also Transportation safety		Roanoke (Va.)	T2—755 791
Road camps		Roanoke County (Va.)	T2—755 792
penology	365.34	Roanoke Island (N.C.)	T2—756 175
see also Correctional		Roanoke River (Va. and N.C.)	T2—756 16
institutions		North Carolina	T2—756 16
Road engineers	625.709 2	Virginia	T2—755 6
occupational group	T7—625	Roarers (Musical instruments)	783.99
Road maintenance	625.761	Roasters	
Road oils	665.538 8	electric cooking	641.586
Road repair	625.761	Roasting	
Road safety	363.125	home cooking	641.71
see also Transportation safety		Robben Island (South Africa)	T2—687 35
Road tests		Robber flies	595.771
automotive	629.282 4	Robbery	364.155 2
Road transportation	388.31	law	345.025 52
international law	341.756 8	Robbery insurance	368.82
law	343.094	*see also* Insurance	
public administration	350.878 31	Robbins Island	T2—946 7
central governments	351.878 31	Robert-Cliche (Quebec)	T2—714 71
local governments	352.918 31	Robert II, King of France	
urban	388.413 1	French history	944.021
Roadability tests		Roberts County (S.D.)	T2—783 12
automotive	629.282 5	Roberts County (Tex.)	T2—764 818
Roadbeds		Robertson (South Africa :	
railroad engineering	625.123	District)	T2—687 3
interurban railroads	625.65	Robertson County (Ky.)	T2—769 415
local railroads	625.65	Robertson County (Tenn.)	T2—768 464
road engineering	625.733	Robertson County (Tex.)	T2—764 239
Roadrunners	598.74	Robeson County (N.C.)	T2—756 332
Roads	388.1	Robins (American)	598.842
agricultural use	631.28	Robinson Gorge National	
area planning	711.7	Park	T2—943 5
engineering	625.7	Robinvale (Vic.)	T2—945 9
forestry	634.93	Robotics	629.892
land economics	333.11	engineering	629.892
landscape architecture	713	Robots	629.892
law	343.094 2	engineering	629.892
military engineering	623.62	factory operations engineering	670.427 2
		social effects	303.483 4

Rodents (continued)
pest control	363.78
social welfare	363.78
technology	628.969 3
agriculture	632.693 23
see also Pest control	
Rodeos	791.84
Rodopi (Greece)	T2—495 7
Rodopi Mountains	T2—497 75
Rodrigues Island (Mauritius)	T2—698 2
Rodríguez, Abelardo L.	
(Abelardo Luján)	
Mexican history	972.082 44
Rods	624.177 4
music	786.82
concussed	786.872
friction	786.862
set	786.862
single	786.888
percussed	786.842
set	786.842
single	786.884 2
plucked	786.85
set	786.85
single	786.887
see also Percussion	
instruments	
structural engineering	624.177 4
Roentgenology	
medicine	616.075 72
Rogaland fylke (Norway)	T2—483
Roger Mills County (Okla.)	T2—766 16
Rogers County (Okla.)	T2—766 94
Roggeveld Range	T2—687 17
Rogue River (Or.)	T2—795 21
Role conflict	302.15
Role playing	
psychiatry	616.891 523
see also Mental illness	
Role-playing games	793.93
Role theory	302.15
Rolette County (N.D.)	T2—784 592
Roll (Aeronautics)	629.132 364
Roll on/roll off shipping	387.544 2
Roller bearings	621.822
Roller painting	751.49
Roller skates	
manufacturing technology	685.362
Roller skating	796.21
Rollers (Agricultural tools)	
manufacturing technology	681.763 1
Rollers (Birds)	598.892
Rolling metals	671.32
decorative arts	739.14
sculpture	731.41
Rolling stock	385.37
engineering	625.2
law	343.095 5

Rolling stock (continued)
military	358.25
engineering	623.633
mining	622.66
monorail	385.5
engineering	625.28
operation	385.204 4
production economics	338.476 252
public administration	351.875 37
rapid transit	388.42
engineering	625.4
special purpose	385.5
engineering	625.3–.6
transportation services	385.37
Rolls	641.815
commercial processing	664.752
cooking	641.815
Rolong (African people)	T5—963 977 5
Rolong dialect	496.397 75
	T6—963 977 5
ROM (Computer memory)	004.53
engineering	621.397 3
Roma (Italy)	T2—456 32
ancient	T2—376
Roma (Italy : Province)	T2—456 3
Roma (Qld.)	T2—943 4
Roman architecture	722.7
Roman calligraphy	745.619 78
Roman Catholic cathedrals	
architecture	726.64
Roman Catholic Church	282
canon law	262.9
church government	262.02
parishes	254.02
conversion to	248.242
doctrines	230.2
catechisms and creeds	238.2
general councils	262.52
guides to Christian life	248.482
Inquisition	272.2
liturgy	264.02
missions	266.2
moral theology	241.042
papacy	262.13
persecution under Queen	
Elizabeth	272.7
public worship	264.02
religious associations	267.182
religious education	268.82
religious orders	255
church history	271
schools	377.82
seminaries	207.112
social teaching	261
theology	230.2
Roman Catholic sacred music	781.712
public worship	782.322 2
music	782.322 2

Roofing	695
Roofing paper	676.289
Roofing tiles	666.732
Roofs	721.5
architecture	721.5
construction	690.15
Rooks (Birds)	598.864
Rooks (Chessmen)	794.143
Rooks County (Kan.)	T2—781 18
Rooming houses	647.94
Roosevelt, Franklin D. (Franklin	
Delano)	
United States history	973.917
Roosevelt, Theodore	
United States history	973.911
Roosevelt County (Mont.)	T2—786 22
Roosevelt County (N.M.)	T2—789 32
Root canal surgery	617.634 205 9
see also Dentistry	
Root celery	641.351 28
botany	583.48
see also Celeriac	
Root crops	
agriculture	635.1
cooking	641.651
food	641.351
Root extraction (Mathematics)	512.923
arithmetic	513.23
Roots (Mathematics)	
number theory	512.72
Roots (Plants)	
anatomy	581.498
physiology	581.104 28
Rope climbing	796.46
Roper River	T2—942 95
Ropes	677.71
knotting and splicing	623.888 2
materials science	620.197
power transmission	621.853
sculpture material	731.2
ship gear	623.862
structural engineering	624.189 7
Roraima (Brazil)	T2—811 4
Rorquals	599.51
Rorschach personality theory	155.264
Rorschach tests	155.284 2
Rosaceae	583.372
Rosales	583.37
Rosary	242.74
Roscher, Wilhelm	
economic school	330.154 2
Roscommon (Ireland :	
County)	T2—417 5
Roscommon County (Mich.)	T2—774 76
Rosé	641.222 3
commercial processing	663.223
Rose apples	583.42
Rose chafers	595.764 9
Rose of Sharon	583.17
Roseau County (Minn.)	T2—776 98
Rosebery (Tas.)	T2—946 6
Rosebud (Vic.)	T2—945 2
Rosebud County (Mont.)	T2—786 32
Rosemaling	745.723
Rosemarie	583.87
Roses	583.372
floriculture	635.933 72
Roses, Wars of the, 1455-1485	942.04
Rosetta stone	493.1
Rosh Hashanah	296.431
customs	394.268 296 431
Rosicrucianism	135.43
Rosicrucians	135.430 92
social group	T7—13
Roskilde amt (Denmark)	T2—489 1
Ross and Cromarty (Scotland)	T2—411 72
Ross County (Ohio)	T2—771 82
Ross Sea	551.469 4
	T2—167 4
Rossarden (Tas.)	T2—946 4
Rossendale (Borough)	T2—427 63
Rossland (B.C.)	T2—711 62
Rostock (Germany : Bezirk)	T2—431 74
Rostov (R.S.F.S.R. : Oblast)	T2—477 7
Rostovskaia oblast	
(R.S.F.S.R.)	T2—477 7
Rostral furniture	
church architecture	726.529 2
Rot	
agricultural diseases	632.4
materials science	620.112 23
Rotary blowers	621.62
Rotary fans	621.62
Rotary files (Records	
management)	651.54
Rotary International	369.5
Rotary International members	369.5
social group	T7—369 5
Rotary pumps	621.66
hydraulic	621.252
Rotary steam engines	621.166
Rotation	
celestial bodies	521
earth	525.35
solid mechanics	531.34
sun	523.73
Rotation groups	512.2
Rotation of crops	
cultivation technique	631.582
economics	338.162
soil conservation	631.452
Rotational flow	532.052
gas mechanics	533.21
liquid mechanics	532.51
ROTC (Reserve training)	355.223 207 11

Rubber industry workers	678.209 2
occupational group	T7—678
Rubber plant (Moraceae)	583.962
Rubber-stamp printing	761
Rubber stamps	
manufacturing technology	681.6
Rubber tree	583.95
Euphorbiaceae	583.95
rubber crop	633.895 2
Rubbings	
graphic arts	760
research technique	739.522
Rubella	
incidence	614.524
medicine	616.916
see also Communicable	
diseases (Human)	
Rubeola	
incidence	614.523
medicine	616.915
pediatrics	618.929 15
see also Communicable	
diseases (Human)	
Rubiales	583.52
Rubidium	669.725
chemical engineering	661.038 4
chemistry	546.384
metallurgy	669.725
see also Chemicals	
Rubies	553.84
economic geology	553.84
jewelry	739.27
mining	622.384
synthetic	666.88
Rubus berries	583.372
horticulture	634.71
Rudders	623.862
aircraft	629.134 33
Rudolf, Lake (Kenya and	
Ethiopia)	T2—676 27
Rudolf II, Holy Roman Emperor	
German history	943.034
Rue (Plant)	583.24
Rugby	796.333
Rugby (England : Borough)	T2—424 85
Rugby players	796.333 092
sports group	T7—796 33
Rugs	645.1
arts	746.7
building construction	698.9
household management	645.1
interior decoration	747.5
manufacturing technology	677.643
Ruhr River (Germany)	T2—435 5
Ruiz Cortines, Adolfo	
Mexican history	972.082 8
Rukwa Region (Tanzania)	T2—678 28
Rule of law	340.11

Rule of the road at sea	
international law	341.756 66
maritime safety technology	623.888 4
transportation law	343.096 6
Ruled surfaces	516.362
Rules of order	060.42
legislatures	328.1
Rum	641.259
commercial processing	663.59
Rumania	949.8
	T2—498
ancient	939.8
	T2—398
Rumanians	T5—59
Rumba form	784.188 8
Ruminantia	599.735
see also Ruminants	
Ruminants	599.735
animal husbandry	636.2
paleozoology	569.73
Rummy	795.418
Rumor	
social psychology	302.24
Runaway young people	305.906 9
	T1—086 9
social group	305.906 9
social welfare	362.74
Rundi (African people)	T5—963 946 5
Rundi language	496.394 65
	T6—963 946 5
Rundi literature	896.394 65
Runes	430
divination	133.33
Runnels County (Tex.)	T2—764 724
Runners (Athletes)	796.420 92
sports group	T7—796 4
Runners (Plants)	
floriculture	635.946
plant propagation	631.533
Running	
human	796.42
physical fitness	613.717 2
sports	796.42
Running boards	629.26
Running gear	
railroad engineering	625.21
Running myrtle (Periwinkle)	583.72
Runnymede (England)	T2—422 11
Runoff (Hydrology)	551.488
Runways (Airports)	
engineering	629.136 3
military airports	623.663
Rupert's Land	971.201
	T2—712
Ruppiaceae	584.742
Rupture strength	
materials science	620.112 6
Rupununi (Guyana : District)	T2—881 8

Rwanda	967.571
	T2—675 71
Rwanda language	496.394 61
	T6—963 946 1
Rwandans	T5—967 571
Ryazan (R.S.F.S.R. : Oblast)	T2—473 1
Rye	641.331 4
botany	584.93
commercial processing	664.725
cooking	641.631 4
food crop	633.14
forage crop	633.254
Ryedale (England : District)	T2—428 46
Ryukyu Islands	T2—522 9
Ryukyuans	T5—956
Ryutekis	788.32
see also Woodwind instruments	
Rzeszow (Poland :	
Voivodeship)	T2—438 6

S

S.A.T. (Aptitude test)	378.166 2
S.D.I. (Information service)	025.525
S.D.I. (Strategic Defense	
Initiative)	358.174
S.E.A.T.O. (Alliance)	355.031 095 9
S.I. (Metric system)	530.812
physics	530.812
social aspects	389.15
S.I.D.S. (Syndrome)	
pediatrics	618.92
S.T.D. (Diseases)	
incidence	614.547
medicine	616.951
see also Communicable	
diseases (Human)	
S.T.O.L. airplanes	
engineering	629.133 340 426
Saanich (B.C.)	T2—711 28
Saanich Peninsula (B.C.)	T2—711 28
Saar River (France and	
Germany)	T2—434 2
Saarbrücken (Germany)	T2—434 21
Saarland (Germany)	T2—434 2
Saba (Netherlands Antilles)	T2—729 77
Sabah	T2—595 3
Sabbath	296.41
Christianity	263.1
Judaism	296.41
Sabbatianism	296.82
Sabbaticals	331.257 63
economics	331.257 63
Sabellian languages	479.7
	T6—797
Sabellian literatures	879.7
Sabellianism	273.3

Sabers	623.441
art metalwork	739.722
Sabiaceae	583.28
Sabie (South Africa)	T2—682 6
Sabie River	T2—682 6
Sabine County (Tex.)	T2—764 177
Sabine Lake	T2—763 52
Sabine language	479.7
	T6—797
Sabine Parish (La.)	T2—763 62
Sabine River (Tex. and La.)	T2—764 14
Sable Island (N.S.)	T2—716 99
Sables	599.744 47
Sabotage	364.164
labor economics	331.893
law	345.026 4
military science	355.343 7
Sabrata (Ancient city)	T2—397 4
Sac County (Iowa)	T2—777 424
Sac fungi	589.23
Sacatepéquez (Guatemala)	T2—728 162
Saccharides	574.192 48
biochemistry	574.192 48
chemistry	547.78
see also Carbohydrates	
Saccharolytic enzymes	574.192 54
see also Enzymes	
Saccharomycetaceae	589.233
Sachs Harbour (N.W.T.)	T2—719 6
Sackville (N.B.)	T2—715 23
Sacoglossa	594.35
paleozoology	564.35
Sacramental furniture	247.1
architecture	726.529 1
Sacramentals	264.9
Sacramentaries	
Roman Catholic	264.020 36
texts	264.023
Sacramento (Calif.)	T2—794 54
Sacramento County (Calif.)	T2—794 53
Sacramento Mountains	T2—789 65
Sacramento River (Calif.)	T2—794 5
Sacramento Valley	T2—794 5
Sacraments	234.16
public worship	265
Anglican	264.030 8
texts	264.035
Roman Catholic	264.020 8
texts	264.025
Sacred books	291.82
Buddhism	294.382
Christianity	220
Latter-Day Saints	289.32
Hinduism	294.592
Islam	297.12
Judaism	296.1
Bible	221

Sailing on ice	796.97
Sailing on land	796.6
Sailing ships	387.204 3
design	623.812 043
engineering	623.820 3
handling	623.881 3
naval equipment	359.832
naval units	359.322
transportation services	387.204 3
see also Ships	
Sailors	387.509 2
merchant seamen	387.509 2
occupational group	T7—387 5
navy personnel	359.009 2
occupational group	T7—359
occupational group	T7—387 5
sports	797.109 2
sports group	T7—797 1
technologists	623.880 92
occupational group	T7—623 8
Sails	623.862
Saint Albans (England : City)	T2—425 85
Saint Arnaud	T2—945 8
Saint-Augustin-de-Desmaures (Quebec)	T2—714 471
Saint Barthélemy	T2—729 76
Saint Bernard (Dog)	
animal husbandry	636.73
see also Dogs	
Saint Bernard Parish (La.)	T2—763 36
Saint Charles County (Mo.)	T2—778 39
Saint Charles Parish (La.)	T2—763 33
Saint Christopher	T2—729 73
Saint Christopher-Nevis	972.973
	T2—729 73
Saint Christopher-Nevis-Anguilla	T2—729 73
Saint Clair, Lake (Mich. and Ont.)	T2—774 39
Michigan	T2—774 39
Ontario	T2—713 31
Saint Clair, Lake (Tas.)	T2—946 3
Saint Clair County (Ala.)	T2—761 69
Saint Clair County (Ill.)	T2—773 89
Saint Clair County (Mich.)	T2—774 41
Saint Clair County (Mo.)	T2—778 466
Saint Clair River (Mich. and Ont.)	T2—774 41
Michigan	T2—774 41
Ontario	T2—713 27
Saint Croix (V.I.)	T2—729 722
Saint Croix County (Wis.)	T2—775 41
Saint Croix River (Me. and N.B.)	T2—741 42
Maine	T2—741 42
New Brunswick	T2—715 33
Saint Croix River (Wis. and Minn.)	T2—775 1
Saint-Denis (Réunion)	T2—698 1
Saint Edmundsbury (England)	T2—426 44
Saint Elmo's fire	551.563 3
Saint-Emile (Quebec)	T2—714 471
Saint Eustatius (Netherlands Antilles)	T2—729 77
Saint-Foy (Quebec)	T2—714 471
Saint Francis County (Ark.)	T2—767 91
Saint Francis River	T2—767 9
Saint Francois County (Mo.)	T2—778 68
Saint-François River (Wolfe-Yamaska, Quebec)	T2—714 5
Saint Gall (Switzerland : Canton)	T2—494 72
Saint George (Qld.)	T2—943 4
Saint George's Channel	551.461 37
	T2—163 37
Saint Helena	997.3
	T2—973
Saint Helena Parish (La.)	T2—763 15
Saint Helens (England : Metropolitan Borough)	T2—427 57
Saint Hyacinthe (Quebec : County)	T2—714 523
Saint James Parish (La.)	T2—763 31
Saint-Jean (Quebec : County)	T2—714 38
Saint John (N.B. : County)	T2—715 32
Saint John (V.I.)	T2—729 722
Saint John River (Me. and N.B.)	T2—715 5
Saint John the Baptist Parish (La.)	T2—763 32
Saint-John's-bread	583.322
orchard crop	634.46
Saint Johns County (Fla.)	T2—759 18
Saint Johns River (Fla.)	T2—759 1
Saint-John's-wort	583.163
Saint Joseph County (Ind.)	T2—772 89
Saint Joseph County (Mich.)	T2—774 19
Saint Joseph religious orders	255.976
church history	271.976
Saint Kitts	T2—729 73
Saint Kitts-Nevis	972.973
	T2—729 73
Saint Kitts-Nevis-Anguilla	T2—729 73
Saint Landry Parish (La.)	T2—763 46
Saint-Laurent, Louis Stephen Canadian history	971.063 3
Saint-Laurent du Maroni (French Guiana)	T2—882
Saint Lawrence, Gulf of	551.461 44
	T2—163 44
Saint Lawrence County (N.Y.)	T2—747 56
Saint Lawrence River	T2—714
New York	T2—747 56
Ontario	T2—713 7
Quebec	T2—714

Saint Lawrence Seaway	386.5	Sak River	T2—687 17
	T2—714	Saka language	491.53
Ontario	T2—713 7		T6—915 3
Quebec	T2—714	Saka literature	891.53
Saint Louis (Mo.)	T2—778 66	Sakai languages	495.93
Saint-Louis (Senegal)	T2—663		T6—959 3
Saint Louis County (Minn.)	T2—776 77	Sakakawea, Lake	T2—784 75
Saint Louis County (Mo.)	T2—778 65	Sakarya Ili (Turkey)	T2—563
Saint Lucia	972.984 3	Sake	641.23
	T2—729 843	commercial processing	663.49
Saint Lucia Bay	T2—684 3	Sakhalin (R.S.F.S.R. : Oblast)	T2—577
Saint Lucia Estuary	T2—684 3	Sakhalin Ula (China and	
Saint Lucia Game Reserve	T2—684 3	R.S.F.S.R.)	T2—577
Saint Lucia Lake	T2—684 3	Sakhalinskaia oblast	
Saint Lucie County (Fla.)	T2—759 29	(R.S.F.S.R.)	T2—577
Saint-Malo, Gulf of	551.461 38	Salad dressings	641.814
	T2—163 38	food technology	664.37
Saint Martin	T2—729 76	home preparation	641.814
Guadeloupe	T2—729 76	Salad greens	641.355
Netherlands Antilles	T2—729 77	commercial processing	664.805 5
Saint Martin Parish (La.)	T2—763 48	cooking	641.655
Saint Mary Parish (La.)	T2—763 42	garden crop	635.5
Saint Marys, Lake	T2—771 415	Salad oils	
Saint Marys County (Md.)	T2—752 41	food technology	664.36
Saint Marys River (Fla.)	T2—759 11	Salads	641.83
Saint Marys River (Mich. and		cooking	641.83
Ont.)	T2—774 91	Salah ad-Din (Iraq : Province)	T2—567 4
Saint-Maurice (Quebec :		Salahuddin (Iraq : Province)	T2—567 4
County)	T2—714 451	Salaj (Romania)	T2—498 4
Saint Paul (Minn.)	T2—776 581	Salamanca (Spain : Province)	T2—462 5
Saint Paul Island	969.9	Salamanders	597.65
	T2—699	Salamandroidea	597.65
Saint-Pierre	971.88	Salaries	
Saint-Pierre and Miquelon		personnel management	658.32
(France)	971.88	armed forces	355.64
	T2—718 8	executives	658.407 2
Saint-Simonism (Socialist		Salary scales	
school)	335.22	personnel management	658.322 2
Saint Tammany Parish (La.)	T2—763 12	Salat	297.52
Saint Thomas (V.I.)	T2—729 722	Salazar, Antonio de Oliveira	
Saint Vincent	T2—729 844	Portuguese history	946.904 2
Saint Vincent and the Grenadines	972.984 4	Salcedo (Dominican	
	T2—729 844	Republic : Province)	T2—729 363
Sainte Genevieve County		Sale (Vic.)	T2—945 6
(Mo.)	T2—778 692	Sale of businesses	
Saintonge (France)	T2—446 4	law	346.065
Saints	291.092	management	658.16
art representation	704.948 63	Sale of real property	
Christian	270.092	law	346.043 63
doctrines	235.2	Salem (Or.)	T2—795 37
specific denominations	280	Salem (Va.)	T2—755 793
religious group	T7—2	Salem County (N.J.)	T2—749 91
religious worship	291.213	Salerno (Italy : Province)	T2—457 4
Saints' days	263.98	Sales	
Saipan	T2—967	law	346.072
Saitama-ken (Japan)	T2—521 34	Sales analysis	
Saite period (Egyptian history)	932.015	marketing management	658.810 1
Saivism	294.551 3		

Sales clerks	381.092
occupational group	T7—381
Sales finance institutions	332.35
Sales forecasting	
marketing management	658.818
Sales management	658.81
	T1—068 8
Sales meetings	658.810 6
Sales personnel	381.092
occupational group	T7—381
organization	658.810 2
Sales planning	658.810 1
Sales promotion	658.82
Sales tax	336.271 3
law	343.055 2
public administration	350.724 7
central governments	351.724 7
local governments	352.135
public finance	336.271 3
Salesmanship	658.85
etiquette	395.53
Salesmen	381.092
occupational group	T7—381
Salford (England : City)	T2—427 32
Salian emperors (German	
history)	943.023
Salicales	583.981
Salientia	597.8
paleozoology	567.8
Salinas River (Calif.)	T2—794 76
Saline County (Ark.)	T2—767 72
Saline County (Ill.)	T2—773 992
Saline County (Kan.)	T2—781 545
Saline County (Mo.)	T2—778 47
Saline County (Neb.)	T2—782 327
Saline water conversion	
water-supply engineering	628.167
Saline waters	553.72
economic geology	553.72
Salinity	
sea water	551.460 1
soil science	631.416
Salisbury (England : District)	T2—423 19
Salisbury (S. Aust.)	T2—942 32
Salisbury Island (N.W.T.)	T2—719 5
Salisbury Plain	T2—423 19
Salishan Indians	T5—979
Salishan languages	497.9
	T6—979
Saliva	
human physiology	612.313
see also Digestive system	
Salivary glands	
human anatomy	611.316
human diseases	
medicine	616.316
human physiology	612.313
see also Digestive system	

Salmon	597.55
commercial fishing	639.275 5
culture	639.375 5
sports fishing	799.175 5
Salmon Arm (B.C.)	T2—711 68
Salmon River (Idaho)	T2—796 82
Salmon River Mountains	T2—796 7
Salmonella	589.95
Salmonella diseases	
incidence	614.511
medicine	616.927
see also Communicable	
diseases (Human)	
Salmoniformes	597.55
Salon orchestras	784.4
Salop (England)	T2—424 5
Salpingitis	
gynecology	618.12
see also Female genital system	
Salsify	
garden crop	635.16
Salt	553.63
animal feed	636.087 7
chemistry	546.382 4
cooking with	641.6
economic geology	553.63
food technology	664.4
metabolism	
human physiology	612.392 6
see also Digestive system	
mineralogy	549.4
mining	622.363
Salt-flat ecology	574.526 5
Salt-free cooking	641.563 2
Salt-free diet	
health	613.28
Salt Lake City (Utah)	T2—792 258
Salt Lake County (Utah)	T2—792 25
Salt-lake ecology	574.526 36
Salt lakes	551.460 9
resource economics	333.916 4
Salt River	T2—769 45
Salta (Argentina : Province)	T2—824 2
Saltarello form	784.188 2
Salto (Uruguay : Dept.)	T2—895 35
Salton Sea (Calif.)	T2—794 99
Saltpeter	553.64
mineralogy	549.732
Salts	546.34
chemical engineering	661.4
chemistry	546.34
metabolism	
human physiology	612.392 6
see also Digestive system	
see also Chemicals	
Saltwater	
desalinization	628.167
Saltwater ecology	574.526 36

San Joaquin Valley — T2—794 8
San Jorge, Gulf of — 551.464 68
— T2—163 68
San Jose (Calif.) — T2—794 74
San José (Costa Rica : Province) — T2—728 63
San José (Uruguay : Dept.) — T2—895 12
San Juan (Argentina : Province) — T2—826 3
San Juan (Dominican Republic : Province) — T2—729 342
San Juan (P.R.) — T2—729 51
San Juan (P.R. : District) — T2—729 51
San Juan County (Colo.) — T2—788 25
San Juan County (N.M.) — T2—789 82
San Juan County (Utah) — T2—792 59
San Juan County (Wash.) — T2—797 74
San Juan Mountains (Colo. and N.M.) — T2—788 3
San Juan River (B.C.) — T2—711 28
San Juan River (Colo.-Utah) — T2—792 59
San Juans (Plants) — 583.143
San languages — 496.1
— T6—961
San Luis (Argentina : Province) — T2—826 2
San Luis Obispo County (Calif.) — T2—794 78
San Luis Potosí (Mexico : State) — T2—724 4
San Luis Valley (Colo. and N.M.) — T2—788 3
San Marcos (Guatemala : Dept.) — T2—728 184
San Marino — 945.49
— T2—454 9
San Martín (Peru : Dept.) — T2—854 5
San Mateo County (Calif.) — T2—794 69
San Matías, Gulf of — 551.464 68
— T2—163 68
San Miguel (El Salvador : Dept.) — T2—728 432
San Miguel County (Colo.) — T2—788 23
San Miguel County (N.M.) — T2—789 55
San Patricio County (Tex.) — T2—764 115
San Pedro (Paraguay : Dept.) — T2—892 136
San Pedro de Macorís (Dominican Republic : Province) — T2—729 382
San Saba County (Tex.) — T2—764 68
San Salvador (El Salvador : Dept.) — T2—728 423
San Salvador Island — T2—729 6
San Sebastián (Spain) — T2—466 1
San Vicente (El Salvador : Dept.) — T2—728 427
Sanaga languages — 496.396
— T6—963 96

Sanborn County (S.D.) — T2—783 33
Sánchez Ramírez (Dominican Republic : Province) — T2—729 368
Sancti Spíritus (Cuba : Province) — T2—729 145
Sanctification (Christian doctrine) — 234.8
Sanctifying grace — 234.1
Sanctions (International law) — 341.582
Sanctions (International politics) — 327.117
Sanctity of Mary — 232.915
Sanctuaries
  architecture — 726.593
Sanctus — 264.36
  music — 782.323 2
Sand — 553.622
  economic geology — 553.622
  materials science — 620.191
  mining — 622.362 2
  petrology — 552.5
Sand casting
  metals — 671.252
  sculpture — 731.45
Sand dollar — 593.95
Sand eel — 597.58
  fishing — 639.275 8
Sand filter
  sewage treatment — 628.352
Sand flea — 595.371
Sand food (Plant) — 583.62
Sand grouse — 598.65
Sand hopper — 595.371
Sand lance — 597.58
  fishing — 639.275 8
Sand painting — 751.49
Sand River — T2—685 3
Sandalwood — 583.94
Sandblasting
  pneumatic engineering — 621.54
Sandblasting glass
  arts — 748.6
Sanders County (Mont.) — T2—786 833
Sandlot baseball — 796.357 62
Sandoval County (N.M.) — T2—789 57
Sandpaper blocks
  music — 786.863
    see also Percussion instruments
Sandpipers — 598.33
Sandstone — 553.53
  building material — 691.2
  economic geology — 553.53
  petrology — 552.5
  quarrying — 622.353
Sandusky Bay — T2—771 214
Sandusky County (Ohio) — T2—771 214
Sandusky River — T2—771 2

Santo Domingo (Dominican
  Republic)   T2—729 375
Santoríni Island (Greece)   T2—499
Santos
  arts   704.948 2
  religious significance   246.53
Santos, José Eduardo dos
  Angolan history   967.304
Sanzas   786.85
  see also Percussion instruments
São Paulo (Brazil : State)   T2—816 1
São Tomé (Sao Tome and
  Principe)   T2—671 5
Sao Tome and Principe   967.15
                                T2—671 5
Sao Tomeans   T5—967 15
Saône-et-Loire (France)   T2—444 3
Saône River (France)   T2—444
Sap   581.113
  forest products   634.986
Sapés   787.85
  see also Stringed instruments
Sapindales   583.28
Sapodilla   583.685
Sapodilla plums
  orchard crop   634.43
Saponification   547.225
  chemical engineering   660.284 425
Saponins   581.192 483
  biochemistry   581.192 483
  chemistry   547.783
  see also Carbohydrates
Sapotaceae   583.685
  orchard crop   634.43
Sapphires   553.84
  economic geology   553.84
  glyptics   736.25
  jewelry   739.27
  mining   622.384
  synthetic   666.88
Saprolegniales   589.256
Saracenic architecture
  medieval   723.3
Saragossa (Spain : Province)   T2—465 53
Saramacca (Surinam :
  District)   T2—883 3
Sarangis   787.6
  see also Stringed instruments
Sarans
  textiles   677.474 4
  see also Textiles
Sarasota County (Fla.)   T2—759 61
Saratoga County (N.Y.)   T2—747 48
Saratov (R.S.F.S.R. : Oblast)   T2—478 5
Saratovskaia oblast
  (R.S.F.S.R.)   T2—478 5
Saravastivada Buddhism   294.391
Sarawak   T2—595 4

Sarcodina   593.11
Sarcoidosis
  medicine   616
  see also Diseases (Human)
Sarcolaenaceae   583.167
Sarcoma
  medicine   616.994
  see also Cancer
Sarcopterygii   597.48
  paleozoology   567.4
Sarcospermataceae   583.685
Sardegna   T2—459
Sardines   597.55
  fishing   639.275 5
Sardinia   T2—459
  ancient   T2—379
Sardinian language   457.91–.94
                                T6—56
Sardinian literature   850
Sardinians   T5—56
Sardis (Ancient city)   T2—392 2
Sardis Lake   T2—762 83
Sargasso Sea   551.464 62
                                T2—163 62
Sargassum   589.45
Sargent County (N.D.)   T2—784 314
Sargentodoxaceae   583.117
Sargodha District (Pakistan)   T2—549 14
Sark (England)   T2—423 45
Sarmatia   T2—395
Sarozs   787.6
  see also Stringed instruments
Sarpy County (Neb.)   T2—782 256
Sarraceniales   583.121
Sarsaparilla   584.323
Sarthe (France)   T2—441 7
Sasakian geometry   516.373
Sashes (Clothing)   391.44
  see also Accessories (Clothing)
Saskatchewan   971.24
                                T2—712 4
Saskatchewan River (Sask.
  and Man.)   T2—712 42
Saskatoon (Sask.)   T2—712 425
Sasolburg (South Africa :
  District)   T2—685 25
Sasquatch   001.944
Sassafras   583.931
  agriculture   633.82
Sassafras tea   641.338 2
  commercial processing   663.96
  cooking with   641.638 2
  home preparation   641.877
Sassanian Empire   935.07
                                T2—35
Sassari (Sardinia : Province)   T2—459 3
Sassou Nguesso, Denis
  Congolese history   967.240 5

Sawyer County (Wis.)	T2—775 16
Saxhorns	788.97
see also Brass instruments	
Saxifragales	583.38
Saxifrage	583.38
Saxon dynasty (Polish history)	943.802 5
Saxon emperors (German history)	943.022
Saxony (Germany)	T2—432 1
Saxony (Prussia)	T2—431 8
Saxony-Anhalt (Germany)	T2—431 8
Saxophones	788.7
see also Woodwind instruments	
Saxophonists	788.709 2
occupational group	T7—788
Say, Jean Baptiste	
economic school	330.153
Sayan Mountains (R.S.F.S.R.)	T2—575
Sayyid dynasty (Indian history)	954.024 2
Scabies	
medicine	616.57
see also Skin	
Scad	597.58
Scalar field theory	515.63
Scalds	
medicine	617.11
Scale insects	595.752
Scale moss	588.33
Scales (Maps)	912.014 8
Scales (Music)	781.246
Scalic formations (Music)	781.246
Scallops	594.11
cooking	641.694
fisheries	639.481 1
food	641.394
commercial processing	664.94
zoology	594.11
Scalp diseases	
medicine	616.546
see also Skin	
Scalping	
war customs	399
Scandinavia	948
	T2—48
Scandinavian languages	439.5
	T6—395
Scandinavian literatures	839.5
Scandinavian religion	293
Scandinavians	T5—395
Scandium	669.290 1
chemical engineering	661.040 1
chemistry	546.401
economic geology	553.494 2
metallurgy	669.290 1
see also Chemicals, Metals	
Scaphopoda	594.2
paleozoology	564.2

Scapolite	
mineralogy	549.68
Scapulas	
human anatomy	611.717
see also Musculoskeletal system	
Scarabaeoidea	595.764 9
Scarabs	
glyptics	736.209 32
Scarborough (England : Borough)	T2—428 47
Scarborough (Ont.)	T2—713 541
Scarlatina	
incidence	614.522
medicine	616.917
see also Communicable diseases (Human)	
Scarlet fever	
incidence	614.522
medicine	616.917
see also Communicable diseases (Human)	
Scarves	391.41
see also Accessories (Clothing)	
Scarves (Table linen)	642.7
arts	746.96
home sewing	646.21
table setting	642.7
Scat	597.58
Scattering (Physics)	539.758
solid state physics	530.416
Scattering of light	
meteorology	551.566
Scenarios	
music	780
treatises	782.002 69
Scene paintings	751.75
Scene understanding	
artificial intelligence	006.37
Scenery	
dramatic performances	792.025
motion pictures	791.430 25
stage	792.025
television	791.450 25
Scenic rivers	333.784 5
law	346.046 784 5
natural resources	333.784 5
Schaffhausen (Switzerland : Canton)	T2—494 58
Schaffhouse (Switzerland : Canton)	T2—494 58
Scheduling	
broadcasting services	
radio	384.544 2
television	384.553 1
production management	658.53
transportation	388.041
air	387.740 42
automobile	388.321

School policy	371	Science	500
School principals	371.200 92	elementary education	372.35
personnel management	371.201 2	folklore	398.26
School psychologists	371.420 92	sociology	398.36
personnel management	371.202 2	law	344.095
School resource centers	371.307 8	literature	808.803 56
School safety patrols	371.775 2	history and criticism	809.933 56
School safety programs	371.77	specific literatures	T3B—080 356
School secretaries	371.200 92	history and criticism	T3B—093 56
personnel management	371.202 3	social effects	303.483
School social workers	371.420 92	sociology	306.45
personnel management	371.202 2	use in agriculture	338.16
School socialization	303.324	Science and religion	291.175
School superintendents	371.200 92	Christianity	261.55
personnel management	371.201 1	natural theology	215
School supervisors	371.200 92	Science fair projects	507.8
personnel management	371.201 3	Science fiction	808.838 762
School systems	371	history and criticism	809.387 62
School tablet paper	676.286	motion pictures	791.436 15
School week	371.24	radio programs	791.446 15
School year	371.23	specific literatures	T3B—308 762
law	344.079 2	individual authors	T3A—3
Schoolcraft County (Mich.)	T2—774 935	television programs	791.456 15
Schooling	370	Science laboratories	
Schools	371	architecture	727.55
	T1—071	Science museums	
accounting	657.832 7	architecture	727.65
area planning	711.57	Science policy	
fire hazards	363.379	economics	338.926
law	344.07	Science projects in schools	507.8
public finance	379.11	Sciences	T1—015
law	344.076	all knowledge	001
Schools (Styles)		art representation	704.949 5
arts	709	information systems	025.065
Schouten Island (Tas.)	T2—946 4	libraries	026.5
Schouten Islands (New		natural sciences	500
Guinea)	T2—957 5	public administration	351.855
Schrader Range	T2—957 3	Scientific instruments	
Schrödinger wave mechanics	530.124	manufacturing technology	681.75
Schuyler County (Ill.)	T2—773 475	Scientific method	001.42
Schuyler County (Mo.)	T2—778 262		T1—072
Schuyler County (N.Y.)	T2—747 81	Scientific principles	500
Schuylkill County (Pa.)	T2—748 17		T1—015
Schuylkill River (Pa.)	T2—748 1	music	781.2
Schwaben (Germany)	T2—433 7	Scientific recreations	793.8
Schweinfurt (Germany)	T2—433 36	Scientific relations	
Schweizer-Reneke (South		international law	341.767
Africa : District)	T2—682 4	Scientific socialism	
Schwerin (Germany : Bezirk)	T2—431 76	economics	335.423
Schwyz (Switzerland :		Scientific surveys	508
Canton)	T2—494 752	Scientific toys	790.133
Sciaridae	595.771	manufacturing technology	688.725
Sciatica		recreation	790.133
medicine	616.87	*see also* Toys	
see also Nervous system		Scientific travels	508
		Scientific writing	808.066 5

Scientists	509.2	Scotland	941.1
Christian polemics	239.8		T2—411
Islamic polemics	297.298	ancient	936.11
occupational group	T7—5		T2—361 1
Scientology	299.936	Scotland. Children's Hearings	345.411 08
Scilly Isles (England)	T2—423 79	Scotland. Court of Appeal	345.411 016 3
Scintillation		Scotland. Court of First Instance	345.411 016 2
atmospheric optics	551.565	Scotland. Court of Session	347.411 023
Scintillation counters		Scotland. Court of Session. Inner	
nuclear physics	539.775	House	347.411 035
Sciomyzidae	595.774	Scotland. Court of Session. Outer	
Scioto County (Ohio)	T2—771 87	House	347.411 024
Scioto River	T2—771 5	Scotland. Court of the Lord Lyon	347.411 04
Sciuromorpha	599.323 2	Scotland. Crown Counsel	345.411 01
Scleras		Scotland. District Court	345.411 012
human anatomy	611.84	Scotland. High Court of	
human physiology	612.841	Justiciary	345.411 016
ophthalmology	617.719	Scotland. House of Lords (Court	
see also Eyes		of last resort)	347.411 039
Scleroderma		Scotland. Licensing Appeals	
medicine	616.544	Court	347.411 04
see also Skin		Scotland. Licensing Courts	347.411 04
Sclerodermatales	589.221	Scotland. Lord Advocate	345.411 01
Scleroproteins	574.192 453	Scotland. Sheriff Court	347.411 021
biochemistry	574.192 453	criminal law	345.411 014
chemistry	547.753	Scotland. Sheriff-Principal	347.411 032
see also Proteins		Scotland. Solicitor-General	345.411 01
Scolioidea	595.798	Scotland County (Mo.)	T2—778 312
Scoliosis		Scotland County (N.C.)	T2—756 335
orthopedics	617.375	Scots	T5—916 3
Scolopacidae	598.33	Scots language (English dialect)	427.941 1
Sconces			T6—21
furniture arts	749.63	Scott County (Ark.)	T2—767 44
Scone (N.S.W.)	T2—944 2	Scott County (Ill.)	T2—773 455
Scooters	388.347 5	Scott County (Ind.)	T2—772 183
engineering	629.227 5	Scott County (Iowa)	T2—777 69
see also Motorcycles		Scott County (Kan.)	T2—781 43
Scopelomorpha		Scott County (Ky.)	T2—769 425
paleozoology	567.5	Scott County (Minn.)	T2—776 54
Score reading	781.423	Scott County (Miss.)	T2—762 655
Scores (Music)	780	Scott County (Mo.)	T2—778 97
cataloging	025.348 8	Scott County (Tenn.)	T2—768 71
library treatment	025.178 8	Scott County (Va.)	T2—755 732
treatises	780.26	Scottburgh (South Africa)	T2—684 5
Scoring systems		Scottish English dialect	427.941 1
contract bridge	795.415 4		T6—21
Scorodite		Scottish Gaelic language	491.63
mineralogy	549.72		T6—916 3
Scorpaeniformes	597.58	Scottish Gaels	T5—916 3
Scorpion fish	597.58	Scottish Highlands (Scotland)	T2—411 5
Scorpion flies	595.744	Scottish literature	
Scorpion venom		English	820
toxicology	615.942	Gaelic	891.63
Scorpions	595.46	Scotts Bluff County (Neb.)	T2—782 98
paleozoology	565.4	Scottsdale (Tas.)	T2—946 4
Scotch broom	583.322	Scouring compounds	668.127
Scotia Sea	551.469 3	Scouts (Boy and girl)	369.409 2
	T2—167 3	social group	T7—369 4

Scows	387.29
design	623.812 9
engineering	623.829
transportation services	387.29
see also Ships	
Scranton (Pa.)	T2—748 37
Scrap metal	363.728 8
metallurgy	669.042
social services	363.728 8
see also Waste control	
Scraped idiophones	786.886
see also Percussion instruments	
Scratch pad paper	676.286
Scratchboard drawing	741.29
Screamers	598.41
Screen process printing	686.231 6
Screening	
chemical engineering	660.284 22
ores	622.74
sewage treatment	628.34
water-supply treatment	628.162 2
Screenplays	791.437
literature	808.823
history and criticism	809.23
specific literatures	T3B—203
individual authors	T3A—2
motion pictures	791.437
music	780
treatises	780.268
rhetoric	808.23
Screens	645.4
church architecture	726.529 6
church furniture	247.1
decorative arts	749.3
see also Furniture	
Screenwriting	808.23
Screven County (Ga.)	T2—758 695
Screw-cutting tools	621.944
Screwdrivers	621.972
Screws	621.882
Script-geometric shorthand	
systems	653.426
Script shorthand systems	653.428
Scripts	
motion pictures	791.437
puppet plays	791.538
radio	791.447
stage productions	792.9
television	791.457
Scripture readings	
public worship	
Christianity	264.34
Scriptures (Religion)	291.82
see also Sacred books	
Scrollwork	
furniture arts	749.5
wood handicrafts	745.51
Scrophulariaceae	583.81

Scrotum	
human anatomy	611.63
human diseases	
medicine	616.67
human physiology	612.61
see also Male genital system	
Scrub typhus	
incidence	614.526 4
medicine	616.922 4
see also Communicable	
diseases (Human)	
Scrummaging	796.333 23
Scuba diving	
sports	797.23
Sculpin	597.58
Sculptors	730.92
occupational group	T7—731
Sculptural stone	553.5
see also Stone	
Sculpture	730
architectural decoration	729.5
elementary education	372.53
Scunthorpe (England)	T2—428 31
Scurry County (Tex.)	T2—764 731
Scurvy	
medicine	616.394
see also Digestive system	
Scyphostegiaceae	583.962
Scyphozoa	593.73
paleozoology	563.73
Scythia	T2—395 1
Scythian languages	491.53
	T6—915 3
Scythians	T5—915
Scytho-Dravidians	T5—948
Scytopetalaceae	583.19
SDI (Information service)	025.525
SDI (Strategic Defense Initiative)	358.174
Sea anemones	593.6
Sea basins	T2—182
Sea bears	599.746
Sea breezes	551.518 5
Sea cows	599.55
Sea cucumber	593.96
Sea fans	593.6
Sea-floor spreading	551.136
Sea forces	359
Sea hare	594.37
Sea ice	551.343
Sea Islands	T2—757 99
Georgia	T2—758 7
South Carolina	T2—757 99
Sea Lake (Vic.)	T2—945 9
Sea lettuce	589.47
Sea-level changes	551.458
Sea life	
music about	781.595
Sea lily	593.91

Seasons (continued)
  music — 781.524
  natural history — 508
Seat belts
  aircraft — 629.134 43
  automobile — 629.276
  law — 343.094 4
Seat ejectors
  aircraft — 629.134 386
SEATO (Alliance) — 355.031 095 9
Seats
  automobile — 629.26
Seattle (Wash.) — T2—797 772
Seatwork
  education — 371.302 82
Seawalls
  flood control — 627.42
  port engineering — 627.24
  shore protection — 627.58
Seawater — 551.460 1
  desalinization — 628.167
  oceanography — 551.460 1
  water-supply evaluation — 628.116
Seawater intrusion
  prevention — 628.114
Seawater supply
  ship sanitation — 623.854 3
Seaweeds — 589.45
  culture — 639.89
Sebaceous glands
  human anatomy — 611.77
  human diseases
    medicine — 616.53
  human physiology — 612.792 1
  see also Skin
Sebastian County (Ark.) — T2—767 36
Seborrhea
  medicine — 616.53
  see also Skin
Secession (United States history) — 973.713
Second-class mail — 383.123
  see also Postal service
Second Coming of Christ — 236.9
Second Empire (French history) — 944.07
Second International — 324.174
Second Republic (French history) — 944.07
Second Republic (Spanish history) — 946.081
Secondary batteries — 621.312 424
Secondary consciousness
  psychology — 154.3
Secondary education — 373
    T1—071 2
  law — 344.074
  public finance — 379.113
    law — 344.076 83

Secondary industries — 338.4
  enterprises — 338.7
  international enterprises — 338.88
  law — 343.078
  mergers — 338.83
  products
    commerce — 380.145
    domestic — 381.45
    foreign — 382.45
    public administration — 350.826 5
      central governments — 351.826 5
      local governments — 352.942 6
  public administration — 350.824
    central governments — 351.824
      cabinet departments — 351.082 4
    local governments — 352.942 4
  restrictive practices — 338.82
Secondary modern schools
  (United Kingdom) — 373.26
Secondary Prakrits — 491.3
    T6—913
Secondary Prakrits literatures — 891.3
Secondary recovery
  oil extraction — 622.338 2
Secondary roads — 388.12
  see also Roads
Secondary school buildings — 373.162
  architecture — 727.2
Secondary school libraries — 027.822 3
Secondary school teachers — 373.11
Secondary schools — 373
    T1—071 2
Secondary storage (Computer) — 004.56
  engineering — 621.397 6
Secondary X rays — 539.722 2
Secondhand stores — 381.19
  management — 658.87
  see also Commerce
Secret agents
  criminal investigation — 363.252
Secret codes
  computer science — 005.82
Secret police — 363.283
Secret societies — 366
Secretarial accounting — 657.2
Secretarial bookkeeping — 657.2
Secretariat (United Nations)
  international law — 341.232 4
  public administration — 354.103
Secretaries — 651.374 109 2
  occupational group — T7—651
  office services — 651.374 1
Secretary birds — 598.915
Secretion — 574.14
  animals — 591.14
  human physiology — 612.4
  plants — 581.14
  see also Endocrine system

Seed-hair fibers	
textiles	677.2
see also Textiles	
Seed industry	338.17
agricultural economics	338.17
Seed shrimp	595.33
Seeding	
silviculture	634.956 2
Seeding clouds	551.687 6
Seedless plants	586
Seedlings	582.033 4
botany	582.033 4
nursery production	631.52
plant propagation	631.536
Seeds	582.130 416 6
anatomy	582.046 7
flowering plants	582.130 446
animal feeds	
commercial processing	664.76
floriculture	635.942
food	
commercial processing	664.7
forest products	634.987
nursery production	631.521
paleobotany	561.14
physiology	582.130 416 6
plant propagation	631.531
silviculture	634.956 2
Seeds oil	665.35
industrial	665.35
Sees	
Christian ecclesiology	262.3
Sefton (England :	
Metropolitan Borough)	T2—427 59
Segmented worms	595.14
Segovia (Spain : Province)	T2—463 57
Segregation in education	370.193 44
educational sociology	370.193 44
law	344.079 8
Seibo, El (Dominican	
Republic : Province)	T2—729 384
Seiches	551.470 23
Seine (France)	T2—443 6
Seine-et-Marne (France)	T2—443 7
Seine-et-Oise (France)	T2—443 6
Seine-Inférieure (France)	T2—442 5
Seine-Maritime (France)	T2—442 5
Seine River (France)	T2—443 4
Seine-Saint-Denis (France)	T2—443 62
Seining	
sports	799.13
Seismic prospecting	622.159 2
Seismic sea waves	551.470 24
Seismic waves	551.22
Seismography	551.220 287
Seismology	551.22
Seistan and Baluchistan	
(Iran : Province)	T2—558 3

Sekgosese (South Africa :	
District)	T2—682 93
Sekhukhuneberg Range	T2—682 93
Sekhukhuneland (South	
Africa : District)	T2—682 93
Selaginaceae	583.87
Selaginellales	587.9
paleobotany	561.79
Selangor	T2—595 1
Selby (England : District)	T2—428 45
Select committees	
legislative bodies	328.365 7
Selected Federal laws	
United States	348.732 4
Selected laws	348.024
Selection procedures	
personnel management	658.311 2
public administration	350.132 5
central governments	351.132 5
local governments	352.005 132 5
Selective dissemination of	
information	025.525
Selective service	355.223 63
law	343.012 2
Selenides	
mineralogy	549.32
Selenium	
chemical engineering	661.072 4
chemistry	546.724
metallurgy	669.79
organic chemistry	547.057 24
applied	661.895
see also Chemicals	
Selenography	919.91
Seleucid Empire	935.06
	T2—35
Self	
literature	808.803 84
history and criticism	809.933 84
specific literatures	T3B—080 384
history and criticism	T3B—093 84
philosophy	126
psychology	155.2
Self-contained communities	307.77
Self-control	179.9
psychology	153.8
development	155.25
see also Virtues	
Self-defense	613.66
military training	355.548
personal safety	613.66
Self-defense (Law)	345.04
Self-determination of states	320.15
Self-development reading	
library science	028.8

Sena language	496.391	Sensory functions (continued)	
	T6—963 91	localization in brain	
Seneca County (N.Y.)	T2—747 69	human physiology	612.825 5
Seneca County (Ohio)	T2—771 24	*see also* Nervous system	
Seneca Lake (N.Y.)	T2—747 69	Sensory influences	
Senegal	966.3	psychology	155.911
	T2—663	Sensory nerves	
Senegal languages	496.321	human physiology	612.811
	T6—963 21	*see also* Nervous system	
Sénégal-Oriental (Senegal :		Sensory perception	152.1
Region)	T2—663	animals	156.21
Senegalese	T5—966 3	epistemology	121.3
Senegambia	966.305	psychological influence	155.911
	T2—663	Sentences (Legal decisions)	345.077
Senekal (South Africa :		penology	364.6
District)	T2—685 1	Sentencing	345.077 2
Senescence		Sentiments	152.4
human physiology	612.67	Senufo (African people)	T5—963 5
Senga-Sena languages	496.391	Senufo language	496.35
	T6—963 91		T6—963 5
Senile dementia		Senyavin Islands	T2—966
geriatrics	618.976 898 3	Sepals	
medicine	616.898 3	anatomy	582.130 446 3
see also Mental illness		Separated persons	305.906 53
Senior citizens	305.26		T1—086 53
	T1—084 6	family relationships	306.89
see also Old persons		social group	305.906 53
Senior high schools	373.238	Separation (Domestic)	306.89
Seniority		law	346.016 6
labor economics	331.259 6	social theology	291.178 358 9
Senna	583.323	Christianity	261.835 89
Senoic languages	495.93	Separation from parents	
	T6—959 3	child psychology	155.44
Sensation	152.1	Separation from service	
epistemology	121.3	personnel management	
Sensationalism		public administration	350.18
philosophy	145	central governments	351.18
Sensations (Art styles)	709.040 7	local governments	352.005 18
Sense organs	591.182	Separation of powers	320.404
animal anatomy	591.48	law	342.044
animal physiology	591.182	Separation processes	
human anatomy	611.8	chemical engineering	660.284 2
human histology	611.018 98	Separatist parties	324.218
human physiology	612.8	Sepik River (New Guinea)	T2—957 5
see also Nervous system		Sepioidea	594.58
Sensitive plants	583.321	Sepiolite	
Sensitivity training		mineralogy	549.67
applied psychology	158.2	Sepoy Mutiny (Indian history)	954.031 7
social psychology	302.14	Sept-Rivières (Quebec)	T2—714 17
Sensitometry	661.808	Septets	
Sensorineural deafness		chamber music	785.17
otology	617.886	vocal music	783.17
see also Ears		Septic tanks	
Sensory functions		technology	628.742
animals	591.182	Septicemia	
human physiology	612.8	incidence	614.577
		medicine	616.944

Septicemia (continued)
  puerperal diseases
    incidence   614.545
    obstetrics   618.74
  see also Communicable
    diseases (Human)
Sepulchral slabs   736.5
Sequatchie County (Tenn.)   T2—768 77
Sequatchie River (Tenn.)   T2—768 77
Sequence   264.36
  music   782.323 5
Sequences (Mathematics)   515.242
  calculus   515.242
Sequences of integers   512.72
Sequencing
  production management   658.53
Sequential analysis   519.54
Sequoia National Park (Calif.)   T2—794 86
Sequoias   585 2
  forestry   634.975 8
Sequoyah County (Okla.)   T2—766 81
Serbia   949.71
    T2—497 1
  ancient   939.8
    T2—398
Serbian language   491.82
    T6—918 2
Serbian literature   891.82
Serbians   T5—918 22
Serbo-Croatian language   491.82
    T6—918 2
Serbo-Croatian literature   891.82
Serbs   T5—918 22
Serenade form   784.185 6
Serengeti National Park
  (Tanzania)   T2—678 27
Serer (African people)   T5—963 21
Serer language   496.321
    T6—963 21
Serfdom   306.365
Serfs   305.563
    T1—086 25
  customs   390.25
  dress   391.025
Sergipe (Brazil)   T2—814 1
Serial publications   050
    T1—05
  see also Serials
Serialism
  music   781.33
Serials   050
    T1—05
  bibliographies   011.34
  cataloging   025.343 2
  indexes   050
  library treatment   025.173 2
  postal handling   383.123
    see also Postal service

Serials (continued)
  publishing   070.572
Sericulture   638.2
Series (Bibliographical)
  bibliographies   011.48
Series (Mathematics)   515.243
Serigraphy   764.8
Sermon on the Mount   226.9
  Christian moral theology   241.53
Sermon outlines   251.02
Sermon preparation   251.01
Sermons   291.43
  Christianity   252
    public worship   264.6
  Judaism   296.42
Serobacterins
  pharmacology   615.372
Serology   616.079 5
  animal immunity   591.295
Serous membranes
  human histology   611.018 7
Serpentine   553.55
  building material   691.2
  economic geology   553.55
  mineralogy   549.67
  petrology   552.4
  quarrying   622.355
Serpentinites   552.58
Serpents   597.96
  paleozoology   567.96
Serpents (Musical instruments)   788.99
  see also Brass instruments
Serrai (Greece : Nome)   T2—495 6
Serres (Greece : Nome)   T2—495 6
Serritia   589.95
Serums
  pharmacology   615.37
Servants
  legal status   346.024
Servian language   491.82
    T6—918 2
Servians   T5—918 22
Service (Tennis)   796.342 21
Service academies
  armed forces   355.007 11
Service-club members   369.509 2
  social group   T7—369 5
Service clubs   369.5
Service comparison   T1—029 7
Service comparisons   T1—029 6
Service contracts   346.024
Service directories   T1—029 4
Service evaluation   T1—029 7
Service evaluations   T1—029 6
Service industries   338.4
  accounting   657.83

Service industries (continued)
  commerce   380.145
    domestic   381.45
    foreign   382.45
  enterprises   338.761
  international enterprises   338.887 1
  law   343.078
  mergers   338.836 1
  production efficiency   338.456 1
  public administration   350.824 3
    central governments   351.824 3
    local governments   352.942 43
  restrictive practices   338.826 1
Service listings   T1—029
Service marks   929.9
     T1—027 5
Service periods (Armed forces)   355.11
Service stations
  automotive engineering   629.286
Service workers
  labor economics   331.793
  labor force   331.119 042
  labor market   331.129 042
Serviceberry   583.372
Serviettes   642.7
  arts   746.96
  home sewing   646.21
  table setting   642.7
Serving at table   642.6
Servites   255.47
  church history   271.47
Servitudes   346.043 5
  international law   341.4
Servomechanisms
  automation engineering   629.832 3
Sesame   583.54
Sesame oil
  food technology   664.369
Sesamoids
  human anatomy   611.718
  see also Musculoskeletal system
Seshego (South Africa :
  District)   T2—682 93
seSotho language   496.397 72
     T6—963 977 2
Sesquilinear forms
  algebraic geometry   516.35
Sessions (Legislative bodies)   328.35
Set idiophones   786.84
  see also Percussion instruments
Set theory   511.322
Sétif (Algeria : Dept.)   T2—655
Sets   511.32
Settat (Morocco : Province)   T2—643
Setters
  animal husbandry   636.752
  see also Dogs

Setting (Literature)   808.802 2
  history and criticism   809.922
  specific literatures   T3B—080 22
    history and criticism   T3B—092 2
Setting (Performances)   792.025
  motion pictures   791.430 25
  stage   792.025
  television   791.450 25
Settlement (Real estate)   346.043 73
Settlement (Sociology)   307.14
Settling
  water-supply treatment   628.162 2
Setúbal (Portugal : District)   T2—469 42
Seven last words on cross   232.963 5
Seven Weeks' War, 1866   943.076
Seven Years' War, 1756-1763   940.253 4
  North American history   973.26
Seveners (Islamic sect)   297.822
Sevenoaks (England :
  District)   T2—422 36
Seventh-Day Adventist Church   286.732
  see also Adventists
Seventh-Day Baptists   286.3
  see also Baptists
Severance pay
  personnel management   658.322 2
Severance tax   336.271 6
  law   343.055
  public finance   336.271 6
Severn River (Wales and
  England)   T2—424
  England   T2—424
  Wales   T2—429 51
Severnaia Zemlia (R.S.F.S.R.)   T2—987
Severnaya Zemlya
  (R.S.F.S.R.)   T2—987
Severo-Osetinskaia A.S.S.R.
  (R.S.F.S.R.)   T2—479 7
Severočeský kraj
  (Czechoslovakia)   T2—437 1
Severomoravský kraj
  (Czechoslovakia)   T2—437 2
Sevier County (Ark.)   T2—767 47
Sevier County (Tenn.)   T2—768 893
Sevier County (Utah)   T2—792 55
Sevilla (Spain)   T2—468 6
Seville (Spain : Province)   T2—468 6
Sewage
  water-pollution engineering   628.168 2
Sewage disposal   363.728 4
  military engineering   623.753
  social services   363.728 4
  technology   628.36
  see also Waste control
Sewage effluent   363.728 4
  disposal technology   628.362
  recharge of groundwater   627.56
  see also Waste control

Sexual harassment of women
labor law — 344.014 133
Sexual intercourse
sociology — 306.77
Sexual love — 306.7
Sexual practices — 306.77
sociology — 306.77
Sexual relations — 306.7
ethics — 176
religion — 291.566
Buddhism — 294.356 6
Christianity — 241.66
Hinduism — 294.548 66
Islam — 297.5
Judaism — 296.385 66
psychology — 155.34
social theology — 291.178 357
Christianity — 261.835 7
sociology — 306.7
technique — 613.96
Sexual reproduction — 574.166
animals — 591.166
plants — 581.166
Sexual selection (Evolution) — 575.5
Sexually transmitted diseases
incidence — 614.547
medicine — 616.951
see also Communicable
diseases (Human)
Seychelles — 969.6
T2—696
Seychellois — T5—969 696
Seyhan Ili (Turkey) — T2—564
Seymour (Vic.) — T2—945 3
Seymour River (Columbia-
Shuswap, B.C.) — T2—711 68
Sgrafitto decoration — 666.45
arts — 738.15
technology — 666.45
Shaanxi Sheng (China) — T2—514 3
Shaba (Zaire) — T2—675 18
Shabuoth — 296.438
customs — 394.268 296 438
Shackelford County (Tex.) — T2—764 734
Shad — 597.55
fishing — 639.275 5
Shadbush — 583.372
Shade plants
floriculture — 635.954
Shades (Furnishings) — 645.3
household management — 645.3
manufacturing technology — 684
Shadow boxes
furniture arts — 749.7
Shadow puppets — 791.53
performing arts — 791.53
Shadow theaters — 791.53

Shadows
art — 701.82
drawing — 742
technical drawing — 604.243
Shafiites (Islamic sect) — 297.812
Shaft currents (Electricity) — 621.310 42
Shafting
ship power plants — 623.873
Shafts (Excavations) — 624.19
mining — 622.25
underground construction — 624.19
Shafts (Mechanisms) — 621.823
Shah Jahan, Emperor of India
Indian history — 954.025 7
Shahada — 297.51
Shahjahan, Emperor of India
Indian history — 954.025 7
Shaivism — 294.551 3
Shaka, Zulu Chief
Natal history — 968.403 9
Shaka language — 496.395
T6—963 95
Shakers — 289.8
biography — 289.809 2
religious group — T7—288
see also Christian
denominations
Shakes (Roofing) — 695
Shakespeare, William — 822.33
Shaktaism — 294.551 4
Shakuhanchis — 788.35
see also Woodwind instruments
Shale oil
processing — 665.4
Shales
petrology — 552.5
Shallots — 584.324
garden crop — 635.26
Shallu — 584.92
food crop — 633.174 7
forage crop — 633.257 47
Shamaliyah (Sudan :
Province) — T2—625
Shamanism — 291
Shamans — 291.092
role and function — 291.62
Shambala languages — 496.391
T6—963 91
Shame — 152.4
Shamisens — 787.85
see also Stringed instruments
Shamrocks — 583.216
Shan — T5—959 1
Shan language — 495.919
T6—959 19
Shan literature — 895.919
Shandong Sheng (China) — T2—511 4
Shang dynasty (Chinese history) — 931.02

Shelby County (Tenn.)	T2—768 19
Shelby County (Tex.)	T2—764 179
Sheldon, William Herbert	
personality theory	155.264
Shelf fungi	589.222 5
Shelf ice	551.342
Shelflisting	
library science	025.428
Shelikof Strait	551.466 34
	T2—164 34
Shell carving	736.6
Shell model (Nuclear physics)	539.743
Shellac	667.79
Shellfish	594
cooking	641.694
culture	639.4
economics	338.371 4
fisheries	639.4
fishing industry	338.372 4
food	641.394
commercial processing	664.94
resource economics	333.955
zoology	594
Shellfishing	
economics	338.372 4
Shelling crops	631.56
Shells (Ammunition)	
artillery	623.451 3
small arms	
military engineering	623.455
Shells (Mollusks)	594.047 1
carving	736.6
handicrafts	745.55
Shells (Structural element)	624.177 62
naval architecture	623.817 762
structural engineering	624.177 62
concrete	624.183 462
Shelter	
social welfare	361.05
Sheltered employment	362.042 5
see also Employment services—	
social services	
Shelving	684.16
household management	645.4
library collections maintenance	025.81
library plant management	022.4
manufacturing technology	684.16
Shenandoah County (Va.)	T2—755 95
Shenandoah National Park	
(Va.)	T2—755 9
Shenandoah River Valley	
(Va. and W. Va.)	T2—755 9
Shengs	788.82
see also Woodwind instruments	
Shensi Province (China)	T2—514 3
Shepherd's purse	583.123
Shepparton (Vic.)	T2—945 4
Shepway (England : District)	T2—422 395

Sherbet	641.863
home preparation	641.863
manufacturing	637.4
Sherbrooke (Quebec :	
County)	T2—714 66
Sherbrooke (Quebec :	
Regional County	
Municipality)	T2—714 66
Sherburne County (Minn.)	T2—776 66
Sheridan County (Kan.)	T2—781 145
Sheridan County (Mont.)	T2—786 218
Sheridan County (N.D.)	T2—784 76
Sheridan County (Neb.)	T2—782 92
Sheridan County (Wyo.)	T2—787 32
Sheriff Court (Scotland)	347.411 021
criminal law	345.411 014
Sheriff-Principal (Scotland)	347.411 032
Sheriffs	
law	347.016
police services	363.282
Sherman County (Kan.)	T2—781 115
Sherman County (Neb.)	T2—782 44
Sherman County (Or.)	T2—795 64
Sherman County (Tex.)	T2—764 813
Sherman's March to the Sea,	
1864	973.737 8
Sherwood, Newark and	
(England : District)	T2—425 24
Sherwood Forest	T2—425 24
Shetland (Scotland)	T2—411 35
Shetland Islands (Scotland)	T2—411 35
Shetland pony	
animal husbandry	636.16
zoology	599.725
Shewa (Ethiopia : Province)	T2—633
Sheyenne River	T2—784 3
Shi language	496.394
	T6—963 94
Shia Islam	297.82
doctrines	297.204 2
Hadith	297.124 8
public worship	297.302
Shiawassee County (Mich.)	T2—774 25
Shielding	
nuclear reactors	621.483 23
Shields (Armor)	623.441
art metalwork	739.752
Shift work	
labor economics	331.257 2
Shifting cultivation	
agricultural technique	631.581 8
Shiga-ken (Japan)	T2—521 85
Shigella	589.95
Shigella diseases	
incidence	614.516
medicine	616.935 5
see also Communicable	
diseases (Human)	

Shock (Pathological)	
result of injury	617.21
symptomatology	616.047
Shock absorbers	
automotive	629.243
Shock resistance	
materials science	620.112 5
Shock-resistant construction	624.176
buildings	693.85
Shock therapy	
psychiatry	616.891 2
see also Mental illness	
Shock tunnels	
aircraft	629.134 52
Shock waves	531.113 3
fluid mechanics	532.059 3
liquid mechanics	532.593
solid mechanics	531.33
Shoe buckles	391.7
customs	391.7
making	739.278
see also Jewelry	
Shoe repairers	685.310 092
occupational group	T7—685 3
Shoemakers	685.310 092
occupational group	T7—685 3
Shoes	391.413
commercial technology	685.31
customs	391.413
see also Clothing	
Shogi	794.18
Shona (African people)	T5—963 975
Shona languages	496.397 5
	T6—963 975
Shona literature	896.397 5
Shooting game	
sports	799.21
Shop technology	670.42
Shoplifting	364.162
law	345.026 2
Shopping	381.1
etiquette	395.53
see also Commerce	
Shopping centers	381.1
architecture	725.21
area planning	711.552 2
management	658.87
see also Commerce	
Shopping malls	381.1
architecture	725.21
area planning	711.552 2
management	658.87
see also Commerce	
Shops (Retail trade)	381.1
architecture	725.21
management	658.87
see also Commerce	

Shoran	621.384 893
marine navigation	623.893 3
Shore, John, Baron Teignmouth	
Indian history	954.031 1
Shore biology	574.909 46
Shore birds	598.33
commercial hunting	639.123
sports hunting	799.243
Shore flies	595.774
Shore protection	333.917 16
engineering	627.58
land economics	333.917 16
Shore reclamation	333.917 53
engineering	627.58
land economics	333.917 53
Shorelands	551.457
	T2—146
geography	910.914 6
geomorphology	551.457
physical geography	910.021 46
recreational resources	333.784
resource economics	333.917
Shorelines	551.458
	T2—146
geography	910.914 6
geomorphology	551.458
physical geography	910.021 46
Shoring	
foundation engineering	624.152
Short-haired cats	
animal husbandry	636.82
see also Cats	
Short-necked lutes	787.8
see also Stringed instruments	
Short-order cooking	641.57
Short range ballistic missiles	358.175 282
military engineering	623.451 952
military equipment	358.175 282
Short-range weather forecasting	551.636 2
Short stories	808.831
history and criticism	809.31
specific literatures	T3B—301
individual authors	T3A—3
Short takeoff and landing	
airplanes	
engineering	629.133 340 426
Short-term capital	332.041 2
financial management	658.152 44
Short-term loans receivable	
financial management	658.152 44
Short-term securities	
public finance	336.32
Shortages	
agricultural economics	338.17
natural resources	333.711
production	338.02
secondary industries	338.47
Shorthand	653

Sibasa (South Africa :
  District)   T2—682 91
Sibaya Lake   T2—684 91
Siberia (R.S.F.S.R.)   957
     T2—57
Siberia, Eastern (R.S.F.S.R.)   T2—575
Siberia, Western (R.S.F.S.R.)   T2—573
Siberian husky
  animal husbandry   636.73
  see also Dogs
Sibiu (Romania : Judet)   T2—498 4
Sibley County (Minn.)   T2—776 33
Siblings   306.875
     T1—085 5
     T7—045
  child care handbooks   649.102 45
  family relationships   306.875
  home care   649.143
  psychology   155.443
Sibyls   291.62
  parapsychology   133.324 8
Sichuan Sheng (China)   T2—513 8
Sicilian dialect   457.8
     T6—51
Siciliano form   784.188 3
Sicily   T2—458
  ancient   T2—378
Sicily, Strait of   551.462 1
     T2—163 81
Sick leave   331.257 62
  economics   331.257 62
  personnel management   658.312 2
Sick persons   305.908 14
     T1—087 7
     T7—081 4
  architecture for   720.43
  church activities for   259.4
  cooking for   641.563 1
  health services   362.1
    see also Health services
  recreation   790.196
    indoor   793.019 6
    outdoor   796.019 6
  social group   305.908 14
  social welfare   362.1
    see also Health services
Sickle cell anemia
  medicine   616.152 7
  see also Cardiovascular system
Sickness   362.1
  medicine   616
  see also Diseases (Human)
Sidama (African people)   T5—935
Sidamo (African people)   T5—935
Sīdamo (Ethiopia)   T2—632
Sīdamo kifle hāger (Ethiopia)   T2—632
Sidamo languages   493.5
     T6—935

Side arms
  art metalwork   739.72
  military engineering   623.44
Side-blown flutes   788.32
  see also Woodwind instruments
Side chapels
  architecture   726.595
Side dishes   641.81
Side drums   786.94
  see also Percussion instruments
Side effects of drugs
  pharmacodynamics   615.704 2
Side-sewing
  bookbinding   686.35
Sideline markets   381.1
  management   658.870 4
  see also Commerce
Sideline stores   381.1
  management   658.870 4
  see also Commerce
Sidereal clocks
  astronomy   522.5
Sidereal day   529.1
Sidereal month
  lunar motion   523.33
Siderite
  mineralogy   549.782
Sideshows   791.35
Sidewalks   388.411
  road engineering   625.88
  transportation services   388.411
Sidi-Bel-Abbes (Algeria :
  Dept.)   T2—651
Sidi Kacem (Morocco :
  Province)   T2—643
Sidings (Railroads)   625.163
Sidings (Walls)
  buildings   698
  wood   674.43
Sidney (B.C.)   T2—711 28
Sidon (Lebanon)   T2—569 2
  ancient   T2—394 4
Sidonian architecture   722.31
SIDS (Syndrome)
  pediatrics   618.92
Siedlce (Poland :
  Voivodeship)   T2—438 4
Siege of Vicksburg, 1863   973.734 4
Siege warfare   355.44
Siemens process   669.142 2
Siena (Italy : Province)   T2—455 8
Sienna   553.662
Sieradz (Poland :
  Voivodeship)   T2—438 4
Sierra County (Calif.)   T2—794 36
Sierra County (N.M.)   T2—789 67
Sierra Leone   966.4
     T2—664

Silistra (Bulgaria : Okrug)	T2—497 77
Silistrenski okrug (Bulgaria)	T2—497 77
Silk books	096.2
Silk-cotton tree	583.19
Silk-screen printing	686.231 6
graphic arts	764.8
textile arts	746.62
Silk textiles	677.39
arts	746.043 9
see also Textiles	
Silk tree	583.321
Silkworms	
culture	638.2
Silky flycatchers	598.853
Silky terrier	
animal husbandry	636.76
see also Dogs	
Sillery (Quebec)	T2—714 471
Sillimanite	
mineralogy	549.62
Sills (Geology)	551.88
Silo machinery	
manufacturing technology	681.763 1
Silos	
agricultural use	633.208 68
Silt	
petrology	552.5
river engineering	627.122
Silting	627.86
Silurian period	551.732
geology	551.732
paleontology	560.172 5
Siluriformes	597.52
Silver	669.23
chemical engineering	661.065 4
chemistry	546.654
economic geology	553.421
materials science	620.189 23
metallography	669.952 3
metallurgy	669.23
metalworking	673.23
mining	622.342 3
physical metallurgy	669.962 3
production economics	338.274 21
see also Chemicals, Metals	
Silver bell (Flower)	583.686
Silver Bow County (Mont.)	T2—786 68
Silver coins	332.404 2
investment economics	332.63
monetary economics	332.404 2
numismatics	737.4
Silver processes	
photography	772.4
Silver standard	332.422 3
Silverfish (Insect)	595.713
Silverpoint drawing	741.25
Silverside	597.53
Silversmithing	739.23

Silverware	
arts	739.238 3
table setting	642.7
Silviculture	634.95
Simane-ken (Japan)	T2—521 96
Simaroubaceae	583.24
Simbu Province (Papua New	
Guinea)	T2—956 7
Simcoe (Ont. : County)	T2—713 17
Simdlangentsha (South	
Africa : District)	T2—684 91
Similarity (Mathematics)	516.2
Simmering	
cooking	641.73
Simmond's disease	
medicine	616.47
see also Endocrine system	
Simonstown (South Africa :	
District)	T2—687 35
Simples	
pharmacognosy	615.321
Simplexes	514.223
Simpson County (Ky.)	T2—769 735
Simpson County (Miss.)	T2—762 585
Simpson Desert	T2—942 91
Simpson Desert National Park	T2—943 7
Simpson Peninsula (N.W.T.)	T2—719 7
Simulation	003
	T1—011
education	371.397
engineering	620.004 4
management decision making	658.403 52
mathematics	511.8
Simuliidae	595.771
Simultaneous play	
chess	794.17
Sin	291.22
Buddhism	294.342 2
Christianity	241.3
Hinduism	294.522
Islam	297.22
Judaism	296.32
moral theology	291.5
Buddhism	294.35
Christianity	241.3
Hinduism	294.548
Islam	297.5
Judaism	296.385
Sinai (Egypt)	953.1
	T2—531
Sinai Campaign, 1956	956.044
Sinai Peninsula (Egypt)	T2—531
ancient	939.48
	T2—394 8
Sinaloa (Mexico : State)	T2—723 2
Sind (Pakistan)	T2—549 18
Sindhi	T5—948

Sirenia	599.55	Siwi language	493.3
paleozoology	569.5		T6—933
Sirenoidea	597.65	Six Days' War, 1967	956.046
Sirens	621.389 2	Six-man football	796.332 8
music	786.99	Sixth-form colleges	373.238
see also Percussion		Siyabuswa (South Africa)	T2—682 95
instruments		Size of enterprise	338.64
warning device	621.389 2	economics	338.64
Siriono language	498.3	microeconomics	338.514 4
	T6—983	Size of farm	
Sisal		economics	338.16
botany	584.43	Size of particles (Nuclear	
fiber crop	633.577	physics)	539.725
Siskiyou County (Calif.)	T2—794 21	Size standards	
Siskiyou Mountains	T2—795 25	commerce	389.62
Sistan (Iran : Province)	T2—558 3	production management	658.562
Sisters	306.875	Sizing	
	T1—085 5	ores	622.74
	T7—045	Sizing coal	662.623
family relationships	306.875	Sizing paper	676.234
Sisters (Nurses)	610.730 92	Sizuoka-ken (Japan)	T2—521 65
occupational group	T7—613	Sjaelland (Denmark)	T2—489 1
role and function	610.730 69	Skagerrak (Denmark and	
see also Nurses		Norway)	551.461 36
Sisters (Women religious)	271.900 2		T2—163 36
ecclesiology	262.24	Skagit County (Wash.)	T2—797 72
guides to Christian life	248.894 3	Skamania County (Wash.)	T2—797 84
Sisters and brothers	306.875 3	Skanderborg amt (Denmark)	T2—489 5
Sisters of Bon Secours	255.94	Skaneatales Lake (N.Y.)	T2—747 65
church history	271.94	Skaraborgs lan (Sweden	T2—486
Sisters of Charity	255.91	Skateboarding	796.21
church history	271.91	Skateboards	796.21
Sisters of Mercy	255.92	manufacturing technology	685.362
church history	271.92	Skates (Fish)	597.35
Sistrums	786.885	commercial fishing	639.273 5
see also Percussion instruments		Skating (Ice)	796.91
siSwati language	496.398	hockey	796.962 2
	T6—963 98	Skating (Roller)	796.21
Sit-down strikes	331.892 6	Skeena Mountains (B.C.)	T2—711 85
see also Strikes (Work		Skeena-Queen Charlotte	
stoppages)		(B.C.)	T2—711 1
Sit-ins		Skeena River (B.C.)	T2—711 85
social conflict	303.61	Skeet shooters	799.313
Sitars	787.82	sports group	T7—799 3
see also Stringed instruments		Skeet shooting	799.313
Site planning		Skeletal muscle tissues	
architecture	720.28	human histology	611.018 6
Site selection		*see also* Musculoskeletal system	
home economics	643.12	Skeletal organs	
Sitka (Alaska)	T2—798 2	animal anatomy	591.471
Sittidae	598.822	human anatomy	611.71
Situation ethics	171.7	human physiology	612.75
Situational influences		*see also* Musculoskeletal system	
psychology	155.93	Skeletal system	591.185 2
Sivas Ili (Turkey)	T2—565	animal anatomy	591.471
Siwa language	493.3	animal physiology	591.185 2
	T6—933		

Skyscrapers (continued)	
construction	690
Slabs	
structural engineering	624.177 2
concrete	624.183 42
Slacks	391
customs	391
home sewing	646.433
see also Clothing	
Slag (Metallurgy)	669.84
Slalom skiing	796.935
Slander	364.156
criminal law	345.025 6
torts	346.034
Slang	417.2
specific languages	T4—7
Slang dictionaries	T1—03
Slash-and-burn agriculture	
techniques	631.581 8
Slate	553.54
building material	691.2
economic geology	553.54
petrology	552.4
quarrying	622.354
Slaughterhouse residues	
use as fertilizer	631.843
Slaughterhouses	
meat processing	664.902 9
Slave kings (Indian history)	954.023 2
Slave labor	331.117 34
Slave River (Alta. and	
N.W.T.)	T2—719 3
Slave trade	
commerce	380.144
criminal law	345.025
criminology	364.15
international law	341.77
Slavery	306.362
ethics	177.5
see also Ethical problems	
labor economics	331.117 34
law	342.087
political science	326
Slaves	305.567
	T1—086 25
customs	390.25
dress	391.025
Slavic languages	491.8
	T6—918
Slavic literatures	891.8
Slavic people	T5—918
Slavonia (Croatia)	T2—497 2
Slavonic languages	491.8
	T6—918
Slavonic literatures	891.8
Slavs	T5—918
Sledding	796.95

Sleep	154.6
human physiology	612.821
physical fitness	613.79
see also Nervous system	
Sleep disorders	
symptomatology	
neurological disease	616.849 8
see also Nervous system	
Sleeper services	388.042
see also Passenger services	
Sleepers (Ties)	625.143
Sleeping bags	
manufacturing technology	685.53
Sleeping cars	385.33
engineering	625.23
see also Rolling stock	
Sleeping pills	
pharmacodynamics	615.782
Sleeping services	388.042
see also Passenger services	
Sleigh bells	786.848
see also Percussion instruments	
Sleuth dogs	
animal husbandry	636.753
see also Dogs	
Slicers	621.93
Slide preparation	502.82
biology	578.6
botany	578.8
zoology	578.9
Slide rules	
manufacturing technology	681.14
mathematics	510.28
Slides (Photography)	778.2
education	371.335 22
Sliding bearings	621.822
Sligo (Ireland)	T2—417 25
Sligo (Ireland : County)	T2—417 2
Slime molds	589.29
Slings	
sports	799.202 82
Slip laws	348.01
United States	348.731
Slip tracing	666.45
arts	738.15
technology	666.45
Slipcovers	
arts	746.95
commercial technology	684.3
home sewing	646.21
household management	645.4
Slips (Plants)	631.535
floriculture	635.948
Sliven (Bulgaria : Okrug)	T2—497 78
Slivenski okrug (Bulgaria)	T2—497 78
Sloan shorthand system	653.425
Slocan Lake (B.C.)	T2—711 62
Slope County (N.D.)	T2—784 93

Smith, Adam
  economic school — 330.153
Smith, Ian Douglas
  Zimbabwean history — 968.910 4
Smith County (Kan.) — T2—781 213
Smith County (Miss.) — T2—762 582
Smith County (Tenn.) — T2—768 52
Smith County (Tex.) — T2—764 225
Smithers (B.C.) — T2—711 82
Smithfield (South Africa :
  District) — T2—685 6
Smithsonite
  mineralogy — 549.782
Smithton (Tas.) — T2—946 5
Smocking
  arts — 746.44
Smog — 363.739 2
  air pollution — 363.739 2
  pollution technology — 628.532
Smoke — 541.345 15
  colloid chemistry — 541.345 15
    applied — 660.294 515
  pollution technology — 628.532
Smoke bombs — 623.451 6
Smoke-canister launchers — 623.445
Smoke pollution — 363.738 7
  see also Pollution
Smoke signals
  social psychology — 302.222
Smoke tree — 583.28
Smoked foods
  cooking — 641.616
Smokeless powder
  military engineering — 623.452 6
Smokers (Apiary equipment)
  use — 638.142
Smokers' supplies — 688.4
Smoking — 394.14
  addiction — 362.296
    medicine — 616.865
    personal health — 613.85
    social welfare — 362.296
    see also Substance abuse
  customs — 394.14
  social problem — 363.4
Smoking foods — 664.028 6
  commercial preservation — 664.028 6
  home preservation — 641.46
Smoking paraphernalia makers — 688.409 2
  occupational group — T7—688
Smoky Hill River — T2—781 5
Smolensk (R.S.F.S.R. :
  Oblast) — T2—476 2
Smolenskaia oblast
  (R.S.F.S.R.) — T2—476 2
Smolianski okrug (Bulgaria) — T2—497 75
Smolyan, Bulgaria (Okrug) — T2—497 75

Smooth muscle tissues
  human histology — 611.018 6
  see also Musculoskeletal system
Smuggling — 364.133
  law — 345.023 3
Smuts — 589.227
  agricultural diseases — 632.427
Smuts, Jan Christiaan
  South African history — 968.053
    1919-1924 — 968.053
    1939-1948 — 968.055
Smyrna (Ancient city) — T2—392 3
Smyrna Ili (Turkey) — T2—562
Smyth County (Va.) — T2—755 723
Snacks — 642
  commercial processing — 664.6
  cooking — 641.53
  customs — 394.15
Snails — 594.3
  cooking — 641.694
  culture — 639.483 8
  food — 641.394
    commercial processing — 664.95
    home preservation — 641.495
Snake flies — 595.747
Snake Island — T2—945 6
Snake plant — 584.43
Snake River (Wyo.-Wash.) — T2—796 1
  Idaho — T2—796 1
  Oregon — T2—795 7
  Washington — T2—797 4
  Wyoming — T2—787 55
Snake venom
  toxicology — 615.942
Snakebirds — 598.43
Snakehead — 597.58
Snakes — 597.96
  cooking — 641.696
  farming — 639.396
  food — 641.396
  small game hunting — 799.257 96
Snap beans — 583.322
  garden crop — 635.652
Snapdragons — 583.81
Snapper — 597.58
  fishing — 639.275 8
Snare drums — 786.94
  see also Percussion instruments
Sneeuberg Range — T2—687 14
Snipe — 598.33
Snipe flies — 595.771
Snipers — 356.162
Snobbishness
  literature — 808.803 53
    history and criticism — 809.933 53
    specific literatures — T3B—080 353
      history and criticism — T3B—093 53
Snohomish County (Wash.) — T2—797 71

Social determinants	
individual psychology	155.234
Social dysfunction	
collective behavior	302.17
individual interactions	302.542
Social education	303.32
Social environment	
psychological influence	155.92
Social equality	305
social theology	291.178 34
Christianity	261.834
Social ethics	170
sociology	303.372
see also Ethical problems	
Social evolution	303.4
Social factors	
influence on crime	364.25
Social forecasts	303.49
Social gerontology	362.6
Social groups	305
	T1—08
	T7—02
influence on crime	364.253
Social history	306.09
Civil War (United States)	973.71
Mexican War	973.621
South African War	968.048 1
Spanish-American War, 1898	973.891
United States Revolutionary War	973.31
Vietnamese War	959.704 31
War of 1812	973.521
World War I	940.31
World War II	940.531
Social inequality	305
Social influence	303.34
psychology	155.92
Social innovation	303.484
Social insurance	368.4
see also Government-sponsored insurance, Insurance	
Social interaction	302
Social justice	303.372
Social justice school	
economics	330.155
Social law	344
Social learning	303.32
Social mobility	305.513
Social movements	303.484
Social norms	306
social control	303.37
Social ownership of means of production	
Marxian theory	335.41
Social participation	302.14
Social pathology	361.1
collective behavior	302.17
individual interactions	302.542
Social pathology (continued)	
influence on crime	364.256
Social perception	302.12
Social planning	361.25
Social policy	361.25
governmental	361.61
Social prediction	303.49
Social pressure	303.3
executive management	658.409 5
Social problems	361.1
social theology	291.178 3
Buddhism	294.337 83
Christianity	261.83
Hinduism	294.517 83
Islam	297.197 83
Judaism	296.387 83
welfare	362.042
Social processes	303
Social progress	303.44
Social protest	303.6
Social psychology	302
Social reform	303.484
Social reformers	303.484 092
occupational group	T7—309
welfare	361.240 92
occupational group	T7—361
Social relations	302
ethics	177
see also Ethical problems	
Social responsibility	
executive management	658.408
Social role	302.15
Social sciences	300
elementary education	372.83
information systems	025.063
Social scientists	300.92
occupational group	T7—3
Social security	362
government-sponsored insurance	368.4
law	344.02
old-age and survivors	368.43
law	344.023
international law	341.76
public administration	351.825 6
social welfare	362
law	344.032
public administration	351.84
United States	368.43
law	344.730 23
see also Insurance	
Social security tax	336.249
accounting	657.46
law	343.052 42
public finance	336.249
Social services	361
see also Welfare services	

Soda niter	553.64
chemistry	546.382 24
economic geology	553.64
mineralogy	549.732
Soda process	
wood pulp	676.124
Sodalities	248.06
Sodas (Chemicals)	546.382 2
chemical engineering	661.32
Sodermanlands lan (Sweden)	T2—487
Sodium	
chemical engineering	661.038 2
chemistry	546.382
metallurgy	669.725
organic chemistry	547.053 82
applied	661.895
see also Chemicals	
Sodium bicarbonate	546.382 22
chemical engineering	661.323
Sodium carbonate	546.382 24
chemical engineering	661.324
Sodium-free salt	
food technology	664.4
Sodium hydroxide	546.382 22
chemical engineering	661.322
Sodium nitrate	553.64
chemistry	546.382 24
economic geology	553.64
Sodium-vapor lighting	621.327 6
Sodomy	306.773
criminal law	345.025 36
criminology	364.153 6
sociology	306.773
Soekarno	
Indonesian history	959.803 5
Sofala (Mozambique : District)	T2—679 4
Sofas	645.4
manufacturing technology	684.12
see also Furniture	
Sofia (Bulgaria : Okrug)	T2—497 73
Soft fiber crops	633.5
Soft rock	781.66
Soft toys	
making	688.724
handicrafts	745.592 4
technology	688.724
see also Toys	
Softball	796.357 8
Softening processes	
water-supply treatment	628.166 6
Software	005.3
Software documentation	
preparation	005.15
text	005.3
Software engineering	005.1
Software maintenance	005.16
Software packages	005.3

Softwoods	674.144
forestry	634.975
Sogdian language	491.53
	T6—915 3
Sogdian literature	891.53
Sogdiana	T2—396
Sogn og Fjordane fylke (Norway)	T2—483
Sohag (Egypt : Province)	T2—623
Soil	631.4
see also Soils	
Soil biochemistry	
soil science	631.417
Soil biology	574.909 48
agriculture	631.46
Soil chemistry	631.41
Soil classification	631.44
Soil conditioners	
chemical engineering	668.64
use	631.82
Soil conservation	333.731 6
agriculture	631.45
land economics	333.731 6
law	346.047 316
public administration	350.823 26
central governments	351.823 26
local governments	352.942 326
Soil ecology	574.526 404
Soil erosion	631.45
agriculture	631.45
engineering	627.5
Soil factors	
floriculture	635.955
Soil formation	551.305
frost action	551.383
Soil mechanics	624.151 36
agriculture	631.43
engineering geology	624.151 36
railroad engineering	625.122
road engineering	625.732
Soil moisture	631.432
Soil physics	
soil science	631.43
Soil pollution	363.739 6
law	344.046 34
public administration	350.823 26
central governments	351.823 26
local governments	352.942 326
social welfare	363.739 6
technology	628.55
see also Pollution	
Soil science	631.4
Soil surveys	631.47
agriculture	631.47
engineering	624.151 7
Soil working	631.51
equipment manufacturing technology	681.763 1

Solifugae	595.48
paleozoology	565.4
Solihull (England :	
Metropolitan Borough)	T2—424 97
Solipsism	
epistemology	121.2
Solitaire	795.43
Solitaries (Birds)	598.65
Solitary confinement	365.644
Solo instruments	786.—.-78 8
bands and orchestras	784
chamber ensembles	785
Solo voices	783.2
Sololá (Guatemala : Dept.)	T2—728 164
Solomon, King of Israel	
Palestinian history	933.02
Solomon Islands	995.93
	T2—959 3
Solomon River (Kan.)	T2—781 2
Solomon Sea	551.465 76
	T2—164 76
Solothurn (Switzerland :	
Canton)	T2—494 35
Solubility	541.342
chemical engineering	660.294 2
Soluble soaps	668.124
Solutes	541.348 3
chemical engineering	660.294 83
Solution chemistry	541.34
applied	660.294
Solution mining	622.22
Solutions	
practical pharmacy	615.42
Solvent extraction	
chemical engineering	660.284 248
Solvents	541.348 2
chemical engineering	660.294 82
organic	661.807
Solway Firth	551.461 37
	T2—163 37
Somali (Ethnic group)	T5—935
Somali (National group)	T5—967 73
Somali Democratic Republic	
people	T5—967 73
Somali-Ethiopian Conflict,	
1977-1979	963.07
Somali-Ethiopian Conflict, 1979-	963.07
Somali language	493.5
	T6—935
Somali literature	893.5
Somalia	967.73
	T2—677 3
Somaliland	967.7
	T2—677
Somaschi	255.54
church history	271.54

Somatization disorders	
medicine	616.852 4
see also Mental illness	
Somatoform disorders	
medicine	616.852 4
see also Mental illness	
Sombrero Island	T2—729 73
Somerset (England)	T2—423 8
Somerset (Tas.)	T2—946 5
Somerset County (Md.)	T2—752 23
Somerset County (Me.)	T2—741 22
Somerset County (N.J.)	T2—749 44
Somerset County (Pa.)	T2—748 79
Somerset East (South Africa :	
District)	T2—687 14
Somerset Island (N.W.T.)	T2—719 5
Somerset West (South	
Africa : District)	T2—687 3
Somervell County (Tex.)	T2—764 521
Somme (France)	T2—442 6
Somnambulism	
medicine	616.849 8
psychology	154.64
see also Nervous system	
Somogy Megye (Hungary)	T2—439 7
Son of God (Christian doctrines)	231.2
Sonar	621.389 5
marine navigation	623.893 8
Sonata forms	784.183
Sonata-rondo form	781.824
instrumental	784.182 4
Sonatina form	784.183 2
Sonderborg amt (Denmark)	T2—489 5
Sonderend Range	T2—687 3
Sonderjyllands amt	
(Denmark)	T2—489 5
Sondrio (Italy : Province)	T2—452 5
Song cycles	782.47
choral and mixed voices	782.547
single voices	783.094 7
Song of Solomon	223.9
Song of Songs	223.9
Song of the Three Children	
(Bible)	229.5
Song-without-words form	784.189 6
Songbirds	598.8
animal husbandry	636.68
Songe languages	496.393
	T6—963 93
Songhai (African people)	T5—965
Songhai Empire	966.201 8
	T2—662
Songhai language	496.5
	T6—965
Songs	782.42
choral and mixed voices	782.542
folk literature	398.87
single voices	783.094 2

Sound effects	792.024	South Africans (Afrikaners)	T5—393 6
see also Special effects—		South Africans (British	
dramatic performances		origin)	T5—28
Sound engineering	620.2	South Africans (National	
Sound engineers	620.209 2	group)	T5—968
occupational group	T7—620 2	South America	980
Sound-induced illness			T2—8
medicine	616.989 6	South American native languages	498
see also Environmental diseases			T6—98
(Human)		South American native literatures	898
Sound processing		South American native	
computer science	006.45	peoples	T5—98
Sound-ranging devices		South Arabic languages	492.9
marine navigation	623.893 8		T6—929
Sound recording systems	621.389 3	South Arabic literatures	892.9
Sound recordings	621.389 32	South Arabic peoples	T5—929
bibliographies	011.38	South Asia	954
cataloging	025.348 2		T2—54
education	371.333 2	South Asians	T5—914
engineering	621.389 32	South Atlantic Ocean	551.464
library treatment	025.178 2		T2—163 5
music	780	South Atlantic States	975
cover illustration	741.66		T2—75
treatises	780.266	South Auckland (N.Z.)	T2—931 22
reviews	028.138	South Australia	T2—942 3
Sound reproducing systems	621.389 3	South Bedfordshire (England)	T2—425 65
Sound synchronization		South Bend (Ind.)	T2—772 89
motion pictures	778.534 4	South Boston (Va.)	T2—755 662
Sound synthesis		South Bucks (England :	
computer science	006.5	District)	T2—425 98
	T1—028 565	South Cambridgeshire	
engineering	621.399	(England)	T2—426 57
Sounding devices		South Carolina	975.7
marine navigation	623.893 8		T2—757
Soundproofing	620.23	South China Sea	551.465 72
aircraft	629.134 42		T2—164 72
buildings	693.834	South Coast (South Africa)	T2—684 5
Soups	641.813	South Cotabato (Philippines :	
cooking	641.813	Province)	T2—599 7
Sour milk cheeses	641.373 56	South Dakota	978.3
cooking	641.673 56		T2—783
processing	637.356	South Derbyshire (England :	
Source species		District)	T2—425 19
animal breeding	636.082 1	South Dobruja	T2—497 77
Souris River	T2—784 6	South Downs	T2—422 6
Sourwood	583.62	South Dravidian languages	494.81
Sousaphones	788.98		T6—948 1
see also Brass instruments		South Dravidian literatures	894.81
South Africa	968	South Dravidians	T5—948 1
	T2—68	South-Eastern State (Nigeria)	T2—669 44
South African Blacks	T5—968	South Esk River	T2—946 4
South African literature		South Frigid Zone	T2—116
Afrikaans	839.36	South Georgia Island	T2—971 1
Bantu languages	896.39	South Glamorgan (Wales)	T2—429 86
English	820	South Hams (England)	T2—423 592
South African Republic	968.204 5	South Herefordshire	
	T2—682	(England : District)	T2—424 45
South African War, 1899-1902	968.048		

Southern States	975	Soybeans (continued)	
	T2—75	garden crop	635.655
Southern Uplands	T2—413 7	Space	T2—19
Southern Yemen	953.35	astronomy	523.111
	T2—533 5	international law	341.47
Southern Yemenis	T5—927 533 5	physical theories	530.1
Southland (N.Z.)	T2—931 57	Space (Abstraction)	
Southport (Qld.)	T2—943 2	philosophy	114
Southwark (London, England)	T2—421 64	Space (Area)	
Southwest, New	979	arts	701.8
	T2—79	drawing	741.018
Southwest, Old	976	Space and time (Relativity	
	T2—76	theory)	530.11
Southwest jazz	781.653	Space art	709.040 79
Southwest Pacific Ocean	551.465 7	sculpture	735.230 479
	T2—164 7	Space artillery	
Southwest Semitic languages	492	military engineering	623.419
	T6—92	Space biology	574.999
Southwestern Turkic languages	494.36	Space colonies	629.442
	T6—943 6	engineering	629.442
Soutpansberg (South Africa :		Space communications	
District)	T2—682 5	engineering	621.382 38
Soutpansberg Range	T2—682 5	radio engineering	621.384 197
Sovereignty	320.15	Space engineering	620.419
international law	341.26	Space exploration	
Sovereignty of God	212.7	unmanned	629.435
Christianity	231.7	Space facilities	
comparative religion	291.211	military engineering	623.69
Soviet Central Asia	958.4	Space flight	
	T2—584	engineering	629.41
Soviet communism	335.43	transportation services	387.8
economics	335.43	Space flight and religion	
Soviet Union	947.084	natural theology	215.25
	T2—47	Space forces (Military science)	358.8
Asia	957	Space forces personnel	358.809 2
	T2—57	occupational group	T7—358
Soviets	T5—917	Space hazards	
Sow bug	595.372	engineering	629.416
Soweto (South Africa)	T2—682 21	Space heaters	697.2
Soweto riots (South African		Space industrialization	338.091 9
history)	968.062 7	in extraterrestrial worlds	338.099 9
Sowing	631.53	Space laboratories	
Soybean flour	664.726	engineering	629.445
Soybean glue	668.33	Space mail	383.144
Soybean meal	664.726	*see also* Postal service	
Soybean milk		Space medicine	616.980 214
commercial processing	663.64	Space photography	778.35
Soybean oil		military engineering	623.72
food technology	664.369	Space physiology	
Soybeans	583.322	human	612.014 5
agricultural economics	338.175 655	Space ports	
botany	583.322	spacecraft	629.478
commercial processing		Space probes	629.435
economics	338.476 648 056 55	Space psychology	155.966
technology	664.805 655	Space rights	
cooking	641.656 55	sale and rental	333.339
field crop	633.34	*see also* Air rights (Real estate)	
food	641.356 55	Space sciences	500.5

Spinal anesthesia	
surgery	617.964
Spinal column	
fractures	
medicine	617.151
human anatomy	611.711
human diseases	
medicine	616.73
human physiology	612.75
orthopedics	617.375
surgery	617.471
see also Musculoskeletal system	
Spinal cord	
human anatomy	611.82
human diseases	
medicine	616.83
human physiology	612.83
surgery	617.482
see also Nervous system	
Spinal deformities	
orthopedics	617.375
see also Musculoskeletal system	
Spinal nerves	
human diseases	
medicine	616.87
human physiology	612.819
see also Nervous system	
Spine	
human diseases	
medicine	616.73
see also Musculoskeletal system	
Spine fungi	589.222
Spinel	
mineralogy	549.526
Spinets	786.4
see also Keyboard instruments	
Spink County (S.D.)	T2—783 217
Spinning (Angling)	799.12
Spinning (Motion)	
solid mechanics	531.34
Spinning machines	
textile technology	677.028 52
Spinning textiles	677.028 22
arts	746.12
manufacturing technology	677.028 22
Spinor algebras	512.57
Spinor analysis	515.63
Spinulosida	593.93
paleozoology	563.93
Spiny anteaters	599.1
Spiny-headed worm	595.13
Spiny-legged flies	595.774
Spiny rats	599.323 4
Spioenkop Dam	T2—684 7
Spiral and curved bacteria	589.9
Spiral gears	621.833 3
Spirals	516.15

Spires	721.5
architecture	721.5
construction	690.15
Spirit leveling	
geodetic surveying	526.36
Spirit photography	133.92
Spirit varnishes	667.79
Spirit writings	133.93
Spiritual beings	291.21
Christianity	235
Spiritual direction	
Christianity	253.53
Spiritual exercises	248.3
Spiritual gifts	
Christian doctrines	234.13
Spiritual healing	
medicine	615.852
Spiritual powers of Mary	232.916
Spiritual renewal	291.3
Christianity	269
Islam	297.3
Judaism	296.4
Spiritual world	
occultism	133.901 3
Spiritualism	133.9
comparative religion	291.21
philosophy	141
Spiritualists	133.909 2
occupational group	T7—13
Spirituality	291.4
Buddhism	294.344
Christianity	248
Hinduism	294.54
Islam	297.4
Judaism	296.7
Spirituals	782.25
choral and mixed voices	782.525
single voices	783.092 5
Spirochaetales	589.99
Spirogyra	589.47
Spirotrichia	593.17
Spitsbergen	T2—981
Spitsbergen Archipelago	T2—981
Spleen	
human anatomy	611.41
human diseases	
medicine	616.41
human physiology	612.41
surgery	617.551
see also Blood-forming system	
Splenic fever	
incidence	614.561
medicine	616.956
see also Communicable	
diseases (Human)	
Splicing	623.888 2
seamanship	623.888 2
Splines	511.42

Spring	
music	781.524 2
natural history	508
see also Seasons	
Spring-flowering plants	
floriculture	635.953
Spring guns	
art metalwork	739.73
Springboard diving	797.24
Springbok (South Africa)	T2—687 2
Springfield (Ill.)	T2—773 56
Springfield (Mass.)	T2—744 26
Springhaas	599.323 2
Springs (Mechanisms)	621.824
automotive	629.243
railroad engineering	625.21
Springs (South Africa :	
District)	T2—682 2
Springs (Water)	551.498
water-supply engineering	628.112
Springtail	595.715
Sprinkler systems	
fire technology	628.925 2
Sprinters	796.422 092
sports group	T7—796 4
Sprints	796.422
Spruce	585.2
Spruce trees	
forestry	634.975 2
lumber	674.144
Spur gears	621.833 1
Spurge (Euphorbiaceae)	583.95
Spurge laurel	583.933
Spurious knowledge	001.9
Sputtering	
solid state physics	530.416
Spy stories	808.838 72
history and criticism	809.387 2
specific literatures	T3B—308 72
individual authors	T3A—3
Squadrons (Air force units)	358.413 1
Squadrons (Naval air units)	359.943 4
Squadrons (Naval units)	359.31
Squads (Military units)	355.31
Squaliformes	597.31
paleozoology	567.3
Squam Lake (N.H.)	T2—742 3
Squamata	597.94
paleozoology	567.94
Squamish (B.C.)	T2—711 31
Squamish-Lillooet (B.C.)	T2—711 31
Squamous epithelia	
human histology	611.018 7
Square books	099
Square dances	793.34
Square root	513.23
Square-wave generators	
electronics	621.381 548

Squares (Geometry)	516.15
Squares (Location)	
area planning	711.55
Squaring the circle	516.204
Squash (Game)	796.343
Squash players	796.343 092
sports group	T7—796 34
Squashes	641.356 2
botany	583.46
commercial processing	664.805 62
cooking	641.656 2
garden crop	635.62
Squatter's right	346.043 2
Squid	594.58
cooking	641.694
fisheries	639.485 8
food	641.394
commercial processing	664.94
Squirrelfish	597.58
Squirrels	599.323 2
small game hunting	799.259 323 2
Sranan language	427.988 3
	T6—21
Sranantonga language	427.988 3
	T6—21
Srê language	495.93
	T6—959 3
Sri Lanka	954.93
	T2—549 3
Sri Lankans	T5—914 13
Śrīharsa	
Indian history	934.07
St. John's (Nfld.)	T2—718 1
St. Matthias Group	T2—958 3
St. Thomas (Ont.)	T2—713 35
St. Thomas Christians	281.5
see also Eastern churches	
Stabiae (Ancient city)	T2—377
Stabiles	731.55
Stability	
aeronautics	629.132 36
foundation soils	624.151 363
Stability theory	515.35
Stabilization ponds	
sewage treatment	628.351
Stabilizers	
aircraft	629.134 33
Stable flies	595.774
Stachyuraceae	583.394
Stackhousiaceae	583.271
Stacks (Library)	
collections maintenance	025.81
plant management	022.4
Stadiums	796.068
architecture	725.827
Staff notation	780.148
Staff tree	583.271

Staphylinoidea	595.764 2
Star apples	583.685
orchard crop	634.43
Star formation	523.88
Star Mountains	T2—954 9
Star-of-Bethlehem	584.324
Star routes	383.143
see also Postal service	
Star wars (Military science)	358.174
Stara Zagora (Bulgaria :	
Okrug)	T2—497 75
Starbuck Island	T2—964
Starch crops	633.68
Starch paste	668.33
Starches	574.192 482
biochemistry	574.192 482
plants	581.192 482
chemistry	547.782
food technology	664.2
see also Carbohydrates	
Starfish	593.93
paleozoology	563.93
Stark County (Ill.)	T2—773 513
Stark County (N.D.)	T2—784 844
Stark County (Ohio)	T2—771 62
Starke County (Ind.)	T2—772 923
Starlings	598.863
Starozagorski okrug	
(Bulgaria)	T2—497 75
Starr County (Tex.)	T2—764 485
Stars	523.8
astrology	133.53
Starting devices	
automotive	629.257
State (Political body)	320.1
State administration	351
United States	353.9
State bankruptcy	336.368
State banks	332.122 4
State colleges	378.053
State courts (United States)	347.733
State flags	929.92
State governments	
public administration	351
United States	353.9
State labor	331.117 32
State libraries	027.5
State-local relations	
law	342.042
public administration	351.093
United States	353.929 3
State planning	
civic art	711.3
economics	338.9
State schools	371.01
secondary education	373.224
State socialism	335
economics	335
State succession	
international law	341.26
State taxation	336.201 3
law	343.043
public administration	351.724
public finance	336.201 3
State universities	378.053
State visits	
customs	394.4
Stateless persons	323.632
international law	341.486
law	342.083
political science	323.632
Staten Island (N.Y.)	T2—747 26
States (Political bodies)	320.1
governing systems	321
international law	341.26
public administration	351
States of matter	530.4
chemical engineering	660.04
chemistry	541.042
physics	530.4
States of the Church	T2—456
States' Rights Party (U.S.)	324.273 3
Static determinacy	624.171 3
Static indeterminacy	624.171 3
Statice	583.672
Statics	531.12
air	533.61
engineering	620.107 3
engineering	620.103
fluids	532.02
engineering	620.106 3
gases	533.12
engineering	620.107 3
liquids	532.2
engineering	620.106 3
particles	531.162
solids	531.2
engineering	620.105 3
Station posters	
transportation advertising	659.134 4
Station wagons	
driving	629.283
engineering	629.222
repair	629.287 2
Stationary processes	519.232
Stationary steam engines	621.16
Stationary targets	
gun sports	799.312
Stationery	676.282 3
Stations of the cross	
Roman Catholic liturgy	264.027 4
Statistical graphs	T1—021
Statistical inference	519.54
Statistical mathematics	519.5
Statistical mechanics	530.13

Stems (Plants)	
anatomy	581.495
physiology	581.104 25
Stenciling	
decorative arts	745.73
Stencils	
mechanical printing technique	686.231 6
office use	652.4
Stenographers	651.374 109 2
office services	651.374 1
Stenographic machines	
manufacturing technology	681.61
Stenography	653.14
Stenolaemata	594.7
Stenomeridaceae	584.27
Stenurida	563.94
Stepbrothers	306.875
	T1—085 5
	T7—045
family relationships	306.875
Stepchildren	306.874
	T1—085 4
	T7—044 1
family relationships	306.874
Stephanite	
mineralogy	549.35
Stephanotis	583.72
Stephen, King of England	
English history	942.024
Stephens County (Ga.)	T2—758 132
Stephens County (Okla.)	T2—766 53
Stephens County (Tex.)	T2—764 546
Stephenson County (Ill.)	T2—773 33
Stepparents	306.874
	T1—085
	T7—043 1
family relationships	306.874
Steppes	551.453
	T2—145
geography	910.914 5
geomorphology	551.453
physical geography	910.021 45
Steps	
landscape architecture	717
Stepsisters	306.875
	T1—085 5
	T7—045
family relationships	306.875
Sterculiaceae	583.19
Stereochemistry	541.223
Stereophonic sound systems	
engineering	621.389 334
Stereoscopic motion-picture	
photography	778.534 1
cinematography	778.534 1
projection	778.554 1
Stereoscopic photography	778.4

Stereotypes	
sociology	303.385
Sterility	
gynecology	618.178
medicine	616.692
see also Genital system	
Sterilization	
public health	614.48
spacecraft	629.477 4
surgery	617.910 1
unmanned spacecraft	629.467 4
Sterilization (Birth control)	
health	613.942
social services	363.97
surgery	
tubal ligation	618.120 59
vasectomy	617.463
see also Birth control	
Sterkfontein Dam	T2—685 1
Sterkstroom (South Africa : District)	T2—687 5
Sterling County (Tex.)	T2—764 871
Sternum	
human anatomy	611.713
human physiology	612.75
medicine	616.71
orthopedics	617.374
surgery	617.471
see also Musculoskeletal system	
Steroids	574.192 43
biochemistry	574.192 43
human	612.015 73
chemistry	547.73
Sterols	574.192 431
biochemistry	574.192 431
chemistry	547.731
Stethoscopes	
manufacturing technology	681.761
use	616.075 4
Steuben County (Ind.)	T2—772 78
Steuben County (N.Y.)	T2—747 83
Stevenage (England)	T2—425 82
Stevens County (Kan.)	T2—781 725
Stevens County (Minn.)	T2—776 42
Stevens County (Wash.)	T2—797 23
Stewardship (Christian practice)	248.6
Stewart (B.C.)	T2—711 85
Stewart County (Ga.)	T2—758 922
Stewart County (Tenn.)	T2—768 35
Stewart Island (N.Z.)	T2—931 575
Stewartia	583.166
Stewartry (Scotland : District)	T2—414 92
Stewing	
cooking	641.73
Stews	641.823
cooking	641.823
Steynsburg (South Africa : District)	T2—687 13

Stomach diseases
  medicine   616.33
  see also Digestive system
Stomata
  plant anatomy   581.42
Stomatopoda   595.382
  paleozoology   565.38
Stone   553.5
  architectural construction   721.044 1
  architectural decoration   729.6
  building construction   693.1
  building materials   691.2
  economic geology   553.5
  foundation materials   624.153 32
  materials science   620.132
  sculpture material   731.2
  structural engineering   624.183 2
Stone Age   930.12
Stone carving   736.5
Stone County (Ark.)   T2—767 283
Stone County (Miss.)   T2—762 162
Stone County (Mo.)   T2—778 794
Stone flies   595.735
Stone lithography   763.22
Stone Mountains   T2—768 99
Stone pavements   625.82
  road engineering   625.82
  sidewalk engineering   625.882
Stone sculpturing   731.463
Stonefish   597.58
Stones Fauna Reserve   T2—945 7
Stonewall County (Tex.)   T2—764 737
Stoneware   666.6
  arts   738.3
  technology   666.6
Stonewort   589.47
Stopwatches
  technology   681.118
Storage
  coal technology   662.624
  gas technology   665.742
  home economics   648.8
  museology   069.53
  negatives and transparencies   771.45
  petroleum technology   665.542
  positives (Photography)   771.46
  warehouse management   658.785
  water-supply engineering   628.13
Storage (Computer)   004.5
                                    T1—028 545
  engineering   621.397
Storage (Mathematics)   519.83
Storage areas
  home economics   643.5
Storage batteries   621.312 424
Storage buildings
  architecture   725.35
  construction   690.535

Storage centers
  library role   021
Storage containers
  warehouse management   658.785
Storage elevators
  architecture   725.36
Storage of office records   651.53
Storage services   388.044
  see also Freight services
Storax   583.686
Store Baelt (Denmark)   551.461 34
                                    T2—163 34
Store detectives   363.289
Stores (Retail trade)   381.1
  architecture   725.21
  management   658.87
  see also Commerce
Storey County (Nev.)   T2—793 56
Storing clothes
  home economics   646.6
Storing crops   631.568
Storing electric power   621.312 6
Storing food
  home use   641.48
Storing household goods   648.8
Storks   598.34
Storm insurance   368.122
  see also Insurance
Storm sewer systems   628.212
Storm surges
  oceanography   551.470 22
Storm water
  recharge of groundwater   627.56
Stormberg Range   T2—687 6
Stormont, Dundas and
    Glengarry (Ont.)   T2—713 75
Storms   551.55
  meteorology   551.55
  social services   363.349 2
  weather forecasting   551.645
  weather modification   551.685
  see also Disasters
Storstroms amt (Denmark)   T2—489 1
Story County (Iowa)   T2—777 546
Storytelling   808.543
  child care   649.58
  elementary education   372.642
  library services   027.625 1
  rhetoric   808.543
Stour River   T2—423 3
Stoves
  ceramic arts   738.8
  heating buildings   697.22
  household appliances   644.1
    manufacturing technology   683.88
  kitchen appliances   641.502 8
Strabane (Northern Ireland :
    District)   T2—416 41

Streak (Optical property)	
minerals	549.125
Stream ecology	574.526 323
Stream of consciousness	
literature	808.802 5
history and criticism	809.925
specific literatures	T3B—080 25
history and criticism	T3B—092 5
Streaming (Education)	371.254
Streamline flow	532.052
gas mechanics	533.21
liquid mechanics	532.51
Streams	551.483
	T2—169 3
engineering	627.12
fish culture	639.313
hydrology	551.483
landscape architecture	714
recreational resources	333.784 5
resource economics	333.916 2
water-supply engineering	628.112
Středočeský kraj	
(Czechoslovakia)	T2—437 1
Středoslovenský kraj	
(Czechoslovakia)	T2—437 3
Street art (Murals)	751.73
Street cleaning	363.729 1
sanitation services	363.729 1
see also Waste control	
technology	628.46
Street cries	398.87
Street fighting (Military tactics)	355.426
Street furniture	
landscape architecture	717
Street markets	381.18
management	658.87
see also Commerce	
Street music	781.532
Street noise	363.741
see also Noise	
Street patterns	
area planning	711.41
Street songs	398.87
Street theater	792.022
Streetcars	388.46
engineering	625.66
transportation services	388.46
Streets	388.411
engineering	625.7
transportation services	388.411
see also Roads	
Strelitziaceae	584.21
Strength	
crystals	548.842
materials science	620.112
Strepsiptera	595.746
paleozoology	565.74
Streptochaeteae	584.93

Streptococcaceae	589.95
Streptomycetaceae	589.92
Streptoneura	
paleozoology	564.32
Stress	
child psychology	155.418
medicine	616.98
psychiatry	616.89
psychology	155.904 2
Stress (Linguistics)	414.6
specific languages	T4—16
Stress-induced diseases	
medicine	616.98
psychiatry	616.89
see also Environmental diseases	
(Human)	
Stresses (Physical forces)	531.38
crystals	548.842
naval architecture	623.817 6
physics	531.38
structural analysis	624.176
Striated muscle tissues	
human histology	611.018 6
see also Musculoskeletal system	
Strickland River	T2—954 9
Strict liability	346.038
Strigiformes	598.97
paleozoology	568.9
Strijdom, Johannes Gerhardus	
South African history	968.057
Strijdom Dam	T2—684 2
Strike insurance	368.815
see also Insurance	
Strike requirements	331.898 2
economics	331.898 2
Strike votes	331.892 1
Strikebreaking	331.894
Strikes (Geology)	551.85
Strikes (Work stoppages)	331.892
economics	331.892
labor law	344.018 92
personnel management	658.315 4
public administration	350.174
central governments	351.174
local governments	352.005 174
women workers	331.479 2
String	677.71
String art	746.047 1
String beans	583.322
garden crop	635.652
String games	793.9
String orchestras	784.7
Stringed instruments	787
bands and orchestras	784
chamber ensembles	785
mixed	785.2–.5
single type	785.7

Stringed instruments (continued)

construction	787.192 3
by hand	787.192 3
by machine	681.87
solo music	787
Strip cropping	
soil conservation	631.456
Strip mining	622.292
law	346.046 8
Stroboscopic photography	621.367
Stroke (Disorder)	
medicine	616.81
see also Nervous system	
Stromatoporoidea	563.78
Stromboli (Italy)	T2—458 11
Strong interaction (Nuclear	
particles)	539.754 8
Strongboxes	683.34
Strontianite	
mineralogy	549.785
Strontium	669.725
chemical engineering	661.039 4
chemistry	546.394
metallurgy	669.725
physical metallurgy	669.967 25
see also Chemicals	
Strophic form	781.823
instrumental	784.182 3
Stroud (England : District)	T2—424 19
Struck board zithers	787.74
see also Stringed instruments	
Struck drums	786.92
see also Percussion instruments	
Struck stringed instruments	787.7
see also Stringed instruments	
Structural analysis	624.171
construction	690.21
naval architecture	623.817 1
Structural chemistry	541.2
Structural clay products	666.73
materials science	620.142
Structural crystallography	548.81
Structural decoration	729
Structural design	624.177 1
naval architecture	623.817 71
Structural elements	
architecture	721
area planning	711.6
construction	690.1
Structural engineering	624.1
Structural engineers	624.109 2
occupational group	T7—624
Structural foam products	668.493
Structural geology	551.8
Structural materials	
construction	691
Structural stone	553.5
see also Stone	

Structural systems (Linguistics)	415
specific languages	T4—5
Structural unemployment	331.137 041
Structuralism	
arts	709.040 77
sculpture	735.230 477
philosophy	149.96
Structure	
philosophy	117
Structured programming	005.113
Structures	720
architecture	720
interior decoration	747.8
landscape architecture	717
Structures (Mathematics)	511.33
combinatorial topology	514.224
geometry	516
topology	514
Struthioniformes	598.51
paleozoology	568.5
Strychnaceae	583.74
Stuarts (British history)	941 06
Stuarts (English history)	942.06
Stuarts (Irish history)	941.506
Stuccowork	693.6
architectural construction	721.044 6
Studbooks	636.082 2
Student activism	371.81
Student activities	371.89
Student aid	371.22
higher education	378.3
law	344.079 5
Student assessment	371.26
Student attitudes	371.81
Student discipline	371.5
law	344.079 3
Student employment	
higher education	378.365
Student exchanges	370.196 2
international law	341.767 3
Student experiments	T1—078
Student government	371.59
Student housing	371.871
Student life	371.8
Student loans	371.22
law	344.079 5
Student mobility	371.291
Student newspapers	371.805
Student organizations	371.83
Student projects	T1—078
Student protest	371.81
Student rights	
law	344.079 3
Student services	371
law	344.079 4
Student-teacher relations	371.102 3
Student teaching	370.733
Student transportation	371.872

Subversive activities (continued)
law	345.023 1
military science	355.343 7
Subversive groups	322.42

Subversive material
postal handling	383.120 5
see also Postal service	

Subway stations
architecture	725.31
Subway transportation	388.428
transportation services	388.428
see also Subways	
Subways	388.428
engineering	625.42
law	343.098 3
public administration	350.878 428
central governments	351.878 428
local governments	352.918 428
transportation services	388.428
Success	646.7
applied psychology	158
home economics	646.7
parapsychology	131
social psychology	302.14
Success in business	650.1
Success runs (Mathematics)	519.84
Successful living	646.7
home economics	646.7
Succession (Law)	346.052
Succubi	133.423

Succulent plants
floriculture	635.955
Suceava (Romania : Judet)	T2—498 1
Suchitepéquez (Guatemala)	T2—728 165
Suckers (Fish)	597.52

Suckers (Plants)
plant propagation	631.533
Sucking lice	595.751 2
Sucre (Bolivia)	T2—842 4
Sucre (Colombia : Dept.)	T2—861 13
Sucre (Venezuela : State)	T2—875 3
Sucrose	574.192 481 5
biochemistry	574.192 481 5
chemistry	547.781 5
see also Carbohydrates	
Suction lipectomy	617.95
Suctoria	593.175
Sud (Haiti)	T2—729 46
Sudan	962.4
	T2—624
Sudan grass	584.92
Sudanese	T5—927 624
Sudanic languages (Chari-Nile)	496.5
	T6—965
Sudbury (Ont. : District)	T2—713 133

Sudden infant death syndrome
pediatrics	618.92
Suddhadvaita (Philosophy)	181.484 4

Sudetenland (Czechoslovakia)	T2—437 1
Suede leather	675.25
Suez (Egypt : Governorate)	T2—621 5
Suez, Gulf of	551.467 33
	T2—165 33
Suez, Isthmus of	T2—621 5
Suez Canal (Egypt)	386.43
	T2—165 33
Suffolk (England)	T2—426 4
Suffolk (Va.)	T2—755 53

Suffolk Coastal (England : District)
	T2—426 46
Suffolk County (Mass.)	T2—744 6
Suffolk County (N.Y.)	T2—747 25

Suffolk horse
animal husbandry	636.15
zoology	599.725
Suffrage	324.62
Suffrages (Liturgy)	264.13
music	782.292
Sufi orders	297.65

Sufis
biography	297.409 2
Sufism	297.4
Sugar	641.336
biochemistry	574.192 481 5
chemistry	547.781 5
commercial processing	664.1
cooking with	641.636
food	641.336
Sugar beets	583.913
agriculture	633.63
Sugar cane	584.92
agricultural economics	338.173 61
agriculture	633.61
Sugar crops	633.6
Sugar maple	583.28
syrup crop	633.64

Sugar substitutes
food technology	664.5

Sugars
biochemistry	574.192 481
chemistry	547.781

Suggestion therapy
medicine	615.851 2
Suhaj (Egypt : Province)	T2—623
Suhl (Germany : Bezirk)	T2—432 26
Sui dynasty (Chinese history)	951.016
Suicidal compulsions	362.28
medicine	616.858 445
social welfare	362.28
see also Mental illness	
Suicide	362.28
criminal law	345.025 22
criminology	364.152 2
customs	394.8

Summer	
music	781.524 4
natural history	508
see also Seasons	
Summer-flowering plants	
floriculture	635.953
Summer school	371.232
Summer systems	
air conditioning	
buildings	697.933 3
Summer theater	792.022 4
Summers County (W. Va.)	T2—754 76
Summit County (Colo.)	T2—788 45
Summit County (Ohio)	T2—771 36
Summit County (Utah)	T2—792 14
Summons	347.072
criminal law	345.072
Sumner County (Kan.)	T2—781 87
Sumner County (Tenn.)	T2—768 47
Sumner's method	
celestial navigation	527.3
Sumo	796.812 5
Sumo Indians	T5—978
Sumo language	497.8
	T6—978
Sumskaia oblast (Ukraine)	T2—477 15
Sumter County (Ala.)	T2—761 41
Sumter County (Fla.)	T2—759 73
Sumter County (Ga.)	T2—758 913
Sumter County (S.C.)	T2—757 69
Sumu Indians	T5—978
Sumu language	497.8
	T6—978
Sumy (Ukraine : Oblast)	T2—477 15
Sun	523.7
	T2—994
astronomy	523.7
religious worship	291.212
Sun bathing	
health	613.193
Sun-dried blocks	
architectural construction	721.044 22
building construction	693.22
Sun flies	595.774
Sun spider	595.48
Sun tables	
earth astronomy	525.38
Sunburn	
medicine	616.5
see also Skin	
Sunbury (N.B.)	T2—715 43
Sunbury (Vic.)	T2—945 2
Sunda Islands	T2—598
Sunda Islands, Lesser	
(Indonesia)	T2—598 6
Sunda Islands seas	551.465 74
	T2—164 74

Sundanese language	499.22
	T6—992 2
Sunday	
Christian observance	263.4
music	781.522 2
Sunday school	268
Judaism	296.68
Sunday school buildings	
administration	268.2
architecture	726.4
Sunday work	
economics	331.257 4
Sundays River (Cape of Good	
Hope)	T2—687 14
Sundays River (Natal, South	
Africa)	T2—684 7
Sunderland (England :	
Metropolitan Borough)	T2—428 71
Sundew	583.121
Sundials	
technology	681.111
Sunfish	597.58
Sunflower	583.55
Sunflower County (Miss.)	T2—762 47
Sung dynasty (Chinese history)	951.024
Sunlight-favoring plants	
floriculture	635.954
Sunn	
fiber crop	633.56
Sunni Islam	297.81
doctrines	297.204 1
public worship	297.301
Sunshine Coast (B.C.)	T2—711 31
Sunshine law	342.066 2
Sunspots	523.74
geomagnetic effects	538.746
Sunwar language	495.49
	T6—954 9
Suomi language	494.541
	T6—945 41
Suomi literature	894.541
Super Bowl (Football)	796.332 648
Super colliders	539.73
Supercomputers	004.11
architecture	004.251
communications	004.611
programming	005.712 1
programs	005.713 1
engineering	621.391 1
graphics programming	006.671
graphics programs	006.681
interfacing	004.611
programming	005.712 1
programs	005.713 1
operating systems	005.441
performance evaluation	004.110 297
for design and improvement	004.251
peripherals	004.711

Supply ships	
military (continued)	
engineering	623.826 5
naval equipment	359.985 83
Supply-side economics	330.15
Support (Domestic relations)	346.016 6
Supporting garments	391.42
commercial technology	687.2
customs	391.42
home sewing	646.42
see also Clothing	
Supporting structures	
mining	622.28
Suppressed books	098.1
Supranational states	321.04
Supreme Court (U.S.)	347.732 6
Supreme court justices	347.035 092
occupational group	T7—342
Supreme Court of Judicature	
(Great Britain)	347.420 29
Supreme courts	347.035
Suras (Koran)	297.122 9
Surety bonds	
insurance	368.84
see also Insurance	
Suretyship	346.074
Surf riding	797.32
Surface-active materials	668.1
Surface chemistry	541.33
applied	660.293
Surface engineering	620.44
Surface finishing	
home woodworking	684.084
wooden furniture	684.104 3
Surface integrals	515.43
Surface-mined lands	333.765
economics	333.765
reclamation technology	631.64
Surface mining	622.292
Surface-painted enamels	
ceramic arts	738.46
Surface physics	
liquids	530.427
solids	530.417
Surface processes (Geology)	551.3
Surface prospecting	622.12
Surface rail transit systems	388.46
engineering	625.6
public administration	350.878 46
central governments	351.878 46
local governments	352.918 46
transportation services	388.46
Surface refinishing	
wooden furniture	684.104 43
Surface tension	541.33
chemical engineering	660.293
physics	530.427
Surface tillage	631.581

Surface-to-air guided missiles	358.174 82
military engineering	623.451 94
military equipment	358.174 82
Surface-to-air missile forces	358.174
Surface-to-surface guided	
missiles	358.171 82
military engineering	623.451 95
military equipment	358.171 82
Surface-to-underwater guided	
missiles	358.176 82
military engineering	623.451 96
military equipment	358.176 82
Surface transportation	
mining	622.69
Surface treatment	
metals	671.7
Surface waters	553.78
	T2—169
economic geology	553.78
hydrology	551.48
Surfaced lumber	674.42
Surfaces	
geometry	516.352
configurations	516.15
differential and integral	516.36
painting material	
arts	751.2
Surfacing roads	625.8
dirt roads	625.75
paved roads	625.8
Surfactants	668.1
Surfers	797.320 92
sports group	T7—797 3
Surfers Paradise (Qld.)	T2—943 2
Surfing	797.32
Surgeons	617.092
law	344.041 2
occupational group	T7—617 1
role and function	617.023 2
Surgery	617
veterinary medicine	636.089 7
Surgery (Topology)	514.72
Surgical abortion	363.46
medicine	618.88
see also Abortion	
Surgical assistants	
role and function	617.023 3
Surgical complications	
medicine	617.01
Surgical dressings	
use	617.93
Surgical gauzes	677.8
manufacturing technology	677.8
use	617.93
Surgical insurance	368.382 2
see also Insurance	
Surgical nursing	
medicine	610.736 77

Sutures	
surgical use	617.917 8
Suurberg Range	T2—687 5
Suwalki (Poland :	
Voivodeship)	T2—438 3
Suwannee County (Fla.)	T2—759 82
Suwannee River (Ga. and	
Fla.)	T2—759 8
Suweida (Syria : Province)	T2—569 14
Svalbard (Norway)	T2—981
Svan language	499.96
	T6—999 6
Svealand (Sweden)	T2—487
Svendborg amt (Denmark)	T2—489 4
Sverdlovsk (R.S.F.S.R. :	
Oblast)	T2—478 7
Sverdlovskaia oblast	
(R.S.F.S.R.)	T2—478 7
Svetambara (Jainism)	294.492
Swabia (Germany)	T2—433 7
Swabian Alps (Germany)	T2—434 73
Swabian dialect	437.37
	T6—33
Swabian Jura (Germany)	T2—434 73
Swahili languages	496.392
	T6—963 92
Swahili literature	896.392
Swahili-speaking peoples	T5—963 92
Swain County (N.C.)	T2—756 96
Swale (England : Borough)	T2—422 33
Swale River	T2—428 48
Swallow tanagers	598.8
Swallows	598.813
Swamp ecology	574.526 325
Swan Hill (Vic.)	T2—945 9
Swan River (W.A.)	T2—941 2
Swans	598.41
animal husbandry	636.681
Swans Lagoon Fauna Reserve	T2—943 6
Swansea (Wales : City)	T2—429 82
Swanskin fabrics	677.624
see also Textiles	
Swarming of bees	
apiculture	638.146
Swartberg Range	T2—687 16
Swartruggens (South Africa :	
District)	T2—682 3
Swat (Pakistan)	T2—549 122
Swatow dialect	495.17
	T6—951 7
Swazi (Ethnic group)	T5—963 98
Swazi (National group)	T5—968 87
Swazi language	496.398
	T6—963 98
Swaziland	968.87
	T2—688 7
Swearing	
customs	394

Swearing (continued)	
ethics	179.5
Sweat glands	
human anatomy	611.77
human diseases	
medicine	616.56
human physiology	612.792 1
see also Skin	
Sweaters	391
commercial technology	687.146
customs	391
home sewing	646.454
see also Clothing	
Sweden	948.5
	T2—485
Swedenborgianism	289.4
see also Christian	
denominations	
Swedenborgians	
biography	289.409 2
religious group	T7—284
Swedes	T5—397
Swedes (Plants)	641.351 26
see also Rutabaga	
Swedish language	439.7
	T6—397
Swedish literature	839.7
Swedish people	T5—397
Swedish turnip	641.351 26
see also Rutabaga	
Sweep	597.58
Sweep generators	
electronics	621.381 548
Sweeping	
housecleaning	648.5
Sweet alyssum	583.123
Sweet bay	583.114
Sweet cider	641.341 1
commercial processing	663.63
cooking with	641.641 1
Sweet clover	583.322
forage crop	633.366
Sweet corn	641.356 72
botany	584.92
commercial processing	664.805 672
cooking	641.656 72
garden crop	635.672
Sweet Grass County (Mont.)	T2—786 64
Sweet gum	583.394
Sweet peas	583.322
Sweet peppers	641.356 43
botany	583.79
commercial processing	664.805 643
cooking	641.656 43
garden crop	635.643
Sweet potatoes	641.352 2
agriculture	635.22
botany	583.79

Symbolic programming	005.1
Symbolic theory of folklore	398.01
Symbolism	
art representation	704.946
literature	808.801 5
history and criticism	809.915
specific literatures	T3B—080 15
history and criticism	T3B—091 5
of divinatory arts	133.3
paintings	753.6
religious significance	291.37
Christianity	246.55
Judaism	296.4
social psychology	302.222
Symbolism (Art style)	709.034 7
painting	759.057
Symbolism in the Bible	220.64
Symbolism in the Talmud	296.120 64
Symbols	302.222
	T1—014 8
cultural institutions	306.4
social psychology	302.222
Symbols (Linguistics)	411
specific languages	T4—11
Symmetallic standards	332.424
Symmetric functions	515.22
Symmetrodonta	569.18
Symmetry	
arts	701.8
Symmetry of particles	539.725
Sympathetic nervous system	
human diseases	
medicine	616.88
human physiology	612.89
see also Nervous system	
Sympathetic strikes	331.892 3
Symphonic poem form	784.184
Symphonions	786.65
see also Mechanical musical	
instruments	
Symphony forms	784.184
Symphony orchestras	784.2
Symphyla	595.63
paleozoology	565.63
Symphyseotomy	
obstetrical surgery	618.85
Symphyta	595.79
Symplocaceae	583.686
Symptoms	
medicine	616.047
Synagogues	296.65
architecture	726.3
Synapsida	567.93
Synbranchiformes	597.58
Syncarida	595.379
paleozoology	565.37
Synchro-cyclotrons	539.735
Synchronic linguistics	410
Synchronized swimming	797.21
Synchronous accelerators	539.735
Synchronous converters	621.313 5
Synchronous generators	621.313 4
Synchronous machinery	621.313 3
Synchroscopes	621.374 9
Synchrotrons	539.735
Synclines	551.86
Syncretism	
philosophy	148
Syndicalism	335.82
economics	335.82
sociology	306.347
Syndicated crime	364.106 8
Syndicates	
banking	332.16
Synecology	574.524
animals	591.524
plants	581.524
Synentognathi	597.53
Synesthesia	
psychology	152.189
Synod of Evangelical Lutheran	
Churches	284.132 3
see also Lutheran church	
Synods	
Christian ecclesiology	262.4
Synonym dictionaries	413.1
specific languages	T4—31
specific subjects	T1—03
Synopses	T1—020 2
music	780
treatises	780.269
vocal music	
treatises	782.002 69
Synoptic Gospels	226
Syntax	415
specific languages	T4—5
Synthesis	
chemical engineering	660.284 4
chemistry	541.39
organic chemistry	547.2
Synthesizers	786.74
see also Electrophones	
Synthetic building materials	666.89
Synthetic chemicals	
organic	
chemical engineering	661.805
Synthetic drugs	
pharmacology	615.31
Synthetic drugs of abuse	362.299
medicine	616.86
personal health	613.8
social welfare	362.299
see also Substance abuse	
Synthetic dyes	667.25
Synthetic fuels	662.66
Synthetic gems	666.88

Synthetic glue	668.31
Synthetic meat	664.64
Synthetic minerals	666.86
Synthetic petroleum	662.662
Synthetism	709.034 7
painting	759.057
Synxiphosura	565.391
Syphilis	
incidence	614.547 2
medicine	616.951 3
see also Communicable	
diseases (Human)	
Syracuse (N.Y.)	T2—747 66
Syracuse (Sicily)	T2—458 14
ancient	T2—378
Syracuse (Sicily : Province)	T2—458 14
Syria	956.91
	T2—569 1
ancient	939.43
	T2—394 3
Syriac language	492.3
	T6—923
Biblical texts	220.43
Syriac literature	892.3
Syrian Desert	T2—569
Jordan	T2—569 54
Saudi Arabia	T2—538
Syria	T2—569 12
Syrian Orthodox Church	281.63
see also Eastern churches	
Syrians	T5—927 569 1
Syrians (Religious order)	255.18
church history	271.18
Syrup crops	633.6
Syrups	641.336
commercial processing	664.1
cooking with	641.636
Syrups (Pharmaceuticals)	
practical pharmacy	615.42
Systellommatophora	594.38
paleozoology	564.38
System identification	003.1
Systematic bibliography	010.44
Système internationale	530.812
physics	530.812
social aspects	389.15
Systemic grammar	415
specific languages	T4—5
Systemic lupus erythematosus	
medicine	616.77
see also Musculoskeletal system	
Systems	003
	T1—011
Systems analysis	003
computer science	004.21
	T1—028 542
engineering	621.392
management use	658.403 2

Systems analysis (continued)	
public administration	350.007 3
central governments	351.007 3
local governments	352.000 473
Systems analysts	003.092
occupational group	T7—090 3
Systems control	003.5
Systems design	003
computer science	004.21
engineering	621.392
Systems engineering	620.001 171
Systems engineers	620.009 2
occupational group	T7—62
Systems of government	321
Systems optimization	003
Systems programming	005.42
Systems programs	005.43
Systems stability	003.5
Systems theory	003
management use	658.403 2
Szabolcs Szatmar Megye	
(Hungary)	T2—439 9
Szczecin (Poland :	
Voivodeship)	T2—438 1
Szechwan Province (China)	T2—513 8
Szolnok Megye (Hungary)	T2—439 8
Szondi tests	155.284 3

T

T cells	596.029
human immunology	616.079
vertebrate immunology	596.029
T formation	796.332 22
T.M.C. (Television)	384.555 4
see also Television	
T.M.J. dysfunction	
regional medicine	617.522
T.N.T. (Explosive)	662.27
military engineering	623.452 7
T.V.	384.55
see also Television	
T.V. dinners	
home serving	642.1
Tabanidae	595.771
Tabasco (Mexico : State)	T2—726 3
Tabby	
building construction	693.22
Tabernacles	247.1
architecture	726.529 1
Tabes dorsalis	
medicine	616.838
see also Nervous system	
Tablas	786.93
see also Percussion instruments	
Tablature	780.148
Table decorations	642.8
Table furnishings	642.7

Table linens	642.7
arts	746.96
home sewing	646.21
table setting	642.7
Table manners	395.54
Table Mountain (Cape of Good Hope, South Africa)	T2—687 355
Table salt	
cooking with	641.6
see also Salt	
Table service	642.6
Table setting	642.6
Table tennis	796.346
Table tennis players	796.346 092
sports group	T7—796 34
Table tipping (Spiritualism)	133.92
Tableaux	793.24
Tablecloths	642.7
arts	746.96
home sewing	646.21
table setting	642.7
Tables (Furniture)	645.4
decorative arts	749.3
manufacturing technology	684.13
outdoor	645.8
see also Outdoor furniture	
see also Furniture	
Tables (Lists)	T1—021 2
Tabletop photography	778.8
Tablets	
practical pharmacy	615.43
Tableware	642.7
earthenware	666.68
arts	738.38
technology	666.68
glass	
arts	748.83
gold	
arts	739.228 3
handicrafts	745.593
ironwork	
arts	739.48
porcelain	666.58
arts	738.28
technology	666.58
pottery	666.3
arts	738
technology	666.3
silver	
arts	739.238 3
table setting	642.7
wood	
arts	736.4
Taboos	390
Tabora Region (Tanzania)	T2—678 28
Tabuaeran Island	T2—964
Tabulated materials	T1—021

Tabulation	
statistical method	001.422 4
Taccaceae	584.29
Tachina	595.774
Tachinidae	595.774
Táchira (Venezuela)	T2—871 2
Tachometers	
technology	681.118
Tackles (Mechanisms)	621.863
Tackling	
American football	796.332 26
Tacna (Peru : Dept.)	T2—853 5
Tacoma (Wash.)	T2—797 788
Tactical exercises (Military training)	355.54
Tactical geography	355.47
Tactical missile forces	358.175 2
Tactical rockets	623.454 3
Tactics (Military science)	355.42
Tactile organs	
human anatomy	611.88
human physiology	612.88
see also Nervous system	
Tactile perception	
psychology	152.182
Tacuarembó (Uruguay : Dept.)	T2—895 32
Tadpole shrimp	595.32
Tadzhik	T5—915 9
Tadzhik language	491.59
	T6—915 9
Tadzhik S.S.R.	958.6
	T2—586
Tadzhiki literature	891.59
Tadzhikistan	958.6
	T2—586
Taeniodontia	569.36
Taeniopteris	
paleobotany	561.597
Taff-Ely (Wales)	T2—429 78
Taft, William H. (William Howard)	
United States history	973.912
Tagalog language	499.211
	T6—992 11
Tagalog literature	899.211
Tagmemics	415
specific languages	T4—5
Tagus River (Spain and Portugal)	T2—469 45
Portugal	T2—469 45
Spain	T2—462 8
Tahiti	T2—962 11
Tahitian language	499.4
	T6—994
Tahoe, Lake (Calif. and Nev.)	T2—794 38
California	T2—794 38
Nevada	T2—793 57

Tambov (R.S.F.S.R. : Oblast)	T2—473 5
Tambovskaia oblast	
(R.S.F.S.R.)	T2—473 5
Tamburas	787.82
see also Stringed instruments	
Tamerlane	
Asian history	950.2
Tameside (England)	T2—427 35
Tami Islands	T2—957 1
Tamil	T5—948 11
Tamil language	494.811
	T6—948 11
Tamil literature	894.811
Tamil Nadu (India)	T2—548 2
Tamilnad (India)	T2—548 2
Tamin (Iraq : Province)	T2—567 4
Tampa (Fla.)	T2—759 65
Tamworth (England)	T2—424 69
Tamworth (N.S.W.)	T2—944 4
Tan-Tan (Morocco :	
Province)	T2—646
Tanagers	598.882
Tanaidacea	595.374
paleozoology	565.37
Tanami Desert Wildlife	
Sanctuary	T2—942 91
Tandem bicycles	
engineering	629.227 6
repair	629.287 76
riding	629.284 76
Tandridge (England : District)	T2— 422 18
Taney County (Mo.)	T2—778 797
T'ang dynasty (Chinese history)	951.017
Tanga Region (Tanzania)	T2—678 22
Tanganyika	967.82
	T2—678 2
Tanganyika, Lake	T2—678 28
Tangible property risks	368.062
Tangier (Morocco : Province)	T2—642
Tangipahoa Parish (La.)	T2—763 13
Tango form	784.188 85
Tank cars	385.34
engineering	625.24
see also Rolling stock	
Tank warfare	358.18
Tankers (Ships)	387.245
engineering	623.824 5
petroleum technology	665.543
see also Ships	
Tanks (Containers)	
water-supply engineering	628.13
Tanks (Vehicles)	358.183
engineering	623.747 52
military equipment	358.183
Tanners	675.230 92
occupational group	T7—675
Tannin-producing plants	
agriculture	633.87

Tanning leather	675.23
Tannins	581.192 483
biochemistry	581.192 483
chemistry	547.783
see also Carbohydrates	
Tano languages	496.338 5
	T6—963 385
Tanoan languages	497.49
	T6—974 9
Tantalum	669.735
chemical engineering	661.052 6
chemistry	546.526
economic geology	553.465
materials science	620.189 35
metallography	669.957 35
metallurgy	669.735
metalworking	673.735
physical metallurgy	669.967 35
see also Chemicals, Metals	
Tantras	
Buddhist	294.385
Hindu	294.595
Tantric Buddhism	294.392 5
Tantric Hinduism	294.551 4
Tanzania	967.8
	T2—678
Tanzanians	T5—967 8
Tanzanite	553.87
Taoism	
art representation	704.948 995 14
religion	299.514
Taoist holidays	299.514 36
customs	394.268 299 514
Taoist philosophy	181.114
Taoist regions	T2—176 951 4
Taoist sacred music	781.795 14
public worship	782.395 14
music	782.395 14
religion	299.514 38
religion	299.514 37
Taoists	
biography	299.514 092
religious group	T7—299 514
Taos County (N.M.)	T2—789 53
Tap dancing	792.7
Tape drives (Computer)	
computer science	004.56
engineering	621.397 6
Tape players	
automobile	629.277
Tape recorders	
education	371.333 3
sound reproduction	621.389 324
Tape recordings	
education	371.333 3
sound reproduction	621.389 324
Tapes (Adhesives)	668.38

Tapes (Computer)
  computer science | 004.56
  engineering | 621.397 6
Tapes (Recording devices) | 621.382 34
Tapes (Sound)
  bibliographies | 011.38
  cataloging | 025.348 2
  library treatment | 025.178 2
Tapes (Textiles) | 677.76
Tapes (Video)
  bibliographies | 011.37
  cataloging | 025.347 3
  library treatment | 025.177 3
Tapestries | 677.64
  manufacturing technology | 677.64
  textile arts | 746.3
Tapestry makers | 746.392
  occupational group | T7—746
Tapestry-woven rugs
  arts | 746.72
  see also Rugs
Tapestry yard goods | 677.642
Tapeworm | 595.121
Tapeworm-caused diseases
  incidence | 614.554
  medicine | 616.964
  see also Communicable
    diseases (Human)
Tapia
  building construction | 693.22
Tapioca | 583.95
  starch crop | 633.682
Tapiridae | 599.727
Tapirs | 599.727
Tapping tools | 621.955
Taproom buildings
  architecture | 725.72
Taps (Valves) | 621.84
Tar
  materials science | 620.196
Tar pavements | 625.85
  road engineering | 625.85
  sidewalk engineering | 625.885
Tar sands | 553.283
  economic geology | 553.283
  mining | 622.338 3
  processing | 665.4
Taranaki (N.Z.) | T2—931 23
Taranto (Italy : Province) | T2—457 55
Taranto, Gulf of | 551.462 6
 | T2—163 86
Tarapacá (Chile : Region) | T2—831 2
Tarascan Indians | T5—97
Tarascan language | 497
 | T6—97
Tarascan literature | 897
Tarasco Indians | T5 —97

Tarasco language | 497
 | T6—97
Tarawa Atoll (Kiribati) | T2—968 1
Tardigrada | 595.187
  paleozoology | 565.1
Tardive dyskinesia
  medicine | 616.83
  see also Nervous system
Taree (N.S.W) | T2—944 2
Target selection
  military gunnery | 623.557
Target shooting | 799.3
Targets
  shooting sports | 799.3
    manufacturing technology | 688.793
Tariff | 382.7
  see also Customs (Tariff)
Tarija (Bolivia : Dept.) | T2—842 5
Tarka (South Africa : District) | T2—687 14
Tarlac (Philippines :
  Province) | T2—599 1
Tarn (France) | T2—448 5
Tarn-et-Garonne (France) | T2—447 5
Tarnobrzeg (Poland :
  Voivodeship) | T2—438 4
Tarnow (Poland :
  Voivodeship) | T2—438 6
Taro | 584.64
  starch crop | 633.68
Tarot | 133.324 24
Taroudant (Morocco :
  Province) | T2—646
Tarpon | 597.55
Tarraconensis | T2—366
Tarragona (Spain : Province) | T2—467 3
Tarrant County (Tex.) | T2—764 531
Tarsals
  human anatomy | 611.718
  see also Musculoskeletal system
Tarsiers | 599.81
Tarsiidae | 599.81
Tartans
  heraldry | 929.6
Tartar horses
  animal husbandry | 636.11
  zoology | 599.725
Tartous (Syria : Province) | T2—569 13
Tarts | 641.865 2
  commercial processing | 664.752 5
  home preparation | 641.865 2
Taruma language | 498.4
 | T6—984
Taseko River (B.C.) | T2—711 75
Task forces (Naval units) | 359.31
Tasman Peninsula (Tas.) | T2—946 4
Tasman Sea | 551.465 78
 | T2—164 78
Tasmania | T2—946

Tasmanian devils 599.2
Tasmanian wolves 599.2
Taste 591.182 6
  animal physiology 591.182 6
  human physiology 612.87
Taste (Aesthetics)
  music 781.17
Taste disorders
  medicine 616.87
  see also Nervous system
Taste perception
  psychology 152.167
Tatar A.S.S.R. (R.S.F.S.R.) T2—478 3
Tatar Empire 950.2
    T2—5
Tatar language 494.3
    T6—943
Tatar Strait (R.S.F.S.R.) 551.465 54
    T2—164 54
Tatar suzerainty (Russian history) 947.03
Tatars T5—943
Tatarskaia A.S.S.R.
  (R.S.F.S.R.) T2—478 3
Tate County (Miss.) T2—762 85
Tatted fabrics 677.663
  see also Textiles
Tatting
  arts 746.436
Tattnall County (Ga.) T2—758 775
Tattooing
  customs 391.65
Tatura (Vic.) T2—945 4
Taung (South Africa :
  District) T2—682 94
Taunton Deane (England :
  District) T2—423 87
Taunus (Germany) T2—434 16
Tauounate (Morocco :
  Province) T2—643
Taurus Mountains (Turkey) T2—564
Tautomerism 541.225 2
Tawhid 297.211
Tawi-Tawi (Philippines) T2—599 9
Tawitawi (Philippines) T2—599 9
Tax accounting 657.46
  income tax law 343.052 044
  law 343.042
Tax administration
  law 343.04
  public administration 350.724
    central governments 351.724
    local governments 352.13
Tax appeals
  law 343.042
Tax assessment 336.2
  income tax law 343.052 042
  law 343.042

Tax assessment (continued)
  public administration 350.724
    central governments 351.724
    local governments 352.13
  public finance 336.2
Tax auditing
  law 343.04
Tax avoidance 336.206
  law 343.04
  public finance 336.206
Tax collection
  law 343.042
  public administration 350.724
    central governments 351.724
    local governments 352.13
Tax consultants
  income tax law 343.052 044
Tax credits 336.206
  income tax law 343.052 3
  public finance 336.206
Tax deductions 336.206
  income tax law 343.052 3
  public finance 336.206
Tax evasion 364.133
  international law 341.77
  law 345.023 3
Tax-exempt organizations
  law 343.066
Tax-exempt securities
  law 346.092 2
Tax exemption 336.206
  income tax law 343.052 3
  public finance 336.206
Tax expenditures 336.206
  public finance 336.206
Tax incentives 336.206
  income tax law 343.052 3
  public finance 336.206
Tax incidence 336.294
Tax law 343.04
Tax limitations
  law 343.034
Tax lists
  genealogy 929.3
Tax loopholes 336.206
Tax planning
  income tax law 343.052
  law 343.04
Tax rebates 336.206
Tax reduction 336.206
  income tax law 343.052 3
  public finance 336.206
Tax reform 336.205
Tax returns
  income tax law 343.052 044
Tax shelters 336.206
  income tax law 343.052 3
  public finance 336.206

Relative Index

Telefax	384.14
engineering	621.382 35
Telegraphy	384.1
communication services	384.1
engineering	621.383
international law	341.757 7
law	343.099 42
military engineering	623.732
nautical engineering	623.856 2
public administration	351.874 1
sociology	302.235
Telegraphy stations	
communication industry	384.15
Telemark fylke (Norway)	T2—482
Telemarketing	381.1
management	658.84
see also Commerce	
Teleology	124
natural theology	210
philosophy	124
Teleorman (Romania)	T2—498 2
Teleostei	597.5
paleozoology	567.5
Telepathists	133.820 92
occupational group	T7—13
Telepathy	133.82
Telephone	384.6
communication services	384.6
engineering	621.385
international law	341.757 7
law	343.099 43
military engineering	623.733
public administration	351.874 6
sociology	302.235
Telephone books	910.25
Telephone calls	384.64
wireless	384.534 2
see also Telephone	
Telephone counseling	361.323
Telephone engineers	621.385 092
occupational group	T7—621 3
Telephone etiquette	395.59
Telephone lines	
communication services	384.65
Telephone-order houses	381.142
management	658.872
see also Commerce	
Telephone selling	381.1
management	658.84
see also Commerce	
Telephone services	384.64
wire	384.64
wireless	384.534
Telephone stations	
communication services	384.65
wireless	384.535

Telephones	621.386
automobile	629.277
office services	651.73
Telephony	384.6
see also Telephone	
Telephotography	778.322
Telescopes	522.2
manufacturing technology	681.412
use	522.2
Teletex	004.692
communication services	384.34
see also Computer communications	
Teletext	004.69
communication services	384.352
see also Computer communications	
Teletype	384.14
wireless	384.524
see also Telegraphy	
Television	384.55
adult education	374.26
	T1—071 53
communication services	384.55
international law	341.757 7
law	343.099 46
public communication	351.874 55
education	371.335 8
engineering	621.388
influence on crime	364.254
journalism	070.195
law	343.099 46
military engineering	623.735
performing arts	791.45
sociology	306.485
production economics	338.476 213 88
sociology	302.234 5
use by local Christian church	
administration	254.3
pastoral theology	253.78
Television advertising	659.143
Television broadcasting	384.55
see also Television	
Television dinners	
home serving	642.1
Television drama	
literature	808.822 5
history and criticism	809.225
specific literatures	T3B—202 5
individual authors	T3A—2
recreation	791.457
rhetoric	808.225
Television engineers	621.388 009 2
occupational group	T7—621 3
Television evangelism	269.26
Television music	781.546
Television news	070.195
Television photography	778.59

Television plays	
literature	808.822 5
history and criticism	809.225
specific literatures	T3B—202 5
individual authors	T3A—2
recreation	791.457
rhetoric	808.225
Television programs	384.553 2
broadcasting	384.553 2
performing arts	791.45
Television recorders	778.599 3
Television recording	778.599 2
Television scripts	
rhetoric	808.066 791
Television selling	381.1
management	658.84
see also Commerce	
Television selling organizations	381.142
management	658.872
see also Commerce	
Television sets	621.388 8
automobile	629.277
Television stations	384.552 2
engineering	621.388 6
facilities	384.552 2
architecture	725.23
organizations	384.550 65
Television studios	
engineering	621.388 6
Television towers	
architecture	725.23
Television transmission	
engineering	621.388 1
Telex	384.14
wireless	384.524
see also Telegraphy	
Telfair County (Ga.)	T2—758 843
Telford pavements	625.86
road engineering	625.86
sidewalk engineering	625.886
Teller County (Colo.)	T2—788 58
Tellurides	
mineralogy	549.32
Tellurium	
chemical engineering	661.072 6
chemistry	546.726
metallurgy	669.79
see also Chemicals	
Telpherage	621.868
Telugu	T5—948 27
Telugu language	494.827
	T6—948 27
Telugu literature	894.827
Tem (African people)	T5—963 5
Tem language	496.35
	T6—963 5
Témiscamingue (Quebec)	T2—714 13
Témiscouata (Quebec)	T2—714 76

Témiscouata (Quebec :	
Regional County	
Municipality)	T2—714 76
Temora (N.S.W.)	T2—944 8
Temotu (Solomon Islands :	
Province)	T2—959 39
Tempera painting	751.43
Temperament (Musical	
instruments)	784.192 8
Temperaments (Psychology)	155.262
Temperance	178
see also Virtues	
Temperate Zones	T2—12
astronomy	525.5
diseases	
medicine	616.988 2
see also Environmental	
diseases (Human)	
Temperature	536.5
biophysics	574.191 6
human	612.014 46
health	613.1
meteorology	551.525
physics	536.5
seawater	551.460 1
meteorological effect	551.524 6
Temperature changes	
effect on materials	620.112 15
geologic work	551.39
Temperature control	
buildings	697.932 2
mining	622.43
ships	623.853
spacecraft	629.477 5
unmanned spacecraft	629.467 5
Temperature-volume-pressure	
relationships	536.41
Tempering glass	666.129
Tempering metals	671.36
Templars	255.791 3
church history	271.791 3
Temple blocks	786.884 3
see also Percussion instruments	
Temples	291.35
architecture	726.1
Buddhist	294.343 5
Hindu	294.535
Islamic	297.35
Jain	294.435
Sikh	294.635
Temporal mandibular joint	
dysfunction	
regional medicine	617.522
Temporal power of pope	262.132
Temporary deformation	
materials science	620.112 32
physics	531.382

Temporary housing
  social welfare   361.05
Temptation of Jesus Christ   232.95
Ten Commandments   222.16
  moral theology
    Christianity   241.52
    Judaism   296.385
Ten kingdoms (Chinese history)   951.018
Ten Thousand Islands   T2—759 44
Tenancy
  land economics   333.53
  law   346.043 4
Tenant-landlord relations
  land economics   333.54
Tenants' liability insurance   368.56
  see also Insurance
Tenda (African people)   T5—963 2
Tenda language   496.32
     T6—963 2
Tende-Tanzi languages   496.396
     T6—963 96
Tender offers (Securities)   332.632 2
  financial economics   332.632 2
  law   346.066 6
  mergers   338.83
  law   346.066 26
Tenderizers
  food technology   664.4
Tendinitis
  medicine   616.75
  see also Musculoskeletal system
Tendon sheaths
  human anatomy   611.75
  human diseases
    medicine   616.76
  human physiology   612.75
  see also Musculoskeletal system
Tendons
  human anatomy   611.74
  human diseases
    medicine   616.75
  human physiology   612.75
  surgery   617.474
  see also Musculoskeletal system
Tendring (England : District)   T2—426 725
Tenebrionoidea   595.764 7
Tenedos Island   T2—562
  ancient   T2—391 1
Tenements   647.92
  architecture   728.314
  household management   647.92
  social provision   363.5
Tenkiller Ferry Reservoir   T2—766 88
Tennant Creek (N.T.)   T2—942 95
Tennessee   976.8
     T2—768

Tennessee River   T2—768
  Alabama   T2—761 9
  Tennessee   T2—768
Tennessee Valley   T2—768
Tennessee Walking Horse
  animal husbandry   636.13
  zoology   599.725
Tennis   796.342
  electronic games   794.863 42
  equipment technology   688.763 42
Tennis courts   796.342 068
Tennis players   796.342 092
  sports group   T7—796 34
Tenor horns   788.974
  see also Brass instruments
Tenor recorders   788.366
  see also Woodwind instruments
Tenor saxophones   788.74
  see also Woodwind instruments
Tenor viols   787.64
  see also Stringed instruments
Tenor voices   782.87
  choral and mixed voices   782.87
  single voices   783.87
Tenos Island (Greece)   T2—499
Tenrecs   599.33
Tensas Parish (La.)   T2—763 79
Tenses (Grammar)   415
  specific languages   T4—5
Tensile stress   531.38
  physics   531.38
Tension
  effect on materials   620.112 41
Tensor algebra   512.57
Tensor analysis   515.63
Tensor calculus   515.63
Tentacles
  plant anatomy   581.47
Tentaculata   593.8
Tenterfield (N.S.W.)   T2—944 4
Tentering textiles   677.028 25
Tents
  manufacturing technology   685.53
Tenure   331.259 6
  economics   331.259 6
  higher education   378.122
  public administration   351.834
  teachers   371.14
Tepo language   496.33
     T6—963 3
Tequila   641.25
  commercial processing   663.5
Tequila (Plant)   584.43
Teraina Island   T2—964
Teramo (Italy : Province)   T2—457 15
Terang (Vic.)   T2—945 7
Teratogenic agents
  medicine   616.043

Teratology	574.22
animals	591.22
medicine	616.043
plants	581.22
Terbium	
chemistry	546.416
see also Rare earths	
Terce	264.1
music	782.324
Terminal ballistics	
military engineering	623.516
Terminal care	362.175
law	344.041 97
medicine	616.029
nursing	610.736 1
social theology	291.178 321 75
Christianity	261.832 175
social welfare	362.175
see also Health services	
Terminals (Computer)	004.75
engineering	621.398 5
graphics	006.62
engineering	621.399
Terminals (Transportation)	388
see also Transportation facilities	
Termination	
insurance	368.016
Terminology	T1—014
Termite damage prevention	691.14
Termite-resistant construction	693.842
Termites	595.736
Ternary form	781.822 3
instrumental	784.182 2
Ternary superconductors	537.623 3
Ternary system (Numeration)	513.5
Terni (Italy : Province)	T2—456 52
Ternopol (Ukraine : Oblast)	T2—477 18
Ternopolskaia oblast	
(Ukraine)	T2—477 18
Terns	598.338
Terpenes	581.192
biochemistry	581.192
chemistry	547.71
Terra-cotta	
architectural construction	721.044 3
building construction	693.3
building materials	691.4
foundation materials	624.153 42
materials science	620.142
Terraba Indians	T5—978
Terraba language	497.8
	T6—978
Terrace (B.C.)	T2—711 85
Terraces	
landscape architecture	717
Terracing	
soil conservation	631.455

Terrariums	
floriculture	635.982 4
Terrebonne (Quebec :	
County)	T2—714 24
Terrebonne Parish (La.)	T2—763 41
Terrell County (Ga.)	T2—758 935
Terrell County (Tex.)	T2—764 922
Terrestrial ecology	574.526 4
Terrestrial gravity	531.14
mechanics	531.14
Terrestrial photogrammetry	526.982 5
Terrestrial radiation	
meteorology	551.527 2
Terriers	
animal husbandry	636.755
see also Dogs	
Terriers (Toy dogs)	
animal husbandry	636.76
see also Dogs	
Territorial property	320.12
international law	341.42
Territorial waters	
international law	341.448
Territoriality	
animal ecology	591.566
human ecology	304.23
Territory of states	320.12
international law	341.42
Terrorism	303.625
criminal law	345.02
criminology	364.1
international law	341.773
prevention	
management	658.473
public safety	363.32
social conflict	303.625
Terry cloth	677.617
Terry County (Tex.)	T2—764 859
Tertiary education	378
see also Higher education	
Tertiary period	551.78
geology	551.78
paleontology	560.178
Tertiary Prakrits	491.4
	T6—914
Tertiary Prakrits literatures	891.4
Tertiary recovery	
oil extraction	622.338 2
Teruel (Spain : Province)	T2—465 51
Tessin (Switzerland)	T2—494 78
Test bias	
education	371.260 13
psychology	150.287
Test construction	371.271
	T1—076
Test design	371.271
Test River	T2—422 732

Texts (Music)	780
treatises	780.268
Textual criticism	
literature	809
specific literatures	T3B—09
theory	801.959
Texture	
materials science	620.112 92
Texture (Music)	781.28
Thaba Nchu (South Africa)	T2—682 94
Thabamoopo (South Africa :	
District)	T2—682 93
Thabankulu (South Africa :	
District)	T2—687 91
Thabazimbi (South Africa :	
District)	T2—682 5
Thai	T5—959 1
Thai language	495.91
	T6—959 11
Thai languages	495.91
	T6—959 1
Thai literatures	895.91
Thailand	959.3
	T2—593
Thailand, Gulf of	551.465 72
	T2—164 72
Thalamus	
human anatomy	611.81
human physiology	612.826 2
see also Nervous system	
Thalassemia	
medicine	616.152
see also Cardiovascular system	
Thalattosauria	567.93
Thaliacea	596.2
Thallium	669.79
chemical engineering	661.067 8
chemistry	546.678
metallurgy	669.79
physical metallurgy	669.967 9
see also Chemicals	
Thallobionta	589
Thallophyta	589
paleobotany	561.9
Thames River (England)	T2—422
Thamesdown (England)	T2—423 13
Thanet (England)	T2—422 357
Thanksgiving	394.268 3
customs	394.268 3
private prayer	
Christianity	242.724
Thao (Taiwan people)	T5—992 5
Thar Desert (India and	
Pakistan)	T2—544
Thasos Island (Greece)	T2—499
ancient	T2—391 1
Thatching grass	584.92
Thayer County (Neb.)	T2—782 335

Theales	583.166
Theater	792
Christian religious education	268.67
elementary education	372.66
influence on crime	364.254
performing arts	792
religious significance	291.37
Christianity	246.7
see also Arts—religious	
significance	
sociology	306.484
Theater etiquette	395.53
Theater-in-the-round	792.022 8
Theater television	384.556
see also Television	
Theaters	
architecture	725.822
area planning	711.558
music	781.538
Theatines	255.51
church history	271.51
Theatrical costumes	792.026
dramatic performances	792.026
home sewing	646.478
see also Costumes	
Theatrical performers	792.028 092
occupational group	T7—792
Theban supremacy (Greek	
history)	938.06
Thebes (Egypt : Ancient city)	T2—32
Thebes (Greece : Ancient	
city)	T2—384
Thecodontia	567.97
Theft	364.162
law	345.026 2
prevention	
management	658.473
museology	069.54
Theft insurance	368.82
see also Insurance	
Theism	211.3
Christianity	231
comparative religion	291.211
Islam	297.211
Judaism	296.311
natural theology	211.3
Thelephoraceae	589.222
Thelon Game Sanctuary	
(N.W.T.)	T2—719 4
Thelon River (N.W.T.)	T2—719 4
Thematic apperception tests	155.284 4
Thematic catalogs	780.216
Theme and variations form	781.825
instrumental	784.182 5
Themes	
musical element	781.248

Thermotherapy	
medicine	615.832
Theromorpha	567.93
Thesauri (Information science)	025.49
Thesauri (Synonym dictionaries)	413.1
specific languages	T4—31
specific subject	T1—03
Thesaurofacets	025.46
Theses	
bibliographies	011.75
rhetoric	808.02
Thesprotia (Greece)	T2—495 3
Thessalonians (Biblical books)	227.81
Thessalonike (Greece : Nome)	T2—495 6
Thessaloniki (Greece : Nome)	T2—495 6
Thessaly (Greece)	T2—495 4
ancient	T2—382
Theta function	515.984
Theunissen (South Africa :	
District)	T2—685 3
Thiazoles	547.594
Thiès (Senegal : Region)	T2—663
Thigh muscles	
human anatomy	611.738
see also Musculoskeletal system	
Thighs	612.98
human physiology	612.98
regional medicine	617.582
surgery	617.582
see also Lower extremities	
(Human)	
Thin-film circuits	621.381 5
Thin-film memory	004.53
engineering	621.397 32
Thin-film technology	621.381 52
Thin films	
liquid state physics	530.427 5
solid state physics	530.417 5
Thin-layer chromatography	543.089 56
Things (Law)	346.04
Things (Philosophy)	111
Thinking	153.42
human physiology	612.82
psychology	153.42
Thinners	
paint technology	667.624
Thinnings	
silviculture	634.953
Thioacids	547.064
chemical engineering	661.896
Thioalcohols	547.063
chemical engineering	661.896
Thioaldehydes	547.065
chemical engineering	661.896
Thiobacteriales	589.96
Thioethers	547.061
chemical engineering	661.896

Thioketones	547.065
chemical engineering	661.896
Thiophenes	547.594
Third-class mail	383.124
see also Postal service	
Third International	324.175
Third Order Regular of St.	
Francis	255.38
church history	271.38
women's	255.973
church history	271.973
Third orders	
religious orders	255.094
church history	271.094
women's	255.909 4
church history	271.909 4
Third Reich (German history)	943.086
Third Republic (French history)	944.081
Third stream jazz	781.657
Third World	T2—171 6
Thirst	
human physiology	612.391
psychology	152.188 6
see also Digestive system	
Thirty Years' War, 1618-1648	940.24
Thismiaceae	584.13
Thisted (Denmark : Amt)	T2—489 5
Thistle	583.55
Thlaping Tlaro (South	
Africa : District)	T2—682 94
Thohoyandou (South Africa)	T2—682 91
Thomas County (Ga.)	T2—758 984
Thomas County (Kan.)	T2—781 132
Thomas County (Neb.)	T2—782 774
Thomist philosophy	189.4
modern	149.91
Thompson (Man.)	T2—712 71
Thompson, John S. D. (John	
Sparrow David), Sir	
Canadian history	971.055
Thompson-Nicola (B.C.)	T2—711 72
Thompson River (B.C.)	T2—711 72
Thomson River	T2—943 5
Thonga (African people)	T5—963 97
Thonga language	496.397
	T6—963 97
Thoracica	595.35
paleozoology	565.35
Thoracostei	597.53
Thorax	
human anatomy	611.94
human physiology	612.94
orthopedics	617.374
regional medicine	617.54
surgery	617.540 59
Thorium	
chemistry	546.422
economic geology	553.493

Thyroid gland
  human anatomy   611.44
  human diseases
    medicine   616.44
  human physiology   612.44
  surgery   617.539
  see also Endocrine system
Thyroxine
  chemistry   547.734 5
Thysanolaeneae   584.93
Thysanoptera   595.731
  paleozoology   565.73
Thysanura   595.713
  paleozoology   565.71
Tianjin Shih (China)   T2—511 54
Tiaras   391.7
  customs   391.7
  making   739.278
  see also Jewelry
Tiaret (Algeria : Dept.)   T2—651
Tiba-ken (Japan)   T2—521 37
Tibet (China)   T2—515
Tibet Autonomous Region
  (China)   T2—515
Tibetan Buddhism   294.392 3
Tibetan language   495.4
     T6—954 1
Tibetan literature   895.4
Tibetan spaniel
  animal husbandry   636.72
  see also Dogs
Tibetan terrier
  animal husbandry   636.72
  see also Dogs
Tibetans   T5—954
Tibeto-Burman languages   495.4
     T6—954
Tibeto-Burman literatures   895.4
Tibias
  human anatomy   611.718
  see also Musculoskeletal system
Ticino (Switzerland)   T2—494 78
Tick typhus
  incidence   614.526 3
  medicine   616.922 3
  see also Communicable
    diseases (Human)
Ticker tapes
  investment analysis   332.632 042
Tickle
  psychology   152.182 8
Ticks   595.42
  disease carriers   614.433
Tidal currents   551.470 8
Tidal power plants   621.312 134
Tidal waves   551.470 24
Tidbinbilla Nature Reserve   T2—947

Tide tables
  navigation aids   623.894 9
Tides   551.470 8
Tidewater (Md.)   T2—752 1
Tidewater (Va.)   T2—755 1
Tie-dyeing
  textile arts   746.664
Tie plates   625.143
Tien Shan   T2—516
  China   T2—516
  USSR   T2—584 3
Tiento form   784.187 6
Tientsin (China)   T2—511 54
Tierra del Fuego (Argentina)   T2—827 6
Tierra del Fuego (Argentina
  and Chile)   T2—827 6
Tierra del Fuego (Chile)   T2—836 46
Tierra del Fuego island   T2—827 6
Ties (Neckwear)   391.41
  see also Accessories (Clothing)
Ties (Railroad)   625.143
Tift County (Ga.)   T2—758 882
Tiger beetle   595.762
Tigerflower   584.24
Tigers   599.744 28
  animal husbandry   636.89
  big game hunting   799.277 442 8
Tigray Kifle Häger (Ethiopia)   T2—634
Tigre (African people)   T5—928
Tigrē (Ethiopia)   T2—634
Tigre language   492.8
     T6—928
Tigre literature   892.8
Tigrinya (African people)   T5—928
Tigrinya language   492.8
     T6—928
Tigrinya literature   892.8
Tikar (African people)   T5—963 6
Tikar language   496.36
     T6—963 6
Tilapra
  culture   639.375 8
Tile drains   666.733
Tile furniture   645.4
  manufacturing technology   684.106
  see also Furniture
Tile piping   666.733
Tiles
  architectural construction   721.044 3
  building construction   693.3
  building materials   691.4
  ceramic arts   738.6
  floor coverings
    building construction   698.9
  foundation materials   624.153 42
  materials science   620.142
  rubber   678.34
  structural engineering   624.183 6

Tioga County (N.Y.)	T2—747 77	Title (Property)	346.043 8
Tioga County (Pa.)	T2—748 56	conveyancing	346.043 8
Tipitaka	294.382	public administration	350.8
Tippah County (Miss.)	T2—762 923	central governments	351.8
Tippecanoe County (Ind.)	T2—772 95	local governments	352.8
Tipperary (Ireland : County)	T2—419 2	Title insurance	368.88
Tipping		law	346.086 88
economics	331.216 6	*see also* Insurance	
etiquette	395.5	Title investigations	346.043 8
Tipton County (Ind.)	T2—772 555	Title manipulation	
Tipton County (Tenn.)	T2—768 17	subject indexing	025.486
Tires	678.32	Titles of honor	
automotive	629.248 2	genealogy	929.7
Tirmidhi, Muhammad ibn Isa		Titling	
Hadith	297.124 4	cinematography	778.535
Tirol (Austria)	T2—436 42	technical drawing	604.243
Tiryns (Ancient city)	T2—388	Titmice	598.824
Tishah b'Ab	296.439	Tito, Josip Broz	
customs	394.268 296 439	Yugoslavian history	949.702 3
Tishomingo County (Miss.)	T2—762 995	Titoism	335.434 4
Tissue banks	362.178 3	economics	335.434 4
see also Health services		political ideology	320.532 309 497
Tissue biology	574.82	Titus (Biblical book)	227.85
animals	591.82	Titus County (Tex.)	T2—764 215
human	611.018	Tiumenskaia oblast	
plants	581.82	(R.S.F.S.R.)	T2—573
Tissue culture	574.072 4	Tiv (African people)	T5—963 6
experimental botany	581.072 4	Tiv language	496.36
experimental zoology	591.072 4		T6—963 6
human	612.028	Tiverton (England : District)	T2—423 54
Tissue grafting		Tivi (African people)	T5—963 6
surgery	617.95	Tivi language	496.36
Tissue paper	676.284 2		T6—963 6
handicrafts	745.54	Tizi-Ouzou (Algeria : Dept.)	T2—653
Tissue regeneration		Tiznit (Morocco : Province)	T2—646
human	611.018	Tlaxcala (Mexico : State)	T2—724 7
Tissue respiration		Tlemcen (Algeria : Dept.)	T2—651
human physiology	612.26	Tlingit Indians	T5—972
see also Respiratory system		Tlingit language	497.2
Titanium	669.732 2		T6—972
chemical engineering	661.051 2	TMC (Television)	384.555 4
chemistry	546.512	*see also* Television	
economic geology	553.462 3	TMJ dysfunction	
materials science	620.189 322	regional medicine	617.522
metallography	669.957 322	TNT (Explosive)	662.27
metallurgy	669.732 2	military engineering	623.452 7
metalworking	673.732 2	Toadfish	597.53
physical metallurgy	669.967 322	Toads	597.87
see also Chemicals, Metals		Toadstools	589.222
Titanium group		Toamasina (Madagascar :	
chemical engineering	661.051	Province)	T2—691
chemistry	546.51	Toasters	
Tithes		electric cooking	641.586
local Christian church	254.8	Toasting	
Titicaca Lake (Peru and		customs	394.1
Bolivia)	T2—841 2	Toasts	
Bolivia	T2—841 2	literature	808.851
Peru	T2—853 6	history and criticism	809.51

Toasts		Toilet training	649.62
literature (continued)		Tok Pisin	427.995 3
specific literatures	T3B—501		T6—21
individual authors	T3A—5	Toka (African people)	T5—963 91
rhetoric	808.51	Toka language	496.391
Tobacco	583.79		T6—963 91
agriculture	633.71	Tokamaks	621.484
customs	394.14	Tokat Ili (Turkey)	T2—565
ethics	178.7	Tokelau Islands	996.15
see also Ethical problems			T2—961 5
manufacturing technology	679.7	Token coins	
toxicology	615.952 379	economics	332.404 3
Tobacco abuse	362.296	Tokens	
medicine	616.865	numismatics	737.3
personal health	613.85	Tokharian language	491.994
social welfare	362.296		T6—919 94
see also Substance abuse		Tokugawa period (Japanese	
Tobacco industry	338.173 71	history)	952.025
agricultural economics	338.173 71	Tokushima-ken (Japan)	T2—523 4
law	343.076 371	Tokusima-ken (Japan)	T2—523 4
manufacturing	338.476 797	Tokyo (Japan)	T2—521 35
Tobacco industry workers	679.709 2	Tolbukhin (Bŭlgarla , Okrug)	T2—497 77
occupational group	T7—679 7	Tolecraft	745.123
Tobacco mosaic virus	576.648 3	Toledo (Belize : District)	T2—728 24
Tobacco substitutes	688.4	Toledo (Ohio)	T2—771 13
Tobago	972.983	Toledo (Spain : Province)	T2—464 3
	T2—729 83	Toledo Bend Reservoir (La.	
Tobias (Deuterocanonical book)	229.22	and Tex.)	T2—763 62
Tobit (Deuterocanonical book)	229.22	Toleration	179.9
Tobogganing	796.95	*see also* Virtues	
Tobote language	496.35	Toliary (Madagascar :	
	T6—963 5	Province)	T2—691
Toccata form	784.189 47	Tolima (Colombia : Dept.)	T2—861 36
Tocharian language	491.994	Tolland County (Conn.)	T2—746 43
	T6—919 94	Tolls	
Tocharish language	491.994	roads	388.114
	T6—919 94	transportation services	388.049
Tochigi-ken (Japan)	T2—521 32	Tollways	388.122
Tocopilla (Chile : Province)	T2—831 32	*see also* Roads	
Toda (Dravidians)	T5—948 1	Tolman, Edward Chace	
Toda language (Dravidian)	494.81	psychological system	150.194 34
	T6—948 1	Tolna Megye (Hungary)	T2—439 7
Toda literature	894.81	Toltec empire	972.017
Todd County (Ky.)	T2—769 77		T2—72
Todd County (Minn.)	T2—776 88	Tom Green County (Tex.)	T2—764 721
Todd County (S.D.)	T2—783 62	Tomahawks	623.441
Todd River	T2—942 91	Tomatoes	641.356 42
Todies	598.892	botany	583.79
Tofu	641.356 55	commercial processing	664.805 642
commercial processing	664.805 655	cooking	641.656 42
cooking	641.656 55	garden crop	635.642
Togaviruses	576.648 4	Tombigbee River (Miss. and	
Togo	966.81	Ala.)	T2—761 2
	T2—668 1	Tombs	
Togolanders	T5—966 81	architecture	726.8
Togolese	T5—966 81	Tomography	
Tōhoku region (Japan)	T2—521 1	medicine	616.075 7
Toilet paper	676.284 2	Tompkins County (N.Y.)	T2—747 71

Tomsk (R.S.F.S.R. : Oblast)	T2—573
Tomskaia oblast (R.S.F.S.R.)	T2—573
Tonal systems (Music)	781.26
Tonality	781.258
Tonbridge and Malling (England)	T2—422 372
Tonder amt (Denmark)	T2—489 5
Tone color	
musical element	781.234
perception	
psychology	152.157
Tone River (Japan)	T2—521 3
Tonga	996.12
	T2—961 2
Tonga (Mozambique and South African people)	T5—963 97
Tonga (Zambian people)	T5—963 91
Tonga language (Inhambane)	496.397
	T6—963 97
Tonga language (Nyasa, Zambesi)	496.391
	T6—963 91
Tongaat (South Africa)	T2—684 4
Tongaland (South Africa)	T2—684 91
Tongan language	499.4
	T6—994
Tongue	
human anatomy	611.313
human physiology	612.312
tasting	612.87
surgery	617.522
see also Digestive system	
Tongue (Scotland)	T2—411 65
Tongue-and-groove products	674.43
Tongue twisters	398.8
Tonguing (Music)	784.193 4
Tongwe languages	496.394
	T6—963 94
Tonic sol-fa	780.148
Toning solutions	
photography	771.54
Tonkin, Gulf of	551.465 72
	T2—164 72
Tonometry	
glaucoma treatment	617.741 075 4
see also Eyes	
Tonsilitis	
medicine	616.314
see also Digestive system	
Tonsils	
human anatomy	611.32
human diseases	
medicine	616.314
human physiology	612.312
surgery	617.532
see also Digestive system	
Tonus	
muscles	
human physiology	612.741
see also Musculoskeletal system	
skin	
human physiology	612.791
see also Skin	
Tooele County (Utah)	T2—792 43
Tool engineers	621.900 92
occupational group	T7—621
Toole County (Mont.)	T2—786 12
Tooling	
bookbinding	686.36
Tools	621.9
Tooma River	T2—944 8
Toombs County (Ga.)	T2—758 782
Tooms Lake Wildlife Sanctuary	T2—946 4
Tooth tissues	
human diseases	
dentistry	617.634
see also Dentistry	
Toothed whales	599.53
Toothpicks	
wooden	674.88
Toothshells	594.2
Toowoomba (Qld.)	T2—943 3
Top-down programming	005.11
Top games	795.2
equipment technology	688.752
Top management	658.42
Topaz	
mineralogy	549.62
Topcoats	391
commercial technology	687.144
customs	391
home sewing	646.452
see also Clothing	
Topectomy	
surgery	617.481
see also Nervous system	
Topeka (Kan.)	T2—781 63
Topiary work	715.1
Topminnow	597.53
Topographic surveying	526.98
Topographical anatomy	
animals	591.49
human	611.9
plants	581.49
Topography	910
city planning	711.42
geographical description	910
geomorphology	551.41
influence on crime	364.22
influence on precipitation	551.577 5
maping	526
military engineering	623.71

Traffic flow (Road)	388.31
urban	388.413 1
Traffic laws	343.094 6
Traffic noise	363.741
see also Noise	
Traffic patterns	
highways	388.314 3
streets	388.413 143
Traffic safety	363.125
law	343.094
see also Transportation safety	
Traffic signals	388.312 2
see also Traffic signs	
Traffic signs	388.312 2
engineering	625.794
law	343.094 6
transportation services	388.312 2
urban	388.413 122
law	343.098 2
Traffic surveys	
roads	388.314
urban	388.413 14
Traffic violations	364.147
law	345.024 7
Traffic volume	
highways	388.314 2
streets	388.413 142
Trafficways	
engineering	629.047
military engineering	623.6
Trafford (England :	
Metropolitan Borough)	T2—427 31
Tragedies (Drama)	792.12
literature	808.825 12
history and criticism	809.251 2
specific literatures	T3B—205 12
individual authors	T3A—2
stage presentation	792.12
Tragedy (Literary quality)	808.801 6
history and criticism	809.916
specific literatures	T3B—080 16
history and criticism	T3B—091 6
Traguloidea	599.735 5
Trail (B.C.)	T2—711 62
Trailer camps	647.94
area planning	711.557
household management	647.94
Trailer parks	647.92
area planning	711.58
household management	647.92
Trailers (Freight)	388.344
engineering	629.224
see also Trucks	
Trailers (Passenger)	388.346
architecture	728.79
engineering	629.226
pulling	629.284 6
recreation	796.79

Trailers (Passenger) (continued)	
repair	629.287 6
see also Motorized homes	
Traill County (N.D.)	T2—784 14
Trails	
forestry	634.93
law	343.098 1
Train accidents	363.122
see also Transportation safety	
Trainable retarded students	371.928 3
Trainers (Aircraft)	
military engineering	623.746 2
Training	
armed forces	355.5
child care	649.6
labor economics	331.259 2
personnel management	658.312 4
	T1—068 3
executives	658.407 124
public administration	350.15
central governments	351.15
local governments	352.005 15
Training personnel	
personnel management	658.312 404
Training plants	631.546
Training programs	
personnel management	658.312 404
Training schools	
penology	365.42
see also Correctional institutions	
Training teachers	T1—07
Trains	385.37
engineering	625.2
sanitation services	363.729 3
see also Waste control	
transportation services	385.37
see also Rolling stock	
Traits	
individual psychology	155.23
Trajectories	531.31
military engineering	623.514
solid mechanics	531.31
Tramp routes	
marine	387.523
Trampolining	796.47
Tramps	305.568
	T1—086 92
Tramways	388.46
engineering	625.6
transportation services	388.46
Trance phenomena	154.772
Tranquilizer abuse	362.299
medicine	616.86
personal health	613.8
social welfare	362.299
see also Substance abuse	

Transmission facilities	
communications engineering	621.382 3
Transmission media	
computer communications	004.64
engineering	621.398 1
Transmission modes	
computer communications	004.66
engineering	621.398 1
Transmission of light	535.3
Transmission of pressure	532.02
fluid mechanics	532.02
gas mechanics	533.12
liquid mechanics	532.2
Transmission of sound	534.2
Transmitters	
radio engineering	621.384 131
Transmitting electricity	621.319
Transmitting heat	
engineering	621.402 2
Transmitting steam	621.185
Transoceanic flights	
engineering	629.130 91
Transonic flow	533.274
air mechanics	533.62
aeronautics	629.132 304
Transpiration	581.129
Transplantation of organs	362.197 95
see also Organ transplants	
Transplanting	
plant propagation	631.536
Transplants (Medical)	362.197 95
see also Organ transplants	
Transport aircraft	
military engineering	623.746 5
Transport phenomena	530.475
chemical engineering	660.284 2
gaseous state physics	530.43
liquid state physics	530.425
physics	530.475
semiconductors	537.622 5
solid state physics	530.415
Transport ships	
military	359.985 83
design	623.812 64
engineering	623.826 4
naval equipment	359.985 83
Transport theory (Statistical	
mechanics)	530.138
Transport workers	388.092
occupational group	T7—388
Transportation	388
coal technology	662.624
fire hazards	363.379
gas technology	665.743
law	343.093
military engineering	623.6
mining	622.6
museology	069.53

Transportation (continued)	
petroleum technology	665.543
public administration	350.875
central governments	351.875
cabinet departments	351.087 5
local governments	352.915
social effects	303.483 2
transportation services	388
Transportation (Spiritualism)	133.92
Transportation accidents	363.12
see also Transportation safety	
Transportation advertising	659.134 4
Transportation diseases	
medicine	616.980 2
see also Environmental diseases	
(Human)	
Transportation engineering	629.04
Transportation equipment	
engineering	629.046
military equipment	355.83
Transportation facilities	388
architecture	725.3
area planning	711.7
construction	690.53
military resources	355.27
Transportation for employees	
personnel management	658.383
Transportation injuries	
medicine	617.102 8
Transportation insurance	368.2
see also Insurance	
Transportation law	343.093
international law	341.756
Transportation liability insurance	368.57
see also Insurance	
Transportation police	363.287
Transportation safety	363.12
law	343.093
public administration	350.875 002 89
central governments	351.875 002 89
local governments	352.915 002 89
social services	363.12
Transportation workers	388.092
occupational group	T7—388
Transporter bridges	388
construction	624.86
see also Bridges	
Transporting animals	
agriculture	636.083
Transposition (Music)	781.436
Transposons	575.2
Transsexual persons	305.908 24
	T1—087 4
	T7—082 4
Transsexuality	305.3
Transuranium elements	546.44
see also Chemicals	

Treinta y Tres (Uruguay :
  Dept.)   T2—895 22
Trellises
  plant training   631.546
Tremandraceae   583.141
Trematoda   595.122
Trematode-caused diseases
  incidence   614.553
  medicine   616.963
  see also Communicable
    diseases (Human)
Tremellales   589.225
Trempealeau County (Wis.)   T2—775 49
Trench fever
  incidence   614.526 6
  medicine   616.922 6
  see also Communicable
    diseases (Human)
Trench mouth
  medicine   616.312
  see also Digestive system
Trench warfare   355.44
Trengganu   T2—595 1
Trent (Italy : Province)   T2—453 85
Trent, River (England)   T2—425
Trentino-Alto Adige (Italy)   T2—453 8
Trento (Italy : Province)   T2—453 85
Trenton (N.J.)   T2—749 66
Treponema   589.99
Trespass (Law)   346.036
Trestle bridges   388
  construction   624.32
  see also Bridges
Treutlen County (Ga.)   T2—758 682
Treviño (Spain)   T2—466 7
Treviso (Italy : Province)   T2—453 6
Trial-and-error learning
  psychology   153.152 4
Trial by jury
  civil right   323.422
Trial of Jesus Christ   232.962
Trial practice   347.075
  criminal   345.075
Trial procedure   347.075
Trials (Law)   347.07
  criminal law   345.07
Triangles   516.15
Triangles (Music)   786.884 2
  see also Percussion instruments
Triangulation
  geodetic surveying   526.33
Triassic period   551.762
  geology   551.762
  paleontology   560.176 2
Tribal communities   307.772
Tribal fighting (Military tactics)   355.425
Tribal government   321.12
Tribal groups   306.08

Tribal land
  economics   333.2
Triboelectricity   537.21
Tribology   621.89
Tribonematales   589.486
Tribulation (Christian doctrine)   236.9
Tribunals
  papal administration   262.136
Trichechiformes
  paleozoology   569.5
Trichiales   589.29
Trichinosis
  incidence   614.562
  medicine   616.965 4
  see also Communicable
    diseases (Human)
Trichomonadida   593.18
Trichomycetes   589.258
Trichopodaceae   584.27
Trichoptera   595.745
  paleozoology   565.74
Trick games   793.5
Trick photography   778.8
  motion pictures   778.534 5
Trick skiing   796.937
Trickling filter
  sewage treatment   628.352
Tricks   793.8
  manufacturing technology   688.726
Tricladida   595.123
Triconodonta   569.17
Tricuspid valve
  human anatomy   611.12
  human diseases
    medicine   616.125
  human physiology   612.17
  see also Cardiovascular system
Tricycles
  engineering   629.227 3
  repair   629.287 73
  riding   629.284 73
Trier (Germany)   T2—434 313
Trier (Germany :
  Regierungsbezirk)   T2—434 31
Trieste (Italy : Province)   T2—453 93
Trifolium clover   583.322
  forage crop   633.32
Trigg County (Ky.)   T2—769 79
Trigger circuits
  electronics   621.381 537
Triggerfish   597.58
Trigoniaceae   583.143
Trigonometric leveling
  geodetic surveying   526.38
Trigonometry   516.24
  Euclidean   516.24
Trihydroxy aromatics   547.633
Trikkala (Greece : Nome)   T2—495 4

Tropisms	
plant physiology	581.183 2
Troposphere	551.513
	T2—161 2
Trotskyism	335.433
economics	335.433
political ideology	320.532 3
Trotskyists	324.175
Trotting horses	
animal husbandry	636.12
zoology	599.725
Troubadour poetry	808.814
history and criticism	809.14
specific literatures	T3B—104
individual authors	T3A—1
Trough zithers	787.72
see also Stringed instruments	
Troughs	
music	786.82
concussed	786.874
friction	786.864
set	786.864
single	786.888
percussed	786.844
set	786.844
single	786.884 4
see also Percussion	
instruments	
Troup County (Ga.)	T2—758 463
Troupials	598.881
Trousdale County (Tenn.)	T2—768 482
Trousers	391
commercial technology	687.113
customs	391
home sewing	646.433
see also Clothing	
Trout	597.55
commercial fishing	639.275 5
culture	639.375 5
sports fishing	799.175 5
Trover and conversion	346.036
Troy (Ancient city)	T2—392 1
Truancy	371.295
law	344.079 2
Trucial States	T2—535 7
Truck accidents	363.125 9
see also Transportation safety	
Truck cavalry	357.54
Truck farming	635
Truck insurance	
inland marine	368.232
see also Insurance	
Truck terminals	388.33
transportation services	388.33
urban	388.473

Truck transportation	388.324
international law	341.756 883
law	343.094 83
public administration	350.878 324
central governments	351.878 324
local governments	352.918 324
transportation services	388.324
urban	388.413 24
law	343.098 2
Truckers	388.324 092
occupational group	T7—388
Trucks	388.344
agricultural use	631.373
driving	629.284 4
engineering	629.224
law	343.094 4
military engineering	623.747 4
operation	388.324 044
urban	388.413 24
repair	629.287 4
Trudeau, Pierre Elliott	
Canadian history	971.064 4
1968-1979	971.064 4
1980-1984	971.064 6
True bugs	595.754
True buzzards	598.916
True frogs	597.89
True lice	595.751 2
True seals	599.748
Truffles	641.358
agriculture	635.8
botany	589.23
commercial processing	664.805 8
cooking	641.658
Trujillo (Venezuela : State)	T2—871 4
Trujillo Molina, Rafael Léonidas	
Dominican history	972.930 53
Truk (Micronesia)	T2—966
Truman, Harry S.	
United States history	973.918
Trumbull County (Ohio)	T2—771 38
Trumpet creeper	583.54
Trumpeters (Birds)	598.31
Trumpeters (Musicians)	788.920 92
occupational group	T7—788
Trumpets	788.92
see also Brass instruments	
Trunks (Luggage)	
manufacturing technology	685.51
Truro (N.S.)	T2—716 12
Truss bridges	388
construction	624.38
see also Bridges	
Trusses (Structural element)	
naval architecture	623.817 73
structural engineering	624.177 3
Trust companies	332.26
Trust services	332.178

Tug Fork	T2—754 4	Tuna (continued)	
Kentucky	T2—769 2	sports fishing	799.175 8
West Virginia	T2—754 4	Tunas, Las (Cuba : Province)	T2—729 162
Tug services		Tunbridge Wells (England :	
inland ports	386.866	Borough)	T2—422 38
law	343.096 7	Tunceli Ili (Turkey)	T2—566 7
ports	387.166	Tundra ecology	574.526 44
Tugboats	387.232	Tundras	551.453
design	623.812 32		T2—145
engineering	623.823 2	geography	910.914 5
see also Ships		geomorphology	551.453
Tugela (South Africa)	T2—684 4	physical geography	910.021 45
Tugela River	T2—684	Tung oil	665.333
Tughluk dynasty (Indian history)	954.023 6	Tung tree	583.95
Tuition	371.206	Tungstates	
higher education	378.02	mineralogy	549.74
private schools	371.206	Tungsten	669.734
public schools	379.13	chemical engineering	661.053 6
Tuktoyaktuk (N.W.T.)	T2—719 6	chemistry	546.536
Tula (R.S.F.S.R. : Oblast)	T2—473 1	economic geology	553.464 9
Tulameen River (B.C.)	T2—711 5	materials science	620.189 34
Tulare County (Calif.)	T2—794 86	metallography	669.957 34
Tularemia		metallurgy	669.734
incidence	614.573 9	metalworking	673.734
medicine	616.923 9	mining	622.346 49
see also Communicable		physical metallurgy	669.967 34
diseases (Human)		*see also* Chemicals, Metals	
Tularosa Valley	T2—789 65	Tungurahua (Ecuador)	T2—866 15
Tulbagh (South Africa :		Tungus	T5—941
District)	T2—687 3	Tungus languages	494.1
Tulbukhinski okrug			T6—941
(Bulgaria)	T2—497 77	Tungus-Manchu languages	494.1
Tulip tree	583.114		T6—941
Tulips	584.324	Tungusic languages	494.1
floriculture	635.934 324		T6—941
Tulle	677.654	Tungusic peoples	T5—941
see also Textiles		Tunica County (Miss.)	T2—762 86
Tully (Qld.)	T2—943 6	Tunicata	596.2
Tulsa County (Okla.)	T2—766 86	paleozoology	566
Tulskaia oblast (R.S.F.S.R.)	T2—473 1	Tuning	784.192 8
Tulums	788.49	Tunis (Tunisia)	T2—611
see also Woodwind instruments		Tunisia	961.1
Tumbes (Peru : Dept.)	T2—851 2		T2—611
Tumbler Ridge (B.C.)	T2—711 87	Tunisians	T5—927 611
Tumbleweed	583.913	Tunnel diodes	621.381 522
Tumbling	796.47	Tunnel engineers	624.193 092
Tumbling flower beetle	595.767	occupational group	T7—624
Tumboa plant	585.1	Tunnel vaults	721.45
Tumbuka (African people)	T5—963 91	architecture	721.45
Tumbuka language	496.391	construction	690.145
	T6—963 91	Tunneling	624.193
Tumors		mining	622.26
incidence	614.599 9	Tunneling (Physics)	530.416
medicine	616.992	semiconductors	537.622 6
see also Diseases (Human)		Tunnels	388
Tumut (N.S.W.)	T2—944 8	architecture	725.98
Tuna	597.58	construction	624.193
commercial fishing	639.275 8	military engineering	623.68

Turmeric	584.21
Turn and bank indicators	629.135 2
Turner, John	
Canadian history	971.064 6
Turner County (Ga.)	T2—758 885
Turner County (S.D.)	T2—783 385
Turneraceae	583.453
Turnices	598.31
Turning tools	621.94
Turnip celery	641.351 28
see also Celeriac	
Turnips	641.351 25
botany	583.123
commercial processing	664.805 125
cooking	641.651 25
garden crop	635.125
Turnouts	
railroad engineering	625.163
Turnover	
personnel management	658.314
Turnover tax	336.27
law	343.055
public administration	350.724 7
central governments	351.724 7
local governments	352.135
public finance	336.27
Turnovski okrug (Bulgaria)	T2—497 76
Turnpikes	388.122
see also Roads	
Turnstones	598.33
Turpentine	665.332
agriculture	633.895 9
chemical technology	665.332
recovery from pulp	676.5
Turquoise mineralogy	549.72
Turtle grass	584.73
Turtles	597.92
farming	639.392
food	641.396
commercial processing	664.95
cooking	641.696
home preservation	641.495
small game hunting	799.257 92
Turun ja Porin lääni (Finland)	T2—489 73
Tuscaloosa County (Ala.)	T2—761 84
Tuscany (Italy)	T2—455
Tuscarawas County (Ohio)	T2—771 66
Tuscarawas River	T2—771 66
Tuscarora Mountain (Pa.)	T2—748 44
Tuscola County (Mich.)	T2—774 45
Tussah silk textiles	677.392
see also Textiles	
Tutankhamen, King of Egypt	
Egyptian history	932.014
Tutoring	371.394
Tuva Autonomous Soviet Socialist Republic (R.S.F.S.R.)	T2—575
Tuvalu	996.82
	T2—968 2
Tuvalu language	499.4
	T6—994
Tuvinskaia A.S.S.R. (R.S.F.S.R.)	T2—575
TV	384.55
see also Television	
TV dinners	
home serving	642.1
Tweed River (Scotland and England)	T2—413 7
Tweeddale (Scotland : District)	T2—413 82
Tweedsmuir Provincial Park (B.C.)	T2—711 82
Tweezers	
manufacturing technology	688.5
Twelve patriarchs	
pseudepigrapha	229.914
Twelve-tone system	781.268
Twelve Tribes (Palestinian history)	933.02
Twelvers (Islamic sect)	297.821
Twentieth century	909.82
history	T1—090 4
Twenty-first century	909.83
history	T1—090 5
Twenty-one (game)	795.42
Twi (African people)	T5—963 385
Twi language (Akan)	496.338 5
	T6—963 385
Twiggs County (Ga.)	T2—758 545
Twilight	525.7
meteorology	551.566
Twill-woven rugs	
arts	746.72
see also Rugs	
Twin Cities Metropolitan Area (Minn.)	T2—776 579
Twin Falls County (Idaho)	T2—796 37
Twines	677.71
Twining	
arts	746.42
plant physiology	581.185
Twins	
family relationships	306.875
psychology	155.444
Twisters (Tornadoes)	551.553
Twisting	
effect on materials	620.112 43
Twisting textiles	677.028 22
arts	746.12
manufacturing technology	677.028 22
Two Mountains (Quebec : County)	T2—714 25

Two Mountains (Quebec :
　Regional County
　Municipality)　　　　　　T2—714 25
Two-way radios
　automobile　　　　　　　629.277
Tyler, John
　United States history　　　973.58
Tyler County (Tex.)　　　　T2—764 163
Tyler County (W. Va.)　　　T2—754 19
Tylopoda　　　　　　　　599.736
　paleozoology　　　　　　569.73
Tympanic membranes
　human anatomy　　　　　611.85
　human physiology　　　　612.854
　otology　　　　　　　　617.85
　see also Ears
Tyndale Bible　　　　　　220.520 1
Tyne and Wear (England)　T2—428 7
Tyne River (England)　　　T2—428 7
Tynedale (England : District)　T2　428 81
Type ornaments　　　　　686.224
Typecasting　　　　　　　686.221
Typefaces　　　　　　　　686.224
Typefounding　　　　　　686.221
Typesetters　　　　　　　686.225 092
　occupational group　　　T7—686 2
Typesetting　　　　　　　686.225
Typewriter art　　　　　　760
Typewriters　　　　　　　652.3
　manufacturing technology　681.61
　office practice　　　　　652.3
Typewriting　　　　　　　652.3
Typewriting analysis
　criminal investigation　　363.256 5
Typhaceae　　　　　　　　584.613
Typhales　　　　　　　　584.61
Typhoid fever
　incidence　　　　　　　614.511 2
　medicine　　　　　　　616.927 2
　see also Communicable
　　diseases (Human)
Typhoons
　meteorology　　　　　　551.552
Typhus
　incidence　　　　　　　614.526 2
　medicine　　　　　　　616.922 2
　see also Communicable
　　diseases (Human)
Typing　　　　　　　　　652.3
Typists　　　　　　　　　651.374 109 2
　occupational group　　　T7—651
　office services　　　　　651.374 1
Typographic masterpieces
　books　　　　　　　　　094.4
Typographical designs
　graphic arts　　　　　　760
Typography　　　　　　　686.22

Typology
　Biblical interpretation　　220.64
　Christian doctrines　　　232.1
　Talmudic interpretation　296.120 64
Typology (Grammar)　　　415
　specific languages　　　T4—5
Typology (Psychology)　　155.26
Tyrannidae　　　　　　　598.811
Tyrant flycatchers　　　　598.811
Tyre (Lebanon)　　　　　T2—569 2
　ancient　　　　　　　　T2—394 4
Tyrell, Lake (Vic.)　　　　T2—945 9
Tyrian architecture　　　　722.31
Tyrol (Austria)　　　　　T2—436 42
Tyrolean zithers　　　　　787.75
　see also Stringed instruments
Tyrone (Northern Ireland)　T2—416 4
Tyrrell County (N.C.)　　T2—756 172
Tyrrhenian Sea　　　　　551.462 3
　　　　　　　　　　　T2—163 83
Tyubu Region (Japan)　　T2—521 6
Tyngoku (Japan)　　　　T2—521 9
Tyumen (R.S.F.S.R. : Oblast)　T2—573
Tzaneen (South Africa)　　T2—682 6

U

U.F.O.s (Objects)　　　　001.942
U.H.F radio systems　　　621.384 151
U.M.T. (Military training)　355.225
U.N. (United Nations)　　341.23
　international law　　　　341.23
　see also United Nations
U.N.E.S.C.O.
　law　　　　　　　　　341.767
U.N.I.C.E.F. (Children's Fund)
　law　　　　　　　　　341.76
U.S.S.R.　　　　　　　　947.084
　　　　　　　　　　　T2—47
Ubangi-Shari　　　　　　967.410 3
　　　　　　　　　　　T2—674 1
Ubangian languages　　　496.36
　　　　　　　　　　　T6—963 6
Ubombo (South Africa :
　District)　　　　　　　T2—684 91
Udine (Italy : Province)　T2—453 91
Udmurt A.S.S.R. (R.S.F.S.R.)　T2—478 1
Udmurt language　　　　494.53
　　　　　　　　　　　T6—945 3
Udmurt literature　　　　894.53
Udmurts　　　　　　　　T5—945 3
Udmurtskaia A.S.S.R.
　(R.S.F.S.R.)　　　　　T2—478 1
UFOs (Objects)　　　　　001.942
Uganda　　　　　　　　967.61
　　　　　　　　　　　T2—676 1
Ugandans　　　　　　　T5—967 61
Ugarit (Ancient city)　　T2—394 3

Ugaritic language	492.6
	T6—926
Ugaritic literature	892.6
Ugrians	T5—945 1
Ugric languages	494.51
	T6—945 1
Ugric literatures	894.51
Ugric peoples	T5—945 1
UHF radio systems	621.384 151
Uíge (Angola : Province)	T2—673 2
Uighur	T5—943
Uighur language	494.3
	T6—943
Uigur	T5—943
Uigur language	494.3
	T6—943
Uillean pipes	788.49
see also Woodwind instruments	
Uinta County (Wyo.)	T2—787 84
Uinta Mountains (Utah and	
Wyo.)	T2—792 14
Uintah County (Utah)	T2—792 21
Uitenhage (South Africa :	
District)	T2—687 5
Ukraine	T2—477 1
Ukrainian language	491.79
	T6—917 91
Ukrainian literature	891.79
Ukrainian Soviet Socialist	
Republic	T2—477 1
Ukrainians	T5—917 91
Ukuleles	787.89
see also Stringed instruments	
Ulama	297.61
Ulawun	T2—958 5
Ulcerations	
skin	
medicine	616.545
see also Skin	
Ulcers	
medicine	616.343
see also Digestive system	
Ulexite	
mineralogy	549.735
Ulianovskaia oblast	
(R.S.F.S.R.)	T2—478 3
Ulladulla (N.S.W.)	T2—944 7
Ulmaceae	583.962
Ulnas	
human anatomy	611.717
see also Musculoskeletal system	
Ulotrichales	589.47
Ulster (Northern Ireland and	
Ireland)	941.6
	T2—416
Ulster County (N.Y.)	T2—747 34
Ultima Esperanza (Chile)	T2—836 42

Ultimatums	
international law	341.58
Ultrafiltration analysis	544.5
Ultrahigh frequency electronics	
physics	537.534 4
Ultrahigh frequency radio	
systems	621.384 151
Ultrahigh-speed photography	778.37
Ultralight airplanes	387.733 43
engineering	629.133 343
transportation services	387.733 43
see also Aircraft	
Ultramicrobes	576.6
medical microbiology	616.019
Ultramicroscopes	502.824
use	502.824
Ultrasonic cardiography	
medicine	616.120 754 3
see also Cardiovascular system	
Ultrasonic diagnosis	
medicine	616.075 43
Ultrasonic testing	
materials science	620.112 74
Ultrasonic therapy	
medicine	615.83
Ultrasonic vibrations	
biophysics	574.191 45
human	612.014 455
engineering	620.28
physics	534.55
Ultrasonic weapons	623.447
Ultrastructure	
cytology	574.873
Ultraviolet photography	
engineering	621.367 2
Ultraviolet radiation	535.014
biophysics	574.191 54
human	612.014 484
chemical engineering	660.295 34
chemistry	541.353 4
engineering	621.364
military engineering	623.042
physics	535.014
therapeutic use	615.831 5
water-supply treatment	628.166 2
Ultraviolet spectroscopes	
manufacturing technology	681.414 4
Ultraviolet spectroscopy	543.085 85
chemical analysis	543.085 85
engineering	621.361 4
physics	535.844
Ulundi (South Africa)	T2—684 91
Uluru National Park	T2—942 91
Ulverstone (Tas.)	T2—946 5
Ulyanovsk (R.S.F.S.R. :	
Oblast)	T2—478 3
Umatilla County (Or.)	T2—795 69
Umbagog Lake (N.H.)	T2—742 1

Umbanda	299.67	Unauthorized strikes	331.892 4
Umbellales	583.48	*see also* Strikes (Work	
Umber	553.662	stoppages)	
Umberto I, King of Italy		Unclaimed estates	346.057
Italian history	945.084	Uncles	306.87
Umbilical cord disorders			T1—085
obstetrics	618.58		T7—046
Umboi Islands	T2—957 1	family relationships	306.87
Umbrella plant (Cyperales)	584.84	Unconscious	
Umbrella plant (Saxifragales)	583.38	philosophy	127
Umbrella tree	583.114	Unconventional warfare	355.343
Umbrellas		Civil War (United States)	973.785
customs	391.44	Mexican War	973.628
manufacturing technology	685	South African War	968.048 8
Umbria (Italy)	T2—456 5	Spanish-American War, 1898	973.898
ancient	T2—374	United States Revolutionary	
Umbrian language	479.9	War	973.385
	T6—799	Vietnamese War	959.704 38
Umbrians	T5—79	War of 1812	973.528 5
Umbumbulu (South Africa :		World War I	940.485
District)	T2—684 91	World War II	940.548 5
Umbundu languages	496 399	Underberg (South Africa :	
	T6—963 99	District)	T2—684 7
Umfolozi Game Reserve	T2—684 91	Undercover police work	363.232
Umhlanga (South Africa)	T2—684 4	Underdeveloped areas	T2—172 4
Umhlanga Rocks (South		Underemployed	331.13
Africa)	T2—684 4	Underemployment	331.13
Umingmaktok (N.W.T.)	T2—719 7	Underglaze painting	666.45
Umlazi (South Africa :		arts	738.15
District)	T2—684 91	technology	666.45
Umm al-Qaiwain (United		Underground architecture	720.473
Arab Emirates : Emirate)	T2—535 7	Underground areas	
Umm al-Qaywayn (United		environmental psychology	155.964
Arab Emirates : Emirate)	T2—535 7	Underground construction	624.19
Umpiring (Recreation)	790.1	Underground disposal	363.728
American football	796.332 3	sewage sludge disposal	628.366
baseball	796.357 3	solid waste technology	628.445 66
Canadian football	796.335 3	*see also* Waste control	
cricket	796.358 3	Underground electrical lines	621.319 23
rugby	796.333 3	Underground mining	622.2
soccer	796.334 3	Underground movements	
Umpqua River	T2—795 29	World War II	940.533 6
UMT (Military training)	355.225	Underground publications	
Umtata (South Africa :		bibliographies	011.56
District)	T2—687 91	Underground railroad	
Umvoti (South Africa :		Civil War (United States)	
District)	T2—684 7	cause	973.711 5
Umzimkulu (South Africa :		Underground railroads	388.428
District)	T2—687 91	*see also* Subways	
Umzinto (South Africa :		Underground shelters	
District)	T2—684 5	military engineering	623.38
UN (United Nations)	341.23	Underground transportation	388.428
international law	341.23	*see also* Subways	
see also United Nations		Underground water	553.79
Unaligned blocs	T2—171 6	economic geology	553.79
Unarmed combat	796.81	water-supply engineering	628.114
military training	355.548	Underpopulation	363.91
sports	796.81		

Understanding (Gift of the Holy
   Spirit)   234.12
Undertaking (Mortuary)   363.75
  customs   393
  economics   338.473 637 5
  funerals   393.9
   see also Funerals—customs
  law   344.045
  social services   363.75
   public administration   350.772
    central governments   351.772
    local governments   352.6
  technology   614.6
  see also Death
Underwater acoustics
  engineering   620.25
Underwater archaeology   930.102 804
Underwater construction   627.702
Underwater demolition
  operations
  naval forces   359.984
Underwater engineering   627.7
Underwater guided missiles   358.981 782
  military engineering   623.451 97
  military equipment   358.981 782
Underwater mining   622.295
Underwater photography   778.73
Underwater prospecting   622.17
Underwater reconnaissance
  operations
  naval forces   359.984
Underwater swimming
  sports   797.23
Underwater tunnels   388
  construction   624.194
  see also Tunnels
Underwear   391.42
  commercial technology   687.2
  customs   391.42
  home sewing   646.42
  see also Clothing
Underweight persons
  cooking for   641.563 4
  health   613.24
Underwriters   368.012 092
  occupational group   T7—368
Underwriting   368.012
Undulant fever
  incidence   614.565
  medicine   616.957
  see also Communicable
   diseases (Human)
Unemployed persons   305.906 94
     T1—086 94
  labor economics   331.137
  social group   305.906 94

Unemployment   331.137
  economics   331.137
  influence on crime   364.2
  sociology   306.361
Unemployment compensation   368.44
  labor economics   331.255
  social law   344.024
  see also Insurance
Unemployment insurance   368.44
  labor economics   331.255
  social law   344.024
  see also Insurance
Unesco
  law   341.767
Unfair economic practices   338.604 8
  see also Restraint of trade
   (Competition)
Ungava Bay Region (Quebec
  and N.W.T.)   T2—714 111
Unguiculata   599.3
  paleozoology   569.3
Unicameral legislatures   328.39
UNICEF (Children's Fund)
  law   341.76
Unicoi County (Tenn.)   T2—768 982
Unicorn plant   583.54
Unicorns
  folklore   398.245 4
   sociology   398.469
  literature   808.803 7
   history and criticism   809.933 7
   specific literatures   T3B—080 37
    history and criticism   T3B—093 7
Unidentified flying objects   001.942
Unification Church   289.96
  see also Christian
   denominations
Unified field theory   530.142
Uniflagellate molds   589.258
Uniform algebras   512.55
Uniform flow   532.052
  gas mechanics   533.21
  liquid mechanics   532.51
Uniform functions   515.223
Uniform spaces   516
  geometry   516
  topology   514.320 2
Uniform titles
  cataloging   025.322
Uniforms   391
  armed forces
   costume   355.14
  commercial technology   687.15
  customs   391
  see also Clothing
Unincorporated banks   332.123

United funds	
social welfare	361.8
United Kingdom	941
	T2—41
United Lutheran Church in	
America	284.133 5
see also Lutheran church	
United Methodist Church (Great	
Britain)	287.53
see also Methodist Church	
United Methodist Church (U.S.)	287.6
see also Methodist Church	
United Methodist Free Churches	287.53
see also Methodist Church	
United Nations	341.23
finance	336.091 63
international law	341.23
public administration	354.103
law	341.233
United Nations. Charter	341.232
United Nations. General	
Assembly	341.232 2
United Nations. Secretariat	
international law	341.232 4
public administration	354.103
United Nations. Secretary-	
General	
international law	341.232 4
public administration	354.103
United Nations. Security Council	
international law	341.232 3
United Nations (Military	
alliance)	
World War II	940.533 2
United Nations Children's Fund	
law	341.76
United Nations Educational,	
Scientific, and Cultural	
Organization	
law	341.767
United Nations International	
Children's Emergency Fund	
law	341.76
United Nations philatelic issues	769.561
United Nations treaties series	341.026 2
United Party (South Africa)	324.268 08
United Pentecostal Church	289.94
see also Christian	
denominations	
United Presbyterian Church in	
the U.S.A.	285.131
see also Presbyterian Church	
United Presbyterian Church of	
North America	285.134
see also Presbyterian Church	

United Provinces of Central	
America	972.804
	T2—728
Costa Rican history	972.860 42
Guatemalan history	972.810 42
Honduran history	972.830 4
Nicaraguan history	972.850 42
Salvadoran history	972.840 42
United Provinces of the	
Netherlands	949.204
	T2—492
United Reformed Church in the	
United Kingdom	285.232
see also Presbyterian Church	
United Society of Believers in	
Christ's Second Appearing	289.8
see also Christian	
denominations	
United South African National	
Party	324.268 08
United States	973
	T2—73
United States. Air Force, Dept. of	
the	353.63
United States. Army, Dept. of the	353.62
United States. Court of Customs	
and Patent Appeals	347.732 8
United States. Defense, Dept. of	353.6
United States. Dept. of Defense	353.6
United States. Dept. of Justice	353.5
United States. Dept. of State	353.1
United States. Dept. of the Air	
Force.	353.63
United States. Dept. of the Army.	353.62
United States. Dept. of the	
Interior	353.3
United States. Dept. of the Navy.	353.7
United States. Dept. of the	
Treasury	353.2
United States. Interior Dept.	353.3
United States. Navy Dept.	353.7
United States. Post Office Dept.	353.4
United States. Supreme Court	347.732 6
reports	348.734 13
United States Code	348.732 3
United States customary	
measurements	530.813
United States federal law reporter	
system for the Atlantic	
region	348.734 22
United States federal reporter	
system for the Northeast	
region	348.734 23
United States federal reporter	
system for the Northwest	
region	348.734 24
United States federal reporter	
system for the Pacific region	348.734 28

United States federal reporter
    system for the South region   348.734 27
United States federal reporter
    system for the Southeast
    region   348.734 25
United States federal reporter
    system for the Southwest
    region   348.734 26
United States government
    public administration   353
United States national reporter
    system   348.734 2
United States of Colombia   986.106 1
    T2—861
United States Pacific seawaters   551.466 32
    T2—164 32
United States people
    (National group)   T5—13
United States Sanitary
    Commission
    Civil War (United States)   973.777
Uniterm indexing   025.484
Uniting Church in Australia   287.93
  see also Christian
    denominations
Unitized cargo services   385.72
  public administration   351.875 72
Unity   111.82
  Christian church   262.72
Unity School of Christianity   289.97
  see also Christian
    denominations
Universal algebra   512
Universal bibliographies   011.1
Universal Decimal Classification   025.432
Universal history   909
Universal joints   621.825
Universal languages   401.3
Universal military training   355.225
  law   343.012 2
Universal priesthood   234
Universal time   389.17
Universalism (Economic school)   330.155
Universalist churches   289.134
  see also Unitarian and
    Universalist churches
Universalists
  biography   289.109 2
  religious group   T7—281
Universals (Philosophy)   111.2
Universe
  astronomy   523.1
Universities   378.155
    T1—071 1
  area planning   711.57
University administrators   378.009 2
  occupational group   T7—371
  role and function   378.112

University buildings
  architecture   727.3
University education   378
  see also Higher education
University libraries   027.7
  administration   025.197 7
  collection development   025.218 77
  use studies   025.587 7
University presidents   378.009 2
  role and function   378.111
University presses
  bibliographies of publications   011.54
  publishing   070.594
University teachers   378.120 92
  occupational group   T7—372
Unjust enrichment   346.029
Unlawful assembly   364.143
  law   345.024 3
Unloading operations
  materials management   658.788 5
  ships   623.888 1
Unmanned space flight
  engineering   629.43
Unmanned spacecraft
  engineering   629.46
  military engineering   623.749
Unmarried couples   306.735
  law   346.015
Unmarried mothers   306.874 3
    T1—086 947
  family relationships   306.874 3
  psychology   155.642 3
  social group   305.489 694 7
  social welfare   362.839 2
    public administration   350.848
     central governments   351.848
     local governments   352.944 8
Unofficial strikes   331.892 4
  see also Strikes (Work
    stoppages)
Unsized papers   676.286
Unskilled workers
  labor economics   331.798
  labor force   331.114 22
  unemployment   331.137 804
Unspecified keyboard
  instruments   786
  see also Keyboard instruments
Unspecified melody instrument   787
  see also Stringed instruments
Unterfranken (Germany)   T2—433 3
Unterwalden (Switzerland :
  Canton)   T2—494 76
Untouchables   305.568
  social theology   291.178 345 6
  Hinduism   294.517 834 56

Unwed parenthood	306.856
social theology	291.178 358 56
Christianity	261.835 856
Upanishads	294.592 18
Upas tree	583.962
Upholstered furniture	645.4
manufacturing technology	684.12
see also Furniture	
Upholstery	645.4
arts	746.95
home sewing	646.21
household management	645.4
interior decoration	747.5
Upholstery fabrics	677.616
see also Textiles	
Upholstery trimmings	677.76
Upington (South Africa)	T2—687 12
Upland rice	584.93
food crop	633.179
Upolu	T2—961 4
Upper Arrow Lake (B.C.)	T2—711 62
Upper atmosphere	551.514
wind systems	551.518 7
Upper Austria (Austria)	T2—436 2
Upper Avon River (England)	T2—424 4
Upper Bavaria (Germany)	T2—433 6
Upper Canada	971.03
	T2—71
Ontario	971.302
	T2—713
Upper classes	305.52
	T1—086 21
education	371.962
Upper Egypt	T2—623
Upper extremities (Human)	612.97
anatomy	611.97
bones	612.75
anatomy	611.717
medicine	616.71
physiology	612.75
surgery	617.471
fractures	
medicine	617.157
joints	
medicine	616.72
surgery	617.57
muscles	
anatomy	611.737
orthopedics	617.397
physiology	612.97
regional medicine	617.57
surgery	617.570 59
Upper Franconia (Germany)	T2—433 1
Upper Guinea	T2—665
Upper houses (Legislative bodies)	328.31
Upper Karoo (South Africa)	T2—687 13
Upper Nile (Sudan : Province)	T2—629 3

Upper Nile (Sudan : Region)	T2—629 3
Upper Palatinate (Germany)	T2—433 4
Upper Peninsula (Mich.)	T2—774 9
Upper Volta	966.25
	T2—662 5
Upper Volta people	T5—966 25
Uppsala lan (Sweden)	T2—487
Upshur County (Tex.)	T2—764 222
Upshur County (W. Va.)	T2—754 62
Upson County (Ga.)	T2—758 486
Upton County (Tex.)	T2—764 863
Ur (Ancient city)	T2—35
Ur period (Mesopotamian history)	935.01
Urabá, Gulf of	551.463 5
	T2—163 65
Ural-Altaic languages	494
	T6—94
Ural-Altaic literatures	894
Ural Mountains (R.S.F.S.R.)	T2—478 7
Uralic languages	494
	T6—94
Uralic literatures	894
Uraninite	
mineralogy	549.528
Uranium	669.293 1
chemical engineering	661.043 1
chemistry	546.431
economic geology	553.493 2
materials science	620.189 293 1
metallography	669.952 931
metallurgy	669.293 1
mining	622.349 32
physical metallurgy	669.962 931
production economics	338.274 932
prospecting	622.184 932
toxicology	615.925 431
see also Chemicals, Metals	
Uranography	522
Urantia	299
Uranus (Planet)	523.47
	T2—992 7
unmanned flights to	629.435 47
Urban areas	T2—173 2
Urban communities	307.76
psychological influence	155.942
Urban development	307.121 6
law	344.06
public administration	350.818
central governments	351.818
local governments	352.941 8
Urban drainage	
sewer systems	628.21
Urban ecology (Biology)	574.526 8
Urban economics	330.917 32
Urban environments	
effect on education	370.193 48
Urban exodus	307.26

Valleys (continued)
physical geography 910.021 44
Valois, House of (French history) 944.025
Valparaíso (Chile : Province) T2—832 55
Valréas (France) T2—449 2
Vals River T2—685 2
Valuation
investment economics 332.632 21
Valuation of assets
accounting 657.73
land economics 333.332
Valuation of businesses
law 346.065
Valuation of real property
law 346.043 7
Valuation theory 515.784
Value T1—013
labor theory
Marxian economics 335.412
microeconomics 338.521
Value-added networks 004.69
computer communication
services 384.33
see also Computer
communications
Value-added tax 336.271 4
law 343.055
public administration 350.724 7
central governments 351.724 7
local governments 352.135
public finance 336.271 4
Value cognition
psychology 153.45
Values
epistemology 121.8
social control 303.372
Valverde (Dominican
Republic : Province) T2—729 357
Valves 621.84
internal-combustion engines 621.437
Valvifera 595.372
Valvular activity
heart
human physiology 612.171
see also Cardiovascular
system
Valvular diseases
medicine 616.125
see also Cardiovascular system
Vampires 133.423
folklore 398.21
sociology 398.45
literature 808.803 75
history and criticism 809.933 75
specific literatures T3B—080 375
history and criticism T3B—093 75
Vampyromorpha 594.55
paleozoology 564.55

Van Allen radiation belts
(Geomagnetism) 538.766
Van Buren, Martin
United States history 973.57
Van Buren County (Ark.) T2—767 29
Van Buren County (Iowa) T2—777 98
Van Buren County (Mich.) T2—774 13
Van Buren County (Tenn.) T2—768 657
Van de Graaff electrostatic
generators 539.732
Van Ili (Turkey) T2—566 2
Van pools 388.413 212
Van Wert County (Ohio) T2—771 413
Van Zandt County (Tex.) T2—764 276
Vanadates
mineralogy 549.72
Vanadinite
mineralogy 549.72
Vanadium 669.732
chemical engineering 661.052 2
chemistry 546.522
economic geology 553.462 6
materials science 620.189 32
metallography 669.957 32
metallurgy 669.732
metalworking 673.732
organic chemistry 547.055 22
applied 661.895
physical metallurgy 669.967 32
see also Chemicals, Metals
Vanadium group
chemical engineering 661.052
chemistry 546.52
Vance County (N.C.) T2—756 532
Vancouver (B.C.) T2—711 33
Vancouver Island (B.C.) T2—711 2
Vandal language 439.9
T6—399
Vandalic language 439.9
T6—399
Vandalism 364.164
law 345.026 4
school problem 371.58
Vandals (Germanic people) T5—39
Vandas
floriculture 635.934 15
Vanderbijlpark (South
Africa : District) T2—682 1
Vanderburgh County (Ind.) T2—772 33
Vanderhoof (B.C.) T2—711 82
Vanga shrikes 598.8
Vanier (Quebec) T2—714 471
Vanilla 641.338 2
agriculture 633.82
botany 584.15
commercial processing 664.52
Vanima (Papua New Guinea) T2—957 7
Vanishing animals 591.529

Vasodilators (Nerves)
  human physiology   612.18
  see also Cardiovascular system
Vasomotors
  human physiology   612.18
  see also Cardiovascular system
Vasopressin   596.014 2
  chemistry   547.734 5
  human physiology   612.492
  pharmacology   615.363
  physiology   596.014 2
  see also Endocrine system
Vasterbottens lan (Sweden)   T2—488
Vasternorrlands lan (Sweden)   T2—488
Vastmanlands lan (Sweden)   T2—487
VAT (Tax)   336.271 4
  see also Value-added tax
Vatican City   945.634
          T2—456 34
Vaucheriales   589.486
Vaucluse (France : Dept.)   T2—449 2
Vaud (Switzerland)   T2—494 52
Vaudeville   792.7
Vaudreuil (Quebec : County)   T2—714 26
Vaudreuil-Soulanges
  (Quebec)   T2—714 26
Vaulting (Gymnastics)   796.44
Vaults   721.43
  architecture   721.43
  construction   690.143
Vaupés (Colombia)   T2—861 65
VCR (Cassette recorders)   384.558
  see also Video recorders
VDP (Disc players)   384.558
  see also Video recorders
Veal   641.362
  commercial processing   664.92
  cooking   641.662
Vector algebra   512.5
Vector analysis   515.63
Vector calculus   515.63
Vector geometry   516.182
Vector processing   004.35
Vector processors   004.35
  engineering   621.391
Vector quantities
  mechanics   531.112
Vector spaces   512.52
Vector-valued functions   515.7
Vectorcardiography
  medicine   616.120 754 7
  see also Cardiovascular system
Vectors (Disease carriers)   614.43
Vedanta (Philosophy)   181.48
Vedas   294.592 1
Vedic language   491.2
          T6—912
Vedic literature   891.2

Vedic period (Indian history)   934.02
Vedic religion   294.509 013
Vega, La (Dominican
  Republic : Province)   T2—729 369
Vegetable arrangements   745.924
Vegetable drugs
  pharmacology   615.32
Vegetable fats   665.3
  food technology   664.3
  industrial   665.3
Vegetable fibers
  textiles   677.54
    see also Textiles
Vegetable gardening   635
Vegetable glue   668.33
Vegetable juices   641.35
  commercial processing   663.63
  cooking with   641.65
  home preparation   641.875
Vegetable manures
  agricultural use   631.87
Vegetable oils   665.3
  industrial   665.3
Vegetable poisons
  toxicology   615.952
Vegetable waxes   665.12
Vegetables   641.35
  commercial preservation   664.8
  commercial processing   664.8
  cooking   641.65
  garden crop   635
  home preservation   641.4
Vegetarian cooking   641.563 6
Vegetarianism
  dietary regimen   613.262
  ethics   179.3
    religion   291.569 3
      Buddhism   294.356 93
      Christianity   241.693
      Hinduism   294.548 693
Vegetation
  influence on precipitation   551.577 5
Vegetation regions   T2—15
Vegetative generation
  animals   591.165
  plants   581.165
Vegetative reproduction   574.165
Vegliote dialect   T6—57
Vegliote literature   850
Vehicle failures   363.120 1
  air transportation   363.124 16
  see also Transportation safety
Vehicles   388
  engineering   629.046
  law   343.093
  military engineering   623.74
  military equipment   355.83
  transportation services   388

Vehicular accidents	363.125
see also Transportation safety	
Vehicular safety	363.125
see also Transportation safety	
Vehicular transportation	
(Automotive)	388.3
law	343.09
public administration	350.878 3
central governments	351.878 3
local governments	352.918 3
transportation services	388.3
urban	388.41
public administration	350.878 41
central governments	351.878 41
local governments	352.918 41
Vei (African people)	T5—963 4
Vei language	496.34
	T6—963 4
Veii (Ancient city)	T2—376
Veins	
human anatomy	611.14
human diseases	
medicine	616.14
human physiology	612.134
surgery	617.414
see also Cardiovascular system	
Veins (Geology)	551.88
economic geology	553.19
mineralogy	549.119
Vejle amt (Denmark)	T2—489 5
Veliko Turnovo okrug	
(Bulgaria)	T2—497 76
Velloziaceae	584.29
Vellum books	096.2
Velocity (Mechanics)	531.112
Velocity of flow	
air mechanics	533.62
fluid mechanics	532.053 2
gas mechanics	533.27
liquid mechanics	532.57
Velocity of light	535.24
Velocity of particles (Nuclear	
physics)	539.725
Velocity of sound	534.202
Velocity theory	
monetary economics	332.401
Velour	677.617
see also Textiles	
Velvet	677.617
see also Textiles	
Velveteen	677.617
see also Textiles	
Venango County (Pa.)	T2—748 96
Venda (African people)	T5—963 97
Venda (South Africa)	T2—682 91
Venda language	496.397
	T6—963 97
Vendée (France)	T2—446 1

Vendettas	
influence on crime	364.256
Vending machines	629.82
Vendor selection	
library acquisitions	025.233
materials management	658.722
Vendors and purchasers	346.043 63
Veneers	674.833
architectural decoration	729.6
Venereal diseases	
incidence	614.547
medicine	616.951
see also Communicable	
diseases (Human)	
Venesection	
therapeutics	615.899
Venetia	T2—373
Venetia (Italy)	T2—453 1
Venetic language	479.4
	T6—794
Veneto (Italy)	T2—453
Venezia (Italy : Province)	T2—453 1
Venezuela	987
	T2—87
Venezuela, Gulf of	551.463 5
	T2—163 65
Venezuelan literature	860
Venezuelans	T5—688 7
Venial sin	241.31
Venice (Italy : Province)	T2—453 1
Venice, Gulf of	551.462 5
	T2—163 85
Venison	641.391
commercial processing	664.92
cooking	641.691
Venoms	
toxicology	615.942
Ventersburg (South Africa :	
District)	T2—685 3
Ventersdorp (South Africa :	
District)	T2—682 4
Venterstad (South Africa :	
District)	T2—687 13
Ventilation	
aircraft	629.134 42
buildings	697.92
household management	644.5
library buildings	022.8
mining	622.42
museums	069.29
plant management	658.25
sewers	628.23
underground construction	624.19
Ventilation engineers	697.920 92
occupational group	T7—697
Ventricles (Heart)	
human anatomy	611.12

Ventricles (Heart) (continued)
human physiology   612.17
  see also Cardiovascular system
Ventriloquism   793.89
Ventura County (Calif.)   T2—794 92
Venus (Planet)   523.42
     T2—992 2
  unmanned flights to   629.435 42
Venus's-flytrap   583.121
Veps   T5—945 4
Veps language   494.54
     T6—945 4
Veps literature   894.54
Veracruz (Mexico : State)   T2—726 2
Veraguas (Panama : Province)   T2—728 722
Verapaz (Guatemala :
  Province)   T2—728 15
Verb tables
  applied linguistics   418
    specific languages   T4—82
Verbal communication   302.224
  psychology   153.6
Verbal intelligence tests   153.933 3
  individual   153.932 3
Verbena   583.88
Verbenales   583.88
Vercelli (Italy : Province)   T2—451 7
Verchères (Quebec : County)   T2—714 36
Verd antique marble   553.55
  economic geology   553.55
  quarrying   622.355
Verdefort (South Africa :
  District)   T2—685 2
Verdicts   347.077
  criminal law   345.075
Verdun, Treaty of, 843   943.02
Vereeniging (South Africa :
  District)   T2—682 1
Verification
  musical instruments   784.192 7
  programming   005.14
Vermicelli
  commercial processing   664.755
Vermicides   668.651
  agricultural use   632.951
  chemical engineering   668.651
Vermiculite   553.678
  economic geology   553.678
  mining   622.367 8
Vermiform appendix
  human anatomy   611.345
  human diseases
    medicine   616.34
  human physiology   612.33
  surgery   617.554 5
  see also Digestive system
Vermilion County (Ill.)   T2—773 65
Vermilion Parish (La.)   T2—763 51

Vermillion County (Ind.)   T2—772 462
Vermont   974.3
     T2—743
Vernon (B.C.)   T2—711 5
Vernon County (Mo.)   T2—778 44
Vernon County (Wis.)   T2—775 73
Vernon Parish (La.)   T2—763 61
Verona (Italy : Province)   T2—453 4
Verrucae
  medicine   616.544
  see also Skin
Versailles Treaty, 1783   973.317
Verse drama
  literature   808.82
    history and criticism   809.2
    specific literatures
      individual authors   T3A—2
      specific literatures   T3B—2
Versification   808.1
Versions
  obstetrical surgery   618.82
Vertebrata   596
  paleozoology   566
Vertebrates   596
  paleozoology   566
Vertical combinations
  (Production economics)   338.804 2
Vertical lift bridges   388
  construction   624.84
  see also Bridges
Vertical lift rotors
  aircraft   629.134 36
Vertical-speed indicators   629.135 2
Vertical takeoff and landing
  aircraft   387.733 5
  engineering   629.133 35
  military engineering   623.746 047
  transportation services   387.733 5
Vertigo
  symptomatology
    neurological diseases   616.841
  see also Nervous system
Vervains   583.88
Verwoerd, Hendrik Frensch
  South African history   968.058
Verwoerd Dam (South Africa)   T2—687 13
Very-high-frequency radio
  systems   621.384 151
Very large scale integration   621.395
Very-low-frequency radio
  systems   621.384 153
Vesicles   574.874
Vesicular eruptions
  medicine   616.52
  see also Skin
Vespers   264.1
  Anglican   264.030 1
    texts   264.034

Vices	179.8	Victualing (continued)	
religion	291.5	transportation services	388.041
Buddhism	294.35	Vicuña wool textiles	677.32
Christianity	241.3	*see also* Textiles	
Hinduism	294.548	Vicuñas	599.736
Islam	297.5	animal husbandry	636.296
Judaism	296.385	Video art	700
Vichada (Colombia)	T2—861 39	fine arts	702.81
Vicksburg, Siege of, 1863	973.734 4	Video cassette recorders	384.558
Victimology	362.88	*see also* Video recorders	
Victims of crime	362.88	Video cassettes	384.558
insurance	368.82	*see also* Video recordings	
law	344.028	Video disc players	384.558
social welfare	362.88	*see also* Video recorders	
public administration	350.848 8	Video discs	384.558
central governments	351.848 8	*see also* Video recordings	
local governments	352.944 88	Video disks (Computer)	
welfare law	344.032 88	computer science	004.56
Victims of political oppression		engineering	621.397 6
social welfare	362.87	Video display screens	
public administration	351.848	computer science	004.77
Victor Emanuel Range	T2—957 7	engineering	621.398 7
Victor Emmanuel II, King of		Video recorders	384.558
Italy		communication services	384.558
Italian history	945.084	engineering	621.388 33
Victor Emmanuel III, King of		photography	778.599 3
Italy		*see also* Television	
Italian history	945.091	Video recordings	384.558
Victor Harbour (S. Aust.)	T2—942 32	communication services	384.558
Victoria	T2—945	engineering	621.388 332
Victoria (B.C.)	T2—711 28	music	780
Victoria (N.B. : County)	T2—715 53	treatises	780.267
Victoria (N.S. : County)	T2—716 93	photography	778.599
Victoria (Ont. : County)	T2—713 64	*see also* Television	
Victoria (Seychelles)	T2—696	Video records	384.558
Victoria, Lake	T2—678 27	*see also* Video recordings	
Victoria, Lake (N.S.W.)	T2—944 8	Video tape players	384.558
Victoria, Queen of Great Britain		*see also* Video recorders	
British history	941.081	Video tapes	384.558
English history	942.081	*see also* Video recordings	
Scottish history	941.108 1	Videocassette players	384.558
Victoria County (Tex.)	T2—764 125	*see also* Video recorders	
Victoria Falls	T2—689 1	Videocassettes	384.558
Victoria Island (Kitikmeot,		*see also* Video recordings	
N.W.T.)	T2—719 7	Videodisc players	384.558
Victoria River	T2—942 95	*see also* Video recorders	
Victoria swine		Videodiscs	384.558
animal husbandry	636.484	*see also* Video recordings	
zoology	599.734	Videorecordings	384.558
Victoria West (South Africa :		*see also* Video recordings	
District)	T2—687 17	Videorecords	384.558
Victorian architecture	724.5	performing arts	791.45
Victualing		*see also* Video recordings	
aircraft	387.736 4	Videotape players	384.558
boats	387.168	*see also* Video recorders	
buses	388.33	Videotapes	384.558
ships	387.168	*see also* Video recordings	
trains	385.26		

Violoncellos	787.4
see also Stringed instruments	
Viols	787.6
see also Stringed instruments	
Viral diseases	574.234
agriculture	632.8
incidence	614.575
medicine	616.925
plant husbandry	632.8
see also Communicable	
diseases (Human)	
Vireonidae	598.871
Vireos	598.871
Virgin birth of Jesus Christ	232.921
Virgin Gorda (V.I.)	T2—729 725
Virgin Islanders	T5—969 729 72
Virgin Islands	972.972
	T2—729 72
Virgin Islands (American)	T2—729 722
Virgin Islands (Danish)	T2—729 722
Virgin Islands, British	T2—729 725
Virgin Islands National Park	
(Saint John, V.I.)	T2—729 722
Virgin Islands of the United	
States	T2—729 722
Virginals	786.4
see also Keyboard instruments	
Virginia	975.5
	T2—755
Virginia (South Africa :	
District)	T2—685 3
Virginia Beach (Va.)	T2—755 51
Virginia City (Nev.)	T2—793 56
Virginia creeper	583.279
Virginia reels	793.34
Virginity of Mary	232.913
Viroids	576.648 3
Virologists	576.640 92
Virology	576.64
medicine	616.019 4
Virtual memory	004.54
systems programs	005.43
Virtual storage access method	
systems programs	005.43
Virtues	179.9
religion	291.5
Buddhism	294.35
Christianity	241.4
Hinduism	294.548
Islam	297.5
Judaism	296.385
Virtues of Mary	232.915
Viruses	576.64
medical microbiology	616.019 4

Visas	323.67
international law	341.484 2
law	342.082
political science	323.67
public administration	351.898
Visayan Islands (Philippines)	T2—599 5
Visceral perception	
psychology	152.188 6
Viscose rayon	677.463
see also Textiles	
Viscosity	531.113 4
fluid mechanics	532.053 3
gas mechanics	533.28
liquid mechanics	532.58
solid mechanics	531.4
Viscous flow	532.053 3
gas mechanics	533.28
liquid mechanics	532.58
Vises	621.992
Viseu (Portugal : District)	T2—469 31
Vishnuism	294.551 2
Visibility	
aeronautics	629.132 4
meteorology	551.568
Visible light	535
biophysics	574.191 53
human	612.014 44
physics	535
spectral region	535.013
Visible light spectroscopes	
manufacturing technology	681.414 3
Visible light spectroscopy	543.085 84
chemical analysis	543.085 84
engineering	621.361 3
physics	535.843
Visigothic domination (Spanish	
history)	946.01
Vision	
artificial intelligence	006.37
arts	701.8
human physiology	612.84
see also Eyes	
Visistadvaita (Philosophy)	181.483
Visitation rights (Domestic law)	346.017
Visitation Sisters	255.975
church history	271.975
Visiting housekeepers	
social welfare	362.828 3
Visiting nurses	610.730 92
medicine	610.734 3
social welfare	362.14
see also Health services	
see also Nurses	
Visual-auditory memory	153.134
Visual binaries (Stars)	523.841
Visual display units	
computer science	004.77
engineering	621.398 7

Voice	
human physiology	612.78
music	783
rhetoric of speech	808.5
Voice disguisers (Musical instruments)	783.99
Voice disorders	
medicine	616.855
see also Communicative disorders	
Voice in preaching	251.03
Voice input devices	006.454
computer engineering	621.399
Voice instruments	783.99
Voice output devices	006.54
computer engineering	621.399
Voice prints	
criminal investigation	363.258
Voice synthesis	006.54
computer engineering	621.399
Voiōtia (Greece)	T2—495 1
Voivodina (Serbia)	T2—497 1
Vojvodina (Serbia)	T2—497 1
Volatilization analysis	545.46
Volcanic eruptions	
social services	363.349 5
see also Disasters	
Volcanic rocks	552.2
Volcanism	551.21
Volcanoes	551.21
Voles	599.323 3
Volga languages, Middle	494.56
	T6—945 6
Volga River (R.S.F.S.R.)	T2—478
Volgograd (R.S.F.S.R. : Oblast)	T2—478 5
Volgogradskaia oblast (R.S.F.S.R.)	T2—478 5
Volition	153.8
Volksrust (South Africa : District)	T2—682 7
Volleyball	796.325
Volleyball players	796.325 092
sports group	T7—796 32
Vologda (R.S.F.S.R. : Oblast)	T2—472 3
Vologodskaia oblast (R.S.F.S.R.)	T2—472 3
Volscian language	479.7
	T6—797
Volsinii (Orvieto, Italy)	T2—374
Volsinii Novi (Bolsena, Italy)	T2—376
Volt-ammeters	621.374 6
Volta-Comoe languages	496.338
	T6—963 38
Volta River (Ghana)	T2—667
Voltage detectors	621.374 3
Voltage multipliers	
nuclear physics	539.732

Voltaic languages	496.35
	T6—963 5
Voltameters	621.374 4
Voltans	T5—966 25
Volterra equations	515.45
Voltmeters	621.374 3
Volume (Sound)	
musical element	781.233
perception	
psychology	152.154
Volume-temperature relationships	536.41
Volumetric analysis	545.2
Voluntarism	
philosophy	141
social psychology	302.14
Voluntary association	302.3
Voluntary enlistment (Military)	355.223 62
Voluntary form	784.189 3
Voluntary movement	
psychology	152.35
Voluntary muscle tissues	
human histology	611.018 6
see also Musculoskeletal system	
Voluntary retail chains	381.12
management	658.870 3
see also Commerce	
Voluntary service agencies	
foreign affairs administration	351.896
Voluntary service groups	
international assistance	361.26
international law	341.759
Volunteer social work	361.37
Volunteer teachers assistants	371.100 92
Volunteer teachers' assistants	
role and function	371.141 24
Volusia County (Fla.)	T2—759 21
Volvocales	589.47
Volyn (Ukraine : Oblast)	T2—477 18
Volynskaia oblast (Ukraine)	T2—477 18
Von Mises, Ludwig	
economic school	330.157
Von Neumann algebras	512.55
Voodooism	299.67
Vorarlberg (Austria)	T2—436 45
Voronezh (R.S.F.S.R. : Oblast)	T2—473 5
Voronezhskaia oblast (R.S.F.S.R.)	T2—473 5
Voroshilovgrad (Ukraine : Oblast)	T2—477 16
Voroshilovgradskaia oblast (Ukraine)	T2—477 16
Vorster, B. J. (Balthazar Johannes)	
South African history	968.062
Vortex motions	532.059 5
fluid mechanics	532.059 5

Waghi River	T2—956 5
Wagner tubas	788.98
see also Brass instruments	
Wagoner County (Okla.)	T2—766 87
Wagons	388.341
agricultural use	631.373
manufacturing technology	688.6
Wagtails	598.854
Wahhabis (Islamic sect)	297.814
Wahkiakum County (Wash.)	T2—797 91
Wakashan Indians	T5—979
Wakashan languages	497.9
	T6—979
Wakayama-ken (Japan)	T2—521 82
Wake	393.9
music	781.588
Wake County (N.C.)	T2—756 55
Wake Island	T2—965
Wakefield (England : City)	T2—428 15
Wakkerstroom (South Africa : District)	T2—682 7
Wakool River	T2—944 8
Wakulla County (Fla.)	T2—759 89
Walachia	T2—498 2
Walbiri language	499.15
	T6—991 5
Walbrzych (Poland : Voivodeship)	T2—438 5
Waldenses	
biography	284.4
religious group	T7—244
Waldensian churches	284.4
heresy	273.6
persecution of	272.3
see also Christian denominations	
Waldo County (Me.)	T2—741 52
Wales	T2—429
ancient	T2—362 9
Wales, North	T2—429 1
Wales, South	T2—429 4
Wales Island (N.W.T.)	T2—719 5
Walgett (N.S.W.)	T2—944 9
Walker County (Ala.)	T2—761 76
Walker County (Ga.)	T2—758 33
Walker County (Tex.)	T2—764 169
Walkie-talkies	621.384 5
Walking	
human physiology	612.04
physical fitness	613.717 6
sports	796.51
equipment technology	688.765 1
Walkingstick (Insect)	595.724
Wall coverings	
household management	645.2
Walla Walla County (Wash.)	T2—797 48
Wallabies	599.2
Wallace County (Kan.)	T2—781 123
Wallachia	T2—498 2
Wallachia (Principality)	949.801 4
	T2—498 2
Wallaga (Ethiopia : Province)	T2—633
Wallaroo (S. Aust.)	T2—942 35
Wallboards	676.183
Wallenpaupack, Lake (Pa.)	T2—748 23
Waller County (Tex.)	T2—764 249
Walleye (Fish)	597.58
sports fishing	799.175 8
Wallflower (Flower)	583.123
Wallis (Switzerland)	T2—494 79
Wallis and Futuna Islands	T2—961 6
Wallo (Ethiopia)	T2—634
Wallonia (Belgium)	T2—493 4
Walloons	T5—42
Wallowa County (Or.)	T2—795 73
Wallowa Mountains	T2—795 73
Wallpaper	676.284 8
handicrafts	745.54
household management	645.2
interior decoration	747.3
Walls (Building element)	721.2
architecture	721.2
construction	690.12
interior decoration	747.3
Walls (Structures)	
agricultural use	631.27
architecture	725.96
Walnut trees	583.973
forestry	634.973 973
Walnuts	641.345 1
botany	583.973
nut crops	634.51
Walras, Léon	
economic school	330.157
Walruses	599.747
Walsall (England)	T2—424 92
Walsh County (N.D.)	T2—784 18
Walthall County (Miss.)	T2—762 22
Waltham Forest (London, England)	T2—421 72
Walton County (Fla.)	T2—759 97
Walton County (Ga.)	T2—758 212
Waltz form	784.188 46
Waltzes	793.33
Walvis Bay (South Africa)	T2—688 1
Walworth County (S.D.)	T2—783 18
Walworth County (Wis.)	T2—775 89
Wambis	787.92
see also Stringed instruments	
Wandering Jew	584.38
Wandsworth (London, England)	T2—421 66
Wangaratta (Vic.)	T2—945 5
Wansbeck (England)	T2—428 86
Wansdyke (England)	T2—423 97
Wapello County (Iowa)	T2—777 93

Warren County (Ky.)	T2—769 74	Washabaugh County (S.D.)	T2—783 64
Warren County (Miss.)	T2—762 29	Washakie County (Wyo.)	T2—787 34
Warren County (Mo.)	T2—778 386	Washboards	
Warren County (N.C.)	T2—756 52	music	786.886
Warren County (N.J.)	T2—749 78	*see also* Percussion	
Warren County (N.Y.)	T2—747 51	instruments	
Warren County (Ohio)	T2—771 763	Washburn County (Wis.)	T2—775 15
Warren County (Pa.)	T2—748 67	Washing clothes	
Warren County (Tenn.)	T2—768 653	home economics	648.1
Warren County (Va.)	T2—755 97	Washing coal	662.623
Warrenton (South Africa :		Washing fabrics	
District)	T2—687 11	home economics	648.1
Warrick County (Ind.)	T2—772 32	Washing machines	
Warrington (England :		manufacturing technology	683.88
Borough)	T2—427 19	Washington	979.7
Warrnambool (Vic.)	T2—945 7		T2—797
Warrumbungle Range	T2—944 4	Washington (D.C.)	975.3
Wars	355.02		T2—753
history	900	Washington (District)	976.803
military analysis	355.48		T2—768
military science	355.02	Washington, George	
social services	363.349 8	United States history	973.41
see also Disasters		1789-1793	973.41
Wars of the Roses, 1455-1485	942.04	1793-1797	973.43
Warsaw (Poland :		Washington County (Ala.)	T2—761 243
Voivodeship)	T2—438 4	Washington County (Ark.)	T2—767 14
Warsaw Pact	355.031 094 7	Washington County (Colo.)	T2—788 79
Warships	359.83	Washington County (Fla.)	T2—759 963
ancient and medieval	359.832	Washington County (Ga.)	T2—758 672
design	623.812 1	Washington County (Idaho)	T2—796 25
engineering	623.821	Washington County (Ill.)	T2—773 88
handling	623.882 1	Washington County (Ind.)	T2—772 22
naval equipment	359.83	Washington County (Iowa)	T2—777 923
naval units	359.32	Washington County (Kan.)	T2—781 273
power-driven	359.83	Washington County (Ky.)	T2—769 493
design	623.812 5	Washington County (Md.)	T2—752 91
engineering	623.825	Washington County (Me.)	T2—741 42
naval equipment	359.83	Washington County (Minn.)	T2—776 59
wind-driven	359.832	Washington County (Miss.)	T2—762 42
design	623.812 25	Washington County (Mo.)	T2—778 64
engineering	623.822 5	Washington County (N.C.)	T2—756 165
Warthogs	599.734	Washington County (N.Y.)	T2—747 49
Warts		Washington County (Neb.)	T2—782 245
medicine	616.544	Washington County (Ohio)	T2—771 98
see also Skin		Washington County (Okla.)	T2—766 96
Warwick (England : District)	T2—424 87	Washington County (Or.)	T2—795 43
Warwick (Qld.)	T2—943 3	Washington County (Pa.)	T2—748 82
Warwickshire (England)	T2—424 8	Washington County (R.I.)	T2—745 9
Warwickshire Avon River		Washington County (Tenn.)	T2—768 97
(England)	T2—424 4	Washington County (Tex.)	T2—764 245
Wasatch County (Utah)	T2—792 23	Washington County (Utah)	T2—792 48
Wasatch Range (Utah and		Washington County (Va.)	T2—755 725
Idaho)	T2—792 2	Washington County (Vt.)	T2—743 4
Idaho	T2—796 44	Washington County (Wis.)	T2—775 91
Utah	T2—792 2	Washington Island	T2—964
Wasco County (Or.)	T2—795 62	Washington Parish (La.)	T2—763 11
Waseca County (Minn.)	T2—776 195	Washita County (Okla.)	T2—766 42
Wash, The	T2—425 3		

Waterfowl	598.41
commercial hunting	639.124
sports hunting	799.244
Waterleaf	583.76
Waterloo (Ont. : Regional	
municipality)	T2—713 44
Watermarks	676.280 27
Watermeal	584.64
Watermelons	641.356 15
botany	583.46
commercial processing	664.805 615
cooking	641.656 15
garden crop	635.615
Waterpower	333.914
economics	333.914
law	343.092 4
Waterproof construction	
buildings	693.892
Waterproof fabrics	677.682
see also Textiles	
Waterspouts (Tornadoes)	551.553
Waterton-Glacier	
International Peace Park	T2—786 52
Alberta	T2—712 34
Montana	T2—786 52
Waterton Lakes National Park	
(Alta.)	T2—712 34
Waterval-Boven (South	
Africa : District)	T2—682 7
Waterways	
hydraulic engineering	627
land economics	333.915
transportation services	386.3—.5
Waterwheels	621.21
Waterwort	583.152
Watford (England)	T2—425 892
Watling Island	T2—729 6
Watonwan County (Minn.)	T2—776 29
Watsonian behaviorism	150.194 32
Watt-hour meters	621.374 5
Wattled crows	598.8
Wattmeters	621.374 6
Waukesha County (Wis.)	T2—775 93
Waupaca County (Wis.)	T2—775 38
Waushara County (Wis.)	T2—775 57
Wave action	551.36
Wave-guide theory of electricity	537.125
Wave guides	
microwave electronics	621.381 331
Wave mechanics	530.124
Wave propagation	
microwave electronics	621.381 31
radio engineering	621.384 11
Wave radiations	
ionization	539.722
Wave theories	530.14
Wave theory of light	535.13

Wave transmission	
microwave electronics	621.381 31
radio engineering	621.384 11
Wavell, Archibald Percival	
Wavell, Earl of	
Indian history	954.035 9
Waveney (England)	T2—426 41
Waveney River	T2—426 19
Waverley (England :	
Borough)	T2—422 19
Waves	
air mechanics	533.62
fluid mechanics	532.059 3
gas mechanics	533.293
liquid mechanics	532.593
mechanics	531.113 3
oceanography	551.470 2
solid mechanics	531.33
Waves (Property of matter)	530.124
Wax beans	583.322
garden crop	635.652
Wax carving	736.93
Wax myrtle	583.974
Wax painting	751.46
Waxes	665.1
biochemistry	574.192 47
chemistry	547.77
sculpture material	731.2
Waxing	
woodwork	
buildings	698.33
Waxwings	598.852
Wayatinah (Tas.)	T2—946 3
Waycross (Ga.)	T2—758 794
Wayne County (Ga.)	T2—758 756
Wayne County (Ill.)	T2—773 792
Wayne County (Ind.)	T2—772 63
Wayne County (Iowa)	T2—777 88
Wayne County (Ky.)	T2—769 64
Wayne County (Mich.)	T2—774 33
Wayne County (Miss.)	T2—762 573
Wayne County (Mo.)	T2—778 92
Wayne County (N.C.)	T2—756 395
Wayne County (N.Y.)	T2—747 87
Wayne County (Neb.)	T2—782 57
Wayne County (Ohio)	T2—771 61
Wayne County (Pa.)	T2—748 23
Wayne County (Tenn.)	T2—768 39
Wayne County (Utah)	T2—792 54
Wayne County (W. Va.)	T2—754 47
Waynesboro (Va.)	T2—755 912
Weak interaction (Nuclear	
particles)	539.754 4
Weakley County (Tenn.)	T2—768 24
Weald of Kent (England)	T2—422 5
Wealden (England : District)	T2—422 51

Wealth	330.16
economic theory	330.16
ethics	178
religion	291.568
Buddhism	294.356 8
Christianity	241.68
Hinduism	294.548 68
Islam	297.5
Judaism	296.385 68
macroeconomics	339.3
distribution	339.2
Wealthy classes	305.523 4
	T1—086 21
customs	390.1
dress	391.01
Weapons	355.82
military engineering	623.4
military equipment	355.82
small arms	683.4
Weapons testing	
international law	341.733
Wear	
machine engineering	621.89
Wear resistance	
materials science	620.112 92
Wear River	T2—428 6
Wear Valley (England :	
District)	T2—428 64
Weasel spider	595.48
Weasels	599.744 47
Weather	551.6
aeronautics	629.132 4
earth sciences	551.6
folklore	398.26
sociology	398.363
health	613.11
influence on crime	364.22
social effects	304.25
transportation hazard	363.120 1
air transportation	363.124 12
see also Transportation safety	
Weather belts	551.62
Weather control	551.68
international law	341.762
public administration	351.823 24
Weather forecasting	551.63
Weather-induced illnesses	
medicine	616.988
see also Environmental diseases	
(Human)	
Weather modification	551.68
international law	341.762
public administration	351.823 24
Weather satellites	
use	551.635 4
Weather services	
armed forces	355.343 2
Weather stripping	678.35

Weathering	551.302
by water	551.352
by wind	551.372
materials science	620.112 23
soil formation	551.305
Weatherization (Housing	
program)	363.583
Weaver finches	598.873
Weaverbirds	598.873
Weaving	677.028 242
arts	746.14
threads and yarns	746.14
vegetable fibers	746.41
manufacturing technology	677.028 242
Webb County (Tex.)	T2—764 462
Weber County (Utah)	T2—792 28
Webster County (Ga.)	T2—758 916
Webster County (Iowa)	T2—777 51
Webster County (Ky.)	T2—769 883
Webster County (Miss.)	T2—762 697
Webster County (Mo.)	T2—778 823
Webster County (Neb.)	T2—782 374
Webster County (W. Va.)	T2—754 65
Webster Parish (La.)	T2—763 96
Weddell Sea (Antarctic regions)	551.469 3
	T2—167 3
Wedding clothes	392.54
commercial technology	687.16
customs	392.54
home sewing	646.47
see also Clothing	
Wedding music	781.587
Weddings	
customs	392.5
dress	392.54
etiquette	395.22
flower arrangements	745.926
handicrafts	745.594 1
interior decoration	747.93
Weed control	
sanitary engineering	628.97
Weed killers	668.654
chemical engineering	668.654
Weeding (Library collections)	025.216
Weeds	
agriculture	632.58
botany	581.652
Weeks	
time interval	529.2
Weenen (South Africa :	
District)	T2—684 7
Weever	597.58
Weevils	595.768
Weight-gaining programs	
health	613.24
Weight lifters	796.410 92
sports group	T7—796 4

Welsh pony	
animal husbandry	636.16
zoology	599.725
Weltwitschiales	585.1
Welwyn Hatfield (England)	T2—425 86
Wenatchee Mountains	T2—797 57
Wendish language	491.88
	T6—918 8
Wendish literature	891.88
Wendish people	T5—918 8
Wends	T5—918 8
Wenlock River	T2—943 8
Wens (Disorder)	
medicine	616.53
see also Skin	
Wentworth (N.S.W.)	T2—944 8
Wepener (South Africa :	
District)	T2—685 6
Werewolves	133.423
folklore	398.245 4
sociology	398.469
Werribee (Vic.)	T2—945 2
Weser-Ems (Germany)	T2—435 91
Wesleyan Conference	287.53
see also Methodist Church	
Wesleyan Methodist Church	287.1
see also Methodist Church	
Wesleyan Reform Union	287.534
see also Methodist Church	
Wesleyan Reformers	287.53
see also Methodist Church	
Wesselsbron (South Africa :	
District)	T2—685 3
Wessex supremacy (English	
history)	942.016
West (U.S.)	978
	T2—78
West Africa	966
	T2—66
West-Atlantic languages (Africa)	496.32
	T6—963 2
West Azerbaijan (Iran :	
Province)	T2—554
West Bank	T2—569 53
West Baton Rouge Parish	
(La.)	T2—763 452
West Bengal (India)	T2—541 4
West Berbice (Guyana :	
District)	T2—881 6
West Berlin (Germany)	T2—431 554
West Branch Susquehanna	
River (Pa.)	T2—748 5
West Cameroon	T2—671 1
West Carroll Parish (La.)	T2—763 83
West Demerara (Guyana :	
District)	T2—881 4
West Derbyshire (England :	
District)	T2—425 13

West Devon (England :	
Borough)	T2—423 53
West Dorset (England :	
District)	T2—423 31
West Feliciana Parish (La.)	T2—763 17
West Flanders (Belgium)	T2—493 12
West Frisian Islands	
(Netherlands)	T2—492 13
West Germanic languages	439
	T6—39
West Germanic literatures	839
West Germany	943.087
	T2—43
West Glamorgan (Wales)	T2—429 81
West Indian steel drums	786.843
see also Percussion instruments	
West Indies	972.9
	T2—729
West Indies, Dutch	T2—729 86
West Indies, French	T2—729 76
West Indies Associated States	T2—729 73
West Iranian languages	
(Ancient)	T6—915 1
West Iranian literatures (Ancient)	891.51
West Irian	T2—951
West Kettle River (B.C.)	T2—711 62
West Lake Region (Tanzania)	T2—678 27
West Lancashire (England :	
District)	T2—427 612
West Lindsey (England :	
District)	T2—425 31
West Lothian (Scotland)	T2—413 3
West Makian language	499.12
	T6—991 2
West Malaysia	T2—595 1
West Midlands (England)	T2—424 9
West New Britain Province	
(Papua New Guinea)	T2—958 7
West New Guinea	T2—951
West Norfolk, King's Lynn	
and (England : Borough)	T2—426 13
West Orange (N.J.)	T2—749 33
West Oxfordshire (England :	
District)	T2—425 71
West Pakistan (Pakistan)	954.910 4
	T2—549 1
West Prussia (Germany)	T2—438 2
West Rand (South Africa)	T2—682 2
West Redonda Island (B.C.)	T2—711 1
West Riding of Yorkshire	
(England)	T2—428 1
West Road River (B.C.)	T2—711 75
West Scandinavian languages	439.6
	T6—396
West Scandinavian literatures	839.6
West Scandinavian literatures	
(Modern)	839.69
West Scandinavians	T5—396

West Semitic languages	492	Western Province (Solomon	
	T6—92	Islands)	T2—959 31
West Semitic peoples	T5—92	Western Province (South	
West Sepik Province (Papua		Africa)	T2—687 3
New Guinea)	T2—957 7	Western Province (Zambia)	T2—689 4
West Slavic languages	491.85	Western Region (Nigeria)	T2—669 2
	T6—918 5	Western Sahara	T2—648
West Slavic literatures	891.85	Western Samar (Philippines :	
West Slavs	T5—918 5	Province)	T2—599 5
West Somerset (England :		Western Samoa	996.14
District)	T2—423 85		T2—961 4
West Suffolk (England)	T2—426 44	Western Samoans	T5—994
West Sussex (England)	T2—422 6	Western Siberia (R.S.F.S.R.)	T2—573
West Thurlow Island (B.C.)	T2—711 1	Western State (Nigeria)	T2—669 2
West Vancouver (B.C.)	T2—711 33	Western States (U.S.)	978
West Virginia	975.4		T2—78
	T2—754	Western stories	808.838 74
West Wiltshire (England :		history and criticism	809.387 4
District)	T2—423 15	specific literatures	T3B—308 74
West Yorkshire (England)	T2—428 1	individual authors	T3A—3
Westbury (Tas.)	T2—946 3	Westerns	
Westchester County (N.Y.)	T2—747 277	motion pictures	791.436 278
Westerlies	551.518 3	radio programs	791.446 278
Western architecture		television programs	791.456 278
ancient	722.6	Westerns (Fiction)	808.838 74
Western art music	781.68	history and criticism	809.387 4
Western Asian international		specific literatures	T3B—308 74
organizations	341.247 7	individual authors	T3A—3
Western Australia	T2—941	Westland (N.Z.)	T2—931 54
Western bloc	T2—171 3	Westmeath (Ireland)	T2—418 15
Western calendars	529.4	Westminster (London,	
Western calligraphy	745.619 7	England)	T2—421 32
Western Canada	T2—712	Westmoreland County (Pa.)	T2—748 81
Western Desert (Egypt)	T2—622	Westmoreland County (Va.)	T2—755 24
Western Equatoria Province		Westmorland (England)	T2—427 8
(Sudan)	T2—629 5	Westmorland (N.B. : County)	T2—715 23
Western Europe	940	Weston County (Wyo.)	T2—787 14
	T2—4	Westonaria (South Africa :	
ancient	936	District)	T2—682 2
	T2—36	Westphalia (Germany)	T2—435 6
Western folk music modes	781.263	Wet-collodion process	772.14
Western front		Wet-weather photography	778.75
World War I	940.414 4	Wetar Island	T2—598 6
Western Hemisphere	T2—181 2	Wetherby (England)	T2—428 19
Western Hemisphere		Wetlands	
international organizations	341.245	freshwater ecology	574.526 325
Western Highlands (Papua		law	346.046 918
New Guinea)	T2—956 5	resource economics	333.918
Western Hindi languages	491.43	saltwater ecology	574.526 36
	T6—914 3	Wetlands ecology	574.526 325
Western Hindi literatures	891.43	Wetting agents	668.14
Western Isles (Scotland)	T2—411 4	Wetzel County (W. Va.)	T2—754 18
Western Mediterranean Sea	551.462 1	Wewak (Papua New Guinea)	T2—957 5
	T2—163 81	Wexford (Ireland)	T2—418 856
Western popular music	781.64	Wexford (Ireland : County)	T2—418 85
Western Province (Kenya)	T2—676 28	Wexford County (Mich.)	T2—774 67
Western Province (Papua		Weymouth and Portland	
New Guinea)	T2—954 9	(England : Borough)	T2—423 35

Whale lice	595.371	Whisk fern	587.4
Whale oil	665.2	Whiskey	641.252
Whalers	639.280 92	commercial processing	663.52
occupational group	T7—639 2	Whist	795.413
Whales	599.5	Whistle (Voices)	782.98
hunting	639.28	choral and mixed voices	782.98
paleozoology	569.5	single voices	783.98
resource economics	333.959	Whistle-blowing (Government)	
Whaling		law	342.068
international law	341.762 2	Whistler (B.C.)	T2—711 31
law	346.046 959	White alder	583.62
production economics	338.372 95	White clover	583.322
technology	639.28	forage crop	633.327
Whaling industry	338.372 95	White-collar crime	364.168
products		law	345.026 8
commerce	380.143 95	White-collar workers	305.556
Whaling ships			T1—086 22
engineering	623.824 8	labor economics	331.792
Wharton County (Tex.)	T2—764 133	labor force	331.119 042
Wharves		labor market	331.129 042
engineering	627.31	labor unions	331.880 41
Whatcom County (Wash.)	T2—797 73	social class	305.556
Wheat	641.331 1	White corpuscles	
botany	584.93	human histology	611.018 5
commercial processing	664.722	human physiology	612.112
cooking	641.631 1	*see also* Cardiovascular system	
food crop	633.11	White County (Ark.)	T2—767 76
forage crop	633.251	White County (Ga.)	T2—758 277
Wheatland County (Mont.)	T2—786 63	White County (Ill.)	T2—773 96
Wheel games	795.2	White County (Ind.)	T2—772 93
equipment technology	688.752	White County (Tenn.)	T2—768 66
Wheelbarrows		White dwarfs (Stars)	523.887
manufacturing technology	688.6	White Horse, Vale of	
Wheelchair basketball	796.323 8	(England)	T2—425 76
Wheeler County (Ga.)	T2—758 835	White-listing (Labor)	331.894
Wheeler County (Neb.)	T2—782 762	White Mountains (N.H. and	
Wheeler County (Or.)	T2—795 81	Me.)	T2—742 2
Wheeler County (Tex.)	T2—764 828	White Nile (Sudan : Province)	T2—626 4
Wheeler Lake	T2—761 98	White Nile River	T2—629 3
Wheeling (W. Va.)	T2—754 14	White peppers	583.925
Wheels		White Pine County (Nev.)	T2—793 15
automotive	629.248	White race	T5—034
railroad engineering	625.21	White River (Ark. and Mo.)	T2—767 2
Whelks	594.32	White River (Ind.)	T2—772 3
Whey	641.373	White River (S.D.)	T2—783 6
cooking	641.673	White River (South Africa :	
processing	637.3	District)	T2—682 6
Whig Party (Great Britain)	324.241 02	White River (Vt.)	T2—743 65
Whig Party (U.S.)	324.273 23	White Rock (B.C.)	T2—711 33
Whip scorpion	595.453 2	White Russia	T2—476 5
Whippet (Dog)		White Russian Soviet	
animal husbandry	636.753	Socialist Republic	T2—476 5
see also Dogs		White Sands National	
Whips		Monument	T2—789 65
music	786.99	White Sea (R.S.F.S.R.)	551.468 4
see also Percussion			T2—163 24
instruments		White slave traffic	364.153 4
Whirligig beetle	595.762	law	345.025 34

Wildcat strikes 331.892 4
  see also Strikes (Work
    stoppages)
Wildebeests 599.735 8
Wilderness (South Africa) T2—687 4
Wilderness areas
  law 346.046 782
  natural resources 333.782
Wildfowl
  cooking 641.691
  food 641.391
Wildlife conservation 333.951 6
  law 346.046 951 6
  technology 639.9
Wildlife reserves 333.951 6
  conservation technology 639.9
    animals 639.95
  economics 333.951 6
  landscape architecture 719.36
  law 346.046 951 6
Wilge River T2—685 1
Wilhelmina, Queen of the
  Netherlands
  Dutch history 949.207 1
Wilhelmshaven (Germany) T2—435 917
Wilkes-Barre (Pa.) T2—748 32
Wilkes County (Ga.) T2—758 172
Wilkes County (N.C.) T2—756 82
Wilkes Land T2—989
Wilkin County (Minn.) T2—776 91
Wilkinson County (Ga.) T2—758 543
Wilkinson County (Miss.) T2—762 25
Will 153.8
  philosophy 128.3
Will County (Ill.) T2—773 25
Willacy County (Tex.) T2—764 493
Willamette River (Or.) T2—795 3
Willamette Valley T2—795 3
Willem Pretorius Game
  Reserve T2—685 3
Willemite
  mineralogy 549.62
William I, German Emperor
  German history 943.083
William I, King of England
  English history 942.021
William II, German Emperor
  German history 943.084
William II, King of England
  English history 942.022
William III, King of England
  British history 941.068
  English history 942.068
  Scottish history 941.106 8

William IV, King of Great Britain
  British history 941.075
  English history 942.075
  Scottish history 941.107 5
Williams County (N.D.) T2—784 73
Williams County (Ohio) T2—771 113
Williams Lake (B.C.) T2—711 75
Williamsburg (Va.) T2—755 425 2
Williamsburg County (S.C.) T2—757 83
Williamson County (Ill.) T2—773 993
Williamson County (Tenn.) T2—768 56
Williamson County (Tex.) T2—764 289
Williamsoniaceae 561.592
Willingdon, Freedman
  Freedman-Thomas,
  Marquess of
  Indian history 954.035 8
Williston (South Africa :
  District) T2—687 17
Williston Lake (B.C.) T2—711 87
Willmore Wilderness
  Provincial Park (Alta.) T2—712 332
Willow 583.981
  basketwork crop 633.58
Willowmore (South Africa :
  District) T2—687 15
Willowvale (South Africa :
  District) T2—687 91
Wills 346.054
  genealogy 929.3
Willy-willies (Hurricanes) 551.552
Wilmington (Del.) T2—751 2
Wilmington (N.C.) T2—756 27
Wilmot Proviso, 1847 973.61
  Civil War cause 973.711 3
Wilpena Pound T2—942 37
Wilson, Woodrow
  United States history 973.913
Wilson cloud chambers
  nuclear physics 539.777
Wilson County (Kan.) T2—781 925
Wilson County (N.C.) T2—756 43
Wilson County (Tenn.) T2—768 54
Wilson County (Tex.) T2—764 445
Wilsons Promontory National
  Park (Vic.) T2—945 6
Wiltshire (England) T2—423 1
Wiluna T2—941 6
Wimborne (England :
  District) T2—423 34
Wimmera (Vic. : District) T2—945 8
Wimmera River T2—945 9
Winburg (South Africa :
  District) T2—685 3
Winchelsea (Vic.) T2—945 2
Winches 621.864
Winchester (England : City) T2—422 735
Winchester (Va.) T2—755 991

Winnipeg (Man.)	T2—712 743	Wirral (England)	T2—427 51
Winnipeg, Lake (Man.)	T2—712 72	Wirt County (W. Va.)	T2—754 26
Winnipegosis, Lake (Man.)	T2—712 72	Wisconsin	977.5
Winnipesaukee, Lake (N.H.)	T2—742 4		T2—775
Winona County (Minn.)	T2—776 12	Wisconsin Evangelical Lutheran	
Winooski River (Vt.)	T2—743 17	Synod	284.134
Winston County (Ala.)	T2—761 74	*see also* Lutheran church	
Winston County (Miss.)	T2—762 692	Wisconsin River (Wis.)	T2—775
Winter		Wisdom (Gift of the Holy Spirit)	234.12
music	781.524 8	Wisdom literature (Bible)	223
natural history	508	Apocrypha	229.3
see also Seasons		Old Testament	223
Winter-flowering plants		pseudepigrapha	229.912
floriculture	635.953	Wisdom of God	212.7
Winter Olympic Games	796.98	Christianity	231.6
Winter systems		comparative religion	291.211
air conditioning		Wisdom of Solomon (Bible)	229.3
buildings	697.933 2	Wise County (Tex.)	T2—764 532
Winteraceae	583.114	Wise County (Va.)	T2—755 743
Winterberg Range	T2—687 5	Wise men (Christian doctrines)	232.923
Wintergreen	583.62	Wisteria	583.322
agriculture	633.82	Witbank (South Africa :	
commercial processing	664.52	District)	T2—682 7
Winter's bark	583.114	Witch hazel (Plant)	583.394
Winton (Qld.)	T2—943 5	Witchcraft	133.43
Wintun language	497.41	criminal law	345.028 8
	T6—974 1	criminology	364.188
Wire communication systems	384.6	literature	808.803 7
communication services	384.6	history and criticism	809.933 7
public administration	351.874 6	specific literatures	T3B—080 37
see also Telephone		history and criticism	T3B—093 7
Wire services		religion	291.33
journalism	070.435	Islam	297.33
Wire-stitching		Witches (Occultists)	133.430 92
bookbinding	686.35	as a group	T7—13
Wire walking		persecution by Church	272.8
sports	796.46	Witches (Religious leaders)	291.092
Wirehaired pointing griffon		role and function	291.62
animal husbandry	636.752	Witham River	T2—425 3
see also Dogs		Witherite	
Wireless communication	384.5	mineralogy	549.785
communication services	384.5	Withholding tax	336.242 2
international law	341.757 7	law	343.052 42
law	343.099 45	public finance	336.242 2
public administration	351.874 5	Withlacoochee River (Fla.)	T2—759 7
Wires		Witness bearing	248.5
electrical circuits	621.319 3	Witnesses	347.066
metal	671.842	police interrogation	363.254
power transmission	621.854	trial procedure	347.075
sculpture material	731.2	Witsieshoek (South Africa :	
structural engineering	624.177 4	District)	T2—685 91
Wires (Sound)		Wittlesea (South Africa)	T2—687 92
bibliographies	011.38	Wittmund (Germany :	
Wiretapping		Landkreis)	T2—435 917
criminal investigation	363.252	Wives	306.872
electronic engineering	621.389 28		T1—086 55
law	345.052	family relationships	306.872
Wireworms	595.765		

Worker security	331.259 6
law	344.012 596
public administration	351.834
Worker self-management	
personnel management	658.315 2
see also Worker control of	
industry	
Workers	305.562
biography	305.562 092
economics	331.11
occupational group	T7—331 7
social class	305.562
Workers' compensation	
insurance	368.41
employers' liability	368.56
government-sponsored	368.41
law	344.021
personnel management	658.325 4
public administration	351.825 6
see also Insurance	
Workhouses	
penology	365.34
see also Correctional	
institutions	
Working capital	332.041 2
financial management	658.152 44
Working-class parties	324.217
international organizations	324.17
Working classes	305.562
	T1—086 23
see also Laboring classes	
Working conditions (Physical)	331.25
see also Work environment	
Working dogs	
animal husbandry	636.73
see also Dogs	
Working environment	331.25
see also Work environment	
Working mothers	
economics	331.44
Working ships	387.2
engineering	623.82
power-driven	387.248
engineering	623.824
transportation services	387.248
small craft	387.204 26
engineering	623.820 26
transportation services	387.204 26
transportation services	387.2
wind-driven	387.226
engineering	623.822 6
transportation services	387.226
see also Ships	
Workmen's compensation	
insurance	368.41
see also Insurance, Workers'	
compensation insurance	

Workplace environment	331.25
see also Work environment	
Workshops	
agriculture	631.304
Workshops (Adult education)	T1—071 52
World Bank	332.153 2
law	341.751
World-circling travel	910.41
World community	
international law	341.2
World Community of al-Islam in	
the West	297.87
World Council of Churches	270.820 601
World Court	341.552
World Cup competition	796.334 668
World fairs	907.4
see also Exhibitions	
World government	321.04
law	341.21
World Party of Socialist	
Revolution	324.175
World series (Baseball)	796.357 646
World views	140
World War I, 1914-1918	940.3
World War II, 1939-1945	940.53
Worm-caused diseases	
incidence	614.552
medicine	616.962
see also Communicable	
diseases (Human)	
Worm culture	639.75
Worm gears	621.833 3
Worms	595.1
agricultural pests	632.651
hunting	639.75
paleozoology	565.1
plant pests	632.651
Worms (Germany)	T2—434 352
Wormwood	583.55
Wororan languages	499.15
	T6—991 5
Worry	152.46
Worship	291.43
Buddhism	294.344 3
Christianity	248.3
Hinduism	294.543
Islam	297.43
Judaism	296.72
see also Public worship	
Worth	
epistemology	121.8
Worth County (Ga.)	T2—758 945
Worth County (Iowa)	T2—777 232
Worth County (Mo.)	T2—778 143
Worthing (England)	T2—422 68
Wounds	
medicine	617.14

X

X-ray spectroscopy	543.085 86
chemical analysis	543.085 86
engineering	621.361 6
physics	537.535 2
X-ray testing	
materials science	620.112 72
X-ray therapy	
medicine	615.842 2
X rays	539.722 2
biophysics	574.191 55
human	612.014 485
physics	539.722 2
X Región (Chile)	T2—835
Xanthe (Greece : Nome)	T2—495 7
Xanthophyceae	589.486
Xanthorrhoeaceae	584.43
Xenon	
chemistry	546.755
economic geology	553.97
gas technology	665.822
see also Chemicals	
Xeroderma	
medicine	616.544
see also Skin	
Xerography	686.44
equipment manufacturing	
technology	681.65
library services	025.12
office use	652.4
technology	686.44
Xhosa (African people)	T5—963 985
Xhosa language	496.398 5
	T6—963 985
Xhosa literature	896.398 5
XI Región (Chile)	T2—836 2
Xiang dialect	495.17
	T6—951 7
XII Región (Chile)	T2—836 4
Xinjiang Weiwuer Zizhiqu	
(China)	T2—516
Xiphosura	595.392
paleozoology	565.392
Xizang Zizhiqu (China)	T2—515
Xoloizuintli	
animal husbandry	636.76
see also Dogs	
Xosa language	496.398 5
	T6—963 985
Xosa literature	896.398 5
Xylariales	589.23
Xylem	
plant anatomy	581.41
Xylophones	786.843
see also Percussion instruments	
Xyridales	584.36

Y

Y.M.C.A. (Association)	267.3
Y.M.H.A. (Association)	296.673
Y.W.C.A. (Association)	267.5
Y.W.H.A. (Association)	296.675
Yacht racing	797.14
Yachting	797.124 6
Yachts	387.204 23
engineering	623.820 23
handling	623.881 23
power-driven	387.231 4
engineering	623.823 14
transportation services	387.231 4
sailing	
design	623.812 23
transportation services	387.204 23
wind-driven	387.223
engineering	623.822 3
transportation services	387.223
see also Ships	
Yadkin County (N.C.)	T2—756 66
Yadkin River (N.C.)	T2—756 68
Yaghnobi language	491.59
	T6—915 9
Yaghnobi literature	891.59
Yahuna language	498.3
	T6—983
Yahya Khan, Aga Muhammad	
Pakistani history	954.904 6
Yajurveda	294.592 14
Yakima County (Wash.)	T2—797 55
Yakima River (Wash.)	T2—797 55
Yaks	599.735 8
Yakut	T5—943
Yakut Autonomous Soviet	
Socialist Republic	
(R.S.F.S.R.)	T2—575
Yakut language	494.3
	T6—943
Yallourn (Vic.)	T2—945 6
Yalobusha County (Miss.)	T2—762 82
Yamagata-ken (Japan)	T2—521 16
Yamaguchi-ken (Japan)	T2—521 97
Yamaguti-ken (Japan)	T2—521 97
Yamal-Nenets National	
Okrug (R.S.F.S.R.)	T2—573
Yamanashi-ken (Japan)	T2—521 64
Yamanasi-ken (Japan)	T2—521 64
Yamaska (Quebec : County)	T2—714 54
Yambol, Bulgaria (Okrug)	T2—497 78
Yamhill County (Or.)	T2—795 39
Yami (Taiwan people)	T5—992 5
Yamoussoukro (Ivory Coast)	T2—666 8
Yams (Dioscorea)	641.352 3
agriculture	635.23
botany	584.27

Yiddish literature	839.09
Yield point (Mechanics)	531.38
Yields	
crop production	631.558
Yin dynasty (Chinese history)	931.02
YMCA	267.3
YMHA (Association)	296.673
Ynys Môn (Wales)	T2—429 21
Yo-Yos®	796.2
Yoakum County (Tex.)	T2—764 849
Yodo River (Japan)	T2—521 83
Yoga	181.45
health	613.704 6
philosophy	181.45
Yogacara Buddhism	294.392
Yogurt	641.371 476
cooking	641.671 476
processing	637.147 6
Yoho National Park (B.C.)	T2—711 68
Yokohama-shi (Japan)	T2—521 364
Yolo County (Calif.)	T2—794 51
Yom Kippur	296.432
customs	394.268 296 432
Yom Kippur War, 1973	956.048
Yonne (France)	T2—444 1
York (England)	T2—428 43
York (N.B.)	T2—715 51
York (Ont.)	T2—713 541
York (Ont. : Regional	
municipality)	T2—713 547
York, House of (English history)	942.04
York, House of (Irish history)	941.504
York County (Me.)	T2—741 95
York County (Neb.)	T2—782 345
York County (Pa.)	T2—748 41
York County (S.C.)	T2—757 43
York County (Va.)	T2—755 423
York River (Va.)	551.461 47
	T2—163 47
Yorke Peninsula (S. Aust.)	T2—942 35
Yorkshire (England)	T2—428 1
Yorkshire coach horse	
animal husbandry	636.14
zoology	599.725
Yorkshire Dales (England)	T2—428 4
Yorkshire terrier	
animal husbandry	636.76
see also Dogs	
Yorkshire Wolds	T2—428 3
Yorkton (Sask.)	T2—712 42
Yoro (Honduras : Dept.)	T2—728 314
Yoruba (African people)	T5—963 33
Yoruba language	496.333
	T6—963 33
Yoruba literature	896.333
Yosemite National Park	
(Calif.)	T2—794 47
Young (N.S.W.)	T2—944 8

Young adult literature	808.899 283
history and criticism	809.892 83
specific literatures	T3B—080 928 3
history and criticism	T3B—099 283
Young adults	305.235
	T1—083 5
	T7—055
etiquette	395.123
health	613.043 3
home care	649.125
human physiology	612.661
journalism for	070.483 3
labor economics	331.34
legal status	346.013 5
libraries for	027.626
mental disorders	616.890 22
over twenty	305.242
	T1—084 2
	T7—056
psychology	155.65
social aspects	305.242
physical fitness	613.704 3
psychology	155.5
publications for	
bibliographies	011.625
reading	
library science	028.535
recreation	790.192
indoor	793.019 2
outdoor	796.019 2
sex hygiene	613.951
social aspects	305.235
Young adults' political	
organizations	324.3
Young animals	591.3
domestic animals	636.07
mammals	599.03
Young County (Tex.)	T2—764 545
Young men	305.235
	T1—083 51
	T7—055
etiquette	395.123 2
grooming	646.704 4
health	613.042 33
journalism for	070.483 36
over twenty	305.242
	T1—084 2
	T7—056
social aspects	305.242
psychology	155.532
publications for	
bibliographies	011.624 1
sex hygiene	613.953
social aspects	305.235
social welfare	362.708 3
Young Men's Christian	
Association camps	796.542 2

Young Men's Christian		Young workers (continued)	
Associations	267.3	public administration	
Young Men's Hebrew		central governments	351.838 2
Associations	296.673	twenty and under	
Young people	305.23	public administration	350.838 2
	T1—083	central governments	351.838 27
	T7—054	local governments	352.943 82
Christian religious associations	267.6	twenty-one and over	
Christian religious education	268.433	public administration	350.838
church activities for	259.2	central governments	351.838 28
guides to Christian life	248.83	local governments	352.943 8
institutional buildings		Young's modulus	531.381
architecture	725.57	Youngstown (Ohio)	T2—771 39
legal status	346.013 5	Youth	305.235
psychology	155.5		T1—083 5
publications for		*see also* Young adults	
bibliographies	011.62	Youth, Isle of	T2—729 125
reviews	028.162	Yozgat Ili (Turkey)	T2—563
reading		Ytterbium	
library science	028.5	chemistry	546.419
social theology	291.178 342 3	*see also* Rare earths	
Christianity	261.834 23	Yttrium	669.290 3
social welfare	362.7	chemical engineering	661.040 3
public administration	350.847	chemistry	546.403
central governments	351.847	metallurgy	669.290 3
local governments	352.944 7	physical metallurgy	669.962 903
sociology	305.23	*see also* Chemicals	
Young people's books		Yttrium-group metals	
bibliographies	011.62	economic geology	553.494 7
Young people's societies	369.4	*see also* Metals	
Young people's society members	369.409 2	Yüan dynasty (Chinese history)	951.025
social group	T7—369 4	Yuat River	T2—957 5
Young People's Society of		Yuba County (Calif.)	T2—794 35
Christian Endeavor	267.613	Yucatán (Mexico : State)	T2—726 5
Young women	305.235	Yucatán Channel	551.463 4
	T1—083 52		T2—163 64
	T7—055	Yucca	584.43
etiquette	395.123 3	Yugoslav Banat	T2—497 1
grooming	646.704 2	Yugoslav communism	335.434 4
health	613.042 43	economics	335.434 4
journalism for	070.483 37	Yugoslavia	949.7
over twenty	305.242		T2—497
	T1—084 2	ancient	939.8
	T7—056		T2—398
social aspects	305.242	Yugoslavs	T5—918 2
psychology	155.533	Yuin-Kuric languages	499.15
publications for			T6—991 5
bibliographies	011.624 2	Yukaghir language	494.6
sex hygiene	613.955		T6—946
social aspects	305.235	Yuki Indians	T5—975
social welfare	362.708 3	Yuki language	497.5
Young Women's Christian			T6—975
Associations	267.5	Yukian Indians	T5—975
Young Women's Hebrew		Yukian languages	497.5
Associations	296.675		T6—975
Young workers		Yukon	T2—719 1
economics	331.34	Yukon Delta National	
personnel management	658.304 2	Wildlife Refuge	T2—798 4

Yukon-Koyokuk Borough
(Alaska)   T2—798 6
Yukon River (Yukon and
Alaska)   T2—798 6
  Alaska   T2—798 6
  Yukon   T2—719 1
Yuma County (Ariz.)   T2—791 71
Yuma County (Colo.)   T2—788 78
Yuman Indians   T5—975
Yuman languages   497.5
    T6—975
Yunnan Province (China)   T2—513 5
Yurak Samoyed language   494.4
    T6—944
Yurok language   497.3
    T6—973
Yvelines (France)   T2—443 66
YWCA   267.5
YWHA (Association)   296.675

Z

Z transform   515.723
Zacapa (Guatemala : Dept.)   T2—728 132
Zacatecas (Mexico : State)   T2—724 3
Zaire   967.51
    T2—675 1
Zaire (Angola : Province)   T2—673 2
Zaire River   T2—675 1
Zairians   T5—967 51
Zakarpatskaia oblast
(Ukraine)   T2—477 18
Zakat   297.54
Zakynthos (Greece)   T2—495 5
Zala Megye (Hungary)   T2—439 7
Zambales (Philippines)   T2—599 1
Zambezi River   T2—679
Zambézia (Mozambique)   T2—679 6
Zambia   968.94
    T2—689 4
Zambians   · T5—968 94
Zamboanga del Norte
(Philippines : Province)   T2—599 7
Zamboanga del Sur
(Philippines)   T2—599 7
Zamora (Spain : Province)   T2—462 4
Zamora-Chinchipe (Ecuador)   T2—866 44
Zamosc (Poland :
Voivodeship)   T2—438 4
Zande (African people)   T5—963 6
Zande language   496.36
    T6—963 6
Zanichelliaceae   584.722
Zanjan (Iran : Province)   T2—551
Zante (Greece)   T2—495 5
Zanzibar   967.81
    T2—678 1
Zanzibaris   T5—967 8

Západočeský kraj
(Czechoslovakia)   T2—437 1
Západoslovenský kraj
(Czechoslovakia)   T2—437 3
Zapata County (Tex.)   T2—764 483
Zaporoshskaia oblast
(Ukraine)   T2—477 17
Zaporozhye (Ukraine :
Oblast)   T2—477 17
Zapotec Indians   T5—976
Zapotec language   497.6
    T6—976
Zapotec literature   897.6
Zaragoza (Spain : Province)   T2—465 53
Zaramo language   496.391
    T6—963 91
Zastron (South Africa :
District)   T2—685 6
Zavala County (Tex.)   T2—764 437
Zaydites (Islamic sect)   297.824
Zealand, Denmark   T2—489 1
Zealots (Judaism)   296.81
Zebra plant   584.21
Zebras   599.725
  animal husbandry   636.18
  big game hunting   799.277 25
Zebus   599.735 8
  animal husbandry   636.291
Zechariah (Biblical book)   224.98
Zeehan (Tas.)   T2—946 6
Zeeland (Netherlands :
Province)   T2—492 42
Zeerust (South Africa)   T2—682 3
Zeewolde (Netherlands)   T2—492 2
Zeiformes   597.58·
Zeil, Mount   T2—942 91
Zelaya (Nicaragua : Dept.)   T2—728 532
Zen Buddhism   294.392 7
Zener diodes   621.381 522
Zenith telescopes
  astronomy   522.4
Zenjan (Iran : Province)   T2—551
Zeolite
  mineralogy   549.68
Zephaniah (Biblical book)   224.96
Zero-base budgeting   658.154
  public administration   350.722 204 3
    central governments   351.722 204 3
    local governments   352.122 043
Zero-memory systems   003.8
Zeta function   515.56
Zhejiang Sheng (China)   T2—512 42
Zhengs   787.72
  see also Stringed instruments
Zhitomir (Ukraine : Oblast)   T2—477 14
Zhitomirskaia oblast
(Ukraine)   T2—477 14
Ziebach County (S.D.)   T2—783 53

Manual

Use of the Manual

The Manual for the Dewey Decimal Classification is intended to serve practicing classifiers and students. It describes the policies and practices of the Decimal Classification Division of the Library of Congress. Outline maps provide a display of key area numbers from Table 2. Users are led from the Schedules and Tables to the Manual by see-Manual notes.

The Manual is arranged in the numerical order of the Tables and Schedules. For certain classes there are several notes which are subarranged in the following sequence:

(A) Notes on problems common to more than one number (the notes for numbers linked by "-" or "and," e.g., 580-590 or 380.1 and 381, 382).

(B) Notes on problems involving only one number (or a single number and its subdivisions).

(C) Notes on differentiating numbers (the notes linked by "vs.," e.g., 300 vs. 600).

These notes may contain sections on specific problems, e.g., the treatment of adaptations in 800 literature.

There is an unusually full note on 780 Music to explain the complete revision of the class introduced in this edition.

An appendix at the end of the Manual describes the policies and procedures of the Decimal Classification Division of the Library of Congress in respect to the following: Segmentation in centrally cataloged records, bracketed DDC numbers on LC bibliographic records, and classifying children's books in the Decimal Classification Division.

Notes on Table Numbers

Table 1. Standard Subdivisions   T1

Table 1. Standard Subdivisions

Standard subdivisions are so called because they are applicable to virtually all classes. There are several kinds of standard subdivisions:

1. Subdivisions which indicate the bibliographic forms that the information may take, e.g., encyclopedias, periodicals, audiovisual treatment.

2. Subdivisions which treat the whole subject but in a restricted situation, e.g., by areas, historical periods, kinds of persons.

3. Subdivisions which identify a specific kind of information about the subject, e.g., illustrations, directories, product lists, identification marks, statistics.

4. Subdivisions which bring the methods of other disciplines to bear on the subject, e.g., management, education, research, scientific principles, auxiliary techniques.

5. Subdivisions which relate the subject to its users, e.g., the subject as a profession, and works for a specific type of users.

6. Miscellaneous subdivisions, e.g., biography, humorous treatment.

The common feature of standard subdivisions is that they identify limited treatment of the subject that may be wanted by users not immediately concerned with the rest of the subject. This feature leads to the first general rule in applying them: in doubtful cases, do not use standard subdivisions, since they serve to segregate specialized material from works of general interest. For example, avoid using the most recent period subdivision in T1—0904 for "state of the art" works on a subject because most users will expect to find such works in the main number.

Some standard subdivisions used in doubtful situations may be annoying as well as superfluous. Any elementary work on a subject may be considered a work for novices, amateurs, laymen, dabblers, the uninitiated, or collectors. However, to add standard subdivision T1—0240909 will not only double the length of the number in most cases, but also might offend more than help the specified users. Similarly, many works in social sciences refer mostly to well-developed countries or to the subject in the West but do not intentionally exclude other areas. Use T1—091722 or T1—091821 sparingly for such works, since few users will be helped by segregating material according to aspects which the authors do not emphasize.

In some cases the standard subdivision may be redundant, or nearly so. For example, T1—024694 indicates the subject for carpenters. It is never used with 694 carpentry, since works on a subject are primarily written for its practitioners. One need not (until the 21st century) use 004.0904 for computers in the 20th century, since the computer is virtually a 20th-century phenomenon. In certain cases a standard subdivision would simply redefine the base discipline, e.g., T1—01 Philosophy and theory in most direct subdivisions of 100 Philosophy. *See also T1—01.*

Use whether or not supplied in the schedules

Standard subdivisions can be used anywhere in the schedules unless there are instructions to the contrary. They are not normally supplied in the number column except where needed to fill out three-digit numbers under the main classes. However, under certain numbers a few standard subdivisions may be supplied when these subdivisions have special meanings or when extended notation is required for the subject in question. The rest of the standard subdivisions (those not supplied) are to be used with their normal meanings as given in this table. For example, in the standard subdivision position under 370 Education the schedule gives only 370.1 and 370.7, which have been given modified or extended meanings; and 370.287, 370.68, and 370.82 which are enclosed in brackets to show that they are not used. The rest of 370.2—.6 and 370.8—.9 are to be used with their normal meanings even though the standard subdivisions are not printed.

Whenever the base digits of a normal standard subdivision are supplied, all further subdivisions found in Table 1 are implied. For example, the regular heading of notation 07 from Table 1 Education, research, related topics is supplied at 507. That entry is followed immediately by 507.2 Research, and 507.8 Use of apparatus and equipment in study and teaching, each with the regular heading found in Table 1. These three standard subdivisions are supplied for technical reasons only: 507 to fill out the three-digit number, 507.2 to supply a reference to 001.4, and 507.8 to supply a note on science projects. In no way do they limit the use of other subdivisions found under T1—07 in Table 1, e.g., 507.24 Experimental research, 507.6 Review and exercise.

Approximating the whole

(The principles explained here apply equally to the use of recurring subdivisions indicated by footnotes.)

Standard subdivisions should be added only when the work in hand applies to the whole, or approximately the whole, of the subject of the number. For example, there is no number for black widow spiders

Table 1. Standard Subdivisions T1

under 595.44, the number for spiders. Do not, therefore, assume that black widows are "just another spider," and start using 595.440972 for an account on black widow spiders in Mexico. Stop at 595.44, where works on black widow spiders have standing room pending further development of the schedule.

The approximate-the-whole restriction need not be applied to a number which, because of the nature of its subject, appears unlikely to be given subdivisions in the future, e.g., 929.3 Genealogical sources. Here the standard subdivisions (as well as the direct area subdivisions 929.33–.39 used in lieu of 929.3093–.3099) may be used for any specific kind of source, e.g., registers, wills, tax lists. In many cases specific instances of a restricted subject are more usefully arranged geographically under T1—09 than by kinds which may not be stable over the years, e.g., hospitals in a given area, whether public, private, church related, or serving veterans and their dependents, should be classed in 362.1109, not 362.11.

A special case of concepts unlikely to be given subdivisions in the future are the elements of a unitary term. Many headings contain two or more parts joined by the word "and." Sometimes the words thus joined are so close in meaning that they are unlikely ever to be separated. These headings (and similar phrases in class-here notes) constitute unitary terms. (See discussion of class-here notes below.) When a unitary term is at issue, standard subdivisions are added even when the work in hand uses only one of the terms and attempts to draw a distinction between the two.

Examples of unitary terms are:

255	Religious congregations and orders
338.9	Economic development and growth
341.5	Disputes and conflicts between states
362.2	Mental and emotional illnesses and disturbances
681.2	Testing and measuring instruments
725.81	Music halls and concert halls

These are not to be confused with related terms which commonly go together to form a larger whole. Such terms may each have its own subdivision (and in the following examples, one or both terms do):

306	Culture and institutions
306.8	Marriage and family
332.8	Interest and discount
347	Civil procedure and courts

Use caution in assuming that subjects will not be subdivided. At present there are few titles on architecture of office buildings in 725.23, leaving it doubtful if a number will ever be provided for medical office buildings. However, the latter constitute a legitimate subject which might eventually be added to make the Classification more useful for architecture libraries. Therefore, class a history of architecture of medical office buildings in 725.23, not 725.2309.

In determining what subject or combination of subjects approximates the whole of a larger subject, the normal rule is that a work covering three subdivisions approximates the whole. If there are only three subdivisions, then normally two subdivisions approximate the whole. However, if a subject consists of a large number of distinct subclasses, e.g., species in zoology or botany, a work on representatives of three or more distinct subdivisions counts as approximating the whole. For example, a work on the grizzly bear, the jackrabbit, and the opossum of North America will be classed in 599.097, e.g., as representative mammals (599) of North America (T1—097).

Class-here notes and approximating the whole

The class-here note, i.e., the instruction note beginning with the words "Class here," is a reliable guide that standard subdivisions may be added to the notation for the term or terms listed. While some terms will refer to subjects larger than the one indicated by the heading, any term in a class here note for a concept smaller than the subject for the heading is regarded as approximating the whole for purposes of classification.

Table of precedence

The table of precedence yields to two other citation order rules: First, when standard subdivisions are displaced to nonzero positions, the rule of zero (paragraph 5.13 in the Introduction to DDC) overrides the table of precedence here, e.g., management of prisons in Great Britain 365.941068, not 365.068 as would normally be the case. (*See also* the section below on Multiple standard subdivisions.) Second, the rule of applications (paragraph 5.6 in the Introduction to DDC) remains basic to sound classification, so teaching financial management in hospital administration is classed in 362.110681, not 362.1107.

Subdivision of displaced standard subdivisions

A displaced standard subdivision is one that has been moved from its normal position, e.g., under 362 standard subdivision T1—09 has been displaced from 362.09 to 362.9 for historical, geographical, persons treatment of social welfare problems and services. A displaced standard subdivision is subdivided as shown in Table 1, except for units

Table 1. Standard Subdivisions **T1**

that have been given a changed or extended meaning (as at 370.71). For example, 340.1 Philosophy and theory of law may be subdivided to yield 340.14 for legal language and communication in the same way that it would be if located beside the rest of the standard subdivisions of law in 340.02–.09. Similarly, 910.01 Philosophy and theory of geography and travel may be subdivided to yield 910.015 for scientific principles of geography. However, see T1—093–099 and T2—3–9 for discussion of an exception to this rule for displaced geographical treatment.

Multiple standard subdivisions

Do not add one standard subdivision to another standard subdivision unless specifically instructed. In the following cases, addition of a second standard subdivisions is allowed:

1. With standard subdivision T1—04, which is actually not a *standard* subdivision, but a special topic subdivision available to permit introduction of new development when there is no suitable vacant notation in direct 1–9 subdivisions.

2. With standard subdivisions which have specially changed or extended meanings, e.g., periodicals on educational psychology 370.1505, on pyrometallurgy 669.028205, on political situations and conditions 320.9005. (In contrast, the periodical subdivision is not added to the true standard subdivisions nearby, e.g., not to metallurgical patents 669.0272 or the history of political science 320.09.)

3. Under standard subdivision T1—09, certain other standard subdivisions are specifically provided, notably for statistics (T1—021); illustrations (T1—022); and museums, collections, exhibits (T1—074). (In the case of T1—074 it is not redundant to add a second area number that is more specific than the first, e.g., to use T1—09810748161 for collections of Brazilian objects in São Paulo.)

4. With standard subdivision concepts displaced to nonzero numbers (usually for geographical treatment), the full range of standard subdivisions is available, e.g., management of penal institutions in Great Britain 365.941068. In contrast, management of hospitals in Great Britain is classed in 362.11068. For encyclopedias on British penal institutions and hospitals the numbers are 365.94103 and 362.110941, respectively, since encyclopedias yield precedence to place. Many of the displaced standard subdivisions date from early editions of the Dewey Decimal Classification, and reflect aspects of unusual importance in particular subjects. Therefore there is often a larger and more diverse literature on these concepts than is normal for the regular standard subdivisions.

Standard subdivisions under synthesized numbers

Take care in using a standard subdivision when the number to which it is to be attached is the result of synthesis. The standard subdivision applies to the entire number that has been synthesized, not to any of its elements. Take the synthesis of clothing and trade numbers as an example. 687 means manufacturing of clothing, a number which is used for products, i.e., clothing. 380.145 means trade in products of secondary industries and services. Add 687 to 380.145 and we have 380.145687 trade in clothing. When T1—05 is added to 687 we get 687.05 periodicals on clothing. We do not then add 687.05 as a unit to the trade number, since we would then create a number for trade in clothing periodicals, an unlikely subject. Rather, we take 380.145687 as a unit and add T1—05 to create a number for periodicals on the clothing trade.

The only exception to the foregoing rule is 016 Bibliography. When we add a synthesized number to 016, we must consider that logically bibliography is like a standard-subdivision concept in that it applies to the whole of the synthesized number plus any attached standard subdivisions. Thus 016.38014568705 is used only for bibliographies of periodicals of the clothing trade; it is not used for a periodical bibliography of the clothing trade. There is no notation to show periodical bibliographies, since T1—05 must be reserved here for the material covered by the bibliography.

Number of zeros

If there is no indication to the contrary, use one zero for standard subdivisions, e.g., history of radiobroadcasting 384.5409. The following kinds of instructions indicate when a different number of zeros must be used:

1. Notation in the number column, e.g., 620.009 for history of engineering.

2. Standard subdivision notes, e.g., the instruction at 324.241 to use 324.241001–.241009 for standard subdivisions gives us 324.241009 for history of political parties in the United Kingdom.

3. Footnotes leading to an add table in which the subdivisions are supplied, e.g., the add table under 616.1–.9 indicates that 001–009 is to be used for standard subdivisions. At 616.1 the heading *Diseases of the cardiovascular system is governed by a note that says add as instructed under 616.1–.9. Thus we get 616.1009 for the history of diagnosis and treatment of cardiovascular diseases.

4. Footnotes directly under an add instruction stipulating the use of extra zeros, e.g., the footnote to the add note under 327.3–.9 which

Table 1. Standard Subdivisions   T1

gives us 327.41009 for the history of foreign policy of the United Kingdom. This footnote cites instructions at the beginning of Table 1 which govern in any case: standard subdivisions must have enough zeros to avoid any possible conflict with a number supplied in the schedules.

T1—01   **Philosophy and theory**

While most subdivisions of T1—01 are easy to understand and apply, T1—01 by itself can cause problems. The term "philosophy and theory" is considered a unitary one, covering the general or abstract principles applied to a field of activity or thought, such as science or art. However, it should not be used where theory constitutes the bulk of the subject matter of a field, e.g., nuclear physics. In philosophy subdivisions in 100, T1—01 is used only in the sense of theory and method of the topic.

A work discussing the discipline itself as a discipline, rather than the subject matter of the discipline, is a likely candidate for use of T1—01. Aspects of a discipline that are likely to be indicated by T1—01 include:

1. The boundaries and limits of a field of study; its nature as an art or science.

2. Schools of thought within a discipline. However, if there is a heavy literature on schools or systems of thought, special provisions may have been made, e.g., 150.19 for psychological schools and 330.1 for economic systems and theories. Numbers for theories found in certain disciplines are often an extension of the work of such schools of thought, e.g., political theories in 320.5, physical theories in 530.1.

3. The ideal state of a discipline, and how far it can be expected to reach its goal, e.g., how close science can come to absolute truth.

4. Techniques and principles of criticism of a discipline. However, the criticism itself is classed with the work criticized, e.g., criticism of Browning's poetry 821.8, of Frank Lloyd Wright's architecture 720.92, of Italian cooking 641.5945.

Note, however, that historical, geographical, and persons treatment of a discipline is classed in T1—09.

T1—0113   **[Computer modeling and simulation] vs. Data**
vs.   **processing   Computer applications**
T1—0285

Use T1—0285 for general works on use of computers, programs, etc., by persons working with a subject. However, use T1—0113 for attempts to represent the subject and to predict outcomes under various hypothetical conditions. In the absence of a specific design number, T1—0113 is also used for computer modeling in design. For example (using microcomputer numbers in each case), ordinary programs for lathe operators 621.9420285536, programs for chemical process simulation in ceramics 666.0113536, programs for research modeling of nuclear structure 539.740113536.

See also 003, T1—011 vs. 510, T1—051.

T1—014 vs.   Language (Terminology) and communication vs. Dictionaries,
T1—03   encyclopedias, concordances

Use T1—014 for discourses on terminology; T1—03 for works systematically arranged for ready reference, e.g., alphabetical and picture dictionaries, thesauruses in classified order. However, use T1—0142 for etymological dictionaries and T1—0148 for lists of abbreviations and symbols.

T1—015 vs.   Scientific principles vs. Works for specific types of users
T1—024

Observe the "table-of-contents" rule to distinguish between the scientific principles of a technology and science written for technology and engineering users. If the table of contents is developed in terms of concepts found in subdivisions of the science (or in the tables of contents of common treatises on the science), class with the science using T1—024. Conversely, if the table of contents is developed in terms of concepts found in subdivisions of the technology (or in the tables of contents of common treatises on the technology), class with the technology using T1—015. If in doubt between science and technology, prefer the technology number.

When not to use either subdivision

Use T1—015 and T1—024 in 500 and 600 only when there is not a direct relationship between a science and a corresponding technology, e.g., do not use 540.2466 for chemistry for chemical engineers, or 660.0154 for chemical principles in chemical engineering.

Do not use T1—0246 in 500 for all the applications of a science, even though the work may be in effect a work for technologists, since such a work is hardly for specific types of users of that subject. Although T1—015 may be used in 600 for all the sciences applied in a technology, use it with caution, since the distinction between the principles of a technology and the principles of science used in a technology are not often observed in practice.

Table 1. Standard Subdivisions   T1

T1—019   **Psychological principles**

Because counseling in a specific subject usually encompasses the entire subject with which the counseling is concerned and not just the psychological aspect, be cautious about using notation 019 for counseling in a specific subject, e.g., investment counseling 332.6, not 332.6019. Note that counseling and interviewing in welfare are classed in 361.32 and often have specific provision in 362–363, using 86 from the table at 362–363, e.g., counseling and guidance of poor people 362.586. Guidance and counseling in education are classed in 371.4 and cognate numbers for specific levels of education.

T1—0222   **Pictures and related material vs. Maps and related forms, plans,**
vs.   **diagrams**
T1—0223

The basic concept in T1—0222 is *picture*, i.e., a naturalistic representation of a subject. It may be sketchy, impressionistic, or detailed, but it is intended to represent what will be seen. In contrast, the basic concept in T1—0223 is *plan*, i.e., a two-dimensional representation such as a ground or floor layout, or a vertical plane representation. The word "diagram" adds to T1—0223 the concept of a graphic design which explains, rather than represents. It shows arrangements and relations among the parts, and need not be limited to a single plane.

Unfortunately, the classifier must work with a number of words which blur the basic distinction of picture vs. plan, e.g., charts, designs, atlases. Use T1—0222 for charts that are basically pictures of things, T1—0223 for charts that are basically plans or diagrams. Use T1—0222 for designs which give a visual impression of what something does or will look like, e.g., architectural drawings; T1—0223 for designs that show details on horizontal or vertical planes (often as a preliminary to construction), or the arrangement and relations of parts showing how something works. Atlases are usually compilations of maps, plans, or diagrams (T1—0223), but be alert for atlases that are simply compilations of pictorial material. Anatomical atlases are so picture-like that they are classed in T1—0222. Also be alert for atlases that are simply heavily illustrated texts on a subject. These are classed in the base number.

Class comprehensive works in T1—0222, e.g., architectural drawings and plans, 720.222. If in doubt, use T1—0222.

T1—0223   **Maps and related forms, plans, diagrams vs. Graphic representations**
vs. 912   **of surface of the world and of extraterrestrial worlds**

Geographical atlases and maps, i.e., atlases and maps which either do not emphasize a subject, or are devoted to any subject in 910 (general geography and travel) are classed in 912. Road atlases and maps, being primarily intended for travelers, are also classed in 912, but railroad atlases will normally be devoted to transportation, so will fall in 385.0223 or in 385.09 with notation 022 from the add tables found under T1—093–099, e.g., railroad atlases in Brazil 385.0981022.

T1—024   **Works for specific types of users**

Do not use T1—024 when it is redundant or nearly so, i.e., when it is directed towards those who would normally be expected to be studying the subject, e.g., engineering for practitioners, students, beginners 620 (not 620.002462, 620.0024375, or 620.00240909, respectively).

Use T1—024 with caution for works that effectively cover the subject for the general reader but simply draw examples from one broad discipline or for one kind of professional user. For example, a work on cardiology for nurses is often just as suitable for patients, relatives, or social workers as for nurses. Therefore, prefer 616.12 over 616.120024613 unless the work emphasizes special instructions for nurses that general readers would not find useful.

The Decimal Classification Division does not use T1—024054 to identify works for children, since such works are usually brought together in special collections.

T1—024 vs.   **Works for specific types of users vs. History and description with**
T1—08   **respect to kinds of persons**

Notation 024 refers primarily to the treatment of a discipline for the instruction of some type of user (usually members of an occupational group) other than its primary students and practitioners, e.g., mathematics for engineers 510.2462. Its emphasis on occupational groups is reflected in the fact that most of its subdivisions (i.e., T1—0241 and T1—0243–0249) are taken up by them.

In contrast, T1—08 refers either to kinds of persons active in the subject, e.g., women aviators 629.13082; or to kinds of persons affected by the subject, especially those personally benefited by the subject. Most how-to books that target specific kinds of persons (except occupational groups that need to learn and use a discipline other than their primary one) call for the T1—08. The emphasis on nonoccupational groups is reflected in the subdivisions: only T1—088 is devoted to the occupational and religious groups which occupy all the direct (nonzero) subdivisions of T1—024. All the other subdivisions of T1—08 (T1—081–087 and T1—089) are devoted to the kinds of persons relegated to zero subdivisions in T1—024 (T1—02403–02408).

If a work uses the word "for" in the sense of "of" or "for the benefit of," then T1—08 is the appropriate subdivision, e.g., success in obtaining jobs for students 650.14088375, social services for children 361.0083, meal planning and table service for shut-in persons

Table 1. Standard Subdivisions T1

642.0877. A work on hair care for women meaning care of women's hair is 646.724082, but a work on hair care for women who may be responsible for the hair of children, parents, husbands, and friends is 646.724024042. A work on diet for mothers may be either 613.20852 if it tells mothers about their own diet, 613.2083 if it tells about their children's diet, or 613.20240431 if it tells mothers about the diet of all members of their families.

T1—028 **Auxiliary techniques and procedures; apparatus, equipment, materials**

Unless specific instructions are given, T1—028 is not used for the techniques and procedures that are basic to a subject. For example, use 640 (not 640.28) for the basic techniques of home economics, 264 (not 264.028) for the conduct of public worship. The subdivision is not normally used for the technology of subjects in 600; however, 610.28 is used for medical technology since the subject does not refer to the basic arts or techniques of medicine, but to the specialized apparatus, equipment, and materials of medicine and their use.

The apparatus, equipment, and materials covered by T1—028 refer to what is used in a subject, not to the products of a subject.

T1—0285 **Data processing** **Computer applications**

Do not use T1—02854 by itself, since the digit 4 simply repeats the meaning of notation 0285. If the applied concept is one for which 004 is the interdisciplinary number, simply stop at T1—0285, e.g., digital computers T1—0285. However, it is not redundant to add 4 plus additional digits to T1—0285, e.g., digital microcomputers T1—0285416.

It is similarly redundant to add only the digit 4 to numbers divided like 004–006 when the base number is limited to data processing and computer concepts, e.g., 651.8, 658.05.

Machine-readable materials and programs

Do not use T1—0285 to indicate that a work is in machine-readable form (e.g., do not use it for census data stored on machine-readable tapes). Notation 028 (Auxiliary techniques and procedures; apparatus, equipment, materials) is not used as a form subdivision. A program, however, may be regarded as a kind of apparatus—a device to make a computer work properly or to accomplish a particular task—and works about programs typically discuss techniques and procedures. Hence T1—028553 and its subdivisions should be used for programs themselves and for works about programs, regardless of form (e.g., programs in machine-readable form, such as disk, or tape, and printed program listings bound into books).

Do not use T1—028553 for items that include both programs and data files, unless the data files are clearly of minor importance (e.g., small files intended merely to help beginners learn to use the programs).

If in doubt, do not use T1—028553.

T1—0285
vs.
T1—068

Data processing   Computer applications vs. Management

Class the management of applied data processing with the application, using T1—0285. It is more common, however, for books to treat data processing applied to management of a subject, in which case T1—068 is used, e.g., data processing applied to the management of hospitals 362.11068.

T1—0294
vs.
T1—074

Trade catalogs and directories vs. Museums, collections, exhibits

While most catalogs of products for sale are classed in T1—0294, catalogs of collections are an exception. The distinction is based upon primary purpose: T1—0294 is used for catalogs whose primary purpose is to promote sale or distribution of products, T1—074 for catalogs whose primary purpose is to promote knowledge or art. However, T1—074 is stretched a little to cover catalogs of replicas, duplicates, and minor items when offered for sale in museum- or exhibit-like settings by noncommercial institutions. It is also used in art (700–770) for auction catalogs, and for catalogs of temporary exhibits of groups of artists, even if a succession of such exhibits provides most of the artists with their primary source of income. If in doubt, prefer T1—074.

T1—0601–
0609

Organizations

Organization subdivisions in T1—06 are primarily used for membership organizations and associations, but are also used for a selection of nonmembership institutions, foundations, and agencies which do not belong to the categories listed under T1—0601–0609. However, before using T1—06 for nonmembership organizations, determine that "organization" is not inherent in the subject. For example, except as indicated below, do not use T1—06 for most subdivisions in 250–280 Christian church, in 355–359 military art and science, or for many subdivisions in 360 for social services. Under such numbers, use T1—09 for the basic organizations in specific areas, and for specific basic organizations, e.g., hospitals in China 362.110951. However, use T1—06 for nonoperating associations of the basic organizations and their staffs, e.g., hospital associations in China 362.1106051.

There remains a small residual use for T1—06 for nonmembership organizations, e.g. for administrative (in contrast to service) histories of hospitals (362.1106) or police agencies (363.206). These histories are not to be confused with how-to works on management, which are identified by T1—068.

Table 1. Standard Subdivisions T1

Do not use T1—06 for membership organizations where "membership organization" is inherent in the subject, e.g., in 366 Association or 061—068 General organizations.

Selection of area number

For membership organizations, use the area that is the chief focus of the membership, e.g., American Medical Association 610.6073. For local affiliated associations or chapters that have their own name, use the area number of the local organization, e.g., Massachusetts Medical Association 610.60744. For offices and chapters that take the name of the parent body, use the number of the parent organization, e.g., the Washington office of the American Medical Association 610.6073 (not 610.60753).

For nonmembership organizations, institutions, foundations, and conferences use the area number of the headquarters. Also use the number of the headquarters for membership organizations whose area cannot be determined, or whose purpose is to support or benefit from a fixed institution.

T1—0601–
0609 vs.
T1—072

Organizations vs. Research

Use T1—072 for organizations that conduct research, e.g., agricultural research stations in the United States 630.72073, but T1—06 for membership organizations which primarily promote research, e.g., the American Association for the Advancement of Science 506.073. If in doubt, class in T1—072.

T1—07 vs.
016, 026

Education, research, related topics vs. Bibliographies and catalogs of works on specific subjects or in specific disciplines vs. Libraries, archives, information centers devoted to specific subjects and disciplines

Notation 07 from Table 1 is used for comprehensive works on resources for study and teaching. Many of the resources are encompassed by subdivisions of T1—07, e.g., schools and laboratories, collections of objects (such as botanical collections), and financial support. Books, manuscripts, recordings, and the like are also resources, but works that describe such resources will normally be classed in 016 or 026 unless the work (a) also describes kinds of resources not found in libraries and archives or (b) emphasizes how to use the library or archival resources for study, teaching, or research. In case of doubt between the subject plus T1—07 from Table 1 and 016 or 026, prefer 016 or 026.

To be classed in 016, a work about resources in a field must describe individual works, such as books and articles. A work about kinds of material not traditionally described in detail, however, is classed in 016 if small units are described, e.g., five shelf feet of correspondence of a particular person on a particular subject. Inventories and calendars of archives are typically classed in 016. Works about resources in a field that give broad descriptions of whole collections held by libraries, archives, and other information organizations are classed in 026. Such works often include directory information about the institutions and organizations. In case of doubt between 016 and 026, prefer 016.

Notation 07 may be used in 016 if the resources being described treat study and teaching, e.g., a bibliography of material on the study and teaching of mathematics 016.5107.

T1—081–087 Specific miscellaneous kinds of persons

Be alert for provisions for certain age, sex, or handicapped groups which were assigned numbers before T1—08 was developed for kinds of persons, e.g., age and sex groups in 613.04; the handicapped, men, women, and children at 646.31–.36 and cognate numbers in 646.4–.7; the handicapped, infirm, and aged in 720.42–.43 and cognate numbers in 721–729.

T1—081, T1—082, T1—08351 and T1—08352   Men [and] Women [and] Young men [and] Young women

Subdivisions for men and women should be used only for works explicitly emphasizing the sex of the people treated. Do not use T1—081 for fire*men* unless the work makes clear that firemen are being contrasted with fire*women*, or T1—08351 for juvenile delinquents (a term often implying young men) unless male delinquents are being contrasted to female delinquents.

T1—0882 vs. T1—09   [Religious groups] vs. Historical, geographical, persons treatment

Treatment of a religious group is classed in T1—0882 even if the group is limited to an area in which it is predominant, e.g., Roman Catholics of Spain T1—08822, not T1—0946, even though Catholics predominate in Spain.

T1—089 vs. T1—09   Racial, ethnic, national groups vs. Historical, geographical, persons treatment

T1—089 takes precedence over T1—09 except for groups which predominate in an area, e.g., French people in Australia T1—08941094, but French people in Paris T1—0944361; Caucasoids in Europe T1—094, but Caucasoids in Africa T1—08903406; Arabs generally T1—089927, Arabs in Egypt T1—0962, Arabs in France T1—089927044. Notation 09174 is not used for groups of persons treatment since such use would practically duplicate the group treatment numbers, e.g., Arabs who are residents of all areas where they

Table 1. Standard Subdivisions   T1

predominate taken together constitute the overwhelming majority of all Arabs, so T1—089927 is used for them, not T1—09174927.

Use T1—09 to identify distinguishing characteristics of a subject rather than T1—089, e.g., Arab architecture 720.9174927, not 720.89927; French pastries 641.8650944, not 641.86508941.

If in doubt, prefer T1—09.

T1—09   **Historical, geographical, persons treatment**

Be alert for distinctions occasionally made between the historical and geographical treatment of a subject and the historical and geographical treatment of the discipline within which the subject is treated.   For example, 364.9 is provided for historical and geographical treatment of crime and its alleviation, while 364.09 is provided for comparable treatment of the discipline. Use 364.9 for area treatment of offenses, offenders, causes, prevention, and treatment (when all are considered together). Use 364.09 for area treatment of the discipline of criminology and of the principles and methods used in analyzing causes and remedies of crime. Where the distinction is not made between the subject and the discipline, use T1—09 for either or both aspects.

T1—0901–   **Historical periods**
0905
Do not use these periods for subjects that had no significant history outside the period indicated, e.g., the history of railroads 385.09 (not 385.0903), but the history of railroads during the 19th century 385.09034. If in doubt, do not use periods, e.g., use 629.1309, not 629.130904, for 20th-century aviation, since aviation hardly existed before the 20th century.

Avoid using the most recent period subdivision in T1—0904 for "state of the art" works on a subject. Most users will expect to find these works in the base number. However, when the nature of the subject requires attention to the changing situation, the latest period number must be used, e.g., 320.9049 for world political conditions in 1990.

Use historical periods only for retrospective works. For example, a work on music theory of the baroque 781.09032, but a reprint of a treatise on music theory written in 1620 when baroque music prevailed 781. Similarly, do not use the latest period for a work on current practice or the state of the art of a subject.

T1—0902   **6th-15th centuries, 500–1499**

The Middle Ages and the Medieval period often refer to European history. However, the medieval record of many subjects outside Europe is poorly documented, so a work attempting worldwide coverage may in fact be predominantly about the subject in Europe. Therefore, one must distinguish between T1—0940902 for works that are clearly limited to Europe, and T1—0902 for works that attempt to cover the whole world during the period.

T1—092   Persons

These instructions apply also to notation 2 from Table 2 when numbers from Table 2 are added directly without the interposition of T1—09.

In the notes below, the word "biography" is used for stylistic convenience; however, the instructions apply fully to description and critical appraisal as well as other "persons" aspects.

T1—092 is not used for the actual works of a person except where so instructed at certain numbers in 700–770.

Comprehensive biography: General

Class a comprehensive biography of a person with the subject of the person's most noted contribution. If the person made approximately equal contributions to a number of fields, class in the subject which provides the best common denominator, giving some extra consideration to the person's occupational commitment. For example, a physicist who became a science teacher, then head of a school of science, but went on to become a university president would be classed in the university's area number under 378. The biography of a person who made significant contributions in political science, in university education, and the study of administrative and economic aspects of utility regulation will be classed in 300.92, since there is no other common denominator for his work. However, a famous woman doctor who also served as a feminist leader, wrote minor novels, and often served as a delegate to political conventions will normally be classed in 610.92 unless there is an obvious emphasis on her avocations. Give weight to designations listed first in biographical dictionaries, but make allowances for the tendency to list occupation first even when a career transcends occupation.

If in doubt between a number for a discipline and a number for a specific subject within the discipline, prefer the number for the discipline, e.g., a mechanical engineer who also did important work in transportation and construction engineering 620.0092 rather than 621.092.

Comprehensive biography: Public figures

Biographies of public figures frequently present difficulties because the figures may have filled several positions which are given varying emphasis by different authors, or may have filled one position which had many facets. For persons who held such positions, prefer history numbers in 930–990 for comprehensive works. However, for biogra-

Table 1. Standard Subdivisions T1

phies that emphasize one position or interest of a person's career, e.g., a biography emphasizing Wayne Morse's promotion of the National Institutes of Health 362.1092, even though he was a U.S. Senator. (See also Partial biography, below.)

There are a number of offices a public figure may hold that afford an opportunity to exert a wide-ranging impact upon the history of the jurisdiction served. For example, Daniel Webster is most famous as a U.S. Senator, although he served twice as Secretary of State. In both positions, as well as in his position as lawyer and orator, he influenced the history of his time, so the best number for his biography is 973.5092, not 328.73092 for his senatorial service, 327.730092 for his foreign relations service, or 349.73092 for his legal activities. However, if a person in a high office of general responsibility concentrated on a single important field, consider a number which identifies that field. For example, Claude Pepper's chief interest while serving in the U.S. Congress, both as Senator, and later as Representative, was the promotion of services to older people. Thus the suitable number for his comprehensive biography might be 362.6092 for his services to the elderly rather than 973.92092 for his impact on the general history of his period or 328.73092 for his legislative work.

For public figures who served in several capacities, give greatest weight to the highest office reached, normally the one in the highest category in the following table. When there is no clear reason to the contrary, use the following table of precedence:

1. 930–990 for kings, presidents, other heads of state, prime ministers, vice presidents, regents using the number for the period during which they held office. Also class here public figures of any position or combination of positions who had a significant impact upon general history, including the king makers and the powers behind the throne, using the period numbers which best approximate their period of influence. Candidates of major parties for the highest office of a country are also assigned history numbers, generally using the period for which they ran for office, e.g., 973.68092 for Stephen Douglas who ran against Lincoln. Sometimes a candidate defeated for party nomination had a significant enough impact to warrant a history number for his comprehensive biography, e.g., 973.923092 for Eugene McCarthy who ran unsuccessfully for the Democratic presidential nomination in 1968.

2. The number for the field of service for cabinet members, e.g., a foreign minister of France 327.440092, a secretary of the treasury 336.092. (These were formerly often classed in 353–354.)

3. 327.3–.9 for ambassadors and pre-World War II ministers plenipotentiary.

4. 328.4–.9 for legislators not warranting a specific subject number, e.g., a floor leader, whip, or member noted for promoting legislative work. Consider, however, that biographers tend to concentrate upon legislators who left their mark on general history, so always weigh the number in 900 for the area the legislature served before assigning another. Only occasionally will a work focus on a legislator's own constituency.

5. 327.3–.9 for diplomats below the level of ambassador or pre-World War II minister plenipotentiary, unless associated with notable events, then with the events.

6. The number for field of service for public administrators not holding cabinet positions, if their contribution to the service was significant, e.g., J. Edgar Hoover, director of the U.S. Federal Bureau of Investigation 363.25092; otherwise 353–354. (These were formerly most often classed in 353–354.)

Give comparable precedence to public figures of state, provincial, and local jurisdictions. Normally national office takes precedence over other levels, but the weight of contributions must be considered. For example, DeWitt Clinton, the famous governor of New York, was briefly U.S. Senator, and was a minor party candidate for President, but his comprehensive biography should be classed in 974.703092 for the state history of his time. Fiorello La Guardia served fourteen years as U.S. Representative, and briefly as chief of the U.S. Office of Civilian Defense and as director of the United Nations Relief and Rehabilitation Administration; but he is more noted as Mayor of New York City, and should be classed in 974.71042092.

Families and close associates of the famous

Class a history of the immediate or extended family of a famous person with the biography of that person if the work strongly emphasizes the famous person. The same rule applies to the biography of a single relative or close associate of a famous person. However, if the relative or associate is important in his own right, or if the famous person is not strongly featured, class the life of the relative in the subject warranted by his own work, e.g., a biography of evangelist Ruth Carter Stapleton, sister of President Jimmy Carter, that treats the president only incidentally 269.2092. If in doubt, do not use the number for a famous person for a relative or close friend; prefer a number warranted by the biographee's own activities. Class a general family history in 929.2.

Partial biography

Each partial biography featuring a specific contribution of a person is classed with the contribution. However, a biography of the portions of

Table 1. Standard Subdivisions T1

a person's life that preceded the activity with which he is chiefly associated is classed in his comprehensive biography number when there is no significant alternative subject emphasis. For example, Justice Byron White's life as an All-American football player 796.332092; but the childhood of Indira Gandhi 954.045092, the number for her period as Prime Minister of India.

Division policies

It is the policy of the Decimal Classification Division to add T1—092 more liberally than any other standard subdivision in cases when a person's work may not approximate the whole of the most specific available number. Similarly, T1—092 is not added to extremely minute subjects, e.g., ball players are classed in the game they played, not in subordinate numbers for specific positions on the field, even if a player filled only one position.

It is also Division policy with individual biography, when a work is not clearly associated with any subject but is clearly associated with a place, to class the biography in the number most nearly covering the history and civilization of the place and time of the activity emphasized, e.g., the diary of a resident of San Francisco during the Gold Rush 979.46104092.

T1—0922	**Collected [persons] treatment**

Treat as collected biography a work on two people collaborating in the same field, e.g., the Wright brothers 629.1300922, Pierre and Marie Curie 530.0922. However, when the focus is strongly on one of the two, use T1—092.

T1—0922 **vs.** **T1—093–** **099**	**Collected [persons] treatment vs. [Geographical] Treatment by specific continents, countries, localities; extraterrestrial worlds**

Persons treatment covers "description and critical appraisal of work," and geographical treatment covers "description by place, by specific instance of the subject." For material limited by persons yet emphasizing area aspects, persons treatment normally takes precedence over geographical treatment. However, when the intent of the author or compiler is to describe works of art characteristic of an area, or simply to describe such works in an area (even though the works may be listed under their producers), the material should be classed in T1—093–099. When the title and front matter does not reveal the intent, any discussion of style is an important indicator. A discussion focusing on the character and style of the individual producers indicates persons treatment; one focusing on the characteristics of the place and times indicates geographical treatment. For example, a book on the style and character of sculptures by Cellini, Donatello, and Michelangelo is classed in 730.92245, but a book illustrating Italian Renaissance sculpture by describing the work of these same men is classed in 730.94509024. If in doubt, prefer T1—0922.

If the text is largely confined to concise descriptions of works of technology or art (or to identifications and illustrations of them), class in the area number in any case, even if persons are indicated in the title, e.g., descriptions of the works of six famous Italian sculptors 730.945.

However, for individual persons use notation 092 for all description and critical appraisal of works they have produced.

T1—093–   **[Table 1 notation for] Treatment by specific continents, countries,**
099 and   **localities; extraterrestrial worlds [and Table 2 notation for] Specific**
T2—3–9   **continents, countries, localities; extraterrestrial worlds**

Change of precedence when area notation is added directly

When area notation from Table 2 is added directly in the schedules rather than through notation 09 from Table 1, while all or most of the other subdivisions are in their regular positions, the rule of zeros (paragraph 5.13 of Introduction to the DDC) changes the precedence of area in respect to many of the standard subdivisions. The table of precedence at the beginning of Table 1 shows areas almost in the middle. They move to the top when there is no zero. As a result, all standard subdivisions (including persons notation 092 if persons has not been moved to the same span as areas) can be added. For example, management of prisons in Great Britain is classed in 365.941068 (not 365.068 as it would be if prisons in Great Britain were 365.0941).

The change of precedence takes place whenever the number of zeros differs, e.g., when areas remain in T1—09 but other subdivisions are displaced to 001–009.

Differences in standard subdivisions added to area notation

While normally one standard subdivision is not added to another standard subdivision, a limited number may be added in notation 09. Special add tables in T1—09 show which of the subdivisions falling below T1—09 subdivisions in the table of precedence may be used in area and history period subdivisions. The special table under T1—093–099 also allows T1—09 to be used to add historical periods and to add area notation to area notation in certain cases.

When the area notation is added directly, the restrictions to the use of standard subdivisions no longer apply. All but T1—092–099 can be used with their normal meanings. Persons notation 092 can be used, but only when the area notation is added directly while the persons notation remains in its standard subdivision position. For example, if all of T1—09 is vacated, as when 365[.09] is moved to 365.9, all biography regardless of area is classed in 365.92, e.g., persons associated

Table 1. Standard Subdivisions   T1

with penal institutions in Europe 365.9224. But if only some of T1—09 is vacated, as when treatment by specific continents, countries, and localities is moved from 373.09 to 373.3–.9, then notation 092 is added to area notation, e.g. secondary educators in Europe 373.40922. Notation 093—099 can be added when the base area notation specifies origin or style, while the added notation identifies the area in which the subject is found or practiced, e.g., French cooking 641.5944, French cooking as practiced in West Africa 641.59440966.

Table 2. Geographic Areas, Historical Periods, Persons

T2—1   **Areas, regions, places in general**

Subdivisions of T2—1 are used only for areas, regions, and places that overlap more than one continent (considering Oceania as a continent), e.g., urban regions of the United States, Europe, and Japan T2—1732. Such regions within one continent but covering several countries are classed with the number for the continent in combination with the appropriate subdivision of T2—1, e.g., urban regions of Europe T2—4091732.

Within a single country or place these general regions are classed in the general number for the country or place; then, in the disciplines of geography and history, the appropriate subdivisions of T2—1 are added, e.g., a history of the urban regions of England 942.009732, geography of the urban regions of England 914.2009732. However, in all other disciplines this is done only as an option that is not followed by the Decimal Classification Division.

See also T2—2 vs. T2—1, T2—3–9.

T2—163   **Atlantic Ocean [and] Pacific Ocean [and] Indian Ocean**
and
T2—164,
T2—165   This table follows the latest thinking of geographers in dividing the world ocean in three parts—Atlantic, Indian, and Pacific Oceans. The "Arctic Ocean" is considered a sea of Atlantic. There is no Antarctic Ocean, but provision in made in T2—167 for the extreme southern portions of the three oceans.

Divisions between the oceans are considered to be as follows:

Atlantic-Pacific: north, Bering Strait; south, a line drawn southeasterly from Cape Horn to the northern tip of Palmer Peninsula, Antarctica.

Pacific-Indian: north, a line from Melville Island to Timor, thence through the islands of Indonesia to Singapore Strait; south, a line drawn south from Cape Howe, Victoria, Australia, on the 150° east meridian.

Indian-Atlantic: north, Suez Canal; south, a line drawn south from Cape Agulhas, South Africa, on the 20° east meridian.

Notes and references throughout show where to class connecting bodies of water, e.g., Bering Strait T2—16451, not T2—16325 or T2—16327.

See also T2—1631 and T2—1635; T2—1644 and T2—1648, T2—1649.

T2—163,
T2—164,
T2—165
vs.
T2—182

Atlantic Ocean [and] Pacific Ocean [and] Indian Ocean vs. Ocean and sea basins

Note that T2—163, T2—164, and T2—165 deal with the oceans and seas themselves, i.e., their waters. Specific lands are classed in T2—3–9, while the total lands around an ocean or sea or surrounded by an ocean or sea are classed in the appropriate subdivision of T2—182.

T2—1631
and
T2—1635

North Atlantic Ocean [and] South Atlantic Ocean

In this table, the division of the North Atlantic Ocean from the South Atlantic Ocean occurs along a line drawn from the Strait of Gibraltar to the Straits of Florida.

Notes and references throughout show where to class connecting bodies of water, e.g., Straits of Florida T2—16363, not T2—16348.

T2—1644
and
T2—1648,
T2—1649

North Pacific Ocean [and] South Pacific Ocean [and] Central Pacific Ocean

In this table, the Pacific Ocean is divided into the North Pacific Ocean, the South Pacific Ocean, and the Central Pacific Ocean.

North Pacific Ocean: the American and Asian coastal waters located in an arc from the Mexico-United States boundary to the southern tip of the Philippines, excluding the South China Sea and the inner seas of the Philippines.

South Pacific Ocean: the American coastal waters from the Mexico-United States boundary to the Strait of Magellan; the coastal water of Antarctica, New Zealand, Australia, and New Guinea; the waters of Melanesia; and the coastal waters west and south of the Philippines, including the South China Sea and the inner seas of the Philippines.

Central Pacific Ocean: the American and Asian non-coastal waters and the waters of Polynesia and isolated islands of the Pacific, such as Wake and Easter Island.

Notes and references throughout show where to class connecting bodies of water, e.g., Formosa Strait T2—16474, not T2—16472.

Table 2. Geographic Areas, Periods, Persons   T2

T2—19 vs. **Space vs. Extraterrestrial worlds**
T2—99

Class in T2—19 only space itself. The various bodies of the universe moving through space are classed in T2—99, e.g., moon rocks 552.09991. The anticipated use of T2—19 is not great.

T2—2 vs. **Persons vs. Areas, regions, places in general [and] Specific**
T2—1, **continents, countries, localities**
T2—3–9

Observe that T2—2 covers persons "regardless of area, region, place," which means that persons are classed here, not in T2—1 or T2—3–9. There are similar instructions in Table 1 for preferring notation 092 over notations T1—091 and T1—093–099.

See also T1—0922 vs. T1—093–099.

T2—3–9 **Specific continents, countries, localities; extraterrestrial worlds**

Parts of oceans and non-inland seas limited by either country or locality are classed in T2—16. For example, Chesapeake Bay, an arm of the Atlantic Ocean that is almost surrounded by Maryland and Virginia, is classed in T2—16347, not in either T2—752 or T2—7551. Be alert that estuaries are sometimes named rivers. Estuaries that are parts of oceans and non-inland seas are classed in T2—16. For example, the York River, an estuary of the Chesapeake Bay, is classed in T2—16347 (not T2—7553).

See also T2—163, T2—163, T2—165 vs. T2—182; T2—2 vs. T2—1, T2—3–9.

T2—3 vs. **The ancient world vs. The modern world; extraterrestrial worlds**
T2—4–9

Under T2—3 "The ancient world" are gathered those parts of the world more or less known *to* classical antiquity, and considered only during the period of "ancient history." The same areas in later times, as well as other areas such as America in both ancient and later times, are classed in T2—4–9. Examples: ancient China T2—31, later China T2—51; ancient Palestine T2—33, later Palestine T2—5694; ancient Gaul T2—364, France T2—44; Yucatán, both ancient and later, T2—7265. The approximate date of demarcation between "ancient" and "later" varies from place to place and may be determined by examination of the terminal dates in classes 931–939, e.g., 931 China to 420, 933 Palestine to 70, 936.4 Celtic regions to 486.

T2—4–9 **The modern world; extraterrestrial worlds**

Physiographic regions and features

Class features not named in the area table and that are wholly or almost wholly contained within a political or administrative unit with the unit, e.g., Mount Washington, New Hampshire T2—7421; Lake Moultrie, South Carolina T2—75793. Class a river with the unit where its mouth is located, e.g., Escanaba River, Michigan T2—77494. However, if the upper part of the stream is more important politically, economically, or culturally, class the river with that part, e.g., Tigris and Euphrates Rivers T2—5674 rather than T2—5675.

Cities, towns, villages

Class cities, towns, and villages not given in Table 2 with the narrowest political or administrative unit that contains them. With certain exceptions, cities are not named in Table 2. The exceptions include:

1. The capital and largest city of each state of the United States, e.g., Pierre and Sioux Falls, South Dakota, at T2—78329 and T2—783371 respectively.

2. Major world cities, usually with their own numbers, e.g., Athens at T2—49512 and Mecca included at T2—538.

3. Smaller cities given their own numbers early in the development of the DDC, e.g., Guelph, Ontario T2—71343.

4. Independent cities, e.g., Alexandria, Virginia T2—755296.

5. United States cities coextensive with their counties (or parishes), e.g., Philadelphia T2—74811, San Francisco T2—79461.

6. Cities, towns, and villages named to help define the boundaries between numbers where none exist in law or on maps, e.g., throughout Australia T2—94 and the western provinces of Canada T2—711–712.

The foregoing explains why many large cities are not named, while many smaller and less important ones are.

Class a metropolitan area with the central city, using notation from Table 1 as needed, e.g., the metropolitan area of Chicago T2—77311.

See also T2—41–42.

Order within notes

More than one kind of geographic area or feature may be given in either an including or class-here note. The kinds are separated by semi-colons and are given in the following order:

1. Large jurisdictions, e.g., districts

2. Small jurisdictions, e.g., towns

   3. Other units with man-made boundaries

      a. Parks

      b. Reserves

   4. Physiographic regions or entities, e.g., islands

   5. Physiographic features

      a. Mountains

      b. Rivers

      c. Lakes

For example, at T2—71187 Peace River-Liard Regional District is the following note:

> Including Dawson Creek, Fort Nelson, Fort St. John, Tumbler Ridge; Finlay, Fort Nelson, Ingenika, Mesilika, Murray, Pine, Sukunka Rivers; *Williston Lake

Dawson Creek, Fort St. John, and Tumbler Ridge are towns. The first Fort Nelson is a town, while the second Fort Nelson is a river.

Changes in geographical concepts

Note that some geographical concepts of an earlier day have been divided by whims of history. Many such concepts are given special notes to show where comprehensive works are to be classed, e.g., Armenia as a whole and Turkish Armenia at T2—5662, Soviet Armenia at T2—4792.

However, in many cases adjustments have been made between recent editions of the DDC to conform to historical changes. For example, Finland, which before World War I was part of the Russian empire, was placed by Melvil Dewey in T2—471, as the first subdivision of Russia. It was not until recently that the DDC relocated works on Finland to T2—4897, thus removing the block of material that had separated comprehensive works on Russia and the Soviet Union in T2—47 from works on their various parts in T2—472–479.

On the other hand, Hawaii, which is not part of North America, is classed in T2—969 under Oceania, separated from the rest of the United States in T2—73–79; and the Asian parts of the U.S.S.R. are classed in T2—57–58, quite apart from the European portion of the U.S.S.R. in T2—47.

T2—41 and T2—42   **British Isles [and] England and Wales**

     In the British Isles, the jurisdiction directly below the County is referred to as either District, Borough, or City. The term "City" does not refer to urban localities. The Districts, Boroughs, and Cities are usually named after an urban locality either within or coextensive with the jurisdiction. If the urban locality is coextensive with the jurisdiction, the locality is given in a Class here note. For example, City of Bristol, the jurisdiction, and Bristol, the urban locality, are coextensive; thus, the table entry:

>   T2—42393   City of Bristol
>
>   Class here Bristol

If the urban locality is not coextensive with the jurisdiction, only the jurisdiction is given. The classifier can assume that if the locality were to be given, the locality would be in an Including note. For example, City of Canterbury, the jurisdiction, and Canterbury, the urban locality, are not coextensive; thus, the table entry:

>   T2—42233   City of Canterbury

See also T2—4—9: Cities, towns, villages.

T2—7193– **Specific regions of Northwest Territories**
7197

Although there seems to be agreement on which communities are situated in which region, the boundaries drawn on available maps do not always agree. The Decimal Classification Division uses the following to define each region:

Fort Smith Region: Area north of 60° N, west of 106° W, south of 65° N (from 106° W to 123° W), and south of 64° N (123° W to the Yukon boundary); and the eastern part of Great Bear Lake and its immediate environs.

Keewatin Region: Mainland between 60° N and 66° N, and east of 106° W; land surrounding Repulse Bay; and Southampton and Coats Island.

Baffin Region: Baffin, Bylot, Mansel, Nottingham, Salisbury, Somerset, and Wales Islands; all other islands north of M'Clure Strait and Viscount Melville and Lancaster Sounds; all islands in Hudson, James, and Ungava Bays and Hudson Strait; and Melville Peninsula.

Inuvik Region: Area between the Yukon boundary and 123° W, and north of 64° N; and Banks Island.

Kitikmeot Region: Victoria, King William, and Prince of Wales Islands; mainland north of 66° N (from 87° W to 106° W) and north of 65° N (from 106° W to 123° W); and excluding Great Bear Lake and its immediate environs.

Maps

Maps

The following outline maps provide a display of key area numbers from Table 2. With the exception of island nations lying beyond the continental maps used, the maps indicate the Dewey Decimal Classification area numbers of members of the United Nations and comparable states. Sub-national areas are shown for the United States, Canada, the British Isles, and Australia.

While DDC area numbers are largely hierarchical, be sure to check Table 2 before using a number for part of a given area. In some instances (as illustrated here with the United States), the numbers for the parts are built on a base other than that of the area as a whole.

Note that certain major regional concepts which do not correspond to delineated areas are listed in the margins.

Table 2. Geographic Areas, Periods, Persons   T2

OCEANS AND CONTINENTS

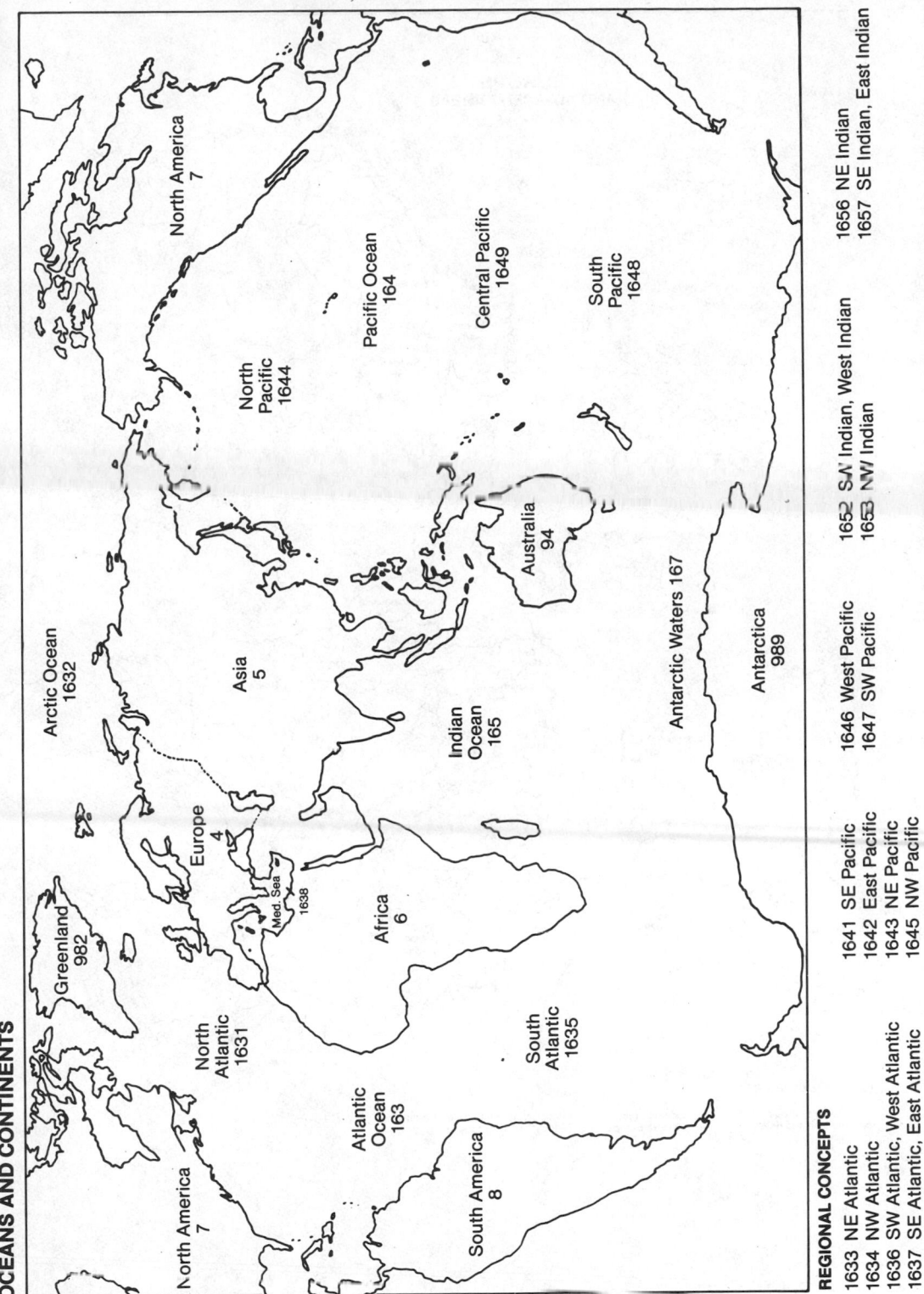

North America
7

Arctic Ocean
1632

Greenland
982

North America
7

North Atlantic
1631

Atlantic
Ocean
163

South America
8

South Atlantic
1635

Europe
4

Med. Sea
1638

Africa
6

Asia
5

Indian
Ocean
165

North
Pacific
1644

Pacific Ocean
164

Central Pacific
1649

Australia
94

Antarctic Waters 167

Antarctica
989

South
Pacific
1648

REGIONAL CONCEPTS

1633 NE Atlantic	1641 SE Pacific
1634 NW Atlantic	1642 East Pacific
1636 SW Atlantic, West Atlantic	1643 NE Pacific
1637 SE Atlantic, East Atlantic	1645 NW Pacific

1646 West Pacific	1652 SW Indian, West Indian
1647 SW Pacific	1653 NW Indian

1656 NE Indian
1657 SE Indian, East Indian

EUROPE
AND ADJACENT AREAS

Iceland
4912

Finland
4897

Norway
481

Sweden
485

Soviet Union
47

Denmark
489

Belorussia
4765

Eire
417

Netherlands
492

United
Kingdom
41

Belgium
493

West
Germany
43

East
Germany
431

Poland
438

Ukraine
4771

Lux.
4935

Czechoslovakia
437

France
44

Switz.
494

Austria
436

Hungary
439

Liechtenstein
43648

Romania
498

Portugal
469

Andorra
4679

Monaco
44949

San Marino
4549

Yugoslavia
497

Turkey
in Europe
4961

Spain
46

Corsica
44945

Italy
45

Bulgaria
4977

Vatican City
45634

Albania
(4965)

Turkey
561

Gibraltar
4689

Balearic
Islands
4675

Sardinia
459

Greece
495

Morocco
64

Algeria
65

Tunisia
611

Sicily
458

Malta
4585

Crete
4998

Cyprus
5645

Libya
612

Egypt
62

REGIONAL CONCEPTS

4	Western Europe	43	Central Europe	48	Northern Europe, Scandinavia
42	England and Wales	47	Eastern Europe	496	Balkan Peninsula

Table 2. Geographic Areas, Periods, Persons   T2

BRITISH ISLES

Orkney 41132

Western Isles 4114

REGIONAL CONCEPTS

41	British Isles, United Kingdom, Great Britain
411	Scotland
4111	Northern Scotland
4112	Islands Authorities
4115	Scottish Highlands
412	Northeastern Scotland
413	Southeastern Scotland, Central Lowlands
414	Southwestern Scotland
415	Ireland
416	Ulster, Northern Ireland
417	Republic of Ireland (Eire)
4171	Connacht
418	Leinster
419	Munster
42	England and Wales, England
421	Greater London
422	Southeastern England, Home Counties, Thames Valley
423	Southwestern England and Channel Islands
424	Midlands, Welsh Marshes, Severn Valley
425	East Midlands, Chilterns, Trent Valley
426	Eastern England, East Anglia
427	Northern England, Northwestern England
428	Northeastern England, Pennines
4281	Yorkshire
429	Wales
4291	North Wales
4294	South Wales

Highland 4115

Grampian 4121

Tayside 4125

Fife 4129

Central 4131

Lothian 4132

Strathclyde 4141

Borders 4137

Dumfries and Galloway 4147

Northumberland 4288

Tyne and Wear 4287

Cleveland 4285

Durham 4286

Cumbria 4278

Donegal 41693

Northern Ireland 416

North Yorkshire 4284

Humberside 4283

Isle of Man 4279

Sligo 4172

Leitrim 4176

Monaghan 41697

Cavan 41698

Louth 41825

Mayo 4173

Roscommon 4175

Longford 41812

Meath 41822

Westmeath 41815

Dublin 4183

Galway 4174

Offaly 4186

Kildare 41835

Laois 4187

Wicklow 4184

Clare 4193

Tipperary 4192

Carlow 41882

Kilkenny 4189

Wexford 41885

Limerick 4194

Kerry 4196

Cork 4195

Waterford 4191

Lancashire 4276

West Yorkshire 4281

Merseyside 4275

Greater Manchester 4273

South Yorkshire 4282

Lincolnshire 4253

Derbyshire 4251

Nottingham-shire 4252

Cheshire 4271

Clwyd 4293

Norfolk 4261

Gwynedd 4292

Staffordshire 4246

Leicestershire 4254

Shropshire 4245

West Midlands 4249

Warwick-shire 4248

Cambridgeshire 4265

Suffolk 4264

Powys 4295

Northampton-shire 4255

Bedford-shire 4256

Hereford and Worcester 4244

Bucking-ham-shire 4258

Hertford-shire 4259

Essex 4267

Dyfed 4296

Gloucestershire 4241

Oxfordshire 4257

Greater London 421

Gwent 4299

Berkshire 4229

West Glamorgan 42981

Avon 4239

Wiltshire 4231

Surrey 4221

Kent 4223

South Glamorgan 42986

Hampshire 4227

West Sussex 4226

East Sussex 4225

Mid Glamorgan 4297

Somerset 4238

Dorset 4233

Isle of Wight 4228

Devon 4235

Cornwall 4237

Scilly Isles 42379

Channel Islands 4234

ASIA, AUSTRALIA, NEW ZEALAND

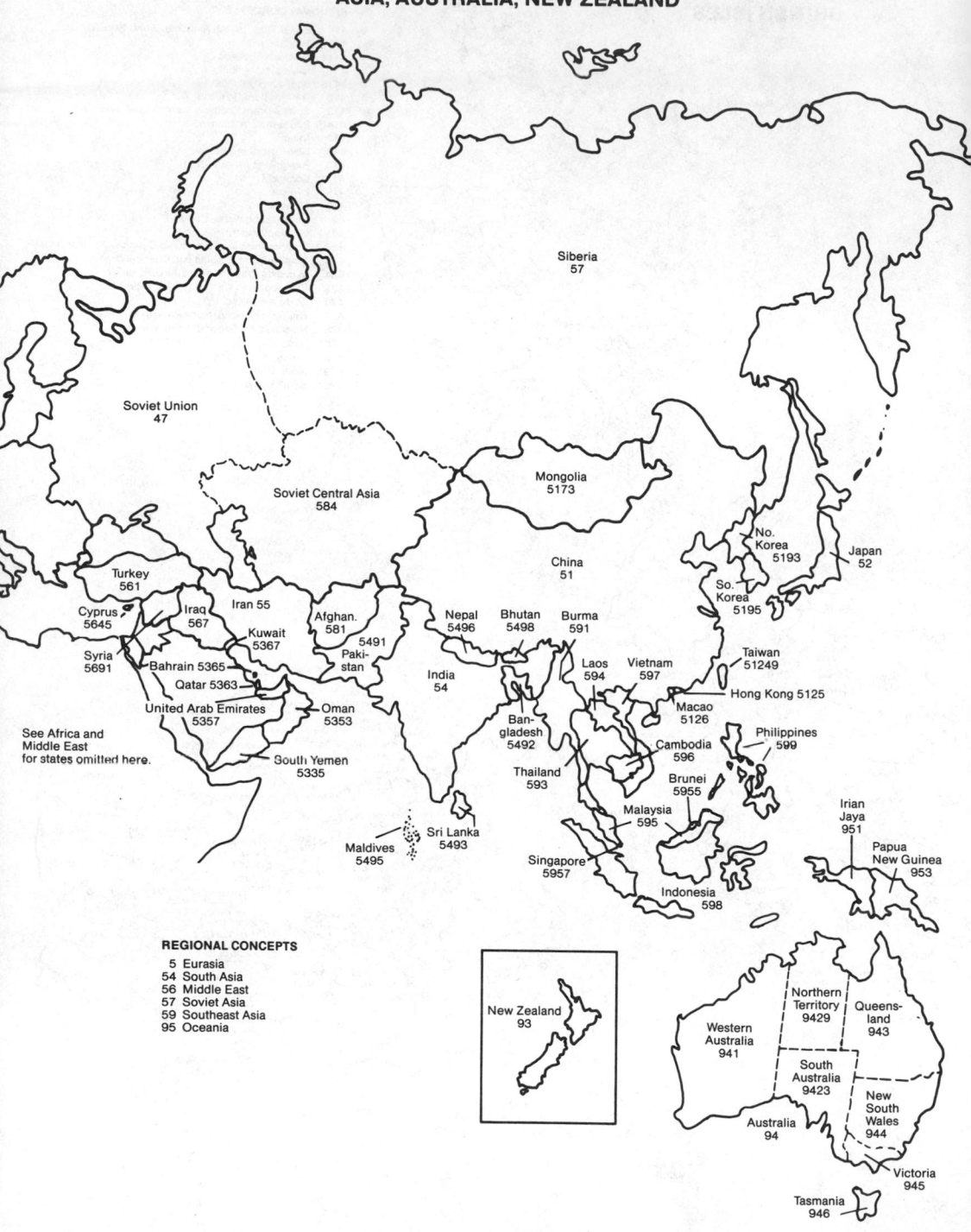

Siberia
57

Soviet Union
47

Soviet Central Asia
584

Mongolia
5173

China
51

No.
Korea
5193

Japan
52

Turkey
561

So.
Korea
5195

Cyprus
5645

Iraq
567

Iran 55

Afghan.
581

Nepal
5496

Bhutan
5498

Burma
591

Taiwan
51249

Kuwait
5367

5491
Paki-
stan

Laos
594

Vietnam
597

Hong Kong 5125

Syria
5691

Bahrain 5365

Qatar 5363

India
54

Macao
5126

United Arab Emirates
5357

Oman
5353

Ban-
gladesh
5492

Cambodia
596

Philippines
599

See Africa and
Middle East
for states omitted here.

South Yemen
5335

Thailand
593

Brunei
5955

Irian
Jaya
951

Malaysia
595

Papua
New Guinea
953

Maldives
5495

Sri Lanka
5493

Singapore
5957

Indonesia
598

REGIONAL CONCEPTS

 5 Eurasia
54 South Asia
56 Middle East
57 Soviet Asia
59 Southeast Asia
95 Oceania

New Zealand
93

Northern
Territory
9429

Queens-
land
943

Western
Australia
941

South
Australia
9423

New
South
Wales
944

Australia
94

Victoria
945

Tasmania
946

Table 2. Geographic Areas, Periods, Persons   T2

AFRICA AND MIDDLE EAST

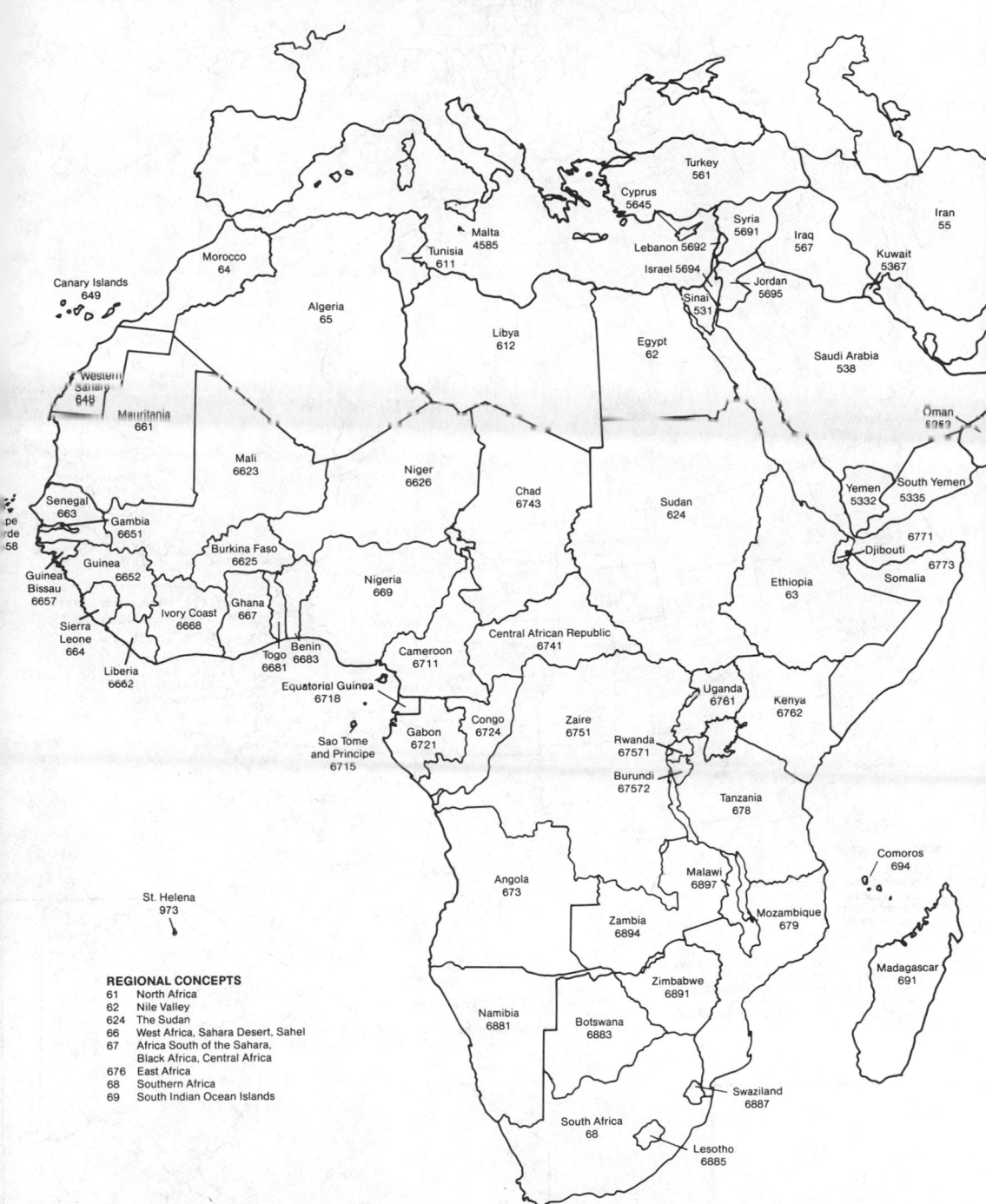

Turkey 561

Cyprus 5645

Iran 55

Syria 5691

Iraq 567

Kuwait 5367

Morocco 64

Malta 4585

Tunisia 611

Lebanon 5692

Israel 5694

Jordan 5695

Canary Islands 649

Sinai 531

Algeria 65

Libya 612

Egypt 62

Saudi Arabia 538

Oman 5952

Western Sahara 648

Mauritania 661

Mali 6623

Niger 6626

Chad 6743

Sudan 624

Yemen 5332

South Yemen 5335

6771

Djibouti

6773

Somalia

Senegal 663

pe rde 58

Gambia 6651

Burkina Faso 6625

Ethiopia 63

Guinea Bissau 6657

Guinea 6652

Nigeria 669

Ivory Coast 6668

Ghana 667

Sierra Leone 664

Togo 6681

Benin 6683

Cameroon 6711

Central African Republic 6741

Liberia 6662

Equatorial Guinea 6718

Uganda 6761

Kenya 6762

Sao Tome and Principe 6715

Gabon 6721

Congo 6724

Zaire 6751

Rwanda 67571

Burundi 67572

Tanzania 678

Comoros 694

St. Helena 973

Angola 673

Malawi 6897

Mozambique 679

Madagascar 691

Zambia 6894

Zimbabwe 6891

Namibia 6881

Botswana 6883

Swaziland 6887

South Africa 68

Lesotho 6885

REGIONAL CONCEPTS
61 North Africa
62 Nile Valley
624 The Sudan
66 West Africa, Sahara Desert, Sahel
67 Africa South of the Sahara,
    Black Africa, Central Africa
676 East Africa
68 Southern Africa
69 South Indian Ocean Islands

UNITED STATES AND CANADA

REGIONAL CONCEPTS

71	Canada
712	Western Canada, Prairie Provinces
713	Eastern Canada
715	Atlantic Provinces, Maritime Provinces
719	Canadian Arctic
7192	Northwest Territories
73	United States as a whole
74	Eastern U.S., Northeast, Appalachian Mountains, New England, Middle Atlantic states
75	The South, Southeast, South Atlantic states
76	South Central states, Gulf Coast states
77	Mississippi Valley, Midwest, North Central states, Great Lakes states, Ohio Valley
78	The West, Great Plains, Missouri Valley, Rocky Mountains
79	Pacific Coast states, Great Basin

Table 2. Geographic Areas, Periods, Persons T2

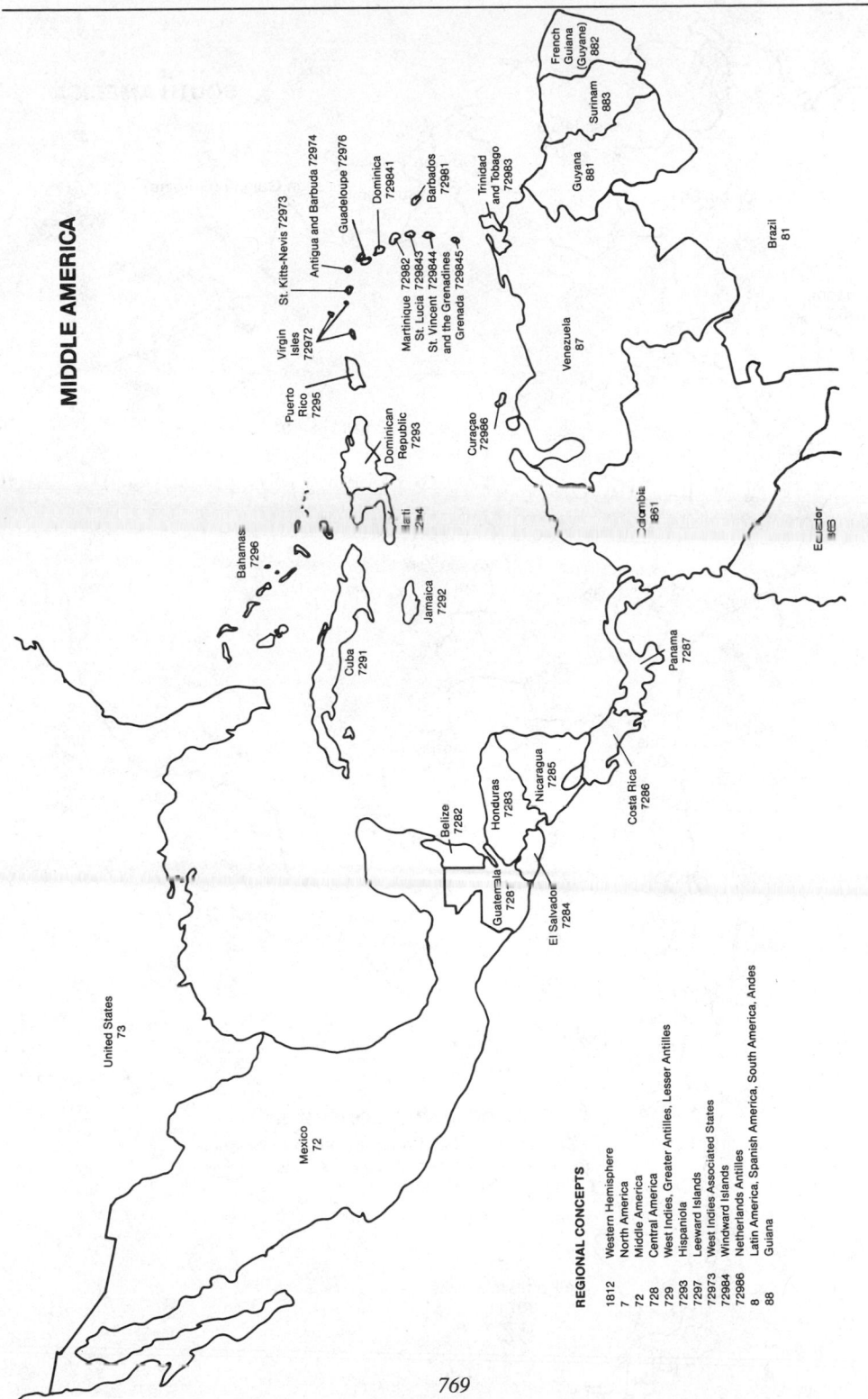

MIDDLE AMERICA

French Guiana (Guyane) 882
Surinam 883
Guyana 881
Brazil 81

Trinidad and Tobago 72983
Barbados 72981
Venezuela 87
Dominica 729841
Guadeloupe 72976
Antigua and Barbuda 72974
St. Kitts-Nevis 72973
Martinique 72982
St. Lucia 729843
St. Vincent 729844 and the Grenadines
Grenada 729845
Virgin Isles 72972
Curaçao 72986
Puerto Rico 7295
Dominican Republic 7293
Colombia 861
Ecuador 866
Haiti 7294
Bahamas 7296
Jamaica 7292
Panama 7287
Cuba 7291
Nicaragua 7285
Costa Rica 7286
Belize 7282
Honduras 7283
Guatemala 7281
El Salvador 7284
United States 73
Mexico 72

REGIONAL CONCEPTS

1812	Western Hemisphere
7	North America
72	Middle America
728	Central America
729	West Indies, Greater Antilles, Lesser Antilles
7293	Hispaniola
7297	Leeward Islands
72973	West Indies Associated States
72984	Windward Islands
72986	Netherlands Antilles
8	Latin America, Spanish America, South America, Andes
88	Guiana

SOUTH AMERICA

Venezuela 87

Guyana 881

Surinam 883

French Guiana (Guyane) 882

Colombia 861

Ecuador 866

Brazil 81

Peru 85

Bolivia 84

Chile 83

Paraguay 892

Argentina 82

Uruguay 895

REGIONAL CONCEPTS

8   Latin America, Spanish America, South America, Andes
88   Guiana

Falklands/Malvinas 9711

770

Table 3. Individual Literatures, Specific Forms   T3

Table 3. Subdivisions for Individual Literatures, for Specific Literary Forms

Here are examples of basic number building for works in an individual language by or about individual authors (with use of Table 3–A) and by or about more than one author (with use of Table 3–B). The following elements are used to build the numbers: base number; form; period; kind, scope, or medium; notation 08 Collections or notation 09 Criticism (plus additional 0s in some cases); subform; additional notation from Table 3–C and other tables. Detailed instructions for building the numbers appear in Tables 3–A and 3–B.

Note: in the following discussion, "T3" refers to both Table 3–A (individual authors) and Table 3–B (more than one author).

More than one form

1. Works by or about more than one author: not restricted by period or form (Table 3–B)

Base no. + notation 08 or 09

81 + 08 = 810.8 (an anthology of American literature)

2. Works by or about more than one author: restricted to a specific period but not to a specific form (Table 3–B)

Base no. + notation 08 or 09 + period

83 + 08 + 006 = 830.8006 (a collection of 18th-century German literture)

Forms T3—1–7

1. Works by or about an individual author: restricted to a specific form and period (Table 3–A)

Base no. + form + period

82 + 1 + 3 = 821.3 (Spenser's *Faerie Queene*)

2. Works by or about more than one author: restricted to a specific form, to a specific kind, scope, or medium, and to a specific period (Table 3–B)

Base no. + form + kind, scope, or medium + notation 08 or 09 + period

84 + 3 + 01 + 08 + 07 = 843.010807 (a collection of 19th-century French short stories)

3. Works by or about more than one author: restricted to a specific form but not to a specific kind, scope, or medium; restricted to a specific period (Table 3–B)

Base no. + form + period + notation 08 or 09

83 + 2 + 914 + 09 = 832.91409 (criticism of German drama of the second half of the 20th century)

Form T3—8 Miscellaneous writings

1. Works by or about an individual author: restricted to a specific form, period, and subform (T3A—8)

Base no. + form + period + subform

81 + 8 + 4 + 02 = 818.402 (a collection of quotations of an individual American author of the later 19th century)

2. Works by or about more than one author: restricted to a specific form, period, and subform (T3B—8)

Base no. + form + period + subform + notation 08 or 09

84 + 8 + 914 + 02 + 08 = 848.9140208 (a collection of quotations of several French authors of the later 20th century)

Affiliated literatures for which period numbers are not used

1. Works by or about an individual author or more than one author: restricted to a specific form and a specific period (Table 3–A or 3–B)

Base no. + form

86 + 1 = 861 (may represent a collection of Spanish-language poetry by an individual Argentine author or criticism of Spanish-language poetry of several Mexican authors)

2. Works by or about more than one author: restricted to a specific form but not to a specific period (Table 3–B)

Base no. + form + notation 008 or 009

82 + 4 + 008 = 824.008 (a collection of essays in English by several Australian authors of several periods)

3. Works by or about more than one author: restricted to a specific form and to a specific kind, scope, or medium; regardless of period (Table 3–B)

Base no. + form + kind, scope, or medium + notation 08 or 09

84 + 2 + 041 + 09 = 842.04109 (criticism of French-Canadian one-act plays)

Table 3. Individual Literatures, Specific Forms   T3

4. Works by or about more than one author: restricted to a specific period but not to a specific form (Table 3–B)

> Base no. + notation 08 or 09
>
> 82 + 08 = 820.8 (an anthology of post-World War II Australian literature in several forms)

5. Works by or about more than one author: not restricted by form or period; place of authorship emphasized (Table 3–B)

> Base no. + notation 080 or 09 + 9 from Table 3–C + area notation from Table 2
>
> (a) 869 + 080 + 9 + 81 = 869.080981 (an anthology of literature in Portuguese in several forms by Brazilian authors)
>
> (b) 81 + 09 + 9 + 7292 = 810.997292 (criticism of literature in English in several forms by Jamaican authors)

Table 3–A. Subdivisions for Works by or about Individual Authors

To determine the comprehensive number for collected works, critical evaluation, or biography of an author, follow the criteria given below on language, form, and literary period.

Language

Class an author with the language in which he writes.

For an author who continues to write in the same language, but who changes his place of residence or national affiliation to a country with a different language, use the language in which he writes. For example, class a novel in Russian by Solzhenitsyn in 891.7344, even if the novel was written while the author was living in the United States.

For an author who changes his national affiliation to a country with the same language as that in which he has been writing, use the literature number for the country of which he is now a citizen. Thus, T.S. Eliot is classed as a British author.

For an author who changes his place of residence, but not his national affiliation, to another country with the same language as that in which he has been writing, continue to use the literature number of his original country. Thus, a New Zealand author living in London, but still retaining New Zealand citizenship, is classed as a New Zealand author.

If information about an author's national affiliation is not readily available in the work being classed or in standard reference books, use the literature number of the author's country of origin, if known; or the literature number of the country in which his earlier works were published.

Class an author who writes in more than one language with the language that he used last, e.g., Samuel Beckett 840. However, if another language is predominant, class with that language. (Individual works of such an author are classed with the language in which they were originally written.)

Literary form

Use the form with which an author is chiefly identified, e.g., Jane Austen 823.7. If the author is not chiefly identified with one form, use form T3A—8 Miscellaneous writings plus literary period plus notation 09 from the table at T3A—81–89. Thus, class a late-20th-century English author who is equally famous as a novelist, dramatist, and poet in 828.91409. (An individual work of such an author, of course, is classed with the form exemplified by the work.)

Literary periods

The literary period for an author and all his works is determined in accordance with scholarly consensus about when an author flourished. Thus an author commonly regarded as an early 19th-century writer is classed as such, even if he published his first literary works at the end of the 18th century. If the classifier cannot determine when an author flourished, however, he should use the date of an author's earliest known separate literary publication, disregarding magazine contributions, isolated student works, and juvenilia.

Biography

Do not use notation 092 from Table 1 for biography. Class literary reminiscences in T3A—8 plus period subdivision plus subdivision 03, e.g., Hemingway's *A Moveable Feast* 818.5203.

Number building

Examples of number building are given in the *Manual* at the beginning of Table 3. The following flow chart is offered as an aid to building numbers and as a supplement to the detailed instructions at Table 3–A.

Table 3–A. Individual Authors   T3A

Flow chart A: Works by or about an individual author

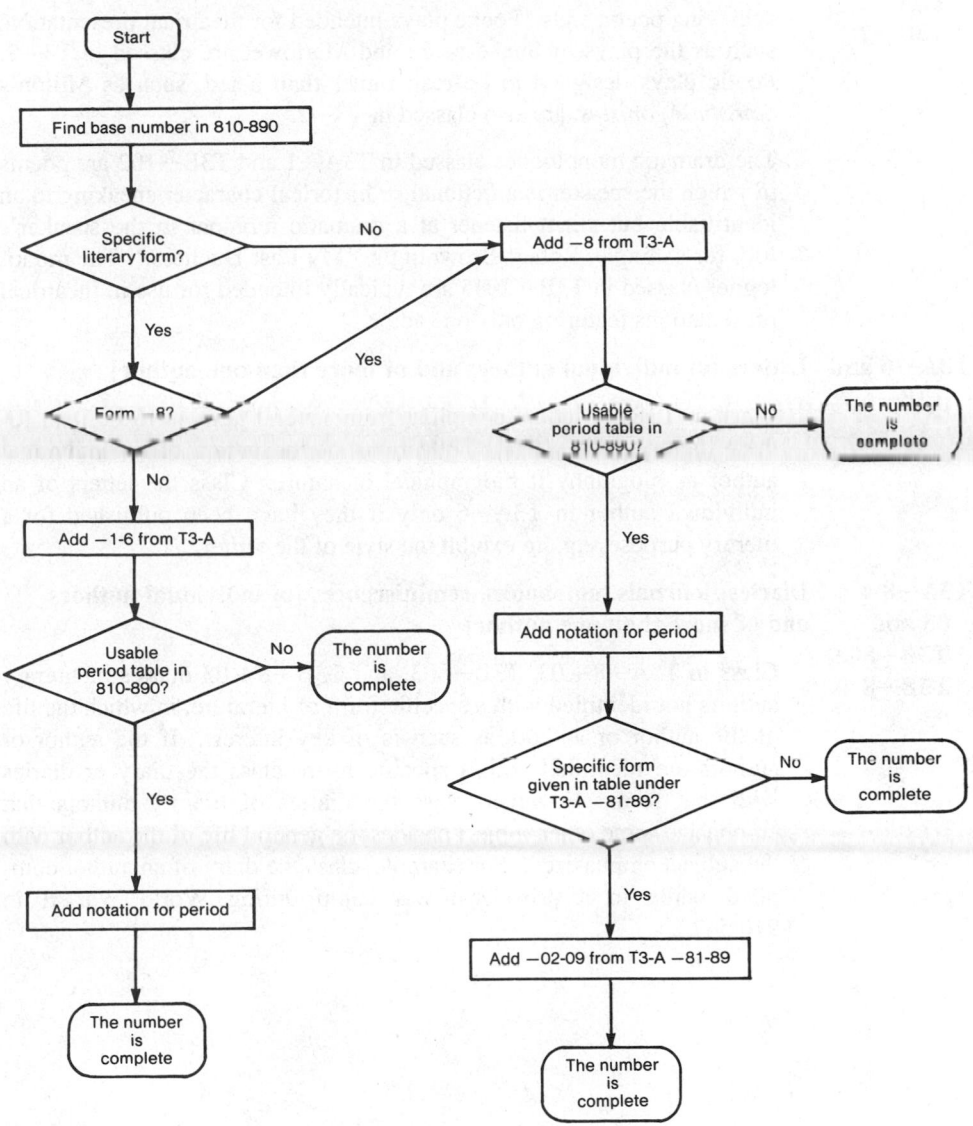

T3A—1,
T3B—102
vs.
T3A—2,
T3B—2

Dramatic poetry vs. Drama

Dramatic poetry in T3A—1 and T3B—102 is poetry that employs dramatic form or some element of dramatic technique as a means of achieving poetic ends. Poetic plays intended for theatrical presentation, such as the plays of Shakespeare and Marlowe, are classed in T3—2. Poetic plays designed to be read rather than acted, such as Milton's *Samson Agonistes*, are also classed in T3—2.

The dramatic monologues classed in T3A—1 and T3B—102 are poems in which the speaker is a fictional or historical character speaking to an identifiable but silent listener at a dramatic moment in the speaker's life, for example, Robert Browning's ''My Last Duchess.'' The monologues classed in T3B—2045 are typically intended for use in theatrical presentations featuring only one actor.

T3A—6 and
T3B—6

Letters [of individual authors and of more than one author]

Class in T3B—6 letters compiled from several authors to be read for their literary value. Class collections of the letters of an individual author as biography if biographical in nature. Class the letters of an individual author in T3A—6 only if they have been published for a literary purpose, e.g., to exhibit the style of the writer.

T3A—8 +
03 and
T3B—803,
T3B—8 +
03

Diaries, journals, notebooks, reminiscences [of individual authors and of more than one author]

Class in T3A—8 + 03, T3B—803, and T3B—8 + 03 diaries of literary authors not identified with a specific form of literature, in which the life of the author or authors as such is of key interest. If the author or authors are identified with a specific form, class the diary or diaries with that form. However, class the diaries of literary authors that emphasize some other subject besides the general life of the author with the subject emphasized. For example, class the diary of an author compiled while in a prisoner-of-war camp during World War II in 940.5472.

Table 3−B. Subdivisions for Works by or about More than One Author

Order of precedence

The order of precedence in case of conflict between literary forms is spelled out at the beginning of the 800 schedule and in Table 3−B under T3B—1−8. In addition, there are orders of precedence in case of conflict among other aspects. The four aspects expressed by means of Table 3−C are used in accordance with the following table of precedence:

Themes and subjects	T3C—3
Elements	T3C—2
Qualities	T3C—1
Persons	T3C—8−9

Thus, for example, a general anthology of poetry about war written by American women poets is classed in 811.0080358, not 811.00809287.

The precedence given to literary period in relation to the four aspects expressed by means of Table 3−C varies: for works treating more than one literature or more than one form in one literature, literary periods have a lower priority than the aspects from Table 3−C; for works treating a specific form in an individual literature, literary periods have a higher priority than the aspects from Table 3−C.

Specific kinds, scopes, media consistently take precedence over both period and the aspects from Table 3−C. The precedence given to scope in relation to kind, however, varies: for drama, scope has a higher precedence; but for fiction, kind has higher precedence.

Here, for example, are complete priority listings for fiction:

More than one literature

1. Specific kinds
2. Specific scopes
3. Specific themes and subjects
4. Specific elements
5. Specific qualities
6. Period

One literature

1. Specific kinds

2. Specific scopes

3. Period

4. Specific themes and subjects

5. Specific elements

6. Specific qualities

7. For and by specific kinds of persons

In all cases, the orders of precedence are the same for collections of literary texts and criticism of the texts.

Sometimes elements low in the priority listings can be added to a number after the higher priority elements. For example, a critical appraisal of later-20th-century American fiction about the sea is classed in 813.540932162: 813 (American fiction) + 54 (period: later 20th century) + 09 (critical appraisal) + 32162 (theme: the sea). The period is given first because it has higher priority than the theme; but the theme can also be expressed. The same order of precedence is used for these additional elements, e.g., for critical appraisal of later-20th-century American fiction about the sea by women, the theme of the sea would be expressed by means of Table 3–C and the authorship by a specific kind of person would not, because themes appear higher in the priority listing.

Sometimes aspects low in the priority listings can be expressed only by means of standard subdivision notation from Table 1. In the example of a critical appraisal of American fiction of the later 20th century about the sea by women, notation 082 from Table 1 could be used to bring out the aspect of women: 813.540932162082. For another example, a collection of 19th-century fiction of several literatures about urban life is classed in 808.83932173209034: 808.839 (collection of fiction from more than one literature displaying specific features) + 321732 (theme: urban life) + 09034 (standard subdivision for the historical period of the 19th century). In the priority listing, theme comes before period; and once the theme has been expressed, there is no way to express the period except by use of the standard subdivision.

See also 808.8, T3B—08–09, and specific forms in Table 3–B for additional priority listings.

Table 3–B. More than One Author   T3B

Number building

Examples of number building are given in the *Manual* at the beginning of Table 3. The following flow charts are offered as an aid to building numbers and as a supplement to the detailed directions at Table 3–B.

Flow chart B: Works by or about more than one author

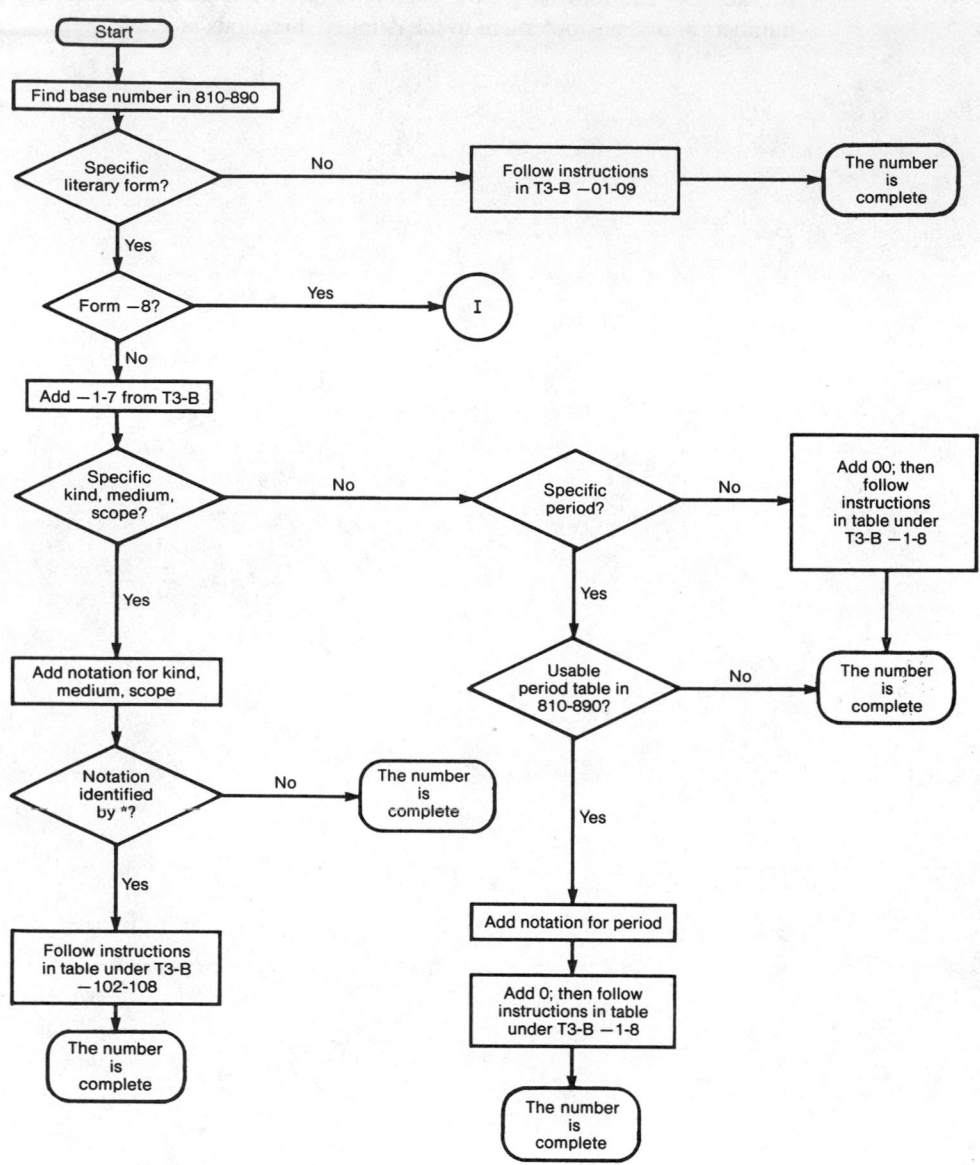

Table 3-B. More than One Author T3B

Flow chart B for notation 3B—8 Miscellaneous writings

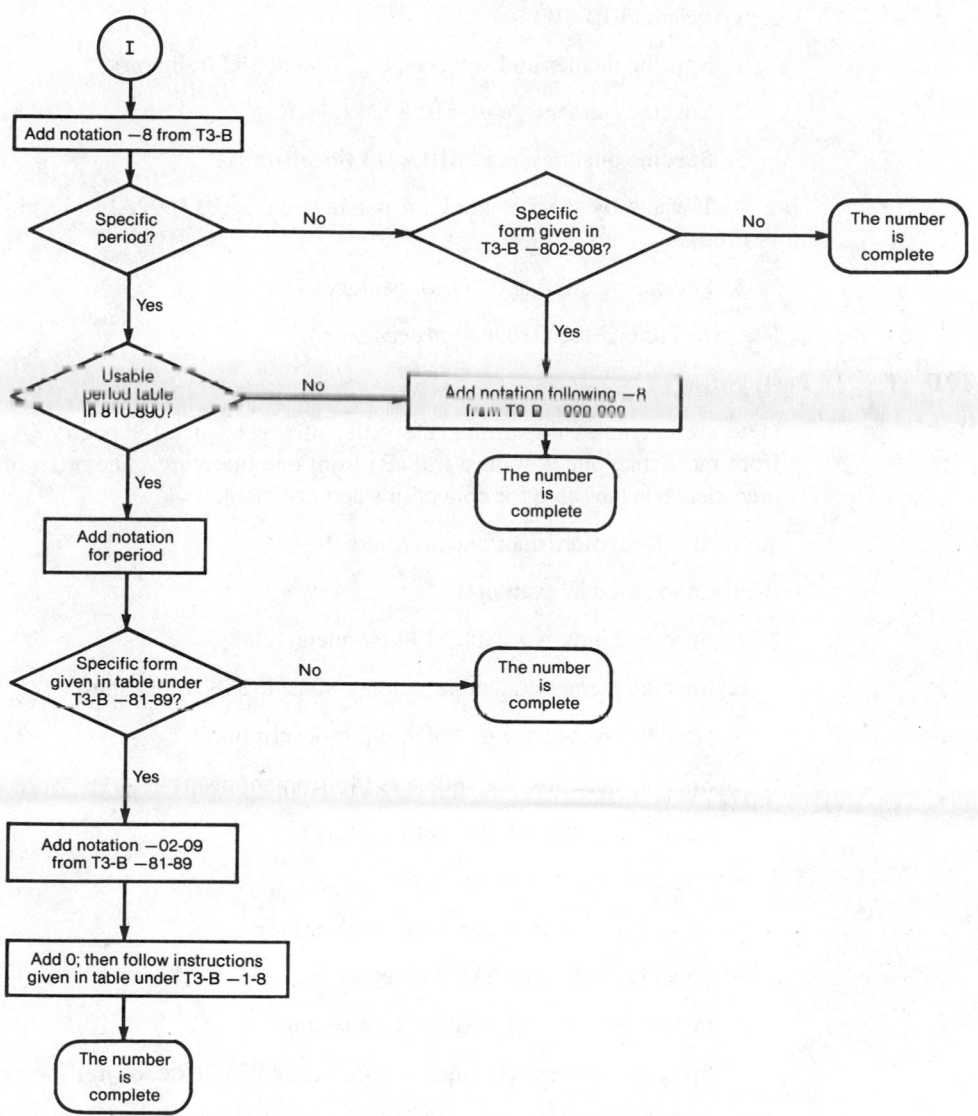

T3B—08 **Collections of literary texts in more than one form**

Here are examples illustrating the order of precedence for collections of texts in more than one form from an individual literature (American literature used for the examples). The order of precedence is the same for criticism (T3B—09).

1. Specific themes and subjects, e.g., 810.80382 (religion)

2. Specific elements, e.g., 810.8024 (plot)

3. Specific qualities, e.g., 810.8013 (idealism)

4. For and by specific kinds of persons, e.g., 810.809282 (for children)

5. Period, e.g., 810.8003 (19th century)

See also Table 3–B: Order of precedence.

T3B—1 **Poetry**

Here are examples illustrating the order of precedence for poetry (A) from more than one literature and (B) from one literature. The order of precedence is the same for collections and criticism.

A. Poetry from more than one literature

(Collections used as example)

1. Specific kinds, e.g., 808.8142 (sonnets)

2. Specific themes and subjects, e.g., 808.819353 (friendship)

3. Specific elements, e.g., 808.81922 (description)

4. Specific qualities, e.g., 808.819145 (romanticism)

5. Period, e.g., 808.81033 (18th century)

B. Poetry from one literature

(Criticism of American poetry used as example)

1. Specific kinds, e.g., 811.032 (epic)

2. Period, e.g., 811.5409 (later 20th century)

3. Specific themes and subjects, e.g., 811.009353 (friendship)

4. Specific elements, e.g., 811.00922 (description)

5. Specific qualities, e.g., 811.00914 (romanticism)

6. For and by specific kinds of persons, e.g., 811.0098924 (by Jews)

See also Table 3–B: Order of precedence.

T3B—102–
108,
T3B—205,
T3B—308
vs.
T3C—1–3

[Specific kinds of poetry, drama, fiction] vs. Literature displaying specific features

The numbers for specific kinds of poetry, drama, and fiction are for works belonging to specific genres, e.g., the genres of historical drama T3B—20514 and realistic fiction T3B—3083. Often the themes and other characteristics that mark specific genres can also be expressed by means of notation 1–3 from Table 3−C, e.g., works about historical themes T3C—358, works displaying realism T3C—12. For works belonging to a specific genre, the genre number always takes precedence over the number derived from Table 3−C; for example, a collection of historical drama is classed in T3B—2051408, not T3B—20080358; criticism of realistic novels in T3B—308309, not T3B—300912. Notation 1–3 from Table 3−C is used primarily for works that display specific features and are not limited to a specific genre, e.g., a discussion of historical themes in serious and comic drama from more than one period T3B—2009358, a discussion of realistic elements in fiction of various kinds from more than one period T3B—300912. Notation 1–3 from Table 3−C may be added to the genre number if it is not redundant. For example, T3C—358 is added for a discussion of historical themes in tragedy (T3B—2051209358), but not for a discussion of historical themes in historical drama.

T3B—2   **Drama**

Here are examples illustrating the order of precedence for drama (A) from more than one literature and (B) from one literature. The order of precedence is the same for collections and criticism.

A. Drama from more than one literature

(Criticism used as example)

     1. Specific media, e.g., 809.225 (television)

     2. Specific scopes, e.g., 809.241 (one-act plays)

     3. Specific kinds, e.g., 809.2512 (tragedy)

     4. Specific themes or subjects, e.g., 809.29351 (Abraham Lincoln)

     5. Specific elements, e.g., 809.2925 (stream of consciousness)

     6. Specific qualities, e.g., 809.29145 (romanticism)

     7. Period, e.g., 809.204 (20th century)

B. Drama from one literature

(Collections of American drama used as example)

1. Specific media, e.g., 812.02508354 (television plays on death)

2. Specific scopes, e.g., 812.04108 (one-act plays)

3. Specific kinds, e.g., 812.051208 (tragedy)

4. Period, e.g., 812.5408 (collection of later 20th century, no focus), 812.540809287 (20th century, by women)

5. Specific themes and subjects, e.g., 812.008036 (weather)

6. Specific elements, e.g., 812.008027 (characters)

7. Specific qualities, e.g., 812.008015 (symbolism)

8. For and by specific kinds of persons, e.g., 812.008092827 (for girls)

See also Table 3–B: Order of precedence.

T3B—3   **Fiction**

Here are examples illustrating the order of precedence for fiction (A) from more than one literature and (B) from one literature. The order of precedence is the same for collections and criticism.

A. Fiction from more than one literature

(Collections used as example)

1. Specific kinds, e.g., 808.8383 (sociological)

2. Specific scopes, e.g., 808.831 (short stories)

3. Specific themes and subjects, e.g., 808.83936 (animals)

4. Specific elements, e.g., 808.83922 (description)

5. Specific qualities, e.g., 808.83913 (idealism)

6. Period, e.g., 808.83034 (19th century)

B. Fiction from one literature

(Criticism of American fiction used as example)

1. Specific kinds, e.g., 813.0876209 (science fiction)

2. Specific scopes, e.g., 813.0109358 (short stories about war)

3. Period, e.g., 813.5409 (later 20th century), 813.540932162 (later 20th century, about the sea)

4. Specific themes and subjects, e.g., 813.009351 (about King Arthur)

Table 3–B. More than One Author   T3B

5. Specific elements, e.g., 813.00927 (characters)

6. Specific qualities, e.g., 813.00912 (naturalism)

7. For and by specific kinds of persons, e.g., 813.009896073 (fiction by Afro-Americans)

See also Table 3–B: Order of precedence.

T3B—308729 Gothic fiction vs. Love and romance

vs.
T3B—3085

Some modern fiction is called Gothic romance even when it does not contain most of the traditional elements of 18th- and 19th-century Gothic fiction, such as the supernatural and the isolated, picturesque setting. This modern romance is classed in T3B—3085. The traditional Gothic romance, however, is classed in T3B—308729. If in doubt, class in T3B—308729.

T3B—7 vs. **Satire and humor vs. Jokes, quotations, epigrams, anecdotes, graffiti**
T3A—8 + **vs. Works without identifiable literary form vs. Humorous treatment**
02,
T3B—802,
T3B—8 +
02,
T3B—807,
T3B—8 +
07,
T1—0207

Jokes are classed in T3B—802 (or T3—8 + 02), humorous literary works without identifiable literary form in T3B—807 (or T3—8 + 07). In T3B—7 are classed *only* collections of satire or humor in more than one literary form (works in a particular form, e.g., poetry or fiction, are classed with the form).

Any subject may be dealt with in a humorous or satirical manner. Works dealing with a subject in such a manner fall in one of the following categories:

1. The humor involved is entirely incidental to the serious treatment of the subject, e.g., a joke injected in a lecture to provide respite from a serious mood;

2. A subject is dealt with in a serious way, but the humorous or satiric treatment of the subject is vital to the author's intent, e.g., political satire grounded in genuine political criticism;

3. The subject merely provides the occasion for humor, the author's primary concern being to amuse, e.g., a collection of jokes about cats.

Only works falling in the third category are classed in literature, usually at T3B—802 (or T3—8 + 02). Works in the second category are classed with the subject plus notation 0207 from Table 1. Works in the first category are classed with the subject without T1—0207.

Table 3–C. Notation to Be Added Where Instructed in Table 3–B and in 808–809

T3C—17 vs. Comedy vs. Satire and humor
T3B—7

> Class in T3C—17 textbooks and teaching collections showing the development of manifestations of comedy in literature of various forms; class collections of humor in various forms to be read for pleasure in T3B—7008.

T3C—93– [Literature] For and by persons resident in specific continents,
99   countries, localities

> Use T3C—93–99 for the following:
>
> 1. Literature in a language by persons from a certain area within a country, e.g., a collection of American literature by residents of Illinois 810.809773.
>
> 2. A specific affiliated literature, e.g., a collection of French poetry by Swiss authors of the later 19th century 841.80809494.
>
> 3. Literature in a language by nonnative residents of a specific country, e.g., a collection of English literature by non-Japanese residents of Japan 820.80952.
>
> 4. Literature in a language by residents of several countries on the same continent from more than one period (only for works in which the literature of one country does not predominate), e.g., French literature by residents of France, Switzerland, Belgium 840.8094; French literature by residents of Africa 840.8096.

Table 4. Subdivisions of Individual Languages

T4—3 vs. Dictionaries of the standard form of the language vs. [Standard
T4—81   usage of] Words

> Works classed in T4—3 are intended for ready-reference use. While specialized dictionaries may be arranged in other ways besides alphabetically (e.g., picture dictionaries in subject order, thesauri in classified order), the order must be appropriate for ready reference.
>
> Works classed in T4—81 are intended to be read or studied in full in order to learn vocabulary. They may be informal and entertaining, e.g., narratives for small children, or they may be formally organized into lessons with quizzes.

Table 4. Subdivisions of Individual Languages   T4

T4—32–39   Bilingual dictionaries

> The Decimal Classification Division classes a bilingual dictionary with entry words in both languages with the language coming later in the sequence 420–490.

T4—7   Historical and geographical variations, modern nongeographical variations

> Remember that a language may have multiple standard forms. A work on standard Australian English pronunciation, for example, is classed in 421.52, not 427.994. A work on Australian English pronunciation is classed in 427.994 only if it stresses the distinctive characteristics that make Australian pronunciation different from British or American pronunciation.

> A specific pidgin or creole is classed as a variation of the source language from which more of its vocabulary comes than from its other source language(s). A pidgin or creole is customarily associated with a specific geographic area and is therefore classed in T4—709 plus the area number from Table 2 or in one of the subdivisions of T4—7 for geographical variations where they are provided in 420–490, e.g., the Krio language of Sierra Leone 427.9664.

T4—864 vs.   [Readers] For those whose native language is different vs. Languages
T1—014   (Terminology) and communication

> Class in T4—864, using notation 024 from Table 1, readers for nonnative speakers intended to instill a knowledge of the special vocabulary of a specific subject or discipline, e.g., science readers for Spanish-speaking people T4—864610245. Class works on the vocabulary of a specific subject or discipline without regard to the language status of the user with the subject or discipline, using notation 014 from Table 1.

Table 5. Racial, Ethnic, National Groups

> Table 5 and Table 6 Languages are similar, both based on the traditional sequence of languages in 420–490. Two tables have been developed, however, because language and nationality do not always match. For example, there are Canadian people (T5—11 in Table 5), but no Canadian language; there is a Yiddish language (T6—37 in Table 6) but no Yiddish people.

> The citation order given at some specific numbers in Table 5 differs from the generally preferred citation order of ethnic group over nationality. For example, for Canadians of French and British origin, the prescribed citation order is nationality first (T5—11 Canadians), then ethnic group: T5—112 for Canadians of British origin, T5—114

for Canadians of French origin. The numbers T5—21071 (T5—21 people of British Isles + [notation from Table 2] T2—71 Canada) and T5—41071 (T5—41 French + T2—71 Canada) are used only for persons of British and French origin in Canada who are not Canadian citizens. In the absence of specific instructions to the contrary, however, use the citation order given at the beginning of the table, e.g., Canadians of Ukrainian descent T5—91791071 (not T5—11). Note that the same number is used for both Canadians of Ukrainian descent and persons of Ukrainian descent who are in Canada but not Canadian citizens. This lumping together of citizens and noncitizens is typical for Table 5 because of the low priority normally given to nationality; the developments for Canadians of British and French descent are atypical.

Normally the same number is used for both the majority ethnic group of a nation and the total population viewed as a national group, e.g., T5—94541 for both ethnic Finns and all citizens of Finland viewed as a national group. In such cases the question of priority between ethnic and national affiliation arises only for minority ethnic groups. Finnish citizens who are ethnic Swedes, a minority ethnic group, are classed in T5—39704897 (T5—397 Swedes + [notation from Table 2] T2—4897 Finland) because their ethnic group takes priority over their nationality. If Finnish citizens who are ethnic Finns move to the United States, their number in Table 5 is T5—94541073 (T5—94541 Finns + [notation from Table 2] T2—73 United States); but if Finnish citizens who are ethnic Swedes move to the United States, their number is T5—397073 (Swedes + United States), the same number for all persons of Swedish descent in the United States. The Finnish national origin is not expressed because of the low priority given to nationality.

Special developments that allow expression of both ethnic and national affiliation are typically made only for the majority ethnic group in a nation, under the rubric "national group." Thus T5—6887 expresses both Spanish American ethnicity and Venezuelan nationality, while T5—9697292 expresses both African ancestry and Jamaican nationality. There is no special development to express both African ancestry and Venezuelan nationality because Blacks are a minority in Venezuela and cannot be called a "national group." The number for Black Venezuelans in England (T5—96042) is the same as the number for Blacks in general in England; the link to Venezuela is not expressed. The numbers for Venezuelans of Spanish origin in England (T5—6887042) and Black Jamaicans in England (T5—9697292042), by contrast, do express the national origins.

An atypical development for United States Blacks (T5—96073) gives extra emphasis to nationality for a minority group, while still preserving the usual citation order of ethnic group before nationality. The full Table 5 number for Black U.S. citizens in New York is

Table 5. Racial, Ethnic, National Groups   T5

T5—960730747, but for Black noncitizens in New York T5—960747. For most ethnic groups in the United States, there are no such special developments; thus, for example, T5—510747 specifies persons of Italian descent in New York regardless of whether they are U. S. citizens. The Table 5 number for United States Blacks in England (T5—96073042) expresses the U. S. national origin, but the number for Italian-Americans in England (T5—51042) is the same as for Italians in England.

In some cases, special developments for national groups lead to the number for a national group being clearly different from the number for the majority ethnic group of the country. For example, the number for the Bhutanese as a national group is T5—91418; but the Bhutia, the majority ethnic group, speak Tibetan dialects and are classed as an ethnic group with the Tibetans in T5—954. In some other cases, the national-group number for a country may be seen as expressing or not expressing the ethnicity of the majority of the population, depending on how one defines that ethnicity. For example, the national-group numbers for all the modern nations of Latin America where Spanish is at least one of the official languages express Spanish-American ethnicity, though the majority of the population in some countries is of native American origin. In Guatemala, 55% of the population is of Mayan origin; but a majority of the people, including some of the Maya, speak Spanish and follow Spanish-American customs. Class works that discuss all the people of a nation in the national-group number specified in the table. Class works that focus on a specific ethnic group with the group. If the national-group number expresses the appropriate ethnicity, use it for a work that focuses on a specific ethnic group. For example, class in T5—687281 works that discuss all the people of Guatemala and works that focus on the Guatemalans who speak Spanish and follow Spanish-American customs; but class in T5—974 works that focus on the Maya of Guatemala.

T5—1   **North Americans**

Use this number and its subdivisions for (a) comprehensive works on all the peoples of North America, (b) the people of Canada (T5—11) and the United States (T5—13) as national groups, (c) North Americans of British origin, and (d) Canadians of French origin (T5—114). Works focusing on other national or ethnic groups in North America are all classed elsewhere in Table 5, e.g., people of French origin in the United States T5—41073, Mexicans as a national group T5—6872, the Inuit T5—971.

T5—201—   **British**   **English**   **Anglo-Saxons [by area] vs. People of the**
209 vs.   **British Isles [by area]**
T5—2101—
2109   Use T5—2101–2109 for persons of British ancestry in an area when
they are or have most recently been citizens of the United Kingdom,
e.g., persons from the United Kingdom in the Third World
T5—2101724. Use T5—201–209 for persons of British ancestry in an
area when many of them are or have most recently been citizens of the
United States, Canada, Australia, and New Zealand, e.g., persons from
the United Kingdom, the United States, Canada, and Australia in the
Third World T5—201724.

T5—914 vs.   **South Asians vs. Dravidians and Scytho-Dravidians**
T5—948
      Speakers of Marathi (T6—9146 in Table 6) and Sindhi (T6—91411 in
Table 6) are classed as Scytho-Dravidians in T5—948 in Table 5.

T5—9141   **National groups**

      As specified in the class-elsewhere note at T5—9141, Trinidadians and
Fijians of South Asian origin are classed according to their nationality
rather than their ethnic origins. Other South Asians, however, are
classed according to the normal citation order for Table 5, which gives
precedence to ethnic origins. For example, South Africans of South
Asian descent are classed in T5—914068 (not T5—968).

T5—9435   **Turks**

      Class here (a) the people of Turkey as a national group; (b) people who
speak, or whose ancestors spoke, Turkish (Osmanli Turks and their des-
cendants), including those who are not Turkish nationals, e.g., Turkish
Cypriots T5—943505645.

Table 6. Languages

T6—9639   **Bantu languages**

      The subdivisions of Bantu languages are adapted from Voegelin's
arrangement of Guthrie's Bantu language zones. See Charles F. and
Florence M. Voegelin, *Classification and Index of the World's
Languages* (New York: Elsevier, 1977), and Malcolm Guthrie, *Com-
parative Bantu; an Introduction to the Comparative Linguistics and
Prehistory of the Bantu languages* (Farnborough: Gregg, 1967–1971).

Notes on Schedule Numbers

000   Generalities

Two categories of works fall within the Generalities class:

(1) Works in "umbrella" or "tool" disciplines, that is, disciplines relating to or applied to many other disciplines, e.g., systems analysis and computer science (003–006), bibliography (010 and 090), library and information sciences (020), museology (069), journalism and publishing (070). In some cases the links between these disciplines and other disciplines may be shown by attachment of a number from the 001–999 span, e.g., 016.54 bibliographies of chemistry, 026.61 medical libraries. In other cases the links may be shown by the use of standard subdivisions notation from Table 1, e.g., systems analysis in civil engineering 624.011, computer applications in business 650.0285.

(2) Multidisciplinary works, e.g., general encyclopedias (030), general periodicals (050), works on general organizations (060), general collections (808). There is parallel standard subdivisions notation in Table 1 for three of these types of works, so that they may be shown in connection with specific subjects:

030 General encyclopedic works

    T1—03 Dictionaries, encyclopedias, concordances

050 General serial publications and their indexes

    T1—05 Serial publications

060 General organizations ...

    T1—06 Organizations ...

001.9 and 130   **Controversial knowledge [and] Paranormal phenomena**

001.9 and 130 both pertain to topics in the twilight realms of half-knowledge, topics that refuse either to be disproved or to be brought into the realm of certain and verifiable knowledge. Certain characteristics of a work are good indicators that they belong in either 001.9 or 130:

    1. A claim of access to secret or occult sources;

    2. A rejection of established authority;

    3. A pronounced reverence for iconoclasts, for laymen-become-experts;

    4. An uncritical acceptance of lay observation of striking phenomena;

5. A fixation on the unexplained, the enigmatic, the mysterious;

6. A confidence verging on certainty in the existence of conspiracies and the working of malevolent forces;

7. An acknowledgment of the powers of extraterrestrial beings or intelligences (other than religious beings).

Phenomena classed in 130 are closely linked to human beings—the human mind, human capabilities and powers, human happiness. Phenomena classed in 001.9 are not closely linked to humans. In case of doubt, and for interdisciplinary works, prefer 001.9.

003   **Systems**

Despite having names that make them sound quite different, systems analysis and operations research often deal with the same problems using the same techniques, especially mathematical models of systems. They are classed in the same numbers because there is not enough difference to justify separate numbers.

Class works treating systems in related disciplines in the appropriate broad number for those disciplines, using notation 011 from Table 1, e.g., systems in medicine, engineering, management, and manufacturing 601.1. To be classed in 003 a work must be applicable to at least three main classes (e.g., 300, 500, 600).

Class use of systems analysis and operations research in management in 658.4032. Be especially careful with works on operations research, because they often appear at first glance to be general, but in fact emphasize management applications.

See also 004.21 vs. 003.

003,
T1—011
vs. 510,
T1—0151

Systems [and Table 1 notation for] Systems vs. Mathematics [and Table 1 notation for mathematical principles]

Many works properly classed in 003 are highly mathematical. What distinguishes them from works properly classed in 510 is that the mathematics is applied to real-world systems.

Some works about systems treat purely mathematical systems, e.g., systems of equations. Such works are of course classed in 510. Beware: the same or similar terms may be applied to both mathematical systems and mathematical descriptions of real-world systems; for example, a work on *dynamical systems* may discuss either mathematics (515.352) or real-world systems (003.85).

Half a work on systems in the 003 sense may be organized according to mathematical concepts, but typically the introduction makes clear that the mathematics is intended as background for systems theory. The systems part of such a work will typically be organized according to specific applications, types of systems, or systems concepts such as control, stability, input-output, feedback, observability, or state estimation.

If in doubt whether or not mathematics is applied to real-world systems, prefer 510.

The distinction between the standard subdivisions for systems and mathematics is more difficult than that between 003 and 510 because works classed with the subject using T1—0151 usually involve mathematics applied to the real world. Use T1—011 for works that clearly stress systems, modeling, forecasting, or other topics named in 003. For works lacking such stress, and in case of doubt, prefer T1—0151.

See also 519.5, T1 015195 vs. 001.422, T1—072.

003.2   **Forecasting and forecasts**

Most works on forecasting and forecasts treat primarily social forecasting; such works are classed in 303.49. Works classed in 003 treat forecasting as applied in a variety of social and nonsocial disciplines. Such works typically focus on methods of forecasting. Interdisciplinary works that stress forecasting in a particular kind of system are classed with the system in 003.7—.8, e.g., forecasting in stochastic systems 003.760112.

003.5 vs.   **Cybernetics vs. Automatic control engineering**
629.8

Class interdisciplinary works on control of living and nonliving systems in 003.5 or with various specific kinds of systems in 003.7—.8. Class automatic control of man-made physical systems in 629.8. If in doubt, prefer 003.5.

003.7   **Kinds of systems**

Many kinds of systems are defined in terms of the equations used to model them, e.g., distributed-parameter systems are defined as systems governed by partial differential equations. Other equations may be used to model the behavior of the same real-world system. Class a work about a specific kind of system according to the way the work describes the system, e.g., a work that discusses applying the mathematics of stochastic (random) processes to systems 003.76.

004–006 vs.   **[Data processing**   **Computer science] vs. [Engineering of]**
   621.39   **Computers**

Works classed in 004–006 treat (a) computer hardware from the user's viewpoint and/or (b) software or firmware. Works classed in 621.39 (a) treat computer hardware solely from the viewpoint of engineering or manufacturing and (b) do not treat software or the program aspect of firmware. A work treating the physical processes of manufacturing firmware chips, not discussing the programs embodied in those chips, would be classed in 621.39. Comprehensive works on the computer science and computer engineering aspects of a computer topic are classed in 004–006.

Works treating 004–006 concepts may be classed in 621.39 only if the 004–006 concepts are applied to 621.39 concepts, as in computer graphics programs to assist in design of computer circuitry 621.3950285668.

621.39 parallels 004 in structure, except for 621.399, which is analogous to 006. Because certain numbers in 621.39 were skipped to minimize reuse of numbers, the parallel to 004 is not as close as it would otherwise be.

Computers in general; comprehensive works on digital computers	004	621.39
Digital supercomputers	004.11	621.3911
Digital mainframe computers	004.12	621.3912
Digital minicomputers	004.14	621.3914
Digital microcomputers	004.16	621.3916
Hybrid and analog computers	004.19	621.3919
Systems analysis and design, computer architecture, performance evaluation	004.2	621.392
Storage	004.5	621.397
Interfacing and communications	004.6	621.3981
Peripherals	004.7	621.3984
Special computer methods	006	621.399

There is no analogue for 004.3 Processing modes in 621.39 because most works focusing on processing modes include treatment of software or the program aspect of firmware and thus are not classed in 621.39. Class general works on the engineering of computers, processors (central processing units), computer systems distinguished by their processing modes in 621.391, specific aspects of such machinery with the aspect, e.g., engineering design of multiprocessors 621.392.

Most works on computer architecture and computer performance evaluation include treatment of software or the program aspect of firmware; hence there are separate subdivisions of 004.2 for these topics (004.22 Computer architecture and 004.24 Performance evaluation), but no such separate subdivisions of 621.392. Works on these topics that truly are limited to computer engineering, however, are classed at 621.392.

Engineering of devices for the special computer methods named in 006 is to be classed in 621.399, whether the devices or methods are named there or not.

There is no analogue in 004 for 621.395 Circuitry because circuitry is strictly an engineering aspect of computers, not something that the computer user needs to understand.

Computer engineering is not part of notation 0285 in Table 1. It is, however, subject to the same rule that applies to electronic engineering in general: a specific application is classed with the application, e.g., electronic engineering of computers in robots 629.892.

004 vs. 005 **Data processing   Computer science vs. Computer programming, programs, data**

Class in 004 works on computer hardware and works treating both computer hardware and the "soft" aspects of computer systems— programs, programming, and data. Class works treating only these "soft" aspects in 005. Exception: Class hardware applied to topics named in 005 with the topic using notation 028 in Table 1, e.g., database machines 005.74028. Exception to the exception: Class hardware for interfacing and data communications in 004.6 (not 005.71).

004.1 **General works on specific types of computers**

In this number, its subdivisions, and analogous numbers elsewhere in 004–006 and 621.39, computers and processors (central processing units) are treated for classification purposes as if they were the same. In fact they are not, but few works about processors can avoid discussing the other parts of the computer with which the processor must interact; hence works about specific types of computers and processors are typically not different enough to justify separate numbers.

Programmable calculators are classed in 510.28541 rather than 004.1 because they are limited-function computers, capable of working only with numbers, not alphabetic data.

004.11–.16 **Digital computers**

Use these numbers and the analogous engineering numbers (621.3911–.3916) with caution: use them only for works that emphasize the specific type of computer, not for works that may refer most of the time to a particular type as an illustration of what computers in general do. For example, use 004, not 004.12, for a general introduction to computers written at a time when the only computers were mainframes. If in doubt, prefer 004 or 621.39 without subdivision.

Supercomputers are the largest, fastest, most powerful, most expensive computers; mainframe computers are next; then minicomputers; finally microcomputers are the smallest, slowest, least powerful and least expensive computers. Specific distinctions among these types of computers have been made, especially in terms of word size, memory size, and speed; but the distinctions vary from authority to authority, manufacturer to manufacturer, and especially over time. Class a particular computer according to the way it is presented in the first work about it that a library acquires (unless it is known that that work presents an atypical view of the computer).

Do not class a work treating more than one computer or processor in a number for specific computers in 004–006 unless:

1. The work treats a single series of very closely related computers or processors (e.g., the IBM 370® series of mainframe computers 004.125 or the Intel 8080® and 8080A® microprocessors 004.165); or

2. The work treats primarily one specific computer or processor but adds that it is also applicable to other similar machines (e.g., a work about programming the IBM PC® that says it can also be used as a guide to programming "IBM-compatible" computers 005.265).

Note: A work that discusses a computer and its processor is in effect a work about the computer and should be treated as such (e.g., a work about the Apple II® computer and the 6502® microprocessor 004.165).

In case of doubt, do not use a number for specific computers.

004.21 vs. 003   **Systems analysis and design vs. Systems**

In addition to the analysis and design of computer-based systems, class in 004.21 systems analysis of a user's problem in order to design a computer-based system to solve it. Class a work on systems analysis and design that is not concerned primarily with computer-based systems in 003 or with the specific system.

004.21 vs. 004.22, 621.392   **Systems analysis and design vs. Computer architecture vs. Systems analysis and design, computer architecture [in computer engineering]**

In 004.21 systems analysis and design of a computer-based system involves a computer, application programs, and procedures, usually also other hardware, often a database and communications network, all working together to accomplish a task for the user.

In 004.22 computer architecture focuses on the design and structure of the computer itself and on the computer in relation to its peripheral devices. Most works on computer architecture treat software or the program aspect of firmware as well as hardware; but in the discussion of programs, the focus is on system programs, which make the computer function properly, rather than on application programs, which accomplish user tasks.

In 621.392 are classed works that treat computer hardware but do not treat software or firmware.

004.24   Performance evaluation

Class here only specialized works treating performance measurement and evaluation as an aid in designing or improving the performance of a computer system. Class general evaluations of computers in the appropriate general works number, e.g., general evaluations of microcomputers 004.16, of the BBC Microcomputer® 004.165. If in doubt, prefer the general works number. Add notation 0297 from Table 1 to the general works number if the emphasis is on evaluation as a consideration in purchasing, e.g., evaluation and purchasing manuals for microcomputers 004.160297.

004.6   Interfacing and communications

It is impossible to make a distinction useful for classification between computer interfacing and computer communications. For example, there are many similarities between (a) the interfacing techniques that link a computer and a printer located next to it and (b) the communications techniques that link a computer and a physically remote printer, terminal, or other computer. The schedule is designed so that the classifier need not distinguish computer interfacing from computer communications. In 004.6, 005.71, and 621.3981, computer interfacing and computer communications are classed in the same numbers.

See also 384.3 vs. 004.6.

004.6 vs.   Interfacing and communications vs. Data communications
005.71

These two numbers are parallel: interfacing is classed in both, and *computer communications* and *data communications* are synonyms. Class in 004.6 selection and use of computer interfacing and communications equipment—"hard" aspects. Class in 005.71 comprehensive works on "soft" aspects—programming, programs, and data in interfacing and communications. (Class specific data aspects of interfacing and communications with the aspect in 005.7–.8, e.g., error-correcting codes 005.72, data compression 005.746, data encryption 005.82.) Class comprehensive works on both the "hard" and "soft" aspects of computer interfacing and communications in 004.6.

005   Computer programming, programs, data

Text processing as classed here is broader than word processing; it includes all computer processing of information coded as characters or sequences of characters (as contrasted with information coded as numbers), e.g., counting word frequency, making concordances, storing and retrieving text, sorting lists alphabetically. Class specific applications of text processing with the application, e.g., alphabetic sorting 005.748, word processing 652.5.

See also 004 vs. 005.

005.1 vs.   Programming vs. Programs
005.3
Class in 005.1 and other programming numbers works on programming to achieve reliability, compatibility, portability, and other ideal qualities. Class in 005.3 and other numbers for programs works that discuss whether existing programs actually have these qualities.

Class in 005.10218 and 005.150218 standards for programs and program documentation that are aimed at programmers and documentation writers, to ensure that they produce good programs and documentation. Class in 005.30218 and other numbers for programs works that discuss standards to help users in selecting from among existing programs and documentation.

Class in 005.14 testing and measurement as part of program development. Class in 005.30287 and other numbers for programs works that discuss ways for users to test or measure programs as an aid in selection.

Class a work devoted equally to programming and programs in 005.1 Programming or 005.2 Programming for specific types of computers.

005.1 vs.   [Computer] Programming vs. Mathematics
510
Certain terms may be used for both a computer science concept and a mathematics concept. *Algorithm*, for example, may be used for processes to solve mathematical problems—with or without the aid of a computer. *Algorithm* may also be used in the context of computer programming for processes to solve many different kinds of problems—information-retrieval and word-processing problems, for example, as well as mathematical problems.

Programming may refer to a branch of applied mathematics that has no necessary connection with computers, though computations necessary for this branch are commonly accomplished with the aid of a computer. For example, *linear programming* refers to the study of maximizing or minimizing a linear function $f(x_1, \ldots, x_n)$ subject to given constraints which are linear inequalities involving the variables of x_i. *Nonlinear programming* refers to the study of maximizing or minimizing a function of several variables, when the variables are constrained to yield values of other functions lying in a certain range, and either the function to be maximized or minimized, or at least one of the functions whose value is constrained, is nonlinear. Works on programming as a branch of applied mathematics are classed in 519.7. *Programming* may also refer to writing instructions to direct the operation of a computer or its peripheral equipment. Programming in this sense is classed in 005.1.

005.101 Philosophy and theory [of programming]

Notation 01 from Table 1 is not used here or with subdivisions of 005.1 for general discussions of logic in programming because logic is inherent in programming and is discussed in nearly every work about programming. Notation 01 from Table 1 may be used for specialized works with an unusually intense focus on logical analysis. Typically such works treat not logic in general but rather symbolic (mathematical) logic, for which notation 015113 is used.

005.11 Special programming techniques

Here are classed special programming techniques as applied to the multiple phases of programming, e.g., works on structured programming that treat program design, coding, and testing 005.113. Special programming techniques applied to only one phase of programming are classed with the phase, e.g., works on structured program design 005.12.

005.136 Machine and assembly languages

Most machine and assembly languages are limited to a specific computer or processor (or at least to a specific type); and most works about specific machine and assembly languages emphasize programming with these languages; hence most works about specific machine and assembly languages are classed in 005.2 Programming for specific types of computers. A work about a specific machine or assembly language that did not emphasize programming would be classed here. Most of the works classed here treat machine or assembly languages in general.

005.15 vs. Preparation of program documentation vs. [Composition of works
808.066005 about programs]

Class in 005.15 comprehensive works on how to prepare program documentation; works on how to prepare the technical documentation needed by the personnel who will maintain, modify, and enhance the program (including such things as program source listings, program comments, flow charts, decision logic tables, file specifications, program function descriptions, program test history records, modification logs); works on how to prepare program users' manuals that focus on content rather than form; works on policies for program documentation.

Class in 808.066005 works that emphasize effective technical writing—that is, works that emphasize such things as organizing for clarity, writing appropriately for the intended audience, using good paragraph structure, preferring the active voice, using consistent terminology. Typically such works are concerned only with users' manuals.

005.3   Programs

Class a program or programs designed to run on two types of computers with the predominant type if there is one, e.g., a program that runs on five mainframe computers and one minicomputer 005.329. If neither of two types is predominant, class with the smaller type, e.g., a program for minicomputers and microcomputers 005.369.

Class programs for a specific application in computer science with the application in 005–006, but never in 004. Among the numbers most frequently used for software besides 005.3 and its subdivisions are 005.43 for systems software and operating systems, 005.713 for interfacing and data communications programs, 005.74 for database management systems, and 006.68 for computer graphics programs.

Programs applied to a particular subject or discipline are classed with the subject or discipline, using notation 028553 from Table 1, e.g., programs for tax accounting 657.46028553.

See also T1—0285; 005.1 vs. 005.3.

005.362   [Programs] In specific programming languages

Class here (and in cognate numbers) programs and works about programs only if the material being classified emphasizes the programming language. For much off-the-shelf software, the user does not need to know in what programming language it was written; such software is classed in subdivisions of 005.3 not devoted to specific programming languages.

005.369   Specific programs

Class here (and in cognate numbers) programs having interdisciplinary applications, such as electronic spreadsheets (which can be used in research, business, personal finance, indeed any time a matrix format is useful) and statistics packages that are used more widely than just in research and that have report formatting or other features beyond statistical capabilities. If a work discussing how to use such a program is a guide that would be helpful to users applying the program in many fields, class it in 005.369 and cognate numbers even if most of the examples come from one field. If a work truly focuses on how to use such a program in a particular field, however, class it with that field, using notation 02855369 from Table 1 and cognate numbers, e.g., use of a particular electronic spreadsheet in financial administration 658.1502855369. In case of doubt, prefer 005.369 and cognate numbers.

005.43   Systems programs   Operating systems

Although there are technical differences between a type of utility program called a text editor and a word processing program, they are both classed in 652.5; however, text editors specially adapted for inputting computer programs, e.g., those that check program grammar, are classed in 005.13.

005.6   Microprogramming and microprograms

Microprogramming does not mean programming for microcomputers, nor does *microprogram* mean a program for a microcomputer. *Microprogramming* means writing programs in which each instruction specifies a minute operation of the computer. Such programs are microprograms. Class programming for microcomputers in 005.26, programs for microcomputers in 005.36.

See also 004 vs. 005; 004–006 vs. 621.39.

005.713   [Data communications] Programs

An example of a program for data communications is one that enables a user with a microcomputer and a modem to transmit and receive data and possibly also to store and manipulate data. The program may also prepare a computer to handle different forms of data, change transmission speeds to suit the hardware, store phone numbers and provide automatic routines so that the user need not repeat the connect process, etc.

005.74   Data files and databases

Although there are technical differences between data files and databases, they are treated as the same for classification.

Class in 005.74 computer science aspects of databases—that is, the narrowly technical issues of designing, programming, and installing databases and database management systems—the kinds of things that system designers and programmers need to know but that users generally do not need to know unless are installing a database on their own computer. Class the subject content of databases (and works discussing that content) as if the databases were books, e.g., encyclopedic databases 030, bibliographic databases 010, nonbibliographic chemistry databases 540. Do not use notation 0285574 from Table 1 except for works that focus on the computer science aspects of the databases rather than the subject content. Class in 025.04 the information science aspects of the automated storage and retrieval systems that make databases available—the kinds of things that users need to know about the systems in order to benefit fully from them. Class in 025.06 the information science aspects of the automated systems that make databases on specific subjects available to users. Class interdisciplinary works on databases in 025.04.

See also 011.3 vs. 011.77, 005.30296.

006.37 vs. 006.42, 621.367, 621.391, 621.399   **Computer vision vs. Optical pattern recognition vs. Technological photography and photo-optics vs. General works on [engineering of] specific types of computers vs. Devices for special computer methods**

Computer vision and optical pattern recognition both involve recognition of forms, shapes, or other optical patterns for the purpose of classification, grouping, or identification; but computer vision makes extensive use of artificial intelligence for the complex interpretation of visual information, whereas optical pattern recognition involves only simple interpretation.

Most works on computer vision and optical pattern recognition give substantial treatment to the computer programs needed to interpret optical patterns; such works are classed in 006.37 and 006.42, as are also works treating computer-vision and optical-pattern-recognition devices from the user's point of view. Class at 621.399 works on designing and manufacturing the hardware for computer vision and optical pattern recognition.

Class in 621.367 works on devices that record and process optical signals while doing virtually no interpreting (either because interpretation is not needed or because interpretation is left to others—computers or humans), e.g., devices for image enhancement.

At 621.391 *optical computer* refers to general-purpose computers in which the central data processing mechanism is based on light (e.g., lasers). Sometimes *optical computer* is used for special-purpose computers designed to process optical data, regardless of the type of central data processing mechanism. Works on such computers are classed in 006.37, 006.42, or 621.399.

011.3 vs. 011.77, 005.30296   **General bibliographies of works published in specific forms vs. [General bibliographies of] Computer programs vs. Commercial miscellany [about computer programs]**

Class general bibliographies of machine-readable works *not limited to software* in 011.3. A general list of *software only*, however, is a list of works with a special content, not merely a special form; yet it is not a list on a specific subject in the 016 sense. Class a general list of software in 011.77. Class annotated lists in 011.77 if the annotations are relatively brief; but class lists with lengthy reviews as buyers' guides in 005.30296, e.g., a collection of reviews of microcomputer software 005.360296.

See also 005.74.

020   Library and information sciences

The order of precedence in the schedule for library and information science is complex. The following table shows precedence among 022, 023, 025, 026, and 027:

025 Operations, such as technical services, e.g., acquisitions, cataloging; readers' services, e.g., reference, circulation

Exceptions: (a) Administration (025.1) has a lower precedence than other operations (see below). (b) Readers' services for special groups and organizations are classed with libraries for special groups and organizations in 027.6, not in 025.5. (c) Comprehensive works on operations in a specific kind of institution are classed with the kind of institution in 026 027, not in 025.

022, 023, 025.1 Administration

026 Institutions devoted to specific disciplines and subjects

027 General institutions

Examples follow:

1. Administration of cataloging

   Operation (cataloging) + administration 025.3 + T1—068 (notation from Table 1) = 025.3068

2. Administration of law libraries

   Administration + institution (law library) 025.19 + 634 (from 026.34) = 025.19634

3. Personnel administration in university libraries

   Personnel administration + institution (university library) 023

   (Note that type of institution cannot be indicated in the number.)

4. Book selection in public libraries

   Operation (book selection) + institution (public library) 025.218 + 74 (from 027.4) = 025.21874

5. Reference services in the corporate library

Library for a special organization (business organization) + operation (reference services) 027.69

(Note that the usual facet order of operation + institution is reversed here because of the exception listed above under 025. Note also that the operation [reference services] cannot be indicated in the number.)

In two contexts in 020, materials by subject or discipline (e.g., chemistry) take precedence over materials by format or special bibliographic characteristics (e.g., sound recordings, serials). Institutions devoted to specific disciplines and subjects (026) take precedence over institutions devoted to materials in special formats or with special bibliographic characteristics (027); selection and acquisition of materials on specific disciplines and subjects (025.27) takes precedence over selection and acquisition of materials in special forms (025.28). In the context of bibliographic control, however, materials in special formats or with special bibliographic characteristics (025.34) take precedence over materials in specific disciplines and subjects (025.46 classification, 025.49 controlled subject vocabularies).

Examples follow:

1. Selection and acquisition of chemistry serials for university libraries

Operation (selection and acquisition) + subject of material (chemistry) + format of material (serial) + institution (university library) 025.27 + 54 (from 540) = 025.2754

(Note that format of material [serial] and type of institution [university library] cannot be indicated in this number. If notation 05 from Table 1 were added to form 025.275405, the number would mean serials on selection and acquisition of chemistry materials, not selection and acquisitions of chemistry serials.)

2. Classifying sound recordings of music

Operation (classifying) + format of material (sound recordings) + subject of material (music) 025.3482

(Note that subject of material [music] cannot be indicated in this number.)

025.3   Bibliographic analysis and control

Most works on bibliographic analysis and control treat some form of standard (e.g., standard cataloging codes, standard lists of subject headings) because standards are inherent in control. For this reason, do not use notation 0218 from Table 1 here or in any subdivision of 025.3–.4.

026–027   **Specific kinds of institutions**

A specific operation in a specific kind of institution is classed with the operation, e.g., collection development in patients' libraries 025.2187662; however, services to special groups and organizations are classed in 027.6, e.g., reader services in patients' libraries 027.662.

Libraries, archives, information centers devoted to specific kinds of special materials are classed in 026–027. Those limited to a specific subject or discipline are classed in 026, e.g., libraries devoted to music scores 026.78026, to maps 026.912.

A general library (1) devoted to a kind of special material and (2) not serving special groups and organizations may be loosely regarded as devoted to a subject and classed in 026 plus the number in 001–999 for the kind of material, e.g., a rare book library 026.09. If, however, a library devoted to a kind of special material is limited to what may be properly called a specific subject or discipline, it is classed with the subject or discipline, e.g., a rare book library devoted to literature 026.8. A general library devoted to a kind of special material and serving special groups and organizations is classed in 027.6, e.g., a braille library 027.663.

027   **General libraries, archives, information centers**

Few archives are sufficiently general to be classed here; most are classed in 026 because they contain primarily material on specific disciplines and subjects, e.g., archives of religious organizations 026.2 (not 027.67).

027.5   **Government libraries**

General government archives for a specific jurisdiction usually contain primarily material reflecting the history and civilization of the place; works on such archives are classed in 026 plus the history number for the jurisdiction, e.g., United States National Archives 026.973.

070.433   **Reporting local, foreign, war news**

General reporting on a specific area is treated as reporting on the history and civilization of the area and is classed in 070.449 plus the history number for the area from notation 909.09 or 940–990, e.g., reporting the local news of London 070.4499421, foreign correspondents reporting on South Africa 070.449968.

080   **General collections**

To be classed here a work must contain a collection of writings, statements, or quotations on a variety of topics. Examples: selected articles of a general nature from one or more periodicals, such as highlights from *The Atlantic*; a collection of quotations by Winston Churchill on various topics.

081–089   [General collections] In specific languages and language families

Collections originally written in one language or language family are classed with that language or language family. Collections originally written in two or more languages or language families are classed with the preponderant language or language family if there is one. If no original language or language family is preponderant, but the work appears in one language as a result of translation, class it with the language in which it appears. Class in 080 collections in which the material appears in multiple languages with none preponderant, even if accompanied by translations into the language of the intended audience.

100   Philosophy, parapsychology and occultism, psychology

Ethics is an exception to the rule that the philosophy of a discipline or subject is classed with the discipline or subject. Class the ethics of a discipline or subject in 172–179. Class ethics within or based on a religious tradition with the religion in 200. For example, class philosophy and theory of international relations in 327.101; the ethics of relations between states in 172.4; the ethics of those relations treated as part of Christian moral theology in 241.624.

100, 109 vs.   Philosophy, parapsychology and occultism, psychology [and]
190   Historical and collected persons treatment of philosophy vs. Modern Western philosophy

To be classed in 100 or 109, works must include (a) discussion of the discipline of philosophy itself or several of philosophy's major questions and branches, as is common in introductory works; or (b) discussion of philosophy broad enough to include non-Western and ancient or medieval as well as modern Western philosophy.

See also 190.

100 vs. 200   Philosophy, parapsychology and occultism, psychology vs. Religion

Both philosophy and religion deal with the ultimate nature of existence and relationships, but religion treats them within the context of revelation, deity, worship. Natural theology (210) does not involve revelation or worship but does examine questions within the context of deity.

Any work that emphasizes revelation, deity, or worship is classed in 200, even if it uses philosophical methods, e.g., a philosophical proof of the existence of God 212.1. Sometimes the thought of a religious tradition is used to examine the questions of philosophy without reference to deity or religious topics, e.g., Jewish philosophy 181.06, Christian philosophy 190. However, class ethics based on a religion in 200. If in doubt, prefer 200.

130 vs. 133   Paranormal phenomena vs. Parapsychology and occultism

Note that 130 by itself is seldom used; most general works on paranormal phenomena in fact focus on parapsychology and occultism and thus are classed in 133, not 130.

133 vs. 200   Parapsychology and occultism vs. Religion

If the author of a work about parapsychological or occult phenomena describes them as religious, or the believers and practitioners consider them to be religious, the work is classed in 200. If parapsychological and occult phenomena are not presented as religious, or if in doubt as to whether they have been so presented, prefer 133.

Class knowledge reputedly derived from secret and ancient religious texts but not applied for religious purposes in 133; however, class editions of the texts in 200, even if annotated from an occultist viewpoint, e.g., discussion of occult traditions derived from the Zohar 135.4, but the text of the Zohar 296.16.

133.129 vs.   Specific haunted places vs. [Historical, geographical, persons
133.109   treatment of Apparitions (Ghosts)]

Use 133.129 only for works that treat one single haunted place, e.g., old Monterey's Hotel del Monte 133.12979476. Use 133.109 for works that treat two or more haunted places during a specific historical period or geographical area, e.g., haunted places in Cornwall 133.1094237.

133.9013 vs.   Personal survival, nature of spiritual world and life after death vs.
129   Origin and destiny of individual souls

Class in 133.9013 accounts of life after death from personal sources or from within the occult tradition. Class in 129 philosophical discussions of personal survival and life after death. If in doubt, prefer 133.9013.

140   Specific philosophical schools and viewpoints

Viewpoints or schools of philosophy are sets of attitudes or presuppositions that a given philosopher or group of philosophers brings to the study of various topics. Topics are the questions studied by philosophy, such as the self 126. Only general works that discuss how a viewpoint or school treats a wide variety of topics are classed in 140, e.g., existentialism 142.78, but existentialist views of the self 126.

140 vs.   Specific philosophical schools and viewpoints vs. Historical,
180–190   geographical, persons treatment of philosophy

Unless other instructions are given, class in 140 specific modern Western schools and viewpoints and comprehensive works on specific schools and viewpoints, but class in 180 ancient, medieval, and Oriental schools and viewpoints, e.g., modern Western idealism, comprehensive works on ancient and modern idealism or on Indian and Western idealism 141, but Indian idealism 181.4. Class in 190 historical and geographical treatment of modern Western philosophy not limited to a specific viewpoint, but class a specific school or viewpoint with the school or viewpoint regardless of time or place, e.g., French philosophy 194, but existentialism in France 142.780944.

Class collected works of an individual philosopher and criticism of his work as a whole in 180–190, even if his work falls entirely within one philosophical viewpoint or serves as the foundation of a school, e.g., the works of Immanuel Kant 193, but Kantianism as a viewpoint espoused by philosophers 142.3.

146.32 vs. **Dialectical materialism [as a philosophic viewpoint] vs. Dialectical**
335.4112 **materialism [as a philosophical foundation of Marxian systems]**

Class in 335.4112 dialectical materialism applied to the economic and political aspects of Marxian systems. Class in 146.32 dialectical materialism as a philosophical viewpoint either not applied to topics outside philosophy or else applied to many different disciplines. If in doubt, prefer 335.4112.

150   Psychology

While application of psychology to any subject is classed with the subject with use of notation 019 from Table 1, application of social psychology to a subject is classed in the social sciences (most often in 302–307) without use of notation 019. For example, class individual psychology of religion in 200.19, social psychology of religion in 306.6.

150 vs. **Psychology vs. [Social psychology]**
302–307

Class in 150 works that focus on the individual, including those that discuss the influence of group behavior on the individual. Class in 302–307 works that focus on group behavior, including those that discuss the role of the individual in group behavior. If in doubt, prefer 302–307.

150.19   **[Psychological] Systems, schools, viewpoints**

Certain schools and systems draw their fundamental principles from a few selected psychological topics. When such topics are used to illustrate a system, class with the system in 150.19, e.g., the subconscious, fantasies, and dreams used to illustrate psychoanalytic principles 150.195 (not 154).

150.195 vs. 616.89   **Psychoanalytic systems vs. Psychiatric disorders**

The psychoanalytic systems classed in 150.195 are the foundation of much of the writing on psychiatric disorders (616.89), and are also the bases of several schools of psychology. Most of the founders of psychoanalytic systems were physicians, so material from psychiatry is heavily used to illustrate the principles of the various psychoanalytic systems. Class comprehensive works on a system or its founder in 150.195. Class applications of a system to specific topics or branches of normal psychology or of both normal and abnormal psychology in the appropriate subdivision of 150. Class applications of a system to psychiatry in 616.89 and related numbers, e.g., psychoanalysis 616.8917. If in doubt, prefer 616.89.

152 vs. 612.8   **[Psychology of] Sensory perception, movement, emotions, physiological drives vs. [Physiology of] Nervous functions   Sensory functions**

Class in 152 works that emphasize awareness, sensation, intentions, meanings, and actions as experienced by the individual or observed and described without reference to the physics or chemistry of the nervous system, e.g., seeing colors, feeling anger. Class in 612.8 works that emphasize the physical and chemical mechanisms and pathways of sensations, emotions, movements, e.g., studies using electrodes to determine what parts of the brain process different kinds of stimuli. Class comprehensive works in 152. If in doubt, prefer 612.8.

152.1 vs. 153.7   **Sensory perception vs. Perceptual processes**

Class in 153.7 comprehensive works on sensory perception and perceptual processes in general; works that focus on the active, interpretative mental processes associated with perception in general or with types of perception that involve more than one sense, e.g., spatial perception 153.752. Class in 152.1 works that focus on the receptive aspects of sensory perception and comprehensive works on perception by a specific sense, e.g., visual perception 152.14. If in doubt, prefer 153.7.

152.384 vs. 153.69   **Expressive movements vs. Nonverbal communication**

Use of 152.384 is limited to noncognitive aspects of expressive movements, e.g., habituation, emotional content. Class the meaning of movements (as in body language) and the cognitive processes involved in interpreting movements in 153.69. If in doubt, prefer 153.69.

153.15 vs. 155.4–.6   **[Psychology of] Learning vs. Psychology of specific ages**

Class a work on the learning psychology of people of a specific age bracket in 155.4–.6 when age is actually the focus of the work. If the reference to age is vague or incidental, class the work in 153.15. If in doubt, prefer 155.4–.6.

**153.15 vs.
370.15**

[Psychology of] Learning vs. Educational psychology

Be careful to distinguish between studies that use students as subjects for research into the fundamental processes of learning, which are classed in 153.15 and related numbers, and studies on the application of learning psychology to education, which are classed in 370.15 and related numbers. In case of doubt, prefer 153.15.

**153.4 vs.
153**

Cognition (Knowledge) vs. Conscious mental processes and intelligence

The terminology in this field is used in a variety of overlapping senses. Many works that claim to be about cognition, thought and thinking, or reasoning also cover such subjects as memory, communication, perception, motivation, and intelligence. These broader works are classed in 153, not 153.4. A book about "cognitive psychology" is more apt to belong at 153 than 153.4.

**153.43 vs.
160**

Reasoning vs. Logic

Class the psychology of reasoning and problem solving in 153.43. Class the science of reasoning and problem solving, that is, the logical processes considered apart from internal mental operations, in 160. If in doubt, prefer 153.43.

153.94

Aptitude tests

Note that 153.94 has priority over other psychology numbers, as shown in the table of precedence at 150. Class in 153.94001–.94999 tests to determine aptitude in specific fields even if drawn from other branches of psychology, e.g., color matching tests for interior decorators 153.94747 (not 152.145), personality tests for social workers 153.943613 (not 155.28). Also class in 153.94 aptitude and vocational interest tests and testing limited to categories of persons defined in 155.3–.6, e.g., vocational interest tests for young adults 153.94000835 (not 155.51394).

**154.6 vs.
612.821**

[Psychology of] Sleep phenomena vs. [Physiology of] Sleep phenomena

Class sleep phenomena in 154.6 if the emphasis is on the overall state of sleep, on the effect of sleep on other psychological activity, or on dreams as phenomena that have meaning in themselves or in the life of the dreamer. Class sleep phenomena in 612.821 if the emphasis is on the chain of bodily activities or on other physiological activity accompanying sleep or dreams, e.g., eye movements, breathing, brain waves. If in doubt, prefer 612.821.

155   Differential and developmental psychology

Some works on the psychology of sensory perception, movement, emotions, physiological drives (152) and conscious mental processes (153) analyze research based on persons belonging to one or several differential categories or subject to one or several environmental influences that are provided for in 155.3–.9. If there is clearly little or no interest in the distinctiveness of the category or influence, class the work in 152–153. This guideline is particularly applicable to ethnic and national groups (155.8), adults (155.6), and social environment (155.92) where the researcher has simply reached out for convenient samples.

Similarly, a study on sex psychology, drawing almost exclusively upon adult middle-class whites, but showing only marginal interest in the class, age, or race of the respondents, is classed in 155.3. Discussion of the class, national, or ethnic bias of such research is classed with the research in 155.3 since the interest is in the validity of the findings about sex psychology.

155.34 vs.   [Individual psychology of] Sexual relations vs. Institutions pertaining
306.7   to relations of the sexes

Most works on the psychology of sexual relations treat social psychological aspects—the interaction between the partners. Such works are classed in 306.7. Only an occasional work emphasizes the psychology of the individual and is therefore classed in 155.34, e.g., a work that focuses on the anxieties of the individual with regard to sexual relations. In case of doubt, prefer 306.7.

155.84 vs.   [Psychology of] Specific racial and ethnic groups vs. National
155.89   psychology

Class in 155.89 the psychology of nations taken as a whole, and the psychology of racial and ethnic groups that are predominant in an area constituting an independent nation. Class in 155.84 the psychology of racial and ethnic groups taken as a whole and the psychology of racial, ethnic, and national groups in areas where they are not predominant. For example, class the national psychology of Malaysia or the psychology of Malays in Malaysia in 155.89595; but class the psychology of Malays taken as a whole in 155.84992, of Malays in Thailand in 155.849920593. If in doubt, class in 155.89.

155.92 vs.   Influence of social environment [on psychology of individual] vs.
158.2,   [Applied psychology of] Interpersonal relations vs. [Social
302–307   psychology]

Class in 155.92 the influence of family, friends, and other people upon the individual. Class in 158.2 the art of getting along with people. Class in 302–307 social interaction regarded as group behavior.

When a work treats both the psychology of social influences (155.92 or 155.94) and social interaction (302–307), prefer 302–307, e.g., the influence of a rural community on individuals and interactions within a rural community 307.72 (not 155.944).

156 vs.
302–307   **Comparative psychology vs. [Social psychology]**

Class in 156 comparative social psychology (sometimes called sociobiology or biosociology) when used to shed light on the behavior of the individual.   Class in 302–307 works considering the social behavior of animals as a background to human social behavior. In case of doubt, prefer 156.

171   **[Ethical] Systems and doctrines**

Class collected works, biography, and critical appraisal of the work of an individual ethicist in 171, if the ethical system represented can be determined (e.g., critical appraisal of the ethics of Jeremy Bentham 171.5092). Otherwise, class such works in 170.92.

174.1   **[Occupational ethics of] Clergy**

Class in 174.1 a discussion of occupational ethics for clergy from a secular or philosophical viewpoint. If the subject is treated as part of the moral theology or ethics of a particular religion, class it with the religion, e.g., a discussion of the occupational ethics of clergy as part of Christian morality 241.641.

180–190   **Historical, geographical, persons treatment of philosophy**

Class single works by individual philosophers with the topic in philosophy. If there is no focus on a specific topic, class a work expressing primarily the philosopher's own viewpoint with the collected works of the philosopher in 180–190. For example, a general work by Hegel, such as *Phenomenology of Spirit*, is classed in 193.

Class a work by an individual philosopher that is primarily a discussion of other philosophers' writings with the other philosophers' writings.

180.938   **[Philosophy of ancient] Greece**

Since most works on ancient philosophy are predominantly concerned with ancient Greek philosophy, 180 is used for both ancient Greek philosophy and ancient philosophy in general. The subdivisions of notation 38 from Table 2 may be added to 180.9 to show philosophy as practiced in one part or city of ancient Greece, e.g., philosophy in ancient Athens 180.9385.

190 Modern Western philosophy

This is the comprehensive number for (a) Christian philosophy; (b) Western philosophy from ancient Greece to the present; (c) modern philosophy, even when both modern Western and modern Oriental philosophies are treated; and (d) European philosophy. For this reason, 190 is used more often than 100 or 109 for what appear to be general works on philosophy.

200 Religion

200 is the comprehensive number for religion in general and for Christianity. 200 and standard subdivisions 200.1–.9 are used for religious thought and the general religious situation and conditions. 201–209 are the standard subdivisions of Christianity in general. 210 is for natural religion and religion based on reason alone. 220 is for the Bible. 230–280 are used for various topics in Christianity. 291 is used for comparative religion and for individual religious topics treated with respect to religions based on revelation or authority. 292–299 are for religions other than Christianity. For any specific topic in religion, the classifier must consider whether the topic is treated within one religion and should be classed in 201–209, 230–280 or 292–299; or whether it is treated from the viewpoint of comparative religion or of various religions and should be classed in 291; or whether it is treated using reason alone and should be classed in 210.

200.1 vs.   **Philosophy and theory [of religion] vs. Natural theology vs.**
210, 291   **Comparative religion**

Comprehensive works on the philosophy of religion are classed in 200.1, but the study of specific topics in religion by use of philosophic methods may be provided for elsewhere, especially in 210 and 291. Natural theology (210) is an older term for the study of religion that excludes divine revelation but uses the methods of philosophy heavily. Hence, abstract questions are nearly always classed in 210, e.g., a philosophical treatment of the existence of God 212.1. Discussions of religious practice and experience nearly always involve the outlook of religions based on revelation, authority, or traditions; these are usually classed in 291 when treated in a philosophical manner, even if the methods of comparative religion are not emphasized. For example, a philosophical treatment of religious rituals would nearly always be classed in 291.3801. Some topics may be treated equally well from the point of view of natural theology or world religions. The reconciliation of science and religion, for example, is classed in 215 if no appeal to revelation, sacred scriptures, or authority is apparent, or in 291.175 if the work assumes revelation. Works comparing or describing three or more religions are classed in 291, e.g., a comparison of the concept of God in Christianity, Islam, and Hinduism 291.211.

207 vs. 268   Education, research, related topics of Christianity vs. [Christian] Religious education

> Class education in and teaching of Christianity as an academic subject in 207, e.g., a course on Christianity in secular secondary schools 207.12. Class in 268 religious education for the purpose of confirming believers in Christian faith and life. It is assumed that this is the purpose of any religious education sponsored by a church, so comprehensive works on religious education are classed in 268. The only exception is that education at the university level is classed in 207.11, including education in universities sponsored by churches.
>
> Study and teaching with regard to any specific topic in 200 is classed with the topic using notation 07 from Table 1, e.g., study and teaching of church history 270.07.

209.2 **[Biography of persons associated with Christianity and Christian thought]**

Use the following table of precedence for comprehensive biographies:

Jesus Christ, Mary, Joseph, Joachim, Anne, John the Baptist	232.9
Other persons in the Bible	220
Founders of denominations	280
Founders of religious orders	271
Higher clergy (e.g., popes, metropolitans, archbishops, bishops) prior to 1054	270.1–.3
Higher clergy subsequent to 1054	280
Theologians	230
Moral theologians	241
Missionaries	266
Evangelists	269.2
Persons noted for participation in associations for religious work	267
Martyrs	272
Heretics	273
Saints	270
Saints prior to 1054	270.1–.3
Saints subsequent to 1054	280
Mystics	248.22
Hymn writers	264.2
Religious educators	268
Members of religious orders	271
Clergy prior to 1054	270.1–.3
Clergy subsequent to 1054	280
Members of the early church to 1054	270.1–.3
Members of denominations	280

This number (209.2) is the last resort for Christian biography. Class here only biographies of persons known not to be members of any church. This number may also be used when it has not been possible to determine whether there is church membership or not. Class in 280 without subdivision church members whose affiliation is not known and members of nondenominational and interdenominational churches.

Do not use 248.2 Religious experience or its subdivisions except 248.22 for comprehensive biographies, e.g., a biography of Teresa of Avila's religious life 282.092, not 248.2092. However, biographical accounts written for devotional purposes, not as comprehensive accounts of a person's life, may be classed in 248.2, e.g., the story of one's conversion 248.246092.

253, 255, and 262.1 are no longer used for biographies of the kinds of persons listed above in the table of precedence.

Certain numbers in the range 220–269 other than those listed in the table of precedence above may be used for comprehensive biographies of persons with specialized religious careers, but are more commonly used for books treating only one aspect of a person's life and work, e.g., 220.092 for a Biblical scholar.

Examples:

270.0922	(Collected biography of saints)
225.92	(New Testament biography) Paul the Apostle
230.2092	(Catholic theology) Saint Thomas Aquinas
232.94	(John the Baptist) John the Baptist
266.2092	(Catholic missions) Saint Francis Xavier
269.2092	(Evangelism) Billy Graham
271.12502	(Trappist order in church history) Thomas Merton
270.2092	(Church history, 325–787) Pope Gregory the Great
283.092	(Anglican churches) Thomas Cranmer
287.092	(Methodist churches) John Wesley

See 291 for non-Christian and comparative religious biographies.

See also 220.92; 230.04 vs. 230.092, 230.1–.9; 232; 280.

212.1 vs. 231.042   **Existence [of God] vs. Ways of knowing God [in Christian theology]**

Class in 212.1 any discussion of proofs of the existence of God based on reason alone, including discussions by Christian theologians, e.g., by Thomas Aquinas. Class proofs of God's existence in 231.042 only if they are treated as part of Christian theology.

220   **Bible**

Biblical theology usually means using the Bible for the basis of Christian or Judaic doctrine and is classed as directed at 220. But if a book on Biblical theology does no more than interpret the text of the Bible, it is classed in 220.6 and cognate numbers in 221–229. The key difference is whether the author adheres to the Biblical text and its meaning, or whether he uses the Biblical text as a springboard to the interpretation of theological concepts.

220.92   **Collected persons [in the Bible]**

Class a comprehensive biography of a Biblical character with the book or books with which the character is most closely associated. In many cases this is the historical part of the Bible in which persons' lives are narrated, e.g., Solomon, King of Israel, in 1st Kings 222.53092. Solomon's association with 223 Poetic books is weaker. However, some Biblical characters are more closely associated with nonhistorical books. For example, class Isaiah and Timothy with the books that bear their names. They appear briefly in historical narratives, but their lives are not narrated in full there. Class the apostles John, Peter, and Paul at 225.92 since each is associated with a number of books in the New Testament, but class the rest of the original Apostles, associated primarily with Gospels and Acts, in 226.092.

See also 209.2

230.04 vs. 230.092, 230.1–.9	**Specific types of Christian theology vs. [Persons treatment of theology] vs. Doctrines of specific denominations and sects**

Use these subdivisions with notation 092 from Table 1 for biography and criticism of individual theologians, e.g., criticism of a United Methodist theologian 230.76092. Class Protestant theologians who are not connected with a specific denomination or who are important and influential enough to transcend their own denominations in 230.044092, e.g., Karl Barth 230.044092. Class theologians not connected with any specific type of theology in 230.092. Class critical appraisal of an individual theologian's thought on a specific topic with the topic, e.g., on justification 234.7092.

230.16–.2	**[Doctrines of Eastern churches, of Roman Catholic Church]**

Class here theology of Eastern and Roman Catholic churches after 1054; for earlier theology, use 230.11–.14.

231.765 vs. 213, 575	**[Christian theology of] Creation vs. Creation [in natural theology] vs. [Organic] evolution and genetics**

Most works on creation science or creationism are classed in 231.765 because they are written by Christians who assume that the Bible provides a chronology of natural history and who attempt to support this interpretation by using arguments from the natural sciences. Works by creationist authors that are limited to criticizing the methods or conclusions of the natural sciences are classed in 500 with the branch of science criticized, even if the criticism is considered unorthodox by most scientists. Works refuting creationism are usually classed in 231.765, unless they take the writings of creationists as a starting point from which to demonstrate the case for evolution. The latter works are classed in 575 or other appropriate numbers in 500.

Other 500 numbers that must sometimes be considered for works of a limited scope concerning evolution are 523.88 (stellar evolution), 551.7 (historical geology), and 560 (paleontology).

Works that consider the relation between divine creation and evolution as a philosophical problem, without appealing to a particular religion or scripture, are classed in 213.

232   Jesus Christ and his family   Christology

Class doctrine and theories about Jesus Christ in 232.1–.8, events in the life of Jesus in 232.9, e.g., the doctrine of the resurrection 232.5, historicity and narration of events surrounding the resurrection 232.97.

Use notation 092 from Table 1 for criticism, biography of Christologists (232.092) and Mariologists (232.91092). Class biography of Jesus, Mary, Joseph, Joachim, Anne, and John the Baptist in 232.9.

241.6 vs.   Specific moral issues vs. Sin and vices [and] Virtues
241.3,
241.4   Class in 241.3–.4 works about sin, about vices and virtues in general, and about specific vices and virtues. Class in 241.6 works treating specific moral issues in such a way that the works cannot be viewed as being about specific vices or virtues. Vices and virtues are habits, e.g., gluttony, temperance. Works on specific moral issues discuss the morality or immorality of specific actions, e.g., whether it is right to eat meat 241.693. In case of doubt, prefer 241.3–.4.

251–254,   Local church [and] Activities of the local church vs. Christian social
259 vs.   and ecclesiastical theology
260
The local church is the group in which individual believers can meet regularly face to face for worship, fellowship, and church activities—for example, a congregation, a college church group.

Among the more recent forms of the local church are the small groups called basic Christian communities or basic ecclesial communities. These are smaller than parishes or congregations, but, like other forms of the local church, are organized for the general religious welfare of their members, not just for special projects or functions. They are classed in the same way as parishes, i.e., comprehensive works are classed in 250 (or in 262.26 when treated as part of ecclesiology) and specific aspects are classed with the aspect in the subdivisions of 250.

Activities undertaken by the church may be classed in 250 or 260, depending on the context. Most of the works in 250 are intended for the individual practitioner in the local setting. The local setting may be as small as a parish youth group or as large as a counseling program that serves a metropolitan area. Class the church's attitude to cultural and social problems, and its activities regarding them in 261 unless the context is limited to the local church, e.g., a practical work for the prison chaplain 259.5, but the church's attitude to the treatment of criminals 261.8336.

Some activities that can be conducted by the local church are classed in 260, e.g., public worship (264–265), religious education (268), spiritual renewal and evangelism (269). The context of works on these subjects is often broader than that of the local church.

Class church organization in 262, unless the scope is limited to administration of the local church (254).

261.5   Christianity and secular disciplines

Class here personal Christian views and church teachings about secular disciplines as a whole, their value, how seriously a Christian should take them, how far the disciplines should affect faith. Class Christian philosophy of a secular discipline or Christian theories within a discipline with the discipline, e.g., a Christian philosophy of psychology 150.1. Be alert for specific uses of secular disciplines for religious purposes, e.g., use of drama 246.7. If in doubt, class with the secular discipline.

Class here works treating generally antagonism between and reconciliation of Christian belief and another discipline. Class antagonism of a specific Christian doctrine and another discipline with the doctrine in 231–239. For example, class the relation between Christian doctrines in general and science in 261.55; but class the relation between Christian doctrine on the soul and modern biology in 233.5.

261.8 vs.   Christianity and socioeconomic problems vs. [Christian] Moral
241   theology

Some topics are covered in both moral and social theology, e.g., family relationships (241.63, 261.83587). Class in 241 works that focus on what conduct is right or wrong. Works classed in 261.8 may discuss right and wrong, but they treat the topic in a broader context as a problem in society and discuss Christian attitudes toward and influence on the problem. Class in 241 works that emphasize what the individual should do; class in 261.8 works that stress what the church's stance should be, or the church's view on problems transcending individual conduct. If in doubt, prefer 241.

280   Denominations and sects of the Christian church

The kinds of biographies to be classed here are shown in the table of precedence for biographies under 209.2.

The Decimal Classification Division classifies biographies with the main branch of the denomination rather than with the most specific organization or area, e.g., a biography of a clergyman of the Lutheran Church in America 284.1092, not 284.133092; of the African Methodist Episcopal Church 287.8092, not 287.83; of a Russian clergyman of the Eastern Orthodox Church 281.9092, not 281.947092; collected biography of Catholics in the United States 282.092273.

280.042 vs. 270.82, 262.0011   **Relations between denominations vs. [Ecumenical movement] vs. Ecumenicalism**

Class in 270.82 the ecumenical movement as part of general church history. Class in 280.042 relations between two or more specific denominations having notation that differs in the first three digits, e.g., relations between Roman Catholics (282) and Lutherans (284.1). Class works about relations among denominations having the same notation in the first three digits in the most specific number that includes them all, e.g., relations among the various Baptist denominations, between Baptists and Disciples of Christ 286. Class works about relations between one denomination and several others with the denomination emphasized, e.g., relations of Baptists with other denominations 286. Class theoretical works on ecumenicalism at 262.0011. Class discussions among denominations with respect to a specific subject with the subject, e.g., the Eucharist 234.163.

281.1–.4   **Early church**

The early church is considered to be undivided by denominations until the schism of 1054. So the history of the Church prior to 1054 is classed in 270.1–.3, not here. The history of specific churches prior to 1054 is classed in 274–279.

283–289   **Protestant and other denominations**

Notation for specific denominations is provided under the general name of some denominations, e.g., Presbyterian churches of United States origin 285.1, specific denominations 285.13. A specific denomination here means a named church body uniting a number of individual local churches, e.g., the Presbyterian Church (U.S.A.) 285.137, the Associate Presbyterian Church of North America 285.13 (the latter denomination is not listed in the schedule). Class specific denominations in the notation provided for them if they are treated with regard to all or nearly all the area they cover. Class specific denominations in the area in which they are treated when they are treated with regard to substantially less area than they cover, e.g., the Hudson River Presbytery 285.17473, a state association of Southern Baptist churches in Tennessee 286.1768. Class individual local churches by area, regardless of the specific denomination to which they belong. Also class a work about several specific denominations in one country by area, e.g., a work describing the various Presbyterian denominations in the United States 285.173, not 285.13.

In several cases, the notation for specific denominations is limited to churches centered in the United States or the United Kingdom, e.g., the numbers following 284.1, 285.1, 285.2 and 287.5. In these cases, specific denominations in other countries are classed by dividing by area. For example, the Evangelical Lutheran Church in America is classed in 284.135, but the Lutheran Church of Sweden is classed in 284.1485 (284.1 plus notation 485 for Sweden from Table 2).

Churches which are centered in the United States or the United Kingdom may have branches in other countries; thus, there are instructions to add any area from Table 2, e.g., at 285.14–.19.

284.143 **Lutheran church in Germany**

Class here Evangelische Kirche in Deutschland, even though some non-Lutheran churches have joined with it.

289.9 **[Other Christian denominations]**

Class nondenominational and interdenominational churches in 280 without subdivision, or at 280.4 if limited to Protestants.

290 **Comparative religion and religions other than Christianity**

290 by itself will never be used, since 291 has been designated as the number for comprehensive works on the non-Christian religions, on Christian and non-Christian religions, and for works on comparative religion.

Note that 200 and standard subdivisions 200.1–.9 are used for religion and religious thought in general, not for the description and analysis of various religions.

291 **Comparative religion**

The subdivisions of the various religions in 292–299 are based on the subdivisions of 291. The order is sometimes different, but all topics in 291 are provided for either explicitly, by synthesis, or by implication under the separate religions included in 292–299. What is said about 291, therefore, will also be true of 292–299.

A comparison of the topics in 291 with the subdivisions of Christianity can sometimes be helpful in determining what goes where. A comparative list follows:

Social theologies	291.17	261
Doctrinal theologies	291.2	230
Public worship	291.3	246–247, 263–265
Religious experience, life, practice	291.4	242, 245, 248
Moral theology	291.5	241
Leaders and organizations	291.6	250, 262, 267
Pastoral theology and work	291.61	253
Missions, religious education	291.7	266, 268
Sources	291.8	220
Denominations, sects, reform movements	291.9	280

A comparison of 291.211 (God, gods, goddesses, other divinities and deities) with 231 (God) shows that 291.211 includes the topics listed at 231 that are not limited to Christianity: ways of knowing God, general concepts of God, attributes, providence, love and wisdom, relation to human experience, justice, and goodness.

Treat the early history of a specific religion before its division into sects as general history of the religion, but class a comprehensive survey of the various sects in the number for the sects of the religion, e.g., the sects and reform movements of Judaism 296.8. A work dealing with both early history and sects is classed in the general number for history of the religion.

Class the history of a specific congregation in the number for the sect to which it belongs, if this can be determined. ("Congregation" here refers to organizations in other religions analogous to the local church in Christianity, e.g., synagogues, mosques.) If the sect cannot be determined, class the work in the broadest number for the sects of the religion. For example, the history of a Jewish synagogue and its congregation, which may have changed sects over the years or whose sect cannot be determined, is classed in 296.83 (modern Jewish sects). In such a case do not add standard subdivisions.

Class religious orders in 291.65 and cognate numbers in 292–299, and not with any sect within the religion to which they may belong.

Biography

Persons associated with the religions in 292–299 are often identified with a number of religious functions and activities. A Hindu guru, for example, may be thought of as a theologian, a teacher, a missionary or a clergyman. If a religious leader cannot be identified primarily with one function, activity, or sect, class his biography in the base number for the religion and add notation 092 from Table 1. For comprehensive biographies of persons of an identifiable function, activity, or sect, use the following table of precedence.

Divinely inspired persons, founders of religions	291.63
Founders of sects	291.9092
Founders of religious orders	291.65
Religious leaders	291.092
Of specific sects	291.9092
Theologians	291.2092
Moral theologians	291.5092
Missionaries	291.7092
Martyrs, heretics, saints	291.092
Of specific sects	291.9092
Teachers	291.7092
Members of religious orders	291.65
Clergy	291.9092
Members of sects and movements	291.9092

Except for founders of religions (291.63) and founders of religious orders (291.65), the subdivisions of 291.6 are not used for biography, but for the nature, role, and function of religious leaders.

Works dealing with only one specialized aspect of a person's career are classed with the aspect, e.g., Muhammad as a moral theologian 297.5092 (not 297.63).

291.09 vs. 294, 299.5   **Historical, geographical, persons treatment [of Comparative religion] vs. Religions of Indic origin vs. [Religions] Of East and Southeast Asian origin**

294 and 299.5 refer to religions that originated in particular geographic areas. Most of these religions have spread beyond the area where they originated. The areas also have adherents of religions that originated elsewhere, e.g., Buddhism (from India) in China. If a work covers various religious traditions in an area, not just the religions that originated there, class it in 291 and use notation 09 from Table 1. For example, the religions of India (including Christianity and Islam) 291.0954, of China (including Christianity and Buddhism) 291.0951.

300 Social sciences

Sociology 301–307 is the study of the processes, interactions, groups, culture, and cultural institutions that give form and purpose to every society. Part of the subject matter of sociology is found in 390 Customs, etiquette, folklore.

Some of the raw data for the study of human society is found in 310 Statistics, which constitutes a displacement of a standard subdivision concept from 300.21. Statistics on specific social subjects, however, are scattered throughout 300, using notation 021 from Table 1, e.g., demographic statistics 304.6021.

In order to maintain internal peace and safety from external threat, societies devise political processes and institutions such as the state and government. These are dealt with in 320 Political science and in 350–354, the latter dealing with the executive branch of government and public administration. The military arm of government is found in 355–359.

The production, distribution, and consumption of the goods and services needed to maintain society are dealt with in 330 Economics. Part of this discipline is also found in 380–382, that part which deals with commerce and trade. Also found in the 380s are two of the major auxiliaries to commerce: communication 383–384 and transportation 385–388.

Law 340 treats the codified social, political, and economic rules that society requires and by which its members agree to live.

No social structure, however good, is perfect. Social problems are inevitable. The nature of these problems, taken together with the services society performs to overcome them, are dealt with in the 360s.

Education 370 is one of the means through which society attempts to socialize the young and to prepare them for a useful role in the life of the society.

300 vs. 600 Social sciences vs. Technology

Many topics can be discussed from either a technological or a social point of view. If a work discusses how to make, operate, maintain, or repair something, it is normally classed in technology. If, on the other hand, it discusses the social implications of a technological operation, it falls in the social sciences, e.g., the economic importance of lumbering 338.17498, not 634.98.

Class the social utilization, the social control, and the social effect of technology in 300. The distinction between social science and technology is especially difficult for works on technology and its use or control, works that fall somewhere along the continuum from technology at one end to social science at the other. This is particularly true of regulatory control and popular works.

The following criteria will be useful in determining what material should be classed in 300 rather than 600:

1. When the emphasis in on the social use of the topic rather than on operating or processing it, e.g., tea drinking in England 394.12, not 641.33720942 or 641.63720942.

2. When the emphasis is on the overall perspective, e.g., the shift from coal to oil in American industry 333.82130973, not 621.4023.

3. When the emphasis is on social control as opposed to the control exercised during the manufacturing process, e.g., standards of drug quality imposed by a government agency or a trade association 363.1946, not 615.19.

4. When the raw statistics are cited, e.g., crop production, acreage, fertilizer consumption, farm size, use 338.1, not 631.

Technical reports

Many technical and research reports actually emphasize procedural technicalities and may refer to economic, legal, administrative, or regulatory complexities. Such reports should be classed in the social sciences. In determining the classification of a report series, and of individual reports in a series, consider the purpose of the writer and the mission of the agency authorizing the reports. If the emphasis is on the exercise of social control over a process, the report is classed in 300, not with the process in technology which is being controlled. For example, water quality monitoring systems are more likely to be 363.739463 than 628.161.

It cannot be stressed too strongly that most of the social sciences are involved in technological processes, but are quite distinct from them. The classifier must go behind the technological vocabulary that often dominates title pages and tables of contents and analyze what is being described. A book on trains is not classed in 625.2 if it describes how railroads serve Argentina, but in 385.0982; and a report on fertilizer and rice is not classed in 633.18891 if it is studying production efficiency in developing countries, but in 338.162.

Interdisciplinary works

Generally speaking, the 300 number is the interdisciplinary number for a phenomenon of social significance; it is used as the place of last resort for general works on a subject lacking disciplinary focus, e.g., a work on industrial archaeology not emphasizing how things were made 338.47609 rather than 609. However, works that emphasize descriptions of products or structures, such as clocks, locomotives, windmills, are classed in technology.

Biography and company history

Works on artisans, engineers, and inventors are normally classed in technology. Works on artisans, engineers, and inventors who are of more interest as entrepreneurs are classed in 338.7, e.g., Henry Ford 338.76292092.

Many works on products concentrate on the products of specific companies, e.g., Seth Thomas clocks or Ferrari automobiles. So long as these works emphasize the description and design of the products, class them in technology (or art 700 if the interest is artistic). But as soon as the organization or history of the company receives significant attention, class the works in 338.7, e.g., Seth Thomas clocks 681.113097461, but the Seth Thomas Clock Company and its clocks 338.7681113097461.

301 **Sociology and anthropology**

Sociology is the description and analysis of social phenomena. A work on social phenomena is classed in 301–307 even if it being studied in a special context, e.g., in a political or economic institution. For instance, a descriptive work on family patterns of members of the executive branch of government is classed at 306.87; on the social role of political institutions in Korea at 306.209519; on the use of power among committee chairmen of a national legislature at 306.23.

See also 305 vs. 306, 909, 930–990 for aspects of anthropology.

301 vs. **Sociology and anthropology vs. Social problems and services**
361–365

To be classed in 301–307 works on social phenomena must deal exclusively, or almost exclusively, with the phenomenon in its pure state, i.e., its social background, its role in the social structure, its effects on society, its innate characteristics and inner structure.

Consideration of social pathology apart from remedial measures is often found in 301–307, but is more likely to be considered in connection with actual and potential remedies found in the 361–365 span. The family as a social phenomenon is classed in 306.85. The dissolution of the family can be classed in either 306.88 or 362.82 depending on the focus of the work. A work discussing the effect of the changing social role of women in bringing about family dissolution is classed at 306.88. Once this topic begins to be considered as a problem about which something should be done, the work is classed in 362.82, e.g., what can or should be done to prevent family dissolution 362.827. If in doubt, prefer 361–365 over 301–307 for social problems.

Note that criminal anthropology (criminal sociology) is found in 364.2.

302–307 Specific topics in sociology and anthropology

Topics in sociology and anthropology are arranged in a sequence that moves from the general to the specific. The most general topics and those most applied to other topics come first, followed in order by the less general and less applied, ending with the ones most often subject to analysis by the preceding topics. Social interaction, covering the basic forms of behavior in groups and between groups is found in 302; social processes that must be maintained so that society can continue, in 303, consideration of environment and population that affects development of all societies, in 304; the social groups, classes, and kinds of persons that make society possible, in 305; the culture and institutions that are the framework within which groups carry on the processes, in 306; and geographically restricted communities studied in various ways but always considered as whole communities, in 307.

302.2308 History and description [of Media (Means of communication)] with respect to kinds of persons

For the effects of mass media upon social groups, the rule that the effect of one subject on another is classed with the subject affected is reversed, since discussion of the social processes of mass media cannot be separated from their effects on society and on the various groups that constitute society. Thus, a work about the effect of television on young people is primarily about the role of television in society (and often about the issues involved in altering the impact of that role), and only secondarily about the effect on young people. This principle holds true for all groups and all media, e.g., the effect of radio on the life style of the middle class 302.234408622.

303.372 vs. 170 Customs and belief systems vs. Ethics (Moral philosophy)

Social ethics may be a subject in either moral philosophy or in methods of social control. Class social ethics in 303.372 when considered as a system of beliefs influencing society and its institutions, but in 170 when considered as a philosophical matter or as a rule of personal conduct. 303.372 is descriptive, while 170 is prescriptive. Class interdisciplinary works in 170.

303.376 vs. **Censorship [as social control] vs. Censorship and control of**
363.31, **information vs. Motion pictures, radio, television**
791.4

Class in 303.376 theories of censorship and sociological studies of censorship of movies, radio, and television. Class in 363.31 censorship of movies and programs after being released or aired. Class in 791.4 censoring films and programs as they are being produced, e.g., censorship through editing. If in doubt, class in 363.31.

303.483 vs. **Development of science and technology [as causes of social change]**
306.45, **vs. Science [and] Technology [as cultural institutions]**
306.46

Class in 303.483 the effects of scientific discoveries and technological innovations upon society, e.g., a work on the transformation of religious, economic, and leisure institutions stemming from the development of electronic media 303.4833. Class in 306.45 or 306.46 the patterns of behavior of the individuals and groups engaged in scientific or technical endeavors, e.g., a description of the milieu which seems to be conducive to technological innovation 306.46. If in doubt between the two subjects, prefer 303.483 and its subdivisions.

304.66 vs. **Demographic effects of population control efforts vs. Population**
363.9 **problems**

Class in 304.66 the effects upon society of control efforts by its members, regardless of whether or not society sanctions the effort, e.g., infanticide practiced in ancient Greece 304.6680938. But class in 363.9 programs or policies that are discussed as population control efforts, e.g., Athenian efforts to promote population growth after the Peloponnesian War 363.9109385. If in doubt, prefer 363.9

305 vs. 306, **Social groups vs. Culture and institutions vs. World history [and]**
909, **History of ancient world, of specific continents, countries, localities;**
930–990 **of extraterrestrial worlds**

305 is the comprehensive number for social groups interacting more or less freely with the rest of society, and is used for the totality of the culture and institutions of specific groups except as provided in 306.08. The role of social groups in specific institutions of society, however, is classed with the institution in 306, using notation 08 from Table 1 if appropriate, e.g., women as a social category 305.4, but women in the family 306.85082; the status of serfs in society 305.563, but serfs in agricultural systems of labor 306.365 (where notation 08625 is redundant); improvement of the status of homosexuals in society, 305.90664, but sexual institutions and orientation of homosexuals 306.766 (where notation 08664 is redundant). The role of social groups in history is classed in 900. The history of specific social groups, particularly that part of their history which is called their civilization, is more troublesome. Class in 900 only accounts of the major events shaping the his-

tory and civilization of a group. Normally, "history" is written only about racial, ethnic, and national groups, while "civilization" of all social groups tends to equate more with their culture (broadly conceived) than with the major events of their history. But be alert for exceptions: histories of major events, and description of nonanthropological civilization can be written for any group. If in doubt between 305 and 900, prefer 305; if in doubt between 305 and 306, prefer 306.

The following table indicates the general relation among these numbers and other related ones:

Anthropology	301
Cultural and social anthropology	306
Of specific groups	305
Unassimilated indigenous ethnic groups	306.08
Physical anthropology	573
Criminal anthropology	364.2
Ethnology, cultural ethnology	305.8
Of unassimilated indigenous ethnic groups	306.08
History of specific ethnic groups	909.04
In specific countries	930–990
Social situation and conditions	306
In specific areas	306.09
Of specific groups	305
Specific unassimilated indigenous ethnic groups	306.08

305.9 vs. 305.5   **Occupational and miscellaneous groups vs. Social classes**

Social classes take precedence over occupational and miscellaneous groups. Therefore, whenever a group found in 305.9 is considered in terms of its specific social status, 305.5 must be used. Use 305.9 for works on its component groups when either

1. There is little or no emphasis on class,

2. The group is well represented in two or more distinct classes, or

3. The group has an indefinite or transitional status.

If in doubt, prefer 305.9 for its component classes.

306.08 vs. 305.8   **[Culture and institutions of] Indigenous racial, ethnic, national groups vs. Racial, ethnic, national groups [as social groups]**

Use 305.8 as the comprehensive number for specific racial, ethnic, national groups which interact more or less freely (whether in a dominant, nondominant, or intermediate position) with the rest of society. Use 306.089 only for indigenous groups living in distinct communities or "tribal areas" not fully integrated into the economic and social life of the nation in which they are (often involuntarily) incorporated. Such groups are normally perceived as culturally autonomous societies with their own distinctive cultures and institutions. If in doubt, prefer 305.8.

306.4 vs.
306

Cultural institutions vs. Culture and institutions

306.4 represents culture in its narrower, more everyday sense, as in "popular culture" or "high culture." It refers to the intellectual, artistic, recreational, and skilled activities of people. In contrast, 306 represents culture in its broadest sense, referring to the sum total of the activities by which society maintains, controls, and directs itself. To be classed in 306.4, a work should largely be limited to what is indicated in subdivisions of the number, and should only incidentally consider other aspects of life, e.g., work and marriage. If in doubt, prefer 306.

307

[Sociology of] Communities

This section includes works on the community in a relatively restricted area as a social phenomenon and works on community planning, development, and redevelopment. These terms are used here in their ordinary meaning to imply the planning for and development of the community as a whole. When specific subjects of community interest are addressed, the work is classed elsewhere in 300, e.g., economic development of the community 338.93–.99, developing hospitals for the community 362.11, planning community housing 363.5525, planning the city water supply 363.61, planning the education system 379.4–.9.

307.336 vs.
307.34,
363.5

Residential use vs. [Community] Redevelopment vs. Housing [problems and services]

Class in 307.336 the descriptive analysis of housing patterns that touches upon problems only in the larger context. Class in 363.5 works on housing problems and solutions addressed specifically to housing. However, class in 307.34 works addressing housing problems in the context of restructuring whole communities. If in doubt, prefer 363.5 over the other two numbers, and 307.34 over 307.336.

320   **Political science (Politics and government)**

The state and government

The concepts of "the state" and "government" are emphasized in varying proportions in the subdivisions in 320–323. The state refers to the politically organized body of people occupying a more or less definite territory, while government (in the sense relevant here) is the organization through which the state exercises its authority and functions. The state may be considered an abstraction, the government its concrete embodiment. Comprehensive works on the abstraction are classed in 320.1; specific kinds of states in 321.01–.08; and the relation of the state to people (and *vice versa*) in 322–323, e.g., civil rights 323.4.

In contrast to "the state," the concept of "government" is more central to political science, and the word is often used loosely as an approximate equivalent of political science, so it has no separate number. However, specific aspects do have separate numbers, notably comparative government in 320.3, structure and functions of government in 320.4, and kinds of government in 321.3–.9.

Most political theories transcend the distinction between the state and government, and are classed in 320.011 or with ideologies in 320.5. *See also 320.011 vs. 320.5.*

320 vs. 302–307

Political science (Politics and government) vs. Specific topics in sociology and anthropology

Some works on major social institutions, processes, and phenomena may have a decidedly political cast, but if they emphasize how the social topics are related to and manifested in political ones, they are classed in 302–307. For example, a work on the relation between the feminist movement and the enfranchisement of women is classed in 305.42, not 324.623.

320 vs. 306.2

Political science (Politics and government) vs. [Sociology of] Political institutions

Be alert for works that discuss not politics and government but the social dynamics of political institutions. The basic thrust of 306.2 is to find out the social sources (e.g., race, class, family) and the social processes of political institutions, or the impact of these institutions and their activity upon the social environment. In addition, it is used for works dealing with political institutions and processes as models for social institutions and processes. In contrast, the objective of 320 is the descriptive, comparative, historical, and theoretical study of political institutions and processes. In these political studies, the social environment is considered only as a background. While 306.2 is the comprehensive number, use 320 if in doubt between the two.

320 vs. 909, 930–990

Political science (Politics and government) vs. World history [and] History of ancient world; of specific continents, countries, localities; of extraterrestrial worlds

Politics

In the subheading "Politics and government," the word "politics" adds to "government" the concepts of adjusting relationships among individuals and groups in a political community, guiding and influencing the policy of government, and winning and holding control of society. More of the subdivisions of 320 are used for politics in the broad sense than are used for state or government. While the number 320 is used for comprehensive works on politics in the broad sense, most works on politics in the sense of party politics fall in 324.

Political history

Political history with an emphasis on major political events typified by the "battles, kings, and dates" school of history is clearly 900. Political history with an emphasis on the mechanics of give and take of political forces and movements and on their internal development is usually classed in 320.9, but if the forces and movements come to power or bring about major changes in society, their successes or failures become general history, and should be classed in 900.

Political activities

The sum total of political activity of a specific period or place is also considered general history, and is classed in 909 and 930–990. Various subdivisions of 320 include material on important political activities when considered in terms of the discipline "political science," but whenever an activity is discussed in a manner which highlights its influence on general events 900 must be considered. The general rule is: Important events and leaders with wide-ranging responsibilities are classed in general history, unless considered primarily in the context of a specific subject. The chief problems concern three numbers: 320.9, 324, and 328:

320.9: Under political situation and conditions there can be works on habitual activities and styles of leading political figures as a group, and on the activities reflecting the adjustment of political forces or the status of political parties and movements. But when the activities are analyzed in terms of their effect on general events, use 900.

324: Party histories are classed in 324.2; and histories of nomination and election campaigns, in 324.5 and 324.9, respectively, but only when they concern largely internal events of the parties and campaigns, or report winners, losers, and votes. A history of how a party or candidate came to power (or almost did), or a discussion of how party and campaign events move nations (or other areas) in certain directions is classed in 900.

328: Histories of specific legislative bodies are classed in 328.4–.9, but only when they are largely limited to what happened within or to the bodies, without significant consideration of what the legislative body did for the political unit it served. The accomplishments of a given legislative session are normally a matter of general history and are classed in 900, but if a work concentrates on the body's internal history it is classed in 328. While the report of proceedings of a legislature (i.e., its motions, debates, actions) may constitute the raw material of history, it is not in itself general history, and remains in 328.

Politics of specific subjects

Political activities relating to specific problems, issues, and organizations are classed with the subject in social science, e.g., the politics of immigration 325.1, of the banking system 332.1, of welfare policy 361.61. However, the politics of an administrative agency is classed in the subject which it administers, not with the subject in public administration (unless there is no alternative), e.g., the politics of the U.S. Federal Aviation Administration 387.7068, not 353.008777.

320.011 vs. **General [political] theory; systems vs. Political ideologies**
320.5

The distinction between general theory and political ideologies is more straightforward than might appear, since in most cases authors define themselves. Class in 320.5 the schools of thought that are more or less prescriptive, and that, at least potentially, provide the rallying themes of political movements seeking to organize or reorganize the state and government in characteristic ways. Class in 320.011 theory that is more analytical, or that attempts to define the purposes of government rather than to recommend how to achieve these purposes. If in doubt between the two for a theory that is not named in 320.5, prefer 320.011.

320.5 vs. **Political ideologies vs. Political situation and conditions vs. The**
320.9, 324 **political process**

The noun "movement" is used in various different senses in each of these numbers, and a given ideological movement may be treated in subdivisions of any one of them depending upon the emphasis of the work. Use 320.5 for works concerning the thought and internal history or dynamics of such movements, 324 for their attempts to achieve power by nonviolent means and their ventures into electoral politics (even as splinter parties with scant chance of success), and 320.9 for the impact of the movements upon the political system and their interaction with other political forces. Class comprehensive works on specific ideological movements in 320.5, but if in doubt, give preference first to 324, then to 320.9. However, also consider history numbers for movements which come to power or directly affect the major events of history.

See also 320 vs. 909, 930–990.

322.1 vs. **[Relation of the state to] Religious organizations and groups vs.**
261.7, **Christianity and political affairs [and] Religions and political affairs**
291.177

The difference lies in the perspective. 261.7, 291.177 and similar numbers in 292–299 are in social theology, and are used for works on the position religious people and organizations take or should take toward political affairs (including the state). 322.1 is used for works with a secular perspective, discussing the relationships between religious organizations or movements and states or governments. If in doubt, class in 322.1.

323.46 vs.
361.614

Economic rights (Property) vs. Welfare and human rights

Use 323.46 for welfare rights when the term refers to economic rights such as equal opportunity to employment; use 361.614 when the term refers to rights to welfare services. Use 361.614 for comprehensive works on welfare rights.

324.1 vs.
324.2,
324.209,
324.21

International party organizations, auxiliaries, activities vs. Political parties [and] Historical, geographical, persons treatment [of political parties and] Kinds of parties

For international treatment of parties, a distinction is made between collected accounts of national parties (324.2, or 324.209 for specific continents or regions and 324.21 for specific kinds of parties), and the organizations which parties and their activists create to promote party activities and influence on an international scale (324.1). The material which belongs in 324.1 is usually quite distinctive, since it concentrates on international organizations and their goals and influence, while generally considering specific national parties only in passing. Comprehensive works on national parties and international organizations are classed in 324.2.

324.24–.29
and
324.209

Parties in specific countries in modern world [and] Historical, geographical, persons treatment [of political parties]

For political parties, the three kinds of areas that are usually treated in a single span (continents, countries, and localities) are treated in three different ways. They are differentiated because the country (nation) is the main effective unit of political activity, and thus of party life and power. In most countries the local party is a branch of the national party, or, at most, a local organization of persons who regard themselves as members of a national party. The order of precedence used to express the subordination of local party organization is country (nation), then topic (party), then locality.

Treatment by continent and by region larger than a specific country is classed in 324.209 (or in 324.21 for specific kind of party). Treatment by country is classed in 324.24–.29, using area notation for country taken directly from Table 2. Treatment by locality within a country is classed in the country number, with use of notation 09 from Table 1 at the appropriate point. In Canada, the United States, and Australia, each of which have strong traditions of autonomy for state and provincial parties, the states and provinces are treated like ''countries'' rather than like ''localities.''

For example, parties of all parts of the United Kingdom are found under 324.241 and its zero subdivisions. The Conservative Party is classed in 324.24104, the Conservative Party in Wales in 324.2410409429 (not 324.242904). Sectionalist and separatist parties are classed by the same rule, but in the absence of a specific number for them the specific local area number cannot be added. A separatist party of Wales is classed simply in 324.241098 (the final 8 being derived from notation 08 in the table under 324.24–.29), of Catalonia in 324.24608. Comprehensive works on parties of a specific part of a nation are classed in the national number, using modified standard subdivision 009, e.g., parties of Wales 324.241009429, of Catalonia 324.246009467.

In the three countries provided with state and provincial spans, regions and localities are subordinated to national or state and provincial numbers depending upon relative size, e.g., the Democratic party in the Midwest 324.27360977, in New York City 324.274706097471.

324.24–.29 Parties in specific countries in modern world

If in doubt between parties identified primarily by position on the right to left spectrum (03–07 from the add table) and other recent parties (08 from the add table), prefer 08.

324.6 vs. 342.07 Election systems and procedures vs. Election law

Use 324.6 for manuals outlining procedures for the conduct of elections. However, if laws or administrative regulations for elections, or legal discussions of them, are discussed to any significant extent, use 342.07. If in doubt, prefer 342.07.

331 vs. 331.8 Labor economics vs. Labor unions (Trade unions), labor-management (collective) bargaining and disputes

Industrial relations in the broad sense of all relations between management and individual employees or employee groups is classed in 331. Industrial relations in the narrow sense of relations between management and labor unions is classed in 331.8.

331.13704 vs. 331.1372 Kinds of unemployment vs. Causes of unemployment

Kinds of unemployment are frequently defined in terms of their causes. Class a specific cause that defines a kind of unemployment with the kind, e.g., structural causes of unemployment 331.137041 (not 331.1372). Class comprehensive works on causes of unemployment in 331.1372.

332 vs. 338, 658.15   **Financial economics vs. Production vs. Financial management**

The choice among 332, 338, and 658.15 depends upon the point of view from which the topics are treated. Class in 332 works treating financial topics from the viewpoint of people or organizations with money to invest and those who serve them—investors, bankers, stock-brokers, and the like. Class in 338 works that treat financial topics from the viewpoint of people concerned with the production of goods and services, people who are interested in capital because it is neces-sary for production. For example, class in 332.6722 (domestic invest-ment in specific types of enterprise) a work discussing whether mining is a safe and profitable field of investment for the general public; but class in 338.23 (financial aspects of extraction of minerals) a work dis-cussing whether the mining industry will attract enough investment to expand production. Class in 658.15 (or with the subject, using notation 0681 from Table 1) works that treat financial topics from the viewpoint of an executive responsible for the financial management of an organi-zation, works that focus narrowly on managerial concerns.

332.024 vs. 640.42   **Personal finance vs. [Personal] Management of money**

Class in 640.42 works that deal only with everyday household finance, e.g., how to control day-to-day expenditures, how to budget for rent and groceries. Class in 332.024 works that are broader in scope, e.g., how to plan for one's financial future, including such topics as insurance and IRAs (Individual Retirement Accounts). Class interdis-ciplinary works in 332.024.

332.41 vs. 339.41, 339.42   **Value of money vs. Income and its relation to consumption [and] Cost of living (Prices)**

Class in 332.41 works on purchasing power that focus on the value of money as measured by the goods and services it can buy. Class in 339.41–.42 works on purchasing power that focus on the ability of con-sumers to buy. If in doubt, prefer 339.41–.42.

332.632044 vs. 332.6323   **General types of securities vs. Bonds**

In American usage the term ''gilt-edged securities'' may refer to any security of exceptionally high quality, or it may refer primarily to high-quality bonds. Works on all types of gilt-edged securities are classed in 332.632044, works on bonds in 332.6323. In British usage the term ''gilt-edged securities'' refers to government bonds. Works on that topic are classed in 332.63232.

332.6322 vs. 332.6323   **Stocks (Shares) vs. Bonds**

In British usage the term ''stocks'' usually refers to bonds rather than shares, but in American usage the term always refers to shares. Class stocks in the sense of shares in 332.6322, stocks in the sense of bonds in 332.6323.

332.7 vs.   **Credit vs. Banks and banking**
332.1

At 332.7 credit is divided by the type of credit, e.g., agricultural credit, home finance, personal loans, credit cards. At 332.1 (including 332.2 and 332.3, which are logically subordinate to 332.1), credit is divided by the type of financial institution offering it as a service, e.g., commercial banks, savings and loan associations, consumer finance institutions, insurance companies. Comprehensive works on a particular type of credit are classed in 332.7, e.g., a work discussing home mortgages as issued by commercial banks, mutual savings banks, savings and loan associations, and insurance companies 332.722. Comprehensive works on the credit offered by a particular type of institution and works discussing only one type of credit offered by a particular type of institution are both classed with the institution in 332.1–.3. For example, a work discussing all the kinds of loans and debit cards available from savings and loan associations and a work discussing the home mortgages available from savings and loan associations are both classed in 332.32. Similarly, comprehensive works on credit cards offered by commercial banks, department stores, oil companies, and travel agencies are classed in 332.765, but works about credit cards issued by commercial banks are classed in 332.178.

333.1–.5 vs.   **Ownership and control of land and other natural resources vs.**
333.73–.78   **[Land]**

Land as property is classed in 333.1–.5, where the central issues are the right to possession and use, and the right to transfer possession and use. The only control of land and resources that belongs in 333.1–.5 is the control that stems from ownership.

Land as a natural resource, as a source of economic goods (chiefly agricultural and mineral), is classed in 333.73–.78. The usage of the land and its resources is classed there, as distinct from the right to use that is classed in 333.1–.5. The controls of usage that hold regardless of who owns the land are classed in 333.73–.78, with notation 17 from the add table under 333.7. Price control and zoning are among the controls covered by notation 17.

Land inventories often focus on land as a resource and land usage; such inventories are classed in 333.73–.78.

Comprehensive works on both 333.1–.5 and 333.73–.78 concepts are classed in 333.

333.1–.5 vs.   **Ownership and control of land and natural resources vs. [Law of]**
346.043   **Real property**

Class economic aspects of the various forms of ownership, use and transfer of land in 333.1–.5. Class legal aspects in 346.043. If in doubt, prefer 346.043.

333.7–.9   **[Natural resources and energy]**

Consumption, development, and control of usage of natural resources are classed in 333.7–.9, with notation from the add table under 333.7. Consequently, some works discussing natural resources that are no longer in their natural state are properly classed in 333.7–.9, e.g., works about the economics of uses of urban lands 333.77.

333.75 vs.   **Forest lands vs. [Products of forestry]**
338.1749

Several of the concepts provided at 333.75 by virtue of the add table under 333.7 potentially conflict with concepts provided at 338.1749. The general distinction is that works classed in 333.75 are primarily concerned with forest land and uncut timber as present and future resources, whereas works classed in 338.1749 are primarily concerned with cut timber as a product to be sold. Class comprehensive works in 338.1749.

Use of add table under 333.7

11   Reserves (Stock, Supply)

Class in 333.7511 the supply of forest land and uncut timber, in 338.17498 the supply of cut timber.

12   Requirements (Need, Demand)

Class in 333.7512 the demand for timber discussed in terms of its effect on the supply of forest land and uncut timber. Class in 338.17498 the demand for timber discussed in terms of how much timber will have to be cut in order to meet the demand.

13   Consumption (Use, Utilization)

Class in 333.7513 use and abuse discussed in terms of the effect it has on the future supply of uncut timber. Class in 338.17498 utilization of forests to provide products for sale.

15   Development

Class in 333.7515 measures to increase the supply of forests as a long-term resource, e.g., reforestation 333.75153. Class in 338.174956 reforestation viewed as a way to produce crops that can be harvested and sold.

333.8 vs.   Subsurface resources vs. Extraction of minerals vs. Economic
338.2, 553   geology

For subsurface resources, class reserves in nature in appropriate subdivisions of 553, e.g., reserves of oil that have never been pumped out of the ground 553.282. Use notation 11 Reserves (Stock, Supply) from the add table at 333.7 with subdivisions of 333.8 only for reserves in storage, e.g., crude oil stored in salt caves as a strategic reserve and crude oil in tanks awaiting refinement both 333.823211. Class works treating equally reserves in nature and in storage in 553. Do not class any sort of reserves in 338.2.

Class requirements (need, demand) for subsurface resources in 333.8, using notation 12 from the add table at 333.7. Do not class demand in 338.2 or 553.

Do not use notation 15 Development from the add table under 333.7 with subdivisions of 333.8, because there is no development of subsurface resources comparable to that possible with other types of resources. New coal mines cannot be grown. What is often referred to as development is almost always some form of extraction, which is classed in 338.2.

333.94 vs.   Space [as a natural resource] vs. [Economics of production in space]
338.0919

Class in 333.94 works that discuss space as a scarce resource analogous to land or air, for example, because there are a limited number of good positions for geostationary satellites, because we cannot afford to fill the space around the earth with orbiting garbage. Class in 338.0919 comprehensive works on the industrialization of space, e.g., works that discuss transportation and manufacturing in space.

333.954 vs   Animal resources vs. [Products derived from nondomesticated
338.37   animals]

Several of the concepts provided at 333.954 (and 333.955–.959) by virtue of the add table under 333.7 potentially conflict with concepts provided at 338.37. To distinguish between the two numbers, apply the same general criteria as explained at 333.75 vs. 338.1749. For example, class the supply of uncaught animals in 333.95411 (333.954 plus notation 11 Reserves [Stock, Supply]). Class the supply of caught animals in 338.37. Works classed in 333.95411 may, however, use statistics of catches as an aid in estimating the population of uncaught animals.

Class measures to increase the supply of animals in nature as a long-term resource in 333.954 or 333.955–.959, using the notation 15 Development, e.g., stocking mountain streams with fish 333.95615. Class the culture of nondomesticated animals viewed as a way to produce crops that can be harvested and sold in 338.371. Do not use

338.372 (Products of fishing, whaling, hunting, trapping) for measures to increase the supply of animals.

335 vs. 320.53, 306.345

Socialism and related systems [of economics] vs. Collectivism and fascism [as political ideologies] vs. [Sociology of] Socialism [as an economic system]

Since socialism and related systems are based upon theories of how the economy does or should work, interdisciplinary works and works on their philosophical foundations are classed in 335. The number is also used for wide-ranging works that do not fit within normal disciplinary boundaries but are clearly about socialism and related systems. Other numbers are used only for works clearly limited to a specific discipline.

Use 320.53 for works that emphasize how political movements intend to introduce socialism and what political forces they expect to harness to attain and keep power, or that discuss political movements and forces without in-depth discussion of the economic dynamics or theory. Works on political ideology often discuss questions such as the class bias or motivation of political forces, the dependability of political allies of different economic background, and progress (or lack of it) toward economic goals, but do not usually get into economics *per se*.

In contrast to 306.345, both the other numbers may include material that is prescriptive, that says how society, the economy, or the political system ought to be organized. 306.345 is intended for sociological studies of how socialist economic systems work out in practice. It should be limited to such studies. Works discussing how another economic system should be reorganized into a socialist system must be classed in 335.

335.4 vs. 335.401, 335.411

Marxian systems vs. Philosophy and related topics [of Marxian systems] vs. Philosophic foundations [of Marxian systems]

General works on theory of Marxian systems are classed in 335.4. Works that emphasize the philosophic foundations of Marxian systems are classed in 335.411. 335.401 is rarely used, except for its subdivisions, e.g., 335.4014 for Marxist terminology. If in doubt, prefer 335.4.

336 vs. 351.72

Public finance vs. [Public] Financial management

Class in 351.72 works focusing on the practical aspects and details of financial management and accounting in the public sector. For example, class budget estimates of expenditures, administrative reports of actual expenditures, and works on how to prepare them in subdivisions of 351.72. Class in 336 works on the economics of public finance, e.g., economic analyses of government spending policy 336.39. Class works treating both public finance and public financial administration in 336.

336.2 vs.
351.724,
343.04

Taxes and taxation vs. Tax administration vs. Tax law

Most works on taxes, especially popular works, are classed in law, because they explain what the law allows and prohibits. For example, a work for taxpayers about U.S. income tax deductions is classed in 343.730523. Tax administration, which includes especially the administration of assessment and collection, is classed in 351.724, e.g., real property tax assessors' manuals 351.72421. Works on the economics of taxes and interdisciplinary works on taxes are classed in 336.2, e.g., an economic and political analysis of U.S. tax policy 336.200973.

336.249 vs.
368.401,
368.4011

Social security taxes [in public finance] vs. [Finance of social security and Rates and rate making for social security]

Class broad economic aspects of social security taxes in 336.249. Class actuarial and administrative aspects of finance for social security in 368.401, of rates and rate making for social security in 368.4011.

337.1 vs.
337.3—.9

Multilateral economic cooperation vs. Foreign economic policies and relations of specific jurisdictions and groups of jurisdictions

Class cooperative relations among the states of multistate groups in 337.1, e.g., cooperation within the European Common Market in 337.142; but class relations between a cooperative group treated as a whole and other countries or groups in 337.3—.9, e.g., economic relations of the Common Market with Japan 337.4052 (not 337.142), economic relations of the Common Market with the rest of the world 337.4 (not 337.142).

338.09 vs.
338.6042,
332.67309,
346.07,
658.11,
658.21,
T1—068

Historical, geographical, persons treatment of production vs. Location [of production] vs. Historical, geographical, persons treatment [of international investment] vs. Commercial law vs. [Management of] Initiation of business enterprises vs. [Management of plant] Location and [Table 1 notation for] Management

Class in 338.09 works showing where industry is in fact located. Class in 338.6042 the rationale for and the process of locating business organizations. A useful device in distinguishing the two is to consider location in 338.09 to be a condition, in 338.6042 an action.

Class in 332.67309 works describing the advantages and disadvantages of making international investments, including establishing international enterprises, in particular areas.

Class in 346.07 laws and regulations for governing investment in and initiation of businesses.

Class in 658.11 or with the subject using notation 0681 from Table 1 works on managerial techniques for locating a new business that treat multiple issues, e.g., tax and labor laws in various jurisdictions, location of markets, location of sources of raw materials and skilled labor. Class in 658.21 or with the subject using notation 0682 from Table 1 works limited to managerial techniques for locating the physical plant itself, with emphasis on a location that will facilitate good plant management, e.g., one with adequate level ground for possible future expansion.

338.372   Products of fishing, whaling, hunting, trapping

Class finfishing and comprehensive works on fin- and shellfishing in 338.3727. Class fishing for mollusks and comprehensive works on shellfishing (mollusks and crustaceans) in 338.3724, fishing for crustaceans in 338.37253.

For geographic treatment of a fishing industry, use the area number for the industry's home base, not the place where the fish or other animals are caught. Thus a fleet based at Los Angeles is classed in 338.37270979494, even though the fish are caught off Lower California. It is not classed in either 338.372709722 Lower California or 338.3727091641 Southeast Pacific Ocean.

338.76   Business enterprises in specific industries and groups of industries

Class here directories of companies in specific industries or groups of industries, using notation 025 from Table 1, e.g., directories of manufacturing companies 338.767025. However, class works called directories that include lists of products and services offered for sale or free distribution (even if the works are arranged by company rather than product or service) with the subject, using notation 029, e.g., lists of manufactured products for sale 670.294.

Biographies of people associated with the development and operation of specific types of enterprises but not confined to a specific industry or group of industries are classed in 338.6–.3, e.g., persons associated with trusts 338.85092. Company directors on the boards of companies in several industries or groups of industries are classed in 338.7092.

338.888–.889 [Foreign-owned enterprises]

Enterprises classed here include those with mixed ownership in which some of the owners are local, but in which the principal owners are foreign.

339 vs. 332,   Macroeconomics and related topics vs. Financial economics [and]
336   Public finance

Macroeconomics is the study of the economy as a whole, especially with reference to its general level of output and income and the interrelationships among sectors of the economy. Some topics appearing in 332 and 336 are considered in macroeconomics (339). These topics, however, will be classed in 339 only when they are clearly discussed in relation to the total economic picture of a country or region. For example, monetary activities of central banks, normally 332.112, are classed in 339.53 when undertaken primarily to carry out macroeconomic policy.

339.32 vs. **Other kinds of national accounts and accounting vs. Personal**
339.22 **distribution of income and wealth**

Personal income as a measure of national income is classed in 339.32. Personal income in relation to distribution of the national income is classed in 339.22

340 Law

Law, one of the chief instruments of social control, consists of the whole body of customs, practices, and rules recognized in a society as binding, and promulgated or enforced by a central authority.

Three general forms of literature may be distinguished in this field:

1. The laws themselves as promulgated by a body officially authorized to do so.

2. Decisions of the courts or other adjudicative bodies on matters of dispute that arise under these laws.

3. Treatises written on various aspects of the laws.

The first two of these, laws and decisions, are considered to be original materials. Treatises are derivative in nature and are considered to be secondary. A special section (348) has been provided for original materials and guides to them when such materials are not confined to any specific branch or topic in law. Original materials that are confined to a specific branch or topic are to be classed with that branch or topic, using the special standard subdivision 026 and its subdivisions. (This standard subdivision is given in detail in Edition 20 under 342–347. Note that there is a similar development of 026 under 341 International law.) Treatises have no special place or designation, but are classed in 349 if dealing with the total law of a jurisdiction, or in the number for the specific branch or topic without further indication.

Terminology

Civil law: This term has two meanings that must be carefully distinguished. In one sense it is the name of a system of law (340.56) derived from Roman law and in use to a greater or lesser extent in most countries in the modern world, e.g., Germany, France, Japan, Brazil, and even in some subordinate jurisdictions of countries that otherwise use another system, e.g., the province of Québec in Canada and the state of Louisiana in the United States. It is frequently used in contrast to other great systems of law, e.g., the common law (340.57), which is derived from the customs and laws of ancient and medieval England and is used in the United Kingdom, the United States, and most countries belonging to the British Commonwealth, e.g., Canada, Australia, New Zealand.

The more common meaning of the term "civil law" is all law that is not criminal law (342–344, 346–347). It is used in stated or implied contrast to criminal law.

Law enforcement: This is not necessarily a police matter, although it may be. Any government agency may enforce the law. A department of education, for instance, is enforcing the law when it sees that the requirements of the law are being met by the schools. Enforcement of law in this sense is classed with the subject outside of law. A work about the law enforcement activities of the department of education mentioned above would be classed in 350.851 and cognate and related numbers in 352–354. Law enforcement by the police is classed in 363.23. It should be noted, however, that laws governing how such enforcement should be carried out are classed in law, e.g., the law governing what measures police may use in enforcing the law 344.0523 (or 345.052 if it pertains to matters of criminal investigation).

Enforcement of the law through the courts is always classed in law, using law standard subdivision 0269 where appropriate, e.g., court enforcement of tax law 343.040269.

Law of countries with federal governments

In federally organized countries, e.g., the United States, Australia, Federal Republic of Germany, there are two sets of laws: those of the central jurisdiction (national laws) and those of subordinate jurisdictions (laws of the provinces or states). Laws of an individual state or province are classed using the area number for the jurisdiction in question, e.g., criminal law of Virginia 345.755, of New South Wales 345.944. However, the laws of the states or provinces taken as a whole are classed in the same numbers as the laws of the federal jurisdiction, e.g., criminal laws of the states of the United States 345.73, of the states of Australia 345.94.

Laws of local jurisdictions (cities, counties, subprovincial jurisdictions) are treated in the same way. For the laws of a specific jurisdiction, use the area number for that jurisdiction; but for the laws of all the localities of a given area, use the area number for the jurisdiction that contains them: tax laws of Chapel Hill, North Carolina 343.75656504; by-laws relating to public parks in Sheffield, England 346.42821046783; but, tax laws of the cities of North Carolina 343.75604, of the cities of the United States 343.7304, laws relating to the public parks of cities in the United Kingdom 346.41046783.

Jurisdiction in time

Laws of an area that was at some point not an independent jurisdiction are classed as follows:

1. If still operative in the now-independent jurisdiction, class with the jurisdiction in question, e.g., the Limitation Act of 1908, which was enacted before Pakistan became independent but is still the currently operating law for Pakistan, is classed in 347.5491052.

2. If the law is not still operative in the now-independent jurisdiction, class with the laws of the jurisdiction that was previously dominant, e.g., a law of 1908 no longer operative in Pakistan is classed with the law of India, using notation 54 from Table 2.

Law and aboriginal groups

Certain groups, such as the aborigines of Australia and the native peoples of the United States, had legal systems of their own prior to their incorporation into the national systems of other groups. Such laws are classed in 340.52 Law of traditional societies, e.g., laws of North American native tribes before becoming a part of the United States 340.5273. Class laws of such groups on a specific subject with the subject in law, using notation 089 from Table 1, e.g., family law of North American native peoples 346.01508997.

Class in international law the relations between aboriginal groups and a nation established in their territory before their incorporation into the nation, e.g., treaties between the United States and native American peoples on territorial matters 341.42026.

Relations between an aboriginal group and a nation established in its territory after its incorporation into the nation are classed in the regular numbers for the law of the jurisdiction, e.g., law regulating nursing services for Australian aborigines 344.940414.

Policy

Policy is not necessarily law and ordinarily is classed with the subject outside of law, e.g., conservation policy 333.72. Only policy embodied in specific laws and court interpretations is classed in law, e.g., a law passed to enforce conservation policy 346.044.

The principle of approximating the whole does not apply to jurisdictions for which there is no specific area number, i.e., subdivisions may be added for a jurisdiction not having its own number, e.g., Flint, Michigan's ordinance governing mental health services to the addicted 344.77437044. Flint is in an including note, which normally means subdivisions may not be added for it. Even if the jurisdiction is not mentioned in a note, subdivisions may be added to it, e.g., a similar ordinance for Mt. Morris, Michigan, a suburb of Flint 344.77437044.

Use of area number for capital districts

Use notation 753 from Table 2 for laws of Washington, D.C., even though some of these laws are passed by the United States Congress. These are, in effect, local laws even though passed by the national legislature. The same situation occurs in Australia, where all laws of the Capital Territory are passed by the national legislative body, for which use notation 947 from Table 2. The same situation may occur in other jurisdictions.

Legal writing

Class works on the composition of legal briefs, law reports, and other documents at 808.06634; however, if the work emphasizes how to make the document comply with the law, class it with the subject in law, e.g., how to draw a legal contract 346.022.

Terminology and notation used

To avoid cumbersome repetition the phrase "the law of" is frequently omitted. Unless otherwise stated, law is understood. If, for example, the phrase "taxes are classed in 343.04" is used, it means that the law of taxes is classed in 343.04. Similarly, when referring to the law of specific topics in 342–348 the number is given as it physically appears in Edition 20, e.g., the law of taxes 343.04. It is to be understood that in most instances, to use the above example, the number will actually be 343 plus notation from Table 2 plus 04.

340.023   **Law as a profession, occupation, hobby**

Distinguish 340.023 carefully from legal practice 347.0504, which deals with the technicalities of conducting a lawsuit. Class in 340.023 such topics as what it is like to be a lawyer, professional relationships, specialities available in the profession, career opportunities, and the like.

340.57   **Common law systems**

The phrase "common law" is used in several ways. (1) Law that is not the result of legislation but rather of custom and judicial decision. (2) The branch of English law which derives from the old English courts of common law as opposed to the branch of law known as equity that grew up in the Court of Chancery. (3) The system of law of England and other countries, such as the United States, whose law is derived from English law. Number one is found here in 340.57. Numbers two and three give form and structure to 342–347.

340.9　　**Conflict of laws**

This topic is usually called private international law, which is something of a misnomer, since it is not the law governing the interrelationships of nations, but is the law governing the conflicts and disputes between private citizens of different nations. Its matter is drawn from private law. The chief point at issue is usually which jurisdiction's laws are to govern the case, hence the term conflict of laws. For example, whose laws will govern in the case of a Canadian citizen married in France to a citizen of Germany and later divorced in Mexico when a dispute arises as to the disposition of jointly owned personal property?

341　　**International law**

International law is defined here as that body of rules, principles, and standards to which independent states (nations) are bound by common consent. It lacks two of the features that commonly characterize law: genuine enforceability and promulgation by a central authority. The validity of international law depends on the good faith of nations, national self-interest, the pressure of world opinion, fear of reprisal, and sanctions imposed by international bodies and other nations. This law is embodied in treaties, protocols, conventions, and other international agreements (analogous to statutes); decisions of international courts; and writings (treatises) by recognized legal scholars.

Note that interdisciplinary works on international organizations and works dealing with the structure and overall functions of such organizations are classed in 341.2, even when no substantial discussion of the organic law establishing such organizations appears in the work under consideration. A specific aspect of one of these organizations is classed with the subject outside of law, e.g., the economic aspects of the European Economic Community 337.142.

Distinguishing between international law and international relations is no easy matter at times. To some extent it might be considered as the difference between what actually is (327) and what ought to be (341). Works on international relations will discuss what is actually transpiring (including the theory as to why things happen as they do), and the effects of what has happened. Works on international law will discuss those standards and principles which it is commonly felt should govern international relations, and will also discuss concrete events from the standpoint of the problems that they pose to this system of order. Included in international law, of course, will also be works on treaties and cases of international courts. If in doubt, prefer 341.

341.026   **Treaties and cases**

Use this extended standard subdivision for the texts of treaties and judicial decisions, not for the discussions, commentaries, or popular works upon them.

Class in international law the approval of a treaty by the legislative body of a nation. However, legislation passed by such a body to enforce the provisions of a treaty within national boundaries is classed with the law of the nation. For example, a work on a treaty between the United States and Canada with respect to fish and wildlife conservation is classed in 341.762, but a work on a fish and game law passed by the United States Congress to enforce the provisions of such a treaty on the citizens of the United States would be classed in 346.73046954.

342–347   **Law of specific jurisdictions**

0262   Preliminary materials

Preliminary materials are documents relating to proposed legislation. Even after passage of the legislation these documents continue to be relevant in law as showing the mind and intention of the legislators responsible for the bill.

The main forms are:

Bills (the proposed laws themselves)

Hearings on the bills

Statements of witnesses

Executive messages with respect to bills

Reports on the hearings

Class in 342–347:

Bills

Including authorizations and appropriation bills that establish government agencies; both of these are classed in law with the subject with which the agency deals, e.g., a bill to establish an education department 344.070262

Hearings, reports, and resolutions relating to bills

Hearings on the proposed appointments of judges

These are classed in 345 or 347, e.g., a hearing on the proposed appointment of a justice to the United States Supreme Court 347.732634

Class in 350–354:

Hearings on authorizations and appropriations

Except for military authorizations and appropriations, class hearings on authorizations in 351.72234, on appropriations for a specific agency with the agency in 351 and cognate numbers in 353–354, e.g., appropriations for hospitals 351.841

Oversight hearings

These are not hearings on a bill, but examinations into the effectiveness with which an agency is doing its job. Class them with the subject with which the agency deals, e.g., an oversight hearing on the U.S. Bureau of Indian Affairs 353.0081497

Class in 355–359:

Military appropriation and authorization bills and the hearings and reports pertaining to them

Class in other places throughout the Classification general hearings and reports on them, reports on legislative investigations not related to proposed legislation, e.g., a congressional investigation (U.S.) into the sale of arms to Iran and the subsequent transfer of the proceeds of the sales to Nicaraguan rebels 364.1310973.

Note that reports are classed with the hearings to which they pertain. Materials containing such statements as "under authority of" or "pursuant to" are not usually classed in law.

See also 350–354: Nomination hearings

342.06   Executive branch of government

Administrative law involves the exercise by the executive branch of certain judicial functions, e.g., settling disputes, imposing fines, specifying certain remedies. When a work deals with such functions, it is classed here. Class administrative law on a specific subject with the subject in law, e.g., the role of the U.S. Federal Aviation Administration in settling a dispute with air traffic controllers 343.730976. Standards set by an agency in connection with a specific subject are classed with the subject outside of law, e.g., standards for safety in health care facilities 363.1562.

343.078 vs.   [Regulation of] Secondary industries and services vs. Regulation of
343.08   trade

In sorting out industrial versus trade regulations, the following may help. When production quotas, quality of the material produced, sizes of products specified, and the like are treated, industrial regulations are involved. When truth-in-labeling, advertising practices, and other aspects of marketing are treated, trade regulations are involved. For instance, what services hotels are permitted to provide, how they are to provide them, what activities are permitted in them, and what rates they may charge are classed in industrial regulation 343.07864794. How hotels may advertise is classed in 343.08564794. If in doubt, prefer 343.078.

345   **Criminal law**

Criminal law deals with actions of so damaging a nature that the interests of society are considered to be directly at stake. For this reason cases in criminal law are always between the state in its capacity as the body politic and the individual charged with a crime. A dispute between two private persons (natural or corporate) becomes a civil law case. Penal action is a possible result of a criminal case. In a civil case damages are awarded or some other remedy is found. It should be noted that the state can also bring a suit at civil law, acting in this case as a juristic person rather than as the body politic.

345.02 vs.   **Crimes (Offenses) vs. Torts (Delicts)**
346.03

It should be noted that certain acts listed as criminal offenses here are also to be found in 346.03 as torts (a part of civil law). Works on these acts should be classed according to the point of view taken in the work or the type of legal action being brought. Thus libel and slander considered from the standpoint of criminal law are classed in 345.0256, considered as a tort in 346.034. It should be further noted that whether a particular act is regarded as a crime or as a tort or as neither will often depend on the jurisdiction in which it is regarded. For example, adultery may be regarded as a crime for which the offender may be prosecuted, a tort for which the offender may be sued, or merely as a fact to be adduced in evidence in a divorce case.

346.02   **Contracts and agency**

A contract is an agreement, implicit or explicit, between two or more parties. The contract itself is not law, but is enforceable at law. The following aspects of contracts are classed in law: their legality and enforceability, disputes concerning them, breach of contract, how to draft contracts so that they will be legal.

347   **Civil procedure and courts**

Care must be taken in determining the jurisdiction involved in procedure and courts. The location of the court does not necessarily determine this. For example, procedure in a court in Boston, Massachusetts, would be classed in 347.744 if a state court, in 347.73 if a United States district court; only a local Boston court, established under and interpreting Boston ordinances, would be classed in 347.74461. Except for local courts, this problem does not usually arise in countries with unitary rather than federal governments, e.g., France.

350   Public administration and military science

The two halves of the 350s are distinct except in the one narrow field where they overlap: the administration of defense forces and departments. Apart from works on departments of defense in 351.06 and related numbers in 353–354, administration of military and defense matters is classed in 355–359. Comprehensive works on military administration are classed in 355.6. Administration of a specific branch or service is classed with the branch or service, usually with use of notation 6 derived from 355.6. Administration of a specific topic is classed with the topic without use of any subdivision.

350–354   [Public administration]

Basis of arrangement

Two basic distinctions are made in the public administration schedule: first between administration in general and administration of specific jurisdictions, and second between administration of central and administration of local jurisdictions.

350 is used for public administration in general, when works refer to matters relating to both central and local administration. Its subdivisions may be divided by area, using notation 09 from Table 1 when discussion refers primarily to principles and practices in a country or region, but does not refer predominately to the central administration of any one country, state, or large province, e.g., local, state, and federal welfare administration in the United States 350.840973.

351 is used for central administration in general, but not for the administration of any specific jurisdiction. Its subdivisions are divided by area only for treatment covering two or more countries. Central administration of specific countries and of their states or state-like provinces is found in 354, except for the United States, which is found in 353.

352 is used for local administration irrespective of jurisdiction, i.e., for local administration in general, in specific countries or regions, or in specific localities.

State and provincial administration

Central administration in 351 and 353–354 includes public administration of states and of provinces in countries that have large provinces encompassing a large number of separate local governments, e.g., Canada and China. Administration of small provinces comparable to counties in the United States or the United Kingdom, i.e., provinces that have relatively few districts or municipalities, is classed as local administration in 352.0073. If in doubt, class administration of a country's provinces in 352.0073.

There is specific provision for administration of states of the United States in 353.9. For any other country, administration of states and of provinces of size equal to states is classed under their area notation in 354, e.g., central administration of Brazil 354.81, of Minas Gerais 354.8151. Comprehensive works on states or provinces of a country in 354 are classed in the number for the country, using subdivisions for specific topics from the add table under 354, e.g., state welfare administration in Brazil 354.810084.

Citation order of jurisdiction vs. topic

The basic citation order for administration of specific central governments is Level + Jurisdiction + Topic. It is switched for local governments to Level + Topic + Jurisdiction. *(See 353–354 for examples with central administration, 352 for examples with local administration.)*

Agencies and their component parts

With the exception of cabinet-level agencies in 351.01–.08 and related numbers in 353–354, no distinction is made between the administration of a function and the administration of an agency designated to perform that function. Administrative reports of specific agencies are classed in the same numbers as independent studies of the functions the agencies perform. However, notation 06 from Table 1 is added for periodic administrative reports if the scope of the agency is approximately the same as the scope of the number. Notation 06 is used even for annual reports, not notation 05 from Table 1. *(See also 351.0006.)*

Specific agencies tend to have a range of responsibilities that do not fit the definitions devised to cover the common patterns. Furthermore, in any specific jurisdiction, the responsibilities tend to shift with time, as agencies are enlarged, reduced, divided, or merged. It is necessary, therefore, to class according to "best fit." A general services agency, for example, may have a wide range of miscellaneous functions, but if its predominant duty concerns property administration, class it in a number derived from 351.713, even if it has sections for archives and personnel training.

In such cases, class works limited to a specific component of a larger agency in the number fitting the component, e.g., an archives section in a general services agency in a number derived from 351.7146, a personnel training section of such an agency in a number derived from 351.15.

When two agencies independently cover the same field, as happens when watchdog or coordinating agencies are created to monitor the activity of other agencies or groups of agencies, the monitoring agencies are classed in the numbers for the functions being monitored, e.g., personnel review boards in 351.1.

Nominal subordination of an agency to a nonexecutive branch of government does not affect classification. For example, the U.S. General Accounting Office is officially part of the legislative branch, but it performs a classical executive function of reviewing accounts and judging the effectiveness of expenditures throughout the government; it is, therefore, classed in 353.007232 (derived from 351.7232).

Public policy

Public policy in specific fields of social concern is normally classed with the specific field in the social sciences, regardless of whether the policy is formulated by legislation, administrative decision, or informal public consensus. For example, economic development and growth policies are classed in 338.9, welfare policies in 361.61. Public policy in matters outside the social sciences generally are classed with the subject in public administration, e.g., art policy 351.854, not 700. However, a policy with civil rights implications will be classed with civil rights in 323, e.g., religious policy 323.442, not 200, 351.811, or 351.857.

Certain policies that have names suggesting one discipline actually concern another. For example, technology policy, technology transfer policy, research and development (R&D) policy, and even science policy are often formulated in terms of promoting economic growth and development. In each case, where the policies are metaphors for growth policies, they should be classed in 338.9.

These remarks refer only to the policies themselves and arguments for and against them, not to policy execution or formulation. How to carry out policy, or how to set up procedures for resolving policy issues is administration. For example, class a work about what civil rights policies are or should be in 323, but a work on how to administer civil rights policies in 351.811.

Nomination hearings

Hearings on nominations for important offices may emphasize either public policy in the field in which an agency is active, the personal philosophy and plans of the nominees, the personal qualifications of the nominees, or the administrative problems of the agency. Hearings emphasizing the first two factors are classed with the subject, usually outside public administration; those emphasizing the last two, with the subject, always in public administration. For example, hearings emphasizing housing policies or the welfare philosophy of potential housing officials in 363.5, but hearings on officials being called in to resolve management problems in housing agencies or on the ability of a housing official being nominated for promotion in 351.865. If in doubt, use the number outside public administration. (Formerly nomination hearings were routinely classed in public administration.)

350–354 vs. **[Public administration] vs. Structure and functions of government**
320.4, **[and] Political situation and conditions**
320.9

The terms "government" and "public administration" can be easily confused and are sometimes used interchangeably. In the Dewey Decimal Classification, however, they are kept quite distinct. Government is limited to top-level considerations: the nature, role, goals, structure of states; their political direction and control; and the critical matter of forms by which central controls are exercised and balanced against each other. Public administration concentrates on public agencies and the procedures used to carry out their goals, policies, and actions in various fields.

Of the several numbers in 320 concerning different aspects of government, 320.4 is the one often confused with public administration. It includes works on the overall structure of governments, emphasizing their chief legislative, judicial, and executive organs. It may be used for works that discuss typical activities of the different branches, e.g., patrolling streets as an illustration of the police function. However, it should not be used for works emphasizing the kind of work that executive agencies perform.

Some works that seem to cover the activities of government are simply discussing the habitual conduct and methods of people in high office, and should be classed in 320.9.

Most works that should be classed in 350–354 will clearly emphasize agencies of the executive branch, or the usual components of administration: planning, organizing, staffing, financing, and equipping agencies to do a job or perform a function. Works on these components will be classed in 350–354 when they apply to any two of the three branches of government. For example, financial administration of the legislative and judicial branches taken together is classed in 351.72 and related numbers. However, when the components apply to only one of the nonexecutive branches, they are classed with the branch, e.g., financial administration of the legislative branch 328.0681, of the judicial branch 347.013.

350–354 vs. **[Public administration] vs. General management [and Standard**
658, **subdivision for] Management**
T1—068

The difference between public administration and management appears obvious at first glance. However, there are specific aspects in which the distinction can be confusing. In the Dewey Decimal Classification "public administration" refers primarily to running government agencies that regulate and exercise control of various fields, while "management" refers to running organizations, public or private, that are directly operating the matters within their scope. In several fields traditionally dominated by public agencies, this operational management is called administration, as in library, hospital, or school administration. Some special provisions for administration were made in the Dewey Decimal Classification before notation 068 in Table 1 was developed, e.g., library administration 025.1, military administration 355.6, educational administration 371.2. In each case, however, "administration" refers to running an operational agency, i.e., an agency providing books, teaching students, or controlling the activities and lives of soldiers, not one telling other agencies or persons how to do so.

The cabinet level departments and their relations with other agencies are classed in public administration even in the three cases where all operational administration and sometimes part of what is considered public administration is found elsewhere. The numbers are 351.06 and related numbers for departments of defense, but 355.6 and other numbers in 355–359 for military administration; 351.0851 for departments of education, but 371.2 and other numbers in 371–378 for school administration and 379 for government regulation, control, and support of education; 351.0873 for postal departments, but 383.068 and other numbers in 383 for postal management.

There are activities where administration of an actual operation is classed in 350–354. These are mostly activities performed by government that have not been provided for outside public administration, e.g., licensing, taxing, and gathering census information. In addition, the administrative management of foreign affairs is classed in 351.89 and cognate numbers in 353–354, not in 327.068 and cognate numbers in 327.4–.9.

"General management" is the comprehensive term. Thus works on both public administration and management are classed in 658. However, management of a specific field is classed with the field (using notation 068 from Table 1, e.g., hospital administration 362.11068), while public administration of a specific field is classed in 350–354. The most important and extensively used subdivisions in public administration are the numbers defining the fields of activity that are administered (found in 351.74–.89 and spans derived from there), e.g., secondary industries 351.824.

Size is not a factor in differentiating between public administration and management. Running a one-person bureau licensing commercial establishments is public administration (using numbers derived from

351.826046), while running a transcontinental nationalized railroad is management (385.068).

There is often both public administration and management in the same field. For example, managing railroads is classed in 385.068, while running agencies that regulate railroads is found in 351.875; administering library systems is classed in 025.1, while administering agencies that regulate and support libraries is found in 351.852. If in doubt, prefer the number outside public administration.

350.0001–.9 **Standard subdivisions; specific aspects of public administration vs.**
vs. 351 **Administration of central governments**

For convenience in number-building throughout 352–354, where numbers for most topics are derived by adding subdivisions shared by 350 and 351, the subdivisions are developed under 351, even though comprehensive works on specific aspects of public administration are normally classed in 350.0001–.9. While 351 is limited to administration of central governments, it is easier to take the many zero subdivisions used in 352–354 from a number ending in 1 than from a number ending in 0. However, the classifier must be aware that the numbers visible in the schedule under 351 are not normally the comprehensive numbers for the topics listed.

Class comprehensive works on specific topics in public administration in 350.001–.9, unless the topic either pertains to a field that is seldom or never assigned to local governments, e.g., foreign affairs (351.89), foreign trade (351.827), primary industries (351.8233–.8238), and financial institutions (351.825); or has little relevance in local administration, e.g., cabinets (351.004) and cabinet departments (351.01–.08). In case of doubt, check the topic in the index: if no 350 number is given, use the cited 351 number for comprehensive works.

351.0006 **Administrative reports**

Notation 06 from Table 1 is used throughout 350–354 for periodic administrative reports, i.e., those primarily covering internal administration of agencies. Reports covering the fields or clients that are the responsibility of agencies are classed with the subject. For example, reports on the internal administration of bureaus of mines are classed in 351.823806, but reports by bureaus of mines on the situation in mines are classed in 338.2 if the thrust of the reports is economic, in 363.119622 if it is safety, in 622 if it is technical. If in doubt, prefer 351.0006 or cognate numbers in 350–354.

352 **Administration of local governments**

The basic citation order for local administration is Level + Topic + Jurisdiction. Jurisdiction is supplied by notation 09 from Table 1, and ranks in its usual order of precedence among the standard subdivisions as spelled out in the table of precedence at the beginning of Table 1. Selected standard subdivision notation can be added to area numbers from the table found at T1—093–099 in Table 1. For example:

1. Property tax assessment in Glasgow is analyzed as Level (city, 352) + Topic (property tax assessment, 13521) + Jurisdiction (Glasgow, 0941443. The number is built 352 + 13521 + 0941443 = 352.135210941443.

2. A periodical on local zoning administration in Texas is analyzed as Level (local, 352) + Topic (zoning, 961) + Jurisdiction (Texas, 09764) + Standard subdivision (periodical, 05). The number is built 352 + 961 + 09764 + 05 = 352.9610976405.

352.03–.09 vs. 352.002– .009 **Treatment [of administration of local governments] by specific continents, countries, localities vs. General topics of local administration**

The following works are classed in 352.03–.09:

1. Works on topics found in 352.002–.009 when discussed in respect to a specific local government, e.g., regulatory agencies of the government of Cook County, Illinois 352.07731 (not 352.0092097731).

2. Comprehensive works on a specific local government, e.g., on the government of Cook County 352.07731, of Chicago 352.077311.

3. Comprehensive works on two or more local governments in a specific area, e.g., on several municipalities in Cook County 352.07731.

However, works on topics found in 352.002–.009 are classed in 352.002–.009 when discussed in respect to two or more local governments in a specific area, e.g., regulatory agencies in several municipalities in Cook County 352.0092097731 (not 352.07731 as is the case for regulatory agencies of the government of Cook County).

Area treatment in 352.1–.9 is completely regular, e.g., budgeting for the Cook County government, for several municipalities in Cook County 352.12097731, for Chicago 352.120977311.

352.2–.9 **Local administration of specific fields**

The instruction at 350–354 vs. 658, T1—068 concerning management of public organizations that are directly delivering the services within their scope apply with particular force for many agencies of local government. Management of agencies actually delivering services is classed with the subject outside public administration, e.g., managing school systems is classed in 371.2 (school administration and management); library systems, in 025.1 (library administration). However, managing local police departments is classed in 352.2, not 363.2068 (which is not used).

The numbers in 352.3–.9 should be used only for two kinds of material:

1. Works on regulation and support of activity in specific fields not performed by the government, e.g., control of private waste collection 352.63, issuance of construction permits 352.92, support for historical commemorations 352.9459.

2. Works emphasizing external managerial relationships of specific agencies and kinds of agencies, e.g., the position of the New York Fire Department in the New York City government 352.3097471. The internal management of the Department is classed in 363.37068, as is comprehensive treatment of management of fire departments.

If in doubt between numbers in 352 and numbers outside public administration, prefer the outside numbers.

353–354   [Administration of specific central governments]

The basic citation order for administration of central governments is Level + Jurisdiction + Topic + Standard subdivision. For example:

1. A discussion of leaves of absence for employees of the government of Spain is analyzed as Level (national, 354) + Jurisdiction (Spain, 46) + Topic (leaves of absence, 00164) + Standard subdivisions (none). The number is built 354 + 46 + 00164 = 354.4600164.

2. The duties of the lieutenant governor of California are analyzed as Level (state, 353.9) + Jurisdiction (California, 794) + Topic (lieutenant governor, 0318) + Standard subdivision (none). The number is built 353.9 + 794 + 0318 = 353.97940318.

3. An annual report of a bureau of mines in Zaire is analyzed as Level (national, 354) + Jurisdiction (Zaire, 6751) + Topic (mines, 0082382) + Standard subdivision (administrative serial, 06). The number is built 354 + 6751 + 0082382 + 06 = 354.6751008238206.

355 vs. 623   Military science vs. Military and nautical engineering

Use 623 for physical description, design, manufacture, operation, and repair of ordnance; use 355–359 for procurement, deployment, and control of the units and services which use the ordnance. Histories of the development of weapons emphasizing the interplay of human and social factors are regarded as procurement history, and are classed in 355.82 and related numbers in 356–359. If in doubt, prefer 355–359.

355.00711 **Military colleges and universities**

In designating area numbers for official service academies, use the notation for the country it serves, e.g., the Royal Military Academy (Sandhurst, England) 355.0071141, the U.S. Naval Academy (Annapolis, Maryland) 359.0071173.

Military schools that are not official training academies, most of whose students (except in wartime) enter civilian occupations, are treated like other higher educational institutions and classed in 378 plus notation for the area where they are located, e.g., Virginia Military Institute (Lexington, Virginia) 378.755853, The Citadel (Charleston, South Carolina) 378.757915.

355.009 vs. **Historical, geographical, persons treatment [of military science] vs.**
930–990 **History of ancient world; of specific continents, countries, localities; of extraterrestrial worlds**

Military topics and war

Use the historical treatment standard subdivisions in 355–359 for works emphasizing military history or topics without consideration of the general course of a war, e.g., changes in tank tactics during the course of World War II 358.18409044. Use numbers in 900 for works on the military history of wars that deal with the outcome of significant events, e.g., the use of tanks on the Eastern Front and how the use affected various battles 940.54217. If in doubt between 355–359 and 930–990, prefer 930–990.

Persons

Use 930–990 for comprehensive works on soldiers chiefly associated with the history of a specific war, e.g., William Tecumseh Sherman 973.73092; use 355.0092 for comprehensive works on soldiers associated with more than one war, or who had long and varied careers, e.g., Douglas MacArthur.

See also 930–990: Wars.

355.07 and **Military research and development of equipment and supplies [and]**
355.8 **Military equipment and supplies (Matériel)**

The word "development" as used here refers to the procurement history of equipment and supplies. Class economic aspects in 338.47355.

355.134092 **[Persons treatment of awards]**

Class here biographies of awardees, e.g., of recipients of the Croix de Guerre 355.1342092. However, do not class a comprehensive biography of an awardee here if the person's life embraces other significant activities; class with the subject for which the person is otherwise famous, e.g., Audie Murphy 791.43028092, not 355.134092.

355.14 vs.
355.81

Uniforms vs. Clothing, food, camp equipment, office supplies

Use 355.14 for military clothing if the emphasis is on cut, style, or color of uniforms; on insignia, identification of units or branches of service; or on the history of uniforms. Use 355.81 if the emphasis is on the function of various articles of clothing, or on supply administration (from development through issue and disposition). If in doubt, prefer 355.81.

355.1409

[Historical, geographical, persons treatment of uniforms]

Class uniforms of several participants in a particular war in the area number corresponding to the one used for the war in general history, e.g., uniforms of the Peninsular War (part of the Napoleonic Wars classed in 940.27) 355.14094, not 355.140946.

Class uniforms of a specific branch of the armed services with the branch, e.g., uniforms of the Royal Air Force 358.41140941.

355.4 vs.
355.02

Military operations vs. War and warfare

Use 355.02 for works on strategy that consider the overall problems and objectives of national policy; use 355.4 for works on strategy that emphasize military operations. If in doubt, prefer 355.02.

355.82

Ordnance

Subdivisions implied by the add instructions are used only for weapons common to two or more land forces, or to at least two of the three major defense forces, e.g., to land and sea forces. Note also that comprehensive works on missiles are found in 358.17182, on aircraft in 358.4183, on ships in 359.83.

356–359

Specific kinds of military forces and warfare

Where the numbers in the add table under 356–359 correspond to one- and two-digit subdivisions of 355, they are subject to qualifications and instructions found under 355.

358.4183

[Air force transportation equipment and supplies]

Use this number for comprehensive works on military aircraft. Aircraft used by a specific force or service are classed with the force or service, e.g., aircraft of fighter forces 358.4383, of naval air forces 359.94834.

359.32 vs.
359.83

Ships as naval units vs. [Ships as] Transportation equipment and supplies

Naval ships may be written about either as units of organization or as items of equipment. When a work on ships focuses on matters normally covered by analogous works on regiments and other military units, class it in 359.32 or cognate numbers in 359.9. Such a work will normally emphasize the crew and its organization, duties, effectiveness, and history. When, in contrast, the work focuses on development, procurement, operation, and actual or potential combat effectiveness of the hardware, class it in 359.83 or cognate numbers in 359.9. Whatever discussion of personnel or personalities such a work has will usually concern persons responsible for development and procurement of ships, e.g., Admiral Rickover's work in developing nuclear submarines 359.93834092. Works about a specific ship will most often consider the ship as a naval unit (unless there is only one ship of a class). If in doubt, prefer 359.32.

Use country numbers in notation 09 from Table 1 for either specific ships, or a number of ships of a specific class employed employed by a specific nation.

359.97 **Coast guard**

The United States Coast Guard is not a part of the military establishment except during time of war. Class comprehensive works on the USCG in 363.2860973, public administration aspects in 353.0074.

361–365 **Social problems and services**

Problems and services in this section of the schedules are often linked terms, and, where one is spelled out, the other is implied. Thus, addictions at 362.29 implies services to the addicted, while services of extended care facilities at 362.16 implies the problems that require such services.

See also 300 vs. 600.

Political, economic, and legal considerations

Many publications give considerable emphasis to the political and legal considerations related to social services. So long as the focus is on the problem or the service, class such publications here. Thus, a discussion of political obstacles to effective poverty programs is classed in 362.5, of the political maneuvering behind the adoption of an act of the United States Congress spelling out a new housing program in 363.580973.

361–365 vs. **Social problems and services vs. [Public administration]**
350–354

Much of the material on social problems and services consists of government reports. Reports about welfare programs and institutions are classed in 361–365. Reports concentrating on the administrative activities of agencies supporting and regulating the programs and institutions are classed in 350–354. If in doubt, class in 361–365; however, prefer 350–354 for administrative annual reports of agencies not actually providing the services.

361 vs. 362   **Social problems and social welfare in general vs. Social welfare problems and services**

361 is used for two kinds of material: comprehensive works on the whole range of problems and services found in 362–363, and works on principles and methods of assessing and solving the problems. The second kind of material normally does not address specific problems but may refer to welfare problems, usually found in 362. Material on the principles and methods of welfare work in general is classed in 361. Application of the principles and methods to a specific problem is classed with the problem, using subdivision 5 from the table under 362–363.

A helpful guide in deciding between 361 and 362 is the table of contents. If it reads like a summary of the subdivisions of 362, class in 362; if like a summary of the subdivisions of 361, class in 361. In the absence of a table of contents or summary, the coverage of topics is a useful guide. If topics in both 361 and 362 are covered, class in 361. If in doubt, class in 361.

361.1 vs.   **Social problems vs. Social [welfare] problems vs. Sociology and**
362.042,   **anthropology**
301

Social problems at 362.042 should be thought of as social welfare problems, a narrower concept than 361.1. 361.1 encompasses any and all kinds of social problems from providing child care to supplying water. Class at 362.042 social problems that apply to individuals as such and the remedial measures for these problems. 361.1 comprises social problems as a background to social action, and should be used sparingly. If in doubt, prefer 361.1.

301 is used for social problems primarily when they are discussed as social phenomena, rather than as matters that society should take action to solve. Usually the emphasis in works on social problems is clearly towards problems to be solved and thus indicates 361.1. If the emphasis is not clear or if in doubt between 301 and 361.1 or 362.042, prefer 301.

361.23–.24   **[Social protest, dissent, reform movements] vs. Reform movements**
vs. 322.44

General discussions about social protest, dissent, and reform movements are classed in 322.44. If the discussion is limited to social action as an aspect of social welfare, it is classed in 361.23–.24. If the discussion is limited to a specific problem, it is classed with the problem. Social protest, dissent, and reform movements as related to a specific social welfare problem are shown by using either 523 or 524 from the table under 362–363. 523 and 524 are based on 361.23 and 361.24.

361.6 vs.
361.7,
361.8

Governmental action vs. Private action vs. Community action

Organizations are classed in 361.6, 361.7, and 361.8 depending upon who has financial control. For example, the Peace Corps, a governmentally funded organization of overseas volunteers, is classed in 361.6; Canadian University Service Overseas, a privately funded organization of overseas volunteers, is classed in 361.763.

The scope of the membership, not the area served, determines whether the organization is national or international. For example, the International Red Cross is classed in 361.77, but the United States Red Cross, a national organization which provides service worldwide, is classed in 361.76340973.

362–363

Specific social problems and services

Add table

These digits are to be added to numbers bearing an asterisk (*) in 362 363. Topics are not usually marked with an asterisk when the concepts in this table have already been provided for in another manner. In such cases the schedule inserts the concepts missing in the earlier editions wherever a convenient place can be found for them. In some cases these concepts have been provided for in another location altogether.

362.1 is a good example of all these contingencies. In general, causes of disease are medical in nature and are classed in 616.1–.9. Strictly social causes are classed in 362.1042, e.g., changes in social attitudes leading to an increase in various diseases. Incidence of disease is ordinarily classed in 614.42, social effects at 362.10422. Control of disease is classed in 614.43 and 614.5, prevention in 614.44–.48 and 614.5. The chief remedial measures are hospital and related services, classed in 362.11–.19 (or direct medical treatment, classed in 616–618). Subdivision 81 Rescue operations is not applicable with respect to diseases. Its closest relative, emergency services, is classed in 362.18. Financial assistance to the sick is classed in 362.104252. (However, class medical insurance in 368.38 and 368.42.) Subdivisions 83–85 are not applicable here. Counseling and guidance are provided for at 362.104256.

When certain subdivisions are not applicable under numbers marked with an asterisk, they will be listed with an instruction that they are not to be used. Subdivisions with altered meanings are also listed. For example, at 362.86, subdivision 82 Financial assistance has been spelled out to carry additional information not found in the table. The listing of only one subdivision does not mean that other subdivisions may not be used. Thus residential care for veterans is classed in 362.8685.

362.1–.4 vs.   **Problems of and services to sick and disabled people vs. Medical**
610   **sciences   Medicine**

Class health services from the social viewpoint in 362.1–.4, from the technological viewpoint in 610. For example, class social measures for the provision of dental care through clinics in 362.1976, but how dentists actually use their skill in 617.6. Class works treating both the medical sciences and the medical social services in 362.1–.4. If in doubt, prefer 362.1–.4.

Biographies

Class in 362.1–.4, using notation 092 from Table 1, biographies and memoirs of the sick, the handicapped, and the dying that lack any other disciplinary focus. The rationale behind this rule is that these biographies illustrate the way society addresses itself to fundamental health problems and their solution. Be alert, however, for significant disciplinary emphasis, e.g., a work offering guidance in the Christian life with respect to health misfortunes is classed in 248.86, Christian meditations in 242.4. Class studies of individual cases designed for the use of researchers, practitioners, and students in the field in the number for the field, without adding notation 092 from Table 1. Class in 616–618 studies of patients describing their illnesses in medical terms rather than their lives in social terms, using subdivision 09 from the table under 616.1–.9, e.g., case studies of heart disease 616.1209. If in doubt, prefer 362; however, prefer 616.8909 and related numbers for psychiatric disorders, since the consideration of external circumstances is generally subordinated to the discussion of the state of mind of the patient.

While most personal and biographical treatment of medical personnel is classed in 610, works on public health doctors or nurses emphasizing their influences on public health services and awareness are classed in 362, e.g., a biography of a doctor noted chiefly for promoting nursing homes 362.16092.

362.17 vs.   **Specific [medical] services vs. Medical sciences   Medicine**
610

Services at 362.17 refer to societal arrangements to make sure that specific kinds of medical work are provided, e.g., services of nurses 362.173. The work actually performed is classed in 610, e.g., the work of nurses 610.73. Interdisciplinary works covering both societal arrangements for medical work and the work itself are classed in 362.17. If in doubt, prefer 610.

363   **Other social problems and services**

Several subdivisions involve the control of technology, particularly under safety (363.1) and environment (363.7). Class in 363 works addressing what must be done, regulating how it is to be done, inspecting to see whether or not it has been done, and investigating when it was not done. Only works dealing with the technological procedures for carrying out a given operation are classed in technology. Finding out what broke is 600; finding out who let it break is 363. Machinery breakdown is 600; institutional breakdown is 363.

A useful clue in choosing the appropriate discipline is the perspective of the author or publishing agency. If the author is interested in social service and social need, the work is classed in 363; in the economics of what we have to live on, 333.7; in how the environment works, 304.2; in how to make things, 620–690; in how organisms survive, 570–590; in how crops survive, 632–635; in physical techniques for controlling pollution, 628.5. In general, commercial publishers and environmental or safety advocacy groups tend to produce works that are classed in the social sciences, e.g., 304.2, 333.7, or 363.

To summarize: class comprehensive works and works oriented toward problems and their solution in 363, resource-oriented material in 333.7, works giving significant consideration to the social dynamics of the problem in 302–307, those emphasizing technology in 600.

See also 300 vs. 600; 301 vs. 361–365.

363 vs. 340, 350–354 **Other social problems and services vs. Law vs. [Public administration]**

Class the work of agencies by which the government carries out the detailed intent of the law in matters of population, safety, the environment, and provision of basic necessities in 363. Class the internal administration of agencies concerned with these fields, including their administrative annual reports, in 350–354. The law itself, draft laws, and enforcement of the law in courts is classed in 341–346. But most of the discussion of policy and most detailed procedures for enforcing law, policy, or regulation are classed in 363. If in doubt, class in 363.

363.1 **Public safety programs**

Note that all the headings in this section, however worded, include the conditions or potential conditions that pose a threat to safety, the measures of prevention and control contemplated or adopted, disasters resulting from the failure or lack of such measures, and the measures of relief and rehabilitation resulting therefrom.

Note also that the word "safety" is used loosely and equivocally in many instances. It may be so broad as to cover most of the social services. In this case the work is classed at 363, or even at 361 if sufficient 362 material is included. On the other hand, it may be so narrow as to comprise only the work of the police and fire departments, in which case the work is classed at 363.2.

Safety regulations

Class safety regulations that spell out operating and construction techniques in explicit detail with the technology involved even if they are in the form of an officially promulgated regulation by a safety authority. In some cases such regulations may not even warrant the addition of notation 0289 from Table 1 for safety measures because they cover more or less the whole construction picture. On the other hand, manuals written by or for safety agencies may discuss, among other things, various technical details useful as background for regulation and inspection of various operations while still focusing primarily on safety services. These are classed in 363.1 and its subdivisions as appropriate, often with numbers using subdivision 6 from the table under 362–363.

Priority of safety

Class the safety aspects of any subject in the social sciences in 363.1 or 363.3 rather than with the subject elsewhere in the social sciences, e.g., railroad safety 363.122, not 385.0289. However, the public administration of safety is classed as instructed at 351.783 and 352.3 in the schedule.

363.1065   **Investigation of specific incidents**

Prefer this and cognate numbers in 363 to numbers in 600 for accident investigations when the investigation implicates large, impersonal agencies (companies or governments) that should have prevented the accident by proper supervision, inspection, or regulation. For example, class a technical description of what went wrong at Three Mile Island in 621.48350974818, but an investigation of why it took so long to find out what went wrong in 363.1799650974818.

363.17   **Hazardous materials**

Note that many works on hazardous materials are not classed in 363 at all. The material as an environmental factor affecting the natural ecology is classed in 574.5222, as a cause of disease or injury in an organism in 574.24, and as a cause of injury to persons in 615.9 (for chemicals) and 616.9897 (for radiation hazards).

363.176 vs. 604.7   **[Control of hazardous materials] vs. Hazardous materials technology**

While the technology of handling hazardous materials is classed in 604.7, be alert for works on "handling" that are addressed to those responsible for monitoring or inspecting the handling, and that may be devoid of engineering considerations. Class such works in 363.176. If in doubt, prefer 363.176.

363.5, 363.6, 363.8 vs. 338 **Housing [and] Public utilities and related services [and] Food supply vs. Production**

363.5, 363.6, and 363.8 deal with the problems of providing the basic necessities of life. Each has economic implications; thus, a careful distinction must be made between these numbers and the economics of industries under 338. If the work deals with the effect of these topics on the economic aspects of society, or the impact of economic conditions on the availability of housing, water, fuel, or food, it is classed in 338. If it deals with broader social factors affecting these commodities, or with social measures to insure an adequate supply, class it in 363.5, 363.6, or 363.8. For example, a study of the effect of a drop in farm prices on the food supply is classed in 338.19; a study of the mismatch between the expected growth of the food supply and of the population is classed in 363.81. If in doubt, prefer 363.5, 363.6, or 363.8.

363.6 vs. 333.7 **Public utilities and related services vs. Natural resources and energy**

Use care in distinguishing between the resources and energy (333.7–.9) and the utilities delivering the resources to customers (363.6). For instance, class in 333.7 comprehensive works on resources, projection of needs and supplies, development, conservation, protection of resources. Class in 363.6 problems and services related to distributing the resources to users. A useful device in distinguishing the two is to consider that ''supply'' as a noun is classed in 333.7, while ''supply'' as a verb is classed in 363.6. If in doubt, class in 333.7.

An exception is made for electrical power companies. Works about these utilities almost always emphasize the problems of developing the ''supply'' as a noun, saying little about the problems of distributing the electricity to customers, and seldom discuss prices without reference to production costs. A work about electrical power utilities focusing on distribution should be classed in 333.7932 with the bulk of works about electrical power companies.

Class the rationing of natural resources still in their natural state at 333.717 and cognate numbers in 333.7–.9, but of final products in 363, e.g., wellhead allocation of natural gas for companies or jurisdictions 333.823317, but rationing of natural gas among consumers or classes of consumers at the other end of the line 363.63.

363.61 **Water supply**

Water reports

Water supply reports concentrating on the supply of water on hand are classed in 553.7; on water used, or needed in the future, in 333.91; on the problem of treating and delivering water to consumers in 363.61; on assuring that waste waters are properly treated in 363.7284; on protection of natural waters in 363.739472.

Water quality monitoring reports serve several purposes. As tools for assuring compliance with water supply standards they are classed in 363.61, for assuring compliance with waste water pollution standards in 363.739463, for determining plant loads and technical difficulties in water treatment in 628.16 (e.g., pollution surveys in specific areas 628.1686), and for checking the effectiveness of sewage treatment works in 628.3. Those reporting the present chemical and biological status of available water, but not focusing on a specific objective, are classed as economic geology in 553.7, using notation 1–9 from Table 2 where appropriate, e.g., a base-line study of the quality of French surface waters 553.780944. The most general works on monitoring "to protect water quality" are classed in 333.9116, e.g., an environmentalist's alert "we must monitor our water supply."

363.7 vs. 333.72, 304.28   **Environmental problems and services vs. Conservation and protection [of natural resources and the environment] vs. Environmental abuse [in human ecology]**

"Environmentalism" refers to two different sets of issues. Use 363.7 when the issues are preserving and restoring the quality of the social living space, i.e., taking care of wastes, pollution, noise, the dead, and pests. Use 333.72 for the broader concept of preserving and protecting the supply as well as the quality of natural resources. Works about the environmental movement that focus on the concerns it shares with the long established conservation movement are classed in 333.72. Use 304.28 for works that emphasize the effect upon society of overuse, misuse, or pollution of the environment. If in doubt between 333.72 and either 363.7 or 304.28, prefer 333.72. If in doubt between 304.28 and 363.7, prefer 304.28.

363.8 vs. 338.19   **[Social problems and services relating to] Food supply vs. [Economics of] Food supply**

363.8 encompasses the whole problem of supplying food to society, while 338.19 concerns the routine economic aspects. Economic problems like poverty and maldistribution are at the root of most food supply and nutrition problems, but most works concerning such problems focus on the resulting social problems and on the social services needed to overcome them, and therefore are classed in 363.8. Requirements of specific segments of the population are also classed in 363.8. For example, total economic demand for food in Nigeria is classed in 338.19669, food requirements of the urban poor in Nigeria in 363.82086942, normal food trade in Nigeria in 381.41, distribution of food during a famine in Nigeria in 363.88309669. If in doubt, prefer 363.8.

364.1 vs.
362–363

Criminal offenses vs. Specific social problems and services

Some human activities can be considered either as social problems or as crimes. An activity as a social problem is classed in 362–363. The activity treated as a crime is classed in 364.1. For example, drug addiction as a social problem is classed in 362.29, but illegal use of drugs is classed in 364.177. Suicide as a social problem is classed in 362.28, but suicide treated as a crime is classed in 364.1522. If in doubt, prefer 362–363.

368.12

Allied fire insurance lines and extended coverage endorsement

Allied fire insurance lines are those miscellaneous lines which have evolved from fire insurance. One example of this is sprinkler leakage insurance; another is crop insurance, a line that historically evolved from a seemingly unrelated type of insurance.

368.382 vs.
362.1042

Health insurance vs. Social aspects [of health services]

Works on health insurance plans that focus on their insurance features are classed in 368.382, e.g., a work on the need to raise prepaid health care rates in California 368.38201109794. Works that focus on their health services features are classed in 362.1042, e.g., a work on the adequacy of prepaid health services in California 362.104209794. If in doubt, class in 362.1042.

368.4 vs.
362

Government-sponsored insurance vs. Social welfare problems and services

Social security as a government-sponsored insurance scheme is classed in 368.4 and cognate numbers, e.g., social security in the United States 368.4300973. Social security that is not insurance classes in 362, e.g., social security in the United Kingdom 362.0941. If in doubt, class in 362.

370   **Education**

Education is here considered to be a social science—the methods and processes involved in the primary effort outside the home to socialize the young and to prepare them to be independent adults.

370.195 vs.
370.9

Comparative education vs. [Historical, geographical, persons treatment of education]

To be classed in 370.195 a work must emphasize the comparison of two or more educational systems. A discussion of the systems of several jurisdictions that does not emphasize the comparison is classed in 370.9 with the appropriate area notation. For example, a comparison of European systems of education is classed in 370.195094, but a description of educational systems of various European countries in 370.94. If in doubt, prefer 370.9.

In either case, use the area notation coming first in Table 2 if only two systems are involved, e.g., a comparison of education between the United Kingdom and the United States 370.1950941. If more than two systems are involved, use the most specific area notation that will contain them all, e.g., schools in Germany, France, and Italy 370.94. If one area predominates, the notation for that area is used even if some systems outside the area are included, e.g., a comparison of education in France, Germany, Italy, the Soviet Union, Spain, and the United States 370.195094.

371.2 vs.
379

School administration and management vs. Government regulation, control, support of education

In 371.2 are found the operations and activities of schools and school systems: how a school is administered, its students bused and taught, its buildings maintained. In 379 are found the activities of the state (government at any level) regarding the regulation, supervision, and support of the schools and school systems under its control or purview: the finance of public and private schools, their standards, evaluation, and accreditation. If in doubt, class in 371.

375

Curriculums

Works on the curriculum of a specific subject will be classed here infrequently inasmuch as two or more levels of education must be treated; the normal mode of curriculum consideration treats of only one level.
If the curriculum is discussed at the elementary level, the work is classed in 372; if discussed at any other level, the work is classed with the subject, using notation 0711–0715 from Table 1, as appropriate.
For example, a mathematics curriculum for the elementary level 372.7043, for the secondary level 510.712, for elementary and secondary levels considered together 375.51.

380

Commerce, communications, transportation

Commerce deals with the distribution of goods and services, and is a part of the discipline of economics. So too is transportation, an activity that adds to the value of the goods moved. Both communication and transportation developed primarily in response to commercial needs and practices, i.e., to trade, banking, accounting, and so on; therefore, they have been placed in 380 with commerce. The technical aspects of commerce, transportation, and communication are classed in 600.

In order of precedence of subjects under 330 in the Manual, commerce and transportation take the same position as production. Therefore, a work on the labor force in transportation would be classed in 331.1251388, but transportation in communist bloc countries 388.09171.

Add table

065 vs. 09 Business organizations vs. Historical and geographical treatment

Use notation 065 when the work discusses the corporate history of the organization, e.g., the corporate history of the Union Pacific Railroad 385.06578. For international companies use the area number for the country which is its home base, e.g., Pan American World Airways 387.706573.

Use notation 09 when the work discusses the system (facilities, activities, services) maintained by the company in a specific area, e.g., railroad transportation provided by the Union Pacific Railroad 385.0978, air transportation provided by Pan American World Airways 387.7.

If in doubt, prefer 09.

380.1 and **Commerce (Trade) [and] Internal commerce (Domestic trade) [and]**
381, 382 **International commerce (Foreign trade)**

In most cases, notation 029 from Table 1 is not to be used with the subdivisions of these numbers. Commercial miscellany of specific products or groups of products are classed with the product, using notation 029 from Table 1, e.g., offers to sell tools 621.900294. Commercial miscellany of a broad range of products, however, are classed here, e.g., offers to sell products of secondary industries 380.145000294, department store catalogs 381.1410294. A noncurrent offer for sale of a broad range of products that is used primarily to illustrate customs of an earlier period is classed in 909 or 930–990.

380.1 vs. **Commerce (Trade) vs. Management of distribution (Marketing)**
658.8

Class in 380.1 the economic aspects of trading and selling goods, what is, in fact, traded and in what amounts. Class managerial techniques for disposing successfully of the products and services of enterprises in 658. If in doubt, prefer 380.1.

383–388 **Communications and transportation**

Class a comprehensive work on the activities, services, and facilities of a system in the number for the system, e.g., radio broadcasting activities, services, and facilities 384.54, not 384.544.

Offers for sale vs. Economic aspects

Notation 0294 from Table 1 is added throughout 384–388 to designate offers for sale made by organizations producing various kinds of services. Provisions for "economic aspects" of the various services listed are given throughout 384–388 (usually in .1 under a given topic, but sometimes in standing room in the general number). In distinguishing between these two concepts the following may be helpful:

1. Class in the "economic aspects" number schedules of rates and fares published by an agency other than the one offering the service, since these are not offers to sell. A listing of railroad fares put out by a government regulatory agency is an example of this, and is classed in 385.1.

2. Class a list of rates and fares published by the agency offering the service in the "economic aspects" number when such a list is no more than a list of charges for various services, even though this is, in a sense, an offer to sell. For example, class in 387.51 a list emanating from a shipping company that gives only destinations and prices.

3. Class in the number for the appropriate activity or service, using notation 0294, a publication containing a more or less full description of the services being offered as well as the information about rates and fares. Thus, if the shipping company were running a passenger liner and put out a brochure describing the various classes of accommodations offered, the kinds of staterooms, the dining facilities, the garage accommodations, and the medical facilities aboard, such a publication would be classed at 387.5420294, not 387.51, even though fares are given.

384.3 vs. 004.6   **Computer communication vs. Interfacing and communications**

Class economic and related aspects of providing computer communication services to the public in 384.3. Class computer communication and its hardware in office and private use, computer science applied to the technological aspects of computer communication, and interdisciplinary works in 004.6. If in doubt, prefer 004.6.

384.34 and 384.352   **Electronic mail [and] Broadcast videotex (Teletext)**

Teletex is not the same as teletext. Teletex is an electronic-mail system linking telex terminals, word processors, and computer terminals. Teletext is a system for transmitting computer-based information in coded form within the standard television signal for display on visual display units or television sets. Teletex is classed in 384.34, teletext in 384.352.

384.54, **384.55,** **384.8 vs.** **791.4**	**Radiobroadcasting [and] Television [and] Motion pictures vs.** **[Performing arts aspects of] Motion pictures, radio, television**

Class works combining aspects of 384 and 791.4 in 384.

Class in 791.4 the various aspects of producing an individual program, e.g., arranging the various acts of a television variety show 791.450232. Class in 384.54, 384.55, and 384.8 the various aspects of presenting the finished program to the general public, e.g., selecting the correct day and time to broadcast a television variety show 384.5531.

The history of a radio, television, or motion picture company is classed using the following criteria:

1. Class in 384, using notation 09 from Table 1, a general history of the organization, e.g., a history of NBC (National Broadcasting Company) Television Network 384.5540973, and the history of the system (facilities, activities, services) maintained by the organization, e.g., stations broadcasting NBC television programs 384.551530973.

2. Class in 384, using notation 065 from the add table under 380, the corporate history of the organization, e.g., the corporate history of the NBC Television Network 384.55406573.

3. Class in 791.4, using notation 09 from Table 1, the history and critical appraisal of the products of the organization, e.g., the history of the television programs provided by NBC 791.450973.

384.5453, **384.5455** **vs.** **384.54065**	**Stations [and] Networks vs. Business organizations (Stations and** **networks)**

The terms "station" and "network" can refer either to the facility used to broadcast the program or the organization in general. Class in 384.5453 and 384.5455 stations and networks as facilities. Class in 384.54065 stations and networks as business organizations. If in doubt, prefer 384.54065.

384.5522, **384.5523** **vs.** **384.55065**	**Stations [and] Networks vs. Business organizations (Stations and** **networks)**

The terms "station" and "network" can refer either to the facility used to broadcast the program or to the business organization. Class in 384.5522 and 384.5523 stations and networks as facilities. Class in 384.55065 stations and networks as business organizations. If in doubt, prefer 384.55065.

See also 384.54, 384.55, 384.8 vs. 791.4

384.555 and   **Pay television [and] Premium (Subscription) television**
384.5554

In this schedule, "cable television" and "pay television" are treated as the same thing, i.e., systems that provide television signals to customers for a fee, and are classed in 384.555. If "pay-cable" is used to mean premium (or subscription television), i.e., the provision of scrambled signals that are decoded for a fee, it is classed in 384.5554.

386.8 vs.   **[Inland] Ports vs. Ports**
387.1

The distinction is based on whether the port is on tidal waters (387.1) or on nontidal waters (386.8), not upon either distance from the sea or the ability to handle ocean-going ships. For example, class the port of New Orleans (110 miles from the mouth of the Mississippi River but on tidal waters) in 387.10976335, the port of Chicago (which can handle ocean-going vessels but is on nontidal waters) in 386.80977311.

388.314 and   **Highway use [and Use of local streets and highways]**
388.41314

Use notation 0723 from Table 1 for works on the techniques of conducting traffic surveys, e.g., how to survey Detroit's highway uses 388.413140723. Use notation 09 from Table 1 to indicate the results of a traffic survey, e.g., a survey of Detroit's highway use 388.413140977434.

390   **Customs, etiquette, folklore**

Customs, etiquette, and folklore are among the raw material of the social sciences, particularly of anthropology and sociology—the descriptive and analytical aspects of the study of the behavior of mankind in general social groups. Melvil Dewey considered customs to be the culmination of social activity and classed them in 390, just before language, the last of the social sciences and a main class requiring a whole digit (4) to itself.

391 vs.   **Costume and personal appearance vs. Clothing and accessories vs.**
646.3,   **[Artistic aspects of] Costume**
746.92

Costume, clothing, and fashion can be treated in terms of customs, home economics, or art. Customs, such as what was worn, what is fashionable, national costumes, are classed in 391, e.g., Edwardian fashion 391.0094109041, Lithuanian national costumes 391.009475. Home economics aspects, such as how to dress on a limited budget, select the best quality clothing, dress correctly for the business world, are classed in 646.3. Artistic aspects, such as clothing as a product of the textile arts, fashion design, are classed in 746.92. If in doubt between 391 and 646.3 or 746.92, prefer 391; between 646.3 and 746.92, prefer 746.92.

394.2682 vs. 263.9, 290   **Religious holidays vs. Church year and other days and times [of Christian religious observance and] Comparative religion and religions other than Christianity**

> Class in 394.2682 the secular customs associated with religious holidays, e.g., Easter egg hunts 394.268283. Class in 263.9 and cognate numbers in 290 the religious customs associated with religious holidays, e.g., sunrise Easter services 263.93. If in doubt, prefer 263.9 and cognate numbers in 290.

394.5 vs. 791.6   **Pageants, processions, parades vs. Pageantry**

> Class in 394.5 works that discuss traditions of pageants, processions, or parades and works that describe the event. Class in 791.6 works that discuss planning, promoting, and staging the event, including such topics as publicity and float construction. If in doubt, prefer 394.5.

395   **Etiquette (Manners)**

> Etiquette includes prescriptive works on rules of conduct designed to make life pleasanter and more seemly and to eliminate causes of friction in the numerous inevitable minor opportunities for conflict or offense in daily life. More important matters of conduct are classed in 170 Ethics.

398.2   **Folk literature**

> There is no notation available for folk literature in 398.2 to distinguish literary forms, collections, or criticism as there is for general literature in 800. In each case, disregard these aspects in classifying, using the most specific number available.

> Standard subdivisions may be added to subdivisions of this number even if the subject of the work does not approximate the whole, e.g., French folk tales about fairies 398.210944. However, do not add standard subdivisions for individual folk tales, e.g., Sleeping beauty 398.21, not 398.210944.

> Minor characters in a tale do not affect the classification. For example, the presence of Morgan le Fay, a fairy, in the tale of King Arthur does not prevent the tale from being classed at 398.22, even though "fairies" is given as a type under 398.21. However, a tale about Morgan le Fay would be classed in 398.21.

398.2 vs. 291.13   **Folklore vs. Mythology and mythological foundations [of religions]**

> Class in 398.2 mythology having a real, legendary, or nonreligious basis. Myths populated by gods, goddesses, quasi-gods, or quasi-goddesses are classed either in 398.2 or 291.13 according to content, mode of presentation, or author's or editor's intention. Thus, mythol-

ogy presented from a strictly theological point of view or presented as an embodiment of the religion of a people would be classed in 291.13.

However, myths or mythology presented in terms of cultural entertainment or, especially, as representatives of the early literary expression of a society class in 398.2. Often the literary or religious focus is clear (e.g., almost all myths retold for a juvenile audience are classed in 398.2); however, if in doubt, prefer 398.2.

Specific myths and legends presented as examples of a people's religion are classed with the subject in religion, e.g., legends of Jesus' coming to Britain 232.9.

**398.21 vs.   Tales and lore of paranatural and legendary beings of human and
398.22   semihuman form vs. Tales and lore of historical and quasi-historical
                persons and events**

Folktales about quasi-historical persons (who may have actually existed), e.g., King Arthur, are classed in 398.22. Tales about purely legendary persons, e.g., Paul Bunyan, are classed in 398.21. If in doubt, prefer 398.21.

Certain types of persons, such as giants, kings, witches, can either be historical or nonhistorical. The listing of such a type in the example notes at either 398.21 or 398.22 does not preclude tales about that type of person from classing in the other number. For example, "Hansel and Gretel" is classed in 398.21 even though "witches" is given in the note at 398.22.

**398.352 vs.   [Historical and quasi-historical] Persons vs. Legendary beings of
398.45   human and semihuman form**

Works discussing the folklore of quasi-historical persons (who may have actually existed), e.g., King Arthur, are classed in 398.352. Works about the folklore of purely legendary persons, e.g., Paul Bunyan, are classed in 398.45. If in doubt, prefer 398.45.

400   Language

Class examples and collections of "text" whose purpose is to display and study a language with the language, even if limited to a particular subject, e.g., a grammar of scientific English 425. Language analysis of a specific work is criticism and is classed with the work.

See also T4—864 vs. T1—014.

400 vs. 800   Language vs. Literature (Belles-lettres) and rhetoric

Many works treating both language and literature are predominantly about literature; such works are classed in 800. Comprehensive works on language and literature, giving equal attention to both, are classed in 400.

400 vs. 909, **Language vs. World history [and] History of ancient world; of**
930–990 **specific continents, countries, localities; of extraterrestrial worlds**

> Class in 400 studies that emphasize language and literature, even though some material on culture and history is included; but class in 900 studies in history and culture that include but do not emphasize language and literature.

401.43 vs. **Semantics vs. Etymology vs. Structural systems (Grammar) vs.**
412, 415, **[Sociology of] Language vs. Psycholinguistics**
306.44,
401.9

> Semantics at 401.43 is the branch of linguistics that deals with meaning in language. In trying to answer the question of what meaning is, semantics deals with such subtopics as synonymy, ambiguity, semantic truth (metalinguistic truth), and entailment. Closely linked with philosophy, semantics is particularly concerned with the underlying logical structure of natural language, i.e., what elements are necessary beyond correct grammar for statements to make sense.

> Etymology at 412 has only a narrow interest in meaning; it studies the history of the meanings of words.

> Grammar at 415 also has only a narrow interest in meaning; it is concerned with meaning only in relation to morphology and syntax.

> The sociology of language at 306.44 is concerned with meaning as it is affected by its sociocultural context. Most works on linguistic pragmatics deal with language in its sociocultural context and are classed in 306.44. The exception would be works on pragmatics that focus on the individual psychological context; such works are classed in 401.9 Psycholinguistics.

407, T1—07 **Education, research, related topics [in language and Table 1 notation**
vs. 410.7, **for] Education, research, related topics [under individual languages]**
418.007, **vs. [Education, research, related topics in] Linguistics vs. [Education,**
T4—8007, **research, related topics in] Standard usage of language [and Table 4**
401.93 **notation for education, research, related topics under individual**
languages] vs. [Psycholinguistics of] Language acquisition

> The basic distinction between prescriptive and nonprescriptive linguistics is explained in the Manual note at 410. Class in 418.007 works on how to study or teach language using a prescriptive approach.

> Class in 407 broad works on language education not limited to the prescriptive approach and comprehensive works on the study and teaching of both language and literature.

> Class in 410.7 works on the study and teaching of linguistics.

Class in notation 8007 from Table 4 works on how to study or teach a specific language using a prescriptive approach, e.g., how to teach basic French 448.007. In Table 4 there is no analogue to 410.7. Class with the specific language, using notation 07 from Table 1 (which is incorporated in Table 4), works on studying and teaching the linguistics of the language, broad works on studying and teaching the language that are not limited to the prescriptive approach, and comprehensive works on studying and teaching both the language and its literature.

Class in 401.93 works on the psychology of learning language informally, as a child learns from its parents, and comprehensive works on the psychology of informal and formal language learning. Class works on the psychology of formal study and teaching of language in the study-and-teaching numbers discussed above, primarily 418.007 and T4—8007. Since notation 019 Psychological principles from Table 1 cannot be added to notation 07 from Table 1, the numbers for works on the psychology of study and teaching of language do not express the psychological aspect.

410   Linguistics

Prescriptive linguistics is concerned with promoting standard or correct usage of language. Anyone trying to learn to speak or write like educated native users of a standard form of a language is involved with prescriptive linguistics. The various nonprescriptive approaches to linguistics (e.g., descriptive, theoretical, comparative linguistics) are concerned with describing or explaining language usage as it does or did exist, without regard to an ideal of correct usage. Most works of prescriptive linguistics are classed in 418 or with the specific language, using notation 8 from Table 4; works of nonprescriptive linguistics are classed elsewhere in 410–490. For example, descriptive works about grammar are classed in 415 and with the specific language, using notation 5 from Table 4; but prescriptive works about grammar are classed in 418 or with the specific language, using notation 8 from Table 4. Dictionaries, however, are classed in 413 or with the specific language, using notation 3 from Table 4, regardless of whether they are prescriptive or descriptive.

General historical (diachronic) linguistics is classed in 417.7. No comparable provision exists for individual languages, although under some languages, subdivisions of notation 7 from Table 4 are provided for specific early forms of the language, e.g., 427.02 Middle English. For general historical linguistics of a specific language, or for historical linguistics of a specific topic, use notation 09 from Table 1 if the work gives a history, but not if the work merely discusses the processes of change in a general way. For example, class a general discussion of grammatical change in 415, a history of grammatical changes in the

English language in 425.09, a history of all kinds of changes in the English language in 420.9.

Class a comparison of two languages with the language requiring local emphasis (usually the language that is less common in the particular setting). For example, a work comparing English and Japanese is classed in 495.6 in English-speaking countries, but in 420 in Japan. If no emphasis is required, class the work with the language coming later in Table 6.

Class a comparison of three or more languages in the most specific number that will contain them all; e.g., class a comparison of Dutch, German, and English at 430 since all are Germanic languages.

If there is no number that will contain them all (e.g., a comparison of French, Hebrew, and Japanese), class the work in 410.

For comparisons of just one feature of various languages, apply the criteria given above, except do not add notation from Table 4 to the number for language families. A comparison of French, Hebrew, and Spanish grammar is classed in 415; a comparison of Dutch, German, and English grammar at 430.

411–418   [Specific elements of linguistics]

Note that most of these topics correspond to those listed in Table 4, although there is not a complete correspondence in the extent to which the notation is developed or applied. For example, a general bibliographic guide to foreign-language texts is classed in 016.418, but a bibliographic guide to English texts for non-English-speaking students is classed in 016.42824.

420–490   Specific languages

The citation order of 420–490 is straightforward and without exception: Language + language subdivision from Table 4 + standard subdivision from Table 1.

1. Grammar of the Hungarian language:

   494.511 + T4—5 = 494.5115

2. History of the Korean language:

   495.7 + T1—09 = 495.709

3. Dictionary of foreign words in the English language:

   42 + T4—24 + T1—03 = 422.403

It frequently happens that one source calls a particular tongue a language, and another calls it a dialect. Consequently, it is common for a tongue to be treated as a dialect in the Dewey Decimal Classification and as a language in the work being classified, or vice versa.

470   Italic languages   Latin

The dates of the Classical Age of Latin are 80 B.C. to 130 A.D. (the Ciceronian Age 80 B.C. to 43 B.C., the Golden Age of Augustan literature 43 B.C. to 18 A.D., the Silver Age 18 A.D. to 130 A.D.). The formal or literary Latin written at any time thereafter that conforms to the standards of that age is classed in 471–475 and 478. However, works on Vulgar Latin, on Old Latin (80 B.C. or earlier), or on Postclassical Latin are classed in 477. The phrase "Postclassical Latin" refers to the nonclassical or vulgarized Latin used from the death of Juvenal (140 A.D.) until the period of renewed interest in the "pure" Latin of the Classical Age in the eleventh and twelfth centuries, and from the fourteenth century onward. Classical Latin did not die out during the interim, however; and a linguistic study written on, say, Latin manuscripts of the monks of Iona is properly classed with Classical Latin.

500 vs. 001   Natural sciences and mathematics vs. Knowledge

Be careful about equating the word "science" with the natural sciences and mathematics in 500. Quite often the word is used to cover the social sciences and the analytical aspects of other disciplines. Class a work in 001 when "science" is used without implying emphasis on "natural science," in 001.2 Scholarship and learning when used to cover disciplines outside 500, and in 500 only when it is clearly used to imply emphasis on the natural sciences. Works on scientific method and scientific research are particularly apt to belong in 001.4 Research rather than 507.2. According to literary warrant, however, "history of science" more often than not relates to the natural sciences and mathematics and is classed in 509.

500 vs. 338.926, 351.855   Natural sciences and mathematics vs. Information policy vs. Science [administration]

"Science policy" generally focuses on what society should do to promote the utilization of science and the growth of industries and activities based on science. Thus, it generally should be regarded as a policy or program to promote economic development and growth (338.926 and cognate numbers in 338.93–.99). Class works on public administration of science policy in 351.855 and cognate numbers in 353–354, unless there is a heavy emphasis on administration of economic development or on specific industries, in which case, prefer 351.82 and cognate numbers. However, in the absence of a focus on the social sciences, use 509 for natural science policy in an area. If in doubt, prefer 338.9.

500 vs. 600   Natural sciences and mathematics vs. Technology (Applied sciences)

The natural sciences (500) describe and attempt to explain the world we live in, while technology (600) consists of utilizing these sciences to manipulate the natural world and its resources for the benefit of mankind. Be alert, however, for certain subdivisions of 500 that consist largely of technology, e.g., surveying and cartography in 526 and celestial navigation in 527 (all of which would fit better in 620 Engineering); and certain subdivisions of 600 which consist largely of natural science, e.g., human anatomy and physiology in 611–612 (which clearly are parts of 599.9 Hominidae).

Class in 500 interdisciplinary works on any science and its applications in technology. For example, a work on space science (500.5), engineering in other worlds and space (620.419), and astronautics (629.4) is classed in 500.5.

**508 vs. 574,   Natural history vs. Biology vs. Geography and travel vs. Human
910, 304.2   ecology**

Use 508 if a work on natural history has significant emphasis on earth sciences phenomena, but use 574 if the work concentrates on various living things and their settings. If a work covers the description of human settlement as well as natural phenomena, class it in 910. If the emphasis is on the relationship between the natural phenomena and human institutions, class it in 304.2. Class interdisciplinary works on natural history and its human settings in 304.2. If in doubt between science and nonscience numbers, prefer science numbers; if in doubt between 508 and 574, prefer 574.

510   Mathematics

The type of mathematics presently taught in elementary and secondary schools of the United States does not usually have three digit numbers. The following is a list of the school subjects and their numbers:

Arithmetic	513
Algebra	512.9
Geometry	516.2
Trigonometry	516.24

Combination of topics

Use the following instructions when classing in 512.1 Algebra combined with other branches of mathematics, 513.1 Arithmetic combined with other branches of mathematics, and 515.1 Analysis and calculus combined with other branches of mathematics and when using "Class here linear algebra combined with analytic geometry'' at 512.5 Linear, multilinear, multidimensional algebras:

1. These sections are designed for works that deal basically with one subject but have some information on another subject either added at the end of the work or interspersed throughout it. For example, class a textbook with ten chapters on algebra and two on Euclidean geometry in 512.12 Algebra and Euclidean geometry.

2. The work must be predominately about the branch first named. For example, the work must be about algebra with some trigonometry added to be classed in 512.13 Algebra and trigometry. If it is about trigonometry with some algebra added, it is classed in 516.24 Trigonometry.

510, **Mathematics [and Table 1 notation for mathematical principles] vs.**
T1—0151 **[Data processing   Computer science] and [Table 1 notation for]**
vs. 004– **Data Processing   Computer applications**
006,
T1—0285

Mathematics is frequently applied to data processing, and data processing is heavily used in mathematics. In each case, class a work with the discipline to which the other discipline is applied, e.g., recursive functions (511.35) used to explain how computers work 004.0151135, computer programs (005.3) used to solve differential equations 515.35028553.

If the application is in a third discipline, the choice between the two standard subdivisions is governed by the same rule of application. However, normally the distinction between the use of computers in a subject heavily dependent on mathematics, and the use of computers in the mathematics of the subject is not made, so the computer standard subdivision is used. For example, a computer program that could not solve astronomical calculations would be of little use to astronomers. Programs which do perform the calculations will normally be found in 522.8553 (522.8 being the irregular notation for standard subdivision T1—028 in astronomy).

519.5, **Statistical mathematics [and Table 1 notation for statistical**
T1—015195 **mathematics] vs. Statistical method [and Table 1 notation for]**
vs. **Research**
001.422,
T1—072

The subject of statistics can be divided into three parts:

1. How to obtain and arrange statistical data.

2. How to manipulate the data by mathematical means to produce information regarding the topic being examined.

3. How to interpret the statistical results.

When a work gives equal treatment to 1, 2, and 3, or contains information about only 1 or 3 or both 1 and 3, class it with statistical method in 001.422 or with the subject, using notation 072 from Table 1. When it contains only 2 or 2 with 1 or 3 or both as incidental information, class the work as statistical mathematics in 519.5 or with the subject, using notation 015195 from Table 1.

In many disciplines a word derived from the discipline name combined with -metrics or -statistics is used for statistical work, e.g., sociometrics, econometrics, biometrics, biostatistics. Commonly works on these subjects concentrate on 2 from the above list, with secondary treatment of 3 or 1 or both. Therefore, they usually require notation 015195 from Table 1. However, note that works of broader treatment, emphasizing 1 or 3 or both 1 and 3, require notation 072.

If in doubt, prefer 519.5 or notation 015195.

See also 003, T1 011 vs. 510, T1 0151.

520 vs. **Astronomy and allied sciences vs. The universe; space, galaxies,**
523.1 **quasars**

Use 520 for works describing the universe in its several distinct components, e.g., as individual planets, stars, galaxies. Use 523.1 for works treating the universe as a single unit. If in doubt, prefer 520.

523.8 vs. **Stars vs. Galaxies**
523.112

Use 523.8 for comprehensive works on stars and galaxies when they are treated as individual astronomical bodies. However, use 523.112 when stars are considered primarily as components of galaxies. If the galaxies and stars are considered primarily in the context of cosmological theories, prefer 523.1; if other astronomical bodies are treated, e.g., planets and comets, use 520.

530 vs. **Physics vs. Physical sciences**
500.2

Physics deals with the ultimate nature and behavior of matter and energy. As originally formulated in what is now called classical physics (exemplified in most of the span 531–538), it deals largely with matter and energy on a visible or palpable scale. Thus, it was logically located between astronomy (520) which deals with matter and energy on an extremely large scale, and chemistry (540) which deals with matter and energy on an extremely small scale. In this classical view the atoms of chemistry were the smallest particles of matter. The three disciplines together constituted the physical sciences, and co-opted mathematics, which had not yet been recognized as a universal tool valid far beyond the domain of the natural sciences.

Over time, chemistry has continued its focus on atoms and their interactions and combinations with each other to form the molecules of solids, liquids, and gases. However, modern physics has outflanked chemistry by developing physical theories about the even smaller components of atoms. Chemistry has borrowed the part of this new physics that explains the behavior of atoms and molecules in chemical reactions, and in the fascinating pathways of these reactions in both the inorganic world and the phenomena of life. It has for the most part left all other physical relationships and reactions to the physicists. Physics, however, has grown to a point where it can be fairly said that chemistry is but a part of physics.

The resulting expansion of physics has created anomalies in the Dewey Decimal Classification schedule. Not only does physics in 530 conceptually outflank chemistry at both the macro and micro levels, but also modern physics, dealing with the smallest of components, appears at the two ends of the 530s, in 530.1–.4 and 539, leaving the classical physics of large scale phenomena in the middle. The classical and modern approaches to sound, light, heat, and electromagnetic phenomena are often combined in 534–538. While 539 is the comprehensive number for modern (quantum) physics, the subject is more often written about either in its parts or in conjunction with classical physics, so the number 539 itself is relatively unused.

The upshot is that 530 and its standard subdivisions are used for comprehensive works on classical physics, on classical and modern physics, and on physics and chemistry. If mathematics *per se* or astronomy, or both, are added to the mix, the result is classed in 500.2 Physical sciences.

530 vs. 540   **Physics vs. Chemistry and allied sciences**

Class works on specific topics common to both physics and chemistry with chemistry when they relate to chemical composition, or to reactions affecting the combination of atoms in chemical processes. Class other works with physics. Clues more useful here than in most DDC disciplines are the occupations of the authors or the fields of the sponsoring organizations, the presumption being that chemists are writing about chemistry and physicists about physics. In cases where these clues give no indication, class with the topic in physics.

530.12 vs.   **Quantum mechanics (Quantum theory) vs. Classical**
531   **mechanics   Solid mechanics**

Quantum mechanics 530.12 is the concept that energy exists in small separate units (quanta) and is not continuous. It is contrasted with continuum or classical mechanics 531, which applies to the large scale phenomena of the solids, liquids, and gases of everyday observation.

Since the two mechanics have practically nothing in common, and are fundamental to modern (sometimes called quantum) and classical physics respectively, class works covering both in 530. Note, however, that the word mechanics by itself is often used when only classical mechanics is being referred to, so check the contents of a work on mechanics to make sure that both 530.12 and 531 are covered before placing it in 530.

530.41 vs. 548   **Solid-state physics vs. Crystallography**

Use 530.41 for works on crystallography and the crystalline state in their broad senses, i.e., when the terms are used to cover atomic arrangement in metals, ceramics, amorphous materials, polymers, or liquids. Use 548 for works on crystals and crystallography when the terms are used in their everyday meaning, i.e., to refer to discrete objects and abstract lattice patterns. While 530.41 is the comprehensive number, use 548 if in doubt between the two numbers for works clearly emphasizing crystals.

530.416 vs. 539.75   **Responsive behavior and energy phenomena vs. Nuclear reactions and interactions**

Many of the topics in responsive behavior and energy phenomena of the solid state overlap similar topics in nuclear reactions and interactions. Some of the examples listed under each topic may be found treated in the other. Class the topics in 530.416 if studied in the context of the condensed (solid and liquid) state, i.e., in answer to the question, what is taking place in condensed matter that makes it behave the way it does. Class them in 539.75 if they are studied in the abstract, or in the context of nuclear structure, i.e., in answer to the question, what makes the atom behave the way it does.

530.475 vs. 531.16, 530.12   **Diffusion and mass transport phenomena vs. Particle mechanics [and] Quantum mechanics (Quantum theory)**

Particle mechanics is a subject which exists in both quantum and classical physics, but is far more basic to the study of quantum physics, where the quanta for which it is named can be considered particles. Particles are particularly important in the study of diffusion and transport phenomena, where the basic mechanism is random oscillation or Brownian motion of particles. Use 530.12 for comprehensive works on particle mechanics but prefer 530.475 or cognate numbers in 530.4 for treatment of particles in diffusion within various states of matter. Also consider other appropriate numbers in modern physics, e.g., 539.725 for orbits of subatomic particles. Use 531.16 only if it is clear that the emphasis is on classical mechanics. If in doubt between 530.475 and either 531.16 or 530.12, prefer 530.475.

Brownian motion usually refers to the random motion of microscopic particles. However, the concept is extended by analogy to a variety of similar random movements, e.g., of prices, of biological populations, of instrumental recordings. Use 530.475 for interdisciplinary works on the concept, and class specific analogies with the subject. Note that many works on Brownian motion have an unstated emphasis on such motion in fluids, and should be classed in 530.425.

536.4 vs.   **Effects of heat on matter vs. Phase changes (Phase transformations)**
530.474

The difference between studies of expansion, melting, incandescence, etc., in 536.4 and in 530.474 is essentially that between classical physics and modern or quantum physics. Class in 536.4 the effects of heat that can be readily observed or measured with simple instruments for determining temperature, expansion, viscosity, luminescence, etc. Class in 530.474 the analysis of what is happening to matter at the molecular and submolecular level. If in doubt, prefer 536.4.

544–545 vs.   **[Qualitative and Quantitative analysis] vs. Analytical chemistry**
543

The distinction between qualitative and quantitative analysis has been rendered largely obsolete by the growing sophistication of techniques. Therefore, prefer numbers in 543.08 over those in 544 or 545 for specific techniques unless qualitative or quantitative use is specifically emphasized.

546 vs. 541   **Inorganic chemistry vs. Physical and theoretical chemistry**

The rule that physical and theoretical chemistry of specific elements or compounds is classed in 546 does not apply when one or two examples drawn from large groupings like metals (546.3) or nonmetals (546.7) are used primarily to study or explain a specific topic in physical or theoretical chemistry. In such cases, use the number in 541, e.g., hydrogen-ion concentration 541.3728, not 546.2.

546 vs. 549   **Inorganic chemistry vs. Mineralogy**

Chemistry and mineralogy are considered to be coordinate subjects. As a result, many topics of physical and theoretical chemistry pertaining to the structure and behavior of homogeneous crystalline solids will not be classed in 546. Use 546 numbers for comprehensive works on the chemistry and mineralogy of specific chemical types, but if in doubt, prefer 549.

548 vs. 549   **Crystallography vs. Mineralogy**

The relation between crystallography and mineralogy is approximately the same as between physical and theoretical chemistry (541) and inorganic chemistry (546). The crystallography of specific minerals is classed in 549 unless used to study or explain a topic in 548, e.g., quartz, feldspar, and related crystals 549.68, but a study of isomorphism using quartz, feldspar, and related crystals 548.3.

549.1   Determinative mineralogy

Topics spelled out in subdivisions of 549.1 (other than meteorites in 549.112 and physical mineralogy in 549.12) should be interpreted narrowly, within the context of techniques of identifying and characterizing minerals. If in doubt between 549.1 and a comprehensive number elsewhere in 540 and 550, prefer the comprehensive number, e.g., minerals in metamorphic rocks 552.4 (not 549.1144).

550 vs. 910   Earth sciences vs. Geography and travel

Geophysics (550) is the analysis of the structure of the earth and the forces shaping it; physical geography (910.02) is the description of the resulting landscape. Descriptions of the results of a specific force or process are classed with the subject in 551; the operation of all forces and processes which combined to create a specific topographic land form is classed with the land form in 551.41–.45; the operation of all the forces and processes taken as a whole in a specific area, especially if emphasizing solid geology, is classed with the area in 554–559. However, when a work treats the whole geographical landscape with only minor consideration of the geophysical processes, it is classed in 910.02 or under the specific area number in 913–919, using notation 02 from the table at 913–919. For example, physical description of surface features in Burma 915.9102, geophysical processes operating in Burma or the geology of Burma 555.91, earthquakes in Burma 551.2209591, mountains in Burma 551.43209591. If in doubt, prefer 550.

Descriptions of surface features for travelers, which usually cover resort accommodations and the ambience as well as the features are also classed in 910, with use of notation 04 from the table under 913–919 as appropriate, e.g., contemporary tourist beaches in Burma 915.91045.

551.302–.307 [General topics of surface and exogenous processes] vs. Geologic
vs. 551.35   work of water

Since water is by far the most important agent in the erosion, transport, and deposit of geological materials, the normal rule of predominance does not apply in choosing between 551.302–.304 and 551.352–.354. Use the latter numbers only for works limited to the work of water or to materials transported by water; prefer 551.302–.304 when the treatment gives due coverage to the work of wind, glaciers, or frost, even if agents other than water take up a small part of the text.

Water is also the most important agent in soil formation (551.305) and mass movement (551.307). However, it almost always acts in conjunction with other agents to produce soil or mass movement, e.g., action of dissolved chemicals, temperature changes, or earthquake vibrations. Therefore, the work of water in these two phenomena is brought together with that of other agents in 551.305 and 551.307.

551.46 vs. 574.92   **Hydrosphere   Oceanography vs. Aquatic biology   Marine biology**

While 551.46 is the number for comprehensive treatment of physical oceanography and marine biology, note that marine biology in 574.92 may include significant consideration of ocean waters as part of the ecology of marine organisms. If in doubt, prefer 574.92.

551.6 vs. 551.5   **Climatology and weather vs. Meteorology**

Meteorology analyzes and describes the properties and phenomena of the atmosphere, and thus explains climate and weather. Meteorology is also the comprehensive subject, encompassing consideration of climatology and weather. Unfortunately, however, some works on the larger subject (meteorology) may be called "climatology," "climate and weather," or simply "climate" or "weather," but must be classed in 551.5 in spite of the words used in the titles. Books so titled are classed in 551.6 only when the words are limited to four senses:

1. The description of phenomena of the atmosphere taken as a whole, weather usually being the short-range description, and climate the long-range description.

2. The prediction of weather, climate, or specific meteorological phenomena, i.e., weather forecasting and forecasts (551.63–.65).

3. The study of climate or meteorology in small areas, i.e., microclimatology or micrometeorology (551.66).

4. The attempt to modify weather or any specific meteorological phenomena (551.68), which is actually a technology.

All other elements, including description (weather reports) of specific phenomena, remain in 551.5, regardless of the terms used in the work in hand. For example, reports of rainfall are classed in 551.577, forecasts of rainfall in 551.6477, a forecast of a rainy day in Singapore in 551.655957, a description of rain belts of Asia in 551.62, a discussion of how weather works 551.5.

551.7   **Historical geology**

It is not anticipated that the periods and epochs presently given in 551.72–.79 will be further subdivided; therefore, standard subdivisions may be added for specific epochs, stages, or formations, e.g., Albian stage (of Lower Cretaceous) in France 551.770944. However, the Precambrian eras may be further divided, so standard subdivisions are used only for works approximating the whole of the given eras.

551.7 vs. 560   **Historical geology vs. Paleontology   Paleozoology**

Paleontology is the study of life in former geologic ages through the interpretation of fossils. It utilizes the same material as historical geology (i.e., the geological record), but only as a record of life and the environment in which life evolved. Historical geology emphasizes the rocks and their strata, using paleontological facts to help date and interpret deposition, movement, and erosion. If in doubt, prefer 551.7.

552 vs. 549   **Petrology vs. Mineralogy**

Rocks can be defined as aggregates of minerals, the minerals being homogenous, usually crystalline grains (large and small) that give rocks their texture. Petrology encompasses the study of rocks and minerals, or of rocks alone. The homogenous minerals studied by themselves are classed in 549. If in doubt, prefer 552.

553   **Economic geology**

Works classed in 553 may include either scientific analysis or economic evaluation or both, and may range from very technical to very superficial. Deposits may be defined in terms of volume, monetary value, years' supply; or simply as good, rich, or promising.

While 553 is the interdisciplinary number for specific nonmetallic materials, be alert for works that emphasize economics of the materials as a whole (not just reserves, stocks, supplies), e.g., a work on the importance of water, not giving much consideration to scientific or other aspects, 333.91 (not 553.7).

Also be alert for works having a heavy but unstated emphasis on metallic deposits: these are classed in 553.4.

559.9   **[Earth sciences in extraterrestrial worlds]**

Use 559.9 and notation 0999 from Table 1 in 551–553 for phenomena of celestial bodies directly comparable to terrestrial phenomena. Generally the analogy with earth holds only if the bodies have distinct lithospheres, otherwise hydrosphere and meteorology are moot concepts. For example, class the atmosphere of Mars (which has a lithosphere) in 551.5099923, but the atmosphere of stars (which do not) in 523.86, the red spot of Jupiter (a planet without a distinct lithosphere) in 523.45.

560 vs. 575   **Paleontology   Paleozoology vs. Evolution and genetics**

Paleontology provides a major part of the evidence for evolution, and many works cover both fields. Class in 575 works that cite paleontological evidence for evolution and works that add significant non-paleontological evidence to the picture. Prefer 560 for works emphasizing the description of extinct organisms and environment as the history of life, and for works on the evolution of extinct taxons. If in doubt, prefer 575.

573.2   **Evolution and genetics of humankind**

Be alert for misleading or equivocal phrases like "evolution of man." They may cover the whole field of evolution (575), review all of paleontology or paleozoology (560), or concentrate on the immediate forebears of modern humankind (573.3).

573.6 vs.   **Anthropometry vs. Human anatomy, cytology (cell biology),**
611   **histology (tissue biology)**

Anthropometry is concerned with measuring human beings to determine variation and presumed evolutionary development. The emphasis is generally on external variation and bone structure, in contrast to anatomy (611), which is more concerned with norms of structure, internal as well as external. Prefer 573.6 for external features and shapes, and gross bone structure (e.g., the comparison of heavy- and thin-boned people, indexes of length and breadth of skeletal features); 611 for all other features.

574.5222 vs.   **Effects of specific aspects of environment on organisms vs. Diseases**
574.24,   **and injuries caused by physical and chemical factors vs.**
363.73   **[Environmental problems and services relating to] Pollution**

In using 574.24 and 574.5222 for studies of the effects of pollution and other deleterious agents, keep in mind that the former is part of pathology (574.2), while the latter is part of ecology (574.5). Therefore, use 574.24 and cognate numbers in 576 and 580–590 for the pathological conditions caused by pollution and other agents in the tissues of organisms. Use 574.5222 and cognate numbers for the more generalized effects upon the community of organisms, e.g., for studies of the presence and absence of indicator organisms, the reduction of species counts, the general vigor and health of surviving species.

However, use biology numbers with caution for pollution studies, because the growth and decline of indicator species is often used to measure the extent and kind of pollution, and are interpreted to suggest the need for remedial measures. Such studies are classed in 363.7363 and cognate numbers in 363.738–.739.

If in doubt between a biology number and 363.73, prefer 363.73; if in doubt between 574.24 and 574.5222, prefer 574.5222.

574.526 vs. [Ecology of] Specific kinds of environments vs. [Biology of areas, 574.909–.92 regions, places in general]

The kinds of environments important in ecology usually have a counterpart number under the span used for biology of kinds of areas. Class in 574.526 works emphasizing the interrelationships among various elements in a specific kind of area, in 574.909–.92 descriptive accounts of organisms characteristic of a kind of area. The latter span may be used to describe characteristic life cycles and behavior of particular kinds of organisms, but stops short of a discussion of interrelationships. In case of doubt, prefer 574.526.

580–590 [Botanical and zoological sciences]

The sequence of taxonomic groups of plants and animals can be described as following the course of the letter U. It begins at one tip of the U with the most highly developed and complex plants (dicotyledons among the flowering plants) and moves down to the base of the U for fungi, algae, and bacteria. The sequence then skips over to 590 to begin up the other arm of the U with the protozoa. After moving up through increasingly complex invertebrates, it reaches the vertebrates, and finally humankind, the most highly developed animal.

580–590 vs. [Botanical and zoological sciences] vs. Agriculture and related 630, 641.3 technologies vs. Food

Interdisciplinary numbers

Numbers from 580–590 are used for interdisciplinary works on plants and animals. However, many works on species known primarily in agriculture emphasize growing and harvesting while giving some biological information as background. Class these works in 630, e.g., a work on cotton that gives enough about the physiology of cotton to explain why it should be cultivated in a certain way 633.51, a work on aquarium fish that tells where they are found in nature but concentrates on how to grow them 639.34.

A complicating consideration is that the interdisciplinary number for food is 641.3. Thus works on the utilization and food value as well as the agriculture and botany of edible plants and animals are classed in 641.3, not in 580–590.

Physiology and Pathology

The classification of physiology and anatomy differs between agricultural plants and animals. Physiology and anatomy of plants is classed in botany (581.1, 581.4, and related numbers); that of animals, in agriculture (636.0891–.0892 and related numbers).

The classification of pathology and diseases is the same for agricultural plants and animals; they are classed in agriculture. The number for plant pathology and diseases (and for comprehensive works of plant and animal pathology and diseases) is 632; for animal pathology and diseases is 636.0896. *(However, see also 591 vs. 610 for experimental work in medicine.)*

581   Botany

Use 581 with caution, since many works on "plants" are in fact limited to spermatophytes (582), angiosperms (comprehensive works 582.13), or dicotyledons (583). Substantial treatment of nonspermatophytic plants must be present to justify the use of 581.

Notes for subdivisions of 574 apply to cognate numbers here.

**582.1 vs.   Nontaxonomic groupings [of seed-bearing plants] vs. Flowers and
635.9   ornamental plants [in agriculture]**

The nontaxonomic groupings of plants in 582.1 are similar to some groupings found in floriculture. Class in 635.9 (often in 635.97 gardening of other groupings) if the emphasis is on plants to be cultivated or appreciated in man-made settings, in 582.1 if the emphasis is on the plants in nature or on their biology. If in doubt, prefer 635.9.

See also 580–590 vs. 630, 641.3.

583–584   Angiospermae (Flowering plants)

The arrangement of larger taxonomic groupings of dicotyledons (583) and of monocotyledons (584) is roughly according to the Engler-Prantl system of classification. However, under the larger groupings, the orders and families are defined according to John Hutchinson's *The Families of Flowering Plants*, 1959. When a family formerly provided under one order is assigned to a different order by Hutchinson, it has not been relocated in this schedule. A cross reference from the order to which Hutchinson places it leads to its number in the schedule.

Exercise caution in identifying orders and families of flowering plants by common names; many such names are used for plants in several unrelated taxonomic groups. Notes in the schedule linking the common names are not exhaustive.

591   Zoology

In zoology it is often difficult to apply the rule that a biological process or system is classed with the type of organism in which it is studied. Often the type of animal is not stated, or each of a compilation of studies uses a different species. When the interest appears to be medical, and in the absence of obvious contrary clues, give the benefit of doubt to 599 and its zero subdivisions, the comprehensive numbers for warm-blooded vertebrates. 599 can be used when warm-blooded animals predominate, even if there is a sprinkling of material on other animals. However, note that works on diseases of humankind are classed in 616–618; diseases of useful animals in 636–639 even if studied experimentally in laboratory animals, not in 599.02 and cognate numbers.

Notes for subdivisions of 574 apply to cognate numbers here.

591 vs. 610   Zoology vs. Medical sciences   Medicine

The results of anatomical and physiological research with animal models are classed in zoology 591–599, but the results of pharmacological, therapeutic, and pathological research with animals and plants are classed in 615–619 if the medical relevance for humans is stated or implied.

591.29 vs.   Immunity [in animals] vs. Immunity (Immunology) [in medical
616.079   sciences]

Class in 616.079 and cognate numbers in 616–618 works emphasizing immunology in relation to diseases and problems in human beings. If in doubt between a 590 number and a 616–618 number, prefer 616–618.

598.81–.88   Passeriformes (Passerine, Perching birds)

Not all the passerine families are provided for in 598.81–.88; use 598.8 for those not listed. Exercise caution in identifying families of passerine birds by common names; many such names are used for birds of several different families. Cautionary notes in the schedule are not exhaustive.

599.03   [Development and maturation of mammals]

Use for pregnancy, lactation, placentas, other concepts brought out in 612.63–.68 (subdivisions of human development and maturation) not brought out under 574.3.

608 vs. 609   Inventions and patents vs. Historical, geographical, persons
treatment [of technology]

Use 608 for works on inventions that are primarily descriptive (and usually arranged topically); 609 for works that emphasize historic factors that led to inventions, or that arrange inventions chronologically. If in doubt, prefer 608.

610.69   Medical personnel

Be careful not to confuse the nature of the duties performed by the personnel with the technology of the operations used to discharge the duties, e.g., the technology of the services of medical technicians 610.737, not 610.6953; of surgeons 617, not 617.0232.

610.73   Nursing and services of medical technicians and assistants

Class here only works that emphasize what the nurse does. As the nursing profession continues to expand its responsibilities and gain recognition for those it already performs, more and more works by and for nurses are about the subjects of medical science in a larger context than intended here. Class such works in other medical numbers, e.g., a survey of medical sciences for nurses 610, not 610.73; a work treating the problems and techniques of surgery written to help nurses understand the context of their duties 617, not 610.73677, even if called surgical nursing. If the broader works contain many special instructions for nurses that general readers would not find useful, add notation 024613 from Table 1 (the subject for nurses), e.g., a general work about surgery that contains many special instructions for nurses 617.0024613.

See also T1—024.

610.9   Historical, geographical, persons treatment [of medical sciences, of medicine]

Class in 610.9 the history of three or more medical sciences. Class the history of a particular medical science with the science, e.g., the history of nursing 610.7309, of surgery 617.09, of internal medicine 616.009. Class histories of major diseases and their distribution in 614.42, and histories of medical service and the resulting medical welfare of people in 362.109. If in doubt, prefer 362.109.

Class works on former medical practices emphasizing therapy in 615.88 Empirical and historical remedies, 615.882 Folk medicine, or 615.899 Ancient and medieval remedies.

611 vs. 612   Human anatomy, cytology (cell biology), histology (tissue biology) vs. Human physiology

Anatomy concerns the form and structure of organs in contrast to their physiology, which deals with how they work. Sometimes works bearing the names of organs emphasize their physiology or treat physiology as well as anatomy; class these works in 612, unless they are limited to the cytological and histological level. Class treatment of anatomy, physiology, and pathology at the cytological and histological level in 611.018.

612 vs. 616   Human physiology vs. Diseases

Class in 612 comprehensive works on physiology and pathological physiology (612 plus 616.07). Class in 616 comprehensive works on diseases that move from a discussion of physiology to a more general consideration of causes of disease, complications, prevention, and therapy. For example, class the normal and pathological conditions of the circulatory system in 612.1, but the physiology, pathology, and therapeutics of the circulatory system in 616.1. If in doubt, prefer 616.

612.1–.8   **Specific functions, systems, organs**

Here is found the basic division of the human body into physiological systems. Parallel subdivisions 1–8 appear elsewhere in shortened or slightly altered form: under human anatomy in 611.1–.8; under pharmacodynamics in 615.71–.78; under diseases in 616.1–.8; under surgery by system in 617.41–.48; and in comparable physiology, anatomy, and disease numbers in biology 574–599.

If in doubt where to class an organ or function not provided for in one of the parallel arrays, use 612.1–.8 as a guide. For example, use 615.74 Drugs affecting the lymphatic and glandular systems for pharmacodynamics of the pituitary gland. This is comparable to 612.4 Secretion, excretion, related functions, where this gland is named at 612.492. In the same manner use 615.73 Drugs affecting the digestive system and metabolism for pharmacodynamics of the pancreas. This is comparable to 612.3 Digestion, where the pancreas is named at 612.34. However, class pharmacodynamics of the kidneys in 615.761, where the urinary system is provided for, even though kidney physiology is at 612.463 under secretions.

612.3923 vs.   **[Metabolism of] Water vs. [Biochemistry of] Fluids**
612.01522
Only water may be considered at 612.3923. Class fluid metabolism in the sense of all the biochemical and metabolic processes taking place in cellular and interstitial fluids in 612.01522. Also class fluid balance and electrolytic balance in 612.01522.

613 vs.   **Promotion of health vs. Specific therapies and kinds of therapies**
615.8
Note that many of the topics in 613 appear also in 615.8, e.g., breathing 613.192 and 615.836, diet 613.2 and 615.854, exercise 613.71 and 615.82. In each case the 613 number refers to the preventive or "staying healthy" aspects, while the 615.8 number refers to the therapeutic or "regaining health" aspects. Class comprehensive works in 613.

613.2 vs.   **Dietetics vs. Food vs. Food supply**
641.3,
363.8
Class comprehensive works on personal aspects of nutrition in 613.2. However, class interdisciplinary works on food in 641.3, on nutrition in 363.8. The essential thrust of 613.2 is to help individuals meet dietary requirements and maintain optimal balanced intake without gaining or losing weight. Also included is material for dietitians in planning diets for individuals. In contrast, the emphasis in 641.3 is on the food itself, and in 363.8 it is on meeting and maintaining the needs of society in general and of various social groups.

613.62 vs.   Industrial and occupational health vs. Occupational and industrial
363.11   hazards

> Use 613.62 for works that emphasize technical measures to be taken for promotion of industrial and occupational health. Use 363.11 for works that emphasize social and institutional arrangements. In case of doubt, prefer 363.11.

613.71 vs.   Exercise and sports activities [for fitness] vs. [Grooming for]
646.75,   Physique and form vs. Athletic and outdoor sports and games [as
796   recreation]

> Exercise and sports activities as means of improving physical fitness are classed in 613.71, as means of improving the appearance of the body in 646.75, as recreation in 796. For example, lifting weights for physical fitness is classed in 613.713, bodybuilding contests in 646.75079, weight lifting as a sport (i.e., contests to determine who can lift the most weight) in 796.41. If in doubt among 613.71, 646.75, and 796, prefer 613.71.

614.4–.5 vs.   [Incidence of and public measures to prevent disease] vs. Problems
362.1–.4   of and services to sick and disabled people

> Studies of epidemics and of the incidence of physical disease (including mental retardation and physical handicaps) are classed in 614 when treated solely from the medical standpoint. Works emphasizing diseases as social problems are classed in 362.1.

> Works on the social provision of services to the physically ill are classed in 362.1. Works on preventive measures, however, are classed in 614.4–.5, regardless of whether the emphasis is medical or social. Thus works on social provision of immunization services are classed in 614.47, as are works on the medical aspects of immunization. Note that the public measures classed in 614.4–.5 are strictly limited to preventive ones. For example, class fluoridation and programs advising people how to avoid cavities in 614.5996, but class programs to identify and treat people with cavities in 362.19767.

> Works about the incidence and prevention of mental illness, mental illness as a social problem, and social provision of services to the mentally ill, are all classed in 362.2.

614.4   Incidence of and public measures to prevent disease

> The term "epidemiology" sometimes refers to a research technique with application outside 614, e.g., in determining etiologies, such as smoking as a cause of cancer 616.994071; in determining the dimensions of social service requirements, such as the boundaries of the mental retardation problem 362.32; in exploring the possible effectiveness

of proposed preventive measures, such as in reducing traffic accidents 363.1257.

614.5 **Incidence of and public measures to prevent specific diseases and kinds of diseases**

When adding notation from Table 1 to numbers built by use of the add notes in 614.526–.598 directing addition of digits from 616, note that two zeros are required for most diseases—those that have an asterisk in 616—while one zero is required for diseases and groups of diseases not marked by an asterisk.

614.5939 vs. **[Incidence of and public measures to prevent nutritional diseases] vs.**
363.82 **[Incidence, extent, severity of food supply problems]**

Class nutrition surveys in 363.82. These surveys sometimes mention prevalence of malnutrition as an indicator of nutrition levels. Only if the emphasis is on the malnutrition problem *per se* should a survey be classed in 614.5939.

615 **Pharmacology and therapeutics**

Note that 615 is seldom used by itself because pharmacology (615.1) and therapeutics (615.5) are usually treated separately or with a preponderance of one or the other.

615.1 vs. **Drugs (Materia medica) vs. Pharmacodynamics**
615.7

"Pharmacology" is often used in the titles of works mainly limited to pharmacodynamics. If the table of contents is arranged by physiological systems (as 615.7 is), the chances are good that the work emphasizes the physiological and therapeutic action of drugs, making 615.7 the appropriate number. If in doubt, prefer 615.1.

615.2–.3 **Specific drugs and groups of drugs**

Note that most drugs are organic (615.3). Class comprehensive works on drugs in 615.1 even if there is a strong predominance of organic drugs so long as coverage of inorganic drugs is in proportion to their importance. However, class in 615.321 comprehensive works on crude drugs and simples (products that serve as drugs with minimal processing, e.g., medicinal teas, baking soda, royal jelly).

615.2–.3 vs. **Specific drugs and groups of drugs vs. Pharmacodynamics**
615.7

The note in the schedule at 615.2–.3 saying to class a specific drug or group of drugs affecting a specific system in 615.7 means that the numbers 615.2–.3 are not used for drugs known primarily for their effect on a single system. For example, digitalis is classed in 615.711 Heart stimulants (or 616.129061 drug therapy for heart failure), not in

615.32381 drugs derived from the Personales order; alcohol in 615.7828, not 615.32.

615.4   **Practical pharmacy**

This number covers only a limited aspect of pharmacy: putting drugs into forms that can be used by human beings. Class works on the larger meaning of pharmacy in 615.1, e.g., managing a pharmacy 615.1068. Follow the same procedure when adding 615 numbers in other disciplines, e.g., economics of the pharmacy industry 338.476151.

615.53   **General therapeutic systems**

Use this number and its subdivisions only when the discussion is historical or theoretical, e.g., a discussion of the theory of naturopathy 615.535. When these systems are discussed in their application to therapy, class them in a therapy number, e.g., the application of chiropractic 615.82. When the therapies are applied to specific conditions, class in 616–618, e.g., chiropractic in musculoskeletal diseases 616.7062.

Be careful about biography. Founders of systems are usually classed with the respective systems, e.g., a biography of Andrew Taylor Still, the founder of osteopathy, 615.533092. Other practitioners of a specific system are usually classed in 610.92. *See also 615.534 for chiropractic.*

615.534   **Chiropractic**

Many chiropractors limit their practice to therapeutic manipulation (615.82) or to manipulation for diseases of the musculoskeletal system (616.7062). For these people, the best biography number is one that emphasizes their special therapeutic system—615.534092. For chiropractors who do not limit their practice, use 610.92 for biographies.

615.7 vs. 615.9   **Pharmacodynamics vs. Toxicology**

Class toxic effects and interactions of drugs primarily of pharmacodynamic interest in 615.704 or with the system affected in 615.71–.78. However, a drug primarily of pharmacodynamic interest may be considered a poison if it is so toxic that a single inadvertent ingestion would cause serious complications or death, e.g., the pharmacodynamics of atropine (belladonna) 615.7 (not in any specific subdivision because it affects several systems), but the toxicology of belladonna 615.952379. If in doubt, prefer 615.7.

615.7 vs. 616–618   **Pharmacodynamics vs. [Diseases, surgery, other branches of medicine]**

Class in 615.7 only general works on the pharmacodynamic action of drugs and their effects on the human body. Class the use of a drug in treatment in 616–618, adding subdivision 061 from the various tables under these numbers. If in doubt, prefer 616–618.

615.8   **Specific therapies and kinds of therapies**

Several therapies listed in 615.8 are usually applied only to certain specific types of disorders, and works on the therapies take such application for granted without highlighting it in the title. Note the unstated emphasis and class accordingly, e.g., radiotherapy emphasizing cancer treatment 616.9940642, not 615.842; music therapy emphasizing psychiatric uses 616.891654, not 615.85154.

615.854   **Dietotherapy**

Use with caution; when a single food element is heavily emphasized, dietotherapy may amount to drug therapy, e.g., a diet distinctive largely by its use of enzymes 615.35, by its use of royal jelly 615.36.

615.8809   **[Historical, geographical, persons treatment of empirical and historical remedies]**

This number is limited to therapy. If pathological or etiological beliefs are also emphasized, e.g., the theory of the four humors or the influence of bad airs, the work must be classed in 610.9.

Class here discussions of old remedies of a specific geographic area that are not limited by the terms of Folk medicine 615.882 or Ancient and medieval remedies 615.899. If in doubt whether to class geographical treatment in 615.8809 or either 615.88209 or 615.89909, prefer 615.8809.

615.882   **Folk medicine**

Class a work of medical folk literature in 398.27 if the emphasis is on the story told; a work on the sociology of medical folklore in 398.353 if the emphasis is on the tales as cultural and social phenomena. Class in 615.882 only if the emphasis is on the medical practice.

Note that 615.882 is under therapy. If a work gives more than token consideration to folk theories on the causes of disease, it must be classed in 610, e.g., folk etiologies and therapies of India 610.954 (or 616.00954 when the material is arranged by class of disease as in 616.1–.9).

See also 615.8809.

616 vs. 610   Diseases vs. Medical sciences   Medicine

Class in 616 comprehensive works on the diseases listed in 616–618. However, if a work contains separate treatment of health, pharmacology, and therapeutics, as well as of diseases, class it in 610.

When the whole of medicine is brought to bear on the concept of diseases in a single treatise that discusses group after group of diseases, class the work in 616. The table of contents usually offers guidance. If it reads like a summary of topics in 610.73–.98, class the work in 610; if it reads like a summary of topics in 616.01–.99 or in 616–618, class the work in 616.

Use notation from Table 1 with caution under 616 except for internal medicine or works clearly limited to the concept of diseases. Prefer 610.3 for medical dictionaries, 610.711 for medical schools, 610.92 for doctors not having a distinct specialty.

616 vs. 616.075   Diseases vs. Diagnosis and prognosis

"Clinical medicine" has two meanings. In one sense it approximates 616, i.e., the application of all branches of medicine to treatment of various diseases. However, just as often it is shorthand for the work of a clinical diagnostic laboratory, and is properly classed at 616.075.

616.01   Medical microbiology

Do not confuse 616.01 with 576.165 Deleterious microorganisms and cognate numbers for the biology of microorganisms in 576, 589, and 593.1. If in doubt between a biology number and numbers in 610 for microorganisms, prefer the biology number.

616.01 vs. 616.9   Medical microbiology vs. Other diseases [communicable diseases]

Do not confuse medical microbiology with the classes of communicable disease in 616.91–.96 caused by various types of microorganisms. The emphasis in 616.01 is on the organism, usually as the cause of disease, while in 616.9 it is on the whole disease and its course, cure, and prevention. Each is comprehensive in its own way, 616.01 as the interdisciplinary number for pathogenic organisms affecting humans and domestic animals, and 616.9 for the resulting diseases. If in doubt, prefer 616.9.

616.0757   Radiological diagnosis

Diagnosticians use the term "radiology" with meanings of differing scope, with the result that three different works on diagnostic radiology may be classed in three different places. Class a work limited to the use of X-rays in 616.07572; a work about the use of X-rays, radioactive materials, other ionizing radiations in 616.0757; and a work about the use of all kinds of radiation, both ionizing and non-ionizing, in 616.0754.

616.1–.9   **Specific diseases**

Add table

071 vs. 01   [Etiology] vs. [Microbiology]

When the etiological agent is known to be a single type of microorganism, use 01 for the work without further subdivision, unless predisposing and contributing factors are emphasized, e.g., microorganisms causing venereal disease 616.95101, predisposing factors leading to severity of venereal disease 616.951071.

616.1–.8   **Diseases of specific systems and organs**

When a disease of one system affects another system so strongly that it is the second system that must be the focus of concern and treatment, class the work with the affected system, e.g., retinal complications of diabetes 617.73 Disease of optic nerves and retinas not 616.462 Diabetes mellitus.

616.123028   **[Intensive care in coronary diseases]**

Use caution with the phrase "coronary care." It often extends to intensive care for any serious heart disease and in that case is classed in 616.12028.

616.932 vs.   **Cholera vs. Diseases of the stomach**
616.33

"Cholera" was formerly a nonspecific term for a variety of gastrointestinal disturbances. Cholera morbus and other choleras using the former meaning of "cholera" are classed in 616.33. Today, "cholera" is limited to the type of viral disease formerly called Asiatic cholera and is classed in 616.932. If in doubt, class in 616.932.

616.992 vs.   **Tumors (Neoplasms and neoplastic diseases) vs. Cancers (Malignant**
616.994   **tumors [neoplasms])**

Many works about neoplasms, tumors, and oncology discuss only or predominantly cancer (616.994). Therefore, before using 616.992, check whether benign tumors (616.993) are significantly represented. If in doubt, prefer 616.994.

616.995   **Tuberculosis**

Many authors writing about tuberculosis concentrate entirely on pulmonary tuberculosis (616.99524); they do not mention this fact because the other forms of tuberculosis are so much less common. Check the front matter for signs of an implicit focus on the disease in the lungs. If no such signs are found, class the work in 616.995.

617   **Miscellaneous branches of medicine   Surgery**

Add table

059   Surgery

For 617 numbers whose meaning is limited to surgery, use 059 only for surgery by specific instrument or technique, e.g., cryosurgery, dialysis, and bypass surgery; and 0592 for plastic surgery, transplantation of organs, implantation of artificial organs.

059 is limited to operative surgery. Class other physical procedures (included in the broader concept of surgery) in 06.

06   Therapy

Do not use 06 by itself under numbers whose meaning is limited to surgery, since surgery is a therapy. Subdivisions of 06 are added to surgery numbers for specific physical therapies used in preparation for or rehabilitation from operative surgery, or for branches of surgery in which operation is not a choice, e.g., whirlpool baths for sprains 617.170653. 06 is used freely under numbers not limited to surgery, e.g., ophthalmological therapy 617.706.

617 vs. 616   **Miscellaneous branches of medicine   Surgery vs. Diseases**

617 contains a mixed set of nonsurgical and surgical specialties. If there is a provision in both 616 and 617 for an organ that defines a specialty, use the 617 number only for surgery. *See also 617.5.*

Class comprehensive works on medical treatment of the handicapped in 617 unless the term is clearly used to cover all disabling diseases, in which case, class in 616. If in doubt whether to class a work on the handicapped in 616 or 617, prefer 617.

617.3 vs.   **Orthopedics vs. Diseases of the musculoskeletal system vs. Regional**
616.7,   **medicine   Regional surgery**
617.5

Use 617.3 only for works covering orthopedics in general, and its subdivisions only for works that emphasize deformities. If in doubt whether to class a work on orthopedics in 617.3 or in 616.7 Diseases of the musculoskeletal system, prefer 616.7. If in doubt between 617.3 and 617.5 regional medicine, prefer 617.5.

617.307 vs.   **Orthopedic appliances vs. Operative surgery and special fields of**
617.9   **surgery**

If in doubt whether to class a work on appliances with orthopedic appliances in 617.307 or with prosthetic equipment or surgical appliances, both in 617.9, prefer 617.9.

617.4 vs.   **Surgery by systems vs. Diseases**
616

617.4 is primarily limited to operative surgery of systems. Nonoperative therapies are usually classed in 616, e.g., therapeutic manipulations of muscles 616.74062, not 617.473062. Nonoperative therapies are classed in 617.4 only if they have some connection with operative surgery, e.g., electrotherapy by heart pacer 617.4120645, since the pacer must be surgically implanted (617.412059).

617.5   **Regional medicine   Regional surgery**

Two quite different concepts are spliced together here: (1) regions, which incorporate parts of several physiological systems, e.g., the abdominal region 617.55; and (2) organs, which are parts of single systems, e.g., the stomach 617.553. Since the numbers for regions are used for regional medicine as well as regional surgery, notation 059 from the add table under 617 must be used for regional surgery, e.g., abdominal surgery 617.55059. However, since the nonsurgical treatment of specific organs is provided for with the system in 616.1–.8, the numbers for specific organs in 617.5 are used only for surgery, and subdivision 059 by itself is not used except for surgery utilizing specific instruments or techniques, e.g., stomach surgery 617.553. Notation 0592 remains valid with organ numbers for plastic surgery, transplantation of tissue and organs, implantation of artificial organs. In the case of regions, resolve doubts in favor of 617.5 numbers. In the case of organs, resolve doubts in favor of 616 numbers or numbers in 617.6–.8 for teeth, eyes, and ears.

617.522 vs.   **[Surgery of] Oral region vs. Surgery [in dentistry]**
617.605

"Oral surgery" is a term much used in the dental profession. Do not class a work so identified in 617.522 unless it covers substantially more than procedures for which one would go to a dentist (617.605).

618.92 vs.   **Pediatrics vs. Diseases vs. Fetal disorders**
616,
618.32

Use caution in classing in 618.92 certain diseases that are most often treated in children, but that remain lifetime problems or threats, e.g., congenital diseases, mumps. Class these in 616 unless actually limited to their occurrence in children.

Works on diagnosing genetic diseases in the fetus, e.g., by amniocentesis, typically focus on immediate measures, not lifetime treatment; class such works in 618.32042.

618.9209 vs.   **Special branches of medicine [in pediatrics] vs. Miscellaneous**
617   **branches of medicine   Surgery**

Class in 618.92097 nonsurgical specialties provided for in 617.5 and 617.7–.8 when applied to children (regional medicine, ophthalmology, otology, audiology). Class surgical specialties applied to children in 617—comprehensive works in 617.98, surgery of a specific organ, system, disorder with the subject. For example, class medicine of the back for children in 618.9209756, but surgery of the back in 617.560083.

Class both medical and surgical aspects of dentistry for children in 617.6—comprehensive works in 617.645, diseases of the teeth and gums in 617.630083, dental surgery in 617.605083. Also class both nonsurgical and surgical aspects of topics provided for in 617.1–.3 in 617 when applied to children, e.g., pediatric sports medicine 617.1027083, pediatric orthopedics 617.30083.

618.977 vs. [Special branches of geriatric medicine] vs. Miscellaneous branches
617   of medicine   Surgery

Class in 618.9775–.9778 nonsurgical specialties provided for in 617.5–.8 when applied to persons in late adulthood (regional medicine, dentistry, ophthalmology, otology, audiology). Class surgical specialties applied to persons in late adulthood in 617—comprehensive works in 617.97, surgery of a specific organ, system, disorder with the subject. For example, class medicine of the back for persons in late adulthood in 618.9775600846, but surgery of the back in 617.5600846; class diseases of the teeth and gums in 618.97763, but dental surgery in 617.6050846.

Class both nonsurgical and surgical aspects of topics provided for in 617.1–.3 in 617 when applied to persons in late adulthood, e.g., injuries in late adulthood 617.100846, geriatric orthopedics 617.300846.

621 vs. 530   Applied physics vs. Physics

When the heading of an applied physics subdivision corresponds to one in physics, use the 621 number when the focus is on technology, even though much of the work is scientific background; use the 530 number when the focus is equally on science and technology. If in doubt, prefer 530.

621.36 vs.   Applied optics and paraphotic engineering vs. Optoelectronics [and]
621.381045, Optical communications
621.3827

Two major applications of engineering optics (specifically of lasers in 621.366 and fiber optics in 621.3692) are optoelectronics and optical communications. On the other hand, an important application of electronics, especially of optoelectronics, is in optics, e.g., in remote sensing technology (621.3678). It is sometimes difficult to determine if a focus on a specific application is intended by an author. The best rule here is not to consider an implied interest in applications: in the absence of a clear emphasis upon a specific kind of application, class a specific topic found in 621.36 in 621.36, and of a specific topic found in 621.38 in 621.38. However, if a process or device of engineering optics is considered as an integral link in an electronics processing system, class the process or device with the system in 621.38, e.g., optical fibers in communication 621.38275.

If electronics or communications is emphasized, class in 621.38. If in doubt, prefer 621.36.

621.381 **Electronics**

The schedule for electronics has been simplified by eliminating distinctions made in earlier editions for certain terms that refer to practically the whole of either "electronics" or "electronic circuits." The terms usually refer to innovations and conceptual formulations that have come to permeate the technology and become symbolic of it. When another important innovation appears, it usually builds upon the former ones rather than replacing them; nevertheless it becomes the new symbol for the subject. For example, works on circuits have at different times emphasized the concepts of microelectronic, integrated, semiconductor, or digital circuits, yet the essential principles and problems addressed have remained the same. Thus works on circuits in general are now all classed in 621.3815 rather than in several subdivisions of 621.38153 and 621.3817 as in Edition 19. Likewise, numbers for electronics in general have all been collapsed into 621.381, even if concepts like shortwave and long-wave electronics or microelectronics are emphasized.

621.382 vs. 621.3981, 004.6 **Communications engineering vs. [Computer] Interfacing and communications devices [and] Interfacing and communications [in computer science]**

Exercise caution in classifying works on digital communication. If they emphasize engineering, they may be either computer data communications (621.3981), digital telecommunications (621.382), or digital aspects of both telecommunications and data communications (also 621.382). If in doubt between the engineering numbers, prefer 621.382.

However, in works that do not emphasize engineering, "digital communications" is apt to refer to communications in computer science 004.6. This number is used for works dealing with telecommunications and data communications engineering plus interfacing and communications in computer science. For the other choices for works not emphasizing engineering, see 004.6 vs. 005.71; 384.3 vs. 004.6.

621.3822 vs. 003.54 **Signal processing [in communications engineering] vs. Information theory**

Information theory was originally developed in the context of communications engineering, then applied as well in other disciplines. Class in

003.54 only interdisciplinary works. Class information theory in communications engineering in 621.3822 or with the specific kind of communication, e.g., radio 621.384 (without using notation 01154 from Table 1 in either case). Class information theory in any other specific subject with the subject, using notation 01154 from Table 1, e.g., information theory in economics 330.01154.

621.38416
vs.
621.38454

Amateur (Ham) radio vs. Citizens band (CB) radio

Both ham and CB are two-way systems for nonprofessionals involving reserved bandwidths not available to commercial stations. However, the word "amateur" has by tradition been reserved for long-distance (usually shortwave) communication regulated by international treaties, with stiff licensing requirements for operators. In contrast, citizens band is local (ca. 10 miles or 15 kilometers), with easier or no licensing requirements. If in doubt, prefer 621.38416.

621.3845 vs.
621.38782

Radiotelephony vs. Long distance systems [in telephone transmission]

Radiotelephony in 621.3845 refers to the use of terminals which both receive and send messages by radio. The use of radio relays (either ground-based or satellite-based) as integral parts of what appear to users to be a wire-based telephone system is classed with telephone transmission systems in 621.38782. If in doubt, prefer 621.3845.

622.7,
622.22 vs.
669, 662.6

Ore dressing [and] In-situ processing vs. Metallurgy [and Chemical engineering of] Fuels

Ore dressing, which refers to physical means of separating more usable ore from the low-grade materials that are dug out of the ground, is classed in 622.7. When means that effect substantial chemical change are applied, the process normally becomes chemical engineering (usually metallurgy, 669). For example, magnetic separation of iron ore is classed in 622.77, but electrodeposition of iron from ores is classed in 669.14.

Since use of high temperatures causes drastic chemical changes, it is counted as chemical engineering, e.g., pyrometallurgy 669.0282.

In-situ processing involves using chemical techniques to get the target materials (or compounds containing the target materials) out of the ground. It is, therefore, usually considered as mining, and is classed in 622.22 or with the specific material in 622.3, e.g., solution mining of uranium 622.34932. However, in-situ processing of a fossil fuel usually transforms the fuel into another form. When there is such a transformation, class the processing in the chemical engineering number for the material produced, e.g., coal gasification 665.772.

624.1 vs. 624 **Structural engineering and underground construction vs. Civil engineering**

Structural engineering may be considered the "general topics" heading for civil engineering. It comprises the specific subdisciplines of civil engineering that have general applicability to all kinds of structures. Since a civil engineer is normally trained in all branches of structural engineering, basic texts on civil engineering emphasize the subject. Use 624.1 only for works that take a narrow view of structural engineering, that is, that do not discuss the various types of structures to which the engineering is applied. If in doubt, prefer 624.

628.44042 vs. 363.7288, 628.445 **[Technology of] Specific kinds of solid wastes vs. [Problems and services concerning] Specific kinds of wastes [and Technology of] Treatment and disposal**

Use 628.44042 with caution, since most works on specific kinds of solid wastes emphasize the context of waste and pollution problems and services, or programs with incentives to recycle materials, and are classed in 363.7288. Of the technological works on specific kinds of solid wastes, many will concentrate on recycling or other treatment and disposal technologies, and will thus be classed in 628.445 or with the specific technology which creates or utilizes the waste, e.g., technology of recycling glass bottles 666.192. Class in 628.44042 only the few works that are primarily technological, and emphasize collection as well as treatment and disposal. If in doubt, prefer 363.7288.

628.7 **Sanitary engineering for rural and sparsely populated areas**

628.7 takes precedence over 628.1–.4. While the goals here are the same as in the main numbers for the subject, the population served is so scattered that it is usually difficult to use all of the methods applied in urban settings.

629.046 vs. 388 **Transportation equipment vs. Transportation   Ground transportation**

The following guidelines help to distinguish between the vehicle numbers in 385–388 and those in 623.74, 623.82, 625.2, 629, and 688.6.

Class in 385–388:

1. Services provided by the vehicle, e.g., transportation of passengers by trains 385.22.

2. Operation (general) of the vehicle, e.g., duties of the ship's captain 387.54044.

3. Economic and social aspects of the vehicle, e.g., a register of the airplanes owned by a company 387.73340216.

Class in 629.046 and related numbers in the 600s:

1. Description of the vehicle, e.g., steam locomotives of the 1930s 625.26109043.

2. Technology of the vehicle, e.g., design tests for ships 623.819.

3. Operation (technical) of the vehicle, e.g., piloting spacecraft 629.4582.

4. Maintenance and repair of the vehicle, e.g., repairing motorcycles 629.28775.

If in doubt, prefer 629.046 and related numbers in the 600s.

629.226 vs. **Motorized homes, campers, trailers (caravans) vs. Special kinds of**
643.2, **housing [and Construction of mobile homes] and [Architecture of]**
690.879, **Mobile homes**
728.79

Use the housing numbers (not 629.226) for what are essentially houses on wheels, i.e., mobile homes that must be towed. Use 629.226 (which is listed under types of motor land vehicles) for what are essentially either automobiles with living accommodations, collapsible living accommodations to be used with trucks or trailers, or trailers with such limited living accommodations that they would not (even when hooked up) serve as permanent homes. Use the housing numbers if in doubt, and use 643.2 for interdisciplinary works on movable homes.

631.47 vs. **Soil and land use surveys vs. Historical, geographical, persons**
631.49 **treatment [of soil science]**

Soil surveys usually involve small areas (the size of a United States county or less), are quite detailed, and are accompanied by numerous detailed maps. Geographical studies of soils normally cover much larger areas and are not so detailed. If in doubt, use 631.49 for large areas, 631.47 for small areas.

631.558 vs. **[Crop] Yields [in agriculture] vs. [Economics of] Agriculture**
338.1

Usually works on crop yields are compilations giving the total production of an area, and are classed in 338.1. Works on yields per unit of area are classed in 338.16 if they are taken as indicators of production efficiency, either of agricultural systems using various methods (e.g., crop rotation) or of agricultural systems prevailing in various areas. If yield studies per unit of area are used in technical tests of varieties or specific production techniques, they are classed with the subject in agriculture, e.g., yield tests of fertilizer use 631.80287. Use of 631.558 is limited to works that have little or no economic or testing implications, e.g., lists of record yields of various crops. If in doubt, class in 338.1.

633–635   **Specific plant crops**

Certain plants are important for two or more quite different crops, and may have different numbers assigned to each. Some of the more important distinctions are:

Cereal grains versus cereal grasses (633.1 vs. 633.25)

Class in 633.1 if grown for grain (even if the fodder is an important by-product), in 633.25 if the whole plant is to be consumed (even if the grain is allowed to ripen).

Legumes (633.3 vs. 635.65)

Class in 633.3 if grown for either the ripened fruit or forage, in 635.65 if the pod is to be picked green or unripened for human consumption.

Other crops

For crops which are listed in only one number use that number if the difference in the crop produced by the farmer is minor, e.g., potatoes grown for food, feed, or starch all look about the same, so are classed in 635.21. However, a hemlock grown for lumber looks quite different when shipped from a hemlock grown for landscaping, so the first is classed in 634.9753, the second in 635.97752. If the crop described in a work does not fit existing numbers where the plant is named, class the work in the closest suitable number, e.g., a legume grown for hard fibers 633.58. If in doubt, prefer the existing number coming first in the schedule.

635.3 vs.   **Edible leaves, flowers, stems vs. Cooking greens and rhubarb vs.**
635.4,   **Salad greens**
635.5

The distinctions which set off cooking greens and salad greens from each other and from edible leaves in general are not rigidly maintained. Class all works on growing a leafy vegetable named in 635.3–.5 in the number where it is named, regardless of any emphasis on its use, e.g., growing kale for cooking 635.347 (not 635.4).

636.088   **Animals for specific purposes**

Several of the terms used in subdivisions of 636.088 apply primarily to one or a few kinds of animals provided for in 636.1–.8. Such terms are listed here primarily for number-building purposes. For example, the numbers for raising cows for milk and raising poultry for eggs are both derived in part from the eggs and milk number 636.08842. The final 42 is added to 636.21 (cattle for specific purposes) giving 636.2142 for dairy farming; to 636.51 (poultry for specific purposes) giving 636.5142 for producing eggs. Since there are few works on producing both milk and eggs or on producing milk from several kinds of animals, and since producing eggs from several kinds of birds is classed in the poultry number, 636.08842 will seldom be used. If in doubt between a subdivision of 636.088 and a derived subdivision under a specific kind of animal, prefer the latter.

636.72–.76   Specific breeds and groups of dogs

The groupings used are those recognized by the American Kennel Club in *The Complete Dog Book*, 1985. Class breeds having pedigrees recognized in other nations that fit within an AKC grouping with the grouping, e.g., European gundog with 636.752. If in doubt about a breed not recognized by the AKC, use 636.7.

643.1 vs.   Housing [in home economics] vs. Housing [in social services]
363.5

A distinction is often made between "housing" and "houses." The term "housing" normally refers to the provision of shelter considered in the abstract, while the term "houses" normally refers to the buildings considered as concrete objects. 643.1 is used for the home economics aspects of either housing or houses. It is also the number for interdisciplinary works on *houses* and their use. However, since works on housing often treat the social aspects of shelter, interdisciplinary works on *housing* are classed in 363.5.

643.7 vs.   Renovation, improvement, remodeling [in home economics] vs.
690   [Construction of] Buildings

The scope note at 643 reading "works for owner-occupants and renters covering activities by members of household" indicates that 643.7 and other numbers in 643 are used for a broad range of material intended for the do-it-yourself enthusiast. Works on home renovation and remodeling for professional builders are classed in 690.80286 or other numbers in 690. (The special standard subdivision notation 0286 is used in 690 only with numbers drawn from 725–728; elsewhere in 690 no standard subdivision is used.) If in doubt, prefer 690.

647.068   Management [of public households]

Use notation 068 from Table 1 with caution here and in subdivisions of 647, because the term "management" often refers to the basic techniques of operating an establishment. Works on basic techniques are classed in the base number without the use of notation 068, regardless of what they are called.

See also 647.96–.99 vs. 658.2, T1—0682.

647.96–.99
vs. 658.2,
T1—0682

Institutional households not primarily used for residence, eating, drinking vs. Plant management [and Table 1 notation for] Plant management

Class in 647.96–.99 strictly housekeeping operations, such as food service and cleaning. Class works of broader scope in 658.2 or with the subject with use of notation 0682 from Table 1. Specific aspects of institutional housekeeping are classed with the aspect in home economics, however, class utilities in 648.9 numbers, not 644.

There are two exceptions for sanitation: Numbers in 648 are used only for the how-to aspects of hospital sanitation; discussion of sanitary services is classed in 362.110682. The whole of industrial sanitation is classed in 628.51.

650 vs. 330

Management and auxiliary services vs. Economics

Works about business can be classed in several places. Most often the choice is between 330 and 650. Use 330 if the work presents general information, economic conditions, financial information (such as interest rates), and reports on what certain companies are doing. Use 650 when the work presents only practical managerial information that covers 651 Office services as well as 658 General management. If the work is limited to general management, use 658. Class comprehensive works on 330 and 650 in 330.

651.7 vs.
808.06665,
658.45

Communication   Creation and transmission of records [as an office service] vs. [Business writing] vs. Communication [in management]

Class in 651.7 such topics as the use of the telephone, techniques of dictation, how to use microcomputer software for form letters, mail-handling techniques—in short, the mechanics of communication. Do not class in 651.7 works that emphasize effective business writing style.

Class in 808.06665 style manuals for business writing and works on how to do effective business writing, whether aimed at secretaries or executives. Class in 808.066651 works on how to write a specific type of communication (e.g., business letters) and model collections of a specific type intended to illustrate good writing style. In case of doubt between 651.7 and 808.06665, prefer 808.06665.

Class in 658.45 works that focus on use of communication to achieve management goals. Often these works emphasize the personal relations aspects of management communication.

657 vs.
658.1511,
658.1512

Accounting vs. Management accounting [and] Use of reports

How to do accounting is classed in 657, use of accounting information by management in 658.1511. How to prepare a financial statement is classed in 657.32, use of a financial statement by management to improve business performance in 658.1512. Design of accounting systems in general and for outside reporting is classed in 657.1. Design of accounting systems with specific emphasis on increasing the internal flow of information to management is classed in 658.1511. If in doubt, prefer 657.

658 and
T1—068
General management [and Table 1 notation for] Management [in specific fields]

Management comprises the conduct of all types of enterprises except government agencies that do not themselves provide direct services. *(See 350–354 vs. 658, T1—068.)* Management is not confined to "business enterprises."

Organizations to be managed may be divided in three ways. First is division by size or scope of the enterprise, which is classed in 658.02. Second is division by the legal form of the enterprise, e.g., corporations, partnerships, etc., which is classed in 658.04. Third, and most important, is division by the kind of work the organization does: selling books, manufacturing light bulbs, carrying freight, caring for the sick, etc. Management of enterprises doing specific kinds of work is classed with the kind of work being done, using notation 068 from Table 1. 658 and its subdivisions are reserved for discussions of management applicable to any type of enterprise. Comprehensive works on management of public enterprises are classed in 351.0092.

For an enterprise's field of work, select if possible a straightforward number for making a product or performing a service. For example, class works on the management of automobile manufacturing in 629.222068, not 338.7629222068, because 338.7629222 is for the economics of automobile manufacturing.

For management of a particular kind of retail store, use a subdivision of 658.87 if there is no emphasis on a specific kind of product. For example, class management of retail chain stores in 658.8702, not 381.12068, since chain stores are a form of management organization. 381.12 is for the economic aspects of such an organization. However, class a retail store marketing a specific product in 381.4 plus notation for the product, e.g., management of a book store 381.45002068. The same holds true for the other subdivisions of 658.87, e.g., management of franchise businesses selling cars 381.45629222068.

Note that specific fields of management are also brought out in this way, e.g., financial management of automobile manufacturing 629.2220681, of chain stores 658.87020681, of book stores 381.450020681.

See also 363.1; 658, T1—068 vs. 302.35.

658,
T1—068
vs. 302.35
General management [and Table 1 notation for] Management [in specific fields] vs. [Social interaction] In hierarchically organized (complex) groups

Class in 658 and T1—068 works that emphasize how to manage. Class in 302.35 works that analyze and describe the social dynamics of how people behave and work in organizations. If in doubt, prefer 302.35.

658.15 and
T1—0681
Financial management [and Table 1 notation for] Organization and financial management [in specific fields]

Financial management deals with money: how to raise funds to initiate or expand an organization, how to invest capital in capital goods or in the securities of other organizations, how to allocate funds to various operations (budgeting), and how to control expenses and costs. These aspects of financial management do not vary greatly from enterprise to enterprise, except with respect to sources of funds. Examples follow:

Financial management of airlines: 387.70681.

Financial management of commercial banks: 332.120681.

Note that a bank's *work* is finance. Notation 0681 from Table 1 can apply only to its internal finance: raising money to start the bank; using money to finance its internal operations, such as paying the employees and the light bills; keeping down costs of operation. The financial services that the bank renders to the public are part of production management, which is discussed at 658.5 and T1—0685.

Financial management of hotels: 647.940681.

Financial management of schools: 371.206.

Financial management of libraries: 025.11.

It should be noted that 658.15 and T1—0681 do not include bookkeeping or accounting for specific types of organizations. Class works on these subjects in 657.8.

658.2 and
T1—0682
Plant management [and Table 1 notation for] Plant management [in specific fields]

Plant management deals with the physical environment and tools requisite to the performance of the organization's work. It includes land, buildings, utilities (light, heat, etc.), and the specific equipment (such as vehicles, machinery, furnishings) necessary to do the work. Acquisition of grounds, buildings, and major equipment is classed in 658.15242, since these are considered to be capital goods. Their maintenance is classed with plant management, as is the use of land, buildings, and utilities. Use of production equipment is classed with production management. Examples follow:

Plant management for airlines: 387.73068.

Note that since 387.73 already implies the plant (as will be clear from an examination of the subdivisions), the notation from Table 1 is T1—068, the 2 being redundant.

Plant management for commercial banks: 332.120682.

Plant management for hotels: 647.940682.

Plant management for schools: 371.6.

Plant management for libraries: 022.

See also 647.96–.99 vs. 658.2, T1—0682.

658.3 and
T1—0683
Personnel management [and Table 1 notation for] Personnel management [in specific fields]

Personnel management deals with people: how to recruit, select, place, train, develop, and motivate them in performing the work of the organization. It also includes pay, hours, leave, retirement, and pensions, as well as subjects like discipline and discharge. Examples follow:

Personnel management in airlines: 387.70683.

Personnel management in commercial banks: 332.120683.

Personnel management in hotels: 647.2.

Personnel management in libraries: 023.9.

658.3 vs.
331
Personnel management vs. Labor economics

Many of the topics in 658.3 are paralleled in 331. Class in 658.3 works written from the viewpoint of management, in 331 works written from the viewpoint of the employee (the worker). Also class in 331 works written from a neutral standpoint, simply describing the phenomena, and comprehensive works including both management and employee views.

658.402 vs.
658.04,
658.114
Internal organization vs. Management of enterprises of specific forms [and] Forms of ownership organization

In 658.402 "organization" means the internal managerial organization of an enterprise, not the legal or ownership organization. Internal organization is concerned with the way that authority and responsibility are apportioned. For example, in line organization a single manager exercises final authority, either directly over production workers or over several supervisors who in turn supervise workers. Class organization by legal and ownership forms (e.g., corporations, partnerships) in 658.04 and 658.114.

658.42 and
658.43

Top management [and] Middle management

Class works in these numbers only if they make a real point of being about top or middle management as opposed to executive management in general. If in doubt, prefer 658.4.

658.455 vs.
658.4038

[Management of] Informational programs vs. Information management

Communication of information by management in order to maintain control of people and processes is classed in 658.455. Gathering of information by management and its use in decision making is classed in 658.4038. If in doubt, prefer 658.4038.

658.5 and
T1—0685

Management of production [and Table 1 notation for] Management of production [in specific fields]

Production management is the management of the work that the organization exists to perform. It concerns itself with the organization of the work flow and the methods to be used in performing individual operations. It also deals with insuring the quality and accuracy of the operations and of their results. It is related to, but not the same as, the technology involved in the operations. It differs radically from one organization to another. Examples follow:

Management of factory production: 658.5.

This is the organization and direction of the processes by which raw materials, parts, and subassemblies are combined and processed through the operation of people and machines to produce such concrete objects as automobiles, bread, toys, etc. This is also known as logistics.

658.5 fits the nature of factory operations better than production management of other kinds of enterprises because it reflects an earlier state of the management art when books of management were chiefly concerned with industrial management. Accordingly, 658.5 is used for production management in factories in general rather than 670.

Production management for airlines: 387.70685.

Note the presence of elements of production management in subdivisions of 387.7, e.g., planning airline routes 387.72; assigning airplanes to routes and scheduling them 387.740420685; planning, organizing and supervising meal services, baggage services, and reservation services 387.7420685.

Production management for book stores: 381.450020685.

Production management for commercial banks: 332.120685.

> This includes planning, organizing, and supervising customer services, maintenance of checking and savings accounts, vault services, trust services, etc.

Production management for hotels: 647.940685.

> This consists of managing the operations directly involved in providing food, entertainment, and clean and attractive rooms and facilities for guests.

Production management for schools: 371.2.

> This is the management of the activities involved in imparting knowledge and attitudes to students, and includes such things as scheduling of classes and grouping students for instruction.

Production management for libraries: 025.1.

**658.7 and   Management of materials [and Table 1 notation for] Management of
T1—0687   materials [in specific fields]**

> Management of materials involves the raw materials, parts, and subassemblies used in creating the final product or service; the supplies necessary for conducting the business, e.g., ink, pens, paper; and other small pieces of equipment, e.g., typewriters, filing cabinets.

> The activities dealing with these materials fall into three distinct categories: acquisition, internal management, and physical distribution.

> Acquisition, or procurement, involves contracts and their negotiation, vendor selection, order work, receiving and unloading shipments, and expediting and tracing when done by the purchaser.

> Internal management involves storage and the maintenance of inventory, checking materials out of inventory for use in the work process, their movement from work station to work station, checking them into storage and storing them prior to sale, and maintaining the inventory at this point. In service organizations, where there is no sale of a final product, the process is complete when materials and supplies are issued for and used in the work process.

> Physical distribution involves processing orders received, matching the orders to items in inventory, checking the items out of inventory, packing them, loading them, selecting carrier and routing, and expediting and tracing when done by the shipper. Note that major equipment is considered to be capital, and its acquisition is classed in 658.15242 and T1—0681. Physical distribution is not a factor in most service organizations.

Materials management for airlines: 387.70687.

Materials management in hotels: 647.940687.

Materials management in schools: 371.209.

Materials management in libraries: 025.1.

However, class management of the acquisition of books and other information media at 025.2068, their internal management in 025.8, their circulation (analogous to physical distribution) in 025.6.

658.8 and   Management of distribution (Marketing) [and Table 1 notation for]
T1—0688   Management of distribution (Marketing) [in specific fields]

Marketing management deals with the sale of the product or service of the organization. This concept also includes credit management. Examples follow:

Marketing management for airlines: 387.70688.

This number is used chiefly for sales promotion and credit management. Most sales effort for such an organization is concentrated in advertising, which is classed in 659.1.

Marketing management for commercial banks: chiefly advertising, which is classed in 659.1.

Marketing management for hotels: 647.940688.

This is usually credit management and other limited applications, e.g., sale of facilities for conventions.

Marketing management for schools: not applicable.

Private schools do some advertising and public relations but these are classed in 659.

Marketing management for libraries: class public relations of libraries in 021.7.

658.8,   Management of distribution (Marketing) [and Table 1 notation for]
T1—0688   Management of distribution (Marketing) [in specific fields] vs.
vs. 659   Advertising and public relations

Marketing (658.8) is the broader concept; it includes sales management, marketing research, channels of distribution, and customer credit management, which are classed in 658.8; it also includes the advertising and public relations that have been drawn off to 659. What belongs in 659 is the publicity used by an organization to present itself and its goods and services to the public. Research focused on advertising or public relations is the only kind of marketing research classed in 659; broader research is classed in 658.83. If in doubt, prefer 658.8.

660.2804 vs. Safety technology [in chemical engineering] vs. Hazardous materials
604.7   technology

Use 660.2804 for consideration of hazardous chemicals during chemical engineering; prefer 604 for comprehensive consideration of hazardous chemicals that includes handling, transporting, and utilization outside the chemical industry.

However, for specific hazardous chemicals, the comprehensive technology number is usually found in 660, e.g., processing, transportation, utilization of natural gas 665.73.

Class interdisciplinary works on hazardous chemicals in 363.17.

669   Metallurgy

Class comprehensive works on alloys of a variety of metals in 669; comprehensive works on a specific alloy, on the alloys of a specific metal in 669.1–.7; the physical and chemical metallurgy of alloys, the process of forming alloys in 669.9.

Class an alloy not listed in 669 with the chief constituent metal if readily ascertainable, e.g., Monel®, a nickel alloy of about 67 percent nickel and 30 percent copper 669.7332, not 669.3. If the chief constituent is not readily ascertainable, class with the metal coming first in the schedule, except class all alloys of steel in 669.142.

670.285 vs. Data processing   Computer applications [in manufacturing] vs.
670.427   Mechanization and automation of factory operations

Works on flexible manufacturing systems are classed in 670.427 if limited to computer-aided manufacture; in 670.285 if including also other computer applications in manufacturing, such as computer-aided design or computer applications in management of manufacturing.

671–679 vs. Manufacture of products from specific materials vs. Manufacture of
680   products for specific uses

The distinction between 671–679 and 680 cannot be drawn consistently because some manufacture by material appears in 680, e.g., leather and fur goods 685; and some products for specific uses appear in 671–679, e.g., paper plates and cups 676.34. In general 671–679 has primary products in contrast to the final products from a given material in 680, e.g., textiles 677, clothing 687; but that distinction is not relevant in many specific cases, e.g., brushes 679.6, combs 688.5. In case of doubt, prefer 671–679.

676 vs.
676.1,
676.2

Pulp and paper technology vs. Pulp vs. Conversion of pulp into paper, and specific types of paper and paper products

Use 676 for the total process of making paper out of logs or other sources of pulp. Use 676.1 for the process of making pulp, through the bleaching of the pulp. Use 676.2 for works about the conversion of pulp into paper or paper products, starting with the beating and refining of the pulp.

680   Manufacture of products for specific uses

The order of the subdivisions of 680 is drawn from that of 670; the 680 numbers usually represent a type of final product related in some general way to the material in the comparable 670 number:

672	682	Ferrous metals [vs.] Small forge work
673	683	Nonferrous metals [vs.] Hardware and household appliances
674	684	Lumber, cork, wood [vs.] Furnishings and home workshops
675	685	Leather and fur [vs.] Leather and fur goods
676	686	Pulp and paper [vs.] Printing
677	687	Textiles [vs.] Clothing

690 vs. 624   **Buildings vs. Civil engineering**

To be classed in 690, the work must limit its discussion to habitable structures (buildings). If other structures are discussed, the work is classed in 624. Works about "building" in the sense of constructing all types of structures are classed in 624, not 690. If in doubt, prefer 624.

The word "construction" in the title usually implies that a work covers more than habitable structures. However, it is sometimes used loosely for construction of 690–type buildings.

700   The arts   Fine and decorative arts

Generally the word "arts," used without a qualifier, is a signal that the area covered is broader than the fine and decorative arts. Literature, music, and the performing arts are the other kinds of arts most often included. A quick check each time that "art" or "arts" is used should establish the area covered.

"Computer art" usually refers to two different uses of computers in the arts. The computer can be a device employed in creating the final art work, as when the computer serves as an aid in composing music to be played on traditional instruments or as an aid in designing or engraving the plates for otherwise traditional prints. Alternatively, the computer can serve as the instrument on which music is performed, as in computer music, or as the display medium for visual art, as when computer graphics works are intended for display on a computer monitor. The computer as a device is classed with other devices using either notation 0285 from Table 1 or specific provisions in the schedule, e.g., computers and the arts 700.285, computers in the graphic arts 760.0285, computer composition of music 781.34. The computer as an instrument or display medium is classed with the type of art, e.g., history of computer art 709.04, computer graphic art 760, computer music 786.76.

700.74   **Museums, collections, exhibits [in the arts]**

When the works of more than one artist are involved, notation 074 from Table 1 may be added to notation 09 from Table 1 when the latter has been used to denote historical period or place of origin, e.g., an exhibition in New York City of the nude in French art 704.942109440747471. However, do not add notation 074 from Table 1 if the period or place of origin does not approximate the full period or area expressed by the notation used for the subject being exhibited.

700.92   **Persons [in the arts]**

The instructions at each major area for the classification of artists varies. Even within one division, the 730s, the treatment varies: 730.92 for a sculptor, 739.2272 for a goldsmith, 730.092 for a sculptor who has also worked in one or more of the other plastic arts.

Works of an artist or artists are designated in one of two ways, either by notation 092 from Table 1 as in sculpture, or by notation for period or place as in drawing 741.92–.99.

704.9   **Iconography**

Iconography takes precedence over historical and geographical treatment, e.g., a general work on Romanesque art 709.0216, Romanesque art of Normandy 709.44209021, but the Virgin Mary and Child in Romanesque art of Normandy 704.948550944209021. However, care should be taken in classifying schools and styles that usually are limited in subject matter, such as early Christian, Byzantine, and Romanesque schools, which usually treat religious themes. Class in 704.9 only if a point is made that iconography or one of its aspects is the focus of the work.

Generally in any use of the iconography numbers, standard subdivisions are added even if the topic does not approximate the whole of the heading. There are three exceptions: 704.9432 Animals, 704.9434 Plants, and notation from Table 2. For instance, if a work covers only dogs in art, a standard subdivision should not be added.

Notation 09 from Table 1 plus notation 3–9 from Table 2 is added to show the nationality or locality of the artists rather than the location of the subject, e.g., Canadian portraits of British royal children 704.94250971. Do not add notation 074 from Table 1 unless the area covered by the work being classed approximates the whole of the area indicated by the notation from Table 2.

709.012–.05 vs. 709.3–.9

Periods of development [of fine and decorative arts] vs. Treatment by specific continents, countries, localities [of fine and decorative arts]

Class the works produced by an artistic school or in a particular style as follows:

1. From the same locality, with the locality in 709.3–.9.

2. From various localities within a specific country, with the country in 709.3–.9.

3. From two countries, with the country coming first in Table 2 in 709.3–.9.

4. From three or more European countries, with the period when the school or style flourished in 709.012–.05.

5. From three or more non-European countries within the same continent, with the continent in 709.3–.9.

6. From three or more countries not within the same continent, with the period when the school or style flourished in 709.012–.05.

If in doubt between classing with country or locality, prefer country; if between 709.012–.05 or 709.3–.9, prefer 709.012–.05.

709.2 vs. 380.1457092

Persons [associated with fine and decorative arts] vs. [Persons associated with the trade of art]

Works about art dealers that focus on the economics of trading in art are classed in 380.1457092. Works that focus on the dealers as a part of the art world, e.g., the artists the dealers knew and works of art they handled, are classed in 709.2. If in doubt, class in 709.2.

711 vs. 307.12

Area planning (Civic art) vs. [Community] Planning

Works that focus on the presentation and analysis of the physical plans, even if some historical and social material is included, are classed in 711. Works that focus on the historical or social aspects are classed in 307.12. If in doubt, class in 307.12.

721

Architectural structure

The note "Class here interdisciplinary works on design and construction" is not meant to broaden the scope of 721 to include all aspects of architecture. Works that are classed here are concerned with the elements included in 721.04 and 721.1–.8. Works about the architecture of buildings as a whole are classed in 720.

721 vs. 690   Architectural structure vs. Buildings

Descriptive details of buildings erected in the past or planned for the future are classed in 721. Principles of engineering design and construction or actual instruction (e.g., for the builder) on how to put structural elements, shapes, and materials together are classed in 690. If in doubt, prefer 721.

726.1   [Architecture of] Temples and shrines

Be as specific as possible in building the number, e.g., a Theravada Buddhist temple in Thailand 726.1439109593. If the branch or sect is not given, add from 292–299 only as far as the information warrants, then add notation from Table 1, e.g., Buddhist temples in Java (sect not specified) 726.143095982; temple forms in southern India (religion not identified) 726.1409548.

729   Design and decoration of structures and accessories

More material is taken out of 729 by notes than is left in. Class in 729 only those general works in which the focus is specifically architectural design. Design and construction treated together are classed in 721. Construction alone is classed in 690. Decoration is classed in 729 only when the subject is being treated as an aspect of architectural decoration rather than as an art object in itself. For example, comprehensive works on murals are classed in 751.73; however, the use of murals as architectural decoration is classed in 729.4.

736–739 vs.   Other plastic arts vs. Sculpture
731–735

The products and techniques of the plastic arts in 736–739 are often difficult to separate from those of sculpture; if in doubt, prefer 731–735. For example, bronze figures are classed in sculpture, but a bronze figure is classed in 739.512 if it was a part (such as a finial or handle) of a larger decorative work.

745.1   Antiques

Class a specific type of antique with the subject in art if a number is provided, e.g., gold coins 737.43, antique New England furniture 749.214.

If there is no available number in 700–799, use the appropriate number in 600–699, e.g., antique passenger automobiles 629.222. If there is a separate technology number for the use of the object in question as opposed to the number for the manufacture of the object, prefer the use number, e.g., thimbles 646.19 rather than 687.8.

If antiques and collectibles fit in neither the art nor the technology numbers, class with the subject with which they are most closely associated, e.g., Shirley Temple collectibles 791.43028092.

745.5 vs. 680

[Artistic] Handicrafts vs. Manufacture of products for specific uses

Handicraft when limited to artistic work is classed in 745.5. In general usage the term "crafts" may be used for country crafts, and cottage industries and trades, such as those of the farrier, the cooper, and the thatcher. Crafts in this sense and handicrafts as the routine way of manufacturing secondary and final products are classed in 680. If in doubt, prefer 680.

745.5928

[Handcrafted] Models and miniatures

Class handcrafted miniatures and models as follows:

Class in 700:

1. If there is a specific number for the model, e.g., paper airplanes 745.592.

2. If there is a specific number for the subject illustrated by the model, e.g., handcrafted miniature furniture 749.0228. (Note: notation 0228 from Table 1 is used to indicate the model or miniature).

3. If there is no number for the model or the subject illustrated in 600. In this case the most specific number possible is chosen.

Class in 600 if there is no specific number in 700–779 *and* either of the following conditions is met:

1. If there is a specific number in 600–699 for the model, e.g., handcrafted model airplanes 629.133134.

2. If there is a specific number for the subject illustrated by the model, e.g., handcrafted miniature reciprocating steam engines 621.1640228. (Note: notation 0228 from Table 1 is used to indicate the model or miniature).

745.67

Illumination of manuscripts and books

Illumination includes not only the manuscripts and books produced in medieval Europe, but Egyptian and Roman survivals from antiquity. In addition, Persian, Mogul, and Indian illuminations often labeled "miniatures" are considered painted illustrations or illuminations and are classed here rather than in 751.77.

753–758

Iconography

Iconography takes precedence over historical and geographical treatment, e.g., a general work on Romanesque painting 759.0216, Romanesque painting of Normandy 759.44209021, but the Virgin

Mary and Child in Romanesque painting of Normandy 755.550944209021. However, care should be taken in classifying schools and styles that usually are limited in subject matter, such as early Christian, Byzantine, and Romanesque schools, which usually treat religious themes. Class in 753–758 only if a point is made that iconography or one of its aspects is the focus of the work.

Generally in any use of the iconography numbers, standard subdivisions are added even if the topic does not approximate the whole of the heading. There are three exceptions: 758.3 Animals, 758.5 Plants, and notation from Table 2. For instance, if a work covers only dogs in painting, a standard subdivision should not be added.

Notation 09 from Table 1 plus notation 3–9 from Table 2 is added to show the nationality or locality of the artists rather than the location of the subject, e.g., Canadian portraits of British royal children 757.50971. Do not add notation 074 from Table 1 unless the area covered by the work being classed approximates the whole of the area indicated by the notation from Table 2.

769.92   **[Printmakers]**

Printmakers who copy other artists or the artists being copied (if only prints are being discussed) are classed here, e.g., prints after Gainsborough 769.92. Prints produced by either a print workshop or studio are classed in 769.93–.99.

778.3 vs.   **Special kinds of photography vs. Technological photography and**
621.367   **photo-optics**

The techniques of producing the picture as an end unto itself are classed in 778.3. The engineering technology underlying the photography and the scientific applications are classed in 621.367. Applications to a specific field of science are classed with the field, e.g., to astronomy 522.63. If in doubt, prefer 778.3.

779   **Photographs**

Notation 092 from Table 1 can be added to 779 and its subdivisions for collections of works by individuals. Class biographies and critical appraisals, which may also contain some photographs, in 770.92. For collections of photographs by several artists from the same area, add notation 09 from Table 1 and notation 1–9 from Table 2 to show the area where the photographers originated.

780   **Music**

The completely revised schedule for music follows the general outline and much of the detail of the schedule found in the 1980 Forest Press publication *Proposed Revision of 780 Music* prepared under the direction of Russell Sweeney and John Clews. (See page 934 for a comparison of the *Proposed Revision* and class 780 in Edition 20.)

Overall structure

780.0001–.0999	Relation of music to other subjects
780.1–.9	Standard subdivisions, regular and modified
781	General principles and musical forms
781.1	Basic principles
781.2	Elements of music
781.3	Composition
781.4	Techniques of music
781.5	Kinds of music (e.g., for specific occasions)
781.6	Traditions of music (e.g., folk, popular)
781.7	Sacred music
781.8	[General] musical forms
782–788	Voices and instruments
782–783	Voices and vocal music
782	Vocal music The voice
783	Music for single voice
784–788	Instruments and their music
784	Instruments and instrumental ensembles and their music
785	Ensembles with only one instrument per part
786–788	Specific instruments and their music
786	Keyboard, mechanical, electrophonic, percussion instruments
787	Stringed instruments
788	Wind instruments

Citation order

The citation order is:

Voices and instruments	782–788
Musical forms	781.8
Sacred music	781.7
Traditions of music	781.6
Kinds of music	781.5
Techniques of music	781.4
Composition	781.3
Elements of music	781.2
Basic principles of music	781.1
Standard subdivisions	780.1–.9

Note that a major facet, the composer, is not indicated in the class number (unless the option at 789 is used for literature about music). A cutter number or other alphabetizing device will perform the role of indicating composer. Notation 092 from Table 1 is used to indicate a biography, a general criticism of the composer, an analysis of a composer's contribution to the development of some aspect of music (such as Haydn's role in the development of the concerto form), and critical works on the body of a composer's work (such as a critique of the piano music of Ravel). Criticism of an individual work by a composer does not receive notation 092 in order that a piece of music and criticism of it will fall at the same class number. Likewise, a collection of analyses of individual pieces of music does not receive T1—092.

Throughout most of the schedule it is possible to show several of the elements in the above list by building numbers. Where instructions to build numbers are given, the classifier can add one part of the schedule to another part, using the digits 0 or 1 to show that a new facet is being introduced. This allows the expression of all relevant facets for a recording of Spanish folk music by a guitarist or for a score for a polonaise for piano. If a library uses the schedule only for treatises and not for scores and recordings, the need to build numbers will not be great. Combining elements can be seen in the following:

Rock and roll Christmas music	781.723166
Christmas day	781.723
Facet indicator	1
Rock and roll	66 (from 781.66)

The 1 is the facet indicator that informs the user that an element from elsewhere in the schedule is about to be introduced.

"Voices" refers to the human voice, "instruments" to the artifact that makes the sound. Both voices and instruments are referred to as executants, i.e., that which makes the sound.

781.2 Elements of music contains the building blocks of sound and time used in making music. Several of the elements better located with compositional techniques have been placed in 781.3. At 781.4 are found performance, recording, and other skills necessary in the performance of music. Music is performed for all sorts of times, places, and reasons. These are found in the span 781.5—.7. In 781.5, for instance, are sea music, patriotic music, music for television, and music for debuts.

In 781.6 are found the traditions of music, such as folk, jazz, and classical. Libraries that prefer to emphasize one tradition, e.g., non-Western art music, may class it and only it throughout 780—788, and class all other traditions in subdivisions of 789.

In 781.7 is found sacred music in general.

In 781.8 Musical forms are found such general categories as rondo, theme and variations, and ostinato. They are to be used only when the item does not specify a voice or instrument. Musical forms specific to voices are found in 782.1—.4, specific to instruments in 784.18.

Note that vocal and instrumental music that represent the categories found in 781 are classed with the executant in 782–788, e.g., sacred music for the organ is classed with the organ.

Literature about music vs. scores and recordings

The major difference between music and other subjects in the whole field of knowledge is the need to distinguish literature about music from music as bibliographic objects in the form of scores and recordings.

Edition 19 provided separate class numbers for literature about music and for music itself. Edition 20 does not provide separate numbers, but libraries may make the distinction by using other devices in the call number (*see the third note at 780 in the schedules*).

Standard subdivisions

Several extended standard subdivisions have been introduced; one, 026 Treatises on music scores, recordings, texts, may cause difficulty. Note that the meaning of 026 is applied differently when used within 780–788 and when used with 780–788 numbers added to other numbers in the Classification. Within 780, 026 is used only for treatises about scores and recordings. The Classification does not distinguish among scores, recordings, and treatises about the music. A library using the DDC has to make the distinction either by applying the optional provision or by some other notational device if it wishes to separate the material on music. When used with numbers from 780–788 added to other numbers in the Classification, 026 is used for scores and recordings and treatises about them. This distinction is made in order to separate scores, recordings, and treatises about them from treatises about the music. For example:

Number	Used for
787.2	A treatise on violin music, AND
787.2	Violin scores, AND
787.2	Recordings of violin music
787.2026	A treatise on violin scores
787.20266	A treatise on recordings of violin music

BUT

016.7872	A bibliography of treatises on violin music
016.7872026	A bibliography of violin scores, AND
016.7872026	A bibliography of treatises on violin scores
016.78720266	A discography of recordings of violin music, AND
016.78720266	A bibliography of treatises on recordings of violin music.

Unlike Edition 19, Edition 20 makes no distinction between the music of a place and music in a place, e.g., Parisian opera and the opera in Paris are both classed in 782.1094436, Viennese music and music played in Vienna are both 780.943613.

782–783 Voices and vocal music

The primary characteristic of arrangement in Edition 19 was that of *character*. That is, vocal music was either dramatic (782) or non-dramatic (783 and 784); nondramatic was either sacred (783) or secular (784). The distinctions are maintained in Edition 20: Vocal music is either dramatic (782.1) or nondramatic (782.2–.4); nondramatic is either sacred (782.2–.3) or secular (782.4). There similarity between the two editions ceases. (Note that staging dramatic music is now classed in 792.5.)

In vocal music 782–783 whether an item is a score, a treatise, or a recording determines how the work is to be classed. The following flowchart is offered as an aid in determining the correct section of vocal music.

Flow chart for choosing correct section within vocal music

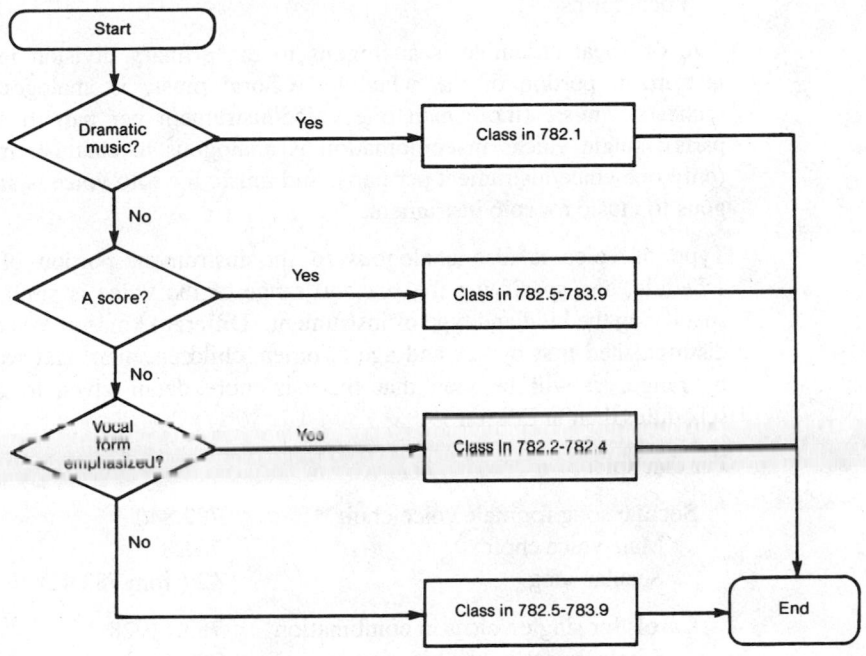

Examples (from applying the flow chart):

Soprano arias from opera [scores]	782.1
Soprano airs not from opera [scores]	783.66
Sacred songs by sopranos [recordings]	782.25
Women's soprano voice [treatise]	783.66

Vocal scores

When dealing with scores, kind and size of voice must be considered. The distinction between 782.5–.9 and 783 is made upon the number of voices per part. That is, in 782.5–.9 go works that treat music having several voices per part (what is usually meant by choral music). In 783 go works that treat music having one voice per part (part songs and solos). The citation order for scores and parts of nondramatic vocal music is:

Size of vocal ensemble (including solos)

Type of voice, e.g., male, high, soprano, child's

Vocal forms

Size of vocal ensemble is analogous to the primary division in the instrument portion of the schedule. Choral music is analogous to orchestral music (more than one voice/instrument per part in some parts); single voices in combination is analogous to chamber music (only one voice/instrument per part); and music for solo voice is analogous to music for solo instrument.

Type of voice is also analogous to the instrument portion of the schedule, and specifying the sex and range of the voice is similar to specifying the kind and type of instrument. Different kinds of voice are distinguished first by sex and age (women, children, men) and second by range. It will be seen that there is more detail given in these schedules than in Edition 19.

For example:

Secular song for male voice choir	782.842
Male voice choir	782.8
Secular song	42 (from 782.42)
Carols for single voices in combination	783.11928
Single voices in combination	783.1
Facet indicator	19
Carols	28 (from 782.28)

784–788 Instruments and their music

Instruments and their music are allotted the span 784–788, which to a substantial degree maintains a large to small arrangement that proceeds from orchestral ensembles (more than one instrument to a part) through chamber music (only one instrument per part) to single instruments.

Because of the intention of the developers of the DDC to internationalize the Classification by making it less reliant on an American or even Western view of the world, and making it applicable to knowledge modified by cultures other than Western, it was imperative that the new schedule for music be hospitable to the music of all cultures. Thus it was essential to find a value-free basis for the classification of instruments. At first glance the orientation of the new schedule appears to be European, as most instruments named or given as examples in the schedule are familiar to Westerners; however, the classification is applicable to all instruments from whatever culture, being based on the solely acoustical arrangement found in the "Systematik der Musikinstrumente; ein Versuch" of E. M. von Hornbostel and C. Sachs, first published in *Zeitschrift fur Ethnologie* 4–5, 1914; and consulted in the translation by A. Baines and K. P. Wachsmann in *Galpin Society Journal* 17:45–63, 1964. (Note that many non-Western instruments are found in the Relative Index, e.g., gaitas, hichirikis, santirs, surunais, and tulums.)

The 780 schedule attempts to reconcile the Sachs-Hornbostel fourfold classification with the divisions of the traditional Western classification with which they are broadly synonymous: percussion (idiophones and membranophones), strings (chordophones), and wind (aerophones). The schedule provides for the functional divisions necessitated by the application of Western technology to musical instruments, by making keyboard and mechanical instruments, however the sound is produced, into primary classes, and by adding a fifth acoustical category of electrophones to the instrumental classification. The order in the schedule is as follows:

Functional categories of instruments

Instruments in combination (orchestral and chamber music)

Keyboard instruments

Mechanical and aeolian instruments

Acoustical categories of instruments

Electrophones (electrical sound producers)

Idiophones (sonorous solids) [Percussion]

Membranophones (drums) [Percussion]

Chordophones (stringed instruments)

Aerophones (wind instruments)

The two main characteristics within instrumental music are the number of instruments per part (the size), e.g., full symphony orchestra, chamber groups, and solo instruments; and instrumental grouping, e.g., orchestra with solo instrument, woodwind ensembles. The two characteristics are enumerated in the schedule, in most cases without the need for building a number. However, where particular instruments are involved in the compound, it may be necessary to specify them from other parts of the schedule, e.g.:

785.8<u>32</u>   Flute ensembles (from 788.32)

785.9<u>62</u>   Clarinet ensembles (from 788.62)

The subdivisions of 784.1 will be heavily used because the numbers for providing for specific musical forms for specific instruments, for performance upon specific instruments, and for the instrument itself are given there. For example:

Breathing techniques in playing the clarinet	788.621932
Clarinet	788.62
Facet indicator	1
Breath technique	932 (from 784.1932)
Organ fugues	786.51872
Organ	786.5
Facet indicator	1
Fugues	872 (from 784.1872)

789 Composers and traditions of music

The optional number 789 may be used for both composers and traditions of music. The citation orders and instructions provided in 780–788 are applicable here when the option is followed.

Comparison of the 1980 Proposed Revision of 780 Music and class 780 in Edition 20

The major changes between the 1980 Proposed Revision and the present schedule are:

The list of composers has been eliminated. Composers are not indicated in the notation (unless the new Option A at 789 is used).

The ability to specify the original instrument or voice has been added to 781.38 Arrangements.

781.52–.58 Music for various specific times, settings, media reduced to 781.52–.54.

781.62 Traditions of music broadened to 781.62–.69. 781.62 is now Folk music.

781.63 Sacred music moved to 781.7.

781.64–.69 Specific kinds of music moved to 781.55–.59.

781.7 Musical forms that are both instrumental and vocal moved to 781.82.

781.8–.9 Instrumental forms moved to 784.183–.189.

In 782.5–.9 accompaniment is no longer a facet used in arranging vocal music. The presence of accompaniment is now indicated by adding 147 (from 781.47).

In 782.5–.9 treatises about and recordings of vocal forms for specific vocal ensembles and for specific kinds of ensembles of single voice moved to 782.1–.4.

787.8 Lutes and guitars rearranged.

788.79 Bagpipes moved to 788.49.

Examples from 780 Music

Works about music

New music vocabulary: a guide to notational signs	780.148
Music notation	780.148
Sound structure in music	781.234
Timbre	781.234
New life in country music	781.642
Western popular music	
Country	781.642
Wagner as man and artist	782.1092
Opera	782.1
General biography and criticism	092 (from Table 1)
Voice production in choral technique	782.5143
Choral music	782.5
Facet indicator	1
Performance technique	43 (from 781.43)
Bartok orchestral music [criticism in general]	784.2092
Orchestra	784.2
Composer	092 (from Table 1)
Bartok orchestral music [criticism of five pieces]	784.2
Orchestra	784.2
Scoring for brass band	784.9138
Brass band	784.9
Facet indicator	1
Arrangement	38 (from 781.38)
Beethoven string quartets [criticism]	785.7194
Chamber group—strings	785.7
Facet indicator	19
Quartet	4 (from 785.14)
The fugue in Beethoven's piano music	786.21872
Piano	786.2
Facet indicator	1
Fugue	872 (from 784.1872)

Scientific piano tuning and servicing	786.21928
Piano	786.2
Facet indicator	1
Tuning	928 (from 784.1928)
The origins of bowing	787.1936909
Bowed stringed instruments	787
Facet indicator	1
Bowing	9369 (from 784.19369)
History	09 (from Table 1)
Pablo Casals; a biography	787.4092
Cello	787.4
Performers	092 (from 780.92)
Discography of zither music	016.78770266
Subject bibliography	016
Zither	787.7
Recordings	0266 (from 780.266)
The organs of London	786.519421
Organ	786.5
Facet indicator	19
London	421 (from Table 2)
The Story of "Silent Night"	782.281723
Carols	782.28
Facet indicator	1
Christmas music	723 (from 781.723)

Scores

Hymns for choirs, arranged for mixed voices and organ by David Willcocks.	782.527
Choral music for mixed voices	782.5
Hymns	27 (from 782.27)
Lees. Breathe on me, breath of God; anthem for 3-part female voice choir unaccompanied	782.6265
Choral music—women's voices	782.6
Anthems	265 (from 782.265)
Schubert song cycles	783.247
Solo voice	783.2
Song cycle	47 (from 782.47)

Brahms. Variations on the St. Anthony Chorale	784.21825
Orchestra	784.2
Facet indicator	1
Variations	825 (from 784.1825)
Berlioz. Romeo and Juliet; a dramatic symphony	784.22184
Orchestra with vocal parts	784.22
Facet indicator	1
Symphony form	84 (from 784.184)
Schuller. Trio: oboe, horn, viola	785.42193
Ensembles of woodwind, brass, strings	785.42
Facet indicator	19
Trios	3 (from 785.13)
Chopin. Mazurka, piano	786.21884
Piano	786.2
Facet indicator	1
Mazurka form	884 (from 784.1884)

780.079 vs. 790.2   **[Music and the performing arts] vs. The performing arts in general**

780.079 is used for works focusing on music in relation to the other performing arts, while 790.2 is used for works on the performing arts as a whole. If in doubt, prefer 780.079.

780.268   **Words and other vocal sounds to be sung or recited with music**

Use this subdivision only for building other numbers; never use it by itself. In most instances it will be used in 782–783, e.g., lyrics of songs 782.420268; however, it can be used in 784–788 when voice is only one element in a predominantly instrumental work, e.g., texts of choral symphonies 784.221840268.

780.269   **Stories, plots, synopses**

Use this subdivision only for building other numbers; never use it by itself. In most instances it will be used in 782–783, e.g., plots of operas 782.10269; however, it can be used in 784–788 when voice is only one element in a predominantly instrumental work, e.g., synopses of choral symphonies 784.221840269.

780.89 vs. 781.62   **Music with respect to specific racial, ethnic, national groups vs. Folk music**

Works discussing a racial, ethnic, or national group in relation to music in general are classed in 780.89, e.g., a work about Afro-American composers, opera singers, jazz conductors is classed in 780.8996073. Works discussing music indigenous to the group is classed in 781.62, e.g., Afro-American music 781.6296073. If in doubt, class in 781.62.

781.382– **[Arrangements] By original voice, instrument, ensemble**
.388

Use these subdivisions only for building other numbers; never use them by themselves. These subdivisions are added to the number for the voice, instrument, or ensemble for which the music was arranged in order to indicate the original voice, instrument, or ensemble. For example, an arrangement of violin music for piano would be classed in 786.213872, 786.2 (piano music) plus 13872 (arrangements of violin music). Arrangements in general either of or for a voice, instrument, or ensemble are classed in 782–788. For example, class in 787.2138 both violin music arranged for various instruments and music of several instruments arranged for the violin.

781.47 **Accompaniment**

When 147 accompaniment (from 781.47) is added to treatises, it indicates how to accompany the work.

(Option: With scores, add 147 to indicate the presence of accompaniment. For example, for treatises, 787.2147 means how to accompany violin music; for scores, 787.2147 means accompanied violin music and 787.2 means unaccompanied violin music.)

784–788 **Instruments and their music**

Add table

092 [Persons associated with instruments and their music]

Class musicians associated with an instrument and its music, or with the music for the instrument, in the number for the instrument and its music plus notation 092 from Table 1, e.g., Isaac Stern (a violinist) 787.2092.

Class persons interested only in the instrument as such in the number for the instrument alone plus notation 092 from Table 1, e.g., Antonio Stradivari (a violin maker) 787.219092.

790 Recreational and performing arts

The original heading for 790 was Amusements. There are two ways of being amused: One can be entertained by others (791 and 792) or one can amuse oneself (793–799). The settings where one can be amused are two: indoors (793–795) and outdoors (796–799). As Dewey made the first number of each span the general number for the activity (i.e., 791, 793, 796), the classifier can usually expect to find in these numbers a broader spectrum of forms of entertainment or amusement.

During the past century participatory amusements have become entertainments as well. Where once golfers were accompanied by only a few individuals who wished to witness this novel recreation, now millions watch them in person or on television. The same is true of most sports. And some outdoor amusements, such as American football, are now played indoors occasionally. Consequently, technology and social values have so altered over the past century that while the location of a subject within the 790s is predictable and reasonable with respect to the original structure of the class, it is neither predictable nor reasonable in the light of modern practices and concepts.

791.092   **Persons [associated with public performances]**

Class the biography of a performer with the activity which the person's career is chiefly identified, e.g., the biography of an opera singer 782.1092. If the person's career involves more than one kind of public performance with no particular predominance, class the biography with the activity that comes first in the following table of precedence:

music	780
dancing	792.8
stage	792
motion pictures	791.43
television	791.45
radio	791.44

For example, class the biography of a stage actor who has also done considerable work in television in 792.028092. Activities listed in the table above take precedence over all other other activities listed in 791.

791.437 and   **Films [and Radio] Programs [and Television] Programs [and] Stage**
791.447,   **productions**
791.457,
792.9   The text of a play is classed in the appropriate number in literature, e.g., the text of Thornton Wilder's *Our Town* 812.52. A production script is classed in either 791 or 792, e.g., the production script for a staged production of *Our Town* 792.92. A production script is distinguished from a literary text in that it contains a variety of directions, e.g., where the furniture is to be placed, where the actors are to stand.

A production recorded in a different medium than the original production is classed with the recording, not with the production. For example, a staged opera recorded for television would class with television in 791.4572, not with staged opera in 792.542.

792.5 vs.   **[Staging] Opera vs. [Musical aspects of] Dramatic vocal forms**
782.1
      Class in 782.1 works that discuss dramatic vocal forms as a type of vocal music, including such topics as tempos, plots, singers, conducting. Class in 792.5 works that discuss dramatic vocal forms as a type

of stage presentation, including such topics as costumes, sets, direction. Works about an opera house and its productions are classed in 792.509, e.g., a history of La Scala, Milan 792.5094521. If in doubt, class in 782.1.

792.8 vs. 793.3   **Ballet and modern dance vs. Social, folk, national dancing**

A social, folk, or national dance can be given in the theater, just as a theatrical dance can become a social dance. A dance is classed in either 792.8 or 793.3 depending upon the focus of the work. For example, the waltz is usually treated as a ballroom dance and is classed in 793.33; but waltzes as an integral part of Balanchine's *Vienna Waltzes,* a ballet, are classed in 792.842.

794.82   **Specific genres of computer games**

Use of 794.82 (introduced in *DC&* 4:3) for comprehensive works on computer games has been discontinued; class in 794.8.

796   **Athletic and outdoor sports and games**

Notation 068 from Table 1 is sometimes used under 796–798 for the description of the playing field, court, or similar facility. The use of the facility is classed with the use. For example, the description of the greens of a golf course is classed in 796.352068; however, how the slope of the greens affects putting is classed in 796.35235.

It is the practice of the Decimal Classification Division to class the biography of sports personnel in the general number for the specific sport regardless of position played or type of game. For example, a quarterback in American professional football is classed by the Division in 796.332092, not 796.33225092 or 796.33264092.

798.2   **Horsemanship**

The cross reference at 798.2 *"For horse racing, see 798.4"* means that horse racing is considered a part of 798.2. Therefore, only works that discuss both riding and racing are classed here. Many works having "horsemanship" in their titles do not cover racing; they are classed in 798.23.

800   Literature (Belles-lettres) and rhetoric

In the following discussion, whenever application of principles to various literatures is being discussed, notation from Table 3 is mentioned. For example, "T3—1" is used to discuss poetry in specific literatures rather than "811, 841, etc." The number "T3—1" refers to both T3A—1 from Table 3–A (individual authors) and T3B—1 from Table 3–B (more than one author). Difficulties arise with the notation for T3—8 Miscellaneous writings because the literary period intervenes between T3—8 and its various subdivisions. When reference is made to this form, it is expressed as T3—8 + the notation for the subdivision, e.g., diaries T3—8 + 03.

Choice between literature and nonliterary subject

The aims of literature, according to Horace, are twofold: to teach and delight. The Dewey Decimal Classification holds to this precept. Works of the imagination intended to delight are classed in 800, but works that are essentially informational are classed according to subject in other parts of the schedule. The discipline of literature is restricted to: (1) works of the imagination that are written in the various literary forms, e.g., fiction, poetry; (2) literary criticism and description; (3) literary history and biography. The exclusion of informational works from the realm of belles-lettres holds regardless of the literary form of a work. Jonathan Swift's *The Drapier's Letters*, therefore, is not classed as a collection of the author's letters, rather as a work on monetary policy in 332.49415.

Essays, speeches, letters, and diaries are commonly used for nonliterary purposes. If in doubt whether a work in one of these forms should be classed as literature in 800 or with a subject elsewhere in the schedule, class with the subject.

The nonfiction novel is a problem for classifiers. This kind of novel uses the techniques of fiction writing to tell the story of actual people and actual events. Class an account of a true event or series of events using the names of the people involved, not inventing characters or distorting facts to enhance an intended artistic effect, not going beyond the information available to the author from investigation and interviews, in the discipline appropriate to the facts described. Truman Capote's *In Cold Blood*, a true account of a multiple murder, has not been assigned a fiction number, but is classed in 364.1523, the criminology number for murder. If, however, the author goes beyond what he learned from investigation and interviews in describing conversations, feelings, thoughts, or states of mind of the people he is writing about, then he is treating them as fictional persons, and the work should be classed as fiction, e.g., Norman Mailer's *The Executioner's Song* 813.54. In case of doubt, class as fiction.

Other kinds of fiction, and poetry and drama are sometimes used as vehicles for conveying factual information. Biographies have been written in verse, and fiction has been employed to teach the fundamentals of mathematics. Prefer 800 for poetry, drama, and fiction unless the form is purely incidental to the explanation of a specific subject, e.g., Harvey's *Circulation of the Blood* (written in Latin verse) 612.13, not 871.04.

An exception to the general rule is made for certain ancient works that have long been classed as literature regardless of the content of the work. For example, Hesiod's *Works and Days* is classed in 881.01, not 631, even though it deals with practical agriculture. These ancient works continue to be classed as literature, but new works whose major purpose is to inform are classed with the subject treated.

A literary study of nonliterary works is classed in 809, e.g., the Bible as literature 809.93522.

Language

Literature always involves the use of language, and language is the basic facet for building numbers in 800.

Class literary works by language, not by country of origin.* A major exception to this rule is that works in English originating in countries of the Western Hemisphere are classed in 810, not in 820 with English literature from the Eastern Hemisphere and comprehensive works on English literature.

Class literary works in the language in which they were originally written. An English translation of a work originally written in Spanish is classed with Spanish literature in 860, not with English literature in 820.

Literature of two or more languages. Works treating literature of two or more languages are usually collections or works of criticism. If two languages are involved, class the work in the number coming first in 820–890, except class Greek and Latin in 880, not 870. If more than two languages are involved, class the work in the most specific number that will contain them all. For instance, class a work including English, German, and Dutch in 830 since these are all Germanic languages. Class a work involving English, French, and Russian in 808 for collections or 809 for criticism. If any one language is predominant, class with that language.

Literary form

The second facet to be applied in literature is form. In literature there are two basic modes of expression: poetry and prose. Drama, whether in poetry or prose, is classed with drama in T3—2. The epigram is classed with miscellaneous writings in T3—8 + 02, regardless of mode. Works in other forms are classed with poetry in T3—1 if written in verse. Only prose works are classed in T3—3 Fiction, T3—4 Essays,

*In certain instances country of origin can be indicated through the use of Table 3–C. *See* T3C—93–99.

T3—5 Speeches, T3—6 Letters, and (except for verse epigrams) T3—8 Miscellaneous writings. The subdivision for prose literature, T3—8 + 08, is used only for prose works in more than one literary form; prose works in a specific form are classed with the form.

Though satire and humor have the number T3B—7 in the span for specific forms, they are neither form nor mode; rather, they are categories of writing marked in the case of satire by ridicule and derision, in the case of humor by a manner of expression that makes a point amusingly. Literary works in a particular form (T3—1–6 and T3—8) exhibiting satire and humor are classed with the form. Table 3–A for individual authors has no notation parallel to T3B—7; a collection of works by an individual author in more than one form exhibiting satire and humor is classed in T3A—8 + 09.

Kinds, scopes, media

For works by more than one author, the major forms can be subdivided. Poetry, drama, fiction, and speeches can be divided by kind, e.g., lyric and narrative poetry, science fiction and historical fiction. Drama and fiction can also be divided by scope, e.g., one-act plays and short stories. Drama can be divided by medium, e.g., plays written for television.

Literary period

The third facet in literature is literary period. Period tables are supplied under the literature of every language where their use is recommended. They are used for the literature of the language from throughout the world and for the literature from the traditional homeland of the language. For instance, French-language poetry of the later 19th century from throughout the world and French-language poetry of the later 19th century from France are both 841.8. The same periods are used for affiliated literatures (literatures in the same language, but from countries other than the traditional homeland) if the affiliated literature emanates from the same continent. Thus Swiss and Belgian French-language poems of the later 19th century are also classed in 841.8.* The periods of Great Britain are used for English-language literature of Ireland, the U.S. periods for English-language literature of Puerto Rico. The Canadian periods 4 and 5, however, are used for Canadian literature in English. Period is usually omitted if the literature emanates from a country on another continent, e.g., French-language poetry of the 19th century from Canada 841.* (Optional periods are sometimes provided for use with such a country if some special device

*In certain instances country of origin can be indicated through the use of Table 3–C. *See* T3C—93–99.

is used to set such literature apart from the literature in general. The options are described at 810–890 in the schedule.)

Other elements

For works by or about more than one author, two key elements are commonly added from Table 3–B: T3B—08 and cognate numbers for collections, T3B—09 and cognate numbers for history, description, and critical appraisal. This notation also serves as a link to Table 3–C, the table that allows for expression of additional features. These features are literary themes or subjects, literary elements (e.g., dialogue), literary qualities (e.g., romanticism), and specific kinds of persons for whom or by whom the literature is written.

Literary criticism

As used here the term "literary criticism" includes textual criticism.

The chief rule to be observed in classing criticism is that it is always classed with the literature being criticized.

Criticism of a specific work is classed with the work, e.g., a critical analysis of Hemingway's *For Whom the Bell Tolls* is classed in 813.52, the same number as the work itself. Criticism of the work of an author in general is classed in the comprehensive number for the author in question, e.g., criticism of Hemingway 813.52.

809 and notation 09 from Table 3–B and cognate numbers under specific forms of literature are used for criticism of all kinds of literature except the works of individual authors. Criticism of several literatures as a whole is classed in 809, criticism of fiction from several literatures in 809.3. Criticism of the literature of the United States in general is classed in 810.9, criticism of fiction of the United States in general in 813.009, criticism of early 20th-century American fiction in 813.5209.

Class criticism of literature in a specific form from more than one literature in 809.1–.7. Class in 801.95 the theory and technique of literary criticism. Class in these numbers also critical works in which the emphasis is on the various forms of literature as such, not on the various authors and literatures that may be used as examples. If in doubt between 801.95 and 809.1–.7, prefer 809.1–.7.

Appreciation of literature is classed in the same manner as other criticism.

*In certain instances country of origin can be indicated through the use of Table 3–C. *See* T3C—93–99.

Criticism of criticism is classed with the criticism being criticized and hence with the original subject of criticism. Criticism of Hemingway is classed in 813.52. If a third person writes a criticism of the criticism of Hemingway, this also is classed in 813.52.

Works about critics are treated in the same manner as works about other authors, i.e., the critic is classed with the kind of literature that he chiefly criticizes. Thus, a man who devoted the major part of his life to criticizing the works of Hemingway is classed in 813.52. A critic of Spanish literature is classed in 860.9.

It should be noted that criticism and critics are classed with the language of the literature they are criticizing, not with the language in which the criticism is written. For example, a French critic writing in French but criticizing American literature is classed in 810.9.

Adaptations

An adaptation may alter the form of a work or modify the content to such an extent in language, scope, or level of presentation that it can no longer be considered a version of the original. An adaptation is classed in the number appropriate to the adaptation, e.g., Lamb's *Tales from Shakespeare* 823.7. *For translations, see 800: Language.*

Note, however, that a prose translation of poetry (which is merely a change in mode) is not treated as an adaptation, e.g., Dante's *Divine Comedy* translated into German prose 851.1.

Excerpts

Treat a collection of excerpts as a collection. However, if the collection is meant to serve as a model for studying another discipline, class with the discipline illustrated. For instance, class in 307 a collection meant to explain what a community is.

800 vs. 398.2   Literature (Belles-lettres) and rhetoric vs. Folk literature

Folk literature consists of brief works in the oral tradition and is classed in 398.2. Whatever literary individuality the folk literature may once have had has been lost to the anonymity that the passage of time brings. Anonymous classics, however, are not considered to be folk literature. Despite the fact that their authorship is unknown, such works have a recognized literary merit, are almost always lengthy, and form a part of the literary canon. Therefore, they are classed in 800, e.g., *Chanson de Roland* 841.1, *Cantar de mio Cid* 861.1, *Kalevala* 894.54111.

Some legendary or historical events or themes, such as the search for the Holy Grail or the battle of Roland with the Saracens, appear as the basis for original works in many literatures, periods, and forms, the medieval works involving them often being anonymous. Although the theme rather than the literature is the binding thread, what is read is a literary work. Consequently, class each retelling of the event or theme with the literature, form, and period in which it was written, e.g., Mary Stewart's Merlin trilogy 823.914. Class works about a specific theme treated in several literatures in 809.933.

If in doubt, prefer 800.

800 vs. 591, 636, 398.245

Literature (Belles-lettres) and rhetoric vs. Zoology vs. Animal husbandry vs. [Folk literature of] Animals

Works about animals intended to contribute to some discipline other than literature are classed in the relevant discipline. Class animal stories in which the author's emphasis is on the habits and behavior of the animal in 591, on the care and training of the animal in 636. Class folk literature of animals in 398.245.

Literary accounts of animals are classed with the appropriate form in literature, e.g., poetry. Such accounts may be either fictional or true. A book about animals is certainly fiction if it contains conversations or thoughts of animals. Literary accounts of actual animals are often in the form of anecdotes or personal reminiscences. Such accounts are usually accommodated in T3—8 Miscellaneous writings. They are to be classed, as appropriate, at T3—8 + 02 for anecdotes, at T3—8 + 03 for reminiscences, diaries, journals; or at T3—8 + 07 for works without identifiable literary form.

800 vs. 741.6

Literature (Belles-lettres) and rhetoric vs. Graphic design, illustration, commercial art

Class illustration in general in 741.6. Class a specific type of illustration with the art form represented if the type is emphasized, e.g., etchings. If the illustrations merely accompany or enhance the literary text, class with the text in literature.

808.001–.7 vs. 070.52

[Rhetoric] vs. [Publishers'] Relations with authors

Three elements combine to produce the finished piece of writing: composition, preparation of the manuscript, and publishing:

1. Composition

   General 808

   How to write for newspapers 808.06607

   How to write about law 808.06634

   How to write plays 808.2

2. Preparation of the manuscript

   General 808.02

   For newspapers 808.06607

   For works about law 808.06634

   For plays 808.2

3. Publishing 070.52

   Class in 070.52 works limited to securing agents, submitting manuscripts, the relations of authors and publishers.

Works combining (2) and (3) are classed in the numbers for preparation of the manuscript (808.02, etc.) unless heavily weighted toward the publishing end:

How to make money in free-lance writing 808.02

Where to market your manuscript 070.52

808.0427   **Study of rhetoric through critical reading**

Readers used in the study of composition are classed here. Readers limited to a particular literary form are classed in the rhetoric number for the form, e.g., short stories 808.31. Academic readers in a subject are classed with the subject.

808.1 vs.   **Rhetoric of poetry vs. Suprasegmental features [in linguistics]**
414.6

Because many studies of prosody are concerned with how to write poetry, general studies of literary prosody are classed in 808.1. However, works on the prosody of a specific literature are classed as criticism of the literature, e.g., a study of the use of language by American poets 811.009, a study of the prose rhythms of a later 19th century French essayist 844.8.

Prosodic studies of a particular language as a whole from the linguist's viewpoint are classed with intonation for the specific language, using notation 16 from Table 4, e.g., 451.6 for prosodic studies of the Italian language. Linguistic studies of prosody across several languages and from the linguist's viewpoint are classed in 414.6.

808.8   **Collections of literary texts from more than one literature**

Here are examples illustrating the order of precedence for collections of texts in more than one form from more than one literature. The order of precedence is the same for criticism (809).

1. Specific themes and subjects, e.g., 808.80382 (religion)

2. Specific elements, e.g., 808.8024 (plot)

3. Specific qualities, e.g., 808.8013 (idealism)

4. For and by specific kinds of persons, e.g., 808.899282 (children)

5. Period, e.g., 808.80033 (18th century)

See also Table 3—B: Order of precedence.

900   Geography, history, and auxiliary disciplines

History is a record of events, their causes and effects, and of the contemporary conditions that clarify and enrich these events. When a work is the story of events that have transpired or an account of the conditions that have prevailed in a particular place or region, it is classed in 900. When it is the history of a specific subject, it is classed in the appropriate discipline, e.g., a history of political developments (such as internal developments in government) without respect to their effect upon the larger society and place where they occur 320.9; of economic events in France 330.944; of warfare 355.0209; of clocks 681.11309.

Political history is a strong component of history because it affects the whole of a particular society. But the history of political developments as they affect the internal activity of parties or other political groups is classed in 320.9 or in the 324 numbers for parties, campaigns, and election history.

History includes the present (situation and conditions), but not the future (projected events). Class projected events at 303.49.

Note that position on the map rather than political affiliation usually determines the number assigned to the history or the geography of a particular place, for while political affiliation may change, position on the earth's surface does not.

Citation order

The citation order in the 900s is straightforward:

History: 9 + place + period + standard subdivision, e.g., a periodical of the history of Jalisco state (Mexico) during the 20th century: 972.350805.

Geography and travel: 91 + place + physical geography, travel, or regional geography + standard subdivision, e.g., an encyclopedia of travel in Italy today: 914.50492803, a periodical about mountains in Italy 914.50914305.

Historic events vs. nonhistoric events

Depending upon their impact, specific events are classed either in 900 or in specific disciplines in 001–899. Events that are important enough to affect the general social life and history of the place are classed with the history of the place regardless of any discipline involved. For example, the sinking of the Lusitania is classed in 940.4514, the assassination of Abraham Lincoln in 973.7092, the San Francisco earthquake in 979.461051.

Other specific events are classed with the history of the discipline to which they relate. For example, the history of a crime is classed in 364, e.g., the Whitechapel murders committed by Jack the Ripper 364.1523. A sporting accident is classed in 796–799, e.g., a fatal accident during an automobile race 796.72.

In applying the above, the classifier should take into account the author's purpose or point of view. For instance, a work about the assassination of John F. Kennedy that is focused on the modus operandi of the crime, the detective work involved in solving it, or both, is classed at 364.1524092, not at 973.922092.

Works about events are more apt to emphasize social aspects than technological aspects and are usually classed in 300 rather than 600. If safety factors are stressed, the work is classed in 363, not with any other discipline involved. For example, a study of the wreck of the Andrea Doria to determine what the causes of the accident were, what preventive measures might be mandated as a result of the incident, is classed at 363.12365.

Collected accounts of events are treated in the same manner, provided that they all pertain to one discipline, e.g., scientific travel 508. Class collected events without such focus in 904.

910 vs. 909, 930–990   **Geography and travel vs. World history [and] History of ancient world; of specific continents, countries, localities**

If a work deals with geography and civilization or travel and civilization, class it in 909 or 930–990; however, if the treatment of geography or travel is predominant, class the work in 910. If in doubt, prefer 909 or 930–990.

If the work deals with the description of the physical earth only, class it in 910.02 or in 913–919, using notation 02 from table under 913–919.

913–919   **Geography of and travel in ancient world and specific continents, countries, localities in modern world; extraterrestrial worlds**

Historic sites and buildings

Except as discussed below, class here works describing historic sites and buildings (and parts thereof) designed for the use of visitors to the sites whether or not the works are designated specifically as guides. Do not use subdivision 04 from the add table unless the area covered by the guides approximates the whole of the area designated by the notation from Table 2. For example, a contemporary guide to the historic houses of England is classed in 914.204858.

Class historic buildings that have become museums or monuments in one of the following ways:

1. If the museum or monument is associated with the life of an individual, class with the biography number for that person, e.g., the home of Thomas Wolfe in Asheville, North Carolina 813.52.

2. If the museum or monument is associated with the history of a place, class with the appropriate number in 930–990, using notation 074 from Table 1 if applicable, e.g., a museum of Canadian history in Windsor, Ontario 971.007471332.

3. If the building is still in use for a specific purpose, class with the purpose, e.g., a guide to the New York Stock Exchange building 332.64273. Buildings for religious and related purposes do not follow this rule but are classed in 726.

Class histories of historical buildings and houses in 930–990, architecture in 720, interior decoration in 747.

Add table

The following flow chart is offered as an aid to building numbers and as a supplement to the detailed directions at 913–919.

Flow chart for geography and travel

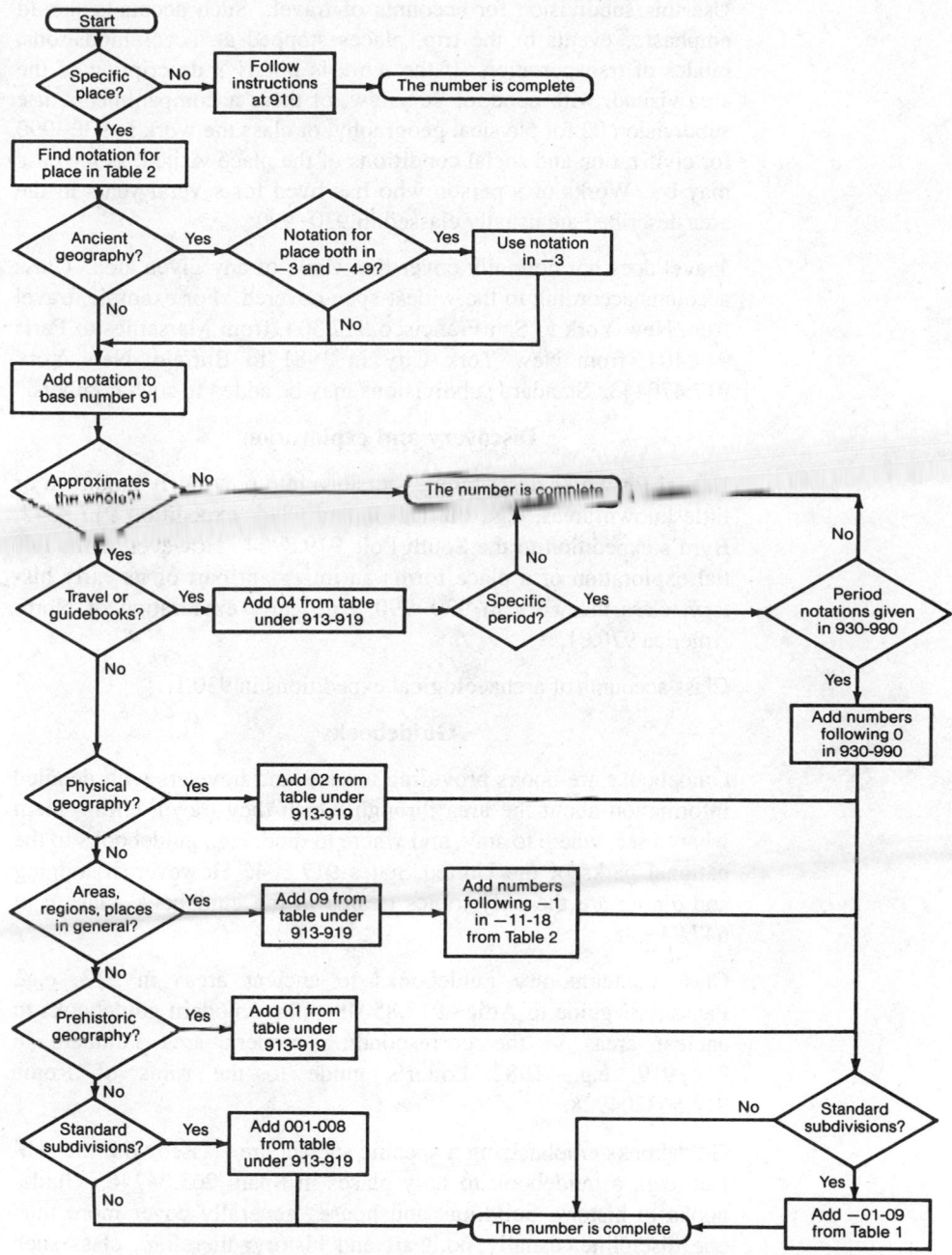

*See also "Approximates the whole" section of Manual notes on Table 1

04   Travel

Use this subdivision for accounts of travel. Such accounts should emphasize events of the trip, places stopped at, accommodations, modes of transportation. If the work is purely a description of the area visited, with none, or very few, of these accompaniments, use subdivision 02 for physical geography, or class the work in 930–990 for civilization and social conditions of the place visited, as the case may be. Works of a person who has lived for several years in the area described are usually classed in 930–990.

Travel does not normally cover the whole of any given area. Class accounts according to the widest span covered. For example, travel from New York to San Francisco 917.304, from Marseilles to Paris 914.404, from New York City in 1981 to Buffalo, New York 917.470443. Standard subdivisions may be added to such numbers.

Discovery and exploration

Use 04 for works describing excursions into previously unknown or little known areas, e.g., the Lewis and Clark expedition 917.8042, Byrd's expedition to the South Pole 919.8904. However, if the initial exploration of a place forms an important part of its early history, class the work in 930–990, e.g., early exploration of North America 970.01.

Class accounts of archaeological expeditions in 930.1.

Guidebooks

Guidebooks are books providing tourists and travelers with detailed information about the area through which they travel, telling them what to see, where to stay, and where to dine, e.g., guidebooks to the national parks of the United States 917.304. However, if lodging and dining are the only topics treated in the guidebook, class it in 647.94–.95.

Class contemporary guidebooks to ancient areas in 913, e.g., Pausanias' guide to Attica 913.85049. Class modern guidebooks to ancient areas in the corresponding modern area numbers in 914–919, e.g., 1982 Fodor's guide to the ruins of Rome 914.563204928.

Guidebooks emphasizing a specific subject are classed with the subject, e.g., a guidebook to holy places in Spain 263.04246. Guidebooks to historic buildings and houses generally cover more than one discipline, usually both art and history; therefore, class such guidebooks in 913–919.

Class a guide for persons moving to another country on a permanent basis in 940–990.

See also 913–919: Historic buildings and houses.

Biography

Notation 092 from Table 1 is added to subdivisions 041–049 for biographies of discoverers, explorers, and travelers, but not for general geographers nor for first-person accounts of travel. Class biographies of general geographers in the base number for the area without further subdivision. Use subdivisions 041–049 for first-person accounts of travel, but do not add notation 092.

929.1 Genealogy

This is the comprehensive number for works providing information about genealogy itself: what it is, where to go to find genealogical records, what to look for, what sources to use, how to obtain these sources, how to trace family trees. The sources themselves are classed in 929.3.

929.2 Family histories

Inasmuch as families disperse from their place of origin, the area number selected for a family history should not be too specific. The Decimal Classification Division adds area numbers only for the country in which the family lives, not for the state, province, or smaller area. For example, the Division classes the history of a Florida family in 929.20973, not 929.209759.

Class a family history with the country in which the family presently lives, not with the country from which the family's ancestors came. For example, class the Duponts, a United States family of French origin, in 929.0973, not 929.0944.

Family histories that give historical information about the area in which the family is located are classed with the history of the area, e.g., prominent families in New York City 974.71

929.2 vs. 929.7 **Family histories vs. Royal houses, peerage, gentry, orders of knighthood**

Family histories of the nobility and gentry are usually classed in 929.2. Family histories that emphasize lineage or descent of the peerage or gentry are classed in 929.7, e.g., *Burke's Peerage* 929.72, *Virginians of Gentle Birth* 929.709755. If in doubt, prefer 929.2.

930–990   **History of ancient world; of specific continents, countries, localities; of extraterrestrial worlds**

Wars

In most instances, the history of a war is classed with the history of the country or region in which most of the fighting took place, e.g., the Vietnam War 959.7043, the Napoleonic wars 940.27, the Falkland Islands War (1982) 997.11. However, some wars are arbitrarily assigned to either the history of one of the principle participants or to the region where the war began. For example, the Spanish-American War is classed with United States history in 973.89. World War II is classed in European history (the area where the war began) at 940.53, and not in world history at 909.824.

Regardless of the area to which a war is assigned, specific battles or actions of a war are classed in the number for the war, not with the number of the place where the action occurred. For example, a battle occurring in the Philippines during the Spanish-American War is classed in 973.8937, not 959.9031; air raids on Tokyo in World War II 940.5425, not 952.135033.

There are two kinds of wartime history that are not classed in the war numbers (unless the area covered coincides with the area used for the war). Routine history of the everyday events of an area, even if during wartime, is classed with the numbers for the area, not with the war, e.g., the history of Maryland during the Civil War 975.203, not 973.709752. The effect of military action on the everyday life and civilization of a place is classed with the history of the place, e.g., the effect of Civil War military actions on Maryland 975.203, not 973.709752. These two kinds of history must be carefully distinguished from the participation of an area in the war because the area's participation in the war is classed with the war, e.g., Maryland's participation in the Civil War 973.709752, not 975.203. Usually, national histories covering a time of war will emphasize the country's participation and will be classed with the war; if there is no such emphasis, the history will be classed in the appropriate national history number. For example, British participation in World War II 940.5341, history of Britain during George VI's reign 941.084.

See also 355.009 vs. 930–990.

Occupied countries

The history of the occupation of a country during time of war is classed with the war, e.g., occupation of countries in World War II 940.5336. Military administration of the government of an occupied country during or following the war is classed in 355.49. International law with respect to occupation is classed in 341.66.

Specific units in a war

The history of specific military units in a war is classed with the numbers for military units under history of the particular war, e.g., military units in World War I 940.412–.413. If there is no specific number for military units, a work on military units is classed in the number for military operations, e.g., military units in the Vietnam War 959.70434.

Class comprehensive works on specific military units and military units in peacetime in 355.3 or cognate numbers in 355–359.

Personal narratives

The personal narratives of participants in a war are classed in the appropriate subdivision of the history numbers for the specific war, e.g., personal narratives of American soldiers in World War II 940.548173. Narratives that focus on a specific campaign, battle, or other subject are classed with the subject, e.g., a personal account of the Battle of Berlin 940.5421092, of Axis intelligence operations in World War II 940.548743092.

The narrative of a person's experiences during time of war, if it does not focus on the war as such, is classed as biography and not in the number for the war. For example, an actor's personal experiences of performing in Scotland during 1940–1942 is classed in 792.092, not 940.5315792092.

Historic preservation

Class comprehensive works on historic preservation and lists of preservation projects to be undertaken in 363.69. However, if such a list is primarily devoted to inventorying or describing the sites, class the list in the appropriate number in 930–990, or, if primarily a description of buildings at the site, class in 720.

Class administrative annual reports of agencies promoting the preservation of historical sites in 351.859 and cognate numbers in 352–354.

Class historic preservation in an architectural context in 720.288 and cognate numbers in 721–729.

Add table

The following flow chart is offered as an aid to building numbers and as a supplement to the detailed instructions at 930–990.

Flow chart for history

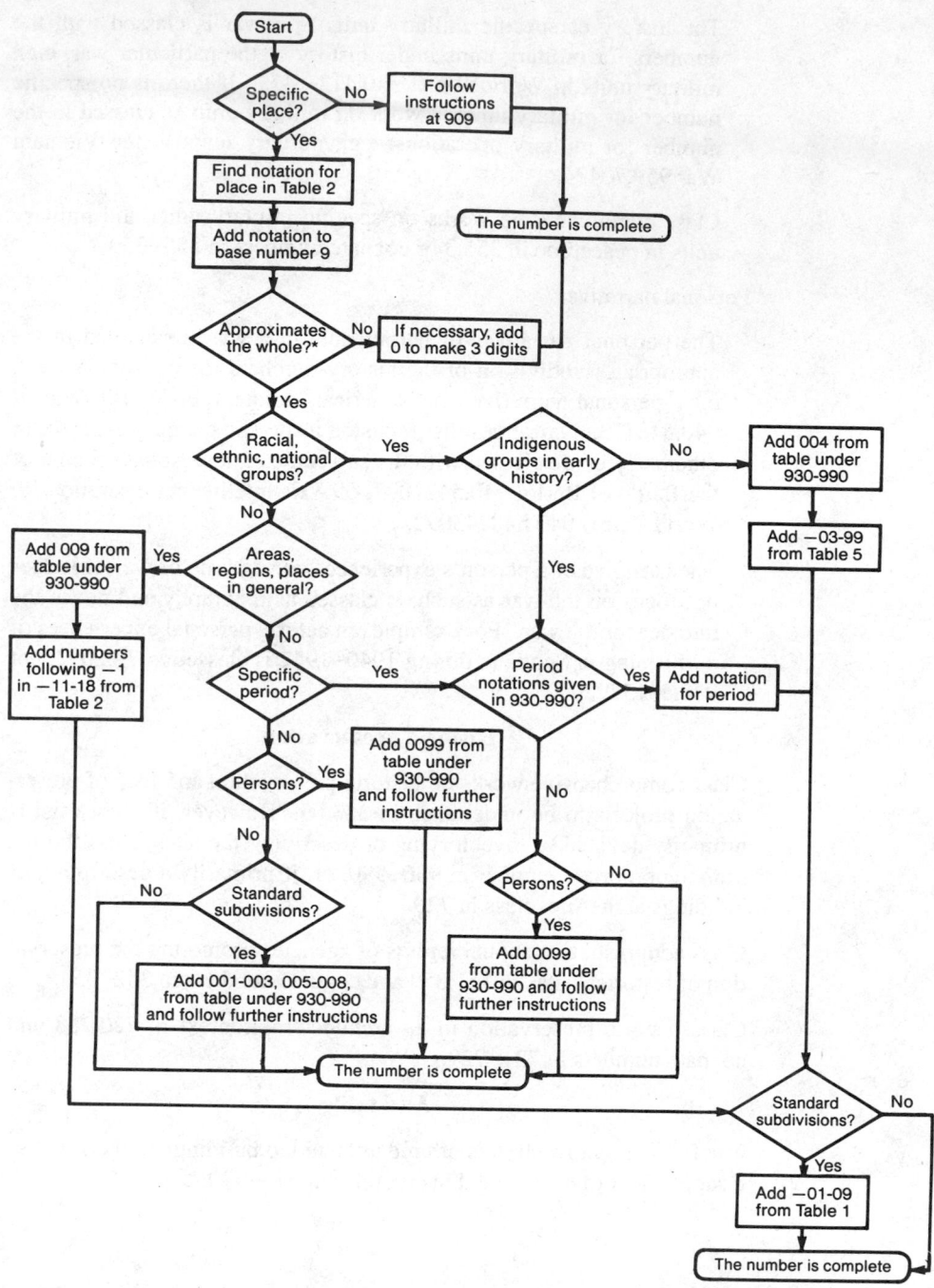

*See also ''Approximates the whole'' of Manual notes on Table 1

01–09	Historical periods

The history of the area is usually subdivided into periods defined by the events that affected the area. The events, whether stated or implied in the heading, rarely occurred on either January 1 or December 31. Thus, the year during which the event occurred will normally be given at two different notations. For example, 1861, the year when Kansas became a state, appears at both 978.102 Territorial period, 1803–1861 and 978.103 Statehood period, 1861–. In like manner, 1945, the year when World War II ended, appears at both 978.1032 1918–1945 and 978.1033 1945–.

The history of the area can also be subdivided by periods of time, such as centuries or decades. Since they start on January 1 and end on December 31, the year either beginning or ending the period will appear in only one notation. For example, in the development for the history of the Western United States, 978.02 1800–1899 and 978.03 1900–. (The DDC uses the convention that a century begins with the year 0 and ends with the year 99.) The name for a particular century is given only if the span of years in the heading is less than 75 years. For example, the 15th century in German history is given in a class-here note at 943.028 Reigns of Albert II and Frederick III, 1438–1493. The 17th century in German history is not given at 943.04 1618–1705.

When adding standard subdivisions to the historical periods, use notation 01–09 from Table 1, not 001–009 from the table under 930–990. However, numbers T1—089 and T1—091 are not used since the provisions for them given at 004 and 0091–0098 in the table under 930–990 take precedence over provisions for historical periods.

941   **[History of the] British Isles**

Class here works on the United Kingdom (England, Wales, Scotland, and Northern Ireland), a political entity, and on Great Britain (England, Wales, and Scotland), a geographical entity. Class in 942 only works dealing with England alone, or with England and Wales. Histories of the period since 1603 (or including this period) will seldom deal with England or England and Wales alone. Histories of the period before 1603 may deal with England or England and Wales alone. Books on the civilization of this area may deal with any combination. The following combinations of two areas will be classed in 941: England and Scotland, England and Ireland, Ireland and Wales.

968   Southern Africa   Republic of South Africa

Period notation for a country or region is added to each geographical subdivision of the country not provided with its own periods, regardless of considerations of sovereignty. Thus, the historical periods of the provinces of Republic of South Africa also apply to the homelands in the area of each province. For example, the historical periods of Natal apply also to KwaZulu, e.g., history of KwaZulu during the reign of Shaka 968.491039, during the prime ministership of P. W. Botha 968.491063.

970.004   [General history of North American] Racial, ethnic, national groups

The principal fact to keep in mind in assigning class numbers to works of the various native American peoples is that they have moved in the course of time from place to place and that these places are often widely scattered.

Therefore, in general, a work on specific peoples is classed in 970.00497, no attempt being made to assign a more specific location. For example, general works on Cherokees class in 970.00497.

If, however, the focus of the work is clearly on the native peoples in a specific place, use the number for the place plus notation 00497 from the table under 930–990.   For example, native races of Canada, 971.00497, Cherokees in North Carolina 975.600497.

Appendix

Policies and Procedures of the
Library of Congress Decimal Classification Division

Segmentation in Centrally Cataloged Records

One aid to reduction of the full DDC number is the segmentation provided in DDC numbers by centralized cataloging services, such as the Decimal Classification Division of the Library of Congress, the British Library, and the National Library of Canada. The segmentation is indicated by a prime mark ('), a slash mark (/), or other comparable indicators.

The segmentation provided by the Decimal Classification Division is applied according to two different principles. A segmentation mark can indicate the end of an abridged number (as found in the Abridged Edition of the DDC), or the beginning of a standard subdivision. Thus, a DDC number can consist of one, two, or three segments. For example:

324.6'23'092		A biography of Susan B. Anthony
324.6		Election systems and procedures; suffrage (the number found in the Abridged Edition)
	23	Women's suffrage (the remainder of the number from the Schedules of the Unabridged Edition)
	092	Persons (from Unabridged Table 1)
323'.025'73		Directory of civil rights leaders and organizations in the United States
323		Civil and political rights (the number found in the Abridged Edition)
.025		Directories (applicable standard subdivision from Abridged Table 1)
73		United States (area notation from Table 2 that can be added to the directories number [025] in Unabridged Table 1)

Bracketed DDC Numbers on LC Bibliographic Records

Libraries using cataloging data provided by the Library of Congress will notice that there are sometimes two or more DDC numbers or non-numeric notation in the DDC field. On LC printed cards, all but the first DDC number is given in brackets ([ ]). The following examples (omitting segmentation marks described above) explain the practices of the Decimal Classification Division with respect to bracketed DDC numbers:

Nonjuvenile Works

A. For works belonging to a monographic series classed as a set but analyzed in full or in part according to the decisions of the Subject Cataloging Division of the Library of Congress, the Decimal Classification Division assigns two numbers:

    081 s   the number for the item if the series is kept together at one class number

    [327.7]   the number for the specific item in the series

B. For biography and works primarily biographical, the Division assigns a number and the letter [B]:

    780.92   the number if the item is added to the classified collection

    [B]   the letter if the item is added to the biography collection

C. Brackets for a monograph in a series and for biography may both be present:

    780.92 s   the number for the series

    [787.66092]   [B]   the number and the letter for a monograph in a series

D. For law, the Division makes the only exception to its practice of eschewing optional numbers. It supplies both the preferred number and the Option B number:

    345.7308   the preferred number

    [347.3058]   the Option B number

E. When works on law belong to analyzed monographic sets, four numbers are supplied. On Library of Congress catalog cards, they are usually printed two by two, with the DDC preferred numbers on the top line and the optional numbers on the bottom line:

    343.41052 s   [343.410523]

    344.10352 s   [344.103523]

Juvenile Works

For juvenile works, bracketed numbers and alphabetical codes (other than [B]) are assigned by the Children's Literature Section of the Library of Congress.

A. Easy books
    1. Easy books without a clearly defined topic in a recognized field of study are assigned [E], e.g., Tommy takes his first trip to the store [E].
    2. Easy books with a discernible topic in a recognized field of study are assigned both an [E] and a DDC number, e.g., Tommy takes his first trip to London 914.2 [E].
    3. Easy fiction, for children K-3 (through eight years old) is assigned [E].

B.   Fiction intended for grades 4–6, or ages 9–11, is assigned [Fic]. Adult fiction that has been deemed appropriate for a juvenile and classes of children's literature that have a continuing adult audience will be assigned [Fic] as well as a class number, e.g., *Treasure Island* 823.8 [Fic].

C.   Biography
       1.   Without subject or disciplinary associations

              One person   [92]
              Several persons   [920]

       2.   With subject or disciplinary association

              One person   509.2   [B]   [92]
              Several persons   509.22   [B]   [920]

Classifying Children's Books in the DCD

The Decimal Classification Division classifies most children's literature processed by the Children's Literature Section of the Library of Congress, except that works designated by [Fic] or [E] are normally sent on without further classification.

The 20th edition of the Dewey Decimal Classification was designed by Lisa Hanifan of Albany, New York. Edition 20 is the first edition to be generated from an online database. Database design, technical support, and programming for this edition were provided by John J. Finni and Cora M. Arsenault from Inforonics, Inc., of Littleton, Massachusetts. Composition was done in Times Roman and Helvetica on a Linotronic L100 under the supervision of Inforonics, Inc. The book was printed and bound by Hamilton Printing Company of Rensselaer, New York.